Wembley

The Complete
Record
1923-2000

Wembley

The Complete Record 1923-2000

Glen Isherwood

SPORTS
BOOKS

Published by SportsBooks Ltd

SportsBooks Limited
PO Box 422
Cheltenham
GL50 2YN
United Kingdom
Tel: 01242 256755
Fax: 01242 254694
e-mail   randall@sportsbooks.ltd.uk
Website   www.sportsbooks.ltd.uk

Photographs supplied by Actionimages

ISBN 1899807 42 X

Printed by Compass Press.

FOREWORD
by Sir Geoff Hurst

WEMBLEY STADIUM has been the stage for some of the greatest sporting dramas of the last century and, for me personally, many of the most memorable moments in my 17 year career as a professional footballer. Naturally, I grew fond of the stadium but I'm an enthusiastic supporter of the new Wembley and hope that one day it will have a history to match the old Empire Stadium.

But that will take a long while. Just why will become obvious as you delve through this exhaustive and fascinating 77 year history of Wembley Stadium. Compiling such a catalogue of matches, both big and small, has clearly been a labour of love but the detail unearthed in this lavish history helps you understand why Wembley Stadium became the Venue of Legends.

Among my most vivid memories, of course, are the big games at Wembley. Like all the groundstaff boys at West Ham in the late fifties I dreamed of one day playing in the great stadium that had become the mecca of world football.

I was just 18 when I went there for the first time. I was one of a crowd of 80,000 that went to see England play Spain, one of the most powerful soccer nations in Europe at the time. Their team was built around players like Gento, di Stefano and Santamaria, all members of the Real Madrid side that won the European Cup five years in succession between 1956-60.

England's team at the time was pretty useful, too. Not surprising when you consider the forward line that day: Bryan Douglas, Jimmy Greaves, Bobby Smith, Johnny Haynes, Bobby Charlton.

Greaves scored in the first minute and England won 4-2 and I can remember going home totally exhilarated by the atmosphere within the stadium.

My first visit as a player, though, was a different matter. I was 23 when West Ham reached the FA Cup Final in 1964 and, although I wasn't usually prone to nerves, the prospect of playing at Wembley for the first time was not something to be treated lightly.

By this time, of course, my friend and West Ham club mate Bobby Moore had played there a few times for England and he was a calming influence in the dressing room beforehand.

To be honest, we struggled that day against Preston North End when we should have won comfortably. West Ham were the favourites from the First Division. Preston were from Division Two.

Even so, Preston twice took the lead. In the 52nd minute I headed a goal that put us level at 2-2 and, in the last moments of the match, Peter Brabrook and I created the winner for Ronnie Boyce. We won 3-2 and although the sympathy and glory went to Preston, nothing could dilute my happiness as I walked up the 39 steps to collect my winners' medal.

The following year I was back at Wembley, this time in the European Cup-winners' Cup Final. We met the German team, TSV Munchen 1860, and the match is still ranked by many as one of the finest Wembley finals.

A wall-to-wall crowd of 100,000 squeezed into the stadium, 30 million more watched on TV throughout Europe, and the two sides provided a memorable match packed with excitement, drama and football's finer arts. West Ham won 2-0, both goals supplied by Alan Sealey. Everything we had worked at on the training pitch came to fruition that day and our manager Ron Greenwood was bubbling in the dressing room afterwards.

I remember him saying: "Our greatest game... a tremendous advert for football."

Two games at Wembley, two wins. I was beginning to enjoy my annual excursion. Looking back, I couldn't have complained had those two finals been the pinnacle of my playing career.

At that time I hadn't played for England, apart from at Under-23 level. Sir Alf Ramsey, the England manager, was busy preparing his side for the World Cup Final in 1966 and, to be honest, I had never dreamt of being selected for the senior team, never mind the World Cup.

Then, one day in January 1966, I was training with the other West Ham players at an indoor gymnasium in Forest Gate. Ron Greenwood called me to one side and told me I had been selected for the England squad for a game against Poland.

I didn't play against the Poles, but a month later Sir Alf selected me again – and this time I played.

It was February 1966. The opposition was West Germany and the venue was Wembley. We won 1-0, Nobby Stiles scoring the goal.

Suddenly, I was in the frame for a World Cup place. The finals were just five months away and, although I played four games in the interim period, it wasn't until Jimmy Greaves was injured against France that I got into the World Cup side.

I scored in the quarter final against Argentina and Sir Alf decided to keep me in the team. We beat Portugal in the semi-final, met West Germany again in the final and the rest, of course, has been well-catalogued.

The three goals I scored changed my career and the course of my life. I was just another First Division footballer until July 1966 when I suddenly became a celebrity.

People still ask me what it was like that day at Wembley. They always ask whether my second goal, the one that gave England a 3-2 lead in extra time, was over the goal line.

My shot, from Alan Ball's cross, hit the underside of the bar. The ball bounced down and out of the net. The Swiss referee consulted his Soviet linesman and awarded the goal.

The Germans claimed the ball had not crossed the line. I believed at the time that it was a goal but the controversy has continued for over thirty years.

What convinced me of the goal's validity at the time was the reaction of Roger Hunt. He was perhaps two yards away when the ball struck the bar and, were there any doubts in his mind, he would have continued his run and pushed the ball into the net.

As it was he wheeled away and acclaimed the goal immediately.

After that 4-2 victory, Wembley became a very special place for me. I visited other great and spectacular stadia – notably the Maracana in Rio – but nothing could ever rival Wembley for its atmosphere.

If it provided the stage for the high points of my career, it also supplied the setting for the single biggest disappointment.

In April 1972 England met West Germany – yes, them again – at Wembley in the European Championship quarter finals. It was my 49th and last England game.

We lost 3-1 and I was substituted by Rodney Marsh. I felt it was the wrong move by Sir Alf. I had the greatest respect for him as a manager, but pulling me out of that game prematurely was a mistake.

I didn't realise it at the time, but that was the end of the road for me as an international. I never played at Wembley again.

Sir Geoff Hurst
October 2005

Acknowledgements

I must acknowledge the help and support I received from the following individuals and organisations over the years (some of whom have probably forgotten, because it was so long ago!):

Colin Timbrell (President Elect of Gloucestershire Northern Senior League), Mike Bondy (MJB Research Services), Mike Simmons & David Cook (English Schools FA), Cliff Butler (Manchester United FC), Gordon Macey (Queens Park Rangers FC), Wally Goss & Mike Taylor (Amateur Football Alliance), Fred Wickers (Ealing Association FC), Colm Kerrigan, David Barber (Football Association), Sarah Fisher and Paul Hughes (Littlewoods Pools), Harold Whiddon (Middlesex County Youth FA), Cambridge University, Oxford University, Northern Ireland Schools FA, Grange Museum of Community History, Ray Spiller and Ron Hockings (Association of Football Statisticians), John Trewick (West Bromwich Albion FC), Scunthorpe United FC, Blackburn Rovers FC, Crystal Palace FC, Everton FC, Wigan Athetic FC, Mauro Pratesi, Mel Aldis (Earl Soham Victoria), Eastleigh FC, Chris Tilbrook (Sizewell FC), Robert Chamberlain (Honiton Clyst), Bill McGregor (West Hendon Ex-Servicemen), Thalia Kenton (Burton Menswear), Paul Johnson, Mark Harrison and Gert Kristiansen (Carlsberg), Leif Pedersen and Kai Kristiansen (Vagns Krostue), Bob Webster and Tony Bowker (Dawlish Town FC), James Wright (Non-League Newsdesk), KNVB (Royal Netherlands Football Association), Erik Aldaeus (Swedish Football Association), Jimmie Thomsen (Danish Football Association), John and Michael Robinson (Soccer Books Ltd), Paul Burns and Ross Cheshire (Britespot Publishing), Jim Cadman (www.intofootball.co.uk), Nick Harris (*The Independent*), Sir Geoff Hurst, Michael Hart (*London Evening Standard*), Chris Palmer and Martin Corrie (Wembley National Stadium Ltd), Peter Young and Chris Goodwin (www.englandfootballonline.com), Chris Warren, Richard Zimmern, Bryan Horsnell, Phil Bird, Colin Cameron (Charlton Athletic FC), Gary Chalk (Southampton FC), Simon Pitts (www.lutonfc.com), George Orr (Blue Blood, Everton FC fanzine), www.borntobeblue.co.uk, www.rsssf.com, www.since1888.co.uk

It would be impossible to list an entire bibliography, because of the sheer volume of publications I have used in my research. These are a few of the most significant:

The Times, Rothmans/Sky Sports Football Yearbook, The Complete Record of the FA Cup (Mike Collett), *Glorious Wembley* (Howard Bass), *The Guinness Book of World Soccer* (Guy Oliver), *England The Complete Post-War Record* (Mike Payne) and *Non-League Football Fact Book* (Tony Williams), Wembley match programmes

Glen Isherwood

INTRODUCTION

FUNNY HOW a random thought can end up dominating your life for almost a quarter of a century.

Well, maybe 'dominating' is too strong a word, but this book is the culmination of 23 years of research, and throughout that period, Wembley's history rarely managed to stray too far from my mind.

It was in 1983 that I casually wondered if all the game's greatest players had played at Wembley. It couldn't be that difficult to find out, could it?. I only had to go through the team line-ups for the cup finals and internationals. How wrong I was.

The details were fairly easy to find. I already had most of the line-ups in books and one trip to the library was all it took to find the foreign team line-ups. My brother's ZX Spectrum was my only option for indexing and that seemed fairly limited, so I set about writing them out instead.

It was taking me longer than I had anticipated, but by 1987, I was wondering if it would make a good book. A few tentative letters to publishers made me realise I had to offer far more, such as match reports and the idea lost a little favour with me.

Then, in 1991, came the turning point. I was 29, single, plenty of time on my hands and disillusioned with women. Turning my work into a proper book would be therapeutic, only I didn't have a clue what would make a good book. I turned to the library for inspiration and found a previous history of Wembley (*Glorious Wembley* by Howard Bass). It was filled with fascinating stories that I had not heard before. I realised that there was far more than just cup finals and internationals to write about. The author had written that a complete history would run to many volumes. I can now confirm that it did. And I only wrote the football history.

His words made me wonder if such a record already existed. I contacted Wembley, who told me that they only had limited records from about 1950, when a fire had destroyed the earlier stuff and that I had set myself 'an impossible task'. It amazed me that such a famous landmark did not have its own definitive history, though I realised that Wembley's primary concern was to sell itself to potential hirers such as the Football Association and concert promoters and to do that, it really only had to remind people about the great events – the 1966 World Cup, Live Aid etc., much as any function room would do, only this was a much grander stage.

I felt obliged to attempt the job myself, unofficially, but I knew I could not do it all myself. What I could do was chase up every mention of the word 'Wembley' I could find in books, magazines, newspapers, programmes and videos, trace it back to an event date and categorise it. I also felt I could not just concentrate on football and, in fact, the other sports and entertainments were a welcome distraction from the endless succession of football matches.

It would not have been right to include all the winners from over 70 years of greyhound races, but I found myself wondering if Evel Knievel did eventually break the world record by clearing 13 buses, after his crash at Wembley in 1975 (he did).

The next two years were spent hunting down every football match, not knowing how many there were. Every organisation had its own records, but there appeared to be several one-offs that I'd find out about from the odd P.S. at the end of a letter and off I'd go on another fact-finding mission. It was from one of my requests for information on a County Youth Cup game that I received a reply from Colin Timbrell, who became a major influence. Colin had kept a close eye on the stadium's events for over 40 years, collecting rare programmes from obscure games and it was thanks to him that I managed to document all the war years, which I was beginning to think would not be possible because of all the local fixtures. There were other games too, such as the University International of 1937, the British Junior Cup Finals after the war and Ealing playing half a season at Wembley in 1928, that I would never have unearthed on my own. This was the local knowledge I needed to convince myself that I was building a unique record and that much of it would have been lost otherwise.

As luck would have it, within six months of devoting my life to this quest, Tracy came along and restored my faith in the female form. Now I had a reason to finish the book. We were married in 1993 and I set about getting my work published. This was no easy task. It ran to four huge volumes and it needed a hook to interest the publishers.

Then came the news that the stadium was to be demolished and rebuilt. *The Independent* newspaper featured my list of games on the eve of the last match, in October 2000. I had also named Tony Adams as the player who made most appearances in the stadium's history and it made back-page headlines as the player himself was unaware of the fact.

Wembley used some of the match details on their website for a while and I became their official historian, but the political wrangling delayed the rebuilding and I wondered if my history would be consigned to gathering dust on a shelf because of the adverse publicity continually attracted by the stadium.

In 2003, Britespot Publishing took the plunge and I managed to release a history of FA Cup Finals, but was there still one last opportunity to publish the complete record? There was, and with the new stadium (slowly) nearing completion, Randall Northam and SportsBooks Ltd stepped in to allow me to fulfil my 23-year mission.

At times, my wife has told me it's like living with Anne Frank and it's probably taken more of my life than I could ever have planned, but I hope it does justice to a fabulous history of a majestic structure.

And the answer to that random thought that sparked off this obsession – just about every famous player you could think of, played at Wembley, apart from the most famous of all, Pele.

Glen Isherwood, June 2006

Contents

A Short History of Wembley's Competitions

WEMBLEY STADIUM was built for the 1924 British Empire Exhibition, but proved to be the ideal size and location for the FA Cup Final, notwithstanding the farcical situation of its first event when the Football Association decided spectators could just turn up on the day, estimating that as the stadium could hold 117,000 there would be no problems. The crowd of more than 200,000 plus the need for police horses to help clear the pitch (Billy, the white horse was not the only one but because of his colour became synonymous with the first match played at the stadium) showed how wrong the association could be. This was easily avoided in future years by making every Cup Final an all-ticket match. The England v Scotland fixture was the next to take place there, in 1924, and the appeal of this biennial pilgrimage by the Scots ensured a full house.

When the Exhibition closed in 1925, the Wembley site faced an uncertain future with its buildings being sold off or demolished. The stadium faced a similar fate until Arthur Elvin's intervention. The significance of his determination to buy the stadium and to make it a viable proposition can never be understated in its history. It was the defining period and without him, Wembley would never have become a name indistinguishable from English football history. His objective was to provide popular entertainment and the introduction of greyhound racing several times a week gave him the foundation and financial stability to make the stadium pay.

There had been an RAF Final played during the Exhibition, but Elvin's first attempt to introduce more football into Wembley's calendar came with Ealing Association's move to the stadium as an experimental home ground in 1928. It was not successful and the vastness of an empty stadium was never going to generate a good atmosphere. A few other amateur games were played that season, but it was back to the drawing board as far as attracting football fans to the stadium on a more regular basis went. The cup final each year and the England v Scotland fixture every other year from 1928 onwards, were secure and Wembley provided the capacity each deserved, but there was plenty of space in the calendar for more. There were a couple of one-off local finals, the Wembley Hospital Cup Final in 1930 and the London Occupational League Final in 1934. Clapton Orient made a couple of Football League appearances in 1930, while their new ground was made available and a University International was staged in 1937, curiously against Germany.

Wembley made its money from other events during this period. It became the premier venue for speedway, with the World Championship being held there annually from 1936. The indoor Empire Pool, part of the Wembley complex, could undergo amazing transformations in order for it to stage swimming, ice-skating and boxing, and it was used for the 1934 British Empire (now Commonwealth) Games.

It was not until the Second World War that football really established itself at the stadium. Even though the FA Cup was suspended, a cup final was still held there each spring. In 1940 and '41, it was the Football League War Cup Final, in 1942 it was the London War Cup Final for the breakaway teams in the London League and for the remaining two years it was the Football League South Cup Final. England had only played seven times at Wembley before the war, all against Scotland, but during the hostilities they made eight appearances (including three against Wales) and then played two Victory Internationals against France and Belgium. The Belgians and Dutch, whose refugees had been housed at the stadium, had played the first game between two foreign teams, in 1941.

Arthur Elvin was very generous to the war effort and made the stadium available on numerous occasions, with proceeds going to war charities. He was knighted in 1946. The Middlesex Charity Cup Final was played at the stadium each year from 1942-45, as well as the Wembley Youth Committee League Cup Finals and a Civil Defence Cup Final. There was also a charity match each year from 1941-45 between the forces and the police, or rather, the professional footballers serving in those organisations.

The end of the war saw an International Trial match held at the stadium in 1946 and the first British Junior Cup Final for youths from the forces' training organisations, plus boys' clubs. This competition held its final at Wembley every year from 1948-56.

Olympic Showpiece

With London awarded the first post-war Olympics, Wembley was the natural choice for the showpiece events. In the football tournament, the semi-finals, final and bronze medal play-off were staged amid the athletics, hockey and equestrianism.

Wembley was now a huge name and the time was right to add more football matches to the schedule. The following year, 1949, saw the FA Amateur Cup Final move to Wembley, just in time for its golden era in the early 1950s, when 100,000 crowds were recorded for five consecutive finals. This competition ran until the demise of the amateur game in 1974, to be replaced by the FA Vase, which staged its finals at Wembley right up to 2000, though crowds were usually below 20,000.

The first schoolboy international played at Wembley was in 1950 and became a popular annual fixture, receiving a boost in the 1970s with live television coverage and a second fixture in 1970, '71 and each year from 1973-95. For the last two years of the stadium, with the FA having taken over the administration of the Under-15 game, the English Schools FA used the stadium for two Under-18 internationals.

Middlesex played their home leg of the 1950 FA County Youth Cup Final at Wembley and the new decade brought even more games to the stadium. The FA had seen that Wembley could attract top crowds to any England games at Wembley and Argentina became the first foreign visitors for a full international at the stadium. After that, the floodgates opened. England played Wales in the British Championship at Wembley for the first time, in 1952 and Northern Ireland were not far behind in 1955. All England's home games were at Wembley from 1966-95 and it became an honour for visiting nations to be invited to play on the hallowed turf. Four amateur internationals between England and Scotland were played at Wembley in the 1950s, hoping to capitalise on the popularity of the amateur game during the period, but these did not quite capture the public's imagination like the Amateur Cup Finals. England lost three of them and they were eventually discarded from the calendar after 1958.

One amateur fixture that did survive was the annual Varsity match between the Cambridge and Oxford Universities. First played at Wembley in 1953, a rearranged fixture after the postponement in December 1952, it ran until 1987, when the sparse crowds could no longer justify use of the stadium.

The FA Cup Final continued to grow in popularity throughout the 1950s and live television coverage meant that the fixture was switched to the week after the end of the league season so as not to affect other attendances. From 1953 onwards it was the only fixture of the day. The clamour for more midweek games led to Wembley installing floodlights in 1955, with a London representative side meeting Frankfurt in the European Fairs Cup, the stadium's first European tie. An Olympic Qualifying tie was played the following year, one of only two in the stadium's history. Strangely, they were both between Great Britain and Bulgaria, though 15 years apart. Wembley's history is littered with one-off games from various competitions. In 1957, the one and only Under-23 international to be held at Wembley was played between England and Romania. This was also the year that England played their first World Cup Qualifying match at the stadium.

First European Cup Final

Sir Arthur Elvin died in 1957 and for the next five years, there were very few additions to the football calendar with seven or eight games being played each year. The Centenary of the FA in 1963 brought about a few changes. Wembley acquired a new roof to cover all the spectators and the stadium saw its first European Cup Final, as well as two youth internationals, the first being the final of the European Youth Tournament. October brought the FA Centenary match between England and a star-studded FIFA line-up.

15

West Ham United won the European Cup-Winners Cup at the stadium in 1965 and the stadium was all set for the big extravaganza the following year. The 1966 World Cup was Wembley's and English football's greatest moment and the stadium staged 17 games during the year which also saw the first European Championship qualifier as two successive British Championships doubled up into Group Eight of the emerging continental competition.

The Football League Cup Final was played at Wembley for the first time in 1967. Though two Third Division sides won it in three years, it did not diminish the status of the competition which acquired European qualification for its winners. By 1982 it had also acquired its first sponsor and became the Milk Cup. Two years later it switched to a Sunday and received live television coverage for the first time. Further sponsors followed in Littlewoods, Rumbelows, Coca-Cola and Worthington.

Manchester United won Wembley's most famous European Cup Final in 1968 and the England v Scotland fixture was moved to the end of the season in 1969, along with the rest of the British Championship. The next addition to the football calendar arrived in 1970. The FA Trophy was introduced to cater for the semi-professional non-league ranks of the English game. Subtle increases to the number of games around this time brought a swift end to the re-emergence of the Wembley Lions speedway team, which required modifications to the corners of the pitch each time they raced.

Scotland fixture killed off

In 1973 Wembley celebrated Britain's entry into the European Economic Community with a game between The Three and The Six, the new and existing members of the Common Market. The following year brought two more competitions to the stadium; the short-lived National Association of Youth Clubs Cup Final and the FA Charity Shield. Live TV coverage of the former failed to prevent its demise after two years but the Charity Shield took on a new lease of life because of Wembley. It was in danger of being shelved after the League Champions and FA Cup winners had declined to take part in the preceding three years, but from 1974 onwards no club would ever refuse again such was the allure of the famous stadium.

Liverpool won the European Cup at Wembley in 1978 and three FA Cup Final replays were staged from 1981-83, but the stadium now slipped into a regular pattern of about thirteen games per year. The British Championship ended in 1984, but the Scotland fixture was played at Wembley as part of the Rous Cup in 1986 and '88 and then twice in the 1990s in the European Championship. Crowd violence and the advent of bigger competitions had killed off the world's oldest international rivalry.

In 1985, further initiatives brought yet more games to Wembley. The

16

Freight Rover Trophy Final arrived first and underwent four changes of names (Sherpa Van Trophy, Leyland Daf Cup, Autoglass Trophy and Auto Windscreens Shield) while still attracting large crowds. Under-16 internationals were introduced as curtain raisers to the FA Charity Shield as a showcase for the FA's new National School at Lilleshall. These ran until 1989, though in 1987 it was an Under-17 international, and the Under-16 game was played prior to the Football League Centenary match. In 1990 a women's international was played before the Charity Shield, the second to be played at Wembley. The first was in 1989 before England's Rous Cup tie with Chile. 1990 was also the year three Under-18 internationals and one Under-17 were played before England's World Cup warm-up matches. An Under-19 international was played the following year.

The Full Members Cup Final was added to the calendar in 1986. This subsequently became the Simod and then Zenith Cup Final, thanks to sponsorship, before its demise in 1992, as English clubs re-established themselves in European competitions following the five-year ban after the Heysel Stadium disaster.

Wembley was also aware of its responsibilities to the local community and was made available in 1987 for Brent Council's annual football festival and the London International Youth Festival, which included an under-14 girls match.

The Football League took over the stadium for a whole weekend in 1988 to organise a 16-team tournament to celebrate its centenary. This was the year when Wembley passed the twenty-games mark for the first time, not including the Football League's tournament but helped by the one-off return of the Middlesex Charity Cup Final and the pre-season Wembley International Tournament sponsored by Makita in the two following years.

There was a rapid increase to a staggering 27 games in 1990 with the pre-match youth internationals and the Football League Play-Off Finals which were generating so much interest that only Wembley could satisfy demand.

Semi-finals at the stadium

The stadium held its first FA Cup Semi-Final in 1991, because nowhere else could effectively stage the north London derby between Arsenal and Tottenham Hotspur. It happened again in 1993 when the same two teams were drawn together and public pressure forced the other semi-final between the two Sheffield clubs to be staged at Wembley as well on the same weekend. It was a controversial decision because some felt it was taking away some of the mystique of the final and the experiment lasted one more year when the futility of staging Manchester United against Oldham Athletic at Wembley became a step too far. The semi-finals did return, however, for one last time in 2000.

Wembley's last European Cup Final was held in 1992 with its second and last Cup-Winners Cup Final the following year which also saw two new competitions reach the stadium. The first of four Anglo-Italian Cup Finals was held but was a much-derided revival of a competition made popular in the 1970s. The Women's League Cup Final was played before the Third Division Play-Off Final in 1993, but received scant coverage and no other senior women's games were played at Wembley apart from the occasional pre-match short exhibition games.

In the mid-1990s Wembley became more alive to the potential of commercial interest, which manifested itself in a number of tournaments held at the stadium for employees of the media and sponsors. The first Carlsberg Pub Cup Final was played at Wembley in 1996, before the FA Vase Final, and the winners returned to contest an international challenge against the Danish Pub Cup winners later in the year.

If Wembley was no longer restricted to the best in the football world, it could still at least put on a great show when the best were in town and 'Euro 96' produced some of the stadium's finest memories. The European Championship revoked the spirit of thirty years earlier and England almost repeated their earlier success. They certainly made their mark on the tournament and were unlucky to lose on penalties.

The stadium never failed to excite with new competitions and in 1998 and '99, an ambitious experiment saw Arsenal playing their home games in the Champions League at Wembley. Sadly, despite some very attractive fixtures and full houses, they failed to progress to the last 16 in both years.

A day of Under-16 internationals for both sexes was also held in 1999 and one more competition made its debut in 2000 six months before the stadium closed. This was the Football League Youth Alliance Cup Final.

Wembley Stadium certainly made a massive contribution to English football history in its 77 years throughout all levels of the game and it is to be hoped the new stadium will continue in the same vein.

The Matches

Every match played at Wembley with reports
and scorers for the bigger ones

1920s	21
1930s	27
1940s	37
1950s	49
1960s	80
1970s	124
1980s	182
1990s	252
2000	349

FA CUP FINAL

Saturday 28th April 1923

Bolton Wanderers   **2-0**   **West Ham United**
Jack 3, J R Smith 54
126,047
Referee: D Asson (West Bromwich)

It is remarkable that this game took place. The FA had decided that no tickets would be issued and that anyone who turned up could pay on the day. They reckoned that Wembley would hold 117,000 but an estimated 200,000 people invaded the stadium, and swarmed all over the pitch.The match kicked off 45 minutes late, when the police finally drove the crowds back to the touchlines. One police horse, Billy, in particular, had more success than most, probably because of its colouring, and the game subsequently became known as 'The White Horse final'.

Bolton scored within three minutes, when David Jack intercepted a clearance from Young, and smashed an unstoppable shot past Hufton. They increased their lead in the second half, when Vizard's cross was volleyed against the underside of the bar, by John Smith. The referee ruled that it had crossed the line, before rebounding back into play.

Neither side had previously won a major trophy, and this was their first meeting. Bolton were appearing in their third final, having lost 4-1 to Notts County at Goodison Park in 1894, and 1-0 to Manchester City at Crystal Palace ten years later. They had knocked out the holders, Huddersfield Town, in the last 16. West Ham had never previously progressed beyond the last 16, but had become the third Second Division side in four years, to reach the final. The other two had lost.

West Ham were in only their fourth season in the league, but the following week clinched promotion, as runners-up on goal average, ahead of Leicester City, despite losing their last match, at home, to Notts County, who went on to win the Second Division Championship.

Bolton were to win the FA Cup twice more in the 1920's. But West Ham had to wait another 41 years before they finally got their hands on the FA Cup, although they did win the Football League War Cup, at Wembley, in 1940.

Bolton: Pym, Haworth, Finney, Nuttall, Seddon, Jennings, Butler, Jack, Smith (J R), Smith (J) – capt, Vizard. manager: Charles Foweraker
West Ham: Hufton, Henderson, Young, Bishop, Kay – capt, Tresadern, Richards, Brown (W), Watson, Moore (W), Ruffell. manager: Syd King

BRITISH CHAMPIONSHIP

Saturday 12th April 1924

England   **1-1**   **Scotland**
Walker 60   Taylor og 40
37,250
Referee: T Dougray (Scotland)

Wales had already won the British Championship, for only the third time, winning all three of their games, including a 2-0 win over Scotland, at Ninian Park and a 2-1 win over England, at Ewood Park. England had also lost 2-1 to Ireland at Windsor Park and needed to win, to avoid finishing bottom, for the first time. Scotland, the British Champions for the previous three years, needed a point to finish runners-up.

The Scots took the lead just before the interval. A Clunas free kick came to Cowan, whose shot hit the post, rebounded against goalkeeper Ted Taylor and went in.

On the hour England were level, when Buchan headed across goal, for Billy Walker to score the equaliser.

Scotland were to regain the British Championship, the following year, and keep it for a further three years. England had to wait until 1927 to beat Scotland again, but not before finishing bottom again, in 1926.

England: Taylor (Huddersfield), Smart (Aston Villa), Wadsworth (Huddersfield), Moss (Aston Villa) – capt, Spencer* (Newcastle), Barton (Birmingham), Butler* (Bolton), Jack (Bolton), Buchan (Sunderland), Walker (Aston Villa), Tunstall (Shefffield U)
Scotland: Harper (Hibernian), Smith* (Ayr Utd), McCloy* (Ayr Utd), Clunas* (Sunderland), Morris (Raith R), McMullan (Partick) – capt, Archibald (Rangers), Cowan* (Newcastle), Harris* (Newcastle), Cunningham (Rangers), Morton (Rangers)
*first cap

Final table	P	W	D	L	F	A	Pts
Wales	3	3	0	0	5	1	6
Scotland	3	1	1	1	3	3	3
Ireland	3	1	0	2	2	4	2
England	3	0	1	2	3	5	1

FA CUP FINAL

Saturday 26th April 1924

Aston Villa　　　　　　　**0-2**　　　**Newcastle United**
　　　　　　　　　　　　　　　　　　　　　Harris 83, Seymour 85

91,695
Referee: W Russell (Swindon)

Aston Villa had won the FA Cup a record six times, including a 2-0 win over Newcastle in the 1905 final, at Crystal Palace. Their sixth win had been in 1920, beating Huddersfield Town 1-0 at Stamford Bridge. The 1905 final was Newcastle's first in a run of five finals in seven years, which only brought one win, in 1910, when they beat Barnsley 2-0, in a replay at Goodison Park. They lost the Cup the following year, 1-0 to Bradford City, in another replayed final, at Old Trafford.

Villa had beaten Newcastle 6-1 five days earlier, but although they had most of the play at Wembley they could not score.

So with seven minutes left, Newcastle broke away and a McDonald shot was saved by Jackson only for Neil Harris to score from the rebound. Within three minutes, the issue was beyond doubt when Stan Seymour struck a brilliant shot past Jackson from another breakaway move.

Newcastle were League Champions three years later and won the Cup again in 1932, but it was another 33 years before Villa won the FA Cup for a record seventh time.

Aston Villa: Jackson, Smart, Mort, Moss – capt, Milne, Blackburn, York, Kirton, Capewell, Walker, Dorrell. manager: George Ramsay
Newcastle: Bradley, Hampson, Hudspeth – capt, Mooney, Spencer, Gibson, Low, Cowan, Harris, McDonald, Seymour. manager: Frank Watt

Friday 2nd May 1924

RAF Manston beat the holders, RAF Cran-well, in the RAF Senior Cup final. It was only the fourth match to be played at the stadium, but the press largely ignored it.

FA CUP FINAL

Saturday 25th April 1925

Cardiff City　　　　　　　**0-1**　　　**Sheffield United**
　　　　　　　　　　　　　　　　　　　　　Tunstall 30

91,763
Referee: G Watson (Nottingham)

In only their fifth season in the League, Cardiff had become the first Welsh club to reach the FA Cup final. United had won the Cup three times previously; the last occasion being in 1915, with a 3-0 victory over Chelsea, in the final at Old Trafford.

Cardiff finished 11th in the First Division, after finishing runners-up on goal average to Huddersfield Town, the previous season. United finished 14th.

The only goal came after half-an-hour. A long pass from Pantling was missed by Cardiff defender Wake and fell to Fred Tunstall, who controlled the ball and stabbed it past Farquharson. Cardiff subsequently failed to break down the United defence.

Cardiff returned two years later to win the FA Cup, but United had reached their peak and were relegated to the Second Division in 1934. This did not stop them reaching Wembley, though, in 1936.

Cardiff: Farquharson, Nelson, Blair, Wake, Keenor – capt, Hardy, Davies (W), Gill, Nicholson, Beadles, Evans. manager: Fred Stewart

Sheffield Utd: Sutcliffe, Cook, Milton, Pantling, King, Green, Mercer, Boyle, Johnson (H), Gillespie – capt, Tunstall. manager: John Nicholson

FA CUP FINAL

Saturday 24th April 1926

Bolton Wanderers   **1-0**   **Manchester City**
Jack 76
91,447
Referee: I Baker (Crewe)

Bolton returned to Wembley after winning the first final at the stadium three years earlier. City had also won the Cup once, in 1904, when, ironically, they beat Bolton, 1-0 at Crystal Palace. In an earlier round, they had thrashed Huddersfield Town, heading for a record third successive League Championship, 4-0.

Bolton finished eighth in the First Division. City, battling against relegation to the Second Division, had not beaten Bolton for three seasons.

Wembley's first Lancashire derby was settled 14 minutes from time, after Bolton 'keeper Dick Pym had performed heroics, to stop the City forwards. A Vizard cross was drilled into the net by David Jack who had scored Wembley's first goal in 1923.

Bolton were back at Wembley for their third FA Cup win in 1929. City missed a penalty in their last match the following week at Newcastle United and were relegated.

But it took them just two years to return to the top flight as Second Division champions and they returned to Wembley in 1933.

Bolton: Pym, Haworth, Greenhalgh, Nuttall, Seddon, Jennings, Butler, Jack, Smith (J R), Smith (J) – capt, Vizard. manager: Charles Foweraker

Manchester C: Goodchild, Cookson, McCloy, Pringle, Cowan, McMullan – capt, Austin, Browell, Roberts, Johnson, Hicks. manager: Peter Hodge

FA CUP FINAL

Saturday 23rd April 1927

Arsenal   **0-1**   **Cardiff City**
                                             Ferguson 74
91,206
Referee: W Bunnell (Preston)

Neither side had previously won a major trophy. Arsenal were appearing in their first final while Cardiff had reached their second final in three years and were once again attempting to take the FA Cup out of England for the first time. They had already knocked out the holders, Bolton Wanderers in the last 16.

The only goal of a defensive game was scored with about a quarter of an hour left, and was a personal disaster for the Arsenal 'keeper Lewis. From a pass by Davies, a seemingly harmless looking shot from Hugh Ferguson squirmed out of the grasp of Lewis and ended up in the net. A sad end to Arsenal's first final. They blamed the mistake on the sheen on the new jersey worn by the hapless goalkeeper, and thereafter, legend has it, Arsenal always washed the jersey of the goalkeeper before a Cup final.

Arsenal reached the semi-finals again the following year and had only to wait a further two years to win the FA Cup for the first time. Cardiff finished bottom of the Third Division South just seven years later and had to apply for re-election to the Football League. They have yet to emulate those glory years of the 1920's.

Arsenal: Lewis (D), Parker, Kennedy (A), Baker, Butler, John, Hulme, Buchan – capt, Brain, Blyth, Hoar. manager: Herbert Chapman
Cardiff: Farquharson, Nelson, Watson, Keenor – capt, Sloan, Hardy, Curtis, Irving, Ferguson, Davies (L), McLachlan. manager: Fred Stewart

BRITISH CHAMPIONSHIP

Saturday 31st March 1928

England	1-5	Scotland

England
Kelly 89
80,868
Referee: W Bell (Scotland)

Scotland
Jackson 3, 65, 85, James 44, 67

Wales had already won the British Championship for the fourth time, beating England, 2-1 at Turf Moor on the way. Ireland had finished runners-up after beating both England and Scotland who were now left to fight for bottom place. Scotland, British Champions for the previous three years, needed a point to avoid finishing bottom for the first time. England, who had shared the Championship the previous year, needed to win to avoid finishing last for the third time in five years.

Scotland humiliated England with skill and speed in very wet conditions to earn the legendary status of 'Wembley Wizards'. The turning point came very early, when a shot from Smith hit the inside of a post. Scotland cleared the ball upfield, and promptly took the lead; Alan Morton's cross being headed in by Alec Jackson. Just before half-time, Alex James beat two men and smashed the ball past Hufton, from outside the box.

In the second half, England were outplayed by Scotland's diminutive forwards. In the 66th minute, James again beat two defenders and his cross was headed in by Jackson. A few minutes later, a Gallacher run was stopped by Jones but the ball fell for James. With five minutes remaining, another Morton cross was met by a spectacular Jackson finish, to complete his hat-trick and England astonishingly, were five goals down. In the dying seconds, Bob Kelly scored for England from a free kick from well outside the box.

England had lost all three of their British Championship games for the first time, and had suffered their heaviest defeat since losing 6-1 to Scotland at the Kennington Oval in 1881. Scotland regained the Championship the following year, beating runners-up England 1-0 at Hampden Park. But it was another ten years before Scotland won again at Wembley and England were to take their revenge in 1930.

England: Hufton (West Ham), Goodall (Huddersfield) – capt, Jones (Blackburn), Edwards (Leeds), Wilson* (Huddersfield), Healless (Blackburn), Hulme (Arsenal), Kelly (Huddersfield), Dean (Everton), Bradford (Birmingham), Smith (Huddersfield)
Scotland: Harkness (Queens Park), Nelson (Cardiff), Law* (Chelsea), Gibson (Aston Villa), Bradshaw* (Bury), McMullan (Man City) – capt, Jackson (Huddersfield), Dunn (Hibernian), Gallacher (Newcastle), James (Preston), Morton (Rangers)
*first cap

Final table	P	W	D	L	F	A	Pts
Wales	3	2	1	0	6	4	5
Ireland	3	2	0	1	4	2	4
Scotland	3	1	1	1	7	4	3
England	3	0	0	3	2	9	0

FA CUP FINAL

Saturday 21st April 1928

Blackburn Rovers   **3-1**   **Huddersfield Town**
Roscamp 1, 85, McLean 22   Jackson 55
92,041
Referee: T Bryan (Willenhall)

Blackburn were aiming to equal Aston Villa's record of six FA Cup wins, but their last had been in 1891 when they beat Notts County 3-1 at Kennington Oval. In the semi-finals they had beaten the previous year's finalists Arsenal. Huddersfield had won the Cup only once, in 1922, when they beat Preston North End 1-0 at Stamford Bridge, and they had just come through a gruelling semi-final with Sheffield United which went to two replays.

Huddersfield were battling with Everton in an attempt to regain the League Championship for the fourth time in five years, having completed the first hat-trick of League Championships two years earlier. Their opponents were becalmed in mid-table.

Wembley's first Roses match got off to a sensational start with Blackburn scoring in the first minute. Healless knocked the ball across, Puddefoot barged into 'keeper Mercer as he came to collect the ball and Jack Roscamp touched it over the line.

Huddersfield fought back, but found themselves two down midway through the first half as Tom McLean struck a great shot from just inside the penalty area. Huddersfield did score in the second half, however, when a fine passing move left Alec Jackson to prod it past Crawford as the 'keeper came out. They pushed men forward, in search of an equaliser, but they were caught on the break in the dying minutes as Roscamp took a pass from Thornewell and rifled his second past Mercer.

This was Blackburn's only highlight in a very long barren spell. Their next final was 32 years later, but they did reach the Football League War Cup final in 1940.

Huddersfield's long season finally caught up with them and they finished League runners-up, for the second year in succession. They reached the semi-finals again the following year and the final again the year after. But they were beginning a steady decline from heights they have not reached since.

Blackburn: Crawford, Hutton, Jones, Healless – capt, Rankin, Campbell, Thornewell, Puddefoot, Roscamp, McLean, Rigby. manager: Bob Crompton
Huddersfield: Mercer, Goodall, Barkas, Redfern, Wilson, Steele, Jackson, Kelly, Brown, Stephenson – capt, Smith. manager: Jack Chaplin

Southern Amateur League
First Division

Saturday 29th September 1928

Ealing Association 1
Woosnam
Hastings and St. Leonards 0

The first amateur match to be held at Wembley Stadium, Ealing's new home ground for an experimental season. They had won the 'double' of Southern Amateur League Championship and Amateur FA Cup in 1927 but they were now in a stage of rebuilding. Martin Woosnam's winner against the previous season's Second Division Champions hid a poor attacking performance which gave warning of troubles ahead.

The 1928-29 season was unique in Wembley's history for this proliferation of amateur matches. It was originally planned that a team formed especially to enter the Football League, called the Argonauts, would play there but they were not elected and Ealing took over the venue. By the following summer the stadium's owner Arthur Elvin had decided speedway was a more lucrative form of paying the bills.

Saturday 13th October 1928

Ealing Association 0
Ipswich Town 4
Gibbs, Rogers 2, Bugg

Ealing were out of their depth again as the eventual runners-up gave them a resounding defeat. Ipswich were elected to the Football League in 1938. They reached the First Division in 1961 and incredibly marked their debut season in the top flight by winning the League Championship. Fifty years after beating Ealing they returned to Wembley to win the FA Cup.

Saturday 20th October 1928

Ealing Association 0
Midland Bank 4
Probyn og, Sugden, Ewer, Irwin

Ealing did not deserve to lose by four goals, but once again their finishing let them down.

Saturday 27th October 1928

Ealing Association 1
Farnfield
Bank Of England 5
Gray 2, Stone 2, Dyson

The third successive four-goal deficit for Ealing and all at Wembley. The Bank of England had also put five past them at Roehampton three weeks before.

Saturday 3rd November 1928

Ealing Association 0
Westminster Bank 3
Grigg 2, Bickel

Ealing gave a much improved performance, but still lacked a goalscorer.

Saturday 10th November 1928

Ealing Association 4
Farnfield, Woosnam 3
Barclays Bank 2
Lewis, Punnett

Ealing were two goals down before at last, finding their scoring touch. Martin Woosnam returned to the side and inspired a spectacular fightback with a hat-trick. Barclays Bank returned to Wembley two months later to beat Old Malvernians in the Amateur FA Cup.

Friendly

Saturday 17th November 1928

Cambridge U 5
Lewis 4, Parker
Casuals 2
Watson, Lowe

Cambridge made the first of what was to become an annual trip to the stadium. They had to come from behind twice before defeating the famous old amateur club. Casuals were to amalgamate with Corinthians 11 years later and the new club appeared at Wembley in the 1956 FA Amateur Cup final.

Southern Amateur League

First Division

Saturday 1st December 1928

Ealing Association 0
Aquarius 3
Finch, Schoffield 2 (1 pen)

Ealing slumped again.

Saturday 8th December 1928

Ealing Association 0
Old Lyonians 3
Noad, Massey 2

Ealing's experiment came to an end. Yet another drubbing, their sixth defeat in eight appearances with 24 goals conceded. They returned to Corfton Road in Ealing but failed to win another point. Not surprisingly, they were relegated to the Second Division for the first time after finishing bottom. Ealing were promoted as Second Division Champions in 1937 and now play in the Amateur Football Combination, having passed their centenary in 1991.

Amateur FA Cup

2nd Round

Saturday 12th January 1929

Old Malvernians 1
Barclays Bank 2

The old boys from Malvern College took advantage of Ealing's departure to use the stadium. But Barclays Bank's second appearance at Wembley brought them more success than the first.

Inter-Varsity Match

Saturday 26th January 1929

London U 0
Cambridge U 3
Grant, Valentine, Kemp-Welch

The first meeting between the two universities gave Cambridge their second Wembley win. But it was to be another 24 years before they appeared again at Wembley.

The holders went on to reach the semi-finals before losing 5-1 to the eventual winners Old Wykehamists at Selhurst Park.

Arthur Dunn Cup

Second Round Replay

Saturday 9th February 1929

Old Malvernians 4
Toppin, Abrams 2, Acheson-Gray
Old Cholmeleians 2
Fabian, Passingham

Schoolboy Charity Match

Saturday 9th March 1929

Middlesex 1
London 5

This fixture was held, to raise money for the National Playing Fields Association.

FA CUP FINAL

Saturday 27th April 1929

Bolton Wanderers   **2-0**   **Portsmouth**
Butler 79, Blackmore 87
92,576
Referee: A Josephs (South Shields)

Bolton were becoming regular visitors following their two earlier FA Cup wins in the 1920's. They had knocked out the holders Blackburn Rovers in the quarter-finals, and the previous year's other finalists Huddersfield Town in the semi-finals.

Portsmouth, by comparison, had never previously been beyond the last 32 in the competition.

Bolton's experience allowed them to control the game, but it was not until 11 minutes from the end that they scored. A run from Billy Butler ended in the winger shooting past Gilfillan and defender Mackie on the line.

Butler laid on the second with three minutes remaining, crossing for Harold Blackmore to blast it past the helpless 'keeper.

Bolton were not to return for a further 24 years but Portsmouth managed to establish themselves as a first division side and reached another final in 1934.

Bolton: Pym, Haworth, Finney, Kean, Seddon – capt, Nuttall, Butler, McClelland, Blackmore, Gibson, Cook. manager: Charles Foweraker
Portsmouth: Gilfillan, Mackie, Bell, Nichol, McIlwaine – capt, Thackeray, Forward, Smith (J), Weddle, Watson, Cook. manager: Jack Tinn

Wembley Hospital Cup Final

Saturday 22nd February 1930

Glacier Sports 4
Page 2, Hutson 2

Harrow St Mary's 5
Todd 3, Sanderson, Tipping
After extra time

The winning goal came two minutes from time. Glacier's 'keeper Heron saved a second half penalty from T Pratt.

BRITISH CHAMPIONSHIP

Saturday 5th April 1930

England   **5-2**   **Scotland**
Watson 11, 28, Rimmer 30, 55, Jack 33   Fleming 49, 62
87,375
Referee: W McLean (Ireland)

For the first time Wembley was to decide the winners of the British Championship as both England and reigning champions Scotland had won both their previous matches. England had not won the championship outright since 1913 but Scotland had won, or shared it, seven times in the previous ten years.

England took the lead when Vic Watson took a pass from Jack and shot past Harkness. Then, in a five-minute spell, towards the end of the first half England scored three goals to destroy Scotland's resistance. Sammy Crooks created them all. First he crossed for Watson to head his second. Then, a cross to the far post found Ellis Rimmer's head. Following this, a corner by Crooks was neatly converted by David Jack

and Scotland were four goals down at the interval.

To their credit, they did not give up. In the second half, Hibbs failed to hold a long shot from Craig and the ball bounced out for Jimmy Fleming to net the rebound. England soon quelled the revival when Rimmer took a pass from Bradford and shot past Harkness without breaking stride. Scotland managed a second with 28 minutes remaining. Morton's cross was converted by Fleming, but Scotland had suffered their heaviest defeat since losing 3-0 to England at Goodison Park in 1895.

This was the first of three successive British Championships for England, although they had to share it with Scotland the following year.

England: Hibbs (Birmingham), Goodall (Huddersfield), Blenkinsop (Sheffield W), Strange* (Sheffield W), Webster* (Middlesbrough), Marsden (Sheffield W), Crooks* (Derby Couty), Jack (Arsenal) – capt, Watson (West Ham), Bradford (Birmingham), Rimmer* (Sheffield W)
Scotland: Harkness (Hearts), Gray (Rangers), Law (Chelsea), Buchanan (Rangers), Meiklejohn (Rangers) – capt, Craig (Rangers), Jackson (Huddersfield), James (Arsenal), Fleming (Rangers), Stevenson (Motherwell), Morton (Rangers)
*first cap

Final table	P	W	D	L	F	A	Pts
England	3	3	0	0	14	2	6
Scotland	3	2	0	1	9	8	4
Ireland	3	1	0	2	8	6	2
Wales	3	0	0	3	2	17	0

FA CUP FINAL

Saturday 26th April 1930

Arsenal   **2-0**   **Huddersfield Town**
James 16, Lambert 88
92,448
Referee: T Crew (Leicester)

Having turned Huddersfield into a great side in the 1920's, their manager Herbert Chapman was about to transform Arsenal from a team without a major honour into one which would dominate the 1930's. The Gunners were in front early on. Alex James took a quick free kick after being fouled, playing the ball out to Bastin on the wing. James moved into the middle where he met the centre to set Arsenal on their way. They sat back in the second half and rode their luck as their 'keeper Preedy made several

errors. As so often happens, though, the dominant side were caught on the break. With two minutes remaining, a long clearance from James sent Jack Lambert clean through to put the ball past Turner. Arsenal had at last won a major trophy. The following year they became the first London club to win the League Championship, and were back at Wembley in 1932. Huddersfield finished as League runners-up to Arsenal in 1934 and reached another final four years later.

Arsenal: Preedy, Parker – capt, Hapgood, Baker, Seddon, John , Hulme, Jack , Lambert, James, Bastin. manager: Herbert Chapman
Huddersfield: Turner, Goodall, Spence, Naylor, Wilson – capt, Campbell, Jackson, Kelly, Davies, Raw, Smith. manager: Clem Stephenson

Football League
Third Division South
Saturday 22nd November 1930

Clapton Orient 3
Cropper 2, Tricker
Brentford 0

Orient had moved to a new ground at Lea Bridge Road but the Football League had declared it unsuitable and they were given permission to use Wembley for home matches while the new ground was undergoing changes. This was a good win in front of 10,300 spectators as Brentford had finished as Third Division South runners-up to Plymouth Argyle the previous season. In 1933, Brentford were to win the Third Division South Championship, winning promotion to the Second Division for the first time while Orient avoided having to apply for re-election to the Football League on goal average. Two years later, Brentford were Second Division Champions.

Clapton Orient: Wood, Morley, Evans, Lawrence, Galbraith, Bolton, Jack , Cropper, Tricker, Fowler, Fletcher. manager: Peter Proudfoot

Brentford: Fox, Stevenson, Adamson, Davies, Bain, Salt, Foster, Lane, Sherlaw, Blakemore, Berry. manager: Harry Curtis

Saturday 6th December 1930

Clapton Orient 3
Fowler 2, Tricker
Southend United 1
Jones

Orient came from behind to win their last match at Wembley before moving to their new ground. The pitch had been described as an 'emerald oasis in a desert of concrete', so sparse was the crowd. Southend finished in their highest ever position, fifth, although by 1935,they would be applying for re-election to the Football League. Orient had been relegated from the Second Division in 1929 and they would have to wait until 11 years after the end of the war to win promotion.

Clapton Orient: Blackwell, Morley, Broadbent, Lawrence, Galbraith, Bolton, Jack, Cropper, Tricker, Fowler, Fletcher. manager: Peter Proudfoot
Southend: Moore, French, Robinson, Ward, Wilson, Johnson, Barnett, Jones, Shankly, Donovan, Crompton. manager: Ted Birnie

FA CUP FINAL

Saturday 25th April 1931

Birmingham 1-2 **West Bromwich Albion**
Bradford 57
92,406
Referee: A Kingscott (Long Eaton)
W G Richardson 25, 58

Birmingham had never been beyond the last 16 before but West Brom had strong Cup traditions. They were appearing in their seventh final and had twice won. Their last win, however, had been 39 years earlier when they beat Aston Villa 3-0 at Kennington Oval.

Birmingham finished 19th in the First Division while West Brom were on the verge of returning to the First Division after four seasons in the Second. The last Second Division team to win the Cup had been Barnsley, in 1912, when, ironically, they beat West Brom.

In very wet conditions the Second Division side took the lead. Billy Richardson got on to the end of a cross from Carter, shot and fell. Barkas blocked it but Richardson managed to scramble it over the line.

Their local rivals drew level after a long ball from Cringan was picked up by Joe Bradford to shoot past Pearson. Within a minute West Brom were back in front. Richardson collected Cringan's attempted back pass and scored his second.

It was 25 years before Birmingham were to reach the final again and they have yet to win the trophy.

West Brom secured promotion the following week to complete a memorable season. They returned to Wembley in 1935.

Birmingham: Hibbs, Liddell, Barkas – capt, Cringan, Morrall, Leslie, Briggs, Crosbie, Bradford, Gregg, Curtis. manager: Leslie Knighton
West Brom: Pearson, Shaw, Trentham, Magee, Richardson (W), Edwards, Glidden – capt, Carter, Richardson (W G), Sandford, Wood. manager: Fred Everiss

BRITISH CHAMPIONSHIP

Saturday 9th April 1932

England	3-0	Scotland

Waring 36, Barclay 80
Crooks 88
92,180
Referee: S Thompson (Ireland)

This was virtually the same situation as in 1930. Both teams had won both their previous matches but now England had been British champions for the past two years. Scotland however, had beaten England 2-0 at Hampden Park the previous year to share the Championship.

Ten minutes before half time, a Houghton corner was punched out by Hamilton, but Pongo Waring headed it down and then shot to put England ahead. England sealed their victory late in the game when Houghton crossed and a shot from Bobby Barclay took a wicked deflection off Craig to send Hamilton the wrong way. In the closing minutes Sammy Crooks, the hero of 1930, scored the best goal of the game to complete the scoring.

England: Pearson* (West Brom), Shaw* (West Brom), Blenkinsop (Sheffield W) – capt, Strange (Sheffield W), O'Dowd* (Chelsea), Weaver* (Newcastle), Crooks (Derby Couty), Barclay* (Shefffield U), Waring (Aston Villa), Johnson (Everton), Houghton (Aston Villa)
Scotland: Hamilton* (Rangers), Crapnell (Airdrie) – capt, Nibloe (Kilmarnock), McNab (Dundee), Craig (Motherwell), Brown (Rangers), Archibald (Rangers), Marshall* (Rangers), Dewar* (Third Lanark), Napier* (Celtic), Morton (Rangers)
*first cap

Final table	P	W	D	L	F	A	Pts
England	3	3	0	0	12	3	6
Scotland	3	2	0	1	6	6	4
Ireland	3	1	0	2	7	9	2
Wales	3	0	0	3	3	10	0

FA CUP FINAL

Saturday 23rd April 1932

Arsenal	1-2	**Newcastle United**

John 15
92,298
Referee: W Harper (Stourbridge)

Allen 38, 72

Arsenal were attempting to regain the FA Cup for the second time in three years, having won it for the first time in 1930. Newcastle had last won the Cup in 1924. Arsenal had won the League Championship for the first time the previous year and were chasing Everton in an attempt to retain it. Newcastle finished 11th in the First Division.

The favourites took the lead when a cross from Hulme was misjudged by the Newcastle defence and Bob John took the easiest of opportunities to score. But Newcastle equalised with one of the most controversial goals ever scored in an FA Cup final.

Davidson's pass down the wing seemed to be too long for Richardson who crossed after the ball had clearly gone over the goal line. As Jack Allen put the ball in the net the Arsenal players stood motionless waiting for the referee to give a goal kick. To their amazement he gave a goal.

It stayed this way until, with 18 minutes left, a Roberts miskick was picked up by Allen. With defenders converging on him he moved out to the left and drove a low shot into the corner past Moss to give Newcastle the Cup.

Arsenal had to concede defeat in the title race the following week and finished runners-up. But they found ample consolation in winning the next three League Championships, so emulating Huddersfield Town's feat of the 1920's. Following this, they returned to win the FA Cup again. Newcastle were relegated to the Second Division two years later, and it was 19 years before they again won the Cup.

Arsenal: Moss, Parker – capt, Hapgood, Jones, Roberts, Male , Hulme, Jack , Lambert, Bastin, John. manager: Herbert Chapman
Newcastle: McInroy, Nelson – capt, Fairhurst, McKenzie, Davidson, Weaver, Boyd, Richardson, Allen, McMenemy, Lang. manager: Andy Cunningham

FA CUP FINAL

Saturday 29th April 1933

Everton   **3-0**   **Manchester City**
Stein 41, Dean 52, Dunn 80
92,950
Referee: E Wood (Sheffield)

Everton were appearing in their fifth final, but their first at Wembley. Their solitary success had been in 1906 when they beat Newcastle United 1-0 at Crystal Palace. The following year they lost the final 2-1 to Sheffield Wednesday at Crystal Palace. City's only FA Cup win had been two years before Everton's but they had appeared at Wembley in 1926.

Everton had had an eventful three years; relegated in 1930, straight back as Second Division Champions in 1931 and then League Champions in their first season back. Their defence of the title, though, saw them drop to 11th in the First Division. City finished 16th, their lowest position since promotion in 1928.

Four minutes before half-time Everton took the lead when from 25 yards out near the touchline Britton tried a speculative lob into the middle. Langford misjudged its flight, coming out too far. He got a touch, but it left Jimmy Stein with an easy tap-in. Seven minutes into the second half Britton tried the same lofted pass from a similar position. This time, Dixie Dean charged Langford and the ball ended up in the net. Geldard's corner was headed in by Jimmy Dunn with ten minutes left for the biggest winning margin in an FA Cup final since 1915.

City returned the following year to win the FA Cup but it was to be another 33 years before Everton lifted the trophy again.

Sir Matt Busby, who was to make his name as manager of City's near neighbours Manchester United, made the first of five playing appearances at Wembley, two for City and three during wartime for Scotland.

Everton: Sagar, Cook, Cresswell, Britton, White, Thomson, Geldard, Dunn , Dean – capt, Johnson, Stein. manager: Thomas McIntosh
Manchester C: Langford, Cann, Dale, Busby, Cowan – capt, Bray, Toseland, Marshall, Herd, McMullan, Brook. manager: Wilf Wild

London Occupational League final

Wednesday 21st March 1934

Greenwich Trafalgar 0
Walthamstow Fellowship 1
Jones

A rare day out, for London's unemployed, with the Prince of Wales presenting the honours. Greenwich goalkeeper, Chalk saved a penalty from Bence.

BRITISH CHAMPIONSHIP

Saturday 14th April 1934

England	**3-0**	**Scotland**

Bastin 43, Brook 75, Bowers 85
92,363
Referee: S Thompson (Ireland)

Wales had already retained the British Championship, beating Scotland 3-2 at Ninian Park and England 2-1 at St James' Park. Scotland had also lost 2-1 to Ireland at Parkhead, and had to win or they would finish bottom for the first time.

Just before half-time Brook passed to Cliff Bastin who let fly with a beauty from 25 yards. The ball was hit hard and low and its swerve was enough to beat Jackson. With 15 minutes remaining an Eric Brook free kick was deflected past Jackson for the second goal. Ten minutes later Brook's cross was headed in by Jack Bowers to repeat the scoreline of 1932 and leave Scotland without a point for the first time.

Scotland recovered to share the Championship the following year after beating them at Hampden Park for the fourth time in succession. Strange that they lost on three successive visits to Wembley during the same period.

England: Moss* (Arsenal), Cooper (Derby Couty) – capt, Hapgood (Arsenal), Stoker (Birmingham), Hart (Leeds), Copping (Leeds), Crooks (Derby Couty), Carter* (Sunderland), Bowers (Derby Couty), Bastin (Arsenal), Brook (Man City)
Scotland: Jackson (Chelsea), Anderson (Hearts), McGonagle (Celtic), Massie (Hearts) – capt, Smith* (Kilmarnock), Miller (St Mirren), Cook* (Bolton), Marshall (Rangers), Gallacher (Chelsea), Stevenson (Motherwell), Connor (Sunderland)
*first cap

Final table	P	W	D	L	F	A	Pts
Wales	3	2	1	0	6	4	5
England	3	2	0	1	7	2	4
Ireland	3	1	1	1	3	5	3
Scotland	3	0	0	3	3	8	0

FA CUP FINAL

Saturday 28th April 1934

Manchester City	**2-1**	**Portsmouth**
Tilson 73, 87		Rutherford 26

93,258
Referee: S Rous (Watford)

City were back to make amends for their performance the previous year. Portsmouth's only previous final had been in 1929.

It was Portsmouth who took the lead when Weddle sent Sep Rutherford away down the left. He cut inside and fired past Swift. They held it until 17 minutes from the end when captain Allen went off injured. City seized their chance. Brook set off on a mazy run, passed to Fred Tilson and the striker, who had netted four times in the semi-final, shot past Gilfillan for the equaliser.

With the game heading for extra time, Herd's pass enabled Tilson to score again with three minutes left.

It was to be 21 years before City returned to Wembley. Portsmouth won for the first time in 1939. Referee Stanley Rous went on to become secretary of the FA, president of FIFA, from 1961-74 and to be knighted.

Manchester C: Swift, Barnett, Dale, Busby, Cowan – capt, Bray, Toseland, Marshall, Tilson, Herd, Brook. manager: Wilf Wild
Portsmouth: Gilfillan, Mackie, Smith (W), Nichol, Allen – capt, Thackeray, Worrall, Smith (J), Weddle, Easson, Rutherford. manager: Jack Tinn

FA CUP FINAL

Saturday 27th April 1935

Sheffield Wed	4-2	West Bromwich Albion

Palethorpe 2, Hooper 70, Rimmer 85, 89
Boyes 21, Sandford 75
93,204
Referee: A Fogg (Bolton)

Wednesday had won the Cup twice, the last occasion being in 1907 when they beat Everton 2-1 at Crystal Palace. They had eliminated Arsenal, heading for their third successive League Championship, in the quarter-final. West Brom had won in 1931.

Wednesday finished third in the First Division – the fourth time in five years. West Brom were ninth, their lowest since returning to the First Division in 1931.

In only the second minute, Jack Palethorpe controlled Hooper's cross before placing it past Pearson to give Wednesday the lead. West Brom drew level when Carter sent Wally Boyes away on a brilliant run which ended with a powerful shot into the net. With 20 minutes remaining Mark Hooper cut in from his wing to receive a ball from Starling and beat Pearson via the post with a swerving shot which barely crossed the line. West Brom came fighting back again, and five minutes later were level again. Boyes' throw-in found Ted Sandford whose shot from the edge of the box spun off Millership's head which took it into the angle of the goal.

Wednesday settled it in the last five minutes. Ellis Rimmer ran on to Sharp's long ball and headed it over the advancing 'keeper. He scored again, in the dying seconds. Wednesday were the first to score four in an FA Cup final since Bury in 1903.

Sheffield W: Brown, Nibloe, Catlin, Sharp, Millership, Burrows, Hooper, Surtees, Palethorpe, Starling – capt, Rimmer. manager: Billy Walker
West Brom: Pearson, Shaw, Trentham, Murphy, Richardson (W), Edwards, Glidden – capt, Carter, Richardson (W G), Sandford, Boyes. manager: Fred Everiss

BRITISH CHAMPIONSHIP

Saturday 4th April 1936

England	1-1	Scotland

Camsell 30
Walker pen 75
93,267
Referee: W Hamilton (Ireland)

Scotland had lost on their last three visits to Wembley but now needed only a point to win the British Championship outright for the first time since 1929. England's 2-1 defeat by Wales at Molineux meant that they had to beat Scotland to win the title.

After half an hour, Bastin dribbled his way along the touchline and put in a great cross which left George Camsell with the simple task of beating Dawson from close range. England held this lead until the 76th minute. Crum was brought down in the box by Hapgood and Tommy Walker made no mistake from the penalty to give Scotland the Championship and end their run of defeats at Wembley.

England: Sagar (Everton), Male (Arsenal), Hapgood (Arsenal) – capt, Crayston (Arsenal), Barker (Derby Couty), Bray (Man City), Crooks (Derby Couty), Barclay (Shefffield U), Camsell (Middlesbrough), Bastin (Arsenal), Brook (Man City)
Scotland: Dawson (Rangers), Anderson (Hearts), Cummings (Aston Villa), Massie (Aston Villa), Simpson (Rangers) – capt, Brown (Rangers), Crum* (Celtic), Walker (Hearts), McCulloch (Brentford), Venters (Rangers), Duncan (Derby Couty)
*first cap

Final table	P	W	D	L	F	A	Pts
Scotland	3	1	2	0	4	3	4
England	3	1	1	1	5	4	3
Wales	3	1	1	1	5	5	3
Ireland	3	1	0	2	5	7	2

FA CUP FINAL

Saturday 25th April 1936

Arsenal	**1-0**	**Sheffield United**

Drake 75
93,384
Referee: H Nattrass (Seaham)

Arsenal were appearing in their fourth final in ten years but had won the Cup only once. United had last won in 1925, their fourth win in the competition.

After winning the League Championship for the previous three years, Arsenal finished a lowly sixth. United had been in the Second Division for two years and had an outside chance of winning promotion.

The only goal came after Bastin's pass to Ted Drake enabled the prolific scorer to get past Johnson for the first time in the match and score with a well hit shot.

United had their chances, but Arsenal held on.

Arsenal won another League Championship two years later before war interrupted. They made two visits during the war and their third FA Cup win came in 1950. United's promotion hopes ended four days later.

They took another three years before winning promotion back to the First Division but they did not appear at Wembley again until the FA Cup Semi-final, of 1993.

Arsenal: Wilson (A), Male, Hapgood, Crayston, Roberts, Copping, Hulme, Bowden, Drake, James – capt, Bastin. manager: George Allison
Sheffield Utd: Smith, Hooper – capt, Wilkinson, Jackson, Johnson (T), McPherson, Barton, Barclay, Dodds, Pickering, Williams. manager: Ted Davison

University International

Thursday 7th January 1937

Great Britain 1
Collins
Germany 0

Two-and-a-half years before the two countries went to war with each other they met in a fairly low-key encounter which the Germans should have won. The British side was composed entirely of players from English universities.

Maurice Edelston went on to play for England at Wembley in a Wartime International in 1942 before embarking on a broadcasting career which saw him commentating for BBC Radio Two on FA Cup finals in the 1970's.

Great Britain: Reed, Hollis, Strasser, Leek, Pettit, Beswick, Mulrenan, Goodyear, Lee, Edelston, Collins

FA CUP FINAL

Saturday 1st May 1937

Preston North End	**1-3**	**Sunderland**

F O'Donnell 44
93,495
Referee: R Rudd (Kenton)

Gurney 52, Carter 70, Burbanks 87

Preston had won the FA Cup once before, way back in 1889 when they beat Wolverhampton Wanderers 3-0 at Kennington Oval. They also won the first League Championship that year. Since then their achievements had been modest. Their last final had been in 1922, when they lost 1-0 to Huddersfield Town at Stamford Bridge. Sunderland's only final had been in 1913 when they lost 1-0 to Aston Villa at Crystal Palace. Sunderland won the League Championship that year, and just failed to equal Preston's earlier 'double'.

Just on halftime Frank O'Donnell took a pass from Dougal and blasted it past Mapson to give Preston the lead. Sunderland came back strongly in the second half. From a 53rd minute corner by Burbanks,

Carter headed on for Bobby Gurney to score. With 20 minutes left, it was Gurney's header which laid on Sunderland's second for Raich Carter to shoot past Burns. Three minutes from the end Eddie Burbanks scored the third when he ran on to meet Gallacher's pass with a powerful drive.

Preston returned the following year to win the FA Cup and Sunderland nearly joined them in a repeat final, but lost in the semi-finals. They were not to win it again for 36 years.

Bill Shankly, the legendary Liverpool manager of the 1960's and '70's, made his Wembley debut.

Preston: Burns, Gallimore, Beattie (A), Shankly, Tremelling – capt, Milne, Dougal, Beresford,O'Donnell (F), Fagan, O'Donnell (H). manager: Tommy Muirhead

Sunderland: Mapson, Gorman, Hall, Thompson, Johnson, McNab, Duns, Carter – capt, Gurney, Gallacher, Burbanks. manager: Johnny Cochrane

Summer of 1937. The stadium was used for the final of a competition contested by the local Feathers clubs, which were organised for juniors, who met regularly for friendship, occupation, and recreation.

BRITISH CHAMPIONSHIP

Saturday 9th April 1938

England	0-1	Scotland
		Walker 6

93,267
Referee: W Hamilton (Ireland)

England had beaten both Ireland and the reigning British Champions Wales, and needed only a point to secure their first outright Championship since 1932. Scotland had lost 2-1 to Wales at Ninian Park and needed to win to share the Championship with England.

The only goal came after a poor clearance from Hapgood was knocked back in by an overhead kick from Milne to O'Donnell. He passed to Tommy Walker who shot past Woodley. England fought back, but there were no further goals and Scotland were good value for their victory.

The legendary Sir Stanley Matthews made his first appearance at Wembley. Matthews was the first Footballer of the Year in 1948 and won it again 15 years later at the unbelievable age of 48. He was also the first European Footballer of the Year in 1956.

England: Woodley (Chelsea), Sproston (Leeds), Hapgood (Arsenal) – capt, Willingham (Huddersfield), Cullis (Wolves), Copping (Arsenal), Matthews (Stoke City), Hall (Tottenham), Fenton* (Middlesbrough), Stephenson* (Leeds), Bastin (Arsenal)

Scotland: Cumming* (Middlesbrough), Anderson (Hearts), Beattie (A) (Preston), Shankly* (Preston), Smith (Preston), Brown (Rangers) – capt, Milne* (Middlesbrough), Walker (Hearts), O'Donnell (Preston), Mutch* (Preston), Reid (Brentford)
*first cap

Final table	P	W	D	L	F	A	Pts
England	3	2	0	1	7	3	4
Scotland	3	2	0	1	5	3	4
Ireland	3	1	0	2	3	8	2
Wales	3	1	0	2	3	4	2

FA CUP FINAL

Saturday 30th April 1938

Huddersfield Town   0-1   **Preston North End**

Mutch pen. 120

After extra time
93,497
Referee: A Jewell (London)

Huddersfield were back for their third Wembley final, having lost in 1928 and 1930. They had beaten the holders Sunderland in the semi-finals and were looking for their second FA Cup win against the team they had beaten in the 1922 final. On that occasion they had won with a penalty given for a foul apparently committed outside the area.

Preston were in their second successive final, having lost the previous year, and had knocked out Arsenal, who were heading for their fifth League Championship in eight years, in the last 16.

Huddersfield were now a shadow of their former selves and were battling against relegation to the Second Division. Preston were having their best season since promotion in 1934 and still had an outside chance of winning the League Championship for the first time since 1890.

A boring match seemed to be heading for a replay when in the very last minute of extra time George Mutch was tripped on the edge of the Huddersfield penalty area by Young. Mutch took the penalty himself and beat Hesford as the ball went in off the bar. As in 1922, the penalty award was disputed but this time the luck had gone Preston's way. It was the first penalty to be awarded in a Wembley FA Cup final.

In an extraordinary end to the league season the following week, Huddersfield escaped relegation by defeating the defending League Champions Manchester City to relegate them in the process. In an incredibly tight finish, the victory lifted them to 14th. They reached the FA Cup semi-finals again the following year, but their decline continued after the war and they were eventually relegated in 1952. They did not appear at Wembley again until the Autoglass Trophy final of 1994.

Preston's Championship hopes faded just two days later, but they returned to Wembley for the Football League War Cup final in 1941. They held on to their First Division status until 1949, returning two years later as Second Division Champions and they were back at Wembley in 1954.

Huddersfield: Hesford, Craig, Mountford, Willingham, Young – capt, Boot , Hulme, Isaac, McFadyen, Barclay, Beasley. manager: Clem Stephenson

Preston: Holdcroft, Gallimore, Beattie (A), Shankly, Smith (T) – capt, Batey, Watmough, Mutch, Maxwell, Beattie (R), O'Donnell (H). chairman: Jim Taylor

FA CUP FINAL

Saturday 29th April 1939

Portsmouth   4-1   **Wolverhampton Wanderers**

Barlow 29, Anderson 43, Parker 46, 71   Dorsett 54
99,370
Referee: T Thompson (Lemington)

Portsmouth were hoping to take the FA Cup south of London for the first time, despite losing their two previous finals. In the quarter-finals they had knocked out the holders Preston North End and in the semi-finals they had eliminated the previous year's other finalists Huddersfield Town.

Wolves had won the Cup twice before; the last occasion being in 1908 when they beat Newcastle United 3-1 in the final at Crystal Palace. Their last of five previous finals had been in 1921 when they went down 1-0 to Tottenham Hotspur at Stamford Bridge.

Portsmouth were a struggling First Division side and finished 17th while Wolves finished as League runners-up for the second year in succession to Everton.

The burden of being overwhelming favourites made Wolves look nervous and Portsmouth took the lead on the half-hour.

Bert Barlow, signed from Wolves, only two months earlier, took a pass from Anderson and struck a great shot past Scott into the corner. Jock Anderson scored the second just before half-time. Collecting Worrall's high cross, and going past Cullis, he shot. Scott got his hands to the ball but only succeeded in pushing it into the top of the net. Any hopes Wolves had of recovering were dashed only a minute into the second half. Scott initially saved from Bar-

low but the ball squirmed out of his grasp. He managed to recover and stopped it with one hand on the line. Unfortunately for him, Cliff Parker ran in and knocked the ball in before he could get his other hand on it.

Wolves struck back when Westcott put Dickie Dorsett through to score but they were never really in the game and Parker completed the scoring with his second, a header, from another Worrall cross.

Britain was at war five months later and Portsmouth could not defend the FA Cup for seven years but they reached the London War Cup final at Wembley in 1942 and won two successive League Championships at the end of the 1940's. Wolves were to win the FA Cup ten years later.

Portsmouth: Walker, Morgan, Rochford, Guthrie – capt, Rowe , Wharton, Worrall, McAlinden, Anderson, Barlow, Parker. manager: Jack Tinn

Wolves: Scott, Morris, Taylor, Galley, Cullis – capt, Gardiner, Burton, McIntosh, Westcott, Dorsett, Maguire. manager: Frank Buckley

---

Wembley Stadium played an important role during the war. Not only did it stage wartime cup finals and internationals for the Red Cross and other charities, but it was a temporary home for refugees. Due to the limited media coverage of these games, some details are missing.

Wartime International

Saturday 13th April 1940

England 0
Wales 1
B Jones 42
40,000
Referee: A Jewell (London)

Victory for the Welsh on their first visit thanks to Bryn Jones' winner, although this was not an official international. Five minutes from the end England had a great opportunity to equalise but Willie Hall's penalty went wide.

England: Bartram (Charlton), Bacuzzi (Fulham), Hapgood (Arsenal) – capt, Willingham (Huddersfield), Cullis (Wolves), Copping (Leeds), Matthews (Stoke City), Hall (Tottenham), Westcott (Wolves), Goulden (West Ham), Compton (Arsenal)

Wales: Sidlow (Wolves), Turner (Charlton) – capt, Williams (Millwall), Green (Charlton), Davies (Nottingham F), Witcomb (West Brom), Hopkins (Brentford), Dearson (Birmingham), Astley (Blackpool), Jones (B) (Arsenal), Jones (L) (Arsenal)

Football League War Cup Final

Saturday 8th June 1940

Blackburn Rovers 0
West Ham United 1
Small 36
42,399

Sam Small's winner made it a memorable occasion for West Ham, helping them to forget their defeat in Wembley's first ever match in 1923. This was a vastly different event, however, with a drastically reduced attendance.

Blackburn: Barron, Hough, Crook – capt, Whiteside, Pryde, Chivers, Rogers, Butt, Weddle, Clarke, Gucat. manager: Bob Crompton

West Ham: Conway, Bicknell – capt, Walker (C), Fenton, Walker (R), Cockcroft, Small, Macaulay, Foreman, Goulden, Foxall. manager: Charlie Paynter

Saturday 10th May 1941

Arsenal 1
D Compton 40
Preston North End 1
McLaren 10

60,000
Referee: F Milner (Wolverhampton)

Leslie Compton hit the foot of a post from a fifth-minute penalty for Arsenal. Preston needed a replay to lift the trophy and made it a 'double' with the Northern Regional League Championship.

Arsenal: Marks, Scott, Hapgood – capt, Crayston, Joy, Collett, Kirchen, Jones, Compton (L), Bastin, Compton (D). manager: George Allison
Preston: Fairbrother, Gallimore, Scott, Shankly, Smith (T) – capt, Beattie (A), Finney, McLaren, Dougal, Beattie (R), O'Donnell (H). chairman: Jim Taylor

Replay:
Saturday 31st May 1941
Arsenal 1
Gallimore og
Preston North End 2
R Beattie 2
(Ewood Park, Blackburn)

Charity Match

Wednesday 4th June 1941

Met Police 3
RAF 6
Referee: H Williams (London)

This was to become an annual fixture in aid of the war charities. Newspapers often failed to report on these midweek evening matches. These were the line-ups which appeared in the programme.

Met Police: Mason (QPR), Bicknell (West Ham) – capt, F Dawes (Crystal P), Forsyth (Millwall), Hiles (Fulham), Weaver (Chelsea), Bonass (QPR), Mangnall (QPR), Compton (L) (Arsenal), A Dawes (Aldershot), Spence (Chelsea)
RAF: Boulton (Derby Couty), Scott (Arsenal), Buchanan (Chelsea), Hunt (Barnsley), Joy (Arsenal), Buckingham (Tottenham), Kirchen (Arsenal), Smith (Crystal P), Mills (Chelsea), Gibbons (Tottenham), Houghton (Aston Villa)

Wartime International

Saturday 4th October 1941

England 2
Welsh 16, Hagan 35
Scotland 0
65,000
Referee: F Milner (Wolverhampton)

Scotland's first defeat at Wembley, since 1934. Joe Mercer, Footballer of the Year in 1950, made his first appearance at Wembley.

England: Marks (Arsenal), Bacuzzi (Fulham), Hapgood (Arsenal) – capt, Goslin (Bolton), Cullis (Wolves), Mercer (Everton), Matthews (Stoke City), Mannion (Middlesbrough), Welsh (Charlton), Hagan (Shefffield U), Compton (D) (Arsenal)
Scotland: Dawson (Rangers), Carabine (Third Lanark) – capt, Beattie (A) (Preston), Shankly (Preston), Dykes (Hearts), McDonald (Celtic), Caskie (Everton), Walker (Hearts), Smith (Rangers), Wallace (Clyde), Williams (Clyde)

Saturday 11th October 1941

Belgium 5
De Busscher 2, Schuermans, Landrieux, Clerinckx
Netherlands 4
Luttmer, Van Elsacker, Van der Gender 2
7,000

Wembley had a special relationship with these two countries as the stadium had been used to house many Belgian and Dutch refugees. A very attacking game saw Netherlands take an early two-goal lead but it was Belgium who proved most prolific on the day.

Saturday 17th January 1942

England 3
Hagan 1, Lawton 53, 65
Scotland 0
64,000
Referee: Ross-Gower (Scots Guards)

England: Marks (Arsenal), Bacuzzi (Fulham), Hapgood (Arsenal) – capt, Willingham (Huddersfield), Cullis (Wolves), Welsh (Charlton), Matthews (Stoke City), Mannion (Middlesbrough), Lawton (Everton), Hagan (Sheffield U), Compton (D) (Arsenal)
Scotland: Dawson (Rangers), Carabine (Third Lanark), Beattie (A) (Preston), Shankly (Preston), Dykes (Hearts), Busby (Liverpool) – capt, Caskie (Everton), Walker (Hearts), Gillick (Everton), Black (Hearts), Johnston (Rangers)

Wednesday 22nd April 1942

The Wembley Youth Committee League staged their Junior Cup final at the stadium between Glacier and Kingsbury, who were to return the following year. The Geipel Cup was presented to the winners.

Charity Match

Wednesday 6th May 1942

Met Police 3
A Dawes, Compton, Spence
RAF 6
Drake 3, Rooke 3
10,000
Referee: W Vickers (London)

The RAF hit six at the stadium in a repeat of the previous year's scoreline with two hat-tricks.

Met Police: Tootill (Crystal P), Bicknell (West Ham) – capt, Dawes (F) (Crystal P), Hiles (Fulham), Ridyard (QPR), Forsyth (Millwall), Fisher (Millwall), Dawes (A) (Crystal P), Compton (L) (Arsenal), Weaver (Chelsea), Spence (Chelsea)
RAF: Boulton (Derby Couty), Hardwick (Middlesbrough), Hapgood (Arsenal) – capt, Oakes (Charlton), Joy (Arsenal), Whittaker (Kingstonian), Kirchen (Arsenal), Smith (J) (Crystal P), Drake (Arsenal), Rooke (Fulham), Smith (L) (Brentford)

London War Cup Final

Saturday 30th May 1942

Brentford 2
Smith 11, 90
Portsmouth 0
71,000

Leslie Smith's goals secured the first London War Cup, a competition set up by a breakaway group of 16 clubs, who had refused to travel to the north for fixtures such were the difficulties involved in fielding full teams. Jackson, Chelsea's goalkeeper, guesting for Brentford, saved a first-half penalty from Portsmouth's Jimmy Guthrie.

Brentford: Jackson (Chelsea), Brown, Poyser, McKenzie (Middlesbrough), James – capt, Sneddon (Swansea), Hopkins, Wilkins, Perry, Hunt (Sheffield W), Smith. manager: Harry Curtis
Portsmouth: Walker, Rookes, Rochford, Guthrie – capt, Flewin, Wharton, Bullock (Barnsley), Griffiths, Black (Hearts), Barlow, Parker. manager: Jack Tinn

Middlesex Charity Cup Final

Wednesday 3rd June 1942

RAF Uxbridge 2
Clements 2
Wealdstone 5
Russell 2, own goal, Morris 2
After extra time
Referee: W Huggett

The stadium played host to a County Cup match for the first time in aid of war charities. Wealdstone twice came from behind to defeat the RAF team which was comprised of several Football League players.

RAF Uxbridge: Clack (Brentford), Forder (Crystal P) – capt, Dale (Portsmouth), McGregor (Man City), Vause (Rochdale), Johnson (Newcastle), Gibson (Watford), Harris (Swansea), Clements (Corinthian-Casuals), Mullinger (Aston Villa), Finch (Barnet)
Wealdstone: Doherty, Kay, Barker, Leeming , Upchurch, Stanton, Moore, Morris, Russell, Wilson, Dolding

Wartime Internationals

Saturday 10th October 1942

England 0
Scotland 0
75,000
Referee: P Stevens (Bedford)

Wembley's first goalless match.

England: Marks (Arsenal), Bacuzzi (Fulham), Hapgood (Arsenal) – capt, Britton (Everton), Cullis (Wolves), Mercer (Everton), Matthews (Stoke City), Edelston (Reading), Lawton (Everton), Hagan (Sheffffield U), Compton (D) (Arsenal)
Scotland: Dawson (Rangers), Carabine (Third Lanark), Beattie (A) (Preston), Shankly (Preston), Corbett (Celtic), Busby (Liverpool) – capt, Waddell (Rangers), Walker (Hearts), Dodds (Blackpool), Bremner (Arsenal), Liddell (Liverpool)

Saturday 27th February 1943
England 5
Carter 2, Westcott 3
Wales 3
Lowrie 3
75,000
Referee: G Reader (Hampshire)

England gained revenge for their 1940 defeat despite George Lowrie's hat-trick. George Reader was the man in the middle when Uruguay beat Brazil to win the World Cup in 1950.

England: Marks (Arsenal), Bacuzzi (Fulham), Hapgood (Arsenal) – capt, Britton (Everton), Cullis (Wolves), Mercer (Everton), Matthews (Stoke City), Carter (Sunderland), Westcott (Wolves), Hagan (Sheffffield U), Compton (D) (Arsenal)
Wales: Poland (Liverpool), Turner (Charlton) – capt, Hughes (Birmingham), Dearson (Birmingham), Jones (T) (Everton), Powell (QPR), Hopkins (Brentford), Lucas (Swindon), Lowrie (Coventry), Jones (B) (Arsenal), Cumner (Arsenal)

Football League South Cup Final

Saturday 1st May 1943

Arsenal 7
Lewis 4, 19, 51, 74, D Compton 8, Drake 26, 47
Charlton Athletic 1
Green pen 13
75,000

A shattering experience for Charlton on their first visit as Reg Lewis developed a taste for scoring goals at Wembley. He was to return seven years later to win the FA Cup for the Gunners. Arsenal also won the Football League South Championship as the breakaway London League from the previous year came back under the auspices of the Football League.

Arsenal: Marks, Scott, Compton (L), Crayston, Joy – capt, Male, Kirchen, Drake, Lewis, Bastin, Compton (D). manager: George Allison
Charlton: Hobbins, Cann, Shreeve, Phipps, Oakes, Davies (Barrow), Green, Mason (Third Lanark), Welsh – capt, Brown, Revell. manager: Jimmy Seed

Charity Match

Wednesday 5th May 1943

Met Police 3
Richardson 2, Brocklebank
RAF 4
Revell, Brocklebank, Smith, Rooke og
15,000
Referee: L Cadwallader (Middlesex)

A closer match for the more experienced RAF side than in their two previous appearances but they still recorded a victory.

Met Police: Tootill (Crystal P), Bicknell (West Ham) – capt, Dawes (F) (Crystal P), Nicholas (Derby Couty), Callaghan (Aston Villa), Mangnall (QPR), Fisher (Millwall), Dawes (A) (Crystal P), Richardson (W G) (West Brom), Brocklebank (Burnley), Spence (Chelsea)
RAF: Marks (Arsenal), Male (Arsenal), Hardwick (Middlesbrough), Shankly (Preston), Joy (Arsenal) – capt, Oakes (Charlton), Revell (Charlton), Smith (Crystal P), Drake (Arsenal), Rooke (Fulham), Cochrane (Bradford PA)

Middlesex Charity Cup Final

Wednesday 12th May 1943

Finchley 1
F Boston
Southall 0
6,500
Referee: T Terry

Another opportunity for local teams to sample the Wembley atmosphere in aid of the war charities. The winning goal came about 20 minutes from the end.

Eddie Baily went on to play for England and won a League Championship medal with Tottenham Hotspur in 1951.

Finchley: Hill, Willis, Taylor, Boston (W) – capt, Holmes, Milne, Baker, Gleave, Hanwell, Baily, Boston (F)
Southall: Green, Froom, Marshall, Clark, Annals, Brown – capt, Breagan, Lawson, Moran, Chudley, Pyne

Geipel Cup Final

Thursday 13th May 1943

Alperton Athletic 4
Kingsbury Juniors 0

Bingham scored twice, while Kingsbury were somewhat unlucky not to get on the scoresheet. They missed a second half penalty.

Rotary Cup Final

ATC 478 Squadron 0
West Hendon 1
Rickett

These were the Wembley Youth Committee League Cup finals. The Geipel Cup was restricted to Second Division teams only, while the Rotary Cup, the senior competition, was open to both divisions.

Wartime Internationals

Saturday 25th September 1943

England 8
Carter 2, Welsh 3, Hagan 2, Compton
Wales 3
Lowrie 2, A Powell
80,000
Referee: C Argent

Another record Wembley scoreline.

When Ivor Powell broke his collar-bone his replacement, Stan Mortensen, was in fact an English reserve. He went on to win 25 caps for England, as well as netting a memorable hat-trick for Blackpool in the 1953 FA Cup final. Wales had arrived at Wembley with just eleven players and Mortensen had to change out of his RAF uniform for the second half.

England: Roxburgh (Blackpool), Scott (Arsenal), Hardwick (Middlesbrough), Britton (Everton), Cullis

(Wolves) – capt, Soo (Stoke City), Matthews (Stoke City), Carter (Sunderland), Welsh (Charlton), Hagan (Shefffield U), Compton (D) (Arsenal)
Wales: Sidlow (Wolves), Lambert (Liverpool), Hughes (Birmingham), Dearson (Birmingham), Jones (Everton) – capt, Powell (I) (QPR), Powell (A) (Leeds), Murphy (Bradford C), Lowrie (Coventry), Burgess (Tottenham), Cumner (Arsenal). sub: Mortensen (Blackpool) for I Powell 46

Saturday 19th February 1944

England 6
Hagan 2, Macaulay og, Lawton, Mercer, Carter
Scotland 2
Dodds 2
80,000
Referee: E Wood (Sheffield)

After a clean sheet on their previous visit in 1942 the Scots succumbed to the England forwards.

England: Ditchburn (Tottenham), Scott (Arsenal), Hardwick (Middlesbrough), Britton (Everton), Cullis (Wolves) – capt, Mercer (Everton), Matthews (Stoke City), Carter (Sunderland), Lawton (Everton), Hagan (Sheffield U), Smith (Brentford)
Scotland: Crozier (Brentford), Kilmarnock (Motherwell), Stephen (Bradford PA), Macaulay (West Ham), Kirton (Stoke City), Busby (Liverpool) – capt, Flavell (Airdrie), Stenhouse (St Mirren), Dodds (Blackpool), Duncanson (Rangers), Caskie (Everton)

Football League South Cup Final

Saturday 15th April 1944

Charlton Athletic 3
Revell 13, 35, Welsh 35
Chelsea 1
Payne pen. 11
85,000

Charlton made amends for the previous year's final after briefly going behind. Ten of the 22 players on view were guests from other clubs. Forty years later Joe Fagan was manager of the Liverpool side which completed a hat-trick of League Championships and also collected both the European Cup and a fourth-successive Milk Cup in a memorable 'treble' season.

Charlton: Bartram, Shreeve, Jobling, Smith, Oakes, Chilton (Man Utd), Robinson (Sunderland), Brown, Revell, Welsh – capt, Duffy (Leith). manager: Jimmy Seed
Chelsea: Woodley, Hardwick (Middlesbrough), Westwood (Man City), Russell (Airdrie), Harris (Wolves) – capt, Foss, Ashcroft (Tranmere), Fagan (Liverpool), Payne, Bowie, Mitten (Man Utd). manager: Billy Birrell

Charity Match

Wednesday 10th May 1944

Combined Services 5
Smith, Drake 3, Edelston
Met Police And Civil Defence 2
A Dawes, Oakes og
15,000
Referee: W Vickers (London)

The fourth successive defeat for the Police at Wembley but the real winners were the war charities that benefited from the proceeds.

Combined Services: Ditchburn (Tottenham), Male (Arsenal), Whateley (Tottenham), White (Tottenham), Oakes (Charlton), Burgess (Tottenham), Kurz (Grimsby), Edelston (Reading), Drake (Arsenal), Rooke (Fulham), Smith (Brentford)
Met Police and Civil Defence: Merrick (Birmingham), Bicknell (West Ham) – capt, Dawes (F) (Crystal P), Owen (Newport), Mangnall (QPR), Callaghan (Aston Villa), Spence (Chelsea), Dawes (A) (Crystal P), Foreman (West Ham), Goulden (West Ham), Thorley (Huddersfield)

Middlesex Charity Cup Final

Wednesday 17th May 1944

QPR Juniors 2
Smith, Ling
Tufnell Park 3
Weston 2, Jones pen

Queens Park Rangers included three players with first team experience, and led 2-1 at half-time, but eventually lost out to the Isthmian League club.

QPR Juniors: Unfortunately the Queens Park Rangers line-up was not recorded although the five listed definitely played. Bird, Alexander, How, Smith, Ling
Tufnell Park: Munday, Lynch – capt, Fennel, Williams (A), Thompson, Williams (F), Penn, Norris, Beuschier, Jones, Weston

Wartime International

Saturday 14th October 1944

England 6
Lawton 3, Goulden, Carter, Smith
Scotland 2
Milne, Walker
90,000
Referee: G Reader (Hampshire)

Eight months on and the same high scoring result between the two rivals.

England: Swift (Man City), Scott (Arsenal), Hardwick (Middlesbrough), Soo (Stoke City), Joy (Arsenal), Mercer (Everton) – capt, Matthews (Stoke City), Carter (Sunderland), Lawton (Everton), Goulden (West Ham), Smith (Brentford)

Scotland: Cumming (Middlesbrough), Stephen (Bradford PA), Cummings (Aston Villa), Thyne (Darlington), Baxter (Middlesbrough) – capt, Macaulay (West Ham), Smith (Hibernian), Walker (Hearts), Milne (Hibernian), Black (Hearts), Caskie (Everton)

Football League South Cup Final

Saturday 7th April 1945

Chelsea 2
McDonald 47, Wardle 52
Millwall 0
90,000

Chelsea emulated Charlton's feat of returning the year after losing the final to lift the trophy. They did, however, need eight guest players, to help them do it.

Chelsea: Black (Aberdeen), Winter (Bolton), Hardwick (Middlesbrough), Russell, Harris (Wolves) – capt, Foss, Wardle (Exeter), Smith (Brentford), Payne, Goulden (West Ham), McDonald (Bournemouth). manager: Billy Birrell
Millwall: Bartram (Charlton), Dudley, Fisher, Ludford (Tottenham), Smith – capt, Tyler, Rawlings, R Brown (Charlton), Jinks, T Brown, Williams (Aberdeen). manager: Jack Cock

Wednesday 18th April 1945
The Wembley Youth Committee once again staged their League Cup finals, at the stadium. Alperton Athletic met Kingsbury Juniors again, in the Geipel Cup final, while Kingsbury Seniors, the League Champions, took on St John Bosco, in the Rotary Cup final.

London Civil Defence Cup Final

Wednesday 25th April 1945

Greenwich 10
Kennell 4, Hall 3, Ethridge 2, Etherton
Paddington 1
Dale
Referee: F Whitewick

Greenwich achieved the unique feat of becoming the only team in the entire history of the stadium to reach double figures in a single match. Kennell's four goals were all scored in the first half while Hall's hat-trick included one direct from a corner. Greenwich retained the trophy for the third year in succession.

Greenwich: Phillips, Braisted – capt, Webb, Lewis, Pearce, Rogers, Ethridge, Kennell, Hall, Etherton, Hooper
Paddington: Bennett (F), Bloxham, Lee, Hyatt, Roberts, Woolf, Smith, Dale, Flory, Bennett (L), Rouse

Charity Match

Wednesday 9th May 1945

Combined Services 3
Mortensen 2, Heathcote
National Police and Civil Defence 1
Goulden
25,000
Referee: W Vine (Middlesex)

The last of these annual fixtures as players would soon return to their professional clubs. The Police team broadened its player base to cover the whole country but still lost for the fifth year in succession.

Combined Services: Marks (Arsenal), Tennant (Chelsea), Lloyd (Wrexham), White (Tottenham), Fenton (West Ham), Buckingham (Tottenham), Kurz (Grimsby), Burgess (Tottenham), Heathcote (QPR), Mortensen (Blackpool), Smith (Brentford)
National Police and Civil Defence: Tootill (Crystal P), Bicknell (West Ham) – capt, Dawes (F) (Crystal P), Owen (Newport), Ridyard (QPR), Wilson (West Ham), Spence (Chelsea), Beasley (Tottenham), Richardson (W G.) (West Brom), Goulden (West Ham), Bastin (Arsenal)

Middlesex Charity Cup Final

Wednesday 16th May 1945

Golders Green 4
Cochrane 16, 85, Bucci 21, 48
Tufnell Park 1
Richards 76

The holders failed to retain the trophy as Golders Green made a winning debut at Wembley. They are now known as Hendon and returned to win the same competition 33 years later after five FA Amateur Cup finals at the stadium.

Golders Green: Roberts, Fisher, Bossoms, Topp , Halton, Gallacher, Stroud, Robshaw, Griffiths, Bucci, Cochrane
Tufnell Park: Moon, Lynch – capt, Norris, Penn, Brophy, Williams (F), Smith, Price, Richards, Williams (A), Weston

Victory International

Saturday 26th May 1945

England 2
Carter 10, Lawton 79
France 2
Vaast 44, Heisserer 90

65,000
Referee: G Reader (Hampshire)

Da Rui saved a first-half penalty from Leslie Smith as the French earned a surprise draw.

England: Williams (Walsall), Scott (Arsenal), Hardwick (Middlesbrough), Soo (Stoke City), Franklin (Stoke City), Mercer (Everton) – capt, Matthews (Stoke City), Carter (Sunderland), Lawton (Everton), Brown (Charlton), Smith (Brentford)
France: Da Rui (Lille), Dupuis (RC Paris), Swiatek (Girondins), Jasseron (RC Paris), Jordan (RC Paris), Samuel (RC Paris), Aston (Red Star Olympique), Heisserer (RC Paris) – capt, Bihel (Lille), Siklo (Lens), Vaast (RC Paris)

Saturday 19th January 1946

England 2
Brown 14, Pye 24
Belgium 0
85,000
Referee: G Reader (Hampshire)

Belgium's second visit, but their first meeting with England at Wembley. The hosts now had a manager, Walter Winterbottom, although the national team would still be selected by committee for another 17 years.

Billy Wright, Footballer of the Year in 1952, made his first appearance at Wembley. He went on to win 105 caps for England.

England: Swift (Man City), Scott (Arsenal), Hardwick (Middlesbrough), Wright (Wolves), Franklin (Stoke City), Mercer (Everton) – capt, Matthews (Stoke City), Pye (Notts County), Lawton (Chelsea), Brown (Charlton), Mullen (Wolves). manager: Walter Winterbottom
Belgium: Daenen (Tilleur), Paverick (Royal Antwerp) – capt, Pannaye (Tilleur), Puttaert (Union St. Gilloise), Vercammen (Lyra), Devos (Beerschot), Lemberechts (Mechelen), Coppens (Mechelen), De Cleyn (Mechelen), Mermans (Anderlecht), Sermon (Anderlecht). Coach: Francois Demol

British Junior Cup Final

Saturday 30th March 1946

ATC 4
Brown 2, Wardhaugh, Mackintosh
NABC 2
Heath 2
15,000
Referee: V Rae
The NABC and the three pre-service training organisations were invited to take part in this national competition sponsored by *The Star* with the final at Wembley. It was to run for ten years. In this first final the NABC were two goals down after nine minutes but came back to equalise before conceding two further goals. The following year they gained their revenge by beating the ATC 6-5 after extra time in the semi-final at New Writtle Street, Chelmsford, before going on to beat the Sea Cadet Corps 7-3 in another goal feast in the final at Stamford Bridge.

International Trial

Saturday 6th April 1946

FA 3
Shackleton 28, Stubbins 52, Elliott 83
Army PTC 5
Lawton 31, Welsh 35, 78, Wardle 40, Compton 50
35,000

An entertaining match with many top stars in action.

FA: Williams (Wolves), Scott (Arsenal), Hardwick (Middlesbrough), Soo (Leicester), Franklin (Stoke City), Mitchell (Birmingham), Elliott (West Brom), Pye (Notts County), Stubbins (Newcastle), Shackleton (Bradford PA), Smith (Aston Villa)
Army Physical Training Corps: Merrick (Birmingham), Beattie (A) (Preston), Cater (West Ham), Wright (Wolves), Smith (Brentford), Mercer (Everton) – capt, Wardle (Exeter), Welsh (Charlton), Lawton (Chelsea), Hagan (Sheffffield U), Compton (D) (Arsenal)

MOST WARTIME APPEARANCES

10 – George Hardwick & Stan Matthews.

TOP SCORERS

8 – Ted Drake & Tommy Lawton.

FA CUP FINAL

Saturday 27th April 1946

Charlton Athletic	**1-4**	**Derby Couty**
H Turner 86		H Turner og 85, Doherty 92
		Stamps 97, 106

After extra time
98,000
Referee: E Smith (Whitehaven)

Charlton had never before been beyond the last 16 of the competition but had won the Football League South Cup in 1944 at Wembley. Derby were appearing in their fourth final but had never won the Cup. Their last final had resulted in a miserable 6-0 defeat by Bury at Crystal Palace in 1903.

The Football League was not to resume again until the following season but both clubs had top First Division sides at the beginning of the war.

The first post-war FA Cup final was dominated by Derby yet they needed extra time to win it. It was almost settled with five minutes remaining when Bert Turner diverted Duncan's shot into his own net. Turner made amends within a minute. His free kick from outside the area was deflected past Woodley into the net for the equaliser. Having had victory snatched from their grasp Derby responded with three more goals in extra time.

Within two minutes of the restart Peter Doherty slotted home the rebound after Bartram had parried a Stamps shot. Doherty then laid on the third for Jack Stamps to finish. In the first minute of the second extra period, Doherty again supplied Stamps with a pass and the striker netted his second.

Raich Carter became the only man to have collected winners' medals before and after the war, having won the Cup with Sunderland in 1937.

Charlton were back the following year to win the Cup, but Derby's glory days were not to return for a quarter of a century. They came back to Wembley to win the FA Charity Shield in 1975.

Charlton: Bartram, Phipps, Shreeve, Turner (H), Oakes, Johnson, Fell , Brown, Turner (A), Welsh – capt, Duffy. manager: Jimmy Seed
Derby: Woodley, Nicholas – capt, Howe, Bullions, Leuty, Musson, Harrison, Carter, Stamps, Doherty, Duncan. manager: Stuart McMillan

BRITISH CHAMPIONSHIP

Saturday 12th April 1947

England	**1-1**	**Scotland**
Carter 56		McLaren 16

98,250
Referee: C Delasalle (France)

England had beaten both Ireland and Wales and needed only a point to secure the first post-war British Championship. Scotland had lost 3-1 to Wales at the Racecourse Ground and could finish joint runners-up at best. They had lost four out of five wartime internationals at Wembley since winning in 1938.

Scotland dominated the first half and took the lead when a pass from Pearson found Andy McLaren who shot past Swift. England's equaliser came from a very quick and incisive move which split the Scottish defence and Mannion provided the in-rushing Raich Carter with the final pass from which he drove the ball past Miller.

England were to retain the British Championship the following year, their fourth successive peacetime title, while Scotland finished bottom without a point. They returned to Wembley in 1949, however, with a much-improved side.

The 1951 Footballer of the Year, Harry Johnston, made his first Wembley appearance.

England: Swift (Man City), Scott (Arsenal), Hardwick (Middlesbrough) – capt, Wright (Wolves), Franklin (Stoke City), Johnston (Blackpool), Matthews (Stoke City), Carter (Derby Couty), Lawton (Chelsea), Mannion (Middlesbrough), Mullen* (Wolves). manager: Walter Winterbottom
Scotland: Miller (Celtic), Young (Rangers), Shaw* (Rangers) – capt, Macaulay* (Brentford), Woodburn* (Rangers), Forbes* (Sheffield U), Smith (Hibernian), McLaren* (Preston), Delaney (Man Utd), Steel* (Morton), Pearson* (Newcastle)
*first cap

Final table	P	W	D	L	F	A	Pts
England	3	2	1	0	11	3	5
Ireland	3	1	1	1	4	8	3
Scotland	3	0	2	1	2	4	2
Wales	3	1	0	2	4	6	2

FA CUP FINAL

Saturday 26th April 1947

Burnley   0-1   **Charlton Athletic**
Duffy 114

After extra time
99,000
Referee: J Wiltshire (Sherborne)

Burnley had won the FA Cup once in 1914, beating Liverpool 1-0 in the final at Crystal Palace. This time they had beaten the same opponents, who were about to win the first post-war League Championship, in the semi-finals. Charlton had never won the Cup, but had lost the previous year's final in extra time and were appearing in their fourth Wembley final in five years.

The first post-war league season had been extended due to a very severe winter. Burnley were well placed in the Second Division promotion race, while Charlton had struggled after three consecutive top four placings before the war.

This was a defensive game and was finally settled with only six minutes of extra time remaining. Robinson's cross was headed on by Welsh to Chris Duffy who fired it past Strong.

Burnley finished as Second Division runners-up to Manchester City and spent the next 24 seasons in the First Division. They returned to Wembley in 1962. Charlton finished 19th in the First Division. Their run of Wembley appearances came to an end with this success and it was to be another 40 years before they were back for the Full Members Cup final.

Burnley: Strong, Woodruff, Mather, Attwell, Brown – capt, Bray, Chew, Morris, Harrison, Potts, Kippax. manager: Cliff Britton
Charlton: Bartram, Croker, Shreeve, Johnson, Phipps, Whittaker, Hurst, Dawson, Robinson, Welsh – capt, Duffy. manager: Jimmy Seed

British Junior Cup Final

Saturday 3rd April 1948

ATC 2
White, Whyte
ACF 0
15,000

The ATC regained the prize for the second time in three years after beating the holders the National Association of Boys Clubs 3-2 after extra time in the semi-final at Western Road, Southall.

FA CUP FINAL

Saturday 24th April 1948

Blackpool   **2-4**   **Manchester United**
Shimwell pen 12, Mortensen 35   Rowley 28, 70, Pearson 80, Anderson 82
99,000
Referee: C Barrick (Northampton)

Blackpool had never been past the quarter-finals before, and had never won a major trophy. United had won the Cup in 1909, beating Bristol City 1-0 in the final at Crystal Palace. They had knocked out the holders Charlton Athletic in the last 16.

Blackpool finished ninth in the First Division while United were League runners-up for the second year in succession to Arsenal.

An exciting game which came to life with the first goal. Mortensen bore down on goal and would have had only the goalkeeper to beat but was tripped from behind by Chilton. Although he fell into the area the foul actually took place outside.

But the referee gave a penalty and Eddie Shimwell hit a poor strike only for it to go straight underneath the diving Crompton.

United were level when from a Delaney lob into the goalmouth a misunderstanding between Hayward and Robinson left Jack Rowley with a simple task to equalise. Seven minutes later Matthews played a free kick across to Kelly who knocked it through for Stan Mortensen to turn and fire past Crompton to put Blackpool back in front.

United began to take control in the second half but there were only 20 minutes left when they finally equalised. A quickly taken free kick from Morris was centred to Rowley whose diving header produced his second. With ten minutes remaining a Mortensen shot was saved by Crompton and United went straight upfield to score again.

An Anderson pass found Stan Pearson whose shot went in off the post. United completed the scoring when a shot from John Anderson was deflected off the head of Kelly into the far corner.

Blackpool reached the final again in 1951. United rebuilt and then proceeded to dominate the mid-1950's, returning to Wembley, in 1957.

Johnny Carey made his only appearance at Wembley. Twelve months later he was voted Footballer of the Year.

Blackpool: Robinson (J), Shimwell, Crosland, Johnston – capt, Hayward, Kelly, Matthews, Munro, Mortensen, Dick, Rickett. manager: Joe Smith
Manchester U: Crompton, Carey – capt, Aston (snr), Anderson, Chilton, Cockburn, Delaney, Morris, Rowley, Pearson (S), Mitten. manager: Matt Busby

Olympic Semi-Finals

Tuesday 10th August 1948

Denmark 2
Seebach 2, J Hansen 75

Sweden 4
Carlsson 18, 44, Rosen 30, 37
20,000
Referee: S Boardman (England)

An impressive performance from the Swedes, who had the game won by half-time, despite conceding the first goal.

Denmark: Nielsen (KB Copenhagen), V Jensen (Esbjerg), Overgaard (B93 Copenhagen), Pilmark (KB Copenhagen), Ornvold (KB Copenhagen), I Jensen (AB Copenhagen), Ploger (Frem), K Hansen (AB Copenhagen) – capt, Praest (Odense), J Hansen (Frem), Seebach (AB Copenhagen)
Sweden: Lindberg (Norrkoping), Leander (AIK Stockholm), Nilsson (Malmo), Rosengren (Norrkoping) – capt, B Nordahl (Degerfors), Andersson (AIK Stockholm), Rosen (Malmo), Gren (IFK Gothenburg), G Nordahl (Norrkoping), Carlsson (AIK Stockholm), Liedholm (Norrkoping)

Wednesday 11th August 1948

Great Britain 1
Donovan 20

Yugoslavia 3
Bobek 19, Velfl 24, Mitic 48
40,000
Referee: K Van der Meer (Netherlands)

A disappointing end to the home team's bid for Olympic gold.

Great Britain: McAlinden (Belfast Celtic & Ireland), Neale (Walton and Hersham & England), McColl (Queens Park & Scotland), McBain (Queens Park & Scotland), Lee (Chester & England), Fright (Bromley & England), Donovan (Pembroke & Wales), Hardisty (Bishop Auckland & England) – capt, McIlvenny (Yorkshire Amateurs & England), Kelleher (Barnet & Ireland), Kippax (Yorkshire Amateurs & England). coach: Matt Busby
Yugoslavia: Sostaric (Partizan Belgrade), Brozovic (Partizan) – capt, Stankovic (Red Star Belgrade), Zl Ciakowski (Partizan), Jovanovic (Partizan), Atanakovic (Partizan), Mihajlovic (Partizan), Mitic (Red Star), Velfl (Dinamo Zagreb), Bobek (Partizan), Ze Ciakowski (Dinamo Zagreb). Coaches: Milorad Arsenijevic and Aleksandar Tirnanic

Olympic Third And Fourth Place

Friday 13th August 1948

Denmark 5
Praest 10, 48, Hansen 13, 79, Sorensen 70
Great Britain 3
Aitkin 5,McIlvenny 33, Amor pen 60
5,000
Referee: K Van der Meer (Netherlands)

The home team made several changes, but it was not enough to win them a medal.

The 17-year-old goalkeeper Ronnie Simpson went on to win a European Cup winners medal with Celtic in 1967 and made his international debut for Scotland at Wembley the same year.

Denmark: Nielsen (KB Copenhagen), V Jensen (Esbjerg), Overgaard (B93 Copenhagen), Pilmark (KB Copenhagen), Ornvold (KB Copenhagen), I Jensen (AB Copenhagen), Ploger (Frem), Lundberg (AB Copenhagen) – capt, Praest (Odense), Hansen (J) (Frem), Sorensen (Odense)
Great Britain: Simpson (Queens Park & Scotland), Neale (Walton and Hersham & England), Carmichael (Queens Park & Scotland), Hardisty (Bishop Auckland & England) – capt, Lee (Chester & England), Fright (Bromley & England), Boyd (Queens Park & Scotland), Aitkin (Queens Park & Scotland), McIlvenny (Yorkshire Amateurs & England), Rawlings (Enfield & England), Amor (Huntley & Palmer's & England). coach: Matt Busby

Olympic Final

Saturday 14th August 1948
Sweden 3
Gren 24, 67 pen, G Nordahl 48
Yugoslavia 1
Bobek 42
60,000
Referee: W Ling (England)

Stankovic was sent off for a reckless foul which gave Sweden their penalty in Yugoslavia's first of four consecutive Olympic finals. They lost the first three, before finally winning in Rome in 1960.

Sweden: Lindberg (Norrkoping), Nordahl (K) (Norrkoping), Nilsson (Malmo), Rosengren (Norrkoping) – capt, B Nordahl (Degerfors), Andersson (Aik Stockholm), Rosen (Malmo), Gren (IFK Gothenburg), Nordahl (G) (Norrkoping), Carlsson (AIK Stockholm), Liedholm (Norrkoping)
Yugoslavia: Lovric (Red Star Belgrade), Brozovic (Partizan Belgrade) – capt, Stankovic (Red Star), Zl Caikowski (Partizan), Jovanovic (Partizan), Atanakovic (Partizan), Cimermancic (Dinamo Zagreb), Mitic (Red Star), Bobek (Partizan), Ze Caikowski (Dinamo Zagreb), Vukas (Hajduk Split). coaches: Milorad Arsenijevic and Aleksandar Tirnanic

British Junior Cup Final

Saturday 19th March 1949

ATC 2
Womersley, Riley og
NABC 2
Leaver 2
After extra time
Referee: H Pearce (Bedfordshire)

Despite leading twice, the ATC could not retain the Junior Cup against the side they had beaten in the first final three years earlier. The NABC were attempting to regain the prize for the second time in three years. Twenty minutes of extra time failed to separate them.

Replay:
ATC 2
NABC 3
(Griffin Park, London)

BRITISH CHAMPIONSHIP

Saturday 9th April 1949

England	**1-3**	**Scotland**
Milburn 75		Mason 29, Steel 52, Reilly 61

98,188
Referee: M Griffiths (Wales)

Both England, the reigning British Champions, and Scotland had won both their previous matches. For England a point would give them their fifth successive peacetime Championship. Scotland had not beaten England since 1938 and had not won the Championship outright since 1936.

For the first 25 minutes it was all England, but the Scotland goalkeeper Jimmy Cowan made save after save to keep them out. Then Scotland struck. Reilly crossed and Jimmy Mason flicked the ball just wide of Swift to give the Scots a surprise lead. With an hour's play gone Scotland were, incredibly, three goals up. First, Billy Steel put Houliston through. Swift was slow in coming off his line but Aston managed to stab the ball away from the attacker before he could shoot only for Steel to net the attempted clearance. Then a Waddell cross was headed in by Lawrie Reilly. England finally got a goal back in the last 15 minutes when Finney laid the ball back for Mortensen whose shot was turned in by Jackie Milburn.

England regained the Championship the following year and qualified for their first World Cup in the process. Scotland finished runners-up after losing 1-0 to England at Hampden Park.

England: Swift (Man City), Aston (Man Utd), Howe (Derby Couty), Wright (Wolves) – capt, Franklin (Stoke City), Cockburn (Man Utd), Matthews (Blackpool), Mortensen (Blackpool), Milburn (Newcastle), Pearson (Man Utd), Finney (Preston). manager: Walter Winterbottom
Scotland: Cowan (Morton), Young (Rangers) – capt, Cox (Rangers), Evans (Celtic), Woodburn (Rangers), Aitken* (East Fife), Waddell (Rangers), Mason (Third Lanark), Houliston (Queen of South), Steel (Derby Couty), Reilly (Hibernian)
*first cap

Final table	P	W	D	L	F	A	Pts
Scotland	3	3	0	0	9	4	6
England	3	2	0	1	8	5	4
Wales	3	1	0	2	3	4	2
Ireland	3	0	0	3	4	11	0

FA Amateur Cup Final

Saturday 23rd April 1949

Bromley 1
Hopper 20
Romford 0
93,000

The final of the amateur game's premier competition was played at Wembley for the first time. Bromley recorded their third victory.

Bromley: Cornthwaite, Cameron, Yenson, Fuller (T), Fuller (C), Fright – capt, Martin, Hopper, Brown, Dunmall, Ruddy
Romford: Ivey, Collier, Fryatt – capt, McKenzie, Barton, Regan, Brooks, Maddick, Bridge, Jennings, Patterson

FA CUP FINAL

Saturday 30th April 1949

Leicester City	**1-3**	**Wolverhampton W**
Griffiths 46		Pye 13, 42, Smyth 68

99,500
Referee: R Mortimer (Huddersfield)

Leicester were appearing in their first final, Wolves in their seventh, but they had not won the Cup since 1908 and were hoping to avenge their humiliating defeat of ten years previously. Leicester were ironically having one of the worst league seasons in their history and were in danger of being relegated to the Third Division South for the first time. Wolves finished sixth in the First Division which, by contrast, was their lowest position since 1936. They had not been beaten by Leicester for 24 years.

Wolves took an expected lead when a cross from Hancocks was headed in by Jesse Pye as he ran in between two defenders. Three minutes before half-time they scored again. Leicester failed to clear a corner properly, a Dunn shot hit his own man and it fell for Pye to score his second.

Leicester came out for the second half with plenty of fighting spirit and quickly scored. Williams saved at the feet of Chisholm but the ball ran loose for Mal Griffiths. Springthorpe tried to head it off the line but only succeeded in heading it against the post and in. Sammy Smyth completed Wolves' third FA Cup win, however, when he scored after a brilliant solo run through the Leicester defence.

Leicester played three games in four days the following week and escaped relegation by a point. They won the Second Division Championship twice in the 1950's and were back at Wembley in 1961. Wolves were League runners-up to Portsmouth the following year and only lost the title on goal average. But by the time they won the FA Cup for the fourth time in 1960 they had won the League Championship three times.

Leicester C: Bradley, Jelly, Scott, Harrison (W), Plummer – capt, King (J), Griffiths, Lee, Harrison (J), Chisholm, Adam. manager: John Duncan
Wolves: Williams, Pritchard, Springthorpe, Crook, Shorthouse, Wright – capt, Hancocks, Smyth, Pye, Dunn, Mullen. manager: Stan Cullis

Schoolboy International

Saturday 15th April 1950

England 8
Clamp, Brown, Haynes 2 (1 pen), Scott 3, Parry
Scotland 2
McDonald 2 (1 pen)
50,000
Referee: A Bailey (Finchley)

Wembley's first schools international produced a record scoreline for the fixture. Scotland played for a time with nine men due to injuries.

Johnny Haynes, who went on to win 56 England caps, made his first Wembley appearance, scoring twice. Dave Mackay, one of the Scottish substitutes, came on for his first appearance at Wembley. Nineteen years later he was joint Footballer of the Year.

England: Ward, Cooper, Spencer – capt, Thwaites, Cope, Clamp, Charlton, Haynes, Brown, Parry, Scott

Scotland: Mortimer, Brown – capt, Milloy, McGowan, Milne, Anderson (J), Anderson (T), Gray, McDonald, Peden, Grassie. Subs: Durnie for Anderson (T), Mackay for Peden

FA Amateur Cup Final

Saturday 22nd April 1950

Bishop Auckland 0
Willington 4
Taylor 12, Rutherford 21, Larmouth 30, Armstrong 75
88,000

Willington's first victory, in the competition, was emphatic revenge, for losing the last pre-war final, to their more illustrious opponents, in 1939.

Bishop Auckland: Washington, Coxon, Farrer, Taylor, Davison, Nimmins, Major, Hardisty, McIlvenny – capt, Gilholme, Palmer
Willington: Snowdon, Craggs, Howe, Leuthwaite, Yeardley, Dodd, Robinson, Taylor – capt, Larmouth, Armstrong, Rutherford

FA CUP FINAL

Saturday 29th April 1950

Arsenal	**2-0**	**Liverpool**

Lewis 18, 63
100,000
Referee: H Pearce (Luton)

Arsenal had last won the Cup in 1936 but had won the Football League South Cup at Wembley in 1943. Liverpool were appearing in only their second final, having lost 1-0 to Burnley at Crystal Palace in 1914 and were appearing at Wembley for the first time.

Arsenal finished sixth in the First Division after winning the League Championship in 1948. Liverpool finished a point behind them in eighth position. They had won the first post-war League Championship in 1947.

The Gunners' first goal started with a pass from Logie which enabled Reg Lewis, who had scored four on his previous Wembley appearance in 1943, to stride through a lethargic Liverpool defence to slot the ball past Sidlow for the opening goal.

They scored again when Cox flicked the ball through for Lewis to get his second. Arsenal won the Cup for the third time after being two goals down in the semi-final just as when they first won it in 1930.

Arsenal reached the final again two years later.

Within four years Liverpool were in the Second Division and after six years of near misses they won promotion and won the FA Cup for the first time in 1965.

Arsenal: Swindin, Scott, Barnes, Forbes, Compton (L), Mercer – capt, Cox, Logie, Goring, Lewis (R), Compton (D). manager: Tom Whittaker
Liverpool: Sidlow, Lambert, Spicer, Taylor – capt, Hughes (L), Jones (W), Payne, Baron, Stubbins, Fagan, Liddell. manager: George Kay

British Junior Cup Final

Saturday 13th May 1950

ACF 1
Spanswick
NABC 4
Henwood, Lythgoe, 2 other scorers

The NABC had beaten the only other previous winners of this competition, the ATC, 1-0 in the semi-final at Western Road, Southall. They went on to become the first team to retain the Junior Cup with their record third win in four years. The ACF lost their second final in three years.

Len Allchurch played for the Army Cadet Force and went on to represent Wales alongside his more famous brother Ivor.

FA County Youth Cup Final

Second Leg

Saturday 20th May 1950

Middlesex 1
Dwight
Essex 2
Kenlay, Seabourne

After extra time
Essex win 4-3 on aggregate

Essex, in their third final in four years, became the first county to win the trophy twice when they came from behind to regain the prize for the second time in three years. Middlesex suffered defeat for the second year in succession despite being two goals up in the first leg at Highbury the previous week.

The Middlesex goal was scored by Roy Dwight, who scored and then broke his leg, in the FA Cup final nine years later. He was an uncle to pop star Sir Elton John who also appeared at the stadium many times.

Also in the Middlesex line-up was Bobby Smith, who was to score in consecutive FA Cup finals in the early 1960's, and was a key member of Tottenham Hotspur's 1961 'double-winning' side.

Schoolboy International

Saturday 7th April 1951

England 3
Parry, Farrall pen, Barnes
Wales 0
53,000

50

The first appearance for the Welsh ended in defeat. Two England schoolboys, Duncan Edwards and David Pegg, who were to lose their lives in the Munich air disaster of 1958, made their first Wembley appearances.

England: Silver, Heyes, Smith, Conroy, May, Edwards, Perrin, Farrall, Barnes, Parry – capt, Pegg
Wales: Jones, Barnes, Williams (A), Roberts, Edwards, Manley, Meakin, Williams (P), Walters, McCarthy, Burder

BRITISH CHAMPIONSHIP

Saturday 14th April 1951

England   2-3   Scotland
Hassall 26, Finney 63   Johnstone 33, Reilly 47, Liddell 54
98,750
Referee: T Mitchell (Northern Ireland)

Once again, both England, the reigning British Champions, and Scotland had beaten both Northern Ireland and Wales and were set to decide the Championship between them. England were still suffering from their embarrassing first round exit from their first World Cup in Brazil the previous year which included a humiliating defeat at the hands of the USA. Scotland had not been beaten at Wembley in the British Championship since 1934.

England were down to ten men from the 11th minute when Mannion went off injured but took the lead when Harold Hassall took a pass from Mortensen and shot past Cowan, the hero of 1949.

Bobby Johnstone put Scotland level from a pass by Reilly.

England were in deep trouble at the start of the second half as Mortensen was suffering from a first half collision and did not re-appear after the interval.

The Scots began to take advantage of the nine men and within two minutes Steel supplied Lawrie Reilly who turned and shot Scotland into the lead.

Mortensen then came back on and England found new inspiration to attack. Scotland soaked up the pressure, however, and increased their lead when Reilly robbed Williams of the ball from a Steel cross leaving Billy Liddell to score the third. England continued to battle and pulled one back when Tom Finney took a pass from Mortensen and lobbed Cowan. They could not muster another and Scotland were British Champions for the second time in three years.

England: Williams (Wolves), Ramsey (Tottenham), Eckersley (Blackburn), Johnston (Blackpool), Froggatt (Portsmouth), Wright (Wolves) – capt, Matthews (Blackpool), Mannion (Middlesbrough), Mortensen (Blackpool), Hassall* (Huddersfield), Finney (Preston). manager: Walter Winterbottom
Scotland: Cowan (Morton), Young (Rangers) – capt, Cox (Rangers), Evans (Celtic), Woodburn (Rangers), Redpath (Motherwell), Waddell (Rangers), Johnstone* (Hibernian), Reilly (Hibernian), Steel (Dundee), Liddell (Liverpool)
*first cap

Final table	P	W	D	L	F	A	Pts
Scotland	3	3	0	0	12	4	6
England	3	2	0	1	10	6	4
Wales	3	1	0	2	5	8	2
Northern Ireland	3	0	0	3	3	12	0

FA Amateur Cup Final

Saturday 21st April 1951

Bishop Auckland 1
Nimmins 87

Pegasus 2
Potts 50, Tanner 80
100,000

A club formed only three years previously from the players of Oxford and Cambridge Universities won the trophy in a full stadium as Bishop Auckland lost their second successive final.

Bishop Auckland: White, Marshall, Farrer, Hardisty, Davison, Nimmins, Taylor, Anderson, McIlvenny – capt, Williamson, Edwards
Pegasus: Brown, Cowan, Maughan, Platt, Shearwood, Saunders – capt, Pawson, Dutchman, Tanner, Carr, Potts

FA CUP FINAL

Saturday 28th April 1951

Blackpool   0-2   **Newcastle United**
                                    Milburn 50, 55

100,000
Referee: W Ling (Cambridge)

Blackpool were back for a further attempt at winning a major trophy for the first time after their gallant failure in 1948. Newcastle were back at Wembley for the first time since their 1932 triumph.

Blackpool finished third in the First Division, their highest ever league position, while Newcastle finished a point and a place behind in only their third season back in the First Division. Blackpool had failed to beat Newcastle throughout that time.

Newcastle broke the deadlock just into the second half. Robledo's pass beat the offside trap and Jackie Milburn was totally free to run on and slot the ball past Farm. He scored again five minutes later. Taylor cleverly back-heeled the ball and Milburn sent a 25-yard bullet flying past the helpless Farm.

Newcastle retained the FA Cup the following year while Blackpool won it the year after.

The 1960 Footballer of the Year, Bill Slater, made his first appearance, at Wembley.

Blackpool: Farm, Shimwell, Garrett, Johnston – capt, Hayward, Kelly, Matthews, Mudie, Mortensen, Slater, Perry. manager: Joe Smith
Newcastle: Fairbrother, Cowell, Corbett, Harvey – capt, Brennan, Crowe, Walker, Taylor, Milburn, Robledo (G), Mitchell. manager: Stan Seymour

INTERNATIONAL

Wednesday 9th May 1951

England   2-1   **Argentina**
Mortensen 79, Milburn 86   Boye 18
99,000
Referee: M Griffiths (Wales)

England were facing foreign opposition at Wembley in an official international for the first time. Argentina had not competed in the previous year's World Cup but had won the South American Championship three years in succession in the mid-1940's and had the best record in the history of the competition. They were coached by Guillermo Stabile, the top scorer in the 1930 World Cup, and this was their first meeting with England.

The home side, wearing red shirts at Wembley for the first time were a goal down when Loustau lured Williams from his goal and chipped the ball up for Mario Boye to head in.

England looked to be heading for defeat but they finally drew level when Stan Mortensen headed in a Finney corner. With four minutes to go they snatched victory when Mortensen headed on a Ramsey free kick for Jackie Milburn to drive home the winner.

England went to Buenos Aires the following year, but the game was abandoned after only 21 minutes without a goal because of torrential rain. Argentina returned to Wembley in 1966 for the World Cup.

England: Williams (Wolves), Ramsey (Tottenham), Eckersley (Blackburn), Wright (Wolves) – capt, Taylor* (Fulham), Cockburn (Man Utd), Finney (Preston), Mortensen (Blackpool), Milburn (Newcastle), Hassall (Huddersfield), Metcalfe* (Huddersfield). manager: Walter Winterbottom*first cap
Argentina: Rugilo (Velez Sarsfield), Colman (Boca Juniors), Figueras (Huracan), Iacono (River Plate) – capt, Faina (Newell's Old Boys), Pescia (Boca), Boye (Racing Club), Mendez (Racing), Bravo (Racing), Labruna (River Plate), Loustau (River Plate). Coach: Guillermo Stabile. sub: Allegri (Newell's Old Boys) for Colman 35

British Junior Cup Final

Saturday 19th May 1951

ACF 2
Rolls, Donnelly

NABC 4
Williams 2, 2 other scorers
25,000
Referee: A Bond (London)

Alf Bond, who refereed the FA Cup final in 1956, was unique in his role as he had only one arm.

A hat-trick of triumphs for the NABC and a second successive final defeat and third in four years for the ACF.

Cliff Jones in the Army Cadet Force side went on to win 59 Welsh international caps and played in the great Tottenham Hotspur 'double-winning' team of 1961.

INTERNATIONAL

Wednesday 28th November 1951

England   **2-2**   **Austria**
Ramsey pen 68, Lofthouse 75   Melchior 47, Stojaspol pen 87
98,000
Referee: J Mowat (Scotland)

England were battling with Wales to regain the British Championship. Austria had not competed in the previous year's World Cup and had beaten England only once in six meetings, 2-1 in Vienna in 1936. They had lost 4-3 on their only previous visit to England at Stamford Bridge in 1932.

All the goals came in the second half. First an Ocwirk free kick cleared the England defence for Ernst Melchior to run in to beat Merrick.

England equalised with a quarter of the game remaining. Ocwirk brought down Baily in the area and Alf Ramsey stepped up to score from the penalty. Seven min-utes later a Ramsey free kick was headed in by Nat Lofthouse on his first Wembley appearance, but three minutes from the end Austria levelled from an Ernst Stojaspol penalty after Eckersley had handled a goal-bound header from Huber.

England went on to share the British Championship with Wales and then went to Vienna the following year and beat Austria 3-2. Nat Lofthouse earned the nickname 'Lion of Vienna' after being knocked unconscious when scoring the winner and then returning for the last five minutes. Lofthouse was Footballer of the Year in 1953 and scored 30 goals for England.

England: Merrick (Birmingham), Ramsey (Tottenham), Eckersley (Blackburn), Wright (Wolves) – capt, Froggatt (Portsmouth), Dickinson (Portsmouth), Milton* (Arsenal), Broadis* (Man City), Lofthouse (Bolton), Baily (Tottenham), Medley (Tottenham). manager: Walter Winterbottom
* first cap
Austria: Zeman (Rapid Vienna), Roeckl (SK Vienna), Happel (Rapid), Hanappi (Rapid), Ocwirk (FK Austria Vienna) – capt, Brinek (Wacker Vienna), Melchior (FK Austria), Gernhardt (Rapid), Huber (FK Austria), Stojaspol (FK Austria), Koerner (Rapid). coach: Walter Nausch

Amateur International

Saturday 15th March 1952

England 1
Noble 79

Scotland 2
Murray 23, Grierson 78
80,000

The first amateur international to be played at Wembley resulted in England's first defeat since 1949 against what was, but for four players, the Queens Park team which was to finish next to bottom of the Scottish Second Division.

George Robb and Bill Slater went on to represent England at full international level.

England: Brown (Pegasus), Charlton (Bromley), Stratton (Walthamstow), Topp (Hendon), Fuller (Bromley), Slater (Brentford), Mortimore (Aldershot), Noble (Leytonstone), Lewis (Walthamstow) – capt, Walton (Man Utd), Robb (Finchley). coach: Walter Winterbottom
Scotland: Ritchie (Alloa), Paterson (Queens Park), Stewart (Queens Park) – capt, Hastie (Queens Park), Caldwell (Kilmarnock), Doherty (Queens Park), Hodge (Albion), Anderson (Bishop Auckland), Cromer (Queens Park), Grierson (Queens Park), Murray (Queens Park).

Schoolboy International

Saturday 5th April 1952

England 1
Bolton

Scotland 0
80,000

Frank Bolton's 21st minute winner was enough to win the game. His captain Duncan Edwards was the only player ever to represent England Schools in three consecutive years.

England: Dodds, Storey, Jones, Bolton, Yeatman, Edwards – capt, Morton, Sykes, Bannister, Asher, Ward
Scotland: Brodie, McMillan, Neil, King – capt, Baillie, Taggart, Brand, Lawlor, Irvine, Dunsmuir, Armour

FA Amateur Cup Final

Saturday 26th April 1952

Leyton 1
Skipp 43

Walthamstow Avenue 2
Lewis 16, Hall 119
After extra time
100,000
Referee: J Sherlock (Sheffield)

Walthamstow won the cup for the first time with a last-minute winner.

Leyton: Sullivan, Dixon, Pullinger, Gardiner, Yenson – capt, Casey, Fitch, Facey, McIntee, Goddard, Skipp
Walthamstow: Gerula, Young, Stratton, Lucas, Brahan, Saunders – capt, Rossiter, Bailey, Lewis, Hall, Camis.

FA CUP FINAL

Saturday 3rd May 1952

Arsenal   **0-1**   **Newcastle United**
                                          G Robledo 84

100,000
Referee: A Ellis (Halifax)

Arsenal were attempting to regain the FA Cup for the second time in three years after winning it in 1950. They had beaten the same semi-final opponents as in 1950, Chelsea, at the same venue, and again after a replay. It was also an opportunity to avenge their controversial defeat by Newcastle in the 1932 final. Newcastle were the holders and aiming to become the first team to retain the FA Cup since Blackburn Rovers (who they had beaten in the semi-final) in 1891. They had already reached a record ninth final.

Arsenal finished third in the First Division their highest position since winning the League Championship in 1948. Newcastle finished eighth, their lowest position since promotion, also in 1948.

The turning point came after 19 minutes. Arsenal had begun well, when Barnes was injured in a tackle with Milburn. He lasted until the 35th minute but then went off. Arsenal's ten men fought magnificently against the marauding Newcastle forwards. But with six minutes left Newcastle finally broke through. Mitchell's cross was headed in off the post by the Chilean George Robledo. Newcastle had won the Cup, but Arsenal had won overwhelming sympathy from the crowd.

Newcastle secured a third FA Cup win in five years in 1955.

Arsenal: Swindin, Barnes, Smith (L), Forbes, Daniel, Mercer – capt, Cox, Logie, Holton, Lishman, Roper. manager: Tom Whittaker
Newcastle: Simpson, Cowell, McMichael, Harvey – capt, Brennan, Robledo (E), Walker, Foulkes, Milburn, Robledo (G), Mitchell. manager: Stan Seymour

British Junior Cup Final

Saturday 10th May 1952

ATC 3
Westerman, Brolls, Collins

NABC 5
Bretland, Barrowcliffe 2, Whitehurst 2 pens

The invincible NABC had thrashed the Sea Cadet Corps 9-1 in a one-sided semi-final at Stompond Lane, Walton, and went on to win the competition for the fourth year in succession and fifth overall. But they had to work for it in the final when their goalkeeper Oldknow was carried off with a knee injury just before half-time.

BRITISH CHAMPIONSHIP

Wednesday 12th November 1952

England	**5-2**	**Wales**
Finney 8, Lofthouse 10, 75,		Ford 15, 49
Bentley 47		

94,094
Referee: D Gerrard (Scotland)

Having made three visits in wartime, Wales now appeared at Wembley in the British Championship for the first time. They had not beaten England in the competition since 1938 but had shared the title with them the previous season. England had already drawn 2-2 with Northern Ireland at Windsor Park, but Wales had lost 2-1 to Scotland at Ninian Park and had to avoid defeat to continue their interest in the Championship.

England scored twice in the opening ten minutes. After some early pressure Tom Finney converted an Elliott centre. The second came from an Elliott corner. This time a flick-on from Redfern Froggatt supplied Nat Lofthouse with a goal.

Within five minutes Wales had pulled one back. Trevor Ford fought off the challenge of Jack Froggatt to shoot past Merrick. Froggatt was later stretchered off but then returned to play out on the wing and then miraculously met Finney's cross with a diving header to score England's third.

In the second half Lofthouse and Finney combined to set up Roy Bentley with a chance to shoot and score from just outside the penalty area.

Wales almost immediately scored again when a Foulkes shot was blocked by Smith but fell to Ford to score his second with a cheeky back-heel. Lofthouse completed the scoring with 15 minutes left when his 25-yard shot went crashing through Shortt's hands.

Wales ruined Northern Ireland's chances by beating them 3-2 at Windsor Park and the Championship was concluded at Wembley.

England: Merrick (Birmingham), Ramsey (Tottenham), Smith (Arsenal), Wright (Wolves) – capt, Froggatt (J) (Portsmouth), Dickinson (Portsmouth), Finney (Preston), Froggatt (R)* (Sheffield W), Lofthouse (Bolton), Bentley (Chelsea), Elliott (Burnley). manager: Walter Winterbottom
Wales: Shortt (Plymouth Argyle), Stitfall* (Cardiff), Sherwood (Cardiff), Paul (Man City), Daniel (Arsenal), Burgess (Tottenham) – capt, Foulkes (Newcastle), Davies (Newcastle), Ford (Sunderland), Allchurch (Swansea), Clarke (Man City)
* first cap.

INTERNATIONAL

Wednesday 26th November 1952

England	**5-0**	**Belgium**
Elliott 4, 48, Lofthouse 42, 86		
R Froggatt 60		

68,333
Referee: L Horn (Netherlands)

Belgium had appeared at Wembley twice before in unofficial internationals. England had never failed to beat them at home but had lost 3-2 in Brussels in 1936. Belgium had not competed in the 1950 World Cup. England took the lead in only the fourth minute. Lofthouse hit a thunderous shot against the bar and Billy Elliott scored from the rebound.

Just before the interval Finney and Bentley neatly prised open the Belgian defence and Nat Lofthouse unleashed another powerful shot which this time went in off the bar. Three minutes after the break, from a Bentley cross, Lofthouse challenged Boogaerts and Elliott slotted in his second. The fourth came after an hour with Redfern Froggatt heading in a Finney free kick. Lofthouse scored the fifth with a header from Bentley's cross.

Their next meeting was to produce an exciting 4-4 draw after extra time in the 1954 World Cup in Basle and Belgium returned to Wembley in 1964.

England: Merrick (Birmingham), Ramsey (Tottenham), Smith (Arsenal), Wright (Wolves) – capt, J Froggatt (Portsmouth), Dickinson (Portsmouth), Finney (Preston), Bentley (Chelsea), Lofthouse (Bolton), R Froggatt (Sheffield W), Elliott (Burnley). manager: Walter Winterbottom
Belgium: Boogaerts (Standard Liege), Diricx (Union St Gilloise), Van Brandt (Lierse), Mees (Royal Antwerp), Carre (FC Liege), Maertens (Antwerp), Lamberechts (Mechelen), Van Der Auwera (Mechelen), Mermans (Anderlecht) – capt, Coppens (Beerschot), Straetmans (White Star). Coach: Bill Gormlie

Inter-Varsity Match

Saturday 7th March 1953

Cambridge U   **0-0**
Oxford U

The Varsity match came to Wembley three months late after being postponed the previous December. It was, however, a disappointing, goalless draw. Cambridge had previously appeared twice at Wembley in the late 1920's.

Schoolboy International

Saturday 28th March 1953

England 3
Charlton 2, Pratt
Wales 3
Rees 2, Hughes
80,500

England failed to win at Wembley for the first time but the record crowd saw a thriller, with the Welsh taking a two-goal lead before a Bobby Charlton-inspired England came storming back to lead themselves, only for Wales to grab a last-minute equaliser. Welsh goalkeeper Brian Thomas damaged his ribs trying to stop Charlton's equaliser, the first of many goalkeepers to dread the name of R Charlton on the opposition teamsheet.

This match marked Charlton's first appearance at Wembley. In 1966 he was both Footballer of the Year and European Footballer of the Year. He went on to win 106 full international caps for England, scoring a record 49 goals.

England: Hawksworth, Moxham, Daly, McGuinness – capt, Titcombe, Smales, Neil, Saxby, Tate, Charlton, Pratt
Wales: Thomas, Smith, Harris, Arnold, Hughes (B), Nurse, Court – capt, Miller, Hughes (M), Davies, Rees. sub: Evans for Thomas 75

FA Amateur Cup Final

Saturday 11th April 1953

Harwick and Parkeston 0
Pegasus 6
Saunders, Sutcliffe 2, Carr 2, Laybourne
100,000

Pegasus won the cup for the second time in three years with a resounding thrashing for their opponents.

Harwich and Parkeston: King, Nightingale, Tyrell – capt, Christie, Bloss, Haugh, Stremp, Pearson, Davies, Cooper, Jennings
Pegasus: Brown, Alexander, McKinna, Vowels, Shearwood, Saunders – capt, Pawson, Carr, Laybourne, Lunn, Sutcliffe

BRITISH CHAMPIONSHIP

Saturday 18th April 1953

England   **2-2**   **Scotland**
Broadis 19, 70   Reilly 55, 90
97,000
Referee: T Mitchell (Northern Ireland)

England had already beaten Wales and drawn with Northern Ireland. Scotland had done likewise. Victory for either side would give them the Championship outright. A draw would mean they would share it. Scotland were still unbeaten at Wembley in the British Championship since 1934 and had won on their last two visits.

Scotland started the stronger but fell behind. The skilful Finney beat three men and passed to Ivor Broadis, who fought off a challenge from Brennan to blast the ball past Farm.

Scotland equalised after Johnstone hit the bar and Lawrie Reilly scored from the rebound, his third in consecutive visits to Wembley. Twenty minutes from the end Finney again provided Broadis with a shooting opportunity which he didn't squander. Cox twisted his ankle in trying to stop Finney and was carried off. With ten men the Scots looked to be beaten. But in the last minute their unbeaten record was saved when Reilly and Johnstone ripped open the England defence for Reilly to shoot home his second.

England won the British Championship outright the following year by beating Scotland at Hampden Park for the fifth successive time in the competition. In so doing England and runners-up Scotland qualified for the World Cup in Switzerland. Scotland's run at Wembley finally came to an end with a crushing defeat in 1955.

England: Merrick (Birmingham), Ramsey (Tottenham), Smith (Arsenal), Wright (Wolves) – capt, Barrass (Bolton), Dickinson (Portsmouth), Finney (Preston), Broadis (Man City), Lofthouse (Bolton), Froggatt (R) (Sheffield W), Froggatt (J) (Portsmouth). manager: Walter Winterbottom

Scotland: Farm (Blackpool), Young (Rangers) – capt, Cox (Rangers), Docherty (Preston), Brennan (Newcastle), Cowie* (Dundee), Wright (Sunderland), Johnstone (Hibernian), Reilly (Hibernian), Steel (Dundee), Liddell (Liverpool).*first cap

Final table	P	W	D	L	F	A	Pts
England	3	1	2	0	9	6	4
Scotland	3	1	2	0	5	4	4
Northern Ireland	3	0	2	1	5	6	2
Wales	3	1	0	2	6	9	2

FA CUP FINAL

Saturday 2nd May 1953

Blackpool   **4-3**   **Bolton Wanderers**
Mortensen 35, 68, 89, Perry 90   Lofthouse 2, Moir 39, Bell 55
100,000
Referee: M Griffiths (Newport)

Blackpool had yet to win a major trophy, and were appearing in their second final in three years. Much media attention was centred on Stan Matthews, who, at 38, was surely going to get no more chances to win an FA Cup winners medal. He had played in Blackpool's two previous finals.

In the quarter-finals Blackpool had knocked out the previous year's finalists and shortly to be League Champions Arsenal on their own ground. Bolton were appearing in their first final since their third FA Cup win of the 1920's.

Bolton took a second minute lead when Nat Lofthouse took a pass from Holden and shot from 25 yards. Farm allowed it to slip through his hands into the net. Bolton began to take control, but suffered a blow when Bell went down injured with a pulled muscle. His team mates reshuffled and Bell was moved out to the wing. With ten minutes to go before half-time Blackpool drew level. Hassall, who had dropped back to defence, deflected a Stan Mortensen shot past Hanson. But within five minutes Bolton had regained the lead. When Langton centred, Farm hesitated, and Willie Moir nodded in Bolton's second.

Blackpool's world fell apart in the tenth minute of the second half. The injured Eric Bell, of all people, rose to head in Holden's centre. Blackpool were 3-1 down, and no team had ever lost a two-goal lead in an FA Cup final.

At this point Matthews began to take charge of proceedings. Faced with an almost certain third runners-up medal he began to pressurize the Bolton full back Banks and started to put dangerous crosses into the penalty area. From one of these Hanson fumbled, and Mortensen ran in to scramble the ball over the line.

Bolton, who had almost lost a four-goal lead in the semi-final, now looked tired and vulnerable. Banks went down with cramp but was still left to mark Matthews. With a minute left from a free kick on the edge of the penalty area Mortensen found a gap at the end of the Bolton defensive wall and blasted in the equaliser to complete his hat-trick. And then, in injury time, Matthews beat Banks and crossed for Bill Perry to knock in Blackpool's winner and complete the most remarkable recovery in the history of the FA Cup.

'The Matthews final', as it became known, still remains the only occasion when Blackpool won a major trophy. They did not appear at Wembley again until 1991 when they reached the Fourth Division Promotion play-off final. Bolton came back to win the FA Cup in 1958.

Blackpool: Farm, Shimwell, Garrett, Fenton, Johnston – capt, Robinson (C), Matthews, Taylor, Mortensen, Mudie, Perry. manager: Joe Smith
Bolton: Hanson, Ball, Banks (R), Wheeler, Barrass, Bell, Holden, Moir – capt, Lofthouse, Hassall, Langton. manager: Bill Ridding

British Junior Cup Final

Saturday 9th May 1953

ATC 1
Hunt
NABC 3
Chapman, Wragg, McParland

The same sides failed to reproduce the drama of the previous year's final (or the previous week's) as the NABC were three goals up after 25 minutes. It was their fifth successive Junior Cup and sixth in all. The ATC only ever lost to the NABC in the history of the competition but their conquerors had now defeated them in each of the past five competitions.

FA 90TH ANNIVERSARY MATCH

Wednesday 21st October 1953

England	**4-4**	**FIFA**
Mortensen 8		Kubala 5 (pen), 64
Mullen 43, 49		Boniperti 15, 39
Ramsey pen. 90		
96,000		
Referee: M Griffiths (Wales)		

England were still unbeaten at home against continental opposition. They had met a Europe side only once before, beating them 3-0 at Highbury in 1938 on the FA's 75th anniversary.

The FIFA select took the lead when Hanappi sent Vukas away down the middle. Eckersley brought him down and Ladislao Kubala scored from the spot. Within three minutes, though, England had equalised. Stan Mortensen took a pass from Lofthouse and ran on to shoot low past Zeman.

But they went behind again when a cross from Zebec was slammed in by Gianpiero Boniperti. Six minutes before half-time Boniperti scored again from a pass by Vukas to leave England's proud record in grave danger. But, just four minutes later, a mix-up between Zeman and Navarro gave Jimmy Mullen an open goal from which to reduce the arrears. FIFA swapped goalkeepers at half-time but the new man Beara could do little about England's second equaliser. From a Matthews cross Mullen scored his second off the post. With 25 minutes remaining FIFA took the lead for the third time. Zebec crossed and Kubala struck a great shot into the corner. England seemed to have met their match but with seconds remaining Cajkovski brought down Mortensen and Alf Ramsey rescued England at the death from a penalty.

England's record was to finally fall in their very next Wembley appearance.

England: Merrick (Birmingham), Ramsey (Tottenham), Eckersley (Blackburn), Wright (Wolves) – capt, Ufton* (Charlton), Dickinson (Portsmouth), Matthews (Blackpool), Mortensen (Blackpool), Lofthouse (Bolton), Quixall (Sheffield W), Mullen (Wolves). manager: Walter Winterbottom
*first cap
FIFA: Zeman (Rapid Vienna & Austria), Navarro (Real Madrid & Spain), Hanappi (Rapid & Austria), Cajkovski (Partizan Belgrade & Yugoslavia), Posipal (Hamburg & W Germany), Ocwirk (FK Austria Vienna & Austria) – capt, Boniperti (Juventus & Italy), Kubala (Barcelona & Spain), Nordahl (Ac Milan & Sweden), Vukas (Hajduk Split & Yugoslavia), Zebec (Partizan & Yugoslavia). Subs: Beara (Hajduk & Yugoslavia) for Zeman 46. coach: Karel Lotsy (Netherlands)

INTERNATIONAL

Wednesday 25th November 1953

England	**3-6**	**Hungary**
Sewell 13		Hidegkuti 1, 20, 53
Mortensen 38		Puskas 24, 29
Ramsey pen 57		Bozsik 50
100,000		

Referee: L Horn (Netherlands)

Hungary were the Olympic Champions. They had beaten England 2-1 in 1934 in Budapest but had suffered heavy defeats in all their other meetings. England still held their proud unbeaten home record against foreign opposition (discounting the mainly British-based players of the Republic of Ireland in 1949 at Goodison Park) but the Hungarians had built a formidable side and they showed it in the opening minute when Nandor Hidegkuti's dummy took Johnston out of the way and enabled him to shoot past Merrick into the top corner.

Hungary kept on the pressure but England broke away to equalise when Johnston intercepted a Hungarian attack and ran upfield, eventually releasing a perfect pass to Mortensen, who provided Jackie Sewell with the chance to drive a low shot past Grosics. This was merely a stay of execution.

Within the next quarter of an hour, England were ripped to shreds by an overwhelming display of world-class skill and finishing. A Czibor cross was flicked on by Kocsis for Hidegkuti to score again. Ferenc Puskas made Wright look amateurish when he pulled the ball back as the defender committed himself and then smashed it into the roof of the net in the same movement. Five minutes later, a Bozsik free kick

was diverted past Merrick by the heel of Puskas.

England, typically, refused to lie down. Stan Mortensen forced his way through to score England's second before the interval but Hungary were just too good for them. A Czibor header was pushed onto the post by Merrick but Jozsef Bozsik drove home the rebound and then Puskas lobbed the ball up for Hidegkuti to complete his hat-trick with a volley.

Fifty six minutes had gone. England were 6-2 down and beginning to face up to the fact that Hungary were in a different class to them.

Alf Ramsey scored a penalty for England four minutes later after Robb had been brought down by Grosics, who went off injured ten minutes from time but the scoreline flattered England and the manner of their defeat made them realise that they would have to change their attitude and approach to succeed in world football.

The Hungarians emphasised their superiority by thrashing England 7-1 in Budapest six months later.

They went to the World Cup in Switzerland as odds-on favourites, but after being unbeaten for four years lost the final to West Germany despite being two goals up after eight minutes.

England: Merrick (Birmingham), Ramsey (Tottenham), Eckersley (Blackburn), Wright (Wolves) – capt, Johnston (Blackpool), Dickinson (Portsmouth), Matthews (Blackpool), Taylor* (Blackpool), Mortensen (Blackpool), Sewell (Sheffield W.), Robb* (Tottenham). manager: Walter Winterbottom
*first cap
Hungary: Grosics (Honved), Buzansky (Dorogi), Lantos (Voros Lobogo), Bozsik (Honved), Lorant (Honved), Zakarias (Voros), Budai (Honved), Kocsis (Honved), Hidegkuti (Voros), Puskas (Honved) – capt, Czibor (Honved). sub: Geller (Voros) for Grosics 80. coach: Gusztav Sebes

Inter-Varsity Match

Saturday 5th December 1953

Cambridge U 1
Wittekind
Oxford U 1
Robinson

Their second meeting of the year produced another draw.

British Amateur Championship

Saturday 27th March 1954

England 1
Lewis
Scotland 4
McQuarrie 2, Omand 2,1 pen

Once again the Scots came to Wembley and won, this time with eight men from Queens Park. England were a goal up at half-time, but were left second best after the turnaround. Scotland finished runners-up to the first British Amateur Champions, Northern Ireland.

England: Brown (Pegasus), Mcghee (Royal Navy), Hunt (Marine), Topp (Hendon), Adams (Hendon) – capt, Taylor (Crook), Lewis (Chelsea), Heckman (Bromley), Oliver (Bishop Auckland), O'connell (Bishop Auckland), Walton (Finchley)
Scotland: Weir (Queens Park), Harnett (Queens Park), Stewart (Bishop Auckland), Cromar (Queens Park), Valentine (Queens Park), Hastie (Queens Park) – capt, Callaghan (St. Mungo's FP), Ward (Queens Park), Murray (Queens Park), Mcquarrie (Billingham), Omand (Queens Park)

Schoolboy International

Saturday 3rd April 1954

England 1
Bennett
Scotland 0

Scotland's third successive defeat at the stadium.

England: Dean, Cooper, Hallett, Horne, Staton – capt, Cox, Sluman, Spears, Oliver, Jeffrey, Bennett
Scotland: Barron, Burns (J), McKay, Hastings, Gay, Burns (F), Crowe, Finlay, Goldie, Alexander, Lornie

FA Amateur Cup Final

Saturday 10th April 1954

Bishop Auckland 2
Dixon 13, Oliver 44
Crook Town 2
Thompson 15, Appleby 55
After extra time
100,000

Bishop Auckland's third Wembley final in five years, but once again they failed to win. When Nimmins broke his leg in the first five minutes, the ten-man Bishops seemed set to lose, but they took the initiative and twice led. Crook were appearing in their first final since 1901 and had a two-goal lead at half-time in the replay. The trophy would have been shared if the third meeting had failed to separate them, but it was Crook who were victorious in the end.

Bishop Auckland: Sharratt, Marshall, Fryer, Hardisty, Cresswell, Nimmins, Major – capt, Dixon, Oliver, O'Connell, Watson
Crook: Jarrie, Riley, Steward, Jeffs, Davison – capt, Taylor, Appleby, Thompson, Harrison, Williamson, McMillan

Replay: Monday 19th April 1954
Bishop Auckland 2
Oliver 2
Crook Town 2
Harrison 2
After extra time
(St. James' Park, Newcastle)

Second Replay: Thursday 22nd April 1954
Bishop Auckland 0
Crook Town 1
Harrison
(Ayresome Park, Middlesbrough)

FA CUP FINAL

Saturday 1st May 1954

Preston North End	**2-3**	**West Bromwich Albion**
Morrison 22		Allen 21, 63 (pen)
Wayman 51		Griffin 87

100,000
Referee: A Luty (Leeds)

Preston had won the FA Cup at Wembley in 1938 and had appeared in the Football League War Cup final in 1941. West Brom had won the Cup in 1931 and had lost the 1935 final. The two teams had met in the 1888 final, with West Brom winning 2-1 at Kennington Oval.

Preston finished 11th in the First Division, their lowest position since promotion in 1951. The previous season they had been League runners-up to Arsenal on goal average. West Brom finished as League runners-up to Wolverhampton Wanderers. This was their highest league position since 1925.

West Brom's opening goal came after Lee blocked a Cunningham clearance, chased after it and crossed. Ronnie Allen was in the centre to beat Thompson.

Within a minute Preston were level, Angus Morrison heading in from a Docherty cross. Early in the second half Preston took the lead. Finney and Foster combined to send Charlie Wayman through. The prolific striker rounded Sanders and scored.

Albion's equaliser came from the penalty spot after Docherty brought down Barlow. Allen made no mistake.

Three minutes remained when West Brom snatched the winner. Frank Griffin took a pass from Ryan, cut inside and slammed it past the 'keeper.

Preston dropped out of the First Division in 1961 but reached the FA Cup final again in 1964. They have not won the Cup since, nor returned to the top flight. It was another 14 years before West Brom won the Cup again, but there was to be a Football League Cup final appearance at Wembley the year before.

Preston: Thompson, Cunningham. Walton, Docherty, Marston, Forbes, Finney – capt, Foster, Wayman, Baxter, Morrison. manager: Scot Symon.

West Brom: Sanders, Kennedy, Millard – capt, Dudley, Dugdale, Barlow, Griffin, Ryan, Allen, Nicholls, Lee. manager: Vic Buckingham

British Junior Cup Final

Saturday 8th May 1954

ATC 1
Frampton

NABC 0
40,000

The same teams appeared in the final for the third year in succession but the NABC suffered their first defeat in six years of the competition in the lowest scoring final. For the ATC it was sweet revenge for five successive defeats at the hands of their opponents and Corporal Frampton's 55th minute winner gave them their third Junior Cup win.

BRITISH CHAMPIONSHIP

Wednesday 10th November 1954

England	**3-2**	**Wales**
Bentley 70, 74, 82		Charles 35, 75

91,112
Referee: C Faultless (Scotland)

England, the reigning British Champions, had already beaten Northern Ireland 2-0 at Windsor Park. Wales had lost 1-0 to Scotland at Ninian Park and, as in 1952, had to avoid defeat to retain their interest in the Championship.

They took the lead when a cross by Allchurch was converted by John Charles.

Wales held this until 20 minutes to go when Roy Bentley headed in from Matthews' centre. Four minutes later King misjudged Byrne's cross and Bentley scored again. Wales took less than a minute to draw level with a clever piece of skill from Charles as he turned swiftly to send a low drive past Wood. England took the points, however, when Blunstone crossed and Bentley came charging in to complete his hat-trick.

Wales avoided finishing bottom by defeating Northern Ireland 3-2 at Windsor Park. England and Scotland were once again left to decide the destiny of the British Championship. The following season Wales beat England for the first time since the war.

England: Wood (Man Utd), Staniforth (Huddersfield), Byrne (Man Utd), Phillips (Portsmouth), Wright (Wolves) – capt, Slater* (Wolves), Matthews (Blackpool), Bentley (Chelsea), Allen (West Brom), Shackleton (Sunderland), Blunstone* (Chelsea). manager: Walter Winterbottom

Wales: King* (Swansea), Williams (West Brom), Sherwood (Cardiff) – capt, Paul (Man City), Daniel (Sunderland), Sullivan (Cardiff), Tapscott (Arsenal), Ford (Cardiff), Charles (Leeds), Allchurch (Swansea), Clarke (Man City).
*first cap

INTERNATIONAL

Wednesday 1st December 1954

England   **3-1**   **West Germany**
Bentley 28, Allen 48, Shackleton 80   Beck 75
100,000
Referee: V Orlandini (Italy)

West Germany had won the World Cup five months earlier with a surprise victory over the mighty Hungarians in Berne but only three members of their winning team were to play at Wembley.

England had reached the quarter-finals where they lost to Uruguay in Basle. This was the first meeting between England and West Germany. They had met a united Germany three times before the war.

The red-shirted England side took the lead after 27 minutes. Matthews crossed and Roy Bentley headed in at the far post. They increased their lead just after half-time.

Herkenrath saved at the feet of Finney but Ronnie Allen scored from the rebound. Seeler provided Alfred Beck with a pass and he shot past Williams to reduce the arrears with a quarter of an hour left. But then Allen passed to Len Shackleton, who drew Herkenrath before delivering an exquisite chip over the 'keeper's head and into the net.

England won by the same scoreline in Berlin in 1956. West Germany finished fourth in their defence of the World Cup in 1958 in Sweden and had lost to England again by the time they returned to Wembley in 1966.

England: Williams (Wolves), Staniforth (Huddersfield), Byrne (Man Utd), Phillips (Portsmouth), Wright (Wolves) – capt, Slater (Wolves), Matthews (Blackpool), Bentley (Chelsea), Allen (West Brom), Shackleton (Sunderland), Finney (Preston). manager: Walter Winterbottom

West Germany: Herkenrath (Rot-Weiss Essen), Posipal (Hamburg) – capt, Kohlmeyer (Kaiserslautern), Erhardt (Schalke), Liebrich (Kaiserslautern), Harpers (Schalke), Kaufhold (Kickers Offenbach), Pfeiffer (Alemania Aachen), Seeler (Hamburg), Derwall (Fortuna Dusseldorf), Beck (St. Pauli). Coach: Sepp Herberger

Inter-Varsity Match

Saturday 4th December 1954

Cambridge U 3
Brough 2, Scanlan

Oxford U 2
Sweeney, Newell og

Oxford were 2-0 up at half-time, but it was Cambridge who secured the first Wembley victory of the annual meeting.

In the Oxford University side was Frank Bough, who went on to present BBC Television's 'Grandstand' from the stadium on many occasions in the 1970's.

BRITISH CHAMPIONSHIP

Saturday 2nd April 1955

England   **7-2**   **Scotland**
Wilshaw 1, 70, 73, 83,   Reilly 10, Docherty 88
Lofthouse 7, 27, Revie 24
96,847
Referee: M Griffiths (Wales)

England had already beaten both Northern Ireland and Wales and needed only a point to retain the Championship. Scotland had failed to beat Northern Ireland at Hampden Park and so needed to win to claim their first outright Championship since 1951.

They were still unbeaten at Wembley in the British Championship since 1934.

England were ahead in the first minute. Blunstone crossed and Martin came out but Dennis Wilshaw slotted the ball into an empty net. They scored again in the seventh minute, Nat Lofthouse hitting the target after good work by Revie and Stan Matthews.

Lawrie Reilly then pulled one back by scoring in his fourth successive game at Wembley when Wright was uncharacteristically hesitant. But Don Revie soon scored when Martin fumbled and before the half hour England had notched their fourth, Matthews crossing for Lofthouse to score.

England now eased off a little but finished with a flourish.

With 20 minutes left a pinpoint centre from Matthews left Wilshaw with a simple header for the fifth. The 40-year-old Matthews was now destroying the Scottish defence almost at will. He sent Wilshaw through to complete his hat-trick and then created another chance yet again for Wilshaw to score.

Tommy Docherty scored a late consolation goal from long range but England had emphatically buried their Scottish jinx with their biggest ever victory over their rivals.

Footballer of the Year Don Revie made his first Wembley appearance, scoring England's third goal.

England: Williams (Wolves), Meadows* (Man City), Byrne (Man Utd), Armstrong* (Chelsea), Wright (Wolves) – capt, Edwards* (Man Utd), Matthews (Blackpool), Revie (Man City), Lofthouse (Bolton), Wilshaw (Wolves), Blunstone (Chelsea). manager: Walter Winterbottom
Scotland: Martin (Aberdeen), Cunningham (Preston) – capt, Haddock* (Clyde), Docherty (Preston), Davidson (Partick), Cumming* (Hearts), McKenzie (Partick), Johnstone (Man City), Reilly (Hibernian), McMillan (Aidrie), Ring (Clyde)
*first cap

Final table	P	W	D	L	F	A	Pts
England	3	3	0	0	12	4	6
Scotland	3	1	1	1	5	9	3
Wales	3	1	0	2	5	6	2
Northern Ireland	3	0	1	2	4	7	1

FA Amateur Cup Final

Saturday 16th April 1955

Bishop Auckland 2
Lewin 2
Hendon 0
100,000

At the fourth attempt, with a goal in each half, Bishop Auckland finally recorded their first victory at Wembley.

Bishop Auckland: Sharratt, Marshall, Stewart, Hardisty, Cresswell, Nimmins, Major – capt, Lewin, Oliver, O'Connell, Edwards
Hendon: Ivey, Fisher, Beardsley, Topp, Adams, Austin, Saffery, Hvidsten, Bahler, Cunningham, Parker

Schoolboy International

Saturday 23rd April 1955

England 6
Bunch, Dawson 2, Wynn 2, Hall
Wales 0
90,000

Alex Dawson, who scored twice, went on to appear in two FA Cup Finals, scoring for Preston North End in 1964.

England: Moore, Feist, Wright, Bunch, Holland, Bradbury – capt, Dawson, Hall, Wynn, Cliss, Pearson
Wales: Twigg, Jones, Parry, Collins, Morgan, Edwards, Thomas (J), Thomas (F), O'Brien, Lovell, Evans

FA CUP FINAL

Saturday 7th May 1955

Manchester City   1-3   **Newcastle United**
Johnstone 44   Milburn 1, Mitchell 53, Hannah 60
100,000
Referee: R Leafe (Nottingham)

City had last won the FA Cup in 1934. Newcastle had won it four times at Wembley in four visits and were aiming to regain it for the third time in five years. Victory would give them a record-equalling sixth Cup win.

Newcastle took the lead in the first minute. White's corner was headed in by Jackie Milburn. The match turned, though, in the 18th minute when City lost Meadows with a knee injury. Just as in 1952 Newcastle had ten men to beat.

Even so they managed to equalise. Hayes crossed and Bobby Johnstone beat Simpson with a diving header. But Newcastle made their experience, and numerical advantage, tell in the second half. First, Bobby

Mitchell took a pass from White and then showed great skill in beating Spurdle, taking the ball to the goal line and shooting from an acute angle. Trautmann, who was expecting a cross, could not get down quick enough and the ball went under him. Seven minutes later Mitchell laid on the third for George Hannah (who joined City three years later) to shoot past Trautmann.

City returned to win the Cup the following year. Newcastle went into decline and were relegated six years later. It was 1974 when they reached their next final.

Bert Trautmann, the German goalkeeper, appeared at Wembley for the first time. Twelve months later he was Footballer of the Year.

Manchester C: Trautmann, Meadows, Little, Barnes (K), Ewing, Paul – capt, Spurdle, Hayes, Revie, Johnstone, Fagan. manager: Les McDowall
Newcastle: Simpson, Cowell, Batty (R), Scoular – capt, Stokoe, Casey, White, Milburn, Keeble, Hannah, Mitchell. manager: Duggie Livingstone

EUROPEAN FAIRS CUP

Wednesday 26th October 1955

London   3-2   **Frankfurt**
Jezzard 46, 70   Pfaff pen 26, Kaufhold 31
Robson 65

London's representative side were two goals down at half-time in Wembley's first match played under floodlights. They went on to win the group and reached the final where they lost to Barcelona almost three years later.

Danny Blanchflower, who went on to

win the Footballer of the Year award twice and captained Tottenham Hotspur to the League and Cup 'double' in 1961, made his first Wembley appearance.

Sir Bobby Robson, future England manager, made a scoring Wembley debut, netting London's equaliser.

London: Ditchburn (Tottenham), Sillett (Chelsea), Willemse (Chelsea), Blanchflower (Tottenham), Hurley (Millwall), Hammond (Charlton), Groves (Leyton Orient), Robson (Fulham), Jezzard (Fulham), Bentley (Chelsea) – capt, Mitten (Fulham)
Frankfurt: Rado (FSV), Sattler (OFC Kickers Offenbach), Magel (OFC), Keim (OFC), Lurz (FSV), Weber (OFC), Kraus (OFC), Kaufhold (OFC), Kress (Eintracht), Pfaff (Eintracht), Herrmann (FSV) – capt

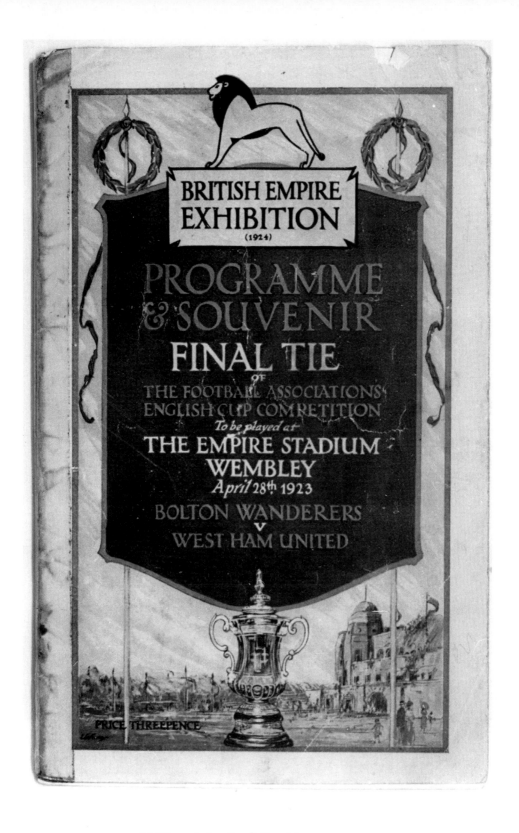

1923 and the first Wembley programme.

1928 and the programme for the game when the Scots became known as the Wembley Wizards.

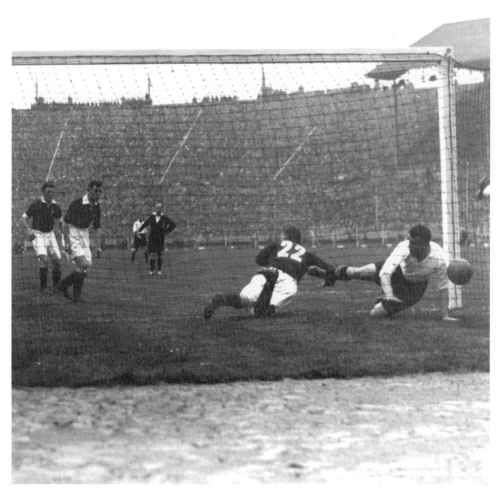

1933. Numbers were worn for the first time. Everton wore 1-11 and Manchester City 12-22. City goalkeeper Len Langford fails to stop the legendary Dixie Dean from scoring. Everton won 3-0.

1947 and Charlton returned to Wembley after losing in 1946. This time they beat Burnley after extra time.

THE IMPORTANT THING IN THE OLYMPIC GAMES IS NOT WINNING BUT TAKING PART. THE ESSENTIAL THING IN LIFE IS NOT CONQUERING BUT FIGHTING WELL.

BARON de COUBERTIN

1948. London was still devastated by the war but Britain staged the 'austerity' Olympics.

1953. A wake up call for English football as Hungary win 6-3. Here goalkeeper Gil Merrick and Bill Eckersley fail to stop Nandor Hidegkuti (out of picture) from scoring while Harry Johnston looks on.

*1954. West Bromwich Albion goalkeeper Jim Sanders cannot bear
to look as Ronnie Allen takes a penalty. He scored and Albion beat
Preston North End 3-2*

1956 and arguably Wembley's most famous injury. Manchester City's German goalkeeper Bert Trautmann (on ground) and Birmingham City's no. 10 Peter Murphy receive treatment. Trautmann broke his neck but carried on playing. City won 3-1.

1958. Nat Lofthouse triumphant after Bolton Wanderers had beaten a Manchester United team patched together after the Munich air crash. Lofthouse scored the first goal.

1961. Tottenham Hotspur lift skipper Danny Blanchflower aloft after the League and Cup double is won. From left: Cliff Jones, Bill Brown, Peter Baker, Terry Dyson, Bobby Smith, Les Allen (looking up) and John White.

*1963. The stadium was used for the heavyweight fight between
the then Cassius Clay (later Muhamed Ali) and Henry Cooper.
The referee was Tommy Little.*

1966. The World Cup final. Geoff Hurst, scorer of a hat-trick in England's 4-2 extra time win over West Germany rises above the defence.

1968. Nobby Stiles and Bobby Charlton celebrate Manchester United's European Cup final victory over Benfica.

1973. Was this the best ever save at Wembley? Sunderland's Jim Montgomery pulls off an astonishing stop as his team provide one of the stadium's biggest shocks by beating Leeds United 1-0 in the FA Cup final.

1973. Sir Alf Ramsey's face tells the story as he walks to the dressing room following England's 1-1 draw with Poland which prevented the team from qualifying for the 1974 World Cup finals.

1975. Malcolm Macdonald looks pensive despite scoring all the goals when England beat Cyprus 5-0.

BRITISH CHAMPIONSHIP

Wednesday 2nd November 1955

England   **3-0**   **Northern Ireland**
Wilshaw 51, 53, Finney 88
62,000
Referee: M Griffiths (Wales)

England were aiming for a third successive outright British Championship, but had already lost 2-1 to Wales at Ninian Park. Northern Ireland had beaten Scotland 2-1 at Windsor Park and were making their first appearance at Wembley. They had not beaten England since 1927 when they won 2-0 at Windsor Park.

The Irish defence held out until just after half-time. A brilliant pass from Haynes left Dennis Wilshaw with only Uprichard to beat which he did with ease. Two min-utes later from Finney's cross, Perry lobbed for Wilshaw to head his second over the 'keeper. In the 89th minute, from a pass by Jezzard, Tom Finney cut inside and shot into the corner for England's third.

This was the only occasion that all four teams shared the British Championship. England had now won a record five succes-sive titles while Northern Ireland's success was their first since 1914. They would be back two years later to secure a memorable victory.

England: Baynham* (Luton), Hall (Birmingham), Byrne (Man Utd), Clayton* (Blackburn), Wright (Wolves) – capt, Dickinson (Portsmouth), Finney (Preston), Haynes (Fulham), Jezzard (Fulham), Wilshaw (Wolves), Perry* (Blackpool). manager: Walter Winterbottom
Northern Ireland: Uprichard (Portsmouth), Cunningham (Leicester), Graham (Doncaster), Blanchflower (Tottenham) – capt, McCavana (Coleraine), Peacock (Celtic), Bingham (Sunderland), McIlroy (Burnley), Coyle (Coleraine), Tully (Celtic), McParland (Aston Villa). manager: Peter Doherty*first cap

Final table	P	W	D	L	F	A	Pts
England	3	1	1	1	5	3	3
Northern Ireland	3	1	1	1	3	5	3
Scotland	3	1	1	1	4	3	3
Wales	3	1	1	1	3	4	3

INTERNATIONAL

Wednesday 30th November 1955

England   **4-1**   **Spain**
Atyeo 12, Perry 13, 60, Finney 59   Arieta 80
95,550
Referee: M Guigue (France)

In 1929 in Madrid Spain had been the first foreign team to beat England. In fact Eng-land had beaten them only once but that was by 7-1 at Highbury two years later. Their last meeting had been a 1-1 draw in Madrid just six months earlier. Spain had failed to qualify for the previous year's World Cup having been eliminated on the drawing of lots after surprisingly failing to beat Turkey.

England missed a penalty in the sev-enth minute. Finney was brought down by Campanal but his spot kick was weakly hit and comfortably saved by Carmelo. They had to wait only another five min-utes, however, for a goal. A neat passing move ended with Clayton touching the ball on for John Atyeo to score. England scored again within a minute and again a fine passing move split open the Spanish defence. This time Lofthouse supplied the final pass for the in-rushing Bill Perry to drive the ball home.

England's third came in the second half. Tom Finney atoned for his penalty miss by speeding away down the wing, cutting in and shooting past the 'keeper as Campanal desperately tried to stop him. Perry headed his second shortly afterwards from a cross by Clayton and then Spain scored in the

81st minute when Arieta headed in from a Gonzalez centre.

Spain also failed to qualify for the 1958 World Cup, finishing runners-up to Scotland in their group, but they did record an emphatic 3-0 win over England in Madrid in 1960 before returning to Wembley later that year.

England: Baynham (Luton), Hall (Birmingham), Byrne (Man Utd), Clayton (Blackburn), Wright (Wolves) – capt, Dickinson (Portsmouth), Finney (Preston), Atyeo* (Bristol C), Lofthouse (Bolton), Haynes (Fulham), Perry (Blackpool). manager: Walter Winterbottom
*first cap
Spain: Carmelo (Athletic Bilbao), Guillamon (Barcelona) – capt, Campanal (Sevilla), Mauri (Bilbao), Garay (Bilbao), Maguregui (Bilbao), Gonzalez (Atletico Madrid), Paya (Real Madrid), Arieta (Bilbao), Domenech (Sevilla), Collar (Atletico Madrid). Coach: Guillermo Eizaguirre

Inter-Varsity Match

Wednesday 7th December 1955

Cambridge U 4
Steward, Pretlove, Howlett 2
Oxford U 2
Roberts, Sweeney

A second successive victory for Cambridge.

British Amateur Championship

Saturday 24th March 1956

England 4
McKenna 2, Bromilow, Oliver
Scotland 2
Devine, Reid
10,000
Referee: W Williams (Belfast)

Despite fielding seven of the side that was to win the Scottish Second Division Championship, the Queens Park influence was not enough this time for Scotland. England earned their first win at Wembley at amateur level and with it they shared the British Championship with Northern Ireland.

England: Pinner (Cambridge U& Pegasus), Alexander (Corinthian-Casuals), Farrer (Walthamstow) – capt, Robinson (Brentford), Prince (Walthamstow), Dodkins (Ilford), Mckenna (Bishop Auckland), Coates (Royal Navy & Kingstonian), Oliver (Bishop Auckland), Bromilow (Southport), Twissell (Royal Navy & Plymouth)
Scotland: Samson (Hamilton), Taylor (Hounslow), Hastie (Queens Park) – capt, Cromar (Queens Park), Robb (Queens Park), Chalmers (Dunfermline), Reid (Queens Park), Mccann (Queens Park), McGrory (Arbroath), Devine (Queens Park), Omand (Queens Park)

FA Amateur Cup Final

Saturday 7th April 1956

Bishop Auckland 1
McKenna 78
Corinthian-Casuals 1
Kerruish 56
After extra time
80,000
Referee: J Clough (Lancashire)

Bishop Auckland, the holders, were in their third successive final, but needed a replay to retain the trophy.

Bishop Auckland: Sharratt, Fryer, Stewart – capt, Hardisty, Cresswell, Nimmins, McKenna, Lewin, Oliver, O'Connell, Edwards
Corinthian-Casuals: Ahm, Alexander, Newton, Shuttleworth, Cowan – capt, Vowels, Insole, Sanders, Laybourne, Citron, Kerruish

Replay: Saturday 14th April 1956
Bishop Auckland 4
Lewin 2, Hardisty, Stewart
Corinthian-Casuals 1
Citron
(Ayresome Park, Middlesbrough)

Schoolboy International

Saturday 21st April 1956

England 1
Bridges
Scotland 2
,McGurk, Gaskell og

England's first defeat at Wembley at this level despite taking the lead in the first thirty seconds. Dave Gaskell fumbled Malcolm's cross into his own net for Scotland's winner, but just six months later he was keeping a clean sheet for Manchester

United as they won the FA Charity Shield at Maine Road against local rivals City. Gaskell had only just turned 16 years of age but was drafted in for his debut when Ray Wood picked up an injury on the day. Seven years later he won an FA Cup winners medal at Wembley.

England's goalscorer Barry Bridges played three times at Wembley for the full international side. His first cap was won in 1965. Ten years later Jimmy Gabriel was in the Everton side that won the FA Cup at Wembley.

England: Gaskell, France, Bentham – capt, Simpson, Smith, Vaissen, Bates, Hobbs, Bridges, Rowlands, Carlin
Scotland: Davie, Sjoberg, W Grant – capt, Gabriel, McConnachie, J Grant, Malcolm, McDonald, McCulloch, Cunningham, McGurk.

FA CUP FINAL

Saturday 5th May 1956

Birmingham City   **1-3**   **Manchester City**
Kinsey 1
Referee: A Bond (Fulham)
Hayes 3, Dyson 65, Johnstone 68

Birmingham's only previous final had been in 1931 and they had still to win a major trophy. City had won the Cup for the second time in 1934 and were eager to make amends for defeat in the previous year's final.

Birmingham finished sixth in the First Division, their highest ever league position. They had been promoted on goal average the previous season but were Second Division Champions as three clubs finished on the same number of points.

City finished fourth, a point ahead of Birmingham, their highest position since they won the League Championship in 1937.

City took only three minutes to score. Clarke's cross found Revie, who back-heeled the ball into the path of Joe Hayes, who had time to steady himself, before driving it past Merrick. Birmingham recovered from this early blow by equalising when a Newman throw-in was flicked on by Brown for Noel Kinsey to blast a shot in

off the post. The game then developed into an exciting end-to-end attacking game. It was City who scored next, 20 minutes into the second half. Barnes put Jack Dyson through to score. Within three minutes City had effectively settled it. A long kick from Trautmann was touched on by Dyson and Bobby Johnstone ran on to score the third. With 15 minutes left Trautmann made a brave save at the feet of Murphy, sustaining an injury which was diagnosed four days later as a broken neck. The heroic German goalkeeper and Footballer of the Year, completed the match, however, without being beaten again.

Birmingham reached the semi-finals again the following year but did not return to Wembley until 1991 when they won the Leyland DAF Cup. They have yet to better their league position of 1956. City were relegated seven years later but returned with a trophy-winning side in the late 1960's. In 1969 they won the FA Cup for the fourth time.

Birmingham: Merrick, Hall, Green, Newman, Smith, Boyd – capt, Astall, Kinsey, Brown, Murphy, Govan manager: Arthur Turner
Manchester C: Trautmann, Leivers, Little, Barnes (K), Ewing, Paul – capt, Johnstone, Hayes, Revie, Dyson, Clarke manager: Duggie Livingstone

INTERNATIONAL

Wednesday 9th May 1956

England   **4-2**   **Brazil**
Taylor 3, 65, Grainger 5, 84
100,000
Referee: M Guigue (France)
Paulinho 53, Didi 55

This was the first meeting between the two countries. Like England, Brazil had reached the World Cup quarter-finals in 1954. They had last won the South American Championship in 1949 and had finished runners-up to Uruguay in the 1950 World Cup in Brazil.

England were two up in just five minutes. Matthews set up the first with Haynes knocking the ball on for Tommy Taylor, who beat Pavao before running on and shooting past Gilmar. Then Colin Grainger raced in and slotted home number two, also from a Haynes pass.

Just after half-time Brazil suddenly sprang to life. A cross from Nilton Santos was reached by Paulinho, whose shot spun off Byrne and over Matthews. Two minutes later, Didi collected a clearance from Wright and deceived Matthews from the edge of the box with a spinning shot to bring Brazil level. After an hour's play, England were given an opportunity to regain the lead when a Haynes free kick was handled by Zozimo in the area. After a long delay, during which Alvaro walked away with the ball, Atyeo's kick was saved by Gilmar. Atyeo soon made amends, however, when he headed on a Matthews cross for Taylor to head his second and put England back in front. England were then awarded another penalty, when a move involving Taylor and Atyeo was stopped by another Zozimo handling offence. Incredibly, Byrne shot wide. It was left to the ever-reliable 41-year-old Stan Matthews to make sure of victory with yet another accurate centre for Grainger to net his second.

England next met Brazil in a goalless draw in the 1958 World Cup in Gothenburg. England were the only team to prevent them from scoring but Brazil went on to mesmerize Europe by winning the World Cup, scoring five in both the semi-final and final. They then beat England twice before returning to Wembley in 1963.

England: Matthews (R) (Coventry), Hall (Birmingham), Byrne (Man Utd), Clayton (Blackburn), Wright (Wolves) – capt, Edwards (Man Utd), Matthews (S) (Blackpool), Atyeo (Bristol C), Taylor (Man Utd), Haynes (Fulham), Grainger* (Sheffield U). manager: Walter Winterbottom
*first cap
Brazil: Gilmar (Corinthians), Santos (D) (Portuguesa), Santos (N) (Botafogo) – capt, Zozimo (Bangu), Pavao (Bangu), Dequinha (Flamengo), Paulinho (Flamengo), Alvaro (Santos), Gino (Sao Paulo), Didi (Botafogo), Canhoteiro (Sao Paulo). coach: Flavio Costa

British Junior Cup Final

Saturday 12th May 1956

ACF 1
Griffiths
NABC 2
Denham, Thewlis
Referee: H Stokes (London)

There had been no competition the previous year, and this was to be the last final. The NABC, fittingly enough, notched up their seventh triumph and received a trophy for the first time. The ACF suffered a fourth final defeat. The match was a curtain-raiser to the Olympic Qualifying match in the evening.

Olympic Qualifying Second Leg

Great Britain 3
Hardisty 2, Lewis pen
Bulgaria 3
Milanov, Prince og, Dimitrov

30,000
Referee: G Bernardi (Italy)
Bulgaria win 5-3 on aggregate

Great Britain, represented by 11 Englishmen, were knocked out by a side containing nine members of the Bulgarian army team CSKA Sofia. This was no disgrace because England's amateurs had held the full-strength Bulgarian national team to a draw.

Six months later Great Britain actually went to the Olympics by invitation after a spate of withdrawals. They reached the quarter-finals in Melbourne before losing 6-1 to Bulgaria!

Great Britain: Pinner (Cambridge U& Pegasus), Alexander (Corinthian-Casuals), Farrer (Walthamstow) – capt, Topp (Hendon), Prince (Walthamstow), Dodkins (Ilford), Lewis (Chelsea), Hardisty (Bishop Auckland), Laybourne (Corinthian-Casuals), Bromilow (Southport), Twissell (Royal Navy & Plymouth)
Bulgaria: Naydenov, Vassilev, Nisheinov, Bozhkov – capt, Rakarov, Patev, Milanov, Dimitrov, Panavotov, Kolev, Yanev

1956

BRITISH CHAMPIONSHIP

Wednesday 14th November 1956

England   **3-1**   **Wales**
Haynes 52, Brooks 55, Finney 75   J Charles 8
93,796
Referee: H Phillips (Scotland)

Wales had beaten England 2-1 at Ninian Park the previous year, their first victory over England since the war. They had only won once at Wembley, during wartime. England had already drawn 1-1 with Northern Ireland at Windsor Park, while Wales had drawn 2-2 with Scotland at Ninian Park. All four teams had shared the previous season's British Championship, but England were aiming for a record sixth successive title. Defeat would eliminate Wales, as in their two previous visits.

The visitors were ahead after only eight minutes. An inch-perfect free kick from Allchurch was headed in by John Charles. Four minutes later, however, they seemed destined to lose their lead when their goalkeeper Kelsey was injured diving at the feet of Finney. Sherwood went in goal. Somehow they managed to hold their lead until half-time. Kelsey came out for the second half for a short while but Sherwood stayed in goal.

Inevitably, England scored. Just after half-time a corner from Grainger was headed on by Finney for Johnny Haynes to volley the equaliser. Johnny Brooks put England in front from a rebound. Then, with half an hour left, England were reduced to ten men when Grainger went off with an injured ankle. The Welsh were still disadvantaged, though, and finally the ageless Matthews crossed for Tom Finney to score the third.

Yet again England and Scotland decided the British Championship. Wales did not return to Wembley until 1960 and they would not beat England again until 1977.

England: Ditchburn (Tottenham), Hall (Birmingham), Byrne (Man Utd), Clayton (Blackburn), Wright (Wolves) – capt, Dickinson (Portsmouth), Matthews (Blackpool), Brooks* (Tottenham), Finney (Preston), Haynes (Fulham), Grainger (Sheffield U). manager: Walter Winterbottom
Wales: Kelsey (Arsenal), Sherwood (Newport) – capt, Hopkins (Tottenham), Harrington (Cardiff), Daniel (Sunderland), Sullivan (Cardiff), Medwin (Tottenham), Charles (M) (Swansea), Charles (J) (Leeds), Allchurch (Swansea), Jones (Swansea)
*first cap

INTERNATIONAL

Wednesday 28th November 1956

England   **3-0**   **Yugoslavia**
Brooks 13, Taylor 65, 89
78,500
Referee: E Harzic (France)

Yugoslavia were unbeaten in their three previous meetings with England. England had lost twice in Belgrade and there had been a 2-2 draw at Highbury in 1950. Yugoslavia had beaten Great Britain in the 1948 Olympic semi-final at Wembley before losing the final. They had also lost the 1952 final 2-0 to Hungary in Helsinki and six of that side were appearing at Wembley. In the 1954 World Cup they had reached the quarter-finals, like England, but lost to the eventual winners West Germany.

England took the lead in the 13th minute. From a pass by Haynes, Johnny Brooks ran in and found the target with a well-hit shot. In the 65th minute Finney expertly drew the defence with a mazy dribble and then passed to substitute Tommy Taylor who scored the second. Ten minutes later Matthews was upended by Stankovic (who had been sent off in the 1948 Olympic final) but Beara saved Byrne's penalty kick, England's fourth Wembley miss in just under 12 months. But in the dying seconds Taylor scored again, this time from Blunstone's pass.

England: Ditchburn (Tottenham), Hall (Birmingham), Byrne (Man Utd), Clayton (Blackburn), Wright (Wolves) – capt, Dickinson (Portsmouth), Matthews (Blackpool), Brooks (Tottenham), Finney (Preston), Haynes (Fulham), Blunstone (Chelsea). sub: Taylor (Man Utd) for Haynes 30 manager: Walter Winterbottom

Yugoslavia: Beara (Red Star Belgrade), Belin (Partizan Belgrade), Stankovic (Red Star), Tasic (Red Star), Horvat (Dinamo Zagreb) – capt, Boskov (Vojvodina), Rajkov (Vojvodina), Conc (Dinamo Zagreb), Toplak (Red Star), Vukas (Hajduk Split), Zebec (Partizan). Coach: Aleksandar Tirnanic

Inter-Varsity Match

Saturday 8th December 1956

Cambridge U 1
Steward

Oxford U 4
King 2, Caddick, Trimby

Oxford were two up after only eight minutes and an injury to Bushell in the 15th minute meant there was little chance of Cambridge preventing Oxford's first win at Wembley.

Schoolboy International

Saturday 30th March 1957

England 2
Woodley, Brookes

Wales 0

Nobby Stiles, who went on to win a World Cup winners medal in 1966 and a European Cup winners medal in 1968, appeared at Wembley for the first time.

Five years later, Bobby Tambling made his full international debut at Wembley against Wales.

England: Smart, Wileman, McCarthy, Stiles, Wood – capt, Jones, Woodley, Sullivan, Tambling, Brooks, Brookes
Wales: Griffiths, Owen, Herrity, Burton, Bryant, Jones, Lloyd, Hughes, Mitchell, Williams, Castle.

BRITISH CHAMPIONSHIP

Saturday 6th April 1957

England	2-1	Scotland
Kevan 63, Edwards 84		Ring 1

97,520
Referee: H Roomer (Netherlands)

England needed only a point for a record sixth successive British Championship, but a draw would mean they shared it with Scotland. Victory for the Scots would give them their first outright win since 1951, when they last beat England. Their previous visit had been a traumatic experience.

In the first minute, Tommy Ring intercepted a clearance from Hall, beat Wright and shot Scotland into the lead. They held it until the second half when Grainger crossed and Derek Kevan dived to head the equaliser. With six minutes left, England snatched victory. From a pass by Matthews, Duncan Edwards hammered home the winner from fully 25 yards out.

The following year, England recorded their biggest ever victory at Hampden Park, Glasgow in the British Championship, when they beat Scotland 4-0.

England: Hodgkinson* (Sheffield U), Hall (Birmingham), Byrne (Man Utd), Clayton (Blackburn), Wright (Wolves) – capt, Edwards (Man Utd), Matthews (Blackpool), Thompson (Preston), Finney (Preston), Kevan* (West Brom), Grainger (Sunderland). manager: Walter Winterbottom
Scotland: Younger (Liverpool), Caldow (Rangers), Hewie (Charlton), McColl (Rangers), Young (Rangers) – capt, Docherty (Preston), Collins (Celtic), Fernie (Celtic), Reilly (Hibernian), Mudie (Blackpool), Ring (Clyde)
*first cap

Final table	P	W	D	L	F	A	Pts
England	3	2	1	0	6	3	5
Scotland	3	1	1	1	4	4	3
Northern Ireland	3	0	2	1	1	2	2
Wales	3	0	2	1	3	5	2

FA Amateur Cup Final

Saturday 13th April 1957

Bishop Auckland 3
Russell 13, Lewin 38, Bradley 70

Wycombe Wanderers 1
Smith 37
90,000
Referee: J Topliss (Lincolnshire)

Records all the way for Bishop Auckland. They completed the only hat-trick in the history of the FA Amateur Cup in their fourth successive final. It was their tenth win overall but it was to be their last appearance at Wembley.

Bishop Auckland: Sharratt, Marshall, Childs, Thursby, Cresswell, Nimmins – capt, Bradley, Lewin, Russell, Hardisty, Edwards
Wycombe: Syrett, Lawson, Westley – capt, Truett (G), Wicks, Truett (J), Worley, Trott, Bates, Tomlin, Smith.

FA CUP FINAL

Saturday 4th May 1957

Aston Villa	2-1	Manchester United
McParland 68, 73		Taylor 83

100,000
Referee: F Coultas (Hull)

For the second year in succession a team from Birmingham met a team from Manchester in the final. Villa's last final had been in 1924 and they were attempting to win the Cup for a record seventh time. United had won the Cup in 1948 for the second time and had defeated the previous year's finalists Birmingham City in the semi-final.

Villa finished 10th in the First Division while United had convincingly retained the League Championship for a second year with a team which was now on the verge of the first League and FA Cup 'double' since 1897 when it had been achieved by Villa. They had also become the first English club to enter the European Cup, reaching the semi-finals where they lost to the holders and eventual winners Real Madrid.

The whole pattern of the game was decided in the sixth minute when United's 'keeper Wood was stretchered off with a fractured cheekbone after being charged by McParland. United reorganised and Blanchflower went in goal. They had such a powerful side, though, that they still gave their opponents a hard game. Wood came back in the 33rd minute but played out on the wing.

Villa at last broke through when Peter McParland, booed almost every time he touched the ball, headed in from Dixon's cross. Five minutes later, he added a second with the rebound from a Dixon shot which had hit the bar. United pulled one back with seven minutes remaining when Tommy Taylor headed in an Edwards corner. Wood went back into goal so United could reorganise in a desperate attempt to snatch an equaliser. But it was not to be and Villa secured the most unpopular of their record seven FA Cup wins.

Villa were relegated two years later, but returned as Second Division Champions the following year. They were, however, a Third Division club when they next appeared at Wembley in 1971. For United, everything paled into insignificance when six of the Wembley team were killed in the Munich air disaster the following February. Incredibly, on a wave of emotion, they reached the FA Cup final again.

Aston Villa: Sims, Lynn, Aldis, Crowther, Dugdale, Saward, Smith, Sewell, Myerscough, Dixon – capt, McParland. manager: Eric Houghton
Manchester U: Wood, Foulkes, Byrne – capt, Colman, Blanchflower, Edwards, Berry, Whelan, Taylor (T), Charlton, Pegg. manager: Matt Busby

WORLD CUP QUALIFYING

Wednesday 8th May 1957

England	**5-1**	**Republic of Ireland**
Taylor 8, 17, 40, Atyeo 38, 90		Curtis 56

52,000
Referee: H Phillips (Scotland)

Both teams had already beaten Denmark at home in Group One. They had met each other only twice before. England had won 1-0 at Dalymount Park, Dublin, in 1946, Ireland surprisingly winning 2-0 at Goodison Park three years later, England's first home defeat by a foreign team. Ireland had yet to qualify for a World Cup.

In the ninth minute of Wembley's first World Cup match Tommy Taylor opened the scoring, taking a pass from Clayton to shoot England in front. Nine minutes later Finney's pass gave Taylor the chance to score again and once more Kelly was beaten. Then Kelly saved from Finney but John Atyeo headed in the rebound.

Taylor completed a first half hat-trick with a header from a Finney corner. England relaxed a little in the second half and the Irish pulled one back when Dermot Curtis headed in a centre from Haverty but in the dying seconds England restored their four-goal advantage when Finney crossed and Atyeo came charging in to score again.

England won the group 11 days later with a 1-1 draw in the return at Dalymount Park. This was only achieved, however, by a last-minute equaliser from Atyeo. It was to be 19 years before the Republic of Ireland appeared at Wembley again.

At the age of 42 Stan Matthews made his 27th and final appearance at Wembley. Strangely he never scored at the stadium.

England: Hodgkinson (Sheffield U), Hall (Birmingham), Byrne (Man Utd), Clayton (Blackburn), Wright (Wolves) – capt, Edwards (Man Utd), Matthews (Blackpool), Atyeo (Bristol C), Taylor (Man Utd), Haynes (Fulham), Finney (Preston). manager: Walter Winterbottom.
Republic of Ireland: Kelly (Drumcondra), Donovan (Everton), Cantwell (West Ham), Farrell (Everton) – capt, Mackey (Shamrock), Saward (Aston Villa), Ringstead (Sheffield U), Whelan (Man Utd), Curtis (Bristol C), Fitzsimons (Middlesbrough), Haverty (Arsenal)

Final table	P	W	D	L	F	A	Pts
England	4	3	1	0	15	5	7
Republic of Ireland	4	2	1	1	6	7	5
Denmark	4	0	0	4	4	13	0

Under-23 International

Wednesday 16th October 1957

England 3
Greaves 1, 20, Curry 60

Romania 2
Georgescu 34, Ene 35

34,381
Referee: Devilliers (France)

England: Hodgkinson (Sheffield U), Armfield (Blackpool), Harris (Wolves), Setters (West Brom), Smith (Birmingham) – capt, Crowther (Aston Villa), Brabrook (Chelsea), Greaves (Chelsea), Curry (Newcastle), Parry (Bolton), A'Court (Liverpool)
Romania: Utu (Dinamo Bucharest), Pahontu (Energia Ploiesti) – capt, Szakacs (Stiinta), Vasile (Dinamo Bucharest), Stanch (Stiinta), Nunweiler (Dinamo Bucharest), Anghel (Dinamo Bucharest), Szeredai (Lokomotiva Bucharest), Ene (Lokomotiva), Georgescu (Lokomotiva), Semenescu (Lokomotiva).

England, in red shirts, won the only international at this level ever to be played at Wembley despite losing the two-goal lead given them by Jimmy Greaves on his first appearance at the stadium. Greaves went on to score 44 goals in 57 full internationals after scoring a record 13 goals in 12 under-23 internationals.

BRITISH CHAMPIONSHIP

Wednesday 6th November 1957

England   **2-3**   **Northern Ireland**

A'Court 58, Edwards 80   McIlroy pen 31, McCrory 59, Simpson 71
42,000
Referee: M Griffiths (Wales)

It had been 30 years since England had lost to Northern Ireland and 41 years since they had lost at home to them. England were aiming for a record seventh successive British Championship and had already beaten Wales 4-0 at Ninian Park. Northern Ireland had drawn 1-1 with Scotland at Windsor Park and needed to avoid defeat to retain any hope of their second British Championship in three years. They were well placed in their World Cup qualifying group to join England in the finals in Sweden the following year.

Northern Ireland took a shock lead. After being brought down by Wright in the penalty area Jimmy McIlroy stepped up himself to take the kick. His shot hit the post and went in off the 'keeper (perhaps it should have been a Hopkinson own goal). It was another half hour before Alan A'Court slotted home the equaliser.

The Irish were soon back in front, how-

ever. Sammy McCrory took advantage of a mix-up between Wright and Edwards and his shot went in off the post. Then, Bingham's cross was headed in by Billy Simpson to give the Irish an incredible 3-1 lead.

England were not finished and Duncan Edwards took a pass from Douglas and beat Gregg with a powerful shot but it was not enough and the Irish held on for a memorable victory.

Northern Ireland threw England a lifeline by failing to beat Wales at Ninian Park. England then gained a share by defeating Scotland 4-0 at Hampden Park but Northern Ireland proved that this result was no fluke by qualifying for the World Cup and performing admirably in Sweden where they bettered England by reaching the quarter-finals. They followed this with a thrilling 3-3 draw with England at Windsor Park and shared the British Championship with them again the following year.

England: Hopkinson (Bolton), Howe (West Brom), Byrne (Man Utd), Clayton (Blackburn), Wright (Wolves) – capt, Edwards (Man Utd), Douglas (Blackburn), Kevan (West Brom), Taylor (Man Utd), Haynes (Fulham), A'Court* (Liverpool). manager: Walter Winterbottom

Northern Ireland: Gregg (Doncaster), Keith* (Newcastle), McMichael (Newcastle), D Blanchflower (Tottenham) – capt, J Blanchflower (Man Utd), Peacock (Celtic), Bingham (Sunderland), McCrory* (Southend), Simpson (Rangers), McIlroy (Burnley), McParland (Aston Villa). manager: Peter Doherty

*first cap

Final table	P	W	D	L	F	A	Pts
England	3	2	0	1	10	3	4
Northern Ireland	3	1	2	0	5	4	4
Scotland	3	0	2	1	2	6	2
Wales	3	0	2	1	2	6	2

INTERNATIONAL

Wednesday 27th November 1957

England   **4-0**   **France**

Taylor 3, 33, Robson 24, 84
64,349
Referee: N Latychev (USSR)

Like England, France had qualified for the following year's World Cup. In 1954 they had failed to progress beyond the first round. They did, however, have two vic-

tories over England and had drawn 2-2 at Wembley in a victory international. The two more recent meetings had ended in a 2-2 draw at Highbury in 1951 and a 1-0

French victory in Paris in 1955. England had not beaten them since 1949 in Paris.

They began redressing the balance very early when Tommy Taylor beat Tylinski to a Bryan Douglas cross to head England in front. Douglas also created the second. Going round Abbes, he pulled the ball back for Bobby Robson to score the second. Nine minutes later an inch-perfect pass across the field from Haynes let Taylor in

to score his second (and sadly his last for England). There was no further scoring until a neat passing move ended with Douglas supplying Robson with his second and England's fourth.

France finished third in the 1958 World Cup and did not return to Wembley until the 1966 competition. Byrne, Edwards and Taylor died at Munich less than three months later.

England: Hopkinson (Bolton), Howe (West Brom), Byrne (Man Utd), Clayton (Blackburn), Wright (Wolves) – capt, Edwards (Man Utd), Douglas (Blackburn), Robson* (West Brom), Taylor (Man Utd), Haynes (Fulham), Finney (Preston). manager: Walter Winterbottom*first cap
France: Abbes (Saint-Etienne), Zitouni (Monaco), Kaelbel (Monaco), Domingo (Saint-Etienne), Tylinski (Saint-Etienne), Bollini (Racing Club), Wiesnieski (Lens), Ujlaki (Nice), Douis (Lille), Piantoni (Reims) – capt, Vincent (Reims). coach: Albert Batteux

Inter-Varsity Match

Saturday 7th December 1957

Cambridge U 1
Scanlan
Oxford U 1
Hurren

British Amateur Championship

Saturday 29th March 1958

England 2
Hamm, Bradley
Scotland 3
Orr 3
6,000
Referee: J Bailey (Wales)

Despite the defeat, with Doug Orr netting a hat-trick, England shared the championship with Scotland and Northern Ireland. It was their fourth, of seven, consecutive titles. But the amateur game had peaked in the early 1950's as far as the public was concerned and dwindling attendances meant that this fixture was never played again at Wembley.

England: Pinner ((Pegasus), Clarke (Walthamstow), Valentine (Loughborough College), Thursby (Bishop Auckland), Prince (Walthamstow), Dodkins (Ilford), Bradley (Bishop Auckland), Robinson (Sutton), Mortimore (Woking), Hamm (Woking), Littlejohn (Woking)
Scotland: Freebairn (Glasgow University), Harnett (Queens Park), Macgregor (Jordanhill TC), Cromar (Queens Park), Neil (Airdrie), Holt (Queens Park), Orr (QPR), Mcdonald (Hounslow), Mcewan (Queens Park), Robb (Queens Park), Perry (Queens Park)

FA Amateur Cup final

Saturday 12th April 1958

Ilford 0
Woking 3
Hebdon 2, Stratton
71,000
Referee: R Clements (Birmingham)

Woking's first final produced a convincing victory.

Ilford: Gibbins, Simmons, Cross, Sharod, Whittall – capt, Dodkins, Durston, Taylor, Winch, Butler, Castle
Woking: Burley, Ellerby, Parsons, Collingwood, Turner, Clacey, Littlejohn, Hebdon, Mortimore – capt, Hamm, Stratton

Schoolboy International

Saturday 26th April 1958

England 3
Murray 2, Chisnall
Scotland 1
Gibson
90,000

England were three up at the interval and Henderson missed a second-half penalty for Scotland.

Billy Bremner, who won 54 full international caps for Scotland and was Footballer of the Year in 1970, made his first Wembley appearance. Terry Venables went on to win youth, amateur, under-23, and full international caps for England, before becoming head coach from 1994-96.

Six years later Ronnie Boyce scored the winner in the FA Cup final for West Ham.

England: Hempsall, More, Mountain, Venables, Greenwood – capt, Gibbens, Chisnall, Boyce, Murray, Thompson, Derrick

Scotland: Mailey, Sharp, McDonald, Hyslop, Crawford, Cullen, Penman, Henderson, Gibson, Bremner, Swanson

FA CUP FINAL

Saturday 3rd May 1958

Bolton Wanderers	2-0	Manchester United

Lofthouse 3, 50
100,000
Referee: J Sherlock (Sheffield)

It had been 29 years since Bolton had last won the FA Cup, and in 1953 they had had victory snatched from their grasp. In the quarter-finals they had knocked out Wolverhampton Wanderers, who were heading for the League Championship.

United had picked themselves up from their unfortunate defeat in the previous year's final and had been contenders in all three competitions until the Munich air disaster which decimated the team. But with overwhelming national sympathy, they had reached the final again with a rebuilt side.

Bolton finished a disappointing 15th in the First Division. United had started out chasing a hat-trick of League Championships but finished ninth, their lowest position for 20 years. The pre-Munich side had also taken them to the European Cup semi-finals for the second year in succession. Milan proved too much for them after the tragedy.

Bolton took the lead when a cross from Edwards fell to Nat Lofthouse who beat Gregg from close range. The result was never really in doubt, and Bolton scored a controversial second.

A shot from Stevens was saved by Gregg, but as he collected the ball Lofthouse came charging in and forced the ball over the line for his second. Gregg was knocked out in the collision but the goal stood.

Bolton were relegated six years later and did not return to Wembley until 1986 for the Freight Rover Trophy final. United were rebuilt once more by Matt Busby after amazingly finishing League runners-up the following year. They won the FA Cup five years after Munich as yet another great side emerged.

Bolton: Hopkinson, Hartle, Banks (T), Hennin, Higgins, Edwards, Birch, Stevens, Lofthouse – capt, Parry, Holden. manager: Bill Ridding
Manchester U: Gregg, Foulkes – capt, Greaves, Goodwin, Cope, Crowther, Dawson, Taylor (E), Charlton, Viollet, Webster. manager: Matt Busby

INTERNATIONAL

Wednesday 7th May 1958

England	2-1	Portugal

Charlton 24, 60
65,000
Referee: A Alsteen (Belgium)

Duarte 50

Portugal had failed to qualify for the World Cup after finishing bottom of Northern Ireland's group. They had beaten England, though, in the last of their four previous meetings, 3-1 in 1955 in Oporto. England had won the first three, scoring 20 goals in the process. Although they had shared the British Championship England had lost three important and influential players at Munich and were struggling to find good replacements for the approaching World Cup.

England were not impressive but went ahead when, from Haynes' pass, Bobby Charlton beat Torres and shot past Gomes from outside the penalty area.

Portugal deservedly drew level when Da Silva showed neat skills and then passed to Carlos Duarte who ran in to equalise. On the hour mark, however, from a centre by

Douglas, Charlton hit a beauty to restore England's lead with his second. They could have increased their lead when Finney was fouled by Martins in the area but Langley hit the post from the penalty. Unbelievably, it was England's fifth consecutive penalty miss at Wembley.

Four days later England were thrashed 5-0 by Yugoslavia in Belgrade. This was the worst possible preparation for the World Cup and England were eliminated in a first round play-off by the USSR in Gothenburg.

Portugal reached the quarter-finals of the first European Championship in 1960 where they lost to Yugoslavia, the eventual finalists. They were back at Wembley in 1961 for a World Cup qualifying match.

England: Hopkinson (Bolton), Howe (West Brom), Langley (Fulham), Clayton (Blackburn), Wright (Wolves) – capt, Slater (Wolves), Douglas (Blackburn), Charlton (Man Utd), Kevan (West Brom), Haynes (Fulham), Finney (Preston). manager: Walter Winterbottom

Portugal: Gomes (Sporting Lisbon), Mendes (Porto) – capt, Martins (Benfica), Graca (Vitoria Setubal), Arcanjo (Porto), Torres (Academica Coimbra), Duarte (Porto), Coluna (Benfica), Augusto (Barreirense), Rocha (Academica), Da Silva (Porto). sub: Travacos (Sporting) for Augusto 46. coach: Jose Maria Antunes.

INTERNATIONAL

Wednesday 22nd October 1958

England	5-0	USSR

Haynes 45, 63, 82, Charlton pen 84
Lofthouse 90
100,000
Referee: M Guigue (France)

Before 1958 England had never met the USSR, but in the space of just over five months they were to meet four times. A 1-1 draw in Moscow in May was followed by 2-2 in the World Cup in Gothenburg. The Soviets, in their first World Cup, then put out England by beating them 1-0 in a play-off, also in Gothenburg. They were then beaten in the quarter-finals by the host nation Sweden. The USSR had only been competing in internationals for six years but had won the Olympic title in 1956. England were looking for revenge after a disappointing World Cup.

Just before half-time from a pass by Douglas, Johnny Haynes gave England the lead. After 63 minutes Kesarev's poor clearance was seized upon by Haynes and England were two up. The Soviet defence crumbled in the last eight minutes and conceded three more goals. From a corner Finney pulled the ball back and Haynes completed his hat-trick from the edge of the area.

Then Kuznetsov brought down Douglas and Bobby Charlton converted the spot kick to end England's run of unsuccessful penalties at Wembley. Nat Lofthouse scored the fifth in the last minute from a pass by Charlton. It was the USSR's worst ever defeat.

The USSR won the first European Championship two years later and reached the World Cup quarter-finals again in 1962. They were back at Wembley for the 1966 World Cup.

England: McDonald (Burnley), Howe (West Brom), Shaw* (Sheffield U), Clayton (Blackburn), Wright (Wolves) – capt, Slater (Wolves), Douglas (Blackburn), Charlton (Man Utd), Lofthouse (Bolton), Haynes (Fulham), Finney (Preston). manager: Walter Winterbottom. *first cap

USSR: Belaev (Dynamo Moscow), Kesarev (Dynamo Moscow), Kuznetsov (Dynamo Moscow), Voinov (Dynamo Kiev), Maslenkin (Spartak Moscow), Tsarev (Dynamo Moscow), Metreveli (Torpedo Moscow), Ivanov (Torpedo), Simonian (Spartak) – capt, Mamedov (Dynamo Moscow), Ilyin (Spartak). Coach: Gavriil Kachalin

Inter-Varsity Match

Saturday 6th December 1958

Cambridge U 1
Bushell

Oxford U 1
Randle

The second successive 1-1 draw, for this fixture.

BRITISH CHAMPIONSHIP

Saturday 11th April 1959

England	1-0	Scotland

Charlton 59
98,329
Referee: J Campos (Portugal)

Victory for Scotland would have given them their first outright British Championship since 1951 when they had last beaten England. The home side had drawn their two previous games and had to win to secure a record eighth successive title. Like England, Scotland had been knocked out of the previous year's World Cup in the first round but the Scots had finished bottom of their group.

The only goal came after almost an hour's play. A high cross from Douglas was met by Bobby Charlton who directed a superb header past Brown. Apart from this it was a poor match to celebrate Billy Wright's 100th cap.

Northern Ireland's 4-1 win over Wales at Windsor Park gave them a share of the Championship for the third time in four years. After gaining a share themselves the following year, Scotland were back at Wembley in 1961 for a game they would never forget.

England: Hopkinson (Bolton), Howe (West Brom), Shaw (Sheffield U), Clayton (Blackburn), Wright (Wolves) – capt, Flowers (Wolves), Douglas (Blackburn), Broadbent (Wolves), Charlton (Man Utd), Haynes (Fulham), Holden* (Bolton). manager: Walter Winterbottom
Scotland: Brown (Dundee), McKay* (Celtic), Caldow (Rangers), Docherty (Arsenal), Evans (Celtic) – capt, Mackay (Tottenham), Leggat (Fulham), Collins (Everton), Herd (Arsenal), Dick* (West Ham), Ormond (Hibernian). manager: Andy Beattie
*first cap

Final table	P	W	D	L	F	A	Pts
England	3	1	2	0	6	5	4
Northern Ireland	3	1	2	0	9	6	4
Scotland	3	1	1	1	5	3	3
Wales	3	0	1	2	3	9	1

FA Amateur Cup Final

Saturday 18th April 1959

Barnet 2
Brown 30, 87

Crook Town 3
Tracey 10, 79, Keating 60
60,000

Crook Town's third victory in the competition.

Barnet: Goymer, Duncan, Cooper, Sleap, D'Arcy (A), Cantwell, Welch, D'Arcy (D) – capt, Brown, Harding, Drake
Crook: Snowball, Gardener, Steward – capt, Carr, Bainbridge, Wilkie, Coates, O'Connell, Keating, Tracey, McMillan

Schoolboy International

Saturday 25th April 1959

England 2
Ashe, Baker pen

West Germany 0
95,000
Referee: C Coppack (Wembley)

England's first schoolboy meeting with foreign opposition at Wembley.

Martin Peters made his Wembley bow and found himself facing Wolfgang Overath. They were to cross swords again seven years later at the same venue in the World Cup final. Peters went on to win 67 full international caps for England.

England's captain Chris Lawler had to wait another 12 years for the first of his four full England caps but scored on his debut against Malta at Wembley. By then he'd also returned to play in two FA Cup finals for Liverpool, winning in 1965.

England: Dixon, Clay, Niblett, Smith, Lawler – capt, Peters, Ashe, Baker, Sharples, Caple, Fortt

FA CUP FINAL

Saturday 2nd May 1959

Luton Town 1-2 **Nottingham Forest**
Pacey 62 Dwight 10, Wilson 14
100,000
Referee: J Clough (Bolton)

Neither side had appeared at Wembley before. Luton had never won a major trophy and had not been beyond the FA Cup quarter-finals before. Forest had won the Cup way back in 1898 when they beat Derby County 3-1 in the final at Crystal Palace. In the quarter-finals they had knocked out the holders Bolton Wanderers.

Forest took an early lead. A low cross from Imlach was blasted into the corner by Roy Dwight. Four minutes later a cross from Gray was headed in by Tommy Wilson and Forest threatened to destroy Luton.

But after 32 minutes Dwight was carried off with a broken leg after a tackle with McNally. Despite the numerical advantage Luton were unable to rescue the game. They did pull a goal back when Hawkes passed through the middle for Dave Pacey to score for Luton but Forest held on.

Luton were relegated the following season and dropped right through the divisions in six years. They eventually fought their way back and returned to Wembley three times in 1988. It took Forest 19 years to win another major trophy but that was to be the beginning of the greatest era in their history.

Footballer of the Year and Luton captain, Syd Owen, made his only appearance at Wembley and then retired to become the club's manager.

Luton T: Baynham, McNally, Hawkes, Groves, Owen – capt, Pacey, Bingham, Brown, Morton, Cummins, Gregory. chairman: Thomas Hodgson
Nottingham F: Thomson, Whare, McDonald, Whitefoot, McKinlay, Burkitt – capt, Dwight, Quigley, Wilson (Th), Gray (W), Imlach. manager: Billy Walker

INTERNATIONAL

Wednesday 6th May 1959

England 2-2 **Italy**
Charlton 26, Bradley 38 Brighenti 56, Mariani 61
91,000
Referee: A Dusch (West Germany)

Italy had failed to qualify for the previous year's World Cup, having been surprisingly knocked out by Northern Ireland. They had never beaten England in six previous meetings and had lost on both their previous visits to England.

Midway through the first half Haynes worked an opening and Bobby Charlton smacked in a low shot from the edge of the area to give England the lead. Twelve minutes later a shot from Haynes was blocked and Warren Bradley turned swiftly to score. Eight minutes into the second half Flowers took a bang on the nose in a heading duel and was carried off. This unsettled England and the Italians seized the initiative. A terrible mix-up between Shaw and Hopkinson allowed Sergio Brighenti in for an easy goal. Then, from a pass by Gratton, Amos Mariani shot past Hopkinson for the equaliser. Flowers returned to learn that they had squandered their two-goal lead.

Italy failed to progress beyond the first round in the 1962 World Cup after a violent confrontation with the hosts Chile and they were not to beat England until 1973.

England: Hopkinson (Bolton), Howe (West Brom), Shaw (Sheffield U), Clayton (Blackburn), Wright (Wolves) – capt, Flowers (Wolves), Bradley* (Man Utd), Broadbent (Wolves), Charlton (Man Utd), Haynes (Fulham), Holden (Bolton). manager: Walter Winterbottom.
*first cap
Italy: Buffon (AC Milan), Robotti (Fiorentina), Castelletti (Fiorentina), Zaglio (Roma), Bernasconi (Sampdoria), Segato (Fiorentina) – capt, Mariani (Padova), Gratton (Fiorentina), Brighenti (Padova), Galli (AC Milan), Petris (Fiorentina)

INTERNATIONAL

Wednesday 28th October 1959

England   **2-3**   **Sweden**
Connelly 9, Charlton 81   Simonsson 52, 60, Salomonsson 75
72,000
Referee: R Davidson (Scotland)

Sweden had reached the World Cup final in their own country the previous year before falling to the mighty Brazilians. They had won the Olympic title at Wembley in 1948 and had won and drawn in their previous two meetings with England.

England started well with a neat passing move ending with Clough crossing for John Connelly to slot home the opener. But just after half time a defensive error involving Charlton and Flowers enabled Berndtsson to supply Agne Simonsson (who had scored in the World Cup final) with a headed equaliser.

Simonsson struck again after an hour's play, beating Hopkinson from an acute angle after Borjesson's shot was blocked. Later Simonsson's skilful ball control killed off the home side as he sent Bengt Salomonsson away to score the third.

Bobby Charlton scored from a pass by Greaves but England had suffered their second defeat at Wembley by a continental side.

Sweden, surprisingly, failed to qualify for the 1962 World Cup, losing a play-off to Switzerland in Berlin. England gained their revenge with a 2-1 win in Gothenburg in 1965 and Sweden were back at Wembley in 1968.

England: Hopkinson (Bolton), Howe (West Brom), Allen (Stoke City), Clayton (Blackburn) – capt, Smith (Birmingham), Flowers (Wolves), Connelly (Burnley), Greaves (Chelsea), Clough (Middlesbrough), Charlton (Man Utd), Holliday (Middlesbrough). manager: Walter Winterbottom
Sweden: Nyholm (Norrkoping), Bergmark (Orebro) – capt, Axbom (Norrkoping), Jonsson (Norrkoping), Johansson (Norrkoping), Parling (Djurgardens), Berndtsson (Gothenburg), Thillberg (Malmo), Simonsson (Orgryte), Borjesson (Orgryte), Salomonsson (Helsingborgs)

BRITISH CHAMPIONSHIP

Wednesday 18th November 1959

England   **2-1**   **Northern Ireland**
Baker 17, Parry 90   Bingham 89
60,000
Referee: L Callaghan (Wales)

They had shared the British Championship between them for the past two years but England were aiming for a record ninth successive title. The Irish were now unbeaten in three meetings with England, including their 1957 win on their previous visit. They had started their British Championship campaign disastrously, however, with a 4-0 thrashing by Scotland at Windsor Park and needed, at least, a point to stay in contention. England had drawn 1-1 with Wales at Ninian Park.

From Allen's free kick, Joe Baker eluded Cunningham's challenge and turned to shoot England in front.

The Irish ought to have equalised on the stroke of half-time when Bingham's pass put McIlroy through to beat three men before being fouled, jointly, by Howe and Brown. But the penalty, taken by McIlroy, was brilliantly saved by Springett. The Irish did equalise two minutes before time when McParland raced away down the wing, cut inside and shot inside the near post. Springett managed to block it, but Billy Bingham pounced on the rebound. But England snatched victory in the very last minute. Baker crossed and Ray Parry slotted in the winner to deprive Northern Ireland of their interest in the Championship.

England secured a share of the British Championship by drawing 1-1 with Scotland at Hampden Park. Northern Ireland finished bottom, without a point, after losing 3-2 to Wales at the Racecourse Ground.

England: Springett* (Sheffield W), Howe (West Brom), Allen (Stoke City), Clayton (Blackburn) – capt, Brown* (West Ham), Flowers (Wolves), Connelly (Burnley), Haynes (Fulham), Baker* (Hibernian), Parry* (Bolton), Holliday (Middlesbrough). manager: Walter Winterbottom

Northern Ireland: Gregg (Man Utd), Keith (Newcastle), McMichael (Newcastle), Blanchflower (Tottenham) – capt, Cunningham (Leicester), Peacock (Celtic), Bingham (Luton), Crossan* (Sparta Rotterdam), Cush (Leeds), McIlroy (Burnley), McParland (Aston Villa). manager: Peter Doherty. *first cap

Final table	P	W	D	L	F	A	Pts
England	3	1	2	0	4	3	4
Scotland	3	1	2	0	6	2	4
Wales	3	1	2	0	5	4	4
Northern Ireland	3	0	0	3	3	9	0

Inter-Varsity Match

Saturday 5th December 1959

Cambridge U 6
Neil 2, Bateson 2, Jacobs 2

Oxford U 2
Smith, R F Jackson

Oxford were two up inside eight minutes but Cambridge eventually overwhelmed them in Wembley's highest scoring university match.

FA Amateur Cup Final

Saturday 23rd April 1960

Hendon 2
Topp 87, Howard 89

Kingstonian 1
Whing 41
60,000
Referee: J Hunt (Hampshire)

Hendon lifted the Amateur Cup for the first time in extremely dramatic circumstances, snatching victory from the jaws of defeat.

Hendon: Shearing, Widdowfield, Harris, Topp, Fisher, Murphy – capt, Candey, Figg, Spector, Quail, Howard

Kingstonian: Groves, Davies, Bird, Richards, Ashworth, Gilson, Harris, Coates – capt, Whing, Lindsay, Oakes

Schoolboy International

Saturday 30th April 1960

England 5
Thwaites, Hewitt, Harris, Fry, Pleat

Scotland 3
Graham, Forrest, Moonie
92,000
Referee: M Graham (Northumberland)

Scotland pulled back from five goals down but ran out of time.

The scorer of Scotland's first goal, George Graham, was a member of Arsenal's 'double-winning' team 11 years later and went on to manage the club to further league and cup success in the 1980's and '90's.

Two other future managers both scored for England; David Pleat, who took Tottenham Hotspur to the FA Cup final in 1987, and Barry Fry, who was in charge of Birmingham City, when they won the Auto Windscreens Shield at Wembley in 1995 and led Peterborough to play-off success in 2000.

Bobby Moncur won 16 full international caps for Scotland and captained them on seven occasions, including at Wembley against England in 1971. Three years later he returned to the stadium as skipper of Newcastle United in the FA Cup final.

England: Kerr, Badger, Dennis – capt, Bloomfield, Turner, Harris, Pleat, Fry, Hewitt, Atkinson, Thwaites

Scotland: Ewington, Parkes, Moncur, Watson, Markie, Combe, Moonie, Willoughby, Forrest, Graham, Mitchell. Sub: Davidson for Ewington

FA CUP FINAL

Saturday 7th May 1960

Blackburn Rovers   **0-3**   **Wolverhampton Wanderers**
McGrath og 41, Deeley 67, 88

100,000
Referee: K Howley (Middlesbrough)

It had been 32 years since Blackburn had won the FA Cup but they were attempting to equal Aston Villa's record of seven wins. They had knocked out Burnley in the quarter-finals. Wolves had last won the Cup in 1949 and had knocked out the previous year's finalists Luton Town in the last 16.

Blackburn finished 17th in only their second season back in the First Division, just three points clear of relegation. Wolves had been chasing a hat-trick of League Championships but were pipped by a point and finished runners-up to Burnley, despite beating them 6-1 in March. They also reached the European Cup quarter-finals before Barcelona beat them comfortably.

Four minutes before half-time Stobart crossed and Mick McGrath diverted it past Leyland for an own goal. Two minutes later Whelan broke his leg when he twisted as he tried to go past Deeley. For Blackburn, with ten men and a goal down, things went from bad to worse in the second half. Norman Deeley scored from Horne's cross midway through the half and two minutes from time netted the rebound when Stobart hit the post. Wolves had their consolation for losing the League title.

Blackburn had to wait until 1987 before appearing at Wembley again when they won the Full Members Cup.

Wolves became England's first representatives in the European Cup-Winners Cup the following season and reached the semi-finals before falling to Rangers. It was to be 14 years before they reached another Wembley final.

Ally McLeod returned to Wembley in 1977 as manager of the Scotland team which famously defeated England before it all turned sour at the following year's World Cup in Argentina.

Blackburn: Leyland, Bray, Whelan, Clayton – capt, Woods, McGrath, Bimpson, Dobing, Dougan, Douglas, McLeod. manager: Dally Duncan
Wolves: Finlayson, Showell, Harris, Clamp, Slater – capt, Flowers, Deeley, Stobart, Murray, Broadbent, Horne. manager: Stan Cullis

INTERNATIONAL

Wednesday 11th May 1960

England   **3-3**   **Yugoslavia**
Douglas 44, Greaves 48, Haynes 88   Galic 31, 60, Kostic 80
70,000
Referee: R Davidson (Scotland)

England's only victory in five meetings with Yugoslavia had been at Wembley in 1956. Yugoslavia had reached the World Cup quarter-finals in 1958 before losing to West Germany just a month after thrashing England 5-0 in Belgrade. They had also reached the quarter-finals of the first European Championship and, three days earlier, had lost the first leg, 2-1 to Portugal in Lisbon.

After half an hour the visitors took the lead when Jerkovic headed on a free kick from Zebec for Milan Galic to knock in the opener. England equalised just before the interval with a similar goal. A free kick from Wilson was headed on by Baker for Bryan Douglas to level. Just after half-time Charlton put Jimmy Greaves through to beat Soskic from a narrow angle but Yugoslavia drew level after an hour's play, Galic getting his second from a pass by Perusic. In the 80th minute Galic created another with a clever back-heel to Borivje Kostic who shot past Springett. Defeat stared England in the face but with just two minutes left Baker hit the bar from Greaves' cross and Johnny Haynes rescued a draw with a header.

Yugoslavia went on to reach the European Championship final but lost 2-1 to the USSR after extra time in Paris. Two years later they reached the World Cup semi-finals in Chile before losing to Czechoslovakia. They were back at Wembley in 1966.

England: Springett (Sheffield W), Armfield (Blackpool), Wilson (Huddersfield), Clayton (Blackburn) – capt, Swan* (Sheffield W), Flowers (Wolves), Douglas (Blackburn), Haynes (Fulham), Baker (Hibernian), Greaves (Chelsea), Charlton (Man Utd). manager: Walter Winterbottom
*first cap
Yugoslavia: Soskic (Partizan Belgrade), Durkovic (Red Star Belgrade), Jusufi (Partizan), Zanetic (Hajduk Split), Zebec (Red Star), Perusic (Dinamo Zagreb), Lipusinovic (Zagreb) – capt, Jerkovic (Zagreb), Sekularac (Red Star), Galic (Red Star), Kostic (Red Star). Sub: Mujic (Velez Mostar) for Jerkovic 41

INTERNATIONAL

Wednesday 26th October 1960

England	4-2	Spain
Greaves 1, Douglas 41, Smith 68, 79		Del Sol 14, Suarez 51

80,000
Referee: M Guigue (France)

Spain had lost on both their previous visits to England, the last occasion being at Wembley in 1955. They had beaten England 3-0 in Madrid, however, just five months earlier. Spain had also reached the European Championship quarter-finals but politics forced them to withdraw from a meeting with the eventual winners, the USSR.

England took a first-minute lead. Smith's pass found Jimmy Greaves who shot low to beat Ramallets. Spain were not behind for long, Luis Del Sol taking a pass from Mateos to equalise.

England regained the lead before the break. Armfield crossed and Bryan Douglas headed home. Spain levelled again just afterwards when Gento broke away, then pulled it back to enable Luis Suarez to shoot past Springett. England were not to be denied, though. Bobby Smith headed them in front once more from Charlton's centre. Then, in the 80th minute, Smith took a pass from Robson and brilliantly lobbed the 'keeper from 25 yards for his second.

Spain finished bottom of their group in the 1962 World Cup in Chile but won the European Championship in their own country in 1964. They returned to Wembley to face the World Cup holders in 1967.

Two European Footballers of the Year, Alfredo Di Stefano (who won it twice) and Luis Suarez (the 1960 winner) who scored their second goal, made their first appearances at Wembley. Only Di Stefano would return, for the FA's Centenary match in 1963.

England: Springett (Sheffield W), Armfield (Blackpool), McNeil (Middlesbrough), Robson (West Brom), Swan (Sheffield W), Flowers (Wolves), Douglas (Blackburn), Greaves (Chelsea), Smith (Tottenham), Haynes (Fulham) – capt, Charlton (Man Utd). manager: Walter Winterbottom
Spain: Ramallets (Barcelona), Marquitos (Real Madrid), Gracia (Barcelona), Sosa (Sevilla), Santamaria (Real Madrid), Verges (Barcelona), Mateos (Real Madrid), Del Sol (Real Madrid), Di Stefano (Real Madrid), Suarez (Barcelona) – capt, Gento (Real Madrid)

BRITISH CHAMPIONSHIP

Wednesday 23rd November 1960

England	5-1	Wales
Greaves 2, 69, Charlton 16, Smith 29, Haynes 61		Leek 75

65,000
Referee: R Davidson (Scotland)

Wales returned to Wembley after two draws in their previous meetings with England and a World Cup quarter-final appearance in 1958 when they were beaten by

1960-61

the eventual winners Brazil. Both sides had won their opening game. Wales defeated Scotland 2-0 at Ninian Park while England beat Northern Ireland 5-2 at Windsor Park. England and Wales had shared the Championship with Scotland the previous season, but England were aiming for a tenth successive title. They had not won it outright, however, since 1957.

As against Spain, England took an early lead. After two minutes, from a pass by Smith, Jimmy Greaves shot past Kelsey in the Welsh goal.

Soon they were two up. Flowers shot from outside the box. Williams blocked it but Bobby Charlton swept home the rebound. By the half-hour mark the Welsh were killed off. An inch-perfect cross from

Greaves was smartly headed in by Bobby Smith.

Johnny Haynes thumped in the fourth after good work by Charlton before they scored the best goal when Greaves beat four men and then Kelsey from an acute angle. With 15 minutes remaining Hodgkinson gifted the Welsh a goal when he dropped a Woosnam cross and Ken Leek seized on the opportunity. It mattered little, however.

Wales thrashed Northern Ireland 5-1 at Windsor Park to finish runners-up but failed to qualify for the 1962 World Cup when they lost to Spain. England had now scored 23 goals in four games. Scotland were to be their next unfortunate victims as England actually increased their scoring rate.

England: Hodgkinson (Sheffield U), Armfield (Blackpool), McNeil (Middlesbrough), Robson (West Brom), Swan (Sheffield W), Flowers (Wolves), Douglas (Blackburn), Greaves (Chelsea), Smith (Tottenham), Haynes (Fulham) – capt, Charlton (Man Utd). manager: Walter Winterbottom
Wales: Kelsey (Arsenal), Harrington (Cardiff), Williams (West Brom), Crowe (Aston Villa) – capt, Nurse (Swansea), Baker (Cardiff), Medwin (Tottenham), Woosnam (West Ham), Leek (Leicester), Vernon (Everton), Jones (Tottenham). manager: Jimmy Murphy

Inter-Varsity Match

Saturday 3rd December 1960

Cambridge U 2
Neil 2

Oxford U 2
Ralph, Igglesden

The fifth draw in nine Wembley meetings. Pat Neil, who played alongside Bobby Charlton for England Schoolboys at Wembley in 1953, scored twice for the second year in succession.

BRITISH CHAMPIONSHIP

Saturday 15th April 1961

England 9-3 **Scotland**
Robson 8, Greaves 18, 28, 83   Mackay 47, Wilson 52, Quinn 7
Douglas 54, Smith 72, 84 Haynes 79, 81
97,350
Referee: M Luquesne (France)

England needed only a point for their tenth successive British Championship. Scotland had to win to gain their second successive share of the title but had lost on their three previous visits to the stadium.

A shot from Bobby Robson, from a pass by Greaves, gave England the lead in the ninth minute. Ten minutes later Jimmy Greaves added a second from Haynes' exquisite pass and Smith's lob. By the

half-hour mark they were three up when Greaves again profited as the floundering Haffey failed to gather Smith's shot. Scotland fought bravely back at the beginning of the second half. Dave Mackay struck a powerful shot which was deflected past Springett and five minutes later Davie Wilson headed in for the second from Mackay's back header. It was a false dawn.

Within two minutes England quelled

the revival. From a Greaves free kick, Bryan Douglas restored England's two-goal lead and Scotland subsequently fell apart. In the last 17 minutes England scored five more goals. Haynes and Greaves provided Bobby Smith with a shooting opportunity for England's fifth.

Scotland briefly replied, with Mackay giving Pat Quinn the opportunity to beat Springett from close range following a corner, but with 11 minutes left, a superb run from Johnny Haynes ended with a shot from the edge of the box.

Two minutes later Haynes scored again, finishing a move involving Douglas and Charlton. Within a minute, Greaves ran from his own half to complete his hat-trick and Haffey's nightmare was complete

when Smith scored England's ninth.

It was England's biggest ever victory over Scotland, who had never before conceded more than seven, and their goalkeeper never again played for his country. Wembley had also never seen as many goals in one match at the stadium. Denis Law, European Footballer of the Year in 1964, had a traumatic Wembley debut.

There was a dramatic transformation the following year as Scotland gained their revenge with a 2-0 win over England at Hampden Park.

It had been 11 years since they had last beaten England. Scotland failed to qualify for their third successive World Cup, however. Czechoslovakia beat them in a play-off in Brussels.

England: Springett (Sheffield W), Armfield (Blackpool), McNeil (Middlesbrough), Robson (West Brom), Swan (Sheffield W), Flowers (Wolves), Douglas (Blackburn), Greaves (Chelsea), Smith (Tottenham), Haynes (Fulham) – capt, Charlton (Man Utd). manager: Walter Winterbottom
Scotland: Haffey (Celtic), Shearer* (Rangers), Caldow (Rangers) – capt, Mackay (Tottenham), McNeill* (Celtic), McCann (Motherwell), MacLeod* (Hibernian), Law (Man City), St John (Motherwell), Quinn* (Motherwell), Wilson (Rangers). manager: Ian McColl
*first cap

Final table	P	W	D	L	F	A	Pts
England	3	3	0	0	19	6	6
Wales	3	2	0	1	8	6	4
Scotland	3	1	0	2	8	13	2
N Ireland	3	0	0	3	5	15	0

FA Amateur Cup Final

Saturday 22nd April 1961

Walthamstow Avenue 2
Groves, Lewis
West Auckland Town 1
Douglas
45,000
Referee: J Williams (Nottinghamshire)

Jim Lewis, with Chelsea when they won the League Championship in 1955, secured Walthamstow's second Wembley win by pouncing on Bowmaker's error with 20 minutes remaining. It was a brave victory as Walthamstow had been left with ten fit men after Saggers was injured early in the game.

Walthamstow: McGuire, Edwards, Bambridge, Andrews, Prince, Keenes, Groves, Minall, Lewis, Saggers, Harvey
West Auckland: Bowmaker, Siddle, Stafford, Mendum, Summerson, Carter, Briggs, Broomfield, Curtis, Skelton, Douglas

Schoolboy International

Saturday 29th April 1961

England 8
Pardoe 4, Sissons 2, Bennett, Prosser pen
Wales 1
Lambourne
95,000
Referee: W Travis (Crewe)

The home side overwhelmed their Welsh opponents, almost emulating the full international side's proficiency in front of goal from two weeks earlier.

Just three years later, John Sissons, who scored twice, became the youngest player to score in an FA Cup final when he netted for West Ham United.

Peter Storey, England's substitute, was a member of Arsenal's 'double' winning side in 1971 and won 19 full international caps for England.

Glyn Pardoe, who scored four, made his name as a full-back but still popped up to score the winner for Manchester City in the 1970 Football League Cup final at Wembley.

England: Ogley, Harcombe, Wright – capt, Parker, Ashcroft, Walker, Bennett, Prosser, Pardoe, Sissons, Kinsey. sub: Storey for Parker

Wales: Black, Griffiths, Girolami, Coldrick, Jones, Edwards, Hughes, Lloyd – capt, Roberts, Lambourne, Humphreys

FA CUP FINAL

Saturday 6th May 1961

Leicester City   **0-2**   **Tottenham Hotspur**
Smith 70, Dyson 77

100,000
Referee: J Kelly (Chorley)

Leicester had lost their only previous final, indeed they had never won a major trophy and had fought their way through a difficult semi-final. Tottenham had won the Cup twice before, but their last victory had been in 1921 with a 1-0 win against Wolverhampton Wanderers at Stamford Bridge. This was their first Wembley appearance.

Leicester finished sixth in the First Division, their highest position since 1929. Tottenham won the League Championship for the second time in their history and were aiming to become the first team to win the 'double' since Aston Villa in 1897.

Yet again an injury determined the course of an FA Cup final. After 18 minutes, Chalmers picked up a leg injury in a tackle with Allen and was reduced to limping on the wing for the rest of the game. Leicester had begun strongly but Tottenham eventually overcame them.

First Bobby Smith took a pass from Dyson, turned brilliantly away from King and hit an unstoppable, rising shot past the 'keeper. Seven minutes later Terry Dyson ran in unmarked to meet Smith's centre with a powerful header past the diving Banks and the 'double' was won.

Because of Tottenham's qualification for the European Cup, Leicester took up their place in the European Cup-Winners Cup but lost in the last 16 to the eventual winners Atletico Madrid. They reached the FA Cup final again though in 1963. Tottenham went on to retain the FA Cup.

Leicester fielded two future Footballers of the Year in goalkeeper Gordon Banks (1972), who won a World Cup winners medal in 1966, and Frank McLintock, who, ironically, won the award in the year he captained Arsenal to the 'double' (1971).

Leicester C: Banks, Chalmers, Norman, McLintock, King (I), Appleton, Riley, Walsh (J) – capt, McIlmoyle, Keyworth, Cheesebrough. manager: Matt Gillies
Tottenham: Brown, Baker, Henry, Blanchflower – capt, Norman, Mackay, Jones, White, Smith, Allen (L), Dyson. manager: Bill Nicholson

INTERNATIONAL

Wednesday 10th May 1961

England   **8-0**   **Mexico**
Hitchens 2, Charlton 12, 62, 73,
Robson 23, Douglas 44, 85
Flowers pen 59
77,000
Referee: R Davidson (Scotland)

The high-scoring British Champions now took on Mexico who had beaten them 2-1 in Mexico City two years earlier in their only previous meeting. Mexico had appeared in every World Cup since the war but had always failed to qualify from their group.

England took just over a minute to score. From a pass by Charlton, Gerry

Hitchens shot and Mota's fumble helped it into the net. The second was not long in coming; Hitchens passed to Bobby Charlton who unleashed a powerful volley past the 'keeper.

Next a fast-flowing move ended with Hitchens supplying Bobby Robson with the chance to make it three. Bryan Douglas netted the fourth from Charlton's pass just before half-time. With half an hour remaining Sepulveda fouled Hitchens and Ron Flowers scored from the spot. Three minutes later, after Hitchens was blocked by three defenders, another thunderbolt

from Charlton nearly broke the Mexican net. In the 74th minute England turned defence into attack and a flick from Douglas gave Charlton his hat-trick as he finished off the move. The eighth and final goal came with five minutes left. Charlton's cross was turned in by Douglas. England's confidence could not be higher.

Mexico qualified for the following year's World Cup but once again failed to progress beyond the first round. Their next meeting with England was in the 1966 World Cup at Wembley where Mexico played all of their matches.

England: Springett (Sheffield W), Armfield (Blackpool), McNeil (Middlesbrough), Robson (West Brom), Swan (Sheffield W), Flowers (Wolves), Douglas (Blackburn), Kevan (West Brom), Hitchens* (Aston Villa), Haynes (Fulham) – capt, Charlton (Man Utd). manager: Walter Winterbottom
*first cap
Mexico: Mota (Oro), Pena (Oro), Jauregui (Atlas), Cardenas (Zacatepec) – capt, Sepulveda (Guadalajara), Portugal (America), Del Aguila (Toluca), Reyes (Guadalajara), Gonzales (Tampico), Flores (Guadalajara), Mercado (Toluca). coach: Ignacio Trelles. sub: Reynoso (Necaxa) for Flores 45

WORLD CUP QUALIFYING

Wednesday 25th October 1961

England	2-0	Portugal

Connelly 5, Pointer 9
98,750
Referee: M Bois (France)

England needed only a point to qualify for Chile after Portugal had lost, amazingly, 4-2 in Luxembourg. Portugal had to win to force a play-off. They had lost on their previous visit to Wembley in 1958 and had drawn 1-1 with England in Lisbon in their earlier meeting in Group Six.

After five minutes, a Wilson free kick rebounded to John Connelly who fired it past Pereira. Four minutes later Haynes' pass found Ray Pointer who hit the back of the net with a stunning drive.

Despite Portugal hitting the woodwork

three times in the second half, the two Burnley players had secured England's passage to the World Cup.

England won 4-3 in Lisbon three years later but Portugal returned to Wembley in 1966 with their best ever team.

Eusebio, European Footballer of the Year in 1965, made the first of his six appearances at Wembley. Only one other foreign-based player made as many visits to the stadium in his career, his team-mate Mario Coluna.

England: Springett (Sheffield W), Armfield (Blackpool), Wilson (Huddersfield), Robson (West Brom), Swan (Sheffield W), Flowers (Wolves), Connelly (Burnley), Douglas (Blackburn), Pointer (Burnley), Haynes (Fulham) – capt, Charlton (Man Utd). manager: Walter Winterbottom
Portugal: Pereira (Benfica), Lino (Sporting Lisbon), Hilario (Sporting), Perides (Sporting), Soares (Sporting), Vicente (Belenenses), Yauca (Belenenses), Eusebio (Benfica), Aguas (Benfica) – capt, Coluna (Benfica), Cavem (Benfica). coach: Fernando Peyroteo

Final table	P	W	D	L	F	A	Pts
England	4	3	1	0	16	2	7
Portugal	4	1	1	2	9	7	3
Luxembourg	4	1	0	3	5	21	2

BRITISH CHAMPIONSHIP

Wednesday 22nd November 1961

England   **1-1**   **Northern Ireland**
Charlton 20   McIlroy 81
30,000
Referee: L Callaghan (Wales)

Northern Ireland had lost their last seven British Championship matches and had been thrashed 6-1 by Scotland at Windsor Park. They had also failed to qualify from a World Cup qualifying group dominated by West Germany. England were aiming for a record 11th successive British Championship and had drawn 1-1 with Wales at Ninian Park.

England opened the scoring when Bobby Charlton took a pass from Haynes and beat Hunter with a typical bullet shot into the corner. Northern Ireland levelled with only nine minutes left. From McAdams' pass, Jimmy McIlroy struck the equaliser to end the Irish run. It was not enough, though, to keep them in the Championship.

Scotland ended England's run with a 2-0 victory at Hampden Park. Northern Ireland finished bottom for the third year in succession and their next visit to Wembley was to be their worst ever.

England: Springett (Sheffield W), Armfield (Blackpool), Wilson (Huddersfield), Robson (West Brom), Swan (Sheffield W), Flowers (Wolves), Douglas (Blackburn), Byrne* (Crystal P), Crawford* (Ipswich), Haynes (Fulham) – capt, Charlton (Man Utd). manager: Walter Winterbottom
Northern Ireland: Hunter* (Coleraine), Magill (Arsenal), Elder (Burnley), Blanchflower (Tottenham) – capt, Neill (Arsenal), Nicholson (Man Utd), Bingham (Everton), Barr* (Linfield), McAdams (Bolton), McIlroy (Burnley), McLaughlin (Shrewsbury. manager: Peter Doherty
*first cap

Final table	P	W	D	L	F	A	Pts
Scotland	3	3	0	0	10	1	6
Wales	3	1	1	1	5	3	3
England	3	0	2	1	2	4	2
N Ireland	3	0	1	2	2	11	1

Inter-Varsity Match

Saturday 9th December 1961

Cambridge U 2
Neil, Flann
Oxford U 0

Pat Neil scored his fifth goal in three matches at Wembley.

INTERNATIONAL

Wednesday 4th April 1962

England   **3-1**   **Austria**
Crawford 8, Flowers pen 38, Hunt 67   Buzek 79
45,500
Referee: P Schwinte (France)

After finishing bottom of England's group in the 1958 World Cup, Austria had decided not to enter the 1962 competition despite reaching the quarter-finals of the first European Championship in 1960. In May 1961 they defeated England 3-1 in Vienna. It was only their second win in ten meetings. Their previous visit to Wembley in 1951 had brought them a draw.

Ray Crawford opened the scoring

after Fraydl pushed Haynes' shot onto the post and he knocked in the rebound. Half an hour later, Connelly was tripped by Stotz and Ron Flowers converted the spot kick.

Midway through the second half England wrapped up the victory. Haynes crossed for Roger Hunt to head past Fraydl.

Austrian consolation came when Johann Buzek dived to head in Hof's centre.

Austria's misfortune continued as the Republic of Ireland surprisingly beat them in the first round of the 1964 European Championship 18 months later. They came back to Wembley, though, in 1965 and pulled off a surprise victory.

England: Springett (Sheffield W), Armfield (Blackpool), Wilson (Huddersfield), Anderson* (Sunderland), Swan (Sheffield W), Flowers (Wolves), Connelly (Burnley), Hunt* (Liverpool), Crawford (Ipswich), Haynes (Fulham) – capt, Charlton (Man Utd). manager: Walter Winterbottom
*first cap
Austria: Fraydl (FK Austria Vienna), Trubrig (Linzer Ask), Hasenkopf (Vienna Sportklub), Oslanski (Sportklub), Stotz (FK Austria), Koller (First Vienna) – capt, Knoll (Sportklub), Hof (Sportklub), Buzek (First), Fiala (FK Austria), Rafrieder (Dornbirn). Sub: Flogel (Rapid Vienna) for Fiala 40. coach: Karl Decker

FA Amateur Cup Final

Saturday 14th April 1962

Crook Town 1
McMillan 66
Hounslow Town 1
Patterson 73
After extra time
43,000
Referee: J Taylor (Wolverhampton)

Both goals were scrappy, with Rhodes fumbling McMillan's cross for the first, and Patterson charging Snowball and the ball over the line for the equaliser. Crook remained unbeaten in their fourth final and finished the job in the replay.

Referee Jack Taylor took charge of the World Cup final in 1974 when West Germany beat Netherlands in Munich. Frank Clark won a European Cup winners medal with Nottingham Forest 17 years later.

Crook: Snowball, Gardener, Clark, Storey, Heatherington, Brown, Sparks, Garbutt, Coates, Pearey, McMillan
Hounslow: Rhodes, MacDonald, Creasey, Evans, Taylor, Digweed, Somers, Fennell, McHattie, Dipper, Patterson

Replay: Saturday 21st April 1962
Crook Town 4
Coates 2, Sparks, McMillan
Hounslow Town 0

(Ayresome Park, Middlesbrough)

Schoolboy International

Saturday 28th April 1962

England 1
Bullock
West Germany 2
Korsikowski, Bechtold
95,000
Referee: L Callaghan (Merthyr Tydfil)

England took the lead in the tenth minute but suffered their first home defeat by a foreign team at schoolboy level.

England: Barnett, Harrop, Hignett, Farrar, Barlow – capt, Adams, Bond, McCulloch, Bullock, Hurst, Maher

FA CUP FINAL

Saturday 5th May 1962

Burnley	1-3	Tottenham Hotspur
Robson 50		Greaves 3, Smith 51, Blanchflower pen 80
100,000		
Referee: J Finney (Hereford)		

Burnley had lost to a late winner in extra time in their only previous Wembley appearance in 1947. They had had a good FA Cup record in more recent years and had lost to Tottenham in the previous year's semi-final. But they had won the Cup only once, in 1914. Tottenham were the holders.

Burnley finished as League runners-up to Ipswich Town, having won the Championship in 1960. Tottenham finished a point, and a place, below them in their defence of the title. They had also reached the European Cup semi-finals before losing to the holders, and eventual winners, Benfica.

Tottenham took a third minute lead. Smith's header sent Jimmy Greaves through, and, finding himself surrounded by defenders, he stopped suddenly and checked back, before brilliantly turning and shooting past Blacklaw.

Burnley equalised five minutes after the interval. From a cross by Harris, Jimmy Robson beat Brown at the near post. But within a minute, White crossed and Bobby Smith turned and fired Tottenham back in front. With ten minutes left it was all over. Medwin's shot was handled on the line by Cummings. Danny Blanchflower sent Blacklaw the wrong way from the penalty and Tottenham had won the Cup for the fourth time.

Burnley gained their revenge by knocking Tottenham out of the FA Cup in their first defence the following year with an emphatic 3-0 away win. But for their next visit to Wembley in the 1988 Sherpa Van Trophy final they were a Fourth Division club.

Tottenham became Britain's first winners of a European trophy the following year when they thrashed the holders Atletico Madrid 5-1 in the final of the European Cup-Winners Cup in Rotterdam. They also finished as League runners-up to Everton. They returned to win the FA Cup again in 1967.

Footballer of the Year, Jimmy Adamson, made his only appearance at Wembley.

Burnley: Blacklaw, Angus, Elder, Adamson – capt, Cummings, Miller, Connelly, McIlroy, Pointer, Robson, Harris. manager: Harry Potts

Tottenham: Brown, Baker, Henry, Blanchflower – capt, Norman, Mackay, Medwin, White, Smith, Greaves, Jones. manager: Bill Nicholson

INTERNATIONAL

Wednesday 9th May 1962

England   **3-1**   **Switzerland**
Flowers 20, Hitchens 21, Connelly 36   Allemann 32
41,000
Referee: D Zariquiegui (Spain)

Switzerland had produced the shock of the World Cup qualifying matches by coming from behind to knock out the 1958 finalists Sweden in a play-off in Berlin. They had beaten England twice before, the last occasion in 1947 by the only goal in Zurich. Their only previous visit to England 18 months later saw them thrashed 6-0 at Highbury. England had just lost the British Championship, for the first time in 11 years, to Scotland.

England went ahead when a free kick from Haynes was turned in by Ron Flowers. Within a minute it was 2-0, as Gerry Hitchens scored from Charlton's cross. Switzerland replied when Anton Allemann smartly beat Springett. But four minutes later, a long ball from Flowers was headed in by John Connelly. Despite their lead England failed to impress and there were no further goals.

Switzerland failed to win a point in the World Cup in Chile while England only reached the quarter-finals on goal average ahead of Argentina. They were beaten by the holders, and eventual winners, Brazil. The following year England had a crushing 8-1 win over Switzerland in Basle.

England: Springett (Sheffield W), Armfield (Blackpool), Wilson (Huddersfield), Robson (West Brom), Swan (Sheffield W), Flowers (Wolves), Connelly (Burnley), Greaves (Tottenham), Hitchens (Internazionale), Haynes (Fulham) – capt, Charlton (Man Utd). manager: Walter Winterbottom

Switzerland: Permunian (Lucerne), Roesch (Servette Geneva), Tacchella (Lausanne-sports), Grobety (Lausanne-sports), Schneiter (Young Boys Berne) – capt, Weber (Basle), Antenen (Chaux-de-Fonds), Vonlanthen (Lausanne-sports), Eschmann (Red Star Olympique Audonien), Allemann (Mantova), Durr (Lausanne-sports). sub: Stettler (Basle) for Permunian 46. coach: Karl Rappan

BRITISH CHAMPIONSHIP

Wednesday 21st November 1962

England   **4-0**   **Wales**
Connelly 7, Peacock 35, 63, Greaves 88
27,500
Referee: S Carswell (Northern Ireland)

Wales had finished runners-up in each of the past two British Championships but this time had already lost 3-2 to the reigning champions Scotland at Ninian Park. They had lost on each of their four previous British Championship visits to Wembley and needed to win to stay in contention. Both teams had entered the European Championship for the first time but suffered disappointing starts.

In the first round first legs England had been held to a 1-1 draw by France at Hillsborough, and Wales had been beaten 3-1 by Hungary in Budapest. England had begun the British Championship, however, with a 3-1 win over Northern Ireland at Windsor Park.

England started smartly; Greaves hit the bar and John Connelly netted the rebound to put England in front. Ten minutes before the interval, from Hill's pass, Alan Peacock caught Millington by surprise with his shot and the goalkeeper pushed it into his own net. Peacock clinched the points just past the hour when he robbed Williams as the Welsh captain received a goal kick from Millington, running on to score his second. Jimmy Greaves put the icing on the cake, in Walter Winterbottom's last match as England manager, when he beat three men and sent a rising shot into the corner with two minutes left.

England and Wales were both knocked out of the European Championship in the second legs while England and Scotland were left to decide the British Championship.

Making his Wembley debut was Bobby Moore, who captained England to their 1966 World Cup triumph. In 1964 he was Footballer of the Year and he went on to win 108 England caps.

Walter Winterbottom was knighted in 1978 and died in 2002 at the age of 88.

England: Springett (Sheffield W), Armfield (Blackpool) – capt, Shaw (Sheffield U), Moore (West Ham), Labone (Everton), Flowers (Wolves), Connelly (Burnley), Hill (Bolton), Peacock (Middlesbrough), Greaves (Tottenham), Tambling* (Chelsea). manager: Walter Winterbottom
Wales: Millington (West Brom), Williams (Southampton) – capt, Sear* (Man City), Hennessey (Birmingham), Nurse (Middlesbrough), Lucas (Leyton Orient), Jones (Swansea), Allchurch (Cardiff), Leek (Birmingham), Vernon (Everton), Medwin (Tottenham). manager: Jimmy Murphy
*first cap

Inter-Varsity Match

Saturday 8th December 1962

Cambridge U 5
Clayton 2, Payne 2, Fitch
Oxford U 2
Jackson, Irvine

Cambridge were two up in seven minutes, and well on their way to their third victory in four years.

European Youth Tournament

Final

Tuesday 23rd April 1963

England 4
Napier og, Sammels, Whittaker, Sissons
Northern Ireland 0
30,500
Referee: R Kreitlein (West Germany)

The hosts won the tournament for the second time without conceding a goal in their five games. They retained it the following year in Netherlands.

The unfortunate Irish goalkeeper was Pat Jennings, Footballer of the Year in 1973, who went on to win a record 119 full international caps for Northern Ireland. His last competitive appearance was on his 41st birthday against Brazil in the World Cup in Mexico, an incredible 23 years after his Wembley debut and 18 months after his last league game.

Also in the Irish team was Dave Clements, who won 48 full international caps and was player-manager of the national team from 1975-76.

John Sissons followed up his two goals for the schoolboys in 1961 with England's fourth goal.

England fielded two future Cup final captains and renowned hard men, Ron Harris and Tommy Smith. Smith also won a full international cap in 1971 at Wembley.

Referee Rudolf Kreitlein was in charge of England's World Cup Quarter-final in 1966 and sent off the Argentinian captain Rattin.

England: Cowen (Chelsea), Badger (Sheffffield U), Shaw (Sheffffield U), Smith (Liverpool), Chatterley (Aston Villa) – capt, Harris (Chelsea), French (Shrewsbury, Sammels (Arsenal), Jones (Bury), Sissons (West Ham), Whittaker (Arsenal)

Northern Ireland: Jennings (Newry), Corbett (Ballyclare), McCurley (Linfield), Nicholl (Coleraine), Napier (Bolton), Todd (Burnley), Dunlop (Coleraine), Guy (Linfield), Clements (Wolves), Ross (Glentoran), McKinney (Glenavon)

BRITISH CHAMPIONSHIP

Saturday 6th April 1963

England   1-2   Scotland
Douglas 79   Baxter 28, (pen) 30
98,606
Referee: L Horn (Netherlands)

Scotland, the reigning British Champions, had won every game in the competition since losing 9-3 on their last visit. They had beaten England 2-0 at Hampden Park the previous year but had to win to retain the Championship outright. Their last Wembley win had been in 1951. They had decided not to enter the European Championship. England also had to win to regain the title, a draw would mean it was shared.

In the sixth minute Wembley's so called injury hoodoo struck again as Smith and Caldow were involved in a collision which saw both players stretchered off. Caldow had a broken leg while Smith returned for the second half. Just before the half hour Scotland took the lead. Armfield lost the ball on the edge of the box to Jim Baxter, who ran on and beat Banks with a rising shot. Two minutes later Flowers brought down Henderson and Baxter sent Banks the wrong way from the penalty spot. Even though Smith was not fully fit, England's extra man began to tell in the second half and it was Smith's long ball, missed by Ure, which left Bryan Douglas in the clear to drive a low shot into the corner with 11 minutes left. Scotland held on, though, to retain the British Championship in the new look stadium, now with cover for all spectators.

Scotland completed their first ever hat-trick of victories over England in the British Championship the following year with a 1-0 win at Hampden Park.

England: Banks* (Leicester), Armfield (Blackpool) – capt, Byrne* (Liverpool), Moore (West Ham), Norman (Tottenham), Flowers (Wolves), Douglas (Blackburn), Greaves (Tottenham), Smith (Tottenham), Melia* (Liverpool), Charlton (Man Utd). manager: Alf Ramsey
Scotland: Brown (Tottenham), Hamilton (Dundee), Caldow (Rangers) – capt, Mackay (Tottenham), Ure (Dundee), Baxter (Rangers), Henderson (Rangers), White (Tottenham), St John (Liverpool), Law (Man Utd), Wilson (Rangers).
manager: Ian McColl
*first cap

Final table	P	W	D	L	F	A	Pts
Scotland	3	3	0	0	10	4	6
England	3	2	0	1	8	3	4
N Ireland	3	1	0	2	6	8	2
Wales	3	0	0	3	3	12	0

Schoolboy International

Saturday 27th April 1963

England 4
Bentley pen, Baker 3

Wales 1
Murphy
90,000
Referee: F Cooper (Salford)

Wales scored first in the 28th minute but still suffered their fourth successive defeat at Wembley. Jimmy Pearce was back, ten years later, when he was in the Spurs side that won the Football League Cup.

England: Macey, Hinton, Bentley, Hart, Curwen – capt, Boot, Wosahlo, Bradley, Baker, Pearce, Husband
Wales: Davies, Derrett, Harris, Raybould – capt, Mallard, Thomas, Carvell, Pearson, Hawkins, Murphy, Curten

FA Amateur Cup Final

Saturday 4th May 1963

Sutton United 2
Goodall, Bladon

Wimbledon 4
Reynolds 4
45,000
Referee: K Dagnall (Lancashire)

All four of Eddie Reynolds' goals were headers as Wimbledon won the trophy for the first and only time. Twenty five years later they were the proud holders of the FA Cup.

Sutton: Roffey, Gamblin, Shears, Shepherd, Price, Clack, Bladon, Osborne, Bates, Hermitage, Goodall
Wimbledon: Kelly, J Martin, Willis, Ardrey, Law, Murphy, Brown, B Martin, Reynolds, Hamm, Williams

INTERNATIONAL

Wednesday 8th May 1963

England	**1-1**	**Brazil**
Douglas 86		Pepe 18

92,000
Referee: L Horn (Netherlands)

Brazil had retained the World Cup the previous year in Chile, beating England 3-1 in the quarter-finals, but their side contained only the goalkeeper Gilmar and Amarildo (who scored in the final) from their winning team.

A car crash in Hamburg two nights earlier had robbed Wembley of the talents of Zito (who also scored in the final) and Pele. This was to be Brazil's only appearance at the stadium in Pele's career. So it was that the man who scored three goals in two World Cup finals 12 years apart never set foot on the famous turf.

He could have played in the FA Centenary Match five months later but his club Santos would not release him.

England's only victory against Brazil had been in their first meeting in 1956. Brazil had been runners-up in the South American Championship three times in the 1950's but had not won it since 1949.

Pepe curled a brilliant free kick past the defensive wall, sending Banks the wrong way, to give Brazil the lead but with four minutes left Armfield's shot was touched on by Charlton and Bryan Douglas rescued England with the equaliser.

A Pele-inspired Brazil thrashed England 5-1 in Rio de Janeiro the following year and they were back at Wembley in 1978.

England: Banks (Leicester), Armfield (Blackpool) – capt, Wilson (Huddersfield), Milne* (Liverpool), Norman (Tottenham), Moore (West Ham), Douglas (Blackburn), Greaves (Tottenham), Smith (Tottenham), Eastham* (Arsenal), Charlton (Man Utd). manager: Alf Ramsey
*first cap
Brazil: Gilmar (Santos) – capt, Lima (Santos), Eduardo (Corinthians), Zequinha (Palmeiras), Dias (Sao Paulo), Rildo (Botafogo), Dorval (Santos), Mengalvio (Santos), Coutinho (Santos), Amarildo (Botafogo), Pepe (Santos). sub: Ney (Corinthians) for Amarildo 40. coach: Aymore Moreira

EUROPEAN CUP FINAL

Wednesday 22nd May 1963

Benfica   **1-2**   **AC Milan**
Eusebio 18   Altafini 58, 70
45,000
Referee: A Holland (Barnsley)

The holders Benfica were on the verge of a hat-trick of European Cup wins. After Real Madrid's five successive victories, they had taken the trophy to Portugal and retained it in the previous year's final by defeating Real Madrid 5-3 in Amsterdam after going two goals down and with Puskas getting a first-half hat-trick.

Milan had reached the final in 1958 and had twice led against Real Madrid in Brussels before losing 3-2 after extra time. They had beaten Ipswich Town in the last 16 and the Scottish League Champions Dundee in the semi-finals. No Italian team had previously won the trophy.

Benfica won the Portuguese League Championship for the third time in four years and for a record 12th time. Milan had failed to retain their Italian League title, finishing third.

The holders took the lead when, from a Torres pass, Eusebio sped through and fired past Ghezzi. Milan drew level in the second half when Rivera put Jose Altafini clear to beat Pereira.

With 20 minutes left Pereira saved from Altafini only for the Brazilian to score his second from the rebound. This was enough to take the European Cup to Italy for the first time.

Benfica lost two more European Cup finals in the 1960's, the second of which was at Wembley in 1968. Internazionale kept the European Cup in Milan for the next two years but AC Milan were to regain it in 1969 after their first European Cup-Winners' Cup success a year earlier. They reappeared at Wembley in 1988 for the Wembley International Tournament.

Making his first appearance at Wembley was Gianni Rivera, European Footballer of the Year in 1969.

Benfica: Pereira, Cavem, Cruz, Humberto, Raul, Coluna – capt, Augusto, Santana, Torres, Eusebio, Simoes. coach: Fernando Riera

AC Milan: Ghezzi, David, Trebbi, Benitez, Maldini – capt, Trapattoni, Pivatelli, Sani, Altafini, Rivera, Mora. coach: Nereo Rocco

FA CUP FINAL

Saturday 25th May 1963

Leicester City   **1-3**   **Manchester United**
Keyworth 80   Law 30, Herd 57, 85
100,000
Referee: K Aston (Ilford)

Leicester were appearing in their third final, their second in three years, although they had yet to win the Cup. United had also lost their previous two finals in 1957 and '58 but had won the Cup twice.

Leicester finished fourth in the First Division their highest position since 1929, while United were still rebuilding after Munich, finishing 19th and narrowly escaping relegation in their worst league season since promotion in 1938.

After half an hour of a final, delayed three weeks because of the severe winter, Crerand's pass came to Denis Law, who turned sharply and shot past Banks. Just before the hour, Charlton's shot was saved by Banks but David Herd netted the rebound. Leicester pulled a goal back with Ken Keyworth's diving header from a McLintock cross ten minutes from time but five minutes later Banks dropped a cross from Giles and Herd scored again. The new United had won their first trophy.

Leicester won their first major trophy, the Football League Cup, the following year and reached another FA Cup final in 1969. United reached the semi-finals in each of the next three years, losing them all. They were League runners-up to Liverpool the following year and knocked the holders Tottenham Hotspur out of the European Cup-Winners Cup before losing a 4-1 first-leg lead to Sporting Lisbon, the eventual winners, in the quarter-finals. But they were League Champions twice in three years, (1965 & '67), and won the European Cup on an emotional night at Wembley in 1968.

Leicester C: Banks, Sjoberg, Norman, McLintock, King , Appleton – capt, Riley, Cross, Keyworth, Gibson, Stringfellow. manager: Matt Gillies
Manchester U: Gaskell, Dunne, Cantwell – capt, Crerand, Foulkes, Setters, Giles, Quixall, Herd, Law, Charlton. manager: Matt Busby

FA CENTENARY MATCH

Wednesday 23rd October 1963

England	2-1	FIFA
Paine 65, Greaves 90		Law 82

100,000
Referee: R Davidson (Scotland)

Ten years after a FIFA side had visited Wembley for the FA's 90th anniversary, England faced a rest of the world select containing six former and future European Footballers of the Year.

England broke the deadlock when Greaves' shot from a cross by Smith was blocked and Terry Paine scored from close range. With eight minutes left, Di Stefano and Puskas worked an opening for Manchester United's Denis Law to fire the equaliser past Banks. But in the last minute Soskic could not hold Charlton's drive and Jimmy Greaves nipped in to secure the victory.

The win gave England high hopes of winning the World Cup in 1966 in their own country.

Making their first appearances at Wembley were Raymond Kopa (European Footballer of the Year in 1958), Josef Masopust (European Footballer of the Year in 1962) and Lev Yashin, who was about to be named European Footballer of the Year for 1963. Yashin was to return in the 1966 World Cup.

England: Banks (Leicester), Armfield (Blackpool) – capt, Wilson (Huddersfield), Milne (Liverpool), Norman (Tottenham), Moore (West Ham), Paine (Southampton), Greaves (Tottenham), Smith (Tottenham), Eastham (Arsenal), Charlton (Man Utd). manager: Alf Ramsey
FIFA: Yashin (Dynamo Moscow & USSR), Santos (Palmeiras & Brazil), Schnellinger (Mantova & W Germany), Pluskal (Dukla Prague & Czechoslovakia), Popluhar (Slovan Bratislava & Czechoslovakia), Masopust (Dukla Prague & Czechoslovakia), Kopa (Reims & France), Law (Man Utd & Scotland), Di Stefano (Real Madrid & Spain) – capt, Eusebio (Benfica & Portugal), Gento (Real Madrid & Spain). subs: Soskic (Partizan Belgrade & Yugoslavia) for Yashin 46, Eyzaguirre (Universidad De Chile & Chile) for Santos 46, Baxter (Rangers & Scotland) for Masopust 46, Puskas (Real Madrid & Hungary) for Eusebio 46, Seeler (Hamburg & W Germany) for Kopa 59. coach: Fernando Riera (Chile)

Youth International

Wednesday 6th November 1963

England 5
Jones, Sissons, Sammels, Smith 2 pens
Rest of United Kingdom 2
Graham , Mitchell

8,000
Referee: W O'Neill (Republic of Ireland)

Another match held to celebrate the FA's centenary. England fielded the team which had won the European Youth Tournament at Wembley seven months earlier. Tommy Smith, who scored two penalties, was in Liverpool's FA Cup-winning side the following season and netted for Liverpool in the European Cup final in 1977.

England: Cowen (Chelsea), Badger (Shefffield U), Shaw (Shefffield U), Smith (Liverpool), Chatterley (Aston Villa) – capt, Harris (Chelsea), French (Swindon), Sammels (Arsenal), Jones (Bury), Sissons (West Ham), Whittaker (Arsenal)
Rest of United Kingdom: Jennings (Watford & N Ireland), Clements (Wolves & N Ireland), Baillie (Hearts & Scotland), Nicholl (Coleraine & N Ireland), Murray (Cardiff & Scotland), Hollywood (Southampton & Scotland), Edwards (Dunfermline & Scotland), Roden (Swansea & Wales), Graham (Aston Villa & Scotland), Mitchell (Dundee U & Scotland), McKinney (Glenavon & N Ireland)

BRITISH CHAMPIONSHIP

Wednesday 20th November 1963

England	**8-3**	**Northern Ireland**
Paine 2, 38, 61, Greaves 20, 30, 60, 65		Crossan 42
Smith 46		Wilson 53, 85
53,000		
Referee: L Callaghan (Wales)		

Northern Ireland had finished bottom in each of the last four British Championships but had drawn on their last visit and had already beaten Scotland, Champions for the past two years, 2-1 at Windsor Park. They had also narrowly lost on aggregate to Spain, the eventual winners, in the European Championship after holding them to a draw in Bilbao. England had beaten Wales 4-0 at Ninian Park.

Mesmerising skill from Charlton, in only the second minute, enabled Terry Paine to open the scoring. England scored again as Jimmy Greaves put the finishing touch to some clever passing through the Irish defence. Ten minutes later he was on the end of a Paine cross and just before half-time, Eastham's cross was volleyed home by Paine for his second as England threatened to reach double figures.

Northern Ireland pulled one back before the interval, Johnny Crossan beating Banks with a diving header from a Magill centre but any hopes of a revival were quashed after the restart. Paine crossed and Bobby Smith headed England's fifth. Harvey put Sammy Wilson through to temporarily reduce the deficit.

But on the hour mark Greaves slammed an unstoppable shot past Gregg from Eastham's pass to complete his hat-trick. Within a minute Armfield combined with Eastham and Paine finished off the move for his hat-trick.

Paine then supplied a pass for Greaves to score the eighth. The scoring was completed when Armfield cleared off the line from a corner only for Wilson to force it back over the line for his second.

Northern Ireland, incredibly, shared the Championship by beating Wales 3-2 at Vetch Field as England lost 1-0 at Hampden Park to Scotland who completed a hat-trick of titles.

England: Banks (Leicester), Armfield (Blackpool) – capt, Thomson* (Wolves), Milne (Liverpool), Norman (Tottenham), Moore (West Ham), Paine (Southampton), Greaves (Tottenham), Smith (Tottenham), Eastham (Arsenal), Charlton (Man Utd). manager: Alf Ramsey
Northern Ireland: Gregg (Man Utd), Magill (Arsenal), Parke (Hibernian), Harvey (Sunderland), Neill (Arsenal), McCullough (Arsenal), Bingham (Port Vale) – capt, Humphries (Coventry), Wilson (Falkirk), Crossan (Sunderland), Hill (Everton). manager: Bertie Peacock
*first cap

Final table	P	W	D	L	F	A	Pts
England	3	2	0	1	12	4	4
N Ireland	3	2	0	1	8	11	4
Scotland	3	2	0	1	4	3	4
Wales	3	0	0	3	3	9	0

Inter-Varsity Match

Saturday 7th December 1963

Cambridge U 4
Cutler 2, Richardson 2

Oxford U 2
Gilliat 2

A third successive victory for Cambridge.

FA Amateur Cup Final

Saturday 18th April 1964

Crook Town 2
Goodfellow, Brown

Enfield 1
Day
37,000
Referee: D Smith (Stonehouse)

Enfield's goalkeeper Mitchell broke his arm in the 26th minute when Enfield were leading.

Thomas took over in goal with Mitchell returning in the second half to play in attack. Crook eventually overcame them to record their second cup win in three years.

Crook: Snowball, McCourt, Reid, Storey, Garbutt – capt, Brown, Weir, Goodfellow, Lumsden, Roughley, McMillan
Enfield: Mitchell, Neale, Harris, D'Arcy – capt, Kingsland, Cantwell, Thomas, Broomfield, Edwards, Day, Howard

Schoolboy International

Saturday 25th April 1964

England 1
Suggett
West Germany 1
Pielken
Referee: W Webster (Torquay)

England failed to gain revenge for their 1962 defeat.

England: Forster, Glozier – capt, Youlden, Luke, Fox, Evans, Brough, McVitie, Bryan, Suggett, Bristow. sub: Davidson for Luke

FA CUP FINAL

Saturday 2nd May 1964

Preston North End	**2-3**	**West Ham United**
Holden 9, Dawson 40		Sissons 10, Hurst 52, Boyce 90

100,000
Referee: A Holland (Barnsley)

Preston had last won the Cup in 1938 and had surrendered a 2-1 lead in the closing stages of the 1954 final. West Ham had never won the Cup and their only final had been back in 1923 in Wembley's first match. They had, however, won the Football League War Cup at Wembley in 1940. In the semi-finals they had beaten the holders Manchester United.

Preston had been in the Second Division for three years and finished third. West Ham finished 14th in the First Division and also reached the Football League Cup semi-finals where they lost to the eventual winners Leicester City.

The Second Division side took a surprise lead. Standen saved from Dawson but Doug Holden knocked the ball in. It lasted only a minute. John Sissons played a one-two with Byrne and drove home the equaliser. Five minutes before the interval Alex Dawson headed in from a Wilson corner

and West Ham were rocking. Just after half-time they equalised again. Kelly stopped Brown's header but Geoff Hurst headed the rebound back towards goal. Kelly managed to push it onto the bar but it hit him on the way out and went over the line. West Ham scored a dramatic winner in injury time. Brabrook's cross found the head of Ronnie Boyce at the far post and the gallant underdogs were beaten.

Preston did not appear at Wembley again for 30 years when they reached the Third Division promotion play-off final. They had dropped into the lower divisions in 1970. West Ham received little praise for their victory but went on to win the European Cup-Winners Cup a year later.

Geoff Hurst made a scoring Wembley debut. Two years later he became the only player ever to score a hat-trick in a World Cup final as England beat West Germany in Wembley's finest moment.

Preston: Kelly, Ross, Smith (J), Lawton – capt, Singleton, Kendall, Wilson, Ashworth, Dawson, Spavin, Holden. manager: Jimmy Milne
West Ham: Standen, Bond, Burkett, Bovington, Brown (K), Moore (R) – capt, Brabrook, Boyce, Byrne, Hurst, Sissons. manager: Ron Greenwood

INTERNATIONAL

Wednesday 6th May 1964

England	**2-1**	**Uruguay**
Byrne 43, 52		Spencer 78

54,000
Referee: I Zsolt (Hungary)

Uruguay had won the World Cup on the first two occasions that they had entered the competition but in 1962 they had been knocked out in the first round.

They had won the South American Championship on ten occasions. It was their first visit to England but they had beaten their hosts in both of their previous meetings. The last occasion had been by 4-2 in Basle in the 1954 World Cup quarter-final.

England took the lead a couple of minutes before half-time, Paine's flick being turned in by Johnny Byrne. After the restart the West Ham centre forward scored again, turning to shoot after Greaves had controlled a cross from Charlton, winning his 50th cap.

Alberto Spencer took a pass from Gil to reduce the deficit late on but England held on for their first victory over Uruguay.

Uruguay comfortably qualified for the 1966 World Cup and opened the tournament against England at Wembley.

England: Banks (Leicester), Cohen* (Fulham), Wilson (Huddersfield), Milne (Liverpool), Norman (Tottenham), Moore (West Ham) – capt, Paine (Southampton), Greaves (Tottenham), Byrne (West Ham), Eastham (Arsenal), Charlton (Man Utd). manager: Alf Ramsey
*first cap
Uruguay: Taibo (Wanderers), Martinez (Rampla) – capt, Diaz (Wanderers), Cincunegui (Danubio), Pereira (Cerro), Pavoni (Defensor), Flores (Defensor), Cortes (Cerro), Spencer (Penarol), Gil (Rampla), Pintos (Cerro)

INTERNATIONAL

Wednesday 21st October 1964

England	**2-2**	**Belgium**
Pickering 32, Hinton 70		Cornelis 22, Van Himst 42

45,000
Referee: C Lo Bello (Italy)

Belgium had lost on their previous visit in 1952 and had beaten England only once in 14 meetings. Like England, they had failed to progress beyond the first round of the last European Championship, losing home and away to Yugoslavia and had also failed to qualify for the last two World Cups.

Belgium took a deserved lead when Vandenberg played the ball back to Jean Cornelis who shot past Waiters. Ten minutes later England were level when Greaves gave Fred Pickering the chance to chip the ball over Nicolay for the equaliser. The visitors regained the lead before the interval, however, as Paul Van Himst's shot was deflected in by Cohen.

But England rescued a draw with 20 minutes to go when Alan Hinton took a pass from Venables and fired the ball home.

Belgium did not return to England for the 1966 World Cup as they lost a play-off to Bulgaria in Florence and they never appeared in the old stadium again.

England: Waiters (Blackpool), Cohen (Fulham), Thomson (Wolves), Milne (Liverpool), Norman (Tottenham), Moore (West Ham) – capt, Thompson (Liverpool), Greaves (Tottenham), Pickering (Everton), Venables (Chelsea), Hinton (Nottingham F). manager: Alf Ramsey
Belgium: Nicolay (Standard Liege), Heylens (Anderlecht), Cornelis (Anderlecht), Sulon (Liege), Vebiest (Anderlecht), Plaskie (Anderlecht), Vermeyen (Lierse), Jurion (Anderlecht) – capt, Van Himst (Anderlecht), Vandenberg (Union St Gilloise), Puis (Anderlecht). coach: Constant Van den Stock

BRITISH CHAMPIONSHIP

Wednesday 18th November 1964

England	**2-1**	**Wales**
Wignall 17, 60		Jones 75

40,000
Referee: T Mitchell (Northern Ireland)

Wales had finished bottom of the last British Championship but had already beaten Scotland 3-2 at Ninian Park. They had, however, lost on all five of their previous British Championship visits to Wembley. England had beaten Northern Ireland 4-3 at Windsor Park in their attempt to win the title outright for the first time since 1961.

Hinton twice had shots blocked before Frank Wignall headed the opening goal past Millington. The Nottingham Forest forward scored again after an hour when he met Hinton's cross with another fine header. Fifteen minutes later Cliff Jones played a one-two with Ron Davies and brought Wales back into the game but England held on.

England now needed only a point against Scotland for the outright Championship. Wales thrashed Northern Ireland 5-0 at Windsor Park but it could only secure them a runners-up spot. They also finished runners-up in their World Cup qualifying group to the USSR and so failed to qualify. Their next visit was in the European Championship in 1966.

England: Waiters (Blackpool), Cohen (Fulham), Thomson (Wolves), Bailey (Charlton), Flowers (Wolves) – capt, Young* (Sheffield W), Thompson (Liverpool), Hunt (Liverpool), Wignall* (Nottingham F), Byrne (West Ham), Hinton (Nottingham F). manager: Alf Ramsey
Wales: Millington (Crystal P), Williams (S) (Southampton), Williams (G) (West Brom), Hennessey (Birmingham), England (Blackburn) – capt, Hole (Cardiff), Rees (Coventry), Davies (R) (Norwich), Davies (W) (Bolton), Allchurch (Cardiff), Jones (Tottenham). manager: Dave Bowen
*first cap

Inter-Varsity Match

Saturday 5th December 1964

Cambridge U 1
Cutler

Oxford U 3
Farr 2, Slater

Oxford's second win at Wembley.

Schoolboy International

Saturday 3rd April 1965

England 3
Shoemark 2, Evans pen

Scotland 0
85,000
Referee: D Howell (Birmingham)

Scotland's third successive defeat at Wembley. The England goalkeeper Peter Shilton was to win a world record 125 full international caps and two European Cup winners medals with Nottingham Forest, keeping clean sheets in both finals.

The Minister for Sport Denis Howell MP added a parliamentary air to the afternoon's proceedings.

England: Shilton, Peaper, Styles, Chambers, Went – capt, Newman, Gould, Evans, Shoemark, Stenson, Moss
Scotland: McNair, Clarke, Weir, Watson, Butler, Manley – capt, Thornton, Howden, Waddell, Cumming, Goodwin

BRITISH CHAMPIONSHIP

Saturday 10th April 1965

England	**2-2**	**Scotland**
R Charlton 24, Greaves 34		Law 40, St John 59

98,199
Referee: I Zsolt (Hungary)

Scotland were aiming for a fourth successive British Championship but needed to beat England for the fourth year in succession to gain a share. England needed only a point to win the title outright for the first time since 1961 when they had last beaten Scotland.

Bobby Charlton's sweetly-struck shot gave England the lead and it was only another ten minutes before he created a second for Jimmy Greaves.

Scotland were back in the game, though, before the interval as Banks failed to stop Denis Law's snap shot. With Wilson carried off injured at half-time and Byrne hobbling throughout the second half, England effectively played the last 45 minutes with only nine fit men. Inevitably, Scotland drew level. With half an hour to go, from a Law corner, Cohen stopped Wilson's

header only for Ian St John to head past Banks. England survived, however, to win the Championship.

England were to beat Scotland the following year at Hampden Park to retain the British Championship. Scotland finished runners-up to Italy in their World Cup qualifying group and so failed to return the following year for the finals in England.

Jack Charlton, elder brother of Sir Bobby and Footballer of the Year two years later, was making his first Wembley appearance.

England: Banks (Leicester), Cohen (Fulham), Wilson (Everton), Stiles* (Man Utd), Charlton (J)* (Leeds), Moore (West Ham) – capt, Thompson (Liverpool), Greaves (Tottenham), Bridges* (Chelsea), Byrne (West Ham), Charlton (R) (Man Utd). manager: Alf Ramsey
Scotland: Brown (Tottenham), Hamilton (Dundee), McCreadie* (Chelsea), Crerand (Man Utd), McNeill (Celtic) – capt, Greig (Rangers), Henderson (Rangers), Collins (Leeds), St John (Liverpool), Law (Man Utd), Wilson (Rangers). manager: Ian McColl
*first cap

Final table	P	W	D	L	F	A	Pts
England	3	2	1	0	10	6	5
Wales	3	2	0	1	9	4	4
Scotland	3	1	1	1	7	7	3
N Ireland	3	0	0	3	5	12	0

FA Amateur Cup Final

Saturday 24th April 1965

Hendon 3
Hyde 2, Quail
Whitby Town 1
Mulvaney
45,000
Referee: G McCabe (Sheffield)

Hendon's second win in the competition. Their manager Ron Burgess had captained Tottenham Hotspur to the League Championship in 1951.

Hendon: Swannell, Hogwood, Sleap, Evans, Riddy, Cantwell - capt, Drake, Slade, Hyde, Quail, Lakey
Whitby: Pybus, Durnall, Nobbs, Kennerley, Barker – capt, Moody, Geldart, McHale, Mulvaney, Edwards, Crosthwaite

FA CUP FINAL

Saturday 1st May 1965

Leeds 1-2 **Liverpool**
Bremner 95   Hunt 93, St John 113
After extra time
100,000
Referee: W Clements (West Bromwich)

Leeds had never been beyond the quarter-finals before and had yet to win a major trophy. In the semi-finals they had beaten Manchester United who were to pip them to the League Championship. Liverpool, appearing in their third final, had still to win the FA Cup. In the semi-finals they had beaten Chelsea, the Football League

Cup winners. Their only previous Wembley appearance had been back in 1950.

Leeds had won the Second Division Championship the previous year but surprised all by only losing the League Championship on goal average. Liverpool finished seventh in their defence of the title and reached the European Cup semi-finals where they lost a 3-1 first-leg lead to the holders and eventual winners Internazionale.

After a bruising 90 minutes, the game was three minutes into extra time when Byrne (who broke his collar bone in the ninth minute) crossed for Roger Hunt to break the deadlock with a low header. With Storrie hobbling on the wing, Leeds looked beaten, but two minutes later, from Charlton's header, the unmarked Billy Bremner volleyed the equaliser past Lawrence.

Liverpool gained the victory they deserved when Callaghan crossed with just seven minutes left, and with Sprake tempted out of his goal, Ian St John dived to head

the winner past Reaney on the line.

Leeds were League runners-up again the following year as Liverpool regained the Championship for the second time in three years. Leeds also reached the European Fairs Cup semi-finals and finally won a major trophy, the Football League Cup, at Wembley in 1968. Liverpool reached the European Cup-Winners Cup final the following year but lost to a Ron Yeats own goal in extra time to Borussia Dortmund at Hampden Park. They were to reach the FA Cup final next in 1971.

Ian Callaghan, the 1974 Footballer of the Year, appeared at Wembley for the first time.

Leeds: Sprake, Reaney, Bell, Bremner, Charlton, Hunter, Giles, Storrie, Peacock, Collins – capt, Johanneson. manager: Don Revie
Liverpool: Lawrence, Lawler, Byrne, Strong, Yeats – capt, Stevenson, Callaghan, Hunt, St John, Smith, Thompson (P). manager: Bill Shankly

INTERNATIONAL

Wednesday 5th May 1965

England 1-0 **Hungary**
Greaves 17
52,000
Referee: P Schwinte (France)

England had been beaten by Hungary three times since their 1953 thrashing, the most recent by 2-1 in the 1962 World Cup in Rancagua. Hungary had finished third in the previous year's European Championship after losing 2-1 to the hosts, and eventual winners, Spain in the semi-final in Madrid.

They were also Olympic Champions for the second time. England, the British Champions, had not beaten Hungary since 1936 when they won 6-2 at Highbury.

The goal which settled it was brilliant. Paine received a pass from Eastham and picked out an unmarked Jimmy Greaves, who just managed to find the net as the 'keeper came out. It proved to be the only goal of the match.

Hungary returned to England the following year for the World Cup. They beat Brazil, the holders, and reached the quarter-finals before losing to the USSR at Roker Park. They would not meet England again until 1978.

England: Banks (Leicester), Cohen (Fulham), Wilson (Everton), Stiles (Man Utd), Charlton (Leeds), Moore (West Ham) – capt, Paine (Southampton), Greaves (Tottenham), Bridges (Chelsea), Eastham (Arsenal), Connelly (Man Utd). manager: Alf Ramsey
Hungary: Gelei (Tatabanya), Matrai (Ferencvaros), Sarosi (Vasas), Nagy (MTK), Meszoly (Vasas), Sipos (Honved) – capt, Gorocs (Ujpesti Dozsa), Varga (Ferencvaros), Bene (Ujpesti Dozsa), Nogradi (Honved), Fenyvesi (Ferencvaros). coach: Lajos Baroti

EUROPEAN CUP-WINNERS CUP FINAL

Wednesday 19th May 1965

TSV Munich **0-2** **West Ham United**
Sealey 69, 71

100,000
Referee: I Zsolt (Hungary)

Munich had come from behind to win a difficult semi-final and become the first German team to reach a European final. Their West German Cup win the previous year had been their first since the war.

West Ham had won the FA Cup for the first time the previous year and both teams were taking part in their first European competition.

In the semi-finals West ham had knocked out the European Fairs Cup holders Real Zaragoza and were hoping to repeat Tottenham Hotspur's success of two years earlier.

The match was deadlocked until midway through the second half when West Ham scored twice in two minutes. First, Alan Sea-ley took a pass from Boyce and fired West Ham into the lead. Then Moore's lofted pass was touched on by Peters, under pressure from Kohlars, for Sealey to beat Radenkovic from close range. In an exciting match, West Ham were finally given the acclaim denied them the previous year.

Munich won the West German League for the first and only time the following year. West Ham reached the semi-finals in their defence of the trophy but lost to the eventual winners Borussia Dortmund. They also reached the Football League Cup final for the first time but lost to West Bromwich Albion. They then had to wait until 1975 to win the FA Cup again.

TSV Munich: Radenkovic, Wagner, Kohlars, Bena, Reich, Luttrop, Heiss, Kuppers, Brunnenmeier – capt, Grosser, Rebele. coach: Max Merkel
West Ham: Standen, Kirkup, Burkett, Peters, Brown (K), Moore (R) – capt, Sealey, Boyce, Hurst, Dear, Sissons.

INTERNATIONAL

Wednesday 20th October 1965

England **2-3** **Austria**
R Charlton 3, Connelly 59   Flogel 53, Fritsch 73, 81
65,000
Referee: P Schwinte (France)

Austria had lost on their previous visit in 1962 and were going through a depressing run at international level. They had already failed to qualify for the following year's World Cup and had never won in England.

In the fourth minute, England took the lead. From Hasil's poor clearance, Paine put Bobby Charlton through to hammer the ball past Fraydl. England threatened to demolish their opponents but were guilty of many missed chances, several of them wasted, uncharacteristically, by Greaves.

It meant that when Hasil scrambled the ball to Rudolf Flogel the Austrians were able to draw level. Six minutes later England restored their lead when John Connelly converted Cohen's cross but Austria were not to be denied.

Springett brilliantly stopped Buzek's free kick only for Anton Fritsch to pounce on the rebound. Having drawn level twice Austria then seized the initiative. Nine minutes remained when Stiles lost the ball to Fritsch who ran on and drove his shot past Springett from fully 30 yards out.

England were left to rue their missed chances.

England: Springett (Sheffield W), Cohen (Fulham), Wilson (Everton), Stiles (Man Utd), J Charlton (Leeds), Moore (West Ham) – capt, Paine (Southampton), Greaves (Tottenham), Bridges (Chelsea), R Charlton (Man Utd), Connelly (Man Utd). manager: Alf Ramsey
Austria: Fraydl (Wacker Innsbruck), Sara (FK Austria), Stamm (Admira), Ullmann (Rapid Vienna), Frank (Schwechat), Ludescher (Wacker Innsburck), Fritsch (Rapid), Buzek (FK Austria) – capt, Hasil (Rapid), Flogel (Rapid), Macek (Austria Salzburg). sub: Dirnberger (FK Austria) for Frank 40 coach: Edi Fruhwirth

BRITISH CHAMPIONSHIP

Wednesday 10th November 1965

England	**2-1**	**Northern Ireland**
Baker 19, Peacock 73		Irvine 21

71,000
Referee: L Callaghan (Wales)

England, the reigning British Champions, had already drawn 0-0 with Wales at Ninian Park. Northern Ireland, who had suffered a humiliating defeat on their last visit, had subsequently failed to win a point in the previous year's British Championship but had already beaten Scotland 3-2 at Windsor Park. They were also battling with Switzerland for a place in the following year's World Cup.

Peacock put Joe Baker through to put England ahead but Moore's error a couple of minutes later enabled Best to supply Willie Irvine with the equaliser.

But England claimed their victory when Stiles' shot was blocked and Alan Peacock, with his back to goal, beat Jennings with an overhead kick.

England retained the British Championship by beating Scotland 4-3 at Hampden Park. Northern Ireland established the runners-up spot with a 4-1 win over Wales at Ninian Park but failed to return to England for the World Cup when they were unexpectedly held to a draw by Albania in Tirana.

George Best, who, three years later, was both Footballer of the Year and European Footballer of the Year, made his first appearance at Wembley.

England: Banks (Leicester), Cohen (Fulham), Wilson (Everton), Stiles (Man Utd), J Charlton (Leeds), Moore (West Ham) – capt, Thompson (Liverpool), Baker (Arsenal), Peacock (Leeds), R Charlton (Man Utd), Connelly (Man Utd). manager: Alf Ramsey
Northern Ireland: Jennings (Tottenham), Magill (Arsenal), Elder (Burnley), Harvey (Sunderland), Neill (Arsenal) – capt, Nicholson (Huddersfield), McIlroy (Stoke City), Crossan (Man City), Irvine (Burnley), Dougan (Leicester), Best (Man Utd). manager: Bertie Peacock

Final table	P	W	D	L	F	A	Pts
England	3	2	1	0	6	4	5
N Ireland	3	2	0	1	8	5	4
Scotland	3	1	0	2	9	8	2
Wales	3	0	1	2	2	8	1

Inter-Varsity Match

Wednesday 8th December 1965

Cambridge U 3
Barnwell, Cutler, Haywood
Oxford U 2
Garofall 2

Oxford drew level twice, but could not repeat the previous year's victory.

INTERNATIONAL

Wednesday 23rd February 1966

England	**1-0**	**West Germany**
Stiles 41		

75,000
Referee: P Roomer (Netherlands)

England had won 1-0 in Nuremberg the previous year, their third successive victory against West Germany. The first had been at Wembley in 1954. West Germany had reached the World Cup quarter-finals in 1962 before losing to Yugoslavia. They had decided not to enter the first two European Championships and had comfortably won their World Cup qualifying group.

Just before half-time Cohen crossed and Hunt's header was saved by Tilkowski, only for Nobby Stiles to drive home the only goal of the game as it landed on the line.

Franz Beckenbauer, twice European Footballer of the Year, and who won the World Cup as both captain and coach of his country, made his Wembley debut.

England: Banks (Leicester), Cohen (Fulham), Newton* (Blackburn), Moore (West Ham) – capt, Charlton (J) (Leeds), Hunter* (Leeds), Ball (Blackpool), Hunt (Liverpool), Stiles (Man Utd), Hurst* (West Ham), Charlton (R) (Man Utd). sub: Wilson (Everton) for Newton 43. manager: Alf Ramsey
*first cap
West Germany: Tilkowski (Borussia Dortmund), Lutz (Eintracht Frankfurt), Lorenz (Werder Bremen), Schulz (Hamburg), Weber (Cologne), Szymaniak (Tasmania Berlin) – capt, Kramer (Duisburg), Beckenbauer (Bayern Munich), Held (Borussia Dortmund), Netzer (Borussia Monchengladbach), Hornig (Cologne). sub: Heiss (TSV Munich) for Hornig 44. coach: Helmut Schoen

FA Amateur Cup Final

Saturday 16th April 1966

Hendon 1
Riddy
Wealdstone 3
Childs 2, Bremmer
45,000
Referee: N Burtenshaw (Great Yarmouth)

Wealdstone came from behind in their first final to beat the holders with two goals in the last two minutes.

Hendon: Swannell, Hogwood, Cooper, Shacklock, Riddy, Cantwell – capt, Churchill, Evans, Swain, Sleap, Hyde
Wealdstone: Goymer, Doyle, Sedgley, Townsend, Ashworth – capt, Dillsworth, Allen, Childs, Cooley, Lindsay, Bremmer

Schoolboy International

Saturday 30th April 1966

England 2
Wilkinson, Thomas
West Germany 1
Hoppe
85,000
Referee: R Willis (Durham)

Steve Bowtell saved a penalty from the German captain Sobieray as England came from behind to inflict on West Germany the second of three Wembley defeats in 1966.

Dave Thomas, who scored England's winner, won eight full international caps in 1974-75, five of them at Wembley.

England: Bowtell, Mitchell, McClelland, Seargeant, Clarke, Merrick – capt, Lowery, Hughes, Wilkinson, Allen, Thomas

INTERNATIONAL

Wednesday 4th May 1966

England   2-0   Yugoslavia
Greaves 9, Charlton (R) 34
54,000
Referee: J Malka (East Germany)

England had beaten Yugoslavia only once in seven meetings at Wembley in 1956. Their two latest clashes had both been draws, 1-1 in Belgrade a year earlier and the six-goal thriller at Wembley in 1960. Yugoslavia had slumped since their fourth place position in the 1962 World Cup. They had failed to qualify for the approaching tournament in England. England had just retained the British Championship.

A rare headed goal by Jimmy Greaves, from Paine's cross, put England in front. Twenty five minutes later Bobby Charlton wrapped it up, giving Soskic no chance with a bullet shot from outside the area. With a two-goal lead England consolidated.

Two years later Yugoslavia beat England 1-0 in Florence in the European Championship semi-finals with a late winner. They then lost the final for the second time to the hosts Italy after a replay. They returned to Wembley in 1972.

England: Banks (Leicester), Armfield (Blackpool) – capt, Wilson (Everton), Peters* (West Ham), Charlton (J) (Leeds), Hunter (Leeds), Paine (Southampton), Greaves (Tottenham), Charlton (R) (Man Utd), Hurst (West Ham), Tambling (Chelsea). manager: Alf Ramsey
*first cap
Yugoslavia: Soskic (Partizan Belgrade), Kuci (Hajduk Split), Jevtic (Red Star Belgrade), Becejac (Partizan), Rasovic (Partizan), Vasovic (Partizan), Samardzic (OFK Belgrade), Musovic (FK Sarajevo), Melic (Red Star), Skoblar (OFK) – capt, Dzajic (Red Star).

FA CUP FINAL

Saturday 14th May 1966

Everton   3-2   Sheffield Wednesday
Trebilcock 59, 64, Temple 80   McCalliog 3, Ford 57
100,000
Referee: J Taylor (Wolverhampton)

It had been over 30 years since either side had last won the FA Cup. Everton had won it for the second time in 1933 and Wednesday had won it for the third time two years later.

Everton had won the League Championship three years earlier but finished only 11th in the First Division, their lowest position for six years. Wednesday finished 17th, their lowest position since promotion in 1959.

After three minutes, Wednesday took the lead when Ford centred and Jim McCalliog's shot was deflected by Wilson past West and just before the hour they appeared to gave made the game safe when David Ford scored Wednesday's second after West had parried Fantham's shot.

Mike Trebilcock had other ideas, though,

and two minutes later took a pass from Temple to fire a shot past Springett and reduce the arrears.

Then a defensive header from Ellis fell to the eager Trebilcock and he wiped out Wednesday's lead.

The Everton winning goal came from a mistake by Young who failed to control a long ball from Harvey, leaving Derek Temple to run on and complete an amazing recovery.

Everton, disappointingly, went out of the European Cup-Winners Cup in the last 16 to Real Zaragoza but they reached the FA Cup final again in 1968. Wednesday were relegated four years later. They reappeared at Wembley for the Football League Centenary Tournament in 1988 and then won the Rumbelows Cup in 1991.

Everton: West, Wright, Wilson (R), Gabriel, Labone – capt, Harris, Scott, Trebilcock, Young, Harvey, Temple. manager: Harry Catterick
Sheffield W: Springett, Smith, Megson – capt, Eustace, Ellis, Young, Pugh, Fantham, McCalliog, Ford, Quinn. manager: Alan Brown

WORLD CUP GROUP ONE

Monday 11th July 1966

England   0-0   Uruguay
87,148
Referee: I Zsolt (Hungary)

Since England had beaten them for the first time in 1964, Uruguay had won their World Cup qualifying group without dropping a point. England, of course, had qualified automatically as hosts and were aiming to go beyond the quarter-finals for the first time. Uruguay had won the competition twice, but not since 1950, and had beaten

England in the 1954 quarter-finals.

Uruguay had come to defend and secured the point they wanted with a well-organised defence which England found impossible to penetrate.

Uruguay followed up this result by beating France 2-1 at White City, returning to Wembley to face Mexico.

England: Banks (Leicester), Cohen (Fulham), Wilson (Everton), Stiles (Man Utd), Charlton (J) (Leeds), Moore (West Ham) – capt, Ball (Blackpool), Greaves (Tottenham), Charlton (R) (Man Utd), Hunt (Liverpool), Connelly (Man Utd). manager: Alf Ramsey
Uruguay: Mazurkiewicz (Penarol), Troche (Cerro) – capt, Manicera (Nacional), Ubinas (Rampla), Goncalvez (Penarol), Caetano (Penarol), Cortes (Penarol), Viera (Nacional), Silva (Penarol), Rocha (Penarol), Perez (Nacional). coach: Ondino Viera

WORLD CUP GROUP ONE

Wednesday 13th July 1966

France   1-1   Mexico
Hausser 61   Borja 48
69,237
Referee: M Ashkenasi (Israel)

France were appearing in their first World Cup match since winning third place in 1958. They had reached the quarter-finals of the European Championship two years earlier and had defeated Mexico twice before in the World Cup, including the very first match of the competition in 1930. They had been soundly beaten 4-0 on their last visit to Wembley in 1957. Mexico had been thrashed 8-0 on their previous visit in 1961 and had never been beyond the first round. They had qualified without losing a match.

Just after half-time Mexico went in front as Padilla's cross found Enrique Borja, who scored at the second attempt.

Thirteen minutes later Chaires unwittingly gave the ball to Gerard Hausser whose shot beat Calderon and went in off the post to leave all four teams with a point each from the opening games in Group One.

France were beaten 2-1 by Uruguay two days later at White City, and then returned to face England. Mexico had to wait just three days to meet their hosts.

France: Aubour (Olympique Lyonnais), Djorkaeff (Olympique Lyonnais), Artelesa (Monaco) – capt, Budzinski (Nantes), De Michele (Nantes), Bonnel (Valenciennes), Bosquier (Sochaux), Combin (Torino), Herbin (Saint-Etienne), Gondet (Nantes), Hausser (Strasbourg). coach: Henri Guerin
Mexico: Calderon (Guadalajara), Chaires (Guadalajara), Nunez (Zacatepec), Hernandez (Atlas), Pena (Oro) – capt, Mercado (Atlas), Diaz (Guadalajara), Reyes (Guadalajara), Fragoso (America), Padilla (Universidad De Mexico), Borja (Universidad De Mexico). coach: Ignacio Trelles

WORLD CUP GROUP ONE

Saturday 16th July 1966

England   2-0   Mexico
Charlton (R) 38, Hunt 74
92,570
Referee: C Lo Bello (Italy)

Both teams had drawn their opening matches in Group One but their last meeting five years earlier had seen the Mexicans thrashed 8-0. England scored their first goal of the World Cup when Bobby Charlton collected the ball from Hunt inside his own half and from 30 yards out sent a screamer into the top corner. The points were secured when Roger Hunt scored from the rebound after Calderon saved Greaves' shot.

Mexico now needed a handsome win against Uruguay three days later to reach the quarter-finals for the first time.

England: Banks (Leicester), Cohen (Fulham), Wilson (Everton), Stiles (Man Utd), Charlton (J) (Leeds), Moore (West Ham) – capt, Paine (Southampton), Greaves (Tottenham), Charlton (R) (Man Utd), Hunt (Liverpool), Peters (West Ham). manager: Alf Ramsey
Mexico: Calderon (Guadalajara), Chaires (Guadalajara), Pena (Oro) – capt, Del Muro (Vera Cruz), Jauregui (Monterrey), Diaz (Guadalajara), Padilla (Universidad De Mexico), Borja (Universidad De Mexico), Nunez (Zacatepec), Reyes (Guadalajara), Hernandez (Atlas). coach: Ignacio Trelles

WORLD CUP GROUP ONE

Tuesday 19th July 1966

Mexico　　　　　**0-0**　　　**Uruguay**
61,112
Referee: B Loow (Sweden)

After losing to England, Mexico needed a convincing victory against Uruguay to have any chance of reaching the quarter-finals for the first time. Uruguay had beaten France 2-1 at White City and only needed a point to reach the last eight. They had won few friends, however, on their previous appearance at the stadium in the opening match.

Once again the Uruguayans relied on strong defence much to the dismay of the crowd. Like England, Mexico could not break through and were eliminated. Antonio Carbajal, the Mexican goalkeeper, became the first player to appear in five World Cups.

Mexico did not return to Wembley until 1997. Uruguayan temperament let them down in the quarter-finals. They had two players sent off and lost 4-0 to the eventual finalists West Germany at Hillsborough. But in 1970 they reached the World Cup semi-finals.

Mexico: Carbajal (Leon), Chaires (Guadalajara), Pena (Oro) – capt, Nunez (Zacatepec), Hernandez (Atlas), Diaz (Guadalajara), Mercado (Atlas), Reyes (Guadalajara), Cisneros (Zacatepec), Borja (Universidad De Mexico), Padilla (Universidad De Mexico). coach: Ignacio Trelles

Uruguay: Mazurkiewicz (Penarol), Troche (Cerro) – capt, Manicera (Nacional), Ubinas (Rampla), Goncalvez (Penarol), Caetano (Penarol), Cortes (Penarol), Viera (Nacional), Sasia (Penarol), Rocha (Penarol), Perez (Nacional). coach: Ondino Viera

WORLD CUP GROUP ONE

Wednesday 20th July 1966

England　　　　　**2-0**　　　**France**
Hunt 38, 75
98,270
Referee: A Yamasaki (Peru)

After losing 2-1 to Uruguay at White City France had to beat England 2-0 to reach the quarter-finals from Group One. They had lost 4-0 in their previous Wembley meeting but had beaten England 6-3 on aggregate in the first round of the 1964 European Championship on their way to the quarter-finals.

The host nation had never failed to reach the last eight and England could lose 1-0 and still qualify. If they won, however, they would win the group and meet the Group Two runners-up at Wembley.

France suffered an early injury to Herbin who played on through his discomfort but England took the lead when Greaves crossed, Jack Charlton headed against the post and Roger Hunt tapped in the rebound despite French appeals for offside. Fifteen minutes from the end, after Simon had come off worst in a tackle with Stiles, Callaghan's cross met the head of Hunt and Aubour's suspect handling helped it into the net.

England: Banks (Leicester), Cohen (Fulham), Wilson (Everton), Stiles (Man Utd), Charlton (J) (Leeds), Moore (West Ham) – capt, Callaghan (Liverpool), Greaves (Tottenham), Charlton (R) (Man Utd), Hunt (Liverpool), Peters (West Ham). manager: Alf Ramsey

France: Aubour (Olympique Lyonnais), Djorkaeff (Olympique Lyonnais), Artelesa (Monaco) – capt, Budzinski (Nantes), Bosquier (Sochaux), Bonnel (Valenciennes), Simon (Nantes), Herbet (Sedan), Gondet (Nantes), Herbin (Saint-Etienne), Hausser (Strasbourg). coach: Henri Guerin

Final table	P	W	D	L	F	A	Pts
England	3	2	1	0	4	0	5
Uruguay	3	1	2	0	2	1	4
Mexico	3	0	2	1	1	3	2
France	3	0	1	2	2	5	1

106

WORLD CUP QUARTER-FINAL

Saturday 23rd July 1966

Argentina   0-1   **England**

Hurst 78

90,584

Referee: R Kreitlein (West Germany)

Argentina had finished as Group Two runners-up to West Germany, the eventual finalists, on goal average. Like England, they were unbeaten in the competition and were appearing in the quarter-finals for the first time since reaching the final in 1930. They had lost on their previous visit to Wembley in 1951. England had beaten them 3-1 in the 1962 World Cup in Chile but Argentina had achieved their first win against England in the Brazilian Jubilee Tournament two years later. England were attempting to reach the semi-finals for the first time.

The match was marred by the 36th minute dismissal of the Argentinian captain Rattin for dissent. This was followed by a delay of eight minutes as his team mates threatened to walk off. Eventually, order was restored, and England won when Peters' cross was met by a glancing header from Geoff Hurst with just 12 minutes left.

Argentina failed to qualify for the 1970 World Cup but appeared again at Wembley in 1974.

Argentina: Roma (Boca Juniors), Ferreiro (Independiente), Perfumo (Racing Club), Albrecht (San Lorenzo), Marzolini (Boca Juniors), Solari (River Plate), Rattin (Boca Juniors) – capt, Gonzalez (Boca Juniors), Artime (Independiente), Onega (River Plate), Mas (River Plate). coach: Juan Carlos Lorenzo

England: Banks (Leicester), Cohen (Fulham), Wilson (Everton), Stiles (Man Utd), Charlton (J) (Leeds), Moore (West Ham) – capt, Ball (Blackpool), Hurst (West Ham), Charlton (R) (Man Utd), Hunt (Liverpool), Peters (West Ham). manager: Alf Ramsey

WORLD CUP SEMI-FINAL

Tuesday 26th July 1966

England   2-1   **Portugal**

Charlton (R) 30, 79   Eusebio pen 82

94,493

Referee: P Schwinte (France)

Portugal had won Group Three, defeating the holders Brazil 3-1 at Goodison Park along the way. In the quarter-finals they had beaten the popular North Koreans at the same venue in a remarkable match, which saw them come back from being three goals down after 22 minutes to win 5-3. They had never previously qualified for a World Cup. Their last appearance at Wembley had been a World Cup qualifying defeat in 1961. They had also lost to England in Lisbon three years later. England were also appearing in the semi-finals for the first time and had yet to concede a goal.

With half an hour gone Pereira saved at the feet of Hunt but Bobby Charlton drove home the rebound. England added a second with 11 minutes remaining. Hurst held off the challenge of Carlos to lay the ball back for Charlton to score again. But within three minutes Portugal had breached England's defence. A cross from Simoes eluded Banks and a header from Torres was punched off the line by Jack Charlton. Eusebio, who had scored four goals in the quarter-final, sent Banks the wrong way from the penalty. England hung on to reach the World Cup final for the first time. A memorable night for Ray Wilson who won his 50th cap.

England: Banks (Leicester), Cohen (Fulham), Wilson (Everton), Stiles (Man Utd), Charlton (J) (Leeds), Moore (West Ham) – capt, Ball (Blackpool), Hurst (West Ham), Charlton (R) (Man Utd), Hunt (Liverpool), Peters (West Ham). manager: Alf Ramsey

Portugal: Pereira (Belenenses), Festa (Porto), Baptista (Sporting Lisbon), Carlos (Sporting Lisbon), Hilario (Sporting Lisbon), Graca (Vitoria Setubal), Coluna (Benfica) – capt, Augusto (Benfica), Eusebio (Benfica), Torres (Benfica), Simoes (Benfica). coach: Manuel De Luz Afonso

WORLD CUP 3RD & 4TH PLACE

Thursday 28th July 1966

Portugal   **2-1**   **USSR**
Eusebio pen 13, Torres 88   Malafeev 43
87,696
Referee: K Dagnall (Bolton)

Portugal were making their second appearance at the stadium in three days. It had still been a successful first World Cup for them, though. The USSR had lost their semi-final 2-1 to West Germany at Goodison Park and had lost heavily to England on their previous visit to Wembley in 1958. Since then they had won the first European Championship in 1960, reached the final again four years later and now had had their best ever World Cup.

Eusebio, the World Cup's top scorer, beat Yashin to give Portugal the lead from the penalty after Khurtsilava handled in the area. The USSR were level just before half-time when Pereira failed to hold Metreveli's shot and Eduard Malafeev brought the Soviets level. Portugal settled it with two minutes remaining. Jose Torres volleyed home from Augusto's header.

Portugal: Pereira (Belenenses), Festa (Porto), Baptista (Sporting Lisbon), Carlos (Sporting Lisbon), Hilario (Sporting Lisbon), Graca (Vitoria Setubal), Coluna (Benfica) – capt, Augusto (Benfica), Eusebio (Benfica), Torres (Benfica), Simoes (Benfica). coach: Manuel De Luz Afonso
USSR: Yashin (Dynamo Moscow) – capt, Ponomarev (CSKA Moscow), Korneev (Spartak Moscow), Khurtsilava (Dynamo Tbilisi), Danilov (Zenit Leningrad), Voronin (Torpedo Moscow), Sichinava (Dynamo Tbilisi), Serebrianikov (Dynamo Kiev), Banichevski (Neftchi Baku), Malafeev (Dynamo Minsk), Metreveli (Dynamo Tbilisi). coach: Nikolai Morozov

WORLD CUP FINAL

Saturday 30th July 1966

England   **4-2**   **West Germany**
Hurst 18, 102, 120, Peters 78   Haller 12, Weber 90
After extra time
96,924
Referee: G Dienst (Switzerland)

England had never previously been beyond the quarter-finals and no host nation had won the World Cup since Italy in 1934. West Germany had won the trophy in 1954, surprisingly beating Hungary 3-2 in the final in Berne. They had never beaten England, though, and had lost at Wembley just five months earlier. England were wearing red shirts for only the third time at Wembley, and the first since 1954 when they beat West Germany.

West Germany went in front when Held's cross was inexplicably headed down by Wilson into the path of Helmut Haller who stroked it past Banks into the corner. England were level within just six minutes. A quick free kick from Moore found the head of Geoff Hurst who directed it into the net.

England did not take the lead until late in the game when from Ball's corner Hurst's shot was deflected by Hottges to leave Martin Peters, in the six-yard box, with a simple chance. England held out until the very last minute when West Germany snatched a desperate equaliser. Emmerich's free kick was blocked by Cohen. It fell to Held who shot. The ball hit Schnellinger's back and ran on to Wolfgang Weber despite England's protests of hand-ball. Weber slid in to beat Wilson and Banks who was scrambling across after diving for Held's shot.

England regained the lead in extra time with arguably the most controversial goal ever scored. Ball crossed, Hurst controlled it and then shot on the turn. The ball struck the underside of the bar and bounced down and out. The referee, unsure as to whether it had gone in or not, consulted his assistant who had not been up with the play. The linesman pointed to the centre circle and the goal was given. None of the numerous camera angles could prove conclusively whether the ball had crossed the line or not and the debate raged for decades. In the dying seconds, with spectators already encroaching onto the pitch, Moore sent Hurst away to beat Tilkowski and become the first man to score a hat-trick in a World Cup final. A historic and dramatic occasion had finally ended in a deserved victory for England.

England's win earned manager Alf Ramsey a knighthood. The controversial third goal should not detract from a magnificent team effort in Wembley's greatest ever football spectacle. Sadly, England have failed to emulate the men of 1966 whereas West Germany won the World Cup twice since then. England's defence of the trophy in 1970 in Mexico ended in the quarter-finals when they were beaten after extra time by West Germany despite taking a two-goal lead. The Germans lost in the semi-finals but by the time they returned to Wembley in 1972 they were on their way to a European Championship and World Cup 'double'.

England: Banks (Leicester), Cohen (Fulham), Wilson (Everton), Stiles (Man Utd), Charlton (J) (Leeds), Moore (West Ham) – capt, Ball (Blackpool), Hurst (West Ham), Charlton (R) (Man Utd), Hunt (Liverpool), Peters (West Ham). manager: Alf Ramsey

West Germany: Tilkowski (Borussia Dortmund), Hottges (Werder Bremen), Weber (Cologne), Schulz (Hamburg), Schnellinger (AC Milan), Haller (Bologna), Beckenbauer (Bayern Munich), Overath (Cologne), Seeler (Hamburg) – capt, Emmerich (Borussia Dortmund), Held (Borussia Dortmund). coach: Helmut Schoen

INTERNATIONAL

Wednesday 2nd November 1966

England   **0-0**   **Czechoslovakia**
75,000
Referee: P Roomer (Netherlands)

After reaching the World Cup final for the second time in 1962, Czechoslovakia had failed to qualify for the 1966 tournament in England from a group won by Portugal. They had beaten England once, by 2-1 in their first meeting in Prague in 1934. England had beaten them twice since then.

England were appearing at Wembley for the first time since their World Cup win just over three months earlier. They were fielding the same eleven that had lifted the trophy.

Despite having 80 per cent of the ball, England could not break down the Czech defence and the match ended goalless.

Czechoslovakia failed to qualify from their European Championship group but beat Olympic Champions Hungary in a play-off to qualify for the 1970 World Cup where England were one of three teams to defeat them. They were back at Wembley for a European Championship match in 1974.

England: Banks (Leicester), Cohen (Fulham), Wilson (Everton), Stiles (Man Utd), Charlton (J) (Leeds), Moore (West Ham) – capt, Ball (Everton), Hurst (West Ham), Charlton (R) (Man Utd), Hunt (Liverpool), Peters (West Ham). manager: Alf Ramsey

Czechoslovakia: Viktor (Dukla Prague), Lala (Slavia Prague), Popluhar (Slovan Bratislava) – capt, Toborsky (Sparta Prague), Horvath (Slovan Bratislava), Geleta (Dukla Prague), Kvasniak (Sparta Prague), Vesely (Slavia Prague), Szikora (Inter Bratislava), Schmidt (Spartak Hradec Kralove), Adamec (Spartak Trnava). Sub: Kuna (Spartak Trnava) for Schmidt 42. coach: Josef Marko

EUROPEAN CHAMPIONSHIP QUALIFYING

Wednesday 16th November 1966

England   **5-1**   **Wales**
Hurst 30, 34, Charlton (R) 43   W Davies 38
Hennessey og 80, Charlton (J) 84
75,380
Referee: T Wharton (Scotland)

For two years the British Championship was to double as European Championship Group Eight. England had already beaten Northern Ireland 2-0 at Windsor Park in their bid to secure their third successive outright British Championship. Wales had drawn 1-1 with Scotland at Ninian Park and needed to avoid defeat for the first time in the British Championship at Wembley to retain their interest in it.

The World Champions took the lead on the half hour. From Peters' pass, Geoff Hurst beat Millington from just outside the area. Four minutes later Hurst headed his second from a Stiles cross. Wales were quick to strike back. Ron Davies supplied the cross for his namesake Wyn to head past Banks but two minutes before half-time Peters set up Bobby Charlton to restore England's two-goal advantage, with a drive which went through Millington's hands. Ten minutes remained when Terry Hennessey converted Hunt's chip into an own goal for England's fourth and then Hurst crossed for Jack Charlton to score the final goal with six minutes left.

Wales still had a chance in the European Championship but the British Championship was to be decided, once again, by England and Scotland.

England: Banks (Leicester), Cohen (Fulham), Wilson (Everton), Stiles (Man Utd), Charlton (J) (Leeds), Moore (West Ham) – capt, Ball (Everton), Hurst (West Ham), Charlton (R) (Man Utd), Hunt (Liverpool), Peters (West Ham). manager: Alf Ramsey

Wales: Millington (Peterborough), Green (Birmingham), Williams (West Brom), Hennessey (Nottingham F), England (Tottenham) – capt, Hole (Blackburn), Rees (Coventry), Davies (W) (Newcastle), Davies (R) (Southampton), Jones (Tottenham), Jarvis (Hull City). manager: Dave Bowen

Inter-Varsity Match

Wednesday 7th December 1966

Cambridge U 1
Phillips
Oxford U 0

Peter Phillips' 11th minute goal secured Cambridge their fifth victory in six years.

FOOTBALL LEAGUE CUP FINAL

Saturday 4th March 1967

Queens Park Rangers   **3-2**   **West Bromwich Albion**
Morgan 64, Marsh 75, Lazarus 82   Clark 7, 36
97,952
Referee: W Crossley (Lancaster)

This was the first Football League Cup final to be played at Wembley. Rangers had never previously progressed beyond the last 64 of the competition. West Brom were the holders, having won at the first attempt the previous year. They had overturned a first-leg deficit to beat West Ham 5-3 on aggregate and had beaten them again in the semi-finals. West Brom had won the FA Cup twice at Wembley, the last occasion in 1954.

Rangers had become the first Third Division club to reach a Wembley final and were heading for promotion for the first time in 15 years. West Brom had reached the last 16 of the European Fairs Cup but had lost the first leg 3-0 in Bologna. Rangers had never previously beaten them.

West Brom were ahead early to no great surprise. Fraser put Clive Clark through to draw Springett before shooting home. Clark had joined West Brom from Rangers in 1961 and was to return to them two years after this final. He scored West Brom's second as well. As Brown was tackled, he laid the ball off to the unmarked Clark. He had also scored in the previous year's final.

Rangers seemed dead and buried, but the second half produced a miraculous transformation. After 63 minutes Allen's free kick was headed in by Roger Morgan. Then Rodney Marsh took a pass from Keen, turned one way and then the other to beat Sheppard with a low shot in off the post.

Now it was the First Division side who

were reeling. Seven minutes later Hunt was put clean through after a one-two with Mark Lazarus and a mix-up between two defenders. Sheppard rushed out and Hunt crashed into him, knocking him out. The ball ran free and Lazarus knocked in the winner.

Despite West Brom's protests that their 'keeper had been fouled, their hold on the trophy had finally been relinquished to a team from two divisions below them. This exciting final had now established the Football League Cup as a major competition.

Rangers won the Third Division Championship by an impressive 12 points. They

were unable to enter the European Fairs Cup because they were not a First Division club but the following year they pipped Blackpool on goal average to finish Second Division runners-up and reached the First Division for the first time. They could not hold their own in the top flight, however, and were relegated straight back. In 1982, they were back at Wembley for their first FA Cup final.

West Brom were knocked out of the European Fairs Cup four days later, losing 3-0 at home to Bologna. They finished 13th in the First Division but the following year returned to Wembley to win the FA Cup.

Queens Park Rangers: Springett, Hazell (A), Langley, Sibley, Hunt, Keen – capt, Lazarus, Sanderson, Allen (L), Marsh, Morgan (R). sub: Morgan (I) (not used). manager: Alec Stock
West Brom: Sheppard, Cram, Williams – capt, Collard, Clarke, Fraser, Brown, Astle, Kaye, Hope, Clark. sub: Foggo (not used) manager: Jimmy Hagan

EUROPEAN CHAMPIONSHIP QUALIFYING

Saturday 15th April 1967

England   **2-3**   **Scotland**
Charlton (J) 84, Hurst 88   Law 27, Lennox 78, McCalliog 87
99,063
Referee: G Schulenburg (West Germany)

The World Champions needed only a point to complete a hat-trick of outright British Championships. Scotland had not lost at Wembley since the 1961 thrashing but needed to win to claim their first outright title since 1963 and go top of European Championship Group Eight for the first time.

England were severely hampered by an 11th minute injury to Jack Charlton, who collided with Lennox and broke his toe. After treatment for 15 minutes, he returned and performed courageously in attack. His presence in defence was missed though, and Scotland took the lead when Wallace shot and Denis Law diverted the ball away from Banks' hands. The 'keeper could only stop it with his feet, but Law swallowed up the rebound.

England fought back but the Scots held out, and, then went two ahead. First, Law

laid the ball back for Bobby Lennox to rush in and fire past Banks for Scotland's second.

Jack Charlton ignored the pain to beat two defenders on the line after a clever back-heel from Greaves put Ball through to round Simpson. England's hopes were dashed immediately, however, when Jim McCalliog played a one-two with Wallace and beat Banks at the near post. Although Geoff Hurst headed in a late consolation from Bobby Charlton's cross, England were beaten for the first time since winning the World Cup by their oldest rivals, who, at times, had toyed and tormented them with arrogant ball skills.

Scotland were to lose their advantage in the European Championship six months later by losing to Northern Ireland in Belfast and were well beaten on their next visit to Wembley.

England: Banks (Leicester), Cohen (Fulham), Wilson (Everton), Stiles (Man Utd), Charlton (J) (Leeds), Moore (West Ham) – capt, Ball (Everton), Greaves (Tottenham), Charlton (R) (Man Utd), Hurst (West Ham), Peters (West Ham). manager: Sir Alf Ramsey
Scotland: Simpson* (Celtic), Gemmell (Celtic), McCreadie (Chelsea), Greig (Rangers) – capt, McKinnon (Rangers), Bremner (Leeds), McCalliog* (Sheffield W), Law (Man Utd), Wallace (Celtic), Baxter (Sunderland), Lennox (Celtic). manager: Bobby Brown
*first cap

111

FA Amateur Cup Final

Saturday 22nd April 1967

Enfield 0
Skelmersdale United 0
After extra time
75,000
Referee: E Jennings (Stourbridge)

Wolstenholme saved a penalty from Alan Bermingham in the last minute of extra time.

Enfield: Wolstenholme, Sedgley, Reid, Payne, D'Arcy – capt, Moxon, Churchill, Connell, Hill, Day, Howard. sub: Adams (not used)
Skelmersdale: Crosbie, Bermingham, Bridge, Unsworth, Wade, Moorcroft – capt, Whitehead, Worswick, Bennett, Burns, Mansley. sub: McDermott (not used)

Replay: Saturday 29th April 1967
Enfield 3
Connell, Hill 2
Skelmersdale United 0
(Maine Road, Manchester)

Schoolboy International

Saturday 29th April 1967

England 0
Scotland 2
Ward 2
85,000
Referee: W Brown (Manchester)

Scotland repeated the success of their seniors a fortnight earlier.

Steve Perryman, Footballer of the Year in 1982 when he was to captain Tottenham Hotspur to a second successive FA Cup win, made his first appearance at Wembley.

Richie Pitt was in the Sunderland side which produced a major shock when they beat Leeds in the 1973 FA Cup final.

England: Cuff, Millerchip, Pitt, Simmonds, Taylor – capt, Towers, Spencer, Perryman, Kenny, Cantello, Jones
Scotland: McInally, Donald, Reekie, Stevenson, Gallacher – capt, Scullion, Sloan, Cruickshank, Ward, McBride, Watson

FA CUP FINAL

Saturday 20th May 1967

Chelsea	1-2	Tottenham Hotspur
Tambling 85		Robertson 40, Saul 67

100,000
Referee: K Dagnall (Bolton)

Chelsea had appeared in only one previous final, losing 3-0 to Sheffield United at Old Trafford in 1915. After two successive semi-final defeats, they had now made it to Wembley for the first time since their two wartime appearances. Tottenham had already won the FA Cup twice in the 1960's and four times in all.

Just before the interval, Mullery's shot from outside the box hit Ron Harris and fell to Jimmy Robertson who put Tottenham in front.

Tottenham were always in control, and midway through the second half, from a pass by Robertson, Frank Saul turned swiftly to beat the startled Bonetti. Chelsea pulled one back with five minutes left.

Boyle crossed and Jennings rushed out when he should have stayed, leaving Bobby Tambling to head home the ball. The scoreline flattered Chelsea as Tottenham's tactics of slowing things down had effectively controlled the game in the first all-London FA Cup final.

Chelsea's FA Cup form finally had its reward in 1970 when they lifted the trophy for the first time after drawing at Wembley. Tottenham went out in the last 16 of the European Cup-Winners Cup to Olympique Lyonnais on away goals despite scoring four in the home leg. In 1971 they won Football League Cup for the first time.

Alan Mullery, the 1975 Footballer of the Year, made his Wembley debut.

Chelsea: Bonetti, Harris (A), McCreadie, Hollins, Hinton, Harris (R) – capt, Cooke, Baldwin, Hateley, Tambling, Boyle. manager: Tommy Docherty. sub: Kirkup (not used)
Tottenham: Jennings, Kinnear, Knowles, Mullery, England, Mackay – capt, Robertson, Greaves, Gilzean, Venables, Saul. manager: Bill Nicholson. sub: Jones (not used)

INTERNATIONAL

Wednesday 24th May 1967

England　　　　　**2-0**　　　**Spain**
Greaves 70, Hunt 75
97,500
Referee: I Zsolt (Hungary)

This match pitted the World Champions against the European Champions. Spain had lost on their two previous visits to Wembley, the last in 1960. In 1965, England had won 2-0 in Madrid.

Less than a year earlier, Spain had been in England for the World Cup but were knocked out in the first round. But in their defence of the European Championship they had played three games without conceding a goal.

The stubborn Spanish defence finally capitulated with 20 minutes remaining. When Ball headed down Hollins' cross, Hunt's shot was blocked, but Jimmy Greaves converted the rebound in an instant. Five minutes later an unmarked Roger Hunt headed past Iribar from Hurst's centre.

Spain were back at Wembley within a year for the first leg of the European Championship Quarter-final.

England: Bonetti (Chelsea), Cohen (Fulham), Newton (Blackburn), Mullery (Tottenham), Labone (Everton), Moore (West Ham) – capt, Ball (Everton), Greaves (Tottenham), Hurst (West Ham), Hunt (Liverpool), Hollins* (Chelsea). manager: Sir Alf Ramsey
*first cap
Spain: Iribar (Athletic Bilbao), Sanchis (Real Madrid), Gallego (Barcelona), Violeta (Real Zaragoza), Reija (Real Zaragoza), Pirri (Real Madrid), Glaria (Atletico Madrid), Amancio (Real Madrid), Grosso (Real Madrid), Jose Maria (Espanol), Gento (Real Madrid) – capt. coach: Domingo Balmanya

EUROPEAN CHAMPIONSHIP QUALIFYING

Wednesday 22nd November 1967

England　　　　　**2-0**　　　**Northern Ireland**
Hurst 44, Charlton 62
83,000
Referee: L Callaghan (Wales)

Although England had lost to Scotland, they had regained the leadership of Group Eight the previous month by beating Wales 3-0 at Ninian Park as Scotland went down 1-0 to Northern Ireland at Windsor Park. The Irish, after two successive defeats at Wembley, had rekindled their own interest but needed to win to have any chance of qualifying.

Victory for either side would give them at least a share of the British Championship.

Northern Ireland gave a good account of themselves but fell behind a minute before half-time. From Charlton's corner and Mullery's pass, Geoff Hurst volleyed past Jennings for the opener. Then Peters' clever back-heel enabled Bobby Charlton to knock Northern Ireland out of the European Championship.

England's 1-1 draw with Scotland at Hampden Park regained the British Championship for them and also ensured their qualification for the European Championship quarter-finals where they met Spain, the reigning champions.

England: Banks (Stoke City), Cohen (Fulham), Wilson (Everton), Mullery (Tottenham), Sadler* (Man Utd), Moore (West Ham) – capt, Thompson (Liverpool), Hunt (Liverpool), Charlton (Man Utd), Hurst (West Ham), Peters (West Ham). manager: Sir Alf Ramsey
Northern Ireland: Jennings (Tottenham), Parke (Sunderland), Elder (Stoke City), Stewart (Glentoran), Neill (Arsenal) – capt, Harvey (Sunderland), Campbell (Dundee), Irvine (Burnley), Wilson (Dundee), Nicholson (Huddersfield), Clements (Coventry). manager: Billy Bingham
*first cap

British Championship						
Final table	P	W	D	L	F	A	Pts
England	3	2	1	0	6	1	5
Scotland	3	1	1	1	4	4	3
N Ireland	3	1	0	2	1	4	2
Wales	3	1	0	2	4	6	2

European Championship						
Final table	P	W	D	L	F	A	Pts
England	6	4	1	1	15	5	9
Scotland	6	3	2	1	10	8	8
Wales	6	1	2	3	6	12	4
N Ireland	6	1	1	4	2	8	3

INTERNATIONAL

Wednesday 6th December 1967

England   **2-2**   **USSR**
Ball 23, Peters 72   Chislenko 42, 44
93,000
Referee: R Kreitlein (West Germany)

England were about to win their European Championship quarter-final place while the USSR had already done so, and quite comfortably. The Soviets had lost on both their previous visits to Wembley, to England in 1958 and to Portugal, in the World Cup Third and Fourth Place the previous year.

As Psenitchnikov saved from Peters, Alan Ball reacted quickest to give England the lead from the rebound. Yet they were behind by half-time.

Anichkin and Voronin combined with Igor Chislenko finishing the move with a shot from outside the box. Chislenko then stunned Wembley by scoring again, this time from a pass by Banichevski, just moments later.

England, at last, drew level when a cross from Wilson was nodded home by Martin Peters.

The teams were to meet again six months later in the European Championship Third and Fourth place in Rome, England winning 2-0. The USSR had been desperately unfortunate to lose their semi-final on the toss of a coin after holding the hosts, and eventual winners, Italy, to a goalless draw after extra time. It was another 17 years before they returned to Wembley.

England: Banks (Stoke City), Knowles* (Tottenham), Wilson (Everton), Mullery (Tottenham), Sadler (Man Utd), Moore (West Ham) – capt, Ball (Everton), Hunt (Liverpool), Charlton (Man Utd), Hurst (West Ham), Peters (West Ham). manager: Sir Alf Ramsey
*first cap
USSR: Psenitchnikov (Pachtakor Tashkent), Istomin (CSKA Moscow), Shesterniev (CSKA Moscow) – capt, Khurtsilava (Dynamo Tbilisi), Anichkin (Dynamo Moscow), Voronin (Torpedo Moscow), Chislenko (Dynamo Moscow), Sabo (Dynamo Kiev), Banichevski (Neftchi Baku), Streltsov (Torpedo Moscow), Malafeev (Dynamo Minsk). coach: Mikhail Yakuschin

Inter-Varsity Match

Wednesday 13th December 1967

Cambridge U 1
Phillips
Oxford U 0

Just as in the previous year's fixture, Peter Phillips scored the only goal of the game, the only difference being that it was three minutes earlier than in 1966. It secured another hat-trick of victories for Cambridge.

FOOTBALL LEAGUE CUP FINAL

Saturday 2nd March 1968

Arsenal   **0-1**   **Leeds**

Cooper 20

97,887

Referee: L Hamer (Horwich)

Arsenal were competing in the League Cup for the second time, having failed to progress beyond the last 32 the previous season. It had been 16 years since they were last at Wembley.

Leeds had never been beyond the last 16 and had never won a major trophy, having lost the 1965 FA Cup final in extra time on their previous visit. They had had three seasons of agonising near misses since promotion in 1964 but had reached the European Fairs Cup quarter-finals for the third year in succession and were also challenging in the league and FA Cup. They had not lost to Arsenal in the four seasons since promotion.

The only goal came from a corner from Gray. Madeley challenged Furnell and the 'keeper went down. Neither touched the inswinger, which was headed off the line by Graham, only for Terry Cooper to find the net past the diving Storey. Despite Arsenal's protests, the goal stood.

Arsenal finished ninth in the First Division and reached the final again the following year. Leeds finished fourth and reached the FA Cup semi-finals for the second year in succession.

But at the beginning of the following season they won the European Fairs Cup to complete a memorable double. In their defence of the European trophy they reached the quarter-finals yet again before losing to the eventual finalists Ujpesti Dozsa of Hungary.

In the league, however, they were almost invincible, losing only twice as they won the Championship for the first time.

Arsenal: Furnell, Storey, McNab, McLintock – capt, Ure, Simpson, Radford, Jenkins, Graham, Sammels, Armstrong. sub: Neill (not used). manager: Bertie Mee

Leeds: Sprake, Reaney, Cooper, Bremner – capt, Charlton, Hunter, Greenhoff, Lorimer, Madeley, Giles, Gray (E). sub: Belfitt for Gray. manager: Don Revie

EUROPEAN CHAMPIONSHIP QUALIFYING
QUARTER-FINAL FIRST LEG

Wednesday 3rd April 1968

England   **1-0**   **Spain**

Charlton (R) 84

100,000

Referee: G Droz (Switzerland)

This was Spain's third defeat at Wembley and they had not beaten England since 1960 in Madrid. While the World Champions were regaining the British Championship to qualify for the quarter-finals, the reigning European Champions were struggling in Group One. They qualified only by virtue of the Republic of Ireland's surprise victory over Czechoslovakia in Prague.

As on their previous visit, Spain had a solid defence and it was not until six minutes from time that England scored. From a free kick by Moore, Bobby Charlton ran wide and then shot past Sadurni to give England a lead to defend in the second leg.

England were much more impressive in the second leg, coming from behind with Norman Hunter (who did not play in the first leg) netting the winner. They went on to finish third in Italy after losing their semi-final 1-0 to Yugoslavia in Florence. Having lost their European Championship title, Spain went into decline. It was to be another ten years before they qualified for another major occasion, the World Cup of 1978. They returned to Wembley in 1981.

England: Banks (Stoke City), Knowles (Tottenham), Wilson (Everton), Mullery (Tottenham), Charlton (J) (Leeds), Moore (West Ham) – capt, Ball (Everton), Hunt (Liverpool), Summerbee (Man City), Charlton (R) (Man Utd), Peters (West Ham). manager: Sir Alf Ramsey
Spain: Sadurni (Barcelona), Saez (Athletic Bilbao), Gallego (Barcelona), Zoco (Real Madrid) – capt, Canos (Elche), Pirri (Real Madrid), Poli (Valencia), Amancio (Real Madrid), Ansola (Valencia), Grosso (Real Madrid), Claramunt (Valencia). coach: Domingo Balmanya

Second Leg
Wednesday 8th May 1968

Spain	1-2	England

Amancio 48   Peters 54, Hunter 82
(Santiago Bernabeu, Madrid)
England won 3-1 on aggregate

FA Amateur Cup Final

Saturday 20th April 1968

Chesham United 0
Leytonstone 1
Gray
52,000
Referee: F Cowen (Lancashire)

Leytonstone, who made a substitution in the fifth minute, were down to ten men after fifteen when substitute Albon broke his leg. They were still the better team, however. The only goal came with 20 minutes left and ten minutes later Leytonstone even survived a penalty when Hadlow saved from Kent.

Chesham: Wells, Thackeray, Smith, Caterer, Burgess, McCaffrey, Ellis, Black, Fruen, Harper, Kent. sub: Frost (not used)
Leytonstone: Hadlow, Tilley, Hames, Andrews, Thomson, Walker, Charles, Gray, Diwell, Minall, Harvey. sub: Albon for Ham

Schoolboy International

Saturday 27th April 1968

England 1
Turner
West Germany 2
Hochheimer, Geyer
Referee: J Caswell (Middlesbrough)

The Germans came from behind to record their second victory at Wembley.

England: Dilnot, Ormrod – capt, English, Jeff, Lewis, Smith, Gough, Holbrook, Nicklin, Young, Turner

FA CUP FINAL

Saturday 18th May 1968

Everton	0-1	West Bromwich Albion

Astle 93

After extra time
100,000
Referee: L Callaghan (Merthyr Tydfil)

Everton were attempting to regain the FA Cup after winning it for the third time in 1966 in dramatic fashion. In the semi-finals they had beaten the Football League Cup winners Leeds. West Brom had last won the Cup in 1954 and had suffered the humiliation of losing the previous year's Football League Cup final to a Third Division club after taking a two-goal lead.

Everton finished fifth in the First Division and had won 6-2 at West Brom two months earlier. West Brom finished eighth.

The winning goal was scored in the fourth minute of extra time. Jeff Astle's first shot, from Fraser's pass, rebounded to him off Harvey but his second flew into the corner, giving West no chance and presenting

116

West Brom with the FA Cup for the fifth time.

Both sides reached the semi-finals the following year. Everton were League Champions in 1970 but did not return to Wembley until the 1977 Football League Cup final. West Brom reached the European Cup-Winners Cup quarter-finals the following year, but they made their third Wembley appearance in four years at the 1970 Football League Cup final.

Everton: West, Wright, Wilson (R), Kendall, Labone – capt, Harvey, Husband, Ball , Royle, Hurst, Morrissey. sub: Kenyon (not used). manager: Harry Catterick

West Brom: Osborne, Fraser, Williams – capt, Brown, Talbut, Kaye, Lovett, Collard, Astle, Hope, Clark. sub: Clarke for Kaye 91. manager: Alan Ashman

INTERNATIONAL

Wednesday 22nd May 1968

England   **3-1**   **Sweden**
Peters 36, Charlton 38, Hunt 72   Andersson 90
72,500
Referee: O Huber (Switzerland)

This was England's last home match before their European Championship semi-final with Yugoslavia in Florence. Sweden had lost in the qualifying stages and had not reached a World Cup since finishing runners-up in their own country in 1958. They were, however, unbeaten at Wembley, winning the Olympic tournament in 1948 and beating England 11 years later. England had won 2-1 in Gothenburg, though, in 1965.

Ten minutes before half-time Hunt's cross hit a defender and Martin Peters beat Kristensson to head England in front. Within two minutes they increased the lead. Moore sent Bobby Charlton through. He beat two men before unleashing a 20-yard piledriver which gave Larsson no chance. Next Knowles hit the bar from a pass by Newton and Roger Hunt swept home the rebound.

Sweden's goalkeeper Larsson was carried off with a fractured skull after an 85th minute collision with Mullery but the visitors gained some consolation in injury time from substitute Rolf Andersson.

England lost their European Championship semi-final to a late winner in Florence. Sweden qualified for the 1970 World Cup and were only eliminated on goal difference but it was to be 20 years before they reappeared at Wembley.

England: Stepney* (Man Utd), Newton (Blackburn), Knowles (Tottenham), Mullery (Tottenham), Labone (Everton), Moore (West Ham) – capt, Bell* (Man City), Peters (West Ham), Charlton (Man Utd), Hunt (Liverpool), Hunter (Leeds). sub: Hurst (West Ham) for Charlton 70. manager: Sir Alf Ramsey
*first cap

Sweden: Larsson (S) (Orebro), Carlsson (Jonkoping), Kristensson (Malmo), Nordqvist (Norrkoping) – capt, Grip (Aik Stockholm), Eriksson (Sirius), Larsson (B) (Stuttgart), Nordahl (Orebro), Ejderstedt (Osters), Lindman (Djurgardens), Persson (Rangers). subs: Andersson (Hammarby) for Ejderstedt, Hult (Malmo) for S Larsson 85 coach: Orvar Bergmark

EUROPEAN CUP FINAL

Wednesday 29th May 1968

Benfica   **1-4**   **Manchester United**
Graca 81   Charlton 52, 98, Best 92, Kidd 97
After extra time
92,000
Referee: C Lo Bello (Italy)

Benfica were appearing in their fifth final in eight years. They had lost in 1963 at Wembley and again, in 1965, to Internazionale in Milan. In 1966 they had lost both home and away to United in the quarter-finals. United's thoughts, inevitably, drifted back to the Munich air disaster ten years earlier when they had just reached the European Cup semi-finals. Matt Busby had rebuilt the team and they had now, at last, reached the European Cup final, the first English club to do so.

Benfica retained the Portuguese League Championship for the seventh time in nine years and a record 16th time. United had failed to win their third League Championship in four years and finished runners-up, two points behind their great rivals Manchester City.

Following a tense first half, United took the lead. Sadler crossed and Bobby Charlton, a survivor from Munich, sent a glancing header past Henrique. Nine minutes from the end Jaime Graca drove home an equaliser after a header down from Torres and Benfica almost snatched victory four minutes from time but Eusebio shot straight at Stepney. United lived again and struck just two minutes into extra time. Stepney's kick downfield was headed on by Kidd. George Best beat Cruz and ran on. He dummied the goalkeeper and then rounded him to score a most extraordinary goal, given the tension and emotion of the occasion. The ease of the finish shattered Benfica. Five minutes later, from Charlton's corner, Sadler headed on to Brian Kidd, whose header was saved by Henrique, only for the 19-year-old to nod the rebound just beyond the reach of the goalkeeper and under the bar. It was from Kidd's cross, a minute later, that Charlton, appropriately, looped his second over Henrique to complete the scoring. United had kept the trophy in Britain after Celtic's win the previous year and there was hardly a dry eye in the house as Matt Busby's dream was fulfilled.

Benfica completed another hat-trick of Portuguese League Championships the following year but it was to be 20 years before they reached another European Cup final. Sadly, they then lost two finals in three years. United reached the semi-finals again the following year, before losing to the eventual winners AC Milan but the victory at Wembley was to be the culmination of ten years' hard work. Busby retired with a knighthood and United went into decline, ending in relegation in 1974. Two years later they were back at Wembley for the FA Cup final.

Benfica: Henrique, Adolfo, Humberto, Jacinto, Cruz, Graca, Coluna – capt, Augusto, Eusebio, Torres, Simoes. coach: Otto Gloria
Manchester U: Stepney, Brennan, Dunne, Crerand, Foulkes, Stiles, Best, Kidd, Charlton – capt, Sadler, Aston (jnr.). manager: Matt Busby

Inter-Varsity Match

Wednesday 4th December 1968

Cambridge U 3
Johnson, Battye, Phillips pen

Oxford U 1
Oxley

Peter Phillips scored in his third consecutive Varsity match as Cambridge made it a Wembley record fourth successive victory.

INTERNATIONAL

Wednesday 11th December 1968

England 1-1 **Bulgaria**
Hurst 36   Asparoukhov 32
80,000
Referee: M Kitabdjian (France)

Bulgaria had met England only once before, a goalless draw in the 1962 World Cup in Rancagua. They had appeared at Wembley, however, for an Olympic Qualifying match in 1956. In the 1966 World Cup in England they had failed to win a point in a tough group won by Portugal but they had gone on to reach the European Championship quarter-finals earlier in the year before losing their first-leg lead to the eventual winners Italy. They had also made a good start to their 1970 World Cup qualifying group by beating the Netherlands 2-0 in Sofia.

The visitors took the lead with a magnificent individual goal. Georgi Asparoukhov outjumped Labone in the middle of the field and then ran the full length of the England half as Newton challenged

strongly to expertly slot the ball past West. But four minutes later Bulgaria's lead was wiped out. In a frantic goalmouth scramble, Simeonov kept out Geoff Hurst until the striker eventually found a way through to hook the ball into the net.

Asparoukhov sadly died in a car crash three years later. Bulgaria qualified for the World Cup but again failed to win a match. England beat them 1-0 in Sofia in 1974 and they were back at the stadium five years later although their Olympic side were given a fright by Great Britain at Wembley in 1971.

England: West* (Everton), Newton (Blackburn), McNab (Arsenal), Mullery (Tottenham), Labone (Everton), Moore (West Ham) – capt, Lee* (Man City), Bell (Man City), Charlton (Man Utd), Hurst (West Ham), Peters (West Ham). sub: Reaney* (Leeds) for Newton 84 .manager: Sir Alf Ramsey
*first cap
Bulgaria: Simeonov (Slavia Sofia), Peshev (Levski Sofia), Dimitrov (Akademik Sofia), Gaganelov (CSKA Sofia) – capt, Penev (CSKA Sofia), Zhechev (Levski Sofia), Popov (Trakia Plovdiv), Bonev (Lokmotiv Plovdiv), Asparoukhov (Levski Sofia), Yakimov (CSKA Sofia), Dermendiev (Trakia Plovdiv). sub: Jekov (CSKA Sofia) for Popov 46 .coach: Stefan Boshkov.

INTERNATIONAL

Wednesday 15th January 1969

England   **1-1**   **Romania**
Charlton (J) 27   Dumitrache pen 74
77,000
Referee: J Callaghan (Scotland)

Romania had met England in Bucharest just two months earlier contesting a goalless draw. Their only previous meeting had been a 2-0 England victory, also in Bucharest, in 1939, but they had appeared at Wembley in 1957 for an Under-23 international.

Romania had not qualified for a World Cup since 1938 and had already lost 3-0 to Portugal in the latest competition. They had finished runners-up to the eventual winners Italy in their European Championship qualifying group for the previous year's tournament.

England took a deserved lead. Jack Charlton headed in a corner from his brother

Bobby who was captaining his country for the first time.

But it was Jack who gave Romania a penalty 15 minutes from the end when Nunweiler's shot hit him on the hand. Florea Dumitrache sent Banks the wrong way from the spot and, once again, a continental defence had held England to a draw.

The teams met the following year in England's first defence of the World Cup in Guadalajara. Geoff Hurst scored the only goal of the game for England. Romania did not qualify for the quarter-finals but denied England at Wembley again in 1981.

England: Banks (Stoke City), Wright (Everton), McNab (Arsenal), Stiles (Man Utd), Charlton (J) (J) (Leeds), Hunter (Leeds), Radford* (Arsenal), Hunt (Liverpool), Charlton (R) (Man Utd) – capt, Hurst (West Ham), Ball (Everton). manager: Sir Alf Ramsey
*first cap
Romania: Gornea (Ut Arad), Satmareanu (Steaua Bucharest), Boc (Dinamo Bucharest), Deleanu (Politehnica Timisoara), Anca (Universitatea Cluj-napoca), Dinu (Dinamo Bucharest), Dembrovski (Dinamo Bacau), Domide (Ut Arad), Dumitrache (Dinamo Bucharest), Nunweiler (Dinamo Bucharest), Lucescu (Dinamo Bucharest) – capt. coach: Angelo Niculescu

INTERNATIONAL

Wednesday 12th March 1969

England   **5-0**   **France**

O'Grady 33, Hurst (pen) 48, 49, (pen) 80
Lee 75
83,000
Referee: I Zsolt (Hungary)

France had lost on their previous visit, in the 1966 World Cup. They had since reached the European Championship quarter-finals before losing 6-2 on aggregate to the eventual finalists Yugoslavia and had made a disastrous start to their World Cup qualifying group by losing to Norway in Strasbourg.

It took England half an hour to take the lead. It was a spectacular goal. From Cooper's cross, Hurst headed the ball back and Mike O'Grady hit the back of the net with a thunderous volley. It was from another O'Grady volley that England increased their lead just after half-time. It was saved by Carnus but Peters was fouled by Bosquier as he moved for the rebound. Geoff Hurst blasted home the penalty. Hurst scored again just a minute later from another Cooper cross. Michel's deflection took the ball into the corner. Fifteen minutes from the end Francis Lee scored a fine individual goal with a brilliant run and shot when put through by O'Grady.

The scoring was completed five minutes later when Rostagni brought down Bell and Hurst, once again, converted the penalty, to complete his hat-trick.

France, as expected, failed to qualify for the following year's World Cup. They were not to meet England again until the 1982 World Cup, when England won 3-1 in Bilbao, and it was a further ten years before France reappeared at Wembley.

England: Banks (Stoke City), Newton (Blackburn), Cooper* (Leeds), Mullery (Tottenham), Charlton (Leeds), Moore (West Ham) – capt, Lee (Man City), Bell (Man City), Hurst (West Ham), Peters (West Ham), O'Grady (Leeds). manager: Sir Alf Ramsey
*first cap
France: Carnus (Saint-Etienne), Djorkaeff (Olympique Marseille), Rostagni (Monaco), Bosquier (Saint-Etienne) – capt, Lemerre (Sedan), Michel (Nantes), Herbert (Sedan), Bonnel (Olympique Marseille), Loubet (Nice), Simon (Girondins Bordeaux), Bereta (Saint-Etienne). coach: Georges Boulogne

FOOTBALL LEAGUE CUP FINAL

Saturday 15th March 1969

Arsenal   **1-3**   **Swindon Town**

Gould 86   Smart 36, Rogers 105, 120
After extra time
98,189
Referee: W Handley (Cannock)

Arsenal were appearing in their second successive final, having lost the previous year to Leeds. It had been 16 years since their last major trophy. Swindon had never been beyond the last 16 before and had never previously appeared at Wembley.

After a long and difficult semi-final with Burnley which went to extra time in the third game, Swindon had become the second Third Division club in three years to reach the final.

They were hoping to emulate Queens Park Rangers' League Cup and Third Division Championship 'double' of 1967 but they had not beaten Arsenal for 58 years.

The pitch was in a terrible state. Drainage problems had left it covered in mud and sand and it was due to be re-laid. Arsenal broke through several times only to be denied by Peter Downsborough in the Swindon goal. Then, Swindon broke away and were gifted a goal.

Ure's poor back pass wrong-footed Wilson who was dispossessed by Noble,. He swivelled and centred with the goal gaping. Simpson slid in to try to clear but the ball ricocheted off Roger Smart agonisingly out of the reach of Wilson as he again lost his footing. It was a bizarre goal.

Arsenal increased their efforts, but time after time, Downsborough saved the underdogs. They almost held out, but four minutes from the end Graham sent Bobby Gould through. Downsborough came out and the ball flew up in the air and Gould beat Burrows to head home a deserved equaliser.

In extra time, though, it was Swindon who proved the stronger on the energy-sapping pitch. At the end of the first half, a goalmouth scramble from Heath's corner ended with Noble's shot hitting Court's back and falling for Don Rogers who, with five defenders between him and the goal, somehow found a way through to put Swindon back in front.

As Arsenal wilted, Smart sent Rogers away to arrogantly round Wilson for his second. Arsenal's humiliation was complete.

Arsenal's disappointment was soon forgotten. They finished fourth in the First Division, their highest position for ten years, and a year later won the European Fairs Cup. They then surpassed that achievement with the League Championship and FA Cup 'double' in 1971.

Swindon could not enter the European Fairs Cup as they were not a First Division club and they lasted just five years in the Second Division before relegation. They won the Second Division Promotion play-off final at Wembley in 1990 but financial irregularities prevented them from appearing in the First Division for the first time.

Arsenal: Wilson (R), Storey, McNab, McLintock – capt, Ure, Simpson, Radford, Sammels, Court, Gould, Armstrong. sub: Graham for Simpson. manager: Bertie Mee
Swindon: Downsborough, Thomas, Trollope, Butler, Burrows, Harland – capt, Heath, Smart, Smith, Noble, Rogers. sub: Penman for Smith. manager: Danny Williams

FA Amateur Cup Final

Saturday 12th April 1969

North Shields 2
Hall, Joicey
Sutton United 1
Mellows
47,500
Referee: P Walters (Somerset)

Sutton took a fourth-minute lead but North Shields fought back to win their first final.

Dario Gradi, who made his name as the long-serving manager of Crewe Alexandra and returned to Wembley twice, including winning the Second Division Promotion play-off final in 1997, was in the Sutton Utd side.

North Shields: Morgan, Driver, Twaddle, Hall, Tatum – capt, Thompson, Wrightson, Lister, Joicey, Cassidy, Rutherford. sub: Orrick for Wrightson
Sutton: Roffey, Garfield, Grose, Brookes, Clarke, Gradi, Bladon – capt, Mellows, Drabwell, Pritchard, Howard. sub: Gane (not used)

Schoolboy International

Saturday 19th April 1969

England 3
Goodlass 2, Guthrie
Wales 0
75,000
Referee: J Hemmings (Chesterfield)

Wales' first appearance at Wembley in six years, but their fifth successive defeat was wrapped up by the third goal just after the interval.

England: Jayes, Pritchard, Martin-Chambers, Marchant – capt, Wilson, Buckley, Smith, Guthrie, Spinner, Stroud, Goodlass
Wales: Hyett, Hines, Hobby, Meyrick, Dwyer – capt, Coombes, McBurney, Newton, Kale, Johnson, Sullivan

FA CUP FINAL

Saturday 26th April 1969

Leicester City　　　　**0-1**　　　**Manchester City**
　　　　　　　　　　　　　　　　　Young 24

100,000
Referee: G McCabe (Sheffield)

Leicester had reached their third final of the decade, their fourth overall, but had still to win the Cup. They had lost to the other Manchester club, United, on their previous visit. In the semi-finals they had beaten the holders West Bromwich Albion. City had last won the Cup in 1956 and had beaten the previous year's finalists Everton in the semi-finals.

Leicester were facing a relegation battle after 12 years in the top flight. City had only been in the First Division for three years but were the reigning League Champions. They finished a miserable 13th, however, in their defence of the title and, in their first European venture, they were surprisingly knocked out in the first round of the European Cup by the Turkish League Champions Fenerbahce.

The only goal came in the middle of the first half. Summerbee's low cross was hammered into the back of the net by Neil Young to give City the FA Cup for the fourth time.

Leicester were left with five league games and were relegated three weeks later when they fell one point short of safety. They bounced back by winning the Second Division Championship two years later but it was 1992 before they returned to Wembley for the Second Division Promotion play-off final and a further five years before they reached another major final in the Coca-Cola Cup. City's trophy-winning habit picked up speed the following year as they won both the Football League Cup and the European Cup-Winners Cup for the first time.

Tony Book, joint Footballer of the Year, appeared at Wembley for the first time at the age of 34, having made his League debut just five years earlier.

Leicester C: Shilton, Rodrigues, Nish – capt, Roberts, Woollett, Cross, Fern, Gibson, Lochhead, Clarke, Glover. sub: Manley for Glover 70. manager: Frank O'Farrell

Manchester C: Dowd, Book – capt, Pardoe, Doyle, Booth, Oakes, Summerbee, Bell, Lee, Young, Coleman. sub: Connor (not used). manager: Joe Mercer

BRITISH CHAMPIONSHIP

Wednesday 7th May 1969

England　　　　　　**2-1**　　　**Wales**
R Charlton 58, Lee 72　　　　　　R Davies 18
72,000
Referee: J Adair (Northern Ireland)

Wales had still to pick up a point in the British Championship at Wembley and had been well beaten on their last visit. Having lost 5-3 to Scotland at the Racecourse Ground four days earlier they needed to beat the reigning British and World Champions to retain their interest in the Championship. They had also got off to a bad start in their World Cup qualifying group, losing to European Champions Italy at Ninian Park and also to East Germany in Dresden. England had defeated Northern Ireland 3-1 at Windsor Park in their defence of the British Championship.

Wales took a surprise lead. Ron Davies heading in Rodrigues' centre. Three minutes later, the same player blocked Astle's header on the line with his hand and although Astle then knocked the ball over the line, the referee had already blown for a penalty.

This was wasted, though, as Lee hit the bar. England, at last, drew level. Bobby Charlton received a return pass from Lee and typically gave Sprake no chance with a powerful shot. Then Astle hit the post but Francis Lee secured the points from the rebound.

England now needed only a point against Scotland three days later to retain the Championship. Wales' goalless draw with Northern Ireland at Windsor Park was not enough to lift them off the bottom.

They did not, as expected, qualify for the following year's World Cup, failing to win a point.

England: West (Everton), Newton (Blackburn), Cooper (Leeds), Moore (West Ham) – capt, Charlton (J) (Leeds), Hunter (Leeds), Lee (Man City), Bell (Man City), Astle* (West Brom), Charlton (R) (Man Utd), Ball (Everton). manager: Sir Alf Ramsey
Wales: Sprake (Leeds), Rodrigues (Leicester), Thomas (Swindon), Durban (Derby County) – capt, Powell (Sheffffield U), Burton (Newcastle), Jones (Cardiff), Davies (R) (Southampton), Toshack (Cardiff), Davies (W) (Newcastle), Moore (Charlton). manager: Dave Bowen
*first cap

BRITISH CHAMPIONSHIP

Saturday 10th May 1969

England
Peters 16, 64, Hurst 20, (pen) 60
89,902
Referee: R Helies (France)

4-1

Scotland
Stein 43

Scotland were unbeaten in their last three visits to Wembley, culminating in their victory over the World Champions in 1967. They had to repeat that victory to regain the British Championship, having been held to a 1-1 draw by Northern Ireland at Hampden Park four nights earlier. A month earlier they had drawn with West Germany in a World Cup qualifying match at Hampden Park which had to be seen as a setback. England needed only a point to retain the Championship.

England went ahead when, from Newton's pass, Martin Peters evaded Murdoch and surprised Herriot with his shot. Four minutes later, Lee supplied Geoff Hurst with the opportunity to notch England's second. Scotland pulled one back just before the interval. Colin Stein headed over Banks, winning his 50th cap, from Gray's cross. The revival was quashed on the hour, however, when Greig brought down Peters in the area. Hurst blasted his second from the penalty. England were now in control and Peters netted his second from Ball's pass four minutes later.

Scotland narrowly lost 3-2 in Hamburg to go out of the World Cup but gained a share of the British Championship the following year.

England: Banks (Stoke City), Newton (Blackburn), Cooper (Leeds), Mullery (Tottenham), Labone (Everton), Moore (West Ham) – capt, Lee (Man City), Ball (Everton), Charlton (Man Utd), Hurst (West Ham), Peters (West Ham). manager: Sir Alf Ramsey
Scotland: Herriot (Birmingham), McCreadie (Chelsea), Gemmell (Celtic), Murdoch (Celtic), McNeill (Celtic), Greig (Rangers), Henderson (Rangers), Bremner (Leeds) – capt, Stein (Rangers), Gilzean (Tottenham), Gray* (Leeds). sub: Wallace (Celtic) for Gilzean 57. manager: Bobby Brown
*first cap

Final table	P	W	D	L	F	A	Pts
England	3	3	0	0	9	3	6
Scotland	3	1	1	1	7	8	3
N Ireland	3	0	2	1	2	4	2
Wales	3	0	1	2	4	7	1

Inter-Varsity Match

Wednesday 3rd December 1969

Cambridge U 1
Emslie
Oxford U 1
Kilty

Oxford brought to an end Cambridge's winning streak but could not win themselves.

INTERNATIONAL

Wednesday 10th December 1969

England   **1-0**   **Portugal**
J Charlton 24
100,000
Referee: M Mouton (France)

Since they had finished third in the 1966 World Cup, Portugal had gone into decline. They had failed to qualify for the 1968 European Championship quarter-finals and then for the forthcoming World Cup, finishing bottom of their qualifying group. They had previously lost three times to England at Wembley, most memorably in the 1966 World Cup semi-final.

The only goal came when, as against Romania almost a year earlier, Jack Charlton headed in at the near post from his brother Bobby's corner.

With 20 minutes left, substitute Peters sent Astle away. The striker was brought down by Henrique as he rounded the 'keeper. The Portuguese protested vehemently and Carlos and Graca were booked but their protests had the desired effect as Lee produced an awful penalty, shooting well wide.

Portugal finished runners-up in each of their next two qualifying groups. They were back at Wembley in the European Championship in 1974.

Emlyn Hughes made his first Wembley appearance. He was Footballer of the Year in 1977, and went on to captain Liverpool to two successive European Cup wins, including one at Wembley in 1978.

England: Bonetti (Chelsea), Reaney (Leeds), Hughes* (Liverpool), Mullery (Tottenham), Charlton (J)(Leeds), Moore (West Ham) – capt, Lee (Man City), Bell (Man City), Astle (West Brom), Charlton (R) (Man Utd), Ball (Everton). sub: Peters (West Ham) for Bell 70. manager: Sir Alf Ramsey
*first cap
Portugal: Henrique (Benfica), Conceicao (Vitoria Setubal), Cardoso (Vitoria Setubal), Carlos (Sporting Lisbon) – capt, Murca (Belenenses), Tome (Vitoria Setubal), Toni (Benfica), Graca (Benfica), Guerreiro (Vitoria Setubal), Antonio (Academica Coimbra), Joao (Vitoria Setubal). subs: Figueiredo (Vitoria Setubal) for Graca 72, Campos (Academica Coimbra) for Antonio 72. coach: Jose Maria Antunes

INTERNATIONAL

Wednesday 14th January 1970

England   **0-0**   **Netherlands**
75,000
Referee: H Siebert (West Germany)

The Netherlands were appearing at Wembley for the first time, apart from a wartime international with Belgium in 1941. They had lost 8-2 to England at Leeds Road, Huddersfield, in 1946 and had not beaten them in four meetings. England had won 1-0 in Amsterdam just two months earlier. The Netherlands had not qualified for a World Cup since 1938.

The visitors greatly impressed with their possession football and neat passing, but the World Champions incurred the wrath of the home supporters for their failure to overcome the emerging Dutch talent.

The Netherlands were on the fringe of great success. They took Europe by storm in the 1970's with their 'total football'. Their club sides, notably Ajax Amsterdam, dominated the European Cup for four years. The national team qualified for the 1974 World Cup, demolishing all before them, including reigning World Champions Brazil to reach the final.

There they met a very professional West German team in Munich and lost 2-1, despite taking a first minute lead. In hindsight, the Wembley crowd had been a little harsh.

Johan Cruyff appeared at Wembley for the first time. He was European Footballer of the Year in 1971 and by 1974 he had become the first to win it three times.

England: Banks (Stoke City), Newton (Everton), Cooper (Leeds), Peters (West Ham), Charlton (J) (Leeds), Hunter (Leeds), Lee (Man City), Bell (Man City), Jones (Leeds), Charlton (R) (Man Utd) – capt, Storey-Moore* (Nottingham F). subs: Mullery (Tottenham) for Lee, Hurst (West Ham) for Jones. manager: Sir Alf Ramsey
*first cap

Netherlands: Van Beveren (Sparta Rotterdam), Drost (Twente Enschede), Israel (Feyenoord), Eijkenbroek (Sparta Rotterdam) – capt, Krol (Ajax), Jansen (Feyenoord), Rijnders (Ajax), Van Hanegem (Feyenoord), Keizer (Ajax), Van Dijk (Ajax), Cruyff (Ajax). subs: Muhren (Ajax) for Rijnders 65, Veenstra (PSV Eindhoven) for Van Hanegem 70. coach: Georg Kessler

FOOTBALL LEAGUE CUP FINAL

Saturday 7th March 1970

Manchester City   **2-1**   **West Bromwich Albion**
Doyle 59, Pardoe 102   Astle 6
After extra time
97,963
Referee: V James (York)

City, who had won the FA Cup the previous year and the League Championship the year before, were hoping to complete a hat-trick of domestic trophies in this, their first League Cup final. In the last 16, they had knocked out Everton, who were to win the League Championship. West Brom were appearing in a record third final in five years.

They were aiming to become the first team to win the League Cup twice, having won it at the first attempt in 1966, but then losing in the final, embarrassingly, to Third Division Queens Park Rangers the following year. They had won the FA Cup, however, in 1968, so were appearing at the stadium for the third time in four years.

Neither side was having a particularly good league season, but four days earlier City had held Academica Coimbra to a goalless draw in the first leg of their European Cup-Winners Cup quarter-final in Portugal.

After just five minutes, a long looping cross from Wilson was met by Jeff Astle who outjumped Corrigan to give West Brom the lead. City fought back and deserved the equaliser. From Pardoe's corner, Summerbee knocked the ball into the goalmouth and Bell headed it back for Mike Doyle to come charging in and beat Osborne at the near post. City scored the winner in the seventh minute of extra time. Lee's great determination took him down the wing. His cross was headed on by Bell and Glyn Pardoe beat Fraser and Osborne to the ball to give City their third domestic trophy in three years.

City would have entered the European Fairs Cup the following year but they overcame Coimbra with a last-minute extra time winner in the second leg and went on to win the European Cup-Winners Cup. Thus, they had to defend it the following year. It was another four years before they were back at Wembley for another League Cup final. West Brom did not return to Wembley until 1993 when they won the Second Division Promotion play-off final.

Manchester C: Corrigan, Book – capt, Mann, Doyle, Booth, Oakes, Heslop, Bell, Summerbee, Lee, Pardoe. sub: Bowyer for Summerbee. manager: Joe Mercer
West Brom: Osborne, Fraser – capt, Wilson, Brown, Talbut, Kaye, Cantello, Suggett, Astle, Hartford, Hope. sub: Krzywicki for Hartford. manager: Alan Ashman

Schoolboy International

Saturday 21st March 1970

England 2
Bradbury, Hornsby
Scotland 0
Referee: J Heron (Newcastle)

England's first victory over the Scots for three years. Frank Gray won a European Cup winners medal with Nottingham Forest ten years later.

England: Ferguson, Donaldson – capt, Bason, Powell, Price, Rodaway, Hornsby, Leman, Bradbury, Clapton, Gannon
Scotland: McKell, Taylor, Brannigan, McCartney, Falconer, McLaughlin, Brolly, McGinley, Brand, Gray, Brown. sub: Adair for Taylor

FA Amateur Cup Final

Saturday 4th April 1970

Dagenham 1
Brooks

Enfield 5
Connell 2, Feely, Adams, Daniels og
33,000
Referee: D Lyden (Birmingham)

In 1967 Enfield had needed a replay to win the cup for the first time. This time the favourites made no mistake at the first attempt.

Dagenham: Huttley, Robertson, Dudley, Daniels, Still, Moore, Leakey, Drake, M Smith, B Smith, Brooks. sub: Scarfe for Robertson
Enfield: Wolstenholme, Clayton, Fry, Payne, Betson, Day – capt, Adams, Connell, Feely, Gray, Hill. sub: D'Arcy for Feely

FA CUP FINAL

Saturday 11th April 1970

Chelsea   **2-2**   **Leeds**
Houseman 41, Hutchinson 86   Charlton 21, Jones 84
After extra time
100,000
Referee: E Jennings (Stourbridge)

Chelsea's FA Cup record in recent years was a good one, yet they had still to win the trophy. They had lost in the final in 1967. Leeds had also still to win the competition, having lost the 1965 final in extra time. They had fought their way through a gruelling semi-final against Manchester United just as in 1965 with Billy Bremner again netting the only goal. This time it was the third game before he broke the deadlock. On their last visit in 1968 Leeds had won the Football League Cup.

Chelsea finished third in the First Division and knocked Leeds out of the Football League Cup. But Leeds, who were reigning League Champions, finished two points above them as runners-up to Everton. They had also reached the European Cup semi-finals at the first attempt but had lost the first leg at home to Celtic, the Scottish League Champions.

The pitch was again in a poor state. It was heavily sanded and caused uneven bounces. The first goal can probably be attributed to it. From Gray's corner, Jack Charlton outjumped Bonetti and his header went over the line underneath McCreadie's foot as he misjudged the bounce. Perhaps it was only fair that Chelsea's equaliser could possibly also have been down to the pitch. Hutchinson headed the ball down for Peter Houseman whose low shot should have been collected easily by Sprake, but the goalkeeper also misjudged the bounce and allowed it to pass through his arms and under his body. With six minutes left, Clarke headed against the post from Giles' cross and Mick Jones drove home the rebound for what seemed to be the winner. But just two minutes later, from a Hollins cross, Ian Hutchinson beat Charlton to head Chelsea level again.

Leeds lost the second leg of their European Cup semi-final four days later and then lost the replay after taking the lead once again. Chelsea's resilience finally won out in extra time in what had become the longest ever FA Cup final.

As in 1965, the unfortunate Leeds had finished runners-up in both league and FA Cup. Chelsea won the European Cup-Winners Cup a year later, also after a replay. They were back at Wembley for the Football League Cup final in 1972, the year Leeds finally won the FA Cup.

Chelsea: Bonetti, Webb, McCreadie, Hollins, Dempsey, Harris (R) – capt, Baldwin, Houseman, Osgood, Hutchinson, Cooke. sub: Hinton for Harris 91. manager: Dave Sexton
Leeds: Sprake, Madeley, Cooper, Bremner – capt, Charlton, Hunter, Lorimer, Clarke, Jones, Giles, Gray (E). sub: Bates (unused). manager: Don Revie

Replay: Wednesday 29th April 1970
Chelsea   **2-1**   **Leeds**
Osgood 78, Webb 104   Jones 35
After extra time
(Old Trafford)

BRITISH CHAMPIONSHIP

Tuesday 21st April 1970

England	**3-1**	**Northern Ireland**
Peters 6, Hurst 57, Charlton 81		Best 50

80,000
Referee: V Pintado (Spain)

England were understandably confident after seven successive wins against Northern Ireland. The only Irish win at Wembley, in 1957, seemed a long time ago. England had drawn 1-1 with Wales at Ninian Park three days earlier. They were aiming to complete a hat-trick of British Championships before leaving for Mexico to defend the World Cup. Northern Ireland had finished runners-up to the USSR in their qualifying group, and so were not going to Mexico. They had lost 1-0 to Scotland at Windsor Park in their opening game and had to avoid defeat to retain their interest in the Championship.

The hosts took the lead in the seventh minute. Charlton, winning his 100th cap, took a corner from which Martin Peters beat Jennings with a simple header. Five minutes into the second half, George Best, who had been sent off against Scotland, received a pass from Clements, beat Stiles and then shot brilliantly past Banks for the equaliser. Geoff Hurst restored England's lead from Newton's cross seven minutes later with a header which Neill diverted past Jennings with his shoulder. Charlton celebrated his century of appearances in some style, sliding in to convert Hughes' cross as Jennings failed to collect it.

England were rather fortunate to hold Scotland to a goalless draw at Hampden Park four days later but it was enough to give them a share of the title. Wales made it a triple tie by inflicting Northern Ireland's third defeat with the only goal at Vetch Field. England recorded their ninth successive victory over Northern Ireland a year later at Windsor Park, but in 1972 the Irish were, at last, victorious at Wembley again.

England: Banks (Stoke City), Newton (Everton), Hughes (Liverpool), Mullery (Tottenham), Moore (West Ham), Stiles (Man Utd), Coates* (Burnley), Kidd* (Man Utd), Charlton (Man Utd) – capt, Hurst (West Ham), Peters (Tottenham). sub: Bell (Man City) for Newton. manager: Sir Alf Ramsey
Northern Ireland: Jennings (Tottenham), Craig (Newcastle), Clements (Coventry), O'Kane (Nottingham F), Neill (Arsenal) – capt, Nicholson (Huddersfield), McMordie (Middlesbrough), Best (Man Utd), Dougan (Wolves), O'Doherty* (Coleraine), Lutton (Wolves). subs: Nelson* (Arsenal) for O'Doherty, Cowan* (Newcastle) for Lutton manager: Billy Bingham
*first cap

Final table	P	W	D	L	F	A	Pts
England	3	1	2	0	4	2	4
Scotland	3	1	2	0	1	0	4
Wales	3	1	2	0	2	1	4
N Ireland	3	0	0	3	1	5	0

FA Trophy Final

Saturday 2nd May 1970

Macclesfield Town 2
Lyon 26, B Fidler 60

Telford United 0
28,000
Referee: K Walker (Kent)

A new competition for the growing number of semi-professional non-league clubs reached its climax at Wembley with player-manager Frank Beaumont's team becoming the first winners.

Telford's player-manager was Ron Flowers, who won 49 caps for England and three League Championship winners medals with Wolverhampton Wanderers.

In goal for Telford was Bobby Irvine, who won eight caps for Northern Ireland in the early 1960's.

Macclesfield: Cooke, Sievwright, Bennett, Beaumont – capt, Collins, Roberts, Lyon, B Fidler, Young, Corfield, D Fidler. sub: Berry (not used)
Telford: Irvine, Harris, Croft, Flowers – capt, Coton, Ray, Fudge, Hart, Bentley, Murray, Jagger. sub: Ball (not used)

Schoolboy International

Saturday 16th May 1970

England 3
Hornsby, Bradbury, Gannon
West Germany 0
55,000

Bradbury and Hornsby again showed a liking for hitting the back of the Wembley net in England's biggest victory over West Germany for five years.

England: Ferguson, Donaldson – capt, Bason, Powell, Rodaway, Cattrell, Hornsby, Leman, Bradbury, Clapton, Gannon

INTERNATIONAL

Wednesday 25th November 1970

England	3-1	East Germany
Lee 12, Peters 21, Clarke 63		Vogel 27

93,000
Referee: R Scheurer (Switzerland)

This was East Germany's first visit to England. They had lost 2-1 to their hosts in their only previous meeting, in 1963 in Leipzig.

They had not yet qualified for a major tournament but had made a good start to their European Championship group, beating the Netherlands in Dresden. England were no longer World Champions, after losing a two-goal lead and succumbing to West Germany after extra time in the World Cup quarter-final in Leon.

A huge kick from Shilton was headed on by Hurst and Francis Lee rounded Croy to put England ahead. Nine minutes later Hurst chested down a Ball free kick and Martin Peters blasted home the second.

Eberhard Vogel brought the Germans back into it when his 25-yard shot from Stein's pass caught Shilton by surprise but then Lee put Allan Clarke through and his shot hit Croy before dropping into the net.

East Germany failed to qualify from their European Championship group but did qualify for the 1974 World Cup. They were back at Wembley in 1984.

England: Shilton* (Leicester), Hughes (Liverpool), Cooper (Leeds), Mullery (Tottenham), Sadler (Man Utd), Moore (West Ham) – capt, Lee (Man City), Ball (Everton), Hurst (West Ham), Clarke (Leeds), Peters (Tottenham). manager: Sir Alf Ramsey
*first cap
East Germany: Croy (Sachsenring Zwickau), Kurbjuweit (Carl Zeiss Jena), Rock (Carl Zeiss Jena), Sammer (Dynamo Dresden), Ganzera (Dynamo Dresden), Strempel (Carl Zeiss Jena), Stein (Carl Zeiss Jena), Irmscher (Carl Zeiss Jena), Ducke (Carl Zeiss Jena) – capt, Kreische (Dynamo Dresden), Vogel (Carl Zeiss Jena). sub: Frenzel (Lokomotive Leipzig) for Strempel 79. coach: Georg Buschner

Inter-Varsity Match

Wednesday 9th December 1970
Cambridge U 1
Wallwork
Oxford U 0

Yet another victory for Cambridge, their eighth in ten years.

FOOTBALL LEAGUE CUP FINAL

Saturday 27th February 1971

Aston Villa	0-2	Tottenham Hotspur
		Chivers 77, 80

100,000
Referee: J Finney (Hereford)

The twin towers with the Post Office Tower in the background.

1977 and the Scottish supporters invade the pitch and break one of the goal frames. Scenes such as this contributed to the demise of the annual fixture between England and Scotland.

1981. Was this Wembley's greatest goal? Ricky Villa scores against Manchester City in the replay after a meandering dribble in the penalty area.

*1985. Manchester United's Kevin Moran looks pleadingly at referee
Peter Willis but still becomes the first player to be sent off in an FA Cup final.*

1986. The first of the two Merseyside FA Cup finals at Wembley. Peter Reid of Everton gets ready to challenge Alan Hansen while Jan Molby looks on.

*1988. Another FA Cup final shock as Wimbledon beat Liverpool 1-0.
Here Andy Thorn jumps on Dave Beasant, the first goalkeeper to
save a penalty in the final.*

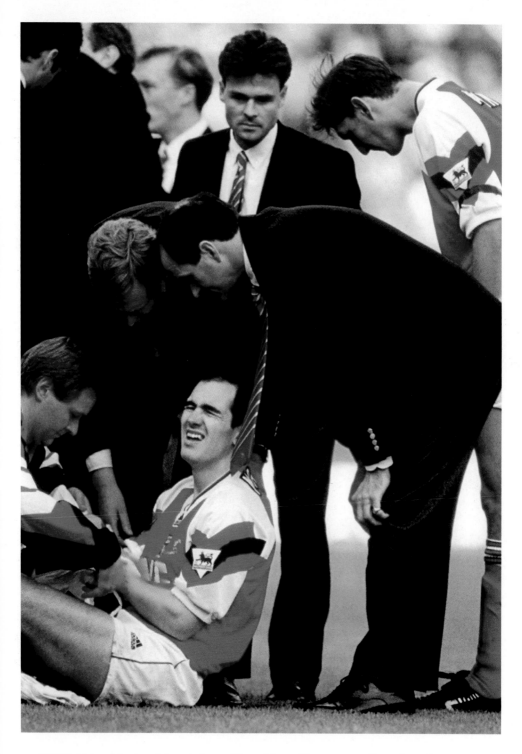

1993. Wembley's oddest injury. The old stadium was often thought to carry an injury jinx but Steve Morrow can be forgiven for thinking he was especially unlucky after scoring the goal which won Arsenal the Coca-Cola Cup. He was picked up by his captain Tony Adams (looking on anxiously with manager George Graham) and dropped, which resulted in a broken arm.

1996. Wembley's oddest celebration followed Paul Gascoigne scoring one of the stadium's greatest goals against Scotland in Euro 96. He laid on his back and teammates mimicked the 'infamous' dentist's chair photographs of England players drinking in a Hong Kong nightclub.

*1998. Sir Stanley Matthews (centre) walks down from the Royal Box
with teammates from the 1953 FA Cup final which became known as
"The Matthews final". They are Bill Perry (front) and Cyril Robinson.
Matthews received an Axa Legend Award.*

1999. Paul Scholes (no. 11) becomes the only player to be sent off at Wembley when representing England. He was cautioned twice against Sweden for two foul tackles. Refereee Jose Maria Encinar waves the card as David Beckham looks on.

*1999 and Alan Shearer gets the first of his hat-trick in a
6-0 rout of Luxembourg*

2000. Wembley's last FA Cup final sees winning Chelsea captain Dennis Wise with son Henry and the FA Cup.

2000. A fan's face tells it all. England have just lost 1-0 to Germany in Wembley's last competitive match.

*2000. Hans Tilkowski, the West German goalkeeper in the 1966 World Cup
final, and Sir Geoff Hurst with the spot where the second goal of his hat-trick,
the famous "did it cross the line?" goal landed.*

2003. The wrecking balls move in on the most iconic stadium in football history.

The "new" Wembley rises above the London skyline.

Villa had been the first winners of the Football League Cup in 1961, overturning a two-goal first-leg deficit to defeat Rotherham United in extra time in the second leg. They reached the final again two years later, but lost to local rivals Birmingham City. They had won the FA Cup at Wembley for a record seventh time in 1957.

Tottenham were appearing in their first League Cup final and had thrashed West Bromwich Albion, the previous year's finalists, 5-0 in the last 16. They had won the FA Cup at Wembley three times in the past decade.

In 1970 Villa had been relegated to the Third Division for the first time, but now, incredibly, had become the third club from that division in five years to reach the League Cup final. The other two, Queens Park Rangers and Swindon Town, had gone on to complete a League Cup and promotion 'double'.

Villa were holding Tottenham fairly comfortably until late in the second half when Dunn parried Neighbour's shot and Martin Chivers stroked it past Turnbull on the line. Three minutes later it was all over. From Mullery's pass, Chivers shrugged off Tiler's challenge and threaded the ball between two defenders and the 'keeper for his second.

Villa finished fourth in the Third Division, missing out on promotion, but the following year they won the Third Division Championship and three years later completed a League Cup and promotion 'double', regaining their First Division place. Tottenham lost to eventual finalists Liverpool after a replay, in the FA Cup, but finished third, in the First Division. The following year, they became the first winners of the renamed UEFA Cup, beating Wolverhampton Wanderers on aggregate in the first all-English European final. A year later, they regained the Football League Cup.

Aston Villa: Dunn, Bradley, Aitken, Godfrey – capt, Turnbull, Tiler, McMahon, Rioch, Lochhead, Hamilton, Anderson. sub: Gibson (not used). manager: Vic Crowe

Tottenham: Jennings, Kinnear, Knowles, Mullery – capt, Collins, Beal, Gilzean, Perryman, Chivers, Peters, Neighbour. sub: Pearce (not used). manager: Bill Nicholson

Schoolboy International

Saturday 6th March 1971

England 1
Morton
Northern Ireland 0
24,000
Referee: R Cocup (Gillingham)

On their first appearance at Wembley, Northern Ireland were beaten by a deflected goal in the 59th minute.

England: Shepherd, Clarkson, Spencer, Powell – capt, Bowtell, Bason, Odeje, Morton, Ayres, Wardrop, Jones. sub: Cameron
Northern Ireland: Dunlop, Aiken, Todd, Welsh, Coyles, Wright, Kennedy, Thompson, Calvert, Sinclair, Nixon. subs: Dougan, McCall

Olympic Qualifying First Leg

Wednesday 24th March 1971

Great Britain 1
Adams 15
Bulgaria 0
3,000
Referee: A.Van Gemert (Netherlands)
A remarkable result, as England's amateurs, plus Scotsman Bill Currie, defeated a team containing seven players who had taken part in the previous year's World Cup in Mexico. They were, however, beaten 5-0, in the second leg in Sofia. This was the last occasion Britain entered the Olympic competition.

Great Britain: Swannell (Hendon), Fuschillo (Wycombe), Currie (Albion), Powell (Wycombe), Gamblin (Leatherhead), Payne (Enfield), Day (Slough), Haider (Hendon), Hardcastle (Skelmersdale), Gray (Enfield), Adams (Slough). sub: Pritchard (Wycombe) for Hardcastle. manager: Charles Hughes
Bulgaria: Yordanov, Zafirov, Kolev, Aladjov, Denev, Penev – capt, Vesselinov, Bonev, Nikodimov, Yakimov, Panov. sub: Vassilev for Bonev

Schoolboy International

Saturday 3rd April 1971

England 5
Morton, Clarkson, Odeje, Bason 2,1 pen
Netherlands 1
De Kruyff
55,000

De Kruyff also missed a penalty on the Netherlands' first visit to Wembley at this level.

England: Gordon, Clarkson, Spencer, Wardrop, Bowtell, Cahill, Ayres, Morton, Odeje, Bason – capt, Cameron. sub: Conroy for Morton 50

EUROPEAN CHAMPIONSHIP QUALIFYING

Wednesday 21st April 1971

England   3-0   **Greece**
Chivers 23, Hurst 68, Lee 87
55,123
Referee: M Hirviniemi (Finland)

This was the first meeting between these two countries. Greece had never qualified for a major tournament, but had finished runners-up to Romania in their last World Cup qualifying group.

England, who had reached the semi-finals in 1968, had already had a single goal victory in Group Three against Malta in Valletta. Greece, however, had lost in Athens to Switzerland.

Martin Chivers put England ahead by beating three men and the goalkeeper in a mazy run. But it was not until midway through the second half that they broke through again, when Geoff Hurst headed home, after good work by Peters and Chivers.

Francis Lee scored the third two minutes from time with a diving header from Storey's cross.

England won the return 2-0 in Athens eight months later. Greece had been knocked out long before then, though. Their next trip to Wembley was also in the European Championship twelve years later.

England: Banks (Stoke City), Storey* (Arsenal), Hughes (Liverpool), Mullery (Tottenham), McFarland (Derby County), Moore (West Ham) – capt, Lee (Man City), Ball (Everton), Chivers (Tottenham), Hurst (West Ham), Peters (Tottenham). sub: Coates (Burnley) for Ball 78. manager: Sir Alf Ramsey
*first cap
Greece: Christidis (Aris Salonika), Gaitatzis (Olympiakos Piraeus), Stathopoulos (AEK Athens), Spyridon (Aris Salonika), Toskas (AEK Athens), Cambas (Panathinaikos), Koudas (PAOK Salonika), Synetopoulos (Olympiakos), Dedes (Panionios), Papaioannou (AEK Athens) – capt, Kritikopoulos (Ethnikos). subs: Haitas (Panionios) for Cambas 75, Delikaris (Olympiakos) for Dedes 88. coach: Lakis Petropoulos

FA Amateur Cup Final

Saturday 24th April 1971

Dagenham 1
Bass
Skelmersdale United 4
Dickin 3, Windsor
45,000
Referee: R Tinkler (Boston)

Ted Dickin's hat-trick secured Skelmersdale's only FA Amateur Cup win as they were in their last season as an amateur club.

It also avenged their last-minute penalty miss in the 1967 final. Dagenham, unfortunately, were thrashed for the second year in succession.

Dagenham: Huttley, Ford, Dudley, Davidson, Still, Moore – capt, Leakey, Fry, Bass, Baker, Dear. sub: Smith for Dear
Skelmersdale: Frankish, Allen, Poole, Turner – capt, Bennett, McDermott, Swift, Wolfe, Dickin, Hardcastle, Clements. sub: Windsor for Swift

FA Trophy Final

Saturday 1st May 1971

Hillingdon Borough 2
Reeve, Bishop
Telford United 3
Owen, Bentley, Fudge
29,500
Referee: D Smith (Gloucestershire)

Telford, who had lost the previous year's final, were two goals down at half-time. Again both bosses were player-managers, although Telford's Ron Flowers had to restrict his contribution to the bench because of injury.

Hillingdon's player-manager, Jim Langley had played for England at Wembley in 1958 and was in Queens Park Rangers' Football League Cup-winning side of 1967. He was 42 years old.

Hillingdon: Lowe, Batt, Langley, Higginson, Newcombe, Moore – capt, Fairchild, Bishop, Reeve, Carter, Knox
Telford: Irvine, Harris, Croft, Ray, Coton, Carr, Fudge, Owen, Bentley, Jagger, Murray

FA CUP FINAL

Saturday 8th May 1971

Arsenal   **2-1**   **Liverpool**
Kelly 101, George 111   Heighway 91
after extra time
100,000
Referee: N Burtenshaw (Great Yarmouth)

It had been 21 years since Arsenal had beaten Liverpool to win the FA Cup for the third time. Since then, they had lost three times at Wembley, including two Football League Cup finals. 1969 had been particularly embarrassing. In the semi-finals against Stoke City, they had come back from being two goals down at half-time. In both 1930 and '50, they had recovered from two-goal semi-final deficits and gone on to win the Cup. The previous year, they had won the European Fairs Cup. Liverpool had won the FA Cup for the first time in 1965.

Just five days earlier, Arsenal had won the League Championship after coming from behind to pip Leeds by a point. They were now on the verge of the 'double'. In their defence of the European Fairs Cup, they had reached the quarter-finals again, but had gone out on away goals, to Cologne. Liverpool finished fifth in the First Division for the second year in succession. They had reached the European Fairs Cup semi-finals for the first time, before losing by the only goal on aggregate to Leeds, the eventual winners.

Neither side could find a breakthrough in the first 90 minutes on a hot day. But in the first minute of extra time, substitute Thompson sent Steve Heighway away on the left and as Wilson prepared for a cross, the winger beat him at the near post to put Liverpool ahead. Arsenal, whose teamwork and resilience was their great strength, were now faced with their sternest test of character.

They responded magnificently. Radford's overhead kick produced a goalmouth scramble. Substitute Eddie Kelly got a touch, which went through Smith's legs and rolled towards Clemence. Graham ran in, swung at the ball and missed, but wrong-footed Clemence and the ball continued on its path under his body and gently rolled into the net. With nine minutes left Arsenal's determination had its reward. Radford played a one-two with Charlie George and then cut inside to return it to the weary striker, whose shot took a slight deflection off Lloyd to elude Clemence's reach. George lay down in exhaustion and triumph after securing the elusive 'double', for a team which refused to accept defeat throughout a remarkable season.

Arsenal reached the final again a year later. As League Champions, they entered the European Cup, leaving Liverpool to take their place in the European Cup-Winners Cup, where they were beaten in the last 16 by Bayern Munich. But Liverpool won both the League Championship and the UEFA Cup in 1973 and then returned in 1974 to win the FA Cup.

Arsenal: Wilson (R), Rice , McNab, Storey, McLintock – capt, Simpson, Armstrong, Graham, Radford, Kennedy (R), George. sub: Kelly for Storey 70. manager: Bertie Mee
Liverpool: Clemence, Lawler, Lindsay, Smith – capt, Lloyd, Hughes (E), Callaghan, Evans, Heighway, Toshack, Hall. sub: Thompson (P) for Evans 70. manager: Bill Shankly

EUROPEAN CHAMPIONSHIP QUALIFYING

Wednesday 12th May 1971

England   **5-0**   **Malta**
Chivers 30, 48, Lee 43, Clarke pen 46
Lawler 75
41,534
Referee: E Roed (Norway)

This was Malta's second entry only into the European Championship and they were already eliminated. England had beaten them 1-0 in Valletta in their first meeting in Group Three three months earlier. The following year they would be entering the World Cup for the first time.

It took England nearly half an hour to make the breakthrough. From a Peters free kick, Martin Chivers left his markers to send a glancing header into the net. Next Coates' corner was met by the head of Peters, and Francis Lee headed the second past three defenders and the goalkeeper on the line. In England's first attack of the second half, Clarke headed the ball towards Peters, but Darmanin controlled it with his arm and a penalty was given. Allan Clarke gave Bonaci no chance.

Chivers scored again two minutes later when he rose to head in Peters' cross. With an hour gone, substitute Ball's shot from Lee's corner, was handled on the line by Grima. Malta's substitute 'keeper Mizzi survived this one, however,, as Clarke drove the penalty wide. But Mizzi was beaten 15 minutes from the end, when Chris Lawler took a pass from Moore and found the net from 35 yards out. The difference in class was emphasised by the fact that England's goalkeeper Banks did not receive the ball from a Maltese player during the whole match.

Malta, not surprisingly, finished bottom and never appeared at Wembley again. England had to catch Switzerland, the pacemakers of the group, if they were to reach the quarter-finals.

England: Banks (Stoke City), Lawler* (Liverpool), Cooper (Leeds), Moore (West Ham) – capt, McFarland (Derby County), Hughes (Liverpool), Lee (Man City), Coates (Tottenham), Chivers (Tottenham), Clarke (Leeds), Peters (Tottenham). sub: Ball (Everton) for Peters 62. manager: Sir Alf Ramsey
*first cap

Malta: Bonaci (Valletta), Pace (Valletta), Grima (Floriana), Camilleri (Floriana), Darmanin (Sliema), Delia (Hibernians), Cocks (Sliema) – capt, Vassallo (Floriana), Bonnet (Sliema), Theobald (Hibernians), Arpa (Floriana). sub: Mizzi (Hibernians) for Bonaci. coach: Carm Borg

BRITISH CHAMPIONSHIP

Wednesday 19th May 1971

England 0-0 Wales
70,000
Referee: M Wright (Northern Ireland)

Wales, who had shared the British Championship with England, the previous year had lost all their eight previous Championship matches at the stadium. Four days earlier, they had fought a goalless draw with the other reigning joint champions, Scotland, at Ninian Park. Defeat would put them out of contention. They had also begun their European Championship group disappointingly, losing to Czechoslovakia at Vetch Field. England had beaten Northern Ireland at Windsor Park by the only goal.

An experimental England side failed to gel as a team and the Welsh secured their first ever British Championship point at Wembley.

England were fortunate to stay top and needed to beat Scotland three days later to win the title outright. Wales lost to Northern Ireland at Windsor Park for the first time since 1959 and completed the Championship without scoring a goal.

In fact, it was another three years before they scored again in the British Championship. They failed to reach the European Championship quarter-finals, but in 1973 they were back at Wembley for a World Cup qualifying match.

England: Shilton (Leicester), Lawler (Liverpool), Cooper (Leeds), Smith* (Liverpool), Lloyd* (Liverpool), Hughes (Liverpool), Lee (Man City), Coates (Tottenham), Hurst (West Ham), Brown* (West Brom), Peters (Tottenham) – capt. sub: Clarke (Leeds) for Coates 72. manager: Sir Alf Ramsey

Wales: Sprake (Leeds), Rodrigues (Sheffield W), Thomas (Swindon), James (Blackpool), Roberts (Arsenal), Yorath (Leeds), Phillips (Cardiff), Durban (Derby County) – capt, Davies (Southampton), Toshack (Liverpool), Reece (Sheffield U). sub: Rees (Nottingham F) for Reece. manager: Dave Bowen
*first cap

BRITISH CHAMPIONSHIP

Saturday 22nd May 1971

England	**3-1**	**Scotland**
Peters 10, Chivers 30, 40		Curran 12

91,469
Referee: J Dorpmans (Netherlands)

Scotland had lost heavily on their last visit, and after losing 1-0 to Northern Ireland at Hampden Park, Glasgow four days earlier, they had to beat England to have any chance of sharing the title for the second year in succession. Defeat would leave them bottom. In the European Championship, they had recently lost in both Belgium and Portugal.

The first goal came from a Ball corner. Chivers flicked the ball on and Martin Peters headed it over Clark towards the goal. Greig, on the line, pushed it against the bar with his hand and it bounced out. The referee mistakenly awarded a goal. But within two minutes, Scotland had scored their first goal of the Championship. Moore blocked Johnstone's pass and Ball headed back to Banks. Suddenly, Hugh Curran appeared from nowhere and raced onto the back-pass. He swung at the ball and this was enough to distract Banks from collecting it. As the ball entered the net Curran took the acclaim, but it is unlikely he touched it. One bizarre goal had cancelled out another. England regained the lead after half an hour's play. Brogan, under pressure from Lee, sent a suicidal pass across goal straight to Martin Chivers, who blasted it past Clark. Five minutes before half-time, Lawler's lofted pass sent Chivers away to lob the 'keeper for his second. Despite numerous second half chances for England, there were no further goals.

Scotland shared the Championship with England the following year despite losing to them again at Hampden Park. They failed to reach the European Championship quarter-finals and England beat them again at Wembley in 1973.

England: Banks (Stoke City), Lawler (Liverpool), Cooper (Leeds), Storey (Arsenal), McFarland (Derby County), Moore (West Ham) – capt, Lee (Man City), Ball (Everton), Chivers (Tottenham), Hurst (West Ham), Peters (Tottenham). sub: Clarke (Leeds) for Lee 73. manager: Sir Alf Ramsey

Scotland: Clark (Aberdeen), Greig (Rangers), Brogan (Celtic), Bremner (Leeds), McLintock (Arsenal), Moncur (Newcastle) – capt, Johnstone (Celtic), Robb (Aberdeen), Curran (Wolves), Green (Blackpool), Cormack (Nottingham F). subs: Jarvie (Airdrie) for Green 80, Munro (Wolves) for Curran 88. manager: Bobby Brown

Final table	P	W	D	L	F	A	Pts
England	3	2	1	0	4	1	5
Northern Ireland	3	2	0	1	2	1	4
Wales	3	0	2	1	0	1	2
Scotland	3	0	1	2	1	4	1

EUROPEAN CUP FINAL

Wednesday 2nd June 1971

Ajax Amsterdam	**2-0**	**Panathinaikos**

Van Dijk 5, Kapsis og 87
83,000
Referee: J Taylor (Wolverhampton)

Ajax were appearing in their second final in three years. They had lost the 1969 final, 4-1 to AC Milan in Madrid and were attempting to keep the trophy in Holland, after Feyenoord's 1970 triumph. In the quarter-finals, they had beaten the previous year's finalists, Scottish Champions Celtic. Panathinaikos had never been beyond the last 16 of any European competition before and no Greek club had ever progressed beyond the quarter-finals. They made Greek history by first eliminating League Champions Everton on away goals to reach a semi-final in which they performed a miraculous recovery, after losing the first leg 4-1 to Red Star Belgrade. Three second-leg goals in Athens took them to Wembley, as the away goals rule again proved their saviour.

Ajax had won the Dutch League Championship four times in the past five years and a record 13 times in all. But this time, they were to lose out, finishing runners-up to Feyenoord. Panathinaikos were chasing a hat-trick of Greek League Championships but finished third.

Wembley's second European Cup final in four years did not quite have the excitement and emotion of 1968, but there was an early goal. Dick Van Dijk headed Ajax in front from Keizer's cross. They did not clinch the victory until three minutes from time. It was created by Cruyff and finished by substitute Haan with Anthimos Kapsis taking it into his own net.

These talented Dutchmen were to complete a hat-trick of European Cup wins, the first since Real Madrid in the late 1950's.

Ajax: Stuy, Vasovic – capt, Suurbier, Hulshoff, Rijnders, Neeskens, Swart, Muhren, Keizer, Van Dijk, Cruyff. subs: Haan for Rijnders 46, Blankenburg for Swart 46. coach: Rinus Michels

Panathinaikos: Economopoulos, Tomaros, Vlahos, Elefterakis, Kamaras, Sourpis, Grammos, Filokouris, Antoniadis, Domazos – capt, Kapsis. coach: Ferenc Puskas

EUROPEAN CHAMPIONSHIP QUALIFYING

Wednesday 10th November 1971

England	**1-1**	**Switzerland**
Summerbee 9		Odermatt 26

90,423

Referee: C Barbulescu (Romania)

Switzerland had lost their last six meetings with England, including the match at Wembley in 1962. In the 1966 World Cup they had failed to win a point and they had failed to qualify in 1970. England had won 3-2 in Basle less than a month earlier through an own goal.

This had put the British Champions top of Group Three on goal difference for the first time. Realistically, Switzerland had to win to have any chance of qualifying for the quarter-finals as England still had to go to Greece. Victory for England would put them through.

It looked as if it would be easy. From Lee's corner, Ramseier's poor header came to Mike Summerbee, who headed into an empty net vacated by Prosperi, when he came for the corner. But the Swiss drew level after 25 minutes. Karl Odermatt took a pass from Kuhn and beat Shilton from 25 yards with a curler. Switzerland held on to the draw, but it was not to be enough.

Three weeks later, England beat Greece 2-0 in Athens to qualify for the quarter-finals where they would meet old rivals West Germany. Switzerland were back at Wembley in 1977.

England: Shilton (Leicester), Madeley (Leeds), Cooper (Leeds), Storey (Arsenal), Lloyd (Liverpool), Moore (West Ham) – capt, Summerbee (Man City), Ball (Everton), Hurst (West Ham), Lee (Man City), Hughes (Liverpool). subs: Chivers (Tottenham) for Summerbee 83, Marsh* (QPR) for Lee 83. manager: Sir Alf Ramsey
*first cap

Switzerland: Prosperi (Lugano), Ramseier (Basle), Stierli (Zurich), Perroud (Servette), Chapuisat (Lausanne), Kuhn (Zurich), Odermatt (Basle) – capt, Blattler (Basle), Balmer (Basle), Kunzli (Zurich), Jeandupeux (Zurich). sub: Meier (Grasshoppers) for Jeandupeux. coach: Louis Maurer

Final table	P	W	D	L	F	A	Pts
England	6	5	1	0	15	3	11
Switzerland	6	4	1	1	12	5	9
Greece	6	1	1	4	3	8	3
Malta	6	0	1	5	2	16	1

Inter-Varsity Match

Wednesday 8th December 1971

Cambridge U 0
Oxford U 0

The first goalless draw since the fixture was first moved to Wembley, in 1953.

FOOTBALL LEAGUE CUP FINAL

Saturday 4th March 1972

Chelsea   **1-2**   **Stoke City**
Osgood 45   Conroy 4, Eastham 74
100,000
Referee: N Burtenshaw (Great Yarmouth)

Chelsea had won the League Cup in 1965, beating the holders Leicester City on aggregate in the final. No team had won the trophy more than once. Chelsea were attempting to add it to the FA Cup they had won in 1970 and the European Cup-Winners Cup which followed in 1971.

A year before Chelsea's League Cup win, Stoke had reached the final, losing to Leicester on aggregate. Now they were at Wembley for the first time, after a marathon semi-final with West Ham United in which they lost the home leg and then had to rely on Footballer of the Year Gordon Banks saving a last minute Geoff Hurst penalty in extra time in the second leg.

Chelsea had suffered a surprise exit in their defence of the European Cup-Winners Cup, losing on away goals in the last 16 to Atvidaberg, of Sweden.

Stoke had not taken a point from Chelsea for three seasons, but were becoming a prolific cup side. They had come agonisingly close to an FA Cup final appearance the previous year and the previous week

had reached the quarter-finals again.

In only the fifth minute, Stoke were ahead from Eastham's cross. Dempsey got to it first and then blocked Smith's shot from the rebound, but it then looped up and Terry Conroy headed it past Bonetti. In the last seconds of the first half, Cooke's ball into the goalmouth was met by Peter Osgood, who fell under pressure from two defenders.

Webb and Bloor battled for possession and it came back to Osgood, who, despite being still on the ground, stroked it past Banks for the equaliser.

Stoke regained the lead some fifteen minutes from time. From Conroy's cross, Ritchie headed it down and Greenhoff shot. Bonetti saved, but George Eastham seized on the rebound and Stoke had won a major trophy for the first time.

Chelsea did not appear at Wembley again until they won the Full Members Cup in 1986. Stoke did not return to Wembley until they won the Autoglass Trophy in 1992, when they were in the Third Division.

Chelsea: Bonetti, Mulligan, Harris (R) – capt, Hollins, Dempsey, Webb, Cooke, Garland, Osgood, Hudson, Houseman. sub: Baldwin for Mulligan. manager: Dave Sexton
Stoke: Banks, Marsh, Pejic, Bernard, Smith, Bloor, Conroy, Greenhoff, Ritchie, Dobing – capt, Eastham. sub: Mahoney for Greenhoff. manager: Tony Waddington

FA Trophy Final

Saturday 15th April 1972

Barnet 0
Stafford Rangers 3
Williams 66, 74 Cullerton 73
24,000
Referee: P Partridge (Middlesbrough)

Once again, the winners were led by a player-manager, Roy Chapman. Milija Aleksic was with Spurs when they won the FA Cup at Wembley in 1981, while his opposite number Jack McClelland won six Northern Ireland caps in the early 1960's.

Barnet: McClelland, Lye – capt, Jenkins, Ward, Embery, King, Powell, Ferry, Flatt, Eason, Plume. sub: Adams for Ferry 78

Stafford: Aleksic, Chadwick – capt, Clayton, Sargeant, Aston, Machin, Cullerton, Chapman, Williams, Bailey, Jones. sub: Barlow (not used)

FA Amateur Cup Final

Saturday 22nd April 1972

Enfield 0
Hendon 2
Smith og, Bass
38,000
Referee: E Wallace (Swindon)

Hendon's third victory in five finals.

Enfield: Williams, Gibson, Hill, Payne, Betson, Smith, Albon, Adams, Butterfield, Gray, Turley. sub: Brooks for Albon
Hendon: Swannell, Jennings, Hand, Deadman, Phillips, Haider, Childs, Connell, Bass, Baker, Jameson

EUROPEAN CHAMPIONSHIP QUALIFYING
QUARTER-FINAL FIRST LEG

Saturday 29th April 1972

England   **1-3**   **West Germany**
Lee 77   Hoeness 26 Netzer pen 84 Muller 88
95,000
Referee: R Helies (France)

West Germany had gained their revenge for their defeat in the 1966 World Cup final with their first two victories against England. Most notable of these was the 1970 World Cup quarter-final in Leon in which England's title was wrested from them after extra time despite being two goals up. West Germany then lost their semi-final to Italy in an extra-time goal feast in Mexico City. Like England, West Germany were unbeaten as they won Group Eight. But they were appearing in the quarter-finals for the first time whereas England had finished third in 1968.

The Germans went ahead when Moore intercepted Held's cross but tried to dribble his way past Held and Wimmer and took the ball straight into the path of Muller. The ace striker held off Hunter and passed to Held who laid it back for Uli Hoeness to beat Banks with the aid of a deflection off Hunter.

England fought back and when they drew level just before the end must have thought they had gained a point. Maier saved from Bell, but Francis Lee tapped in the rebound. The comeback stuttered to a halt seven minutes later when Moore brought down Held and Gunter Netzer beat Banks from the spot. England could not respond and West Germany scored again. England were caught in possession. Hughes slipped and Held played it through to Hoeness who cut inside. He played a short pass to the unmarked Gerd Muller who had time to turn and shoot past Banks into the corner. England were a well beaten side, but terrible defensive blunders had made the situation worse.

This defeat drove home the fact that England were no longer one of the best teams in the world. West Germany won the European Championship with a crushing 3-0 victory over the USSR in the final in Brussels. Two years later they won the World Cup in their own country. They next appeared at Wembley in 1975.

Gerd Muller, making his first appearance at Wembley, was a name which conjured up bad memories for England. The 1970 European Footballer of the Year had scored West Germany's extra-time winner against England in the 1970 World Cup.

Now he had dealt the killer blow in the European Championship and went on to score twice in the final. Two years later, he scored the winner in the World Cup final against the Netherlands.

England: Banks (Stoke City), Madeley (Leeds), Hughes (Liverpool), Bell (Man City), Moore (West Ham) – capt, Hunter (Leeds), Lee (Man City), Ball (Arsenal), Chivers (Tottenham), Hurst (West Ham), Peters (Tottenham). sub: Marsh (Man City) for Hurst 60. manager: Sir Alf Ramsey

West Germany: Maier (Bayern Munich), Hottges (Werder Bremen), Breitner (Bayern Munich), Schwarzenbeck (Bayern Munich), Beckenbauer (Bayern Munich) – capt, Wimmer (Borussia Monchengladbach), Grabowski (Eintracht Frankfurt), Hoeness (Bayern Munich), Muller (Bayern Munich), Netzer (Borussia Monchengladbach), Held (Kickers Offenbach). coach: Helmut Schoen

Second Leg: Saturday 13th May 1972
West Germany 0-0 England
(Olympiastadion, Berlin)
West Germany won 3-1 on aggregate

FA CUP FINAL

Saturday 6th May 1972

Arsenal   **0-1**   **Leeds United**
Clarke 53

100,000
Referee: D Smith (Gloucester)

Arsenal were the holders, after winning the 'double' the previous year. In the last 16 they had beaten Derby County, who were to succeed them as League Champions, despite losing goalkeeper, Bob Wilson to injury for the last 15 minutes; and they had defeated the Football League Cup winners Stoke City, in the semi-finals. Just as in the previous year, Stoke succumbed after a replay.

Leeds were appearing in their second final in three years, having drawn at Wembley in 1970. They had still to win the FA Cup. In an earlier round they had knocked out the previous year's finalists Liverpool. Leeds had beaten Arsenal at Wembley in the 1968 Football League Cup final.

Arsenal finished fifth in their defence of the League Championship and reached the European Cup quarter-finals, before losing both legs to the holders and eventual winners Ajax Amsterdam. Leeds, having won the European Fairs Cup the previous year, went out in the first round of the renamed UEFA Cup. They rested the first team for the second leg at home and lost 4-0 to Lierse after winning 2-0 in Belgium. After finishing League runners-up for two successive years, Leeds had been demolishing their opponents in the league and surely had the greatest team in their history. They were one point away from the League Championship.

The FA Cup, in its centenary year, was won by a single goal early in the second half. A cross from Jones (who was to dislocate his shoulder in the last attack of the match) was met by a diving header from Allan Clarke. Leeds had won the trophy for the first time, repeating their League Cup win of 1968 by the same score.

Arsenal reached the semi-finals for the third consecutive year in 1973, but they did not reach the final again until 1978. Leeds failed to emulate Arsenal's 'double' of the previous year. Just two days after Wembley, needing only a point to win the League Championship on goal average, they were surprisingly beaten by Wolverhampton Wanderers, and Derby County lifted the title. Leeds were runners-up for the third year in succession. They reached the FA Cup final again the following year and also reached the European Cup-Winners Cup final, losing to AC Milan in Salonika. Their victory at Wembley was sadly overshadowed by their numerous near misses.

Arsenal: Barnett, Rice, McNab, Storey, McLintock – capt, Simpson, Armstrong, Ball, George, Radford, Graham. sub: Kennedy (R) for Radford 80. manager: Bertie Mee

Leeds: Harvey, Reaney, Madeley, Bremner – capt, Charlton, Hunter, Lorimer, Clarke, Jones, Giles, Gray (E). sub: Bates (not used). manager: Don Revie

Schoolboy International

Saturday 20th May 1972

England 4-0
Trewick 16, Stronach (pen) 56, 65, Rostron 70

West Germany
67,000
Referee: L Bartels (Westcliff-on-Sea)

West Germany's heaviest defeat at Wembley.

Ray Wilkins went on to win 84 full international caps for England and scored at Wembley for Manchester United in the 1983 FA Cup final before collecting his winners medal after the replay.

The scorer of the first goal, John Trewick, was in the Oxford United side which won the Milk Cup at Wembley in 1986.

England: Danson, Ross, Pashley – capt, Corcoran, Sparrow, Wilkins, Cooper, Pimblett, Trewick, Stronach, Rostron. sub: Chalklin for Wilkins

BRITISH CHAMPIONSHIP

Tuesday 23rd May 1972

England 0-1 **Northern Ireland**
Neill 33

43,000
Referee: W Gow (Wales)

Northern Ireland had not beaten England since 1957 and had lost their last nine matches against them. They had, however, finished runners-up to England in the previous year's British Championship. Three days earlier, they had lost 2-0 to Scotland at Hampden Park while England were beating Wales 3-0 at Ninian Park as they chased their fifth successive title. Northern Ireland, therefore, had to win to retain their interest in the Championship. They had failed to qualify from a European Championship group won by the eventual finalists, the USSR.

The one goal came from a mistake by Shilton. He fumbled Hegan's corner and McMordie headed it down for player-manager Terry Neill to score. The Irish withstood all England's subsequent pressure and pulled off a shock victory.

By beating Scotland 1-0 at Hampden Park four days later England still managed to share the Championship. Northern Ireland failed to gain a share by only drawing 0-0 with Wales at the Racecourse Ground although they had been forced to play all their games away from home because of the troubles in the province. England beat them 2-1 at Goodison Park the following year.

England: Shilton (Leicester), Todd* (Derby County), Hughes (Liverpool), Storey (Arsenal), Lloyd (Liverpool), Hunter (Leeds), Summerbee (Man City), Bell (Man City) – capt, Macdonald (Newcastle), Marsh (Man City), Currie* (Sheffield U). subs: Peters (Tottenham) for Currie 58, Chivers (Tottenham) for Macdonald 69. manager: Sir Alf Ramsey
Northern Ireland: Jennings (Tottenham), Rice (Arsenal), Nelson (Arsenal), Neill (Hull City), Hunter (Ipswich), Clements (Sheffield W), Hegan (Wolves), McMordie (Middlesbrough), Dougan (Wolves) – capt, Irvine (Brighton), Jackson (Nottingham F). player-manager: Terry Neill
*first cap

Final table	P	W	D	L	F	A	Pts
England	3	2	0	1	4	1	4
Scotland	3	2	0	1	3	1	4
Northern Ireland	3	1	1	1	1	2	3
Wales	3	0	1	2	0	4	1

INTERNATIONAL

Wednesday 11th October 1972

England 1-1 **Yugoslavia**
Royle 40 Vladic 50
50,000
Referee: A Angonese (Italy)

Yugoslavia had lost on their last visit to Wembley in 1966 but two years later they had beaten England in the European Championship semi-finals in Florence. They had not qualified for a World Cup since 1962, but like England they had reached the recent European Championship quarter-finals, where they lost to the eventual finalists the USSR.

England opened the scoring when Chan-

non's cross fell to Ball who drew out the keeper before side-footing the ball to Joe Royle who blasted it past two defenders between him and the goal to give England the lead. The second half was only five minutes old when Yugoslavia drew level. From a centre by Petkovic, Bajevic headed it down for an unmarked Franjo Vladic, on his international debut, to head past Shilton.

They met again in Belgrade two years later, and honours were again even at 2-2. Yugoslavia were not to return to Wembley, though, until a European Championship pairing brought them in 1986. They reached the last eight of the 1974 World Cup where they failed to win a point in their second round group.

England: Shilton (Leicester), Mills* (Ipswich), Lampard* (West Ham), Storey (Arsenal), Blockley* (Arsenal), Moore (West Ham) – capt, Ball (Arsenal), Channon* (Southampton), Royle (Everton), Bell (Man City), Marsh (Man City). manager: Sir Alf Ramsey
*first cap

Yugoslavia: Maric (Velez Mostar), Krivokuca (Red Star Belgrade), Katalinski (Zeljeznicar), Paunovic (Partizan Belgrade), Pavlovic (Red Star), Stepanovic (OFK Belgrade), Acimovic (Red Star), Vladic (Velez Mostar), Petkovic (OFK), Bajevic (Velez Mostar), Dzajic (Red Star) – capt. subs: Holcer (Hajduk Split) for Katalinski 46, Rajkovic (Radnicki Nis) for Pavlovic 60. coach: Vujadin Boskov

Inter-Varsity Match

Wednesday 6th December 1972

Cambridge U 2
Hook, Powell

Oxford U 1
Glover

Cambridge were a goal down at half-time, but came back in an exciting match.

EEC Celebration Match

Wednesday 3rd January 1973

The Three 2
Jensen 47, Stein 69

The Six 0
36,500
Referee: N Burtenshaw (Great Yarmouth)

A match held to celebrate the entry of the United Kingdom, Republic of Ireland and Denmark (The Three) into the EEC. The existing six members were Belgium, France, the Netherlands, Italy, Luxembourg and West Germany.

Captaining The Three on his 50th and last appearance at Wembley, over a 20-year period, was Bobby Charlton. His 25 goals at the stadium made him the all-time top scorer. In 1994, he was knighted for his services to the game.

Dino Zoff, who came on as substitute for the second half, captained Italy to their third World Cup win in 1982 at the age of 40.

The Three: Jennings (Tottenham & N Ireland), Storey (Arsenal & England), Hughes (Liverpool & England), Bell (Manchester C & England), Hunter (Ipswich & N Ireland), Moore (West Ham & England), Lorimer (Leeds & Scotland), Giles (Leeds & Republic of Ireland), Stein (Coventry & Scotland), Charlton (Manchester U & England) – capt, Jensen (Borussia Monchengladbach & Denmark). subs: Ball (Arsenal & England) for Jensen 60, Olsen (Utrecht & Denmark) for Bell 74. coach: Sir Alf Ramsey (England)

The Six: Piot (Standard Liege & Belgium), Tresor (Olympique Marseille & France), Vogts (Borussia Monchengladbach & W Germany), Blankenburg (Ajax & Netherlands), Beckenbauer (Bayern Munich & W Germany), Neeskens (Ajax & Netherlands), Grabowski (Eintracht Frankfurt & W Germany), Van Hanegem (Feyenoord & Netherlands), Muller (Bayern Munich & W Germany), Netzer (Borussia Monchengladbach & W Germany) – capt, Bereta (Saint-Etienne & France). subs: Zoff (Juventus & Italy) for Piot 46, Suurbier (Ajax & Netherlands) for Tresor 46, Krol (Ajax & Netherlands) for Beckenbauer 46, Wimmer (Borussia Monchengladbach & W Germany) for Van Hanegem 46. coach: Helmut Schoen (W Germany)

WORLD CUP QUALIFYING

Wednesday 24th January 1973

England　　1-1　　**Wales**
Hunter 42　　Toshack 23
62,273
Referee: M Wright (Northern Ireland)

On their last visit, Wales had picked up their first ever British Championship point at Wembley, but had failed to score in the last two British Championships. They had already lost 1-0 to England at Ninian Park in the opening match of Group Five three months earlier. England were having to compete in a World Cup qualifying group for the first time in twelve years due to hosting and then being the holders.

Wales took a surprise lead. James whipped in a low cross and John Toshack slotted it past Clemence.

Three minutes before half-time Toshack's attempted clearance fell to Norman Hunter who scored only his second goal for England, ironically against his Leeds teammate Sprake, who had no chance as England drew level.

Welsh marking was to frustrate England in the second half and their finishing, once again, let them down. Wales' resurgence continued with a 2-0 win over Poland at Ninian Park two months later and they returned to Wembley for the British Championship two months after that.

Kevin Keegan, Footballer of the Year in 1976 and twice European Footballer of the Year, made his first Wembley appearance. His last was also the stadium's last, when he resigned as England's coach after losing to Germany in 2000.

England: Clemence (Liverpool), Storey (Arsenal), Hughes (Liverpool), Hunter (Leeds), McFarland (Derby County), Moore (West Ham) – capt, Keegan (Liverpool), Bell (Man City), Chivers (Tottenham), Marsh (Man City), Ball (Arsenal). manager: Sir Alf Ramsey

Wales: Sprake (Leeds), Rodrigues (Sheffield W), Thomas (Swindon), Hockey (Sheffield U), England (Tottenham) – capt, Roberts (Birmingham), Evans (Swansea), Mahoney (Stoke City), Toshack (Liverpool), Yorath (Leeds), James (Burnley). sub: Page (Birmingham) for Rodrigues. manager: Dave Bowen

FOOTBALL LEAGUE CUP FINAL

Saturday 3rd March 1973

Norwich City	0-1	Tottenham Hotspur
		Coates 72

100,000
Referee: D Smith (Gloucestershire)

Both sides were aiming to become the first club to win the trophy twice. Norwich had won the League Cup in its second season in 1962 when they were in the Second Division. They convincingly beat Rochdale 4-0 on aggregate. This was their first appearance at Wembley. In the semi-finals they had defeated the previous year's finalists Chelsea. Tottenham, the UEFA Cup holders, were attempting to regain the League Cup for the second time in three years, having won it for the first time in 1971. In the quarter-finals they had beaten the eventual League Champions Liverpool.

Norwich had won the Second Division Championship the previous year but were struggling in their first ever season in the First Division. Tottenham had reached the UEFA Cup quarter-finals again in their attempt to retain the trophy.

A poor match was settled in the second half when a clearance from Cross fell to Ralph Coates, a first-half substitute, on the edge of the area. His first-time shot found the corner past Keelan's despairing dive.

Norwich finished 20th, in the First Division, escaping relegation by two points. It was only a stay of execution, however. They finished bottom a year later and were relegated.

They also reached the League Cup semi-finals again. But they were promoted straight back in 1975 and reached the League Cup final for the second time in three years. Tottenham finished eighth and reached the UEFA Cup semi-finals before losing on away goals to the eventual winners Liverpool. A year later, they reached the UEFA Cup final again, losing to Feyenoord on aggregate. After a short stay in the Second Division they reached the FA Cup final in 1981.

Norwich: Keelan, Payne, Butler, Stringer, Forbes – capt, Briggs, Livermore, Blair, Cross, Paddon, Anderson. sub: Howard for Blair. manager: Ron Saunders

Tottenham: Jennings, Kinnear, Knowles, Pratt, England, Beal, Gilzean, Perryman, Chivers, Peters – capt, Pearce. sub: Coates for Pratt. manager: Bill Nicholson

Schoolboy International

Saturday 7th April 1973

England 3
Scanlan Pen, Penny 2
Netherlands 1
Jansen
52,000

Slight improvement by the Dutch on their first visit two years earlier.

Alan Curbishley played at Wembley only as a schoolboy, but was manager of Charlton Athletic when they won promotion to the Premiership at Wembley in 1998 against Sunderland after one of the greatest ever promotion play-off finals.

England: Fletcher, Wade, Scott, Bradley, Higgins, Curbishley, Botham, Scanlan – capt, Langley, Storey, Penny. sub: McLean for Botham 68, Ellis for Fletcher

FA Amateur Cup Final

Saturday 14th April 1973

Slough Town 0
Walton And Hersham 1
Connell 87
41,000
Referee: H New (Bristol)

Roger Connell's late winner against his old club gave Walton the cup in their first final. They had not conceded a goal in the whole competition (eight games).

Twenty years later Walton's captain Dave Bassett took Sheffield United to Wembley as manager for the FA Cup Semi-final.

Slough: Wolstenholme, Reid , Eaton, Mead, D'Arcy, Reardon, Day, Gaine, Chatterton, O'Sullivan, Anthony. sub: Jamieson for D'Arcy
Walton: Teale, Thomas, Lambert, Donaldson, Edwards, Bassett – capt, Woffinden, Smith, Connell, Somers, Morris. sub: Foskett (not used)

FA Trophy Final

Saturday 28th April 1973

Scarborough 2
Leask 12, Thompson 116
Wigan Athletic 1
Rogers 89
after extra time
24,000
Referee: H Hackney (Sheffield and Hallamshire)

Scarborough won the Trophy for the first time on the 50th anniversary of Wembley's first event.

Scarborough: Garrow, Appleton, Shoulder – capt, Dunn (H), Siddle, Fagan, Donoghue, Franks, Leask, Thompson, Hewitt. sub: Barmby for Leask
Wigan: Reeves, Morris, Sutherland, Taylor, Jackson – capt, Gillibrand, Clements, Oates, Rogers, King, Worswick. sub: McCunnell for Oates

FA CUP FINAL

Saturday 5th May 1973

Leeds United   0-1   Sunderland
Porterfield 32

100,000
Referee: K Burns (Stourbridge)

Leeds, the holders, were appearing in their third final in four years. The previous year had seen their first FA Cup win. Sunderland's only previous Wembley visit was in winning the FA Cup for the first time in 1937. It had been 42 years since a Second Division club had won the trophy (West Bromwich Albion), but in the semi-finals, Sunderland had prevented Arsenal from becoming the first club to reach three consecutive Wembley FA Cup finals.

Leeds finished third in the First Division, incredibly their lowest position in five years. They had also reached the final of the European Cup-Winners Cup. Sunderland finished sixth in the Second Division in their third season since relegation. They had begun badly, but new manager, Bob Stokoe had revitalised the team.

Very few outside Sunderland dared to predict an upset. Leeds were overwhelming favourites but then Sunderland went ahead. Hughes' corner fell to Halom, who knocked it forward. Ian Porterfield controlled it with his knee and had time to turn and blast it over Harvey's head into the roof of the net.

Leeds fought back, but were up against a Sunderland team which defended magnificently. The most memorable moment came 20 minutes from the end, when Jim Montgomery saved from Cherry and left Lorimer with an open goal. With an amazing display of agility, the goalkeeper managed to throw himself from his prone position to deflect Lorimer's shot onto the underside of the bar and out again. Leeds' players stared in disbelief and this save more than the goal convinced them that it was not going to be their day. Sunderland had pulled off possibly the biggest shock in the history of the FA Cup.

Eleven days later Leeds lost the European Cup-Winners Cup final in suspicious circumstances to AC Milan in Salonika. There were allegations that the Greek referee had been bribed. It was the ninth time in nine years that Leeds had finished runners-up in a major competition. One of their great traits, however, was their powers of recovery and the following season they set a new league record of 29 games unbeaten from the start of the season. This time they went on to win the League Championship for the second time. They returned for Wembley's first FA Charity Shield. Sunderland went out in the last 16 of the following season's European Cup-Winners Cup to Sporting Lisbon and it was not until 1976 that they won the Second Division Championship to return to the top flight. They were back at Wembley for the Milk Cup final in 1985.

Leeds: Harvey, Reaney, Cherry, Bremner – capt, Madeley, Hunter, Lorimer, Clarke, Jones, Giles, Gray (E). sub: Yorath for Gray 78. manager: Don Revie

Sunderland: Montgomery, Malone, Guthrie, Horswill, Watson, Pitt, Kerr – capt, Hughes, Halom, Porterfield, Tueart. sub: Young (not used). manager: Bob Stokoe

BRITISH CHAMPIONSHIP

Tuesday 15th May 1973

England	**3-0**	**Wales**

Chivers 23, Channon 30, Peters 67
38,000
Referee: J Paterson (Scotland)

Wales had drawn on their two previous visits but had not scored in the last two British Championships. Three days earlier they had lost 2-0 to Scotland at the Racecourse Ground while England were beating Northern Ireland 2-1 at Goodison Park, thus beginning their bid to win their sixth successive British Championship. Wales had to win to maintain their interest. It was the fourth meeting between the two in the past year. Their World Cup qualifying group was to be decided by their forthcoming matches with Poland.

This was a comfortable win. First, a Channon header gave Martin Chivers the chance to volley the opening goal for England. Seven minutes later, Mike Channon took a pass from Ball, beat Roberts and Thomas, and fired past Phillips in the Welsh goal. Martin Peters scored the third midway through the second half, taking Channon's pass and firing home from just outside the area. It was England's first win in six games at Wembley but they would have swapped it for an extra World Cup point from their meeting four months earlier.

Scotland lost at home to Northern Ireland the following night, leaving England needing only a point against them to win the Championship outright. Wales' goal drought continued as they finished bottom again without a point and a 3-0 defeat in Chorzow by Poland four months later put them out of the World Cup.

England: Shilton (Leicester), Storey (Arsenal), Hughes (Liverpool), Bell (Man City), McFarland (Derby County), Moore (West Ham) – capt, Ball (Arsenal), Channon (Southampton), Chivers (Tottenham), Clarke (Leeds), Peters (Tottenham). manager: Sir Alf Ramsey

Wales: Phillips* (Chelsea), Rodrigues (Sheffield W), Thomas (Swindon), Hockey (Sheffield U), England (Tottenham) – capt, Roberts (J) (Birmingham), James (Burnley), Mahoney (Stoke City), Toshack (Liverpool), Page (Birmingham), Evans (Swansea). subs: Roberts (D) (Oxford) for England, Emanuel* **(Bristol C)** for Page. manager: Dave Bowen
*first cap

BRITISH CHAMPIONSHIP

Saturday 19th May 1973

England   **1-0**   **Scotland**
Peters 54
95,950
Referee: K Tschenscher (West Germany)

Scotland had lost on their last two visits and had also been thrashed 5-0 by England in the Scottish FA Centenary match at Hampden Park three months earlier. Their 2-1 defeat at Hampden Park by Northern Ireland three days earlier meant they had to win to retain the Championship.

England, who were also defending the title, needed only a point to win it outright in their third home game of the Championship. Scotland were battling with Czechoslovakia for a place in the following year's World Cup.

Peter Shilton was in top form, keeping out many Scottish attacks and ten minutes after half-time it was England who scored. From Ball's free kick, Martin Peters appeared unmarked at the far post to head the only goal past Hunter.

Scotland qualified for the World Cup for the first time since 1958 and beat England for the first time in seven years at Hampden Park a year later.

In the World Cup in Germany they went out in the first round on goal difference despite remaining unbeaten. Although they held the reigning champions Brazil to a goalless draw in Frankfurt they were punished for an inadequate 2-0 victory over minnows Zaire in Dortmund. They suffered their fourth successive defeat at Wembley in 1975.

This was Kenny Dalglish's first appearance at Wembley. Twice Footballer of the Year he scored the only goal of the 1978 European Cup final for Liverpool at Wembley. Dalglish won a record 102 Scotland caps and as player-manager of Liverpool led them to the League Championship and FA Cup 'double' in 1986.

England: Shilton (Leicester), Storey (Arsenal), Hughes (Liverpool), Bell (Man City), McFarland (Derby County), Moore (West Ham) – capt, Ball (Arsenal), Channon (Southampton), Chivers (Tottenham), Clarke (Leeds), Peters (Tottenham). manager: Sir Alf Ramsey
Scotland: Hunter (Celtic), Jardine (Rangers), McGrain (Celtic), Bremner (Leeds) – capt, Holton (Man Utd), Johnstone (Rangers), Morgan (Man Utd), Macari (Man Utd), Dalglish (Celtic), Hay (Celtic), Lorimer (Leeds). subs: Jordan* (Leeds) for Macari 74, Stein (Coventry) for Lorimer 80. manager: Willie Ormond
*first cap

Final table	P	W	D	L	F	A	Pts
England	3	3	0	0	6	1	6
Northern Ireland	3	2	0	1	4	3	4
Scotland	3	1	0	2	3	3	2
Wales	3	0	0	3	0	6	0

Schoolboy International

Saturday 9th June 1973

England 2
Bradley, Storey

Scotland 4
Brown 2, Henderson, McCluskey 32,500

England were well beaten as they conceded four at Wembley for the first time. This was the first Schoolboy International to be shown live on television, bringing the potential stars of the future to an audience of millions. Its success prompted ITV to broadcast at least one international each season for over 20 years.

England: Ellis, Wade, Scott, Bradley, Higgins, Curbishley, McLean, Scanlan – capt, Langley, Storey, Penny. sub: Holman
Scotland: Lorimer, Brogan, Jamieson, Boyd – capt, Mowat, Carroll, Casey, Brown, McCluskey, Henderson, Ross. sub: Robertson for McCluskey

INTERNATIONAL

Wednesday 26th September 1973

England   **7-0**   **Austria**

Channon 8, 48, Clarke 28, 43
Chivers 61, Currie 64, Bell 87
48,000
Referee: C Corver (Netherlands)

Austria had won on their last visit in 1965 but England had beaten them 1-0 in Vienna two years later. They had not qualified for the World Cup since 1962 and had finished runners-up to reigning champions Italy in their recent European Championship group.

In the World Cup they had completed their qualifying matches and were top of their group but had let Sweden in with a chance four months earlier by losing to them in Gothenburg. Sweden now had only to beat Malta by two clear goals in Valletta to pip Austria on goal difference. England, the British Champions, were also in danger of not qualifying for the World Cup after losing to Poland in Chorzow three months earlier.

The rout started early. In the ninth minute, from Peters' cross, Chivers headed the ball down and it went in off the heel of Mike Channon. Just before the half hour England were two up. Currie crossed to Allan Clarke, who sent Sara one way, went the other and gave Koncilia no chance with a fine shot. He scored again two minutes before half-time. From Bell's cross Koncilia saved from Clarke who followed up his own shot to give England a three-goal lead at the interval. Clarke almost notched his hat-trick in the third minute of the second half. Again the goalkeeper could not hold his shot, but Channon tapped in his second after the ball hit the post. Martin Chivers scored a simple fifth after an hour from Currie's low centre. Tony Currie got the next himself, controlling the ball on his chest from Channon's nod down and finding the corner with his shot. The rout was completed when Colin Bell found himself on the end of a move involving the four previous scorers.

This result fired England with confidence for their forthcoming World Cup qualifying match with Poland. Sweden could only win 2-1 in Malta and so had to play-off with Austria in Gelsenkirchen, for a chance to return to Germany the following year. The Austrians failed to take advantage of their reprieve and lost 2-1. They did, however, qualify for the 1978 World Cup, reaching the last eight. In 1979, they beat England 4-3 in Vienna but never played at the old Wembley again.

England: Shilton (Leicester), Madeley (Leeds), Hughes (Liverpool), Bell (Man City), McFarland (Derby County), Hunter (Leeds), Currie (Sheffield U), Channon (Southampton), Chivers (Tottenham), Clarke (Leeds), Peters (Tottenham) – capt. manager: Sir Alf Ramsey
Austria: Koncilia (Wacker Innsbruck), Sara (FK Austria Vienna), Krieger (FK Austria), Schmidradner (Kickers Offenbach), Eigenstiller (Wacker Innsbruck) – capt, Hattenberger (Wacker Innsbruck), Starek (Rapid Vienna), Krankl (Rapid), Kreuz (Sparta Rotterdam), Ettmayer (Stuttgart), Jara (Valencia). subs: Gombasch (Wacker Innsbruck) for Hattenberger 46, Kreiss (Wacker Innsbruck) for Eigenstiller 67. coach: Leopold Stastny

WORLD CUP QUALIFYING

Wednesday 17th October 1973

England   **1-1**   **Poland**

Clarke pen 63   Domarski 55
100,000
Referee: V Loraux (Belgium)

Poland, the Olympic Champions, were visiting Wembley for the first time. Their only previous trip to England had earned them a 1-1 draw at Goodison Park in 1966. Six months later they had lost 1-0 to England in Chorzow but had beaten them 2-0 at the same venue four months before the Wembley meeting. Thus they needed only a point to qualify for the World Cup for the first time since 1938. In the recent European

Championship they had finished runners-up in their group to the eventual winners West Germany. England had to win to top Group Five. They had never failed to qualify for a World Cup since entering for the first time in 1950.

This was a most extraordinary match. England dominated the game from start to finish. Poland's goalkeeper Jan Tomaszewski made save after save to deny them. Many of them were desperate blocks, but England were so unfortunate not to break through. Ten minutes into the second half England were caught out by a counter attack. Hunter lost the ball to Lato who played it across to Jan Domarski who shot through Hughes' legs and under Shilton's dive to stun the home supporters. England finally broke through eight minutes later. Peters was brought down by Musial and Allan Clarke at last beat Tomaszewski from the spot. England now had less than half an hour to score again. Once again they bombarded the Polish goal but unbelievably the defence kept them out with scrambled goal-line clearances and there were agonisingly close near misses. At the final whistle England's players were devastated and the nation was stunned while Poland were celebrating their incredible achievement.

Whereas the 1966 World Cup win had earned England manager Alf Ramsey a knighthood, this result was to cost him his job. The sad irony was that England had played brilliantly and luck had been against them. But they were not to qualify for another World Cup until 1982. Poland's confidence soared after this result. They went on to finish third in Germany, losing only to the host nation and eventual winners by 1-0 in Frankfurt. Tomaszewski saved two penalties in the tournament. They reached the Olympic final again in 1976 and were regular World Cup qualifiers until their next visit to Wembley in 1989.

England: Shilton (Leicester), Madeley (Leeds), Hughes (Liverpool), Bell (Man City), McFarland (Derby County), Hunter (Leeds), Currie (Sheffield U), Channon (Southampton), Chivers (Tottenham), Clarke (Leeds), Peters (Tottenham) – capt. sub: Hector* (Derby County) for Chivers 88. manager: Sir Alf Ramsey
*first cap
Poland: Tomaszewski (Lodz), Gorgon (Gornik Zabrze), Szymanowski (Wisla Krakow), Bulzacki (Lodz), Musial (Wisla Krakow), Kasperczak (Stal Mielec), Deyna (Legia Warsaw) – capt, Cmikiewicz (Legia Warsaw), Lato (Stal Mielec), Domarski (Stal Mielec), Gadocha (Legia Warsaw). coach: Kazimierz Gorski

Final table	P	W	D	L	F	A	Pts
Poland	4	2	1	1	6	3	5
England	4	1	2	1	3	4	4
Wales	4	1	1	2	3	5	3

European Amateur Championship
Qualifying

Wednesday 31st October 1973

England 1
Searle 66

West Germany 0
3,200

Substitute, Keith Searle came on to score the only goal in Wembley's last amateur international, to secure England's first win against the Germans, at amateur level, for 60 years. England lost the return 3-1 in Bielefeld, five months later. West Germany won the group on goal difference from England and qualified for the final tournament, in Rijeka, the following year. In the semi-final, they defeated the Netherlands on penalties, after extra time, but the final against the hosts, Yugoslavia, was postponed because the pitch was unplayable. The Championship was shared between them.

England: Swannell (Hendon), Deadman (Hendon), Powell (Sutton), Preston (Kingstonian), Eaton (Enfield), Pritchard (Wycombe), Bass (Bishop's Stortford), Haider (Hendon), Smith (Walton and Hersham), Day (Enfield), Butterfield (Enfield). sub: Searle (Enfield) for Butterfield 46. manager: Charles Hughes
West Germany: Wienhold, Baltes, Traser (E), Traser (H), Schmitt, Koerbel, Kraus, Kalb, Hammes, Krause, Schneider. subs: Koestner for Hammes 46, Mueller for Krause 46

INTERNATIONAL

Wednesday 14th November 1973

England   **0-1**   **Italy**
Capello 86

88,000
Referee: F Lobo (Portugal)

Italy had drawn on their only previous visit to Wembley, but they had beaten England at the ninth attempt by 2-0 in Turin five months earlier. The Italians had reached the 1970 World Cup final before going down 4-1 to the mighty Brazilians in Mexico City and they had won their recent qualifying group without conceding a goal. Dino Zoff was unbeaten in Italy's last nine matches. The previous year they had reached the European Championship quarter-finals, before losing on aggregate to Belgium. This was England's first match since their devastating World Cup elimination.

Once again, England could not break down the opposition's defence and as against Poland they were caught out by a breakaway goal. With just four minutes remaining, Moore, winning his record 108th and last England cap, was beaten for pace by Chinaglia whose low drive was parried by Shilton. Fabio Capello netted the rebound to give Italy their first victory at Wembley.

After two more clean sheets, Zoff was finally beaten in the following year's World Cup by underdogs, Haiti. Italy won the match 3-1 but were eliminated in the first round on goal difference by Argentina after losing to England's conquerors Poland.

They failed to qualify for the 1976 European Championship quarter-finals from a tough group involving the Netherlands and Poland and then stood in England's way to qualification for the 1978 World Cup.

England: Shilton (Leicester), Madeley (Leeds), Hughes (Liverpool), Bell (Man City), McFarland (Derby County), Moore (West Ham) – capt, Currie (Sheffield U), Channon (Southampton), Osgood (Chelsea), Clarke (Leeds), Peters (Tottenham). sub: Hector (Derby County) for Clarke 74. manager: Sir Alf Ramsey
Italy: Zoff (Juventus), Spinosi (Juventus), Facchetti (Internazionale) – capt, Benetti (AC Milan), Bellugi (Internazionale), Burgnich (Internazionale), Causio (Juventus), Capello (Juventus), Chinaglia (Lazio), Rivera (AC Milan), Riva (Cagliari). coach: Feruccio Valcareggi

Inter-Varsity Match

Wednesday 5th December 1973

Cambridge U 0
Oxford U 0

The second goalless draw in three years.

FOOTBALL LEAGUE CUP FINAL

Saturday 2nd March 1974

Manchester City   **1-2**   **Wolverhampton Wanderers**
Bell 60   Hibbitt 43, Richards 85
100,000
Referee: E Wallace (Crewe)

City had won the League Cup once, in 1970. Wolves had reached the semi-finals for the first time the previous year taking the eventual winners Tottenham Hotspur, to extra time in the second leg. This time they had beaten the previous year's other finalists Norwich City in the semi-finals, after knocking out Liverpool (who went on to win the FA Cup) in the quarter-finals. Having also reached the FA Cup semi-finals the previous year and the UEFA Cup final in 1972 Wolves were gaining a reputation of nearly men. Their previous Wembley appearance had been back in 1960 when they had won the FA Cup.

For both sides this was their last chance

to win something in the current season. Wolves had gone out in the last 32 of the UEFA Cup on away goals to Lokomotive Leipzig after bravely pulling back a three-goal deficit from the first leg in Germany.

Wolves went ahead two minutes before half-time. Palmer's cross reached Kenny Hibbitt who gave MacRae no chance with his strike. City's feared strike force began to hit form in search of an equaliser, but Gary Pierce in the Wolves goal was performing heroically. He was beaten on the hour, however, after great skill by Marsh out on the wing. It ended with a perfect cross which eluded all the Wolves defenders and found Colin Bell with only the

'keeper to beat. City were level and had the upper hand. Yet Pierce kept them out and with five minutes left Sunderland's cross hit Marsh on the heel and fell perfectly for John Richards to fire home the winner.

City finished 14th, in the First Division, their lowest position for seven years, but they were back to win the League Cup two years later.

Wolves finished a point and two places above City. In the following season's UEFA Cup they went out in the first round to Porto and in 1976 they were relegated to the Second Division. But they came straight back as Champions and won the League Cup again in 1980.

Manchester C: MacRae, Pardoe, Donachie, Doyle, Booth, Towers, Summerbee – capt, Bell, Lee, Law, Marsh. sub: Carrodus (not used). manager: Ron Saunders
Wolves: Pierce, Palmer, Parkin, Bailey – capt, Munro, McAlle, Sunderland, Hibbitt, Richards, Dougan, Wagstaffe. sub: Powell for Wagstaffe. manager: Bill McGarry

Schoolboy International

Saturday 6th April 1974

England 5
Mabbutt 2, 24, Coyne 17, 60, 87
France 2
Remy 18, 33
42,000

Kevin Mabbutt's first goal went in off the goalkeeper Daviau's back as the ball rebounded from the bar. With Peter Coyne scoring a hat-trick, France were well beaten in the end on their first visit to Wembley.

Kenny Sansom went on to win 86 full international caps for England and captained Arsenal to their 1987 Littlewoods Cup success at Wembley.

England: New, Haverson, Sansom, Clark, Higgins – capt, Savill, Coyne, Patching, Bailey, Mabbutt, Hale. sub: Deakin for Hale 41

FA Amateur Cup Final

Saturday 20th April 1974

Bishop's Stortford 4
Lawrence, Murphy, Leakey, Smith pen
Ilford 1
Drabwell
30,500
Referee: D Turner (Cannock)

After 80 years, the last FA Amateur Cup was won by Bishop's Stortford in their

first and only final. It was a great celebration for their centenary year and for their manager Ted Hardy who had been on the wrong end of two final thrashings while in charge of Dagenham. Amateur clubs could no longer sustain a competition of their own. The following season would see a new competition, the FA Vase, for smaller clubs.

Bishop's Stortford: Moore, Gibson, Coombes, Lawrence – capt, Still, Payne, Leakey, Dear, Bass, Smith, Murphy. sub: Scott (not used)
Ilford: James, Bowhill, Bennett, Betson – capt, Anderson, Day, Bookman, Butterfield, Drabwell, McDermid, Turley. sub: Guiver for Day 13

FA Trophy Final

Saturday 27th April 1974

Dartford 1
Cunningham 90
Morecambe 2
Richmond 18, Sutton 21
19,000
Referee: J Homewood (Sunbury-on-Thames)

Dartford: Morton, Read , Payne, Carr, Burns – capt, Binks, Light, Glozier, Robinson, Cunningham, Halliday. sub: Hearne for Robinson
Morecambe: Coates, Pearson, Bennett, Sutton, Street, Baldwin – capt, Done, Webber, Roberts, Kershaw, Richmond. sub: Galley for Roberts 67

FA CUP FINAL

Saturday 4th May 1974

Liverpool	**3-0**	**Newcastle United**

Keegan 57, 88, Heighway 74
100,000
Referee: G Kew (Amersham)

Liverpool's only FA Cup win had been in 1965, but they had lost the 1971 final in extra time and had gone on to win a League Championship and UEFA Cup 'double', in 1973. Newcastle had not appeared at Wembley since their three FA Cup wins in five years in the 1950's, but they were unbeaten at the stadium and were aiming to equal Aston Villa's record seven FA Cup wins.

In their defence of the League Championship, Liverpool finished runners-up to Leeds, their ninth successive season in the top five. They were disappointing in the European Cup, however, losing both legs to Red Star Belgrade in the last 16. They also reached the quarter-finals of the Football League Cup before losing to the eventual winners Wolverhampton Wanderers. Newcastle finished 15th, in the First Division, their lowest position for seven years, and escaped relegation by only two points.

Liverpool could not score until the second half but then Hall ducked underneath Smith's cross and the ball fell for Kevin Keegan to tee it up and then fire past McFaul. Liverpool's second settled it. From Clemence's kick, Toshack's back-header

was picked up by Steve Heighway who ran on to notch the second with an expert finish. With two minutes left, the demoralised Newcastle side were ripped apart for the final time as Liverpool put on an exhibition display of 11 consecutive passes around the pitch culminating in Smith's low cross which eluded McFaul and left Keegan to tap in his second.

Liverpool's great manager Bill Shankly retired after leading them out for the FA Charity Shield at Wembley three months later. Incredibly, his successor Bob Paisley was to surpass his achievements although in the following season's European Cup-Winners Cup they went out in the last 16 to Ferencvaros on away goals. Newcastle were back at Wembley two years later for their first Football League Cup final.

Terry McDermott joined Liverpool, six months later and in 1980 was Footballer of the Year. He also scored for the Reds at Wembley in successive Charity Shields.

Alan Kennedy also signed for Liverpool, in 1978 and has the distinction of twice scoring European Cup winning goals for them, as well as a couple of League Cup final goals at Wembley.

Liverpool: Clemence, Smith, Lindsay, Thompson (PB), Cormack, Hughes (E) – capt, Keegan, Hall, Heighway, Toshack, Callaghan. sub: Lawler (not used). manager: Bill Shankly
Newcastle: McFaul, Clark, Kennedy, McDermott, Howard, Moncur – capt, Smith, Cassidy, Macdonald, Tudor, Hibbitt. sub: Gibb for Smith 70. manager: Joe Harvey

BRITISH CHAMPIONSHIP

Wednesday 15th May 1974

England	**1-0**	**Northern Ireland**

Weller 73
45,500
Referee: R Davidson (Scotland)

Northern Ireland had won on their previous Wembley visit, but had lost 2-1 to England at Goodison Park in 1973.

England had gone on to claim their sixth successive British Championship with Northern Ireland finishing runners-up for the second time in three years. Four days

earlier, the Irish had beaten Scotland 1-0 at Hampden Park while England had defeated Wales 2-0 at Ninian Park in Joe Mercer's first match as caretaker-manager following the sacking of Sir Alf Ramsey. This meant that victory for either side would give them at least a share of the title.

1974

It had been ten years since Northern Ireland had achieved that feat. Like England, they had failed to qualify for the World Cup but because of the troubles in Northern Ireland, they had been forced to play all their home games in England.

England finally found a way past Jennings. Channon crossed, substitute Worthington headed it back and Keith Weller nodded it past the Irish 'keeper for the only goal of the game.

Three days later, England went down to two own goals against Scotland at Hampden Park and had to share the title with them. Northern Ireland failed to gain a share when they conceded Wales' first British Championship goal for four years, at the Racecourse Ground.

England: Shilton (Leicester), Nish (Derby County), Pejic (Stoke City), Hughes (Liverpool) – capt, McFarland (Derby County), Todd (Derby County), Keegan (Liverpool), Weller (Leicester), Channon (Southampton), Bell (Man City), Bowles (QPR). subs: Hunter (Leeds) for McFarland 36, Worthington* (Leicester) for Bowles 55. caretaker-manager: Joe Mercer
Northern Ireland: Jennings (Tottenham), Rice (Arsenal), Nelson (Arsenal), O'Kane (Nottingham F), Hunter (Ipswich), Clements (Everton) – capt, Hamilton (Ipswich), Cassidy (Newcastle), Morgan (Aston Villa), McIlroy (Man Utd), McGrath (Tottenham). subs: Jackson (Nottingham F) for Nelson, O'Neill (Nottingham F) for Hamilton. manager: Terry Neill
*first cap

Final table	P	W	D	L	F	A	Pts
England	3	2	0	1	3	2	4
Scotland	3	2	0	1	4	1	4
Northern Ireland	3	1	0	2	1	2	2
Wales	3	1	0	2	1	4	2

INTERNATIONAL

Wednesday 22nd May 1974

England   **2-2**   **Argentina**
Channon 44, Worthington 53   Kempes 57, (pen) 89
68,000
Referee: A Ithurralde (Argentina)

This was their first meeting since the infamous World Cup Quarter-final of 1966, the Argentinians' second defeat at Wembley, and they were allowed to have a referee from their own country to prevent any feelings of injustice. Argentina had not won the South American Championship since 1959, but had qualified for their first World Cup since 1966 fairly comfortably.

Just before the interval, Mike Channon gave England the lead, from a pass by Bell. Eight minutes after half-time it was 2-0. Bell's shot struck the bar and Frank Worthington netted from the rebound. But four minutes later the visitors were back in the game. Hughes deflected Ayala's cross to Mario Kempes who shot past Shilton. England looked as if they would hold on, but with a minute left, Kempes was fouled by Hughes and drove home the penalty himself to rescue the draw. Unfortunately, it had been another bad-tempered clash between the two and unlikely to improve relations.

In 1978 Argentina won the World Cup in their own country, beating the Netherlands in the final. They drew 1-1 with England in Buenos Aires in 1977, and came to Wembley as World Champions in 1980.

Mario Kempes, Argentina's two-goal hero, scored twice in the 1978 World Cup final to win the trophy for his country.

England: Shilton (Leicester), Hughes (Liverpool) – capt, Lindsay* (Liverpool), Todd (Derby County), Watson (Sunderland), Bell (Man City), Keegan (Liverpool), Channon (Southampton), Worthington (Leicester), Weller (Leicester), Brooking (West Ham). caretaker-manager: Joe Mercer
*first cap
Argentina: Carnevali (Las Palmas), Perfumo (Cruzeiro) – capt, Sa (Independiente), Glaria (San Lorenzo), Telch (San Lorenzo), Bargas (Nantes), Balbuena (Independiente), Brindisi (Huracan), Kempes (Rosario Central), Squeo (Racing Club), Ayala (Atletico Madrid). subs: Wolff (River Plate) for Glaria 46, Houseman (Huracan) for Brindisi 67. coach: Vladislao Cap

149

Schoolboy International

Saturday 1st June 1974

England 4
Coyne 36, 56, 58, Mabbutt 69
West Germany 0
40,000
Referee: J Hudson (Lincolnshire)

Although the West German national team were European Champions and about to win the World Cup their Schoolboys suffered a third successive thrashing at Wembley as Peter Coyne scored his second Wembley hat-trick.

England: New, Kingston, Sansom, Clark, Higgins – capt, Savill, Coyne, Patching, Bailey, Mabbutt, Gardner. sub: Deakin for Sansom 77

NABC Cup Final

Sunday 9th June 1974

Plymouth 3
Horrocks 6, Snelson 15, Mallett 90
Sheffield 1
Morris 76
10,000
Referee: J.Homewood (Sunbury-on-Thames)

Wembley's first cup final to be played on a Sunday was won by the Devonport Dockyard Apprentices Association, who proved too strong for Sheffield's Christ Church Youth Club. Switching the final to Wembley elevated the status of this competition together with live television coverage of the second half.

FA CHARITY SHIELD

Saturday 10th August 1974

Leeds United	**1-1**	**Liverpool**
Cherry 70		Boersma 19

Liverpool won 6-5 on penalties
(Lorimer 1-0, Lindsay 1-1, Giles 2-1, Hughes 2-2, Gray 3-2, Hall 3-3, Hunter 4-3, Smith 4-4, Cherry 5-4, Cormack 5-5, Harvey missed, Callaghan 5-6)
67,000
Referee: R Matthewson (Bolton)

After three FA Charity Shields, in which the League Champions and FA Cup holders had declined to appear, the match was switched to Wembley and promptly rekindled interest. Leeds had lost the previous year's FA Cup final on their last visit, but had started the season with a record 29-match unbeaten run in the league.

After a late stumble, they had won the League Championship by five points from runners-up Liverpool. Their only previous Charity Shield had seen them beat Manchester City in 1969. Liverpool had received compensation for losing the league title by winning the FA Cup three months earlier. They had won the Charity Shield only once outright, beating Everton in 1966. The teams had met before at Wembley, in the 1965 FA Cup final. Both clubs had surprisingly lost their managers in the close season. Don Revie had left Leeds to take over England, while Bill Shankly had retired, although he led the team out at Wembley.

Liverpool went ahead when Harvey fumbled Keegan's cross and Phil Boersma scrambled the ball over the line. The match was marred by a flare-up after an hour. Billy Bremner, the Leeds captain, and Kevin Keegan were sent off for fighting, the first British players to be dismissed at Wembley.

Leeds fought back and equalised, Trevor Cherry outjumping Thompson to head in from Lorimer's through ball, and the stadium saw its first penalty shoot-out. Leeds' goalkeeper, Harvey stepped up and shot wide leaving Ian Callaghan to beat Harvey and secure the Shield for Liverpool.

Liverpool won the FA Charity Shield again two years later and the teams met again in the Charity Shield in 1992.

Leeds: Harvey, Reaney, Cherry, Bremner – capt, McQueen, Hunter, Lorimer, Clarke, Jordan, Giles, Gray (E). sub: McKenzie for Clarke. manager: Brian Clough
Liverpool: Clemence, Smith, Lindsay, Thompson (P B), Cormack, Hughes (E) – capt, Keegan, Hall, Heighway, Boersma, Callaghan. manager: Bob Paisley

EUROPEAN CHAMPIONSHIP QUALIFYING

Wednesday 30th October 1974

England　　　　　**3-0**　　　**Czechoslovakia**
Channon 72, Bell 80, 83
83,858
Referee: M Kitabdjian (France)

Czechoslovakia had prevented England from scoring in their only previous Wembley appearance in 1966. England had beaten them in the 1970 World Cup in Guadalajara and 1973 had seen a 1-1 draw in Prague. They had reached the semi-finals of the first European Championship in 1960, but, like England, had failed to qualify for the recent World Cup, finishing runners-up in their qualifying group to Scotland. This was the opening match in Group One and England's first under new manager, Don Revie.

England, in their new red, white and blue kit, created several chances, but the Czechs held out until a cross from substitute Thomas was met with a superb header from Mike Channon. Viktor was rooted to the spot as the ball flew past him. Eight minutes later, Channon split the Czech defence and Colin Bell stretched to stab the ball past Viktor for the second. Within three minutes, Channon had crossed for Bell to rise above the defence and score again. After holding out for so long the Czechs had crumbled.

Following such a convincing victory, it was difficult to believe that Czechoslovakia would go on to win the European Championship, two years later after beating England 2-1 in the return in Bratislava, the following year. In the final, they beat West Germany, the reigning World and European Champions, on penalties in Belgrade. Yet Scotland, once again, prevented them from qualifying for the World Cup, in 1978. Later that year, the European Champions returned to Wembley.

England: Clemence (Liverpool), Madeley (Leeds), Hughes (Liverpool) – capt, Dobson (Everton), Watson (Sunderland), Hunter (Leeds), Bell (Man City), Francis* (QPR), Worthington (Leicester), Channon (Southampton), Keegan (Liverpool). subs: Brooking (West Ham) for Dobson 64, Thomas* (QPR) for Worthington 64. manager: Don Revie
*first cap
Czechoslovakia: Viktor (Dukla Prague), Pivarnik (Slovan Bratislava) – capt, Capkovic (Slovan Bratislava), Ondrus (Slovan Bratislava), Varadin (Spartak Trnava), Bicovsky (Union Teplice), Pekarik (Slovan Bratislava), Gajdusek (Dukla Prague), Masny (Slovan Bratislava), Svehlik (Slovan Bratislava), Stratil (Union Teplice). subs: Vojacek (Banik Ostrava) for Capkovic 64, Kuna (Spartak Trnava) for Bicovsky 70. coach: Vaclav Jezek

EUROPEAN CHAMPIONSHIP QUALIFYING

Wednesday 20th November 1974

England　　　　　**0-0**　　　**Portugal**
84,461
Referee: A Bucheli (Switzerland)

Portugal had lost four times at Wembley to England, the most recent in 1969, but seven months earlier they had been involved in a goalless draw with England in Lisbon. The Portuguese, like England, had failed to qualify for the recent World Cup, finishing runners-up in their qualifying group to Bulgaria. It was their second successive failure. This was the second match in Group One, following England's great start three weeks earlier.

Portugal defended well and restricted England's chances to a bare minimum. Unlike the opening game, England failed to score and Portugal won the point they came for. A year later, the return game was drawn 1-1 in Lisbon by which time Portugal had lost 5-0 in Prague to Czechoslovakia, while England's chances were also slipping away. Portugal did not return to Wembley until 1995, but beat England in Monterrey in the 1986 World Cup after reaching the European Championship semi-finals two years earlier.

England: Clemence (Liverpool), Madeley (Leeds), Cooper (Leeds), Watson (Sunderland), Hughes (Liverpool) – capt, Brooking (West Ham), Francis (QPR), Bell (Man City), Thomas (QPR), Channon (Southampton), Clarke (Leeds). subs: Todd (Derby County) for Cooper 23, Worthington (Leicester) for Clarke 70. manager: Don Revie

Portugal: Damas (Sporting Lisbon), Artur (Benfica), Alhinho (Sporting Lisbon), Humberto (Benfica) – capt, Osvaldinho (Vitoria Guimaraes), Octavio (Vitoria Setubal), Martins (Benfica), Alves (Boavista), Texeira (Porto), Nene (Benfica), Chico (Sporting Lisbon). subs: Oliveira (Porto) for Nene, Romeu (Vitoria Guimaraes) for Chico. coach: Jose Maria Pedroto

Inter-Varsity Match

Wednesday 4th December 1974

Cambridge U 1
Nixon

Oxford U 3
Costello, Smith, Price

Oxford came from behind to record their first win in this fixture for ten years, and only their third at Wembley.

FOOTBALL LEAGUE CUP FINAL

Saturday 1st March 1975

Aston Villa   1-0   **Norwich City**
Graydon 80
100,000
Referee: G Hill (Leicester)

Villa were appearing in a record fourth final and, as in 1971, had reached Wembley from outside the First Division. Their only League Cup win had been in the very first competition in 1961. Four years before that had come their only Wembley victory in the FA Cup.

Villa's manager Ron Saunders had achieved the remarkable feat of reaching his third successive final with his third different club, after losing with Norwich and Manchester City. Norwich's second final in three years made this the first all-Second Division Wembley final. In the semi-final they had beaten Manchester United, who were to win the Second Division Championship. Norwich had won the second League Cup in 1962 but were chasing their first win at Wembley.

A dull game was settled with ten minutes left. From Hamilton's corner, Keelan was left stranded when Nicholl headed for goal. Machin turned the ball round the post with his hand and a penalty was given. Ray Graydon stepped up but Keelan brilliantly turned his shot onto the post. Unfortunately for the 'keeper, it came back to Graydon, who had time to control it before beating Keelan at the other side. Norwich had lost their second final in three years.

Both sides were promoted at the end of the season. Villa finished as Second Division runners-up to Manchester United to complete a memorable double in only their third season since promotion from the Third Division. The following season, they reached the UEFA Cup quarter-finals, before losing on aggregate to Barcelona. In 1977 they reached the League Cup final again. Norwich finished third to win promotion straight back to the First Division after relegation the previous year. Their second spell in the top flight was to last longer than their first. Ten years later they won the Milk Cup at Wembley.

Aston Villa: Cumbes, Robson, Aitken, Ross – capt, Nicholl, McDonald, Graydon, Little, Leonard, Hamilton, Carrodus. sub: Evans (not used). manager: Ron Saunders

Norwich: Keelan, Machin, Sullivan, Morris, Forbes – capt, Stringer, Miller, MacDougall, Boyer, Suggett, Powell. sub: Steele (not used). manager: John Bond

INTERNATIONAL

Wednesday 12th March 1975

England   **2-0**   **West Germany**
Bell 25, Macdonald 66
98,000
Referee: R Schaut (Belgium)

World and European Champions West Germany arrived at Wembley with only five of the team which had won the World Cup the previous year. Their 2-1 victory over the Netherlands in Munich had completed their rise to domination of world football. England had been their victims in 1972 and they had not beaten them since the 1966 World Cup final. West Germany had had a shaky start to their defence of the European Championship, but were still unbeaten in the competition since 1967.

England took the lead in Wembley's 100th full international when Hudson's free kick was driven home by Colin Bell, via a deflection off Koerbel.

Hudson gave a superb debut performance in midfield with some brilliant passes but it was Ball's cross that was headed in at the far post by Malcolm Macdonald for the second and final goal.

West Germany went on to reach the European Championship final again the following year but lost on penalties to Czechoslovakia in Belgrade.

Both teams had recently lost to England at Wembley. West Germany also lost the World Cup in 1978 in Argentina after beating England 2-1 in Munich earlier in the year. But they were European Champions again when they next visited Wembley in 1982.

England: Clemence (Liverpool), Whitworth* (Leicester), Gillard* (QPR), Bell (Man City), Watson (Sunderland), Todd (Derby County), Ball (Arsenal) – capt, Channon (Southampton), Macdonald (Newcastle), Hudson* (Stoke City), Keegan (Liverpool). manager: Don Revie
*first cap
West Germany: Maier (Bayern Munich), Beckenbauer (Bayern Munich) – capt, Bonhof (Borussia Monchengladbach), Koerbel (Eintracht Frankfurt), Vogts (Borussia Monchengladbach), Wimmer (Borussia Monchengladbach), Cullmann (Cologne), Flohe (Cologne), Ritschel (Kickers Offenbach), Kostedde (Kickers Offenbach), Holzenbein (Eintracht Frankfurt). subs: Kremers (Schalke) for Wimmer, Heynckes (Borussia Monchengladbach) for Kostedde 75. coach: Helmut Schoen

Schoolboy International

Saturday 22nd March 1975

England 4
Seacole 2, Hurley 2

Netherlands 0
40,000

A third successive defeat for the Dutch at Wembley.

England: Field, Ranson, Rogers, Gilbert – capt, Totty, Murphy, Ingram, Coles, Hurley, Seacole, Leahy. subs: Staniforth for Coles, Waddington for Hurley

EUROPEAN CHAMPIONSHIP QUALIFYING

Wednesday 16th April 1975

England   **5-0**   **Cyprus**
Macdonald 2, 35, 48, 53, 88
68,245
Referee: M Hirviniemi (Finland)

In the first meeting between the two countries, England were completing their home fixtures in Group One before any other team had played a home game. They had already experienced success and disappointment. Cyprus were beginning their third European Championship and had never been remotely close to qualifying for the World Cup. It took England less than two minutes to score. Hudson sent a free kick into the middle, where Malcolm Macdonald rose to head the opener. Ten minutes before the interval, Keegan pulled the ball back from the goal line for Macdonald to notch his second.

He completed his hat-trick early in the second half. A long ball from Madeley was headed back by Keegan and Macdonald headed home. Five minutes later, Thomas came on as substitute and immediately crossed for Macdonald to power home his fourth with yet another header. Cyprus changed goalkeepers when Alkiviades was kicked on the hand by Beattie. But his replacement Constantinou was left stranded by another Thomas cross as Macdonald rose to head the last and became the first England player for 37 years to score five goals in one match.

Cyprus lost 4-0 in Prague to Czechoslovakia four days later, but England could only beat them by one goal in the return in Limassol the following month. The resurgent Czechs beat England in Bratislava, six months later to pip them for a quarter-final place. They went on to win the European Championship on penalties after drawing with West Germany in the final. Cyprus failed to score a goal or win a point and have not met England since.

England: Shilton (Stoke City), Madeley (Leeds), Beattie* (Ipswich), Bell (Man City), Watson (Sunderland), Todd (Derby County), Ball (Arsenal) – capt, Channon (Southampton), Macdonald (Newcastle), Hudson (Stoke City), Keegan (Liverpool). sub: Thomas (QPR) for Channon 53. manager: Don Revie
*first cap
Cyprus: Alkiviades (EPA Larnaca), Kovis (Anorthosis Famagusta), Kyzas (Paralimni), Pantziaras (Apoel Nicosia), Koureas (Ethnikos Pireaus), Theodorou (EPA Larnaca), Michael (Apoel Nicosia), Marcou (Apoel Nicosia), Charalambous (Omonia Nicosia), Savva (Omonia Nicosia), Stylianou (Apoel Nicosia) – capt. subs: T.Constantinou (AEK Athens) for Charalambous 46, A.Constantinou (AEL Limassol) for Alkiviades 58. coach: Panicos Iacovou

Final table	P	W	D	L	F	A	Pts
Czechoslovakia	6	4	1	1	15	9	9
England	6	3	2	1	11	3	8
Portugal	6	2	3	1	5	7	7
Cyprus	6	0	0	6	0	16	0

FA Vase Final

Saturday 19th April 1975

Epsom and Ewell 1
Wales 82

Hoddesdon Town 2
Sedgewick 15, 45
9,500
Referee: R Toseland (Northamptonshire)

This competition was inaugurated to replace the FA Amateur Cup for the smaller clubs. Epsom's fancied young side, led by player-manager Pat O'Connell, conceded two first-half goals and could not respond in time. Dick Sedgewick, Hoddesdon's heroic goalscoring captain, had delayed an operation on his fractured cheekbone to take part.

Epsom: Page, Bennett, Webb, Wales – capt, Worby, Jones, O'Connell, Walker, Tuite, Eales, Lee. sub: Ritman for Webb 59
Hoddesdon: Gulvin, Green, Hickey, Maybury, Stevenson, Wilson, Bishop, Picking, Sedgewick – capt, Nathan, Schofield. sub: Bidwell for Bishop 89

FA Trophy Final

Saturday 26th April 1975

Matlock Town 4
Oxley, Dawson, T Fenoughty, N Fenoughty

Scarborough 0
21,000
Referee: K Styles (Barnsley)

Matlock's player-manager Peter Swan led his team, including the three Fenoughty brothers, to a record victory, although Scarborough were a little unlucky to lose so heavily. Errors in defence and attack cost them dearly.

Swan, an ex-England international, had spent seven years out of the game and received a four-month prison sentence for his part in a bribery scandal while playing for Sheffield Wednesday in 1962.

Matlock: Fell, McKay, Smith, Stuart, Swan, Dawson, Oxley, Fenoughty (N), Scott, T Fenoughty (T) – capt, Fenoughty (M)
Scarborough: Williams, Hewitt, Pettit, Dunn (H), Marshall, Todd, Houghton, Woodall, Davidson, Barmby, Aveyard.

FA CUP FINAL

Saturday 3rd May 1975

Fulham   0-2   **West Ham United**
A Taylor 60, 64

100,000
Referee: P Partridge (Bishop Auckland)

Fulham, appearing in their first final, had never played at Wembley and had never won a major trophy. They had knocked West Ham out of the Football League Cup earlier in the season, though. West Ham had won the FA Cup once before, in 1964, and had returned to Wembley the following year to win the European Cup Winners Cup.

Fulham finished ninth in the Second Division, the best they had managed since promotion from the Third Division in 1971. They were the third club from the Second Division to reach a Wembley final that season and they were hoping to match Sunderland's feat two years earlier. West Ham finished 13th in the First Division, a considerable improvement on the previous year when they had escaped relegation by a point.

The underdogs had played well in the first half, but fell behind on the hour. Cutbush lost the ball to Holland, who sent Jennings away to shoot. Mellor palmed out the ball, but Alan Taylor sent the rebound through his legs and into the net. Four minutes later, Mellor failed to hold Paddon's shot and Taylor was there again.

Taylor, who had started the season with Fourth Division Rochdale, had scored twice in the quarter-finals, the semi-finals and now the final as The Hammers lifted the trophy for the second time.

Five years later, Fulham dropped back into the Third Division and were never to play at the old Wembley again. West Ham reached the following year's European Cup-Winners Cup final, losing 4-2 to Anderlecht in an exciting game in Brussels.

Although Bobby Gould never left the bench, he was manager of Wimbledon when they sensationally lifted the trophy in 1988.

Fulham: Mellor, Cutbush, Lacy, Mullery – capt, Fraser, Moore, Conway, Slough, Mitchell, Busby, Barrett. sub: Lloyd (not used). manager: Alec Stock
West Ham: Day, McDowell, Lampard, Bonds – capt, Taylor (T), Lock, Jennings, Paddon, Taylor (A), Brooking, Holland. sub: Gould (not used). manager: John Lyall

BRITISH CHAMPIONSHIP

Wednesday 21st May 1975

England   2-2   **Wales**
Johnson 10, 85   Toshack 55 Griffiths 66
53,000
Referee: J Paterson (Scotland)

Wales were attempting to beat England at Wembley in the British Championship at the eleventh attempt. They had surrendered a two-goal half-time lead to draw with Scotland at Ninian Park four days earlier. England had opened with a goalless draw against Northern Ireland at Windsor Park and had still to concede a goal after six matches under Don Revie. Wales had to avoid defeat to stay in contention. In the European Championship, they had recovered from an early defeat to Austria in Vienna to complete a 'double' over Hungary and were still in with a chance of reaching the quarter-finals.

After ten minutes, Viljoen's cross struck Phillips and David Johnson had only to head the ball over the line to give England the lead. Ten minutes into the second half, the Welsh drew level as England's defence was at last breached. James' corner was flicked on by Smallman and Griffiths' header was scrambled off the line by Clemence only for his club colleague John Toshack to hook it into the net. England's defence crumbled again as Toshack challenged Watson for a high ball. It hit Gillard, but Arfon Griffiths was on hand to beat Clemence and give Wales a shock lead.

They were five minutes away from a historic victory when substitute Little's cross found the head of Johnson who outjumped Davies to rescue England with his second.

Wales' chances were ended by a single-goal defeat by Northern Ireland two nights later at Windsor Park. But they went on to defeat Austria 1-0 at the Racecourse Ground to reach the European Championship quarter-finals for the first time.

They were the only British qualifiers. Wales lost on aggregate to Yugoslavia but secured that elusive Wembley victory in 1977. England had to beat Scotland three days later to win their eighth title in succession.

England: Clemence (Liverpool), Whitworth (Leicester), Gillard (QPR), Francis (QPR), Watson (Sunderland), Todd (Derby County), Ball (Arsenal) – capt, Channon (Southampton), Johnson* (Ipswich), Viljoen (Ipswich), Thomas (QPR). sub: Little* (Aston Villa) for Channon 71. manager: Don Revie

Wales: Davies (Everton), Thomas (Derby County), Page (Birmingham), Mahoney (Stoke City), Roberts (Birmingham) – capt, Phillips (Aston Villa), Griffiths (Wrexham), Flynn (Burnley), Smallman (Everton), Toshack (Liverpool), James (Burnley). sub: Showers* (Cardiff) for Smallman 60. manager: Mike Smith

*first cap

BRITISH CHAMPIONSHIP

Saturday 24th May 1975

England	**5-1**	**Scotland**
Francis 3, 63, Beattie 5, Bell 40, Johnson 73		Rioch pen 41

98,241

Referee: R Gloeckner (East Germany)

Scotland had lost on their three previous visits to Wembley and had not won there since their famous 1967 victory. But they had beaten England the previous year at Hampden Park by virtue of two own goals to share the Championship with them. To retain it, they needed only a point which would give them their first outright title in eight years. England had to win to make sure of their eighth successive title. In the European Championship, Scotland had lost to Spain at Hampden Park, but had earned a 1-1 draw in the return in Valencia and were still in contention.

England took less than four minutes to silence the thousands of Scottish supporters who had made the long trip south. Gerry Francis took a pass from Channon, ran into space and found the corner of the net with a 20-yard shot which took Kennedy by surprise. Two minutes later, from Keegan's cross, Kevin Beattie outjumped Jardine and once again Kennedy was slow to react as the ball headed for the corner. The luckless goalkeeper was beaten once more with the interval approaching.

Francis played a series of one-twos with Beattie, Channon and Keegan, the ball eventually coming to Colin Bell who rode a McGrain tackle before firing home the third. A minute later, Scotland gained some reward. Todd handled as MacDougall tried to find a way through and Bruce Rioch gave Clemence no chance from the penalty.

But England restored their three-goal advantage when Ball tapped a free kick through Bell's legs and Francis' shot was deflected by Munro onto the post and in. The Scots' misery was completed ten minutes later. Ball sent another free kick into the goalmouth, Keegan headed against the bar and Watson hit the post from the rebound. But David Johnson was following up to make no mistake.

Both England and Scotland failed to qualify for the European Championship quarter-finals. Scotland gained some revenge by beating England a year later to win the British Championship a year later, at Hampden Park. They followed that with victory at Wembley in 1977.

England: Clemence (Liverpool), Whitworth (Leicester), Beattie (Ipswich), Bell (Man City), Watson (Sunderland), Todd (Derby County), Ball (Arsenal) – capt, Channon (Southampton), Johnson (Ipswich), Francis (QPR), Keegan (Liverpool). sub: Thomas (QPR) for Keegan 85. manager: Don Revie

Scotland: Kennedy (Rangers), Jardine (Rangers) – capt, McGrain (Celtic), Munro (Wolves), McQueen (Leeds), Rioch (Derby County), Dalglish (Celtic), Conn (Tottenham), Parlane (Rangers), MacDougall (Norwich), Duncan (Hibernian). subs: Hutchison (Coventry) for Duncan 61, Macari (Man Utd) for MacDougall 71. manager: Willie Ormond

Final table	P	W	D	L	F	A	Pts
England	3	1	2	0	7	3	4
Northern Ireland	3	1	1	1	1	3	3
Scotland	3	1	1	1	6	7	3
Wales	3	0	2	1	4	5	2

Schoolboy International

Saturday 7th June 1975

England 0
Scotland 1
McCluskey 50

John McCluskey's spectacular individual goal secured Scotland's second successive victory at Wembley.

England: Field, Ranson, Gilbert – capt, Totty, Rogers, Murphy, Staniforth, Seacole, Ingram, Hurley, Leahy. sub: Waddington for Staniforth
Scotland: Tulloch, Russell, Anderson, Stuart, Johnston, Cribbes, Bett, Robertson, Strickland, Kerr, McCluskey. sub: Kennedy for Robertson

NABC Cup Final

Saturday 14th June 1975

Merseyside 1
Lawrence 84
Plymouth 3
Krac 20 Knowles 55, 59
Referee: C White (London)

The Devonport Dockyard Apprentices Association retained the trophy in an emotional final. They were watched by Doug Holt, their wheelchair-bound 21-year-old striker, who had lost a leg after breaking it in the semi-final. His goal had settled that match and thus their return visit to Wembley. Alan Krac, his replacement, opened the scoring and captain Andy Knowles secured the victory, before Holt was helped up to the Royal Box to receive his medal. The drama unfolded before a live television audience and would have been cancelled but for the late sponsorship of Thorn Electrical.

Billy Liddell, scorer of Scotland's winning goal at Wembley in 1951, was the Merseyside team's coach.

FA CHARITY SHIELD

Saturday 9th August 1975

Derby County　　2-0　　**West Ham United**
Hector 19, McFarland 42
59,000
Referee: G Kew (Amersham)

Derby were competing in their first FA Charity Shield, after coming from behind to win their second League Championship by two points from Liverpool and Ipswich Town. They had played at Wembley only once before when winning the FA Cup in 1946. Three months earlier West Ham had won the FA Cup for the second time. They had shared the Charity Shield with Liverpool in 1964. West Ham had not beaten Derby for four seasons.

George, making his debut for Derby after leaving Arsenal, flicked the ball on to Kevin Hector and Day could not get down to the striker's low shot. Derby increased their lead just before the interval. Day failed to collect Lee's header as Hector back-heeled it into the path of Roy McFarland who had a simple task to score.

It was a special moment for the Derby captain, who had missed most of the previous season because of a bad injury sustained at Wembley for England against Northern Ireland.

West Ham could not break down Derby's defence and the Rams won the Shield for the first time.

Derby finished fourth in their defence of the League Championship and lost out in the last 16 of the European Cup, failing in extra time to beat Real Madrid, despite a 4-1 first leg victory. They also reached the FA Cup semi-finals where they lost to Manchester United. In 1980 they were relegated to the Second Division and did not appear at Wembley again until the 1993 Anglo-Italian Cup final. West Ham finished a disappointing 18th in the First Division despite reaching the European Cup-Winners Cup final. They were relegated two years later, but won the FA Cup as a Second Division side in 1980.

Derby: Boulton, Thomas, Nish, Rioch, McFarland – capt, Todd, Newton, Gemmill, Lee, Hector, George. manager: Dave Mackay
West Ham: Day, McDowell, Lampard, Holland – capt, Taylor (T), Lock, Taylor (A), Paddon, Jennings, Brooking, Gould. subs: Coleman for Jennings, Robson for Gould. manager: John Lyall

Inter-Varsity Match

Wednesday 3rd December 1975

Cambridge U 0

Oxford U 2
Smith, Thomas

Oxford achieved back-to-back victories for the first time at Wembley.

FOOTBALL LEAGUE CUP FINAL

Saturday 28th February 1976

Manchester City	2-1	Newcastle United
Barnes 12, Tueart 46		Gowling 36

100,000
Referee: J Taylor (Wolverhampton)

City were appearing in their second final in three years after losing to Wolves' late winner in 1974. They had won the League Cup in 1970. In an early round they had eliminated Norwich City, the previous year's finalists. Newcastle had never before been beyond the quarter-finals but had also appeared at Wembley in 1974 in a disappointing FA Cup final. They had won the FA Cup for the sixth time, however, when they beat City at Wembley in 1955.

City took the lead when Hartford's lofted free kick was headed into the goalmouth by Doyle. Craig and Keeley collided as they tried to stop Royle from heading the ball and it fell for Peter Barnes to drive it past Mahoney. Alan Gowling equalised when he stabbed home Macdonald's cross just ahead of Watson.

But in the very first minute of the second half Newcastle were beaten by a most spectacular goal. Donachie's cross was headed into the middle by Booth, and Dennis Tueart, despite being surrounded by three defenders, performed an exquisite overhead kick to send the ball out of the goalkeeper's reach and into the corner.

City were beaten in the following season's UEFA Cup first round by Juventus, the eventual winners, but finished the season as League runners-up – ahead of Ipswich Town on goal average but only a point behind Liverpool. It was 1981 before they were back at Wembley again, for the FA Cup final.

Newcastle next appeared at Wembley in the Football League Centenary Tournament in 1988. It was to be a further eight years before they made a full appearance in the FA Charity Shield.

Manchester C: Corrigan, Keegan, Donachie, Doyle – capt, Watson, Oakes, Barnes (P), Booth, Royle, Hartford, Tueart. sub: Clements (not used). manager: Tony Book
Newcastle: Mahoney, Nattrass, Kennedy, Barrowclough, Keeley, Howard, Burns, Cassidy, Macdonald, Gowling, Craig – capt. sub: Cannell (not used). manager: Gordon Lee

Schoolboy International

Saturday 20th March 1976

England 4
Brignull, Ritchie 2, McGrath

Wales 1
Lewis

Hansen, the Welsh goalkeeper, broke his leg in the last minute to complete a miserable afternoon for him.

England's substitute was Clive Allen, the Footballer of the Year in 1987 when he scored his 49th goal of the season for Tottenham Hotspur in the FA Cup final.

Wayne Clarke scored the only goal of the 1987 FA Charity Shield at Wembley for Everton.

Kevin Ratcliffe won 59 full international caps for Wales and captained Everton to their 1984 FA Cup win at Wembley.

England: Foyster, Wardle, Sisman, Ormsby, Brignull, Fillery, Clarke, Walker – capt, Ritchie, Jasper, McGrath. sub: Allen for Jasper
Wales: Hansen, Martin, Minney, Ratcliffe, Piper, Lucas, Haggett, Wilkins, Lewis, Micallef, Lloyd. subs: Plunkett for Hansen, Botto for Minney, Davies for Micallef

FA Vase Final

Saturday 10th April 1976

Billericay Town 1
Aslett 99

Stamford 0
After extra time

11,858
Referee: A Robinson (Fareham)

Ex-England youth international Geoff Aslett broke the deadlock to win the Vase for Billericay in a very tight game.

Billericay: Griffiths, Payne, Foreman, Pullin, Bone, Coughlan – capt, Geddes, Aslett, Clayden, Scott, Smith
Stamford: Johnson, Kwiatkowski, Marchant, Crawford, Downs, Hird, Barnes, Walpole, Smith, Russell, Broadhurst

FA Trophy Final

Saturday 24th April 1976

Scarborough 3
Woodall, Abbey, Marshall pen

Stafford Rangers 2
Jones 2
After extra time
21,000
Referee: R Challis (Tonbridge)

In a dramatic final, their third in four years, Scarborough twice came from behind and became the first club to win the Trophy twice. Their 1973 winner had been late but Sean Marshall settled this one with the second penalty of the extra half-hour in the second minute of injury time. Arnold had saved Woodall's penalty in the first half of extra time.

Scarborough: Barnard, Jackson, Marshall, Dunn (H), Ayre, Dunn (H A), Dale, Barmby, Woodall, Abbey, Hilley. sub: Donoghue for Barmby
Stafford: Arnold, Ritchie (R) – capt, Richards, Sargeant, Seddon, Morris, Chapman, Lowe, Jones, Hutchison, Chadwick. sub: Ritchie (J) for Hutchison

FA CUP FINAL

Saturday 1st May 1976

Manchester United 0-1 **Southampton**
Stokes 83

100,000
Referee: C Thomas (Treorchy)

United had reached the semi-finals four times since winning the FA Cup in 1963, and they had won the European Cup at Wembley in 1968. Southampton were the second successive Second Division club to reach the final and the third in four years. They had never won the Cup but as a Southern League club at the turn of the century had reached two finals in three years. In the second of these, in 1902, they took Sheffield United to a replay before losing 2-1 at Crystal Palace.

United had won the Second Division Championship the previous year and in their first season back in the top flight finished third, their highest position since 1968. Southampton finished sixth in the Second Division after relegation with United two years earlier. The clubs had therefore finished in the same league positions as Leeds United and Sunderland in the famous giantkilling final of 1973. Was it an omen? Southampton had not beaten United, though, since 1970.

Although they were in the Second Division, Southampton had more players with big-match experience. They did their homework and nullified United's young strikeforce. Then, with seven minutes left, McCalliog sent Bobby Stokes away to outpace United's defenders and shoot past Stepney into the corner. Another sensational victory for the underdogs had given Southampton their first major trophy although United still argue Stokes was offside.

United knocked Southampton out of the following year's FA Cup and went on to win the trophy as underdogs themselves. Southampton reached the European Cup-Winners Cup quarter-finals.

Manchester U: Stepney, Forsyth, Houston, Daly, Greenhoff (B), Buchan – capt, Coppell, McIlroy, Pearson (JS), Macari, Hill. sub: McCreery for Hill 66. manager: Tommy Docherty

Southampton: Turner, Rodrigues – capt, Peach, Holmes, Blyth, Steele, Gilchrist, Channon, Osgood, McCalliog, Stokes. sub: Fisher (not used). manager: Lawrie McMenemy

BRITISH CHAMPIONSHIP

Tuesday 11th May 1976

England   **4-0**   **Northern Ireland**
Francis 35, Channon (pen) 36, 77, Pearson 60
48,000
Referee: C Thomas (Wales)

Northern Ireland's last two visits had produced only one goal on each occasion, for the Irish in 1972 and for England in 1974. England were chasing their ninth successive British Championship after a disappointing exit in the European Championship at the hands of the eventual winners Czechoslovakia. Three days earlier they had beaten Wales by the only goal at Ninian Park and this was their first match at Wembley for almost a year.

Northern Ireland had also failed to qualify for the European Championship quarter-finals, after finishing runners-up to Yugoslavia but ahead of Sweden on goal difference. They had begun the British Championship with a 3-0 drubbing by Scotland at Hampden Park and needed to win to have any chance of sharing the title.

It took England more than half an hour to break down the Irish and then Mills crossed and Channon's back-heel put Gerry Francis through to round Jennings and put England ahead. A minute later, Cassidy brought down Mike Channon who got up to score the penalty himself.

Stuart Pearson hit the third on the hour when he snapped up the rebound after Jennings had stopped Kennedy's shot. The scoring was completed when, from Todd's cross, Keegan's shot was blocked by substitute Scott but it fell to Channon who waited for Jennings to commit himself before firing his second into the net.

Northern Ireland ended up without a goal or a point after losing 1-0 to Wales at Vetch Field three nights later.

England's run of British Championships came to an end a day after that when they were beaten 2-1 by Scotland at Hampden Park.

England: Clemence (Liverpool), Todd (Derby County), Mills (Ipswich), Thompson (Liverpool), Greenhoff (Man Utd), Kennedy (Liverpool), Keegan (Liverpool), Channon (Southampton), Pearson (Man Utd), Francis (QPR) – capt, Taylor (Crystal P). subs: Towers (Sunderland) for Taylor 61, Royle (Man City) for Keegan. manager: Don Revie

Northern Ireland: Jennings (Tottenham), Rice (Arsenal), Nelson (Arsenal), Clements (New York Cosmos) – capt, Hunter (Ipswich), Nicholl (Aston Villa), Hamilton (Everton), Cassidy (Newcastle), McCreery (Man Utd), Spence (Bury), McIlroy (Man Utd). sub: Scott (York City) for Nelson 61. player-manager: Dave Clements

Final table	P	W	D	L	F	A	Pts
Scotland	3	3	0	0	8	2	6
England	3	2	0	1	6	2	4
Wales	3	1	0	2	2	4	2
Northern Ireland	3	0	0	3	0	8	0

Schoolboy International

Saturday 5th June 1976

England 6-1
Ritchie, Walker 2, (1 pen), Fillery 2, Brignull

France
Buscher

Referee: R Lane (Kent)

England's biggest victory over the French.

England: Foyster, Wardle, Sisman, Ormsby, Brignull, Fillery, Clarke, Walker – capt, Ritchie, Carter, Allen. subs: McGrath for Clarke, Dibble for Carter

FA CHARITY SHIELD

Saturday 14th August 1976

Liverpool   1-0   **Southampton**
Toshack 50
76,500
Referee: J Homewood (Middlesex)

Liverpool were League Champions for a record ninth time. They had won the title by a point from Queens Park Rangers after coming from behind to win their last game at Wolverhampton Wanderers. This had followed two seasons as runners-up after winning the FA Charity Shield for the second time outright on their last visit, albeit on penalties. They had also won the UEFA Cup despite being two goals down in the home leg of the final against Bruges. It was the second time that they had achieved that particular 'double'.

Southampton had won their first major trophy three months earlier despite only finishing sixth in the Second Division.

The only goal of a poor game arrived just after half-time – Keegan headed on Callaghan's pass to John Toshack who slammed it past Turner.

Liverpool finished the season with another 'double' and it was almost the 'treble'. They retained the League Championship, their third in five years and a record tenth overall, they became only the second English club to win the European Cup and this amazing team reached the FA Cup final as well. Southampton had to wait another year before winning promotion back to the First Division but once there reached the Football League Cup final for the first time.

Liverpool: Clemence, Neal, Jones (J), Thompson (PB), Kennedy (R), Hughes (E) – capt, Keegan, Case, Heighway, Toshack, Callaghan. manager: Bob Paisley
Southampton: Turner, Rodrigues – capt, Peach, Holmes, Blyth, Steele, Gilchrist, Channon, Osgood, McCalliog, Stokes. sub: Fisher for Blyth. manager: Lawrie McMenemy

INTERNATIONAL

Wednesday 8th September 1976

England   1-1   **Republic of Ireland**
Pearson 45   Daly pen 52
51,000
Referee: H Alexander (Scotland)

The Republic of Ireland had still not qualified for a major tournament. They had been thrashed on their only previous visit to Wembley in 1957 and had been beaten 3-1 in their last meeting, seven years later, at Dalymount Park.

Stuart Pearson gave England the lead at the end of the first half, meeting Keegan's cross with a shot that Kearns could not stop. But the Irish deservedly levelled seven minutes after the interval. Heighway was brought down by Wilkins and Gerry Daly tucked home the equaliser from the resultant penalty.

The Republic of Ireland finished bottom of their World Cup qualifying group after defeats in France and Bulgaria. They were paired with England in the 1980 European Championship and were back at Wembley for the final qualifying match.

England: Clemence (Liverpool), Todd (Derby County), Madeley (Leeds), Cherry (Leeds), McFarland (Derby County), Greenhoff (B) (Man Utd), Keegan (Liverpool) – capt, Wilkins (Chelsea), Pearson (Man Utd), Brooking (West Ham), George* (Derby County). sub: Hill (Man Utd) for George 66. manager: Don Revie

Republic of Ireland: Kearns (Walsall), Mulligan (West Brom), Holmes (Coventry), Martin (West Brom), O'Leary* (Arsenal), Brady (Arsenal), Daly (Man Utd), Conroy (Stoke City), Heighway (Liverpool), Giles (West Brom) – capt, Givens (QPR). player-manager: Johnny Giles

* First cap

WORLD CUP QUALIFYING

Wednesday 13th October 1976

England 2-1 Finland
Tueart 4, Royle 52   Nieminen 48
87,000
Referee: U Eriksson (Sweden)

Finland arrived at Wembley for the first time after four defeats by England in Helsinki. Four months earlier, England had beaten them 4-1 in the opening match of Group Two. But three weeks before this return match Finland had trounced Luxembourg by 7-1, also in Helsinki, to go top of the group on goal difference. Finland had never been close to qualifying for a major tournament.

From Brooking's fifth minute corner, Royle's header was handled on the line by Ranta. Dennis Tueart slammed the rebound into the net before a penalty could be given. England missed several chances and were punished for it before the second half was very old. Aki Heiskanen sent Jyrki Nieminen through to beat Clemence for the equaliser. But four minutes later England were back in front, when Joe Royle headed home Channon's cross. This was all they could manage.

The following month, England lost to Italy in Rome and began to realise that goal difference was going to be vitally important in determining if they were to avoid missing their second consecutive World Cup. Italy were to eliminate Finland from the competition and beat them much more convincingly than England did. Finland failed by just a point to qualify for the 1980 European Championship and returned to Wembley for another World Cup qualifying match in 1984.

England: Clemence (Liverpool), Todd (Derby County), Beattie (Ipswich), Thompson (Liverpool), Greenhoff (Man Utd), Wilkins (Chelsea), Keegan (Liverpool) – capt, Channon (Southampton), Royle (Man City), Brooking (West Ham), Tueart (Man City). subs: Mills (Ipswich) for Brooking 75, Hill (Man Utd) for Tueart 75. manager: Don Revie

Finland: Enckelman (TPS Turku), Heikkinen (OTP Oulu), Vihtila (Ilves Tampere), Makynen (VPS Vaasa), Ranta (Haka Valkeakoski), Jantunen (Reipas Lahti), Suomalainen (KPT Kuopio), Toivola (HJK Helsinki), Nieminen (HJK Helsinki), Heiskanen (A) (KPT Kuopio), Paatelainen (Haka Valkeakoski) – capt. subs: Heiskanen (E) (KuPS Kuopio) for Jantunen 61, Pyykko (OPS Oulu) for Suomalainen 67. coach: Aulis Rytkonen

Inter-Varsity Match

A drab match extended Oxford's unbeaten run at Wembley to four games.

Wednesday 8th December 1976

Cambridge U 0
Oxford U 0

INTERNATIONAL

Wednesday 9th February 1977

England 0-2 Netherlands
                        Peters 29, 38
90,260
Referee: W Eschweiler (West Germany)

England's decline in world football had coincided with the rise to prominence of the Netherlands. After holding England on their previous visit in 1970 they had reached the World Cup final in 1974 and the European Championship semi-finals two years later. In the World Cup final they had taken a first minute lead before succumbing to West Germany in Munich.

In the European Championship semi-final they had lost in extra time to Czechoslovakia, England's conquerors and the eventual winners in Zagreb. They had never beaten England, however, in five meetings and had been held to a 2-2 draw in their World Cup qualifying group by Northern Ireland in Rotterdam four months earlier.

After half an hour the England defence was split wide open by Cruyff and Neeskens' for Jan Peters to run on and beat the advancing Clemence. Nine minutes later Peters took a pass from Hovenkamp, sidestepped Beattie and drove his second past Clemence. England were mesmerised by the Dutch passing and were powerless to respond.

The Netherlands's 2-0 win over Belgium in Antwerp the following month set them on their way to their second successive World Cup. They reached the final again but unfortunately, met another host nation and lost in extra time to Argentina in Buenos Aires. Their ageing stars had missed their opportunities for the ultimate prize and when in 1982 they arrived at Wembley again they had failed to qualify for that year's World Cup.

England's confidence was at an all-time low after their first-hand experience of just how far behind the world's best they were.

England: Clemence (Liverpool), Clement (QPR), Beattie (Ipswich), Doyle (Man City), Watson (Man City), Madeley (Leeds), Keegan (Liverpool) – capt, Greenhoff (Man Utd), Francis* (Birmingham), Bowles (QPR), Brooking (West Ham). subs: Todd (Derby County) for Greenhoff 40, Pearson (Man Utd) for Madeley 74. manager: Don Revie
*first cap

Netherlands: Schrijvers (Ajax Amsterdam), Suurbier (Ajax), Rijsbergen (Feyenoord), Krol (Ajax), Hovenkamp (Alkmaar), Van de Kerkhof (W) (PSV Eindhoven), Neeskens (Barcelona), Peters (NEC Nijmegen), Rep (Valencia), Cruyff (Barcelona) – capt, Rensenbrink (Anderlecht). sub: Kist (Alkmaar). for Rep 75 coach: Jan Zwartkruis

FOOTBALL LEAGUE CUP FINAL

Saturday 12th March 1977

Aston Villa   0-0   Everton
100,000
Referee: G Kew (Middlesbrough)

Villa had reached their second final in three years and a record fifth overall. They had won the League Cup as a Second Division club in 1975 and had begun their attempt to become the first to win it three times by beating the holders Manchester City 3-0. Everton had never been beyond the quarter-finals and had not appeared at Wembley since their extra-time defeat in the 1968 FA Cup final. They had been starved of success since winning the League Championship in 1970 but in the quarter-finals, they had won 3-0 away to Manchester United, who went on to win the FA Cup. Everton manager Gordon Lee had taken Newcastle United to the previous year's final.

A dreadful match passed by almost without incident as the only winners were the players' nerves. The lack of extra time only increased the feeling of anti-climax.

The replay was four days later and Villa almost won with an own goal but Everton levelled with two minutes remaining. The week ended with Villa losing to Manchester United, the eventual winners, in the FA Cup and Everton winning through to the semi-finals, where they were to lose after a replay to their great rivals Liverpool. The League Cup final was won and lost just over a month after it had begun.

This time Villa came from behind in what had become the longest domestic cup final of all-time. Brian Little, who had scored a hat-trick in the semi-final replay, scored twice, including the winner in the very last minute of extra time. Wembley had undoubtedly seen the worst of their exchanges. Villa finished fourth in only their second season back in the First Division and four years later they were League Champions as they returned to Wembley for the FA Charity Shield. It was another seven years before Everton again reached Wembley in what was then the Milk Cup final.

Aston Villa: Burridge, Gidman, Robson, Phillips, Nicholl – capt, Mortimer, Deehan, Little, Gray, Cropley, Carrodus.
sub: Cowans (not used). manager: Ron Saunders
Everton: Lawson, Jones, Darracott, Lyons – capt, McNaught, King, Hamilton, Dobson, Latchford, McKenzie, Goodlass.
sub: Telfer (not used). manager: Gordon Lee

Replay: Wednesday 16th March 1977
Aston Villa   1-1   **Everton**
Kenyon og 79   Latchford 88
After extra time
(Hillsborough)

Second Replay: Wednesday 13th April 1977
Aston Villa   3-2   **Everton**
Nicholl 80, Little 81, 120   Latchford 37 Lyons 83
After extra time
(Old Trafford)

Schoolboy International

Saturday 19th March 1977

England 2
Rees 16, Mills 86

Scotland 0
Referee: B Hill (Northamptonshire

After two successive wins at Wembley the Scots were beaten. Gary Mills made sure of victory with an astonishing 40-yard free kick. Just three years later, at the age of 18, he was to win a European Cup winners medal with Nottingham Forest.

Mark Chamberlain made his full international debut at Wembley in 1982 as a substitute and scored for England against Luxembourg.

England: Foyster, Mills, Bennett, Pittaway – capt, Law, Brandon, Rees, Thomas, Merry, Wray, Chamberlain. sub: Lilley for Merry
Scotland: Walker, Turnbull, Kettings, McStay, Skene, Dorman, Kay, McGee, Lorimer, Bell, Walsh. sub: McKenna for Lorimer

WORLD CUP QUALIFYING

Wednesday 30th March 1977

England   5-0   **Luxembourg**
Keegan 10, Francis 58, Kennedy 65
Channon 69, 81 (pen)
81,718
Referee: P Bonett (Malta)

England had won all their three previous meetings with Luxembourg, including a 9-0 away win in 1960 in a World Cup qualifying match. Luxembourg lost 4-1 in the return match at Highbury the following year, their only previous visit to England and the last meeting between them. For Luxembourg to win a point in international competition was rare. For them to win a qualifying group was almost impossible, although they had reached the European Championship quarter-finals in 1964. England's 2-0 defeat by Italy in Rome four months earlier left them needing to build up a large goal difference if they were to qualify from Group Two assuming Italy beat Finland and Luxembourg.

England had the ideal start. Watson's header across goal was met by Kevin Keegan, who rose to beat Zender for the opener. Then things began to go wrong. England struggled against a well-organised defence and it was not until just before the hour that they scored again. From a Hill corner, Keegan set up Trevor Francis.

Seven minutes later, substitute Mariner met Gidman's cross and the ball ran loose for Ray Kennedy to fire past the 'keeper. At last the visitors began to wilt. Another Hill corner ended up in the net as Mike Channon scrambled the ball over the line and with nine minutes left Channon was brought down by Fandel even though he was running the ball out of play and the

Southampton striker rose to send Zender the wrong way from the penalty spot. With four minutes remaining, Gilbert Dresch was sent off for a foul on Channon. Apart from the last half-hour, it was not a convincing performance by England.

England were back on top of the group, but they could only manage a 2-0 win in the return in Luxembourg seven months later.

Three days after that Italy thrashed Finland 6-1 in Turin and England were left praying for a miracle.

Luxembourg failed to win a point but returned to Wembley in the European Championship in 1982.

England: Clemence (Liverpool), Gidman* (Aston Villa), Cherry (Leeds), Kennedy (Liverpool), Watson (Man City), Hughes (Liverpool), Keegan (Liverpool) – capt, Channon (Southampton), Royle (Man City), Francis (Birmingham), Hill (Man Utd). sub: Mariner* (Ipswich) for Royle 46. manager: Don Revie
*first cap

Luxembourg: Zender (Red Black Pfaffenthal), Fandel (Aris Bonnevoie), Margue (Progres Niedercorn), Mond (Jeunesse Esch), Pilot (Racing Jet Brussels) – capt, Zuang (Stade Dudelange), Di Domenico (Red Boys Differdange), Dresch (Avenir Beggen), Braun (Metz), Philipp (Royale Union Forest), Dussier (Nancy-Lorraine). sub: Orioli (Alliance Dudelange) for Di Domenico 76. coach: Gilbert Legrand

FA Vase Final

Saturday 30th April 1977

Billericay Town 1
Clayden 56
Sheffield 1
Coughlan og 13
After extra time
14,000
Referee: J Worrall (Cheshire)

The holders needed a replay to beat the oldest club in Britain and become the first club to win the Vase twice.

Billericay: Griffiths, Payne, Bone, Coughlan – capt, Pullin, Scott, Wakefield, Aslett, Clayden, Woodhouse, McQueen. sub: Whettell for McQueen 106
Sheffield: Wing, Gilbody, Lodge, Hardisty, Watts – capt, Skelton, Kay, Travis, Pugh, Thornhill, Haines. sub: Strutt for Thornhill 97

Replay: Wednesday 4th May 1977

Billericay Town 2
Aslett, Woodhouse
Sheffield 1
Thornhill
(City Ground, Nottingham)

FA Trophy Final

Saturday 14th May 1977

Dagenham 1
Harris
Scarborough 2
H A Dunn pen, Abbey
20,500
Referee: G Courtney (Spennymoor)

Scarborough were gaining a reputation for dramatic Trophy finals. Their record third win in five years was again thanks to a late winner. This time they were a goal down with five minutes left and their winning goal came in the third minute of injury time. Scarborough were appearing in their third successive final and their fourth in five years, and they had also become the first club to retain the trophy.

Frank Saul had scored for Tottenham Hotspur in the FA Cup final ten years earlier.

Dagenham: Huttley, Wellman, P.Currie, Dunwell, Moore – capt, W.Currie, Harkins, Saul, Fox, Harris, Holder. sub: Scales for Harkins
Scarborough: Chapman, Smith, Marshall, Dunn (H), Ayre, Deere, Aveyard, Donoghue, Woodall, Abbey, Dunn (H A). sub: Barmby for Marshall

FA CUP FINAL

Saturday 21st May 1977

Liverpool	1-2	Manchester United
Case 53		Pearson 51, J Greenhoff 55
100,000		
Referee: R Matthewson (Bolton)		

Liverpool had won the FA Cup for the second time in 1974 and had twice won the FA Charity Shield at Wembley since then. They had retained the League Championship as well and were now on the verge of an amazing 'treble', having also reached the European Cup final

United were appearing in their second successive final and had knocked out Southampton, the holders, in the last 16 to avenge their shock defeat of the previous year. In the quarter-finals, they had beaten Aston Villa, who were to win the Football League Cup. Their third and last FA Cup win had been in 1963.

United finished sixth in their second season back in the First Division but they had not beaten Liverpool since 1972.

After a goalless first half United struck the first blow when Jimmy Greenhoff's header sent Stuart Pearson through to beat Clemence at the near post with a low drive. But two minutes later Liverpool, typically, were level. Jones crossed and Jimmy Case collected it on his thigh before turning sharply to blast an unstoppable shot past Stepney. After a further two minutes United restored their lead with a fortunate deflection. As Jimmy Greenhoff and Smith battled for possession in the penalty area, the ball fell for Macari, whose shot would have gone wide had it not hit Greenhoff's chest and looped over Clemence into the net. Liverpool fought back strongly, but the 'double' and consequently, the 'treble' slipped away.

Liverpool responded like the champions they were four days later. by beating Borussia Monchengladbach 3-1 in Rome to win the European Cup. The only other English club to win the trophy had been United, nine years earlier.

Liverpool: Clemence, Neal, Jones (J), Smith, Kennedy (R), Hughes (E) – capt, Keegan, Case, Heighway, Johnson, McDermott. sub: Callaghan for Johnson 64. manager: Bob Paisley
Manchester U: Stepney, Nicholl, Albiston, McIlroy, Greenhoff (B), Buchan – capt, Coppell, Greenhoff (J), Pearson (JS), Macari, Hill. sub: McCreery for Hill 81. manager: Tommy Docherty

BRITISH CHAMPIONSHIP

Tuesday 31st May 1977

England   0-1   **Wales**
James pen 44

48,000
Referee: J Gordon (Scotland)

Wales had not beaten England for 22 years and, apart from a wartime victory at Wembley, had not won in England since 1936, a 2-1 win at Molineux. In the 1970's they had earned three draws at Wembley and were five minutes away from victory on their last visit in 1975. But England had won twice in Wales in 1976.

Three days earlier Wales had drawn 0-0 with Scotland at the Racecourse Ground while England came from behind to beat Northern Ireland 2-1 at Windsor Park. Wales were top of their World Cup qualifying group on goal difference after deservedly beating European Champions Czechoslovakia 3-0 at the Racecourse Ground two months earlier. They had reached the quarter-finals of the European Championship the previous year.

With half-time approaching, Yorath's ball into the area found its way through to Leighton James as Hughes left it, expecting Shilton to collect.

The goalkeeper was forced to haul down James who took the penalty himself to give Wales the lead. This incident summed up the lack of confidence in the England squad and the Welsh held out for a historic victory.

Wales' 1-1 draw with Northern Ireland at Windsor Park, three nights later meant they could not win the title outright, but it did give England an opportunity to salvage a share if they could beat Scotland.

England: Shilton (Stoke City), Neal (Liverpool), Mills (Ipswich), Greenhoff (B) (Man Utd), Watson (Man City), Hughes (Liverpool), Keegan (Liverpool) – capt, Channon (Southampton), Pearson (Man Utd), Brooking (West Ham), Kennedy (Liverpool). sub: Tueart (Man City) for Brooking 79. manager: Don Revie
Wales: Davies (Everton), Thomas (Derby County), Jones (Liverpool), Mahoney (Stoke City), Phillips (Aston Villa), Evans (Crystal P), Sayer (Cardiff), Flynn (Burnley), Yorath (Coventry) – capt, Deacy (PSV Eindhoven), James (Derby County). sub: Roberts (Hull City) for Phillips. manager: Mike Smith

BRITISH CHAMPIONSHIP

Saturday 4th June 1977

England	**1-2**	**Scotland**
Channon 87 (pen)		McQueen 43 Dalglish 59
98,103		

Referee: K Palotai (Hungary)

Scotland needed only a point to retain the Championship by sharing it with Wales but victory would give them the title outright for the second year in succession. They had lost, however, on each of their last four visits to Wembley, including a 5-1 thrashing in 1975. It had been ten years since their last win at Wembley.

The Scots delighted their thousands of supporters in the stadium by taking the lead two minutes before half-time. Gordon McQueen rose above the England defence to power a header past Clemence from Hartford's free kick. Scotland sealed the Championship when Johnston's cross was headed back into the middle by Rioch and substitute Macari's flick found Kenny Dalglish, whose first attempt was blocked by Neal. But Dalglish stretched to force the rebound over the line as Hughes chal-lenged. Three minutes from time England gained some consolation when Francis was brought down by McQueen and Mike Channon converted the penalty. But it was too late to prevent their second home defeat in four days and the first time in 49 years that they had lost two home games in the Championship. The Scottish supporters invaded the pitch at the end just as they had done ten years earlier, although this time there was more damage and both crossbars were snapped by people climbing them.

Scotland were undoubtedly Britain's top team and went on to qualify for their second successive World Cup by beating both Czechoslovakia and Wales again. England were showing signs of recovery under new management and they beat Scotland at Hampden Park the following year.

England: Clemence (Liverpool), Neal (Liverpool), Mills (Ipswich), Greenhoff (Man Utd), Watson (Man City), Hughes (Liverpool) – capt, Francis (Birmingham), Channon (Southampton), Pearson (Man Utd), Talbot (Ipswich), Kennedy (Liverpool). subs: Cherry (Leeds) for Greenhoff 57, Tueart (Man City) for Kennedy 67. manager: Don Revie
Scotland: Rough (Partick), McGrain (Celtic), Donachie (Man City), Forsyth (Rangers), McQueen (Leeds), Rioch (Everton) – capt, Masson (QPR), Dalglish (Celtic), Jordan (Leeds), Hartford (Man City), Johnston (West Brom). subs: Macari (Man Utd) for Jordan 43, Gemmill (Derby County) for Masson 83. manager: Ally McLeod

Final table	P	W	D	L	F	A	Pts
Scotland	3	2	1	0	5	1	5
Wales	3	1	2	0	2	1	4
England	3	1	0	2	3	4	2
Northern Ireland	3	0	1	2	2	6	1

Schoolboy International

Saturday 18th June 1977

England 1
Rees 29

West Germany 2
Wuttke 44 Brummer 48
Referee: R Richardson (Stoke-on-Trent)

After three successive heavy defeats at Wembley, swift counter-attacks cancelled out England's half-time lead and gave the Germans a long-awaited victory.

England: Foyster, Banfield, Bennett, Pittaway – capt, Law, Mills, Rees, Thomas, Merry, Chandler, Chamberlain. sub: Butterworth for Merry

FA CHARITY SHIELD

Saturday 13th August 1977

Liverpool   0-0   **Manchester United**
82,000
Referee: K Styles (Barnsley)

Liverpool had won the League Championship by a point for the second year in succession. It was their third in five years and a record tenth overall. They had also won the European Cup four days after losing the FA Cup final to United. Liverpool were the Charity Shield holders, having won it twice at Wembley.

United had finished sixth in the First Division but had surprisingly prevented Liverpool from winning the 'treble'. This was their first match under new manager, Dave Sexton. They had not won the Shield outright since beating Aston Villa 4-0 in 1957, but had shared it with Liverpool after a 2-2 draw in 1965.

It was a fine competitive match but it was also the first ever goalless FA Charity Shield. Unlike in 1974 the Shield was shared, giving Liverpool their third triumph in four years and United their third share since their last outright victory, but a record eighth overall.

Liverpool failed to complete a hat-trick of League Championships, finishing runners-up to First Division newcomers, Nottingham Forest.

They did retain the European Cup, however. But before that they met Nottingham Forest in their first Football League Cup final. In 1979 United reached their third FA Cup final in four years.

Liverpool: Clemence, Neal, Jones (J), Thompson (PB), Kennedy (R), Hughes (E) – capt, Dalglish, Case, Fairclough, McDermott, Callaghan. manager: Bob Paisley
Manchester U: Stepney, Nicholl, Albiston, McIlroy, Greenhoff (B), Buchan – capt, Coppell, Greenhoff (J), Pearson (J S), Macari, Hill. sub: McCreery for Greenhoff (J). manager: Dave Sexton

INTERNATIONAL

Wednesday 7th September 1977

England   0-0   **Switzerland**
42,000
Referee: G Konrath (France)

After England's dismal showing in the British Championship, and their disappointing World Cup prospects, manager Don Revie had quit and Ron Greenwood took over, initially as caretaker-manager until the end of the World Cup qualifying games.

Switzerland had avoided defeat at Wembley, for the first time, on their last visit, in 1971, but had lost 2-1 to England in Basle in 1975.

They had not beaten England for 30 years and were already out of the World

Cup, having lost all three qualifying matches to date.

Greenwood used six of Liverpool's European Cup winning team to mould a successful side at international level. But it failed to produce a goal and England had now gone six matches without a win, their worst run since 19 years earlier when the Munich air disaster robbed them of key players.

Switzerland found themselves in England's World Cup qualifying group, returning to Wembley in 1980.

England: Clemence (Liverpool), Neal (Liverpool), Cherry (Leeds), McDermott* (Liverpool), Watson (Man City), Hughes (Liverpool) – capt, Keegan (Hamburg), Channon (Man City), Francis (Birmingham), Kennedy (Liverpool), Callaghan (Liverpool). subs: Hill (Man Utd) for Channon 46, Wilkins (Chelsea) for Callaghan 81. caretaker-manager: Ron Greenwood
*first cap
Switzerland: Burgener (Lausanne), Trinchero (Servette), Fischbach (Zurich), Barberis (Servette), Chapuisat (Zurich), Bizzini (Servette) – capt, Hasler (Neuchatel Xamax), Demarmels (Basle), Kuttel (Young Boys), Elsener (Grasshoppers), Botteron (Zurich). subs: Von Wartburg (Basle) for Demarmels 46, Sulser (Grasshoppers) for Kuttel 57, Brechbuhl (Young Boys) for Hasler 78, Rieder (Etoile Carouge) for Elsener 85. coach: Roger Vonlanthen

168

WORLD CUP QUALIFYING

Wednesday 16th November 1977

England   **2-0**   **Italy**
Keegan 11, Brooking 80
92,000
Referee: K Palotai (Hungary)

Having lost 2-0 to Italy in Rome the year before, England needed to win by four goals to have a realistic chance of qualifying for their first World Cup since 1970. Italy's 6-1 win over Finland in Turin the previous month had virtually assured their qualification as they had only a home game with Luxembourg after Wembley.

They had won on their last visit, in 1973 and were unbeaten at Wembley. England's last victory over Italy had been in New York in the American Bicentennial Tournament 18 months earlier when the Italians had been two goals up at half-time. Like England, Italy had failed to qualify for the previous year's European Championship quarter-finals

England's early lead came as a result of a Brooking centre and Kevin Keegan's glancing header sailed over Zoff into the net. With nothing to lose England attacked Italy down the flanks but did not score again until ten minutes from the end.

Although he was hacked down by Benetti, Keegan returned the favour, playing the ball through for Trevor Brooking to side-foot the second. It was a memorable night for Emlyn Hughes, winning his 50th cap, but it was all too late.

Italy needed only to beat Luxembourg in Rome the following month. They won 3-0 and England went out on goal difference. Italy returned to Wembley in 1989.

England: Clemence (Liverpool), Neal (Liverpool), Cherry (Leeds), Wilkins (Chelsea), Watson (Man City), Hughes (Liverpool) – capt, Keegan (Hamburg), Coppell* (Man Utd), Latchford* (Everton), Brooking (West Ham), Barnes* (Man City). subs: Pearson (Man Utd) for Latchford 75, Francis (Birmingham) for Keegan 83. caretaker-manager: Ron Greenwood
*first cap
Italy: Zoff (Juventus), Tardelli (Juventus), Gentile (Juventus), Benetti (Juventus), Mozzini (Torino), Facchetti (Internazionale) – capt, Causio (Juventus), Zaccarelli (Torino), Graziani (Torino), Antognoni (Fiorentina), Bettega (Juventus). subs: Sala (Torino) for Graziani 46, Cuccureddu (Juventus) for Facchetti 83. coach: Enzo Bearzot

Final table	P	W	D	L	F	A	Pts
Italy	6	5	0	1	18	4	10
England	6	5	0	1	15	4	10
Finland	6	2	0	4	11	16	4
Luxembourg	6	0	0	6	2	22	0

Inter-Varsity Match

Wednesday 7th December 1977

Cambridge U 0
Oxford U 4
Hall, Smith, Allanson, Price

Oxford's biggest ever victory at Wembley.

Schoolboy International

Saturday 4th March 1978
England 3
Bolton, Brooks, Gibson
France 3
Derzakarian pen, Perrez, Sonor

England were three goals up with just over half an hour remaining, but the French came back in an absorbing match.

Ian Muir made his Wembley debut at the tender age of 14 and went on to score five goals beneath the twin towers, including a brace for Tranmere Rovers against Nottingham Forest in the Football League Centenary Tournament in 1988.

Kevin Brock was in the Oxford United side, which won the Milk Cup at Wembley in 1986, while Ian Dawes was in the Queens Park Rangers side they beat.

England: Lowe, Dawes, Caton, Lee, Robinson, Gibson, Brock, Brooks – capt, Muir, Wiggan, Bolton. sub: Neill for Muir

FOOTBALL LEAGUE CUP FINAL

Saturday 18th March 1978

Liverpool 0-0 **Nottingham Forest**

After extra time
100,000
Referee: P Partridge (Durham)

This was a first League Cup final for both teams. Liverpool had never been beyond the quarter-finals, while Forest had beaten the holders Aston Villa to reach the quarter-finals for the first time. Liverpool were becoming regular visitors to Wembley, although Manchester United had stopped them winning on their last two appearances. Forest's only previous visit was for their second FA Cup win in 1959.

The teams were also involved in the battle for the League Championship. Liverpool were chasing a hat-trick of titles but Forest, who had won promotion only in third place the previous year, were setting the pace. Liverpool were also defending the European Cup and three days earlier had reached the semi-finals again. Three months before that they had become the first British club to win the European Super Cup.

But the season's two form sides gave a disappointing display and the final was goalless for the second year in succession. Liverpool should have won, but were kept out by a remarkable performance from Chris Woods, Forest's 18-year-old goalkeeper, who had still to make his league debut and was playing only because Peter Shilton was cup-tied, having turned out for Stoke City earlier in the competition.

Forest won the replay four days later with a controversial penalty. The foul had taken place just outside the area, but guts and determination had overcome the mighty Liverpool and Woods gave another inspired performance.

Forest were to become Liverpool's main challengers for honours over the next two years. They convincingly won the League Championship for the first time to complete a remarkable 'double' and won the FA Charity Shield four months later. They retained the League Cup the following year without a replay. Liverpool recovered to retain the European Cup at Wembley.

Footballer of the Year, Kenny Burns made his first appearance at Wembley and then captained Forest to victory in the replay in the absence of the injured John McGovern.

Liverpool: Clemence, Neal, Smith, Thompson (PB), Kennedy (R), Hughes (E) – capt, Dalglish, Case, Heighway, McDermott, Callaghan. sub: Fairclough for Kennedy. manager: Bob Paisley
Nottingham F: Woods, Anderson, Clark, McGovern – capt, Lloyd, Burns, O'Neill, Bowyer, Withe, Woodcock, Robertson. sub: O'Hare for McGovern. manager: Brian Clough

Replay: Wednesday 22nd March 1978

Liverpool 0-1 **Nottingham Forest**
                    Robertson 54 (pen)

(Old Trafford)

INTERNATIONAL

Wednesday 19th April 1978

England 1-1 **Brazil**
Keegan 70   Gil 9
92,500
Referee: C Corver (Netherlands)

Since the draw on Brazil's last visit in 1963 the South Americans had beaten England four times. But the previous year England had avoided defeat in Brazil for the first time, a goalless encounter in Rio de Janeiro. England's only victory against Brazil had been in their first meeting back in 1956. There had been nine games since then.

England had renewed confidence under Ron Greenwood who had been rewarded with a new, permanent, contract.

Brazil went ahead inside ten minutes. Gil took a pass from Rivelino and fooled Corrigan by beating him at the near post. The Brazilians then proceeded to show the more physical side of their football with some reckless challenges. Twenty minutes from the end Kevin Keegan gave England a deserved equaliser from a free kick, bending the ball round the Brazilian defensive wall.

Brazil went through the World Cup without losing a game but still finished only third. They went out on goal difference to Argentina, the hosts and eventual winners. Brazil were back at Wembley, just three years later.

England: Corrigan (Man City), Mills (Ipswich), Cherry (Leeds), Greenhoff (Man Utd), Watson (Man City), Currie (Leeds), Keegan (Hamburg) – capt, Coppell (Man Utd), Latchford (Everton), Francis (Birmingham), Barnes (Man City). manager: Ron Greenwood

Brazil: Leao (Palmeiras), Ze Maria (Corinthians), Abel (Vasco da Gama), Amaral (Guarani), Edinho (Fluminense), Cerezo (Atletico Mineiro), Rivelino (Fluminense) – capt, Dirceu (Vasco da Gama), Zico (Flamengo), Nunes (Santa Cruz), Gil (Botafogo). sub: Batista for Nunes 60. coach: Claudio Coutinho

FA Vase Final

Saturday 22nd April 1978

Barton Rovers 1
Smith 19
Blue Star 2
Dunn 24 Crumplin 89
16,391
Referee: T Morris (Leeds)

Blue Star, from Newcastle, became the first northern club to win the FA Vase but they had to come from behind and missed a penalty on the hour when James Thompson hit the bar. But they secured victory with Ian Crumplin's 89th minute winner.

Barton: Blackwell, Stephens, Crossley, Evans – capt, Harris, Dollimore, Dunn, Harnaman, Fossey, Turner, Smith. sub: Cox (not used)
Blue Star: Halbert, Feenan, Thompson, Davidson, Dixon (S), Beynon – capt, Storey, Dixon (P), Crumplin, Callaghan, Dunn. sub: Diamond (not used)

FA Trophy Final

Saturday 29th April 1978

Altrincham 3
Rogers 3, Johnson 16, King 48
Leatherhead 1
Cook 86
20,000
Referee: A Grey (Great Yarmouth)

A first victory for the famous non-league club from Cheshire.

Altrincham: Eales, Allan, Crossley, Bailey, Owens, King – capt, Morris, Heathcote, Johnson, Rogers, Davison. sub: Flaherty for Morris 71
Leatherhead: Swannell, Cooper, Eaton, Davies, Reid, Malley – capt, Cook, Salkeld, Kelly, Baker, Doyle. sub: Bailey (not used)

FA CUP FINAL

Saturday 6th May 1978

Arsenal 0-1 **Ipswich Town**
Osborne 77

100,000
Referee: D Nippard (Christchurch)

Arsenal were appearing in their third final of the decade, having won the 'double' in 1971 and then lost in the final the following year. This was the first final for Ipswich, but they had previously appeared at Wembley 50 years earlier in the Southern Amateur League, beating Ealing Association 4-0.

Arsenal finished fifth, in the First Division, their highest position since finishing runners-up in 1973. They also reached the Football League Cup semi-finals. Ipswich had been only a point away from the League Championship, the previous year, but finished 18th, their lowest position since 1971 and just three points clear of relegation.

Surprisingly Ipswich dominated the match, hitting the woodwork three times before finally breaking through. A low cross from Geddis went behind the Arsenal defence and Young could only turn it into the path of Roger Osborne, who drove it past Jennings. The emotion of the occasion was too much for Osborne and he immediately went off exhausted to be substituted. But his one moment of glory had given Ipswich a very popular and deserved victory.

Arsenal returned to win the FA Cup, the following year in one of the most dramatic finals in the history of the competition. Ipswich reached the quarter-finals of the European Cup-Winners Cup before losing a first leg lead to Barcelona. They went out on away goals and Barcelona went on to win the trophy.

Arsenal: Jennings, Rice – capt, Nelson, Price, O'Leary, Young, Brady, Hudson, Macdonald, Stapleton, Sunderland. sub: Rix for Brady 65. manager: Terry Neill
Ipswich: Cooper, Burley, Mills – capt, Talbot, Hunter, Beattie, Osborne, Wark, Mariner, Geddis, Woods. sub: Lambert for Osborne 79. manager: Bobby Robson

EUROPEAN CUP FINAL

Wednesday 10th May 1978

Bruges	0-1	Liverpool
		Dalglish 66

92,000
Referee: C Corver (Netherlands)

Bruges had become the first Belgian club to reach the semi-finals, where they had beaten the UEFA Cup holders Juventus. Two years earlier the Belgians had reached the UEFA Cup final and had lost a two-goal first-half lead in the first leg at Liverpool, finally succumbing 4-3 on aggregate. They were now aiming for revenge and their first European trophy.

Holders Liverpool were aiming for their third successive European trophy and a British record fourth in six years. Victory would make them the first British club to win the European Cup twice.

Bruges completed a hat-trick of Belgian League Championships, winning their fourth in six years while Liverpool had missed out on a League hat-trick, finishing as runners-up to newly-promoted, Nottingham Forest. They had also lost the Football League Cup final to them, after failing to press home their apparent superiority at Wembley. Liverpool had, however, become the first British club to win the European Super Cup when they thrashed European Cup-Winners Cup holders Hamburg 6-0 in the second leg.

The Belgians had come to defend but it was Liverpool who scored the only goal. A Souness through ball left Kenny Dalglish with only Jensen, having a fine match, to beat. The cool Scot waited for the 'keeper to commit himself before calmly chipping it over him. There was never the drama of Manchester United's victory ten years earlier but this was equally significant.

No Belgian club has reached a European Cup final since and Bruges have still to reach another European final.

Liverpool's incredible European run and their hopes of a European Cup hat-trick came to an abrupt end in the first round of the following season's competition when Nottingham Forest once again got the better of them before going on to win the competition themselves. Liverpool returned to Wembley to regain the FA Charity Shield.

Bruges: Jensen, Bastijns – capt, Krieger, Leekens, Maes, Cools, De Cubber, Vandereycken, Ku, Simoen, Sorensen. subs: Volders for Maes, Sanders for Ku. coach: Ernst Happel
Liverpool: Clemence, Neal, Hansen, Thompson (PB), Kennedy (R), Hughes (E) – capt, Dalglish, Case, Fairclough, McDermott, Souness. sub: Heighway for Case 65. manager: Bob Paisley

BRITISH CHAMPIONSHIP

Tuesday 16th May 1978

England   **1-0**   **Northern Ireland**
Neal 44
48,000
Referee: J Gordon (Scotland)

Northern Ireland, like England, had failed to qualify for the World Cup and had lost on their last two visits to Wembley as well as finishing bottom of the last two British Championships. They were chasing their first win in the British Championship in three years. Three days earlier, they had held the reigning champions, Scotland, to a 1-1 draw at Hampden Park, but had to win to stay in contention. England had not won the title since 1975, but had already beaten Wales 3-1 at Ninian Park.

England took until a minute before the interval to break through the Irish defence. From a Wilkins corner, Watson headed down for Phil Neal to slot the only goal past Platt. It was a comfortable win, but they could not add to their score.

After two successive Scottish titles, England regained the British Championship, with a surprise 1-0 win over Scotland at Hampden Park, four days later. Northern Ireland finished bottom for the third year in succession, after losing 1-0 to Wales at the Racecourse Ground three nights after Wembley.

Once again they had played all their games away from home. They were back at Wembley the following year in the European Championship.

England: Clemence (Liverpool), Neal (Liverpool), Mills (Ipswich), Wilkins (Chelsea), Watson (Man City), Hughes (Liverpool) – capt, Currie (Leeds), Coppell (Man Utd), Pearson (Man Utd), Woodcock* (Nottingham F), Greenhoff (Man Utd). manager: Ron Greenwood
Northern Ireland: Platt (Middlesbrough), Hamilton (Millwall) – capt, Scott (York City), Nicholl (C) (Southampton), Nicholl (J) (Man Utd), McIlroy (Man Utd), McCreery (Man Utd), O'Neill (Nottingham F), Anderson (Peterborough), Armstrong (Tottenham), McGrath (Man Utd). sub: Cochrane (Burnley) for McGrath. manager: Danny Blanchflower
*first cap

Final table	P	W	D	L	F	A	Pts
England	3	3	0	0	5	1	6
Wales	3	1	1	1	3	4	3
Scotland	3	0	2	1	2	3	2
Northern Ireland	3	0	1	2	1	3	1

BRITISH CHAMPIONSHIP

Wednesday 24th May 1978

England   **4-1**   **Hungary**
Barnes 11, Neal pen 30, Francis 32,   Nagy 62
Currie 77
74,000
Referee: R Vigliani (France)

Since losing to England on their last visit to Wembley, the Hungarians had shown little sign of repeating the heady days of the 1950's when they demolished England 6-3. Although they finished fourth in the 1972 European Championship they had just qualified for their first World Cup since 1966. In 1970 they had lost a play-off and in 1974 they had missed out on goal difference. England were the new British Champions and were enjoying an upturn in their fortunes after failing to qualify for the World Cup.

England took the lead with an opportunist goal. Watson got his head to Gujdar's clearance and sent Keegan away. Keegan played the ball across for Peter Barnes to knock it in.

At the half-hour mark Gujdar, under pressure from Keegan, failed to collect Barnes' cross and a surprised Toth caught the ball. It was a clear penalty and Phil Neal increased England's lead. Brooking's free kick was headed across goal by Watson for Trevor Francis to head the third two minutes later.

Hungary started the second half more positively and pulled one back just after the hour. Laszlo Nagy took a pass from Nyilasi and beat Shilton with a superb curling shot. But England notched a fourth goal when Barnes' cross was touched on by Brooking for substitute Tony Currie to blast an unstoppable shot past the 'keeper.

Hungary did not win a point in the World Cup, which began the following week. England were left to wonder what would have happened had they qualified. They were to meet Hungary again, in qualification for the next World Cup in 1981.

England: Shilton (Nottingham F), Neal (Liverpool), Mills (Ipswich), Wilkins (Chelsea), Watson (Man City), Hughes (Liverpool) – capt, Keegan (Hamburg), Coppell (Man Utd), Francis (Birmingham), Brooking (West Ham), Barnes (Man City). subs: Greenhoff (Man Utd) for Watson, Currie (Leeds) for Coppell 73. manager: Ron Greenwood
Hungary: Gujdar (Honved), Torok (Vasas), Kocsis (Honved), Toth (Ujpesti Dozsa), Zombori (Vasas), Kereki (Haladas), Fazekas (Ujpesti Dozsa) – capt, Nyilasi (Ferencvaros), Torocsik (Ujpesti Dozsa), Pinter (Honved), Nagy (Ujpesti Dozsa). sub: Csapo (Tatabanya) for Fazekas. coach: Lajos Baroti

Schoolboy International

Saturday 27th May 1978

England 3
Gibson 44, Bolton 55, Muir 74

Scotland 0
61,000
Referee: A Lees (Somerset)

Unlike the match two months earlier England held on to their three-goal lead this time.

England: Lowe, Dawes, Gernon, Lee, Caton, Brock, Gibson, Brooks – capt, Bolton, Kelly, Muir. sub: Robinson
Scotland: Cowan, Gorrie, Docherty, McGeachie, Landells, McIntyre, Hume, King, Ferguson, Burke, Speirs. sub: Hewitt for King

FA CHARITY SHIELD

Saturday 12th August 1978

Ipswich Town   **0-5**   **Nottingham Forest**
O'Neill 10, 76 Withe 27 Lloyd 47 Robertson 88

64,438
Referee: P Reeves (Leicester)

Ipswich had been thrashed at home by Tottenham Hotspur in their only previous FA Charity Shield in 1962 when they were League Champions. This time they were FA Cup winners, their first final, although in the League they escaped relegation to the Second Division by three points. Forest had taken everyone by surprise, winning their first League Championship in such a convincing manner by seven points from European Champions Liverpool, who had been chasing a hat-trick of titles. It was difficult to believe that Forest had won promotion from the Second Division by only a point, the previous year.

Brian Clough had become only the second manager (after Herbert Chapman) to win the Championship with two different clubs (Derby County in 1972 had been his first). To cap a memorable season, Forest had also beaten Liverpool to win the Football League Cup for the first time. Their only previous FA Charity Shield had been in 1959 when they lost to Wolverhampton Wanderers.

Forest took the lead with a scrappy goal, Martin O'Neill stabbing the ball in off the post after Gates had blocked Withe's attempts. Next Robertson mesmerised a depleted Ipswich defence until Gates got in a tackle. The ball fell to Barrett whose headed pass was headed over Cooper by Peter Withe.

After just a minute of the second half, Robertson's free kick was dummied by Withe and Larry Lloyd hammered the third past Cooper from close range. Robertson also created the fourth. Another cross and O'Neill fired his second. With two minutes left John Robertson himself produced an appropriate ending, collecting a wayward pass from Mills and beating Cooper from just outside the area. It was Ipswich's second Charity Shield thrashing.

Ipswich made one further appearance at Wembley in the very last Promotion play-off final beneath the twin towers in 2000. Forest's meteoric rise continued and they won the European Cup at the first attempt, beating Malmo by a single goal in the final in Munich.

Despite Forest setting a new Football League record of 42 games unbeaten, Liverpool took the League Championship from them. Forest were runners-up but did retain the Football League Cup.

Ipswich: Cooper, Burley, Mills – capt, Talbot, Osman, Wark, Parkin, Gates, Mariner, Whymark, Woods. sub: Turner for Whymark. manager: Bobby Robson

Nottingham F: Shilton, Anderson, Barrett, McGovern – capt, Lloyd, Burns, O'Neill, Gemmill (A), Withe, Woodcock, Robertson. sub: Needham for O'Neill. manager: Brian Clough

INTERNATIONAL

Wednesday 29th November 1978

England   **1-0**   **Czechoslovakia**
Coppell 69
92,000
Referee: E Linemayr (Austria)

Czechoslovakia had begun their defence of the European Championship with a fine 3-1 win against Sweden in Stockholm. They had failed to qualify for the last two World Cups, however, each time finishing group runners-up to Scotland. The Czechs had lost on their previous visit to Wembley in 1974 in the European Championship but had beaten England in Bratislava a year later when they went on to win the competition. This was England's first match at Wembley since regaining the British Championship.

On an icy pitch, England's winning goal was created by Anderson's run down the right wing which opened up a shooting opportunity for Currie. Michalik could not hold the ball and Steve Coppell had merely to knock it over the line.

Czechoslovakia qualified for the European Championship but lost their grip on the trophy two years later when the eventual winners West Germany beat them 1-0 in the opening game in Rome.

England beat them 2-0 in the 1982 World Cup in Bilbao but it was 1990 before they returned to Wembley.

England: Shilton (Nottingham F), Anderson* (Nottingham F), Cherry (Leeds), Thompson (Liverpool), Watson (Man City), Wilkins (Chelsea), Keegan (Hamburg) – capt, Coppell (Man Utd), Woodcock (Nottingham F), Currie (Leeds), Barnes (Man City). sub: Latchford (Everton) for Woodcock 41. manager: Ron Greenwood
*first cap

Czechoslovakia: Michalik (Banik Ostrava), Barmos (Dukla Prague), Vojacek (Banik Ostrava), Jurkemik (Inter Bratislava), Gogh (Slovan Bratislava), Stambacher (Dukla Prague), Kozak (Lokomotiva Kosice), Gajdusek (Dukla Prague), Jarusek (Zbrojovka Brno), Masny (Slovan Bratislava), Nehoda (Dukla Prague) – capt. sub: Panenka (Bohemians Prague) for Jarusek 76. coach: Josef Venglos

Inter-Varsity Match

Wednesday 6th December 1978

Cambridge U 2
Cox, McGuire

Oxford U 1
Hannon

Cambridge came from behind to record their first win in six years, with the winning goal coming from the substitute with three minutes left.

EUROPEAN CHAMPIONSHIP QUALIFYING

Wednesday 7th February 1979

England   4-0   **Northern Ireland**
Keegan 25, Latchford 46, 63,
Watson 49
92,000
Referee: U Eriksson (Sweden)

Northern Ireland arrived at Wembley as Group One leaders, unbeaten in three games and having not conceded a goal in Dublin and Sofia, their two away games. England were also unbeaten in two away games (Copenhagen and Dublin).

Northern Ireland had lost on each of their last three visits to Wembley in the British Championship and had been beaten in the European Championship 12 years earlier.

The scoring started when Kevin Keegan outjumped Jennings to head in Coppell's cross. It was Keegan who made the second goal in the first minute of the second half. His cross was headed in by Bob Latchford. Three minutes later yet another headed goal killed off the Irish. This time Dave Watson beat Armstrong to meet Brooking's corner and found the net. England's fourth came after another Brooking corner was flicked on by Keegan and Latchford hammered home his second from inside the six yard box.

England's win took them back to the top of the group on goal difference with a game in hand. England went on to beat the Ulstermen in the British Championship at Windsor Park three months later before returning five months after that for the European Championship return which they won 5-1. Northern Ireland were eliminated by that result, yet still finished as runners-up.

England: Clemence (Liverpool), Neal (Liverpool), Mills (Ipswich), Currie (Leeds), Watson (Man City), Hughes (Liverpool) – capt, Keegan (Hamburg), Coppell (Man Utd), Latchford (Everton), Brooking (West Ham), Barnes (Man City). manager: Ron Greenwood
Northern Ireland: Jennings (Arsenal) – capt, Rice (Arsenal), Nelson (Arsenal), C.Nicholl (Southampton), J.Nicholl (Man Utd), McCreery (Man Utd), O'Neill (Nottingham F), McIlroy (Man Utd), Armstrong (Tottenham), Caskey (Derby County), Cochrane (Middlesbrough). subs: Spence (Blackpool) for Caskey 50, McGrath (Man Utd) for Cochrane 81. manager: Danny Blanchflower

FOOTBALL LEAGUE CUP FINAL

Saturday 17th March 1979

Nottingham Forest   3-2   **Southampton**
Birtles 50, 78, Woodcock 82   Peach 16 Holmes 87
100,000
Referee: P Reeves (Leicester)

Forest, the holders, were attempting to become the first club to retain the League Cup. Since winning it for the first time they had returned to Wembley to win the FA Charity Shield. Southampton had never been beyond the quarter-finals before, but had been to Wembley three years earlier to pull off one of the FA Cup's biggest shocks when as a Second Division club they won their first major trophy. The Saints had returned three months later but lost in the Charity Shield.

Forest were also battling again with Liverpool to retain the League Championship after setting a new Football League record of 42 games unbeaten. Assistant manager, Peter Taylor led them out on to the pitch as Brian Clough had wanted to honour his partner's contribution to Forest's success. They had already ended Liverpool's hopes of completing a European Cup hat-trick by beating them in the first round and had built up a 4-1 lead against Grasshoppers from the first leg of their quarter-final. Southampton had finished Second Division runners-up to Bolton Wanderers the previous year. Just five days earlier they had fought their way through extra time to beat West Bromwich Albion and reach the FA Cup quarter-finals.

Southampton took a surprise lead after David Peach passed to Ball and ran undetected to meet his return before coolly rounding Shilton but it was Forest who came out for the second half on the attack.

Within five minutes they had equalised. Robertson's ball into the middle was blocked by Nicholl but he hesitated for a fatal moment and Garry Birtles nipped in to smash it into the roof of the net. Forest dominated the rest of the game but did not score again until Woodcock sent Birtles away to beat Nicholl and then Gennoe to claim his second.

With eight minutes left a superb Gemmill through ball left Tony Woodcock needing only to blast the ball over Gennoe and it was 3-1. Southampton raised their hopes briefly when Curran teed up the ball for Nick Holmes to fire a fine shot past Shilton but it was too late.

Forest drew 1-1 in Zurich, four days later in the second leg to reach the European Cup semi-finals and amazed the whole of Europe by winning the competition at the first attempt without losing a game, only the third club to win it unbeaten. It was England's third successive European Cup. Forest did not retain the League Championship, however, finishing runners-up to Liverpool. But the following year, they were chasing a hat-trick of League Cup wins when they reached the final again.

In 1984 Southampton were League runners-up themselves, beaten by Liverpool. But they did not reach Wembley again until the 1992 Zenith Cup final when, coincidentally, they met Forest again.

Nottingham F: Shilton, Barrett, Clark, McGovern – capt, Lloyd, Needham, O'Neill, Gemmill (A), Birtles, Woodcock, Robertson. sub: Bowyer (not used). manager: Brian Clough
Southampton: Gennoe, Golac, Peach, Williams, Nicholl, Waldron, Ball – capt, Boyer, Hayes, Holmes, Curran. sub: Sealy for Hayes. manager: Lawrie McMenemy

Schoolboy International

Saturday 24th March 1979

England 1
Wood

Wales 1
Bowen

After six successive defeats Wales avoided defeat at Wembley for the first time in 26 years. They never played at Wembley again at this level.

Mark Hughes went on to score many vital goals for Manchester United and Wales, winning 72 caps. He won a Wembley-record four FA Cup winners medals and scored the semi-final equaliser – plus one in the final – when United won the 'double' in 1994. Hughes also managed his country for five years at the turn of the millennium.

Clayton Blackmore also represented Wales, winning 39 full international caps, and was a scorer at Wembley for Manchester United in the 1990 FA Charity Shield.

Trevor Steven scored for Everton against Manchester United in the 1985 FA Charity Shield at Wembley and was capped 36 times by England.

Mark Bowen, who gave Wales a half-time lead, was the son of former Welsh team manager, Dave Bowen. He went on to win 41 full international caps and scored in the penalty shootout for Charlton Athletic when they dramatically won promotion to the Premiership at Wembley in 1998.

Mark Walters won a single cap for England, in New Zealand in 1991.

England: Oakley, May, Hutchinson, Wood – capt, Ash, Cook, Walters, Steven, Annon, Lane, Rollock. subs: Tierney for Cook, Dykes for Annon
Wales: Mullen, Blackmore, Holtham, Sanders, Bee, Hughes, Taylor, Bowen, Jones (S), Jones (J), Rees

FA Vase Final

Saturday 28th April 1979

Almondsbury Greenway 1
Price 49

Billericay Town 4
Young 11, 70, 87 Clayden 33
16,792

Doug Young's hat-trick gave Billericay a record third FA Vase in four years.

Almondsbury: Hamilton, Bowers (Ph), Scarrett, Sullivan, Tudor, Wookey, Bowers (Pe), Shehean, Kerr, Butt, Price. sub: Kilbaine for Tudor
Billericay: Norris, Blackaller, Bingham, Whettell, Bone – capt, Reeves, Pullin, Scott, Clayden, Young, Groom. sub: Carrigan for Groom 89

FA CUP FINAL

Saturday 12th May 1979

Arsenal   **3-2**   **Manchester United**
Talbot 12, Stapleton 43, Sunderland 89   McQueen 86 McIlroy 88
100,000
Referee: R Challis (Tonbridge)

These two sides were evenly matched, with a wealth of experience between them. Arsenal had been well beaten in the previous year's final and were hell bent on winning the Cup for the first time since the 'double' triumph of 1971. In the last 16 they had won away at Nottingham Forest who went on to win both the Football League Cup and the European Cup. United were appearing in their third final in four years. After ending Liverpool's 'treble' dreams in 1977 and drawing with them in the FA Charity Shield three months later, they had beaten them again in the semi-finals.

Arsenal opened the scoring when Liam Brady worked an opening before passing to Stapleton on the wing. Stapleton's through ball enabled Price to draw Bailey out of his goal and lay the ball back for two attackers and two defenders to fight for. Brian Talbot, who had helped Ipswich beat Arsenal in the previous year's final, just beat Buchan and Coppell – as well as Sunderland, his own team mate – to force the ball past Nicholl on the line. A second goal appeared to have settled it for Arsenal. Brady's supremely accurate cross was headed in by an unmarked Frank Stapleton, who was to score for United in the 1983 final.

Thus, Arsenal were coasting to victory with four minutes left when the whole stadium was thrown into turmoil. United suddenly scored. Coppell's free kick was knocked back into the goalmouth by Jordan, and Gordon McQueen fired past Jennings, despite being surrounded by five Arsenal defenders. United threw everything into attack; Arsenal panicked and United equalised less than two minutes later. Coppell sent Sammy McIlroy away down the right. The Irishman cut inside, beating off desperate lunges from O'Leary and Walford (who had come on as substitute only five minutes earlier), before slipping the ball under the advancing Jennings. Pandemonium ensued. Arsenal were stunned, United euphoric. Yet there was to be a final twist. Brady galvanised Arsenal back into action, passing to Rix out on the left. Rix's cross tempted out Bailey, but he failed to reach it and Alan Sunderland slid in just ahead of Albiston to restore Arsenal's lead. For United, it was a desperately cruel result.

The last four incredible minutes were in complete contrast to a rather drab match which had been played out until then. Comparisons were drawn with the 1953 final but never had such emotions of triumph and despair been packed into such a short space of time and still been completely exhausting.

The following year Arsenal became the first club to reach three successive FA Cup finals at Wembley. They also reached the European Cup-Winners Cup final, but lost 5-4 on penalties following a goalless draw after extra time with Valencia in Brussels. United were League runners-up to Liverpool the following year, and came back to Wembley in 1983 for their first Milk Cup final.

Arsenal: Jennings, Rice – capt, Nelson, Talbot, O'Leary, Young, Brady, Sunderland, Stapleton, Price, Rix. sub: Walford for Price 83. manager: Terry Neill
Manchester U: Bailey, Nicholl, Albiston, McIlroy, McQueen, Buchan – capt, Coppell, Greenhoff (J), Jordan, Macari, Thomas. sub: Greenhoff (B) (not used) manager: Dave Sexton

FA Trophy Final

Saturday 19th May 1979

Kettering Town 0
Stafford Rangers 2
A Wood 34, 65
32,000
Referee: D Richardson (Great Harwood)

Two goals from much-travelled Alf Wood gave Stafford their second FA Trophy win.

Kettering: Lane, Ashby, Lee, Easthall, Dixey, Suddards, Flannagan, Kellock, Phipps, Clayton, Evans. sub: Hughes (not used)
Stafford: Arnold, Wood (F), Willis, Sargeant, Seddon, Ritchie (R) – capt, Secker, Chapman, Wood (A), Cullerton, Chadwick. sub: Jones (not used)

BRITISH CHAMPIONSHIP

Wednesday 23rd May 1979

England   0-0   **Wales**
70,220
Referee: M Moffatt (Northern Ireland)

England had not beaten Wales at Wembley since 1973 and had lost to them on their previous visit. Curiously England had won their last six matches in Wales. Four days earlier, England had begun their defence of the British Championship by beating Northern Ireland 2-0 at Windsor Park. Wales had impressively beaten Scotland 3-0 at Ninian Park. In the European Championship Wales had completed their home fixtures to lead the group on goal difference. Three weeks earlier they had lost 2-0 to the eventual winners West Germany at the Racecourse Ground.

England fielded an experimental line-up and once again failed to pierce the Welsh rearguard.

Two nights later Wales drew 1-1 with Northern Ireland, at Windsor Park leaving England needing to beat Scotland a day later to retain the British Championship. In the European Championship, Wales lost 5-1 to West Germany in Cologne and failed to qualify. But the following year they beat England 4-1 at the Racecourse Ground to record their highest ever victory against them and in 1981 kept another clean sheet at Wembley.

England: Corrigan (Man City), Cherry (Leeds), Sansom* (Crystal P), Wilkins (Chelsea), Watson (Man City), Hughes (Liverpool) – capt, Keegan (Hamburg), Currie (Leeds), Latchford (Everton), McDermott (Liverpool), Cunningham* (West Brom). subs: Coppell (Man Utd) for Keegan 68, Brooking (West Ham) for Wilkins 75. manager: Ron Greenwood
Wales: Davies (Wrexham), Stevenson (Leeds), Jones (Wrexham), Phillips (Swansea), Dwyer (Cardiff), Mahoney (Middlesbrough), Yorath (Coventry) – capt, Flynn (Leeds), James (Swansea), Toshack (Swansea), Curtis (Swansea). sub: Harris (Leeds) for Toshack 80. manager: Mike Smith
*first cap

BRITISH CHAMPIONSHIP

Saturday 26th May 1979

England   3-1   **Scotland**
Barnes 45, Coppell 63, Keegan 70   Wark 21
100,000
Referee: A Garrido (Portugal)

Although Scotland had won at Wembley, two years earlier, England had gained their revenge at Hampden Park a year later and now needed to win to retain the British Championship. A draw would make Wales the first British Champions on goal difference while Scotland had to win 5-0 to regain the title for the third time in four years. In the European Championship Scotland were striving to restore lost pride after the previous year's humiliating World Cup exit but they had lost in Vienna and Lisbon, and only had a narrow home win against Norway to show for their efforts.

Scotland struck first. A teasing Graham cross went behind the England defenders. Dalglish knocked it back in and John Wark tapped it into the empty net. It was

the first goal conceded by Ray Clemence in eight games at Wembley for club and country. Scotland were good value for their lead but lost it in first-half injury time. Keegan's pass was flicked on by Brooking to Peter Barnes who was given too much time and space to control it on the edge of the area and fire a shot which crept into the corner past Wood.

England took a fortunate lead when Wood fumbled Wilkins' shot and Steve Coppell nipped in between the goalkeeper and Hegarty to score. Seven minutes later, England wrapped up the Championship. Kevin Keegan played a brilliant one-two with Brooking to split open the Scottish defence and ran on to tuck the ball under the advancing goalkeeper. Scotland had not played badly but England's clinical finishing at crucial times had killed them off.

Scotland failed to qualify for the European Championship and England completed a hat-trick of victories against them at Hampden Park the following year. But Scotland had their revenge at Wembley in 1981.

England: Clemence (Liverpool), Neal (Liverpool), Mills (Ipswich), Thompson (Liverpool), Watson (Man City), Wilkins (Chelsea), Keegan (Hamburg) – capt, Coppell (Man Utd), Latchford (Everton), Brooking (West Ham), Barnes (Man City). manager: Ron Greenwood

Scotland: Wood (Everton), Burley (Ipswich), Gray (Leeds), Wark (Ipswich), McQueen (Man Utd), Hegarty (Dundee U.), Dalglish (Liverpool) – capt, Souness (Liverpool), Jordan (Man Utd), Hartford (Man City), Graham (Leeds). manager: Jock Stein

Final table	P	W	D	L	F	A	Pts
England	3	2	1	0	5	1	5
Wales	3	1	2	0	4	1	4
Scotland	3	1	0	2	2	6	2
Northern Ireland	3	0	1	2	1	4	1

Schoolboy International

Saturday 9th June 1979

England 2
Rollock, Rideout

West Germany 2
Laschkowski 2

The Germans went ahead for the second time, with six minutes left but England fought back well and equalised again through Paul Rideout. His goal began an amazing Wembley scoring sequence for him. He scored four times, including a hat-trick, for England Schoolboys the following year and then in 1995 notched the only goal of the FA Cup final for Everton.

England: Farnworth, May, Hutchinson, Wood – capt, Ash, Tierney, Walker, Rideout, Reader, Walters, Rollock. sub: Cook

FA CHARITY SHIELD

Saturday 11th August 1979

Arsenal   1-3   Liverpool
Sunderland 86   McDermott 39, 67 Dalglish 64
91,550
Referee: G Courtney (Spennymoor)

Arsenal had won the FA Charity Shield a record seven times outright, but their last victory was in 1953, when they beat Blackpool – their last appearance in the fixture. Their extremely dramatic fifth FA Cup win three months earlier had come at the end of a season in which they finished seventh in the First Division.

Liverpool were aiming for their third Shield in four years, but the first outright since 1976. Their last appearance at Wembley had been when retaining the European Cup but they were appearing as a result of a record-breaking 11th League Championship, their third in four years, won with a record 68 points and the loss of only 16 goals in 42 league games, another record. It was the third meeting at Wembley between the two sides, Arsenal winning two previous FA Cup finals.

Liverpool took most of the first half to penetrate Arsenal's defence. Ray Kennedy's pass gave Terry McDermott the opportunity to run into space and shoot past Jennings. Two more classy goals midway through the second half wrapped up the match. The first saw Kenny Dalglish run on to Hansen's through ball, evade Walford's lunge and drive expertly past the goalkeeper.

Three minutes later it was McDermott running on to a Dalglish pass to score his second. Late on Alan Sunderland scored for Arsenal, after Stapleton had returned his pass but it hardly had the effect of his previous goal at Wembley.

Arsenal reached the European Cup-Winners Cup final for the first time and their third successive FA Cup final after beating Liverpool in a marathon semi-final which went to four games. Liverpool surprisingly went out in the European Cup first round for the second year in succession, losing to Dynamo Tbilisi.

But they retained the League Champion- ship and reached the semi-finals of both the FA Cup, again, and the Football League Cup. They also retained the FA Charity Shield, the following year.

Arsenal: Jennings, Rice – capt, Nelson, Talbot, O'Leary, Walford, Brady, Sunderland, Stapleton, Price, Rix. subs: Young for Nelson, Hollins for Price. manager: Terry Neill

Liverpool: Clemence, Neal, Kennedy (A), Thompson (PB) – capt, Kennedy (R), Hansen, Dalglish, Case, Johnson, McDermott, Souness. manager: Bob Paisley

EUROPEAN CHAMPIONSHIP QUALIFYING

Wednesday 12th September 1979

England   1-0   Denmark
Keegan 18
82,000
Referee: C Correia (Portugal)

Denmark had beaten Great Britain at Wembley to win bronze at the 1948 Olympics, but had only avoided defeat against England once in six previous meetings. That was a goalless draw in their first encounter in Copenhagen just a month after their Olympic appearance.

England's only previous home game against Denmark had been a World Cup qualifying match in 1956 at Molineux which England had won 5-2. England were top of Group One on goal difference from Northern Ireland, but had two games in hand and were unbeaten in their four games.

They had begun twelve months earlier by beating Denmark 4-3 in an entertaining game in Copenhagen. Denmark were three points behind England from two more games and had to win to maintain their slim hopes of qualification. They had reached the semi-finals in 1964 but had never qualified for a World Cup.

England were unimpressive but won the match when, from Neal's cross, Kevin Keegan hammered the ball past Jensen. The Danes could not convert their chances into goals and went out.

By the time England met Bulgaria, two months later, they had already qualified. Denmark's 3-0 defeat in Sofia the following month left them bottom of their qualifying group for the fourth successive European Championship.

They met England again in the European Championship in 1983 and gave them quite a shock at Wembley.

Allan Simonsen, the 1977 European Footballer of the Year, made his first appearance at Wembley.

England: Clemence (Liverpool), Neal (Liverpool), Mills (Ipswich), Thompson (Liverpool), Watson (Werder Bremen), Wilkins (Man Utd), Keegan (Hamburg) – capt, Coppell (Man Utd), McDermott (Liverpool), Brooking (West Ham), Barnes (West Brom). manager: Ron Greenwood

Denmark: Jensen (B) (Bruges), Hojgaard (KB Copenhagen), Busk (Maastricht), Ziegler (Hvidovre) – capt, Olsen (RWD Molenbeek), Lerby (Ajax Amsterdam), Arnesen (Ajax), Nielsen (Anderlecht), Jensen (H) (Ajax), Simonsen (Barcelona), Elkjaer (Lokeren). subs: Bertelsen (Esbjerg) for Nielsen 68, Bjerg (Aalborg) for Elkjaer 81. coach: Sepp Piontek

EUROPEAN CHAMPIONSHIP QUALIFYING

Thursday 22nd November 1979

England   2-0   Bulgaria
Watson 9, Hoddle 68
71,491
Referee: E Fredriksson (Sweden)

The Republic of Ireland's defeat by Northern Ireland at Windsor Park the previous day meant England had won Group One with two matches still to play, both home games. After drawing at Wembley in 1968, England had recorded their first two victories over

Bulgaria, the second of which had been by 3-0 in Sofia five months earlier. Bulgaria had never beaten England and lost to Great Britain at Wembley in an Olympic Qualifying match in 1971. They had failed to qualify for the previous year's World Cup, after losing their final match in Paris.

They had been quarter-finalists in the 1968 European Championship, but had avoided finishing bottom of the current group only by beating Denmark 3-0 the previous month in Sofia. This was their last match, which was delayed a day because of fog.

Woodcock's tenth minute corner led to England taking the lead. A superb cross from Hoddle found Dave Watson heading home. Glenn Hoddle then capped a fine debut half way through the second half by sidefooting home the second from the edge of the area, after a Francis pass.

Bulgaria did not meet England again, until 1996.

England: Clemence (Liverpool), Anderson (Nottingham F), Sansom (Crystal P), Thompson (Liverpool) – capt, Watson (Southampton), Wilkins (Man Utd), Reeves* (Norwich), Hoddle* (Tottenham), Francis (Nottingham F), Kennedy (Liverpool), Woodcock (Cologne). manager: Ron Greenwood
*first cap
Bulgaria: Christov (Pirin Blagoevgrad), Karakolev (Marek Stanke Dimitrov), G.Dimitrov (CSKA Sofia), Bonev (Lokomotiv Sofia), Iliev (Slavia Sofia), B.Dimitrov (Lokomotiv Sofia), Barzov (Levski Spartak), Markov (CSKA Sofia), Velichkov (Lokomotiv Sofia), Jeliazkov (Slavia Sofia) – capt, Tzvetkov (Slavia Sofia). subs: Kostadinov (Trakia Plovdiv) for Tzvetkov 29, Manolov (Trakia Plovdiv) for Velichkov 87. coach: Dragomir Taschkov

Inter-Varsity Match

Wednesday 5th December 1979

Cambridge U 1
Cox

Oxford U 3
Bennett, Sadler, Hannon

Maurice Cox scored Wembley's quickest ever goal when he gave Cambridge the lead in the first 15 seconds, but they were second best on the day.

EUROPEAN CHAMPIONSHIP QUALIFYING

Wednesday 6th February 1980

England   **2-0**   **Republic of Ireland**
Keegan 35, 75
90,299
Referee: K Scheurell (East Germany)

This was the last match in Group One. England had already qualified for the European Championships in Italy and had dropped just one point, a 1-1 draw with the Republic at Lansdowne Road two years earlier.

England had won their three previous home games in the group without conceding a goal. Ireland needed to win to finish runners-up on goal difference from Northern Ireland. They had still never qualified for a major tournament.

Kevin Keegan's first goal was scored with the help of a deflection off Grimes from McDermott's cross and Johnson's nod down, which took the ball past Peyton. The goalkeeper had to go off with an injured arm after a collision with Johnson in the 62nd minute and Healy, his replacement, was beaten by a superb goal.

Keegan outjumped Brady to pick up a loose ball, beat Lawrenson and, finding himself surrounded by four Irish defenders, spotted Healey off his line to produce an unexpected lob, which sailed into the net. A delightful finish but it left England wondering what they would do without him.

England: Clemence (Liverpool), Cherry (Leeds), Sansom (Crystal P), Thompson (Liverpool), Watson (Southampton), Robson* (West Brom), Keegan (Hamburg) – capt, McDermott (Liverpool), Johnson (Liverpool), Woodcock (Cologne), Cunningham (Real Madrid). sub: Coppell (Man Utd) for Johnson 62. manager: Ron Greenwood
Republic of Ireland: Peyton (Fulham), Hughton (Tottenham), Grimes (Man Utd), Lawrenson (Brighton), O'Leary (D) (Arsenal), Brady (Arsenal) – capt, Daly (Derby County), Grealish (Luton Town), Heighway (Liverpool), Stapleton (Arsenal), O'Brien (Philadelphia Fury). subs: Healey (Cardiff) for Peyton 62, O'Leary (P) (Shamrock) for O'Leary (D). manager: Johnny Giles
*first cap

Final table	P	W	D	L	F	A	Pts
England	8	7	1	0	22	5	15
Northern Ireland	8	4	1	3	8	14	9
Rep of Ireland	8	2	3	3	9	8	7
Bulgaria	8	2	1	5	6	14	5
Denmark	8	1	2	5	13	17	4

FOOTBALL LEAGUE CUP FINAL

Saturday 15th March 1980

Nottingham Forest   **0-1**   **Wolverhampton Wanderers**

Gray 67

100,000
Referee: D Richardson (Great Harwood)

Forest were attempting to become the first club to complete a hat-trick of League Cup wins, having become the first to retain the trophy the previous year. This time they were led out by coach Jimmy Gordon, Brian Clough again giving up his honour to one of his staff.

Wolves had won the League Cup for the first time on their previous Wembley visit, in 1974. Since then, they had spent a season in the Second Division, winning promotion as Champions in 1977, as Forest secured promotion by a point in third place. Forest had beaten European Cup-Winners Cup holders Barcelona the previous month, to add the European Super Cup to their surprise European Cup win the pre-

vious year. They had reached the European Cup quarter-finals in their defence, but were in grave danger of losing the crown after Dynamo Berlin had beaten them 1-0 at the City Ground ten days earlier.

Wolves ended Forest's grip on the trophy when Daniel sent a hopeful ball towards the Forest penalty area. Shilton came out to collect, but Needham, who had not heard his goalkeeper's shout, chested it back to where he thought Shilton would be. But sadly for Forest, it left Andy Gray with a simple tap-in to an empty net.

Four days later, Forest went to Berlin and won the second leg 3-1 to reach the European Cup semi-finals, eventually retaining the trophy, England's fourth successive win.

Nottingham F: Shilton, Anderson, Gray (F), McGovern – capt, Needham, Burns, O'Neill, Bowyer, Birtles, Francis, Robertson. sub: O'Hare (not used). manager: Brian Clough
Wolves: Bradshaw, Palmer, Parkin, Daniel, Berry, Hughes – capt, Carr, Hibbitt, Gray, Richards, Eves. sub: Brazier (not used). manager: John Barnwell

Schoolboy International

Saturday 22nd March 1980

England 2
Bray, Rideout
Switzerland 0

England's first victory over Switzerland in their second meeting at schoolboy level.

England: Lara, Queenan, McClure – capt, Byrom, McGinty, Donald, Bray, Parris, Wimbleton, Rideout, Brown. sub: Jones

FA Vase Final

Saturday 26th April 1980
Guisborough Town 0
Stamford 2
Alexander 68 McGowan 74
11,500
Referee: N Midgley (Manchester)

Stamford's victory avenged their extra-time defeat in 1976.

Guisborough: Cutter, Scott, Thornton, Angus, Maltby, Percy, Skelton, Coleman, McElvaney, Sills, Dilworth – capt. sub: Harrison (not used)
Stamford: Johnson, Kwiatkowski, Ladd, McGowan, Bliszczak (I) – capt, Mackin, Broadhurst, Hall, Czarnecki, Potter, Alexander. sub: Bliszczak (S) (not used)

FA CUP FINAL

Saturday 10th May 1980

Arsenal   0-1   **West Ham United**
                                            Brooking 13

100,000
Referee: G Courtney (Spennymoor)

Arsenal, the holders, became the first club since Blackburn Rovers in 1886 to reach three successive FA Cup finals. In the longest semi-final of all time, which went to four matches, they had eventually beaten League Champions Liverpool to avenge their defeat in the FA Charity Shield the previous year.

Their fifth FA Cup win the year before had seen one of the most dramatic climaxes in the history of the competition. West Ham had won the Cup for the second time in 1975 but had lost in the Charity Shield three months later.

In an exhausting season Arsenal had also reached the European Cup-Winners Cup final for the first time and finished fourth in the First Division, their highest position since finishing runners-up in 1973.

Having been relegated two years previously and finishing only seventh in the Second Division, West Ham were aiming to become the lowest-placed club to win the FA Cup since Wolverhampton Wanderers in 1908.

West Ham began well on an extremely hot day and scored what was to be the game's only goal when Devonshire's cross was pushed over to the far post by Jennings. Cross's shot was blocked by Young, only for the rebound to fall to Pearson whose shot flew across goal where Trevor Brooking stooped to divert the ball past Jennings with his head. Arsenal looked jaded and West Ham held on for a surprise FA Cup win.

Four days later Arsenal lost on penalties to Valencia following a goalless draw after extra time in the European Cup-Winners Cup final in Brussels.

They did not win silverware again until 1987 when they captured the Littlewoods Cup for the first time. West Ham reached the European Cup-Winners Cup quarter-finals the following year where they lost to the eventual winners, Dynamo Tbilisi despite winning the second leg in Georgia.

Arsenal: Jennings, Rice – capt, Devine, Talbot, O'Leary, Young, Brady, Sunderland, Stapleton, Price, Rix. sub: Nelson for Devine 61. manager: Terry Neill

West Ham: Parkes, Stewart, Lampard, Bonds – capt, Martin, Devonshire, Allen, Pearson, Cross, Brooking, Pike. sub: Brush (not used). manager: John Lyall

INTERNATIONAL

Tuesday 13th May 1980

England   3-1   **Argentina**
Johnson 42, 50, Keegan 69   Passarella pen 55
90,000
Referee: B McGinlay (Scotland)

Argentina had recovered from a two-goal deficit on their last visit to Wembley in 1974 but had not beaten England since 1964. Their last meeting had ended in a 1-1 draw in Buenos Aires in 1977. The following year Argentina won the World Cup for the first time, beating the Netherlands 3-1 after extra time in the final in Buenos Aires. This was a good test for the re-emerging England who had just qualified with ease for the European Championship.

The visitors were fielding six of the side that won the World Cup but it was the 19-year-old Maradona who caught the eye. England, however, scored when a superb cross from Coppell was met by a diving header from David Johnson which gave Fillol no chance from close range. Five minutes after the interval, England scored again. Fillol got to Kennedy's centre but could only push it up to the far post where Johnson just beat Tarantini to knock the ball over the line.

Argentina pulled one back just five minutes

later when Maradona was brought down by Sansom and Daniel Passarella stepped up to leave Clemence rooted to the spot from the penalty. But England secured their victory when Johnson crossed for Coppell to trap the ball and Kevin Keegan to charge in and hammer the third into the corner as three defenders converged on him. A famous victory to celebrate Dave Watson's 50th cap.

Two years later these two countries clashed in the Falklands and Argentina would not return to Wembley until 1991.

Argentina fielded two World Cup-winning captains. Daniel Passarella, scorer of their goal, had led them to victory two years earlier, while in 1986 it was Diego Maradona who was to score twice against England – one blatantly handled, the other a fantastic individual effort – in the quarter-final in Mexico City before lifting the World Cup again.

England: Clemence (Liverpool), Neal (Liverpool), Sansom (Crystal P), Thompson (Liverpool), Watson (Southampton), Wilkins (Man Utd), Keegan (Hamburg) – capt, Coppell (Man Utd), Johnson (Liverpool), Woodcock (Cologne), Kennedy (Liverpool). subs: Brooking (West Ham) for Kennedy 72, Cherry (Leeds) for Neal 76, Birtles* (Nottingham F) for Johnson 76. manager: Ron Greenwood
*first cap

Argentina: Fillol (River Plate), Van Tuyne (Rosario Central), Tarantini (River Plate), Olguin (Independiente), Gallego (Newell's Old Boys), Passarella (River Plate) – capt, Santamaria (Newell's), Barbas (Racing), Luque (River Plate), Maradona (Argentinos Juniors), Valencia (Talleres). subs: Diaz (River Plate) for Santamaria 18, Ischia (Velez Sarsfield) for Barbas 51, Simon (Newell's) for Van Tuyne. coach: Cesar Luis Menotti

FA Trophy Final

Saturday 17th May 1980

Dagenham 2
Duck 17, Maycock 82

Mossley 1
Smith
26,000
Referee: K Baker (Birmingham)

After three defeats at Wembley in the 1970's, Dagenham began the new decade with the sweet taste of victory thanks to a late winner.

Dagenham: Huttley, Wellman, Scales, Dunwell, Moore – capt, Maycock, Durrell, Horan, Duck, Kidd, Jones. sub: Holder (not used)

Mossley: Fitton, Brown, Vaughan, Gorman, Salter, Pollitt, Smith, Moore, Skeete – capt, O'Connor, Keelan. sub: Wilson for Moore

BRITISH CHAMPIONSHIP

Tuesday 20th May 1980

England   1-1   **Northern Ireland**
Johnson 81   Cochrane 83
33,676
Referee: G Owen (Wales)

England had won their last six matches against Northern Ireland, including a European Championship 'double' in the recent qualifying group won. Northern Ireland had failed to score at Wembley since 1972, their last victory. They had finished bottom of the last four British Championships but had already recorded their first victory in the competition since 1975 when they beat Scotland 1-0 four nights earlier at Windsor Park.

England's hopes of completing a hat-trick of British Championships had taken a severe blow the next day when they went down 4-1 to Wales at the Racecourse Ground, their heaviest ever defeat by the Welsh. Another defeat would put them out in their last home match before the European Championship in Italy.

This was a scrappy game which did not liven up until the last ten minutes. Hughes' cross was touched on by Sansom and David Johnson's challenge on Brotherston resulted in the ball finding the net. Johnson was credited with it although Brotherston appeared to get the final touch. This was a more resilient Irish side than in recent years, however, and they equalised within two minutes. Substitute Terry Cochrane got on the end of Jimmy Nicholl's long ball to fire past Corrigan.

Northern Ireland's 1-0 win over Wales at

Ninian Park three nights later gave them the British Championship for the first time outright since 1914 and only their second overall.

Sadly, they could not defend the title the following year because of the troubles in Northern Ireland, but they had entered a new era which brought success in the 1982 World Cup. England's 2-0 win over Scotland at Hampden Park four days later gave them the consolation of finishing runners-up. Northern Ireland never scored again at the old Wembley and were heavily beaten on their next visit.

England: Corrigan (Man City), Cherry (Leeds), Sansom (Crystal P), Hughes (Wolves) – capt, Watson (Southampton), Wilkins (Man Utd), Reeves (Man City), McDermott (Liverpool), Johnson (Liverpool), Brooking (West Ham), Devonshire* (West Ham). sub: Mariner (Ipswich) for Reeves 70. manager: Ron Greenwood

Northern Ireland: Platt (Middlesbrough), J.Nicholl (Man Utd), Donaghy (Luton Town), C.Nicholl (Southampton), O'Neill (Leicester), Cassidy (Newcastle), McIlroy (Man Utd) – capt, Hamilton (Burnley), Armstrong (Tottenham), Finney (Cambridge), Brotherston (Blackburn). subs: McCreery (QPR) for Cassidy 73, Cochrane (Middlesbrough) for Hamilton 73. manager: Billy Bingham

*first cap

Final table	P	W	D	L	F	A	Pts
Northern Ireland	3	2	1	0	3	1	5
England	3	1	1	1	4	5	3
Wales	3	1	0	2	4	3	2
Scotland	3	1	0	2	1	3	2

Schoolboy International

Saturday 7th June 1980

England 4
Rideout 3, Wimbleton

Scotland 5
McStay 2, Sludden 2, Dick
69,000
Referee: M Taylor (Deal)

In one of the most entertaining games seen at Wembley at any level, England conceded five at the stadium for the first time despite Paul Rideout's powerful shooting at the other end. Millions watching live on TV were enthralled by the game.

Paul McStay, who scored twice, made his full international debut for Scotland at the age of 18 and went on to win 76 caps, seven as captain.

England: Lara, Queenan, McGinty, McClure – capt, Byrom, Donald, Wimbleton, Willis, Rideout, Parris, Jones. subs: Hollier for Donald, Thompson for Willis Brown for Jones

Scotland: Bruce, MacDonald, O'Connor, Plenderleith, Coyle, Nicholas, Robertson, McStay, Sludden, Rae, Dick. subs: Currie for Nicholas, McKay for Sludden

FA CHARITY SHIELD

Saturday 9th August 1980

Liverpool	1-0	West Ham United

McDermott 17
90,000
Referee: J Hunting (Leicester)

Both clubs had beaten Arsenal at Wembley in the past year. Liverpool had begun the previous season by defeating the Gunners in the Charity Shield and were now aiming for their fourth Shield in five years. Their fourth League Championship in five years, a record twelfth overall, had been won by just two points from Manchester United. This overcame the disappointments of losing in the semi-finals of both the FA Cup and the Football League Cup.

West Ham had pulled off a major shock to beat Arsenal in the FA Cup final three months earlier. They had shared the FA Charity Shield with Liverpool in 1964 after a 2-2 draw but had lost in the fixture 11 years later at Wembley.

Liverpool could not produce the same exhibition football which had swept aside Arsenal the previous year. but they retained the Shield when Parkes could not hold Alan Kennedy's shot and Terry McDermott nipped in for the winner.

Liverpool again missed out on a League Championship hat-trick, finishing fifth, their lowest position for ten years, but they still managed to regain the European Cup for a British record third time in five years, beating Real Madrid 1-0 in Paris. It was England's fifth successive victory.

Two months earlier Liverpool again met West Ham, in the Football League Cup final. West Ham ran away with the Second Division Championship, winning it by a massive 13 points and their performances in Europe and the League Cup proved that their FA Cup win was no fluke.

Liverpool: Clemence, Neal, Kennedy (A), Thompson (PB) – capt, Kennedy (R), Hansen, Dalglish, Case, Johnson, McDermott, Souness. manager: Bob Paisley

West Ham: Parkes, Stewart, Brush, Bonds – capt, Martin, Devonshire, Allen, Holland, Cross, Brooking, Pike. sub: Morgan for Pike 73. manager: John Lyall

WORLD CUP QUALIFYING

Wednesday 10th September 1980

England	4-0	Norway

McDermott 37 (pen), 75, Woodcock 66,
Mariner 85
48,250
Referee: M Van Langenhove (Belgium)

England returned from the European Championship in Italy after failing to reach the last four. The host nation had beaten them with a late winner in Turin. They began their attempt to reach the World Cup by entertaining Norway at Wembley for the first time in the opening game of Group Four. Their four previous meetings had all been comfortable victories for England. Norway's only previous trip to England had resulted in a 4-0 deficit at St James' Park in 1938. They had appeared in the World Cup earlier that year but had not qualified for a major tournament since.

A Rix free kick was expertly volleyed into the net by Terry McDermott to give England the lead but they did not extend it until midway through the second half when Thompson's cross found Mariner's head for Tony Woodcock to drive the second past Jacobsen. The Norwegians began to crumble and nine minutes later McDermott scored his second from the penalty spot after Mariner had been fouled by Aas. With five minutes left, Paul Mariner scored the goal of the night after a mazy run ended with a fine shot for England's fourth.

A good start for England, but they could not envisage the dramas they would have to endure before the qualifying group was decided. A year later Norway pulled off a huge shock, winning the return 2-1 in Oslo, their first ever victory over England. It was England's third defeat and it left them relying on the results of others. Norway eventually finished bottom of the group but certainly left their mark on the teams who finished above them. They returned to Wembley in 1992 for another World Cup qualifying match.

England: Shilton (Nottingham F), Anderson (Nottingham F), Sansom (Arsenal), Thompson (Liverpool) – capt, Watson (Southampton), Robson (West Brom), Gates* (Ipswich), McDermott (Liverpool), Mariner (Ipswich), Woodcock (Cologne), Rix* (Arsenal). manager: Ron Greenwood
*first cap

Norway: T.Jacobsen (Valerengens), Berntsen (Viking Stavanger), Kordahl (Lillestrom), Aas (Bayern Munich), Grondalen (Rosenborg) – capt, Albertsen (Den Haag), Hareide (Molde), Dokken (Lillestrom), Larsen-Okland (Bayer Leverkusen), P.Jacobsen (Hamarkameratene), Erlandsen (Lillestrom). sub: Ottesen (Bayer Leverkusen) for Erlandsen 83. coach: Tor Roste Fossen

WORLD CUP QUALIFYING

Wednesday 19th November 1980

England	**2-1**	**Switzerland**
Tanner og 22, Mariner 36		Pfister 76

69,000
Referee: J Keizer (Netherlands)

Switzerland had not qualified for the World Cup since 1966 and had begun Group Four three weeks earlier with a disastrous 2-1 defeat against Norway in Berne. Romania now led the group on goal difference from the Norwegians following a 2-1 victory over England in Bucharest the previous month. England were a point behind while Hungary had yet to play. Switzerland had secured draws on each of their last two visits to Wembley in 1971 and 1977.

England eventually broke down the Swiss when Markus Tanner accidentally sent Coppell's cross past his own 'keeper. Paul Mariner headed the second from Brooking's free kick and England were well on top, but the visitors came fighting back in the second half. Hans-Jorg Pfister scored from Wehrli's cross with 14 minutes left and it was the Swiss who finished strongest and England, rather worryingly, just held on to go back to the top of the group.

Six months later, in the return in Basle, Switzerland beat England for the first time in 34 years by 2-1.

It was England's second defeat in the group and alarm bells were beginning to ring. Switzerland failed to qualify and made very little impression on international football until they reached the 1994 World Cup. They did not appear at Wembley again until 1995.

England: Shilton (Nottingham F), Neal (Liverpool), Sansom (Arsenal), Robson (West Brom), Watson (Southampton), Mills (Ipswich) – capt, Coppell (Man Utd), McDermott (Liverpool), Mariner (Ipswich), Brooking (West Ham), Woodcock (Cologne). sub: Rix (Arsenal) for Brooking 82. manager: Ron Greenwood
Switzerland: Burgener (Lausanne), Wehrli (Grasshoppers), Hermann (Grasshoppers), Ludi (Zurich), Geiger (Sion), Barberis (Monaco), Pfister (Grasshoppers), Tanner (Basle), Schonenberger (Young Boys), Elsener (Zurich), Botteron (Cologne) – capt. subs: Marti (Basle) for Schonenberger 37, Egli (Grasshoppers) for Tanner 46. coach: Leon Walker

Inter-Varsity Match

Wednesday 10th December 1980

Cambridge U 0

Oxford U 2
Bennett 2

A goal in each half gave Oxford their second successive victory at Wembley.

FOOTBALL LEAGUE CUP FINAL

Saturday 14th March 1981

Liverpool	**1-1**	**West Ham United**
A Kennedy 117		Stewart pen 120

After extra time
100,000
Referee: C Thomas (Porthcawl)

Liverpool's only previous League Cup final had been three years earlier when they failed to break down a determined Nottingham Forest defence. Forest again got the better of them two years later in the semi-finals in another famous meeting. Since then, Liverpool had won the European Cup at Wembley and the FA Charity Shield twice. Their second Shield victory had been seven months earlier against West Ham.

The Hammers' only previous final had been back in 1966, when their first leg lead was wiped out by West Bromwich Albion who won 5-3 on aggregate. Now they were making their third appearance at Wembley in ten months, a remarkable achievement for a Second Division club. The first was their FA Cup win the previous year. In the quarter-finals, West Ham had knocked out Tottenham Hotspur, who were to succeed them as FA Cup winners. Both clubs had reached the quarter-finals of a European competition. Ten days earlier in the European Cup, Liverpool had convincingly beaten CSKA Sofia 5-1 in the first leg, while in the European Cup-Winners Cup West Ham had suffered a 4-1 home defeat at the hands of the eventual winners Dynamo Tbilisi in their first leg.

Liverpool were still in contention for a League Championship hat-trick denied them by Nottingham Forest three years earlier. Meanwhile, West Ham were dominating the Second Division.

Neither side could find a breakthrough until three minutes from the end of extra time. Irwin's header into the middle was headed out by Bonds under pressure from Lee, who fell and lay motionless in an offside position.

Martin attempted an overhead clearance but the ball went only as far as Alan Kennedy who hammered it past Parkes. The referee decided that Lee was not interfering with play, although he appeared to look up and then duck his head as the ball passed over him, and gave the goal despite West Ham's vehement protests. Liverpool, it seemed, would win the League Cup at last.

But West Ham came back from the dead with a last desperate attack. A corner from Neighbour was headed towards goal by Martin, but McDermott pushed it onto the bar with his hand and a penalty was given. Ray Stewart sent Clemence the wrong way with the very last kick of the match as West Ham won a reprieve, perhaps deservedly, given the controversy surrounding Liverpool's goal.

The replay was played the following month and Liverpool came from behind to win the League Cup for the first time, a long overdue success in relation to their other honours.

It was to be the first of a record four successive wins in the competition, each of which curiously went to extra time at least. Liverpool regained the European Cup for a British record third time in five years, but they once again failed to capture that League Championship hat-trick, slumping uncharacteristically to fifth, their lowest position in the First Division for ten years.

West Ham, as expected, won the Second Division Championship by a runaway 13 points, reclaiming their rightful place in the First Division after three years absence. They never played at the stadium again.

Liverpool: Clemence, Neal, Kennedy (A), Irwin, Kennedy (R) – capt, Hansen, Dalglish, Lee, Heighway, McDermott, Souness. sub: Case for Heighway 65. manager: Bob Paisley

West Ham: Parkes, Stewart, Lampard, Bonds – capt, Martin, Devonshire, Neighbour, Goddard, Cross, Brooking, Pike. sub: Pearson for Goddard 109. manager: John Lyall

Replay: Wednesday 1st April 1981

Liverpool	2-1	West Ham United
Dalglish 26, Hansen 29		Goddard 10
(Villa Park, Birmingham)		

INTERNATIONAL

Wednesday 25th March 1981

England	1-2	Spain
Hoddle 26		Satrustegui 6, Zamora 32
71,840		

Referee: W Eschweiler (West Germany)

Spain had lost on each of four previous visits to Wembley and they had lost their last seven matches with England,since beating them 3-0 in Madrid in 1960. England had also beaten them twice in the past year. Almost a year earlier to the day, England had won 2-0 in Barcelona and then, three months later, defeated Spain 2-1 in the

European Championship in Naples. Spain finished bottom of the group with England a place above them. The World Cup was to be held in Spain the following year and as hosts they did not have to qualify. In 1978 they had failed to progress beyond the first round.

The Spanish took advantage of an

uncertain England defence very early in the match and Zamora found himself with only Clemence to beat. He laid the ball off for Jesus Satrustegui to provide the finishing touch. England equalised with a spectacular goal. Robson's cross was headed out by Maceda, but Glenn Hoddle volleyed it superbly past Arconada.

But England's defenders could not cope with the Spanish attack, however, and Spain restored their lead when Jesus Zamora ran forward but stopped the ball dead for Juanito to pick up. Zamora then ran unmarked to receive a return pass from where, as Butcher chased in vain, he slotted the winner past Clemence.

Their next meeting resulted in a goalless draw in Madrid in the following year's World Cup. Both teams were eliminated in the last twelve. Spain reached the European Championship final in 1984, where they lost to the hosts France in Paris, but England beat them 4-2 in Madrid in 1987 and they did not return to Wembley until the 1996 European Championship Quarter-final.

England: Clemence (Liverpool), Neal (Liverpool), Sansom (Arsenal), Robson (West Brom), Butcher (Ipswich), Osman (Ipswich), Keegan (Southampton) – capt, Francis (Nottingham F), Mariner (Ipswich), Brooking (West Ham), Hoddle (Tottenham). subs: Wilkins (Man Utd) for Brooking 70, Barnes (West Brom) for Francis 81. manager: Ron Greenwood
Spain: Arconada (Real Sociedad) – capt, Camacho (Real Madrid), Gordillo (Real Betis), Maceda (Sporting Gijon), Tendillo (Valencia), Victor (Real Zaragoza), Juanito (Real Madrid), Alonso (Sporting Gijon), Satrustegui (Real Sociedad), Zamora (Real Sociedad), Marcos (Real Santander). subs: Montero (Sevilla) for Victor 68, Dani (Athletic Bilbao) for Juanito 84. coach: Jose Santamaria

Victory Shield

Schoolboy International

Saturday 28th March 1981

England 4
Sinton, Lambert 2, Kerslake
Northern Ireland 0
Referee: A Bell (Sheffield)

This was the first time that a match in the schoolboys' equivalent of the British Championship had been staged at Wembley. England went on to win the Shield without dropping a point or conceding a goal and it was the first of three successive 4-0 victories against the Irish, who never played at Wembley again.

Andy Sinton won twelve full international caps for England, but only one at Wembley, against Brazil. He also won a Worthington Cup winners medal with Tottenham Hotspur as a substitute in 1999.

England captain and goalscorer, David Kerslake was in the unfortunate Swindon Town side, which won the Second Division Promotion play-off final in 1990, but were denied promotion to the top flight because of financial irregularities.

England: Hope, Parkin, Aldridge, Robinson, Macowat, Kerslake – capt, Neal, Booth, Sinton, Cooper, Lambert. subs: Wynter for Neal, Jones for Cooper
Northern Ireland: Quinn, Agnew, Scott, Rafferty, Roxborough, Mills, Shearer, Atkinson, Kelly, Kennedy, Clarke. subs: Leckey for Roxborough, Baxter for Clarke

FA Vase Final

Saturday 25th April 1981

Whickham 3
Scott, Williamson, Peck og
Willenhall Town 2
Smith, Stringer
After extra time
12,000
Referee: R Lewis (Great Bookham)

Willenhall were two up inside ten minutes but their goalkeeper, Steve Newton was carried off with a head injury in the 26th minute after Whickham had pulled a goal back. They tried two different replacements.

First striker, Gary Matthews held the fort until Whickham equalised after 56 minutes. Then Martin Woodall took over and was only beaten in extra time when he saved Cawthra's shot, which then cruelly rebounded off Peck and the post for an own goal, after he had kept Whickham at bay for 45 minutes.

Whickham: Thompson, Scott, Knox, Williamson, Cook, Ward, Carroll, Diamond, Cawthra, Robertson, Turnbull. sub: Allon for Robertson
Willenhall: Newton, White, Dams, Woodall, Heath, Fox, Peck, Price, Matthews, Smith, Stringer. sub: Trevor for Newton

WORLD CUP QUALIFYING

Wednesday 29th April 1981

England 0-0 **Romania**
62,500
Referee: H Aldinger (West Germany)

Six months earlier Romania had beaten England for the first time by 2-1 in Bucharest and were a point behind them in Group Four with a game in hand. Like England they had not qualified for the World Cup since 1970 and their last three major qualifying groups had all been won by Spain. In 1969 on their only previous visit to England they had held the then World Champions to a draw.

England, in red shirts, were out of luck and lacking in confidence but the Romanians were delighted with the point as England failed to break through.

England had dropped three vital points to the unbeaten Romanians and now faced three difficult away games before the decider with Hungary seven months later. Romania were on the brink of qualifying when they unexpectedly lost to Switzerland in Bucharest, just one of many strange results in this group.

That one, miraculously, threw England a lifeline and the Romanians missed out by a point.

Romania were again paired with England for their next World Cup qualifying group and met them at Wembley in 1985.

England: Shilton (Nottingham F), Anderson (Nottingham F), Sansom (Arsenal), Robson (West Brom), Watson (Southampton) – capt, Osman (Ipswich), Wilkins (Man Utd), Brooking (West Ham), Coppell (Man Utd), Francis (Nottingham F), Woodcock (Cologne). sub: McDermott (Liverpool) for Brooking 70. manager: Ron Greenwood
Romania: Iordache (Steaua Bucharest), Negrila (Universitatea Craiova), Munteanu (Sportul Studentesc), Sames (Steaua), Stefanescu (Universitatea Craiova) – capt, Beldeanu (Universitatea Craiova), Crisan (Universitatea Craiova), Iordanescu (Steaua), Camataru (Universitatea Craiova), Stoica (Steaua), Balaci (Universitatea Craiova). coach: Valentin Stanescu

FA CUP FINAL

Saturday 9th May 1981

Manchester City 1-1 **Tottenham Hotspur**
Hutchison 30   Hutchison og 80
After extra time
100,000
Referee: K Hackett (Sheffield)

Both clubs had last won the FA Cup in the 1960s; City in 1969 and Tottenham in 1967. They had each won the League Cup twice in the 1970's, City in 1970 and 1976, and Tottenham in 1971 and 1973.

City denied Tottenham the space their creative midfield skills needed and drew first blood after half an hour of the 100th FA Cup final. From Ranson's cross, Aleksic could not prevent Tommy Hutchison's diving header finding the corner of the net. Tottenham came back into it in the second half but their equaliser ten minutes from the end was bad luck for the man whose

goal separated the sides. A free kick on the edge of the area was taken by Ardiles. The Argentinian, who had won a World Cup winners medal three years earlier, tapped it to Perryman. The captain steadied the ball for Hoddle to chip it over the defensive wall. Hutchison, anticipating, left the wall but the ball struck his shoulder and gave Corrigan no chance. Neither side could find a winner as several players collapsed with cramp in extra time.

The teams lined up again five days later for Wembley's first ever FA Cup final replay.

Manchester C: Corrigan, Ranson, McDonald, Reid, Power – capt, Caton, Bennett, Gow, Mackenzie, Hutchison, Reeves. sub: Henry for Hutchison 82. manager: John Bond
Tottenham: Aleksic, Hughton, Miller, Roberts, Perryman – capt, Villa, Ardiles, Archibald, Galvin, Hoddle, Crooks. sub: Brooke for Villa 68. manager: Keith Burkinshaw

INTERNATIONAL

Tuesday 12th May 1981

England   **0-1**   **Brazil**

Zico 12

75,000
Referee: E Linemayr (Austria)

Since the bruising encounter on their last visit to Wembley in 1978 Brazil had concentrated on building a more traditional, skilful team. They had already qualified for the following year's World Cup without dropping a point and they were unbeaten in the World Cup since 1974. England were chasing their first win against them since 1956.

The South Americans took the lead through Zico. From Edevaldo's cross, the Flamengo striker was too quick for England's defenders and shot past Clemence as Sansom challenged him. At times Brazil were breathtaking. They could not add to their score but they taught the red-shirted England players a few lessons.

Brazil won a whole new generation of fans in the following year's World Cup in Spain. They reached only the last twelve but scored some astonishing goals from long range. Comparing favourably with the brilliant 1970 team, Brazil came up against an Italian side hitting form at just the right moment. They lost narrowly in a classic match and Italy went on to win the World Cup.

England: Clemence (Liverpool) – capt, Neal (Liverpool), Sansom (Arsenal), Robson (West Brom), Martin* (West Ham), Wilkins (Man Utd), Coppell (Man Utd), McDermott (Liverpool), Withe* (Aston Villa), Rix (Arsenal), Barnes (West Brom). manager: Ron Greenwood
*first cap
Brazil: Waldir Peres (Sao Paulo), Edevaldo (Fluminense), Oscar (Sao Paulo), Luisinho (Atletico Mineiro), Junior (Flamengo), Socrates (Corinthians) – capt, Cerezo (Atletico Mineiro), Zico (Flamengo), Paulo Isidoro (Gremio), Reinaldo (Atletico Mineiro), Eder (Atletico Mineiro). coach: Tele Santana

FA CUP FINAL REPLAY

Thursday 14th May 1981

Manchester City   **2-3**   **Tottenham Hotspur**

Mackenzie 11, Reeves pen 50   Villa 8, 77, Crooks 70
92,000
Referee: K Hackett (Sheffield)

City had been so close to winning the Cup for the fifth time five days earlier but Tottenham's own-goal equaliser had maintained their unbeaten record in FA Cup finals, and at Wembley. They were aiming for a sixth victory in the competition.

Wembley's first ever FA Cup final Replay sprung to life with two goals in the first 11 minutes. After eight minutes, an Ardiles shot hit Archibald, who then had a strike himself. Corrigan stopped it only for the ball to hit Caton and fall for Ricardo Villa to fire Tottenham in front.

City hit back within three minutes. A headed pass from Hutchison was spectacularly volleyed into the corner of the net by Steve Mackenzie. It was so quick and powerful that Aleksic never saw it. Five minutes after the interval City took the lead.

Bennett and Miller tussled for possession and Bennett went down as Hughton also challenged. A penalty was given and Kevin Reeves found the corner of the net.

Once again, Tottenham had to fight back. With 20 minutes remaining a superb Hoddle lob was controlled by Archibald and Garth Crooks stabbed it past Corrigan for the equaliser. But it took a flash of inspiration to win the 100th FA Cup. With time running out, Galvin ran down the wing before passing to Villa. The Argentinian was surrounded by five City defenders, but he beat both Caton and Ranson and then cut in between them. As Caton lunged, Villa fired the ball through Corrigan's legs for a brilliant individual goal. It was a fitting end to a highly entertaining game.

City were next at Wembley in 1986.They

reached the first Full Members Cup final. Tottenham were back at Wembley to defend the FA Cup in their second successive final.

Manchester C: Corrigan, Ranson, McDonald, Reid, Power – capt, Caton, Bennett, Gow, Mackenzie, Hutchison, Reeves. sub: Tueart for McDonald 79. manager: John Bond

Tottenham: Aleksic, Hughton, Miller, Roberts, Villa, Perryman – capt, Ardiles, Archibald, Galvin, Hoddle, Crooks. sub: Brooke (not used) manager: Keith Burkinshaw

FA Trophy Final

Saturday 16th May 1981

Bishop's Stortford 1
Sullivan 90

Sutton United 0
22,578
Referee: J Worrall (Warrington)

Terry Sullivan's last-minute winner made Bishop's the first club to win both the FA Amateur Cup (1974) and the FA Trophy. John Radford had been a member of Arsenal's 'double-winning' side, ten years earlier.

Bishop's Stortford: Moore, Blackman – capt, Brame, Smith, Bradford, Avery, Sullivan, Knapman, Radford, Simmonds, Mitchell. sub: Worrell for Smith
Sutton: Collyer, Rogers, Green, Rains (J), Rains (A), Stephens, Waldon, Pritchard, Cornwell, Parsons, Dennis. sub: Sunnucks for Stephens

BRITISH CHAMPIONSHIP

Wednesday 20th May 1981

England   0-0   **Wales**
34,280
Referee: B McGinlay (Scotland)

The British Championship was declared void after the last-minute withdrawals of both England and Wales from their matches with Northern Ireland in Belfast due to the recent troubles. Nevertheless, the remaining matches went ahead although the Irish could not defend their Championship. Wales had beaten Scotland 2-0 at Vetch Field four days earlier and were unbeaten at Wembley in their last three visits, England failing to score in the last two.

Wales had thrashed England 4-1 at the Racecourse Ground the previous year, their biggest ever victory against them. England had last beaten Wales in 1978 in Cardiff and not at Wembley since 1973. Wales led their World Cup qualifying group by four points after winning all four of their games without conceding a goal.

This was a poor game, with Wales keeping a clean sheet for the sixth time in seven matches. England missed their Ipswich Town and Liverpool players who were involved in European finals.

England had now gone three matches at Wembley without a goal, a feat they had never managed before. Three days later, they entertained Scotland in the final match of the meaningless Championship. Wales had completed their fixtures without conceding a goal. They extended their great defensive record ten days later to seven clean sheets in eight games after a goalless World Cup qualifying match against the USSR, at Ninian Park. But the following season, they won only one more point and were knocked out on goal difference behind group runners-up Czechoslovakia. Their Wembley run came to an end in 1983.

Ian Rush, a Welsh substitute, made his first appearance at Wembley. He became a regular visitor, scoring in major cup finals and was Footballer of the Year in 1984.

England: Corrigan (Man City), Anderson (Nottingham F), Sansom (Arsenal), Robson (West Brom), Watson (Southampton) – capt, Wilkins (Man Utd), Coppell (Man Utd), Hoddle (Tottenham), Withe (Aston Villa), Rix (Arsenal), Barnes (West Brom). sub: Woodcock (Cologne) for Withe 82. manager: Ron Greenwood
Wales: Davies (Wrexham), Jones (Wrexham), Ratcliffe (Everton), Nicholas (Arsenal), Phillips (Swansea), Price (Luton Town), Harris (Leeds United), Flynn (Leeds United) – capt, Walsh (Crystal P), Thomas (Man Utd), James (Swansea). subs: Giles (Swansea) for Harris 60, Rush (Liverpool) for James 65 manager: Mike England

BRITISH CHAMPIONSHIP

Saturday 23rd May 1981

England　　　　　　**0-1**　　　**Scotland**
　　　　　　　　　　　　　　　　　　　　Robertson pen 64

90,000
Referee: R Wurtz (France)

England had won their last three games against Scotland including in 1979 at Wembley, but had not scored in their last three internationals – all at Wembley. Scotland had beaten the reigning British Champions Northern Ireland 2-0 at Hampden Park four days earlier after losing to Wales the previous week.

They were the only team to complete their scheduled fixtures in the decimated British Championship. Scotland led their World Cup qualifying group by two points from Northern Ireland and were unbeaten in five games, although they had twice dropped points at home, to Portugal and Northern Ireland.

It was a better performance from England but still they could not find the net. They were beaten by a penalty after Robson brought down Archibald. John Robertson sent Corrigan the wrong way from the spot.

England had now gone four games at Wembley without a goal and five without a win, disastrous form to precede crucial World Cup qualifying matches in Switzerland and Hungary.

Scotland qualified for their third successive World Cup by winning their group but lost to England at Hampden Park the following year and at Wembley in 1983.

England: Corrigan (Man City), Anderson (Nottingham F), Sansom (Arsenal), Wilkins (Man Utd), Watson (Southampton) – capt, Robson (West Brom), Coppell (Man Utd), Hoddle (Tottenham), Withe (Aston Villa), Rix (Arsenal), Woodcock (Cologne). subs: Martin (West Ham) for Watson 46, Francis (Nottingham F) for Woodcock 46. manager: Ron Greenwood
Scotland: Rough (Partick), Stewart (West Ham), Gray (Nottingham F), McGrain (Celtic) – capt, McLeish (Aberdeen), Miller (Aberdeen), Provan (Celtic), Archibald (Tottenham), Jordan (Man Utd), Hartford (Everton), Robertson (Nottingham F). subs: Narey (Dundee U) for Hartford 27, Sturrock (Dundee U) for Provan 80. manager: Jock Stein

Schoolboy International

Saturday 13th June 1981

England 1
West

West Germany 2
Lorch, Ehreiser

75,000
Referee: A Parsons (Bedfordshire)
The Germans' third successive game at Wembley without defeat.

England: Hope, Parkin, Aldridge, Robinson, Macowat, Kerslake – capt, Lambert, McDonald, West, Jones, Cooper. subs: Lovatt for West, Sinton for Cooper

FA CHARITY SHIELD

Saturday 22nd August 1981

Aston Villa　　　　　**2-2**　　　**Tottenham Hotspur**
Withe 30, 52　　　　　　　　　　　　Falco 43, 47
92,500
Referee: A Grey (Great Yarmouth)

Villa were appearing in their fourth FA Charity Shield still searching for their first goal. Their last appearance was in 1972, when as Third Division Champions they lost 1-0 at home to Manchester City. In the 1970's, they had appeared at Wembley in three Football League Cup finals, the first

of which they had lost to Tottenham.

They had won the League Cup twice in three years, after drawing in 1977, their last visit. Now they were League Champions for the first time in 71 years, their seventh title having been won by four points from Ipswich Town.

Tottenham had won the Charity Shield in successive years in the early 1960's and had last appeared in a 3-3 draw with Manchester United in 1967. They had won the FA Cup for the sixth time in a thrilling replay, three months earlier.

Ray Clemence, making his debut for Tottenham after signing from Liverpool, gifted Villa a goal after half an hour. He fumbled Morley's corner and Peter Withe had a simple chance to fire the League Champions in front.

But Tottenham equalised two minutes before half-time. Mark Falco received the ball from Ardiles on the edge of the area with his back to goal and marked by Gibson. But he flicked the ball up and turned swiftly to send a superb shot flying past Rimmer into the corner. Falco then turned the game in Tottenham's favour by converting Galvin's cross just two minutes into the second half.

Villa responded five minutes later when Clemence again got into difficulties. Challenged by Geddis for Morley's cross the goalkeeper left Withe to head home. There were no more goals and the Shield was shared after an entertaining game.

Villa finished 11th, in their defence of the League Championship, their lowest position since 1976 and Tottenham knocked them out of the FA Cup, but they surprisingly won the European Cup at the first attempt, beating Bayern Munich by a single goal in the Rotterdam final. It was England's sixth successive triumph and they did not concede a goal from the quarter-finals onwards (five matches).

All this after manager, Ron Saunders had resigned in February. The following year, they won the European Super Cup, but only four years later were relegated to the Second Division.

They appeared at Wembley in the Football League Centenary Tournament in 1988 as they were winning promotion straight back to the First Division and returned for the Makita Tournament two years later. In 1994 they won the Coca-Cola Cup.

Tottenham were to make four more Wembley appearances in the next twelve months, beginning with the Football League Milk Cup final and ending with the following year's FA Charity Shield.

Aston Villa: Rimmer, Swain, Gibson, Evans, McNaught, Mortimer – capt, Bremner, Geddis, Withe, Cowans, Morley. sub: Blair for Mortimer. manager: Ron Saunders

Tottenham: Clemence, Hughton, Miller, Roberts, Villa, Perryman – capt, Ardiles, Archibald, Galvin, Hoddle, Falco. manager: Keith Burkinshaw

WORLD CUP QUALIFYING

Wednesday 18th November 1981

England   1-0   Hungary
Mariner 14
92,000
Referee: G Konrath (France)

Group Four had seen many a strange result and it was remarkable that England had lost three games out of seven, yet only needed a point from their last game at home to qualify for Spain on goal difference from Romania.

England's 3-1 win in Budapest five months earlier had put them back on the right track after defeat in Basle the week before. But they then lost alarmingly to the underdog, Norway in Oslo in the biggest shock of the group. Switzerland rescued them by winning in Bucharest and taking three points from Romania who had looked set to qualify.

Hungary, meanwhile, had already won the group but had lost on each of their last two visits to Wembley – in 1965 and 1978.

England were determined not to slip up this time but their goal was somewhat fortunate. Brooking's poor shot was heading wide until Paul Mariner diverted it past Meszaros with an ungainly stumble.

But they all count and very few goals were as important as this one. England had at last qualified for their first World Cup since 1970 and Mariner's goal also brought to an end England's run of four games at Wembley without scoring and five without a win.

England: Shilton (Nottingham F), Neal (Liverpool), Mills (Ipswich), Thompson (Liverpool), Martin (West Ham), Robson (Man Utd), Keegan (Southampton) – capt, Coppell (Man Utd), Mariner (Ipswich), McDermott (Liverpool), Brooking (West Ham). sub: Morley* (Aston Villa) for Coppell 64. manager: Ron Greenwood
*first cap
Hungary: Meszaros (Sporting Lisbon), Martos (Waterschei), Balint (Toulouse), Garaba (Honved), Toth (Ujpesti Dozsa) – capt, Sallai (Debrecen), Muller (Hercules Alicante), Csapo (Tatabanya), Fazekas (Royal Antwerp), Torocsik (Ujpesti Dozsa), Kiss (Vasas). subs: Kerekes (Debrecen) for Fazekas 46, Szanto (Ferencvaros) for Csapo 79. coach: Kalman Meszoly

Final table	P	W	D	L	F	A	Pts
Hungary	8	4	2	2	13	8	10
England	8	4	1	3	13	8	9
Romania	8	2	4	2	5	5	8
Switzerland	8	2	3	3	9	12	7
Norway	8	2	2	4	8	15	6

Inter-Varsity Match

Oxford completed their first Wembley hat-trick. Each win was by a two-goal margin.

Wednesday 9th December 1981

Cambridge U 0
Oxford U 2
Husselbee 2

BRITISH CHAMPIONSHIP

Tuesday 23rd February 1982

England   **4-0**   **Northern Ireland**
Robson 1, Keegan 49, Wilkins 84,
Hoddle 86
54,900
Referee: G Owen (Wales)

On the same night three months earlier both teams had qualified for the forthcoming World Cup, with Northern Ireland finishing runners-up to Scotland. On their last visit to Wembley two years earlier the Irish had ended a run of six successive defeats by England. That helped them win the British Championship for the first time outright since 1914 and this was their first defence as the previous year's competition was declared void.

In the first minute, a sharp Francis found space to cross hard and low and Bryan Robson gave Jennings little hope from inside the six-yard box. Four minutes into the second half another inch-perfect Francis cross gave England a second goal. This time he found the head of Kevin Keegan who guided the ball into the corner. Six minutes from the end Hoddle's corner led to England's third. Watson's shot was blocked by Nelson but Ray Wilkins fired home the rebound via the full back's shoulder. Two minutes after that Jennings failed to gather Sansom's shot and Glenn Hoddle was quicker than Nelson to sweep home the loose ball. A great boost for English confidence and a crushing blow for the Irish.

England regained the British Championship without conceding a goal, with victories in Cardiff (their first in four games against Wales) and Glasgow. Northern Ireland finished bottom in a miserable defence of their title but stunned everyone in the World Cup in Spain by winning their first round group and beating the host nation in Valencia. They finally lost to France in the last twelve.

England: Clemence (Tottenham), Anderson (Nottingham F), Sansom (Arsenal), Wilkins (Man Utd), Watson (Stoke City), Foster* (Brighton), Keegan (Southampton) – capt, Robson (Man Utd), Francis (Man City), Hoddle (Tottenham), Morley (Aston Villa). subs: Regis* (West Brom) for Francis 65, Woodcock (Cologne) for Morley 77. manager: Ron Greenwood

Northern Ireland: Jennings (Arsenal), Nicholl (J) (Man Utd), Nelson (Brighton), Donaghy (Luton Town), Nicholl (C) (Southampton), O'Neill (J) (Leicester), Brotherston (Blackburn), O'Neill (M) (Norwich) – capt, Armstrong (Watford), McIlroy (Stoke City), Hamilton (Burnley). subs: Cochrane (Middlesbrough) for Brotherston 65, McCreery (Tulsa Roughnecks) for O'Neill (M) 77. manager: Billy Bingham
*first cap

Final table	P	W	D	L	F	A	Pts
England	3	3	0	0	6	0	6
Scotland	3	1	1	1	2	2	3
Wales	3	1	0	2	3	2	2
Northern Ireland	3	0	1	2	1	8	1

MILK CUP FINAL

Saturday 13th March 1982

Liverpool   **3-1**   **Tottenham Hotspur**
Whelan 87, 111, Rush 120   Archibald 11
After extra time
100,000
Referee: P Willis (Meadowfield)

Having won the League Cup for the first time the previous year, holders Liverpool were now appearing in their third final in five years – this time the competition had new sponsors – but they had still to win the competition at Wembley after two draws.

Tottenham had won the League Cup twice in the 1970's and had reached the final without conceding a goal in seven matches. Having won the FA Cup for the sixth time the previous year, they were aiming to extend their unbeaten domestic final record to nine. They were also joint holders of the FA Charity Shield from their last Wembley visit.

In their defence of the European Cup, Liverpool had reached the quarter-finals and ten days earlier they had beaten CSKA Sofia by a single goal in the first leg. They were also chasing their fifth League Championship in seven years.

Tottenham also had other distractions. The previous week, three days after beating Eintracht Frankfurt 2-0 in the first leg of their European Cup-Winners Cup quarter-final, they had reached the FA Cup semi-finals in defence of the trophy.

Spurs scored first after Hoddle sent Steve Archibald away to hold off Lawrenson's challenge and slide the ball under the advancing Grobbelaar. They held the lead until three minutes from the end. Substitute Johnson fired in a low cross and Ronnie Whelan drove home the equaliser past Clemence (who had helped Liverpool win the trophy the previous year).

There were nine minutes left in extra time when the Irish youngster scored again. A mistake by Ardiles let Rush in to supply Dalglish who ran to the byeline and waited for support. When Whelan arrived, Dalglish made a short pass and Whelan dispatched it into the roof of the net above a grasping Clemence.

Tottenham pushed up for the equaliser but were caught on the break in the last minute when Lee sent Ian Rush away in acres of space.

As Price came to challenge, Rush cut inside and passed to Johnson who had only Clemence to beat. The 'keeper saved brilliantly but had no defensive support and Johnson had time to collect the ball, look up and play it back to Rush who hammered it past Price on the line.

Four days after the final Liverpool lost 2-0 in Sofia and crashed out of the European Cup. On the same night in Frankfurt Tottenham lost 2-1 but went through to the European Cup-Winners Cup semi-finals, where they were beaten by eventual winners Barcelona.

Liverpool: Grobbelaar, Neal, Kennedy (A), Lawrenson, Whelan, Thompson (PB), Dalglish, Lee, Rush, McDermott, Souness – capt. sub: Johnson for McDermott. manager: Bob Paisley
Tottenham: Clemence, Hughton, Miller, Price, Hazard, Perryman – capt, Ardiles, Archibald, Galvin, Hoddle, Crooks. manager: sub: Villa for Hazard. Keith Burkinshaw

Schoolboy International

Saturday 27th March 1982

England 7
Beckford, Purdie 2, Priest, Hutchings, Keen,
Fairbrother pen

Netherlands 0
44,000
Referee: B Chubb (East Riding)

All seven goals came in the first 50 minutes, with six different goalscorers in England's biggest ever win against the Dutch.

Michael Thomas won his second and last full England cap at Wembley in 1989, the same year he scored a dramatic injury-time goal at Liverpool to grab the Championship for Arsenal. Having shattered the Reds' 'double' dreams, he went on to score for Liverpool in the 1992 FA Cup final at Wembley.

Fraser Digby was twice in goal for Swindon Town when they won Promotion play-off finals at Wembley in 1990 and 1993.

England: Digby, Spiers, Thomas, Seagraves – capt, Wynter, Priest, Hutchings, Fairbrother, Beckford, Keen, Purdie. subs: Heyes for Digby, Beresford for Thomas, Sankey for Keen

FA Vase Final

Saturday 8th May 1982

Forest Green Rovers 3
Leitch 22, 63, Norman 70

Rainworth Miners Welfare 0

12,500
Referee: K Walmsley (Thornton)

A comfortable first victory for Forest Green, settled by the expert finishing of Andy Leitch.

Forest Green: Moss, Norman – capt, Day, Turner, Higgins, Jenkins, Burns, Guest, Millard, Leitch, Doughty. sub: Dangerfield for Higgins
Rainworth: Watson, Hallam, Hodgson, Slater, Sterland, Oliver, Knowles, Raine, Radzki, Reah, Comerford. sub: Robinson for Knowles

FA Trophy Final

Saturday 15th May 1982

Altrincham 0
Enfield 1
Taylor 113
After extra time
18,678
Referee: B Stevens (Stonehouse)

Paul Taylor's 25-yard volley in the closing stages of a dour match enabled Enfield to emulate Bishop's Stortford's feat by adding the FA Trophy to their two FA Amateur Cup wins.

Altrincham: Connaughton, Crossley, Davison, Bailey, Cuddy, King – capt, Allan, Heathcote, Johnson, Rogers, Howard. sub: Whitbread for King
Enfield: Jacobs, Barrett, Tone, Jennings, Waite, Ironton, Ashford, Taylor, Holmes, Oliver, King. sub: Flint for Oliver

FA CUP FINAL

Saturday 22nd May 1982

Queens Park Rangers	1-1	Tottenham Hotspur
Fenwick 115		Hoddle 109

After extra time
100,000
Referee: C White (Harrow)

Rangers had never progressed beyond the quarter-finals of the FA Cup but they had won the League Cup at Wembley as a Third Division club back in 1967. Holders Tottenham were aiming to equal Aston Villa's record of seven FA Cup wins. It was 20 years since any club had retained the FA Cup but Tottenham had been the last to do it.

Rangers were hoping to become the fourth Second Division club in the past decade to win the FA Cup. Tottenham had had an exhausting season. They had reached the European Cup-Winners Cup semi-finals before losing to the eventual winners Barcelona and they almost won the Football League Milk Cup, losing in extra time to holders Liverpool.

Spurs had become the first club to reach both the League Cup and FA Cup finals in the same season and the last thing they wanted was another replay.

They were the stronger side but could not find a way past Peter Hucker and Wembley seemed set for its first goalless FA Cup final. But in the second period of extra time, Glenn Hoddle played a one-two with Roberts and his shot deflected off Currie to beat Hucker.

Rangers forced a replay, however, with just five minutes remaining. From Stainrod's throw, Hazell backheaded the ball into the middle for Terry Fenwick to head over Clemence from inside the six yard box.

So, for the second year in succession, Tottenham faced an FA Cup final Replay to be held five days later.

Queens Park Rangers: Hucker, Fenwick, Gillard, Waddock, Hazell (R), Roeder – capt, Currie, Flanagan, Allen (C), Stainrod, Gregory. sub: Micklewhite for Allen 50. manager: Terry Venables

Tottenham: Clemence, Hughton, Miller, Price, Hazard, Perryman – capt, Roberts, Archibald, Galvin, Hoddle, Crooks. sub: Brooke for Hazard 104. manager: Keith Burkinshaw

INTERNATIONAL

Tuesday 25th May 1982

England 2-0 Netherlands
Woodcock 48, Mariner 53
69,000
Referee: P Bergamo (Italy)

The Netherlands had not conceded a goal against England at Wembley in their two previous clashes. In 1977 they had beaten them far more convincingly than the 2-0 scoreline suggested. England's last victory over them was in 1969. The Netherlands had finished runners-up in each of the last two World Cups but were now in decline after failing by a point to qualify for the forthcoming World Cup in Spain.

England broke the deadlock shortly after half-time, Tony Woodcock taking advantage of Van Breukelen's fumble from Thompson's centre. Five minutes later from substitute, Rix's pass, Paul Mariner scored the second with a curling shot to secure victory for England in Ron Greenwood's last match in charge at Wembley.

In 1988 a new Holland emerged, ready to conquer Europe.

England: Shilton (Nottingham F) – capt, Neal (Liverpool), Sansom (Arsenal), Thompson (Liverpool), Foster (Brighton), Robson (Man Utd), Wilkins (Man Utd), Devonshire (West Ham), Mariner (Ipswich), McDermott (Liverpool), Woodcock (Cologne). subs: Rix (Arsenal) for Devonshire 46, Barnes (Leeds United) for Mariner 82. manager: Ron Greenwood
Netherlands: Van Breukelen (Utrecht), Ophuf (Ajax Amsterdam), Van de Korput (Torino), Krol (Napoli) – capt, Metgod (Alkmaar), Boeve (Ajax), Peters (Alkmaar), Muhren (Ipswich), La Ling (Ajax), Kieft (Ajax), Tahamata (Standard Liege). subs: Van de Kerkhof (R) (PSV Eindhoven) for Peters 63, Rijkaard (Ajax) for Metgod 71, Van Kooten (Go Ahead Eagles) for La Ling 71. coach: Kees Rijvers

FA CUP FINAL REPLAY

Thursday 27th May 1982

Queens Park Rangers 0-1 Tottenham Hotspur
Hoddle pen 6

90,000
Referee: C White (Harrow)

Tottenham had almost retained the FA Cup, five days earlier, but Rangers had refused to give in and produced a late equaliser.

In just six minutes, Currie brought down Roberts and Glenn Hoddle sent Hucker the wrong way from the penalty spot to give Tottenham the best possible start. But unlike the first game, it was Rangers who impressed the most as they fought gallantly for the equaliser. This time it was not to be, despite creating several chances and Tottenham held out for a fortunate victory. Perhaps their endeavours over the season, however, warranted their reward at the end.

In 1986, Rangers were back at Wembley for the Milk Cup final.

Queens Park Rangers: Hucker, Fenwick, Gillard, Waddock, Hazell (R), Neill, Currie – capt, Flanagan, Micklewhite, Stainrod, Gregory. sub: Burke for Micklewhite 84. manager: Terry Venables

Tottenham: Clemence, Hughton, Miller, Price, Hazard, Perryman – capt, Roberts, Archibald, Galvin, Hoddle, Crooks. sub: Brooke for Hazard 67. manager: Keith Burkinshaw

Schoolboy International

Saturday 5th June 1982

England 0
Scotland 0
61,000
Referee: P Tracey (Northumberland)

Jim Morrow bowed out after twelve years as England's manager with Wembley's first scoreless schoolboy game.

England: Heyes, Spiers, Seagraves, Ratcliffe – capt, Thomas, Sankey, Gordon, Fairbrother, Keen, Beckford, Daws. subs: Wynter for Ratcliffe, Priest for Keen
Scotland: Donaldson, Nelson, Robertson, Traynor, McGee, Shepherd – capt, Ferguson, Cameron, Muirhead, Winnie, McGuire. subs: Riddell for Winnie, Fraser for McGuire

FA CHARITY SHIELD

Saturday 21st August 1982

Liverpool   1-0   **Tottenham Hotspur**
Rush 33
82,500
Referee: N Ashley (Cheshire)

Liverpool were hoping to regain the FA Charity Shield for the fifth time in seven years and a record ninth overall. Their two previous victories had been against London clubs. Five months earlier they had come from behind with a late equaliser to beat Tottenham after extra time to win the Football League Milk Cup, their second successive victory in the competition. Two months later they were to beat Tottenham to win their fifth League Championship in seven years and a record 13th overall. This impressive 'double' was achieved despite several new players coming in and the club languishing in mid-table at Christmas.

Tottenham were making an unprecedented seventh appearance at Wembley in just over 15 months – England had only made six appearances in the same period. Tottenham had had a long season which began with them sharing the Charity Shield in an entertaining encounter, the previous year. They had last won the Shield outright in 1962.

Their record-equalling seventh FA Cup win had been at the expense of a replay for the second year in succession, but they had become the first team to retain the FA Cup since they themselves achieved it in 1962. This was not one of Wembley's better games and it was settled when Ian Rush ran on to Thompson's pass and rounded Clemence.

Liverpool comfortably retained the League Championship and were back at Wembley to defend the Charity Shield the following year. They also repeated their 'double' by winning the Milk Cup again.

Tottenham had to wait five years for their next Wembley appearance.

Liverpool: Grobbelaar, Neal, Kennedy (A), Thompson (PB), Lawrenson, Hansen, Dalglish, Lee, Rush, Whelan, Souness – capt. sub: Hodgson for Dalglish. manager: Bob Paisley
Tottenham: Clemence, Hughton, Miller, O'Reilly, Hazard, Lacy, Mabbutt, Archibald, Galvin, Hoddle – capt, Crooks. subs: Perryman for O'Reilly 66, Falco for Hazard. manager: Keith Burkinshaw

INTERNATIONAL

Wednesday 13th October 1982

England   1-2   **West Germany**
Woodcock 85   Rummenigge 73, 82
67,500
Referee: K Palotai (Hungary)

West Germany had lost on their last visit to Wembley in 1975, but had come from behind to win in Munich in 1978. In the summer's World Cup they had drawn 0-0 with England at the Bernabéu, eventually pipping them by a point and going on to lose to Italy in the final.

This was England's first match at Wembley with Bobby Robson as manager, Ron Greenwood retiring after the World Cup.

England had a good first half despite fielding several newcomers but the reigning European Champions came good after the break. The turning point came with 20 minutes left as the Germans introduced Littbarski as a substitute. He had scored a hat-trick the previous night when England beat West Germany on aggregate in the final of the European Under-21 Championship in Bremen.

Three minutes later, Karl-Heinz Rummenigge received the ball from Allofs and brilliantly chipped it over Shilton to give West Germany the lead. With eight minutes left, Littbarski crossed and Rummenigge beat Shilton at the near post as Butcher challenged. Three minutes later, substitute Tony Woodcock pulled one back from a corner from Rix, another substitute, but the Germans had done enough to become the first foreign country to beat England twice at Wembley. By 1991, it was a united Germany that returned to Wembley.

West Germany fielded two European Footballers of the Year. Karl-Heinz Rummenigge had won the award twice (1980 and 1981), while Lothar Matthaus was to win it in 1990. Only Matthaus was to make a return visit to Wembley.

England: Shilton (Southampton), Mabbutt* (Tottenham), Sansom (Arsenal), Thompson (Liverpool), Butcher (Ipswich), Wilkins (Man Utd) – capt, Hill (Luton Town), Regis (West Brom), Mariner (Ipswich), Armstrong (Southampton), Devonshire (West Ham). subs: Woodcock (Arsenal) for Mariner 80, Blissett* (Watford) for Regis 81, Rix (Arsenal) for Armstrong 81. manager: Bobby Robson
*first cap
West Germany: Schumacher (Cologne), Kaltz (Hamburg), Strack (Cologne), Forster (K) (Stuttgart), Forster (B) (Stuttgart), Dremmler (Bayern Munich), Briegel (Kaiserslautern), Matthaus (Borussia Monchengladbach), Meier (Werder Bremen), Allofs (Cologne), Rummenigge (Bayern Munich) – capt. subs: Hieronymus (Hamburg) for Forster (K) 5, Littbarski (Cologne) for Meier 69, Engels (Cologne) for Allofs 89. coach: Jupp Derwall

Inter-Varsity Match

Wednesday 8th December 1982

Cambridge U 2
Lewis, Walsh

Oxford U 4
Hayes 2, Husselbee 2
6,300

This was Oxford's fourth consecutive win, their most successful run at Wembley in the fixture. Husselbee scored twice for the second year in succession. It was, however, to be their last Wembley victory.

EUROPEAN CHAMPIONSHIP QUALIFYING

Wednesday 15th December 1982

England   9-0   **Luxembourg**
Moes og 18, Coppell 21, Woodcock 34,
Blissett 43, 62, 86, Chamberlain 72,
Hoddle 88, Neal 90
33,980
Referee: H Jonsson (Iceland)

England were top of Group Three on goal difference from Denmark after two games although Hungary had still to play a match. Luxembourg had lost both their opening games at home to Greece and Denmark. They had lost all five previous meetings with England, including at Wembley five

years earlier. It had been ten years since they had won a competitive fixture.

It took nearly 20 minutes for Luxembourg's defence to crumble. From Blissett's cross, Bossi's attempted clearance went in off goalkeeper Jeannot Moes. Steve Coppell headed the second three minutes later from another Blissett cross. Next Butcher headed on Coppell's corner and Tony Woodcock dived to head the third. Two minutes before the break, Robson crossed and Woodcock's shot was saved by Moes, only for Luther Blissett to score from the rebound.

It took England 17 minutes of the second half to score the fifth. Again, Blissett dispatched a rebound from a Woodcock shot, this time off the bar. England surged forward mercilessly. Substitute Mark Chamberlain headed the sixth from a Butcher cross.

They then finished with a late goal-flourish. Blissett completed his hat-trick with a header from Woodcock's cross with four minutes left. Within two minutes, from Chamberlain's pass, Glenn Hoddle, the other substitute, unleashed a 25-yard volley, which gave Moes no chance. In the last minute, Sansom sent Phil Neal away up the wing. His poor cross was too close to the goalkeeper, but Moes managed to fumble it and took it over the line to give England their biggest ever win at Wembley.

England won the return by only 4-0 in Luxembourg the following year but they were already out. Luxembourg's chances had evaporated long before and they had to wait until 1999 for their final appearance at Wembley.

England: Clemence (Tottenham), Neal (Liverpool), Sansom (Arsenal), Lee (Liverpool), Butcher (Ipswich), Martin (West Ham), Robson (Man Utd) – capt, Mabbutt (Tottenham), Blissett (Watford), Woodcock (Arsenal), Coppell (Man Utd). subs: Chamberlain* (Stoke City) for Coppell 65, Hoddle (Tottenham) for Mabbutt 74. manager: Bobby Robson
*first cap
Luxembourg: Moes (Avenir Beggen) – capt, Girres (Union Luxembourg), Bossi (Progres Niedercorn), Rohmann (San Diego Sockers), Meunier (Progres Niedercorn), Hellers (Metz), Weis (Reims), Clemens (Spora Luxembourg), Dresch (Avenir Beggen), Di Domenico (Red Boys Differdange), Reiter (Saarbrucken). sub: Nurenberg (Progres Niedercorn) for Di Domenico 46. coach: Louis Pilot

BRITISH CHAMPIONSHIP

Wednesday 23rd February 1983

England	2-1	Wales
Butcher 39, Neal pen 78		Rush 14

24,000
Referee: R Valentine (Scotland)

Wales had not lost at Wembley since 1973 and had not conceded a goal in their last three visits, but England, the reigning British Champions, had beaten them the previous year at Ninian Park. This was the opening match and England's first defence. In the European Championship, Wales were joint-top of their qualifying group with Norway but had a game in hand.

England started well, but it was Wales who scored first. Davies crossed and Robbie James' mis-kick caused enough confusion to allow Ian Rush, under pressure from Butcher, to stab the ball past Shilton. Six minutes before half-time England drew level. From Devonshire's cross, Terry Butcher hammered home the equaliser. The points were secured with only twelve minutes left. Flynn brought down Cowans and Phil Neal made no mistake from the penalty.

Wales also lost to Scotland three months later at Ninian Park before beating Northern Ireland at Windsor Park but this was to be their last visit to Wembley as the British Championship came to an end the following year.

Welsh goalkeeper, Neville Southall made his first appearance at Wembley. Two years later, he was Footballer of the Year.

England: Shilton (Southampton) – capt, Neal (Liverpool), Statham* (West Brom), Lee (Liverpool), Martin (West Ham), Butcher (Ipswich), Blissett (Watford), Mabbutt (Tottenham), Mariner (Ipswich), Cowans* (Aston Villa), Devonshire (West Ham). manager: Bobby Robson
Wales: Southall (Everton), Jones (Chelsea), Ratcliffe (Everton), Flynn (Burnley), Price (Tottenham) – capt, Jackett (Watford), Davies (Fulham), James (R) (Swansea), Rush (Liverpool), Thomas (Stoke City), Mahoney (Swansea). subs: Berry (Stoke City) for Jones 44, James (L) (Sunderland) for Mahoney 80. manager: Mike England
*first cap

Schoolboy International

Saturday 19th March 1983

England 1
Rimmer

West Germany 0

Neil Rimmer's 64th minute goal secured the Germans' first defeat at Wembley since 1974 in Ralph O'Donnell's first appearance at the stadium as England's new manager. Gavin Peacock hit both goals for Chelsea at Wembley 11 years later in the FA Cup Semi-final.

England: Pressman, Thomas – capt, Crumpton, Parsons, O'Brien, Peacock, Rimmer, Bogie, White, Scott, Goddard. sub: Nesbit for Bogie 69

MILK CUP FINAL

Saturday 26th March 1983

Liverpool   **2-1**   **Manchester United**
Kennedy 75, Whelan 99   Whiteside 13
After extra time
100,000
Referee: G Courtney (Spennymoor)

All-conquering Liverpool were now attempting to succeed where Nottingham Forest had failed in 1980, by completing a first hat-trick of League/Milk Cup wins. The previous year they had left it late to come from behind and retain the trophy in extra time.

United were appearing in their first final. In the late 1970's they had appeared in three FA Cup finals in four years and their only win had been against Liverpool in 1977. Three months later, they had drawn with them in the Charity Shield.

Liverpool were once more dominating the League Championship and set to retain it, but they had been knocked out in the European Cup quarter-finals for the second year in succession ten days earlier by Widzew Lodz. United were also going well in the league and, after reaching the FA Cup semi-finals, were aiming to become the first club to win both domestic knock-out competitions in the same season.

United scored first. Norman Whiteside received the ball on his chest from McQueen's long pass, turned one way and then swiftly back the other. This gave him just enough space ahead of Hansen to strike the ball past Grobbelaar and give United the lead. Great skill for a 17-year-old who thus became the youngest player to score in a Wembley final.

Liverpool created many chances but were unable to break through until 15 minutes from the end. United had needed to reshuffle their defence after Moran went off injured seven minutes earlier and then McQueen tore a hamstring. Liverpool's equaliser came out of the blue. Lee played the ball square and Alan Kennedy shot from 25 yards. The ball bounced before it reached Bailey and then hit the net.

United, without both their central defenders, hung on grimly but nine minutes into extra time their resolve was broken. Kennedy made a short pass to Ronnie Whelan and then sprinted for the middle for the return. Whelan tried to play it through Stapleton's legs, but the striker, playing in defence, blocked it. It came back to Whelan, who curled it beyond Bailey's reach into the corner for a truly wonderful goal to add to his two the previous year. At the end, Liverpool manager Bob Paisley was sent up to receive the Milk Cup on his last appearance at Wembley before retirement.

Liverpool won the League Championship for a record 14th time to repeat their 'double' of the previous year. So, once again, they forfeited their UEFA Cup place to chase the European Cup. They met United again at Wembley in the FA Charity Shield before reaching the Milk Cup final yet again the following year. United emulated Tottenham's feat of 1982 by appearing in the FA Cup final two months later. They finished third in the First Division for the second year in succession.

Liverpool: Grobbelaar, Neal, Kennedy (A), Lawrenson, Whelan, Hansen, Dalglish, Lee, Rush, Johnston, Souness – capt. sub: Fairclough for Johnston 83. manager: Bob Paisley
Manchester U: Bailey, Duxbury, Albiston, Moses, Moran, McQueen, Wilkins – capt, Muhren, Stapleton, Whiteside, Coppell. sub: Macari for Moran 68. manager: Ron Atkinson

EUROPEAN CHAMPIONSHIP QUALIFYING

Wednesday 30th March 1983

England   **0-0**   **Greece**
44,051
Referee: D Krchnak (Czechoslovakia)

This was Greece's third fixture in Group Three. After winning in Luxembourg, they had lost 3-0 to England in Salonika four months earlier. England had beaten Greece three times in all without conceding a goal. Each previous encounter was in the European Championship.

Their only previous meeting at Wembley was in 1971. Greece had qualified for the last European Championship in 1980, their first major tournament, but they picked up only one point in Italy although it was against the eventual winners West Germany in Turin.

The Greeks were determined to better their performance in Salonika and packed their defence. England eventually ran out of ideas and dropped a vital point.

Greece were eliminated eight months later as Denmark beat them in Athens to win the group. Six years later they scored their first goal against England from a penalty in Athens before losing 2-1, but they did not qualify for another major tournament until the 1994 World Cup, appearing at Wembley again in the same year.

England: Shilton (Southampton) – capt, Neal (Liverpool), Sansom (Arsenal), Lee (Liverpool), Martin (West Ham), Butcher (Ipswich), Coppell (Man Utd), Mabbutt (Tottenham), Francis (Sampdoria), Woodcock (Arsenal), Devonshire (West Ham). subs: Blissett (Watford) for Woodcock 72, Rix (Arsenal) for Devonshire 72. manager: Bobby Robson
Greece: Sarganis (Olympiakos), Gounaris (Olympiakos) – capt, Karoulias (Panathinaikos), Galitzios (Larissa), Michos (Olympiakos), Xanthopoulos (Iraklis), Kousoulakis (Olympiakos), Kouis (Aris Salonika), Anastopoulos (Olympiakos), Mitropoulos (Olympiakos), Kostikos (PAOK Salonika). sub: Dontas (Panathinaikos) for Mitropoulos 46, Ardizoglou (AEK Athens) for Anastopoulos 85. coach: Christos Archondidis

EUROPEAN CHAMPIONSHIP QUALIFYING

Wednesday 27th April 1983

England   **2-0**   **Hungary**
Francis 30, Withe 70
54,000
Referee: P D'Elia (Italy)

England had won their last four games against Hungary, ending with the important World Cup qualifying match in 1981 and they led Group Three by two points from Hungary, who had two games in hand, having twice beaten Luxembourg 6-2 in their only two outings so far.

After half an hour, Cowans' free kick was headed in at the near post by Trevor Francis. The game was sewn up 20 minutes from the end when a long ball from Lee sent Peter Withe away to fire home the second.

This was the first of four successive defeats for Hungary, which put them out of contention. The following month, they surprisingly lost 3-2 to Greece in Budapest and they were eliminated when England defeated them 3-0 in Budapest, six months after their Wembley visit. Denmark emerged as England's only real challengers in the group and visited Wembley a month earlier. Hungary next appeared at Wembley in 1990.

England: Shilton (Southampton) – capt, Neal (Liverpool), Sansom (Arsenal), Lee (Liverpool), Martin (West Ham), Butcher (Ipswich), Mabbutt (Tottenham), Francis (Sampdoria), Withe (Aston Villa), Blissett (Watford), Cowans (Aston Villa). manager: Bobby Robson
Hungary: Katzirz (Pecsi Munkas) – capt, Martos (Waterschei), Kocsis (Lierse), Toth (Ujpesti Dozsa), Hannich (Raba Gyor), Garaba (Honved), Varga (Honved), Nyilasi (Ferencvaros), Kiss (Vasas), Kardos (Ujpesti Dozsa), Hajszan (Raba Gyor). subs: Burcsa (Raba Gyor) for Martos 68, Torocsik (Ujpesti Dozsa) for Kiss 68. coach: Kalman Meszoly

FA Vase Final

Saturday 30th April 1983

Halesowen Town 0
Valley Sports Rugby 1
Crawley 47
13,700
Referee: B Daniels (Brentford)

A strong defensive display gave Rugby the Vase for the first time in the first final between clubs from the same division. But it was Halesowen who won the West Midlands Premier League Championship.

Halesowen: Caldicott, Penn, Edmonds, Lacey, Shilvock, Randle, Hazlewood, Moss, Woodhouse, Joinson (P), Joinson (L). sub: Smith for Joinson (L)
VS Rugby: Burton, McGinty, Harrison, Preston, Knox, Evans, Ingram, Setchell, Owen, Beecham, Crawley. sub: Haskins for Crawley

FA Trophy Final

Saturday 14th May 1983

Northwich Victoria 1
Bennett 76
Telford United 2
Mather 46, 60
22,071
Referee: B Hill (Kettering)

Telford's first FA Trophy win since 1971. Northwich manager John King would become a regular visitor to Wembley at the beginning of the 1990's as manager of Tranmere Rovers, while Stan Storton, the victorious Telford boss, would lead the men from Shropshire to the last 16 of the FA Cup two years later.

Northwich V: Ryan, Fretwell, Murphy, Jones, Forshaw, Ward, Anderson, Abel, Reid, Chesters, Wilson. sub: Bennett for Abel
Telford: Charlton, Lewis, Turner, Mayman, Walker, Eaton, Barnett, Williams, Mather, Hogan, Alcock. sub: Joseph for Mayman

FA CUP FINAL

Saturday 21st May 1983

Brighton and Hove Albion   2-2   Manchester United
Smith 14, Stevens 87   Stapleton 55, Wilkins 72
After extra time
100,000
Referee: A Grey (Great Yarmouth)

Brighton had pulled off a sensational away win against League Champions and Milk Cup holders Liverpool to reach the quarter-finals of the FA Cup for the first time. By contrast, United had won the FA Cup four times. Their last win in 1977 had been in the middle of a run of three finals in four years. They had emulated Tottenham's feat of the previous year by reaching the FA Cup final after losing the Milk Cup final in extra time two months earlier.

Brighton finished bottom of the First Division and were relegated after four seasons in the top flight. No club had ever won the FA Cup in a relegation season. United finished third, for the second successive year.

The Seagulls had nothing to lose and took a shock lead. Howlett's cross went beyond Moran and Gordon Smith headed it beyond Bailey's reach. But United equalised ten minutes into the second half. Duxbury crossed and Whiteside dived to head the ball past Moseley and across the goalmouth where Frank Stapleton beat Stevens to fire the ball into the roof of the net. Stapleton had also scored against United in the 1979 final for Arsenal. Seventeen minutes later, Muhren found Ray Wilkins in the clear with a long ball and the influential midfielder cut inside as Pearce came to challenge and curled a superb shot which gave Moseley no chance and United the lead.

The underdogs seemed beaten, but three minutes from the end, Case's corner found Grealish outside the area. Gary Stevens ran on to his short pass, steadied himself and fired a dramatic equaliser to force extra time. In the last minute of the extra half-hour, Robinson found an unmarked Smith with only Bailey to beat but a poor shot was safely gathered by the 'keeper and United heaved a massive sigh of relief.

For the third year in succession, the FA Cup final opponents returned to Wembley five days later.

Brighton: Moseley, Ramsey, Pearce, Grealish – capt, Stevens, Gatting, Case, Howlett, Robinson, Smith, Smillie. sub: Ryan for Ramsey 56. manager: Jimmy Melia
Manchester U: Bailey, Duxbury, Albiston, Wilkins, McQueen, Moran, Robson – capt, Muhren, Stapleton, Whiteside, Davies. sub: Grimes (not used). manager: Ron Atkinson

FA CUP FINAL REPLAY

Thursday 26th May 1983

Brighton and Hove Albion 0-4 Manchester United
Robson 25, 44, Whiteside 30, Muhren pen 62

92,000
Referee: A Grey (Great Yarmouth)

The replay was totally different from the first game. Bryan Robson fired United ahead from a Davies pass and it was Davies who again crossed for the second goal five minutes later. Norman Whiteside rose to head powerfully past Moseley and Grealish on the line. Brighton tried to respond, but found themselves three goals down at the interval.

Stapleton's header across goal just eluded McQueen and Foster, but Robson ran in unchallenged at the back post to destroy Brighton with his second. After 61 minutes, Robson was held back by Stevens, and Dutchman, Arnold Muhren beat Moseley from the penalty spot to complete an emphatic victory for United.

Brighton dropped into the Third Division four years later, but were promoted straight back and returned to Wembley for the Second Division Promotion play-off final in 1991.

Brighton: Moseley, Gatting, Pearce, Grealish, Foster – capt, Stevens, Case, Howlett, Robinson, Smith, Smillie. sub: Ryan for Howlett 74. manager: Jimmy Melia
Manchester U: Bailey, Duxbury, Albiston, Wilkins, McQueen, Moran, Robson – capt, Muhren, Stapleton, Whiteside, Davies. sub: Grimes (not used). manager: Ron Atkinson

BRITISH CHAMPIONSHIP

Wednesday 1st June 1983

England 2-0 Scotland
Robson 13, Cowans 54
83,000
Referee: E Fredriksson (Sweden)

Each side had beaten the other 1-0 away from home in their last two encounters. Scotland's victory had been two years earlier at Wembley. Since then, the Scots had been eliminated in the World Cup first round on goal difference for the third tournament in succession in 1982. They were already out of the European Championship after defeats in Berne and Brussels, but a draw would give them the British Championship on goal difference from England for the first time since 1977. England had to win to retain the title.

Bryan Robson continued from where he had left off the previous week, by putting England ahead. Sansom's long throw was flicked on by Butcher's head and Robson ghosted in to force the ball over the line.

The second goal came when Francis crossed, Gordon Cowans could not control the ball, but it fell to Neal who was tackled by Souness. However, Cowans was following up and fired England's second past Leighton. At the other end, Peter Shilton, winning his 50th cap, kept another clean sheet.

Scotland finished bottom of their European Championship group, but qualified for their fourth successive World Cup in 1986. This was their last appearance at Wembley in the British Championship as the competition came to an end the following year. But it was not the end of this fixture and in 1986 they returned for the Rous Cup.

Gordon Strachan appeared at Wembley for the first time. He was Footballer of the Year in 1991.

England: Shilton (Southampton), Neal (Liverpool), Sansom (Arsenal), Lee (Liverpool), Roberts (Tottenham), Butcher (Ipswich), Robson (Man Utd) – capt, Francis (Sampdoria), Withe (Aston Villa), Hoddle (Tottenham), Cowans (Aston Villa). subs: Mabbutt (Tottenham) for Robson 25, Blissett (Watford) for Withe 46. manager: Bobby Robson
Scotland: Leighton (Aberdeen), Gough (Dundee U), Gray (F) (Leeds United), Narey (Dundee U), McLeish (Aberdeen), Miller (Aberdeen), Strachan (Aberdeen), Souness (Liverpool) – capt, Gray (A) (Wolves), Nicholas (Celtic), Bannon (Dundee U). subs: Brazil (Tottenham) for Bannon 55. Wark (Ipswich) for Nicholas 67. manager: Jock Stein

Final table	P	W	D	L	F	A	Pts
England	3	2	1	0	4	1	5
Scotland	3	1	1	1	2	2	3
Wales	3	1	0	2	2	4	2
Northern Ireland	3	0	2	1	0	1	2

Schoolboy International

Saturday 11th June 1983

England 3
Scott 36, Rimmer 40, Moulden 66

Scotland 3
Miller 65, Murray 73, Kelly 77
46,000
Referee: D Scoble (Devon)

England squandered a two-goal half-time lead and the Scots completed their third successive game at Wembley without defeat.

England substitute Julian Darby scored Bolton Wanderers' equaliser at Wembley in the 1989 Sherpa Van Trophy final which they went on to win.

England: Pressman, Thomas – capt, Crumpton, Murphy, O'Brien, Peacock, Rimmer, Scott, White, Nesbit, Moulden. subs: Bogie for Nesbit 62, Darby for Peacock 66
Scotland: Smith, Philliben, Whyte, Walsh, Redpath, Kirkwood, McGuire, Murray – capt, Fraser, McLeod, Miller. subs: Kelly for Fraser 50, Kean for Redpath 57

FA CHARITY SHIELD

Saturday 20th August 1983

Liverpool	0-2	Manchester United
		Robson 23, 61

92,000
Referee: A Robinson (Waterlooville)

Liverpool, holders of the Shield after beating Tottenham Hotspur the previous year, were attempting to win it for the seventh time in ten years and a record tenth overall. They were unbeaten in nine matches at Wembley since losing to United in the 1977 FA Cup final. Their run had begun three months later, with a goalless draw against United, in the FA Charity Shield. They were now League Champions for the sixth time in eight years and a record 14th overall. They had retained the title by 11 points from Watford and they had also retained the Milk Cup, coming from behind to beat United in extra time. This completed an astonishing hat-trick of 'doubles', having won both the European Cup and the first of their hat-trick of Football League/Milk Cups in 1981. Their new manager, Joe Fagan had a lot to live up to after the retirement of Bob Paisley.

United had not won the Charity Shield outright since 1957 but had shared it three times since, twice with Liverpool. Their FA Cup win, three months earlier, had been their fifth and required a replay before their emphatic victory. They finished third, in the First Division for the second year in succession and this was their fourth appearance at Wembley in five months.

The first of Bryan Robson's goals came after he played a one-two with Wilkins, went round Grobbelaar and held off Kennedy's challenge to give United the lead. He scrambled in the second after Lee cleared Stapleton's header from Graham's corner off the line. It was his fifth goal in his last three appearances at Wembley.

Joe Fagan's reign as Liverpool's manager had got off to a bad start, but what happened over the season was beyond his wildest dreams. Liverpool finally achieved the elusive hat-trick of League Championships. They were back at Wembley again for the Milk Cup final and they regained the European Cup for a fourth time, a British record. In the final, they beat Roma in their own stadium in Rome on penalties following a 1-1 draw after extra time. It equalled Real Madrid's record of six European trophy wins. They also returned to Wembley for the following year's FA Charity Shield.

United's defence of the FA Cup resulted in an embarrassing defeat at Third Division Bournemouth, but in 1985 they were back to regain the trophy.

Liverpool: Grobbelaar, Neal, Kennedy (A), Lawrenson, Thompson (PB), Hansen, Dalglish, Lee, Rush, Robinson, Souness – capt. subs: Johnston for Thompson 60, Hodgson for Robinson 60. manager: Joe Fagan

Manchester U: Bailey, Duxbury, Albiston, Wilkins, Moran, McQueen, Robson – capt, Muhren, Stapleton, Whiteside, Graham. sub: Gidman for Muhren. manager: Ron Atkinson

EUROPEAN CHAMPIONSHIP QUALIFYING

Wednesday 21st September 1983

England	0-1	Denmark
		Simonsen pen 39

82,500
Referee: A Ponnet (Belgium)

These two had drawn 2-2 in the opening match of Group Three in Copenhagen twelve months earlier. That had ended a run of six successive England victories against the Danes, including at Wembley in the last European Championship in 1979.

This was expected to be the group decider. England were top, a point ahead of Denmark who had a game in hand. Denmark had failed to qualify for the previous year's World Cup despite beating the eventual winners Italy 3-1 in Copenhagen.

England were very poor and seemed afraid of the Danes. The one goal resulted from a handball from Neal, winning his 50th and last cap. Allan Simonsen sent Shilton the wrong way from the penalty. This was enough to give Denmark victory. Denmark, were back at Wembley in 1988.

John Barnes made his Wembley debut. Five years later he was to win the first of his two Footballer of the Year awards in three years.

England: Shilton (Southampton), Neal (Liverpool), Sansom (Arsenal), Wilkins (Man Utd) – capt, Osman (Ipswich), Butcher (Ipswich), Francis (Sampdoria), Lee (Liverpool), Mariner (Ipswich), Gregory (QPR), Barnes (Watford). subs: Chamberlain (Stoke City) for Barnes 70, Blissett (AC Milan) for Lee 77. manager: Bobby Robson

Denmark: Kjaer (Esbjerg), Rasmussen (Hertha Berlin), Busk (La Gantoise), Olsen (M) (Anderlecht) – capt, Nielsen (Feyenoord), Simonsen (Vejle), Bertelsen (Seraing Liege), Lerby (Bayern Munich), Berggreen (Pisa), Laudrup (M) (Lazio), Olsen (J) (Ajax Amsterdam). subs: Elkjaer (Lokeren) for Laudrup 46, Molby (Ajax) for Olsen (M) 86. coach: Sepp Piontek

Final table	P	W	D	L	F	A	Pts
Denmark	8	6	1	1	17	5	13
England	8	5	2	1	23	3	12
Greece	8	3	2	3	8	10	8
Hungary	8	3	1	4	18	17	7
Luxembourg	8	0	0	8	5	36	0

Inter-Varsity Match

Wednesday 7th December 1983

Cambridge U 2
Aspinwall 2

Oxford U 2
Varty, Husselbee
6,800

The 100th meeting fittingly ended in a draw, thanks to Oxford 'keeper, Rutledge saving a late penalty from Walsh. Husselbee netted his fifth in three visits.

Schoolboy International

Saturday 17th March 1984

England 1
Burke 24
Scotland 0
40,000
Referee: N Midgley (Manchester)

After three games unbeaten at Wembley, Scotland lost for the first time since their 1978 appearance.

Billy McKinlay was capped 29 times at full international level for Scotland, but never played again at Wembley.

England: Martin, Hall, Harvey, Derry, Garwood – capt, Harding, Tomlinson, Wilson, Benali, Jeffers, Burke. sub: Reddington for Garwood
Scotland: Tait, Peters, Strain, Whyte, Deas, McPherson, McEntaggart, McKinlay, Fertacz, Wilson, Hunter. subs: Ferguson for Wilson, Feeney for Hunter

MILK CUP FINAL

Sunday 25th March 1984

Everton   0-0   **Liverpool**
After extra time
100,000
Referee: A Robinson (Portsmouth)

Everton were appearing in their first final since 1977 when they had taken part in possibly Wembley's worst game before losing in a second replay. They had never won the League Cup and had not won a major trophy since the League Championship in 1970. Liverpool were bidding to become the first club to win a domestic competition four years in succession. Each of their three previous victories had required them to come from behind and they had all gone to extra time. However, they had been beaten on their last Wembley visit in the previous year's FA Charity Shield.

Everton had started the season poorly but were now in top form and had also reached the FA Cup semi-finals. Four days earlier Liverpool had reached the semi-finals of the European Cup for the first time since 1981 when they last won the trophy. They were also chasing a League Championship hat-trick and had not lost to Everton for three seasons.

Wembley's first major final to be played on a Sunday was also the first all-Mersey-side final. Everton had more possession, but could not find the final touch to defeat their local rivals despite a penalty appeal after six minutes when Heath's goal-bound shot was blocked by Hansen's hand.

Three days later, Liverpool retained the Milk Cup with a single goal victory, but Everton had given them ample warning that they would challenge again for honours. Indeed, two months later they won the FA Cup. Liverpool completed the League Championship hat-trick and also won the European Cup on penalties for an unprecedented 'treble' in manager Joe Fagan's first season. But they would meet Everton again in the FA Charity Shield five months later.

Everton: Southall, Stevens, Bailey, Ratcliffe – capt, Mountfield, Reid, Irvine, Heath, Sharp, Richardson, Sheedy. sub: Harper for Sheedy 67. manager: Howard Kendall
Liverpool: Grobbelaar, Neal, Kennedy (A), Lawrenson, Whelan, Hansen, Dalglish, Lee, Rush, Johnston, Souness – capt. sub: Robinson for Johnston 91. manager: Joe Fagan

Replay: Wednesday 28th March 1984
Everton   0-1   **Liverpool**
Souness 21

(Maine Road, Manchester)

BRITISH CHAMPIONSHIP

Wednesday 4th April 1984

England	**1-0**	**Northern Ireland**

Woodcock 40
24,000
Referee: R Bridges (Wales)

Northern Ireland had been well beaten on their last visit, but had contested a goalless draw with England at Windsor Park in 1983. This was Wembley's last British Championship match as the competition came to a close in its centenary year.

The Irish had already beaten Scotland 2-0 at Windsor Park while this was England's first match in their bid to complete a final hat-trick of British Championships. Northern Ireland had narrowly failed to qualify for the forthcoming European Championship despite beating the reigning champions West Germany, both at Windsor Park and in Hamburg. They finished as runners-up to the Germans on goal difference.

Barely more than a practice match, which England won with a goal in the 41st minute. Platt saved from Anderson but Tony Woodcock nodded home from the rebound.

England lost 1-0 to Wales at the Racecourse Ground the following month, and all four teams ended on the same number of points, perhaps fittingly for the last Championship. But, unlike in 1956, the only other occasion it had happened, this one was decided by goal difference for the first and only time. Northern Ireland secured their third outright title and were back at Wembley, the following year, for a World Cup qualifying match.

England: Shilton (Southampton), Anderson (Nottingham F), Roberts (Tottenham), Butcher (Ipswich), Kennedy* (Liverpool), Lee (Liverpool), Wilkins (Man Utd), Robson (Man Utd) – capt, Rix (Arsenal), Francis (Sampdoria), Woodcock (Arsenal). manager: Bobby Robson
Northern Ireland: Platt (Ballymena), Nicholl (Rangers), McClelland (Rangers), McElhinney (Bolton), Donaghy (Luton Town), Armstrong (Real Mallorca), O'Neill (Notts County) – capt, Hamilton (Burnley), Whiteside (Man Utd), McIlroy (Stoke City), Stewart (QPR). manager: Billy Bingham
*first cap

Final table	P	W	D	L	F	A	Pts
Northern Ireland	3	1	1	1	3	2	3
Wales	3	1	1	1	3	3	3
England	3	1	1	1	2	2	3
Scotland	3	1	1	1	3	4	3

FA Vase Final

Saturday 28th April 1984

Stamford 2
Waddicor, Allen
Stansted 3
Holt, Gillard, Reading
8,125
Referee: T Bune (Newbury)

A surprise win for Stansted who had never progressed beyond the first round of the competition before.

Stamford: Parslow, Smitheringale, Blades, Mackin – capt, McIlwain, Lyon, Robson, Beech, Genovese, Allen, Waddicor
Stansted: Coe, Hilton, Williams, Simpson – capt, Cooper, Reading, Callanan, Holt, Reeves, Doyle, Gillard

Saturday 12th May 1984

Bangor City 1
Whelan 54
Northwich Victoria 1
Chesters 73
After extra time
14,200
Referee: J Martin (Alton)

Northwich came from behind twice to win the Trophy for the first time in their second successive final thanks to John Anderson's injury-time replay winner.

Bangor: Letheran, Cavanagh, Gray, Whelan, Banks, Lunn – capt, Urquhart, Morris, Carter, Howat, Sutcliffe. sub: Westwood for Sutcliffe 105

Northwich: Ryan, Fretwell, Dean, Jones – capt, Forshaw, Bennett, Anderson, Abel, Reid, Chesters, Wilson. sub: Power for Forshaw 65

Replay: Tuesday 15th May 1984

Bangor City 1
Lunn 18

Northwich Victoria 2
Chesters pen 34, Anderson 90
(Victoria Ground, Stoke)

FA CUP FINAL

Saturday 19th May 1984

Everton　　2-0　　**Watford**
Sharp 38, Gray 51
100,000
Referee: J Hunting (Leicester)

Like Tottenham Hotspur and Manchester United in the two preceding years, the Milk Cup runners-up had returned to contest the FA Cup final. Everton had held their mighty neighbours Liverpool to a goalless draw after extra time two months earlier before losing the replay. This was their first FA Cup final since 1968 when they lost in extra time. Their last victory had been in 1966 when they came back from two goals down. Everton's last major trophy had been the League Championship in 1970.

Watford were appearing in their first final never before having played at Wembley. In the last 16 they had beaten the previous year's finalists Brighton and Hove Albion. Six years earlier Watford had been Fourth Division Champions to begin a meteoric rise up the Football League which saw them finish runners-up in the top two divisions in successive years.

Everton's first goal came from a cross from Richardson – transferred to Watford two years later – which was headed out by Sinnott but Steven knocked it back in to a now unmarked Graeme Sharp who fired in off the post. Six minutes into the second half the contest was effectively over in controversial circumstances. Sherwood leapt backwards to collect Steven's high cross but Andy Gray headed it into the net before he could gather it. It could be argued that Gray had headed it out of Sherwood's hands but the goal stood and Watford were beaten.

Everton won the European Cup-Winners Cup the following year with a 3-1 win against Rapid Vienna in Rotterdam and reached the FA Cup final again. Watford had reached their peak and were relegated back to the Second Division four years later. They were not to return to top-flight football until 1999 when they won the play-offs at Wembley.

Everton: Southall, Stevens, Bailey, Ratcliffe – capt, Mountfield, Reid, Steven, Heath, Sharp, Gray, Richardson. sub: Harper (not used). manager: Howard Kendall
Watford: Sherwood, Bardsley, Price, Taylor – capt, Terry, Sinnott, Callaghan, Johnston, Reilly, Jackett, Barnes. sub: Atkinson for Price 58. manager: Graham Taylor

INTERNATIONAL

Saturday 2nd June 1984

England　　0-2　　**USSR**
　　　　　　　　Gotsmanov 53, Protasov 90
38,125
Referee: M Vautrot (France)

The Soviets had earned a draw on their last visit to Wembley 17 years earlier, but six years later England won 2-1 in Moscow, their last meeting. Only once had they beaten England, back in the 1958 World Cup. In 1972 the USSR had become the first team to reach three European Championship finals, but they had then gone ten years without qualifying for a major tournament.

The visitors took the lead when Duxbury slipped, leaving substitute Sergei Gotsmanov free to run on and beat Shilton. The scoreline was doubled in the last minute. Blokhin's shot was saved by Shilton but Oleg Protasov netted the rebound having just come on as a substitute.

England had their revenge with a 1-0 win in Tbilisi in 1986. Two years after that,

the USSR reached a record fourth European Championship final, beating England along the way and were back at Wembley in 1991.

Oleg Blokhin made his only appearance at Wembley. Nine years earlier, he had been European Footballer of the Year.

England: Shilton (Southampton), Duxbury (Man Utd), Sansom (Arsenal), Wilkins (Man Utd), Roberts (Tottenham), Fenwick (QPR), Robson (Man Utd) – capt, Chamberlain (Stoke City), Francis (Sampdoria), Blissett (AC Milan), Barnes (Watford). subs: Hunt (West Brom) for Barnes 66, Hateley* (Portsmouth) for Francis 70. manager: Bobby Robson
*first cap
USSR: Dasaev (Spartak Moscow), Sulakvelidze (Dynamo Tbilisi), Chivadze (Dynamo Tbilisi) – capt, Baltacha (Dynamo Kiev), Demianenko (Dynamo Kiev), Aleinikov (Dynamo Minsk), Litovchenko (Dnepr), Oganesian (Ararat Yerevan), Zygmantovich (Dynamo Minsk), Rodionov (Spartak Moscow), Blokhin (Dynamo Kiev). subs: Gotsmanov (Dynamo Minsk) for Zygmantovich 20, Pozdnyakov (Spartak Moscow) for Aleinikov 86, Protasov (Dnepr) for Rodionov 87. coach: Eduard Malofeyev

Schoolboy International

Saturday 9th June 1984

England 4
Burke 10, 40, 62, Bell 74

Netherlands 1
Alma 61

35,000
Referee: P Cobby (Gloucestershire)

A Mark Burke hat-trick secured another England victory.

England: Martin, Mills, Harvey, Berry, Garwood – capt, Reddington, Tomlinson, Wilson, Benali, Bell, Burke. subs: Harding for Wilson 69, Hall for Garwood 75

FA CHARITY SHIELD

Saturday 18th August 1984

Everton   1-0   **Liverpool**
Grobbelaar og 55
100,000
Referee: K Hackett (Sheffield)

Everton had not lifted the FA Charity Shield since winning at Chelsea in 1970 and they had lost at home to Liverpool in the 1966 fixture. This was their second meeting at Wembley following their goalless Milk Cup final encounter after extra time five months earlier. Liverpool had won the replay, but Everton had gone on to win the FA Cup, two months later.

The Reds had lost the previous year's Charity Shield and were once again chasing a record tenth win in their third successive appearance in the fixture. They had last won it in 1982. The previous season had been momentous even by Liverpool's standards. Apart from their record fourth successive League/Milk Cup win, they had regained the European Cup for a British record fourth time and they had completed the first League Championship hat-trick

in 49 years, all in Joe Fagan's first season as manager. It was also the fourth successive season in which they had won at least two trophies. The league title had been their seventh in nine years and a record 15th overall.

Everton served notice for the approaching season by beating their local rivals with a goal which was scrappy, to say the least. Bruce Grobbelaar saved from Sharp but the striker hit the rebound back towards goal. Hansen cleared off the line but drove the ball against the Zimbabwean goalkeeper as he scrambled back and in it went.

Liverpool failed to become the first club to win four successive League Championships, but the title did stay on Merseyside as Everton won it for the first time since 1970. Liverpool were runners-up. Everton also won the European Cup-Winners Cup, their first European trophy, and reached their second successive FA Cup final before retaining the FA Charity Shield.

Liverpool had their first season without a trophy for ten years. They reached the FA Cup semi-finals, before losing to the eventual winners Manchester United after extra time and a replay.

Independiente beat them in the World Club Championship in Tokyo and they then lost the European Super Cup to Juventus in Turin, before the season finished on a disastrous note.

Liverpool reached the European Cup final for the second year in succession and were all set to face Juventus again in Brussels when rioting spectators caused an hor-

rific crush against a wall which eventually gave way and 39 people, mostly Juventus fans, lost their lives.

The fact that the match was still played and Liverpool lost to a penalty when the foul was clearly committed outside the box, was irrelevant.

English clubs were immediately withdrawn from European competitions and were not to return for five long years. Liverpool thus concentrated all their efforts on domestic competition and clinched the League Championship and FA Cup 'double' a year later at Wembley.

Steve Nicol made his first appearance at Wembley. In 1989 he was Footballer of the Year.

Everton: Southall, Stevens, Bailey, Ratcliffe – capt, Mountfield, Reid, Steven, Heath, Sharp, Bracewell, Richardson. manager: Howard Kendall

Liverpool: Grobbelaar, Neal – capt, Kennedy (A), Lawrenson, Whelan, Hansen, Dalglish, Lee, Rush, Nicol, Wark. sub: Walsh for Lee. manager: Joe Fagan

INTERNATIONAL

Wednesday 12th September 1984

England   **1-0**   **East Germany**
Robson 82
23,951
Referee: A Thomas (Netherlands)

Ten years before East Germany had avoided defeat against England for the first time with a 1-1 draw in Leipzig. They had then gone on to reach the last eight of the World Cup after beating neighbours and eventual winners West Germany in a group match. Since then they had failed to qualify for every major tournament. Their previous trip to Wembley had been in 1970.

With eight minutes left, England found the finishing touch which had been lacking throughout the game. Sansom's high

cross was headed back across goal by Wilkins and Bryan Robson volleyed it past Muller for a spectacular winner. It was a disappointment for Joachim Streich, who was winning his 100th cap.

East Germany missed out on the 1986 World Cup by just a point from a group won by European Champions France. But this was their last meeting with England as, six years later, Germany became united and the unified nation visited Wembley for the first time, in 1991.

England: Shilton (Southampton), Duxbury (Man Utd), Sansom (Arsenal), Williams (Southampton), Wright (Southampton), Butcher (Ipswich), Robson (Man Utd) – capt, Wilkins (AC Milan), Mariner (Arsenal), Woodcock (Arsenal), Barnes (Watford). subs: Hateley (AC Milan) for Mariner 80, Francis (Sampdoria) for Woodcock 80. manager: Bobby Robson

East Germany: Muller (Lokomotive Leipzig), Kreer (Lokomotive Leipzig), Dorner (Dynamo Dresden) – capt, Stahmann (Magdeburg), Zotzsche (Lokomotive Leipzig), Liebers (Lokomotive Leipzig), Troppa (Dynamo Berlin), Ernst (Dynamo Berlin), Steinbach (Magdeburg), Streich (Magdeburg), Minge (Dynamo Dresden). subs: Richter (Lokomotive Leipzig) for Streich 76, Raab (Carl Zeiss Jena) for Ernst 89. coach: Bernd Stange

WORLD CUP QUALIFYING

Wednesday 17th October 1984

England   **5-0**   **Finland**
Hateley 29, 49, Woodcock 40,
Robson 70, Sansom 85
47,234
Referee: A Suchanek (Poland)

England had won each of their six previous meetings with Finland.

Finland had already beaten Northern Ireland 1-0 in Pori in the opening match of Group Three five months earlier but had still to qualify for a major tournament.

England, in red shirts, broke the deadlock when Barnes hit the bar and Mark Hateley converted the rebound.

Five minutes before half-time Tony Woodcock scrambled the ball over the line after Huttunen had saved his shot and Pekonen had cleared the resulting loose ball off the line only to hit Kymalainen, which enabled Woodcock to complete the job.

Second-half substitute Stevens laid on the third for Hateley to score his second just after the interval and with 20 minutes left Hateley headed Barnes' cross into the path of Bryan Robson,who made no mistake.

The scoring was completed when a cross from Chamberlain, the other substitute, was deposited into the back of the net from 25 yards by Kenny Sansom.

Five months later in the Helsinki return, Finland held England for the first time – a 1-1 draw. The Finns remained unbeaten at home, but it was not enough to qualify. This was their last trip to Wembley.

England: Shilton (Southampton), Duxbury (Man Utd), Sansom (Arsenal), Williams (Southampton), Wright (Southampton), Butcher (Ipswich), Robson (Man Utd) – capt, Wilkins (AC Milan), Hateley (AC Milan), Woodcock (Arsenal), Barnes (Watford). subs: Stevens* (Tottenham) for Duxbury 46, Chamberlain (Stoke City) for Robson 75. manager: Bobby Robson
*first cap
Finland: Huttunen (Haka Valkeakoski), Pekonen (Kuusysi Lahti), Kymalainen (TPS Turku) – capt, Lahtinen (Notts County), Petaja (TPS Turku), Haaskivi (Cleveland Force), Houtsonen (KuPS Kuopio), Ukkonen (Cercle Bruges), Ikalainen (Orgryte), Rautiainen (Arminia Bielefeld), Valvee (Vasalund). subs: Turunen (KuPS Kuopio) for Haaskivi 46, Hjelm (Ilves Tampere) for Valvee 70. coach: Martti Kuusela

Inter-Varsity Match

Wednesday 12th December 1984

Cambridge U 4
Elliott, Whyte, Harper, Marshall
Oxford U 2
Husselbee pen, Hunter

Husselbee's sixth goal in four matches could not prevent Cambridge's first win in the fixture since 1978 despite Oxford pulling back a two-goal deficit at one stage.

Schoolboy International

Saturday 16th March 1985

England 0
West Germany 1
Koerner pen 12
35,761

Despite the presence in the team of seven students from the Football Association's new National School at Lilleshall, England suffered their first defeat at Wembley under Ralph O'Donnell.

Eight years later Steve Tutill came on as a substitute for York City at Wembley in the Third Division Promotion play-off final and gave away the last-minute penalty from which Crewe equalised. Fortunately for him York won on penalties.

England: Elliott, Kelly – capt, Atkin, Tutill, Docker, Esqulant, Darby, Murray, Ward, Thomas, Beckford. subs: Hutchinson for Murray, Starkey for Ward

MILK CUP FINAL

Sunday 24th March 1985

Norwich City   **1-0**   **Sunderland**
Chisholm og 46
100,000
Referee: N Midgley (Salford)

Norwich had won the League Cup in 1962 but had never won at Wembley, having lost two finals in three years in the 1970's. Sunderland were appearing in their first League Cup final, but had won the FA Cup twice at Wembley, the most famous of which was the 1973 shock defeat of mighty Leeds United, when Sunderland were in the Second Division.

Both sides were fighting relegation battles at the foot of the First Division.

Norwich took the lead in the first minute of the second half. Sunderland's young defender Corner, who had made his first full league appearance at Norwich the previous week, tried to shield the ball as it ran out for a goal kick. But Deehan stopped it on the line and crossed to Channon.

The experienced England international was dispossessed by Gordon Chisholm but the ball fell to Hartford, playing in his third final for his third different club. Hartford's shot deflected off Chisholm's chest to give Turner no chance.

Sunderland had a golden opportunity to level within two minutes when Van Wyk handled in the area. But Walker's spot-kick hit the foot of the post and Woods, Not-tingham Forest's hero at 18 in the 1978 final, once again kept his goal intact.

Both these clubs were relegated to the Second Division two months later. Norwich were also denied their first ever place in Europe by the riot and subsequent tragedy at the European Cup final which led to the withdrawal of all English clubs from the following season's European competitions.

In the Screen Sport Super Cup introduced to fill the fixture gaps in the following season Norwich reached the semi-finals, before losing to the eventual winners Liverpool, who also went on to win the 'double'. Norwich won the Second Division Championship and were promoted straight back to the top flight, although they never returned to Wembley.

Two years later Sunderland were relegated to the Third Division for the first time. They came straight back as Third Division Champions, also appearing in the Football League Centenary Tournament at Wembley. They returned again for the Second Division Promotion play-off final in 1990, before reaching the FA Cup final again in 1992.

Norwich: Woods, Haylock, Van Wyk, Bruce, Mendham, Watson – capt, Barham, Channon, Deehan, Hartford, Donowa. sub: Devine (not used). manager: Ken Brown
Sunderland: Turner, Venison – capt, Pickering, Bennett, Chisholm, Corner, Daniel, Wallace, Hodgson, Berry, Walker. sub: Gayle for Corner 63. manager: Len Ashurst

INTERNATIONAL

Tuesday 26th March 1985

England   **2-1**   **Republic of Ireland**
Steven 45, Lineker 76   Brady 88
34,793
Referee; G Smith (Scotland)

The Republic of Ireland had lost to two Kevin Keegan goals on their last visit in 1980 and had beaten England only once back in 1949. They had never qualified for a major tournament and had already lost in both Oslo and Copenhagen in their World Cup qualifying group.

England scored at the end of the first half. Hateley headed on Butcher's cross for Trevor Steven to shoot past Bonner. With 14 minutes left, Gary Lineker took a pass from substitute Davenport and chipped the 'keeper for England's second. The Irish pulled one back two minutes from time.

From Stapleton's pass, a shot from Liam Brady, winning his 50th cap, was fumbled by Bailey at the near post and found its way into the net.

The Republic failed to qualify for the following year's World Cup but did appear in the 1988 European Championship, their first major tournament.

In fact, they beat England 1-0 in Stuttgart in their first match of the finals. Both teams failed to qualify for the semi-finals,

but they met again in two 1-1 draws before the Irish returned to Wembley in 1991 in the European Championship.

Gary Lineker scored on his Wembley debut. This was to become a familiar sight in a career which saw him twice named Footballer of the Year and in 1986, he was the World Cup's top scorer.

Chris Waddle, the 1993 Footballer of the Year, also made his Wembley debut.

England: Bailey* (Man Utd), Anderson (Arsenal), Sansom (Arsenal), Steven (Everton), Wright (Southampton), Butcher (Ipswich), Robson (Man Utd) – capt, Wilkins (AC Milan), Hateley (AC Milan), Lineker (Leicester), Waddle* (Newcastle). subs: Hoddle (Tottenham) for Robson 67, Davenport* (Nottingham F) for Hateley 73. manager: Bobby Robson
Republic of Ireland: Bonner (Celtic), Hughton (Tottenham), Beglin (Liverpool), Lawrenson (Liverpool), McCarthy (Man City), Whelan (Liverpool), Waddock (QPR), Brady (Internazionale), O'Keefe (Port Vale), Stapleton (Man Utd) – capt, McGrath (Man Utd). subs: O'Callaghan (Ipswich) for Whelan 70, Byrne* (QPR) for O'Keefe 79, O'Leary (Arsenal) for McGrath 46. manager: Eoin Hand
*first cap

FA Vase Final

Saturday 27th April 1985

Fleetwood Town 1
Moran 90

Halesowen Town 3
Moss 11, L Joinson 50, 79
16,715
Referee: C Downey (Hounslow)

Lee Joinson had been carried off injured in the 1983 final but made up for it as his goals secured a first victory for Halesowen.

Fleetwood: Dobson, Moran, Hadgraft, Strachan, Robinson, Milligan, Hall, Trainor, Taylor, Cain, Kennerley. sub: Whitehouse for Taylor
Halesowen: Caldicott, Penn, Sherwood, Warner, Randle, Heath, Hazelwood, Moss, Woodhouse – capt, Joinson (P), Joinson (L). sub: Smith for Moss

FA Trophy Final

Saturday 11th May 1985

Boston United 1
Cook 48

Wealdstone 2
Graham 2, Holmes 28
20,775
Referee: J Bray (Hinckley)

Wealdstone, winners of the FA Amateur Cup at Wembley 19 years earlier, completed the first 'double' of Gola League Championship and FA Trophy, the two major non-league competitions.

They could even afford to miss a penalty when Kevin Blackwell, now manager of Leeds United, saved from Dennis Byatt in the 16th minute of a first half dominated by Wealdstone. Sadly, their ground was not up to Football League standard and they did not win the non-league nomination for election to the league.

Boston's manager Arthur Mann had been in the Manchester City side which won the 1970 Football League Cup at Wembley.

Boston: Blackwell, Casey, O'Brien, Laverick, Ladd, Creane, Thomson, Simpson, Lee, Cook, Gilbert. sub: Mallender for Laverick
Wealdstone: Iles, Perkins, Davies, Byatt, Bowgett – capt, Wainwright, Greenaway, Holmes, Cordice (A), Graham, Donnellan. sub: Cordice (N) for Graham

FA CUP FINAL

Saturday 18th May 1985

Everton   0-1   **Manchester United**
Whiteside 110

After extra time
100,000
Referee: P Willis (Meadowfield)

Everton were the FA Cup holders and were hoping for as comfortable a victory as in the previous year's final. Since then they had won the FA Charity Shield at Wembley. United were attempting to regain the FA Cup for the second time in three years, after a convincing replay victory in 1983. Like Everton a year later, they had followed it up by beating Liverpool in the Charity Shield.

Everton had won the League Championship for the first time since 1970 and were aiming to become the first team to win the 'double' since Arsenal in 1971. Three days earlier they had beaten Rapid Vienna in Rotterdam to win the European Cup-Winners Cup, their first European trophy, and so hoped to repeat Liverpool's three trophy wins of the previous year.

United finished fourth in the First Division for the second year in succession. They lost at home to Everton in the Milk Cup, but reached the UEFA Cup quarter-finals before losing on penalties to Videoton, the eventual finalists.

The sides had cancelled each other out when a 79th minute incident transformed the game. Kevin Moran became the first player to be sent off in an FA Cup final after a cynical foul chopped down Reid as he was clean through on goal.

United's players were incensed with the harshness of the decision and were galvanised into action. With ten minutes left in extra time, Hughes sent Norman Whiteside away down the right wing. The young Irishman cut inside and, faced with Van den Hauwe, managed to curl the ball round him and beyond Southall's dive for a magnificent goal. Everton's memorable season had finally caught up with them and their numerical advantage could not match United's determination.

Everton reached their third successive final the following year. United were denied the opportunity of competing in the European Cup-Winners Cup by the Heysel Stadium disaster in Brussels 11 days later and in the competition set up to fill the fixture gaps, the Screen Sport Super Cup, United were beaten home and away by the eventual finalists Everton.

Everton: Southall, Stevens, Van den Hauwe, Ratcliffe – capt, Mountfield, Reid, Steven, Gray, Sharp, Bracewell, Sheedy. sub: Harper (not used). manager: Howard Kendall
Manchester U: Bailey, Gidman, Albiston, Whiteside, McGrath, Moran, Robson – capt, Strachan, Hughes, Stapleton, Olsen. sub: Duxbury for Albiston 91. manager: Ron Atkinson

Freight Rover Trophy Final

Saturday 1st June 1985

Brentford 1
Cooke

Wigan Athletic 3
Newell, Kelly, Lowe
39,897
Referee: T Bune (Newbury)

The competition for Third and Fourth Division clubs, the Associate Members Cup, found a sponsor and with it, a memorable day out at Wembley. It was Brentford's first appearance at the stadium since winning the London War Cup in 1942. They had beaten holders Bournemouth in the quarter-finals and thrashed Newport County 6-0 in the semi-finals.

Wigan had overcome Mansfield Town on penalties to reach Wembley for the first time since the FA Trophy final in 1973. Substitute Paul Jewell took Wigan into the Premiership as manager for the first time in 2005.

Brentford: Phillips, Salman, Murray, Millen, Wignall, Hurlock, Kamara, Cooke, Booker, Cassells, Roberts. sub: Bullivant for Booker. manager: Frank McLintock
Wigan: Tunks, Cribley, Knowles, Kelly, Walsh, Methven – capt, Lowe, Barrow, Bennett, Newell, Langley. subs: Aspinall for Bennett, Jewell for Newell. manager: Bryan Hamilton

Schoolboy International

Saturday 8th June 1985

England 2
Murray 55, Ebbrell 73
Switzerland 0
31,653
Referee: J Gardener (Durham)

England's seventh successive victory against the Swiss was secured by two second-half goals.

England: Elliott, Kelly, Docker, Tutill, Atkin, Atherton, Thomas, Greene, Murray, Starkey, Ebbrell – capt. subs: Beckford for Starkey 65, Wright for Kelly 76

Under-16 International

Saturday 10th August 1985

England 3
Esqulant, Pearson, Williams
Yugoslavia 2
Lukic, Katic
Referee: B Hill (Northamptonshire)

In the curtain-raiser to the FA Charity Shield, the boys from the new FA school recovered from being two goals down at half-time to win Wembley's first international at this level.

Substitute, Mark Robins made four more appearances at Wembley, all as substitute, but scored Manchester United's FA Cup semi-final winner in 1990.

England: Miller, Wright, Teasdale, Walkington, Darby, Esqulant, Cam, Pearson, Osbourne, Beckford, King. subs: Kelly for Darby 41, Williams for Osbourne 41, Robins for King 41, Elliott for Miller 48, Pitcher for Teasdale 48

FA CHARITY SHIELD

Saturday 10th August 1985

Everton   **2-0**   **Manchester United**
Steven 26, Heath 82
82,000
Referee: J Worrall (Warrington)

Both sides had beaten Liverpool in the last two Charity Shields, United in 1983 and Everton a year later. Everton had won their first League Championship since 1970, with United fourth for the second year in succession. But three months earlier United had ended Everton's hopes of the 'double' by regaining the FA Cup for the second time in three years. But Everton won the European Cup-Winners Cup.

Everton's first goal arrived after Mc-Grath lost the ball to Sheedy who crossed for Trevor Steven to give Everton the lead. They retained the Shield with a second goal scored with eight minutes left. Bailey fumbled a Van den Hauwe centre and substitute Adrian Heath took advantage to score.

Everton were chasing the 'double' again, at the end of the season, but finished as runners-up to Liverpool in both their defence of the League Championship and in their third successive FA Cup final. They were invited back to go for a hat-trick of Charity Shields the following year. But Everton could not compete in the European Cup because English clubs were now banned from European competitions.

The clubs that had qualified for Europe competed in the Screen Sport Super Cup instead. Everton beat United home and away, and reached the final where they lost, inevitably, to Liverpool. United began the season with a determined run and won their first ten league games but could not win the Championship. They finished fourth again. In 1988, they finished League runners-up to Liverpool and were back at Wembley for the Football League Centenary Tournament in which they beat Everton. Later that year, they reached the Football League Centenary Trophy final which they lost to Arsenal and in 1990, they were in the FA Cup final again.

Everton: Southall, Stevens, Van den Hauwe, Ratcliffe – capt, Mountfield, Reid, Steven, Sharp, Lineker, Bracewell, Sheedy. subs: Heath for Lineker 76, Bailey for Van den Hauwe 88. manager: Howard Kendall
Manchester U: Bailey, Gidman, Albiston, Whiteside, McGrath, Hogg, Robson – capt, Duxbury, Hughes, Stapleton, Olsen. sub: Moses for Duxbury 61. manager: Ron Atkinson

WORLD CUP QUALIFYING

Wednesday 11th September 1985

England   **1-1**   **Romania**
Hoddle 25   Camataru 60
59,500
Referee: K Tritschler (West Germany)

England led Group Three by a point from Northern Ireland who had drawn with Turkey in Izmir earlier in the day. But England, who had completed their away fixtures and were unbeaten, knew that victory over Romania would probably be enough for them to qualify. The Romanians, a point behind the Irish, would then only be able to catch them on goal difference and that seemed unlikely with only two matches remaining after this.

Romania had never lost at Wembley and had held England in a World Cup qualifying match in 1981. Their earlier meeting in this group had been a tough goalless draw in Bucharest four months earlier. They had almost eliminated England in the last World Cup but blew their chance by losing to Switzerland in Bucharest.

England opened the scoring with a fine goal. From Sansom's free kick, Glenn Hoddle timed his run perfectly and beat the offside trap before expertly bending the ball around Lung. The Romanians always looked dangerous and equalised on the hour. Coras passed to Rodion Camataru, who held off the challenge of Wright and Stevens to fire past Shilton and maintain their unbeaten record at Wembley.

It was a point dropped for England but they were still comfortably placed with two home games left. Romania were also looking confident, yet once again they blew it. The following month they lost to Northern Ireland in Bucharest and eventually missed out by a point for the second World Cup in succession. They were back at Wembley in 1994.

England: Shilton (Southampton), Stevens (Everton), Sansom (Arsenal), Hoddle (Tottenham), Wright (Southampton), Fenwick (QPR), Robson (Man Utd) – capt, Reid (Everton), Hateley (AC Milan), Lineker (Everton), Waddle (Tottenham). subs: Barnes (Watford) for Waddle 69, Woodcock (Arsenal) for Lineker 76. manager: Bobby Robson
Romania: Lung (Universitatea Craiova), Stefanescu (Universitatea Craiova) – capt, Negrila (Universitatea Craiova), Ungureanu (Universitatea Craiova), Rednic (Dinamo Bucharest), Iovan (Steaua Bucharest), Coras (Sportul Studentesc), Klein (Corvinul Hunedoara), Camataru (Universitatea Craiova), Boloni (Steaua), Hagi (Sportul Studentesc). subs: Gabor (Corvinul Hunedoara) for Coras 82, Mateut (Corvinul Hunedoara) for Klein 87. coach: Mircea Lucescu

WORLD CUP QUALIFYING

Wednesday 16th October 1985

England   **5-0**   **Turkey**
Waddle 15, Lineker 18, 43, 54,
Robson 35
52,500
Referee: A Milchenko (USSR)

England now led Group Three on goal difference from Northern Ireland who earlier in the day had surprisingly beaten Romania 1-0 in Bucharest. The Romanians could now catch England only on goal difference which was highly unlikely. A point would mathematically secure England's qualification for Mexico. Turkey were making their first visit to England, having suffered an 8-0 annihilation in their first meeting in Istanbul, the previous year, England's biggest away win for 20 years. Turkey had

only once qualified for the World Cup – in 1954 – and had picked up only one point from this group, against Northern Ireland in Izmir the previous month.

England took the field in an unusual combination of red shirts and blue shorts, but gained an expected lead, a fine individual effort from Chris Waddle who began the move in his own half and meandered his way around before sidestepping two defenders and firing low past Yasar. Three minutes later Gary Lineker headed home

Stevens' cross for England's second. Ten minutes before half-time Bryan Robson hit the post and Lineker lobbed the rebound up to Hateley whose header was saved, only for Robson to score off the post. Lineker, then, scored his second, heading in from another cross from Stevens two minutes before the break, and completed his hat-trick in the second half from Waddle's pass. The victory virtually ensured that England would win the group.

Turkey returned to Wembley two years later in the European Championship.

England: Shilton (Southampton), Stevens (Everton), Sansom (Arsenal), Hoddle (Tottenham), Wright (Southampton), Fenwick(QPR), Robson (Man Utd) – capt, Wilkins (AC Milan), Hateley (AC Milan), Lineker (Everton), Waddle (Tottenham). subs: Steven (Everton) for Robson 66, Woodcock (Arsenal) for Hateley 84. manager: Bobby Robson
Turkey: Yasar (Fenerbahce), Ismail (Galatasaray), Yusuf (Kocaelispor), Rasit (Galatasaray), Sedat (Bursaspor) – capt, Abdulkerim (Fenerbahce), Huseyin (Fenerbahce), Mujdat (Fenerbahce), Senol (Fenerbahce), Hasan Vezir (Trabzonspor), Selcuk (Fenerbahce). sub: Hasan Sengun (Trabzonspor) for Senol 37. coach: Coskun Ozari

WORLD CUP QUALIFYING

Wednesday 13th November 1985

England   0-0   Northern Ireland
70,500
Referee: E Fredriksson (Sweden)

With Romania expected to beat Turkey in Izmir, Northern Ireland needed a point to qualify for their second successive World Cup.

England were defending the only un-beaten record in the European qualifying groups, but as long as they avoided a 9-0 defeat they would win Group Three. If the Irish lost, a Romanian victory in Izmir would qualify them on goal difference. Northern Ireland had lost on each of their last two visits to Wembley but had recovered from their defeat the previous year to win the last British Championship.

Although a draw was quite acceptable to both teams England did their utmost to score. The reason they did not was because of a typically battling Irish side, with Pat Jennings performing heroics in goal even though he had not played a league game for a year.

Seven months later in the World Cup against Brazil, and on his 41st birthday, Jennings made his record 119th and last appearance for Northern Ireland. England and Northern Ireland were paired together again in the next European Championship and met the following year.

England: Shilton (Southampton), Stevens (Everton), Sansom (Arsenal), Wilkins (AC Milan) – capt, Wright (Southampton), Fenwick (QPR), Bracewell (Everton), Lineker (Everton), Dixon (Chelsea), Hoddle (Tottenham), Waddle (Tottenham). manager: Bobby Robson
Northern Ireland: Jennings (Tottenham), Nicholl (West Brom), Donaghy (Luton Town), O'Neill (Leicester), McDonald (QPR), McCreery (Newcastle), Penney (Brighton), McIlroy (Man City) – capt, Quinn (Blackburn), Whiteside (Man Utd), Stewart (Newcastle). subs: Armstrong (West Brom) for Penney 59, Worthington (Sheffield W.) for Stewart 72. manager: Billy Bingham

Final table	P	W	D	L	F	A	Pts
England	8	4	4	0	21	2	12
Northern Ireland	8	4	2	2	8	5	10
Romania	8	3	3	2	12	7	9
Finland	8	3	2	3	7	12	8
Turkey	8	0	1	7	2	24	1

Inter-Varsity Match

Wednesday 11th December 1985

Cambridge U 2
Evans, Earl

Oxford U 0
Referee: D Frampton (Dorset)

A comfortable second successive victory for Cambridge.

1986

Schoolboy International

Saturday 8th March 1986

England 1
Thomas 35

Netherlands 0
21,650

Sixth visit by the Dutch and this was their best result, so far. Rod Thomas' experience from the previous year came to fruition as he rounded the 'keeper to score the only goal of the game.

England: Marriott, Jenkins, Hall, Masters, Duffy, Donnelly, Thomas, Small, Blake, Murray – capt, Parrott. sub: Wratten for Small

Full Members Cup Final

Sunday 23rd March 1986

Chelsea 5
Speedie 23, 51, 58, Lee 36, 79

Manchester City 4
Kinsey 9, Lillis 85, (pen) 90, Rougvie og 88
68,000
Referee: A Saunders (Newcastle)

The Full Members Cup was a new competition for First and Second Division clubs, excluding those qualified for Europe. However, 17 clubs decided not to enter. The 21 remaining, with only five from the First Division, were split into northern and southern sections, with Chelsea beating the eventual Milk Cup Winners Oxford United in the southern final. Chelsea were appearing at Wembley for the first time since the 1972 Football League Cup final. They had not won at the stadium since lifting the Football League South Cup in 1945. City had last appeared in the FA Cup final replay in 1981. Their last victory had been in the Football League Cup final in 1976. Both sides had been forced to play league games away from home, the previous day, Chelsea winning 1-0 at Southampton, while City had held their great rivals Manchester United to a 2-2 draw.

City took the lead when Steve Kinsey turned McCarthy's cross past Francis. But David Speedie rose above McCarthy to head home a Nevin cross and equalise. Colin Lee gave Chelsea a half-time lead before the break, scoring from the rebound after Nixon saved from Bumstead. Chelsea then appeared to kill off City with three more goals. Speedie scored again just after half time before completing his hat-trick. With ten minutes left, City faced humiliation as Lee bagged his second.

But in the last five minutes, City launched an astonishing fightback which almost forced extra time. Substitute Simpson crossed and Mark Lillis sent a firm header past Francis. Three minutes later, another Simpson cross was headed into his own net by Doug Rougvie. In the last minute, May was upended by Spackman in the box and Lillis scored from the penalty.

Chelsea: Francis, Wood, Rougvie, Pates – capt, McLaughlin, Bumstead, Nevin, Spackman, Lee, Speedie, McAllister. subs: Hazard, Jones (not used). manager: John Hollins
Manchester C: Nixon, Reid, Power – capt, Redmond, McCarthy, Phillips, Lillis, May, Kinsey, McNab, Wilson. subs: Simpson for Reid 59, Baker for Phillips 59. manager: Billy McNeill

LEAGUE CUP FINAL

Sunday 20th April 1986

Oxford United 3-0 Queens Park Rangers
Hebberd 39, Houghton 52, Charles 86
90,396
Referee: K Hackett (Sheffield)

Oxford had been a Football League club only since 1962 and they had never previously progressed beyond the quarter-finals of the competition. Rangers had won the League Cup in 1967 as a Third Division club and in 1982, as a Second Division club, in their first FA Cup final, they had narrowly lost in a replay.

This was Oxford's first season in the First Division, after they had become the first club to win the Third and Second Division Championships in successive years. But they were fighting a battle against an immediate return to the Second Division, mindful of the fact that both the previous year's Milk Cup finalists had been relegated at the end of that season.

It was an emotional day for Rangers manager Jim Smith, who had taken Oxford from the Third to the First Division and then left to join Rangers at the beginning of the season.

After 39 minutes of the last final to be sponsored by the National Dairy Council, Aldridge's flick-on sent Trevor Hebberd away. McDonald chased, but missed his tackle as Hebberd checked. McDonald lunged again, but unsighted his 'keeper and Hebberd shot through McDonald's legs to beat Barron at the near post. Hebberd was also involved in the second goal, a few minutes after half-time.

Passing to Ray Houghton, he beat the offside trap to run on to the return ball, before a short pass gave Houghton the chance to sidefoot home past Barron. With four minutes left, Barron saved from Aldridge but Jeremy Charles scored from the rebound to complete the biggest ever winning margin in a League Cup final.

Oxford: Judge, Langan, Trewick, Phillips, Briggs, Shotton – capt, Houghton, Aldridge, Charles, Hebberd, Brock. sub: Thomas (not used). manager: Maurice Evans

Queens Park Rangers: Barron, McDonald, Dawes, Neill, Wicks, Fenwick – capt, Allen (M), James, Bannister, Byrne, Robinson. sub: Rosenior for Allen 61. manager: Jim Smith

ROUS CUP

Wednesday 23rd April 1986

England	**2-1**	**Scotland**
Butcher 27, Hoddle 39		Souness pen 57

68,357

Referee: M Vautrot (France)

Scotland were the Rous Cup holders after a single goal victory over England in the inaugural fixture at Hampden Park the previous year. They had lost on their last visit to Wembley in the 1983 British Championship. Both sides had qualified for the approaching World Cup. For Scotland, it would be their fourth successive appearance.

England scored their first Rous Cup goal following Hodge heading into the middle where Terry Butcher leapt above Gough to put the home side ahead. Six minutes before the break, a long shot from Sansom was palmed out by Rough, only for Glenn Hoddle to send a diving header past him from the rebound. Scotland came back in the second half and Graeme Souness reduced the arrears with a penalty after Butcher had brought down Nicholas but they could not score again.

England: Shilton (Southampton), Stevens (MG) (Everton), Sansom (Arsenal), Hoddle (Tottenham), Watson (Norwich), Butcher (Ipswich), Hodge (Aston Villa), Wilkins (AC Milan) – capt, Hateley (AC Milan), Francis (Sampdoria), Waddle (Tottenham). subs: Reid (Everton) for Wilkins 46, Stevens (G) (Tottenham) for Hodge 75. manager: Bobby Robson

Scotland: Rough (Hibernian), Gough (Dundee U), Malpas (Dundee U), Souness (Sampdoria) – capt, McLeish (Aberdeen), Miller (Aberdeen), Nicol (Liverpool), Speedie (Chelsea), Nicholas (Arsenal), Aitken (Celtic), Bannon (Dundee U). sub: Nevin (Chelsea) for Nicholas 58. caretaker-manager: Alex Ferguson

FA Vase Final

Saturday 26th April 1986

Halesowen Town 3
Moss 35, 76, L Joinson 74

Southall 0

18,340

Referee: D Scott (Burnley)

The same players notched the goals, as Halesowen retained the Vase in their third final in four years. Southall had previously appeared at Wembley in the Middlesex Charity Cup final, back in 1943.

Southall's Les Ferdinand went on to win 17 caps for England, 11 of them at Wembley, scoring three times beneath the twin towers. He was also in Tottenham Hotspur's 1999 Worthington Cup-winning side.

Halesowen: Pemberton, Moore, Sherwood, Lacey, Randle, Heath, Penn, Moss, Woodhouse – capt, Joinson (P), Joinson (L). sub: Rhodes for Randle 85

Southall: Mackenzie, James, Holland, McGovern, Croad, Powell, Rowe, Richardson, Sweales, Pierre, Ferdinand. sub: Richmond for Powell 70

FA CUP FINAL

Saturday 10th May 1986

Everton   **1-3**   **Liverpool**
Lineker 28   Rush 57, 84, Johnston 63
98,000
Referee: A Robinson (Waterlooville)

For the first time at Wembley, the FA Cup final was contested between the top two teams in the league. Everton were appearing in their third successive final and hoping to regain the Cup for the second time in three years. They had comfortably beaten Watford in 1984, but failed to win the 'double', being beaten by the ten men of Manchester United a year later. Liverpool had won the League Championship for the eighth time in 11 years by two points.

No player-manager had won a major honour, but Kenny Dalglish was now poised to lead his team to the first 'double' since Arsenal in 1971. Remarkably it was his first season in management after taking over following the trauma of the Heysel Stadium the previous year.

The Merseyside rivals had met two years earlier, in the Milk Cup final, with Liverpool winning the replay but Everton had beaten them in the first of their two successive FA Charity Shield wins five months later. Liverpool were appearing in their first final since 1977, despite winning many other trophies since. Their last FA Cup win had been in 1974.

Everton were determined to make up for losing the league title to Liverpool the previous week and took the lead when a superb long ball from Reid found Gary Lineker with only Grobbelaar to beat as Hansen gave chase.

The 'keeper saved Lineker's first effort but despite a brave dive could not stop the rebound. Everton tried to finish Liverpool off by pushing for a second, but a Molby pass transformed the game. It freed Ian Rush to beat the offside trap, take the ball round Mimms and equalise against the run of play.

Once Liverpool were back in the game there was no stopping them. Six minutes later, Stevens' tackle on Molby, as he was about to centre, forced the ball behind Dalglish where it found Craig Johnston. He fired Liverpool into the lead.

Everton pushed forward and Liverpool broke away to score a third with six minutes left. Yet another important pass from Molby sent Whelan away down the left. He checked and lobbed the ball across to the unmarked Rush who fired home his second.

Liverpool and Everton met in the Screen Sport Super Cup final which was held over until the following season.

One again Liverpool came out on top with a crushing 7-2 aggregate victory. With Liverpool also winning at Everton in the Littlewoods Cup quarter-finals the following year, they appeared to have the upper hand, but Everton would have their revenge in the league.

Everton: Mimms, Stevens, Van den Hauwe, Ratcliffe – capt, Mountfield, Reid, Steven, Lineker, Sharp, Bracewell, Sheedy. sub: Heath for Stevens 65. manager: Howard Kendall

Liverpool: Grobbelaar, Lawrenson, Beglin, Nicol, Whelan, Hansen – capt, Dalglish, Johnston, Rush, Molby, MacDonald. sub: McMahon (not used). player-manager: Kenny Dalglish

FA Trophy Final

Saturday 17th May 1986

Altrincham 1
Farrelly 43

Runcorn 0
15,700
Referee: A Ward (Southgate)

Altrincham, who had won an FA Cup tie away at First Division Birmingham City four months earlier, secured their second Trophy win thanks to defender Mike Farrelly's strike. After the game, Altrincham's manager, John King resigned and was replaced by Runcorn boss John Williams.

Altrincham: Wealands, Gardner, Densmore, Johnson, Farrelly, Conning, Cuddy, Davison – capt, Reid, Ellis, Anderson. sub: Newton (not used)

Runcorn: McBride, Lee, Roberts, Jones, Fraser, Smith, Crompton (S), Imrie, Carter, Mather, Carrodus. sub: Crompton (A) for Crompton (S) 64

Freight Rover Trophy Final

Saturday 24th May 1986

Bolton Wanderers 0
Bristol City 3
Riley 2, Pritchard
54,502
Referee: G Tyson (Sunderland)

In the semi-finals, Bolton beat the holders Wigan Athletic to reach Wembley for the first time since winning the FA Cup in 1958. Bristol City were two goals down to Hereford United after the first leg of their semi-final but went on to lift the trophy with a resounding victory.

Phil Neal had won a record eight League Championship medals with Liverpool and four European Cup winners medals, a British record. He also scored in two of the finals and won 50 England caps.

Asa Hartford won 50 caps for Scotland and produced the only goal of the previous year's Milk Cup final for Norwich City.

Bolton: Farnworth, Scott, Phillips, Sutton, Came, Thompson, Neal – capt, Oghani, Caldwell, Hartford, Gavin. sub: Bell for Thompson. player-manager: Phil Neal
Bristol C: Waugh, Newman, Williams, Curle, Moyes, Riley, Pritchard, Hutchinson – capt, Harle, Walsh, Neville. manager: Terry Cooper

Schoolboy International

Saturday 31st May 1986

England 2
Blake, Thomas
Italy 1
Capellini
Referee: H Taylor (Leicestershire)

The first meeting between these two countries at this level was memorable for a skilful England performance with Rod Thomas in particular, catching the eye.

England: Marriott, Didlick, Donnelly, Duffy, Hall, Masters, Small, Murray – capt, Cormack, Blake, Thomas. sub: Jenkins for Didlick 73

Under-16 International

Saturday 16th August 1986

England 0
France 1
Roche 3
Referee: M Bodenham (Sussex)

England were caught out by an early goal in the match played immediately before the FA Charity Shield. Graham Stuart was in the Everton side that beat Manchester United in the 1995 FA Cup final.

England: Marriott, Bond, Drysdale, Duffy, McKeown, Stuart, Parker, Cormack, Bullimore, Thomas, Morris. subs: Hall for Drysdale, Soloman for Duffy. Shepstone for Bullimore, Littlejohn for Morris, all a 41

FA Charity Shield

Saturday 16th August 1986

Everton   **1-1**   **Liverpool**
Heath 80   Rush 89
88,231
Referee: N Midgley (Manchester)

Everton were aiming to become the first club to complete a hat-trick of outright Charity Shield wins. In 1984, against Liverpool, they had won with a bizarre own goal and they had retained it a year later. They were competing by invitation only, however, after finishing runners-up in both league and FA Cup. This was their fourth meeting with Liverpool at Wembley in two years.

Liverpool had not won the Shield since 1982, but they had won it a record nine times. Their record 16th League Championship was their eighth in 11 years and was won by just two points from Everton as Kenny Dalglish became the first player-manager to win a major trophy. It was his goal at Chelsea in their last match which clinched the title. A week later they won the FA Cup for the third time to become only the third team of the 20th century to win the 'double'.

Liverpool changed goalkeepers after 55 minutes, when Grobbelaar went off with a stomach strain. His substitute Hooper was beaten with ten minutes left by Adrian

Heath after a pass from Sharp, but in the last minute, Ian Rush once again denied Everton, turning in his manager's cross. Dalglish had brought himself on as a substitute for the last half-hour.

Everton had their revenge by winning the League Championship for the second time in three years with Liverpool, inevitably, runners-up. Everton returned to win a record fourth successive Charity Shield, the following year. Liverpool were surprisingly to have another barren year, despite winning at Everton in the Littlewoods Cup quarter-finals and reaching the final.

Everton: Mimms, Harper, Power, Ratcliffe – capt, Marshall, Langley, Steven, Heath, Sharp, Richardson, Sheedy. subs: Adams for Sheedy 57, Wilkinson for Adams 82. manager: Howard Kendall
Liverpool: Grobbelaar, Venison, Beglin, Lawrenson, Whelan, Hansen – capt, McMahon, Johnston, Rush, Molby, MacDonald. subs: Hooper for Grobbelaar 56, Dalglish for MacDonald 60. player-manager: Kenny Dalglish

EUROPEAN CHAMPIONSHIP QUALIFYING

Wednesday 15th October 1986

England　　　　3-0　　　Northern Ireland
Lineker 33, 80 Waddle 78
35,300
Referee: A Constantin (Belgium)

Northern Ireland had twice lost European Championship matches at Wembley in 1967 and 1979, but had held England to a goalless draw the previous year to qualify for their second successive World Cup. They had not beaten England since 1972 and had not scored in their last five meetings. This was the opening match in Group Four. In the last European Championship, the Irish had been knocked out on goal difference by reigning champions West Germany despite beating them in both Belfast and Hamburg. England had also failed to qualify.

Ten minutes before half time Hoddle's corner found its way to Gary Lineker via Anderson and Butcher and the recent World Cup top scorer made no mistake from close range. Chris Waddle added a second from Beardsley's cross. Then, with ten minutes left, Lineker took a pass from Beardsley, held off McClelland and beat Hughes with a brilliant chip which went in off the near post.

Six months later, England beat Northern Ireland 2-0 at Windsor Park. The Irish then lost at home to Yugoslavia and were out. They did not appear again at the old Wembley.

England: Shilton (Southampton), Anderson (Arsenal), Sansom (Arsenal), Hoddle (Tottenham), Watson (Everton), Butcher (Rangers), Robson (Man Utd) – capt, Hodge (Aston Villa), Beardsley (Newcastle), Lineker (Barcelona), Waddle (Tottenham). sub: Cottee (West Ham) for Beardsley 84. manager: Bobby Robson
Northern Ireland: Hughes* (Bury), Fleming* (Nottingham F), McDonald (QPR), McClelland (Watford) – capt, Worthington (Sheffield W), Donaghy (Luton Town), Whiteside (Man Utd), Penney (Brighton), Clarke (Southampton), Campbell (Nottingham F), Stewart (Newcastle). subs: Quinn (Blackburn) for Penney 74, McIlroy (Man City) for Whiteside 84. manager: Billy Bingham
*first cap

Wednesday 12th November 1986

England　　　　2-0　　　Yugoslavia
Mabbutt 21, Anderson 57
60,000
Referee: F Woehrer (Austria)

Two weeks earlier, Yugoslavia had beaten Turkey 4-0 in Split in their opening match in Group Four. England had already beaten Northern Ireland, so these two had emerged as early favourites. Yugoslavia had not lost to England since 1966 at Wembley. Their last two meetings had been draws in the 1970's (1972 at Wembley). Yugoslavia had pipped Wales by a point to reach the 1984 European Championship but had failed to win a point in France. They then failed to make it to Mexico for the World Cup.

England took the lead through Gary Mabbutt who headed Hoddle's corner past Ravnic but Yugoslavia proved very dangerous opponents and England needed a second goal just after half time from Viv Anderson who connected with Waddle's low centre.

Almost a year later England won 4-1 in Belgrade to qualify for the European Championship. Yugoslavia finished group runners-up, three points behind. They lost again at Wembley in 1989.

England: Woods (Rangers), Anderson (Arsenal), Sansom (Arsenal), Hoddle (Tottenham), Wright (Southampton), Butcher (Rangers) – capt, Mabbutt (Tottenham), Hodge (Aston Villa), Beardsley (Newcastle), Lineker (Barcelona), Waddle (Tottenham). subs: Steven (Everton) for Waddle 79, Wilkins (AC Milan) for Hodge 82. manager: Bobby Robson
Yugoslavia: Ravnic (Rijeka), Vujovic (Zo) (Bordeaux), Baljic (Zeljeznicar), Sabanadzovic (Zeljeznicar), Elsner (Red Star Belgrade), Hadzibegic (Real Betis), Katanec (Partizan), Jankovic (Red Star), Skoro (Zeljeznicar), Sliskovic (Olympique Marseille), Vujovic (Zl) (Bordeaux) – capt. subs: Tuce (Velez Mostar) for Skoro 71, Juric (Velez Mostar) for Tuce 73. coach: Ivica Osim

Inter-Varsity Match

Wednesday 10th December 1986

Cambridge U 4
Bradley 2, Craggs, Palmer
Oxford U 3
Hunter, Burns 2
7,200

Oxford equalised twice, but Cambridge still notched their first hat-trick of wins since 1973.

Schoolboy International

Saturday 14th March 1987

England 2
Cole 44, 54
West Germany 0
25,000
Referee: E Hannah

Andrew Cole netted twice as England beat the Germans for the first time in four years. He was a member of Manchester United's 'treble' winning side in 1999 and scored the goal against Tottenham that settled the Premiership title. Alan Wright was in the Aston Villa side, which won the Coca-Cola Cup at Wembley in 1996.

England: Winters, Kavanagh, Wright, Phillips, Halstead, Cole, Murray, Turner – capt, Ross, Walters, Crosby. sub: Houghton for Murray

Full Members Cup Final

Sunday 29th March 1987

Blackburn Rovers 1
Hendry 85
Charlton Athletic 0

43,789
Referee: B Stevens (Stonehouse)

The Full Members Cup had survived for a second season. It was no longer regionalised, but eight clubs still decided not to enter. Blackburn had entered for the first time.

Blackburn had not appeared at the stadium since losing the 1960 FA Cup final, while Charlton's last visit had been in 1947 when they won the FA Cup for the first, and so far, only time.

Blackburn were the first Second Division club to reach the final and they had escaped relegation to the Third Division by just three points, the previous year. Charlton had finished Second Division runners-up to Norwich the previous year despite giving up their ground to share with Crystal Palace.

Colin Hendry, who had joined Blackburn from Dundee less than three weeks before, became an instant hero, scoring the only goal of an dull game with just five minutes left. Miller crossed, and with Bolder and Humphrey getting in a tangle, Colin Hendry drove home the winner. It was their first Wembley win for 59 years.

Blackburn were back at Wembley for the following year's Football League Centenary Tournament and appeared in the Second Division Promotion play-offs for three consecutive years without success. But in 1992 they finally won promotion at Wembley, and were back two years later for the FA Charity Shield as Premiership runners-up.

Blackburn: O'Keefe, Price, Sulley, Barker, Keeley – capt, Mail, Miller, Ainscow, Hendry, Garner, Sellars. subs: Patterson for Sellars, Branagan (not used). manager: Don Mackay
Charlton: Bolder, Humphrey, Reid, Peake, Thompson – capt, Miller, Milne, Lee, Melrose, Walsh, Shipley. subs: Gritt, Shirtliff (not used). manager: Lennie Lawrence

LEAGUE CUP FINAL

Sunday 5th April 1987

Arsenal   **2-1**   **Liverpool**
Nicholas 28, 83   Rush 22
96,000
Referee: L Shapter (Torquay)

This was the fourth Wembley meeting between these two. Arsenal had won FA Cup finals (in 1950 and 1971) while Liverpool had won the 1979 FA Charity Shield. The Milk Cup had been replaced by the Littlewoods Cup, but Arsenal were aiming to win the competition for the first time after losing two successive League Cup finals at the end of the 1960s. It was remarkable that they reached the final for they had lost the home leg of their semi-final to Tottenham Hotspur and had gone two down on aggregate in the away leg. Then in the replay, also away from home, they had been behind with eight minutes left. Their last visit to Wembley had been their third successive FA Cup final in 1980. Liverpool were appearing in their fifth final in seven years, having won it a record four years in succession in the early 1980s, although only two had been won at Wembley.

Arsenal had a good young side which had made an impression in the League Championship race. Liverpool had gained a share of the Charity Shield and had won the Screen Sport Super Cup. They were once again contesting the League Championship with great rivals Everton whom they had beaten into second place to win the 'double' the previous year.

They scored first when Molby sent McMahon through. As O'Leary came to challenge, McMahon released Ian Rush who nonchalantly sidefooted past Lukic.

Arsenal were behind for just six minutes, equalising after a goalmouth scramble. Sansom found full-back partner Anderson in the area. A short pass followed to Adams, whose shot hit Gillespie's hand. Charlie Nicholas drove the rebound against the post but Anderson crossed it again and Nicholas netted. Arsenal went on to settle it with seven minutes left. Substitute Groves cut in from the wing and passed to Nicholas whose shot took a wicked double deflection off Whelan's legs and crept inside the near post as Grobbelaar dived in vain.

Arsenal were back at Wembley the following year, to defend the trophy. Liverpool lost the League Championship to Everton, finishing without a trophy for the second time in three years. But they were not finished. The following season they dominated the League Championship, returned to Wembley for the Football League Centenary Tournament and reached the FA Cup final in an attempt to take the 'double' for the second time in three years.

Arsenal: Lukic, Anderson, Sansom – capt, Williams, O'Leary, Adams, Rocastle, Davis, Quinn, Nicholas, Hayes. subs: Groves for Quinn 73, Thomas for Hayes 83. manager: George Graham
Liverpool: Grobbelaar, Gillespie, Venison, Spackman, Whelan, Hansen – capt, Walsh, Johnston, Rush, Molby, McMahon. subs: Dalglish for Walsh 73, Wark for McMahon 83. player-manager: Kenny Dalglish

FA Vase Final

Saturday 25th April 1987

St Helens Town 3
Layhe 4, 67, Rigby 8
Warrington Town 2
Reid 54, Cook 89
4,254
Referee: T Mills (Barnsley)

St Helens won their first FA Vase, against a club from six miles away.

St Helens: Johnston, Benson, Wilson, Lowe, Brendon, Cummins, O'Neil – capt, Collins, Rigby, McComb, Layhe.

sub: Gledhill for Collins 88, Deakin (not used)
Warrington: O'Brien, Gratton, Reid, Hunter, Copeland, Cook, Hughes, Kinsey, Brownbill, Looker, Whalley. subs: Hill for Brownbill 68, Woodyer for Looker 73

FA Trophy Final

Saturday 9th May 1987

Burton Albion 0
Kidderminster Harriers 0
After extra time
23,617
Referee: D Shaw (Sandbach)

The first goalless FA Trophy final. Kidderminster survived when Jim Arnold saved Bancroft's 87th minute penalty.

Burton: New, Kamara, Simms, Vaughan, Essex, Land, Groves, Bancroft, Gauden, Redfern, Dorsett. subs: Patterson, Wood (not used)
Kidderminster: Arnold, Barton, Collins, Boxall, Brazier, Woodall, Mackenzie – capt, Casey, Davies, Tuohy, O'Dowd. subs: Pearson for Collins 90, Hazlewood (not used)

Replay: Tuesday 12th May 1987
Burton Albion 1
Groves
Kidderminster Harriers 2
Davies 2
(The Hawthorns, West Bromwich)

FA CUP FINAL

Saturday 16th May 1987

Coventry City   **3-2**   **Tottenham Hotspur**
Bennett 9, Houchen 63, Mabbutt og 96   Allen (C) 2, Kilcline og 40
After extra time
98,000
Referee: N Midgley (Salford)

Coventry had never previously progressed beyond the quarter-finals; they had never appeared at Wembley nor won a major trophy. By contrast Tottenham were aiming to become the first club to win the FA Cup eight times. They had never lost a final and were chasing their third Cup win of the decade after replay wins in 1981 and 1982. Their last appearance had been in losing the 1982 FA Charity Shield.

Tottenham struck first when Waddle crossed and Clive Allen outjumped Peake to head the opener. But within seven minutes, Coventry had struck back. Downs' cross was flicked on by Houchen and seemed to be falling harmlessly for Clemence to collect, but Dave Bennett nipped in to take the ball round him and fire past the covering Hodge. Just before the interval, Tottenham, rather fortunately regained the

lead. Ogrizovic came for Hoddle's floated free kick, but checked and left himself in 'no man's land'. Mabbutt attempted to shoot but connected instead with the back of Brian Kilcline's foot which forced the ball over the line. Tottenham kept threatening, but the next goal was a Coventry equaliser. Keith Houchen played the ball wide to Bennett and then dived to meet the cross and send a powerful header past Clemence. Coventry secured a popular victory in extra time. Gary Mabbutt did well to cut out McGrath's cross but the ball flew up off his knee and looped over Clemence for the winning goal.

Tottenham returned the following year, for the Wembley International Tournament where they met great rivals Arsenal, and in 1991, they faced Arsenal again in Wembley's first FA Cup semi-final.

Coventry: Ogrizovic, Phillips, Downs, McGrath, Kilcline – capt, Peake, Bennett, Gynn, Regis, Houchen, Pickering. subs: Rodger for Kilcline 88, Sedgley (not used). chief coach: John Sillett
Tottenham: Clemence, Hughton, Thomas, Hodge, Gough – capt, Mabbutt, Allen (C), Allen (P), Waddle, Hoddle, Ardiles. subs: Stevens for Ardiles 91, Claesen for Hughton 97. manager: David Pleat

ROUS CUP

Tuesday 19th May 1987

England   **1-1**   **Brazil**
Lineker 35   Mirandinha 36
92,000
Referee: M Vautrot (France)

Brazil were invited to compete in the Rous Cup, now a triangular tournament. On their last visit in 1981 they had beaten England but England had won 2-0 in Rio de Janeiro in 1984, their first victory in Brazil. Both teams had been quarter-finalists

in the previous year's World Cup. England were the Rous Cup holders after beating Scotland the previous year.

An impressive England took the lead when from Beardsley's cross, with Carlos at the near post, Gary Lineker found space to send a diving header into the empty net. But within a minute, Brazil were level. Shilton could not hold Muller's low centre and Mirandinha fired home the equaliser. He was to return to England three months later to join Newcastle United.

Four days later, England were involved in a goalless draw with Scotland at Hampden Park. Brazil then beat the Scots 2-0 at Hampden Park to take the Rous Cup to South America. Two years later Brazil won the South American Championship for the first time in 40 years. They were back at Wembley in 1990.

England: Shilton (Southampton), Stevens (Everton), Pearce* (Nottingham F), Reid (Everton), Adams (Arsenal), Butcher (Rangers), Robson (Man Utd) – capt, Barnes (Watford), Beardsley (Newcastle), Lineker (Barcelona), Waddle (Tottenham). sub: Hateley (AC Milan) for Lineker 76, manager: Bobby Robson
*first cap

Brazil: Carlos (Corinthians), Josimar (Botafogo), Geraldao (Cruzeiro) – capt, Rocha (Guarani), Douglas (Cruzeiro), Nelsinho (Sao Paulo), Muller (Sao Paulo), Silas (Sao Paulo), Mirandinha (Palmeiras), Edu (Portuguesa), Valdo (Gremio). subs: Dunga (Vasco da Gama) for Silas 82, Rai (Botafogo) for Edu 83. coach: Carlos Alberto Silva

Freight Rover Trophy Final

Sunday 24th May 1987

Bristol City 1
Riley 87

Mansfield Town 1
Kent 58
After extra time
Mansfield Town won 5-4 on penalties.
(Williams 1-0, Kearney 1-1, Newman 2-1, Cassells missed, MacPhail 3-1, Stringfellow 3-2, Curle 4-2, Pollard 4-3, Owen saved, Kent 4-4, Moyes saved, Kenworthy 4-5)
58,586
Referee: A Gunn (Burgess Hill)

Holders Bristol City forced the game into extra time by equalising with three minutes left. Glyn Riley, the previous year's two-goal hero, rescued them, but it was Mansfield who triumphed in Wembley's first penalty competition for 13 years.

Gordon Owen was in a great position to retain the trophy for City, but the winger saw his kick saved by Kevin Hitchcock's legs. Hitchcock saved with his legs again from David Moyes, and Tony Kenworthy made sure Mansfield won the trophy for the first time.

Joe Jordan had won 52 caps for Scotland and had scored in three consecutive World Cups.

Bristol C: Waugh, Newman, Williams, Moyes, MacPhail, Llewellyn, Owen, Marshall, Riley, Walsh, Jordan – capt. subs: Curle for Walsh 70, Fitzpatrick for Marshall 116. manager: Terry Cooper
Mansfield: Hitchcock, Graham, Garner, Lowery, Foster – capt, Kenworthy, Kent, Danskin, Whatmore, Cassells, Kearney. subs: Stringfellow for Whatmore 65, Pollard for Danskin 91. manager: Ian Greaves

Victory Shield

Saturday 30th May 1987

England 1
Murray

Scotland 1
McGreish
Referee: K Dunn (Birmingham)

The point was enough to give England the Victory Shield with Scotland runners-up.

Craig Burley went on to win 46 full international caps for Scotland. His last appearance at Wembley was when Scotland beat England in the European Championship in 1999.

England: Winters, Kavanagh, Wright – capt, Seymour, Phillips, Halstead, Houghton, Walters, Murray, Awford, McVey. sub: Cole for McVey
Scotland: Reid, Dunn, Bollan, Siegel – capt, Salton, McGreish, McBride, Burley, Gallacher, Christie, Sermanni. subs: Buchanan for Gallacher, Roddie for Christie

Sunday 31st May 1987

Brent Council held their own football festival at the stadium. Junior and women's teams competed in local cup finals, with the highlight being Brent Leisure's Action Sport Cup final. The day became an annual event.

Thursday 16th July 1987

The London International Youth Festival held the opening ceremony at Wembley, the highlight being a girls' under-14 match between Cincinatti Cardinals and Millwall Lionesses. Although the game lasted for only half an hour, the players became the first female footballers to play at the stadium. The team from Ohio were the winners.

U-17 International

Saturday 1st August 1987

England 3
Murray, Cormack, Thomas

Netherlands 1
Sas
Referee: R Milford (Bristol)

Wembley's first Under-17 International (the AC Delco Challenge) preceded the FA Charity Shield and saw a convincing home win. Shaun Murray and Rod Thomas followed up their Schoolboy International goals at the stadium as England were three goals up at the interval.

England: Marriott (Arsenal), Garland (Tottenham), Hall (Tottenham), Wratten (Man Utd), Soloman (Watford), Blake (Aston Villa), Cormack (Southampton), Thomas (Watford), Stuart (Chelsea), Murray (Tottenham) – capt, Parrott (Aston Villa). subs: Bond (Coventry) for Garland 41, McKeown (Arsenal) for Parrott 65, Duffy (Aston Villa) for Soloman 75, Masters (Southampton) for Cormack 78

FA CHARITY SHIELD

Saturday 1st August 1987

Coventry City	0-1	Everton
		Clarke 44

88,000
Referee: R Lewis (Great Bookham)

Everton were attempting to become the first club to win four successive Charity Shields, after sharing the trophy with Liverpool the previous year. They had regained the League Championship, their second in three years, by nine points from Liverpool, but their manager, Howard Kendall had now departed to join Athletic Bilbao, leaving his assistant Colin Harvey to take the reins.

An unusually early start to the season meant neither side was at its best, but Everton retained the Shield when Wayne Clarke was left unmarked to run on to Steven's pass and fire past Ogrizovic.

Coventry never appeared at the old stadium again. Everton appeared at the Football League Centenary Tournament at Wembley and, in 1989, they reached both the Simod and FA Cup finals.

Coventry: Ogrizovic, Phillips, Downs, McGrath, Kilcline – capt, Peake, Bennett, Gynn, Speedie, Houchen, Pickering. subs: Sedgley for McGrath, Borrows for Gynn. manager: John Sillett
Everton: Mimms, Harper, Power, Ratcliffe – capt, Watson, Reid, Steven, Clarke, Sharp, Heath, Sheedy. sub: Pointon for Sheedy 46. manager: Colin Harvey

U-16 International

Saturday 8th August 1987

England 2
Hung Dang 2,1 pen

Denmark 1
Bronsted
Referee: D Hedges (Oxford)

Vietnamese refugee Hung Dang secured victory for the youngsters in the curtain-raiser to the Football League's Centenary Match.

Ian Walker went on to win four full international caps for England and kept goal in a World Cup Qualifying Match against Italy at Wembley in 1997.

England: Walker, Charlton, Alexander, Towler, Kavanagh, Walters, Houghton, Hung Dang, Morah, Turner, Small. subs: Seymour for Morah 41, Williams for Houghton 65, Hancock for Small 70, Stanger for Walker 75, Sinclair for Charlton 75

230

FOOTBALL LEAGUE CENTENARY MATCH

Saturday 8th August 1987

Football League   **3-0**   **Rest of the World**
Robson 24, 89, Whiteside 58
61,000
Referee: K Hackett (Sheffield)

With 13 substitutions taking place this could not be seen as a serious contest but there was a host of big names on view, including Diego Maradona, who, almost single-handedly, had eliminated England from the previous year's World Cup! The Rest of the World side contained two European Footballers of the Year making their first appearances at Wembley. Igor Belanov was the current holder of the award, while Michel Platini was the only man to win the award three years in succession and came out of retirement to make his only Wembley visit. Also in the visitors line-up was England's Gary Lineker, the 1986 World Cup's top scorer now playing for Barcelona.

Football League: Shilton (Derby & England), Gough (Tottenham & Scotland), McClelland (Watford & N Ireland), Sansom (Arsenal & England), McGrath (Man Utd & Republic of Ireland), Brady (West Ham & Republic of Ireland), Robson (Man Utd & England) – capt, Webb (Nottingham F), Allen (Tottenham & England), Beardsley (Liverpool & England), Waddle (Tottenham & England). subs: Whiteside (Man Utd & N Ireland) for Allen 46, Ogrizovic (Coventry) for Shilton 60, Nevin (Chelsea & Scotland) for Brady 67, Ardiles (Tottenham & Argentina) for Webb 76, Smith (Arsenal) for Beardsley 83, Clarke (Chelsea) for Gough. coach: Bobby Robson

Rest of the World: Dasaev (Spartak Moscow & USSR), Josimar (Botafogo & Brazil), Celso (Porto & Brazil), Alberto (Barcelona & Spain), Hysen (Fiorentina & Sweden), Bagni (Napoli & Italy), Berthold (Verona & W. Germany), Lineker (Barcelona & England), Platini (France). Maradona (Napoli & Argentina) – capt, Futre (Atletico Madrid & Portugal). subs: Zubizarreta (Barcelona & Spain) for Dasaev 46, Elkjaer (Verona & Denmark) for Lineker 46, Detari (Eintracht Frankfurt & Hungary) for Josimar 61, Stojkovic (Red Star Belgrade & Yugoslavia) for Celso 70, Belanov (Dynamo Kiev & USSR) for Bagni 70, Larsson (Gothenburg & Sweden) for Platini 70, Zavarov (Dynamo Kiev & USSR) for Futre 83. coach: Terry Venables

EUROPEAN CHAMPIONSHIP QUALIFYING

Wednesday 14th October 1987

England   **8-0**   **Turkey**
Barnes 2, 28, Lineker 8, 42, 71,
Robson 59, Beardsley 62, Webb 88
42,528
Referee: A Thomas (Netherlands)

After two heavy World Cup qualifying defeats in Istanbul and at Wembley, Turkey had held England to a draw for the first time, a goalless encounter in Izmir, six months earlier. They now needed to beat them for the first time to stay in contention in Group Four which England led by a point from Yugoslavia, who had beaten Northern Ireland 3-0 in Sarajevo, earlier in the day.

With barely a minute gone, a superb curling cross from Webb was sidefooted home by John Barnes. Three more goals followed before half time.

A sloppy clearance by Semih was picked up by Sansom who crossed for Gary Lineker to slot the second past Fatih. Barnes got the third after good work by Beardsley, while Lineker got number four.

England did not add a fifth until almost an hour had passed. Barnes' corner was headed out by substitute, Savas, but the goalkeeper had also gone for it and was left way out of position as Webb drove it through Butcher's legs and Bryan Robson casually back-heeled it into the net.

The sixth, three minutes later, came about when Lineker ran on to Robson's pass and stopped the ball dead, allowing Hoddle, behind him, to chip the ball into the middle where Peter Beardsley headed past Fatih. Lineker ran on to another Robson pass in the 72nd minute and lobbed the 'keeper, to complete his second Wembley hat-trick against Turkey.

Two minutes from time, Hoddle's cross from the byeline was volleyed in by Neil Webb for a deserved goal.

So, in driving rain throughout, England had repeated their 8-0 victory in Istanbul of three years earlier.

Turkey finished bottom again, after losing their last two games, to Northern Ireland in Belfast and Yugoslavia in Izmir. They returned to Wembley in 1991, again in the European Championship.

England needed only a point from their last game, against Yugoslavia in Belgrade the following month. They scored four goals in the first 25 minutes and won 4-1 to qualify for Germany with ease.

England: Shilton (Derby County), Stevens (Everton), Sansom (Arsenal), Steven (Everton), Adams (Arsenal), Butcher (Rangers), Robson (Man Utd) – capt, Webb (Nottingham F), Beardsley (Liverpool), Lineker (Barcelona), Barnes (Liverpool). subs: Hoddle (Monaco) for Steven 46, Regis (Coventry) for Beardsley 73. manager: Bobby Robson
Turkey: Fatih (Samsunspor), Riza (Besiktas), Semih (Galatasaray), Ali Coban (Karsiyaka), Erhan (Galatasaray) – capt, Gultiken (Besiktas), Ugur (Galatasaray), Muhammed (Galatasaray), Kayhan (Fenerbahce), Erdal (Sariyer), Iskender (Trabzonspor). sub: Savas (Galatasaray) for Gultiken 34, Tanju (Galatasaray) for Kayhan 46. coach: Denizli Mustafa

Final table	P	W	D	L	F	A	pts
England	6	5	1	0	19	1	11
Yugoslavia	6	4	0	2	13	9	8
Northern Ireland	6	1	1	4	2	10	3
Turkey	6	0	2	4	2	16	2

Inter-Varsity Match

Wednesday 9th December 1987

Cambridge U 2
Craggs, Palmer pen
Oxford U 1
Zis
Referee: P Helsby

After 36 games at Wembley this poorly attended fixture finally proved too expensive to stage. Cambridge came from behind to win their fourth successive Varsity match with an injury-time penalty by Steve Palmer, who joined Ipswich Town, two years later. It equalled their best run at Wembley.

Schoolboy International

Saturday 12th March 1988

England 2
Mulrain 14, Clark pen 46
Brazil 0
54,900
Referee: M Thompson (Kent)

England's first meeting with South American opposition at this level, but it was the home team under new manager Dave Bushell that demonstrated the better skills.

England: Sheppard, Hancock, Price, Reed, Burton, Clark – capt, Christian, Flitcroft, Mulrain, McDonough, Stewart. subs: Davies for Christian 46, Morah for Mulrain 79

INTERNATIONAL

Wednesday 23rd March 1988

England   2-2   Netherlands
Lineker 13, Adams 61   Adams og 20, Bosman 25
74,590
Referee: A Prokop (East Germany)

The Netherlands' last two visits had produced a 2-0 win in 1977 and a defeat by the same scoreline five years later. After failing to qualify for the 1984 European Championship on goal difference and the 1986 World Cup on away goals, the Dutch, like England, had qualified for the forthcoming European Championship unbeaten.

England began positively and were rewarded in the 14th minute. A typically alert Gary Lineker ran on to Stevens' pass, held off Silooy's desperate challenge to beat Van Breukelen as the 'keeper advanced. The Dutch came roaring back; Gullit was about to knock in Wouters' low cross when Tony Adams unwittingly beat him to it.

The Netherlands then took control. An array of passing moves left England chasing shadows. The Dutch waited for an opening and then struck with deadly accuracy. Gullit outjumped Sansom to head out to Van Aerle who crossed. John Bosman held off Watson to send a diving header past Shilton from close range.

For all their superiority, the Dutch could not add a third and England equalised after an hour. Adams met Stevens' free kick with a glancing header to score at the right end. A highly entertaining game which whetted the appetite for their European Champion-

ship clash three months later.

The Netherlands went on to win the European Championship, beating the USSR, who had beaten them in the opening match, in the final in Munich. They were back at Wembley for a World Cup qualifying match in 1993.

Ruud Gullit, the 1987 European Footballer of the Year, made his Wembley debut. But in 1997 he became the first foreign coach to win the FA Cup when Chelsea lifted the trophy at Wembley.

England: Shilton (Derby County), Stevens (Everton), Sansom (Arsenal), Steven (Everton), Adams (Arsenal), Watson (Everton), Robson (Man Utd) – capt, Webb (Nottingham F), Beardsley (Liverpool), Lineker (Barcelona), Barnes (Liverpool). subs: Hoddle (Monaco) for Webb 69, Hateley (Monaco) for Beardsley 70, Wright (Derby County) for Watson 72, manager: Bobby Robson

Netherlands: Van Breukelen (PSV Eindhoven), Troost (Feyenoord), Silooy (RC Paris), Koeman (PSV), Van Aerle (PSV), Wouters (Ajax Amsterdam), Vanenburg (PSV), Muhren (Ajax), Bosman (Ajax), Gullit (AC Milan) – capt, Van't Schip (PSV). subs: Kruzen (Den Bosch) for Gullit 60, Koot (Feyenoord) for Van't Schip 83. coach: Rinus Michels

Simod Cup Final

Sunday 27th March 1988

Luton Town 1
Harford 13

Reading 4
Gilkes 20, Beavon pen 26, Tait 57, Smillie 66
61,740
Referee: J Martin (Alton)

The Full Members Cup received its first sponsor, but there were still four exemptions from the competition. Luton had decided to enter and had reached Wembley for the first time since the 1959 FA Cup final. This was only the second time Reading had been eligible for the competition and in the previous season they had failed to reach the last 16. They were hoping to emulate Blackburn Rovers' 1987 win from the Second Division.

Luton were due back at Wembley twice in the following month. They had qualified for the Football League Centenary Tournament and also reached the Littlewoods Cup final for the first time. They had also reached the FA Cup semi-finals and were hoping to make an unprecedented fourth appearance, as well.

Reading had not beaten Luton for over half a century so Luton were odds-on favourites. And when Mick Harford opened the scoring with a headed goal from a full-length dive they must have thought they were on easy street. Not so. Seven minutes later, from Beavon's pass, Michael Gilkes tried to lob Sealey. The 'keeper got his

hands to it but it dropped into the back of the net for the equaliser. Reading were fortunate to take the lead when Gilkes was brought down by Breacker outside the area only for the referee to give the penalty. Stuart Beavon made no mistake. Reading added a third after 57 minutes when a brilliant run from Smillie took him into the middle where he set up Mick Tait to fire past Sealey. Luton gave a dreadful defensive display which was summed up by Reading's fourth goal. Jones ran at the defence and Luton just stood off. Eventually Grimes attempted a tackle but the ball fell to the unmarked Neil Smillie who completed Luton's humiliation.

Luton lost in the FA Cup semi-finals to eventual winners Wimbledon but a week after the Football League Centenary Tournament they won the Littlewoods Cup for the first time. Reading were unable to defend the Simod Cup as they finished 21st and were relegated back to the Third Division. It took them six years to win promotion and they almost made it to the Premiership before losing a classic play-off final in 1995 at Wembley.

Luton: Sealey, Breacker, Grimes, McDonough, Foster – capt, Donaghy, Wilson, Stein (B), Harford, Stein (M), Allinson. subs: Johnson for Stein (B), Black for Stein (M). manager: Ray Harford

Reading: Francis, Bailie, Richardson, Beavon, Hicks – capt, Curle, Jones, Taylor, Tait, Gilkes, Smillie. subs: Williams for Jones, Peters for Tait. manager: Ian Branfoot

FOOTBALL LEAGUE CENTENARY TOURNAMENT

To celebrate 100 years of the Football League a knockout competition, sponsored by Mercantile Credit, was organised for 16 clubs from all four divisions. Qualification was based on results from 15 league games played between November 1987 and February 1988.

The tournament was completed over two days with 40-minute matches in the first two rounds and 60-minute matches for the semi-finals and final. Unfortunately it was poorly attended. There were 41,500 on the first day and only 17,000 for the semi-finals and final on the Sunday.

Details for this tournament are surprisingly difficult to find. Consequently the line-ups for Crystal Palace and Wimbledon are educated guesses.

Saturday 16th April 1988

Top Half
First Round

Tranmere Rovers 1
Martindale 27
Wimbledon 0

Kicking off at 10am, with only about 7,000 in the stadium, Fourth Division Tranmere provided the first shock on their first appearance at Wembley. Wimbledon were appearing for the first time since winning the FA Amateur Cup 25 years earlier and had reached their first FA Cup final the previous week.

Tranmere: Nixon, Higgins, McCarrick, Martindale, Moore, Vickers, Morrissey, Harvey – capt, Steel, Muir, Mungall. manager: John King
Wimbledon: Beasant – capt, Scales, Phelan, Ryan, Young, Cawley, Gibson, Cork, Fashanu, Hazel, Wise. manager: Bobby Gould

Liverpool 0
Newcastle United 0
Newcastle United won 1-0 on penalties.
(McMahon saved, McDonald 0-1)

This was the first of six goalless draws over the weekend due to such short games. Liverpool had reached their second FA Cup final in three years the previous week and were to win their seventh League Championship in ten years the following week, but Gary Kelly saved Steve McMahon's penalty and Neil McDonald scored to knock them out.

Newcastle thus gained some minor revenge for their humiliating 3-0 defeat in the 1974 FA Cup final at Wembley.

A very small crowd witnessed the Wembley debut of Paul Gascoigne who was later to score two of the greatest goals ever seen at the stadium.

Three years later he struck a bullet free-kick for Tottenham Hotspur in Wembley's first FA Cup semi-final and then in 1996 he settled England's victory against Scotland in the European Championship with a sublime chip and volley.

Liverpool: Hooper, Nicol – capt, Ablett, Johnston, Gillespie, Watson, McMahon, MacDonald, Aldridge, Barnes, Staunton. subs: Durnin for Aldridge 23, Beardsley for Barnes 38. manager: Kenny Dalglish
Newcastle: Kelly, McDonald, Tinnion, McCreery, Anderson, Roeder – capt, Mirandinha, Gascoigne, Goddard, O'Neill, Wharton. sub: Stephenson for McCreery 26. manager: Willie McFaul

Leeds United 0
Nottingham Forest 3
Carr 8, Pearce pen 15, Parker 37

Forest had lost their FA Cup semi-final to Liverpool the previous week but recovered to win the most one-sided match of the weekend. Their manager Brian Clough decided to stay away much to the disappointment of the organisers.

Leeds: Day, Williams, Aizlewood – capt, Ashurst, Batty, Sheridan, Baird, Adams, Taylor, Grayson, Rennie. subs: Snodin for Adams 10, Pearson for Taylor 30. manager: Billy Bremner
Nottingham F: Sutton, Fleming, Pearce – capt, Chettle, Foster, Wilson, Crosby, Webb, Clough, Carr, Rice. sub: Glover for Crosby 34, Parker for Webb 36. assistant manager: Ronnie Fenton

Aston Villa 0
Blackburn Rovers 0
Aston Villa won 2-1 on penalties.
(Evans 1-0, Archibald 1-1, Gray saved, Sellars saved, Platt 2-1, Hendry missed)

Nothing to choose between the two Second Division promotion chasers. When Terry Gennoe saved from Villa substitute Stuart Gray in the penalty shoot-out, Scott Sellars had only to score to put Blackburn in the quarter-finals; but Nigel Spink saved his kick.

David Platt then put Villa back in front and Colin Hendry, who had scored Blackburn's winner in the previous year's Full Members Cup final at Wembley, fired over the bar to put his team out. Blackburn missed promotion by a point behind Villa and lost in the play-offs to Chelsea, the first of three successive play-off defeats.

Aston Villa: Spink, Gage, Norton, Gray (A), Evans – capt, Keown, Williams, Platt, Thompson, Daley, Aspinall. sub: Gray (S) for Gray (A) 21. manager: Graham Taylor
Blackburn: Gennoe, Price, Millar, Reid – capt, Hendry, Mail, Miller, Archibald, Ardiles, Garner, Sellars. manager: Don Mackay

Quarter-finals

Newcastle United 0
Tranmere Rovers 2
Morrissey 7, Muir pen 17

Tranmere's incredible success story continued as the top half entered the quarter-final stage. Newcastle were destroyed by a team from three divisions below them and even missed a late penalty when Eric Nixon brilliantly saved from Neil McDonald, Newcastle's first round penalty hero. Tranmere deservedly earned an unexpected, but very popular passage, into the following day's semi-finals.

Newcastle: Kelly, McDonald, Tinnion, Stephenson, Anderson, Roeder – capt, Mirandinha, Gascoigne, Goddard, O'Neill, Wharton. sub: Cornwell for Stephenson. manager: Willie McFaul
Tranmere: Nixon, Higgins, McCarrick, Martindale, Moore, Vickers, Morrissey, Harvey – capt, Steel, Muir, Mungall. sub: McKenna for Muir. manager: John King

Aston Villa 0
Nottingham Forest 0
Nottingham Forest won 1-0 on penalties.
(Pearce 0-1, Evans missed)

Villa went out of the tournament without conceding a goal in their two matches. Stuart Pearce converted his second penalty of the day and Forest were through to the semi-finals.

Aston Villa: Spink, Gage, Gallacher, Gray (A), Evans – capt, Keown, Birch, Platt, Thompson, Gray (S), Aspinall. manager: Graham Taylor
Nottingham F: Sutton, Fleming, Pearce – capt, Chettle, Foster, Wilson, Crosby, Webb, Clough, Carr, Rice. subs: Glover for Crosby, Gaynor for Rice. assistant manager: Ronnie Fenton

Bottom Half
First Round

Everton 1
Clarke 3
Wolverhampton Wanderers 1
Dennison 27
Everton won 3-2 on penalties.
(Clarke 1-0, Chard 1-1, Reid 2-1, Thompson 2-2, Heath saved, Bellamy saved, Harper 3-2, Mutch saved)

The longest penalty shoot-out of the weekend, as the clubs in the bottom half began their matches. Wayne Clarke added to his FA Charity Shield goal at Wembley the previous year but Robbie Dennison's stunning 35-yard screamer brought the eventual Fourth Division Champions level. When Mark Kendall saved from Adrian Heath, Gary Bellamy had an opportunity to send a second Fourth Division team into the quarter-finals but Neville Southall saved and after Alan Harper had netted for Everton, Southall also stopped Andy Mutch's kick to send Everton through. Wolves returned the following month to win the Sherpa Van Trophy.

Everton: Southall, Stevens, Pointon, Van den Hauwe, Watson – capt, Reid, Harper, Heath, Clarke, Snodin, Wilson. sub: Power for Wilson. manager: Colin Harvey
Wolves: Kendall, Thompson, Streete, Robertson – capt, Robinson, Chard, Bull, Mutch, Dennison, Bellamy, Holmes. manager: Graham Turner

Luton Town 0
Manchester United 2
McClair 21, Davenport 30

A comfortable win as Luton's season continued to fall apart. They had lost their FA Cup semi-final the previous week and had been humiliated in the previous month's Simod Cup final. But just a week later they won a remarkable Littlewoods Cup final at Wembley to win their first major trophy.

Luton: Dibble, Breacker, Foster – capt, Donaghy, Harvey, Hill, Johnson (R), Wilson, Black, Stein (B), Harford. subs: Johnson (M) for Donaghy 23, Stein (M) for Harford 35. manager: Ray Harford
Manchester U: Turner, Duxbury, Gibson, Bruce, McGrath, Whiteside, Robson – capt, Strachan, McClair, Davenport, Olsen. manager: Alex Ferguson

Sunderland 0
Wigan Athletic 0
Wigan Athletic won 2-1 on penalties.
(MacPhail 1-0, McEwan 1-1, Pascoe saved, Cook 1-2)

The two Third Division sides were drawn together but failed to produce a goal between them. Paul Cook put Wigan in the quarter-finals after Phil Hughes had saved from Colin Pascoe. Sunderland went on to win the Third Division Championship however, at the first attempt after relegation.

Sunderland: Carter, Kay, Gray, Ord, MacPhail, Owers, Lemon, Pascoe, Gates, Gabbiadini, Armstrong. manager: Denis Smith
Wigan: Hughes, Senior, Kennedy, Hamilton, McEwan, Beesley, Thompson (D), Thompson (C), Campbell, Jewell, Cook. manager: Ray Mathias

Crystal Palace 0
Sheffield Wednesday 0
Sheffield Wednesday won 2-1 on penalties.
(Redfearn 1-0, Sterland 1-1, Barber saved, Megson 1-2)

Yet another stalemate settled by penalties as Kevin Pressman stopped Phil Barber's kick with his leg and Gary Megson converted the last kick of the first round. Palace won the Second Division Promotion play-offs the following year and joined Wednesday in the top flight.

Crystal Palace: Suckling, Finnigan, Burke, Pennyfather, Nebbeling, Cannon – capt, Redfearn, Thomas, Bright, Wright, Barber. manager: Steve Coppell
Sheffield Wed: Pressman, Sterland – capt, Worthington, Madden, Cranson, Proctor, Megson, Chapman, Hirst, Jonsson, Galvin. subs: Fee for Cranson 33, West for Hirst 37. manager: Howard Wilkinson

Quarter-finals

Everton 0
Manchester United 1
Bruce 18

United repeated their 1985 FA Cup final victory over Everton with Steve Bruce's goal. Everton were back the following year reaching two cup finals.

Everton: Southall, Stevens, Pointon, Van den Hauwe, Watson – capt, Reid, Harper, Heath, Clarke, Snodin, Wilson. subs: Adams for Harper, Power for Wilson. manager: Colin Harvey
Manchester U: Turner, Duxbury, Gibson, Bruce, McGrath, Whiteside, Robson – capt, Strachan, McClair, Davenport, Olsen. subs: Blackmore for Duxbury 17, O'Brien for Whiteside. manager: Alex Ferguson

Sheffield Wednesday 1
Worthington 3
Wigan Athletic 1
Thompson (C) 22
Sheffield Wednesday won 3-2 on penalties.

(McEwan 0-1, Sterland 1-1, Cook 1-2, Megson 2-2, Campbell missed, Worthington 2-3)

Third Division Wigan remained unbeaten but bowed out of the competition in the final match of an exhausting day which had begun ten hours earlier. Both sides had needed penalties in the first round and once again their top two penalty-takers hit the net. But then Bobby Campbell shot wide and Nigel Worthington ensured Wednesday would return the following day with his second goal of the contest.

Sheffield Wed: Pressman, Sterland – capt, Worthington, Madden, May, Proctor, Megson, Chapman, Hirst, Jonsson, Galvin. subs: West for Hirst 23, Bradshaw for Jonsson 26. manager: Howard Wilkinson
Wigan: Hughes, Senior, Kennedy, Hamilton, McEwan, Beesley, Thompson (D), Thompson (C), Campbell, Jewell, Cook. manager: Ray Mathias

Sunday 17th April 1988

Semi-Finals

Nottingham Forest 2
Clough 47, Carr 52
Tranmere Rovers 2
Muir 13, 51
Nottingham Forest won 1-0 on penalties.
(Muir saved, Pearce 1-0)

Tranmere's fairytale finally came to an end but not before Ian Muir had twice put them ahead. Sadly it was Muir who missed the first penalty after scoring one in the quarter-final and Steve Sutton's save was followed by Stuart Pearce's third successful penalty of the festival.

Tranmere were to return in 1990 for the first of four visits in just over a year.

Nottingham F: Sutton, Fleming, Pearce – capt, Chettle, Foster, Wilson, Crosby, Webb, Clough, Carr, Glover. sub: Gaynor for Crosby. assistant manager: Ronnie Fenton
Tranmere: Nixon, Higgins, McCarrick, Martindale, Moore, Vickers, Morrissey, Harvey – capt, Steel, Muir, Mungall. manager: John King

Manchester United 1
Davenport pen 30
Sheffield Wednesday 2
Sterland pen 40, West 55
Referee: D Axcell (Southend)

No penalty shoot-out, but the game still featured two spot-kicks while Wednesday substitute Colin West scored a spectacular winner. United went on to finish League runners-up to Liverpool.

Manchester U: Turner, Blackmore, Gibson, Bruce, McGrath, Whiteside, Robson – capt, Strachan, McClair, Davenport, Olsen. subs: Moses for Strachan, O'Brien for Olsen. manager: Alex Ferguson

Sheffield Wed: Pressman, Sterland – capt, Worthington, Madden, May, Proctor, Megson, Chapman, Hirst, Jonsson, Galvin. subs: Bradshaw for Jonsson 31, West for Galvin 31. manager: Howard Wilkinson

Final

Nottingham Forest 0
Sheffield Wednesday 0

Nottingham Forest won 3-2 on penalties.
Referee: B Hill (Kettering)
(Pearce 1-0, Sterland 1-1, Clough 2-1, Megson 2-2, Webb 3-2, Worthington saved)

The Festival came to a tired conclusion with the inevitable penalties. The two captains – Stuart Pearce and Mel Sterland – each converted their fourth spot-kick of the tournament, but Steve Sutton saved from Nigel Worthington, Wednesday's quarter-final hero, to give Forest the trophy.

Nottingham F: Sutton, Fleming, Pearce – capt, Chettle, Foster, Wilson, Carr, Webb, Clough, Gaynor, Rice. subs: Glover for Gaynor 40, Crossley, Crosby, Parker, Wassall (not used). assistant manager: Ronnie Fenton

Sheffield Wed: Pressman, Sterland – capt, Worthington, Madden, May, Proctor, Hazel, Megson, Chapman, Bradshaw, West. subs: Jonsson for Proctor 38, Hirst for Chapman 40, Hodge, Fee, Galvin (not used). manager: Howard Wilkinson

FA Vase Final

Saturday 23rd April 1988

Colne Dynamoes 1
Anderson 97

Emley 0
After extra time
15,146
Referee: A Seville (Birmingham)

Victory at Wembley for a club that was rap-idly working its way up through the minor leagues. Two years later they were denied entry to the Vauxhall Conference because their ground was not up to standard. Sadly the club disbanded and one of the great non-league success stories was ended.

Colne: Mason, McFadyen, Dunn, Westwell – capt, Bentley, Whitehead, Roscoe, Anderson, Wood, Rodaway, Diamond. subs: Burke for Whitehead 59, Coates for Wood 74

Emley: Dennis, Hirst, Fielding, Mellor, Codd, Green, Bramald, Francis, Devine, Carmody, Gartland. subs: Burrows for Hirst 78, Cook for Gartland 108

LEAGUE CUP FINAL

Sunday 24th April 1988

Arsenal	2-3	Luton Town
Hayes 71, Smith 74		B Stein 13, 90, Wilson 81

95,732
Referee: J Worrall (Warrington)

Arsenal were the Littlewoods Cup holders, having come from behind to beat Liverpool in the previous year's final. Luton had not been beyond the quarter-finals before and in the previous season had been banned from the competition for refusing to allow visiting supporters into their ground.

In the league, Arsenal once again had not quite had the credentials to challenge for the Championship. Luton had been humiliated in the previous month's Simod Cup final and had lost in the first round of the Football League Centenary Tournament the previous week. They had also reached the FA Cup semi-finals where they lost to the eventual winners, Wimbledon.

This was one of Wembley's most exciting and dramatic finals with the underdogs taking the lead. Preece's free kick was floated into the middle, Harford got his head to it but was crowded out by three Arsenal defenders. Fortunately for him, Foster picked up the loose ball and played a great flick through to Brian Stein who drove it past Lukic. Luton assumed control and almost increased their lead early in the second half when Lukic pulled off an unbelievable save from a Brian Stein header.

Then, with 18 minutes left, the game took a dramatic twist. Thomas took a free kick for Arsenal and played it back to Davis who chipped it into the area. Foster rose above Adams, but headed it down only to Martin Hayes. The Arsenal substitute played it to Smith, who fell as he shot wildly. But the ball went through the legs of both Donaghy and Foster, and there was Hayes to force the ball in under Dibble's diving body. Three minutes later, Alan Smith took a pass from Thomas and gave Arsenal the lead as Dibble appeared to dive under his shot.

In the next five minutes Arsenal launched a furious onslaught on the Luton goal in an attempt to kill off the game. It was in complete contrast to the first 70 minutes.

The main reason Arsenal did not score again was the goalkeeping heroics of Andy Dibble, who kept out further attempts by the two men who had just beaten him. He turned Smith's header onto the bar and Hayes, with an open goal at his mercy, somehow managed to hit the post. From the resultant corner, Hayes' point blank header was tipped over the bar by Dibble and Luton were clinging on desperately.

But after Dibble had saved once again, at the feet of Smith, it seemed all over, with ten minutes left, when Rocastle was tripped by Donaghy and Arsenal were awarded a penalty. Winterburn hit it well enough, but Dibble turned it round the post. This was the final turning point.

Two minutes later, Caesar stumbled as he attempted to clear and Black raced in. He crossed to Brian Stein whose close range shot was brilliantly blocked by Lukic. But the rebound hit Adams and came back to Stein who drove it across to where Danny Wilson headed it over the line for an equaliser that seemed impossible only five minutes earlier.

The transformation was completed in the very last minute. Substitute Grimes crossed and, as Winterburn challenged, Stein turned it past Lukic for his second. Luton had deservedly won their first major trophy in a breathless final in which they had come as close to losing as any team could do before coming back to win.

Arsenal soon forgot about defeat. They won the Wembley International Tournament on goal difference four months later and then the Football League Centenary Trophy.

The following year they won the League Championship in the most dramatic of all finishes and retained what was now the Makita Tournament before returning to Wembley for the FA Charity Shield. Luton reached the final again the following year.

Arsenal: Lukic, Winterburn, Sansom, Thomas, Caesar, Adams – capt, Rocastle, Davis, Smith (A), Groves, Richardson. subs: Hayes for Groves 60, Quinn (not used). manager: George Graham

Luton: Dibble, Breacker, Johnson, Hill, Foster – capt, Donaghy, Wilson, Stein (B), Harford, Preece, Black. subs: Stein (M) for Harford 64, Grimes for Preece 77. manager: Ray Harford

FA Trophy Final

Saturday 7th May 1988

Enfield 0
Telford United 0
After extra time
20,061
Referee: R Dilkes (Mossley)

This was the second successive goalless FA Trophy final. Once again, it took a visit to The Hawthorns to produce the goals.

Enfield: Pape, Cooper, Sparrow, Howell – capt, Keen, Francis, Lewis, Cottington, Furlong, Harding, King. subs: Edmonds for Lewis 104, Hayzleden for Sparrow 112
Telford: Charlton, McGinty, Wiggins, Mayman, Nelson, Storton, Joseph, Biggins, Norris, Sankey, Stringer. subs: Griffiths for Stringer 28, Cunningham (not used)

Replay: Thursday 12th May 1988
Enfield 3
Howell, Furlong 2

Telford United 2
Biggins, Norris pen
(The Hawthorns, West Bromwich)

FA CUP FINAL

Saturday 14th May 1988

Liverpool   **0-1**   **Wimbledon**
Sanchez 36

98,203
Referee: B Hill (Kettering)

Liverpool had won the League Championship for the seventh time in ten years, losing only two league games all season, and they seemed set to win the 'double' for the second time in three years, having won it at Wembley in 1986. Since then, they had failed to win at the stadium, losing the previous year's Littlewoods Cup final and making an early exit on penalties from the previous month's Football League Centenary Tournament.

Wimbledon represented, surely, the most remarkable 'rags to riches' story. Twenty five years earlier they had won the FA Amateur Cup at Wembley. They had been in the Football League for just 11 years and only five years earlier they had been Fourth Division Champions.

While Wimbledon could not match Liverpool for skill, their team spirit was second to none and, allied to clever tactics, they were more than a handful for anyone. Thus, they overcame a team that had been virtually unbeatable all season. The one goal came when Lawrie Sanchez rose above the Liverpool defence to head home Wise's free kick.

Liverpool should have equalised in the 61st minute when they were awarded a penalty after Aldridge went down in the box although Goodyear appeared to have taken the ball. Aldridge took the kick himself, but Dave Beasant pulled off a brilliant diving save, Wembley's first in an FA Cup final.

Liverpool were well beaten in the end, but it was still the most unlikely result in an FA Cup final since Sunderland's 1973 win. It meant the Londoners were the first club to win the FA Cup and FA Amateur Cup. Liverpool won the FA Cup, the following year but had to overcome tragedy before the final.

Liverpool: Grobbelaar, Gillespie, Ablett, Nicol, Spackman, Hansen – capt, Beardsley, Aldridge, Houghton, Barnes, McMahon. subs: Johnston for Aldridge 63, Molby for Spackman 72. manager: Kenny Dalglish

Wimbledon: Beasant – capt, Goodyear, Phelan, Jones, Young, Thorn, Gibson, Cork, Fashanu, Sanchez, Wise. subs: Cunningham for Cork 56, Scales for Gibson 63. manager: Bobby Gould

ROUS CUP

Saturday 21st May 1988

England   **1-0**   **Scotland**
Beardsley 10
70,480
Referee: J Quiniou (France)

Scotland had not won at Wembley since 1981, but had to win to have a realistic chance of regaining the Rous Cup for the first time since the inaugural competition in 1985. Four days earlier, they had been held to a goalless draw by Colombia in the opening match at Hampden Park. England had only won the Rous Cup once – in 1986.

England took an 11th minute lead, when Peter Beardsley ran on to Barnes' pass and shot past the advancing Leighton. England had many more chances, but could not beat Leighton again.

England now needed only a point against Colombia three days later to regain the Rous Cup. They beat Scotland again the following year but the long run of annual meetings came to an end and the countries did not meet again until the 1996 European Championship.

England: Shilton (Derby County), Stevens (Everton), Sansom (Arsenal), Webb (Nottingham F), Watson (Everton), Adams (Arsenal), Robson (Man Utd) – capt, Steven (Everton), Beardsley (Liverpool), Lineker (Barcelona), Barnes (Liverpool). sub: Waddle (Tottenham) for Steven 72. manager: Bobby Robson

Scotland: Leighton (Man Utd), Gough (Rangers), Nicol (Liverpool), Aitken (Celtic) – capt, McLeish (Aberdeen), Miller (Aberdeen), Simpson (Aberdeen), McStay (Celtic), McCoist (Rangers), MacLeod (Borussia Dortmund), Johnston (Nantes). subs: Burns (Celtic) for Simpson 74, Gallacher (Dundee U) for McCoist 77. manager: Andy Roxburgh

Tuesday 24th May 1988

England   1-1   Colombia

Lineker 21   Escobar 65

25,756

Referee: K Assenmacher (West Germany)

After beating Scotland three days earlier, England needed only a point to regain the Rous Cup for the second time in three years. Colombia had held Scotland to a goalless draw at Hampden Park the previous week and had to win to keep the trophy in South America after Brazil's victory the previous year. They had met England just once before, losing 4-0 in Bogota in 1970.

In the 22nd minute, Waddle crossed and Gary Lineker put England in front with a glancing header. But the South Americans demonstrated brilliant ball skills and deservedly equalised in the 66th minute. Andres Escobar headed in off the bar from substitute Trellez's corner, but it was not enough to prevent the red-shirted England team from lifting the trophy. Glenn Hoddle came on as a late substitute to win his 50th cap.

Colombia appeared at Wembley again in 1995.

England: Shilton (Derby County), Anderson (Man Utd), Sansom (Arsenal), McMahon (Liverpool), Wright (Derby County), Adams (Arsenal), Robson (Man Utd) – capt, Waddle (Tottenham), Beardsley (Liverpool), Lineker (Barcelona), Barnes (Liverpool). subs: Hoddle (Monaco) for Waddle 73, Hateley (Monaco) for Beardsley 73. manager: Bobby Robson

Colombia: Higuita (Nacional), Escobar (Nacional), Herrera (Nacional), Hoyos (Deportivo Cali), Arango (Nacional), Garcia (Independiente Santa Fe), Valderrama (C) (Deportivo Cali) – capt, Redin (Deportivo Cali), Alvarez (Nacional), Perea (Nacional), Iguaran (Millonarios). sub: Trellez (Nacional) for Arango 58, Valderrama (A) (Nacional) for Iguaran 78. coach: Francisco Maturana

Schoolboy International

Saturday 28th May 1988

England 4

Clark (pen) 16, 48, 50, Mulrain 40

Italy 1

Rizzioli 67

31,504

Referee: J Key (Rotherham)

Lee Clark's hat-trick gave England their biggest victory over the Italians.

England: Sheppard, Davies, Price, Reed, Holden, Clark – capt, Flitcroft, Clements, Mulrain, McDonough, Stewart. subs: Hancock for Stewart 63, Morah for McDonough 79

Sherpa Van Trophy Final

Sunday 29th May 1988

Burnley 0
Wolverhampton Wanderers 2

Mutch 22, Dennison 51

80,841

Referee: R Milford (Bristol)

Robbie Dennison, who had scored for Wolves in the Football League Centenary Tournament the previous month, confirmed the Sherpa Van Trophy for the Fourth Division Champions. Burnley were also from the Fourth Division, although in 1960 these two sleeping giants had taken the top two placings in the Football League.

This first final, after the renaming of the Freight Rover Trophy, attracted a record crowd for two Fourth Division teams.

Burnley's substitute, Leighton James won 54 caps for Wales and scored the penalty which beat England at Wembley in 1977.

Burnley: Pearce, Daniel, Deakin – capt, Britton, Davis, Gardner, Farrell, Oghani, Taylor, Comstive, McGrory. subs: James for McGrory 62, Hoskin (not used). manager: Brian Miller

Wolves: Kendall, Bellamy, Thompson, Streete, Robertson – capt, Robinson, Dennison, Downing, Bull, Mutch, Holmes. subs: Vaughan for Holmes 45, Gallagher for Robertson 47. manager: Graham Turner

Middlesex Charity Cup Final

Thursday 2nd June 1988

Hendon 2
Dowie 29, Drummy 86
Wembley 0
3,715
Referee: J Abbott (Northolt)

Thanks to astrologer Russell Grant's sponsorship, the Middlesex Charity Cup final returned to the stadium for the first time since 1945 when Hendon won under the name of Golders Green. They had appeared in five FA Amateur Cup finals since but this was the first visit for the local side from Wembley.

Iain Dowie, scorer of the first goal, won his first cap for Northern Ireland two years later and went on to make 59 appearances for his country.

Hendon: Root, Smart, Furneaux, Wade – capt, Campbell, Gridelet, Drummy, Henry, Dowie, Tate, Wolstenholme. subs: Smith for Wade 75, Kiely, Robotham, Roughan (not used)
Wembley: Fanner, Flaherty, Simpson, Murphy – capt, Janaway, Smith, Bhatia, Brown, Dolling, Cadogan, O'Connor. subs: Williams for Brown 86, Pacquette for Dolling 86, McGrath, Ray (not used)

International Tournament

Saturday 13th August 1988

Arsenal 4
Merson 32, Marwood 75, 82, Smith 88
Tottenham Hotspur 0
Referee: J Worrall (Cheshire)

The first meeting at the stadium of the north London rivals kicked off Wembley's new tournament, an attempt to compensate for the lack of European competition due to the ban on English clubs. The attendance for the day was 30,468. Tottenham would have their revenge in the FA Cup semi-finals, three years later.

Arsenal: Lukic, Dixon, Winterburn, Thomas, O'Leary, Adams – capt, Rocastle, Davis, Smith (A), Merson, Marwood. subs: Hayes for Merson 74, Bould for O'Leary 75. manager: George Graham
Tottenham: Mimms, Allen (P), Stimson, Fenwick, Fairclough, Mabbutt – capt, Walsh, Gascoigne, Waddle, Stewart, Samways. subs: Gray for Stewart 74, Howells for Samways 74. manager: Terry Venables

Bayern Munich 0
AC Milan 1
Virdis 33
Referee: N Midgley (Lancashire)

Milan, the Italian League Champions for the first time since 1979, were appearing at Wembley for the first time since winning the 1963 European Cup. After three successive West German League Championships, Bayern Munich had finished runners-up to Werder Bremen. Pietro Virdis' first-half goal was enough to win the points but Arsenal were top overnight on goal difference.

Marco Van Basten had destroyed England's European Championship ambitions the previous month with a hat-trick in Dusseldorf. He scored a spectacular second for the Netherlands in the final against the USSR in Munich and won the first of three European Footballer of the Year awards in five years. This was his Wembley debut.

Bayern Munich: Aumann, Nachtweih, Pflugler, Grahammer, Augenthaler – capt, Flick, Kogl, Reuter, Wohlfarth, Thon, Ekstrom. subs: Wegmann for Thon, Eck for Ekstrom. coach: Jupp Heynckes
AC Milan: Galli, Tassotti, Mussi, Colombo, Costacurta, Baresi – capt, Donadoni, Rijkaard, Van Basten, Evani, Virdis. subs: Cappellini for Evani, Massaro for Virdis. coach: Arrigo Sacchi

Sunday 14th August 1988

AC Milan 2
Virdis 12, Van Basten 14
Tottenham Hotspur 1
Fenwick 60
Referee: G Courtney (Durham)

Milan scored two early goals in just over a minute and left Arsenal needing another victory to win the tournament on goal difference. Only 27,369 turned up for the second and final day. The Italians, with their three famous Dutchmen (Frank Rijkaard, Marco Van Basten and the injured Ruud Gullit) went on to win the European Cup for the next two years although Internazionale took the Italian League Championship from them.

AC Milan: Galli, Tassotti, Mussi, Colombo, Costacurta, Baresi – capt, Donadoni, Rijkaard, Van Basten, Evani, Virdis. subs: Bianchi for Mussi, Massaro for Colombo. coach: Arrigo Sacchi
Tottenham: Mimms, Thomas, Hughton, Fenwick, Fairclough, Mabbutt – capt, Walsh, Gascoigne, Waddle, Stewart, Allen (P). sub: Moran for Walsh. manager: Terry Venables

Arsenal 3
Smith 72, 77, Dixon 86
Bayern Munich 0
Referee: K Hackett (Sheffield)

Arsenal did not score until 18 minutes from the end, but then the Germans collapsed and the Gunners won the first Wembley International Tournament. Two months later, they won the Football League Centenary Trophy and finished the season as League Champions before returning to defend the tournament, now sponsored by Makita.

Arsenal: Lukic, Dixon, Winterburn, Thomas, Bould, Adams – capt, Rocastle, Davis, Smith (A), Merson, Marwood. subs: Richardson for Rocastle, Hayes for Merson. manager: George Graham
Bayern Munich: Aumann, Nachtweih, Pflugler, Johnson, Augenthaler – capt, Bayerschmidt, Eck, Reuter, Wegmann, Thon, Ekstrom. subs: Flick for Bayerschmidt, Wohlfarth for Ekstrom. coach: Jupp Heynckes

U-16 International
Saturday 20th August 1988

England 1
Flitcroft 69
Israel 1
Stanger og 37
Referee: A Gunn (South Chailey)

Gary Flitcroft saved his goalkeeper's blushes in this Vauxhall Challenge by equalising after Jonathan Stanger had punched the ball into his own net from a corner.

England substitute Trevor Sinclair won 12 full international caps, but did not win his first until he was 28 years old after Wembley had closed. He did, however, appear twice as a substitute in successive play-off finals for Blackpool in 1991-92.

England: Stanger, Hancock, Fowler, Flitcroft, Price, Reed, Fuller, Clements, Morah, Joseph, Flatts. subs: Makin for Hancock, Schonberger for Fowler, Gaunt for Price, Sinclair for Fuller, Kenton for Morah

FA CHARITY SHIELD
Saturday 20th August 1988

Liverpool   2-1   Wimbledon
Aldridge 23, 68   Fashanu 17
54,887
Referee: J Martin (near Alton)

Liverpool were chasing a record 11th Charity Shield, but they had not won it outright for six years. In 1986, their last appearance in the fixture, they had gained a share with a late equaliser. Liverpool had won the League Championship for the seventh time in ten years and a record 17th overall. It had been one of their most convincing seasons. They did not lose until their 30th game, equalling Leeds United's 1974 record, and lost only two games all season. They won the title by nine points from Manchester United and would have become the first team to win the 'double' twice but for Wimbledon in the FA Cup.

Wimbledon took an 18th minute lead, when Wise crossed and John Fashanu headed past Grobbelaar. But this time Liverpool took just six minutes to equalise. Tracey, who had yet to make his league debut, came out of his area to head the ball clear but it went straight to Barnes. He laid it off for John Aldridge to score as the 'keeper scrambled back. After 68 minutes, a Barnes cross was met by Aldridge, who controlled it before scoring with an acrobatic scissors kick. Aldridge had gone some way towards redressing the balance after his penalty miss in the FA Cup final.

Liverpool were back for next year's FA Cup final but Wimbledon never appeared at Wembley again.

Liverpool: Grobbelaar, Gillespie, Venison, Ablett, Whelan – capt, Watson, Beardsley, Aldridge, Houghton, Barnes, McMahon. manager: Kenny Dalglish
Wimbledon: Tracey, Scales, Phelan, Ryan, Young, Cawley, Gibson, Fairweather, Fashanu, Sanchez, Wise – capt. subs: Clement for Scales 70, Turner for Fashanu 79. manager: Bobby Gould

INTERNATIONAL

Wednesday 14th September 1988

England　　　　　**1-0**　　　**Denmark**
Webb 28
25,837
Referee: A Ponnet (Belgium)

Both England and Denmark had flopped in the recent European Championships, finishing bottom of their respective groups without a point between them.

Denmark had won on their last visit, to Wembley, five years earlier. The only goal came in the 29th minute. Rasmussen stopped Robson's shot, but Neil Webb volleyed home the rebound. This restored some confidence to the England team, after a disastrous summer. Three new caps were introduced, while at half-time Woods took over from Shilton in goal.

The teams drew 1-1 in Copenhagen the following year, and Denmark returned to Wembley in 1990 after failing to qualify for the World Cup.

England: Shilton (Derby County), Stevens (Rangers), Pearce (Nottingham F), Rocastle* (Arsenal), Adams (Arsenal), Butcher (Rangers), Robson (Man Utd) – capt, Webb (Nottingham F), Harford (Luton Town), Beardsley (Liverpool), Hodge (Nottingham F). subs: Woods (Rangers) for Shilton 46, Walker* (Nottingham F) for Adams 65, Cottee (Everton) for Harford 70, Gascoigne* (Tottenham) for Beardsley 85. manager: Bobby Robson
*first cap
Denmark: Rasmussen (Aarhus), Jensen (Brondby), Nielsen (Brondby), Olsen (Brondby) – capt, Bartram (Brondby), Molby (Liverpool), Helt (Lyngby), Hansen (Odense), Vilfort (Brondby), Elstrup (Odense), Laudrup (M) (Juventus). subs: Heintze (PSV Eindhoven) for Jensen 66, Kristensen (Aarhus) for Bartram 85, Jorgensen (Naestved) for Vilfort 85.
coach: Sepp Piontek

WORLD CUP QUALIFYING

Wednesday 19th October 1988

England　　　　　**0-0**　　　**Sweden**
65,628
Referee: G Biguet (France)

Since losing on their last visit to Wembley 20 years earlier, Sweden had reached the last eight of the World Cup in 1974, but had failed to qualify for the last two World Cups, each time by a point.

They had finished runners-up to Italy in their recent European Championship qualifying group. In their last two meetings, both in Stockholm, England had failed to score. This was one of the opening matches in Group Two.

England did not have much luck in front of goal and subsequently dropped a vital point.

The following year in Stockholm, the return match also ended goalless. Sweden won the group by a point from England, but in the World Cup in Italy they failed surprisingly to win a point.

Sweden did not appear at Wembley again until 1999 for a European Championship match.

England: Shilton (Derby County), Stevens (Rangers), Pearce (Nottingham F), Webb (Nottingham F), Adams (Arsenal), Butcher (Rangers), Robson (Man Utd) – capt, Beardsley (Liverpool), Waddle (Tottenham), Lineker (Barcelona), Barnes (Liverpool). subs: Walker (Nottingham F) for Adams 64, Cottee (Everton) for Barnes 79. manager: Bobby Robson
Sweden: Ravelli (Osters), Nilsson (R) (Gothenburg), Hysen (Fiorentina) – capt, Larsson (Ajax Amsterdam), Ljung (Malmo), Thern (Malmo), Stromberg (Atalanta), Prytz (Atalanta), Nilsson (J) (Malmo), Holmqvist (Cesena), Pettersson (Ajax). subs: Ekstrom (Bayern Munich) for Holmqvist 63, Schiller (Lillestrom) for Nilsson (R) 77. coach: Olle Nordin

Schoolboy International

Saturday 11th March 1989

England 3
Barmby 16, 58, Wilson pen 46

Belgium 1
Pierre 26
23,988
Referee: J Watson (Northumberland)

Foster saved a last minute penalty on Belgium's first appearance at Wembley.

England captain Ryan Wilson is better known now as Ryan Giggs. Just two years later, he became Wales' youngest ever full international, going on to great club success with Manchester United. He was a member of the 'treble' winning side in 1999. In 2005, he was captain of Wales and won his 50th cap.

Nick Barmby, who scored twice, went on to win 23 full England caps, nine of them at Wembley. He never scored again beneath the twin towers, but he did achieve the unusual distinction of scoring the first goal for two different England managers, Glenn Hoddle in 1996 and Sven-Goran Eriksson in 2001.

England: Foster (M), Foster (J), Harriott, Hall, Wilson – capt, Marlowe, Charlton, Mike, Jamfy, Barmby, Durrant. subs: Basham for Mike 76, Brocklehurst for Jamfy 53

LEAGUE CUP FINAL

Sunday 9th April 1989

Luton Town	**1-3**	**Nottingham Forest**
Harford 36		Clough (pen) 55, 76, Webb 67

76,130
Referee: R Milford (Bristol)

After losing to ten-man Forest in the 1959 FA Cup final, Luton had waited 29 years to return to Wembley. They then made three appearances in a month, the highlight of which was winning their first major trophy, the Littlewoods Cup, in a tremendously exciting final.

In 1979 Forest had been the first club to retain the League Cup but had lost the following year's final. Their last appearance had been in winning the Football League Centenary Tournament on penalties the previous year.

Luton were battling against relegation to the Second Division. Forest were still in contention for a historic cup 'treble'. They would be returning three weeks later for their first Simod Cup final, having emulated Luton's feat of the previous year and they had also reached the FA Cup semi-finals for the second year in succession.

Just before half-time Mick Harford out-jumped Chapman and headed Preece's corner out to Wilson. The cross was returned and the centre forward leapt above four static Forest defenders to power a header past Sutton. Forest equalised from the spot after Sealey charged out of his goal to bring down Hodge. Nigel Clough, the manager's son, sent Sealey the wrong way from the penalty.

Twelve minutes later Forest's Neil Webb timed his run to perfection and side-footed the ball past the 'keeper. Forest embellished their victory when Gaynor again supplied the crucial pass from which Clough fired through Foster's legs and beyond Sealey's despairing dive for his second.

Forest went on to win the Simod Cup at the end of the month and retained the Littlewoods Cup, the following year.

Luton: Sealey, Breacker, Grimes, Preece, Foster – capt, Beaumont, Wilson, Wegerle, Harford, Hill, Black. subs: McDonough for Grimes 76, Meade (not used). manager: Ray Harford
Nottingham F: Sutton, Laws, Pearce – capt, Walker, Wilson (Te), Hodge, Gaynor, Webb, Clough, Chapman, Parker. subs: Chettle, Glover (not used). manager: Brian Clough

WORLD CUP QUALIFYING

Wednesday 26th April 1989

England	**5-0**	**Albania**

Lineker 5, Beardsley 12, 64,
Waddle 72, Gascoigne 88
60,602
Referee: E Halle (Norway)

England were top of Group Two on goal difference from Sweden after two matches, although Poland were a point behind after one match. England had won 2-0 in Tirana the previous month in the first meeting between the two countries. Albania had been competing sporadically in international competition since 1963 and had experienced little success. They had lost all three games in the current group.

In the sixth minute, Waddle crossed but Jera leapt above Rocastle to get his head to it. Unfortunately, he headed the ball into the path of Gary Lineker, who could not miss and so headed the opening goal. Seven minutes later, Lineker crossed to an unmarked Peter Beardsley and England were two up.

It was the 65th minute before the third goal was scored. Pearce's high centre was headed down by Webb, Lineker controlled it and Beardsley drove home his second. It was another Pearce cross headed across goal that led to England's fourth eight minutes later. This time, substitute Gascoigne's touch left the goalkeeper undecided and Chris Waddle dived to head in. Then, in the 89th minute, the other substitute Parker supplied Paul Gascoigne and the rising star ran through the Albanian defence to shoot low into the corner.

Albania were eliminated 11 days later when Sweden beat Poland in Stockholm and they failed to win a point in the group. They were in the middle of their worst ever run as they suffered 17 consecutive defeats in international competitions, before beating Iceland in Tirana in the European Championship two years later.

England: Shilton (Derby County), Stevens (Rangers), Pearce (Nottingham F), Webb (Nottingham F), Walker (Nottingham F), Butcher (Rangers), Robson (Man Utd) – capt, Rocastle (Arsenal), Beardsley (Liverpool), Lineker (Barcelona), Waddle (Tottenham). subs: Gascoigne (Tottenham) for Rocastle 66, Parker* (QPR) for Stevens 76. manager: Bobby Robson
*first cap
Albania: Nallbani (Partizani Tirana), Zmijani (Vllaznia Shkoder), Bubeqi (Flamurtari Vlore), Hodja (Nentori) – capt, Gega (Partizani Tirana), Jera (Vllaznia Shkoder), Shehu (Partizani Tirana), Lekbello (Nentori), Millo (Partizani Tirana), Hasanpapa (Nentori), Demollari (Dinamo Tirana). sub: Noga (Partizani Tirana) for Hasanpapa 34. coach: Shyqyri Rreli

Simod Cup Final

Sunday 30th April 1989

Everton 3
Cottee 8, 101, Sharp 60
Nottingham Forest 4
Parker 33, 70, Chapman 92, 118
After extra time
46,606
Referee: A Gunn (South Chailey)

Everton had never been beyond the quarter-finals of the competition, but had won their fourth successive FA Charity Shield at Wembley two years earlier and reached the quarter-finals of the Football League Centenary Tournament in 1988 on their last visit. Forest had entered the competition for the first time the previous year.

Everton had also reached their fourth FA Cup final in six years and would be returning, three weeks later. Forest had won the Littlewoods Cup three weeks earlier and were aiming to become the first club to win two domestic trophies at Wembley in the same season.

Tony Cottee ran on to Steven's long ball, sprinted between Laws and Walker, and shot through Sutton's legs to give Everton an early lead. But Forest levelled when Gaynor's corner was flicked on by Chapman and reached Garry Parker whose volley bounced up where Southall's touch took it past Sheedy who was on the line behind him.

Everton restored their lead on the hour. This time it was Sheedy's long ball which sent Graeme Sharp racing between Laws and Wilson to half-volley it over Sutton with a stunning finish. But ten minutes later, a swift Forest counter-attack brought them level again. Walker passed to Clough, who played the ball into the middle for Parker who ran the length of the pitch to fire his second past Southall.

In the second minute of extra time, Lee Chapman lost his markers as he ran on to Clough's pass and chipped Southall to put Forest in front for the first time. Nine minutes later, Cottee headed Nevin's cross beyond Sutton's reach and Everton were level. Everton almost won when Sharp's shot was pushed onto the bar by Sutton. The goalkeeper then caught it one-handed on the line and almost carried it over. But it was Forest who won with two minutes left. Carr had just come on as substitute when he crossed for Chapman to score his second.

The following week, Forest lost the FA Cup semi-final to Liverpool who went on to beat Everton in the final. Forest returned the following year to retain the Littlewoods Cup.

Everton: Southall, McDonald, Van den Hauwe, Ratcliffe – capt, Watson, Bracewell, Nevin, Steven, Sharp, Cottee, Sheedy. sub: McCall for Bracewell 105, Clarke (not used). manager: Colin Harvey
Nottingham F: Sutton, Laws, Pearce – capt, Walker, Wilson (Te), Hodge, Gaynor, Webb, Clough, Chapman, Parker. subs: Chettle for Hodge 107, Carr for Gaynor 117. manager: Brian Clough

FA Vase Final

Saturday 6th May 1989

Sudbury Town 1
Hubbick 5
Tamworth 1
Devaney 49
After extra time
26,487
Referee: D Vickers (Ilford)

A record attendance for this final saw Sudbury's Mike Henry sent off after clashing

with Russell Gordon during the changeover midway through extra time. Paul Smith missed a penalty in the replay as Tamworth took the Vase.

Sudbury: Garnham, Henry, Thorpe, Barker (G), Boyland, Barker (D), Oldfield, Klug, Hubbick, Smith, Barton. subs: Hunt for Oldfield, Money for Barton
Tamworth: Belford, Lockett, McCormack, Atkins – capt, Cartwright, Devaney, Myers, Finn, Stanton, Gordon, Moores. subs: Heaton for McCormack, Rathbone for Moores

Replay: Wednesday 10th May 1989
Sudbury Town 0
Tamworth 3
Moores, Stanton 2
(London Road, Peterborough)

FA Trophy Final

Saturday 13th May 1989

Macclesfield Town 0
Telford United 1
Crawley 96
After extra time
18,106
Referee: T Holbrook (Walsall)

In Telford's second successive and record fifth final they gained revenge for losing the very first final to Macclesfield back in 1970. For the third year in succession the FA Trophy final went into extra time without a goal, but this time it was settled by substitute Ian Crawley, who had scored the only goal of the 1983 FA Vase final for VS Rugby. The crowd was 8,000 less than for the previous week's Vase final.

Macclesfield: Zelem, Roberts, Hardman, Edwards, Tobin, Hanlon, Askey, Timmons, Lake, Burr, Imrie. subs: Derbyshire for Askey, Kendall for Imrie
Telford: Charlton, Lee, Wiggins, Mayman, Brindley, Hancock, Joseph, Grainger, Stringer, Lloyd, Nelson. sub: Crawley for Mayman 70, Griffiths for Lloyd

FA CUP FINAL

Saturday 20th May 1989

Everton   2-3   **Liverpool**
McCall 89, 102   Aldridge 4, Rush 94, 104
After extra time
82,800
Referee: J Worrall (Warrington)

The FA Cup had been overshadowed by the tragedy at Liverpool's semi-final at Hillsborough when 96 people lost their lives on an overcrowded terrace. Three weeks later the match was played and Liverpool beat the Littlewoods and Simod Cup winners Nottingham Forest for the second successive year to set up the second all-Merseyside FA Cup final and their fifth Wembley meeting with Everton in five years.

Everton had knocked out the holders Wimbledon in the quarter-finals and had reached their fourth final in six years. But they had not won the Cup since 1984. They had beaten Liverpool in the FA Charity Shield, three months later, but had surrendered their half-time lead to them in the 1986 FA Cup final. Three months after that, in their last Wembley meeting, in another Charity Shield, it had finished all square.

Liverpool were appearing in their third final in four years. They had been the victims of a shock result in the previous year's final, but had gained revenge in the Charity Shield three months later.

Everton had been involved in the Simod Cup final thriller three weeks earlier. Having failed to win the 'double' the previous year, Liverpool were making yet another attempt to win it for the second time. To retain the League Championship they had to overcome Arsenal in their final match.

Liverpool took the lead in their first attack. McMahon ran on to Nicol's long ball and played it into the middle where John Aldridge, in the clear, shot past Southall. It was a sweet moment after the previous year's penalty miss. Liverpool could not add to their score and brought on Rush for Aldridge in the hope of producing a winner, but it was Everton's substitute who res-

cued them in the last minute. Grobbelaar could not hold Watson's shot and Stuart McCall just beat Nicol to stab the ball over the line.

Nicol was involved in the move four minutes into extra time which led to Liverpool's second. He crossed, Ian Rush controlled the ball on his chest, shielded it from Ratcliffe and swivelled to hit the roof of the net.

Everton still would not give up and Ratcliffe's free kick was headed out by Hansen. McCall took it on his chest and volleyed it over the defence and into the corner to become the first substitute to score twice in an FA Cup final. Liverpool's own scoring substitute was not to be denied, however. Rush beat Southall again with a glancing header from Barnes' cross and so the man who had destroyed Everton with two goals in the 1986 final had repeated the dose.

Everton returned to Wembley two years later for the Zenith Cup final but were losers yet again. It seemed a formality that Liverpool would win their second 'double' when they beat West Ham United 5-1 three days later. This meant that they had only to avoid a two-goal defeat at home to Arsenal in their final match three days after that to retain the League Championship. But Michael Thomas, last to play for Liverpool, grabbed an injury time goal to give Arsenal victory and the title.

The Gunners beat Liverpool again in the Makita Tournament final at Wembley two months later.

Everton: Southall, McDonald, Van den Hauwe, Ratcliffe – capt, Watson, Nevin, Steven, Bracewell, Sharp, Cottee, Sheedy. subs: McCall for Bracewell 58, Wilson (I) for Sheedy 77. manager: Colin Harvey

Liverpool: Grobbelaar, Nicol, Ablett, Staunton, Whelan – capt, Hansen, Beardsley, Aldridge, Houghton, Barnes, McMahon. subs: Rush for Aldridge 72, Venison for Staunton 91. manager: Kenny Dalglish

Women's International

Tuesday 23rd May 1989

England 0
Sweden 2
Sundhage 7, Videkull 64
Referee: B Hill (Kettering)

Defeat for England women on their first appearance at Wembley. Sweden's first goal was scored by Pia Sundhage who went on to win 146 international caps. England's goalkeeper Theresa Wiseman was winning her 50th cap. This game was watched by around 3,000 people and was followed by

an international involving England's male counterparts.

England returned to Wembley the following year, to play an international against Italy prior to the FA Charity Shield.

England: Wiseman, Broadhurst, Murray, Bampton, Sherrard, Sempare, Powell, Coulthard, Spacey, Davis, Stanley. subs: Harper for Murray 49, Curl for Spacey 54, Davidson for Wiseman 69, Walker for Davis 73

Sweden: Leidinge, Fors, Hansson, Zeikfalvy, Persson, Johansson (I), Karlsson, Sundhage, Johansson (H), Videkull, Kalte. subs: Hultin for Kalte 54, Swedberg for Persson 55, Syren for Hansson 56, Andersson for Karlsson 63

ROUS CUP

Tuesday 23rd May 1989

England   0-0   **Chile**

15,628

Referee: E Fredriksson (Sweden)

England were aiming to become the first team to retain the Rous Cup against a team appearing at Wembley for the first time. The last meeting between the two countries had been a goalless draw in Santiago in 1984, but England had won their two earlier meetings.

In front of a record low attendance for a Wembley international, Chile used every possible opportunity to disrupt England's flow and entertainment was in short supply.

This match did little for the image of the Rous Cup and turned out to be the last at Wembley. Four days later England beat Scotland 2-0 at Hampden Park and Scotland's subsequent 2-0 victory against Chile at the same venue gave England the last Rous Cup.

Chile returned to Wembley in 1998.

England: Shilton (Derby County), Parker (QPR), Pearce (Nottingham F), Webb (Nottingham F), Walker (Nottingham F), Butcher (Rangers), Robson (Man Utd) – capt, Gascoigne (Tottenham), Clough* (Nottingham F), Fashanu* (Wimbledon), Waddle (Tottenham). sub: Cottee (Everton) for Fashanu 71. manager: Bobby Robson
*first cap

Chile: Rojas (Sao Paulo) – capt, Reyes (Universidad de Chile), Hurtado (Universidad Catolica), Contreras (La Serena), Gonzalez (Colo Colo), Pizarro (Colo Colo), Rubio (Bologna), Ormeno (Colo Colo), Espinoza (Colo Colo), Covarrubias (Cobreloa), Astengo (Gremio). subs: Letelier (Cobreloa) for Covarrubias 46, Vera (OFI Crete) for Hurtado 60. coach: Orlando Aravena

Sherpa Van Trophy Final

Sunday 28th May 1989

Bolton Wanderers 4

Darby, Chandler, Crombie, Morgan

Torquay United 1

Edwards

46,513

Referee: G Courtney (Spennymoor)

Bolton recovered from a goal down to lift the Trophy in style. Torquay had knocked out the holders and runaway Third Division Champions Wolverhampton Wanderers after losing the home leg of their semi-final. The previous year, Bolton had pipped Torquay by a point to win promotion straight back to the Third Division after relegation a year earlier. In the mid-1980s, Torquay had finished bottom of the Football League in consecutive years and then escaped relegation on goal difference in 1987, with an injury-time equaliser in their last match. They had recovered to reach the Fourth Division Promotion play-off final, a year later. Torquay lost to Swansea City, but were to win promotion at Wembley in 1991.

Bolton: Felgate, Brown – capt, Cowdrill, Savage, Crombie, Winstanley, Chandler, Thompson, Thomas, Morgan, Darby. sub: Storer for Chandler. manager: Phil Neal
Torquay: Allen, Pugh, Kelly, McNicol, Elliott, Loram, Airey, Lloyd, Edwards, Weston, Morrison. subs: Smith for Airey, Joyce for Weston. manager: Cyril Knowles

WORLD CUP QUALIFYING

Saturday 3rd June 1989

England   3-0   **Poland**

Lineker 24, Barnes 69, Webb 82

69,203

Referee: L Agnolin (Italy)

This was Poland's first visit to Wembley since knocking England out of the World Cup in 1973. Since then, they had twice finished third in the World Cup, but England had gained their revenge with a 3-0 win in Monterrey in the 1986 World Cup. Poland had never previously lost in England.

This was England's last home match in

Group Two, which they led on goal difference from Sweden. Poland were three points behind with a game in hand after losing in Stockholm the previous month.

England dominated the early play and scored when Gary Lineker took a pass from Barnes. His first shot was blocked by Lukasik and Bako, but he stretched to convert the rebound from a seemingly impossible angle.

With 21 minutes left, a superb cross from Stevens eluded the Polish defence and John Barnes volleyed in at the far post. England wrapped up the points when Lineker intercepted Wojcicki's back pass and passed to substitute Rocastle. The 'keeper got a touch to Rocastle's attempted cross to the other substitute Smith. Matysik also got a touch, but the ball ran through leaving Neil Webb with an open goal.

Two goalless draws in Stockholm and Chorzow meant England completed the group four months later without conceding a goal, but it was Sweden who won the group by winning in Chorzow two weeks after England's draw there.

England qualified with eventual winners West Germany as the best runners-up in the groups with four teams. Poland were eliminated when they drew with England, but they were back at Wembley the following year in the European Championship.

England: Shilton (Derby County), Stevens (Rangers), Pearce (Nottingham F), Webb (Nottingham F), Walker (Nottingham F), Butcher (Rangers), Robson (Man Utd) – capt, Waddle (Tottenham), Beardsley (Liverpool), Lineker (Barcelona) – capt, Barnes (Liverpool). subs: Rocastle (Arsenal) for Waddle 75, Smith (Arsenal) for Beardsley 75. manager: Bobby Robson

Poland: Bako (LKS Lodz), Wijas (GKS Katowice), Wojcicki (Hamburg), Wdowczyk (Legia Warsaw), Lukasik (Lech Poznan), Matysik (Auxerre), Prusik (Slask Wroclaw) – capt, Urban (Gornik Zabrze), Furtok (Hamburg), Warzycha (K) (Ruch Chorzow), Lesniak (Bayer Leverkusen). subs: Kosecki (Legia Warsaw) for Lesniak 58, Tarasiewicz (Slask Wroclaw) for Urban 70. coach: Wojciech Lazarek

Final table	P	W	D	L	F	A	pts
Sweden	6	4	2	0	9	3	10
England	6	3	3	0	10	0	9
Poland	6	2	1	3	4	8	5
Albania	6	0	0	6	3	15	0

Schoolboy International

Saturday 10th June 1989

England 1
Mike 22
West Germany 3
Nowotny 3, Thiele pen 39, Reis 73
Referee: P Foakes (Essex)

The Germans' fourth win in seven visits to Wembley.

England: Thomson, Foster, Basham, Hall, Wilson – capt, Marlowe, Mike, Barmby, Lee, Durrant, Read. subs: Brocklehurst for Lee, Harriott for Durrant, Charlton for Read

Makita Tournament

Wembley's international club tournament was sponsored for the first time and changed to a simple knockout format.

Semi-finals

Saturday 29th July 1989

Arsenal 1
Demol og 42
Porto 0
Referee: J Worrall (Cheshire)

Two years earlier, Porto had become the first Portuguese team to win the European Cup for 25 years, coming from behind to defeat Bayern Munich in Vienna. They had gone on to win both the European Super Cup and the World Club Championship. But after three Portuguese League Championships in four years they had finished runners-up to Benfica and now lost to the holders and England's League Champions by a first-half own goal. A disappointing attendance of 20,374 was recorded for both semi-finals.

Arsenal: Lukic, Dixon, Winterburn, Thomas, O'Leary, Adams – capt, Rocastle, Richardson, Smith (A), Bould, Merson. sub: Hayes for Rocastle, Campbell for Smith. manager: George Graham

Porto: Baia, Pinto – capt, Bandeirinma, Demol, Pereira, Moraio, Magalhaes, Madjer, Marito, Couto, Andre. coach: Artur Jorge

Dynamo Kiev 0

Liverpool 2

Barnes pen 62, Aldridge 69
Referee: N Midgley (Lancashire)

Dynamo Kiev had finished as Soviet League runners-up to Dnepr Dnepropetrovsk the previous year and had qualified for the UEFA Cup, but they were defeated by the FA Cup holders.

Dynamo Kiev: Chanov, Bessonov, Zaets, Kuznetsov, Schmatovalenko, Rats, Gorily, Litovchenko, Yaremchuk, Luzhny, Belanov. subs: Kanchelskis, Salenko. coach: Valeri Lobanovsky
Liverpool: Grobbelaar, Venison, Burrows, Nicol, Whelan – capt, Hansen, Beardsley, Houghton, Rush, Barnes, McMahon. subs: Aldridge for Beardsley 67, Molby for McMahon 67. manager: Kenny Dalglish

Third And Fourth Place

Sunday 30th July 1989

Dynamo Kiev 1

Kanchelskis 38

Porto 0

Referee: K Hackett (Sheffield)

Revenge for Dynamo Kiev, who had lost to Porto in the European Cup semi-finals two years earlier. Andrei Kanchelskis, who scored the only goal, was in Manchester United's 'double' winning side in 1994. Kiev finished third in the Soviet League, while both clubs reached the last 16 of the UEFA Cup, Kiev losing to eventual finalists Fiorentina. Porto regained the Portuguese League Championship.

Final

Sunday 30th July 1989

Arsenal 1

Bould 13

Liverpool 0

23,026
Referee: G Courtney (Durham)

A rehearsal for the FA Charity Shield two weeks later, with Arsenal winning their fourth out of five Wembley meetings with Liverpool to retain the trophy. For the second year in succession, they had not conceded a goal but it was too early in the season to read much into it. The following year they would return to go for the hat-trick.

Arsenal: Lukic, Dixon, Winterburn, Thomas, O'Leary, Adams – capt, Rocastle, Richardson, Smith (A), Bould, Merson. subs: Caesar for Winterburn 46, Hayes for Bould 90. manager: George Graham
Liverpool: Grobbelaar, Venison, Burrows, Nicol, Whelan – capt, Gillespie, Ablett, Aldridge, Molby, Barnes, McMahon. subs: Rush for McMahon 46, Beardsley for Aldridge 69. manager: Kenny Dalglish

U-16 International

Saturday 12th August 1989

England 2

Newcombe, Nguyen

Scandinavia 1

Benediktsson

England had won the Vauxhall Nordic Cup for the first time the previous day and their opponents were selected from four of the countries they had been competing with over the previous week. The combined efforts of Denmark, Finland, Iceland and Sweden could not overcome their hosts just as the individual countries had failed to do so. This was England's sixth game in eight days.

England: Foster, Fancutt, Hughes, Basham, Harriott, Caskey, Newcombe, Berry, Nguyen, Barmby, Myers. subs: Stephenson for Foster, Jackson for Fancutt, Everingham for Hughes, Burke for Berry, Lee for Myers

FA CHARITY SHIELD

Saturday 12th August 1989

Arsenal	0-1	**Liverpool**
		Beardsley 32

63,149
Referee: A Gunn (Sussex)

Two weeks after the Makita Tournament final, these two teams met for the sixth time at Wembley. Arsenal had won four, but Liverpool had won the 1979 FA Charity Shield, now sponsored by Tennent's. In their last major final, Arsenal had come from behind to win the 1987 Littlewoods Cup. Arsenal had also won the Football League Centenary Trophy, beating Liverpool in the semi-finals, as well as retaining the Makita Tournament.

Liverpool's League Championship defeat three months earlier came as a big shock at the end of a traumatic season in which they had witnessed a second major disaster in the late 1980's. Six days before their title defeat they had won an exciting FA Cup final. Earlier in the season, they had beaten Arsenal in the Littlewoods Cup in a tie which went to three games. Liverpool were the holders of the Charity Shield, having come from behind to beat Wimbledon the previous year. They were now chasing a record 12th Shield.

The only goal came in the 33rd minute. Peter Beardsley collected Venison's cross and had time to steady himself before firing the winner past Lukic. For the second year in succession, Liverpool had used the Charity Shield to gain their revenge on the team which had denied them the 'double'.

Arsenal gained their revenge over Liverpool in the Littlewoods Cup. They returned to Wembley, the following year, to chase a hat-trick of Makita Tournament wins and in 1991 took part in Wembley's first FA Cup semi-final. Liverpool regained the League Championship and, once again, threatened to win the 'double'. But their defence of the FA Cup ended in the semi-finals. They were back at Wembley chasing a hat-trick of Charity Shields, the following year.

Arsenal: Lukic, Dixon, Winterburn, Thomas, O'Leary, Adams – capt, Rocastle, Richardson, Smith (A), Caesar, Merson. subs: Marwood for Caesar 60, Quinn for Smith 79. manager: George Graham

Liverpool: Grobbelaar, Hysen, Burrows, Nicol, Whelan, Hansen – capt, Beardsley, Venison, Rush, Barnes, McMahon. manager: Kenny Dalglish

INTERNATIONAL

Wednesday 15th November 1989

England   0-0   **Italy**
67,500
Referee: H Forstinger (Austria)

Italy had lost at Wembley for the first time on their last visit in 1977 but they had beaten England twice since then.

There were too few goalscoring chances to excite the crowd and England were involved in their third successive goalless draw. At half-time, Beasant replaced Shilton to make his international debut in goal.

They met again the following year, in the World Cup third and fourth place in Bari. Both had lost semi-finals on penalties. Italy took third place with a 2-1 victory. They

did not appear at Wembley again until a World Cup Qualifying match in 1997.

Italian substitute, Roberto Baggio made his first appearance at Wembley. In 1993 he was European Footballer of the Year. The following year his goals took Italy to the World Cup final in Los Angeles, but his penalty miss gave the trophy to Brazil.

Gianluca Vialli joined Chelsea in 1996 and was manager when they won the last FA Cup final beneath the twin towers, in 2000.

England: Shilton (Derby County), Stevens (Rangers), Pearce (Nottingham F), McMahon (Liverpool), Walker (Nottingham F), Butcher (Rangers), Robson (Man Utd) – capt, Waddle (Olympique Marseille), Beardsley (Liverpool), Lineker (Tottenham), Barnes (Liverpool). subs: Beasant* (Chelsea) for Shilton 46, Phelan* (Man Utd) for Robson 46, Winterburn* (Arsenal) for Pearce 67, Hodge (Nottingham F) for McMahon 67, Platt* (Aston Villa) for Beardsley 78. manager: Bobby Robson
*first cap

Italy: Zenga (Internazionale), Bergomi (Internazionale) – capt, Maldini (AC Milan), Baresi (AC Milan), Ferri (Internazionale), Berti (Internazionale), Donadoni (AC Milan), De Napoli (Napoli), Vialli (Sampdoria), Giannini (Roma), Carnevale (Napoli). subs: Serena (Internazionale) for Carnevale 76, Baggio (Fiorentina) for Vialli 82. coach: Azeglio Vicini

INTERNATIONAL

Wednesday 13th December 1989

England	**2-1**	**Yugoslavia**
Robson 1, 70		Skoro 17

34,796

Referee: D Pauly (West Germany)

England had beaten Yugoslavia at Wembley and in Belgrade in qualifying for the previous year's European Championship, and like England they had qualified for the following year's World Cup without defeat.

After three goalless matches, England scored after 38 seconds. It was the quickest international goal ever scored at Wembley. From Waddle's free kick, Bryan Robson's header went under the 'keeper. Robson had scored England's fastest ever World Cup goal in 1982.

The visitors equalised in the 18th minute. Haris Skoro took a pass from Susic and beat Shilton from 25 yards. It was the first goal in England's net in seven Wembley matches. For the second match in succession, Beasant replaced Shilton at half-time. England restored their lead in the 71st minute. Parker played a one-two with Lineker and crossed. Bull back-heeled it into the path of Robson, who drove it into the corner for his second.

Yugoslavia never played England again.

England: Shilton (Derby County), Parker (QPR), Pearce (Nottingham F), Thomas (Arsenal), Walker (Nottingham F), Butcher (Rangers), Robson (Man Utd) – capt, Rocastle (Arsenal), Bull (Wolves), Lineker (Tottenham), Waddle (Olympique Marseille). subs: Beasant (Chelsea) for Shilton 46, Dorigo* (Chelsea) for Pearce 46, Platt (Aston Villa) for Thomas 67, Hodge (Nottingham F) for Rocastle 67, McMahon (Liverpool) for Robson 75. manager: Bobby Robson *first cap

Yugoslavia: Ivkovic (Sporting Lisbon), Stanojkovic (Partizan Belgrade), Spasic (Partizan), Brnovic (Metz), Hadzibegic (Sochaux) – capt, Vulic (Real Mallorca), Skoro (Torino), Susic (Paris Saint-Germain), Mihajlovic (Bayern Munich), Stojkovic (Red Star Belgrade), Savevski (AEK Athens). subs: Panadic (Dinamo Zagreb) for Brnovic 75, Prosinecki (Red Star) for Susic 75, Petric (Partizan) for Spasic 80. coach: Ivica Osim

Schoolboy International

Saturday 10th March 1990

England 1
Forrester 4

France 1
Bedrossian 55

Referee: I Bogart

France's first visit for twelve years earned them a share of the spoils.

England substitute, Nicky Butt made his Wembley debut and went on to become a member of Manchester United's 'treble' winning side in 1999.

Kevin Sharp, captain when England next played at Wembley three months later, became one of the few players to be sent off at the stadium while playing for Wigan Athletic in the Second Division play-off final in 2000.

England: Reeves, Turner, Tinkler – capt, Pugh, Brydon, Boachie, Sharp, Smith, Clarke, Binks, Forrester. subs: Dichio for Boachie, Cotterell for Clarke, Butt for Binks

Zenith Cup Final

Sunday 25th March 1990

Chelsea 1
Dorigo 25

Middlesbrough 0
76,369

Referee: R Milford (Bristol)

Chelsea had won the first Full Members Cup, now sponsored by Zenith Data Systems, four years earlier, in a nine-goal thriller. Middlesbrough had never been beyond the quarter-finals before and were making their Wembley debut.

'Boro had sacked manager Bruce Rioch only two weeks earlier, his assistant, Colin Todd replacing him. But their injured club captain, Tony Mowbray, led them out at Wembley. The Simod Cup had been replaced by the Zenith Cup and the competition had reverted back to northern and southern sections. There were three more exemptions than the previous year.

Wembley was now all seated and saw a spectacular winning goal. Chelsea won a free kick 25 yards out, and Tony Dorigo curled it round the Middlesbrough wall. Pears got a hand to it but could not keep it out.

Chelsea returned to Wembley for the FA Cup semi-final in 1994. Middlesbrough reached the Coca-Cola Cup final in 1997.

Chelsea: Beasant, Hall, Dorigo, Bumstead, Johnsen, Monkou, McAllister, Nicholas – capt, Dixon, Durie, Wilson (K). subs: Lee, Wilson (C) (not used). manager: Bobby Campbell

Middlesbrough: Pears, Parkinson, Cooper, Kernaghan, Coleman, McGee, Slaven, Proctor – capt, Ripley, Brennan, Davenport. subs: Kerr, Mohan (not used). manager: Colin Todd

Youth International

Wednesday 28th March 1990

England 0
Denmark 0
Referee: B Hill (Northamptonshire)

Wembley's first Under-18 International for 27 years failed to produce a goal in the curtain-raiser to the full international.

England: Walker (Tottenham), Hendon (Tottenham), Minto (Charlton), Hayward (Derby County), Tuttle (Tottenham), Awford (Portsmouth), Houghton (Tottenham), Rouse (Rangers), Cole (Arsenal), Harkness (Liverpool), Small (Aston Villa). subs: Clark (Newcastle) for Hayward, Newhouse (Wimbledon) for Cole. manager: Dave Burnside

INTERNATIONAL

Wednesday 28th March 1990

England	1-0	Brazil

Lineker 36
80,000
Referee: K Peschel (East Germany)

Brazil were South American Champions for the first time in 40 years and like England they had qualified for the forthcoming World Cup without defeat. Their last visit three years earlier had seen the points shared in a Rous Cup match with Brazil going on to win the trophy. They had avoided defeat on their last four trips to Wembley after losing the first back in 1956. England's only other win had been in 1984 in Rio de Janeiro.

For the third international in succession, Shilton did not make it to the second half, but this time he went off injured in the 12th minute after an accidental clash of heads with Walker. Woods proved a very able deputy and England scored after 36 minutes. Barnes, winning his 50th cap, headed on Beardsley's corner and Gary Lineker stooped to head home from close range. Midway through the second half, substitute Muller rounded Woods and Pearce blocked the ball on the line with his hand, but the referee failed to spot it and Brazil were denied a certain penalty.

Brazil were back at Wembley in 1992.

England: Shilton (Derby County), Stevens (Rangers), Pearce (Nottingham F), McMahon (Liverpool), Walker (Nottingham F), Butcher (Rangers) – capt, Platt (Aston Villa), Waddle (Olympique Marseille), Beardsley (Liverpool), Lineker (Tottenham), Barnes (Liverpool). subs: Woods (Rangers) for Shilton 11, Gascoigne (Tottenham) for Beardsley 78. manager: Bobby Robson

Brazil: Taffarel (Internacional), Jorginho (Montpellier), Mozer (Olympique Marseille), Galvao (Botafogo), Branco (Porto), Ricardo Gomes (Benfica) – capt, Bebeto (Vasco da Gama), Dunga (Fiorentina), Careca (Napoli), Silas (Sporting Lisbon), Valdo (Benfica). subs: Alemao (Napoli) for Silas 46, Muller (Torino) for Bebeto 64, Aldair (Benfica) for Mozer 79, Bismarck (Vasco da Gama) for Valdo 79. coach: Sebastiao Lazaroni

Youth International

Wednesday 25th April 1990

England 1
Cole

Czechoslovakia 1
unknown
Referee: A Gunn (Sussex)

Andrew Cole added to his Schoolboy goals at Wembley three years earlier.

England: Walker (Tottenham), Hendon (Tottenham), Ullathorne (Norwich), Hayward (Derby County), Tuttle (Tottenham), Awford (Portsmouth), Houghton (Tottenham), Rouse (Rangers), Cole (Arsenal), Harkness (Liverpool), Small (Aston Villa). sub: Taylor (Wolves) for Ullathorne.

INTERNATIONAL

Wednesday 25th April 1990

England   **4-2**   **Czechoslovakia**
Bull 18, 55, Pearce 23, Gascoigne 89   Skuhravy 10, Kubik 81
21,342
Referee: M Girard (France)

After losing at Wembley in 1978, the then European Champions Czechoslovakia had gone into decline. They finished third in the 1980 European Championships and lost to England in the 1982 World Cup, their last major tournament. Now they were threatening a comeback after qualifying for the forthcoming World Cup.

Czechoslovakia scored their first goal in four appearances at Wembley when an inch-perfect cross from Knoflicek was headed in by Tomas Skuhravy from between Butcher and Walker. Seven minutes later, Gascoigne dropped a superb pass onto the chest of Steve Bull who hammered it into the net for the equaliser.

England then took the lead from Gascoigne's corner. West Ham goalkeeper, Miklosko came for it, but Kocian had already beaten Butcher to head it back to the far post. Lineker was crowded out by Kubik and Hasek, who could only back-head it to Stuart Pearce and the full-back drove it through Bielik's legs on the line.

At half-time, Seaman went in goal as Shilton was replaced for the fourth successive international, despite it being his 50th Wembley appearance for England.

England scored again, and again it was Gascoigne who created it. A powerful run and cross ended with Bull rising majestically, although virtually unchallenged, to give Miklosko no chance with his second. England were now brimming with confidence, but it was the Czechs who hit back with nine minutes left. Lubos Kubik's free kick was curled around the England wall and beyond Seaman's reach into the corner. But with a minute to go, Paul Gascoigne took a pass from substitute Dorigo and, with an electrifying burst of speed, ran through the Czech defence to put the seal on an immaculate performance by firing home England's fourth.

Two years later, England drew 2-2 with the Czechs in Prague, their last meeting before the country split into the Czech Republic and Slovakia.

England: Shilton (Derby County), Dixon* (Arsenal), Pearce (Nottingham F), Steven (Rangers), Walker (Nottingham F), Butcher (Rangers), Robson (Man Utd) – capt, Gascoigne (Tottenham), Bull (Wolves), Lineker (Tottenham), Hodge (Nottingham F). subs: Seaman (QPR) for Shilton 46, Dorigo (Chelsea) for Pearce 46, Wright (Derby County) for Walker 46, McMahon (Liverpool) for Robson 75. manager: Bobby Robson
*first cap
Czechoslovakia: Miklosko (West Ham), Bielik (Sparta Prague), Straka (Borussia Monchengladbach), Hasek (Sparta Prague) – capt, Kocian (St. Pauli), Kinier (Slovan Bratislava), Bilek (Sparta Prague), Kubik (Fiorentina), Knoflicek (St. Pauli), Skuhravy (Sparta Prague), Moravcik (Nitra). subs: Griga (Feyenoord) for Knoflicek 60, Kadlec (Vitkovice) for Straka 68, Weiss (Inter Bratislava) for Skuhravy 71. coach: Josef Venglos

LEAGUE CUP FINAL

Sunday 29th April 1990

Nottingham Forest   **1-0**   **Oldham Athletic**
Jemson 48
74,343
Referee: J Martin (near Alton)

Forest were the holders and were aiming to equal Liverpool's record of four League Cup wins, although in the last two finals the holders had lost each time. Forest had come from behind to win the Littlewoods Cup the previous year and had followed it

with the Simod Cup three weeks later. It had taken Oldham 28 years to reach the last 16 of the competition and now, two years later, they had reached Wembley for the first time. Oldham had become the first Second Division club since West Ham

United in 1981 to reach the final.

Forest were having a mediocre league season, but Oldham still harboured ambitions of reaching the play-offs for the first time since 1987. They had also reached the FA Cup semi-finals and twice took eventual winners Manchester United to extra time.

The holders scored the only goal in the third minute of the second half. Clough took Warhurst away from the middle, then played the ball back in, leaving Nigel Jemson with a clear run at goal. Rhodes blocked his shot with his legs, but Jemson was there to convert the rebound.

Forest reached the FA Cup final the following year. Oldham next appeared at Wembley in the FA Cup semi-final in 1994.

Nottingham F: Sutton, Laws, Pearce – capt, Walker, Chettle, Hodge, Crosby, Parker, Clough, Jemson, Carr. subs: Gaynor, Wilson (Te) (not used). manager: Brian Clough
Oldham: Rhodes, Irwin, Barlow, Henry, Barrett, Warhurst, Adams, Ritchie, Bunn, Milligan – capt, Holden. subs: Palmer for Bunn 68, Williams (not used). manager: Joe Royle

FA Vase Final

Saturday 5th May 1990

Bridlington Town 0
Yeading 0
After extra time
7,932
Referee: R Groves (Weston-super-Mare)

The first goalless FA Vase final and defences were again on top in the replay, with only Paul Sweales making the scoresheet.

Bridlington: Taylor, Pugh, Freeman, McNeil, Warburton, Brentano, Wilkes, Noteman, Gauden, Whiteman, Brattan. subs: Hall for Wilkes, Brown for Brattan
Yeading: Mackenzie, Wickens, Turner, Whiskey, Croad – capt, Denton, Matthews, James, Sweales, Impey, Cordery. subs: McCarthy for Whiskey, Charles for James

Replay: Monday 14th May 1990
Bridlington Town 0
Yeading 1
Sweales
(Elland Road, Leeds)

FA CUP FINAL

Saturday 12th May 1990

Crystal Palace   **3-3**   **Manchester United**
O'Reilly 18, Wright 69, 91   Robson 35, Hughes 61, 112
After extra time
80,000
Referee: A Gunn (South Chailey)

Palace had beaten the holders and eventual League Champions Liverpool to reach their first final. Their only previous appearances at Wembley had been, briefly, in the Football League Centenary Tournament in 1988. United were aiming to equal the record of seven FA Cup wins set by Aston Villa and equalled by Tottenham Hotspur. They had won the trophy twice in the 1980's, but in the past five years they had found little success, losing the 1985 FA Charity Shield, reaching the semi-finals of the Football League Centenary Tournament in 1988 and finishing as League runners-up, the same year, to Liverpool.

Palace had won promotion the previous year by winning the play-offs with an extra-time winner against Blackburn Rovers.

It was Palace who struck first. Barber's free kick was headed in off Pallister's head by Gary O'Reilly as Leighton came out too far. United equalised ten minutes before the break. McClair crossed and Bryan Robson's header was deflected past Martyn at the near post by Pemberton. United were fortunate again when they took the lead. Webb blocked Thorn's attempted clearance and it fell for Mark Hughes who gave Martyn no chance with his shot.

United appeared to have it won, but eight minutes later Palace struck back. From Bright's pass, Ian Wright, on as substitute just three minutes earlier, raced away between Phelan and Pallister. Shrugging off Phelan's lunge, he wrong-footed Pallister and strode on to blast the equaliser past Leighton.

Extra time produced more thrills. After only a minute, Salako's cross left Leighton in no man's land again and Wright charged in to volley Palace back in front. Now the pendulum swung Palace's way, but with only seven minutes remaining Hughes ran on to Wallace's pass and tucked it into the corner past the advancing Martyn as O'Reilly challenged.

Crystal Palace: Martyn, Pemberton, Shaw, Gray, O'Reilly, Thorn, Barber, Thomas – capt, Bright, Salako, Pardew. subs: Wright for Barber 69, Madden for Gray 117. manager: Steve Coppell
Manchester U: Leighton, Ince, Martin, Bruce, Phelan, Pallister, Robson – capt, Webb, McClair, Hughes, Wallace. subs: Blackmore for Martin 88, Robins for Pallister 93. manager: Alex Ferguson

Youth International

Tuesday 15th May 1990

England 3
Harkness, Houghton, Newhouse

Poland 0
Referee: D Axcell (Essex)

A convincing victory for the youngsters.

England: Walker (Tottenham), Hendon (Tottenham), Titterton (Coventry), Hayward (Derby County), Tuttle (Tottenham), Awford (Portsmouth), Houghton (Tottenham), Rouse (Rangers), Cole (Arsenal), Newhouse (Wimbledon), Harkness (Liverpool). subs: Livingstone (Aston Villa) for Walker, Honeywood (Ipswich) for Hendon, Small (Aston Villa) for Houghton, Burnett (Leyton Orient) for Rouse, Taylor (Wolves) for Cole. manager: Dave Burnside

INTERNATIONAL

Tuesday 15th May 1990

England   **1-0**   **Denmark**
Lineker 54
27,643
Referee: J McCluskey (Scotland)

Denmark's three previous visits to Wembley had all resulted in 1-0 scorelines. Two were in England's favour (in 1979 and 1988), with Denmark winning a European Championship match in 1983. This was their third meeting in two years. They had drawn 1-1 in Copenhagen the previous year.

Nine minutes into the second half, Barnes took a quick free kick to Hodge who whipped in a low cross. Gary Lineker beat Aston Villa's Nielsen to it and stabbed it against the underside of the bar and in to give victory. Chris Waddle won his 50th cap, while Woods replaced Shilton at half-time in England's fifth successive goalkeeping substitution.

Denmark returned to Wembley in 1994 to again lose 1-0.

England: Shilton (Derby County), Stevens (Rangers), Pearce (Nottingham F), McMahon (Liverpool), Walker (Nottingham F), Butcher (Rangers) – capt, Hodge (Nottingham F), Gascoigne (Tottenham), Waddle (Olympique Marseille), Lineker (Tottenham), Barnes (Liverpool). subs: Woods (Rangers) for Shilton 46, Dorigo (Chelsea) for Pearce 46, Rocastle (Arsenal) for Waddle 70, Bull (Wolves) for Lineker 70, Platt (Aston Villa) for McMahon 77. manager: Bobby Robson
Denmark: Schmeichel (Brondby), Sivebaek (Saint-Etienne), Nielsen (Aston Villa), Olsen (Brondby) – capt, Andersen (Anderlecht), Bartram (Bayer Uerdingen), Jensen (Brondby), Vilfort (Brondby), Povlsen (PSV Eindhoven), Laudrup (M) (Barcelona), Laudrup (B) (Bayer Uerdingen). subs: Bruun (Silkeborg) for Povlsen 70, Jakobsen (Odense) for Laudrup (M) 70. coach: Richard Moller Nielsen

FA CUP FINAL REPLAY

Thursday 17th May 1990

Crystal Palace   **0-1**   **Manchester United**
                                              Martin 59

80,000
Referee: A Gunn (South Chailey)

Five days earlier, the lead had changed hands three times with United goalkeeper, Jim Leighton being blamed for two of Palace's goals. He was dropped and never played for United again. His replacement Les Sealey, on loan from Luton Town, was making only his third appearance.

Palace tried to unnerve him in the opening exchanges with some physical challenges, but the goalkeeper shrugged them off and gave a faultless display.

The only goal came when Lee Martin, substituted in the first game, charged into the box with Gray in pursuit. He took Webb's pass on his chest and blasted the winner into the roof of the net. This time Wright could not make the same impact and United were worthy winners as they equalled the FA Cup record.

The following year, Palace won the Zenith Cup at Wembley. For United, it was the beginning of a glorious run of success. Two months later, the ban on English clubs in European competitions was lifted, and United, who had missed out in 1985, when they last won the FA Cup, appropriately took part in and amazingly won the European Cup-Winners Cup.

Crystal Palace: Martyn, Pemberton, Shaw, Gray, O'Reilly, Thorn, Barber, Thomas – capt, Bright, Salako, Pardew. subs: Wright for Barber 64, Madden for Salako 79. manager: Steve Coppell

Manchester U: Sealey, Ince, Martin, Bruce, Phelan, Pallister, Robson – capt, Webb, McClair, Hughes, Wallace. subs: Blackmore, Robins (not used). manager: Alex Ferguson

FA Trophy Final

Saturday 19th May 1990

Barrow 3
Gordon 45, 60, Cowperthwaite 57

Leek Town 0
19,011
Referee: T Simpson (Halifax)

Barrow served notice that they intended to regain the Football League status they had lost in 1972. Kenny Gordon scored twice in his last match before emigrating to Australia.

Barrow: McDonnell, Higgins, Chilton, Skivington, Gordon, Proctor, Doherty, Farrell, Cowperthwaite, Lowe, Ferris. subs: Burgess for Doherty, Gilmore for Farrell
Leek: Simpson, Elsby, Pearce, McMullen, Clowes – capt, Coleman, Mellor, Somerville, Sutton, Millington, Norris. subs: Russell for Coleman 59, Smith for Elsby 61

Leyland DAF Cup Final

Sunday 20th May 1990

Bristol Rovers 1
White

Tranmere Rovers 2
Muir, Steel
48,402
Referee: V Callow (Solihull)

The Associate Members Cup had acquired its fourth different name. Bristol Rovers had won the Third Division Championship to return to the Second Division for the first time since 1981, despite playing all their home games at Bath.

Tranmere were the sensations of the Football League Centenary Tournament and Ian Muir, who scored three goals then, set them on their way to a surprise victory. They would have swapped it, however, for a win the following week when they were beaten in the Third Division play-off final.

Bristol R: Parkin, Alexander, Twentyman, Yates, Mehew, Jones – capt, Holloway, Reece, White, Saunders, Purnell. subs: Nixon for Alexander, McClean for Purnell. manager: Gerry Francis
Tranmere: Nixon, Garnett, Mungall, McNab, Hughes, Vickers, Malkin, Harvey – capt, Steel, Muir, Thomas. manager: John King

U-17 International

Tuesday 22nd May 1990

England 1
Clark

France 3
Cassese, Williams o.g., Rabesandratana
Referee: J Moules (Kent)

Despite Lee Clark's fifth goal in four Wembley appearances, England fell to three goals in a four-minute second half spell.

Jamie Redknapp won 17 full caps for England and was in the Liverpool side, which won the Coca-Cola Cup in 1995.

England: Livingstone (Aston Villa), Hancock (West Ham), Fowler (Arsenal), Makin (Oldham), Webster (Arsenal), Flitcroft (Man City), Flatts (Arsenal), Sinclair (Blackpool), Morah (Tottenham), Clark (Newcastle), Doling (Portsmouth). subs: Stanger (Man Utd) for Livingstone, Burton (Sheffield W) for Webster. Williams (Aston Villa) for Flitcroft, Thompson (Ipswich) for Morah, Redknapp (Bournemouth) for Williams

INTERNATIONAL

Tuesday 22nd May 1990

England   **1-2**   **Uruguay**
Barnes 50   Ostolaza 26, Perdomo 61
38,751
Referee: P D'Elia (Italy)

This was England's last home match before the World Cup. Uruguay had not visited England since the 1966 World Cup, when they were involved in two goalless draws at Wembley, against England and Mexico, on their way to the quarter-finals. England won in Montevideo in 1969, but lost there in 1984, their last meeting.

England, in new-style red shirts, were shocked by a Uruguayan goal in the 27th minute. Alzamendi's cross was headed in by Santiago Ostolaza. John Barnes scored a stunning equaliser after 50 minutes.

Taking a cross from Pearce on his chest, he gave Pereira no chance with a superb shot. Uruguay broke again 11 minutes later, though, and Jose Perdomo converted a free kick. Gary Lineker failed to make the scoresheet to mark his 50th cap and England lost for the first time since the 1988 European Championship in Bobby Robson's last home match as manager.

Uruguay reached the last 16 of the World Cup again, before losing to the hosts, Italy. England were to reach the semi-finals. Five years later, Uruguay returned to Wembley.

England: Shilton (Derby County), Parker (QPR), Pearce (Nottingham F), Hodge (Nottingham F), Walker (Nottingham F), Butcher (Rangers), Robson (Man Utd) – capt, Gascoigne (Tottenham), Waddle (Olympique Marseille), Lineker (Tottenham), Barnes (Liverpool). subs: Beardsley (Liverpool) for Hodge 77, Bull (Wolves) for Lineker 77. manager: Bobby Robson
Uruguay: Pereira (Nacional), Gutierrez (Verona), De Leon (River Plate), Herrera (Figueras), Perdomo (Genoa), Dominguez (Penarol), Alzamendi (Logrones), Ostolaza (Nacional), Francescoli (Olympique Marseille) – capt, Paz (Genoa), Sosa (Lazio). sub: Martinez (Defensor) for Sosa 80. coach: Oscar Tabarez

Play-off Finals

Fourth Division

Saturday 26th May 1990

Cambridge United 1
Dublin 77
Chesterfield 0
26,404
Referee: G Courtney (Spennymoor)

For the fourth year in succession the club finishing sixth in the Fourth Division won promotion. Cambridge had also equalled the Fourth Division record by reaching the FA Cup quarter-finals. They had missed out on the play-offs by three points, the previous year, as Chesterfield were relegated from the Third Division.

Dion Dublin's winner took Cambridge into the Third for the first time in five years. Cambridge reached the Second Division Promotion play-offs in 1992 before being relegated a year later. Chesterfield won promotion via the play-offs in 1995 as Cambridge were relegated back to the bottom division.

Cambridge: Vaughan, Fensome, Kimble, Bailie, Chapple – capt, O'Shea, Cheetham, Leadbitter, Dublin, Taylor, Philpott. subs: Claridge for Taylor 61, Cook for Leadbitter 85. manager: John Beck
Chesterfield: Leonard, Francis, Ryan, Dyche, Brien, Gunn – capt, Plummer, Hewitt, Chiedozie, Rogers, Morris. subs: Waller for Chiedozie 79, Shaw (not used). manager: Paul Hart

Third Division

Sunday 27th May 1990

Notts County 2
Johnson 31, Short 62
Tranmere Rovers 0
29,252
Referee: R Milford (Bristol)

The Leyland DAF Cup winners from the previous week were no match for Notts County, who had lost in the semi-finals. County returned to the Second Division for the first time since 1985, after losing to the play-off winners Walsall in 1988. Tranmere could not really complain after their meteoric rise from the foot of the Fourth Division in three years. The following year, County won the Second Division play-offs, while Tranmere returned to win the Third Division play-offs and also reached the Leyland DAF Cup final again.

Notts County: Cherry, Palmer, Platnauer, Short, Yates, Robinson, Thomas, Turner – capt, Bartlett, Lund, Johnson. subs: Draper, Norton (not used). manager: Neil Warnock
Tranmere: Nixon, Garnett, Mungall, McNab, Hughes, Vickers, Malkin, Harvey – capt, Steel, Muir, Thomas. subs: Bishop for Harvey 68, Fairclough for Mungall 76. manager: John King

Second Division

Monday 28th May 1990

Sunderland 0
Swindon Town 1
McLoughlin 27
72,873
Referee: J Martin (near Alton)

When Gary Bennett deflected Alan McLoughlin's shot for the only goal of the game, Swindon appeared to have completed a remarkable rise, which began when they won the Fourth Division Championship in 1986. A year after, they won the Third Division Promotion play-offs and in 1989 they lost to the Second Division play-off winners Crystal Palace.

But the week after this Wembley victory, Swindon were found guilty of making irregular payments to players and Sunderland, who finished sixth, were promoted in their place to complete their own rapid rise.

Sunderland were to spend only one season in the First Division, but reached the FA Cup final in 1992. Swindon won the play-offs again in 1993.

Sunderland: Norman, Kay, Agboola, Bennett – capt, MacPhail, Owers, Bracewell, Armstrong, Gates, Gabbiadini, Pascoe. subs: Atkinson for Pascoe 68, Hauser for Gates 71. manager: Denis Smith
Swindon: Digby, Kerslake, Bodin, McLoughlin, Calderwood – capt, Gittens, Jones, Shearer, White, MacLaren, Foley. subs: Hockaday, Simpson (not used). manager: Osvaldo Ardiles

Schoolboy International

Saturday 2nd June 1990

England 1
Thompson 52
Netherlands 0
Referee: G Lyner (Lincolnshire)

Ian Thompson ensured the Netherlands lost their seventh successive schoolboy international at Wembley.

In goal for the Netherlands was Sander Westerveld, Liverpool's 'keeper in 2001, when they won their unprecedented cup 'treble' of UEFA Cup, FA Cup and Worthington Cup.

England: Reeves, Powell, Binks, Tinkler, Pugh, Brydon, Thompson, Smith, Clarke, Sharp – capt, Irving. sub: Thornley for Irving

Makita Tournament
Semi-finals

Friday 10th August 1990

Real Sociedad 1
Larranaga 26
Sampdoria 1
Vialli 29
Sampdoria won 5-3 on penalties.
Referee: J Worrall (Cheshire)

Three months earlier, Sampdoria had won the European Cup-Winners Cup in their second successive final. They began Wembley's third and last pre-season tournament by defeating the Spaniards, who had two ex-League Champions in John Aldridge and Kevin Richardson, thanks to Gianluca Pagliuca saving Bengoechea's penalty in the shoot-out.

Real Sociedad: Gonzalez, Bengoechea, Alaba, Larranaga, Gorriz, Gajate, Fuentes, Aldridge, Menchaga, Richardson, Lumbreras. subs: Lasa for Lumbreras 52, Dadie for Richardson 76. coach: Marco Boronat
Sampdoria: Pagliuca, Mannini, Bonetti, Pari, Vierchowod, Invernizzi, Katanec, Cerezo, Vialli, Mancini – capt, Dossena. subs: Branca for Katanec 46, Dal Ingai for Vialli 61. coach: Vujadin Boskov

Arsenal 2
Limpar 35, Campbell 75
Aston Villa 0
20,063
Referee: N Midgley (Lancashire)

Arsenal were chasing a hat-trick of wins in this competition and comfortably disposed of the club which had finished as League runners-up to Liverpool. New Swedish signing, Anders Limpar opened the scoring.

Arsenal: Seaman, Dixon, Winterburn, Thomas, Linighan, Adams – capt, Rocastle, Davis, Smith (A), Merson, Limpar. subs: Campbell for Merson 68, Groves for Rocastle 73. manager: George Graham

259

Aston Villa: Spink, Price, Gray – capt, McGrath, Mountfield, Nielsen, Daley, Gage, Yorke, Cowans, Cascarino. subs: Comyn for Nielsen 46, Olney for Price 79. manager: Josef Venglos

Third and Fourth Place

Saturday 11th August 1990

Aston Villa 0
Real Sociedad 1
Larranaga pen 67
Referee: K Hackett (Sheffield)

A good experience for Villa, who were competing in the UEFA Cup the following month following the ban on English clubs being lifted.

Aston Villa: Spink, Gage, Gray – capt, Blake, Mountfield, Comyn, Daley, Olney, Yorke, Cowans, Cascarino. subs: Ormondroyd for Blake, Birch for Yorke. manager: Josef Venglos
Real Sociedad: Gonzalez, Bengoechea, Alaba, Larranaga, Gorriz, Dadie, Irozoki, Lumbreras, Lionaz, Richardson, Menchaga. subs: Aguirre for Lumbreras, Martinez for Lionaz. coach: Marco Boronat

Final

Saturday 11th August 1990

Arsenal 0
Sampdoria 1
Dossena 43
21,542
Referee: G Courtney (Durham)

Just 17 hours after beating Aston Villa, Arsenal reappeared and conceded their first goal in three years of this competition. It was enough to take the trophy abroad for the first time. Sampdoria denied Arsenal the hat-trick, and then proceeded to win a hat-trick of tournaments themselves. Because of dwindling attendances, this was the last to be held at Wembley.

Arsenal regained the League Championship for the second time in three years, losing only one game and they reached the FA Cup semi-finals. They were to regain the last Makita Tournament, on their own ground in 1994.

Arsenal: Seaman, Dixon, Winterburn, Thomas, Linighan, Adams – capt, Rocastle, Davis, Smith (A), Merson, Limpar. subs: Bould for Linighan 70, Campbell for Merson 70. manager: George Graham
Sampdoria: Pagliuca, Mannini, Carboni, Pari, Invernizzi, Lanna, Katanec, Cerezo, Vialli, Mancini – capt, Dossena. subs: Branca for Cerezo 63, Lombardo for Katanec 76. coach: Vujadin Boskov

FA CHARITY SHIELD

Saturday 18th August 1990

Liverpool	1-1	Manchester United
Barnes pen 51		Blackmore 45

66,558
Referee: G Courtney (Durham)

This was the fifth meeting at Wembley between these giants. United had won two of their previous clashes, including the 1983 FA Charity Shield, their last meeting at the stadium. Liverpool had beaten United to win the Milk Cup the same year and they had fought out a goalless draw in the 1977 Charity Shield. If successful, Liverpool would become the first club to win a hat-trick of Shields outright, a feat they had denied Everton in 1986. They had beaten Wimbledon two years later and retained the trophy against Arsenal the previous year, their record 12th Charity Shield.

United's last appearance in this fixture was in losing to Everton in 1985. After losing the League Championship on goal difference, the previous year, Liverpool had regained it for the tenth time in 15 years

and a record 18th overall. They had won it by nine points from Aston Villa and also reached the FA Cup semi-finals for the fifth time in six years in their defence of the trophy. United had needed a replay, three months earlier, to win their record-equalling seventh FA Cup.

United went ahead deservedly in the last minute of the first half. Hughes failed to connect with a Phelan cross, but Clayton Blackmore scored at the far post. Liverpool took just six minutes of the second half to draw level. Pallister was adjudged to have fouled John Barnes. Television suggested he had made a clean tackle, but Barnes made no mistake from the penalty and the Shield was shared.

Liverpool finished as League runners-up to Arsenal, and United knocked them out of the Rumbelows Cup on their way to the final. Liverpool won the FA Cup, however, in 1992. United finished a much-improved sixth, in the First Division, and won the European Cup-Winners Cup in a triumphant return to Europe for English clubs.

Liverpool: Grobbelaar, Hysen, Burrows, Venison, Whelan – capt, Ablett, Beardsley, Houghton, Rush, Barnes, McMahon. sub: Rosenthal for Beardsley 78. manager: Kenny Dalglish
Manchester U: Sealey, Irwin, Donaghy, Bruce – capt, Phelan, Pallister, Blackmore, Ince, McClair, Hughes, Wallace. sub: Robins for Wallace 25. manager: Alex Ferguson

INTERNATIONAL

Wednesday 12th September 1990

England   1-0   Hungary
Lineker 44
51,459
Referee: E Fredriksson (Sweden)

England came back from the World Cup with a creditable fourth place, their best performance in a World Cup apart from the 1966 triumph. They had needed extra time twice to progress and eventual winners West Germany beat them only on penalties following an enthralling 1-1 draw after extra time in the semi-final in Turin. The host nation then beat them 2-1 in Bari to take third place.

England now had a new manager, Graham Taylor replacing Bobby Robson. Their opponents had lost on their last four visits to Wembley, but their last meeting, two years earlier, had been a goalless draw in Budapest. Hungary had failed to qualify for the recent World Cup from a group involving Northern Ireland and the Republic of Ireland.

The only goal of a one-sided game came a minute before the interval. Platt ran wide and then produced a fine shot which Petry could not hold. Gascoigne prevented Garaba from making a clearance and the ball fell invitingly for new captain Gary Lineker to slot past the diving goalkeeper.

Hungary continued their run of disappointing results. They returned to Wembley in 1996.

England: Woods (Rangers), Dixon (Arsenal), Pearce (Nottingham F), Parker (QPR), Walker (Nottingham F), Wright (Derby County), Platt (Aston Villa), Gascoigne (Tottenham), Bull (Wolves), Lineker (Tottenham) – capt, Barnes (Liverpool). subs: Dorigo (Chelsea) for Pearce 46, Waddle (Olympique Marseille) for Bull 74. manager: Graham Taylor
Hungary: Petry (Honved), Monos (Veszpremi), Disztl (MTK Budapest), Keller (Ferencvaros), Limperger (Ferencvaros), Garaba (Ferencvaros) – capt, Kozma (Dunfermline), Bucs (Videoton), Gregor (Veszpremi), Berczy (MTK), Kovacs (Auxerre). subs: Simon (Ferencvaros) for Monos 68, Aczel (Honved) for Garaba 71, Balog (MTK) for Bucs 80. coach: Kalman Meszoly

EUROPEAN CHAMPIONSHIP QUALIFYING

Wednesday 17th October 1990

England   2-0   Poland
Lineker pen 39, Beardsley 89
77,040
Referee: T Lanese (Italy)

England had beaten Poland in a World Cup qualifying match the previous year and knocked them out of the competition with a goalless draw in Chorzow four months later. Earlier in the day, the Republic of Ireland had thrashed Turkey 5-0 at Lansdowne Road in the opening match in Group Seven.

England took 39 minutes to break down the Poles. Gary Lineker's goalbound header was handled on the line by Nawrocki and Lineker took the penalty himself, sending Wandzik the wrong way. But England did not secure the points until the last minute. Substitute Peter Beardsley ran on to Dixon's pass and everyone expected a cross.

But the goalkeeper had strayed from his line and Beardsley drove a brilliant curling shot in at the near post.

A 1-1 draw in Poznan the following year took England through to the Euro-pean Championship in Sweden. They were drawn with Poland yet again in the next World Cup and beat them again at Wembley in 1993.

England: Woods (Rangers), Dixon (Arsenal), Pearce (Nottingham F), Parker (QPR), Walker (Nottingham F), Wright (Derby County), Platt (Aston Villa), Gascoigne (Tottenham), Bull (Wolves), Lineker (Tottenham), Barnes (Liverpool). subs: Waddle (Olympique Marseille) for Bull 57, Beardsley (Liverpool) for Lineker 57. manager: Graham Taylor
Poland: Wandzik (Panathinaikos), Czachowski (Stal Mielec), Wdowczyk (Celtic), Szewczyk (GKS Katowice), Kaczmarek (Auxerre) – capt, Nawrocki (GKS Katowice), Tarasiewicz (Nancy-Lorraine), Warzycha (R) (Gornik Zabrze), Furtok (Hamburg), Ziober (Montpellier), Kosecki (Legia Warsaw). subs: Warzycha (K) (Panathinaikos) for Furtok 76, Kubicki (Lech Poznan) for Kosecki 86. coach: Andrzej Strejlau

INTERNATIONAL

Wednesday 6th February 1991

England   2-0   Cameroon
Lineker (pen) 20, 60
61,075
Referee: J Blankenstein (Netherlands)

Cameroon were the first African side to visit England for a full international. The previous year, they had become the first African team to reach the World Cup quarter-finals and led against England in Naples before two Gary Lineker extra time penalties put them out. It had been a memorable World Cup for Cameroon, beginning with victory against holders Argentina in Milan. In 1988, they had won the African Championship for the second time.

After 20 minutes on a freezing night, Gary Lineker was tripped by the goalkeeper as he went round him and once again the striker drove a penalty into the back of the Cameroon net. The Africans were disappointing, offering very little resistance and causing no problems at all to the home defence.

The match was settled when Pearce's corner was headed on by Mark Wright and Lineker tapped in his second past Pagal on the line.

Cameroon went on to qualify for their second successive World Cup in 1994, but could not repeat their 1990 exploits and won only one point. They were back at Wembley in 1997.

England: Seaman (Arsenal), Dixon (Arsenal), Pearce (Nottingham F), Steven (Rangers), Walker (Nottingham F), Wright (M) (Derby County), Robson (Man Utd) – capt, Gascoigne (Tottenham), Wright (I)* (Crystal P), Lineker (Tottenham), Barnes (Liverpool). subs: Hodge (Nottingham F) for Gascoigne 67, Pallister (Man Utd) for Robson 70. manager: Graham Taylor
*first cap
Cameroon: Bell (Bordeaux), Ebwelle (Prevoyance Yaounde), Onana (Canon Yaounde), Kunde (Prevoyance Yaounde), Tataw (Tonnerre Yaounde) – capt, Mfede (Figueras), Mbouh (Vitoria Guimaraes), Pagal (Saint-Etienne), Kana Biyik (Le Havre), Omam Biyik (Rennes), Ekeke (Valenciennes). subs: Libih (Tonnerre Yaounde) for Kana Biyik 42, Tapoko (Panthere Bangangte) for Ekeke 78. coach: Philippe Redon

Victory Shield

Saturday 9th March 1991

England 2
Murray 49, Irving 50

Scotland 1
Fotheringham 70
Referee: D Elleray (Middlesex)

Richard Irving's spectacular goal secured victory. Scotland recovered to share the Shield with England and Wales.

England: Pettinger, Bowder, Vaughan, Murray – capt, Ryan, Strong, Irving, Geraghty, Goodwin, Gallen, Walker. sub: Beech for Geraghty 41
Scotland: McKenzie, Caldwell, Laidlaw, Nicholson, Ritchie – capt, Riley, Callaghan, Carberry, Harper, Fotheringham, Paterson. subs: McDonald for Callaghan 68, Coyle for Carberry 78

1991

EUROPEAN CHAMPIONSHIP QUALIFYING

Wednesday 27th March 1991

England 1-1 **Republic of Ireland**
Dixon 9 — Quinn 28
77,753
Referee: K Rothlisberger (Switzerland)

The Republic of Ireland had become a major force since losing at Wembley in 1985. They had beaten England in the 1988 European Championship in Stuttgart and then reached the World Cup quarter-finals in Italy. They had begun their first World Cup the previous year by drawing 1-1 with England in Cagliari and lost only to the host nation in Rome. Five months later, they had remained at the top of Group Seven on goal difference from England after another 1-1 draw at Lansdowne Road.

England took a rather fortunate lead when Staunton headed away Pearce's cross, only for the ball to go straight to Lee Dixon, whose shot was deflected by the Irish left back past Bonner. Twenty minutes later Niall Quinn converted McGrath's centre to level. England struggled to cope with Ireland's aerial bombardment and the Republic should really have taken both points. But they missed a number of chances which, ultimately, was to prove costly.

The Republic finished as runners-up to England after dropping a point against Poland two months later at Lansdowne Road, but they then went on to qualify for their second successive World Cup in 1994, just pipping European Champions Denmark, on goal difference. They went out in the last 16, despite beating the eventual finalists Italy in New York.

England: Seaman (Arsenal), Dixon (Arsenal), Pearce (Nottingham F), Adams (Arsenal), Walker (Nottingham F), Wright (M) (Derby County), Robson (Man Utd) – capt, Platt (Aston Villa), Beardsley (Liverpool), Lineker (Tottenham), Barnes (Liverpool). subs: Sharpe* (Man Utd) for Adams 46, Wright (I) (Crystal P) for Lineker 76. manager: Graham Taylor *first cap
Republic of Ireland: Bonner (Celtic), Irwin (Man Utd), Staunton (Liverpool), O'Leary (Arsenal), Moran (Blackburn) – capt, Townsend (Chelsea), McGrath (Aston Villa), Houghton (Liverpool), Quinn (MAn City), Aldridge (Real Sociedad), Sheedy (Everton). sub: Cascarino (Aston Villa) for Aldridge 70. manager: Jack Charlton

Zenith Cup Final

Sunday 7th April 1991

Crystal Palace 4
Thomas 67, Wright 101, 115, Salako 113

Everton 1
Warzycha 69
After extra time
52,460
Referee: G Courtney (Spennymoor)

Palace had reached the semi-finals of the competition in each of the previous two years, losing to the eventual winners each time. But they had reached their first FA Cup final the previous year, losing after a replay. Everton had reached the final in 1989 under its previous name, the Simod Cup, and lost a seven-goal thriller in extra time. They had then lost the FA Cup final three weeks later, also after extra time. They had not competed in the Zenith Cup the previous year but this time there were two fewer exemptions even though English clubs had been re-admitted to the European competitions.

Midway through the second half of a bruising encounter Palace went ahead. A corner from Salako was met by Young and Keown, but Geoff Thomas dived to head the opener. Three minutes later, Polish international Robert Warzycha took a pass from Newell and beat Martyn for the equaliser which took the match into extra time. Palace regained the lead when Ian Wright ran on to Martyn's clearance, evaded Hinchcliffe and drove past Southall. They settled it with two more goals in the second period of extra time. John Salako headed the third after Bright had got his head to a McGoldrick cross and Bright also created the opening for Wright to repeat his double in the previous year's FA Cup final. The goalkeeper was not impressed and refused to go up to collect his runners-up medal after the game.

Palace returned to Wembley for two successive Football League Promotion Play-Off finals, in 1996 and 1997. They lost the first

263

to a last minute winner in extra time, but won the second with their own last minute winner. Everton had now lost five successive Wembley finals. Their dismal run ended, however, when they won the FA Cup in 1995.

Crystal P: Martyn, Humphrey, Shaw, Gray, Young, Thorn, Salako, Thomas – capt, Bright, Wright, Pardew. subs: McGoldrick for Gray 55, Thompson for Young 116. manager: Steve Coppell

Everton: Southall, McDonald, Hinchcliffe, Keown, Watson – capt, Milligan, Warzycha, McCall, Newell, Cottee, Sheedy. subs: Ratcliffe for Keown 80, Nevin for Newell 69. manager: Colin Harvey

FA Cup Semi-final

Sunday 14th April 1991

Arsenal 1
Smith 44

Tottenham Hotspur 3
Gascoigne 5, Lineker 11, 75
77,893
Referee: R Lewis (Great Bookham)

This was Wembley's first FA Cup semi-final. The two north London rivals had previously met at the stadium in the opening match of the International Tournament in 1988, with Arsenal winning comfortably by 4-0. Arsenal had gone on to win the tournament on goal difference with Tottenham finishing bottom.

The Gunners had become regular visitors to Wembley because of the Makita Tournament, as it was now known. On their last visit, the previous year, they had lost the final to Sampdoria. They had last reached the FA Cup semi-finals in 1983, when they lost to Manchester United, the eventual winners, at Villa Park, and the final in 1980.

Tottenham's last final had been in 1987 when they were runners-up for the first time, after a joint record seven wins. Their last appearance at Wembley was the day af-

ter their drubbing by Arsenal. They lost to a Milan side, which was about to win two successive European Cups.

Arsenal were on course for their second 'double', having lost only one league game so far, although they had been surprisingly thrashed 6-2 at home in the last 16 of the Rumbelows Cup by eventual finalists Manchester United who went on to win the European Cup-Winners Cup.

Arsenal did not know what had hit them. Tottenham got off to a flying start when Paul Gascoigne hammered a 30-yard free kick into the top corner. He was also involved in the second with a flick which sent Allen away down the right. His cross went behind the defence, hitting Smith in the side, but Gary Lineker just got ahead of Adams to stab the ball past Seaman. Arsenal clawed their way back and scored in the last minute of the first half. From Dixon's cross, Alan Smith leapt above Mabbutt to send a fine header beyond the reach of Thorstvedt. Arsenal threatened an equaliser after the break, but it was Tottenham who broke away to score a third. Mabbutt's pass sent Lineker away and England's star striker took the ball wide with Adams in hot pursuit. His shot appeared to go through Seaman's hands and secured a very sweet victory indeed for Tottenham.

Arsenal met Tottenham again in the FA Charity Shield four months later. Their very next FA Cup tie, the following year, was an embarrassing defeat at the hands of Wrexham, who had finished bottom of the Football League 91 places below Arsenal. Tottenham went on to win a record eighth FA Cup.

Arsenal: Seaman, Dixon, Winterburn, Thomas, Bould, Adams – capt, Campbell, Davis, Smith (A), Merson, Limpar. sub: Groves for Limpar. manager: George Graham

Tottenham: Thorstvedt, Edinburgh, Van den Hauwe, Sedgley, Howells, Mabbutt – capt, Stewart, Gascoigne, Samways, Lineker, Allen (P). subs: Nayim for Gascoigne, Walsh for Samways. manager: Terry Venables

LEAGUE CUP FINAL

Sunday 21st April 1991

Manchester United   0-1   Sheffield Wednesday
Sheridan 38

77,612
Referee: R Lewis (Great Bookham)

United had reached the final once before, in 1983, while Wednesday were the second successive Second Division club to get that

far following Oldham Athletic. This was their first final.

The original Football League Cup was to

be presented to the winners under its new name, the Rumbelows Cup.

United were making their fourth visit to Wembley in less than a year, having won the FA Cup after a replay and then drawn the FA Charity Shield three months later.

Wednesday were aiming to become the first Second Division club for 16 years to win the trophy and they had waited 56 years since their last major honour, the FA Cup. They had appeared at Wembley since, however. In 1966, they reached another FA Cup final and in 1988 they had beaten United at Wembley to reach the final of the Football League Centenary Tournament, losing on penalties to Nottingham Forest.

Of added spice was the fact that Wednesday's manager Ron Atkinson had twice taken United to FA Cup wins in the mid-1980's, before being sacked in 1986.

Wednesday were not overawed by their higher ranked opponents and took the lead when Worthington's free kick was headed out of the penalty area by Pallister. But John Sheridan followed up to hammer the ball past Sealey as McClair lunged. The goal-keeper got his hands to it but could only push it onto the post and in. Wednesday held firm, kept their goal intact and deserved their victory.

United were compensated three days later, when they drew 1-1 with Legia Warsaw to reach their first European final for 23 years. They went on to win the European Cup-Winners Cup. The following year, they won the Rumbelows Cup for the first time.

Wednesday won promotion straight back to the First Division and completed a memorable 'double'. Two years later, they made an incredible four visits to Wembley in two months, beginning with an all-Sheffield FA Cup semi-final.

Manchester U: Sealey, Irwin, Blackmore, Bruce, Webb, Pallister, Robson – capt, Ince, McClair, Hughes, Sharpe. subs: Phelan for Webb 56, Donaghy (not used). manager: Alex Ferguson

Sheffield W: Turner, Nilsson, King, Harkes, Shirtliff, Pearson – capt, Wilson, Sheridan, Hirst, Williams, Worthington. subs: Madden for Harkes 88, Francis (not used). manager: Ron Atkinson

FA Vase Final

Saturday 4th May 1991

Gresley Rovers 4
Rathbone 32, Smith 48, 90, Stokes pen 95

Guiseley 4
Tennison 2, 31, Walling 9, Roberts (A) 119
After extra time
11,314
Referee: C Trussell (Liverpool)

This was the third successive drawn FA Vase final, but by far the most exciting.

Gresley: Aston, Barry, Elliott, Denby, Land, Astley, Stokes, Smith, Acklam, Rathbone, Lovell. subs: Adcock for Elliott 55, Weston for Lovell 72
Guiseley: Maxted, Bottomley, Hogarth, Tetley, Morgan, McKenzie, Atkinson, Tennison, Walling, Roberts (A), Roberts (W). subs: Adams for Atkinson 81, Annan for Roberts (W) 76

Replay: Tuesday 7th May 1991
Gresley Rovers 1
Astley
Guiseley 3
Tennison, Walling, Atkinson
(Bramall Lane, Sheffield)

FA Trophy Final

Saturday 11th May 1991

Kidderminster Harriers 1
Hadley 59

Wycombe Wanderers 2
Scott 16, West 64
34,842
Referee: J Watson (Whitley Bay)

Mark West, scorer at Wembley for England Schoolboys ten years earlier, bagged the winner with a diving header as Wycombe, managed by Martin O'Neill, European Cup winner with Nottingham Forest in 1980, took the Trophy for the first time. The following year they were denied promotion to the Football League on goal difference by Colchester United after finishing runners-up in the Vauxhall Conference.

Steve Guppy worked his way up from non-league to the Premiership, with a little help from O'Neill and at the age of 30 in 1999 won a full international cap for England against Belgium at Sunderland.

Kidderminster: Jones, Kurila, McGrath, Weir, Barnett, Forsyth, Joseph – capt, Howell, Hadley, Lilwall, Humphreys. subs: Wilcox for Joseph, Whitehouse for Howell
Wycombe: Granville, Crossley, Cash, Kerr, Creaser - capt, Carroll, Bryan, Stapleton, West, Scott, Guppy. sub: Hutchinson for Guppy

FA CUP FINAL

Saturday 18th May 1991

Nottingham Forest   1-2   **Tottenham Hotspur**
Pearce 15   Stewart 53, Walker og 94
After extra time
80,000
Referee: R Milford (Bristol)

Although this was Forest's first final since their second FA Cup win in 1959 they had become regular visitors to Wembley in recent years. Since 1988, they had won the Football League Centenary Tournament, the Simod Cup and two Littlewoods Cups. They had not lost at Wembley since the 1980 Football League Cup final. Tottenham were hoping to secure a record eighth FA Cup win and their first since 1982.

After his stunning free kick goal in the semi-final, all eyes were on Paul Gascoigne to make his mark again, but the hyped-up character made the headlines for all the wrong reasons. The second of two horrific fouls on Forest players put him out of football for over a year with a serious knee injury. Worse still for Tottenham was that Forest scored from the resultant free kick. Stuart Pearce curled it into the corner although he was helped somewhat by Glover pushing Mabbutt off the end of the wall to leave a gap for the shot.

After Gascoigne had been stretchered off, Tottenham set about getting back into the game. In the 32nd minute, Lineker ran on to Stewart's through ball and was brought down by Crossley as he went round the 'keeper. Unfortunately for Lineker, Crossley brilliantly turned his penalty over the bar. Tottenham deservedly levelled, however, after eight minutes of the second half. Allen laid the ball off to Paul Stewart who fired past Crossley.

Tottenham sensed victory, but Forest held out until extra time. Then, Spanish substitute Nayim's corner was headed across to the far post by Stewart. Des Walker held off Mabbutt, but sadly headed it into his own net. It proved to be the winner and maintained Tottenham's curious record of winning a major trophy in a year ending in the figure '1'. It was the fifth decade in succession they had done this.

This defeat did not stop Forest from winning cup ties. They were back at Wembley twice more the following year, winning the Zenith Cup and reaching the Rumbelows Cup final. Tottenham reached the quarter-finals of the European Cup-Winners Cup, before losing to Feyenoord.

Roy Keane, making his Wembley debut, went on to captain Manchester United.

Nottingham F: Crossley, Charles, Pearce – capt, Walker, Chettle, Keane, Crosby, Parker, Clough, Glover, Woan. subs: Hodge for Woan 62, Laws for Glover 108. manager: Brian Clough
Tottenham: Thorstvedt, Edinburgh, Van den Hauwe, Sedgley, Howells, Mabbutt – capt, Stewart, Gascoigne, Samways, Lineker, Allen (P). subs: Nayim for Gascoigne 18, Walsh for Samways 82. manager: Terry Venables

INTERNATIONAL

Tuesday 21st May 1991

England   3-1   **USSR**
Smith 16, Platt (pen) 43, 89   Wright (M) og 9
23,789
Referee: E Aladren (Spain)

The USSR won at Wembley for the first time in 1984 and had convincingly beaten England 3-1 in Frankfurt on their way to a record fourth European Championship final in 1988. England were aiming to beat them for the first time since a 1-0 win in Tbilisi in 1986.

The visitors took a fortunate lead when Tatarchuk's shot hit Mark Wright, on his first appearance as captain, to give Woods no chance. It was the first goal the England goalkeeper had conceded at Wembley in nine appearances for club and country.

England equalised soon after when

Uvarov punched out Parker's free kick under pressure from Mark Wright. Thomas knocked the ball back for Alan Smith to turn it between two defenders on the line. Two minutes before half-time England scored again when Tseviba was adjudged to have tripped David Platt although there appeared to be no contact. Platt took the kick and sent the 'keeper the wrong way.

The final goal came in the last minute after some neat passing by England. Substitute Beardsley's final pass was almost collected by Chernishkov but he could not control it and Platt fired his second into the corner.

This was the first match of a three-team tournament called the England Challenge Cup. Two nights later, the USSR drew 1-1 with Argentina at Old Trafford.

England: Woods (Rangers), Stevens (Rangers), Dorigo (Chelsea), Wise (Chelsea), Parker (QPR), Wright (M) (Derby County) – capt, Platt (Aston Villa), Thomas (Crystal P), Smith (Arsenal), Wright (I) (Crystal P), Barnes (Liverpool). subs: Batty* (Leeds United) for Wise 70, Beardsley (Liverpool) for Wright (I) 70. manager: Graham Taylor
*first cap

USSR: Uvarov (Dynamo Moscow), Chernishkov (Dynamo Moscow), Kulkov (Spartak Moscow), Tseviba (Dynamo Kiev), Galiamin (CSKA Moscow), Shalimov (Spartak Moscow), Mikhailichenko (Sampdoria) – capt, Kanchelskis (Shakhtyor Donetsk), Kolyvanov (Dynamo Moscow), Tatarchuk (Dynamo Kiev), Kuznetsov (CSKA Moscow). sub: Mostovoi (Spartak Moscow) for Tatarchuk 50, Korneyev (CSKA Moscow) for Shalimov 66. coach: Anatoly Bishovets

Under-19 International

Saturday 25th May 1991

England 1
Awford 22

Spain 1
Rodriguez 44
Referee: J Carter (Hampshire)

This was the last of Wembley's pre-match youth internationals but the first at under-19 level. Three weeks later Spain defeated England in the World Youth Cup in Faro.

England substitute Steve McManaman scored both Liverpool's goals when they won the Coca-Cola Cup at Wembley four years later. He won 37 caps for England and two European Cup winners medals with Real Madrid, scoring for them in the 2000 final.

Another of England's substitutes, Darren Anderton, won 30 full caps and was in the Tottenham Hotspur side which won the Worthington Cup at Wembley in 1999.

England: Walker (Tottenham), Watson (Newcastle), Minto (Charlton), Tuttle (Tottenham), Hendon (Tottenham) – capt, Awford (Portsmouth), Hayward (Derby County), Rouse (Rangers), Cole (Arsenal), Bart-Williams (Leyton Orient), Harkness (Liverpool). subs: McManaman (Liverpool) for Cole 46, Houghton (Tottenham) for Bart-Williams 46, Kavanagh (Derby County) for Watson 58, Anderton (Portsmouth) for Hayward 69, Phillips (Derby County) for Hendon 74, Livingstone (Aston Villa) for Walker 78, Myers (Chelsea) for Harkness 78. manager: Dave Burnside

Spain: Ferrer (J), Rios, De Quintana, Juanlu, Santi, Justo, Marquez, Garcia, Casas, Urzaiz, Rodriguez. subs: Israel for Rodriguez 50, Acosta for Marquez 51, Navaero for Casas 60, Ferrer (R) for Justo 66, Martinez for Ferrer (J) 77, Angel for Garcia 77

INTERNATIONAL

Saturday 25th May 1991

England   2-2   Argentina
Lineker 15, Platt 50   Garcia 66, Franco 70
44,497
Referee: Z Petrovic (Yugoslavia)

Argentina had been well beaten in 1980, their last visit to Wembley, but had knocked out England in the quarter-finals in Mexico City on their way to winning their second World Cup in 1986. Diego Maradona, scorer of the controversial 'hand of God' goal in that match, was now banned from football for drug offences after leading his team

to their second successive World Cup final the previous year.

This was the last game of the three-team tournament for the England Challenge Cup. Two days earlier, Argentina had drawn 1-1 with the USSR at Old Trafford.

Gary Lineker's header to put England, wearing red shirts, in front came from a

Pearce free kick from just inside England's half. After the interval, Pearce's cross was headed brilliantly past Goycochea by David Platt and the England Challenge Cup appeared to be comfortably in the bag.

But midway through the second half, substitute Mohammed's corner was headed in by the unmarked Claudio Garcia. Then,

a corner from the same player was headed in by Dario Franco in almost identical fashion. Just as in their 1974 visit, Argentina had pulled back a two-goal deficit but it was England who won the tournament.

Argentina did not appear at Wembley again until 2000.

England: Seaman (Arsenal), Dixon (Arsenal), Pearce (Nottingham F), Batty (Leeds Utd), Walker (Nottingham F), Wright (Derby County), Platt (Aston Villa), Thomas (Crystal P), Smith (Arsenal), Lineker (Tottenham) – capt, Barnes (Liverpool). sub: Clough (Nottingham F) for Barnes 62. manager: Graham Taylor
Argentina: Goycochea (Racing Club), Vazquez (Ferro Carril Oeste), Enrique (River Plate), Basualdo (River Plate), Gamboa (Newell's Old Boys), Ruggeri (Velez Sarsfield) – capt, Garcia (Racing Club), Franco (Newell's), Simeone (Pisa), Martellotto (Monterrey), Boldrini (Newell's). sub: Mohammed (Huracan) for Martellotto 60. coach: Alfio Basile

Leyland DAF Cup Final

Sunday 26th May 1991

Birmingham City 3
Sturridge, Gayle 2

Tranmere Rovers 2
Cooper, Steel
58,756
Referee: J Martin (near Alton)

Holders Tranmere pulled back a two-goal deficit but lost their trophy to an overhead kick from John Gayle five minutes from time. Tranmere returned six days later for their second successive Third Division Promotion play-off final.

Birmingham: Thomas, Clarkson, Frain, Yates, Overson – capt, Matthewson, Peer, Gayle, Robinson, Gleghorn, Sturridge. subs: Bailey for Sturridge, Hopkins (not used). manager: Lou Macari
Tranmere: Nixon – capt, Higgins, Brannan, McNab, Hughes, Vickers, Morrissey, Irons, Steel, Cooper, Thomas. subs: Malkin for McNab, Martindale for Vickers. manager: John King

Play-off Finals

Fourth Division
Friday 31st May 1991

Blackpool 2
Groves 6, Curran og 68

Torquay United 2
Saunders 28, Edwards pen 37
After extra time
Torquay United won 5-4 on penalties.
(Loram saved, Rodwell saved, Holmes (M) 0-1, Taylor 1-1, Saunders 1-2, Gore 2-2, Holmes (P) 2-3, Groves 3-3, Myers 3-4, Garner 4-4, Howells 4-5, Bamber missed)
21,615
Referee: G Courtney (Spennymoor)

After four successive sixth placed clubs had won promotion from the Fourth Division, Torquay achieved the feat after finishing seventh. This was the first play-off final to be decided on penalties.

Blackpool had been relegated from the Third Division the previous year and had missed promotion straight back by a point. It was their first Wembley appearance since their famous FA Cup win of 1953.

Torquay had lost the play-off final to Swansea City in 1988 and had been defeated in the final of the Sherpa Van Trophy a year later – their first visit to Wembley. Their manager, Dave Smith had retired when it seemed their promotion bid had faded. John Impey had taken over the previous month and they were back on course for promotion until Chris Curran sliced the ball into his own net to take the game into extra time and subsequently the dreaded penalty shoot-out.

Both teams missed with their first spot kicks. Steve McIlhargey saved from Mark Loram and Gareth Howells from Tony Rodwell. But the next nine penalties were all successful, until after Howells converted a kick himself, Dave Bamber, whose handling offence had given Torquay a penalty during the game, then shot wide and Torquay were back in the Third Division for the first time since 1972.

Blackpool won the following year's play-off final, also after a penalty shoot-out.

Blackpool: McIlhargey, Davies, Wright, Groves, Horner, Gore, Rodwell – capt, Taylor, Bamber, Garner, Eyres. subs: Sinclair for Davies 103, Richards (not used). manager: Billy Ayre
Torquay: Howells, Curran, Holmes (P), Saunders – capt, Elliott, Joyce, Myers, Holmes (M), Evans, Edwards, Loram. subs: Hall for Edwards 87, Rowland for Evans 115. manager: John Impey

Third Division
Saturday 1st June 1991

Bolton Wanderers 0
Tranmere Rovers 1
Malkin 97
After extra time
30,217
Referee: K Hackett (Sheffield)

In their fourth appearance at Wembley in just over a year, Tranmere returned to the Second Division for the first time in 52 years. After losing the previous year's final to Notts County and then winning the Leyland DAF Cup, this time Tranmere lost the final of the Cup the previous week but won the match they wanted most.

Bolton had missed promotion on goal difference behind Grimsby Town after finishing five points ahead of Tranmere. They had lost to Notts County in the previous year's semi-finals and had been relegated to the Fourth Division by the play-offs in 1987.

Two years after this final, they won promotion as runners-up to Stoke City and two years after that, in 1995, they won promotion to the Premiership via the play-offs, as well as reaching the Coca-Cola Cup final. The winner came from Chris Malkin, who had come on as a substitute after just 14 minutes.

Bolton: Felgate, Brown – capt, Cowdrill, Comstive, Seagraves, Stubbs, Storer, Thompson, Cunningham, Philliskirk, Darby. subs: Reeves for Cunningham 68, Green for Storer 100. manager: Phil Neal
Tranmere: Nixon – capt, Higgins, Brannan, Irons, Hughes, Garnett, Morrissey, Martindale, Steel, Cooper, Thomas. subs: Malkin for Steel 14, Harvey for Martindale 74. manager: John King

Second Division
Sunday 2nd June 1991

Brighton and Hove Albion 1
Wilkins 89

Notts County 3
Johnson 29, 59, Regis 71
59,940
Referee: D Elleray (Harrow)

For the second year in succession, Tommy Johnson set Notts County on their way to promotion in a play-off final. This convincing victory took them into the First Division for the first time since 1984, when they had plummeted straight down to the Third Division with two successive relegations.

Now they had returned with two successive promotions. Alas, there was no happy ending – County were relegated straight back to the Second Division.

This was Brighton's second successive drubbing at Wembley. They had been outclassed in the FA Cup final replay, eight years before.

Brighton: Digweed, Chivers, Gatting, Wilkins – capt, Bissett, Pates, Barham, Iovan, Small, Codner, Walker. subs: Byrne for Gatting 62, Chapman for Iovan 62. manager: Barry Lloyd
Notts C: Cherry, Palmer, Paris, Short, Yates, O'Riordan, Thomas, Turner – capt, Regis, Draper, Johnson. subs: Harding for Draper 81, Bartlett for Regis 85. manager: Neil Warnock

Schoolboy International
Saturday 8th June 1991

England 1
Gallen 22
West Germany 3
Fensch 14, Ratkowski 70, Hahn 80
Referee: D Allison (Lancashire)

Although Germany was now a unified country, the schoolboy squad was still made up of players from the west.

England: Pettinger, Bowder, Vaughan, Murray – capt, Strong, Irving, Gallen, Walker, Faulkner, Beech, Johnson. subs: Geraghty for Murray 53, Goodwin for Johnson 74, Jackson for Gallen 76

FA CHARITY SHIELD

Saturday 10th August 1991

Arsenal   0-0   Tottenham Hotspur
65,483
Referee: T Holbrook (Staffordshire)

Neither side had won the FA Charity Shield outright at Wembley, although Tottenham had shared it in 1981. Arsenal had twice lost to Liverpool (in 1979 and 1989) and had not won it since 1953. Tottenham had also lost to Liverpool on their last appearance in the fixture, in 1982, and had not won it outright since 1962.

These north London rivals had notched a win apiece against each other at Wembley. Arsenal had won 4-0 in the International Tournament in 1988, but Tottenham had won Wembley's first FA Cup semi-final. That result had ended Arsenal's hopes of their second 'double', but they went on to regain the League Championship for the second time in three years, losing only one game. They finished seven points clear of Liverpool, despite having two points de-ducted for their part in a brawl in October at Manchester United.

Tottenham had won an entertaining FA Cup final three months earlier. This was their first match with new manager, Peter Shreeves in charge. Terry Venables had become chief executive.

A well organised Tottenham defence denied Arsenal once again and the Shield was shared for the second year in succession.

Arsenal and Tottenham were back at Wembley, two years later, for another FA Cup semi-final.

Arsenal: Seaman, Dixon, Winterburn, Hillier, O'Leary, Adams – capt, Rocastle, Davis, Smith (A), Merson, Campbell. subs: Thomas for Rocastle 78, Cole for Campbell 78. manager: George Graham

Tottenham: Thorstvedt, Fenwick, Van den Hauwe, Sedgley, Howells, Mabbutt – capt, Stewart, Nayim, Samways, Lineker, Allen (P). manager: Peter Shreeves

INTERNATIONAL

Wednesday 11th September 1991

England 0-1 Germany
Riedle 45

59,493
Referee: A Spirrin (USSR)

Both East and West Germany had visited Wembley in the early 1980's. Now Germany was united again and England were meeting them for the first time since a 6-3 win in Berlin in 1938. West Germany had won the 1990 World Cup, beating Argentina with a late penalty in Rome in their third successive final. In a dramatic semi-final in Turin, they had beaten England on penalties following a 1-1 draw after extra time.

Germany secured their first victory against England at the end of the first half, when Karl-Heinz Riedle headed in a cross from Doll, a former East German. It was also enough to inflict on England their first defeat under Graham Taylor.

This was the third German team to win at Wembley and the following month they thrashed Wales 4-1 in Nuremberg. They went on to reach the European Championship final in Gothenburg the following year but lost 2-0 to the surprise winners Denmark.

In 1993, Germany again beat England, by 2-1, in the US Cup in Detroit. They were back at Wembley in the 1996 European Championship and were involved in yet another dramatic match with England in the semi-final.

German substitute Jurgen Klinsmann was transferred to Tottenham Hotspur three years later. Although he only stayed for one season, he was voted the 1995 Footballer of the Year. The following year, he captained his country to European Championship success at Wembley.

England: Woods (Sheffield W), Dixon (Arsenal), Dorigo (Leeds Utd), Batty (Leeds Utd), Pallister (Man Utd), Parker (Man Utd), Platt (Bari), Steven (Olympique Marseille), Smith (Arsenal), Lineker (Tottenham) – capt, Salako (Crystal P). subs: Stewart* (Tottenham) for Steven 67, Merson* (Arsenal) for Salako 67. manager: Graham Taylor
*first cap
Germany: Illgner (Cologne), Binz (Eintracht Frankfurt), Brehme (Internazionale), Kohler (Juventus), Effenberg (Bayern Munich), Buchwald (Stuttgart), Moller (Eintracht Frankfurt), Hassler (Roma), Riedle (Lazio), Matthaus (Internazionale) – capt, Doll (Lazio). sub:- Klinsmann (Internazionale) for Doll 82. coach: Berti Vogts

EUROPEAN CHAMPIONSHIP QUALIFYING

Wednesday 16th October 1991

England   **1-0**   **Turkey**
Smith 21
50,896
Referee: A Navarette (Spain)

Group Seven was developing into a tight struggle. England were level on points with Poland and the Republic of Ireland who had drawn 3-3 in Poznan earlier in the day after the Irish had led 3-1. England were behind Ireland on goal difference, but knew that a big win over Turkey in this game in hand would put on the pressure. Five months earlier, England had eliminated the Turks in Izmir by the only goal and Turkey had still to score against England after five meetings. On each of their previous visits to Wembley (in 1985 and 1987) Gary Lineker had scored hat-tricks. Although they had not scored or won a point in their four matches played so far in this group, they had missed qualifying for the previous year's World Cup by only two points behind Austria.

The one goal came after Pearce's cross tempted Hayrettin from his goal. The ball sailed over him and Alan Smith headed in.

The following month England's 1-1 draw against Poland in Poznan earned them the trip to Sweden. They had to thank Gary Lineker again for an equaliser 13 minutes from time without which the Republic of Ireland, also unbeaten, would have qualified on goal difference. Sadly, England flopped in the championship. Turkey were back at Wembley five months after the finals for a World Cup qualifying match.

England: Woods (Sheffield W), Dixon (Arsenal), Pearce (Nottingham F), Batty (Leeds Utd), Walker (Nottingham F), Mabbutt (Tottenham), Robson (Man Utd), Platt (Bari), Smith (Arsenal), Lineker (Tottenham) – capt, Waddle (Olympique Marseille). manager: Graham Taylor
Turkey: Hayrettin (Galatasaray), Recep (Besiktas), Ogun (Trabzonspor), Gokhan (Besiktas), Tugay (Galatasaray), Turhan (Fenerbahce), Feyyaz (Besiktas), Riza (Besiktas), Unal (Trabzonspor), Oguz (Fenerbahce), Orhan (Trabzonspor). sub: Hami (Trabzonspor) for Feyyaz 76. coach: Sepp Piontek

Final table	P	W	D	L	F	A	Pts
England	6	3	3	0	7	3	9
Republic of Ireland	6	2	4	0	13	6	8
Poland	6	2	3	1	8	6	7
Turkey	6	0	0	6	1	14	0

INTERNATIONAL

Wednesday 19th February 1992

England   **2-0**   **France**
Shearer 44, Lineker 73
58,723
Referee: A Schmidhuber (Germany)

France had last played at Wembley back in 1969, when the then World Champions thrashed them 5-0. More recently the French had experienced much more success than England. In their last meeting, in 1984 in Paris, France won 2-0 and four months later won the European Championship in the same Parc des Princes stadium by beating Spain in the final. They had also reached the World Cup semi-finals twice, being beaten on each occasion by West Germany.

They were unbeaten in 19 games since losing to the Scots in 1989. England broke the French rearguard on the stroke of half-time. Wright got up to Clough's corner and headed it down, where Alan Shearer confidently turned and fired the opening goal. England brought on Gary Lineker for the second half and he made his mark with a typical poacher's goal. Clough met Shearer's cross with a superb volley, Rousset blocked it, but it veered up and Lineker got above two defenders to head the rebound against the bar. But Lineker did not give up. With Rousset lying on his back in the goal, the ball bounced invitingly and even though Boli was, literally, on Lineker's back, the ace marksman dived to head it over the line. This was Lineker's last goal at Wembley.

This was a psychological blow for France, as they were drawn against England in the forthcoming European Championship. Their meeting in Malmo four months later ended in a goalless draw, but both teams surprisingly failed to qualify for the semi-finals.

England beat France again in 1997 – 1-0 in Montpellier – but by the time the French next appeared at Wembley in 1999 they were World Champions.

Alan Shearer, scorer of the first goal, was named Footballer of the Year in 1994.

Eric Cantona became a regular visitor to Wembley with Manchester United and was named Footballer of the Year in 1996, year in which he scored the only goal of the FA Cup final as United sealed their second 'double' in three years. He also scored two penalties in the 1994 final when they won their first 'double'.

Jean-Pierre Papin, the 1991 European Footballer of the Year, made his Wembley debut.

Amara Simba returned to Wembley at the age of 37 in 1999 to play for Leyton Orient in the Third Division play-off final and scored Kingstonian's winner in Wembley's last FA Trophy Final in 2000.

England: Woods (Sheffield W), Jones* (Liverpool), Pearce (Nottingham F) – capt, Keown* (Everton), Walker (Nottingham F), Wright (Liverpool), Webb (Man Utd), Thomas (Crystal P), Clough (Nottingham F), Shearer* (Southampton), Hirst (Sheffield W). sub: Lineker (Tottenham) for Hirst 46
*first cap
France: Rousset (Olympique Lyonnais), Amoros (Olympique Marseille) – capt, Angloma (Marseille), Boli (Marseille), Blanc (Napoli), Casoni (Marseille), Deschamps (Marseille), Fernandez (Cannes), Papin (Marseille), Perez (Paris Saint-Germain), Cantona (Leeds Utd). subs: Durand (Marseille) for Fernandez 71, Simba (Paris Saint-Germain) for Perez 71. coach: Michel Platini

Schoolboy International

Saturday 7th March 1992

England 0
Netherlands 0
20,443

The Dutch avoided defeat at Wembley for the first time, but it was one of the worst schoolboy games played at the stadium. It was England's first match at Wembley under new manager, Steve Avory.

Phil Neville was a member of Manchester United's 'treble-winning' side in 1999 alongside elder brother, Gary, also his England team-mate. Phil won his 50th full international cap at the 2004 European Championship. Danny Murphy won his first full international cap in 2001 after Wembley had closed, but he did play for Crewe Alexandra when they won the Second Division play-offs at the stadium in 1997.

Stephen Hughes played for Arsenal at Wembley in the Champions League in 1998.

In the Dutch squad was Boudewijn Zenden, who appeared as an injury-time substitute for Barcelona against Arsenal in the Champions League at Wembley in 1999, before scoring for Middlesbrough when they won the Carling Cup in 2004.

England: Cutler, Black, Smith, Neville, Brunskill, Howell – capt, Hughes, Taylor, Ellis, Murphy, Beresford. subs: Power, Clarke

Zenith Cup Final

Sunday 29th March 1992

Nottingham Forest 3
Gemmill 14, 113, Black 45
Southampton 2
Le Tissier 64, Moore 68
After extra time
67,688
Referee: K Hackett (Sheffield)

Forest had won the Zenith Data Systems Cup in 1989, when it was known as the Simod Cup. They had played in two Wembley finals since then, losing the previous year's FA Cup final on their last visit.

Southampton had last appeared at Wembley 13 years before when they lost the Football League Cup final 3-2 to Forest. They had never been beyond the last 16 of the competition before and two seasons earlier had even declined to enter it.

The scoring started when a long throw from Crosby was headed on by Keane and Scot Gemmill sent a superb volley past Flowers and in off the post. His father, Archie, had played against Southampton in the 1979 Football League Cup final.

Forest increased their lead with virtually the last kick of the first half. Kingsley Black, who had played against Forest in the 1989 Littlewoods Cup final, took a pass from Gemmill and beat Flowers with a low shot.

Southampton fought their way back to level the match at full-time. First a brilliant cross from Ruddock into the heart of the defence was headed in by Matthew Le Tissier. Four minutes later they grabbed a sensational equaliser. This time it was Le Tissier who was the creator with a corner. Kevin Moore rose above a static Forest defence to head in off the bar.

But Forest wrapped it up in extra time. A centre from Charles found an unmarked Gemmill who, once again, volleyed home. Because Stuart Pearce had gone off injured after 15 minutes, Des Walker took on the armband and went up to collect the cup.

This was the fifth trophy Forest had won at Wembley in four years and they returned just two weeks later for the Rumbelows Cup final.

Teddy Sheringham made his first Wembley appearance. In a long and successful career, he scored in both the FA Cup final and the Champions League final, when Manchester United won the 'treble' in 1999 and in 2001 he was Footballer of the Year.

It was to be the last Zenith Cup.

Nottingham F: Marriott, Charles, Pearce – capt, Walker, Wassall, Keane, Crosby, Gemmill (S), Clough, Sheringham, Black. subs: Chettle for Pearce 15, Glover (not used). manager: Brian Clough
Southampton: Flowers, Kenna, Benali, Horne, Moore, Ruddock, Le Tissier, Cockerill – capt, Shearer, Dowie, Hurlock. subs: Lee, Wood (not used) manager: Ian Branfoot

LEAGUE CUP FINAL

Sunday 12th April 1992

Manchester United   **1-0**   **Nottingham Forest**
McClair 13
76,810
Referee: G Courtney (Spennymoor)

United were appearing in their second successive final but had never won the League Cup, sponsored by Rumbelows. The previous year they had suffered an embarrassing defeat at the hands of Second Division Sheffield Wednesday.

Forest were aiming to win the League Cup for a record fifth time by regaining it for the third time in four years. They wanted to repeat their 1989 'double', when the two trophies were known as the Littlewoods and Simod Cups.

The one goal came early. Giggs bore down on goal, feinted to shoot, but passed to Brian McClair who slotted the ball past

Marriott as Williams made a desperate lunge. United held on comfortably but did not add to their score.

United were back at Wembley for the following year's FA Charity Shield, but Forest astounded most pundits by finishing bottom of the Premier League. Brian Clough then retired, having taken them back to the division he had found them in some 18 years earlier.

After two European Cup wins and numerous other trophies, it was a sad epitaph for a great manager. They were promoted straight back the following year however, as runners-up to Crystal Palace.

Manchester U: Schmeichel, Parker, Irwin, Bruce – capt, Phelan, Pallister, Kanchelskis, Ince, McClair, Hughes, Giggs. subs: Sharpe for Kanchelskis 75, Webb (not used). manager: Alex Ferguson
Nottingham F: Marriott, Charles, Williams, Walker – capt, Wassall, Keane, Crosby, Gemmill, Clough, Sheringham, Black. subs: Laws for Charles 23, Glover (not used). manager: Brian Clough

FA Vase Final

Saturday 25th April 1992

Guiseley 3
Noteman 14, 51, Colville 90

Wimborne Town 5
Richardson 27, Sturgess 30, 78, Killick 42, 57
10,772
Referee: M Bodenham (Looe)

Wimborne became the first team to hit five in an FA Vase final as holders Guiseley were involved in an eight-goal feast for the second year in succession.

Guiseley: Maxted, Atkinson, Hogarth, Tetley, Morgan, Brockie, Roberts (A), Tennison, Noteman, Annan, Roberts

(W). subs: Wilson for Tetley, Colville for Noteman 79
Wimborne: Leonard, Langdown, Beacham, Allan, Taplin, Arnes, Richardson – capt, Bridle, Killick, Sturgess, Lynn. subs: Wilkins for Langdown, Lovell for Sturgess

FA CUP FINAL

Saturday 9th May 1992

Liverpool   2-0   **Sunderland**
Thomas 47, Rush 68
79,544
Referee: P Don (Hanworth Park)

The teams were competing for a new trophy after the old one was retired after 81 years.

Liverpool coach Ronnie Moran led out the team as manager Graeme Souness had undergone a triple heart by-pass operation the previous month although he watched the game from the bench.

They had reached their fourth final in seven years by beating Second Division Portsmouth in the first semi-final to be decided on penalties. The last two of their four FA Cup wins had both been against Everton (in 1986 and 1989). They had won their tenth League Championship in 15 years in 1990 and shared the FA Charity Shield on their last Wembley visit but had won nothing since.

Sunderland had twice won the FA Cup, their 1973 triumph as a Second Division

club providing great drama. They, too, had last appeared at Wembley in 1990 when, although they lost the Second Division Promotion play-off final to Swindon Town, they were still promoted because of financial irregularities at the Wiltshire club.

Sunderland had looked dangerous in the first half, but it was Liverpool who scored just after half-time. Michael Thomas waited for McManaman's cross to bounce and then smacked a spectacular rising shot past Norman. Thomas had played against Liverpool three times at Wembley for Arsenal.

Sunderland could not respond and Thomas then ran on to Saunders' through ball, took it round Ball and into the path of Ian Rush who tucked it past Norman into the corner. It was his fifth FA Cup final goal, a new record.

Liverpool: Grobbelaar, Jones (R), Burrows, Nicol, Molby, Wright – capt, Saunders, Houghton, Rush, McManaman, Thomas. subs: Marsh, Walters (not used). manager: Graeme Souness
Sunderland: Norman, Owers, Ball, Bennett, Rogan, Rush, Bracewell – capt, Davenport, Armstrong, Byrne, Atkinson. subs: Hardyman for Rush 69, Hawke for Armstrong 77. manager: Malcolm Crosby

FA Trophy Final

Sunday 10th May 1992

Colchester United 3
Masters 5, Smith 19, McGavin 90
Witton Albion 1
Lutkevitch 57
27,806
Referee: K Barratt (Coventry)

Colchester had won the Vauxhall Conference Championship on goal difference from Wycombe Wanderers to return to the Football League after relegation two years earlier. They acquired the FA Trophy as well, despite having Jason Cook sent off for throwing a punch at Witton substitute McCluskie.
Colchester: Barrett, Donald, Roberts, Kinsella, English,

Martin, Cook, Masters, McDonough – capt, McGavin, Smith. sub: Bennett for McDonough
Witton: Mason, Halliday, Coathup, McNeilis, Connor (Ja), Anderson, Thomas, Rose, Alford, Grimshaw, Lutkevitch. subs: Connor (Jo) for Grimshaw, McCluskie for Lutkevitch

Autoglass Trophy Final

Saturday 16th May 1992

Stockport County 0
Stoke City 1
Stein 64
48,339
Referee: R Hart (Darlington)

Although the Leyland DAF Cup had a new sponsor, the competition was won for the second year in succession by the same manager, Lou Macari, and the same captain, Vince Overson. The previous year it was Birmingham City they led to victory. Stoke beat the holders in a group match and went on to reach Wembley for the first time in 20 years.

Stockport lost their opening match of the competition 4-0 at Carlisle United but subsequently knocked them out with a 3-1 away win in the next round.

This was the third meeting of the week between these teams as Stockport had won 2-1 on aggregate in the Third Division Promotion play-off semi-finals.

Stockport would be returning to Wembley the following week for the final. But

Stoke gained their revenge by beating them for the first time in 67 years.

Adrian Heath scored for Everton in consecutive FA Charity Shields at Wembley in the mid-1980's and was on the winning side against Stockport again when Burnley beat them in the Second Division Promotion play-off final two years later.

Stockport: Edwards, Knowles, Todd, Frain, Barras, Williams (W), Gannon, Ward – capt, Francis, Beaumont, Wheeler. subs: Williams (P) for Wheeler 76, Thorpe for Frain 82. manager: Danny Bergara

Stoke: Fox, Butler, Kevan, Cranson, Overson – capt, Sandford, Kelly, Foley, Stein, Biggins, Heath. subs: Barnes, Grimes (not used). manager: Lou Macari

INTERNATIONAL

Sunday 17th May 1992

England 1-1 **Brazil**
Platt 49
Bebeto 25
53,428
Referee: J McCluskey (Scotland)

Brazil had not beaten England since 1981 and their status in world football was declining. This was England's last home match before the European Championship in Sweden and they took to the field in red shirts.

After nine minutes of Wembley's first international to be played on a Sunday, Lineker ran on to Stevens' pass and was brought down by Carlos, connecting dangerously with the striker's neck. The England captain got up to take the penalty. Had he scored, he would have equalled Sir Bobby Charlton's record of 49 goals for England but Lineker was too casual. He tried to chip the 'keeper and fluffed it. Carlos blocked the

shot with his leg and then caught the ball. Lineker would regret this opportunity. He never again scored for England.

Brazil took advantage of the reprieve and scored when Stevens made a hash of a Renato cross, Bebeto firing past Woods. England were poor, but equalised four minutes after the interval. Brazilian substitute Charles, in trying to clear, headed straight to David Platt who volleyed past Carlos. It was a match of many errors.

The following year, England again drew 1-1 with Brazil in the US Cup in Washington. In 1995 Brazil were back at Wembley again, contesting the Umbro Cup.

England: Woods (Sheffield W), Stevens (Rangers), Dorigo (Leeds Utd), Palmer (Sheffield W), Walker (Nottingham F), Keown (Everton), Daley (Aston Villa), Steven (Olympique Marseille), Platt (Bari), Lineker (Tottenham) – capt, Sinton (QPR). subs: Webb (Man Utd) for Steven 46, Rocastle (Arsenal) for Sinton 46, Pearce (Nottingham F) for Dorigo 72, Merson (Arsenal) for Daley 72. manager: Graham Taylor

Brazil: Carlos (Palmeiras), Winck (Vasco da Gama), Mozer (Olympique Marseille), Ricardo Gomes (Paris Saint-Germain), De Silva (Bragantino), Branco (Genoa), Bebeto (Vasco da Gama), Henrique (Palmeiras), Renato (Botafogo), Rai (Sao Paulo) – capt, Valdo (Paris Saint-Germain). subs: Charles (Flamengo) for Winck 46, Paulo Sergio (Corinthians) for Valdo 66, Valdeir (Botafogo) for Henrique 74, Junior (Flamengo) for Renato 78. coach: Carlos Alberto Parreira

EUROPEAN CUP FINAL

Wednesday 20th May 1992

Barcelona 1-0 **Sampdoria**
Koeman 111
After extra time
70,827
Referee: A Schmidhuber (Germany)

This was the first European Cup final to be held at Wembley for 14 years.

Barcelona had never won the European Cup, having lost the 1986 final on penalties to Steaua Bucharest following a goalless draw after extra time in Seville. Barcelona could not even convert a penalty. Although they were more successful in the European Cup-Winners Cup. Three years earlier, they had beaten Sampdoria 2-0 in Berne to become the first team to win the competition three times. Two years later, they reached the final again but lost 2-1 to Manchester United in Rotterdam.

No Spanish team had won the European Cup since Real Madrid's record sixth victory, back in 1966. The last Italian winners had been AC Milan in 1990. Sampdoria had reached their second successive European Cup-Winners Cup final in 1990 and beat Anderlecht 2-0 after extra time in Gothenburg. Three months later, they won the Makita Tournament at Wembley

and they retained it at Arsenal in 1991, after winning the Italian League Championship for the first time.

Barcelona were the more adventurous, with Sampdoria looking dangerous on the counter-attack. But the final looked to be heading for penalties for the second year in succession when with nine minutes of extra time left Barcelona won a free kick 25 yards out. Stoichkov took it, playing a short pass to Bakero, who stopped the ball. Ronald Koeman then unleashed an unstoppable drive, almost breaking the net.

Barcelona had at long last become champions of Europe and to celebrate the historic event the entire squad changed into their traditional red and blue striped shirts to receive the trophy and medals, having had to wear a change strip of all orange for the game.

Hristo Stoichkov, making his Wembley debut, won the European Footballer of the Year award, two years later.

Barcelona: Zubizarreta, Nando, Ferrer, Koeman, Juan Carlos – capt, Bakero, Salinas, Stoichkov, Laudrup, Guardiola, Eusebio. subs: Goicoechea for Salinas 64, Alexanco for Guardiola 113. coach: Johan Cruyff

Sampdoria: Pagliuca, Mannini, Katanec, Pari, Vierchowod, Lanna, Lombardo, Cerezo, Vialli, Mancini – capt, Bonetti. subs: Invernizzi for Bonetti 72, Buso for Vialli 100. coach: Vujadin Boskov

Play-off Finals

Fourth Division

Saturday 23rd May 1992

Blackpool 1
Bamber 41
Scunthorpe United 1
Daws 53
After extra time
Blackpool won 4-3 on penalties.
(Hamilton 0-1, Cook 1-1, Longden 1-2, Groves 2-2, Elliott 2-3, Garner 3-3, Alexander saved, Eyres 4-3, White missed)
22,741
Referee: K Hackett (Sheffield)

For the second successive year, Blackpool's fate was decided by penalty kicks. They had missed promotion by a point again, after losing their last match to two penalties at Lincoln City. Dave Bamber had missed the crucial penalty in the previous year's final but this time he put them ahead.

Scunthorpe, appearing in the play-offs for the fourth time in five years, in their first final and paying their first visit to Wembley, saw the day end in heartbreak when Steve

McIlhargey saved from substitute Graham Alexander and David Eyres netted for Blackpool. Jason White, their other substitute, fired over the bar and succeeded Bamber as the saddest sight of the season.

Blackpool: McIlhargey, Burgess, Cook, Groves – capt, Davies, Gore, Rodwell, Horner, Bamber, Garner, Eyres. subs: Murphy for Davies 69, Sinclair for Horner 90. manager: Billy Ayre
Scunthorpe: Samways, Joyce – capt, Longden, Hill, Elliott, Humphries, Martin, Hamilton, Daws, Buckley, Helliwell. subs: White for Daws 105, Alexander for Buckley 105. manager: Bill Green

Third Division

Sunday 24th May 1992

Peterborough United 2
Charlery 52, 89
Stockport County 1
Francis 87
35,087
Referee: M Bodenham (Looe)

Peterborough had been denied a place in the Fourth Division Promotion play-offs in 1988 on goal difference by eventual winners Swansea City. Three years later they won promotion and moved straight up to the new First Division after spending their entire Football League career of 32 years in the lower divisions.

Stockport, who had reached Wembley for the first time the previous week, had finished as Fourth Division runners-up to Darlington the previous year and had been promoted with Peterborough after 21 years in the Fourth Division.

But it was Peterborough who secured promotion this time with a last minute winner from Ken Charlery, although his first goal did not appear to cross the line.

Stockport reached the final again in 1994.

Peterborough: Barber, Luke, Robinson (R), Halsall – capt, Robinson (D), Welsh, Sterling, Ebdon, Adcock, Charlery, Barnes. subs: Howarth for Welsh 80, Cooper (not used). manager: Chris Turner

Stockport: Edwards, Knowles, Todd, Frain, Barras, Williams, Gannon, Ward – capt, Francis, Beaumont, Preece. subs: Wheeler for Ward 81, Thorpe (not used). manager: Danny Bergara

Second Division

Monday 25th May 1992

Blackburn Rovers 1
Newell pen 45

Leicester City 0
68,147
Referee: G Courtney (Spennymoor)

Blackburn had finished only sixth in the Second Division but were appearing in the play-offs for the fourth time in five years. In 1988 they had missed promotion by a point. In 1989, they had lost the final to Crystal Palace after extra time, despite winning the first leg 3-1. In 1990 they had lost to the eventual winners Swindon Town, who were subsequently denied promotion because of financial irregularities.

Leicester had escaped relegation to the Third Division by two points the previous year. It was their first appearance at Wembley since the 1969 FA Cup final but it was to be their fifth successive defeat at the stadium.

Blackburn, who had played at Wembley in the Football League Centenary Tournament in 1988, took their place in the new FA Premier League thanks to a penalty at the end of the first half from Mike Newell who had left Leicester in 1989.

In 1985 he had scored the opening goal of Wembley's first Freight Rover Trophy final for Wigan Athletic. Six minutes from the end, Blackburn won another penalty but Carl Muggleton saved from Newell. Still Blackburn held on to regain their top flight place after a gap of 26 years.

The Blackburn players put their more traditional blue and white halved shirts on top of their change kit of all yellow to go up to receive the trophy.

Leicester reached the final again the following year while Blackburn moved on to new heights. They appeared in the 1994 FA Charity Shield and went on to win the FA Carling Premiership in 1995.

Gordon Cowans had won a European Cup winners medal with Aston Villa ten years earlier. He was to play against Leicester again as Derby County captain in the 1994 play-off final.

Blackburn: Mimms, May, Wright, Cowans, Moran – capt, Hendry, Price, Atkins, Speedie, Newell, Sellars. subs: Richardson for Sellars 85, Wegerle (not used). manager: Kenny Dalglish

Leicester: Muggleton, Mills, Whitlow, Hill, Walsh – capt, James, Thompson, Grayson, Wright, Ormondroyd, Russell. subs: Gee for James 67, Oldfield (not used). manager: Brian Little

Schoolboy International

Saturday 6th June 1992

England 1
Goodridge 75

Italy 1
Totti pen 1
44,000
Referee: R Groves (Weston-super-Mare)

The Italians avoided defeat at Wembley for the first time. Their scorer Francesco Totti starred for his country at the European Championship eight years later when they were seconds away from lifting the trophy in Rotterdam, France snatching it from their grasp.

England: Cutler, Blaney, Power, Neville, Brunskill, Howell – capt, Hughes, Taylor, Ellis, Murphy, Beresford. subs: Smith for Blaney 41, Goodridge for Power 61, Clarke for Murphy 72

FA CHARITY SHIELD

Saturday 8th August 1992

Leeds United	**4-3**	**Liverpool**

Cantona 25, 77, 87, Dorigo 43
61,291
Referee: D Elleray (Harrow)

Rush 34, Saunders 65, Strachan og 89

Leeds and Liverpool had been the participants in Wembley's first FA Charity Shield in 1974 but unlike that match when Billy Bremner and Kevin Keegan were dismissed for fighting there was excitement of a different order.

Leeds had only won the Shield once, in 1969, and their only Wembley appearance since 1974 had been a forgettable first round exit in the Football League Centenary Tournament in 1988.

In only their second season back in the First Division they had won their third League Championship by four points from Manchester United who had faltered at the end when they seemed set to win the title themselves.

Liverpool, who had beaten Leeds in the 1965 FA Cup final, were chasing a record 14th Charity Shield and had completed their second hat-trick, albeit sharing it in 1990. After finishing sixth in the First Division, their lowest position for 27 years, they had salvaged the season with a fifth FA Cup win.

Leeds broke the deadlock when Batty found Wallace in acres of space on the left. Wallace took the ball into the area, checked back and played it across to Eric Cantona whose shot took a deflection off Burrows to beat Grobbelaar.

The equaliser came from Ian Rush's head but Leeds regained the lead just before half-time with another deflection. From a free kick just outside the area, Batty tapped the ball to Speed, who steadied it for Tony Dorigo whose shot deflected off Rosenthal,

on the end of the wall, and into the corner of the net.

Liverpool equalised again when Whyte blocked Walters' shot only for it to hit Fairclough and fall invitingly for Dean Saunders to drill past Lukic. This unusually entertaining Charity Shield swung Leeds' way again when Cantona got up to McAllister's free kick. His header hit Fairclough but came back to him and he fired his second through Wright's legs and past Grobbelaar. It was the first time Liverpool had conceded three goals at Wembley in 32 visits.

They then let in a fourth with three minutes left. Tanner's headed clearance rebounded off the corner flag and with Liverpool's defence in momentary disarray, Wallace crossed. Grobbelaar came for it, but missed and left Cantona to rise above Wright and head into the empty net. He became the first foreign player to score a hat-trick at Wembley since Nandor Hidegkuti for Hungary in 1953.

Still, the scoring was not complete. Kozma, Liverpool's Hungarian substitute, took a corner in the last minute. Lukic, under pressure, could palm the ball only to Wright whose shot was blocked on the line by substitute Gordon Strachan. In his anxiety to clear he accidentally back-heeled it into his own net for a bizarre consolation goal in Wembley's highest scoring FA Charity Shield.

It was another four years before Leeds returned to Wembley for the Coca-Cola Cup final. It was to be another three years before Liverpool returned to win the Coca-Cola Cup.

Leeds: Lukic, Newsome, Dorigo, Batty, Fairclough, Whyte, Cantona, Wallace, Chapman, McAllister – capt, Speed.
subs: Hodge for Chapman 80, Strachan for Newsome 86. manager: Howard Wilkinson
Liverpool: Grobbelaar, Tanner, Burrows, Marsh, Whelan, Wright – capt, Saunders, Stewart, Rush, Rosenthal, Walters.
subs: Hutchison for Marsh 70, Kozma for Rosenthal 85. manager: Graeme Souness

WORLD CUP QUALIFYING

Wednesday 14th October 1992

England   **1-1**   **Norway**
Platt 55   Rekdal 76
51,441
Referee: A Brizio Carter (Mexico)

Norway had lost 4-0 at Wembley in a World Cup qualifying match in 1980, but had shocked England by winning the return in Oslo the following year, their first victory against them.

They had not qualified for a major tournament since the 1938 World Cup but had already won their first three games in Group Two, including a 10-0 win over San Marino and a 2-1 victory against the Netherlands, both in Oslo.

England took a deserved lead ten minutes after half-time. From Pearce's free kick, David Platt, England's lone scorer from the European Championship in which they had finished bottom of their group, got the touch to beat the Tottenham Hotspur 'keeper Thorstvedt.

The Norwegians drew level, however, with Kjetil Rekdal taking Sorloth's cross on his chest and with England's defence standing off, unleashed a 25-yard screamer which gave Woods no chance. Their only real mistake had cost England a vital point.

Norway won the return, 2-0 in Oslo the following year, a defeat which was as crippling to England's World Cup prospects as the 1981 loss. The Norwegians went on to win the group and qualified for their first World Cup since 1938. Before flying to the USA, they met England again at Wembley.

England: Woods (Sheffield W), Dixon (Arsenal), Pearce (Nottingham F) – capt, Batty (Leeds Utd), Walker (Sampdoria), Adams (Arsenal), Platt (Juventus), Gascoigne (Lazio), Shearer (Blackburn), Wright (Arsenal), Ince (Man Utd). subs: Merson (Arsenal) for Wright 68, Palmer (Sheffield W) for Dixon 89. manager: Graham Taylor
Norway: Thorstvedt (Tottenham), Nilsen (Viking Stavanger), Pedersen (Gothenburg), Bratseth (Werder Bremen) – capt, Bjornebye (Rosenborg), Ingebrigtsen (Rosenborg), Mykland (Start Kristiansand), Rekdal (Lierse), Halle (Oldham), Sorloth (Rosenborg), Jakobsen (Young Boys). subs: Berg (Lillestrom) for Pedersen 19, Flo (Sogndal) for Mykland 78. coach: Egil Olsen

Wednesday 18th November 1992

England   **4-0**   **Turkey**
Gascoigne 16, 62, Shearer 28, Pearce 61
42,984
Referee: B Karlsson (Sweden)

England had dropped to fourth in Group Two after Turkey's 4-1 win against San Marino in Ankara three weeks earlier. The Turks had kept England down to one goal in each of their last two meetings in the recent European Championship. Their performance at Wembley the previous year gave them hope that they would score their first goal against England in this their seventh meeting.

It was a better performance from England than that match and they were ahead after Bulent took too long to clear. He was tackled by Ince and the ball fell for Paul Gascoigne who calmly tucked it away.

The second goal was superb. Wright broke down the left and crossed. Alan Shearer intelligently stayed back until the last moment when he ran around Ogun to send a diving header past Hayrettin. Stuart Pearce added a third from a second half free kick which struck a Turkish foot in the wall and flew up past the 'keeper.

Within a minute it was 4-0. Shearer could not connect with a cross from Walker, winning his 50th cap, but Gascoigne could and he waltzed round the 'keeper before slotting in his second.

England won 2-0 in Izmir, the following year as the Turks still could not find a way past England's defence. Turkey finished fifth in the group, but returned to England in 1996 when they qualified for the European Championship for the first time although they failed to score or win a point. Their football was on the rise, however, and by 2002 they were playing Brazil in a World Cup semi-final.

England: Woods (Sheffield W), Dixon (Arsenal), Pearce (Nottingham F) – capt, Palmer (Sheffield W), Walker (Sampdoria), Adams (Arsenal), Platt (Juventus), Gascoigne (Lazio), Shearer (Blackburn), Wright (Arsenal), Ince (Man Utd). manager: Graham Taylor
Turkey: Hayrettin (Galatasaray), Recep (Besiktas), Bulent (Galatasaray), Gokhan (Besiktas), Ogun (Trabzonspor), Orhan (Trabzonspor), Hami (Trabzonspor), Unal (Trabzonspor) – capt, Mehmet (Besiktas), Oguz (Fenerbahce), Hakan (Galatasaray). subs: Ugur (Galatasaray) for Mehmet 46, Riza (Besiktas) for Hami 69. coach: Sepp Piontek

Wednesday 17th February 1993

England   6-0   San Marino

Platt 13, 24, 67, 83, Palmer 77
Ferdinand 86
51,154
Referee: R Phillipi (Luxembourg)

The only change to the Group Two table after England's victory against Turkey was that the Netherlands had moved up to third, behind England on goal difference, having played a game more. Norway were still four points clear at the top, but England now had an opportunity to close the gap and at the same time increase their goal difference.

San Marino had been involved in international competition for only three years. They had still to win a point after 11 competitive fixtures and had scored only their second goal in Ankara against Turkey four months earlier. Their first ever World Cup tie had seen them suffer a crushing 10-0 defeat by Norway in Oslo.

The rout started when Barnes got a touch to Gascoigne's corner for David Platt to head in at the far post. When Batty crossed, another Platt header put England further ahead although Benedettini appeared to have stopped it from crossing the line.

Platt completed his hat-trick midway through the second half when he rounded the 'keeper after Ferdinand had got his head to a Dorigo free kick. Ferdinand also laid on the fourth: Carlton Palmer thundering in with a diving header to meet his cross.

Platt grabbed his fourth, diverting a Dixon shot past Benedettini after Adams had centred and then, with four minutes left, Dixon crossed, Adams headed against the underside of the bar and Les Ferdinand dived to head home England's sixth.

It should have been seven when Manzaroli brought down Dorigo in the dying seconds but Benedettini pulled off a fine save from Platt's penalty to deny the England captain his opportunity to equal Malcolm Macdonald's five-goal Wembley record set in 1975.

England beat San Marino 7-1 in Bologna in their final match of the group nine months later but by then it was too late for England.

England: Woods (Sheffield W), Dixon (Arsenal), Dorigo (Leeds Utd), Palmer (Sheffield W), Walker (Sampdoria), Adams (Arsenal), Platt (Juventus) – capt, Gascoigne (Lazio), Ferdinand* (QPR), Barnes (Liverpool), Batty (Leeds Utd). manager: Graham Taylor
*first cap
San Marino: Benedettini (Juvenes), Muccioli (Novafeltria), Gennari (Juvenes), Zanotti (Juvenes), Canti (Juvenes), Guerra (Calcio San Marino), Manzaroli (Calcio San Marino), Mazza (M) (Cerveteri), Bacciocchi (Calcio San Marino), Bonini (Bologna) – capt, Francini (Santarcangiolese). subs: Mazza (P) (Maremmana) for Bacciocchi 64, Matteoni (Calcio San Marino) for Francini 81. coach: Giorgio Leoni

Victory Shield

Saturday 13th March 1993

England 1
Cassidy

Scotland 2
O'Brien, Pollock pen

Scotland reversed a half-time deficit to record their first Wembley win since the 5-4 thriller of 1980. The Scots went on to win the Victory Shield.

England: Dungey, Futcher, Hilton, Millett, Curtis, Broomes, Wynter, Hodges, Ducros, Cassidy, Omoyinmi. subs: Clemence for Wynter, Fotiadis for Ducros
Scotland: McCondichie, Canning, McDonald, Pollock, Horn, Gaughan, Macdonald, Mullen, O'Brien, Harty, McShane. sub: Rice for Mullen

Anglo-Italian Cup Final

Saturday 27th March 1993

Cremonese 3
Verdelli 9, Maspero pen 49, Tentoni 83
Derby County 1
Gabbiadini 21
37,024
Referee: J Velasquez (Spain)

The Anglo-Italian Cup was revived after 16 years to be competed for by clubs from the new First Division of the Barclays League and the Italian Second Division. Cremonese had won 3-1 at Derby in an earlier group match.

Derby had reached the final only on away goals after losing their semi-final second leg at home to Brentford and on their first Wembley appearance since their 1975 FA Charity Shield win they were well beaten by the Italians.

Cremonese also missed a first half penalty, when Martin Taylor saved from Nicolini. They were unable to defend the trophy as they finished runners-up to Reggiana and were promoted to the Italian First Division for the third time in five years.

Cremonese: Turci, Gualco, Pedroni, Cristiani, Colonnese, Verdelli – capt, Giandebiaggi, Nicolini, Tentoni, Maspero, Florjancic. subs: Dezotti for Florjancic 75, Montorfano for Tentoni 85. coach: Luigi Simoni
Derby: Taylor, Patterson, Forsyth, Nicholson, Coleman, Pembridge, Micklewhite, Goulooze, Kitson, Gabbiadini, Johnson. subs: Simpson for Johnson 80, Hayward for Goulooze 82. manager: Arthur Cox

FA Cup Semi-finals

Saturday 3rd April 1993

Sheffield United 1
Cork 43
Sheffield Wednesday 2
Waddle 1, Bright 106
After extra time
75,364
Referee: K Morton (Bury St. Edmunds)

This was a historic day for the city of Sheffield. United had not appeared at Wembley for 57 years.

Wednesday had twice reached the semi-finals in the 1980's but their last final had been in 1966.

United had twice slipped into the lower divisions in the 1980's but were now in their third season in the top flight, although they were fighting against relegation.

Wednesday had won the League Cup as a Second Division club two years earlier and had reached the final again and would be returning to Wembley to face Arsenal in two weeks time. They were also to reach the FA Cup final, again against the Londoners.

Just as in 1991, Wembley's first semi-final, the game came to life with a spectacular free kick early in the game. In the second minute, Chris Waddle curled a powerful shot past Kelly to give Wednesday a fantastic start.

United equalised at the end of the first half. A fine pass from Carr found Alan Cork who tucked the ball away past Woods. Wednesday created far more chances than United but had to wait until extra time to clinch it. Harkes' corner was headed in by an unchallenged Mark Bright.

Sheffield U: Kelly, Gage, Whitehouse, Gannon, Gayle – capt, Pemberton, Carr, Ward, Cork, Deane, Hodges. subs: Littlejohn for Ward, Hoyland for Hodges. manager: Dave Bassett
Sheffield W: Woods, Nilsson, Worthington, Palmer, Harkes, Anderson – capt, Wilson, Waddle, Warhurst, Bright, Sheridan. subs: Hirst for Warhurst, Hyde for Sheridan. manager: Trevor Francis

Sunday 4th April 1993

Arsenal 1
Adams 79
Tottenham Hotspur 0
76,263
Referee: P Don (Hanworth Park)

This was the fourth Wembley meeting in five years for the north London rivals.

Arsenal had won their first clash in the International Tournament of 1988 but Tottenham had beaten them in the stadium's first FA Cup semi-final three years later. They then drew in the FA Charity Shield three months later.

Arsenal had not reached the final since 1980 but were already in the Coca-Cola Cup final and would be returning to Wembley two weeks later.

Arsenal gained their revenge for their 1991 defeat but the only goal did not arrive until late. Tony Adams rose at the far post to head Merson's free kick past Thorstvedt. With five minutes left, Lee Dixon was sent off for a foul on Edinburgh, his second bookable offence. The suspension caused him to miss the Coca-Cola Cup final.

Tottenham had to wait another six years for their next visit to Wembley. Arsenal were to face Sheffield Wednesday in both the Coca-Cola Cup final and the FA Cup final. It was the first time that the same two teams had reached both of the major domestic finals.

Arsenal: Seaman, Dixon, Winterburn, Hillier, Linighan, Adams – capt, Parlour, Wright, Campbell, Merson, Selley. subs: Morrow for Wright, Smith (A) for Campbell. manager: George Graham

Tottenham: Thorstvedt, Austin, Edinburgh, Samways, Mabbutt – capt, Ruddock, Sedgley, Nayim, Anderton, Sheringham, Allen (P). subs:- Barmby for Samways, Bergsson for Sedgley. coach: Doug Livermore

LEAGUE CUP FINAL

Sunday 18th April 1993

Arsenal　　　2-1　　　Sheffield Wednesday
Merson 18, Morrow 68　　　　　　Harkes 9
74,007
Referee: A Gunn (South Chailey)

Arsenal were in their first final since their two successive Littlewoods Cup finals in the late 1980's. Wednesday were attempting to regain the trophy for the second time in three years, having won the Rumbelows Cup as a Second Division club. Coca-Cola had now taken over the sponsorship of the competition.

Just two weeks earlier, both clubs had won FA Cup semi-finals at the stadium and would be returning to face each other again in the following month's final.

Wednesday took the lead early when King received Sheridan's free kick and crossed. O'Leary cleared but only to John Harkes who drove in a low shot.

The equaliser came from another free kick. Morrow tapped it back to Davis whose chip into the middle was headed out by Bright. Paul Merson volleyed the ball back with a wicked swerve to beat Woods.

Midway through the second half Merson crossed and Palmer should have cleared. But he lost control and the ball ran to Steve Morrow who beat Woods from close range to score his first goal for the club.

Arsenal held on comfortably after this but their celebrations were somewhat muted when Morrow broke his arm after Adams, his captain, playfully threw him over his shoulder. Morrow was stretchered off in agony as his team-mates went up to receive the trophy and medals. The freak accident caused him to miss the FA Cup final.

Arsenal: Seaman, O'Leary, Winterburn, Parlour, Adams – capt, Linighan, Morrow, Merson, Wright, Campbell, Davis. subs: Selley, Smith (A) (not used). manager: George Graham

Sheffield W: Woods, Nilsson, King, Palmer, Anderson – capt, Harkes, Wilson, Waddle, Warhurst, Bright, Sheridan. subs: Hirst for Wilson 74, Hyde for King 83. manager: Trevor Francis

WORLD CUP QUALIFYING

Wednesday 28th April 1993

England　　　2-2　　　Netherlands
Barnes 1, Platt 23　　　　　　Bergkamp 34, Van Vossen pen 85
73,163
Referee: P Mikkelsen (Denmark)

Norway now led Group Two only on goal difference from England and the Netherlands, although the Dutch had played a game more.

The Netherlands had lost their opening match in Oslo and had been two goals down to Poland in Rotterdam before salvaging a point. Their last visit to Wembley five years earlier had resulted in an entertaining 2-2 draw. Three months later they had won the European Championship, beating England 3-1 in Dusseldorf on the way. In the 1990 World Cup the Netherlands had lost in the last 16 to eventual winners West Germany after an earlier goalless draw with England in Cagliari.

England had not beaten the Dutch since 1982 at Wembley but they took a spectacular lead after just a minute, John Barnes curling a 25-yard free kick into the top corner.

England increased their lead when Gascoigne's miscue led to Ferdinand hitting the post for David Platt to stab the rebound into the net.

The Dutch soon began the fightback and a lob from Wouters was volleyed over Woods by Dennis Bergkamp. Two years later Bergkamp was transferred to Arsenal and won the Footballer of the Year award in 1998 as his goals helped them win the 'double'.

England had almost secured a famous victory but with just five minutes left Overmars headed for goal and had his shirt pulled by Walker. Although the original contact took place outside the box, Overmars fell in the area and a penalty was given. Substitute Peter Van Vossen sent Woods the wrong way to rescue a vital point.

Six months later England lost the return 2-0 in Rotterdam and the Netherlands qualified as runners-up to Norway a month later by winning 3-1 in Poznan. In 1996 they returned to Wembley for the European Championship.

England: Woods (Sheffield W), Dixon (Arsenal), Keown (Arsenal), Palmer (Sheffield W), Walker (Sampdoria), Adams (Arsenal), Platt (Juventus) – capt, Gascoigne (Lazio), Ferdinand (QPR), Barnes (Liverpool), Ince (Man Utd). sub: Merson (Arsenal) for Gascoigne 46. manager: Graham Taylor

Netherlands: De Goey (Feyenoord), Blind (Ajax Amsterdam), De Boer (F) (Ajax), Wouters (Bayern Munich), Witschge (Feyenoord), Winter (Lazio), Bergkamp (Ajax), Rijkaard (AC Milan), Bosman (Anderlecht), Gullit (AC Milan) – capt, Overmars (Ajax). subs: De Wolf (Feyenoord) for Bosman 46, Van Vossen (Anderlecht) for Gullit 69. coach: Dick Advocaat

FA Vase Final

Saturday 8th May 1993

Bridlington Town 1
Radford 63

Tiverton Town 0
9,061
Referee: R Hart (Darlington)

Bridlington made amends for their 1990 final defeat with Alan Radford's deflected winner.

Bridlington: Taylor, Brentano, McKenzie, Harvey, Bottomley, Woodcock, Grocock, Roberts, Jones, Radford, Parkinson. sub: Tyrell for Radford
Tiverton: Nott, Smith (J), Saunders (N), Saunders (M), Short, Steele – capt, Annunziata, Smith (K), Everett, Daly, Hynds. subs: Scott for Short, Rogers for Hynds

Autoglass Trophy Final

Sunday 9th May 1993

Runcorn 1
Shaughnessy 41

Wycombe Wanderers 4
Cousins 2, Kerr 20, Thompson 59, Carroll 89
32,968
Referee: J Borrett (Harleston)

Yet another curling free kick in the opening minutes of a game at Wembley. This time it was Jason Cousins who put Wycombe in the driving seat. Martin O'Neill's men regained the Trophy for the second time in three years and injured club captain Glyn Creaser was sent up to receive it. After missing out on promotion to the Football League on goal difference, the previous year, Wycombe made no mistake this time. They won the Vauxhall Conference by a runaway 15 points and so repeated Colchester United's 'double' of the previous year.

Runcorn: Williams, Bates, Robertson, Hill, Harold, Anderson, Brady, Brown, Shaughnessy, McKenna, Brabin. subs: Connor for Harold, Parker for Brady
Wycombe: Hyde, Cousins, Cooper, Kerr – capt, Crossley, Thompson, Carroll, Ryan, Hutchinson, Scott, Guppy. subs: Hayrettin for Hutchinson 65, Casey (not used)

EUROPEAN CUP-WINNERS CUP FINAL

Wednesday 12th May 1993

Parma	3-1	**Royal Antwerp**
Minotti 9, Melli 30, Cuoghi 84		Severeyns 11

37,393
Referee: K Assenmacher (Germany)

This was Wembley's first Cup-Winners Cup final for 28 years. Parma had been in the Italian First Division for only three years and had reached a final in only their second entry into Europe.

Antwerp had won the previous year's Belgian Cup on penalties, their first win since 1955. They had never previously progressed beyond the last 16 of any European competition.

Parma finished third in the Italian First Division, their highest ever.

The Italians were ahead early. Stojanovic, who had been Red Star Belgrade's penalty shoot-out hero in the European Cup final two years earlier, came out for Osio's corner but could only punch it out to Lorenzo Minotti who slammed a spectacular half-volley into the net.

The lead did not last long. After another two minutes, Zorrato's attempted clearance hit Czerniatynski in the chest and the Belgian international took advantage to supply Francis Severeyns who expertly fired past Ballotta for the equaliser.

Parma regained the lead as Stojanovic was again tempted from his line for Osio's cross but he was too slow and was left helpless as Alessandro Melli outjumped Taeymans to head into the unguarded net.

The Italians deservedly won their first European trophy with six minutes left. Stefano Cuoghi beat the offside trap to reach Grun's long ball and had only the 'keeper to beat. He waited for Stojanovic to commit himself and then found the net.

Parma reached the final again the following year., losing by a single goal to Arsenal in Copenhagen. They reached their third consecutive European final in 1995 and won the UEFA Cup for the first time. Antwerp are still searching for their first European success.

Parma: Ballotta, Benarrivo, Di Chiara, Minotti – capt, Apolloni, Grun, Melli, Zoratto, Osio, Cuoghi, Brolin. subs: Pin for Zoratto 27, Pizzi for Osio 65. coach: Nevio Scala

Royal Antwerp: Stojanovic, Kiekens, Broeckaert, Taeymans, Smidts – capt, Jakovljevic, Van Rethy, Segers, Severeyns, Lehnhoff, Czerniatynski. subs: Van Veirdeghem for Jakovljevic 58, Moukrim for Segers 86. coach: Walter Meeuws

FA CUP FINAL

Saturday 15th May 1993

Arsenal   1-1   **Sheffield Wednesday**
Wright 20   Hirst 61
After extra time
79,347
Referee: K Barratt (Coventry)

This was Arsenal's first final since 1980 when they were defending the trophy won the year before. But they were by no means strangers to Wembley. They had made 13 appearances since 1980, which included two semi-finals against their north London rivals Tottenham Hotspur.

It was Wednesday's first final since 1966 and it had been 58 years since they last won the FA Cup.

Arsenal had beaten Wednesday in the previous month's League Cup final.

Arsenal scored first. A Davis free kick into the box was headed across goal by Linighan. It went beyond Warhurst to Ian Wright who powered a header past Woods.

The Londoners stayed in control until half-time. Wednesday came out more determined after the interval and were rewarded when Sheridan's cross was flicked on by Bright to Harkes. As Dixon came to challenge Harkes unselfishly headed the ball across to David Hirst who slid in the equaliser as Seaman advanced.

Wednesday had chances to win it, but this disappointing final could produce no winning goal. Five days later they met for the replay, their third match at Wembley in two months.

Arsenal: Seaman, Dixon, Winterburn, Davis, Linighan, Adams – capt, Jensen, Wright, Campbell, Merson, Parlour. subs: Smith (A) for Parlour 66, O'Leary for Wright 91. manager: George Graham

Sheffield W: Woods, Nilsson, Worthington, Palmer, Anderson – capt, Warhurst, Harkes, Waddle, Hirst, Bright, Sheridan. subs: Hyde for Anderson 85, Bart-Williams for Waddle 112. manager: Trevor Francis

REPLAY

Thursday 20th May 1993

Arsenal 2-1 **Sheffield Wednesday**

Wright 34, Linighan 119 Waddle 68
After extra time
62,267
Referee: K Barratt (Coventry)

Having drawn five days earlier, and with Arsenal having beaten Wednesday in the previous month's Coca-Cola Cup final, there was little these two teams did not know about each other. None of the games had been very entertaining, however, and the attendance was the lowest ever for an FA Cup tie at Wembley.

The replay followed a similar pattern to the first game. After 34 minutes, Smith sent Ian Wright away. Woods hesitated and Wright tucked the ball past him. It was his fourth FA Cup final goal in four appearances, although he did not complete a match in any of them.

Once again Wednesday came back in the second half. Bright and Linighan went up for a cross from Harkes and the ball hit Linighan's shoulder. It bounced off Dixon's knee to Chris Waddle whose shot then deflected off the full back's leg to beat Seaman for a bizarre equaliser.

Again Wednesday had chances to win but the final was heading for its first penalty shoot-out when Arsenal won a corner in the last minute of extra time. Merson found the head of Andy Linighan who powered a header to which Woods got his hands but could not keep out. Linighan had broken his nose and a finger when colliding with Bright's elbow in the 18th minute and he became the hero with the most dramatic of winners. Wednesday ended with nothing but really should have taken their chances.

After becoming the first club to win both major domestic knockout trophies in the same season, Arsenal went on to win the European Cup-Winners Cup the following year. In the Copenhagen final they defeated the holders Parma by a single goal. They almost retained the trophy in 1995 but lost the final to Real Zaragoza in Paris, the winner coming from ex-Tottenham player Nayim's speculative 50-yard lob in the last minute of extra time.

Wednesday's unsuccessful hunt for a trophy continued and they were relegated from the Premiership in 2000.

Arsenal: Seaman, Dixon, Winterburn, Davis, Linighan, Adams – capt, Jensen, Wright, Smith (A), Merson, Campbell.
subs: O'Leary for Wright 81, Selley (not used). manager: George Graham
Sheffield W: Woods, Nilsson, Worthington, Harkes, Palmer – capt, Warhurst, Wilson, Waddle, Hirst, Bright, Sheridan.
subs: Hyde for Wilson 62, Bart-Williams for Nilsson 118. manager: Trevor Francis

FA Trophy Final

Saturday 22nd May 1993

Port Vale 2
Kerr, Slaven

Stockport County 1
Francis
35,885
Referee: D Elleray (Harrow)

It was the fourth year in succession that a finalist in this competition had also reached the play-off final with Port Vale being the team due a quick second visit to the stadium.

For Stockport it was a case of déja vu. The previous year they had lost to Stoke in the Autoglass Trophy final after beating them in the play-off semi-finals. But this time they did not have a play-off final to look forward to and suffered their third Wembley defeat in just over a year. Sadly for them the nightmare was to continue. They reached the play-off final again the following year and lost.

Port Vale: Musselwhite, Aspin, Kent, Porter, Swan, Glover (D) – capt, Slaven, Van der Laan, Foyle, Kerr, Taylor. subs: Billing for Van der Laan, Cross (not used). manager: John Rudge
Stockport: Edwards, Todd, Wallace, Finley, Miller, Williams, Gannon, Ward – capt, Francis, Beaumont, Duffield. subs:- Preece for Beaumont, Frain (not used). manager: Danny Bergara

Women's League Cup Final

Saturday 29th May 1993

Arsenal 3
Ball 2, Coulling

Knowsley United 0

In the curtain-raiser to the first play-off final, Naz Ball scored twice as Arsenal went one better than their male counterparts and completed the 'treble'. They had already won both the League Championship and the FA Cup.

This was the first full-length women's club match to be played at the stadium. Only a few dozen spectators saw the whole game, with Crewe and York fans not being allowed in until midway through the first half.

Arsenal: Shipp, Pealling, Few, Slee, Wylie – capt, Barber, Williams, Bampton, Churchman, Coulling, Ball. subs: Sneddon for Churchman, Mulligan for Coulling
Knowsley: Thomas, Critchley, Markey, Taylor, Moss, Hayward, Burke, Gore, Harper – capt, Davies, Maxwell. subs: Coughlin for Critchley, McDonald for Markey

Play-off Finals

Third Division
Saturday 29th May 1993

Crewe Alexandra 1
McKearney pen 119

York City 1
Swann 104

After extra time
York City won 5-3 on penalties.
(McCarthy 0-1, McKearney 1-1, Barnes 1-2, Smith (S) 2-2, Canham 2-3, Whalley saved, Pepper 2-4, Ward 3-4, Hall 3-5)
22,416
Referee: A Gunn (South Chailey)

For the third year in succession, a heartbreaking penalty shoot-out was necessary to decide the last promotion spot in the bottom division. York appeared to have won it when Gary Swann, who had put them in the final with his first goal for the club, scored in extra time. But substitute Steve Tutill handled a last minute Crewe corner and Dave McKearney levelled from the spot and Tutill looked to have wrecked his team-mates' season.

But when Dean Kiely saved from Gareth Whalley in the shootout, it put York back in control and Wayne Hall's kick ended their five-year spell in the bottom division. Alan Little had been York's manager for just two months.

The following year Crewe won promotion after three years in the bottom division. Although York reached the Second Division play-offs they were in the Nationwide Conference in 2004.

Crewe: Smith (M), McKearney, Smith (S), Evans – capt, Carr, Whalley, Ward, Naylor, Lennon, Walters, Edwards. subs: Woodward for Edwards 70, Clarkson for Walters 104. manager: Dario Gradi
York: Kiely, McMillan, Hall, Pepper, Stancliffe – capt, Atkin, McCarthy, Canham, Barnes, Swann, Blackstone. subs: Tutill for Stancliffe 108, Borthwick (not used). manager: Alan Little

Second Division

Sunday 30th May 1993

Port Vale 0

West Bromwich Albion 3
Hunt 66, Reid 82, Donovan 90
53,471
Referee: R Milford (Bristol)

Port Vale, the Autoglass Trophy winners from the previous week, had missed promotion by a point. Their hopes of completing a 'double' and repeating their play-off victory of 1989 evaporated after Peter Swan was sent off on the hour for bringing down Bob Taylor when he was through on goal. West Brom scored three in the last quarter of the game to secure promotion back to the division they had left in 1991.

For their manager Osvaldo Ardiles it was a proud moment as he had taken Swindon Town to promotion in 1990 via the play-offs, only to be disqualified because of financial irregularities. He was to leave West Brom to manage Tottenham Hotspur the following season.

Vale finished as Second Division runners-up to Reading and returned to the division they had left in 1992.

Port Vale: Musselwhite, Aspin, Kent, Porter, Swan, Glover (D) – capt, Slaven, Van der Laan, Foyle, Kerr, Taylor. subs: Billing for Kent 63, Cross for Van der Laan 81. manager: John Rudge
West Brom: Lange, Reid, Lilwall, Bradley – capt, Raven, Strodder, Hunt, Hamilton, Taylor, McNally, Donovan. subs: Garner for Hunt 88, Robson (not used). manager: Osvaldo Ardiles

First Division

Monday 31st May 1993

Leicester City 3
Joachim 56, Walsh 68, Thompson 69

Swindon Town 4
Hoddle 41, Maskell 47, Taylor 53, Bodin pen 84
73,802
Referee: D Elleray (Harrow)

After their disqualification in 1990, Swindon had almost been relegated the following year, escaping by two points. They recovered and at last won promotion to the top flight for the first time in their history in front of a crowd that was more than 11,500 bigger than at the FA Cup final replay 11 days earlier.

Player-manager, Glenn Hoddle opened the scoring and Swindon were three up eight minutes after the interval. But Leicester, in their second successive final, stormed back to level with three goals in 13 minutes. Swindon weathered the storm, however, and won their passage into the FA Carling Premiership with a late penalty. It meant that Leicester manager, Brian Little was unable to complete a unique family double after brother Alan had won the Third Division final with York two days earlier.

Leicester had lost to a penalty the previous year and this was their sixth consecutive defeat at Wembley in a spell spanning 44 years. The following year Leicester finally broke the longest Wembley record without a victory by winning the play-offs. This meant that all three beaten play-off finalists secured promotion a year later.

Swindon lasted only one season in the Premiership, finishing bottom and dropped right through into the Second Division although they halted the slide by winning the Second Division Championship at the first attempt and promotion straight back to the First Division in 1996.

Glenn Hoddle won 53 caps for England and scored the only goal of the 1982 FA Cup final Replay. He left Swindon to become Chelsea's player-manager after the play-offs and by 1996 he was England's coach, taking them to the 1998 World Cup before being sacked because of ill-judged comments to the press.

Leicester: Poole, Mills – capt, Whitlow, Smith, Walsh, Hill, Oldfield, Thompson, Joachim, Agnew, Philpott. subs: Gibson, Ormondroyd (not used). manager: Brian Little
Swindon: Digby, Summerbee, Bodin, Hoddle, Calderwood – capt, Taylor, Moncur, MacLaren, Mitchell, Ling, Maskell. subs: White for Maskell 78, Hazard for Moncur 88. player-manager: Glenn Hoddle

Schoolboy International

Saturday 5th June 1993

England 0
Germany 0
30,000
Referee: G Lee (Northamptonshire)

The first visit to Wembley by a unified German schoolboy side. England created several chances, but could not break through.

England: Dungey, Hilton, Millett, Curtis, Broomes, Hodges, Fotiadis, Cassidy, Kyte, Clemence, Teather. subs: Omoyinmi for Kyte 71, Bell for Fotiadis 78

FA CHARITY SHIELD

Saturday 7th August 1993

Arsenal   1-1   Manchester United
Wright 44   Hughes 8
Manchester United won 5-4 on penalties.
(Ince 0-1, Winterburn 1-1, Bruce 1-2, Jensen 2-2, Irwin saved, Campbell 3-2, Keane 3-3, Merson 4-3, Cantona 4-4, Wright missed, Robson 4-5, Seaman missed)
66,519
Referee: G Ashby (Worcester)

This was Arsenal's third FA Charity Shield in five years. They had failed to score in their previous two and had not won the Shield outright since 1953. In 1948 Arsenal had beaten United in a seven-goal thriller to win the Shield after they had won the League Championship and United the FA Cup. Their most famous meeting had been the 1979 FA Cup final when Arsenal had lost a two-goal lead to United before winning the trophy with a last minute winner.

Three months earlier Arsenal had once again won the FA Cup with a last minute winner after also winning the Coca-Cola Cup. Both matches were won 2-1 against Sheffield Wednesday with the FA Cup final going to extra time in the replay.

Arsenal were making their fifth appearance at Wembley in just over four months. United had shared the Charity Shield in 1990 but had not won it outright since 1983. They had followed up their League Cup triumph the previous year by winning the first Premier League Championship by ten points from Aston Villa.

United struck first. Irwin's cross fell to Cantona and the Frenchman, who had scored a hat-trick for Leeds United in the previous year's Charity Shield, lobbed it back into the middle where Mark Hughes fired an acrobatic volley past Seaman.

Arsenal drew level with an equally spec-tacular goal. Davis headed on a loose ball to Ian Wright who left Schmeichel, United's Danish keeper, rooted to the spot with a breathtaking shot.

Both teams seemed to settle for the draw but the Shield was decided on penalties for the first time since 1974. At 4-4 in the shootout Ian Wright had only to score to give Arsenal the Shield but he fired wide and substitute Bryan Robson put United back in front. Arsenal's goalkeeper David Seaman then stepped up but his opposite number, Peter Schmeichel made a comfort-able save to give United the Shield.

Arsenal did not appear at Wembley for another five years when they again reached the FA Cup final.

United returned to Wembley for the Coca-Cola Cup final. They would also be back to defend the Charity Shield.

Arsenal: Seaman, Dixon, Winterburn, Davis, Linighan, Adams – capt, Campbell, Wright, Limpar, Mersen, Jensen. subs: Keown for Dixon 46, McGoldrick for Limpar 74. manager: George Graham

Manchester U: Schmeichel, Parker, Irwin, Bruce – capt, Kanchelskis, Pallister, Cantona, Ince, Keane, Hughes, Giggs. sub: Robson for Giggs 68. manager: Alex Ferguson

WORLD CUP QUALIFYING

Wednesday 8th September 1993

England   3-0   Poland

Ferdinand 5, Gascoigne 49, Pearce 53
71,220
Referee: F Van den Wijngaert (Belgium)

Poland were appearing at Wembley in their third successive qualifying competition, having been well beaten on the two previous visits. England had since earned two draws in Poland with late equalisers including one in Chorzow four months earlier. Four days after that Norway had beaten a poor England side in Oslo and now led Group Two by three points from England and the Netherlands with the Poles a point below them but with two games in hand. Qualification was going to be tight.

England got off to a perfect start. Les Ferdinand controlled Platt's pass and tucked it neatly into the corner as Bako advanced. Ferdinand also had a hand in England's second as he headed down Jones' free kick to Paul Gascoigne who turned and smashed it into the net.

A superb free kick move secured the points. Sharpe tapped it to Gascoigne, who steadied the ball and a typical Stuart Pearce strike soared past Bako as Wright drew a defender from the wall.

After five matches unbeaten, Poland lost all their last five, with defeat in Poznan the following month to group winners Norway finally ending their qualifying hopes and relegating them to fourth. On that night England lost 2-0 in Rotterdam and were themselves eliminated when the Dutch won in Poznan a month later. England's manager Graham Taylor resigned.

Poland were drawn against England yet again in the next World Cup and returned to Wembley three years later.

England: Seaman (Arsenal), Jones (Liverpool), Pearce (Nottingham F) – capt, Sharpe (Man Utd), Adams (Arsenal), Pallister (Man Utd), Platt (Sampdoria), Gascoigne (Lazio), Ferdinand (QPR), Wright (Arsenal), Ince (Man Utd). manager: Graham Taylor

Poland: Bako (Lech Poznan), Czachowski (Legia Warsaw), Brzeczek (Gornik Zabrze), Kozminski (Udinese), Lesiak (Wacker Innsbruck), Warzycha (R) (Everton), Swierczewski (Saint-Etienne), Adamczuk (Dundee), Furtok (Eintracht Frankfurt), Kosecki (Atletico Madrid) – capt, Lesniak (Wattenscheid). subs: Ziober (Montpellier) for Furtok 46, Bak (Lech Poznan) for Adamczuk 78. coach: Andrzej Strejlau

Final table	P	W	D	L	F	A	Pts
Norway	10	7	2	1	25	5	16
Netherlands	10	6	3	1	29	9	15
England	10	5	3	2	26	9	13
Poland	10	3	2	5	10	15	8
Turkey	10	3	1	6	11	19	7
San Marino	10	0	1	9	2	46	1

INTERNATIONAL

Wednesday 9th March 1994

England 1-0 Denmark
Platt 16
71,970
Referee: J Uilenberg (Netherlands)

Terry Venables' first match in charge of England was against the European Champions who, like England, had failed to qualify for the forthcoming World Cup. Denmark had lost their last qualifying match in Seville and had been pipped to a place in the USA by the Republic of Ireland. Their points and goal differences had been equal, but the Republic had scored four more goals.

They had also missed out on the 1990 World Cup after losing their last match, making their 1992 European Championship success in Sweden all the more remarkable. Denmark had been last minute entrants as Yugoslavia were forced to pull out and their opening match was a goalless draw with England in Malmo. Despite losing their second match to the hosts in Stockholm they went on to lift the trophy. They had lost 1-0 in three of their previous four visits to Wembley, but they had won by the only goal in the European Championship in 1983.

With over two years before England's next competitive match as hosts of the European Championship, Venables could afford to experiment. He introduced three new caps and recalled Peter Beardsley for his 50th appearance.

The one goal was created by Shearer threading a pass through to David Platt who shot on the turn and beat Manchester United's Schmeichel. England should have scored more but were happy with the victory.

Denmark would return to England to defend the European Championship two years later but they were eliminated in the first round after Croatia beat them 3-0 at Hillsborough.

England: Seaman (Arsenal), Parker (Man Utd), Le Saux* (Blackburn), Ince (Man Utd), Adams (Arsenal), Pallister (Man Utd), Platt (Sampdoria) – capt, Gascoigne (Lazio), Shearer (Blackburn), Beardsley (Newcastle), Anderton* (Tottenham). subs: Batty (Blackburn) for Ince 66, Le Tissier* (Southampton) for Gascoigne 66. coach: Terry Venables *first cap
Denmark: Schmeichel (Man Utd), Dethlefsen (Odense), Rieper (Brondby), Olsen (Seraing) – capt, Kjeldbjerg (Chelsea), Larsen (Waldhof Mannheim), Jensen (Arsenal), Vilfort (Brondby), Christensen (Olympiakos), Laudrup (M) (Barcelona), Laudrup (B) (AC Milan). subs: Hogh (Brondby) for Vilfort 71, Frederiksen (Silkeborg) for Christensen 71. coach: Richard Moller Nielsen

Schoolboy International

Saturday 12th March 1994

England 3
Gower 4, 11, Wilson 42

Switzerland 0
Referee: P Durkin (Dorset)

England should have had many more against a very poor Swiss side. This was their first win at Wembley under Steve Avory after two years in charge.

Goalkeeper Nicky Weaver was Manchester City's penalty shoot-out hero five years later as they won the Second Division play-offs with a dramatic recovery.

England: Weaver, Perry, Curtis – capt, Culshaw, Clement, Marshall, Staton, Gower, Platts, Branch, Wilson. subs: Brightwell for Platts 64, Sullivan for Branch, Bunn for Wilson 64

Anglo-Italian Cup Final

Sunday 20th March 1994

Brescia 1
Ambrosetti 60

Notts County 0
17,185
Referee: A Cakar (Turkey)

Brescia kept the trophy in Italy by winning it at the first attempt. They had been relegated from the Italian First Division the previous year by Udinese in a play-off in Bologna after only one season in the top flight.

County had lost 3-1 at Brescia in an earlier group match and had needed penalties to defeat Southend United in the semi-finals. This was their first Wembley defeat from three appearances in five years, having won two successive Football League Promotion play-offs at the beginning of the 1990's.

Brescia were promoted straight back to the First Division, emulating the feat of the previous year's winners Cremonese but they finished bottom the following year and found themselves back in the Second Division once more. County would return the following year to win the competition.

Seven months later Georghe Hagi made his second appearance against England at Wembley for Romania.

Brescia: Landucci, Marangon, Giunta, Domini, Baronchelli, Bonometti – capt, Schenardi, Sabau, Ambrosetti, Hagi, Gallo. subs: Neri for Schenardi 46, Piovanelli for Ambrosetti 75. coach: Mircea Lucescu

Notts C: Cherry, Wilson, Dijkstra, Turner – capt, Johnson, Palmer, Devlin, Draper, Lund, McSwegan, Legg. sub: Agana for McSwegan 72. manager: Mick Walker

LEAGUE CUP FINAL

Sunday 27th March 1994

Aston Villa	3-1	Manchester United
Atkinson 25, Saunders 75, (pen) 89		Hughes 83

77,231
Referee: K Cooper (Pontypridd)

Villa's manager Ron Atkinson was attempting to complete a second League Cup final victory against his old club, after guiding Sheffield Wednesday to the Rumbelows Cup as a Second Division club in 1991. Goalkeepers Bosnich and Sealey were also pitted against their old clubs.

Villa were attempting to equal the League Cup record by securing their fourth victory, but had not won it since 1977 after the first drawn final at Wembley. After drawing the 1981 FA Charity Shield at the stadium they had ended that season by surprisingly winning the European Cup at the first attempt. However, their more recent visits to the stadium had failed to produce a goal. They had lost on penalties in the Football League Centenary Tournament of 1988 and suffered two defeats in the 1990 Makita Tournament.

United were attempting to regain the trophy for the second time in three years and this was their third final in four years and they were mounting a serious assault on all three major domestic trophies. After lifting the Charity Shield on penalties, they had led the FA Carling Premiership all season. They had also reached the FA Cup semi-finals and would be returning to Wembley two weeks later. United had won a major trophy in each of the past four years with Villa finishing runners-up to them in the previous year's title race.

Villa had met United at Wembley before in the 1957 FA Cup final when United were poised to win the 'double'. But an early injury to United's goalkeeper Ray Wood swung the match Villa's way.

The Midlanders knew they would have to be at their best to win but they also knew what it was like to beat United in the Coca-Cola Cup, having done it the year before.

Fortunately for them their manager had his tactics spot on. Villa took a surprise lead when Dalian Atkinson ran on to Saunders' pass to flick it past the advancing Sealey. Villa worked hard to deny United the space their rich skills required and just as the favourites began to put the pressure on they snatched a second.

Richardson's free kick took everyone by surprise as it headed towards the near post. Dean Saunders stuck out a foot and turned it into the net. Seven minutes remained when United finally broke through. Keane fired in a cross which Mark Hughes tried to back-heel past Bosnich, Villa's Australian goalkeeper who was to rejoin United five years later. The ball stuck between the legs of Hughes but he reacted quickest and managed to stab it under the 'keeper and past Fenton on the line.

United pushed up and were caught out in the last minute. Daley hit the post and Atkinson's shot from the rebound was handled on the line by Andrei Kanchelskis. The Russian international was sent off and the dismissal cost him a place in the FA Cup semi-final. Saunders fired the penalty straight down the middle for his second and Villa secured a remarkable win in which, the goals apart, they had never really created chances.

Two years later Villa regained the Coca-Cola Cup. United were back at Wembley two weeks later for the FA Cup semi-final.

Aston V: Bosnich, Barrett, McGrath, Teale, Staunton, Atkinson, Townsend, Richardson – capt, Fenton, Daley, Saunders. sub: Cox for Staunton 79, Spink (gk), Houghton (not used). manager: Ron Atkinson
Manchester U: Sealey, Parker, Bruce – capt, Pallister, Irwin, Kanchelskis, Keane, Ince, Giggs, Cantona, Hughes. subs: Sharpe for Giggs 61, McClair for Bruce, Walsh (gk) (not used). manager: Alex Ferguson

FA Cup Semi-finals

Saturday 9th April 1994

Chelsea 2
Peacock 13, 47
Luton Town 0
59,989
Referee: R Dilkes (Mossley)

Chelsea had knocked out the previous year's finalists Sheffield Wednesday and had now reached their first semi-final since they won the trophy in 1970 following Wembley's first drawn final.

Their last Wembley appearance had been in winning the Zenith Cup in 1990. As in the 1970 semi-finals, when they beat Watford 5-1 at White Hart Lane, they were facing a team from a division below them. Luton had twice reached semi-finals in the 1980's but had not appeared in the final since 1959, and had never won the trophy. Since their successive Littlewoods Cup finals in the late 1980's they had been relegated and had only avoided dropping straight down to the Second Division by two points the previous year.

Despite showing great potential in winning the previous year's Makita Tournament, Chelsea had been at the wrong end of the table.

Chelsea scored early; Sinclair's free kick from his own half was headed on by Cascarino via Spencer to Gavin Peacock who fired into the corner past Luton's American goalkeeper Sommer. Two minutes after the interval Peacock played a one-two with

Spencer and once again found the corner of the net. Chelsea subsequently cruised to their first Wembley win in the FA Cup.

Chelsea: Kharine, Clarke, Johnsen, Kjeldbjerg, Sinclair, Burley, Peacock, Newton, Wise – capt, Cascarino, Spencer. subs: Barnard for Burley 41, Hitchcock (gk), Hopkin (not used). manager: Glenn Hoddle
Luton: Sommer, Linton, Peake – capt, Dreyer, James, Hughes, Preece, Harper, Telfer, Oakes, Dixon. sub: Hartson for Linton 66, Thomas and Petterson (gk) (not used). manager: David Pleat

Sunday 10th April 1994

Manchester United 1
Hughes 119
Oldham Athletic 1
Pointon 106
After extra time
56,399
Referee: P Don (Hanworth Park)

When United won their seventh FA Cup in 1990 they had beaten Oldham in an exciting semi-final which twice went to extra time. Oldham were then in the Second Division and appeared in the Littlewoods Cup final in the same month but they had never won a major trophy nor reached the FA Cup final.

United's recent disappointing form continued as Oldham held them at bay. Then in extra time Schmeichel rose to collect Holden's corner and dropped it as Bruce accidentally ran in to him. Neil Pointon fired it into the corner to give Oldham a shock lead.

United's season looked to be falling

apart after they had promised so much. They must have had flashes of their League Cup final defeat by Aston Villa, but in a last desperate attack in the dying seconds McClair flicked the ball over the Oldham defence and Mark Hughes lunged ahead of Fleming to gave Hallworth no chance with an incredible volley.

Hughes' equaliser was to have far reaching consequences. It became the turning point for both teams. Three days later in the replay, United hit Oldham with two early goals and secured their return to Wembley, the following month. Oldham never recovered from being so close to their first final and were relegated to the First Division after finishing 21st.

Manchester U: Schmeichel, Parker, Bruce – capt, Pallister, Irwin, Sharpe, McClair, Ince, Giggs, Hughes, Dublin. subs: Robson for Dublin 73, Butt for Parker 109, Sealey (gk) (not used). manager: Alex Ferguson

Oldham: Hallworth, Makin, Jobson, Fleming, Pointon, Bernard, Milligan – capt, Henry, Holden, Beckford, Sharp. subs: Gerrard (gk), Brennan, Ritchie (not used). manager: Joe Royle

Replay: Wednesday 13th April 1994
Manchester United 4
Irwin, Kanchelskis, Robson, Giggs

Oldham Athletic 1
Pointon
(Maine Road)

Autoglass Trophy Final

Sunday 24th April 1994

Huddersfield Town 1
Logan 60

Swansea City 1
McFarlane 7
After extra time
Swansea City won 3-1 on penalties.
(Mitchell hit post, Cornforth 0-1, Scully 1-1, Ampadu 1-2, Starbuck hit bar, Torpey 1-3, Cowan saved)
47,733
Referee: J Rushton (Stoke-on-Trent)

Swansea took the trophy to Wales for the first time after their first match at Wembley. Both sides had recently narrowly missed Wembley trips after losing in the Football League Promotion play-off semi-finals to the eventual winners.

Huddersfield had won at Stockport County in the quarter-finals to end their bid to reach their third successive final. Swansea had knocked out the holders Port Vale in the last 16. Huddersfield's last appearance at Wembley, in the 1938 FA Cup final, had seen them lose to a last minute penalty in extra time. Fifty six years later the penalty kick was again to prove their downfall. Roger Freestone settled the issue by saving Tom Cowan's kick.

Huddersfield's consolation came a year later when they won promotion at Wembley via the play-offs. Swansea were relegated back to the Third Division in 1996.

Huddersfield: Francis, Billy, Mitchell, Scully, Cowan, Baldry, Robinson, Logan, Bullock, Booth, Starbuck. sub: Dunn for Bullock 45. manager: Neil Warnock

Swansea: Freestone, Jenkins, Basham, Harris, Clode, Bowen, Pascoe, Cornforth – capt, Ampadu, McFarlane, Hodge. subs: Ford for Clode 69, Torpey for Hodge 83, Jones (gk) (not used). manager: Frank Burrows

FA Vase Final

Saturday 7th May 1994

Diss Town 2
Gibbs pen 90, Mendham 109

Taunton Town 1
Fowler 12
After extra time
13,450
Referee: K Morton (Bury St. Edmunds)

Taunton had victory snatched from their grasp when Diss, astonishingly, equalised from Paul Gibbs' penalty in the tenth minute of injury time. Diss went on to win the Vase for the first time, after an extra half-hour.

Peter Mendham, who scored Diss' extra-time winner, played for Norwich City when they won the Milk Cup at Wembley in 1985.

Diss: Woodcock, Carter, Hartle, Smith, Wolsey, Casey, Mendham, Barth, Warne, Miles, Gibbs. subs: Musgrave for Wolsey, Bugg for Casey

Taunton: Maloy, Morris, Graddon, Palfrey, Walsh, Ewens, West, Perett, Fowler, Durham, Jarvis. subs: Hendy for West, Ward for Perett 54

FA CUP FINAL

Saturday 14th May 1994

Chelsea   **0-4**   **Manchester United**

Cantona pens. 60, 66, Hughes 69, McClair 90

79,634
Referee: D Elleray (Harrow)

Chelsea had won the Cup only once previously, in 1970, after drawing the final at Wembley, although they had won the Full Members Cup and the Zenith Cup at the stadium.

Chelsea had knocked out the previous year's finalists Sheffield Wednesday. United had beaten the same team in the semi-finals, Oldham Athletic, as when they last won the Cup, in 1990 and they had again needed a replay to beat them. They were now aiming to equal Tottenham Hotspur's record of eight FA Cup wins.

United retained the Premier League championship, winning by eight points from Blackburn Rovers. They were favourites to win the first 'double' since Liverpool's 1986 success. United had also reached the Coca-Cola Cup final, but had lost to Aston Villa although their big disappointment was in losing on away goals to Galatasaray in the last 16 of the European Cup.

Chelsea had completed a league 'double' over United without conceding a goal and again showed the qualities that had produced those two shock victories. But whereas Aston Villa in the Coca-Cola Cup final had used similar tactics to stifle United and broke away to score, Chelsea failed to break through and one rush of blood after an hour's play was to prove their undoing.

Newton upended Irwin in the area and Eric Cantona sent Russian goalkeeper Kharine the wrong way from the penalty spot to give United the lead. Chelsea panicked and pushed players forward in an attempt to grab a quick reply, but this proved fatal as United now had the space previously denied them.

Twice they broke and ripped Chelsea's defence wide open. First Kanchelskis broke away and was knocked over by Sinclair's challenge. Although contact appeared to be outside the area, another penalty was given and Cantona again sent Kharine the other way.

Three minutes later, Sinclair's misery was complete as he slipped in the wet conditions when attempting a clearance and accidentally put Mark Hughes through to fire into the corner. Hughes was to join Chelsea, the following year.

In nine minutes Chelsea had abandoned their previously successful game plan and paid the ultimate price. They bravely created more chances and were cruelly caught out again in injury time. This time it was Ince who broke away, rounded Kharine and left substitute Brian McClair with an open goal. The scoreline was incredibly harsh on Chelsea but United were always capable of over-running teams and the 'double' was just reward for a talented side.

As United were again competing in the European Cup, Chelsea took their place in the European Cup-Winners Cup and surprisingly reached the semi-finals, where they were beaten by the eventual winners, Real Zaragoza. United reached the FA Cup final again the following year while Chelsea won the cup on their next visit in 1997.

Chelsea: Kharine, Clarke, Sinclair, Johnsen, Kjeldbjerg, Wise – capt, Peacock, Burley, Newton, Spencer, Stein. subs: Hoddle for Burley 65, Cascarino for Stein 78, Hitchcock (gk) (not used). player-manager: Glenn Hoddle
Manchester U: Schmeichel, Parker, Irwin, Bruce – capt, Pallister, Kanchelskis, Ince, Keane, Giggs, Hughes, Cantona. subs: Sharpe for Irwin 84, McClair for Kanchelskis 84, Walsh (gk) (not used). manager: Alex Ferguson

INTERNATIONAL

Tuesday 17th May 1994

England   **5-0**   **Greece**

Anderton 23, Beardsley 37
Platt (pen) 44, 55, Shearer 65
23,659
Referee: J McCluskey (Scotland)

293

Greece had surprisingly held England to a goalless draw on their last visit, in the European Championship in 1983, the only occasion they had avoided defeat in five meetings. Their solitary goal against England had been a penalty in Athens in 1989. The following month, Greece would be competing in their first ever World Cup, having qualified without defeat.

England, wearing all red for the first time at Wembley, broke through when Karkamanis failed to hold Le Saux's cross. Darren Anderton was quickest and prodded it into the empty net.

A brilliant piece of skill from Platt resulted in the lead being doubled. It took him to the byeline and a simple lay back left Peter Beardsley with a tap-in.

The match was over as a contest by

half-time when Shearer was tripped by Kalitzakis and David Platt sent Karkamanis the wrong way from the penalty. After the interval, a long kick from Flowers put Anderton through. The 'keeper came out to block, but Shearer lobbed the rebound over him and Platt outjumped Apostolakis to head over substitute Karataidis on the line.

The scoring was completed when Alan Shearer took a pass from Beardsley and fired home. This completed a miserable night for Karkamanis who failed to grasp the ball as the shot passed through them.

This crushing win made England's failure to qualify for the following month's World Cup, all the more inexplicable, especially as the Greeks failed to win a point or score a goal in the tournament.

England: Flowers (Blackburn), Jones (Liverpool), Adams (Arsenal), Bould* (Arsenal), Le Saux (Blackburn), Anderton (Tottenham), Richardson* (Aston Villa), Merson (Arsenal), Platt (Sampdoria) – capt, Beardsley (Newcastle), Shearer (Blackburn). subs: Le Tissier (Southampton) for Anderton 65, Wright (Arsenal) for Beardsley 70, Pearce (Nottingham F) for Jones 82. coach: Terry Venables
*first cap
Greece: Karkamanis (Aris Salonika), Apostolakis (Panathinaikos), Karagiannis (AEK Athens), Kolitsidakis (Apollon), Kalitzakis (Panathinaikos), Tsalouchidis (Olympiakos) – capt, Hantzidis (Olympiakos), Nioplias (Panathinaikos), Machlas (OFI Crete), Kofidis (Aris Salonika), Tsiantakis (Olympiakos). subs: Karataidis (Olympiakos) for Kolitsidakis 46, Mitropoulos (AEK Athens) for Hantzidis 46, Saravakos (Panathinaikos) for Machlas 46, Kostis (Iraklis Salonika) for Kofidis 70. coach: Alketas Panagulias

FA Trophy Final

Saturday 21st May 1994

Runcorn 1
Shaw pen 75
Woking 2
Brown (D) 19, Hay 29
15,818
Referee: P Durkin (Portland)

Runcorn's second successive final defeat and their third overall. Woking marked their first Wembley appearance since winning the 1958 FA Amateur Cup with a long overdue victory.

Clive Walker had missed a penalty for Sunderland at Wembley in the 1985 Milk Cup final but now, in the week of his 37th birthday, he was about to embark on an astonishing run of four FA Trophy wins in five years. The first three were with Woking and his last winners' medal was won with Cheltenham Town, nine days before his 41st birthday.

Runcorn: Williams, Bates, Lee – capt, Brabin, Robertson, Shaw, Anderson, Connor, McKenna, McInerney, Thomas. sub: Hill for McInerney 71
Woking: Batty, Berry, Brown (K) – capt, Tucker, Wye, Clement, Brown (D), Steele, Fielder, Hay, Walker. subs: Rattray for Brown (D) 32, Puckett for Hay 46

INTERNATIONAL

Sunday 22nd May 1994

England   0-0   **Norway**
64,327
Referee: K Nielsen (Denmark)

Norway had won England's World Cup qualifying group to reach their first tournament since 1938 and would be taking their

place in the USA the following month. The point they had picked up at Wembley two years earlier, together with a 2-0 win in

1994

Oslo, the following year had played a major part in England's failure to qualify and this was an ideal opportunity for revenge.

The Norwegians, with eight English-based players, proved their World Cup qualification was no fluke as they again proved difficult to beat. England failed to break through their well-organised defence.

Norway were too defensive in the World Cup and finished bottom of a very tight group. They beat the group winners Mexico in Washington but a goalless draw with the Republic of Ireland in New York left all four teams level on points and goal difference. Norway had only scored one goal and were eliminated.

The following year in Oslo England contested another goalless draw.

England: Seaman (Arsenal), Jones (Liverpool), Bould (Arsenal), Adams (Arsenal), Le Saux (Blackburn), Anderton (Tottenham), Ince (Man Utd), Wise (Chelsea), Platt (Sampdoria) – capt, Beardsley (Newcastle), Shearer (Blackburn). subs: Le Tissier (Southampton) for Anderton 76, Wright (Arsenal) for Ince 76. coach: Terry Venables
Norway: Thorstvedt (Tottenham), Berg (H) (Blackburn), Johnsen (Chelsea), Bratseth (Werder Bremen) – capt, Nilsen (Sheffield U), Flo (Sheffield U), Berg (O) (Basle), Rekdal (Lierse), Bohinen (Nottingham F), Jakobsen (Lierse), Fjortoft (Swindon). subs: Haaland (Nottingham F) for Nilsen 46, Sorloth (Bursaspor) for Fjortoft 46, Ingebrigtsen (Stromsgodset) for Berg (O) 67, By Rise (Rosenborg) for Thorstvedt 86. coach: Egil Olsen

Play-off Finals

Third Division

Saturday 28th May 1994

Preston North End 2
Bryson 32, Raynor 37
Wycombe Wanderers 4
Thompson 33, Garner 47, Carroll 57, 72
40,109
Referee: K Cooper (Pontypridd)

Preston's first appearance at Wembley since the 1964 FA Cup final started well. They held a 2-1 half-time lead but Wycombe crowned their first season in the Endsleigh League with promotion to the Second Division after a stirring second half performance.

Steve Thompson and Dave Carroll had both scored for Wycombe in the previous year's FA Trophy final and they did it again to secure Wycombe's third Wembley win in four years.

Preston had reached the play-offs in the old Third Division in 1989 but had lost to the eventual winners Port Vale. In 1996, they won the Third Division Championship and at last got their promotion.

Preston's captain David Moyes was manager when they reached the First Division play-off final in 2001 before losing to Bolton Wanderers at the Millennium Stadium. He moved on to manage Everton.

Preston: Woods, Fensome, Kidd, Cartwright, Squires, Moyes – capt, Ainsworth, Whalley, Raynor, Ellis, Bryson. subs: Conroy, Lucas, Berryman (gk) (not used). manager: John Beck

Wycombe: Hyde, Cousins, Titterton, Crossley, Creaser – capt, Ryan, Carroll, Thompson, Reid, Garner, Guppy. subs: Brown, Hemmings, Moussaddik (gk) (not used). manager: Martin O'Neill

Second Division

Sunday 29th May 1994

Burnley 2
Eyres 28, Parkinson 65
Stockport County 1
Beaumont 2
44,806
Referee: D Elleray (Harrow)

Burnley had finished only sixth, twelve points behind Stockport. Yet they came from behind to win at Wembley for the first time. In the semi-finals they had won at Plymouth Argyle who had also finished twelve points above them. This completed their rise from the lower divisions which they had dropped into in 1983.

After losing the 1988 Sherpa Van Trophy final at Wembley, they had lost in the old Fourth Division play-off semi-finals in 1991 to the eventual winners Torquay United. But a year later they won the Fourth Division Championship and now secured a surprise second promotion in three years.

Stockport were developing a Wembley jinx. It was their fourth successive defeat there in just over two years. It was also their third successive play-off failure and their second final defeat in three years.

But they had only themselves to blame. Leading after two minutes, they had Michael Wallace sent off for spitting at Ted McMinn twelve minutes later and their

295

scorer, Chris Beaumont was dismissed for stamping on Les Thompson after an hour. They were the only team in the history of the stadium to have two players sent off in the same game.

These self-inflicted wounds handed promotion to Burnley on a plate but the Clarets were relegated straight back to the Second Division, the following year. Stockport took another three years before they won promotion as Second Division runners-up to Bury after 59 years in the lower divisions.

Burnley: Beresford, Parkinson, Thompson, Davis, Pender – capt, Joyce, McMinn, Deary, Heath, Francis, Eyres. subs: Farrell for Francis 15, Lancashire, Williams (gk) (not used). manager: Jimmy Mullen
Stockport: Keeley, Todd, Wallace, Connelly, Flynn, Williams, Gannon, Ward – capt, Francis, Beaumont, Frain. subs: Preece for Williams 59, Miller for Gannon 81, Ironside (gk) (not used). manager: Danny Bergara

First Division

Monday 30th May 1994

Derby County 1
Johnson 27
Leicester City 2
Walsh 40, 86
73,671
Referee: R Milford (Bristol)

As Stockport County's Wembley jinx continued the previous day so Leicester's ended after 45 years at the seventh attempt. Like the other play-off winners they came from behind. It was Leicester's third successive final and despite having fewer points than in each of the two previous years they secured their return to the top flight after a gap of seven years.

Derby had been relegated in 1991 and had lost in the play-offs to the eventual winners Blackburn Rovers a year later. This was their second successive Wembley defeat.

They had lost the previous year's Anglo-Italian Cup final and were beaten again despite Tommy Johnson's fourth goal in three play-off finals. His other three had been for Notts County.

After all their efforts to get there, though, Leicester spent a miserable season in the FA Carling Premiership and were relegated back to the Endsleigh League the following year. They won promotion again, however, by winning the play-offs two years later in even more dramatic fashion. Derby also won promotion to the Premiership in 1996 by finishing as Endsleigh League runners-up to Sunderland.

John Harkes had become the first American to score in a major cup final when he netted for Sheffield Wednesday in the previous year's Coca-Cola Cup final. He won over 50 caps for the USA.

Derby: Taylor, Charles, Forsyth, Harkes, Short, Williams, Cowans – capt, Johnson, Gabbiadini, Pembridge, Simpson. sub: Kitson for Forsyth 88, Kavanagh, Sutton (gk) (not used). manager: Roy McFarland
Leicester: Ward, Grayson – capt, Whitlow, Willis, Coatsworth, Carey, Gibson, Blake, Walsh, Roberts, Ormondroyd. subs: Joachim for Roberts 56, Thompson for Coatsworth 68, Poole (gk) (not used). manager: Brian Little

Schoolboy International

Saturday 11th June 1994

England 2
Bunn, Platts
France 1
Massac

A spectacular injury-time free kick winner from Mark Platts meant that England completed their season by winning all eight fixtures for the first time.

England: O'Toole, Dickman, Clement, Curtis – capt, Morris, Gower, Branch, Marshall, Platts, Bunn, Perry. sub: Wilson for Marshall

FA CHARITY SHIELD

Sunday 14th August 1994

Blackburn Rovers	0-2	Manchester United
		Cantona pen 21, Ince 80

60,402
Referee: P Don (Hanworth Park)

Blackburn had won the FA Charity Shield way back in 1912, beating Queens Park Rangers 2-1 at White Hart Lane and had made their last appearance in the fixture

16 years later. Since then their only major success had been the Full Members Cup win of 1987. Five years later, they had won promotion to the FA Premier League

at Wembley and now made a return visit after finishing as Premiership runners-up, their highest position since their second League Championship in 1914. They were appearing because United had won the coveted 'double' of FA Carling Premiership (by eight points from Blackburn) and FA Cup, three months earlier.

It was their second successive Premiership title and they were also the holders of the Charity Shield, having won it on penalties the previous year. Only their defeat in the Coca-Cola Cup final kept them from completing the first ever clean sweep of domestic honours.

United took the lead after Hendry brought down Ince and Eric Cantona strode up to send Flowers the wrong way from the spot, just as he had done twice in the FA Cup final. Ten minutes from the end they made sure of victory. From Giggs' corner, Hendry headed out only for Cantona to backhead it into the middle where Paul Ince powered a spectacular overhead kick between a stunned Flowers and Wilcox.

Blackburn pipped United by a point to win the FA Carling Premiership the following year, thus returning for the Charity Shield.

United returned to Wembley for the following year's FA Cup final, but suffered defeat.

Blackburn: Flowers, Berg, Hendry, Gale, Le Saux, Slater, Atkins, Sherwood – capt, Wilcox, Ripley, Pearce. sub: Thorne for Atkins 64. manager: Kenny Dalglish

Manchester U: Schmeichel, May, Pallister, Bruce – capt, Sharpe, Kanchelskis, McClair, Ince, Giggs, Cantona, Hughes. manager: Alex Ferguson

INTERNATIONAL

Wednesday 7th September 1994

England **2-0** **USA**
Shearer 33, 40
38,629
Referee: A Lopez Nieto (Spain)

The Americans arrived in England for the first time, fresh from hosting the World Cup in which they reached the last 16 before losing to the eventual winners Brazil by the only goal in San Francisco.

Their previous meetings with England could be summarised by four heavy defeats and two sensational victories. The first win had been by a single goal in their first meeting in the 1950 World Cup in Belo Horizonte but the most recent had been the previous year, a 2-0 success in the US Cup in Boston.

England took more than half-an-hour to break down the Americans. Then Alan Shearer took a pass from Anderton, ran at the defence and beat Friedel at the near post. Seven minutes later, Shearer got ahead of his markers and dived to head Le Saux's cross beyond the keeper's dive and into the corner of the net. England should have scored more but settled for two.

The USA qualified for the World Cup in 1998, but were hugely disappointing and failed to win a point.

England: Seaman (Arsenal), Jones (Liverpool), Le Saux (Blackburn), Venison* (Newcastle), Adams (Arsenal), Pallister (Man Utd), Platt (Sampdoria) – capt, Barnes (Liverpool), Shearer (Blackburn), Sheringham (Tottenham), Anderton (Tottenham). subs: Wright (Arsenal) for Shearer 80, Ferdinand (QPR) for Sheringham 80. coach: Terry Venables
*first cap

USA: Friedel (Brondby), Agoos (Los Angeles Salsa), Balboa (USSF), Caligiuri (USSF), Lalas (Padova), Dooley (Bayer Leverkusen) – capt, Jones (Coventry), Sorber (USSF), Reyna (Bayer Leverkusen), Perez (USSF), Stewart (Willem II Tilburg). subs: Wynalda (Bochum) for Perez 46, Lapper (Wolfsburg) for Agoos 70, Sommer (Luton Town) for Friedel 81, Klopas (USSF) for Reyna 81, Moore (Saarbrucken) for Stewart 81. coach: Bora Milutinovic

INTERNATIONAL

Wednesday 12th October 1994

England	**1-1**	**Romania**

Lee 45   Dumitrescu 36
48,754
Referee: J Quiniou (France)

The last three meetings between these two had been draws. The three previous Wembley clashes had also seen honours even, with England's last victory against Romania back in 1970.

In the current European Championship, Romania had held France to a goalless draw in St. Etienne four nights earlier and were unbeaten from their first two games.

A skilful Romanian side scored the first goal against Terry Venables' England. Popescu's cross was turned in by an unmarked Ilie Dumitrescu.

England drew level at the end of the first half. A long cross from Le Saux was headed down by Shearer to Robert Lee who stabbed it past Stelea as Prodan lunged. Once again,

neither side could manage a winner. The Romanians brought on a substitute 'keeper, with three minutes left, the third successive Wembley international in which the visitors had changed their goalkeeper during the game.

Romania went on to win their European Championship group despite losing 3-1 to France in Bucharest the following year. In the finals in England in 1996, they failed to win a point from a group won by France. They did beat England, however, in each of the next two major tournaments; 2-1 in Toulouse in the 1998 World Cup and 3-2 in Charleroi to knock England out of the 2000 European Championship.

England: Seaman (Arsenal), Jones (Liverpool), Adams (Arsenal) – capt, Pallister (Man Utd), Le Saux (Blackburn), Lee* (Newcastle), Ince (Man Utd), Barnes (Liverpool), Le Tissier (Southampton), Wright (Arsenal), Shearer (Blackburn). subs: Pearce (Nottingham F) for Jones 60, Wise (Chelsea) for Lee 71, Sheringham (Tottenham) for Wright 71. coach: Terry Venables
*first cap

Romania: Stelea (Samsunspor), Belodedici (Valencia), Petrescu (Sheffield W), Prodan (Steaua Bucharest), Munteanu (Cercle Bruges), Popescu (Tottenham), Lupescu (Bayer Leverkusen), Dumitrescu (Tottenham), Hagi (Barcelona) – capt, Lacatus (Steaua), Raducioiu (Espanol). subs: Selymes (Cercle Bruges) for Hagi 46, Timofte (Samsunspor) for Raducioiu 78, Cirstea (National Bucharest) for Lacatus 81, Prunea (Dinamo Bucharest) for Stelea 86. coach: Anghel Iordanescu

INTERNATIONAL

Wednesday 16th November 1994

England	**1-0**	**Nigeria**

Platt 41
37,196
Referee: L Sundell (Sweden)

This was the first meeting between the two countries. Nigeria had followed up their second African Championship success, seven months earlier, by reaching the last 16 of their first World Cup. After winning their first round group on goal difference, they came agonisingly close to eliminating the eventual finalists Italy in Boston but a last minute equaliser and an extra-time winner finally knocked them out.

Nigeria were very impressive early on but could not find the target. Four minutes before the interval they paid the price. David Platt, on his 50th international appearance, rose to head a Wise free kick past Rufai. It was enough.

The rise of Nigerian football was further emphasised two years later when they became Olympic Champions, the first African nation to win the gold.

England: Flowers (Blackburn), Jones (Liverpool), Howey* (Newcastle), Ruddock* (Liverpool), Le Saux (Blackburn), Wise (Chelsea), Lee (Newcastle), Platt (Sampdoria) – capt, Barnes (Liverpool), Beardsley (Newcastle), Shearer

(Blackburn). subs: McManaman* (Liverpool) for Lee 26, Le Tissier (Southampton) for Beardsley 78, Sheringham (Tottenham) for Shearer 78. coach: Terry Venables
*first cap
Nigeria: Rufai (Farense) – capt, Okafor (Uniao Lieira), Eguavoen (Kortrijk), Okechukwu (Fenerbahce), Iroha (Vitesse Arnhem), George (Ajax Amsterdam), Adepoju (Racing Santander), Okocha (Eintracht Frankfurt), Amunike (Sporting Lisbon), Amokachi (Everton), Yekini (Olympiakos). subs: Ikpeba (Monaco) for Amokachi 60, Ekoku (Wimbledon) for Yekini 60, Kanu (Ajax) for Adepoju 85. coach: Amadu Shuaibu

Schoolboy International

Saturday 11th March 1995

England 1
Owen 75
Brazil 0
32,514
Referee: J Brandwood (Staffordshire)

A tight game with few chances but England, under new manager, John Owens, maintained their 100 per cent record against the South Americans.

Michael Owen made a goalscoring Wembley debut. Three years later, he became England's youngest full international of the 20th century and went on to win the European Footballer of the Year award in 2001, after scoring the goals that won Liverpool the FA Cup at the Millennium Stadium on their way to a cup 'treble'.

Michael Ball won a single full international cap six years later as a substitute in Sven-Goran Eriksson's first England selection.

England: Stewart, Cooper, Haslam – capt, Brown (W), Ball, Lunt, Hibburt, Day, Jones, Owen, Brown (A). subs: Burt for Jones 56, O'Brien for Brown (A) 58

Anglo-Italian Cup Final

Sunday 19th March 1995

Ascoli 1
Mirabelli 32
Notts County 2
Agana 12, White 45
11,704
Referee: C Agius (Malta)

County had lost the previous year's final and began this competition by drawing 1-1 at Ascoli. They ended it by securing the Football League's first victory since the competition was revived two seasons earlier. For the second year in succession they had needed penalties to reach the final after a goalless semi-final with Stoke City. For the third year in succession the holders would be unable to defend the trophy.

But whereas the two previous Italian League winners had won promotion, County finished bottom of the First Division and were relegated to the Second Division. They nearly won promotion straight back but lost the following year's play-off final at Wembley. Ascoli, too, would not be entering the following year's competition as they were also relegated to the Italian Third Division, a drop into regionalised football. Not a great advert for the quality of the competition and the size of the crowd reflected this.

Oliver Bierhoff did not drop into the Italian Third Division with Ascoli and just two years later he scored the 'golden goal' that won the European Championship for Germany at Wembley. It was his second of the final.

Ascoli: Bizzarri, Benetti, Mancuso, Marcato, Pascucci, Zanoncelli, Binotto, Bosi, Favo, Mirabelli, Bierhoff. subs: Milana for Mancuso 61, Menolascina for Binotto 76. coach: Albertino Bigon
Notts C: Cherry, Short, Mills, Turner – capt, Murphy, Johnson, Devlin, Simpson, Legg, White, Agana. subs: Reece for Cherry 74, Emenalo for Johnson 74, Gallagher for Agana 86. manager: Howard Kendall

INTERNATIONAL

Wednesday 29th March 1995

England   **0-0**   **Uruguay**
34,849
Referee: H Krug (Germany)

Uruguay had not been beaten at Wembley since 1964 and on their last visit in 1990, they had won for the first time. Like England, they had failed to qualify for the previous year's World Cup from a group topped by the eventual winners Brazil.

Not for the first time, Uruguay came to Wembley to defend and England soon ran out of ideas.

Gustavo Poyet scored both Chelsea's goals when in 2000 they won the last FA Cup semi-final to be played at the stadium before helping the Blues to lift the trophy in the last final a month later.

England: Flowers (Blackburn), Jones (Liverpool), Le Saux (Blackburn), Adams (Arsenal), Pallister (Man Utd), Venison (Newcastle), Anderton (Tottenham), Platt (Sampdoria) – capt, Barnes (Liverpool), Beardsley (Newcastle), Sheringham (Tottenham). subs: McManaman (Liverpool) for Le Saux 46, Barmby* (Tottenham) for Beardsley 65, Cole* (Man Utd) for Sheringham 71. coach: Terry Venables
*first cap
Uruguay: Ferro (Penarol), Lopez (River Plate), Aguirregaray (Penarol), Gutierrez (Nacional), Montero (Atalanta), Dorta (Penarol), Cedres (River Plate, Argentina), Bengoechea (Penarol) – capt, Poyet (Real Zaragoza), Francescoli (River Plate, Argentina), Fonseca (Roma). sub: Debray (Penarol) for Francescoli 85. coach: Hector Nunez

LEAGUE CUP FINAL

Sunday 2nd April 1995

Bolton Wanderers **1-2** **Liverpool**
Thompson 69   McManaman 37, 68
75,595
Referee: P Don (Hanworth Park)

Bolton were appearing in their first League Cup final and had not won a major trophy since the 1958 FA Cup. They had made three Wembley appearances since, however, the last being a Football League Promotion play-off final in 1991.

Liverpool had gone through a period of rebuilding after lifting the FA Cup three years earlier and then losing the FA Charity Shield on their last appearance three months later. They were now chasing a record fifth League Cup win to add to their four successive triumphs in the early 1980's. But they had lost in 1987.

Bolton were not overawed by the occasion despite being underdogs but it was Liverpool who struck first. From Barnes' pass, Steve McManaman ran down the middle. At the edge of the box he moved to his right and accelerated past Stubbs with McAteer in pursuit.

A little nudge took him past Green and he then slotted the ball under Branagan's right foot to give Liverpool a spectacular lead. Bolton again threatened to score but Liverpool rode the storm to hit the First Division side with another spectacular goal. Redknapp supplied McManaman out on the left wing. This time he stopped, cut inside Green, left Seagraves standing and placed his shot just beyond Branagan's reach, for his second.

Within two minutes, Bolton were back in it. The Finnish international Paatelainen got up to back-head a cross from Icelandic substitute Bergsson who came on after Liverpool's second goal. Alan Thompson took it on his chest, turned and fired an unstoppable shot past James. Liverpool held out but Bolton could be proud of their performance in a highly entertaining game.

Bolton were back at Wembley the following month to win promotion to the Premiership in a classic play-off final. Another play-off final followed in 1999 before their last appearance at the stadium, in the FA Cup semi-finals of 2000. Liverpool reached the FA Cup final the next year.

Bolton: Branagan, Green, Phillips, McAteer, Seagraves, Stubbs – capt, Lee, Sneekes, Paatelainen, McGinlay, Thompson. subs: Bergsson for Green 68, Patterson, Davison (gk) (not used). manager: Bruce Rioch
Liverpool: James, Jones (R), Bjornebye, Scales, Babb, Ruddock, McManaman, Redknapp, Barnes, Fowler, Rush – capt. subs: Thomas, Walters, Chamberlain (gk) (not used). manager: Roy Evans

Wembley Challenge Tournament

Saturday 15th April 1995

This was an Easter tournament for the media. It began at 10 a.m. with matches that lasted 25 minutes each. The players were all writers, editors, photographers and broadcasters, plus employees from Littlewoods Pools (the new sponsors of the FA Cup) and the Football Association. It was a dream come true for the players who were watched by friends and family. Each team had a squad of between 15 and 20 and substitutions were made frequently.

Quarter-finals

Crusaders 1
Jobson
Telegraph Guardians 0

Macho Mails 1
Walker og
Mirror Warriors 0

Littlewoods FM 0
News Internationals 2
Williams 2

Magnificent XI 1
Pearce
Television Tigers 1
Sloane
Magnificent XI won 3-2 on penalties.

Semi-finals

Crusaders 1
Kelly
Macho Mails 3
Bloomfield, Scott, Facey

Magnificent XI 3
Pearce, Pelham og, Bigwood
News Internationals 1
Williams

Final

Macho Mails 0
Magnificent XI 0
Macho Mails won 3-2 on penalties.

Auto Windscreens Shield

Sunday 23rd April 1995

Birmingham City 1
Tait 103
Carlisle United 0
In extra time
76,633
Referee: P Foakes (Clacton-on-Sea)

This was the first match at Wembley to be decided by a 'sudden-death' winner in extra time. The new sponsors of the competition, Auto Windscreens, must have been pleased to see two successful clubs reach the final. Both went on to win their respec-

tive divisions. Substitute Paul Tait's winner meant that Birmingham became the first club to win the competition twice, having lifted the Leyland DAF Cup in 1991.

This time they would not be able to defend the Shield because their subsequent Second Division Championship win took them back to the First Division.

In the quarter-finals, they had knocked out the holders Swansea City with another 'golden goal', as it became known.

Carlisle's consolation was the Third Division Championship which promoted them after eight years in the basement division although they were relegated straight back the following year.

Birmingham: Bennett, Poole, Barnett, Daish – capt, Cooper, Hunt, Ward, Shearer, Otto, Claridge, Francis. subs: Tait for Shearer 62, Donowa for Francis 76, Price (gk) (not used). manager: Barry Fry
Carlisle: Caig, Edmondson, Walling, Mountfield, Gallimore, Hayward, Prokas, Conway, Thomas, Reeves – capt, Currie. sub: Thorpe for Prokas 91, Robinson for Mountfield 100, Elliott (gk) (not used). director of coaching: Mick Wadsworth

FA Vase Final

Saturday 13th May 1995

Arlesey Town 2
Palma 25, Gyalog 79
Oxford City 1
Fontaine (S) 55
13,670
Referee: G Willard (Worthing)

Arlesey pulled off a surprise win, having recovered from a three-goal deficit in the first leg of the semi-final.

Arlesey: Young, Cardines, Hull, Gonsalves, Bambrick, Gyalog, Cox, O'Keefe – capt, Marshall, Palma, Kane. subs: Nicholls for Marshall, Ward for Palma
Oxford C: Fleet, Brown, Hume, Shepherd, Muttock, Hamilton, Thomas – capt, Spittle, Fontaine (C), Sherwood, Fontaine (S). subs: Fisher for Brown, Kemp for Hamilton

FA Trophy Final

Sunday 14th May 1995

Kidderminster Harriers 1
Davies 47
Woking 2
Steele 1, Fielder 118
After extra time
17,815
Referee: D Gallagher (Banbury)

Scott Steele scored in the first minute, but Woking had to wait until two minutes from the end of extra time, before Colin Fielder's header secured the Trophy, now sponsored by Umbro, for the second year in succession.

Kidderminster: Rose, Hodson, Bancroft, Webb, Brindley, Forsyth, Deakin, Yates, Humphreys, Davies, Purdie. subs: Cartwright for Brindley 93, Hughes for Humphreys 106
Woking: Batty, Tucker, Wye (L), Fielder, Brown (K) – capt, Crumplin, Wye (S), Ellis, Steele, Hay, Walker. subs: Rattray for Crumplin 46, Newbery for Hay 111

FA CUP FINAL

Saturday 20th May 1995

Everton 1-0 Manchester United
Rideout 30
79,592
Referee: G Ashby (Worcester)

Everton had lost five consecutive Wembley finals since their last FA Cup win in 1984. Their unfortunate run began in 1985 when a single goal in extra time was enough for United to win the FA Cup, despite Kevin Moran being sent off.

Everton gained their revenge three months later in the FA Charity Shield but a single goal was again enough for United to beat them in the Football League Centenary Tournament in 1988.

Everton appeared in two other losing FA Cup finals, both to Liverpool, in the late 1980's and had not won a major trophy since the 1987 League Championship, the year they also won their fourth successive Charity Shield.

United had won the FA Cup twice since beating Everton in 1985. The last triumph had been 1994, their best ever domestic year as they won the 'double'. But United's attempt to lift the FA Cup for a record ninth time was their last chance to avoid their first barren season for six years.

The only goal came on the half-hour mark. Stuart hit the underside of the bar when given a glorious opportunity to score from Jackson's pass. Fortunately for him, Paul Rideout rose to head the rebound past Schmeichel and Bruce, who was struggling with a pulled hamstring and was substituted at half-time.

Rideout's goal was his sixth at Wembley in four games, the other five being at schoolboy level. United came back in the second half, but Neville Southall was on top form in Everton's goal. The holders ran out of ideas and finished the match looking jaded. For Joe Royle, Everton's manager, it was sweet revenge. United had twice beaten his previous club Oldham Athletic in semi-finals.

United recovered in spectacular style and returned the following year on the verge of an unprecedented second 'double' in three years.

Everton: Southall, Jackson, Watson – capt, Unsworth, Ablett, Limpar, Horne, Parkinson, Hinchcliffe, Stuart, Rideout. subs: Ferguson for Rideout 51, Amokachi for Limpar 69, Kearton (gk) (not used). manager: Joe Royle
Manchester U: Schmeichel, Neville (G), Bruce – capt, Pallister, Irwin, Butt, Keane, Ince, Sharpe, McClair, Hughes. subs: Giggs for Bruce 46, Scholes for Sharpe 72, Walsh (gk) (not used). manager: Alex Ferguson

Play-off Finals

Third Division

Saturday 27th May 1995

Bury 0
Chesterfield 2
Lormor 23, Robinson 41
22,814
Referee: P Adcock (Redhill)

Chesterfield had lost Wembley's first promotion play-off final in 1990 and it took them a further five years to rise from the bottom division to which they had been relegated in 1989. They had missed out on the play-offs by two points the previous year. But this time Phil Robinson, on his sixth Wembley appearance for his fifth different club, confirmed promotion to the Second Division with a first half header.

Although this was Bury's first appearance at Wembley they were in the play-offs for the fourth time in six years. In the early 1990's they had reached the old Third Division play-offs in successive years but were relegated in 1992. The following year, they were beaten by eventual play-off winners York City. Bury were to make amends just a year after this defeat by winning promotion and the Second Division Championship in successive years.

Bury: Kelly, Woodward, Stanislaus, Daws, Lucketti, Jackson, Mulligan, Carter, Stant, Rigby, Pugh – capt. subs: Paskin for Carter 46, Hughes for Mulligan 61, Bracey (gk) (not used). manager: Mike Walsh
Chesterfield: Stewart, Hewitt, Rogers, Curtis, Carr, Law – capt, Robinson, Howard, Lormor, Morris, Hazel. subs: Perkins for Howard 77, Davies for Lormor 85, Brown (gk). manager: John Duncan

Second Division

Sunday 28th May 1995

Bristol Rovers 1
Stewart 45
Huddersfield Town 2
Booth 44, Billy 81
59,175
Referee: C Wilkes (Gloucester)

Huddersfield finally experienced victory at Wembley on their fifth visit. The previous year they had lost the Autoglass Trophy final to Swansea City on penalties.

Rovers had now spent a remarkable nine years playing their home games at Bath but their first Wembley trip since losing the Leyland DAF Cup final to Tranmere Rovers in 1990 was to prove fruitless.

Huddersfield manager Neil Warnock recorded his third Wembley play-off victory, after successes with Notts County in the early 1990's. He was to join Plymouth Argyle after the match and was back at Wembley the following year for yet another play-off victory.

Bristol R: Parkin, Pritchard, Clark, Tillson, Gurney, Sterling, Miller, Skinner – capt, Channing, Taylor, Stewart. subs: Browning for Taylor 80, Archer for Channing 82, Collett (gk) (not used) manager: John Ward
Huddersfield: Francis, Trevitt, Sinnott – capt, Scully, Cowan, Billy, Duxbury, Bullock, Crosby, Jepson, Booth. subs: Dyson for Trevitt 56, Dunn for Crosby 80, Blackwell (gk) (not used). manager: Neil Warnock

First Division

Monday 29th May 1995

Bolton Wanderers 4
Coyle 75, De Freitas 86, 118, Paatelainen 105
Reading 3
Nogan 4, Williams 12, Quinn 119

After extra time
64,107
Referee: P Foakes (Clacton-on-Sea)

This was one of Wembley's greatest matches and gave Bolton their second promotion in three years to take them back into the top flight they had left in 1980. It also capped a memorable season for them, as the previous month they had played their part in an entertaining Coca-Cola Cup final.

But they had to go through hell to finish victorious. If Keith Branagan had not saved Stuart Lovell's first half penalty, Bolton would have been three goals down and facing almost certain defeat. But Reading, who had finished as Endsleigh League runners-up to Middlesbrough, tired in the second half and Bolton's attacking style finally overwhelmed them.

Dutch substitute Fabien De Freitas snatched a dramatic equaliser and scored again in extra time to kill off Reading's challenge, although joint player-manager substitute Jimmy Quinn's late goal ensured the tension remained right to the end.

Reading had never played in the top division. They had won the Second Division Championship the previous year, and narrowly failed to add a second Wembley triumph to their 1988 Simod Cup success.

This was the second time in three years that the First Division final had produced a seven-goal thriller and just as the victors in 1993 Swindon Town had failed to hold on to their manager so did Bolton who could not stop Bruce Rioch taking charge at Arsenal.

Without him, Bolton were relegated straight back to the Football League the following year. In 1997 they won the Football League Championship by a mammoth 18 points, scoring 100 goals in the process and strode back into the Premiership only to suffer relegation on goal difference, a year later.

Reading, meanwhile, had reached their peak and finished bottom of the First Division three years later, suffering relegation back to the Second Division.

Bolton: Branagan, Green, Phillips, McAteer, Bergsson, Stubbs – capt, McDonald, Coyle, Paatelainen, McGinlay, Thompson. subs: De Freitas for McDonald 45, Dreyer, Shilton (gk) (not used). manager: Bruce Rioch
Reading: Hislop, Bernal, Osborn, Wdowczyk, Williams – capt, McPherson, Gilkes, Gooding, Nogan, Lovell, Taylor. subs: Quinn for Nogan 63, Hopkins for Bernal 68, Sheppard (gk) (not used). player-managers: Mick Gooding and Jimmy Quinn

UMBRO CUP

Saturday 3rd June 1995

England	**2-1**	**Japan**
Anderton 48, Platt pen 88		Ihara 62

21,142
Referee: J Uilenberg (Netherlands)

The Umbro Cup was a four-team tournament designed to give England competition before hosting the following year's European Championship.

Japan had won the Asian Championship for the first time in 1992 as hosts and now became the first team from that continent to visit Wembley. They were meeting England for the first time during one of the most successful periods in their history. The Japanese had missed out on the previous year's World Cup on goal difference, South Korea preventing them from qualifying for the first time.

A dismal first half with the Japanese defence easily keeping England at bay was followed by a goal just after the interval. Darren Anderton played a one-two with Shearer and his shot from the edge of the box took a deflection off Ihara which was enough to beat Maekawa.

The visitors struck back when Miura's corner was met by Masami Ihara at the near post and a glancing header past Flowers atoned for his unfortunate deflection at the other end.

England looked to be heading for an embarrassing draw and Japan for a glorious point but with two minutes left England managed to grab a victory they scarcely deserved. With his goalkeeper still on his knees after pushing David Platt's header onto the post in a goalmouth scramble, Hashiratani stopped Scales' shot with his hand. The Japanese captain was sent off for his handling offence and Platt tucked the penalty into the corner.

England almost lost their unbeaten record under Terry Venables five days later but two late goals brought them a 3-3 draw with Sweden at Elland Road.

Japan went down 3-0 to Brazil at Goodison Park three days after Wembley. They picked up their only point in a 2-2 draw with Sweden at the City Ground, Nottingham, the following week and finished bottom of the table. England were left to contest the Umbro Cup with Brazil. Two years later, Japan beat Iran in Kuala Lumpur with an extra time 'golden goal' to qualify for their first World Cup although they failed to win a point in France, the following year.

England: Flowers (Blackburn), Neville (G)* (Man Utd), Scales* (Liverpool), Unsworth* (Everton), Pearce (Nottingham F), Batty (Blackburn), Anderton (Tottenham), Platt (Sampdoria) – capt, Beardsley (Newcastle), Collymore* (Nottingham F), Shearer (Blackburn). subs: Gascoigne (Lazio) for Batty 68, McManaman (Liverpool) for Beardsley 68, Sheringham (Tottenham) for Collymore 76. coach: Terry Venables
*first cap

Japan: Maekawa (Sanfrecce Hiroshima), Hashiratani (Verdy Kawasaki) – capt, Tasaka (Bellmare Hiratsuka), Ihara (Yokohama Marinos), Narahashi (Bellmare Hiratsuka), Kitazawa (Verdy Kawasaki), Yamaguchi (Yokohama Flugels), Morishima (Cerezo Osaka), Souma (Kashima Antlers), Miura (Genoa), Nakayama (Jubilo Iwata). subs: Kurosaki (Kashima Antlers) for Nakayama 65, Yanagimoto (Sanfrecce Hiroshima) for Souma 74, Fukuda (Urawa Red Diamonds) for Morishima 81. coach: Shu Kamo

Schoolboy International

Saturday 10th June 1995

England 2
Owen, Kell

Germany 4
Falk 2,1 pen, Endres, Goller
Referee: R Lewis

The first victory at Wembley by a unified German schoolboy team and a very emphatic one at that, as they became the first foreign side to score four against England at the stadium. There was only one highlight for England, that of Michael Owen's record 12th goal of the season.

England: Stewart, Cooper, Haslam – capt, Brown (W), Ball, Lunt, Hibburt, Owen, Day, Jones, Burt. subs: Brown (A) for Lunt 66, Bradley for Jones 66, Kell for Burt 66, Thurrock for Stewart 75, O'Brien for Ball 75

UMBRO CUP

Sunday 11th June 1995

Brazil	**3-1**	**England**
Juninho 54, Ronaldo 61, Edmundo 76		Le Saux 38
67,318		

Referee: P Pairetto (Italy)

England needed to beat Brazil for the first time since 1990 to win the Umbro Cup after scraping a 3-3 draw against Sweden at Elland Road three days earlier. The World Champions needed a point, having disposed of both Sweden and Japan without conceding a goal.

They had not beaten England since 1981 and their last two meetings had been draws, at Wembley in 1992 and in Washington in the US Cup a year later. Brazil were fielding five of the side that beat Italy on penalties in Los Angeles to win the previous year's World Cup, a record fourth victory.

England, in all-red, attacked the World champions and deserved their half-time lead. Jorginho cleared Pearce's free kick with a diving header, but Graeme Le Saux took it on his chest and from 25 yards sent a superb dipping shot over the 'keeper into the corner.

Brazil were stunned, but struck back after the break. Juninho, who was to join Middlesbrough five months later, curled a free kick from just outside the area over the wall and past Flowers.

This was the turning point. Seven minutes later, Ronaldo timed his run perfectly to meet Juninho's pass. He took the ball calmly around Flowers and fired Brazil in front. Class now began to tell. A long ball from Carlos just flicked off Pearce's head. This was enough to leave Edmundo racing clear with Cooper in pursuit.

The Brazilian rubbed salt in the wound by slotting it through Flowers' legs. England had conceded three goals at Wembley for the first time in 23 years. They could have no complaints. Their first defeat under Terry Venables was to a better team. England could take heart from the fact that they had competed well against the best in the world and they would not have to face Brazil in the following year's European Championship.

Brazil beat England, by a single goal, two years later in Paris in a tournament that had already been won by England and they regained the South American Championship the following month. In 2000 they were one of the last visitors to the old Wembley.

Ronaldo, scorer of Brazil's second goal, was twice a winner of the European Footballer of the Year award. He was the first man from his country to win the honour and in 2002 his goals led Brazil to their record fifth World Cup win with Ronaldo being the tournament's top scorer.

Brazil: Zetti (Sao Paulo), Jorginho (Kashima Antlers), Aldair (Roma), Marcio Santos (Fiorentina), Roberto Carlos (Palmeiras), Cesar Sampaio (Yokohama Flugels), Juninho (Sao Paulo), Dunga (Stuttgart) – capt, Zinho (Yokohama Flugels), Ronaldo (PSV Eindhoven), Edmundo (Palmeiras). subs: Giovanni (Santos) for Ronaldo 76, Leonardo (Kashima Antlers) for Juninho 84, Ronaldao (Shimizu S-Pulse) for Aldair 90. coach: Mario Zagallo

England: Flowers (Blackburn), Neville (G) (Man Utd), Scales (Liverpool), Cooper (Nottingham F), Pearce (Nottingham F), Anderton (Tottenham), Platt (Sampdoria) – capt, Batty (Blackburn), Le Saux (Blackburn), Shearer (Blackburn), Sheringham (Tottenham). subs: Gascoigne (Lazio) for Batty 79, Collymore (Nottingham F) for Sheringham 79, Barton (Newcastle) for Scales 90. coach: Terry Venables

Final table	P	W	D	L	F	A	Pts
Brazil	3	3	0	0	7	1	9
England	3	1	1	1	6	7	4
Sweden	3	0	2	1	5	6	2
Japan	3	0	1	2	3	7	1

FA CHARITY SHIELD

Sunday 13th August 1995

Blackburn Rovers	**0-1**	**Everton**
		Samways 58

40,149
Referee: D Gallagher (Banbury)

Blackburn had lost the previous year's Charity Shield when appearing by invitation. This time they had qualified by right, having won the FA Carling Premiership by a point from Manchester United.

Blackburn's title was their first for 81 years and was achieved three years after winning promotion in the play-offs. It also meant that Kenny Dalglish became only the third man to manage two different clubs to the title (he had taken Liverpool to three titles in five years). Dalglish had since become Director of Football and Ray Harford had taken over as manager. Blackburn had won the Charity Shield only once before, in 1912.

Everton's fifth FA Cup win three months earlier had deprived Manchester United of a chance to complete a hat-trick of Charity Shields. Everton themselves held the record of four consecutive Shields, the last of which was in 1987. They won their first Shield back in 1928, when as League Champions they beat the FA Cup holders Blackburn 2-1 at Old Trafford.

The only goal came just before the hour. Vinny Samways ran on to Ablett's long ball down the wing. As Pearce came across to challenge, Samways pushed the ball through his legs and over Flowers and it looped in at the far post. A strange goal, but Everton made the most of it and stifled Blackburn's attempts to get back into the game. Although he had played only for the second half, club captain Dave Watson went up to receive the Shield.

Blackburn: Flowers, Kenna, Pearce, Sutton, Le Saux, Ripley, Batty, Sherwood – capt, Gallagher, Newell, Shearer. subs: Atkins for Kenna 30, Makel for Ripley 68, Marker for Gallacher 80. manager: Ray Harford
Everton: Southall, Barrett, Unsworth, Ablett, Hinchcliffe, Grant, Horne – capt, Parkinson, Samways, Limpar, Rideout. sub: Watson for Grant 46. manager: Joe Royle

INTERNATIONAL

Wednesday 6th September 1995

England	**0-0**	**Colombia**

20,038
Referee: M Batta (France)

Colombia had drawn at Wembley on their only previous visit, in the Rous Cup in 1988. Their only other meeting had been an England victory back in 1970. Unlike England, the Colombians had qualified for each of the last two World Cups.

England hit the woodwork three times but the abiding memory of this match was an extraordinary 'scorpion kick' by Colombia's eccentric 'keeper Rene Higuita who allowed a speculative shot from Redknapp to drop over his head before diving forward and kicking it back out with both feet from behind him.

Three years later England beat Colombia 2-0 in Lens to qualify for the last 16 of the World Cup, eliminating the South Americans in the process.

England: Seaman (Arsenal), Neville (G) (Man Utd), Howey (Newcastle), Adams (Arsenal) – capt, Le Saux (Blackburn), Wise (Chelsea), Redknapp* (Liverpool), Gascoigne (Rangers), McManaman (Liverpool), Barmby (Middlesbrough), Shearer (Blackburn). subs: Lee (Newcastle) for Redknapp 74, Barnes (Liverpool) for Gascoigne 74, Sheringham (Tottenham) for Shearer 74. coach: Terry Venables
*first cap
Colombia: Higuita (Nacional), Santa (Nacional), Bermudez (America de Cali), Mendoza (Junior), Perez (America de Cali), Lozano (Palmeiras), Alvarez (America de Cali), Asprilla (Parma), Valderrama (Junior) – capt, Rincon (Real Madrid), Valenciano (Junior). sub: Quinonez (Caladas) for Lozano 46. coach: Hernan Gomez

INTERNATIONAL

Wednesday 15th November 1995

England   **3-1**   **Switzerland**
Pearce 45, Sheringham 56, Stone 78   Knup 41
29,874
Referee: S Puhl (Hungary)

Switzerland were making their first visit to Wembley since losing a World Cup qualifying match in 1980. They had won the return match in Basle the following year but in 1988 had lost to England in their last meeting by the only goal in Lausanne.

The Swiss took the lead when Turkyilmaz crossed and Adrian Knup beat Adams to send a glancing header past Seaman. England were level at the break, however. Gascoigne's corner was played short to McManaman who moved it on to Stuart Pearce and a deflection off Quentin took it over Pascolo's head for the equaliser. Ten minutes after the interval, Teddy Sheringham rose to meet Stone's cross and head England in front. Victory was secured twelve minutes from the end. Pascolo failed to hold Shearer's shot and Steve Stone, who had come on as substitute after only six minutes, slotted home the rebound.

Switzerland were back at Wembley, the following year to face England in the opening match of the European Championship.

England: Seaman (Arsenal), Neville (G) (Man Utd), Pallister (Man Utd), Adams (Arsenal) – capt, Pearce (Nottingham F), Lee (Newcastle), Redknapp (Liverpool), Gascoigne (Rangers), McManaman (Liverpool), Sheringham (Tottenham), Shearer (Blackburn). sub: Stone (Nottingham F) for Redknapp 6. coach: Terry Venables

Switzerland: Pascolo (Servette), Hottiger (Newcastle), Geiger (Grasshoppers) – capt, Henchoz (Hamburg), Quentin (Sion), Ohrel (Saint-Etienne), Fournier (Sion), Sforza (Bayern Munich), Sutter (Bayern Munich), Turkyilmaz (Galatasaray), Knup (Karlsruhe). subs: Wolf (Lucerne) for Fournier 69, Grassi (Rennes) for Sutter 80, Vega (Grasshoppers) for Quentin 82. coach: Roy Hodgson

INTERNATIONAL

Tuesday 12th December 1995

England   **1-1**   **Portugal**
Stone 44   Alves 58
28,592
Referee: R Pedersen (Norway)

After drawing at Wembley in the European Championship in 1974, Portugal had had few moments of glory. In 1984 they had lost a dramatic European Championship semi-final in Marseille to hosts and eventual winners France, who won with a last minute goal in extra time. They went on to beat England 1-0 in Monterrey in their last meeting in the 1986 World Cup, although they failed to win another point.

Since then, they had failed to qualify for major tournaments until the previous month when they secured their place in England at the 1996 European Championship by winning a group which included both Northern Ireland and the Republic of Ireland.

Steve Stone gave England the lead with a hard, low shot after Ferdinand had chested down Pearce's cross. Portugal were no pushovers, however, and equalised in the second half when two substitutes combined to beat Seaman. Dominguez attempted a short pass to Sa Pinto which ran behind the striker into the path of Paulo Alves who ended a strong run by firing home despite Adams' lunge.

Luis Figo made his Wembley debut. In 2000 when the stadium closed its doors for the last time he was named European Footballer of the Year.

England: Seaman (Arsenal), Neville (G) (Man Utd), Pearce (Nottingham F), Wise (Chelsea), Adams (Arsenal) – capt, Howey (Newcastle), Barmby (Middlesbrough), Gascoigne (Rangers), Shearer (Blackburn), Ferdinand (Newcastle), Stone (Nottingham F). subs: Beardsley (Newcastle) for Ferdinand 68, Le Saux (Blackburn) for Pearce 79, Southgate* (Aston Villa) for Wise 79, McManaman (Liverpool) for Barmby 79. coach: Terry Venables
*first cap

Portugal: Neno (Vitoria Guimaraes), Secretario (Porto), Dimas (Benfica), Jorge Costa (Porto), Couto (Parma) – capt, Paulo Sousa (Juventus), Figo (Barcelona), Joao Pinto (Benfica), Sa Pinto (Sporting Lisbon), Helder (Benfica), Folha (Porto). subs: Alves (Sporting Lisbon) for Paulo Sousa 46, Dominguez (Sporting Lisbon) for Figo 46, Dani (Sporting Lisbon) for Joao Pinto 60, Barbosa (Sporting Lisbon) for Folha 67. coach: Antonio Oliveira

Wembley Challenge Tournament
Saturday 2nd March 1996

For the second year in succession the men from the media enjoyed their own tournament on the hallowed turf. This time, however, there were only six teams competing, two fewer than the previous year, and they were split into two groups with 'sudden death' penalties deciding drawn games.

Group One

Littlewoods 0
Television Tigers 0
Television Tigers won 1-0 on penalties.

Associates 0
Littlewoods 1

Associates 0
Television Tigers 2

Group Two

Crusaders 0
News International 0
Crusaders won 3-2 on penalties.

Mirror Warriors 0
News International 0
Mirror Warriors won 1-0 on penalties.

Crusaders 0
Mirror Warriors 0
Crusaders won 1-0 on penalties.

Final

Crusaders 1
Television Tigers 0

At least the final did not go to penalties. The newspaper men won the tournament without conceding, although their scrambled winner from a corner was the only goal they scored and was only the fourth in the entire tournament of seven matches.

Schoolboy International
Saturday 9th March 1996

England 2
Standing, Jeffers

Spain 3
scorers not known
Referee: D Morrall (Sheffield)

The first meeting between the two at this level brought an unexpected home defeat. England never recovered from three first-half Spanish goals.

Goalscoring substitute Francis Jeffers went on to equal Alan Shearer's record of 13 goals for the England Under-21 side. He came on as a substitute to score on his full international debut against Australia at Upton Park in 2003 although he has yet to win another cap.

England: Ghent, Weston, Nicholson - capt, Foster, Cannoville, Holmes, Parker, Standing, Taylor, Wheatcroft, Biggins. subs: Fitzpatrick, Jeffers

Anglo-Italian Cup Final
Sunday 17th March 1996

Genoa 5
Ruotolo 12, 54, 66, Galante 21, Montella 39
Port Vale 2
Foyle 68, 82
12,683
Referee: I Koho (Finland)

Port Vale were taught a footballing lesson as the trophy returned to Italy for the third time in four years. Genoa had been relegated to the Italian Second Division the previous year. The teams had met in a goalless draw earlier in the competition at Vale Park. Vale were appearing at Wembley for the third time in four years but they were to suffer their second successive three-goal defeat. It could have been much worse as they did not find the net until Genoa had scored five. This was to be the last final as interest in the competition had dwindled.

Genoa: Pastine, Carri, Cavallo, Galante, Magoni, Ruotolo - capt, Bortolazzi, Onorati, Nicola, Montella, Nappi. subs: Torrente for Onorati 46, Van't Schip for Nicola 50, Spagnulo for Pastine 75. coach: Gaetano Salvemini
Port Vale: Musselwhite, Hill, Griffiths, Aspin, Stokes, McCarthy, Porter - capt, Bogie, Guppy, Foyle, Glover (L). subs: Walker for Stokes 37, Naylor for Glover 60, Talbot for Guppy 87. manager: John Rudge

LEAGUE CUP FINAL

Sunday 24th March 1996

Aston Villa　　　　**3-0**　　　**Leeds United**
Milosevic 20, Taylor 54, Yorke 89
77,056
Referee: R Hart (Darlington)

Villa were aiming to follow Liverpool's success of the previous year by securing their fifth League Cup win. It would be their second in three years.

The following year, though, they had escaped relegation to the Endsleigh League by just three points.

Leeds were appearing in their first final since 1968, their only success in this competition. They had won the FA Charity Shield on their last visit, in 1992 but had disappointed since then.

In a much improved season, Villa would be competing in the following week's FA Cup semi-finals. Their manager Brian Little was making his fourth visit in five years, having taken Leicester City to three successive play-off finals. Leeds were having a disappointing season in the league and had been well beaten in the UEFA Cup by PSV Eindhoven.

Villa dominated from the start and struck after Townsend intercepted Speed's pass to McAllister and played it to Savo Milosevic. The Serbian ran at the Leeds defence and as Pemberton finally tried to block him unleashed a powerful drive which sailed beyond Lukic.

Leeds began to threaten after the interval, but Villa doubled their lead when a deep cross from Wright was hooked out by an acrobatic overhead kick from Radebe under pressure from Milosevic. Unfortunately for him, the ball dropped neatly for Ian Taylor to volley past the diving Wetherall on the line.

Leeds were woefully out of touch and Villa added a third in the last minute. Milosevic broke away and again Pemberton backed off. This time he had Dwight Yorke alongside him and a quick lay-off gave the Tobagan the opportunity to fire in off the bar.

Villa lost their FA Cup semi-final, the following week, but finished a creditable fourth, in the FA Carling Premiership and won at Leeds in their first defence of the Coca-Cola Cup. They had to wait another four years to return to Wembley, for an FA Cup semi-final. Leeds slumped to 13th, in the Premiership.

Aston V: Bosnich, Ehiogu, McGrath, Southgate, Charles, Draper, Taylor, Townsend – capt, Wright, Milosevic, Yorke. subs: Johnson, Staunton, Oakes (gk) (not used). manager: Brian Little
Leeds: Lukic, Wetherall, Pemberton, Radebe, Kelly, Ford, McAllister – capt, Palmer, Speed, Gray (A), Yeboah. subs: Deane for Ford 46, Brolin for Radebe 66, Worthington (not used). manager: Howard Wilkinson

INTERNATIONAL

Wednesday 27th March 1996

England　　　　　　**1-0**　　　**Bulgaria**
Ferdinand 7
29,708
Referee: G Benko (Austria)

Bulgaria were visiting Wembley during the most successful spell in their history. Two years earlier they had reached the World Cup semi-finals by defeating the holders Germany 2-1 in New York after five previous World Cup tournaments in which they had failed to register a single win.

They followed up this success by qualifying for the European Championship and would be returning to England three months later. They had beaten Germany again in the qualifying group in Sofia, but finished as runners-up to them. Bulgaria had never beaten England and had scored only once against them – at Wembley in 1968.

England, who broke with tradition to take the field in an all-greyish kit, took little time to break the deadlock. A long pass from Sheringham from just inside the Bulgarian half put Les Ferdinand away. The big striker took the ball on his chest, held off Ivanov's challenge and slipped it under Mikhailov. The Reading goalkeeper got his hands to the ball but could not prevent it going in. England played well, especially in the first half. The Bulgarians gave a better performance in the second half, but England were deserved winners.

Bulgaria had a disappointing European Championship and failed to reach the quarter-finals. They returned to Wembley in the next European Championship two years later.

England: Seaman (Arsenal), Neville (G) (Man Utd), Howey (Newcastle), Southgate (Aston Villa), Pearce (Nottingham F) – capt, Stone (Nottingham F), Ince (Internazionale), Gascoigne (Rangers), McManaman (Liverpool), Sheringham (Tottenham), Ferdinand (Newcastle). subs: Lee (Newcastle) for Sheringham 68, Platt (Arsenal) for Gascoigne 76, Fowler* (Liverpool) for Ferdinand 76. coach: Terry Venables
*first cap
Bulgaria: Mikhailov (Reading) - capt, Houbtchev (Hamburg), Yankov (Bayer Uerdingen), Ivanov (Rapid Vienna), Kremenliev (Olympiakos), Lechkov (Hamburg), Kiriakov (Anorthosis), Guinchev (Denizlispor), Iordanov (Sporting Lisbon), Penev (Atletico Madrid), Kostadinov (Bayern Munich). subs: Popov (CSKA Sofia) for Mikhailov 46, Guentchev (Luton Town) for Guinchev 46, Borimirov (TSV Munich) for Iordanov 46, Kishishev (Neftochimik) for Kremenliev 85, Sirakov (Slavia Sofia) for Penev 85. coach: Dimitar Penev

Auto Windscreens Shield

Sunday 14th April 1996

Rotherham United 2
Jemson 2

Shrewsbury Town 1
Taylor
35,235
Referee: D Allison (Lancaster)

Nigel Jemson had scored the only goal of the 1990 Littlewoods Cup final for Nottingham Forest and furthered his Wembley reputation by deciding this match between two clubs appearing at the stadium for the first time.

Rotherham had won both legs of their semi-final against the previous year's finalists Carlisle United, but had not beaten Shrewsbury in the 1990's.

Jemson was on loan from Notts County and was to join Oxford United at the beginning of the following season. By 2000 the much-travelled striker would be playing for Shrewsbury. Both sides were in the lower reaches of the Second Division and Shrewsbury escaped relegation only by a point. A year later, they were both relegated back to the Third Division.

Rotherham: Clarke - capt, Blades, Hurst, Garner, Richardson, Breckin, Jemson, Goodwin, Berry, Goater, Roscoe. managers: Archie Gemmill and John McGovern
Shrewsbury: Edwards, Kay, Withe, Taylor, Whiston, Scott, Robinson, Stevens, Spink, Walton, Berkley. subs: Anthrobus for Spink 46, Lynch for Robinson 75. manager: Fred Davies

INTERNATIONAL

Wednesday 24th April 1996

England   0-0   Croatia
33,650
Referee: Z Przesmycki (Poland)

This was the first meeting between these two, as Croatia had begun competing only two years earlier following the break-up of Yugoslavia.
They were fancied to do well on their return to England two months later for the European Championship, having surprisingly won their qualifying group on aggregate from Italy, after pulling off a shock 2-1 win against the 1994 World Cup finalists in Palermo.

England had won their last three meetings with Yugoslavia and hoped to continue the run against the Croatians.
A disappointing game as the Croatians were not as adventurous as was hoped and England could not convert any of several chances.

Croatia effectively ended Denmark's reign as European Champions two months later by beating them 3-0 at Hillsborough and went on to reach the quarter-finals before losing 2-1 at Old Trafford to the eventual winners Germany. Two years later they beat Germany 3-0 in Lyon to reach the World Cup semi-finals where they then lost to the hosts and eventual winners France in Paris.

England: Seaman (Arsenal), Neville (G) (Man Utd), Wright (Liverpool), Pearce (Nottingham F), Ince (Internazionale), Stone (Nottingham F), Gascoigne (Rangers), Platt (Arsenal) – capt, McManaman (Liverpool), Sheringham (Tottenham), Fowler (Liverpool). coach: Terry Venables
Croatia: Mrmic (Varteks Varazdin), Jerkan (Real Oviedo), Bilic (West Ham), Stimac (Derby County), Pavlicic (Hercules Alicante), Asanovic (Hajduk Split), Boban (AC Milan) - capt, Prosinecki (Barcelona), Jarni (Real Betis), Boksic (Lazio), Suker (Sevilla). subs: Stanic (Bruges) for Boban 46, Soldo (Croatia Zagreb) for Stimac 58, Parnic (Osijek) for Boksic 71, Mladenovic (Gamba Osaka) for Pavlicic 75. coach: Miroslav Blazevic

FA CUP FINAL

Saturday 11th May 1996

Liverpool 0-1 **Manchester United**
Cantona 85

79,007
Referee: D Gallagher (Banbury)

This game brought back memories of the 1977 final – the first Wembley meeting between the teams – when United denied Liverpool the 'double'. There had been five matches at the stadium between them since then and Liverpool's only victory was in the 1983 Milk Cup final.

After two barren seasons without a trophy, Liverpool had lifted the Coca-Cola Cup the previous year and were now hoping to notch their sixth FA Cup win.

United were appearing in their third successive final and were attempting to win the competition for a record ninth time. Two years earlier they had secured the 'double' at Wembley by dispatching Chelsea. The previous season had ended in extreme disappointment, a low key United losing the FA Cup final a week after failing to complete a hat-trick of Premiership titles.

Liverpool finished third, in the FA Carling Premiership, their best position for five years while United had astonished all their critics the previous week by clinching their third Premiership title in four years.

Victory at Wembley would give them a record second 'double' in three years.

A final which promised so much delivered little. Neither team got into their stride and extra time loomed when one moment settled the issue. With five minutes remaining Beckham's corner was punched out by James but hit substitute Rush on the shoulder and fell to Eric Cantona. With most of the Liverpool team between him and the goal he took a step backwards and fired the ball with poise and precision between Jones and Scales into the net.

It was the culmination of a remarkable transformation in Cantona's career. He had begun the season by completing an eight-month ban for attacking a spectator at Crystal Palace the previous season and ended it as a reformed character. He had become the first French winner of the Footballer of the Year award and had captained a remarkable team to an unprecedented second 'double'.

United had secured it with six of the team that had clinched the first 'double', two years earlier.

Liverpool: James, McAteer, Scales, Wright, Babb, Jones, McManaman, Redknapp, Barnes – capt, Collymore, Fowler. subs: Rush for Collymore 74, Thomas for Jones 85, Warner (gk) (not used). manager: Roy Evans
Manchester U: Schmeichel, Irwin, May, Pallister, Neville (P), Beckham, Butt, Keane, Giggs, Cantona – capt, Cole. subs: Scholes for Cole 65, Neville (G) for Beckham 89, Sharpe (not used). manager: Alex Ferguson

FA Vase Final

Sunday 12th May 1996

Brigg Town 3
Stead (C) 36 pen, 64, Lampkin og 86
Clitheroe 0
7,340
Referee: S Lodge (Barnsley)

A convincing victory sealed the Vase for

Brigg for whom substitute David Mail had been in Blackburn Rovers' Full Members Cup-winning side in 1987 at Wembley.

Brigg: Gawthorpe, Thompson, Buckley - capt, Greaves, Rogers, Elston, McLean, Stead (C), Stead (N), Roach, Flounders. subs: Mail for Buckley 19, Clay for Greaves 84, McNally for Stead (N) 89
Clitheroe: Nash, Rowbotham, Baron, Westwell – capt, Lampkin, Grimshaw, Butcher, Rouine, Hill, Darbyshire, Taylor. subs: Dunn for Hill 60, Otley for Rowbotham 74, Smith for Taylor 74

INTERNATIONAL

Saturday 18th May 1996

| **England** | **3-0** | **Hungary** |

Anderton 38, 62, Platt 52
34,184
Referee: M Merk (Germany)

England's last home match before hosting the European Championship saw them entertain Hungary who had a very poor record against them in recent times. They had failed to score against England in their last six meetings and had lost eight of the last nine. It was now ten years since they had qualified for a major tournament and they had never really been in contention for a place in the forthcoming European Championship.

It still took England a while to break the deadlock. But then Darren Anderton at the far post slid in Sheringham's cross. His second came after Banfi could only deflect Lee's cross with his head towards his own goalmouth. Under pressure from Ferdi-

nand, Petry flapped and the ball dropped for Anderton to put Hungary out of their misery with a shot that Mracsko whacked into the roof of the net in a desperate attempt to clear. The second ten minutes earlier arrived when Ince took a quick free kick to David Platt. Petry came out and blocked him only for the ball to rebound into the net off the England captain.

Hungary did manage to score in their next meeting, a 1-1 draw in Budapest three years later but qualifying success still eluded them. They reached a play-off for the 1998 World Cup but were on the receiving end of a 12-1 aggregate thrashing by Yugoslavia.

England: Seaman (Arsenal), Neville (G) (Man Utd), Wright (Liverpool), Pearce (Nottingham F), Ince (Internazionale), Anderton (Tottenham), Lee (Newcastle), Platt (Arsenal) – capt, Wilcox* (Blackburn), Sheringham (Tottenham), Ferdinand (Newcastle). subs: Southgate (Aston Villa) for Wright 12, Walker* (Tottenham) for Seaman 65, Campbell* (Tottenham) for Ince 65, Wise (Chelsea) for Platt 65, Shearer (Blackburn) for Ferdinand 77. coach: Terry Venables
*first cap
Hungary: Petry (Genclerberligi), Hahn (Kispest-Honved), Banfi (Eendracht Aalst) – capt, Plokai (Kispest-Honved), Balog (Charleroi), Mracsko (Bekescsaba), Urban (Gyor), Sebok (Ujpesti Dozsa), Nagy (Ferencvaros), Horvath (Zalaegerszeg), Vincze (BVSC Dreher). subs: Illes (MTK) for Balog 61, Egressy (Ujpesti Dozsa) for Vincze 79, Telek (Ferencvaros) for Mracsko 81, Aranyos (BVSC) for Nagy 81, Lisztes (Ferencvaros) for Horvath 81. coach: Janos Csank

FA Trophy Final

Sunday 19th May 1996

Macclesfield Town 3
Payne 18, Burgess og 28, Hemmings 81
Northwich Victoria 1
Williams 52
8,672
Referee: M Reed (Birmingham)

The first winners of the FA Trophy, Macclesfield took 26 years to win it again, this time by defeating their Cheshire rivals who had Derek Ward sent off for a second bookable offence after a late tackle on Tony Hemmings. This happened two minutes after Hemmings had clinched victory for Macclesfield. Their manager was Sammy McIlroy who had played 13 times at Wembley for Manchester United and Northern Ireland.

1996

The previous year Macclesfield had won the Vauxhall Conference Championship but had been denied promotion to the Football League because their ground was not the required standard, although Chester City had been using it as their home in the Third Division up until 1992. They were not to be denied, however, and a year after their Wembley success they regained the Conference title with a ground that was passed fit for them to take their place in the Football League.

Macclesfield: Price, Edey, Howarth - capt, Payne, Gardiner, Lyons, Sorvel, Wood, Hemmings, Coates, Power. subs: Hulme for Wood 84, Cavell for Hemmings 89
Northwich: Greygoose, Ward, Abel, Burgess, Duffy, Williams, Butler, Walters, Vicary, Cooke, Humphreys. subs: Steele for Abel 77, Simpson for Burgess 85

Play-off Finals

Third Division
Saturday 25th May 1996

Darlington 0
Plymouth Argyle 1
Mauge 65
43,431
Referee: W Burns (Scarborough)

Before a crowd bigger than for the following day's Second Division final, Plymouth clinched promotion a year after being relegated from the Second Division. They defeated Darlington for the first time in ten years, despite the club from the opposite end of the country completing a league double over them during the season. Plymouth's manager Neil Warnock won his fourth play-off in seven years – two wins with Notts County and the previous year with Huddersfield Town.

Darlington: Newell, Brumwell, Barnard, Appleby, Crosby - capt, Gregan, Bannister, Gaughan, Painter, Blake, Carss. subs: Carmichael for Gaughan 85, Mattison, Twynham (not used). manager: Jim Platt
Plymouth: Cherry, Patterson, Williams, Mauge, Heathcote - capt, Barlow, Leadbitter, Logan, Littlejohn, Evans, Curran. subs: Baird, Billy, Corazzin (not used). manager: Neil Warnock

Second Division
Sunday 26th May 1996

Bradford City 2
Hamilton 8, Stallard 73
Notts County 0

39,972
Referee: G Singh (Wolverhampton)

Despite visiting Wembley for the third year in succession (after two Anglo-Italian Cup finals) and for the fifth time in seven years, County were well beaten, thus failing to bounce back to the First Division at the first attempt following the previous year's relegation in bottom place.

City had lost in extra time in the old Second Division play-offs in 1988 to eventual winners Middlesbrough and were relegated two years later.

This was their first appearance at Wembley and was secured although they had lost 2-0 at home to Blackpool in the first leg of their semi-final. The following year, City escaped relegation by two points but two years later, they were Football League runners-up to Sunderland and won promotion to the Premiership.

Meanwhile, County took a long time to recover from this defeat and dropped into the Third Division after finishing bottom. But they ran away with the Third Division Championship in 1998 to secure promotion straight back.

Bradford C: Gould, Huxford, Jacobs, Mitchell, Mohan, Youds - capt, Kiwomya, Duxbury, Shutt, Stallard, Hamilton. subs: Ormondroyd for Hamilton 73, Wright for Kiwomya 78, Tolson (not used). manager: Chris Kamara
Notts County: Ward, Derry, Baraclough, Murphy, Strodder - capt, Richardson, Finnan, Rogers, Martindale, Battersby, Agana. subs: Jones for Battersby 84, Hogg, Pollitt (not used). manager: Colin Murphy

First Division
Monday 27th May 1996

Crystal Palace 1
Roberts 14
Leicester City 2
Parker pen 76, Claridge 120
After extra time
73,573
Referee: D Allison (Lancaster)

The play-off weekend was brought to a dramatic climax yet again as Leicester won promotion to the FA Carling Premiership for the second time in three years – their fourth final in five years.

Palace had been relegated with them the previous year after winning promotion with them in 1994. Leicester's first promotion had been secured by a late winner: this time it was even more sensational. As a penalty shoot-out loomed, Leicester man-

313

ager Martin O'Neill introduced 6ft 7in Australian goalkeeper Zeljko Kalac in the last minute. He had played only one league game beforehand, in November.

Perhaps Palace momentarily lost concentration following such an unusual replacement although Kalac did not touch the ball. Whatever, Steve Claridge struck an injury-time winner to give O'Neill his fourth Wembley success in six years – after two FA Trophy wins and a play-off victory with Wycombe Wanderers. Kalac never played again for Leicester but more success was to follow for both teams a year later. Palace gained promotion by winning the play-offs, ironically with a last minute winner at Wembley. Leicester, meanwhile, won the Coca-Cola Cup.

Garry Parker scored twice at Wembley for Nottingham Forest, when they won the 1989 Simod Cup.

Crystal P: Martyn, Edworthy, Brown, Roberts, Quinn, Hopkin - capt, Pitcher, Houghton, Freedman, Ndah, Tuttle. subs: Veart for Hopkin 71, Dyer for Freedman 99, Rodger for Tuttle 102. manager: Dave Bassett
Leicester: Poole, Grayson, Whitlow, Watts, Walsh - capt, Izzet, Lennon, Taylor, Claridge, Parker, Heskey. subs: Robins for Taylor 101, Hill for Walsh 118, Kalac for Poole 119. manager: Martin O'Neill

EUROPEAN CHAMPIONSHIP

Saturday 8th June 1996

England	1-1	Switzerland
Shearer 22		Turkyilmaz pen 82

76,567
Referee: M Vega (Spain)

A historic day as the finals of the European Championship were held in England for the first time. It was also the first time that 16 nations had competed in the tournament. England were hoping to reach the final for the first time while Switzerland were happy to appear in the tournament for the first time.

The countries had met previously in the competition. In 1971 England won 3-2 in Basle with the return drawn 1-1 at Wembley as England went on to reach the quarter-finals. Their most recent meeting had been the previous year, with England winning again. They had not lost to the Swiss for 15 years.

The host nation got the goal they wanted when Alan Shearer laid off a short ball to Ince and then ran on to a superb return pass, leaving him with only the 'keeper to beat. The sheer power of his shot left Pascolo without a hope.

England looked tired in the second half and Switzerland forced their way back into the game. With eight minutes left, Pearce put his hands up to protect himself from Grassi's shot and gave away a penalty. Kubilay Turkyilmaz sent Seaman the wrong way to ruin the party.

Switzerland failed to win another point or score another goal and finished bottom of the group. England now had to face Scotland, the following week, with added pressure to win.

England: Seaman (Arsenal), Neville (G) (Man Utd), Pearce (Nottingham F), Adams (Arsenal) – capt, Southgate (Aston Villa), Ince (Internazionale), Anderton (Tottenham), Gascoigne (Rangers), Shearer (Blackburn), Sheringham (Tottenham), McManaman (Liverpool). subs: Barmby (Middlesbrough) for Sheringham 68, Stone (Nottingham F) for McManaman 68, Platt (Arsenal) for Gascoigne 76. coach: Terry Venables
Switzerland: Pascolo (Servette), Jeanneret (Neuchatel Xamax), Vega (Grasshoppers), Henchoz (Hamburg), Quentin (Sion), Geiger (Grasshoppers) – capt, Sforza (Bayern Munich), Vogel (Grasshoppers), Bonvin (Sion), Turkyilmaz (Grasshoppers), Grassi (Rennes). subs: Chapuisat (Borussia Dortmund) for Geiger 68, Koller (Grasshoppers) for Bonvin 68. coach: Artur Jorge

Saturday 15th June 1996

England	2-0	Scotland
Shearer 52, Gascoigne 78		

76,864
Referee: P Pairetto (Italy)

Another historic moment as two British teams met in the finals of a major tournament for the first time. Both sides had drawn their opening games in Group A. England may have disappointed against Switzerland but Scotland had held the mighty Netherlands to a goalless draw at Villa Park two days later, and were now fired up to face their oldest rivals. They had not played England since the 1989 Rous Cup and had not visited Wembley since 1988. It had been 15 years since their last win at the stadium.

With the Netherlands having beaten Switzerland at Villa Park two days earlier to seize the initiative victory was absolutely vital. Defeat would mean almost certain elimination for either side. Scotland had qualified for their second successive European Championship fairly comfortably.

After a dull first half, England began to apply some pressure and they were rewarded when Neville's cross sailed over Goram's head and Alan Shearer came in at the far post to head England in front. Scotland fought back and won a penalty when Ad-ams upended Durie. But to Scotland's dismay, Seaman saved McAllister's kick with his elbow and just a minute later dismay turned to despair, as England clinched victory with a goal which would have demoralised the best of teams.

Paul Gascoigne ran on to Anderton's pass, flicked it over Hendry and volleyed it past Goram. The brilliance of the goal was matched only by the timing of it and McAllister was devastated.

England sat proudly at the top of Group A on goals scored from the Netherlands knowing a draw against the Dutch three days later would take them both through to the quarter-finals. Scotland added yet another hard-luck story to their long history of major tournament heartache. They beat Switzerland at Villa Park on the same night with their only goal of the tournament but were eliminated on goals scored by the Dutch.

Three years later, Scotland were back to contest Wembley's last match of the century with a place in the next European Championship at stake.

England: Seaman (Arsenal), Neville (G) (Man Utd), Pearce (Nottingham F), Southgate (Aston Villa), Adams (Arsenal) – capt, Ince (Internazionale), Anderton (Tottenham), Gascoigne (Rangers), Shearer (Blackburn), Sheringham (Tottenham), McManaman (Liverpool). subs: Redknapp (Liverpool) for Pearce 46, Stone (Nottingham F) for Ince 79, Campbell (Tottenham) for Redknapp 84. coach: Terry Venables

Scotland: Goram (Rangers), McKimmie (Aberdeen), Boyd (Celtic), Calderwood (Tottenham), Hendry (Blackburn), McKinlay (Celtic), Collins (Celtic), McCall (Rangers), Spencer (Chelsea), McAllister (Leeds Utd) - capt, Durie (Rangers). subs: McCoist (Rangers) for Spencer 66, Burley (Chelsea) for McKinlay 82, Jess (Coventry) for Durie 86. coach: Craig Brown

Tuesday 18th June 1996

England   4-1   Netherlands
Shearer (pen) 22, 57, Sheringham 51, 62   Kluivert 77
76,798
Referee: G Grabher (Austria)

Both sides needed just a draw to qualify for the quarter-finals from Group A. Defeat for either team would leave them dependent on the result from the group's other match being played simultaneously between Scotland and Switzerland at Villa Park. The draw would be good enough for England to win the group on goals scored and meet the Group B runners-up Spain at Wembley rather than having to travel to meet the Group B winners France which would happen if they lost and still qualified.

Netherlands, the 1988 European Champions, had effectively knocked England out of the last World Cup at the qualifying stage by beating them 2-0 in Rotterdam in 1993. Their last two visits to Wembley had been 2-2 draws (in 1988 and 1993) and England had not beaten them since 1982. In the Netherlands' last three major tournaments, the eventual winners had eliminated them each time. But they had struggled to qualify for this championship, pipping Norway for the runners-up spot in their group by beating them in their last match in Rotterdam. This took them to a play-off with the Republic of Ireland at Anfield which they won 2-0.

Midway through the first half a clever flick from Ince won England a penalty as he was tripped by Blind. Alan Shearer fired a confident kick past Van der Sar to score in his third successive match in the championship. In the second half England increased their lead as Teddy Sheringham outjumped Winter to head Gascoigne's corner into the corner of the net. Six minutes later the victory was secured as the mighty Dutch defence was sliced wide open by some superb passing moves. Gascoigne shrugged off Winter's challenge and unselfishly laid the ball across to Sheringham as Blind blocked his path. Sheringham feigned to shoot and caused substitute De Kock to stumble by unexpectedly playing it to his right to Shearer who powered it past the 'keeper.

The home fans were astonished by the breathtaking performance by England and it got even better as they added a fourth. Van de Sar managed to stop Anderton's shot even though it deflected off the back of Blind but Sheringham was quick to react and just beat Bogarde to fire home his second.

The Dutch were torn apart and suddenly faced elimination on goal difference as Scotland were beating Switzerland. However, with 13 minutes left, Bergkamp played a brilliant lob into Patrick Kluivert's path and the Dutch substitute slotted it through Seaman's legs for a priceless goal. It took the Netherlands through to the quarter-finals on goals scored from Scotland.

For England it was a magical night which left the whole country believing that they had a real chance of becoming European Champions for the first time.

England had four days to get back down to earth and prepare for their quarter-final with Spain. The Dutch had four days in which to recover from their heaviest ever defeat in a major tournament but they tightened their defence in a goalless draw with France after extra time at Anfield, scene of their play-off victory, the previous year. The French defeated them on penalties though and the Netherlands headed dejectedly for home.

England: Seaman (Arsenal), Neville (G) (Man Utd), Pearce (Nottingham F), Adams (Arsenal) – capt, Southgate (Aston Villa), Ince (Internazionale), Gascoigne (Rangers), McManaman (Liverpool), Anderton (Tottenham), Shearer (Blackburn), Sheringham (Tottenham). subs: Platt (Arsenal) for Ince 67, Fowler (Liverpool) for Shearer 75, Barmby (Middlesbrough) for Sheringham 75. coach: Terry Venables

Netherlands: Van der Sar (Ajax Amsterdam), Reiziger (Ajax), Blind (Ajax) – capt, Bogarde (Ajax), Winter (Lazio), Seedorf (Sampdoria), Witschge (Bordeaux), De Boer (R) (Ajax), Cruyff (Barcelona), Bergkamp (Arsenal), Hoekstra (Ajax). subs: De Kock (Roda JC Kerkrade) for Witschge 46, Kluivert (Ajax) for De Boer 71, Cocu (PSV Eindhoven) for Hoekstra 71. coach: Guus Hiddink

Final table	P	W	D	L	F	A	Pts
England	3	2	1	0	7	2	7
Netherlands	3	1	1	1	3	4	4
Scotland	3	1	1	1	1	2	4
Switzerland	3	0	1	2	1	4	1

QUARTER-FINAL

Saturday 22nd June 1996

England   0-0   Spain

After extra time
England won 4-2 on penalties.
(Shearer 1-0, Hierro hit bar, Platt 2-0, Amor 2-1, Pearce 3-1, Belsue 3-2, Gascoigne 4-2, Nadal saved)
75,440
Referee: M Batta (France)

Spain had won on their last appearance at Wembley 15 years before and had also beaten England by a single goal in their last encounter, in 1992 in Santander. Spain's last defeat at Wembley had, ironically, been as champions in the first leg of the European Championship quarter-final in 1968. England won the second leg in Madrid as well and so the then World Cham-pions knocked out the defending European Champions. England lost to Yugoslavia in the semi-finals and neither side had won a trophy since, although Spain reached the final again in 1984. Their current squad was a strong one and they had not been beaten since they lost 2-1 to eventual finalists Italy in the World Cup quarter-final in Boston two years earlier. They qualified to

1996

face England at Wembley by finishing as Group B runners-up to France, just pipping Bulgaria with a late winner against Romania at Elland Road four days earlier.

England did not reach the heights of the Dutch game of four days earlier and neither side could conjure up the vital goal. It became the first major international to go to 'sudden-death' extra time, but the tension and fear of losing prevented any real chances and penalties were required for the first time in a Wembley international. Stuart Pearce overcame his personal demons to wipe out the memory of his 1990 World Cup miss and his typically rousing celebration got the crowd behind the host nation. David Seaman became a hero by saving a penalty for the second week in succession, this time from Miguel Nadal, and England took their place in the semi-finals.

Spain could count themselves unlucky to be eliminated without losing in open play. England's win sparked wild celebrations. Four days later, their great rivals, Germany stood between them and a place in the final.

England: Seaman (Arsenal), Neville (G) (Man Utd), Pearce (Nottingham F), Adams (Arsenal) – capt, Southgate (Aston Villa), Platt (Arsenal), Gascoigne (Rangers), Shearer (Blackburn), Sheringham (Tottenham), Anderton (Tottenham), McManaman (Liverpool). subs: Stone (Nottingham F) for Sheringham 108, Fowler (Liverpool) for Anderton 108, Barmby (Middlesbrough) for McManaman 108. coach: Terry Venables
Spain: Zubizarreta (Valencia), Belsue (Real Zaragoza), Alkorta (Real Madrid), Abelardo (Barcelona), Hierro (Real Madrid) – capt, Sergi (Barcelona), Kiko (Atletico Madrid), Manjarin (Deportivo La Coruna), Amor (Barcelona), Salinas (Sporting Gijon), Nadal (Barcelona). subs: Caminero (Atletico Madrid) for Manjarin 46, Alfonso (Real Betis) for Salinas 46, Lopez (Atletico Madrid) for Alkorta 73. coach: Javier Clemente

SEMI-FINAL

Wednesday 26th June 1996

England	**1-1**	**Germany**
Shearer 2		Kuntz 15

After extra time
Germany won 6-5 on penalties.
(Shearer 1-0, Hassler 1-1, Platt 2-1, Strunz 2-2, Pearce 3-2, Reuter 3-3, Gascoigne 4-3, Ziege 4-4, Sheringham 5-4, Kuntz 5-5, Southgate saved, Moller 5-6)
75,862
Referee: S Puhl (Hungary)

Germany had beaten England twice since the re-unification of the country, including at Wembley in 1991. England's last win was in 1985, but now with the whole country willing them to win on a wave of emotion they had high hopes of reaching their first European Championship final. Germany had won Group C with ease, beating eventual finalists the Czech Republic 2-0 at Old Trafford in their opening match. They also defeated Croatia 2-1 at Old Trafford in the quarter-finals, and were hoping to reach their second successive final after losing to Denmark in Gothenburg in 1992.

Anglo-German confrontations had a long tradition of dramatic matches in major competitions. England, of course, had beaten West Germany to win the World Cup at Wembley in 1966, but since then the Germans had won all the important clashes. In 1972, on their way to their first European Championship, they had destroyed England in the quarter-final at Wembley. More recently, though, and most painful of all for England had been their defeat on penalties in the 1990 World Cup semi-final in Turin. That was their last meeting with West Germany who went on to win their third World Cup.

With Germany's two main strikers out injured, England, wearing their all-grey kit, knew they were never going to get a better chance to beat them and they attacked from the start. Incredibly, it took them just two minutes to score. Gascoigne's corner was headed on by Adams and Alan Shearer headed it through Kopke's legs to secure his position as the tournament's top scorer. He was two goals clear of any other player with five and this after going almost two years without an international goal.

Germany, though, were renowned for their powers of recovery and struck back quickly. Helmer crossed and Stefan Kuntz got ahead of Pearce to fire past Seaman from close range.

From then on it was stalemate. 'Sudden-death' extra time produced some incredible near misses with Anderton hitting the post for England. The drama reached almost unbearable proportions as both sides took it in turns to create chances. Gascoigne was inches away from a touch that would have taken England into the final but the match ended without a winning goal.

Once again an Anglo-German semi-final went to penalties and two nations held their breath. Five kicks each were converted. The unfortunate Gareth Southgate's poor kick was then saved by Andreas Kopke and Andreas Moller broke millions of English hearts by putting Germany through to their second successive final. It was his last kick of the tournament as he was suspended for the final, having picked up a second booking during the game. Stefan Reuter had also converted a penalty knowing he would also be suspended for the final. These two typified the ice-cool German temperament. They had won through despite injuries to key men and a home crowd urging England to victory for over two hours.

This brought to an end Terry Venables' two-year reign in charge of England. He had transformed a deflated squad, which had failed to qualify for the 1994 World Cup into a team which had lifted the whole country by matching the best in Europe and coming within inches of their first major final for 30 years. They held their heads high unbeaten in open play, and began to plan for the next World Cup. The Germans had now won four consecutive penalty shoot-outs in major tournaments. They had perfected the art to such an extent that they never missed. England's chance had effectively gone when the final whistle blew. The Czech Republic were now the only team left to challenge Germany.

England: Seaman (Arsenal), Pearce (Nottingham F), Ince (Internazionale), Adams (Arsenal) – capt, Southgate (Aston Villa), Platt (Arsenal), Gascoigne (Rangers), Shearer (Blackburn), Sheringham (Tottenham), Anderton (Tottenham), McManaman (Liverpool). coach: Terry Venables

Germany: Kopke (Eintracht Frankfurt), Reuter (Borussia Dortmund), Freund (Borussia Dortmund), Helmer (Bayern Munich), Sammer (Borussia Dortmund), Moller (Borussia Dortmund) – capt, Scholl (Bayern Munich), Kuntz (Besiktas), Babbel (Bayern Munich), Ziege (Bayern Munich), Eilts (Werder Bremen). subs: Hassler (Karlsruhe) for Scholl 76, Bode (Werder Bremen) for Helmer 109, Strunz (Bayern Munich) for Freund 118. coach: Berti Vogts

FINAL

Sunday 30th June 1996

Czech Republic	**1-2**	**Germany**
Berger pen 58		Bierhoff 73, 95

In extra time
73,611
Referee: P Pairetto (Italy)

The final brought together two teams who had met in their opening match of the tournament. Germany had won 2-0 at Old Trafford and went on to win Group C with the Czechs runners-up on aggregate after their surprise victory over 1994 World Cup finalists Italy at Anfield. The Czechs went on to defeat Portugal by a single goal at Villa Park and their appearance in the final was a major shock. They had had four players suspended for the semi-final against France at Old Trafford but they won on penalties.

Comparisons were made with Denmark's sensational triumph four years earlier. The unfancied Czechs were competing in their first competition after the break-up of the old Czechoslovakia three years earlier. The united country had previously had a good record in this competition, the highlight of which was in 1976 when they won a memorable tournament by defeating West Germany on penalties after extra time following a 2-2 draw in Belgrade.

Germany were appearing in their second successive final after losing 2-0 to the Danes in Gothenburg in 1992. They, too, had gone through political change. West Germany had won the competition in 1972 and 1980, sandwiching that 1976 defeat. By 1996 no other country had won the Championship twice. But West Germany's last sucess had been six years previously, the last of their three World Cups, and pressure was on a unified Germany to win something. Wembley Stadium, scene of West Germany's World Cup final defeat in 1966, was the ideal place to do it.

The Czechs were much stronger than in their opening match defeat by Germany and a fairytale win was on the cards when they took the lead just before the hour. Poborsky was brought down by Sammer and although the foul looked to be outside the area, Patrik Berger fired the penalty under Kopke's body. The course of the match was changed by a German substitution ten minutes later. Oliver Bierhoff, who had not played since the first round, came on and within five minutes had headed his country level. He got into the six-yard box ahead of the Czech defence to meet Ziege's free kick and give Kouba no chance.

The Czech Republic had found like England in the semi-final that you could not afford defensive lapses against the Germans. Two quarter-finals and both semi-finals had failed to produce a winner in 'sudden-death' extra time, but the final was all over after just five minutes of the additional half-hour, a major international being decided for the first time by a 'golden goal'. Klinsmann crossed to Bierhoff who had his back to goal.

Despite being closely marked by Rada he managed to turn and shoot. The ball was deflected by Hornak and although Kouba got his hands to the ball it squirmed in off the post. Kuntz was in an offside position, but was deemed not to be interfering with play.

One of the scrappiest goals of the tournament had given Germany their first Championship as a unified nation.

The Germans had ridden their luck, especially in the semi-final, but their class and professionalism brought its reward. They were about to slide from their lofty perch, however. Four years later, their defence of the Championship ended in the last 16 after a 30-year run of consistently reaching at least the quarter-finals in every World Cup and European Championship. They were back at Wembley in 2000 for the stadium's last match, a World Cup qualifier.

The Czech Republic returned to Wembley two years later to face England.

Czech Republic: Kouba (Sparta Prague), Suchoparek (Slavia Prague), Nedved (Sparta Prague), Kadlec (Kaiserslautern) - capt, Nemec (Schalke), Poborsky (Slavia Prague), Kuka (Kaiserslautern), Bejbl (Slavia Prague), Berger (Borussia Dortmund), Hornak (Sparta Prague), Rada (Sigma Olomouc). sub: Smicer (Slavia Prague) for Poborsky 88. coach: Dusan Uhrin

Germany: Kopke (Eintracht Frankfurt), Helmer (Bayern Munich), Sammer (Borussia Dortmund), Scholl (Bayern Munich), Hassler (Karlsruhe), Kuntz (Besiktas), Babbel (Bayern Munich), Ziege (Bayern Munich), Klinsmann (Bayern Munich) – capt, Strunz (Bayern Munich), Eilts (Werder Bremen). subs: Bode (Werder Bremen) for Eilts 46, Bierhoff (Udinese) for Scholl 68. coach: Berti Vogts

FA CHARITY SHIELD

Sunday 11th August 1996

Manchester United   4-0   Newcastle United
Cantona 25, Butt 30, Beckham 86, Keane 88
73,214
Referee: P Durkin (Portland)

Manchester United stood proudly at the top of English football, having completed their second FA Carling Premiership and FA Cup 'double' in three years three months earlier.

With Newcastle twelve points clear of United in January the title looked to have been settled. But Newcastle slumped and United's youngsters flourished, beating them both home and away. And although the FA Cup final had been a drab affair, it proved United's pedigree under pressure. United were now aiming for a record ninth outright Charity Shield and their third in four years, having last won it in 1994.

Newcastle were appearing by invitation, having looked odds-on to secure their first title since 1927. They could still be proud of their highest placing since then which brought them to their first big Wembley occasion for 20 years. They lost the League Cup final on their last major visit in 1976, although they did make a brief appearance at the Football League Centenary Tournament in 1988. Major trophies were still a distant memory though. They had won the Charity Shield just once beating Northampton Town 2-0 at Stamford Bridge in 1909, and lost on four occasions since, including by 4-2, away to United in 1952.

Manchester United were ahead when Beckham found Eric Cantona, who had been suspended until October, in an embarrassing amount of space. He had only to side-foot the ball past Srnicek to score his fifth Charity Shield goal in four appearances. Five minutes later, Cantona cheekily back-heeled to Beckham who crossed for Nicky Butt to get ahead of a static Newcastle defence to notch United's second with a flying header.

Newcastle fought back after the break, but they were caught out again with four minutes left and the same two players were involved again. Just inside his own half, Cantona waited for the right moment before chipping over the Newcastle defence to David Beckham who was clean through. Once again, Srnicek's defence had deserted him and a simple lob left him with no chance. Newcastle's humiliation was completed when Giggs' free kick from the edge of the box was played across to Roy Keane who fired United's fourth with no defender near him.

United had emphasised their superiority and given warning that they were still hungry for success. Newcastle's defence had been virtually non-existent. All four goals found them at fault and they were taught a harsh lesson.

United returned to Wembley to defend the Charity Shield the following year having won the championship by seven points.

Newcastle's manager, Kevin Keegan surprisingly resigned in January, but his replacement, Kenny Dalglish, guided them to a second successive runners-up placing, pipping Arsenal and Liverpool on goal difference. In 1998, Newcastle reached the FA Cup final.

David Ginola made his Wembley debut. Three years later he became only the second French winner of the Footballer of the Year award, following Cantona.

Manchester U: Schmeichel, Irwin, May, Pallister, Neville (P), Beckham, Keane, Butt, Giggs, Cantona – capt, Scholes. subs: Poborsky for Butt 41, Neville (G) for Irwin 46, Cruyff for Scholes 65. manager: Alex Ferguson
Newcastle: Srnicek, Watson, Peacock, Albert, Beresford, Beardsley - capt, Batty (D), Lee, Ginola, Shearer, Ferdinand. subs: Asprilla for Beardsley 75, Gillespie for Ginola 77. manager: Kevin Keegan

Calrsberg Pub International

Sunday 22nd September 1996

Brigade Bodega 1
Eriksen 80

Dawlish Town 0
Referee: R Milford (Bristol)

Four months earlier Dawlish Town Sports and Social Club had won the first Carlsberg Pub Cup at Wembley, 4-2 on penalties following a goalless 60-minute final with Grimethorpe Miners Welfare prior to the FA Carlsberg Vase final. This time player-manager, Tony Bowker's team were second best as their Danish counterparts scored from Peter Eriksen's free kick to lift the first International trophy.

Dawlish: Armitage, Cleave, Bloomfield, Shears, Billings, Shwenn, Carter, Holland, Nardiello, Ross, Rackley. subs: Day for Armitage, Phillips for Bloomfield, Dunston for Shears, Clifford for Billings, Bowker for Carter

WORLD CUP QUALIFYING

Wednesday 9th October 1996

England 2-1 Poland
Shearer 24, 37   Citko 6
74,663
Referee: H Krug (Germany)

England were facing Poland in their fourth consecutive qualifying competition. All the games in Poland had been drawn with England winning all three at Wembley, including their last World Cup fixture at the stadium, in 1993. Poland had not scored at Wembley since the famous draw in 1973 and it had now been ten years since they had last qualified for a major tournament. England had begun Group Two, after the summer's euphoria, with a new man in charge – Glenn Hoddle. They had already won convincingly in Chisinau.

A capacity crowd was stunned after just a

few minutes when Poland took the lead. Warzycha failed to connect with Baluszynski's cross as it passed between his legs but the ball ran through to Marek Citko who calmly beat Seaman.

England equalised thanks to the Polish goalkeeper's poor judgement. Wozniak came charging out in an attempt to meet Beckham's high ball into the area but Alan Shearer got to it first ahead of Wojtala and headed his team level. England scored again before half-time. Shearer's shot deflected off Wojtala's chest into the midriff of Ferdinand who did well to recover and touch ball back while holding off Jozwiak's challenge. It was a perfect touch for Shearer who hammered it into the net as Zielinski threw himself into a last-ditch tackle.

England ended Poland's interest in the competition with a 2-0 victory in Chorzow, the following year. Poland finished third but were back three years later in the European Championship.

England: Seaman (Arsenal), Neville (G) (Man Utd), Pearce (Nottingham F), Southgate (Aston Villa), Hinchcliffe (Everton), Beckham (Man Utd), Gascoigne (Rangers), Shearer (Newcastle) – capt, Ferdinand (Newcastle), McManaman (Liverpool), Ince (Internazionale). sub: Pallister (Man Utd) for Southgate 51. coach: Glenn Hoddle

Poland: Wozniak (Porto), Michalski (Widzew Lodz), Wojtala (Widzew Lodz), Jozwiak (Guingamp), Zielinski (Legia Warsaw), Waldoch (Bochum), Hajto (Gornik Zabrze), Baluszynski (Bochum), Warzycha (K) (Panathinaikos), Nowak (TSV Munich) – capt, Citko (Widzew Lodz). sub: Saganowski (Feyenoord) for Warzycha 75. coach: Antoni Piechniczek

Wednesday 12th February 1997

England 0-1 Italy
Zola 18

75,055

Referee: S Puhl (Hungary)

England had won all three of their Group Two fixtures while Italy had won both theirs. They were meeting in a World Cup Qualifying match for the first time since 1977, England's last win against them. Italy had beaten England in the 1990 World Cup third and fourth place match in Bari with a late penalty. As beaten finalists in 1994 they were expected to be formidable opponents. However, their record in England was not good. They had twice made first round exits in major tournaments. Eventual finalists the Czech Republic had knocked them out of the previous year's European Championship and 30 years before they had been humiliated when losing to North Korea in the World Cup. Italy had not scored at Wembley since beating England in 1973 and their last visit in 1989 had ended in a draw.

The only goal came when Gianfranco Zola collected a long ball from Costacurta and took the ball between Campbell and Pearce. Campbell's challenge succeeded only in deflecting the Chelsea star's shot over Walker's dive at the near post.

Gianfranco Zola had bitten the hand that fed him by severely denting England's World Cup hopes on his Wembley debut. Chelsea's fans whose club had signed him in November forgave him and he went on to become the first Italian winner of the Footballer of the Year award, helping Chelsea to their first FA Cup win for 27 years.

The Italians then brought to bear their experienced defensive capabilities and England were limited to a few half-chances. Their failure to score meant they suffered their first ever World Cup defeat at home.

England still led the group on goal difference but Italy, with a game in hand, were now in command. The Italians then managed to fritter away their advantage by dropping vital away points. A goalless draw in Rome eight months after the Wembley meeting ensured England won the group by a point, despite Italy conceding only one goal in their eight matches. The Italians still went on to qualify, however, by beating Russia in a play-off and reached the quarter-finals in France where they were beaten on penalties by the hosts in Paris.

England: Walker (Tottenham), Neville (G) (Man Utd), Campbell (Tottenham), Pearce (Nottingham F), Beckham (Man Utd), Batty (Newcastle), Ince (Internazionale), Le Saux (Blackburn), McManaman (Liverpool), Le Tissier (Southampton), Shearer (Newcastle) - capt. subs: Ferdinand (Newcastle) for Le Tissier 60, Merson (Arsenal) for McManaman 76, Wright (Arsenal) for Batty 88. coach: Glenn Hoddle

Italy: Peruzzi (Juventus), Di Livio (Juventus), Ferrera (Juventus), Cannavaro (Parma), Costacurta (AC Milan), Maldini (AC Milan) – capt, Baggio (Parma), Albertini (AC Milan), Di Matteo (Chelsea), Casiraghi (Lazio), Zola (Chelsea). subs: Ravanelli (Middlesbrough) for Casiraghi 76, Fuser (Lazio) for Zola 90. coach: Cesare Maldini

INTERNATIONAL

Saturday 29th March 1997

England   **2-0**   **Mexico**
Sheringham pen 19, Fowler 56
48,076
Referee: V Pereira (Portugal)

Mexico were making their first visit to Wembley since the 1966 World Cup when they drew twice and lost to England. Since then they had beaten England in Mexico City in 1985 but the following year England had won their last meeting 3-0 in Los Angeles.

In the 1994 World Cup Mexico had gone out in the last 16 to Bulgaria on penalties in New York after topping the Republic of Ireland's group on goals scored.

The deadlock at Wembley's first Easter international was broken when Ince was brought down by Pardo. Teddy Sheringham confidently gave England the lead from the penalty spot. He went off injured before the interval, the first of a spate of substitutions, which effectively ruined the match as a contest.

England secured the victory when Wright, Sheringham's replacement, met Le Saux's cross with a header. Rios could only palm it onto Robbie Fowler's head and from inside the six-yard box he was not going to miss the opportunity to score his first goal for his country.

England: James* (Liverpool), Keown (Arsenal), Southgate (Aston Villa), Pearce (Nottingham F), Lee (Newcastle), Ince (Internazionale) – capt, Batty (Newcastle), McManaman (Liverpool), Le Saux (Blackburn), Sheringham (Tottenham), Fowler (Liverpool). subs: Wright (Arsenal) for Sheringham 37, Redknapp (Liverpool) for Batty 53, Butt* (Man Utd) for McManaman 68. coach: Glenn Hoddle
*first cap.
Mexico: Rios (Veracruz), Pardo (Atlas), Suarez (Guadalajara), Davino (UA de Guadalajara), Ramirez (R) (Guadalajara), Alfaro (Toluca), Coyote (Guadalajara), Galindo (Santos Laguna), Garcia Aspe (Necaxa) - capt, Hermosillo (Cruz Azul), Alves (Atlante). subs: Pelaez (Necaxa) for Hermosillo 46, Hernandez (Necaxa) for Alves 46, Bernal (Toluca) for Galindo 55, Pineda (America) for Rios 60, Ramirez (N) (Santos Laguna) for Coyote 66. coach: Bora Milutinovic

LEAGUE CUP FINAL

Sunday 6th April 1997

Leicester City   **1-1**   **Middlesbrough**
Heskey 118   Ravanelli 95
After extra time
76,757
Referee: M Bodenham (Looe)

Leicester had won the Football League Cup back in 1964 with a 4-3 aggregate victory against Stoke City, their only major trophy. Until 1994 they had the unenviable distinction of losing six Wembley finals, but two play-off victories in three years had changed their luck and they were now making a fifth Wembley visit in just six years.

Middlesbrough were appearing in their first final despite losing the home leg of their semi-final to Second Division Stockport County. Their only previous Wembley visit had been in the 1990 Zenith Cup final, when they lost to Chelsea.

A fascinating final of contrasting styles went into extra time with both sides unable to find a goal. As so often happens the extra half-hour brought the breakthrough. It took only five minutes for Middlesbrough's expensive foreign imports to prove their big-match pedigree. The little Brazilian Juninho played a one-two with his Italian team-mate Fabrizio Ravanelli who stabbed the ball between Prior's legs only to stumble over the ball as a gap opened up. Lennon managed to get a foot in and in the blink of an eye Ravanelli, who had scored for Juventus in the previous year's

European Cup final, fired a blinding shot through Lennon's legs which beat Keller at the near post.

Leicester's great strength was their battling team spirit and with two minutes left they equalised in an almighty goalmouth scramble. Substitute Robins crossed at the second attempt after Pearson had blocked the first. Walsh headed into the six-yard box where Emile Heskey beat Schwarzer with a header that hit the bar. It bounced down for Claridge to try to bundle it in. Middlesbrough's other Italian, Festa, hooked it off the line only for the ball to hit Mustoe's leg and rebound back off Festa to Heskey. He stabbed the ball over the line just as Schwarzer was getting to his feet.

Middlesbrough were involved in more extra-time drama the following week as they had to claw back a two-goal deficit against Chesterfield, a Second Division club, to force a replay. Victims of their own cup success, they were now facing a horrendous backlog of fixtures and with relegation a very real possibility every game they played was like a cup final. The last thing they needed was more extra time against a team that never gave them an inch.

Alas for Middlesbrough, ten days after the final Leicester wore them down and won thanks to a goal from Steve Claridge, who had put them in the Premiership with a last-minute winner at Wembley, the previous year. Leicester reached the final again two years later.

Middlesbrough's exhausting season sadly ended in relegation. However they still managed to reach their first FA Cup final as well and a year later they reached the Coca-Cola Cup final again.

Leicester: Keller, Grayson, Whitlow, Prior, Walsh (S) – capt, Kaamark, Izzet, Lennon, Parker, Claridge, Heskey. subs: Robins for Whitlow 105, Taylor for Izzet 108, Poole (gk) (not used). manager: Martin O'Neill

Middlesbrough: Schwarzer, Cox, Fleming, Festa, Pearson - capt, Hignett, Mustoe, Emerson, Juninho, Beck, Ravanelli. subs: Blackmore, Moore, Vickers (not used). manager: Bryan Robson

Replay: Wednesday 16th April 1997
Leicester City   1-0   Middlesbrough
Claridge
After extra time
(Hillsborough)

Auto Windscreens Shield

Sunday 20th April 1997

Carlisle United 0
Colchester United 0
After extra time
Carlisle United won 4-3 on penalties.
(Wilkins 0-1, Conway 1-1, Adcock 1-2, Archdeacon saved, Greene 1-3, Walling 2-3, Duguid saved, Aspinall 3-3, Cawley saved, Hayward 4-3)
45,077
Referee: J Kirkby (Sheffield)

The first final between teams from the bottom division of the Football League since 1988 was also the first goalless final. Colchester were at Wembley for the first time since their FA Trophy win of 1992 and it was their first ever visit as a Football League club. Carlisle had won away against the previous year's finalists Shrewsbury Town in the quarter-finals.

Colchester had twice progressed via a 'golden goal' in extra time, including in the semi-final where they came back from a two-goal first-leg deficit to beat Peterborough United. Carlisle had lost the final two years earlier to Birmingham City by a 'golden goal'.

Neither side could manage one in this game and penalties settled the issue.

It was Carlisle captain Steve Hayward who completed their comeback with a successful spot kick.

The following year these teams swapped divisions as Colchester won the play-offs at Wembley and Carlisle were relegated for the second time in three years. After two last day escapes in successive years, the Cumbrians eventually dropped into the Nationwide Conference in 2004 although they were promoted straight back.

Carlisle: Caig, Delap, Walling, Varty, Pounewatchy, Archdeacon, Hayward – capt, Conway, Aspinall, Smart, Peacock. subs: Thomas for Smart 23, Jansen for Thomas 94. manager: Mervyn Day

Colchester: Emberson, Dunne, Greene, Cawley - capt, Gibbs, Abrahams, Gregory (D), Whitton, Wilkins, Sale, Adcock. subs: Locke for Gregory 84, Duguid for Abrahams 91, Fry for Gibbs 105. manager: Steve Wignall

323

WORLD CUP QUALIFYING

Wednesday 30th April 1997

England	**2-0**	**Georgia**

Sheringham 42, Shearer 90
71,206
Referee: R Harrel (France)

Italy were now four points clear at the top of Group Two although England had a game in hand and they expected to keep the pressure on for Georgia's first visit to England.

The Georgians had lost both their fixtures so far, including a 2-0 defeat in Tbilisi the previous year in the first ever match with England. It was Georgia's first ever entry in the World Cup and they were still searching for their first goal. They had only begun competing independently after the break-up of the USSR three years earlier and had finished a respectable third, in a European Championship qualifying group won by Germany, the eventual winners.

They held out until just before the inter- val when Teddy Sheringham got ahead of Shelia to power a header past Zoidze from Shearer's cross. Not an impressive perform- ance by England but they ended on a high note by clinching the points in the third minute of added time. Zoidze gave away a free kick in the six-yard box by picking up a pass back from Shekiladze. Even though Georgia put seven defenders on the goal- line with the goalkeeper, Sheringham touched the ball back to Alan Shearer who fired England's second over the wall.

Italy beat Poland 3-0 on the same night in Naples to maintain their four-point lead. Georgia's interest ended two months later when they went down to a 4-1 defeat in Chorzow. They finished fourth.

England: Seaman (Arsenal), Neville (G) (Man Utd), Campbell (Tottenham), Batty (Newcastle), Adams (Arsenal), Le Saux (Blackburn), Beckham (Man Utd), Ince (Internazionale), Shearer (Newcastle) – capt, Sheringham (Tottenham), Lee (Newcastle). subs: Redknapp (Liverpool) for Ince 77, Southgate (Aston Villa) for Adams 87. coach: Glenn Hoddle
Georgia: Zoidze (Dynamo Tbilisi), Shekiladze (Batumi), Tskhadadze (Alania Vladikavkaz) - capt, Shelia (Alania Vladikavkaz), Chikradze (Shakhtar Donetsk), Machavariani (Dynamo Tbilisi), Nemsadze (Trabzonspor), Jamarauli (Trabzonspor), Ketsbaia (AEK Athens), Kinkladze (Manchester C.), Arveladze (S) (Trabzonspor). subs: Gogrichiani (Zhemchuzhina) for Machavariani 33, Gakhokidze (Alania Vladikavkaz) for Kinkladze 61, Arveladze (A) (Trabzonspor) for Gogrichiani 76. coach: David Kipiani

Carlsberg Pub Cup Final

Saturday 10th May 1997

Corby Caledonian 1
Martin 82
Poulton Victoria 3
Galloway 71, Jones (S) 76, Lewis 81
Referee: R Milford (Bristol)

The Pub Cup had been such a success in the previous year's inaugural competition that the final was extended to a full 90 minutes. The Cheshire side ran out comfortable winners. Poulton went on to beat the Dan- ish winners of the Pub Cup, Udstigen on penalties in Copenhagen and became the first English winners of the Carlsberg Pub Cup International.

FA Vase Final

Saturday 10th May 1997

North Ferriby United 0
Whitby Town 3
Logan, Williams, Toman
11,098
Referee: G Poll (Tring)

Whitby had lost the FA Amateur Cup fi- nal at Wembley back in 1965 but this time they made no mistake, lifting the FA Vase for the first time.

North Ferriby: Sharp, Deacey, Walmsley, Brentano, Smith (A), Harrison, Smith (M), Phillips, Tennison, France, Flounders. subs: Horne for Harrison 64, Milner for Phillips 69, Newman for France 75
Whitby: Campbell, Goodchild, Pearson, Cook, Williams, Hodgson, Goodrick, Toman, Logan, Robinson, Pitman. subs: Borthwick for Goodrick 78, Pyle for Toman 84, Hall for Pitman 86

FA CUP FINAL

Saturday 17th May 1997

Chelsea　　　　　**2-0**　　　　**Middlesbrough**

Di Matteo 1, Newton 82
79,160
Referee: S Lodge (Barnsley)

It had been 27 years since Chelsea's only FA Cup win and the drawn final had meant they had never lifted the trophy at Wembley. They had made five visits since then, winning two other competitions and winning an FA Cup semi-final. Chelsea also wanted to avenge their crushing defeat in the 1994 final.

Middlesbrough had never previously reached the semi-finals and having got there they very nearly became the victims of the most sensational FA Cup run of all time. With Vladimir Kinder sent off in the first half, they went two goals behind to Second Division Chesterfield. No club from the lower divisions had ever reached an FA Cup final but Middlesbrough fought back and after a replay booked a second Wembley meeting with Chelsea. A single goal had been enough to settle the 1990 Zenith Cup final in the Londoners' favour.

Chelsea finished sixth in the FA Carling Premiership, their highest position for seven years. Middlesbrough were about to complete the most eventful season by far, in their history. What should have been a proud and joyous end to an unforgettable season was now their only hope of consolation amid tears of heartbreak and frustration. The previous month in their first Coca-Cola Cup final they had been three minutes away from victory when it was snatched away. They lost an exhausting replay three days after the FA Cup semi-final and their two magnificent cup runs meant league fixtures were piling up in their battle against relegation.

They were forced to play their last four matches in the space of nine days and despite remaining unbeaten they finished 19th and were relegated to the Football League after two years in the top flight. Their last match six days before the FA Cup final saw them finish two points adrift of safety, a fact even more heartbreaking because they had been deducted three points for postponing a fixture at Blackburn in December due to illness and injury.

The quickest ever goal in a Wembley FA Cup final got the match off to a sensational start. Chelsea's Roberto Di Matteo, one of five Italians in this final, received the ball in his own half from Wise and ran straight down the middle. Hughes bundled Festa out of the way and from 30 yards Di Matteo unleashed a vicious dipping shot which sailed over Roberts and in off the crossbar. It was timed at 42 seconds.

Middlesbrough's recent bad luck continued to kick them in the teeth. Two players went off injured in the first half-hour, including the influential Ravanelli, and although the goal was all that divided the teams until eight minutes from the end, Middlesbrough never really threatened.

Eddie Newton started the move that sunk Middlesbrough for the last time and left their fans in tears. He passed to Petrescu who crossed to the far post where Zola's exquisite backheeled-flick set up Newton to beat Roberts via a deflection off Pearson's arm. It was a sweet moment for the scorer, who had conceded the crucial first penalty in the 1994 final.

Chelsea went on to win the European Cup-Winners Cup in Stockholm the following year with a single goal victory against Stuttgart. It was their first European trophy since winning the same competition in 1971.

Middlesbrough bounced straight back to the Premiership the following year by finishing as runners-up and they also returned to Wembley to face Chelsea yet again in their second successive Coca-Cola Cup final.

Chelsea: Grodas, Sinclair, Leboeuf, Clarke, Minto, Petrescu, Newton, Di Matteo, Wise – capt, Zola, Hughes. sub: Vialli for Zola 88, Myers, Hitchcock (gk) (not used). manager: Ruud Gullit
Middlesbrough: Roberts, Blackmore, Pearson – capt, Festa, Fleming, Stamp, Emerson, Mustoe, Hignett, Juninho, Ravanelli. subs: Beck for Ravanelli 23, Vickers for Mustoe 28, Kinder for Hignett 74. manager: Bryan Robson

FA Trophy Final

Sunday 18th May 1997

Dagenham and Redbridge 0
Woking 1
Hay 99
After extra time
24,376
Referee: J Winter (Stockton-on-Tees)

Substitute Darran Hay, who had also scored in the 1994 final, gave Woking their third FA Trophy in four years. Dagenham had won the Trophy in 1980 and five years after their amalgamation with Redbridge Forest they defended well against the favourites. But they had Tony Rogers sent off in the 62nd minute for elbowing Robin Taylor and finally fell to an experienced Woking side in extra time.

Dagenham: Gothard, Culverhouse, Conner, Creaser - capt, Jacques, Davidson, Pratt, Parratt, Broom, Rogers, Stimson. subs: John for Stimson 65, Double for Jacques 75, Naylor for Pratt 81
Woking: Batty, Brown (K) - capt, Howard, Foster, Taylor, Wye (S), Thompson, Ellis, Steele, Walker, Jackson. subs: Hay for Jackson 77, Wye (L) for Steele 108, Jones for Thompson 115

Play-off Finals

Third Division
Saturday 24th May 1997

Northampton Town 1
Frain 90
Swansea City 0
46,804
Referee: T Heilbron (Newton Aycliffe)

A twice-taken free kick in the fourth minute of added time gave Northampton their first promotion since they won the old Fourth Division Championship ten years earlier.

For the second year in succession, the Third Division final attracted a bigger crowd than the following day's Second Division final. Northampton's Wembley debut saw them clinch promotion just three years after finishing bottom of the Football League when they only survived relegation because the ground of Vauxhall Conference Champions Kidderminster Harriers was not the required standard.

Swansea had last won promotion in 1988 via the play-offs and had lost in the Second Division play-offs five years later to

eventual winners West Bromwich Albion.

An Autoglass Trophy win at Wembley on penalties followed in 1994 before relegation two years later and, despite beating Northampton twice in the league, they failed to win promotion straight back.

Northampton reached the Second Division final the following year but were beaten while Swansea reached the play-offs in 1999 only to lose to the eventual winners Scunthorpe United after extra time. In 2000, both these teams won promotion from the Third Division, Swansea as Champions.

Swansea's player-manager, Danish international Jan Molby, had been a key member of Liverpool's 'double-winning' side in 1986.

Northampton: Woodman, Sampson, Rennie, Warburton - capt, Clarkson, Hunter, Parrish, Frain, Lee, Gayle, Grayson. subs: Peer for Rennie 40, White for Gayle 76, Gibb (not used). manager: Ian Atkins
Swansea: Freestone, Walker, Edwards, Moreira, Thomas, Penney - capt, Molby, Ampadu, Coates, Torpey, Heggs. subs: Brown for Thomas 83, Chapple, Lacey (not used). player-manager: Jan Molby

Second Division
Sunday 25th May 1997

Brentford 0
Crewe Alexandra 1
Smith 34
34,149
Referee: U Rennie (Sheffield)

A landmark match for Crewe as they reached a status they had not enjoyed for 101 years. In 1896 they finished bottom of the Football League and failed to win re-election although there were then only two divisions. They rejoined the League 25 years later and had frequented the lower divisions ever since. This was their fourth appearance in the play-offs in five years and in the year they did not contest them they had won promotion.

In 1993 Crewe lost the Third Division final on penalties and two years later they lost the Second Division semi-final on away goals. This time, they made no mistake and became the fourth successive club in this division to win the play-offs from the lowest qualifying position.

The sending off of Brian Statham for a foul on substitute Steve Garvey, his second bookable offence, did not help Brentford's cause. It was the Londoners first Wembley appearance since losing the 1985 Freight Rover Trophy final and it was their first play-off final.

They had won the championship of the old Third Division in 1992 only to be relegated the following year. Then in 1995, despite finishing as Second Division runners-up to Birmingham City, they appeared in the play-offs again and lost on penalties to the eventual winners Huddersfield Town. This Wembley defeat was to have a demoralising effect, however, and they were relegated to the Third Division the following year, although they won promotion straight back as Third Division Champions in 1999.

Brentford: Dearden, Hurdle, Hutchings, Bates - capt, Anderson, Bent, Smith, Statham, Asaba, Taylor, McGhee. subs: Canham for Bent 46, Ashby for Hurdle 74, Fernandes (gk) (not used). manager: David Webb

Crewe: Kearton, Unsworth, Westwood, Macauley, Smith, Little, Murphy, Charnock, Whalley – capt, Adebola, Rivers. subs: Garvey for Rivers 69, Johnson for Murphy 86, Lightfoot for Charnock 88. manager: Dario Gradi

First Division
Monday 26th May 1997

Crystal Palace 1
Hopkin 89
Sheffield United 0
64,383
Referee: N Barry (Scunthorpe)

All three play-off finals were decided by a single goal and this was the second to be won with virtually the last kick of the match. As was now becoming traditional, the last match of the season brought the play-offs to a dramatic conclusion. David Hopkin's superb curling shot into the corner erased the bitter memory of losing the previous year's final in added time at the end of extra time to Leicester City.

Steve Coppell, the most successful manager in Palace's history, had rejoined them only three months earlier when Dave Bassett left to join Nottingham Forest, who ironically were relegated to the Nationwide League with Palace taking their Premiership place.

Two first-half substitutions forced Unit-

ed to reorganise and they were unable to find a way past Carlo Nash.

In front of Nash was Andy Linighan who had scored the dramatic last minute winner in extra time for Arsenal against Sheffield Wednesday in the 1993 FA Cup final replay.

Palace's 'keeper had conceded three goals against Brigg Town in the previous year's FA Vase final at Wembley and his move from Clitheroe had catapulted him to stardom.

Palace finished bottom of the Premiership and were relegated straight back again to the Football League. Nash never played in the top flight for them and also returned to the First Division by joining Stockport County.

United again scraped into the play-offs, this time on goals scored, but lost in the semi-finals.

Crystal P: Nash, Edworthy, Gordon, Roberts, Tuttle, Linighan, Muscat, Hopkin – capt, Shipperley, Dyer, Rodger. subs: Houghton, McKenzie, Veart (not used). manager: Steve Coppell

Sheffield U: Tracey, Ward, Nilsen, Hutchison, Tiler, Holdsworth - capt, White, Spackman, Fjortoft, Katchouro, Whitehouse. subs: Taylor for Katchouro 25, Sandford for Hutchison 46, Walker for Spackman 90. manager: Howard Kendall

Schoolboy International

Saturday 7th June 1997

England 2
Osman 30, Armstrong 64
Germany 1
Bansch 36
39,000
Referee: R Dodge (Bedfordshire)

For the first time in ten years England beat the Germans at Wembley.

Joe Cole made his full international debut for England in 2001.

England: Evans, Hanson, McReady, Maley, O'Brien, Warnock, Standing, Osman, Armstrong, Cole, Mike. subs: Taylor for Mike 60, Bingham for Evans 69, Flitcroft for Standing 69, Burke for Armstrong 76, Knight for O'Brien 77

FA CHARITY SHIELD

Sunday 3rd August 1997

Chelsea	**1-1**	**Manchester United**
Hughes 52		Johnsen 57

Manchester United won 4-2 on penalties.
(Sinclair saved, Scholes 0-1, Zola 1-1, Irwin 1-2, Di Matteo missed, Keane 1-3, Leboeuf 2-3, Butt 2-4)
73,636
Referee: P Jones (Loughborough)

Chelsea's FA Cup win gave them the opportunity to take part in their third Charity Shield but their first at Wembley. They had won the Shield in 1955 with a 3-0 home win against Newcastle United but lost in 1970 after their previous FA Cup win. Now they faced the all-powerful United, who had beaten them 4-0 in the 1994 FA Cup final and were aiming to extend their record number of outright Charity Shield victories to ten. They were the holders and had retained the Premiership title, their fourth in five years, by seven points despite faltering in the closing stages.

An unusually early start to the season surprisingly produced a highly competitive match reflecting the close rivalry between these teams. Chelsea were anxious to prove they were capable of matching United and scored first. Zola took a short corner to Wise, who steadied the ball for the Italian to cross to the far post where Mark Hughes left his marker and headed home between a static Neville and the post, with Schmeichel arriving just too late. Hughes' had scored five times for United at Wembley, the first being against Chelsea in the 1994 FA Cup final.

Five minutes later United equalised also with a header from a corner. Ronny Johnsen rose confidently to direct Giggs' kick downwards past De Goey, Chelsea's new Dutch goalkeeper, who could only help the ball into the roof of the net.

There were no further goals, the game going to penalties. Frank Sinclair, who had conceded a penalty against United at Wembley, three years earlier, had his kick saved by Peter Schmeichel, while Roberto Di Matteo, Chelsea's Cup final hero, hit his over the bar. It was left to Nicky Butt to give United their fourth Shield in five years, matching their Premiership record.

The penalties were but a minor hiccup for Chelsea. They finished the season in fourth place, their best since 1970. They also won the European Cup-Winners Cup for the second time and returned to Wembley for the Coca-Cola Cup final. United, by their standards, had a poor season, but still finished as Premiership runners-up, again failing to complete a hat-trick of titles by one point. Although they failed to win a trophy for only the second time in the 1990's, they were back at Wembley the following year chasing a hat-trick of Charity Shields against 'double' winners Arsenal.

Chelsea: De Goey, Sinclair, Leboeuf, Clarke, Granville, Morris, Wise – capt, Di Matteo, Poyet, Zola, Hughes. subs: Petrescu for Morris 46, Vialli for Hughes 76. manager: Ruud Gullit

Manchester U: Schmeichel, Irwin, Johnsen, Pallister, Neville (P), Scholes, Keane – capt, Butt, Giggs, Sheringham, Cole. subs: Beckham for Giggs 72, Cruyff for Sheringham 72. manager: Alex Ferguson

WORLD CUP QUALIFYING

Wednesday 10th September 1997

England	**4-0**	**Moldova**
Scholes 28, Wright 46, 90,		
Gascoigne 80		

74,102
Referee: K Nilsson (Sweden)

Earlier in the day, Italy had been held to a goalless draw in Tbilisi. Although this returned their lead at the top of Group Two to two points, it meant that England could go back on top by beating Moldova. Like Georgia, Moldova was a former Soviet republic competing for the first time in the World Cup. In their previous European

Championship qualifying campaign they had registered some notable victories in a group won by eventual winners Germany but they were still searching for their first World Cup point and were out of contention. England had beaten them 3-0 in Chisinau, the previous year.

Both teams were wearing black ribbons in memory of the Princess of Wales who had died in a car crash ten days earlier and there was an extremely emotional atmosphere. England gave a very professional performance and took the lead when Beckham's corner was punched back to him by Romanenco. He crossed and Paul Scholes dived full length to score with a flying header.

The second goal arrived in the first minute of the second half. Ian Wright ran on to Gascoigne's pass and fired past Romanenco at the near post. The same two combined to give England a third. Paul Gascoigne worked an opening, laid it off to Wright and ran on to the return pass to send the 'keeper the wrong way.

England added a fourth when substitute Collymore sent Wright, played onside by the injured Rebeja, clean through. Another clinical finish put the seal on a fine performance which left England needing a point to qualify for the World Cup.

England had now become very confident and they went to Rome, the following month without fear. The game ended goalless and England qualified for France as group winners, sweet revenge for their earlier defeat by Italy at Wembley. Moldova failed to win a point.

England: Seaman (Arsenal) – capt, Neville (G) (Man Utd), Neville (P) (Man Utd), Campbell (Tottenham), Southgate (Aston Villa), Batty (Newcastle), Beckham (Man Utd), Gascoigne (Rangers), Scholes (Man Utd), Ferdinand (Tottenham), Wright (Arsenal). subs: Ripley (Blackburn) for Beckham 68, Butt (Man Utd) for Ripley 75, Collymore (Aston Villa) for Ferdinand 83. coach: Glenn Hoddle

Moldova: Romanenco (Zimbru), Fistican (Zimbru), Tistimitanu (Zimbru), Culibaba (Zimbru), Spinu (Zimbru), Stroenco (Tiligul), Curteian (Widzew Lodz) - capt, Sischin (Constructorul), Miterev (Zimbru), Rebeja (Zimbru), Rogaciov (Olimpia). subs: Suharev (Zimbru) for Culibaba 53, Popovici (Tiligul) for Sischin 61, Cebotari (Zimbru) for Rogaciov 74. coach: Ion Caras

Final table	P	W	D	L	F	A	Pts
England	8	6	1	1	15	2	19
Italy	8	5	3	0	11	1	18
Poland	8	3	1	4	10	12	10
Georgia	8	3	1	4	7	9	10
Moldova	8	0	0	8	2	21	0

INTERNATIONAL

Saturday 15th November 1997

England   **2-0**   **Cameroon**
Scholes 44, Fowler 45
46,176
Referee: T Hauge (Norway)
England: Martyn (Leeds Utd), Campbell (Tottenham), Southgate (Aston Villa), Hinchcliffe (Everton), Beckham (Man

England, fresh from World Cup qualification, welcomed Cameroon, who had qualified for their third successive World Cup, an African record. They had disappointed, though, on their last visit to Wembley six years earlier and since their second African Championship success, in 1988, and their classic World Cup quarter-final with England two years later, they had made little impression.

England scored twice at the end of the first half to effectively end this African challenge. Gascoigne created the first,

beating three men. Ipoua got to his pass first and would have cleared it but for an over-anxious Kalla, who blocked the clearance, leaving Paul Scholes to run on and chip over the advancing Ongandzi. Two minutes into added time Robbie Fowler met Beckham's cross with a downward header into the corner.

The following year Cameroon finished bottom of their first round group for the second successive World Cup but two years later they became African and Olympic Champions.

Utd), Ince (Liverpool) – capt, Gascoigne (Rangers), Neville (P) (Man Utd), Scholes (Man Utd), McManaman (Liverpool), Fowler (Liverpool). subs: Ferdinand* (West Ham) for Southgate 37, Lee (Newcastle) for Gascoigne 72, Sutton* (Blackburn) for Scholes 79. coach: Glenn Hoddle
*first cap
Cameroon: Ongandzi (Unisport de Bafang), Kalla (Pananaki Patras), Song (Metz) - capt, Mimboe (Olympic Mvolye), Wome (Lucchese), Ipoua (Rapid Vienna), Etame (Bastia), Foe (Lens), Etchi (Coton Sport), Mboma (Gambo Osaka), Job (Olympique Lyonnais). subs: Billong (Saint-Etienne) for Ipoua 46, Olembe (Nantes) for Etame 72, Geremi (Genclerbirligi) for Mboma 76. coach: Jean Manga Onguene

INTERNATIONAL

Wednesday 11th February 1998

England	0-2	Chile

Salas 45, (pen) 79

65,228
Referee: R Wojcik (Poland)

It had been nine years since their last meeting, a forgettable goalless draw in the Rous Cup. Chile had just qualified for the forthcoming World Cup on goal difference at the expense of Peru. It would be their first tournament since 1982.

An experimental England side was stunned by a superb goal at the end of the first half. Chile broke out of defence and Sierra's long ball from the halfway line found Marcelo Salas who had got beyond Batty. The talented striker took it on his knee before turning to fire past Martyn all in one movement.

England could not find a way through the Chilean defence and conceded another goal towards the end. Again it was the skills of Salas which undid England. Campbell tripped him in the area and Salas got up to send Martyn the wrong way from the penalty spot. It gave his country their first victory against England. Chile had served notice that they were going to the World Cup to make an impact.

Alas, they failed to win a match in the World Cup, but still reached the last 16 before losing 4-1 to the holders and eventual finalists Brazil in Paris.

England: Martyn (Leeds Utd), Neville (G) (Man Utd), Neville (P) (Man Utd), Campbell (Tottenham), Adams (Arsenal) - capt, Batty (Newcastle), Lee (Newcastle), Butt (Man Utd), Dublin* (Coventry), Owen* (Liverpool), Sheringham (Man Utd). subs: Le Saux (Chelsea) for Neville (P) 46, Ince (Liverpool) for Batty 62, Shearer (Newcastle) for Sheringham 62. coach: Glenn Hoddle
*first cap
Chile: Tapia (Universidad Catolica), Villarroel (Santiago Wanderers), Reyes (Colo Colo), Fuentes (Universidad de Chile), Margas (Universidad Catolica), Rojas (Colo Colo), Parraguez (Universidad Catolica), Acuna (Universidad de Chile), Sierra (Colo Colo), Barrera (Universidad de Chile), Salas (River Plate, Argentina) - capt. subs: Carreno (Deportes Concepcion) for Barrera 77, Valenzuela (America) for Sierra 88. coach: Nelson Acosta

Schoolboy International

Saturday 14th March 1998

England 0
Brazil 0

50,787
Referee: G Courtney (Spennymoor)

Brazil avoided defeat against England for the first time in Dave Parnaby's only Wembley appearance as England's manager.

Rubinho became not only the first ever schoolboy international to be sent off at Wembley, but the first goalkeeper when he handled outside his area nine minutes into the second half. This was Wembley's last Under-15 schoolboy international after 48 years and 74 games.

Jermain Defoe scored on his full international debut for England in 2004.

Referee George Courtney was making a record 15th Wembley appearance at the age of 57. Incredibly, it was not his last.

England: Evans, Clark, O'Brien, Clarke, Bewers, Hamshaw, Parnaby, Dodd, Tapp, Defoe, Bothroyd. subs: Logan for Bothroyd 64, Nardiello for Dodd 74, Szmid for Tapp 74, Davis for Hamshaw 80

LEAGUE CUP FINAL

Sunday 29th March 1998

Chelsea   2-0   **Middlesbrough**
Sinclair 95, Di Matteo 107
After extra time
77,698
Referee: P Jones (Loughborough)

For the second year in succession these sides faced each other in a major Wembley final, their third meeting in a final at the stadium. Chelsea won both previous encounters, with Middlesbrough failing to score. Chelsea had won this competition 33 years earlier but their only Wembley final had been in 1972 when they were beaten. Now they were blossoming into a powerful trophy-winning team and had beaten the eventual 'double' winners Arsenal in the semi-finals.

Middlesbrough were appearing in their second successive final after a late equaliser in extra time had robbed them of their first major trophy the previous year. This was their third successive major final and showed that relegation had not adversely affected them.

Chelsea were on course to better the previous season's sixth place in the FA Carling Premiership and although they had lost the FA Charity Shield on penalties, they had reached the semi-finals of the European Cup-Winners Cup. Middlesbrough had reacted to the previous year's relegation back to the Football League with typical determination and were to go on and win promotion.

Chelsea's new player-manager Gianluca Vialli, who had taken over when Ruud Gullit had been surprisingly sacked prior to the semi-final second leg, caused a shock by leaving himself out.

Without his skills at centre forward his side failed to find the net in 90 minutes and a second successive final went to extra time without a goal. The crowd had to wait only another five minutes for the breakthrough. Wise almost ran the ball out but managed to get in a cross and Frank Sinclair sent a powerful downward header past Schwarzer to give Chelsea the lead.

Two minutes into the second half of extra time, Roberto Di Matteo met Zola's corner to sidefoot home at the near post, thus adding to his first minute opener in the previous year's FA Cup final. Vialli was sent up by his players to receive the trophy while Middlesbrough were left to reflect on a third successive cup final defeat.

Chelsea finished fourth, in the Premiership, their highest position for 28 years, and their amazing trophy-winning habit continued when they lifted the European Cup-Winners Cup, repeating their 1971 success.

They followed that by beating European Cup holders Real Madrid in Monaco to win the European Super Cup for the first time, their fourth trophy in 15 months. The following year failed to bring them any silverware but they were back in 2000 in pursuit of the FA Cup.

Chelsea: De Goey, Sinclair, Duberry, Leboeuf, Le Saux, Petrescu, Wise – capt, Newton, Di Matteo, Zola, Hughes. subs: Clarke for Petrescu 75, Flo for Hughes 83, Hitchcock (gk) (not used). manager: Gianluca Vialli
Middlesbrough: Schwarzer, Festa, Pearson – capt, Vickers, Kinder, Merson, Maddison, Mustoe, Townsend, Ricard, Branca. subs: Gascoigne for Ricard 65, Beck for Maddison 102, Fleming (not used). manager: Bryan Robson

Auto Windscreens Shield

Sunday 19th April 1998

Bournemouth 1
Bailey 31
Grimsby Town 2
Glass og 75, Burnett 112
In extra time
62,432
Referee: M Pierce (Portsmouth)

Both sides were appearing at Wembley for the first time although Bournemouth had been the first winners of the competition back in 1984 when they won 2-1 at Hull in the pre-sponsorship days of the Associate Members Cup – the only final not to be played at Wembley.

Grimsby had been relegated to the Second Division the previous year but would complete a notable 'double' by clinching promotion straight back to the First Division via the play-offs at Wembley the following month which meant they would not be able to defend the Shield.

Grimsby cancelled out Bournemouth's first half lead, when Jimmy Glass inadvertently turned Kingsley Black's effort into his own net. The following year, Glass went up the other end of the field and scored the last minute goal which kept Carlisle United in the Nationwide League.

Kingsley Black had scored for Notting-ham Forest in the last Zenith Cup final in 1992 at Wembley. He also won 30 caps for Northern Ireland.

Bournemouth: Glass, Young, Cox, Howe, Vincent, Bailey, Beardsmore, Robinson, Warren, Stein, Fletcher. subs: Brissett for Warren 90, O'Neill for Beardsmore 105, Rolling (not used). manager: Mel Machin
Grimsby: Davison, McDermott, Handyside, Lever, Gallimore, Donovan, Groves - capt, Burnett, Smith, Nogan, Clare. subs: Black for Gallimore 55, Livingstone for Clare 55, Jobling for Nogan 93. manager: Alan Buckley

---

⬛ INTERNATIONAL

Wednesday 22nd April 1998

England	3-0	Portugal

Shearer 5, 65, Sheringham 46
63,463
Referee: M Vega (Spain)

England had not beaten Portugal since 1969 but this was a much more confident performance from England and a good evening for Tony Adams to celebrate winning his 50th cap.

They took just five minutes to get off the mark. From Le Saux's curling cross, Alan Shearer sent a glancing header into the corner. The lead was doubled when a pass from Ince deflected fortuitously off the referee to put Teddy Sheringham through with only Baia to beat and he gently chipped over the diving goalkeeper.

Shearer fired England's third when he volleyed in from Batty's lobbed pass. Por-tugal substitute, Capucho was sent off for foul and abusive language with nine minutes left, the first to be dismissed at Wembley for that offence.

Portugal got over their World Cup disappointment and qualified for their second successive European Championship in 2000 where they began by beating England 3-2 in Eindhoven after being two goals down. They went on to reach the semi-finals for the first time since 1984. They eventually lost to the World Champions France who needed an extra time penalty to defeat them in Brussels before going on to win the Championship.

England: Seaman (Arsenal), Neville (G) (Man Utd), Le Saux (Chelsea), Campbell (Tottenham), Adams (Arsenal), Ince (Liverpool), Batty (Newcastle), Beckham (Man Utd), Scholes (Man Utd), Shearer (Newcastle) – capt, Sheringham (Man Utd) subs: Merson (Middlesbrough) for Beckham 46, Owen (Liverpool) for Sheringham 77, Neville (P) (Man Utd) for Neville (G) 81. coach: Glenn Hoddle
Portugal: Baia (Barcelona) – capt, Xavier (Real Oviedo), Dimas (Juventus), Beto (Sporting Lisbon), Couto (Barcelona), Paulo Sousa (Internazionale), Figo (Barcelona), Joao Pinto (Benfica), Calado (Benfica), Santos (Porto), Cadete (Celta Vigo). subs: Barbosa (Sporting Lisbon) for Dimas 54, Capucho (Porto) for Joao Pinto 68, Oceano (Toulouse) for Paulo Sousa 75. coach: Humberto Coelho

---

⬛ Carlsberg Pub Cup Final

Saturday 9th May 1998

Honiton Clyst 1
Evans og 80

West Hendon Ex-Servicemen 1
Newing 88

West Hendon Ex-Servicemen won 3-1 on penalties.
(Wilson saved, Dale (P) 0-1, Pears saved, Elliott 0-2, Carpenter saved, Roche missed, Taylor 1-2, Dale (A) 1-3)

Having equalised with just two minutes left, the Ex-Servicemen went on to win the Pub Cup with Keith Harvey saving Honiton's first three penalties before Andy Dale sent the Cup to West Hendon.

Manager, Bill McGregor was sent up to receive the trophy and their victory gave them the opportunity to return to Wembley the following month when they beat the winners of the Danish equivalent of the Pub Cup.

FA Vase Final

Saturday 9th May 1998

Tiverton Town 1
Varley 80

Tow Law Town 0
13,193
Referee: M Riley (Leeds)
Tiverton had lost the 1993 final but returned to win the Vase for the first time, substitute, Peter Varley grabbing the only goal. Tow Law then had Tony Nelson sent off in the last minute for punching Waters.

Tiverton: Edwards, Fallon, Saunders, Tatterton, Smith (J), Conning, Nancekivell, Smith (K) - capt, Everett, Daly, Leonard. subs: Varley for Smith (K) 74, Rogers for Nancekivell 84, Waters for Leonard 86
Tow Law: Dawson, Pickering, Darwent, Bailey, Hague, Moan, Johnson, Nelson, Suddick, Laidler, Robinson. sub: Bennett for Laidler 84

FA CUP FINAL

Saturday 16th May 1998

Arsenal   **2-0**   **Newcastle United**
Overmars 23, Anelka 69
79,183
Referee: P Durkin (Portland)

Arsenal had twice lost FA Cup finals to Newcastle either side of the war but faced them on this occasion as overwhelming favourites. It had been five years since they had last won the Cup. They had suddenly struck a rich vein of form to wrest the Premiership title from Manchester United and now stood on the verge of emulating United's two 'double' triumphs. Arsenal had taken a tough route to Wembley, twice progressing on penalties away from home and they also won away against the previous year's finalists Middlesbrough.

Newcastle's last Cup win had been back in 1955 and their more recent Wembley visits had been woeful. They were humiliated in the 1974 final and suffered an even worse fate in the 1996 Charity Shield.

As Arsenal, European Cup-Winners Cup winners in 1994, were sprinting towards their first title since 1991, Newcastle were finishing 13th, their lowest position since promotion in 1993. This was a big disappointment after two successive runners-up placings had raised hopes of long overdue silverware.

Arsenal broke through when Petit, who was to clinch the World Cup for France two months later, sent Marc Overmars through. The Dutchman held off Pistone to slot the opener through Given's legs. The 'double' was clinched when young striker Nicolas Anelka ran on to Parlour's long ball and fired into the corner.

Arsenal's second 'double' was secured by an unexpected but unstoppable run of form in the second half of the season. They won both honours comfortably in the end unlike their 1971 counterparts who had to battle and come from behind to triumph.

There was nearly a repeat of this final the following year, when both sides reached the semi-finals again but only Newcastle made it back to Wembley.

Arsenal: Seaman, Dixon, Keown, Adams – capt, Winterburn, Parlour, Vieira, Petit, Overmars, Wreh, Anelka. sub: Platt for Wreh 63, Bould, Grimandi, Wright, Manninger (gk) (not used). manager: Arsene Wenger
Newcastle: Given, Pistone, Dabizas, Howey, Pearce, Barton, Lee – capt, Batty, Speed, Ketsbaia, Shearer. subs: Andersson for Pearce 72, Watson for Barton 77, Barnes for Ketsbaia 85, Albert, Hislop (gk) (not used). manager: Kenny Dalglish

FA Trophy Final

Sunday 17th May 1998

Cheltenham Town 1
Southport 0
Eaton 79
26,837
Referee: G Willard (Worthing)

Cheltenham's first visit to Wembley brought them consolation for missing out on promotion to the Football League after finishing second in the Conference to Halifax Town.

Thanks to Jason Eaton's winner in a hard fought game with Southport, who were also making their debut at the stadium, Clive Walker won his fourth FA Trophy winners medal in five years.

He was 40, seven years older than his manager Steve Cotterill, who was the youngest boss (apart from player-managers) to win silverware at Wembley. Southport's player-manager was ex-England Under-21 international, Paul Futcher.

A year later Cheltenham won the Conference and joined the league.

Cheltenham: Book, Duff, Victory, Freeman, Banks - capt, Knight, Howells, Bloomer, Eaton, Walker, Watkins. subs: Milton for Knight 78, Smith for Walker 78
Southport: Stewart, Farley, Formby, Horner, Futcher, Ryan, Kielty, Butler, Thompson, Ross, Gamble. subs: Whittaker for Formby 81, Bolland for Thompson 87

Play-offs

Third Division
Friday 22nd May 1998

Colchester United 1
Gregory (D) pen 22
Torquay United 0
19,486
Referee: M Fletcher (Warley)

For the third year in succession a single goal was enough to settle the Third Division final.

Colchester had lost the previous year's Auto Windscreens Shield final on penalties and David Gregory had put them in this final with an extra time penalty against Barnet in the semi-final while Torquay had last won promotion at Wembley in 1991 on penalties. So it was inevitable that a spot kick would decide the issue.

Colchester's victory took them to their highest division since 1981 and this was their first appearance in the play-offs for 11 years. Torquay had reached the play-offs in 1994, two years after relegation, but lost their semi-final in extra time to Preston North End.

Colchester: Emberson, Dunne, Betts, Skelton, Greene, Forbes, Wilkins - capt, Buckle, Sale, Gregory (N), Gregory (D). subs: Lock for Gregory (N) 70, Duguid for Skelton 82, Abrahams (not used). manager: Steve Wignall
Torquay: Gregg, Gurney, Gibbs, Robinson, Gittens, Watson - capt, Clayton, Leadbitter, Jack, McFarlane, McCall. subs: Bedeau for McCall 72, Thomas for McFarlane 84, Hill (not used). head coach: Kevin Hodges

INTERNATIONAL

Saturday 23rd May 1998

England   0-0   **Saudi Arabia**
63,733
Referee: D Jol (Netherlands)

Saudi Arabia made their first visit to England as reigning Asian Champions having won three of the last four tournaments and having reached the final of the other. They had also qualified for their second successive World Cup and like England would appear in France the following month.

Four years earlier in the USA they had surprisingly reached the last 16. England had played them just once, ten years earlier in a 1-1 draw in Riyadh.

This was a mediocre match. As the home team England were the most disappointing, bereft of ideas.

England: Seaman (Arsenal), Neville (G) (Man Utd), Adams (Arsenal), Southgate (Aston Villa), Anderton (Tottenham), Beckham (Man Utd), Batty (Newcastle), Scholes (Man Utd), Hinchcliffe (Sheffield W.), Sheringham (Man Utd), Shearer (Newcastle) – capt. subs: Gascoigne (Middlesbrough) for Beckham 60, Wright (Arsenal) for Sheringham 60, Neville (P) (Man Utd) for Hinchcliffe 71, Ferdinand (Tottenham) for Shearer 74. coach: Glenn Hoddle
Saudi Arabia: Al Deayea (Al-Tae), Al Jahni (Al-Ahli), Al Khlaiwi (Al-Ittihad), Zebramawi (Al-Ahli), Solaimani (Al-Ahli), Al Owairan (K) (Al-Hilal), Al Shahrani (Al-Ahli), Amin (Al-Shabab) - capt, Al Muwalid (Al-Ahli), Al Owairan (S) (Al-Shabab), Al Jaber (Al-Hilal). subs: Al Dosary (Al-Wehda) for Amin 77, Al Temiyat (Al-Hilal) for Al Owairan (S) 77. coach: Carlos Alberto Parreira

Play-offs

Second Division
Sunday 24th May 1998

Grimsby Town 1
Donovan 19

Northampton Town 0
62,988
Referee: T Heilbron (Newton Aycliffe)

Because of the previous day's international the play-offs were spread over four days. Grimsby became the first team to win both the Auto Windscreens Shield and the play-offs, an exhausting but rewarding season which also saw them knock holders, Leicester City out of the Coca-Cola Cup.

They may have been able to relax a little for the last 14 minutes had Kevin Donovan not missed an opportunity to add to his first half goal but Andy Woodman saved his penalty. Five years earlier Donovan had scored for West Bromwich Albion in this same final.

Grimsby had been relegated from the First Division the previous year and were appearing in the play-offs for the first time. Northampton had won the Third Division play-offs a year earlier to the day.

Despite a remarkable comeback from three goals down at Bristol Rovers in the semi-final first leg, they could not quite complete a second successive promotion which would have taken them out of the lower divisions for the first time since 1967.

A year after this defeat they were relegated back to the Third Division but won promotion straight back to the Second Division in 2000.

This was the fifth successive play-off final to be settled by a single goal. The following day would bring a dramatic end to that sequence.

Grimsby: Davison, McDermott, Gallimore, Handyside, Lever, Burnett, Donovan, Smith, Nogan, Lester, Groves - capt. subs: Livingstone for Nogan 60, Black for Smith 66, Jobling (not used). manager: Alan Buckley
Northampton: Woodman, Clarkson, Frain, Sampson, Warburton – capt, Hunt, Peer, Heggs, Freestone, Gayle, Hill. subs: Seal for Gayle 56, Gibb for Hill 60, Dozzell (not used). manager: Ian Atkins

First Division
Monday 25th May 1998

Charlton Athletic 4
Mendonca 23, 71, 103, Rufus 85

Sunderland 4
Quinn 50, 73, Phillips 58, Summerbee 99
After extra time
Charlton Athletic won 7-6 on penalties.
(Mendonca 1-0, Summerbee 1-1, Brown 2-1, Johnston 2-2, Jones (K) 3-2, Ball 3-3, Kinsella 4-3, Makin 4-4, Bowen 5-4, Rae 5-5, Robinson 6-5, Quinn 6-6, Newton 7-6, Gray saved)
77,739
Referee: E Wolstenholme (Blackburn)

Wembley had twice seen seven-goal thrillers in First Division finals but this surpassed them in a game packed with high drama and heart-stopping tension.

Charlton had arrived for their first Wembley appearance since losing the 1987 Full Members Cup final after a run of nine games without conceding a goal. And although their Macedonian goalkeeper Sasa Ilic conceded four goals, he ultimately became the hero as Charlton restored top flight football to the Valley for the first time since 1957.

They had been in the old First Division since, but during their last spell, which ended in 1990, they were ground sharing with Crystal Palace.

Sunderland had lost this final in 1990 yet still won promotion thanks to Swindon Town's financial irregularities. Sunderland reached the FA Cup final two years later after relegation and they were Football League Champions in 1996 only to go down straight away again.

The First Division promotion race had been close run and Sunderland had missed out with 90 points, the most by any team failing to win promotion. They had not beaten Charlton for five years but led three times including in extra time.

But they could not repel the Londoners and a stunning Clive Mendonca hat-trick meant a place in the Premiership was decided on penalties for the first time. Even then, it took 14 attempts before the unfortunate Michael Gray's weak effort was held by Ilic.

Mark Bright had scored the extra time winner for Sheffield Wednesday in Wembley's all-Sheffield FA Cup semi-final in 1993.

Niall Quinn, who scored twice, scored against England at Wembley for the Republic of Ireland in 1991.

The teams swapped places the following year; Charlton suffering relegation while Sunderland made no mistake this time bagging a record 105 points, a massive 18 clear of their nearest challengers. In 2000, Charlton succeeded them as Football League Champions to earn their second promotion in three years.

Charlton: Ilic, Mills, Bowen, Jones (K), Rufus, Youds, Newton, Kinsella - capt, Bright, Mendonca, Heaney. subs: Jones (S) for Heaney 65, Robinson for Mills 76, Brown for Bright 93. manager: Alan Curbishley
Sunderland: Perez, Holloway, Gray, Clark, Craddock, Williams, Summerbee, Ball - capt, Quinn, Phillips, Johnston. subs: Makin for Holloway 46, Dichio for Phillips 73, Rae for Clark 100. manager: Peter Reid

Calrsberg Pub International

Saturday 13th June 1998

Vagns Krostue 0
West Hendon Ex-Servicemen 1
Newing 81
Referee: A Young

West Hendon followed up the previous month's Pub Cup victory by becoming the second successive English team to win the International trophy. Torrential rain throughout meant the pitch was water-logged and at times the conditions were farcical. Steve Newing, also Edgware Town's player-manager, had scored West Hendon's late equaliser on their previous visit and popped up again with a late winner to defeat the Danish Pub Cup winners.

West Hendon: Harvey, Newing - capt, Evans, Elliott, Dale (A), Valenti, Alger, Instone, Roche, Dale (P), Murray. subs: Davey for Alger, Grant for Dale (P), Spellman for Murray

FA CHARITY SHIELD

Sunday 9th August 1998

Arsenal   **3-0**   **Manchester United**
Overmars 33, Wreh 56, Anelka 71
67,342
Referee: G Poll (Tring)

Arsenal had a poor recent Charity Shield record and had not won it outright since 1953. They had twice met United in this fixture, with a win apiece. United's had been in 1993 on penalties in Arsenal's last appearance in the season's curtain raiser.

Now, though, as champions and FA Cup holders Arsenal took the field with one of their strongest teams. They had won their first title since 1991 with an incredible run of ten consecutive wins. They had previously beaten United at Wembley in the dramatic FA Cup final of 1979.

Between them these two had won three 'doubles' in five years. United, the Charity Shield holders, had become accustomed to qualifying for this fixture but this third successive appearance, the fifth in six years, was by invitation after they finished as Premiership runners-up a point behind Arsenal. They were chasing a record 11th outright Shield. The previous year they had needed penalties to defeat Chelsea but another win would make them the first to register a hat-trick of outright victories.

The Gunners scored when Bergkamp, the Footballer of the Year who had missed the FA Cup final through injury, back-heeled the ball into the goalmouth. Johnsen, under pressure from Anelka, could only turn it to the edge of the area from where Marc Overmars hammered it into the net.

Arsenal's multi-national team increased their lead after the interval. Anelka sent Christopher Wreh through and although Schmeichel saved his first effort the Liberian substitute stayed calm to keep the rebound low as he fired it into the net.

The result was put beyond doubt when Nicolas Anelka ran on to Parlour's pass, held off the challenge of United's new defender Stam and beat Schmeichel at the near post. Arsenal had begun the season as they had left off while United seemed lethargic as they suffered their heaviest ever Wembley defeat.

Arsenal ended the season without a trophy. Although their defence of the Premiership went to the last match they finished runners-up by a point as United reclaimed the title for the fifth time in seven years.

United also beat Arsenal in an FA Cup semi-final after a titanic struggle which twice went to extra time. And four days after United's appearance in the FA Cup final, they lifted the European Cup for the first time since 1968.

This final, as in 1968, went into added time before United astonishingly conjured two goals from substitutes to shatter Bayern Munich. United would meet Arsenal again in the following year's Charity Shield.

Arsenal: Seaman, Dixon, Winterburn, Adams – capt, Keown, Parlour, Petit, Vieira, Overmars, Bergkamp, Anelka. subs: Wreh for Bergkamp 46, Boa Morte for Petit 72, Bould for Adams 79, Grimandi for Vieira 83. manager: Arsene Wenger
Manchester U: Schmeichel, Neville (G), Stam, Johnsen, Irwin, Beckham, Keane – capt, Butt, Giggs, Scholes, Cole. subs: Solskjaer for Butt 53, Cruyff for Giggs 70, Neville (P) for Scholes 70, Sheringham for Cole 70, Berg for Keane 75. manager: Alex Ferguson

UEFA Champions League

Wednesday 30th September 1998

Arsenal 2
Adams 64, Keown 72

Panathinaikos 1
Mauro 87
73,455
Referee: A Lopez Nieto (Spain)

Arsenal's experimental move to Wembley for their Champions League campaign kicked off 25 minutes late because of traffic problems but thanks to goals from their two central defenders it brought them their third victory of the year at the stadium.

In their opening match in Group E, two weeks earlier, they had conceded a last minute equaliser in Lens to the French League Champions but this win took them to the top of the table.

Panathinaikos were still the only Greek club to reach a European final, losing in 1971 at Wembley in this competition to Ajax Amsterdam. Their appearance in the Champions League this time was as league runners-up to Olympiakos and they had already beaten the Ukrainian League champions Dynamo Kiev in Athens. A late strike from their Brazilian substitute was not enough to keep them at the top of the group, however, and they would eventually finish bottom after Arsenal beat them again, in Athens two months later.

Arsenal: Seaman, Dixon, Winterburn, Adams – capt, Keown, Vieira, Garde, Petit, Overmars, Bergkamp, Anelka. sub: Vivas for Garde 79. manager: Arsene Wenger
Panathinaikos: Wandzik, Apostolakis - capt, Milojevic, Asanovic, Goumas, Lagonikakis, Mykland, Strandli, Konstantinidis, Liberopoulos, Kiassos. subs: Kola for Kiassos 70, Mauro for Strandli 84, Sypniewski for Liberopoulos 84. coach: Vasilis Daniel

EUROPEAN CHAMPIONSHIP QUALIFYING

Saturday 10th October 1998

England   0-0   **Bulgaria**
72,974
Referee: L Vagner (Hungary)

Both teams had begun Group Five with defeats. England's confidence had slumped after a disappointing World Cup exit in the last 16 to Argentina in St Etienne. It was their third penalties defeat of the 1990's in a major tournament and a huge blow following a memorable 2-2 draw after extra time. They had given a heroic performance after David Beckham was sent off at the beginning of the second half.

Meanwhile Bulgaria, with an ageing side, had picked up just one point, lost 6-1 to Spain in Lens and left the tournament after finishing bottom of their first round group. They had never beaten England and two years earlier they had lost at Wembley.

In their first match England had surrendered an early lead to lose 2-1 in Stockholm the previous month while the Bulgarians had suffered a humiliating 3-0 reversal to Poland in Sofia the following night.

Once again, England were unable to break down an organised defence. Their disjointed approach play and lack of aggression caused their fans to boo the red-shirted home players from the field.

A few hours later Poland went clear at the top of the table by defeating Luxembourg 3-0 in Warsaw. Bulgaria's hopes ended when the return also ended in a draw, 1-1 in Sofia, the following year. They finished fourth.

England: Seaman (Arsenal), Hinchcliffe (Sheffield W.), Neville (G) (Man Utd), Campbell (Tottenham), Southgate (Aston Villa), Lee (Newcastle), Redknapp (Liverpool), Anderton (Tottenham), Scholes (Man Utd), Owen (Liverpool), Shearer (Newcastle) – capt. subs: Le Saux (Chelsea) for Hinchcliffe 34, Batty (Newcastle) for Anderton 67, Sheringham (Man Utd) for Scholes 76. coach: Glenn Hoddle
Bulgaria: Zdravkov (Istanbulspor), Kishishev (Liteks Lovech), Zagorchich (Liteks), Naidenov (CSKA Sofia), Iordanov (Sporting Lisbon), Iankov (Adanaspor), Kirilov (Liteks), Stoichkov (Kashiva Reysol) – capt, Hristov (Kaiserslautern), Petkov (CSKA), Iliev (AEK Athens). subs: Bachev (Slavia Sofia) for Stoichkov 60, Gruev (Neftochimik) for Iliev 62, Ivanov (CSKA) for Hristov 90. coach: Dimitar Dimitrov

UEFA Champions League

Wednesday 21st October 1998

Arsenal 1
Bergkamp 73
Dynamo Kiev 1
Rebrov 90
73,256
Referee: R Wojcik (Poland)

These clubs had both appeared at Wembley in the 1989 Makita Tournament although not against each other. Kiev were then a member of the USSR but now returned as Ukrainian League champions for the sixth successive year. They had also won the Ukrainian Cup for the second time in three years. In the European Cup, however, success was more elusive. They had qualified for the Champions League group stage on penalties after being behind on aggregate for 173 minutes of their two-leg clash with Sparta Prague. In Group E they had picked up just one point and doubled their tally thanks to a last minute equaliser.

Arsenal were fortunate to go ahead but conceded a late goal for the third successive Champions League match. They maintained their lead at the top of the table, however, on goals scored from Lens but Kiev won all their remaining games to win the group.

Andriy Shevchenko, the 2004 European Footballer of the Year, made his first Wembley appearance.

Arsenal: Seaman, Dixon, Adams – capt, Keown, Winterburn, Overmars, Parlour, Hughes, Garde, Anelka, Bergkamp. sub: Vivas for Anelka 84. manager: Arsene Wenger
Dynamo Kiev: Shovkovski, Luzhny - capt, Holovko, Vaschuk, Dmitrulin, Kaladze, Kossovski, Shevchenko, Rebrov, Husin, Bialkevich. sub: Kardash for Husin 82. coach: Valeri Lobanovsky

INTERNATIONAL

Wednesday 18th November 1998

England   **2-0**   **Czech Republic**
Anderton 22, Merson 39
38,535
Referee: U Meier (Switzerland)

England had met Czechoslovakia on ten occasions but had never before played the Republic. They had performed remarkably well in their first tournament, the 1996 European Championship, culminating in a narrow defeat in extra time in the final at Wembley. They had disappointed since then, however, and failed to qualify for the recent World Cup. In the current European Championship they led their qualifying group with maximum points from three games.

England needed a victory to boost morale and scored midway through the first half, Wright's cross being tucked into the corner by Darren Anderton. Six minutes before the interval another superb cross from Wright was flicked on by Dublin's head and Paul Merson fired past Kouba for England's second.

A much improved performance from the home side restored some confidence at the end of a disappointing year.

The Czech Republic became the first team to win all ten of their European Championship qualifying fixtures and won their group by twelve points from Scotland. They came unstuck in the finals although they were placed in an extremely tough group, won by the hosts, the Netherlands with the World Champions and eventual winners France finishing runners-up.

England: Martyn (Leeds Utd), Campbell (Tottenham) – capt, Keown (Arsenal), Ferdinand (West Ham), Le Saux (Chelsea), Butt (Man Utd), Beckham (Man Utd), Anderton (Tottenham), Dublin (Aston Villa), Wright (West Ham), Merson (Aston Villa). subs: Fowler (Liverpool) for Wright 70, Hendrie* (Aston Villa) for Merson 76. coach: Glenn Hoddle
*first cap
Czech Republic: Kouba (Viktoria Zizkov), Latal (Schalke), Votava (Sparta Prague), Novotny (Sparta Prague), Repka (Fiorentina), Berger (Liverpool), Nemec (Schalke) - capt, Poborsky (Benfica), Kuka (Nuremberg), Smicer (Lens), Bejbl (Atletico Madrid). subs: Baranek (Sparta Prague) for Latal 46, Lokvenc (Sparta Prague) for Novotny 46, Vonasek (Lokeren) for Nemec 46, Kotulek (Olomouc) for Smicer 46, Sloncik (Banik Ostrava) for Kuka 73. coach: Jozef Chovanec

UEFA Champions League

Wednesday 25th November 1998

Arsenal 0
Lens 1
Debeve 72
73,707
Referee: A Frisk (Sweden)

Arsenal had lost 3-1 in Kiev three weeks earlier and going into their last home game in this tight Group E there was just one point separating the four clubs.

Lens had won the French League Championship for the first time, on goal difference from Metz, and ended Arsenal's Champions League hopes with Michael Debeve's winner.

Tempers were lost in added time, when first Arsenal's Ray Parlour was sent off for kicking Cyril Rool. As the game was about to restart Tony Vairelles clashed with Lee Dixon and was also shown the red card.

Arsenal were left at the bottom of the table but a 3-1 win in Athens against Panathinaikos the following month lifted them above their Greek opponents. At the same time Lens lost their last match, 3-1 at home to Dynamo Kiev who thus clinched a place in the quarter-finals. Lens finished runners-up by virtue of their victory against Arsenal who had drawn level on points with them and had a better goal difference. The following season, Arsenal got their revenge by beating Lens home and away in the UEFA Cup semi-finals.

Arsenal: Seaman, Dixon, Winterburn, Adams – capt, Keown, Garde, Parlour, Hughes, Overmars, Wreh, Anelka. subs: Bould for Adams 46, Vivas for Garde 67. manager: Arsene Wenger
Lens: Warmuz, Sikora, Lachor, Magnier, Rool, Debeve, Nyarko, Vairelles, Dehu - capt, Smicer, Nouma. subs: Eloi for Nouma 59, Moreira for Smicer 80. coach: Daniel Leclercq

INTERNATIONAL

Wednesday 10th February 1999

England 0-2 **France**
Anelka 69, 76

74,111
Referee: H Krug (Germany)

England suffered the worst possible preparation for the visit of the World Champions. Glenn Hoddle had been sacked the previous week after some ill-judged comments about the disabled in The Times and Howard Wilkinson had been installed hurriedly as caretaker for one match only.

France had been beaten on their last visit to Wembley, in 1992 and also by England five years later in Montpellier in a tournament won by England. But 1998 brought the greatest moment in the history of French football as they hosted and surprisingly won the World Cup.

In the final in Paris they beat the holders Brazil by an astonishing 3-0 scoreline, the heaviest ever World Cup defeat experienced by the South Americans in the 68-year history of the competition. In their current European Championship qualifying group, France were two points behind the leaders the Ukraine.

The French brought their strongest line-up with eight of the World Cup winning team starting the match and two more coming on as substitutes. England played well in the first half, creating a few chances but if they were beginning to feel they could get the better of the World Champions they were sadly mistaken. Martyn replaced Seaman in England's goal at half-time and had to face the might of a very confident French team who were to dominate the second half.

The star was Arsenal's Nicolas Anelka who almost grabbed a hat-trick. First, he was unlucky when his shot hit the bar and bounced down onto the line according to the officials. Six minutes later, Zidane lobbed the ball into his path over the static England defence and Anelka coolly beat Martyn to put the French ahead. The Arsenal striker then nipped in between Adams and Le Saux to slide his second into the corner from substitute Dugarry's cross. He was substituted eight minutes later but the damage had been done and the 19-year-old striker had now scored four times at Wembley in nine months.

England were outplayed by a team fielding five Premiership players and another eight of those on view later played in the

Premiership. France had proved they were worthy World Champions. They had recorded their first Wembley victory and Howard Wilkinson unfortunately handed over the reins without registering a goal.

Robert Pires joined Arsenal the following year and was in their 'double-winning' side of 2002 when he was voted Footballer of the Year. In 2003 he scored the only goal of the FA Cup final at the Millennium Stadium.

France also went on to take the European Championship as well, a 'double' previously achieved only by West Germany in the 1970's.

England, to their credit, managed to hold the French to a 1-1 draw in Paris in their hosts' first match as World and European Champions.

England: Seaman (Arsenal), Dixon (Arsenal), Le Saux (Chelsea), Keown (Arsenal), Adams (Arsenal), Ince (Liverpool), Redknapp (Liverpool), Anderton (Tottenham), Beckham (Man Utd), Owen (Liverpool), Shearer (Newcastle) – capt. subs: Martyn (Leeds Utd) for Seaman 46, Cole (Man Utd) for Owen 64, Ferdinand (West Ham) for Dixon 71, Wilcox (Blackburn) for Keown 84, Scholes (Man Utd) for Redknapp 84. acting head coach: Howard Wilkinson

France: Barthez (Monaco), Lizarazu (Bayern Munich), Blanc (Olympique Marseille), Thuram (Parma), Desailly (Chelsea), Petit (Arsenal), Zidane (Juventus), Deschamps (Juventus) – capt, Djorkaeff (Internazionale), Pires (Olympique Marseille), Anelka (Arsenal). subs: Leboeuf (Chelsea) for Blanc 46, Dugarry (Olympique Marseille) for Pires 46, Wiltord (Bordeaux) for Djorkaeff 83, Vieira (Arsenal) for Anelka 83, Candela (Roma) for Deschamps 90. coach: Roger Lemerre

LEAGUE CUP FINAL

Sunday 21st March 1999

Leicester City   **0-1**   **Tottenham Hotspur**

Nielsen 90

77,892

Referee: T Heilbron (Newton Aycliffe)

The most famous meeting between Leicester and Tottenham was in 1961 when Tottenham clinched the 'double' by winning the FA Cup. Leicester were now appearing at Wembley for the sixth time in eight years, having won the competition two years earlier after a drawn game at the stadium.

Tottenham were in their first final since 1982 and had to go back a further nine years for their last victory in the competition. They had made numerous other Wembley appearances in the past two decades, but had not graced the famous turf since an FA Cup semi-final in 1993.

Both sides were mid-table, with Tottenham acquiring the services of George Graham as manager six months earlier. The man who had led their closest rivals

Arsenal to numerous trophies, including the League Cup twice, had revitalised Tottenham and they had reached the FA Cup semi-finals as well.

Worthington had replaced Coca-Cola as the sponsors and saw a disappointing game come to life after 63 minutes when Justin Edinburgh was sent off after a clash with Robbie Savage.

A few unsavoury incidents followed, but it was Tottenham who snatched the winner two minutes into added time. Iversen broke down the right. Keller got a hand to his low cross, but Allan Nielsen dived full-length to head it into the net.

Leicester returned to win the Worthington Cup the following year in Wembley's last final.

Leicester: Keller, Ullathorne, Elliott, Walsh (S) – capt, Taggart, Izzet, Savage, Lennon, Guppy, Cottee, Heskey. subs: Marshall for Heskey 75, Zagorakis for Savage 90, Campbell, Kaamark, Arphexad (gk) (not used). manager: Martin O'Neill

Tottenham: Walker, Carr, Edinburgh, Campbell – capt, Vega, Nielsen, Freund, Anderton, Ginola, Iversen, Ferdinand. subs: Sinton for Ginola 90, Armstrong, Dominguez, Young, Baardsen (gk) (not used). manager: George Graham

EUROPEAN CHAMPIONSHIP QUALIFYING

Saturday 27th March 1999

England   **3-1**   **Poland**
Scholes 11, 21, 70   Brzeczek 28
73,836
Referee: V Pereira (Portugal)

Poland were becoming regular visitors to Wembley because of being continually drawn in the same qualifying group as England. This was their fifth visit in ten years and while they had lost the previous four they confidently led Group Five on goal difference from Sweden. England were two points behind, having played a game more. So victory was essential.

Kevin Keegan had taken over from Howard Wilkinson until the end of the season while also leading Fulham to a runaway Second Division Championship title as Chief Operating Officer. The country waited to see if he could revive England's fortunes at the same time.

Keegan had to wait only 11 minutes to see his new team, in red shirts, take the lead. As Shearer approached the edge of the area, three defenders converged on him. Zielinski got a foot to the ball but it cannoned off Bak's leg into the path of Paul Scholes who lifted it over Matysek as the goalkeeper advanced from his line.

England rather fortunately increased their lead when a superb Beckham cross was headed in by Scholes after it first hit his arm. Poland were allowed back into the game when slack defending enabled Jerzy Brzeczek to slot Trzeciak's cross past Seaman but England wrapped up the points with 20 minutes left. Gary Neville's long throw was headed on by Shearer and Scholes completed a hat-trick by rising to power a header into the corner.

Sweden took advantage by securing a 2-0 win against Luxembourg in Gothenburg and went back to the top of the group. Four days later the Swedes won 1-0 in Chorzow and built up a five-point lead over England. When Poland entertained England in the return in Warsaw six months later victory would have secured them runners-up spot. It ended goalless and England pipped them to the play-off position on aggregate, although they had to wait another month for Poland to lose their final game in Stockholm.

England: Seaman (Arsenal), Neville (G) (Man Utd), Keown (Arsenal), Campbell (Tottenham), Le Saux (Chelsea), Beckham (Man Utd), Scholes (Man Utd), Sherwood* (Tottenham), McManaman (Liverpool), Shearer (Newcastle) – capt, Cole (Man Utd). subs: Parlour* (Arsenal) for McManaman 69, Neville (P) (Man Utd) for Beckham 77, Redknapp (Liverpool) for Scholes 82. caretaker head coach: Kevin Keegan
*first cap

Poland: Matysek (Bayer Leverkusen), Hajto (Duisburg), Zielinski (Legia Warsaw), Lapinski (Widzew Lodz), Ratajczyk (Rapid Vienna), Swierczewski (Gamba Osaka), Bak (Olympique Lyonnais), Brzeczek (Maccabi Haifa) – capt, Siadaczka (FK Austria), Iwan (PSV Eindhoven), Trzeciak (Atletico Osasuna). subs: Klos (Auxerre) for Swierczewski 46, Kowalczyk (Las Palmas) for Siadaczka 64, Juskowiak (Wolfsburg) for Trzeciak 82. coach: Janusz Wojcik

Auto Windscreens Shield

Sunday 18th April 1999

Millwall 0
Wigan Athletic 1
Rogers 90
55,349
Referee: C Wilkes (Gloucester)

Paul Rogers struck the winner in the third minute of added time and Wigan won the competition for the second time. They had triumphed in the first Wembley final back in 1985 and their only success since then had been in winning the Third Division Championship in 1997 on goals scored from Fulham. Their last Wembley appearance though was when reaching the quarter-finals of the Football League Centenary Tournament in 1988 when they lost on penalties to eventual finalists Sheffield Wednesday.

Millwall's only previous visit was in the Football League South Cup final of 1945.

Wigan were hoping to emulate Grimsby Town's 'double' of the previous year when they sneaked into the play-offs for the first time in twelve years but they were defeated in the semi-finals by the eventual winners Manchester City.

Millwall: Roberts, Lavin, Nethercott - capt, Dolan, Stuart, Ifill, Cahill, Newman, Reid, Harris, Sadlier. subs: Bircham, Bowry, Shaw (not used) manager: Keith Stevens
Wigan: Carroll, Bradshaw - capt, McGibbon, Greenall, Balmer, Sharp, Rogers, O'Neill, Liddell, Haworth, Barlow. subs: Lee for Barlow 88, Green, Jones (not used). manager: Ray Mathias

Forest Green: Shuttlewood, Hedges, Kilgour, Forbes, Drysdale, Honor, Wigg, Bailey, Sykes, McGregor, Mehew. subs: Winter for Honor 58, Cook for Wigg 58, Smart for Bailey 76
Kingstonian: Farrelly, Stewart, Crossley - capt, Harris, Mustafa, Patterson, Pitcher, Luckett, Rattray, Leworthy, Akumoah. sub: Francis for Leworthy 86

Under 18 Schools International

Saturday 8th May 1999

England 1
Foster pen
Netherlands 2
Houwing, Longuet
33,012
Referee: E Lomas (Manchester)

In Wembley's first International at Under-18 level the Netherlands fielded their under-17 side who were all with professional clubs but Dave Cook's team held them until two minutes from the end.

England: Smith, Burden, Duffy, Feely, Morris, Fletcher, Foster - capt, Taylor, Dawson, Onochie, Rummery. subs: Rogers for Smith, Hughes, Sobey, Allison

FA Trophy

Saturday 15th May 1999

Forest Green Rovers 0
Kingstonian 1
Mustafa 48
20,037
Referee: A Wilkie (Chester-le-Street)

Forest Green failed in their attempt to become the first team to win both the FA Vase and the FA Trophy as Kingstonian finally atoned for their dramatic collapse at the FA Amateur Cup final of 1960. For manager Geoff Chapple it was a fourth FA Trophy win in six years, the other three having been won with Woking.

Carlsberg Pub Cup Final

Sunday 16th May 1999

Sizewell 2
Smith 11, Fryer 39
West Hendon Ex-Servicemen 0
Referee: M Fletcher (Warley)

West Hendon were unable to match their double Wembley triumph of the previous year as the side from Suffolk wrested away the trophy. Sizewell Sports and Social Club could not repeat West Hendon's success in the International Pub Tournament in Copenhagen although they reached the final after beating the eventual winners.

FA Vase Final

Sunday 16th May 1999

Bedlington Terriers 0
Tiverton Town 1
Rogers 88
13,878
Referee: W Burns (Scarborough)

Tiverton retained the Vase and again it was a substitute who scored the only goal late in the game. This time it was Scott Rogers.

Bedlington: O'Connor, Pike, Teasdale - capt, Melrose, Bowes, Boon, Middleton, Cross, Bond, Gibb, Milner. subs: Renforth for Boon 90, Ludlow for Middleton 90, Cameron, Gowans, Pearson (not used)
Tiverton: Edwards, Fallon, Tallon, Tatterton, Saunders - capt, Leonard, Conning, Daly, Nancekivell, Everett, Varley. subs: Pears for Conning 70, Rogers for Nancekivell 70, Grimshaw, Hynds, Tucker (not used)

FA CUP FINAL

Saturday 22nd May 1999

Manchester United   2-0   Newcastle United
Sheringham 11, Scholes 53
79,101
Referee: P Jones (Loughborough)

Manchester United were chasing their fourth FA Cup win of the decade and a record tenth overall. Six days earlier they had secured their fifth Premiership title in seven years, by a point from Arsenal the previous year's 'double' winners. Now

United had the opportunity to secure an unbelievable third 'double' and all within the 1990's.

Their opponents, Newcastle were appearing in their second successive final and were again attempting to prevent the 'double' being achieved. In the previous year's final they had been outplayed and were anxious to avoid another Wembley defeat. They had not won the Cup since 1955 and United had destroyed them in the 1996 FA Charity Shield.

In the semi-finals United's Peter Schmeichel saved an added time penalty in the replay against Arsenal which would have put them out. They went on to beat the holders thanks to an incredible individual goal from Ryan Giggs in extra time.

United lost captain Roy Keane, injured after only nine minutes, and it was his substitute who put them ahead less than two minutes later. Teddy Sheringham played a one-two with Scholes before firing through Harper's legs as Charvet made a desperate lunge.

After a brief Newcastle revival at the beginning of the second half the same players combined to add United's second. With his back to goal Sheringham laid the ball into the path of Paul Scholes whose sweetly struck shot went through Charvet's legs before beating Harper. United then strolled to victory and their third 'double'. Keane went up to receive the Cup – his last act of the season, as he was suspended from the European Cup final.

Alex Ferguson had built a team which was rewriting the record books. Three – Schmeichel, Keane and Giggs – had played in all three Cup finals which clinched the 'doubles', while only Johnsen and Solskjaer, of the starting 11, had not played in the 1996 final. Ferguson's policy of resting key players at various points of the season had reaped its rewards.

United had been unbeaten in all competitions during 1999 and had ended the season in unstoppable form. Their greatest triumph came four days later.

In the European Cup final in Barcelona they were a goal down to Bayern Munich in added time when the two substitutes Sheringham and Solskjaer scored to snatch victory from the Germans. United had won the 'treble' and the following month their manager was rewarded with a knighthood. Their European Cup success meant that they would not defend the FA Cup, competing instead in FIFA's Club World Championship in Brazil.

Newcastle were back at Wembley the following year attempting to reach their third successive final.

Manchester U: Schmeichel, Neville (G), May, Johnsen, Neville (P), Beckham, Keane – capt, Scholes, Giggs, Solskjaer, Cole. subs: Sheringham for Keane 9, Yorke for Cole 61, Stam for Scholes 77, Blomqvist, Van der Gouw (gk) (not used). manager: Alex Ferguson

Newcastle: Harper, Griffin, Charvet, Dabizas, Domi, Lee, Hamann, Speed, Solano, Shearer – capt, Ketsbaia. subs: Ferguson for Hamann 46, Maric for Solano 68, Glass for Ketsbaia 79, Barton, Given (gk) (not used). manager: Ruud Gullit

Play-offs

Third Division
Saturday 29th May 1999

Leyton Orient 0
Scunthorpe United 1
Calvo-Garcia 6
36,985
Referee: C Wilkes (Gloucester)

Alex Calvo-Garcia decided this fourth successive final to be won with a single goal. Scunthorpe had lost the 1992 final in the old Fourth Division on penalties, their only previous Wembley appearance. They were now elevated to a level they had not attained since 1984.

Orient had been relegated to the Third Division in 1995 after winning the last Fourth Division play-offs not held at Wembley in 1989. They had appeared at Wembley, however, as Clapton Orient in two Third Division South games in 1930 when their ground was considered unsuitable.

Unfortunately for Scunthorpe, just as in their two previous promotions, they were relegated straight back to the Third Division, the following year.

Leyton Orient: Barrett, Joseph, Smith - capt, Hicks, Clark, Richards, Beall, Ling, Lockwood, Watts, Simba. subs: Maskell for Hicks 46, Inglethorpe for Richards 46, Stimson (not used). manager: Tommy Taylor

Scunthorpe: Evans, Wilcox, Logan, Hope - capt, Harsley, Walker, Calvo-Garcia, Dawson, Sheldon, Forrester, Gayle. subs: Housham for Calvo-Garcia 76, Stamp for Gayle 78, Bull for Forrester 85. manager: Brian Laws

Second Division
Sunday 30th May 1999

Gillingham 2
Asaba 81, Taylor 86

Manchester City 2
Horlock 89, Dickov 90
After extra time
Manchester City won 3-1 on penalties.
(Horlock 0-1, Smith saved, Dickov hit post, Pennock missed, Cooke 0-2, Hodge 1-2, Edghill 1-3, Butters saved)
76,935
Referee: M Halsey (Welwyn Garden City)

In front of the biggest crowd of the play-off weekend City won promotion back to the First Division following their first ever season in the lower divisions. It came after an astonishing climax in which they appeared to be beaten.

Gillingham were at Wembley for the first time. They had never played in the First Division but had reached this final before in 1987, the first year of the play-offs. Gillingham had been two goals up on aggregate at half-time in the second leg but eventually lost after a replay with Swindon Town. Two years later, they were relegated.

The action was packed into the last ten minutes. Gillingham scored twice and appeared to have beaten their opponents for the first time. City pulled a goal back in the last minute and equalised in the fifth minute of added time. It was strangely reminiscent of their mighty rivals Manchester United's European Cup victory with two added time goals just four days earlier.

Gillingham were shell-shocked and the first Second Division final to go to penalties saw it end in heartbreak for them. Horlock added to his goal with the first spot kick. The next three penalties were all missed as nerves were frayed. Paul Dickov turned from hero to villain when he hit both posts following his glorious equaliser but when Nicky Weaver saved from Guy Butters City had earned their first Wembley success since winning the League Cup in 1976. Robert Taylor, who thought he had clinched Gillingham's promotion with their second goal joined City six months later, and helped them continue their meteoric rise by finishing as Nationwide League runners-up to Charlton Athletic.

Gillingham were also celebrating the following year as they won the play-offs in another dramatic final.

Gillingham: Bartram, Ashby, Pennock, Butters, Patterson, Smith, Hessenthaler – capt, Galloway, Southall, Taylor, Asaba. subs: Saunders for Galloway 56, Carr for Asaba 87, Hodge for Patterson 105. manager: Tony Pulis
Manchester C: Weaver, Crooks, Morrison – capt, Wiekens, Edghill, Cooke, Brown, Whitley, Horlock, Goater, Dickov subs: Vaughan for Morrison 61, Bishop for Brown 61, Taylor for Crooks 85. manager: Joe Royle

First Division
Monday 31st May 1999

Bolton Wanderers 0
Watford 2
Wright 38, Smart 89
70,343
Referee: T Heilbron (Newton Aycliffe)

Former England manager Graham Taylor won his seventh promotion and his fifth with Watford in two spells at the club. After taking them to the FA Cup final in 1984 he had left before they were relegated four years later. In 1989 they reached the play-offs but lost on away goals in the semi-finals.

Relegation to the Second Division followed in 1996 but they were promoted as champions two years later and now completed an unexpected second successive promotion to return to the top flight.

Nick Wright's overhead kick in the first half and a breakaway second in the last minute from substitute Allan Smart brought to an end Bolton's recent yo-yo existence between the top two divisions. In 1995 they had won this final after pulling back from two goals down but for the first time in five years, they would stay in the same division.

The following year, Bolton reached the FA Cup semi-finals at Wembley and appeared in the play-offs again only to lose again, this time to Ipswich who went on to win the final. Watford, sadly but predictably, were out of their depth in the Premiership. They finished bottom and were relegated.

Bolton: Banks, Cox, Elliott, Frandsen, Todd, Fish – capt, Johansen, Jensen, Gudjohnsen, Taylor, Gardner. subs: Sellars for Johansen 66, Hansen for Gardner 89, Bergsson (not used). manager: Colin Todd
Watford: Chamberlain, Bazeley, Kennedy, Page – capt, Palmer, Robinson, Ngonge, Hyde, Mooney, Johnson, Wright. subs: Smart for Ngonge 75, Hazan for Wright 87, Day (gk) (not used). manager: Graham Taylor

EUROPEAN CHAMPIONSHIP QUALIFYING

Saturday 5th June 1999

England　　　　　**0-0**　　　**Sweden**
75,824
Referee: J Encinar (Spain)

Sweden arrived at Wembley with a commanding four-point lead at the top of Group Five from Poland, who had moved back above England the previous night by defeating Bulgaria 2-0 in Warsaw. England had to win to regain second spot and to keep Sweden within catching distance. They had not beaten the Swedes since 1968 and their last visit to Wembley, in 1988, had been goalless. Sweden had won all their four qualifying fixtures to date, beginning with a 2-1 victory against England in Stockholm the previous year after England had taken an early lead. But with Paul Ince sent off, the visitors were well beaten in the end.

This game was a depressingly familiar story for England who now had a full-time coach again as Kevin Keegan had given up his role at Fulham. Although they ended Sweden's winning run, the visitors were rarely threatened and maintained their stranglehold on the group leadership. It was disappointing for Alan Shearer winning his 50th cap but more so for Paul Scholes whose foul on Stefan Schwarz in the 51st minute was his second bookable offence and he became the only player to be sent off at Wembley for England.

Four days later England could only draw 1-1 in Sofia as Poland won in Luxembourg which left England three points adrift of the runners-up spot. Sweden won their remaining three games to win the group by nine points. They were hugely disappointing in the following year's tournament, however. Only one point was gained in a group won by the eventual finalists Italy.

England: Seaman (Arsenal), Neville (P) (Man Utd), Keown (Arsenal), Campbell (Tottenham), Le Saux (Chelsea), Beckham (Man Utd), Batty (Leeds Utd), Sherwood (Tottenham), Scholes (Man Utd), Cole (Man Utd), Shearer (Newcastle) – capt. subs: Ferdinand (West Ham) for Keown 34, Gray (Sunderland) for Le Saux 46, Parlour (Arsenal) for Beckham 75. head coach: Kevin Keegan
Sweden: Hedman (Coventry), Nilsson (Helsingborgs), Andersson (P) (Borussia Monchengladbach) – capt, Bjorklund (Valencia), Kaamark (Leicester), Schwarz (Valencia), Mild (Gothenburg), Mjallby (Celtic), Ljungberg (Arsenal), Andersson (K) (Bologna), Larsson (Celtic). subs: Alexandersson (Sheffield W.) for Mild 6, Svensson (Viking Stavanger) for Larsson 69, Andersson (D) (Bari) for Mjallby 82. Coach: Tommy Soderberg

Under-16 Girls' International

Sunday 4th July 1999

England 5
Gomersall, Anderton, Hunn, Whewell, Ritchie

Scotland 0

An afternoon of Under-16 Internationals for both sexes began with England Girls' first ever home game at this level. The highlight was a superb individual goal from Alexa Hunn.

England: Hart, Champ, Sudan, Williams, Gomersall - capt, Luke, Cox, Hunn, Anderton, De La Salle, McDougal. subs: Holdsworth for Hart, Ritchie for Luke, Maggs for Anderton, Whewell for De La Salle, Smith for McDougal. coach: Hope Powell
Scotland: Harris, Kennedy, Orrick, McConnell, Halliday, Donachie, Bruce, Cullen, Hamill, Gallacher, James. subs: Wyles for Kennedy, Ward for Halliday, Tebay for Bruce, Young for Gallacher, McVey for James

Under-16 International

Sunday 4th July 1999

England 2
Howard 21, Chopra 74

Argentina 1
Lizardia 65
14,000

This was the final match of a tournament also involving France. England had been held to 1-1 in the opening match and Argentina had then eliminated France by a single goal. They came here needing a point to win. But England went on to win Wembley's first match at this level for ten years.

England: Allaway, Hylton, Clark - capt, Bowditch, Sherman, Johnson, Spicer, Chopra, Howard, Pennant, Moore. subs: Ostemobor for Johnson 54, Muirhead for Howard 57, Brown for Moore 63, Prince for Pennant 69

FA CHARITY SHIELD

Sunday 1st August 1999

Arsenal   **2-1**   **Manchester United**
Kanu pen 67, Parlour 77   Beckham 36
70,185
Referee: G Barber (Tring)

This was the first occasion that two club sides had faced each other in consecutive Charity Shields. United had a score to settle after Arsenal's emphatic victory the previous year but they still held the record of ten outright wins, the last of which was in 1997.

Although they were the holders, Arsenal had finished the previous season without a trophy as United won the' treble'. United had won the FA Carling Premiership for the fifth time in seven years by a point from Arsenal. The Gunners had won the previous year's title by a point from United, emphasising the fact that these two teams were very closely matched.

Despite the early start to the season, United were much sharper than in the previous year's fixture and took the lead with a superb free kick from 30 yards from David Beckham which hit the bar and bounced down over the line.

Midway through the second half Arsenal won a penalty when Irwin stopped Vieira by pulling the Frenchman's shirt. Nwankwo Kanu sent Bosnich the wrong way from the spot. Ten minutes later Kanu sent Ray Parlour through to beat Bosnich, the ball going in off a post. It was enough to give United their first defeat of 1999 and Arsenal their second successive Charity Shield.

Arsenal were back at Wembley three times before the end of the year but they again flopped in the Champions League, this time failing to reach the last 16. Their consolation was entry into the UEFA Cup, where they reached the final, before losing on penalties to Galatasaray in Copenhagen, following a disappointing goalless draw after extra time.

United became the first British club to win the World Club Championship when they defeated South American Champions Palmeiras 1-0 in Tokyo. They lost the European Super Cup to Lazio in Monaco but went on to retain the Premiership by a record 18 points from Arsenal, runners-up for the second successive year.

Arsenal: Manninger, Dixon, Keown, Grimandi, Winterburn - capt, Parlour, Vieira, Petit, Silvinho, Kanu, Ljungberg. subs: Boa Morte for Silvinho 64, Luzhny for Parlour 89. manager: Arsene Wenger
Manchester U: Bosnich, Neville (P), Berg, Stam, Irwin - capt, Beckham, Scholes, Butt, Cruyff, Yorke, Cole. subs: May for Stam 46, Solskjaer for Cruyff 61, Sheringham for Butt 81. manager: Sir Alex Ferguson

EUROPEAN CHAMPIONSHIP QUALIFYING

Saturday 4th September 1999

England   **6-0**   **Luxembourg**
Shearer (pen) 12, 28, 34,
McManaman 30, 44, Owen 90
68,772
Referee: S Shmolik (Belarus)

England lay third, in Group Five and their only realistic hope was to qualify for the play-offs as runners-up. To do that they had first to dispose of little Luxembourg as they had in every previous meeting. It was Luxembourg's first visit since their humiliating 9-0 defeat in 1982. England had won 3-0 in Luxembourg the previous year and the minnows were still searching vainly for their first point.

Hopes were fading that they could reproduce their achievement from the previous European Championship when, for the first time in their history they did not finish bottom of a qualifying group. The highlight of that campaign was an astonishing 1-0 victory against the eventual finalists the Czech Republic in Luxembourg.

The expected goal rush began when Dyer was tripped in the area by Birsens. Alan Shearer calmly tucked the penalty into the opposite corner to the 'keeper.

Shearer's second came when he took a pass from Fowler and the power of his shot was too much for Felgen. Luxembourg began to crumble and within two minutes they were three goals down. Shearer tried to flick on Parlour's low cross at the near post with his heel but the ball ran to Steve McManaman who slotted it into an empty net.

England scored again when Shearer got ahead of his markers to turn in Dyer's cross for a first half hat-trick. Just before the interval, McManaman headed his second from Batty's chipped cross. All five goals had come from the right. Substitute Michael Owen then wrapped up things in added time, playing a one-two with McManaman before superbly curling it past Felgen.

Sweden's victory over Bulgaria in Stockholm a few hours later ended England's remote mathematical chance of winning the group and left them contesting the runners-up spot with Poland. A goalless draw in Warsaw four days later proved enough for England but they had to wait a further month for Poland to lose their last game in Stockholm before qualifying for the play-offs on aggregate.

Although they had scraped through England could at least point to the facts that they were top scorers in the group and they were the only team to take a point from Sweden. Luxembourg again failed to win a point. As fate would have it Scotland now stood between England and a place in 'Euro 2000'.

England: Martyn (Leeds Utd), Dyer* (Newcastle), Pearce (West Ham), Adams (Arsenal), Keown (Arsenal), Parlour (Arsenal), Beckham (Man Utd), Batty (Leeds Utd), McManaman (Real Madrid), Shearer (Newcastle) – capt, Fowler (Liverpool). subs: Neville (G) (Man Utd) for Dyer 46, Neville (P) (Man Utd) for Adams 65, Owen (Liverpool) for Beckham 65. head coach: Kevin Keegan
*first cap.

Luxembourg: Felgen (Jeunesse Esch), Birsens (Union Luxembourg) – capt, Funck (Dudelange), Schauls (Jeunesse Esch), Ferron (Etzella Ettelbruck), Vanek (Avenir Beggen), Saibene (Swift Hesperange), Theis (Spora Luxembourg), Posing (Dudelange), Schneider (Jeunesse Esch), Christophe (Mondercange). subs: Alverdi (Grevenmacher) for Schneider 46, Zaritski (Agios Nikolaos) for Christophe 61, Deville (Mondercange) for Posing 82. coach: Paul Philipp

Final table	P	W	D	L	F	A	Pts
Sweden	8	7	1	0	10	1	22
England	8	3	4	1	14	4	13
Poland	8	4	1	3	12	8	13
Bulgaria	8	2	2	4	6	8	8
Luxembourg	8	0	0	8	2	23	0

UEFA Champions League

Wednesday 22nd September 1999

Arsenal 3
Ljungberg 27, Henry 89, Suker 90

AIK Stockholm 1
Nordin 52
71,227
Referee: V Pereira (Portugal)

Despite the disappointments of the previous year, Arsenal again moved to Wembley for their Champions League campaign. In the now greatly expanded competition, they had begun Group B by drawing in Florence although Kanu had missed a penalty. Stockholm, meanwhile, had surrendered all three points at home to Barcelona despite leading with five minutes left.

The previous year's Swedish League Champions had won their title by scoring fewer goals than the team finishing bottom of the Swedish First Division so were expected to be more defensive. But they were breached in the first half by a Swedish international, Freddie Ljungberg.

They equalised through Nordin and held Arsenal until added time, when substitute Thierry Henry and Davor Suker, the Croatian who was top scorer at the previous year's World Cup, finally broke through. It made a pleasant change for Arsenal who had three times conceded late goals in the previous year's competition. They beat AIK in the final match of the group in Stockholm two months later, as the Swedes finished bottom.

Arsenal: Manninger, Dixon, Winterburn, Adams – capt, Keown, Grimandi, Vieira, Ljungberg, Overmars, Bergkamp, Suker. subs: Silvinho for Grimandi 55, Henry for Ljungberg 68, Kanu for Overmars 68. manager: Arsene Wenger
AIK Stockholm: Asper, Kaamark, Nordin - capt, Lagerlof, Andersson (O), Brundin, Andersson (A), Novakovic, Gustafsson, Tjernstrom, Ljung. subs: Kjolo for Kaamark 46, Aslund for Novakovic 81, Corneliusson for Andersson (O) 89. coach: Stuart Baxter

347

Tuesday 19th October 1999

Arsenal 2
Bergkamp 44, Overmars 84

Barcelona 4
Rivaldo pen 15, Luis Enrique 16, Figo 56, Cocu 69
73,091
Referee: U Meier (Switzerland)

Barcelona returned to the scene of their greatest triumph with a two point lead over Arsenal at the top of Group B. The 1992 winners had been held at home to a 1-1 draw by the Gunners the previous month but this was to be a night where they got the breaks to qualify for the last 16.

Barcelona were Spanish League Champions for the second year in succession and had won a fourth European Cup-Winners Cup in 1997, a record that could never be beaten because the competition was now defunct.

They got off to a perfect start at Wembley when Tony Adams was adjudged to have fouled Philip Cocu although television suggested it was outside the box and that there was no contact. They doubled the lead seconds later when Adams slipped, allowing Luis Enrique to score. Adams' misery was complete when he later missed an open goal while Cocu wrapped up the points for the visitors. The goals from Arsenal's own Dutch stars came too late.

Barcelona's adventurous counter-attacking paid dividends in an open game, packed with goalmouth incidents. They won the group, the following week, and finished with twelve goals in their last three games. Arsenal were left to battle for the runners-up spot in the group with Fiorentina who had gone above them on goal difference on the same night and were

due at Wembley, the following week.

Arsenal: Seaman, Dixon, Winterburn, Keown, Adams – capt, Parlour, Vieira, Ljungberg, Overmars, Kanu, Bergkamp. subs: Upson for Keown 73, Suker for Ljungberg 76, Henry for Kanu 76. manager: Arsene Wenger
Barcelona: Arnau, Abelardo, Bogarde, Sergi, Reiziger, Guardiola - capt, Luis Enrique, Cocu, Rivaldo, Figo, Kluivert. subs: Gabri for Luis Enrique 70, Dehu for Guardiola 90, Zenden for Cocu 90. coach: Louis Van Gaal

Wednesday 27th October 1999

Arsenal 0
Fiorentina 1
Batistuta 75
73,336
Referee: M Lubos (Slovakia)

Arsenal crashed out of the competition after a powerful shot from Gabriel Batistuta inflicted on them their second home defeat in successive weeks. Fiorentina thus clinching the runners-up spot to Barcelona.

Kanu had missed a penalty in Florence in the goalless opening game of the group, but again it was their Wembley form which let them down. They finished with a win the following week in Stockholm having already secured the third place which allowed them to enter the UEFA Cup.

The Wembley experiment had come to a disappointing end. Arsenal returned to Highbury for a more successful UEFA Cup campaign, which ended when they lost the final on penalties to Galatasaray after extra time in Copenhagen.

Arsenal: Seaman, Dixon, Winterburn, Adams – capt, Keown, Petit, Vieira, Parlour, Overmars, Bergkamp, Kanu. subs: Ljungberg for Parlour 56, Vivas for Petit 59, Suker for Dixon 73. manager: Arsene Wenger
Fiorentina: Toldo, Repka, Firicano, Heinrich, Rossitto, Cois, Di Livio, Pierini, Rui Costa, Batistuta – capt, Chiesa. sub: Adani for Cois 46. coach: Giovanni Trapattoni

---

EUROPEAN CHAMPIONSHIP QUALIFYING

Play-off Second Leg

Wednesday 17th November 1999

England	0-1	Scotland
		Hutchison 38

England win 2-1 on aggregate.
75,848
Referee: P Collina (Italy)

Wembley's last international of the century was fittingly between the two countries which had contested Wembley's first international in 1924. England's 2-0 victory at Hampden Park, Glasgow in the first leg four days earlier had taken some of the

---

edge off this fixture as England were now expected to cruise through to the following year's European Championship in Belgium and the Netherlands.

England reached this position after struggling through their group on aggregate from Poland nine points behind the group winners Sweden. Scotland arrived at the stadium, where their hopes in the last European Championship had been all but extinguished, hoping to at least restore some pride. They had not beaten their rivals since the 1985 Rous Cup and had not won at Wembley since 1981.

They had been hoping to reach their third successive European Championship after finishing runners-up to the Czech Republic in Group Nine. Scotland finished twelve points behind the Czechs but in Prague five months earlier had been the only team to take the lead against them when they went two goals up before losing 3-2. The Czechs won every game, but Scotland finished seven points clear of the rest of the group.

With seven minutes remaining in the first half, Scotland got themselves right back into the tie by taking the lead. Don Hutchison rose above Adams to reach McCann's cross and send a downward header past Seaman. It was Scotland's first goal against England in six matches.

The rest of the match was played on a knife edge for the home side and with so much at stake they gave a very nervous performance. But Scotland could not muster a second, so despite their first defeat under Kevin Keegan England limped into the finals.

Scotland took great pride from their first Wembley victory for 18 years but they were left to concentrate on qualifying for the 2002 World Cup. England now had to convince the country that they could make an impression in 'Euro 2000'.

One odd thing to note was that this was the last occasion that England wore white shirts at Wembley. For each of the remaining four games in the following year they wore red.

England: Seaman (Arsenal), Campbell (Tottenham), Neville (P) (Man Utd), Ince (Middlesbrough), Adams (Arsenal), Southgate (Aston Villa), Beckham (Man Utd), Scholes (Man Utd), Shearer (Newcastle) – capt, Owen (Liverpool), Redknapp (Liverpool). subs: Heskey (Leicester) for Owen 64, Parlour (Arsenal) for Scholes 89. head coach: Kevin Keegan
Scotland: Sullivan (Wimbledon), Weir (Everton), Davidson (Blackburn), Dailly (Blackburn), Hendry (Rangers) – capt, Ferguson (Rangers), Dodds (Dundee Utd), Burley (Celtic), McCann (Rangers), Hutchison (Everton), Collins (Everton). sub: Burchill (Celtic) for McCann 74. coach: Craig Brown

Thursday 25th November 1999

The second Burton Wembley Challenge Tournament was won by the News of the World who beat GQ, the holders, by a single goal in the final. This was another corporate tournament held at the stadium for employees of newspapers and magazines plus the sponsors Burton Menswear. In the previous year's event, there were no newspapers represented and Esquire and FHM competed with GQ and the sponsors.

INTERNATIONAL

Wednesday 23rd February 2000

England	0-0	Argentina

74,008
Referee: M Merk (Germany)

Argentina's first visit since 1991 brought back vivid memories of the latest in a classic series of World Cup encounters. The South Americans had beaten England in St Etienne on penalties after extra time in the last 16 of the 1998 tournament in which England had bravely battled on with ten men after David Beckham was sent off for kicking out at Diego Simeone at the beginning of the second half. Both players took part in this match.

It was now almost 20 years since England had last beaten Argentina but Wembley's first match of the new century saw a much improved England from the team which struggled against Scotland their last match of the previous millennium.

They were much sharper and they created some good chances, as did their opponents but neither side could find that vital touch to break the deadlock.

England: Seaman (Arsenal), Campbell (Tottenham), Keown (Arsenal), Southgate (Aston Villa), Dyer (Newcastle), Wilcox (Leeds Utd), Wise (Chelsea), Beckham (Man Utd), Scholes (Man Utd), Heskey (Leicester), Shearer (Newcastle) – capt. subs: Ferdinand (West Ham) for Keown 46, Neville (P) (Man Utd) for Dyer 58, Parlour (Arsenal) for Beckham 72, Phillips (Sunderland) for Shearer 77, Cole (Man Utd) for Heskey 79. head coach: Kevin Keegan
Argentina: Cavallero (Espanol), Sensini (Lazio) - capt, Arruabarrena (Boca Juniors), Zanetti (Internazionale), Chamot (AC Milan), Ayala (AC Milan), Simeone (Lazio), Veron (Lazio), Gonzalez (Valencia), Batistuta (Fiorentina), Ortega (Parma). subs: Pochettino (Espanol) for Sensini 34, Crespo (Parma) for Batistuta 56, Vivas (Celta Vigo) for Arruabarrena 67, Lopez (Celta Vigo) for Ortega 90. coach: Marcelo Bielsa

LEAGUE CUP FINAL

Sunday 27th February 2000

Leicester City	2-1	Tranmere Rovers

Elliott 29, 81 — Kelly 77
74,313
Referee: A Wilkie (Chester-le-Street)
sub: P Richards (Preston) 57

Although this was Leicester's third final in four years and their seventh Wembley appearance in nine years, they had yet to win a major trophy at the stadium. They had won two play-off finals at Wembley and had twice won the competition previously, first over two legs and then after a replay. In the previous year's final they had conceded an added time winner despite playing against ten men for the last half-hour.

Tranmere were appearing in their first ever major final although they had appeared at Wembley several times before and their semi-final victory had been at the expense of Bolton Wanderers, the team they had beaten on their last Wembley visit in the 1991 Third Division play-off final. Tranmere had never played in the top division and were attempting to become the lowest placed club to win the League Cup for 31 years.

So Leicester were favourites and went ahead when Matt Elliott darted around the penalty box to avoid Challinor and met Guppy's corner with a header which hit the bar but spun into the net off Murphy's hand. Referee Alan Wilkie went off injured with a pulled calf muscle in the second half and his replacement took just seven minutes to make his mark when he sent off Clint Hill for bringing down Emile Heskey. The odds were now to be stacked against the First Division club but with 13 minutes left Jones headed on Roberts' free kick to David Kelly who beat Flowers at the near post to equalise.

As in the previous year's final Leicester were struggling to beat ten men but they were soon back in front. Once again Elliott outjumped Challinor to another Guppy corner to head the winner at the unguarded far post.

Leicester: Flowers, Sinclair, Elliott – capt, Taggart, Guppy, Savage, Lennon, Izzet, Oakes, Heskey, Cottee. subs: Impey for Oakes 77, Marshall for Cottee 89, Gilchrist, Zagorakis, Arphexad (gk) (not used). manager: Martin O'Neill
Tranmere: Murphy, Hazell, Challinor, Hill, Roberts, Parkinson, Henry, Taylor, Jones, Mahon, Kelly - capt. subs: Yates for Parkinson 66, Black, Morgan, Thompson, Achterberg (gk) (not used). manager: John Aldridge

Under-18 Schools International

Saturday 25th March 2000

England 0
Hungary 1
Szabo 30
Referee: S Hames (Aberdare)

The first Hungarian team to win at Wembley since the great 1953 side brought the curtain down on matches at this level at the stadium after only two fixtures. England lost both although once again they were pitted against a nation's finest young professionals already signed up by top clubs. England's players, by contrast, were still in full-time education and were only beaten by a swerving shot, which the goalkeeper Ben Williams failed to gather.

England: Williams, Burke, Coyle - capt, Feely, Nicholls, Thompson, Onions, Willock, Barkley, Borley, Schofield. subs: Potter for Williams 56, Barrett for Onions 65, Rowland for Borley 72, Ward for Schofield 72, Rhodes for Barkley 82

FA Cup Semi-finals

Sunday 2nd April 2000

Aston Villa 0
Bolton Wanderers 0

After extra time
Aston Villa won 4-1 on penalties.
(Stone 1-0, Holdsworth 1-1, Hendrie 2-1, Johnston saved, Barry 3-1, Johansen saved, Dublin 4-1)
62,828
Referee: D Elleray (Harrow)

Villa's last trip to Wembley was in 1996 when they won their second Coca-Cola Cup in three years. Their last FA Cup appearance at the stadium was in 1957, their last victory. Bolton had been Wembley's first winners in 1923 and had hopes too of being the last in front of the twin towers. Their last FA Cup win had been in 1958. They had not reached the semi-finals since.

Bolton were chasing promotion back to the Premiership after relegation in 1998. They had appeared at Wembley in the previous year's play-off final but lost to Watford.

Wembley's first semi-final for six years was a drab affair and it took 109 minutes to come to life when Villa's Mark Delaney was sent off, his foul on Allan Johnston being his second bookable offence. Bolton saw their chance to become the first finalists from outside the top division since 1992 and within two minutes Holdsworth had hit the post from the free kick. Then, in their next attack he astonishingly fired over the bar when it looked easier to score. Gudjohnsen had rounded James and left Holdsworth with Southgate and Barry to beat on the line. Villa hit the post themselves but it was penalties which finally decided the tie.

Holdsworth showed he could find the net but David James saved from both Johnston and Michael Johansen and it was left for substitute Dion Dublin to fire Villa into their first final for 43 years.

Aston V: James, Ehiogu, Southgate – capt, Barry, Delaney, Taylor, Boateng, Wright, Merson, Joachim, Carbone. subs: Stone for Taylor 13, Dublin for Carbone 70, Hendrie for Boateng 119, Samuel, Enckelman (gk) (not used). manager: John Gregory

Bolton: Jaaskelainen, Bergsson, Fish – capt, Ritchie, Whitlow, Johansen, Jensen, Elliott, Johnston, Gudjohnsen, Holdsworth. subs: Warhurst for Jensen 62, O'Kane for Bergsson 91, Hansen, Passi, Banks (gk) (not used). manager: Sam Allardyce

Sunday 9th April 2000

Chelsea 2
Poyet 17, 72
Newcastle United 1
Lee 66
73,876
Referee: D Gallagher (Banbury)

Chelsea had won a Wembley semi-final on the last occasion they had been played at the stadium six years earlier to the day and they had won the trophy as recently as 1997. They had followed that with a Coca-Cola Cup final victory a year later.

Newcastle were attempting to reach their third successive final after two very disappointing displays and a string of other Wembley defeats stretching back to 1974.

Despite an array of top internationals, Chelsea had disappointed in the Premiership and faced a battle to match their third place of the previous year. They had reached the Champions League quarter-finals, however, in their first ever appearance in the competition and four days earlier they had beaten Barcelona (conquerors of Arsenal at Wembley) 3-1 in the first leg. Newcastle, with their third manager in as many years, were again in mid-table.

Quick passing ended with Weah putting Gustavo Poyet through and the Uruguayan lobbed Given to put Chelsea ahead. Newcastle, anxious to avoid a third successive Wembley defeat in the FA Cup, fought their way back and deservedly equalised when Robert Lee met Shearer's cross to head home.

Chelsea were to cruelly deny them, however, and six minutes later Poyet rose to power Harley's cross past Given for his second. Newcastle could not find another goal and Chelsea, rather fortunately, held on to win despite being outplayed at times.

Ten days later, Chelsea lost the second leg in Barcelona, 5-1 after extra time, leaving the FA Cup final the following month as their last chance of a trophy.

Chelsea: De Goey, Ferrer, Desailly, Leboeuf, Harley, Di Matteo, Deschamps, Wise – capt, Poyet, Sutton, Weah. subs: Flo for Sutton 46, Petrescu for Ferrer 75, Zola for Weah 79, Hogh, Cudicini (gk) (not used). manager: Gianluca Vialli

Newcastle: Given, Barton, Howey, Dabizas, Hughes, Solano, Lee, Speed, Dyer, Shearer – capt, Ferguson. subs: Domi for Ferguson 39, Ketsbaia for Hughes 79, Gavilan, Goma, Harper (gk) (not used). manager: Bobby Robson

Auto Windscreens Shield

Sunday 16th April 2000

Bristol City 1
Spencer 73
Stoke City 2
Kavanagh 31, Thorne 81
75,057
Referee: K Lynch (Kirk Hammerton)

Bristol City became the first club to reach three finals in this competition, although it was their first since 1987, when as holders they were beaten on penalties. But Stoke went on to lift the Shield, having previously won the competition in 1992. This was the last final to be played at the old stadium which had given so many lower division clubs the opportunity to taste Wembley glory.

Bristol C: Mercer, Carey, Jordan, Millen - capt, Bell, Murray, Holland, Tinnion, Brown, Thorpe, Beadle. subs: Spencer for Brown 68, Amankwaah for Carey 87, Burnell, Hill, Phillips (gk) (not used). manager: Tony Fawthrop
Stoke: Ward, Hansson, Mohan, Gunnarsson, Clarke, Gudjonsson, Kavanagh, O'Connor, Gunnlaugsson, Thorne, Lightbourne. subs: Dryden for Gunnlaugsson 62, Iwelumo for Lightbourne 89, Jacobsen, Melton, Muggleton (gk) (not used). manager: Gudjon Thordarson

Youth Alliance Cup Final

Sunday 16th April 2000

Scunthorpe United 0
West Bromwich Albion 0
West Bromwich Albion won 3-2 on penalties.
(Mulchinock 1-0, Ball saved, Masson 2-0, Briggs 2-1, Sparrow saved, Richards 2-2, Barwick saved, Morris 2-3, Anderson hit post)

An hour or so after the end of the Auto Windscreens Shield final, the stadium staged its first and only Youth Alliance Cup final with about 700 allowed in to see it. West Brom's Mark Briggs hit the bar in added time but they looked out of it in the penalties when Leigh Herrick saved from Jamie Ball and Scunthorpe went two up.

Elliott Morris then proved a real hero by stopping Scunthorpe's next two from Matt Sparrow and Terry Barwick before netting himself.

Mark Anderson hit the post with Scunthorpe's fifth and West Brom were the winners. Their coach John Trewick had been in Oxford United's Milk Cup winning side at Wembley in 1986.

Scunthorpe: Herrick, Pugh, Ridley (S), Cotterill, McCombe, Ridley (L) - capt, Graves, Barwick, Anderson, Marsh, Sparrow. subs: Maddison for Graves 60, Burraway for Cotterill 71, Masson for Marsh.
West Brom: Morris, Watson, Ball, Chambers (A), Mkaudaware, Adams, Collins, Briggs, Perry, Richards, McFarland. subs: Chambers (J) for Chambers (A), Iezzi for Collins, Scott for Perry. coach: John Trewick

Carlsberg Pub Cup Final

Saturday 6th May 2000

Earl Soham Victoria 2
Aldis (R), Yeomans
Eastleigh 1
Fernandez
Referee: G Courtney (Spennymoor)

Wembley's last Pub Cup final was played prior to its last FA Vase final and saw the trophy stay in Suffolk after Earl Soham had knocked out the holders Sizewell in an early round.

In the final, their defence had to be at its best to withstand some fierce attacks from Hampshire's Eastleigh Social Club.

Like Sizewell, Earl Soham went on to reach the final of the European Pub Cup in Arnhem the following month before losing to a Swedish team.

It was the 16th and last Wembley refereeing experience for referee George Courtney, now 59.

FA Vase Final

Saturday 6th May 2000

Chippenham Town 0
Deal Town 1
Graham 87
20,083
Referee: D Laws (Whitley Bay)

For the third year in succession a single late goal was enough to win the Vase. This last Wembley final after 25 years was settled by Roly Graham's fine volley.

Chippenham: Jones, James, Murphy, Burns - capt, Andrews, Collier, Woods, Charity, Brown, Tweedle, Godley. subs: Cutler for Godley 69, Tiley for James 89, Godwin for Brown 90
Deal: Tucker, Monteith, Best, Kempster, Ash, Seager, Martin - capt, Graham, Ribbens, Marshall, Lovell. subs: Roberts for Monteith 10, Turner for Lovell 58, Warden for Ash 73

FA Trophy Final

Saturday 13th May 2000

Kettering Town 2
Vowden 55, Norman pen 64

Kingstonian 3
Akuamoah 40, 69, Simba 75
20,034
Referee: S Dunn (Gloucester)

An exciting last final at the stadium after 30 years saw holders Kingstonian take the lead but then fall behind, before coming back to retain the Trophy. The winner was scored by 38-year-old Amara Simba, a French International who had appeared as a substitute against England at Wembley in 1992 and was on loan from Leyton Orient with whom he had played in the previous year's Third Division play-off final.

Kingstonian's victory was a fifth in seven years for manager Geoff Chapple, who won three times with Woking. For Kettering it was their second Trophy final defeat.

Kettering: Solitt, Perkins, Vowden – capt, Norman, Shutt, Brown, Fisher, Adams, Setchell, McNamara, Watkins. subs: Hudson for Watkins 46, Diuk for Norman 73, Hopkins for Setchell 80
Kingstonian: Farrelly, Stewart, Crossley – capt, Harris, Mustafa, Pitcher, Kadi, Luckett, Simba, Akuamoah, Green. subs: Saunders for Stewart 75, Leworthy for Kadi 82, Basford for Green 85

FA CUP FINAL

Saturday 20th May 2000

Aston Villa 0-1 **Chelsea 1**
Di Matteo 72

78,217
Referee: G Poll (Tring)

After 77 years of magical memories Wembley Stadium hosted its last FA Cup final before being rebuilt. Villa had not won the trophy since 1957, their seventh victory. Chelsea had won it twice, most recently in 1997.

Sadly, the old Wembley's last Cup final was not memorable. The first half was poor but Chelsea began to pressurise Villa after the interval and deservedly scored after Zola sent a free kick into a crowded penalty area. James managed to reach it but his punch rebounded off Southgate and Roberto Di Matteo crashed it into the roof of the net.

Wembley was a happy place for the Italian. He had scored a sensational first minute goal in the 1997 final and had netted in the following year's Coca-Cola Cup final. Sadly Roberto Di Matteo's career was ended the following season when against St Gallen in the UEFA Cup his leg was badly broken and he was forced to retire at the age of 30.

Villa failed to reply but at least Wembley could proudly claim that it never staged a goalless FA Cup final. Chelsea's captain Dennis Wise took his four-month-old son up to the Royal Box with him to receive the Cup.

Chelsea reached the final again in 2002 in Cardiff, but by the time the new Wembley was ready they had grown into an unstoppable Premiership force.

Aston V: James, Ehiogu, Southgate – capt, Barry, Delaney, Boateng, Merson, Taylor, Wright, Dublin, Carbone. subs: Stone for Taylor 79, Joachim for Carbone 79, Hendrie for Wright 88, Samuel, Enckelman (gk) (not used). manager: John Gregory
Chelsea: De Goey, Melchiot, Desailly, Leboeuf, Babayaro, Poyet, Wise – capt, Deschamps, Di Matteo, Zola, Weah. subs: Flo for Weah 87, Morris for Zola 90, Harley, Terry, Cudicini (gk) (not used). manager: Gianluca Vialli

Play-offs

Third Division
Friday 26th May 2000

Darlington 0
Peterborough United 1
Clarke 74

33,383
Referee: M Dean (Heswall)

On a very wet night the fifth successive 1-0 scoreline for this final took Peterborough into the Second Division after three years in the basement. Darlington had been the unfortunate losers in 1996, while Peterborough had won promotion to the First Division via the play-offs on their only previous visit in 1992.

The north-east of England was one region happy to see Wembley demolished. Since Sunderland's 1973 FA Cup win, four of the league clubs from that area had not managed a single win between them in 15 visits. Newcastle United had lost six, Middlesbrough and Sunderland three apiece and Darlington twice. Only Boro had managed a draw and then lost the replay.

Darlington: Collett, Liddle, Tutill, Aspin, Heckingbottom, Gray, Oliver, Atkinson, Heaney, Gabbiadini - capt, Duffield. subs: Naylor for Heckingbottom 68, Nogan for Duffield 83, Holsgrove for Atkinson 86, Brumwell, Samways (gk) (not used). manager: David Hodgson

Peterborough: Tyler, Drury, Scott, Edwards - capt, Farrell, Clarke, Cullen, Jelleyman, Castle, Rea, Oldfield. subs: Hanlon for Drury 43, Green for Clarke 89, Gill, Wicks, Griemink (gk) (not used). manager: Barry Fry

INTERNATIONAL

Saturday 27th May 2000

England	1-1	Brazil

Owen 38

Franca 44

73,956

Referee: R Wojcik (Poland)

England welcomed the winners of the last two South American Championships for their last Wembley visit before the old stadium was knocked down. Brazil had won their last two meetings, in the 1995 Umbro Cup and in Paris two years later and they had not lost to England since 1990.

Following a delay of half an hour because of congestion on the London Underground, England scored a superb opener. Gary Neville's long throw was headed on by Beckham to Shearer who chested down before slipping the ball through the legs of Aldair to Michael Owen.

The young striker showed his class when, instead of shooting with his left foot, he trapped it with his right, sending Ze Roberto off in the wrong direction, and in an instant turned sharply to fire under the despairing dive of Dida. Owen had scored against Brazil Schoolboys at Wembley five years earlier.

England's defence then went to sleep and conceded an equaliser right on halftime. Seaman came out to meet Rivaldo's corner but the ball sailed over him to Franca whose header beat Gary Neville at the far post. There was no further scoring but England were satisfied by holding the Brazilians.

Two years later Owen scored against Brazil in the World Cup quarter-final in Shizuoka but Seaman was caught out by another lofted set-piece, this time from Ronaldinho, and Brazil went on to regain the World Cup.

England: Seaman (Arsenal), Neville (G) (Man Utd), Keown (Arsenal), Campbell (Tottenham), Neville (P) (Man Utd), Beckham (Man Utd), Scholes (Man Utd), Ince (Middlesbrough), Wise (Chelsea), Shearer (Newcastle) – capt, Owen (Liverpool). subs: Parlour (Arsenal) for Ince 60, Fowler (Liverpool) for Shearer 84, Phillips (Sunderland) for Owen 84, Barmby (Everton) for Parlour 90. head coach: Kevin Keegan

Brazil: Dida (Corinthians), Cafu (Roma) - capt, Antonio Carlos (Roma), Aldair (Roma), Silvinho (Arsenal), Cesar Sampaio (Palmeiras), Emerson (Bayer Leverkusen), Ze Roberto (Bayer Leverkusen), Rivaldo (Barcelona), Amoroso (Parma), Franca (Sao Paulo). subs: Roberto Carlos (Real Madrid) for Silvinho 60, Denilson (Real Betis) for Amoroso 68, Carvalho (Portuguesa) for Antonio Carlos 81. coach: Wanderley Luxemburgo

Play-offs

Second Division
Sunday 28th May 2000

Gillingham 3
McGibbon og 35, Butler 114, Thomson 118

Wigan Athletic 2
Haworth 52, Barlow pen 99

After extra time
53,764
Referee: R Styles (Waterlooville)

With both sides determined to win promotion to the First Division for the first time drama was almost guaranteed and with more heavy rain cutting up the Wembley turf they did not disappoint.

Gillingham's fans had endured terrible heartbreak, the previous year when losing the final on penalties to Manchester City despite holding a two-goal lead in the last minute. They were again to experience a wide range of emotions before finally fulfilling their dream in a thrilling match.

Wigan had lost to Manchester City in the previous year's semi-finals but had beaten Millwall at Wembley in the 1999 Auto Windscreens Shield final and defeated them again to secure a return to Wembley.

When Kevin Sharp was sent off for a late tackle on Nicky Southall four minutes from the end,with the score 1-1 it looked like the game had tilted in Gillingham's favour and so it proved although it was Wigan who surprisingly struck first.

Then two goals in the last six minutes put Gillingham in the First Division and left Wigan to reflect on a game snatched from their grasp in a similar vein to the previous year's final.

Gillingham manager, Peter Taylor left to join Leicester City in the Premiership shortly afterwards but they survived his departure and held their own in the First Division.

In 2003 Wigan finally achieved their goal in style by winning the Second Division Championship and as Gillingham were returning to what was now League One in 2005, Wigan were securing promotion to the Premiership for the first time.

Gillingham: Bartram, Pennock - capt, Edge, Ashby, Butters, Southall, Hessenthaler, Lewis, Gooden, Asaba, Onuora. subs: Smith for Edge 61, Thomson for Onuora 97, Butler for Ashby 105, Nosworthy, Mautone (gk) (not used). manager: Peter Taylor

Wigan: Stillie, Green, McGibbon, Balmer - capt, De Zeeuw, Sharp, Kilford, Redfearn, Sheridan, Haworth, Liddell. subs: Barlow for Redfearn 84, Bradshaw for Liddell 105, Peron for Haworth 106, Griffiths, Carroll (gk) (not used). manager: John Benson

First Division
Monday 29th May 2000

Barnsley 2
R Wright og 6, Hignett pen 78

Ipswich Town 4
Mowbray 28, Naylor 52, Stewart 58, Reuser 90
73,427
Referee: T Heilbron (Newton Aycliffe)

Wembley's last play-off final before the stadium's demolition maintained its reputation for high drama. Barnsley were ahead after six minutes on their first Wembley visit when Craig Hignett's shot rebounded from the bar and the goalkeeper before going in. They then had a glorious chance in first-half added time to regain the lead but Richard Wright saved Darren Barnard's penalty.

Ipswich, on their first trip to the stadium since a Charity Shield thrashing 22 years earlier were appearing in the play-offs for the fourth year in succession. Having finally reached Wembley, they seized the opportunity and overpowered Barnsley in the second half with two substitutes scoring and Marcus Stewart, who had scored for Bristol Rovers in the 1995 Second Division final, getting the other.

Although Barnsley converted a second penalty, Martijn Reuser scored Ipswich's fourth in added time and they could rightly claim that justice had been done, after two successive finishes in third place.

Of the previous ten winners of this play-off only two had avoided relegation the following year but Ipswich were to buck the trend. They finished fifth and even qualified for the UEFA Cup although in 2002 they were relegated back to the Nationwide League as Barnsley dropped into the Second Division.

Five days after this match, Richard Wright made his England debut in Malta and conceded two more penalties. The first rebounded off the post and Wright before going in and he saved the second.

Barnsley: Miller, Curtis, Morgan, Chettle, Brown, Barnard, Tinkler, Hignett - capt, Appleby, Dyer, Shipperley. subs: Thomas for Tinkler 60, Hristov for Dyer 64, Eaden for Curtis 71, Jones, Sheron (not used). manager: Dave Bassett

Ipswich: Wright (R), Croft, McGreal, Mowbray, Venus, Clapham, Holland - capt, Magilton, Wright (J), Johnson, Stewart. subs: Naylor for Johnson 22, Reuser for Stewart 83, Wilnis for Wright (J) 89, Brown, Branagan (gk) (not used). manager: George Burley

INTERNATIONAL

Wednesday 31st May 2000

England	**2-0**	**Ukraine**

Fowler 44, Adams 67
55,975
Referee: L Michel (Slovakia)

In England's last home match before travelling to the Netherlands to begin their European Championship campaign they took on the Ukraine for the first time although Ukrainians had previously played against England for the USSR. They had been competing only since 1992 but were getting ever closer to qualifying for a major tournament.

The eventual semi-finalists Croatia had beaten them on aggregate in a play-off for a place in the last World Cup and the fact that they would not be competing in the following month's European Championship came as a shock after they were unbeaten in their qualifying group. They finished runners-up, a point behind World Champions and eventual winners, France, who failed to score against them in their two drawn meetings. The Ukraine then surprisingly lost again in a play-off, this time to Slovenia on aggregate.

A minute before the interval, England took the lead from a Beckham corner. Kernozenko could not hold Shearer's header and Robbie Fowler was on hand to tap the ball in. Another Beckham corner led to England's second when the 'keeper's punch hit Shearer on the arm but fell to Tony Adams making a record 59th Wembley appearance. He fired it past Popov on the line.

Ukraine lost yet another play-off the following year to the eventual finalists Germany and missed out on another World Cup before eventually qualifying for the 2006 tournament in Germany.

England: Martyn (Leeds Utd), Southgate (Aston Villa), Adams (Arsenal), Campbell (Tottenham), Beckham (Man Utd), Gerrard* (Liverpool), Scholes (Man Utd), Neville (P) (Man Utd), McManaman (Real Madrid), Shearer (Newcastle) – capt, Fowler (Liverpool). subs: Heskey (Liverpool) for Fowler 46, Barmby (Everton) for Scholes 74, Barry* (Aston Villa) for Neville 74, Dyer (Newcastle) for Gerrard 82. head coach: Kevin Keegan
*first cap
Ukraine: Kernozenko (Dynamo Kiev), Luzhny (Arsenal) – capt, Dmitrulin (Dynamo Kiev), Vaschuk (Dynamo Kiev), Tymoschuk (Shakhtar Donetsk), Popov (Shakhtar Donetsk), Kandaurov (Benfica), Holovko (Dynamo Kiev), Husin (Dynamo Kiev), Shevchenko (AC Milan), Rebrov (Dynamo Kiev). subs: Moroz (Krivbas) for Kandaurov 63, Vorobey (Shakhtar Donetsk) for Popov 70, Levitski (Shakhtar Donetsk) for Kernozenko 84. coach: Valeri Lobanovsky

Saturday 3rd June 2000

Wembley Stadium became Nike Park for eight days when more than 40,000 children were given the opportunity to take part in coaching sessions and football tournaments on the famous pitch. The most successful teams were invited back to play on the final day.

FA CHARITY SHIELD

Sunday 13th August 2000

Chelsea	**2-0**	**Manchester United**

Hasselbaink 22, Melchiot 72
65,148
Referee: M Riley (Leeds)

Chelsea's third FA Cup win enabled them to take part in the old stadium's last club fixture. They had won the Charity Shield just once before, in 1955 following a 3-0 home win against Newcastle United.

Chelsea's fifth place in the FA Carling Premiership had been a disappointment but they had reached the Champions League quarter-finals on their first entry into the competition before losing to Barcelona after extra time. United had become the first British club to lift the World Club Championship the previous year when beating the South American champions

Palmeiras 1-0 in Tokyo but they were no longer European champions having also lost at home in the quarter-finals to eventual winners Real Madrid. They were still, however, dominating the English game and had retained the Premiership by a record 18 points from Arsenal – their sixth title in eight years. They were also the first team to appear in five consecutive Charity Shields although they had not won it since beating Chelsea in 1997. They had lost the last two to Arsenal, but still held the record of ten outright victories.

Chelsea took a deserved lead when Jimmy Floyd Hasselbaink marked his debut with a goal. A desperate lunge from Stam, who had been on the pitch for only three minutes, deflected the ball over his new 'keeper, Barthez, fresh from winning the European Championship with France the previous month.

United were reduced to ten men after 61 minutes when captain Roy Keane was sent off for cynically chopping down Poyet from behind. Mario Melchiot made it a Dutch 'double' when he took a pass from Stanic, the Croatian making his debut. The defender then made the most of the space to slot the ball into the corner through Stam's legs and beyond the 'keeper's dive for his first goal for the club.

Despite winning five trophies in less than two-and-a-half years, Gianluca Vialli was sacked as Chelsea's manager the following month. He was replaced by Claudio Ranieri, another Italian, and they finished sixth in the Premiership. Chelsea had big ambitions, though, and by 2005 they would be all powerful.

United unwittingly set another record by becoming the first team to lose three successive Charity Shields but, just as they had followed the two previous defeats by winning the Premiership, they ended the season by finally completing a hat-trick of titles, only the fourth club to do so. They finished ten points clear of Arsenal and it was their seventh Premiership title in nine years.

They began the following season at the Millennium Stadium in a record sixth successive Charity Shield but lost to Liverpool, extending their record run of defeats to four. And Arsenal were to stop them taking a fourth successive Premiership.

Chelsea: De Goey, Melchiot, Desailly, Leboeuf, Babayaro, Stanic, Wise – capt, Di Matteo, Poyet, Hasselbaink, Zola. subs: Morris for Di Matteo 70, Gudjohnsen for Zola 73, Le Saux for Poyet 76. manager: Gianluca Vialli
Manchester U: Barthez, Neville (G), Johnsen, Silvestre, Irwin, Beckham, Keane – capt, Scholes, Giggs, Solskjaer, Sheringham. subs: Stam for Silvestre 19, Fortune for Giggs 77, Cole for Solskjaer 69, Yorke for Sheringham 69. manager: Sir Alex Ferguson

WORLD CUP QUALIFYING

Saturday 7th October 2000

England 0-1 Germany
Hamann 14

76,377
Referee: S Braschi (Italy)

Wembley Stadium's last match was fittingly between the nations involved in its most famous event, the 1966 World Cup final. The Germans had been Wembley's most successful foreign visitors, having won three times before breaking English hearts in the European Championship semi-final in 1996. Germany went on to win the final at Wembley to replace any bitter memories of thirty years earlier.

In their recent defence of the European Championship they had uncharacteristically finished bottom of their first round group, winning only one point, their worst performance in the competition for 32 years. England had beaten them in a major tournament for the first time since 1966, by 1-0 in Charleroi, but this was their only success and they also took a first round exit. Germany had already beaten Greece 2-0 in Hamburg the previous month but this was England's opening match in Group Nine.

England's defence was caught sleeping after 14 minutes. Paul Scholes was caught in possession 35 yards out and committed a foul in trying to atone. With Seaman still trying to organise his defenders, Dietmar Hamann shot hard and low. The 'keeper could not get down quick enough and only helped the ball into the net. In a match played in driving rain, England failed to rise to the occasion and the Liverpool midfielder's goal was enough to win the points for Germany.

It was a miserable end to 77 years of magical memories and the performance also signalled the end of Kevin Keegan's time in charge as he resigned immediately after the match. At this stage, the prospects looked very gloomy for England but England's first foreign coach, Sven Goran Eriksson, was appointed the following year and confidence was immediately restored. Eleven months after this defeat, England won the return 5-1 in Munich with a scarcely believable display of attacking prowess. It was Germany's heaviest home defeat ever in a major competition.

England stumbled in their final game, drawing with Greece at Old Trafford, but they won the group on goal difference from Germany. The Germans recovered as usual beat the Ukraine in a play-off and went on to reach the final where they lost to Brazil in Yokohama. England were beaten in Shizuoka also by Brazil.

England: Seaman (Arsenal), Neville (G) (Man Utd), Keown (Arsenal), Adams (Arsenal) – capt, Le Saux (Chelsea), Beckham (Man Utd), Barmby (Liverpool), Scholes (Man Utd), Southgate (Aston Villa), Owen (Liverpool), Cole (Man Utd). subs: Dyer (Newcastle) for Neville 46, Barry (Aston Villa) for Le Saux 77, Parlour (Arsenal) for Beckham 82. head coach: Kevin Keegan

Germany: Kahn (Bayern Munich), Linke (Bayern Munich), Rehmer (Hertha Berlin), Nowotny (Bayer Leverkusen), Ramelow (Bayer Leverkusen), Deisler (Hertha Berlin), Hamann (Liverpool), Scholl (Bayern Munich), Bode (Werder Bremen), Ballack (Bayer Leverkusen), Bierhoff (AC Milan) – capt. sub: Ziege (Liverpool) for Bode 86. coach: Rudi Voeller

Final table	P	W	D	L	F	A	Pts
England	8	5	2	1	16	6	17
Germany	8	5	2	1	14	10	17
Finland	8	3	3	2	12	7	12
Greece	8	2	1	5	7	17	7
Albania	8	1	0	7	5	14	3

The next few weeks saw a hectic schedule of corporate and charity matches played behind closed doors and the famous turf took a battering during a very wet autumn. More than two years passed before work began on the demolition due to financial and political wranglings and the neglected stadium looked a sad sight. Eventually, in September 2002, the bulldozers rolled in and the world-famous Empire Stadium, Wembley, which had stood for almost 80 years, was reduced to a pile of rubble.

As the new stadium was being built, all the FA Cup finals were played at the Millennium Stadium. Arsenal appeared four times and won three. The Worthington Cup final, which became the Carling Cup final in 2004, was also played in Cardiff, with Liverpool winning there twice. In 2002, the FA Charity Shield became the FA Community Shield and Arsenal lifted it twice on four consecutive appearances. The Promotion play-off finals also relocated to Cardiff, as did the LDV Vans Trophy final (formerly the Auto Windscreens Shield final) and was won twice in three years by Blackpool, who also won a play-off final. Villa Park hosted the FA Trophy finals, while the FA Vase final was played at Villa Park for the first two years and then at West Ham, Birmingham and Tottenham.

England went on a nationwide tour, which proved very popular, taking in the following venues:

Villa Park (v Spain 2001, Portugal 2002, Netherlands 2005)

Anfield (v Finland 2001, Paraguay 2002, Uruguay 2006)

Pride Park (v Mexico 2001)

White Hart Lane (v Netherlands 2001)

St James' Park (v Albania 2001, Ukraine 2004, Azerbaijan 2005)

Elland Road (v Italy 2002)

St Mary's Stadium (v Macedonia 2002)

Upton Park (v Australia 2003)

Stadium of Light (v Turkey 2003)

Walkers Stadium (v Serbia and Montenegro 2003)

Riverside Stadium (v Slovakia 2003)

Portman Road (v Croatia 2003)

City of Manchester Stadium (v Japan 2004, Iceland 2004)

The remaining fixtures were all played at Old Trafford.

The Players

Big Match index
An A-Z of all the British
and Irish-based players
who have played in
Wembley's big games

Top 20 scorers at Wembley

Wembley dismissals

Key to competitions

Full list of matches

The Teams

The records of all the
League Clubs to have
played at Wembley

Records of all
teams to have
played at Wembley

Not just a football stadium…

BIG MATCH PLAYER INDEX

This index covers all the British and Irish-based players who appeared in at least one of the following competitions:

Full peacetime internationals, FA Cup Semi-Finals, Finals and Replays, Football League Cup Finals, Full Members Cup Finals, FA Charity Shields, European Cup Finals and European Cup-Winners Cup Finals.

Their appearances in other competitions and as a manager/coach are also included.

Foreign-based players are also included if they made at least one big match appearance while with a British club.

The full list of abbreviations of competitions referenced in this index is as follows:

AC	FA Amateur Cup Final
AI	Amateur International
AIC	Anglo-Italian Cup Final
AT	Autoglass Trophy Final
AWS	Auto Windscreens Shield Final
BAC	British Amateur Championship
BC	British Championship
CEN	FA Centenary Match
CHA	Charity Matches
CCC	Coca-Cola Cup Final
CS	FA Charity Shield
CYC	FA County Youth Cup Final Second Leg
D3S	Football League Third Division South
EACQ	European Amateur Championship Qualifying
EC	European Cup
ECH	European Championship
ECQ	European Championship Qualifying
ECW	European Cup-Winners Cup Final
EEC	European Economic Community Celebration Match
EFC	European Fairs Cup
EYT	European Youth Tournament Final
FAC	FA Cup
FAT	FA Trophy Final
FAV	FA Vase Final
FLC	Football League Cup Final
FLWC	Football League War Cup Final
FMC	Full Members Cup Final
FRT	Freight Rover Trophy Final
INT	Internationals
IT	International Trial
IV	Inter-Varsity Matches
LC	Littlewoods Cup Final
LCEN	Football League Centenary Match
LCT	Football League Centenary Tournament
LDC	Leyland Daf Cup Final
LSC	Football League South Cup Final
LWC	London War Cup Final

MC	Milk Cup Final
MCC	Middlesex Charity Cup Final
MT	Makita Tournament
NIN	FA 90th Anniversary Match
OLY	Olympic Games
OQ	Olympic Qualifying
PPO	Football League Promotion Play-Off Final
RC	Rous Cup
RLC	Rumbelows Cup Final
SC	Simod Cup Final
SI	Schoolboy Internationals
SVT	Sherpa Van Trophy Final
UC	Umbro Cup
UI	University International
U16I	Under-16 Internationals
U17I	Under-17 Internationals
U18SI	Under-18 Schoolboy Internationals
U19I	Under-19 International
U23I	Under-23 International
VI	Victory International
VS	Victory Shield Schoolboy Internationals
WC	World Cup
WCQ	World Cup Qualifying
WI	Wartime Internationals
WIT	Wembley International Tournament
WLC	Worthington Cup
YAC	Football League Youth Alliance Cup Final
YI	Youth Internationals
ZC	Zenith Cup Final

Numbers in brackets after player's name are totals - (appearances, goals).

For each player's appearance, the details included are:

Competition abbreviation (FAC, INT etc), followed by last two digits of the year, any major contributions to the game in brackets (C – captain, S – came on as a substitute, W – withdrawn and substituted, D – dismissed and/or a number representing the goals scored in that match) and the result, with the player's team listed first.

Ablett, Gary (8, 0)

LCT88	**Liverpool**	0-0	Newcastle Utd
FAC88	**Liverpool**	0-1	Wimbledon
CS88	**Liverpool**	2-1	Wimbledon
FAC89	**Liverpool**	3-2	Everton
MT89	**Liverpool**	0-1	Arsenal
CS90	**Liverpool**	1-1	Man Utd
FAC95	**Everton**	1-0	Man Utd
CS95	**Everton**	1-0	Blackburn

A'Court, Alan (2, 1)

U23I57	**England**	3-2	Romania
BC57 (1)	**England**	2-3	N Ireland

Adam, Charlie (1, 0)

FAC49	**Leicester C**	1-3	Wolves

Adamczuk, Dariusz (1, 0)

WCQ93 (W)	**Poland**	0-3	England

Adams, Neil (3, 0)

CS86 (S, W)	**Everton**	1-1	Liverpool
LCT88 (S)	**Everton**	0-1	Man Utd
LC90	**Oldham**	0-1	Nottm F

Adams, Tony (60, 4)

LC87	**Arsenal**	2-1	Liverpool
RC87	**England**	1-1	Brazil
ECQ87	**England**	8-0	Turkey
INT88 (1)	**England**	2-2	Netherlands
LC88 (C)	**Arsenal**	2-3	Luton
RC88	**England**	1-0	Scotland
RC88	**England**	1-1	Colombia
WIT88 (C)	**Arsenal**	4-0	Spurs
WIT88 (C)	**Arsenal**	3-0	Bayern Munich
INT88 (W)	**England**	1-0	Denmark
WCQ88 (W)	**England**	0-0	Sweden
MT89 (C)	**Arsenal**	1-0	Porto
MT89 (C)	**Arsenal**	1-0	Liverpool
CS89 (C)	**Arsenal**	0-1	Liverpool
MT90 (C)	**Arsenal**	2-0	Aston Villa
MT90 (C)	**Arsenal**	0-1	Sampdoria
ECQ91 (W)	**England**	1-1	R of Ireland
FAC91 (C)	**Arsenal**	1-3	Spurs
CS91 (C)	**Arsenal**	0-0	Spurs
WCQ92	**England**	1-1	Norway
WCQ92	**England**	4-0	Turkey
WCQ93	**England**	6-0	San Marino
FAC93 (C, 1)	**Arsenal**	1-0	Spurs
CCC93 (C)	**Arsenal**	2-1	Sheffield W
WCQ93	**England**	2-2	Netherlands
FAC93 (C)	**Arsenal**	1-1	Sheffield W
FAC93 (C)	**Arsenal**	2-1	Sheffield W
CS93 (C)	**Arsenal**	1-1	Man Utd
WCQ93	**England**	3-0	Poland
INT94	**England**	1-0	Denmark
INT94	**England**	5-0	Greece
INT94	**England**	0-0	Norway
INT94	**England**	2-0	USA
INT94 (C)	**England**	1-1	Romania
INT95	**England**	0-0	Uruguay
INT95 (C)	**England**	0-0	Colombia
INT95 (C)	**England**	3-1	Switzerland
INT95 (C)	**England**	1-1	Portugal
ECH96 (C)	**England**	1-1	Switzerland
ECH96 (C)	**England**	2-0	Scotland
ECH96 (C)	**England**	4-1	Netherlands
ECH96 (C)	**England**	0-0	Spain
ECH96 (C)	**England**	1-1	Germany
WCQ97 (W)	**England**	2-0	Georgia
INT98 (C)	**England**	0-2	Chile
INT98	**England**	3-0	Portugal
FAC98 (C)	**Arsenal**	2-0	Newcastle Utd
INT98	**England**	0-0	Saudi Arabia
CS98 (C, W)	**Arsenal**	3-0	Man Utd
EC98 (C, 1)	**Arsenal**	2-1	Panathinaikos
EC98 (C)	**Arsenal**	1-1	Dynamo Kiev
EC98 (C, W)	**Arsenal**	0-1	Lens
INT99	**England**	0-2	France
ECQ99 (W)	**England**	6-0	Luxembourg
EC99 (C)	**Arsenal**	3-1	AIK Stockholm
EC99 (C)	**Arsenal**	2-4	Barcelona
EC99 (C)	**Arsenal**	0-1	Fiorentina
ECQ99	**England**	0-1	Scotland
INT00 (1)	**England**	2-0	Ukraine
WCQ00 (C)	**England**	0-1	Germany

Adamson, Jimmy (1, 0)

FAC62 (C)	**Burnley**	1-3	Spurs

Ainscow, Alan (1, 0)

FMC87	**Blackburn**	1-0	Charlton

Aitken, Charlie (2, 0)

FLC71	**Aston Villa**	0-2	Spurs
FLC75	**Aston Villa**	1-0	Norwich

Aitken, George (1, 0)

BC49	**Scotland**	3-1	England

Aitken, Roy (2, 0)

RC86	**Scotland**	1-2	England
RC88 (C)	**Scotland**	0-1	England

Albert, Philippe (1, 0)

CS96	**Newcastle Utd**	0-4	Man Utd

Albiston, Arthur (9, 0)

FAC77	**Man Utd**	2-1	Liverpool
CS77	**Man Utd**	0-0	Liverpool
FAC79	**Man Utd**	2-3	Arsenal
MC83	**Man Utd**	1-2	Liverpool
FAC83	**Man Utd**	2-2	Brighton
FAC83	**Man Utd**	4-0	Brighton
CS83	**Man Utd**	2-0	Liverpool
FAC85 (W)	**Man Utd**	1-0	Everton
CS85	**Man Utd**	0-2	Everton

Aldis, Peter (1, 0)

FAC57	**Aston Villa**	2-1	Man Utd

Aldridge, John (9, 4)

MC86	**Oxford**	3-0	QPR
LCT88 (W)	**Liverpool**	0-0	Newcastle Utd
FAC88 (W)	**Liverpool**	0-1	Wimbledon
CS88 (2)	**Liverpool**	2-1	Wimbledon
FAC89 (1, W)	**Liverpool**	3-2	Everton
MT89 (S, 1)	**Liverpool**	2-0	Dynamo Kiev
MT89 (W)	**Liverpool**	0-1	Arsenal
MT90	**Real Sociedad**	1-1	Sampdoria
ECQ91 (W)	**R of Ireland**	1-1	England

As Manager

WLC00   **Tranmere** 1-2 Leicester

Aleksic, Milija (3, 0) (Gk)
FAT72   **Stafford R** 3-0 Barnet
FAC81   **Spurs** 1-1 Man City
FAC81   **Spurs** 3-2 Man City

Alexandersson, Niclas (1, 0)
ECQ99 (S)   **Sweden** 0-0 England

Allchurch, Ivor (5, 0)
BC52   **Wales** 2-5 England
BC54   **Wales** 2-3 England
BC56   **Wales** 1-3 England
BC62   **Wales** 0-4 England
BC64   **Wales** 1-2 England

Allen, Clive (5, 1)
SI76 (S)   **England** 4-1 Wales
SI76   **England** 6-1 France
FAC82 (W)   **QPR** 1-1 Spurs
FAC87 (1)   **Spurs** 2-3 Coventry
LCEN87 (W) **Football League** 3-0 Rest of World

Allen, Jack (1, 2)
FAC32 (2)   **Newcastle Utd** 2-1 Arsenal

Allen, Jim (1, 0)
FAC34 (C)   **Portsmouth** 1-2 Man City

Allen, Les (2, 0)
FAC61   **Spurs** 2-0 Leicester C
FLC67   **QPR** 3-2 WBA

Allen, Martin (1, 0)
MC86 (W)   **QPR** 0-3 Oxford

Allen, Paul (9, 0)
FAC80   **West Ham** 1-0 Arsenal
CS80   **West Ham** 0-1 Liverpool
FAC87   **Spurs** 2-3 Coventry
WIT88   **Spurs** 0-4 Arsenal
WIT88   **Spurs** 1-2 Ac Milan
FAC91   **Spurs** 3-1 Arsenal
FAC91   **Spurs** 2-1 Nottm F
CS91   **Spurs** 0-0 Arsenal
FAC93   **Spurs** 0-1 Arsenal

Allen, Ronnie (3, 3)
FAC54 (2)   **WBA** 3-2 PNE
BC54   **England** 3-2 Wales
INT54 (1)   **England** 3-1 West Germany

Allen, Tony (2, 0)
INT59   **England** 2-3 Sweden
BC59   **England** 2-1 N Ireland

Allinson, Ian (1, 0)
SC88   **Luton** 1-4 Reading

Amokachi, Daniel (2, 0)
INT94 (W)   **Nigeria** 0-1 England
FAC95 (S)   **Everton** 1-0 Man Utd

Anderson, Andrew (3, 0)
BC34   **Scotland** 0-3 England
BC36   **Scotland** 1-1 England
BC38   **Scotland** 1-0 England

Anderson, Jock (1, 1)
FAC39 (1)   **Portsmouth** 4-1 Wolves

Anderson, John (1, 1)
FAC48 (1)   **Man Utd** 4-2 Blackpool

Anderson, Stan (1, 0)
INT62   **England** 3-1 Austria

Anderson, Terry (1, 0)
FLC73   **Norwich** 0-1 Spurs

Anderson, Trevor (1, 0)
BC78   **N Ireland** 0-1 England

Anderson, Viv (19, 1)
FLC78   **Nottm F** 0-0 Liverpool
CS78   **Nottm F** 5-0 Ipswich Town
INT78   **England** 1-0 Czechoslovakia
ECQ79   **England** 2-0 Bulgaria
FLC80   **Nottm F** 0-1 Wolves
WCQ80   **England** 4-0 Norway
WCQ81   **England** 0-0 Romania
BC81   **England** 0-0 Wales
BC81   **England** 0-1 Scotland
BC82   **England** 4-0 N Ireland
BC84   **England** 1-0 N Ireland
INT85   **England** 2-1 R of Ireland
ECQ86   **England** 3-0 N Ireland
ECQ86 (1)   **England** 2-0 Yugoslavia
LC87   **Arsenal** 2-1 Liverpool
RC88   **England** 1-1 Colombia
FAC93 (C)   **Sheffield W** 2-1 Sheffield Utd
CCC93 (C)   **Sheffield W** 1-2 Arsenal
FAC93 (C, W) **Sheffield W** 1-1 Arsenal

Anderson, Willie (1, 0)
FLC71   **Aston Villa** 0-2 Spurs

Andersson, Andreas (1, 0)
FAC98 (S)   **Newcastle Utd** 0-2 Arsenal

Anderton, Darren (20, 5)
U19I91 (S)   **England** 1-1 Spain
FAC93   **Spurs** 0-1 Arsenal
INT94 (S)   **England** 1-0 Denmark
INT94 (1, W)   **England** 5-0 Greece
INT94 (W)   **England** 0-0 Norway
INT94   **England** 2-0 USA
INT95   **England** 0-0 Uruguay
UC 95 (1)   **England** 2-1 Japan
UC 95   **England** 1-3 Brazil
INT96 (2)   **England** 3-0 Hungary
ECH96   **England** 1-1 Switzerland
ECH96   **England** 2-0 Scotland
ECH96   **England** 4-1 Netherlands
ECH96 (W)   **England** 0-0 Spain
ECH96   **England** 1-1 Germany
INT98   **England** 0-0 Saudi Arabia
ECQ98 (W)   **England** 0-0 Bulgaria
INT98 (1)   **England** 2-0 Czech Republic
INT99   **England** 0-2 France
WLC99   **Spurs** 1-0 Leicester C

Anelka, Nicolas (6, 4)
FAC98 (1)   **Arsenal** 2-0 Newcastle Utd
CS98 (1)   **Arsenal** 3-0 Man Utd
EC98   **Arsenal** 2-1 Panathinaikos
EC98 (W)   **Arsenal** 1-1 Dynamo Kiev
EC98   **Arsenal** 0-1 Lens
INT99 (2, W)   **France** 2-0 England

Angus, John (1, 0)
FAC62   **Burnley** 1-3 Spurs

Appleton, Colin (2, 0)
FAC61   **Leicester C** 0-2 Spurs
FAC63 (C)   **Leicester C** 1-3 Man Utd

Archibald, Sandy (2, 0)
BC24   **Scotland** 1-1 England
BC32   **Scotland** 0-3 England

Archibald, Steve (9, 1)
FAC81   **Spurs** 1-1 Man City
FAC81   **Spurs** 3-2 Man City
BC81   **Scotland** 1-0 England
CS81   **Spurs** 2-2 Aston Villa
FLC82 (1)   **Spurs** 1-3 Liverpool
FAC82   **Spurs** 1-1 QPR
FAC82   **Spurs** 1-0 QPR
CS82   **Spurs** 0-1 Liverpool
LCT88   **Blackburn** 0-0 Aston Villa

Ardiles, Osvaldo (7, 0)
FAC81   **Spurs** 1-1 Man City
FAC81   **Spurs** 3-2 Man City
CS81   **Spurs** 2-2 Aston Villa
FLC82   **Spurs** 1-3 Liverpool
FAC87 (W)   **Spurs** 2-3 Coventry
LCEN87 (S)   **Football League** 3-0 Rest of World
LCT88   **Blackburn** 0-0 Aston Villa
As Manager:
PPO90   **Swindon** 1-0 Sunderland
PPO93   **WBA** 3-0 Port Vale

Armfield, Jimmy (16, 0)
U23I57   **England** 3-2 Romania
INT60   **England** 3-3 Yugoslavia
INT60   **England** 4-2 Spain
BC60   **England** 5-1 Wales
BC61   **England** 9-3 Scotland
INT61   **England** 8-0 Mexico
WCQ61   **England** 2-0 Portugal
BC61   **England** 1-1 N Ireland
INT62   **England** 3-1 Austria
INT62   **England** 3-1 Switzerland
BC62 (C)   **England** 4-0 Wales
BC63 (C)   **England** 1-2 Scotland
INT63 (C)   **England** 1-1 Brazil
CEN63 (C)   **England** 2-1 FIFA
BC63 (C)   **England** 8-3 N Ireland
INT66 (C)   **England** 2-0 Yugoslavia

Armstrong, David (1, 0)
INT82 (W)   **England** 1-2 West Germany

Armstrong, George (4, 0)
FLC68   **Arsenal** 0-1 Leeds United
FLC69   **Arsenal** 1-3 Swindon
FAC71   **Arsenal** 2-1 Liverpool
FAC72   **Arsenal** 0-1 Leeds United

Armstrong, Gerry (6, 0)
BC78   **N Ireland** 0-1 England
ECQ79   **N Ireland** 0-4 England
BC80   **N Ireland** 1-1 England
BC82   **N Ireland** 0-4 England
BC84   **N Ireland** 0-1 England

WCQ85 (S)   **N Ireland** 0-0 England

Armstrong, Gordon (3, 0)
LCT88   **Sunderland** 0-0 Wigan Athletic
PPO90   **Sunderland** 0-1 Swindon
FAC92 (W)   **Sunderland** 0-2 Liverpool

Armstrong Ken (1, 0)
BC55   **England** 7-2 Scotland

Ashworth, Alec (1, 0)
FAC64   **PNE** 2-3 West Ham

Asprilla, Faustino (2, 0)
INT95   **Colombia** 0-0 England
CS96 (S)   **Newcastle Utd** 0-4 Man Utd

Astall, Gordon (1, 0)
FAC56   **Birmingham** 1-3 Man City

Astle, Jeff (5, 2)
FLC67   **WBA** 2-3 QPR
FAC68 (1)   **WBA** 1-0 Everton
BC69   **England** 2-1 Wales
INT69   **England** 1-0 Portugal
FLC70 (1)   **WBA** 1-2 Man City

Aston, John Jnr (1, 0)
EC68   **Man Utd** 4-1 Benfica

Aston, John Snr (2, 0)
FAC48   **Man Utd** 4-2 Blackpool
BC49   **England** 1-3 Scotland

Atkins, Mark (3, 0)
PPO92   **Blackburn** 1-0 Leicester C
CS94 (W)   **Blackburn** 0-2 Man Utd
CS95 (S)   **Blackburn** 0-1 Everton

Atkinson, Brian (3, 0)
PPO90 (S)   **Sunderland** 0-1 Swindon
FAC92   **Sunderland** 0-2 Liverpool
PPO00 (W)   **Darlington** 0-1 Peterborough

Atkinson, Dalian (1, 1)
CCC94 (1)   **Aston Villa** 3-1 Man Utd

Atkinson, Paul (1, 0)
FAC84 (S)   **Watford** 0-2 Everton

Attwell, Reg (1, 0)
FAC47   **Burnley** 0-1 Charlton

Atyeo, John (3, 3)
INT55 (1)   **England** 4-1 Spain
INT56   **England** 4-2 Brazil
WCQ57 (2)   **England** 5-1 R of Ireland

Austin, Billy (1, 0)
FAC26   **Man City** 0-1 Bolton

Austin, Dean (1, 0)
FAC93   **Spurs** 0-1 Arsenal

Babayaro, Celestine (2, 0)
FAC00   **Chelsea** 1-0 Aston Villa
CS00   **Chelsea** 2-0 Man Utd

Babb, Phil (2, 0)
CCC95   **Liverpool** 2-1 Bolton
FAC96   **Liverpool** 0-1 Man Utd

Bailey, Gary (8, 0)
FAC79   **Man Utd** 2-3 Arsenal
MC83   **Man Utd** 1-2 Liverpool
FAC83   **Man Utd** 2-2 Brighton

FAC83	**Man Utd** 4-0 Brighton	
CS83	**Man Utd** 2-0 Liverpool	
INT85	**England** 2-1 R of Ireland	
FAC85	**Man Utd** 1-0 Everton	
CS85	**Man Utd** 0-2 Everton	

Bailey, John (4, 0)

MC84	**Everton** 0-0 Liverpool
FAC84	**Everton** 2-0 Watford
CS84	**Everton** 1-0 Liverpool
CS85 (S)	**Everton** 2-0 Man Utd

Bailey, Mike (2, 0)

BC64	**England** 2-1 Wales
FLC74 (C)	**Wolves** 2-1 Man City

Bailie, Colin (2, 0)

SC88	**Reading** 4-1 Luton
PPO90	**Cambridge Utd** 1-0 Chesterfield

Baily, Eddie (2, 0)

MCC43	**Finchley** 1-0 Southall
INT51	**England** 2-2 Austria

Baker, Alf (2, 0)

FAC27	**Arsenal** 0-1 Cardiff
FAC30	**Arsenal** 2-0 Huddersfield

Baker, Colin (1, 0)

BC60	**Wales** 1-5 England

Baker, Graham (1, 0)

FMC86 (S)	**Man City** 4-5 Chelsea

Baker, Joe (3, 2)

BC59 (1)	**England** 2-1 N Ireland
INT60	**England** 3-3 Yugoslavia
BC65 (1)	**England** 2-1 N Ireland

Baker, Peter (2, 0)

FAC61	**Spurs** 2-0 Leicester
FAC62	**Spurs** 3-1 Burnley

Baldwin, Tommy (3, 0)

FAC67	**Chelsea** 1-2 Spurs
FAC70	**Chelsea** 2-2 Leeds
FLC72 (S)	**Chelsea** 1-2 Stoke

Ball, Alan (33, 1)

INT66	**England** 1-0 W Germany
WC66	**England** 0-0 Uruguay
WC66	**England** 1-0 Argentina
WC66	**England** 2-1 Portugal
WC66	**England** 4-2 W Germany
INT66	**England** 0-0 Czechoslovakia
ECQ66	**England** 5-1 Wales
ECQ67	**England** 2-3 Scotland
INT67	**England** 2-0 Spain
INT67 (1)	**England** 2-2 USSR
ECQ68	**England** 1-0 Spain
FAC68	**Everton** 0-1 WBA
INT69	**England** 1-1 Romania
BC69	**England** 2-1 Wales
BC69	**England** 4-1 Scotland
INT69	**England** 1-0 Portugal
INT70	**England** 3-1 E Germany
ECQ71 (W)	**England** 3-0 Greece
ECQ71 (S)	**England** 5-0 Malta
BC71	**England** 3-1 Scotland

ECQ71	**England** 1-1 Switzerland
ECQ72	**England** 1-3 W Germany
FAC72	**Arsenal** 0-1 Leeds
INT72	**England** 1-1 Yugoslavia
EEC73 (S)	**The Three** 2-0 The Six
WCQ73	**England** 1-1 Wales
BC73	**England** 3-0 Wales
BC73	**England** 1-0 Scotland
INT75 (C)	**England** 2-0 W Germany
ECQ75 (C)	**England** 5-0 Cyprus
BC75 (C)	**England** 2-2 Wales
BC75 (C)	**England** 5-1 Scotland
FLC79 (C)	**Southampton** 2-3 Nottm F

Ball, John (1, 0)

FAC53	**Bolton** 3-4 Blackpool

Ball, Kevin (2, 0)

FAC92	**Sunderland** 0-2 Liverpool
PPO98 (C)	**Sunderland** 4-4 Charlton

Banks, Gordon (34, 0)

FAC61	**Leicester** 0-2 Spurs
BC63	**England** 1-2 Scotland
INT61	**England** 1-1 Brazil
FAC63	**Leicester** 1-3 Man Utd
CEN63	**England** 2-1 FIFA
BC63	**England** 8-3 N Ireland
INT64	**England** 2-1 Uruguay
BC65	**England** 2-2 Scotland
INT65	**England** 1-0 Hungary
BC65	**England** 2-1 N Ireland
INT66	**England** 1-0 W Germany
INT66	**England** 2-0 Yugoslavia
WC66	**England** 0-0 Uruguay
WC66	**England** 2-0 Mexico
WC66	**England** 2-0 France
WC66	**England** 1-0 Argentina
WC66	**England** 2-1 Portugal
WC66	**England** 4-2 W Germany
INT66	**England** 0-0 Czechoslovakia
ECQ66	**England** 5-1 Wales
ECQ67	**England** 2-3 Scotland
ECQ67	**England** 2-0 N Ireland
INT67	**England** 2-2 USSR
ECQ68	**England** 1-0 Spain
INT69	**England** 1-1 Romania
INT69	**England** 5-0 France
BC69	**England** 4-1 Scotland
INT70	**England** 0-0 Netherlands
BC70	**England** 3-1 N Ireland
ECQ71	**England** 3-0 Greece
ECQ71	**England** 5-0 Malta
BC71	**England** 3-1 Scotland
FLC72	**Stoke** 2-1 Chelsea
ECQ72	**England** 1-3 W Germany

Banks, Ralph (1, 0)

FAC53	**Bolton** 3-4 Blackpool

Banks, Tommy (1, 0)

FAC58	**Bolton** 2-0 Man Utd

Bannister, Gary (2, 0)

MC86	**QPR**	0-3 Oxford Utd
PPO96	**Darlington**	0-1 Plymouth

Bannon, Eamonn (2, 0)

BC83 (W)	**Scotland**	0-2 England
RC86	**Scotland**	1-2 England

Barber, Phil (2, 0)

LCEN88	**C Palace**	0-0 Sheffield W
FAC90 (W)	**C Palace**	3-3 Man Utd
FAC90 (W)	**C Palace**	0-1 Man Utd

Barclay, Bobby (4, 1)

BC32 (1)	**England**	3-0 Scotland
BC36	**England**	1-1 Scotland
FAC36	**Sheffield Utd**	0-1 Arsenal
FAC38	**Huddersfield**	0-1 PNE

Bardsley, David (1, 0)

FAC84	**Watford**	0-2 Everton

Barham, Mark (2, 0)

MC85	**Norwich**	1-0 Sunderland
PPO91	**Brighton**	1-3 Notts County

Barkas, Ned (2, 0)

FAC28	**Huddersfield**	1-3 Blackburn
FAC31 (C)	**Birmingham**	1-2 WBA

Barker, John (1, 0)

BC36	**England**	1-1 Scotland

Barker, Simon (1, 0)

FMC87	**Blackburn**	1-0 Charlton

Barlow, Andy (1, 0)

LC90	**Oldham**	0-1 Nottm F

Barlow, Bert (2, 1)

FAC39 (1)	**Portsmouth**	4-1 Wolves
LWC42	**Portsmouth**	0-2 Brentford

Barlow, Ray (1, 0)

FAC54	**WBA**	3-2 PNE

Barmby, Nick (13, 2)

SI89 3-1 (2)	**England**	3-1 Belgium
SI89	**England**	1-3 W Germany
U16I89	**England**	2-1 Scandinavia
FAC93 (S)	**Spurs**	0-1 Arsenal
INT95 (S)	**England**	0-0 Uruguay
INT95	**England**	0-0 Colombia
INT95 (W)	**England**	1-1 Portugal
ECH96 (S)	**England**	1-1 Switzerland
ECH96 (S)	**England**	4-1 Netherlands
ECH96 (S)	**England**	0-0 Spain
INT00 (S)	**England**	1-1 Brazil
INT00 (S)	**England**	2-0 Ukraine
WCQ00	**England**	0-1 Germany

Barnard, Darren (2, 0)

FAC94 (S)	**Chelsea**	2-0 Luton
PPO00	**Barnsley**	2-4 Ipswich

Barnes, John (41, 7)

ECQ83 (W)	**England**	0-1 Denmark
FAC84	**Watford**	0-2 Everton
INT84 (W)	**England**	0-2 USSR
INT84	**England**	1-0 E Germany
WCQ84	**England**	5-0 Finland
WCQ85 (S)	**England**	1-1 Romania

RC87	**England**	1-1 Brazil
ECQ87 (2)	**England**	8-0 Turkey
INT88	**England**	2-2 Netherlands
LCT88 (W)	**Liverpool**	0-0 Newcastle Utd
FAC88	**Liverpool**	0-1 Wimbledon
RC88	**England**	1-0 Scotland
RC88	**England**	1-1 Colombia
CS88	**Liverpool**	2-1 Wimbledon
WCQ88 (W)	**England**	0-0 Sweden
FAC89	**Liverpool**	3-2 Everton
WCQ89 (1)	**England**	3-0 Poland
MT89 (1)	**Liverpool**	2-0 Dynamo Kiev
MT89	**Liverpool**	0-1 Arsenal
CS89	**Liverpool**	1-0 Arsenal
INT89	**England**	0-0 Italy
INT90	**England**	1-0 Brazil
INT90	**England**	1-0 Denmark
INT90 (1)	**England**	1-2 Uruguay
CS90 (1)	**Liverpool**	1-1 Man Utd
INT90	**England**	1-0 Hungary
ECQ90	**England**	2-0 Poland
INT91	**England**	2-0 Cameroon
ECQ91	**England**	1-1 R of Ireland
INT91	**England**	3-1 USSR
INT91 (W)	**England**	2-2 Argentina
WCQ93	**England**	6-0 San Marino
WCQ93 (1)	**England**	2-2 Netherlands
INT94	**England**	2-0 USA
INT94	**England**	1-1 Romania
INT94	**England**	1-0 Nigeria
INT95	**England**	0-0 Uruguay
CCC95	**Liverpool**	2-1 Bolton
INT95 (S)	**England**	0-0 Colombia
FAC96 (C)	**Liverpool**	0-1 Man Utd
FAC98 (S)	**Newcastle Utd**	0-2 Arsenal

Barnes, Ken (2, 0)

FAC55	**Man City**	1-3 Newcastle Utd
FAC56	**Man City**	3-1 Birmingham

Barnes, Peter (12, 3)

FLC76 (1)	**Man City**	2-1 Newcastle Utd
WCQ77	**England**	2-0 Italy
INT78	**England**	1-1 Brazil
INT78 (1)	**England**	4-1 Hungary
INT78	**England**	1-0 Czechoslovakia
ECQ79	**England**	4-0 N Ireland
BC79 (1)	**England**	3-1 Scotland
ECQ79	**England**	1-0 Denmark
INT81 (S)	**England**	1-2 Spain
INT81	**England**	0-1 Brazil
BC81	**England**	0-0 Wales
INT82 (S)	**England**	2-0 Netherlands

Barnes, Walley (2, 0)

FAC50	**Arsenal**	2-0 Liverpool
FAC52	**Arsenal**	0-1 Newcastle Utd

Barnett, Geoff (2, 0)

SI62	**England**	1-2 W Germany
FAC72	**Arsenal**	0-1 Leeds

Barnett, Laurie (1, 0)

FAC34	**Man City**	2-1 Portsmouth

Baron, Kevin (1, 0)
FAC50   **Liverpool** 0-2 Arsenal
Barr, Hugh (1, 0)
BC61   **N Ireland** 1-1 England
Barrass, Malcolm (2, 0)
BC53   **England** 2-2 Scotland
FAC53   **Bolton** 3-4 Blackpool
Barrett, Colin (2, 0)
CS78   **Nottm F** 5-0 Ipswich
FLC79   **Nottm F** 3-2 Southampton
Barrett, Earl (3, 0)
LC90   **Oldham** 0-1 Nottm F
CCC94   **Aston Villa** 3-1 Man Utd
CS95   **Everton** 1-0 Blackburn
Barrett, Les (1, 0)
FAC75   **Fulham** 0-2 West Ham
Barron, Paul (1, 0)
MC86   **QPR** 0-3 Oxford Utd
Barrowclough, Stewart (1, 0)
FLC76   **Newcastle Utd** 1-2 Man City
Barry, Gareth (4, 0)
FAC00   **Aston Villa** 0-0 Bolton
FAC00   **Aston Villa** 0-1 Chelsea
INT00 (S)   **England** 2-0 Ukraine
WCQ00 (S)   **England** 0-1 Germany
Barthez, Fabien (2, 0)
INT99   **France** 2-0 England
CS00   **Man Utd** 0-2 Chelsea
Barton, Harold (1, 0)
FAC36   **Sheffield Utd** 0-1 Arsenal
Barton, Percy (1, 0)
BC24   **England** 1-1 Scotland
Barton, Warren (3, 0)
UC95 (S)   **England** 1-3 Brazil
FAC98 (W)   **Newcastle Utd** 0-2 Arsenal
FAC00   **Newcastle Utd** 1-2 Chelsea
Bartram, Sam (5, 0)
WI40   **England** 0-1 Wales
LSC44   **Charlton** 3-1 Chelsea
LSC45   **Millwall** 0-2 Chelsea
FAC46   **Charlton** 1-4 Derby
FAC47   **Charlton** 1-0 Burnley
Bart-Williams, Chris (3, 0)
U19I91 (W)   **England** 1-1 Spain
FAC93 (S)   **Sheffield W** 1-1 Arsenal
FAC93 (S)   **Sheffield W** 1-2 Arsenal
Bastin, Cliff (9, 1)
FAC30   **Arsenal** 2-0 Huddersfield
FAC32   **Arsenal** 1-2 Newcastle Utd
BC34 (1)   **England** 3-0 Scotland
BC36   **England** 1-1 Scotland
FAC36   **Arsenal** 1-0 Sheffield Utd
BC38   **England** 0-1 Scotland
FFLWC41   **Arsenal** 1-1 PNE
LSC43   **Arsenal** 7-1 Charlton
CHA45   **N Police** 1-3 C Services

Batey, Bob (1, 0)
FAC38   **PNE** 1-0 Huddersfield
Batty, David (24, 0)
LCT88   **Leeds** 0-3 Nottm F
INT91 (S)   **England** 3-1 USSR
INT91   **England** 2-2 Argentina
INT91   **England** 0-1 Germany
ECQ91   **England** 1-0 Turkey
CS92   **Leeds** 4-3 Liverpool
WCQ92   **England** 1-1 Norway
WCQ93   **England** 6-0 San Marino
INT94 (S)   **England** 1-0 Denmark
UC95 (W)   **England** 2-1 Japan
UC95 (W)   **England** 1-3 Brazil
CS95   **Blackburn** 0-1 Everton
CS96   **Newcastle Utd** 0-4 Man Utd
WCQ97 (W)   **England** 0-1 Italy
INT97 (W)   **England** 2-0 Mexico
WCQ97   **England** 2-0 Georgia
WCQ97   **England** 4-0 Moldova
INT98 (W)   **England** 0-2 Chile
INT98   **England** 3-0 Portugal
FAC98   **Newcastle Utd** 0-2 Arsenal
INT98   **England** 0-0 Saudi Arabia
ECQ98 (S)   **England** 0-0 Bulgaria
ECQ99   **England** 0-0 Sweden
ECQ99   **England** 6-0 Luxembourg
Batty, Ron (1, 0)
FAC55   **Newcastle Utd** 3-1 Man City
Baxter, Jim (3, 2)
BC63 (2)   **Scotland** 2-1 England
CEN63 (S)   **FIFA** 1-2 England
ECQ67   **Scotland** 3-2 England
Baxter, Jimmy (1, 0)
FAC54   **PNE** 2-3 WBA
Baynham, Ron (3, 0)
BC55   **England** 3-0 N Ireland
INT55   **England** 4-1 Spain
FAC59   **Luton** 1-2 Nottm F
Beadles, Harry (1, 0)
FAC25   **Cardiff** 0-1 Sheffield Utd
Beal, Phil (2, 0)
FLC71   **Spurs** 2-0 Aston Villa
FLC73   **Spurs** 1-0 Norwich
Beardsley, Peter (34, 7)
ECQ86 (W)   **England** 3-0 N Ireland
ECQ86   **England** 2-0 Yugoslavia
RC87   **England** 1-1 Brazil
LCEN87 (W)   **Football League** 3-0 Rest of World
ECQ87 (1, W)   **England** 8-0 Turkey
INT88 (W)   **England** 2-2 Netherlands
LCT88 (S)   **Liverpool** 0-0 Newcastle Utd
FAC88   **Liverpool** 0-1 Wimbledon
RC88 (1)   **England** 1-0 Scotland
RC88 (W)   **England** 1-1 Colombia
CS88   **Liverpool** 2-1 Wimbledon
INT88 (W)   **England** 1-0 Denmark
WCQ88   **England** 0-0 Sweden
WCQ89 (2)   **England** 5-0 Albania

FAC89	**Liverpool**	3-2 Everton
WCQ89 (W)	**England**	3-0 Poland
MT89 (W)	**Liverpool**	2-0 Dynamo Kiev
MT89 (S)	**Liverpool**	0-1 Arsenal
CS89 (1)	**Liverpool**	1-0 Arsenal
INT89 (W)	**England**	0-0 Italy
INT90 (W)	**England**	1-0 Brazil
INT90 (S)	**England**	1-2 Uruguay
CS90 (W)	**Liverpool**	1-1 Man Utd
ECQ90 (S, 1)	**England**	2-0 Poland
ECQ91	**England**	1-1 R of Ireland
INT91 (S)	**England**	3-1 USSR
INT94	**England**	1-0 Denmark
INT94 (1, W)	**England**	5-0 Greece
INT94	**England**	0-0 Norway
INT94 (W)	**England**	1-0 Nigeria
INT95 (W)	**England**	0-0 Uruguay
UC95 (W)	**England**	2-1 Japan
INT95 (S)	**England**	1-1 Portugal
CS96 (C, W)	**Newcastle Utd**	0-4 Man Utd

Beasant, Dave (5, 0)

LCT88 (C)	**Wimbledon**	0-1 Tranmere Rovers
FAC88 (C)	**Wimbledon**	1-0 Liverpool
INT89 (S)	**England**	0-0 Italy
INT89 (S)	**England**	2-1 Yugoslavia
ZC90	**Chelsea**	1-0 Middlesbrough

Beasley, Pat (1, 0)

FAC38	**Huddersfield**	0-1 PNE

Beattie, Andy (8, 0)

FAC37	**PNE**	1-3 Sunderland
BC38	**Scotland**	1-0 England
FAC38	**PNE**	1-0 Huddersfield
FLWC41	**PNE**	1-1 Arsenal
WI41	**Scotland**	0-2 England
WI42	**Scotland**	0-3 England
WI42	**Scotland**	0-0 England
IT46	**Army PT Corps**	5-3 FA
As Manager		
BC59	**Scotland**	0-1 England

Beattie, Bobby (2, 0)

FAC38	**PNE**	1-0 Huddersfield
FLWC41	**PNE**	1-1 Arsenal

Beattie, Kevin (5, 1)

ECQ75	**England**	5-0 Cyprus
BC75 (1)	**England**	5-1 Scotland
WCQ76	**England**	2-1 Finland
INT77	**England**	0-2 Netherlands
FAC78	**Ipswich**	1-0 Arsenal

Beaumont, Dave (1, 0)

LC89	**Luton**	1-3 Nottm F

Beavon, Stuart (1, 1)

SC88 (1)	**Reading**	4-1 Luton

Beck, Mikkel (3, 0)

CCC97	**Middlesbrough**	1-1 Leicester
FAC97 (S)	**Middlesbrough**	0-2 Chelsea
CCC98 (S)	**Middlesbrough**	0-2 Chelsea

Beckford, Darren (3, 1)

SI82 (1)	**England**	7-0 Netherlands
SI82	**England**	0-0 Scotland
FAC94	**Oldham**	1-1 Man Utd

Beckham, David (24, 2)

FAC96 (W)	**Man Utd**	1-0 Liverpool
CS96 (1)	**Man Utd**	4-0 Newcastle Utd
WCQ96	**England**	2-1 Poland
WCQ97	**England**	0-1 Italy
WCQ97	**England**	2-0 Georgia
CS97 (S)	**Man Utd**	1-1 Chelsea
WCQ97 (W)	**England**	4-0 Moldova
INT97	**England**	2-0 Cameroon
INT98 (W)	**England**	3-0 Portugal
INT98 (W)	**England**	0-0 Saudi Arabia
CS98	**Man Utd**	0-3 Arsenal
INT98	**England**	2-0 Czech Republic
INT99	**England**	0-2 France
ECQ99 (W)	**England**	3-1 Poland
FAC99	**Man Utd**	2-0 Newcastle Utd
ECQ99 (W)	**England**	0-0 Sweden
CS99 (1)	**Man Utd**	1-2 Arsenal
ECQ99 (W)	**England**	6-0 Luxembourg
ECQ99	**England**	0-1 Scotland
INT00 (W)	**England**	0-0 Argentina
INT00	**England**	1-1 Brazil
INT00	**England**	2-0 Ukraine
CS00	**Man Utd**	0-2 Chelsea
WCQ00 (W)	**England**	0-1 Germany

Beglin, Jim (3, 0)

INT85	**R of Ireland**	1-2 England
FAC86	**Liverpool**	3-1 Everton
CS86	**Liverpool**	1-1 Everton

Belfitt, Rod (1, 0)

FLC68 (S)	**Leeds**	1-0 Arsenal

Bell, Colin (27, 6)

INT68	**England**	3-1 Sweden
INT68	**England**	1-1 Bulgaria
INT69	**England**	5-0 France
FAC69	**Man City**	1-0 Leicester
BC69	**England**	2-1 Wales
INT69 (W)	**England**	1-0 Portugal
INT70	**England**	0-0 Netherlands
FLC70	**Man City**	2-1 WBA
BC70 (S)	**England**	3-1 N Ireland
ECQ72	**England**	1-3 W Germany
BC72 (C)	**England**	0-1 N Ireland
INT72	**England**	1-1 Yugoslavia
EEC73 (W)	**The Three**	2-0 The Six
WCQ73	**England**	1-1 Wales
BC73	**England**	3-0 Wales
BC73	**England**	1-0 Scotland
INT73 (1)	**England**	7-0 Austria
WCQ73	**England**	1-1 Poland
INT73	**England**	0-1 Italy
FLC74 (1)	**Man City**	1-2 Wolves
BC74	**England**	1-0 N Ireland
INT74	**England**	2-2 Argentina
ECQ74 (2)	**England**	3-0 Czechoslovakia
ECQ74	**England**	0-0 Portugal
INT75 (1)	**England**	2-0 W Germany
ECQ75	**England**	5-0 Cyprus
BC75 (1)	**England**	5-1 Scotland

Bell, Eric (1, 1)
FAC53 (1)   **Bolton** 3-4 Blackpool
Bell, Thomas (1, 0)
FAC29   **Portsmouth** 0-2 Bolton
Bell, Willie (1, 0)
FAC65   **Leeds** 1-2 Liverpool
Benali, Francis (3, 0)
SI84   **England** 1-0 Scotland
SI84   **England** 4-1 Netherlands
ZC92   **Southampton** 2-3 Nottm F
Bennett, Dave (4, 1)
FAC81   **Man City** 1-1 Spurs
FAC81   **Man City** 2-3 Spurs
FAC87 (1)   **Coventry** 3-2 Spurs
CS87   **Coventry** 0-1 Everton
Bennett, Gary (2, 0)
MC85   **Sunderland** 0-1 Norwich
PPO90 (C)   **Sunderland** 0-1 Swindon
FAC92   **Sunderland** 0-2 Liverpool
Bentley, Roy (5, 5)
BC52 (1)   **England** 5-2 Wales
INT52   **England** 5-0 Belgium
BC54 (3)   **England** 3-2 Wales
INT54 (1)   **England** 3-1 W Germany
EFC55 (C)   **London** 3-2 Frankfurt
Beresford, Joe (1, 0)
FAC37   **PNE** 1-3 Sunderland
Beresford, John (2, 0)
SI82 (S)   **England** 7-0 Netherlands
CS96   **Newcastle Utd** 0-4 Man Utd
Berg, Henning (5, 0)
WCQ92 (S)   **Norway** 1-1 England
INT94   **Norway** 0-0 England
CS94   **Blackburn** 0-2 Man Utd
CS98 (S)   **Man Utd** 0-3 Arsenal
CS99   **Man Utd** 1-2 Arsenal
Berger, Patrik (2, 1)
ECH96 (1)   **Czech Republic** 1-2 Germany
INT98   **Czech Republic** 0-2 England
Bergkamp, Dennis (8, 3)
WCQ93 (1)   **Netherlands** 2-2 England
ECH96   **Netherlands** 1-4 England
CS98 (W)   **Arsenal** 3-0 Man Utd
EC98   **Arsenal** 2-1 Panathinaikos
EC98 (1)   **Arsenal** 1-1 Dynamo Kiev
EC99   **Arsenal** 3-1 AIK Stockholm
EC99 (1)   **Arsenal** 2-4 Barcelona
EC99   **Arsenal** 0-1 Fiorentina
Bergsson, Gudni (4, 0)
FAC93 (S)   **Spurs** 0-1 Arsenal
CCC95 (S)   **Bolton** 1-2 Liverpool
PPO95   **Bolton** 4-3 Reading
FAC00 (W)   **Bolton** 0-0 Aston Villa
Bernard, Mike (1, 0)
FLC72   **Stoke** 2-1 Chelsea
Bernard, Paul (1, 0)
FAC94   **Oldham** 1-1 Man Utd

Berry, George (2, 0)
FLC80   **Wolves** 1-0 Nottm F
BC83 (S)   **Wales** 1-2 England
Berry, John (1, 0)
FAC57   **Man Utd** 1-2 Aston Villa
Berry, Steve (1, 0)
MC85   **Sunderland** 0-1 Norwich
Best, George (3, 2)
BC65   **N Ireland** 1-2 England
EC68 (1)   **Man Utd** 4-1 Benfica
BC70 (1)   **N Ireland** 1-3 England
Bilic, Slaven (1, 0)
INT96   **Croatia** 0-0 England
Bimpson, Louis (1, 0)
FAC60   **Blackburn** 0-3 Wolves
Bingham, Billy (6, 1)
BC55   **N Ireland** 0-3 England
BC57   **N Ireland** 3-2 England
FAC59   **Luton** 1-2 Nottm F
BC59 (1)   **N Ireland** 1-2 England
BC61   **N Ireland** 1-1 England
BC63 (C)   **N Ireland** 3-8 England
As Manager
ECQ67   **N Ireland** 0-2 England
BC70   **N Ireland** 1-3 England
BC80   **N Ireland** 1-1 England
BC82   **N Ireland** 0-4 England
BC84   **N Ireland** 0-1 England
WCQ85   **N Ireland** 0-0 England
ECQ86   **N Ireland** 0-3 England
Birch, Brian (1, 0)
FAC58   **Bolton** 2-0 Man Utd
Birtles, Garry (3, 2)
FLC79 (2)   **Nottm F** 3-2 Southampton
FLC80   **Nottm F** 0-1 Wolves
INT80 (S)   **England** 3-1 Argentina
Bishop, Sid (1, 0)
FAC23   **West Ham** 0-2 Bolton
Bjornebye, Stig Inge (1, 0)
CCC95   **Liverpool** 2-1 Bolton
Black, Kingsley (8, 1)
SC88 (S)   **Luton** 1-4 Reading
LCT88   **Luton** 0-2 Man Utd
LC88   **Luton** 3-2 Arsenal
LC89   **Luton** 1-3 Nottm F
ZC92 (1)   **Nottm F** 3-2 Southampton
RLC92   **Nottm F** 0-1 Man Utd
AWS98 (S)   **Grimsby** 2-1 Bournemouth
PPO98 (S)   **Grimsby** 1-0 Northampton
Blackburn, George (1, 0)
FAC24   **Aston Villa** 0-2 Newcastle Utd
Blacklaw, Adam (1, 0)
FAC62   **Burnley** 1-3 Spurs
Blackmore, Clayton (7, 1)
SI79   **Wales** 1-1 England
LCT88 (S)   **Man Utd** 1-0 Everton
LCT88   **Man Utd** 1-2 Sheffield W
FAC90 (S)   **Man Utd** 3-3 C Palace

369

CS90 (1)   **Man Utd** 1-1 Liverpool
RLC91   **Man Utd** 0-1 Sheffield W
FAC97   **Middlesbrough** 0-2 Chelsea

Blackmore, Harold (1, 1)
FAC29 (1)   **Bolton** 2-0 Portsmouth

Blair, Andy (1, 0)
CS81 (S)   **Aston Villa** 2-2 Spurs

Blair, Jim (1, 0)
FLC73 (W)   **Norwich** 0-1 Spurs

Blair, Jimmy (1, 0)
FAC25   **Cardiff** 0-1 Sheffield Utd

Blanchflower, Danny (7, 1)
EFC55   **London** 3-2 Frankfurt
BC55 (C)   **N Ireland** 0-3 England
BC57 (C)   **N Ireland** 3-2 England
BC59 (C)   **N Ireland** 1-2 England
FAC61 (C)   **Spurs** 2-0 Leicester
BC61 (C)   **N Ireland** 1-1 England
FAC62 (C, 1)   **Spurs** 3-1 Burnley
As Manager
BC78   **N Ireland** 0-1 England
ECQ79   **N Ireland** 0-4 England

Blanchflower, Jackie (2, 0)
FAC57   **Man Utd** 1-2 Aston Villa
BC57   **N Ireland** 3-2 England

Blenkinsop, Ernie (2, 0)
BC30   **England** 5-2 Scotland
BC32 (C)   **England** 3-0 Scotland

Blissett, Luther (8, 3)
INT82 (S)   **England** 1-2 W Germany
ECQ82 (3)   **England** 9-0 Luxembourg
BC 83   **England** 2-1 Wales
ECQ83 (S)   **England** 0-0 Greece
ECQ83   **England** 2-0 Hungary
BC 83 (S)   **England** 2-0 Scotland
ECQ83 (S)   **England** 0-1 Denmark
INT84   **England** 0-2 USSR

Blockley, Jeff (1, 0)
INT72   **England** 1-1 Yugoslavia

Bloor, Alan (1, 0)
FLC72   **Stoke** 2-1 Chelsea

Blunstone, Frank (3, 0)
BC54   **England** 3-2 Wales
BC55   **England** 7-2 Scotland
INT56   **England** 3-0 Yugoslavia

Blyth, Billy (1, 0)
FAC27   **Arsenal** 0-1 Cardiff

Blyth, Jim (2, 0)
FAC76   **Southampton** 1-0 Man Utd
CS76 (W)   **Southampton** 0-1 Liverpool

Boa Morte, Luis (2, 0)
CS98 (S)   **Arsenal** 3-0 Man Utd
CS99 (S)   **Arsenal** 2-1 Man Utd

Boateng, George (2, 0)
FAC00 (W)   **Aston Villa** 0-0 Bolton
FAC00   **Aston Villa** 0-1 Chelsea

Boersma, Phil (1, 1)
CS74 (1)   **Liverpool** 1-1 Leeds

Bohinen, Lars (1, 0)
INT94   **Norway** 0-0 England

Bolder, Bob (1, 0)
FMC87   **Charlton** 0-1 Blackburn

Bond, John (1, 0)
FAC64   **West Ham** 3-2 PNE
As Manager
FLC75   **Norwich** 0-1 Aston Villa
FAC81   **Man City** 1-1 Spurs
FAC81   **Man City** 2-3 Spurs

Bonds, Billy (4, 0)
FAC75 (C)   **West Ham** 2-0 Fulham
FAC80 (C)   **West Ham** 1-0 Arsenal
CS80 (C)   **West Ham** 0-1 Liverpool
FLC81 (C)   **West Ham** 1-1 Liverpool

Bonetti, Peter (5, 0)
FAC67   **Chelsea** 1-2 Spurs
INT67   **England** 2-0 Spain
INT69   **England** 1-0 Portugal
FAC70   **Chelsea** 2-2 Leeds
FLC72   **Chelsea** 1-2 Stoke

Bonner, Pat (2, 0)
INT85   **R of Ireland** 1-2 England
ECQ91   **R of Ireland** 1-1 England

Book, Tony (2, 0)
FAC69 (C)   **Man City** 1-0 Leicester
FLC70 (C)   **Man City** 2-1 WBA
As Manager
FLC76   **Man City** 2-1 Newcastle Utd

Boot, Eddie (1, 0)
FAC38   **Huddersfield** 0-1 PNE

Booth, Tommy (4, 0)
FAC69   **Man City** 1-0 Leicester
FLC70   **Man City** 2-1 WBA
FLC74   **Man City** 1-2 Wolves
FLC76   **Man City** 2-1 Newcastle Utd

Borrows, Brian (1, 0)
CS87 (S)   **Coventry** 0-1 Everton

Bosnich, Mark (3, 0)
CCC94   **Aston Villa** 3-1 Man Utd
CCC96   **Aston Villa** 3-0 Leeds
CS99   **Man Utd** 1-2 Arsenal

Bould, Steve (10, 1)
WIT88 (S)   **Arsenal** 4-0 Spurs
WIT88   **Arsenal** 3-0 Bayern Munich
MT89   **Arsenal** 1-0 Porto
MT89 (1, W)   **Arsenal** 1-0 Liverpool
MT90 (S)   **Arsenal** 0-1 Sampdoria
FAC91   **Arsenal** 1-3 Spurs
INT94   **England** 5-0 Greece
INT94   **England** 0-0 Norway
CS98 (S)   **Arsenal** 3-0 Man Utd
EC98 (S)   **Arsenal** 0-1 Lens

Boulton, Colin (1, 0)
CS75   **Derby** 2-0 West Ham

Bovington, Eddie (1, 0)
FAC64   **West Ham**   3-2   PNE

Bowden, Ray (1, 0)
FAC36   **Arsenal**   1-0   Sheffield Utd

Bowers, Jack (1, 1)
BC34 (1)   **England**   3-0   Scotland

Bowles, Stan (2, 0)
BC74 (W)   **England**   1-0   N Ireland
INT77   **England**   0-2   Netherlands

Bowyer, Ian (3, 0)
FLC70 (S)   **Man City**   2-1   WBA
FLC78   **Nottm F**   0-0   Liverpool
FLC80   **Nottm F**   0-1   Wolves

Boyce, Ronnie (3, 1)
SI58   **England**   3-1   Scotland
FAC64 (1)   **West Ham**   3-2   PNE
ECW65   **West Ham**   2-0   TSV Munich

Boyd, Jimmy (1, 0)
FAC32   **Newcastle Utd**   2-1   Arsenal

Boyd, Len (1, 0)
FAC56 (C)   **Birmingham**   1-3   Man City

Boyd, Tommy (1, 0)
ECH96   **Scotland**   0-2   England

Boyer, Phil (2, 0)
FLC75   **Norwich**   0-1   Aston Villa
FLC79   **Southampton**   2-3   Nottm F

Boyes, Wally (1, 1)
FAC35 (1)   **WBA**   2-4   Sheffield W

Boyle, John (1, 0)
FAC67   **Chelsea**   1-2   Spurs

Boyle, Tommy (1, 0)
FAC25   **Sheffield Utd**   1-0   Cardiff

Brabrook, Peter (2, 0)
U23I57   **England**   3-2   Romania
FAC64   **West Ham**   3-2   PNE

Bracewell, Paul (9, 0)
CS84   **Everton**   1-0   Liverpool
FAC85   **Everton**   0-1   Man Utd
CS85   **Everton**   2-0   Man Utd
WCQ85   **England**   0-0   N Ireland
FAC86   **Everton**   1-3   Liverpool
SC89 (W)   **Everton**   3-4   Nottm F
FAC89 (W)   **Everton**   2-3   Liverpool
PPO90   **Sunderland**   0-1   Swindon
FAC92 (C)   **Sunderland**   0-2   Liverpool

Bradford, Joe (3, 1)
BC28   **England**   1-5   Scotland
BC30   **England**   5-2   Scotland
FAC31 (1)   **Birmingham**   1-2   WBA

Bradley, Bill (1, 0)
FAC24   **Newcastle Utd**   2-0   Aston Villa

Bradley, Gordon (1, 0)
FAC49   **Leicester**   1-3   Wolves

Bradley, Keith (1, 0)
FLC71   **Aston Villa**   0-2   Spurs

Bradley, Warren (3, 3)
AC57 (1)   **B Auckland**   3-1   Wycombe

BAC58 (1)   **England**   2-3   Scotland
INT59 (1)   **England**   2-2   Italy

Bradshaw, Paul (1, 0)
FLC80   **Wolves**   1-0   Nottm F

Bradshaw, Thomas (1, 0)
BC28   **Scotland**   5-1   England

Brady, Liam (8, 1)
INT76   **R of Ireland**   1-1   England
FAC78 (W)   **Arsenal**   0-1   Ipswich
FAC79   **Arsenal**   3-2   Man Utd
CS79   **Arsenal**   1-3   Liverpool
ECQ80 (C)   **R of Ireland**   0-2   England
FAC80   **Arsenal**   0-1   West Ham
INT85 (1)   **R of Ireland**   1-2   England
LCEN87 (W)   **Football League**   3-0   Rest of World

Brain, Jimmy (1, 0)
FAC27   **Arsenal**   0-1   Cardiff

Branagan, Keith (2, 0)
CCC95   **Bolton**   1-2   Liverpool
PPO95   **Bolton**   4-3   Reading

Branca, Marco (1, 0)
CCC98   **Middlesbrough**   0-2   Chelsea

Bray, George (1, 0)
FAC47   **Burnley**   0-1   Charlton

Bray, Jack (3, 0)
FAC33   **Man City**   0-3   Everton
FAC34   **Man City**   2-1   Portsmouth
BC36   **England**   1-1   Scotland

Bray, John (1, 0)
FAC60   **Blackburn**   0-3   Wolves

Brazil, Alan (1, 0)
BC83 (S)   **Scotland**   0-2   England

Breacker, Tim (4, 0)
SC88   **Luton**   1-4   Reading
LCT88   **Luton**   0-2   Man Utd
LC88   **Luton**   3-2   Arsenal
LC89   **Luton**   1-3   Nottm F

Bremner, Billy (11, 1)
SI58   **Scotland**   1-3   England
FAC65 (1)   **Leeds**   1-2   Liverpool
ECQ67   **Scotland**   3-2   England
FLC68 (C)   **Leeds**   1-0   Arsenal
BC69 (C)   **Scotland**   1-4   England
FAC70 (C)   **Leeds**   2-2   Chelsea
BC71   **Scotland**   1-3   England
FAC72 (C)   **Leeds**   1-0   Arsenal
FAC73 (C)   **Leeds**   0-1   Sunderland
BC73 (C)   **Scotland**   0-1   England
CS74 (C, D)   **Leeds**   1-1   Liverpool
As Manager
LCT88   **Leeds**   0-3   Nottingham F

Bremner, Des (1, 0)
CS81   **Aston Villa**   2-2   Spurs

Brennan, Frank (3, 0)
FAC51   **Newcastle Utd**   2-0   Blackpool
FAC52   **Newcastle Utd**   1-0   Arsenal
BC53   **Scotland**   2-2   England

Brennan, Mark (1, 0)
ZC90   **Middlesbrough** 0-1 Chelsea

Brennan, Shay (1, 0)
EC68   **Man Utd** 4-1 Benfica

Bridges, Barry (4, 1)
SI56 (1)   **England** 1-2 Scotland
BC65   **England** 2-2 Scotland
INT65   **England** 1-0 Hungary
INT65   **England** 2-3 Austria

Bright, Mark (9, 1)
LCT88   **C Palace** 0-0 Sheffield W
FAC90   **C Palace** 3-3 Man Utd
FAC90   **C Palace** 0-1 Man Utd
ZC91   **C Palace** 4-1 Everton
FAC93 (1)   **Sheffield W** 2-1 Sheffield Utd
CCC93   **Sheffield W** 1-2 Arsenal
FAC93   **Sheffield W** 1-1 Arsenal
FAC93   **Sheffield W** 1-2 Arsenal
PPO98 (W)   **Charlton** 4-4 Sunderland

Briggs, Gary (1, 0)
MC86   **Oxford Utd** 3-0 QPR

Briggs, George (1, 0)
FAC31   **Birmingham** 1-2 WBA

Briggs, Max (1, 0)
FLC73   **Norwich** 0-1 Spurs

Britton, Cliff (1, 0)
FAC33   **Everton** 3-0 Man City
As Manager
FAC47   **Burnley** 0-1 Charlton

Broadbent, Peter (3, 0)
BC59   **England** 1-0 Scotland
INT59   **England** 2-2 Italy
FAC60   **Wolves** 3-0 Blackburn

Broadis, Ivor (2, 2)
INT51   **England** 2-2 Austria
BC53 (2)   **England** 2-2 Scotland

Brock, Kevin (3, 0)
SI78   **England** 3-3 France
SI78   **England** 3-0 Scotland
MC86   **Oxford Utd** 3-0 QPR

Brogan, Jim (1, 0)
BC71   **Scotland** 1-3 England

Brolin, Tomas (2, 0)
ECW93   **Parma** 3-1 Royal Antwerp
CCC96 (S)   **Leeds** 0-3 Aston Villa

Brook, Eric (4, 1)
FAC33   **Man City** 0-3 Everton
BC34 (1)   **England** 3-0 Scotland
FAC34   **Man City** 2-1 Portsmouth
BC36   **England** 1-1 Scotland

Brooke, Gary (3, 0)
FAC81 (S)   **Spurs** 1-1 Man City
FAC82 (S)   **Spurs** 1-1 QPR
FAC82 (S)   **Spurs** 1-0 QPR

Brooking, Sir Trevor (24, 2)
INT74   **England** 2-2 Argentina
ECQ74 (S)   **England** 3-0 Czechoslovakia

ECQ74   **England** 0-0 Portugal
FAC75   **West Ham** 2-0 Fulham
CS75   **West Ham** 0-2 Derby
INT76   **England** 1-1 R of Ireland
WCQ76 (W)   **England** 2-1 Finland
INT77   **England** 0-2 Netherlands
BC77 (W)   **England** 0-1 Wales
WCQ77 (1)   **England** 2-0 Italy
INT78   **England** 4-1 Hungary
ECQ79   **England** 4-0 N Ireland
BC79 (S)   **England** 0-0 Wales
BC79   **England** 3-1 Scotland
ECQ79   **England** 1-0 Denmark
FAC80 (1)   **West Ham** 1-0 Arsenal
INT80 (S)   **England** 3-1 Argentina
BC80   **England** 1-1 N Ireland
CS80   **West Ham** 0-1 Liverpool
WCQ80 (W)   **England** 2-1 Switzerland
FLC81   **West Ham** 1-1 Liverpool
INT81 (W)   **England** 1-2 Spain
WCQ81 (W)   **England** 0-0 Romania
WCQ81   **England** 1-0 Hungary

Brooks, Johnny (2, 2)
BC56 (1)   **England** 3-1 Wales
INT56 (1)   **England** 3-0 Yugoslavia

Brotherston, Noel (2, 0)
BC80   **N Ireland** 1-1 England
BC82 (W)   **N Ireland** 0-4 England

Browell, Tommy (1, 0)
FAC26   **Man City** 0-1 Bolton

Brown, Alan (1, 0)
FAC47 (C)   **Burnley** 0-1 Charlton
As Manager
FAC66   **Sheffield W** 2-3 Everton

Brown, Allan (1, 0)
FAC59   **Luton** 1-2 Nottm F

Brown, Bill (5, 0)
BC59   **Scotland** 0-1 England
FAC61   **Spurs** 2-0 Leicester
FAC62   **Spurs** 3-1 Burnley
BC63   **Scotland** 2-1 England
BC65   **Scotland** 2-2 England

Brown, Billy (1, 0)
FAC23   **West Ham** 0-2 Bolton

Brown, Eddie (1, 0)
FAC56   **Birmingham** 1-3 Man City

Brown, George (1, 0)
FAC28   **Huddersfield** 1-3 Blackburn

Brown, George (3, 0)
BC32   **Scotland** 0-3 England
BC36   **Scotland** 1-1 England
BC38 (C)   **Scotland** 1-0 England

Brown, Jack (1, 0)
FAC35   **Sheffield W** 4-2 WBA

Brown, Ken (3, 0)
BC59   **England** 2-1 N Ireland
FAC64   **West Ham** 3-2 PNE
ECW65   **West Ham** 2-0 TSV Munich

Brown, Robert (6, 1)
LSC43	**Charlton**	1-7 Arsenal
LSC44	**Charlton**	3-1 Chelsea
LSC45	**Millwall**	0-2 Chelsea
VI45	**England**	2-2 France
VI46 (1)	**England**	2-0 Belgium
FAC46	**Charlton**	1-4 Derby

Brown, Tony (4, 0)
FLC67	**WBA**	2-3 QPR
FAC68	**WBA**	1-0 Everton
FLC70	**WBA**	1-2 Man City
BC71	**England**	0-0 Wales

Bruce, Steve (15, 1)
MC85	**Norwich**	1-0 Sunderland
LCT88	**Man Utd**	2-0 Luton
LCT88 (1)	**Man Utd**	1-0 Everton
LCT88	**Man Utd**	1-2 Sheffield W
FAC90	**Man Utd**	3-3 C Palace
FAC90	**Man Utd**	1-0 C Palace
CS90 (C)	**Man Utd**	1-1 Liverpool
RLC91	**Man Utd**	0-1 Sheffield W
RLC92 (C)	**Man Utd**	1-0 Nottm F
CS93 (C)	**Man Utd**	1-1 Arsenal
CCC94 (C, W)	**Man Utd**	1-3 Aston Villa
FAC94 (C)	**Man Utd**	1-1 Oldham
FAC94 (C)	**Man Utd**	4-0 Chelsea
CS94 (C)	**Man Utd**	2-0 Blackburn
FAC95 (C, W)	**Man Utd**	0-1 Everton

Brush, Paul (1, 0)
CS80	**West Ham**	0-1 Liverpool

Buchan, Charlie (2, 0)
BC24	**England**	1-1 Scotland
FAC27 (C)	**Arsenal**	0-1 Cardiff

Buchan, Martin (4, 0)
FAC76 (C)	**Man Utd**	0-1 Southampton
FAC77 (C)	**Man Utd**	2-1 Liverpool
CS77 (C)	**Man Utd**	0-0 Liverpool
FAC79 (C)	**Man Utd**	2-3 Arsenal

Buchanan, John (1, 0)
BC30	**Scotland**	2-5 England

Bull, Steve (8, 2)
LCT88	**Wolves**	1-1 Everton
SVT88	**Wolves**	2-0 Burnley
INT89	**England**	2-1 Yugoslavia
INT90 (2)	**England**	4-2 Czechoslovakia
INT90 (S)	**England**	1-0 Denmark
INT90 (S)	**England**	1-2 Uruguay
INT90 (W)	**England**	1-0 Hungary
ECQ90 (W)	**England**	2-0 Poland

Bullions, Jim (1, 0)
FAC46	**Derby**	4-1 Charlton

Bumstead, John (2, 0)
FMC86	**Chelsea**	5-4 Man City
ZC90	**Chelsea**	1-0 Middlesbrough

Bunn, Frankie (1, 0)
LC90	**Oldham**	0-1 Nottm F

Burbanks, Eddie (1, 1)
FAC37 (1)	**Sunderland**	3-1 PNE

Burchill, Mark (1, 0)
ECQ99 (S)	**Scotland**	1-0 England

Burgess, Ron (4, 0)
WI43	**Wales**	3-8 England
CHA44	**C Services**	5-2 Met Police
CHA45	**C Services**	3-1 N Police
BC52 (C)	**Wales**	2-5 England
As Manager		
AC65	**Hendon**	3-1 Whitby Town

Burke, Steve (1, 0)
FAC82 (S)	**QPR**	0-1 Spurs

Burkett, Jack (2, 0)
FAC64	**West Ham**	3-2 PNE
ECW65	**West Ham**	2-0 TSV Munich

Burkitt, Jack (1, 0)
FAC59 (C)	**Nottm F**	2-1 Luton

Burley, Craig (4, 0)
FAC94 (W)	**Chelsea**	2-0 Luton
FAC94 (W)	**Chelsea**	0-4 Man Utd
ECH96 (S)	**Scotland**	0-2 England
ECQ99	**Scotland**	1-0 England

Burley, George (3, 0)
FAC78	**Ipswich**	1-0 Arsenal
CS78	**Ipswich**	0-5 Nottm F
BC79	**Scotland**	1-3 England
As Manager		
PPO00	**Ipswich**	4-2 Barnsley

Burns, Kenny (3, 0)
FLC78	**Nottm F**	0-0 Liverpool
CS78	**Nottm F**	5-0 Ipswich
FLC80	**Nottm F**	0-1 Wolves

Burns, Mick (1, 0)
FAC37	**PNE**	1-3 Sunderland

Burns, Micky (1, 0)
FLC76	**Newcastle Utd**	1-2 Man City

Burns, Tommy (1, 0)
RC88 (S)	**Scotland**	0-1 England

Burridge, John (1, 0)
FLC77	**Aston Villa**	0-0 Everton

Burrows, David (6, 0)
MT89	**Liverpool**	2-0 Dynamo Kiev
MT89	**Liverpool**	0-1 Arsenal
CS89	**Liverpool**	1-0 Arsenal
CS90	**Liverpool**	1-1 Man Utd
FAC92	**Liverpool**	2-0 Sunderland
CS92	**Liverpool**	3-4 Leeds

Burrows, Frank (1, 0)
FLC69	**Swindon**	3-1 Arsenal
As Manager		
AT94	**Swansea City**	1-1 Huddersfield

Burrows, Horace (1, 0)
FAC35	**Sheffield W**	4-2 WBA

Burton, Ollie (2, 0)
SI57	**Wales**	0-2 England
BC69	**Wales**	1-2 England

Burton, Stan (1, 0)
FAC39	**Wolves**	1-4 Portsmouth

Busby, Sir Matt (5, 0)

FAC33	**Man City** 0-3 Everton	
FAC34	**Man City** 2-1 Portsmouth	
WI42 (C)	**Scotland** 0-3 England	
WI42 (C)	**Scotland** 0-0 England	
WI44 (C)	**Scotland** 2-6 England	

As Manager

FAC48	**Man Utd** 4-2 Blackpool
OLY48	**Great Britain** 1-3 Yugoslavia
OLY48	**Great Britain** 3-5 Denmark
FAC57	**Man Utd** 1-2 Aston Villa
FAC58	**Man Utd** 0-2 Bolton
FAC63	**Man Utd** 3-1 Leicester
EC68	**Man Utd** 4-1 Benfica

Busby, Viv (1, 0)

FAC75	**Fulham** 0-2 West Ham

Butcher, Terry (28, 2)

INT81	**England** 1-2 Spain
INT82	**England** 1-2 W Germany
ECQ82	**England** 9-0 Luxembourg
BC83 (1)	**England** 2-1 Wales
ECQ83	**England** 0-0 Greece
ECQ83	**England** 2-0 Hungary
BC83	**England** 2-0 Scotland
ECQ83	**England** 0-1 Denmark
BC84	**England** 1-0 N Ireland
INT84	**England** 1-0 E Germany
WCQ84	**England** 5-0 Finland
INT85	**England** 2-1 R of Ireland
RC86 (1)	**England** 2-1 Scotland
ECQ86	**England** 3-0 N Ireland
ECQ86 (C)	**England** 2-0 Yugoslavia
RC87	**England** 1-1 Brazil
ECQ87	**England** 8-0 Turkey
INT88	**England** 1-0 Denmark
WCQ88	**England** 0-0 Sweden
WCQ89	**England** 5-0 Albania
RC89	**England** 0-0 Chile
WCQ89	**England** 3-0 Poland
INT89	**England** 0-0 Italy
INT89	**England** 2-1 Yugoslavia
INT90 (C)	**England** 1-0 Brazil
INT90	**England** 4-2 Czechoslovakia
INT90 (C)	**England** 1-0 Denmark
INT90	**England** 1-2 Uruguay

Butler, Billy (4, 1)

FAC23	**Bolton** 2-0 West Ham
BC24	**England** 1-1 Scotland
FAC26	**Bolton** 1-0 Man City
FAC29 (1)	**Bolton** 2-0 Portsmouth

Butler, Geoff (1, 0)

FLC73	**Norwich** 0-1 Spurs

Butler, Jack (1, 0)

FAC27	**Arsenal** 0-1 Cardiff

Butler, Joe (1, 0)

FLC69	**Swindon** 3-1 Arsenal

Butt, Nicky (12, 1)

SI90 (S)	**England** 1-1 France
FAC94 (S)	**Man Utd** 1-1 Oldham

FAC95	**Man Utd** 0-1 Everton
FAC96	**Man Utd** 1-0 Liverpool
CS96 (1, W)	**Man Utd** 4-0 Newcastle Utd
INT97 (S)	**England** 2-0 Mexico
CS97	**Man Utd** 1-1 Chelsea
WCQ97 (S)	**England** 4-0 Moldova
INT98	**England** 0-2 Chile
CS98 (W)	**Man Utd** 0-3 Arsenal
INT98	**England** 2-0 Czech Republic
CS99 (W)	**Man Utd** 1-2 Arsenal

Byrne, Gerry (2, 0)

BC63	**England** 1-2 Scotland
FAC65	**Liverpool** 2-1 Leeds

Byrne, John (4, 0)

INT85 (S)	**R of Ireland** 1-2 England
MC86	**QPR** 0-3 Oxford Utd
PPO91 (S)	**Brighton** 1-3 Notts County
FAC92	**Sunderland** 0-2 Liverpool

Byrne, Johnny (5, 2)

BC61	**England** 1-1 N Ireland
FAC64	**West Ham** 3-2 PNE
INT64 (2)	**England** 2-1 Uruguay
BC64	**England** 2-1 Wales
BC65	**England** 2-2 Scotland

Byrne, Roger (13, 0)

BC54	**England** 3-2 Wales
INT54	**England** 3-1 W Germany
BC55	**England** 7-2 Scotland
BC55	**England** 3-0 N Ireland
INT55	**England** 4-1 Spain
INT56	**England** 4-2 Brazil
BC56	**England** 3-1 Wales
INT56	**England** 3-0 Yugoslavia
BC57	**England** 2-1 Scotland
FAC57 (C)	**Man Utd** 1-2 Aston Villa
WCQ57	**England** 5-1 R of Ireland
BC57	**England** 2-3 N Ireland
INT57	**England** 4-0 France

Caesar, Gus (3, 0)

LC88	**Arsenal** 2-3 Luton
MT89 (S)	**Arsenal** 1-0 Liverpool
CS89 (W)	**Arsenal** 0-1 Liverpool

Calderwood, Colin (3, 0)

PPO90 (C)	**Swindon** 1-0 Sunderland
PPO93 (C)	**Swindon** 4-3 Leicester
ECH96	**Scotland** 0-2 England

Caldow, Eric (4, 0)

BC57	**Scotland** 1-2 England
BC59	**Scotland** 0-1 England
BC61 (C)	**Scotland** 3-9 England
BC63 (C)	**Scotland** 2-1 England

Callaghan, Ian (10, 0)

FAC65	**Liverpool** 2-1 Leeds
WC 66	**England** 2-0 France
FAC71	**Liverpool** 1-2 Arsenal
FAC74	**Liverpool** 3-0 Newcastle Utd
CS74	**Liverpool** 1-1 Leeds
CS76	**Liverpool** 1-0 Southampton
FAC77 (S)	**Liverpool** 1-2 Man Utd

CS77   **Liverpool** 0-0 Man Utd
INT77 (W)   **England** 0-0 Switzerland
FLC78   **Liverpool** 0-0 Nottm F

Callaghan, Nigel (1, 0)
FAC84   **Watford** 0-2 Everton

Campbell, Austin (2, 0)
FAC28   **Blackburn** 3-1 Huddersfield
FAC30   **Huddersfield** 0-2 Arsenal

Campbell, Billy (1, 0)
ECQ67   **N Ireland** 0-2 England

Campbell, David (1, 0)
ECQ86   **N Ireland** 0-3 England

Campbell, Kevin (10, 0)
MT89 (S)   **Arsenal** 1-0 Porto
MT90 (S, 1)   **Arsenal** 2-0 Aston Villa
MT90 (S)   **Arsenal** 0-1 Sampdoria
FAC91   **Arsenal** 1-3 Spurs
CS91 (W)   **Arsenal** 0-0 Spurs
FAC93 (W)   **Arsenal** 1-0 Spurs
CCC93   **Arsenal** 2-1 Sheffield W.
FAC93   **Arsenal** 1-1 Sheffield W.
FAC93   **Arsenal** 2-1 Sheffield W.
CS93   **Arsenal** 1-1 Man Utd

Campbell, Sol (17, 0)
INT96 (S)   **England** 3-0 Hungary
ECH96 (S)   **England** 2-0 Scotland
WCQ97   **England** 0-1 Italy
WCQ97   **England** 2-0 Georgia
WCQ97   **England** 4-0 Moldova
INT97   **England** 2-0 Cameroon
INT98   **England** 0-2 Chile
INT98   **England** 3-0 Portugal
ECQ98   **England** 0-0 Bulgaria
INT98 (C)   **England** 2-0 Czech Republic
WLC99 (C)   **Spurs** 1-0 Leicester
ECQ99   **England** 3-1 Poland
ECQ99   **England** 0-0 Sweden
ECQ99   **England** 0-1 Scotland
INT00   **England** 0-0 Argentina
INT00   **England** 1-1 Brazil
INT00   **England** 2-0 Ukraine

Camsell, George (1, 1)
BC36 (1)   **England** 1-1 Scotland

Cann, Sydney (1, 0)
FAC33   **Man City** 0-3 Everton

Cantello, Len (2, 0)
SI67   **England** 0-2 Scotland
FLC70   **WBA** 1-2 Man City

Cantona, Eric (8, 8)
INT92   **France** 0-2 England
CS92 (3)   **Leeds** 4-3 Liverpool
CS93   **Man Utd** 1-1 Arsenal
CCC94   **Man Utd** 1-3 Aston Villa
FAC94 (2)   **Man Utd** 4-0 Chelsea
CS94 (1)   **Man Utd** 2-0 Blackburn
FAC96 (C, 1)   **Man Utd** 1-0 Liverpool
CS96 (C, 1)   **Man Utd** 4-0 Newcastle Utd

Cantwell, Noel (2, 0)
WCQ57   **R of Ireland** 1-5 England
FAC63 (C)   **Man Utd** 3-1 Leicester

Capewell, Len (1, 0)
FAC24   **Aston Villa** 0-2 Newcastle Utd

Carbone, Benito (2, 0)
FAC00 (W)   **Aston Villa** 0-0 Bolton
FAC00 (W)   **Aston Villa** 0-1 Chelsea

Carey, Johnny (1, 0)
FAC48 (C)   **Man Utd** 4-2 Blackpool

Carr, Franz (7, 2)
LCT88 (1)   **Nottm F** 3-0 Leeds
LCT88   **Nottm F** 0-0 Aston Villa
LCT88 (1)   **Nottm F** 2-2 Tranmere
LCT88   **Nottm F** 0-0 Sheffield W
SC89 (S)   **Nottm F** 4-3 Everton
LC90   **Nottm F** 1-0 Oldham
FAC93   **Sheffield Utd** 1-2 Sheffield W

Carr, Stephen (1, 0)
WLC99   **Spurs** 1-0 Leicester

Carr, Willie (1, 0)
FLC80   **Wolves** 1-0 Nottm F

Carrodus, Frank (3, 0)
FLC75   **Aston Villa** 1-0 Norwich
FLC77   **Aston Villa** 0-0 Everton
FAT86   **Runcorn** 0-1 Altrincham

Carter, Joe (2, 0)
FAC31   **WBA** 2-1 Birmingham
FAC35   **WBA** 2-4 Sheffield W

Carter, Raich (9, 9)
BC34   **England** 3-0 Scotland
FAC37 (C, 1)   **Sunderland** 3-1 PNE
WI43 (2)   **England** 5-3 Wales
WI43 (2)   **England** 8-3 Wales
WI44 (1)   **England** 6-2 Scotland
WI44 (1)   **England** 6-2 Scotland
VI45 (1)   **England** 2-2 France
FAC46   **Derby** 4-1 Charlton
BC47 (1)   **England** 1-1 Scotland

Cascarino, Tony (5, 0)
MT90   **Aston Villa** 0-2 Arsenal
MT90   **Aston Villa** 0-1 Real Sociedad
ECQ91 (S)   **R of Ireland** 1-1 England
FAC94   **Chelsea** 2-0 Luton
FAC94 (S)   **Chelsea** 0-4 Man Utd

Case, Jimmy (10, 1)
CS76   **Liverpool** 1-0 Southampton
FAC77 (1)   **Liverpool** 1-2 Man Utd
CS77   **Liverpool** 0-0 Man Utd
FLC78   **Liverpool** 0-0 Nottm F
EC78 (W)   **Liverpool** 1-0 Bruges
CS79   **Liverpool** 3-1 Arsenal
CS80   **Liverpool** 1-0 West Ham
FLC81 (S)   **Liverpool** 1-1 West Ham
FAC83   **Brighton** 2-2 Man Utd
FAC83   **Brighton** 0-4 Man Utd

Casey, Tom (1, 0)
FAC55   **Newcastle Utd** 3-1 Man City

Caskey, Billy (1, 0)
ECQ79 (W)   **N Ireland** 0-4 England
Cassidy, Tommy (5, 0)
FAC74   **Newcastle Utd** 0-3 Liverpool
BC74   **N Ireland** 0-1 England
FLC76   **Newcastle Utd** 1-2 Man City
BC76   **N Ireland** 0-4 England
BC80 (W)   **N Ireland** 1-1 England
Catlin, Ted (1, 0)
FAC35   **Sheffield W** 4-2 WBA
Caton, Tommy (4, 0)
SI78   **England** 3-3 France
SI78   **England** 3-0 Scotland
FAC81   **Man City** 1-1 Spurs
FAC81   **Man City** 2-3 Spurs
Cawley, Peter (3, 0)
LCT88   **Wimbledon** 0-1 Tranmere
CS88   **Wimbledon** 1-2 Liverpool
AWS97 (C)   **Colchester United** 0-0 Carlisle
Challinor, Dave (1, 0)
WLC00   **Tranmere** 1-2 Leicester
Chalmers, Len (1, 0)
FAC61   **Leicester** 0-2 Spurs
Chamberlain, Mark (6, 1)
SI77   **England** 2-0 Scotland
SI77   **England** 1-2 W Germany
ECQ82 (S, 1)   **England** 9-0 Luxembourg
ECQ83 (S)   **England** 0-1 Denmark
INT84   **England** 0-2 USSR
WCQ84 (S)   **England** 5-0 Finland
Channon, Mike (23, 10)
INT72   **England** 1-1 Yugoslavia
BC73 (1)   **England** 3-0 Wales
BC73   **England** 1-0 Scotland
INT73 (2)   **England** 7-0 Austria
WCQ73   **England** 1-1 Poland
INT73   **England** 0-1 Italy
BC74   **England** 1-0 N Ireland
INT74 (1)   **England** 2-2 Argentina
ECQ74 (1)   **England** 3-0 Czechoslovakia
ECQ74   **England** 0-0 Portugal
INT75   **England** 2-0 W Germany
ECQ75 (W)   **England** 5-0 Cyprus
BC75 (W)   **England** 2-2 Wales
BC75   **England** 5-1 Scotland
FAC76   **Southampton** 1-0 Man Utd
BC76 (2)   **England** 4-0 N Ireland
CS76   **Southampton** 0-1 Liverpool
WCQ76   **England** 2-1 Finland
WCQ77 (2)   **England** 5-0 Luxembourg
BC77   **England** 0-1 Wales
BC77 (1)   **England** 1-2 Scotland
INT77 (W)   **England** 0-0 Switzerland
MC85   **Norwich** 1-0 Sunderland
Chapman, Lee (7, 2)
LCT88   **Sheffield W** 0-0 C Palace
LCT88   **Sheffield W** 1-1 Wigan Athletic
LCT88   **Sheffield W** 2-1 Man Utd

LCT88 (W)   **Sheffield W** 0-0 Nottm F
LC89   **Nottm F** 3-1 Luton
SC89 (2)   **Nottm F** 4-3 Everton
CS92 (W)   **Leeds** 4-3 Liverpool
Charles, Gary (5, 0)
FAC91   **Nottm F** 1-2 Spurs
ZC92   **Nottm F** 3-2 Southampton
RLC92 (W)   **Nottm F** 0-1 Man Utd
PP094   **Derby** 1-2 Leicester
CCC96   **Aston Villa** 3-0 Leeds
Charles, Jeremy (1, 1)
MC86 (1)   **Oxford** 3-0 QPR
Charles, John (2, 3)
BC54 (2)   **Wales** 2-3 England
BC56 (1)   **Wales** 1-3 England
Charles, Mel (1, 0)
BC56   **Wales** 1-3 England
Charlton, Sir Bobby (50, 27)
SI53 (2)   **England** 3-3 Wales
FAC57   **Man Utd** 1-2 Aston Villa
FAC58   **Man Utd** 0-2 Bolton
INT58 (2)   **England** 2-1 Portugal
INT58 (1)   **England** 5-0 USSR
BC59 (1)   **England** 1-0 Scotland
INT59 (1)   **England** 2-2 Italy
INT59 (1)   **England** 2-3 Sweden
INT60   **England** 3-3 Yugoslavia
INT60   **England** 4-2 Spain
BC60 (1)   **England** 5-1 Wales
BC61   **England** 9-3 Scotland
INT61 (3)   **England** 8-0 Mexico
WCQ61   **England** 2-0 Portugal
BC61 (1)   **England** 1-1 N Ireland
INT62   **England** 3-1 Austria
INT62   **England** 3-1 Switzerland
BC63   **England** 1-2 Scotland
INT63   **England** 1-1 Brazil
FAC63   **Man Utd** 3-1 Leicester
CEN63   **England** 2-1 FIFA
BC63   **England** 8-3 N Ireland
INT64   **England** 2-1 Uruguay
BC65 (1)   **England** 2-2 Scotland
INT65 (1)   **England** 2-3 Austria
BC65   **England** 2-1 N Ireland
INT66   **England** 1-0 W Germany
INT66 (1)   **England** 2-0 Yugoslavia
WC66   **England** 0-0 Uruguay
WC66 (1)   **England** 2-0 Mexico
WC66   **England** 2-0 France
WC66   **England** 1-0 Argentina
WC66 (2)   **England** 2-1 Portugal
WC66   **England** 4-2 W Germany
INT66   **England** 0-0 Czechoslovakia
ECQ66 (1)   **England** 5-1 Wales
ECQ67   **England** 2-3 Scotland
ECQ67 (1)   **England** 2-0 N Ireland
INT67   **England** 2-2 USSR
ECQ68 (1)   **England** 1-0 Spain
INT68 (1, W)   **England** 3-1 Sweden

EC68 (C, 2)	**Man Utd** 4-1 Benfica
INT68	**England** 1-1 Bulgaria
INT69 (C)	**England** 1-1 Romania
BC69 (1)	**England** 2-1 Wales
BC69	**England** 4-1 Scotland
INT69	**England** 1-0 Portugal
INT70 (C)	**England** 0-0 Netherlands
BC70 (C,1)	**England** 3-1 Northern Ireland
EEC73 (C)	**The Three** 2-0 The Six

Charlton, Jack (25, 5)

BC65	**England** 2-2 Scotland
FAC65	**Leeds** 1-2 Liverpool
INT65	**England** 1-0 Hungary
INT65	**England** 2-3 Austria
BC65	**England** 2-1 N Ireland
INT66	**England** 1-0 W Germany
INT66	**England** 2-0 Yugoslavia
WC66	**England** 0-0 Uruguay
WC66	**England** 2-0 Mexico
WC66	**England** 2-0 France
WC66	**England** 1-0 Argentina
WC66	**England** 2-1 Portugal
WC66	**England** 4-2 W Germany
INT66	**England** 0-0 Czechoslovakia
ECQ66 (1)	**England** 5-1 Wales
ECQ67 (1)	**England** 2-3 Scotland
FLC68	**Leeds** 1-0 Arsenal
ECQ68	**England** 1-0 Spain
INT69 (1)	**England** 1-1 Romania
INT69	**England** 5-0 France
BC69	**England** 2-1 Wales
INT69 (1)	**England** 1-0 Portugal
INT70	**England** 0-0 Netherlands
FAC70 (1)	**Leeds** 2-2 Chelsea
FAC72	**Leeds** 1-0 Arsenal

As Manager

ECQ91	**R of Ireland** 1-1 England

Charvet, Laurent (1, 0)

FAC99	**Newcastle Utd** 0-2 Man Utd

Cheesebrough, Albert (1, 0)

FAC61	**Leicester** 0-2 Spurs

Cherry, Trevor (13, 1)

FAC73	**Leeds** 0-1 Sunderland
CS74 (1)	**Leeds** 1-1 Liverpool
INT76	**England** 1-1 R of Ireland
WCQ77	**England** 5-0 Luxembourg
BC77 (S)	**England** 1-2 Scotland
INT77	**England** 0-0 Switzerland
WCQ77	**England** 2-0 Italy
INT78	**England** 1-1 Brazil
INT78	**England** 1-0 Czechoslovakia
BC79	**England** 0-0 Wales
ECQ80	**England** 2-0 R of Ireland
INT80 (S)	**England** 3-1 Argentina
BC80	**England** 1-1 N Ireland

Chettle, Steve (9, 0)

LCT88	**Nottm F** 3-0 Leeds
LCT88	**Nottm F** 0-0 Aston Villa
LCT88	**Nottm F** 2-2 Tranmere
LCT88	**Nottm F** 0-0 Sheffield W
SC89 (S)	**Nottm F** 4-3 Everton
LC90	**Nottm F** 1-0 Oldham
FAC91	**Nottm F** 1-2 Spurs
ZC92 (S)	**Nottm F** 3-2 Southampton
PPO00	**Barnsley** 2-4 Ipswich

Chew, Jack (1, 0)

FAC47	**Burnley** 0-1 Charlton

Chilton, Allenby (2, 0)

LSC44	**Charlton** 3-1 Chelsea
FAC48	**Man Utd** 4-2 Blackpool

Chisholm, Gordon (1, 0)

MC85	**Sunderland** 0-1 Norwich

Chisholm, Ken (1, 0)

FAC49	**Leicester** 1-3 Wolves

Chivers, Martin (13, 9)

FLC71 (2)	**Spurs** 2-0 Aston Villa
ECQ71 (1)	**England** 3-0 Greece
ECQ71 (2)	**England** 5-0 Malta
BC71 (2)	**England** 3-1 Scotland
ECQ71 (S)	**England** 1-1 Switzerland
ECQ72	**England** 1-3 W Germany
BC72 (S)	**England** 0-1 N Ireland
WCQ73	**England** 1-1 Wales
FLC73	**Spurs** 1-0 Norwich
BC73 (1)	**England** 3-0 Wales
BC73	**England** 1-0 Scotland
INT73 (1)	**England** 7-0 Austria
WCQ73 (W)	**England** 1-1 Poland

Claesen, Nico (1, 0)

FAC87 (S)	**Spurs** 2-3 Coventry

Clamp, Eddie (2, 1)

SI50 (1)	**England** 8-2 Scotland
FAC60	**Wolves** 3-0 Blackburn

Claridge, Steve (4, 1)

PPO90 (S)	**Cambridge Utd** 1-0 Chesterfield
AWS95	**Birmingham** 1-0 Carlisle
PPO96 (1)	**Leicester** 2-1 C Palace
CCC97	**Leicester** 1-1 Middlesbrough

Clark, Bobby (1, 0)

BC71	**Scotland** 1-3 England

Clark, Clive (2, 2)

FLC67 (2)	**WBA** 2-3 QPR
FAC68	**WBA** 1-0 Everton

Clark, Frank (4, 0)

AC62	**Crook** 1-1 Hounslow
FAC74	**Newcastle Utd** 0-3 Liverpool
FLC78	**Nottm F** 0-0 Liverpool
FLC79	**Nottm F** 3-2 Southampton

Clarke, Allan (15, 6)

FAC69	**Leicester** 0-1 Man City
FAC70	**Leeds** 2-2 Chelsea
INT70 (1)	**England** 3-1 E Germany
ECQ71 (1)	**England** 5-0 Malta
BC71 (S)	**England** 0-0 Wales
BC71 (S)	**England** 3-1 Scotland
FAC72 (1)	**Leeds** 1-0 Arsenal
FAC73	**Leeds** 0-1 Sunderland

BC73	**England**	3-0 Wales
BC73	**England**	1-0 Scotland
INT73 (2)	**England**	7-0 Austria
WCQ73 (1)	**England**	1-1 Poland
INT73 (W)	**England**	0-1 Italy
CS74 (W)	**Leeds**	1-1 Liverpool
ECQ74 (W)	**England**	0-0 Portugal

Clarke, Colin (1, 0)

ECQ86	**N Ireland**	0-3 England

Clarke, Dennis (2, 0)

FLC67	**WBA**	2-3 QPR
FAC68 (S)	**WBA**	1-0 Everton

Clarke, Roy (3, 0)

BC52	**Wales**	2-5 England
BC54	**Wales**	2-3 England
FAC56	**Man City**	3-1 Birmingham

Clarke, Steve (6, 0)

LCEN87 (S)	**Football League**	3-0 Rest of World
FAC94	**Chelsea**	2-0 Luton
FAC94	**Chelsea**	0-4 Man Utd
FAC97	**Chelsea**	2-0 Middlesbrough
CS97	**Chelsea**	1-1 Man Utd
CCC98 (S)	**Chelsea**	2-0 Middlesbrough

Clarke, Wayne (5, 2)

SI76	**England**	4-1 Wales
SI76 (W)	**England**	6-1 France
CS87 (1)	**Everton**	1-0 Coventry
LCT88 (1)	**Everton**	1-1 Wolves
LCT88	**Everton**	0-1 Man Utd

Clayton, Ronnie (17, 0)

BC55	**England**	3-0 N Ireland
INT55	**England**	4-1 Spain
INT56	**England**	4-2 Brazil
BC56	**England**	3-1 Wales
INT56	**England**	3-0 Yugoslavia
BC57	**England**	2-1 Scotland
WCQ57	**England**	5-1 R of Ireland
BC57	**England**	2-3 N Ireland
INT57	**England**	4-0 France
INT58	**England**	2-1 Portugal
INT58	**England**	5-0 USSR
BC59	**England**	1-0 Scotland
INT59	**England**	2-2 Italy
INT59 (C)	**England**	2-3 Sweden
BC59 (C)	**England**	2-1 N Ireland
FAC60 (C)	**Blackburn**	0-3 Wolves
INT60 (C)	**England**	3-3 Yugoslavia

Clemence, Ray (42, 0)

FAC71	**Liverpool**	1-2 Arsenal
WCQ73	**England**	1-1 Wales
FAC74	**Liverpool**	3-0 Newcastle Utd
CS74	**Liverpool**	1-1 Leeds
ECQ74	**England**	3-0 Czechoslovakia
ECQ74	**England**	0-0 Portugal
INT75	**England**	2-0 W Germany
BC75	**England**	2-2 Wales
BC75	**England**	5-1 Scotland
BC76	**England**	4-0 N Ireland
CS76	**Liverpool**	1-0 Southampton

INT76	**England**	1-1 R of Ireland
WCQ76	**England**	2-1 Finland
INT77	**England**	0-2 Netherlands
WCQ77	**England**	5-0 Luxembourg
FAC77	**Liverpool**	1-2 Man Utd
BC77	**England**	1-2 Scotland
CS77	**Liverpool**	0-0 Man Utd
INT77	**England**	0-0 Switzerland
WCQ77	**England**	2-0 Italy
FLC78	**Liverpool**	0-0 Nottm F
EC78	**Liverpool**	1-0 Bruges
BC78	**England**	1-0 N Ireland
ECQ79	**England**	4-0 N Ireland
BC79	**England**	3-1 Scotland
CS79	**Liverpool**	3-1 Arsenal
ECQ79	**England**	1-0 Denmark
ECQ79	**England**	2-0 Bulgaria
ECQ80	**England**	2-0 R of Ireland
INT80	**England**	3-1 Argentina
CS80	**Liverpool**	1-0 West Ham
FLC81	**Liverpool**	1-1 West Ham
INT81	**England**	1-2 Spain
INT81 (C)	**England**	0-1 Brazil
CS81	**Spurs**	2-2 Aston Villa
BC82	**England**	4-0 N Ireland
FLC82	**Spurs**	1-3 Liverpool
FAC82	**Spurs**	1-1 QPR
FAC82	**Spurs**	1-0 QPR
CS82	**Spurs**	0-1 Liverpool
ECQ82	**England**	9-0 Luxembourg
FAC87	**Spurs**	2-3 Coventry

Clement, Andy (2, 0)

CS88 (S)	**Wimbledon**	1-2 Liverpool
FAT94	**Woking**	2-1 Runcorn

Clement, Dave (1, 0)

INT77	**England**	0-2 Netherlands

Clements, Dave (7, 0)

EYT63	**N Ireland**	0-4 England
YI63	**Rest of UK**	2-5 England
ECQ67	**N Ireland**	0-2 England
BC70	**N Ireland**	1-3 England
BC72	**N Ireland**	1-0 England
BC74 (C)	**N Ireland**	0-1 England
BC76 (C)	**N Ireland**	0-4 England

As Player-Manager

BC76	**N Ireland**	0-4 England

Clough, Brian (1, 0)

INT59	**England**	2-3 Sweden

As Manager

CS74	**Leeds**	1-1 Liverpool
FLC78	**Nottm F**	0-0 Liverpool
CS78	**Nottm F**	5-0 Ipswich
FLC79	**Nottm F**	3-2 Southampton
FLC80	**Nottm F**	0-1 Wolves
LC89	**Nottm F**	3-1 Luton
SC89	**Nottm F**	4-3 Everton
LC90	**Nottm F**	1-0 Oldham
FAC91	**Nottm F**	1-2 Spurs
ZC92	**Nottm F**	3-2 Southampton
RLC92	**Nottm F**	0-1 Man Utd

Clough, Nigel (13, 3)

LCT88	**Nottm F**	3-0 Leeds
LCT88	**Nottm F**	0-0 Aston Villa
LCT88 (1)	**Nottm F**	2-2 Tranmere
LCT88	**Nottm F**	0-0 Sheffield W
LC89 (2)	**Nottm F**	3-1 Luton
SC89	**Nottm F**	4-3 Everton
RC89	**England**	0-0 Chile
LC90	**Nottm F**	1-0 Oldham
FAC91	**Nottm F**	1-2 Spurs
INT91 (S)	**England**	2-2 Argentina
INT92	**England**	2-0 France
ZC92	**Nottm F**	3-2 Southampton
RLC92	**Nottm F**	0-1 Man Utd

Clunas, Billy (1, 0)

BC24	**Scotland**	1-1 England

Coates, Ralph (5, 1)

BC70	**England**	3-1 N Ireland
ECQ71 (S)	**England**	3-0 Greece
ECQ71	**England**	5-0 Malta
BC71 (W)	**England**	0-0 Wales
FLC73 (S, 1)	**Spurs**	1-0 Norwich

Cochrane, Terry (4, 1)

BC78 (S)	**N Ireland**	0-1 England
ECQ79 (W)	**N Ireland**	0-4 England
BC80 (S, 1)	**N Ireland**	1-1 England
BC82 (S)	**N Ireland**	0-4 England

Cockburn, Henry (3, 0)

FAC48	**Man Utd**	4-2 Blackpool
BC49	**England**	1-3 Scotland
INT51	**England**	2-1 Argentina

Cockerill, Glenn (1, 0)

ZC92 (C)	**Southampton**	2-3 Nottm F

Cohen, George (19, 0)

INT64	**England**	2-1 Uruguay
INT64	**England**	2-2 Belgium
BC64	**England**	2-1 Wales
BC65	**England**	2-2 Scotland
INT65	**England**	1-0 Hungary
INT65	**England**	2-3 Austria
BC65	**England**	2-1 N Ireland
INT66	**England**	1-0 W Germany
WC66	**England**	0-0 Uruguay
WC66	**England**	2-0 Mexico
WC66	**England**	2-0 France
WC66	**England**	1-0 Argentina
WC66	**England**	2-1 Portugal
WC66	**England**	4-2 W Germany
INT66	**England**	0-0 Czechoslovakia
ECQ66	**England**	5-1 Wales
ECQ67	**England**	2-3 Scotland
INT67	**England**	2-0 Spain
ECQ67	**England**	2-0 N Ireland

Cole, Andrew (19, 3)

SI87 (2)	**England**	2-0 W Germany
VS87 (S)	**England**	1-1 Scotland
YI90 (W)	**England**	0-0 Denmark
YI90 (1)	**England**	1-1 Czechoslovakia
YI90 (W)	**England**	3-0 Poland

U19I91 (W)	**England**	1-1 Spain
CS91 (S)	**Arsenal**	0-0 Spurs
INT95 (S)	**England**	0-0 Uruguay
FAC96 (W)	**Man Utd**	1-0 Liverpool
CS97	**Man Utd**	1-1 Chelsea
CS98 (W)	**Man Utd**	0-3 Arsenal
INT99 (S)	**England**	0-2 France
ECQ99	**England**	3-1 Poland
FAC99 (W)	**Man Utd**	2-0 Newcastle Utd
ECQ99	**England**	0-0 Sweden
CS99	**Man Utd**	1-2 Arsenal
INT00 (S)	**England**	0-0 Argentina
CS00 (S)	**Man Utd**	0-2 Chelsea
WCQ00	**England**	0-1 Germany

Coleman, Keith (1, 0)

CS75 (S)	**West Ham**	0-2 Derby

Coleman, Simon (2, 0)

ZC90	**Middlesbrough**	0-1 Chelsea
AIC93	**Derby**	1-3 Cremonese

Coleman, Tony (1, 0)

FAC69	**Man City**	1-0 Leicester

Collard, Ian (2, 0)

FLC67	**WBA**	2-3 QPR
FAC68	**WBA**	1-0 Everton

Collins, Bobby (4, 0)

BC57	**Scotland**	1-2 England
BC59	**Scotland**	0-1 England
BC65	**Scotland**	2-2 England
FAC65 (C)	**Leeds**	1-2 Liverpool

Collins, John (2, 0)

ECH96	**Scotland**	0-2 England
ECQ99	**Scotland**	1-0 England

Collins, Peter (1, 0)

FLC71	**Spurs**	2-0 Aston Villa

Collymore, Stan (4, 0)

UC95 (W)	**England**	2-1 Japan
UC95 (S)	**England**	1-3 Brazil
FAC96 (W)	**Liverpool**	0-1 Man Utd
WCQ97 (S)	**England**	4-0 Moldova

Colman, Eddie (1, 0)

FAC57	**Man Utd**	1-2 Aston Villa

Compton, Denis (10, 4)

WI40	**England**	0-1 Wales
FLWC41 (1)	**Arsenal**	1-1 PNE
WI41	**England**	2-0 Scotland
WI42	**England**	3-0 Scotland
WI42	**England**	0-0 Scotland
WI43	**England**	5-3 Wales
LSC43 (1)	**Arsenal**	7-1 Charlton
WI43 (1)	**England**	8-3 Wales
IT46 (1)	**Army PTC**	5-3 FA
FAC50	**Arsenal**	2-0 Liverpool

Compton, Leslie (5, 1)

FLWC41	**Arsenal**	1-1 PNE
CHA41	**Met Police**	3-6 RAF
CHA42 (1)	**Met Police**	3-6 RAF
LSC43	**Arsenal**	7-1 Charlton
FAC50	**Arsenal**	2-0 Liverpool

Conn, Alfie (1, 0)
BC75	**Scotland**	1-5 England

Connelly, John (11, 5)
INT59 (1)	**England**	2-3 Sweden
BC59	**England**	2-1 N Ireland
WCQ61 (1)	**England**	2-0 Portugal
INT62	**England**	3-1 Austria
FAC62	**Burnley**	1-3 Spurs
INT62 (1)	**England**	3-1 Switzerland
BC62 (1)	**England**	4-0 Wales
INT65	**England**	1-0 Hungary
INT65 (1)	**England**	2-3 Austria
BC65	**England**	2-1 N Ireland
WC66	**England**	0-0 Uruguay

Connor, Jimmy (1, 0)
BC34	**Scotland**	0-3 England

Conroy, Terry (2, 1)
FLC72 (1)	**Stoke**	2-1 Chelsea
INT76	**R of Ireland**	1-1 England

Conway, Jimmy (1, 0)
FAC75	**Fulham**	0-2 West Ham

Cook, Bill (1, 0)
FAC25	**Sheffield Utd**	1-0 Cardiff

Cook, Billy (1, 0)
FAC33	**Everton**	3-0 Man City

Cook, Fred (1, 0)
FAC29	**Portsmouth**	0-2 Bolton

Cook, Willie (2, 0)
FAC29	**Bolton**	2-0 Portsmouth
BC34	**Scotland**	0-3 England

Cooke, Charlie (3, 0)
FAC67	**Chelsea**	1-2 Spurs
FAC70	**Chelsea**	2-2 Leeds
FLC72	**Chelsea**	1-2 Stoke

Cookson, Sam (1, 0)
FAC26	**Man City**	0-1 Bolton

Cooper, Colin (2, 0)
ZC90	**Middlesbrough**	0-1 Chelsea
UC95	**England**	1-3 Brazil

Cooper, Paul (2, 0)
FAC78	**Ipswich**	1-0 Arsenal
CS78	**Ipswich**	0-5 Nottm F

Cooper, Terry (12, 1)
FLC68 (1)	**Leeds**	1-0 Arsenal
INT69	**England**	5-0 France
BC69	**England**	2-1 Wales
BC69	**England**	4-1 Scotland
INT70	**England**	0-0 Netherlands
FAC70	**Leeds**	2-2 Chelsea
INT70	**England**	3-1 E Germany
ECQ71	**England**	5-0 Malta
BC71	**England**	0-0 Wales
BC71	**England**	3-1 Scotland
ECQ71	**England**	1-1 Switzerland
ECQ74 (W)	**England**	0-0 Portugal

As Manager
FRT86	**Bristol C**	3-0 Bolton
FRT87	**Bristol C**	1-1 Mansfield

Cooper, Tom (1, 0)
BC34 (C)	**England**	3-0 Scotland

Cope, Ron (2, 0)
SI50	**England**	8-2 Scotland
FAC58	**Man Utd**	0-2 Bolton

Coppell, Steve (24, 3)
FAC76	**Man Utd**	0-1 Southampton
FAC77	**Man Utd**	2-1 Liverpool
CS77	**Man Utd**	0-0 Liverpool
WCQ77	**England**	2-0 Italy
INT78	**England**	1-1 Brazil
BC78	**England**	1-0 N Ireland
INT78 (W)	**England**	4-1 Hungary
INT78 (1)	**England**	1-0 Czechoslovakia
ECQ79	**England**	4-0 N Ireland
FAC79	**Man Utd**	2-3 Arsenal
BC79 (S)	**England**	0-0 Wales
BC79 (1)	**England**	3-1 Scotland
ECQ79	**England**	1-0 Denmark
ECQ80 (S)	**England**	2-0 R of Ireland
INT80	**England**	3-1 Argentina
WCQ80	**England**	2-1 Switzerland
WCQ81	**England**	0-0 Romania
INT81	**England**	0-1 Brazil
BC81	**England**	0-0 Wales
BC81	**England**	0-1 Scotland
WCQ81 (W)	**England**	1-0 Hungary
ECQ82 (1, W)	**England**	9-0 Luxembourg
MC83	**Man Utd**	1-2 Liverpool
ECQ83	**England**	0-0 Greece

As Manager
LCT88	**C Palace**	0-0 Sheffield W
FAC90	**C Palace**	3-3 Man Utd
FAC90	**C Palace**	0-1 Man Utd
ZC91	**C Palace**	4-1 Everton
PPO97	**C Palace**	1-0 Sheffield Utd

Copping, Wilf (4, 0)
BC34	**England**	3-0 Scotland
FAC36	**Arsenal**	1-0 Sheffield Utd
BC38	**England**	0-1 Scotland
WI40	**England**	0-1 Wales

Corbett, Bobby (1, 0)
FAC51	**Newcastle Utd**	2-0 Blackpool

Cork, Alan (3, 1)
LCT88	**Wimbledon**	0-1 Tranmere
FAC88 (W)	**Wimbledon**	1-0 Liverpool
FAC93 (1)	**Sheffield Utd**	1-2 Sheffield W

Cormack, Peter (3, 0)
BC71	**Scotland**	1-3 England
FAC74	**Liverpool**	3-0 Newcastle Utd
CS74	**Liverpool**	1-1 Leeds

Corner, David (1, 0)
MC85 (W)	**Sunderland**	0-1 Norwich

Corrigan, Joe (9, 0)
FLC70	**Man City**	2-1 West Brom
FLC76	**Man City**	2-1 Newcastle Utd
INT78	**England**	1-1 Brazil
BC79	**England**	0-0 Wales
BC80	**England**	1-1 N Ireland

FAC81	**Man City** 1-1 Spurs	
FAC81	**Man City** 2-3 Spurs	
BC81	**England** 0-0 Wales	
BC81	**England** 0-1 Scotland	

Cottee, Tony (9, 2)
ECQ86 (S)	**England** 3-0 N Ireland	
INT88 (S)	**England** 1-0 Denmark	
WCQ88 (S)	**England** 0-0 Sweden	
SC89 (2)	**Everton** 3-4 Nottm F	
FAC89	**Everton** 2-3 Liverpool	
RC89 (S)	**England** 0-0 Chile	
ZC91	**Everton** 1-4 C Palace	
WLC99	**Leicester** 0-1 Spurs	
WLC00 (W)	**Leicester** 2-1 Tranmere	

Court, David (1, 0)
FLC69	**Arsenal** 1-3 Swindon	

Cowan, Billy (2, 0)
BC24	**Scotland** 1-1 England	
FAC24	**Newcastle Utd** 2-0 Aston Villa	

Cowan, Jim (2, 0)
BC49	**Scotland** 3-1 England	
BC51	**Scotland** 3-2 England	

Cowan, John (1, 0)
BC70 (S)	**N Ireland** 1-3 England	

Cowan, Sam (3, 0)
FAC26	**Man City** 0-1 Bolton	
FAC33 (C)	**Man City** 0-3 Everton	
FAC34 (C)	**Man City** 2-1 Portsmouth	

Cowans, Gordon (8, 1)
CS81	**Aston Villa** 2-2 Spurs	
BC83	**England** 2-1 Wales	
ECQ83	**England** 2-0 Hungary	
BC83 (1)	**England** 2-0 Scotland	
MT90	**Aston Villa** 0-2 Arsenal	
MT90	**Aston Villa** 0-1 Real Sociedad	
PPO92	**Blackburn** 1-0 Leicester	
PPO94 (C)	**Derby** 1-2 Leicester	

Cowell, Bobby (3, 0)
FAC51	**Newcastle Utd** 2-0 Blackpool	
FAC52	**Newcastle Utd** 1-0 Arsenal	
FAC55	**Newcastle Utd** 3-1 Man City	

Cowie, Doug (1, 0)
BC53	**Scotland** 2-2 England	

Cox, Freddie (2, 0)
FAC50	**Arsenal** 2-0 Liverpool	
FAC52	**Arsenal** 0-1 Newcastle Utd	

Cox, Neil (3, 0)
CCC94 (S)	**Aston Villa** 3-1 Man Utd	
CCC97	**Middlesbrough** 1-1 Leicester	
PPO99	**Bolton** 0-2 Watford	

Cox, Sammy (3, 0)
BC49	**Scotland** 3-1 England	
BC51	**Scotland** 3-2 England	
BC53	**Scotland** 2-2 England	

Coyle, Fay (1, 0)
BC55	**N Ireland** 0-3 England	

Craig, Allan (1, 0)
BC32	**Scotland** 0-3 England	

Craig, Ben (1, 0)
FAC38	**Huddersfield** 0-1 PNE	

Craig, David (1, 0)
BC70	**N Ireland** 1-3 England	

Craig, Tommy (1, 0)
BC30	**Scotland** 2-5 England	

Craig, Tommy (1, 0)
FLC76 (C)	**Newcastle Utd** 1-2 Man City	

Cram, Bobby (1, 0)
FLC67	**WBA** 2-3 QPR	

Crapnell, Jimmy (1, 0)
BC32 (C)	**Scotland** 0-3 England	

Crawford, Jock (1, 0)
FAC28	**Blackburn** 3-1 Huddersfield	

Crawford, Ray (2, 1)
BC61	**England** 1-1 N Ireland	
INT62 (1)	**England** 3-1 Austria	

Crayston, Jack (4, 0)
BC36	**England** 1-1 Scotland	
FAC36	**Arsenal** 1-0 Sheffield Utd	
FLWC41	**Arsenal** 1-1 PNE	
LSC43	**Arsenal** 7-1 Charlton	

Crerand, Pat (3, 0)
FAC63	**Man Utd** 3-1 Leicester	
BC65	**Scotland** 2-2 England	
EC68	**Man Utd** 4-1 Benfica	

Cresswell, Warney (1, 0)
FAC33	**Everton** 3-0 Man City	

Cringan, Jimmy (1, 0)
FAC31	**Birmingham** 1-2 WBA	

Croker, Peter (1, 0)
FAC47	**Charlton** 1-0 Burnley	

Crompton, Jack (1, 0)
FAC48	**Man Utd** 4-2 Blackpool	

Crook, Wally (1, 0)
FAC49	**Wolves** 3-1 Leicester	

Crooks, Garth (6, 1)
FAC81	**Spurs** 1-1 Man City	
FAC81 (1)	**Spurs** 3-2 Man City	
FLC82	**Spurs** 1-3 Liverpool	
FAC82	**Spurs** 1-1 Queens Park R.	
FAC82	**Spurs** 1-0 Queens Park R.	
CS82	**Spurs** 0-1 Liverpool	

Crooks, Sammy (4, 1)
BC30	**England** 5-2 Scotland	
BC32 (1)	**England** 3-0 Scotland	
BC34	**England** 3-0 Scotland	
BC36	**England** 1-1 Scotland	

Cropley, Alex (1, 0)
FLC77	**Aston Villa** 0-0 Everton	

Crosbie, Johnny (1, 0)
FAC31	**Birmingham** 1-2 WBA	

Crosby, Gary (8, 0)
LCT88 (W)	**Nottm F** 3-0 Leeds	
LCT88 (W)	**Nottm F** 0-0 Aston Villa	
LCT88 (W)	**Nottm F** 2-2 Tranmere	
LC90	**Nottm F** 1-0 Oldham	

FAC91	**Nottm F**	1-2 Spurs
ZC92	**Nottm F**	3-2 Southampton
RLC92	**Nottm F**	0-1 Man Utd
PPO95	**Huddersfield**	2-1 Bristol R

Crosland, Johnny (1, 0)

FAC48	**Blackpool**	2-4 Man Utd

Cross, David (4, 0)

FLC73	**Norwich**	0-1 Spurs
FAC80	**West Ham**	1-0 Arsenal
CS80	**West Ham**	0-1 Liverpool
FLC81	**West Ham**	1-1 Liverpool

Cross, Graham (2, 0)

FAC63	**Leicester**	1-3 Man Utd
FAC69	**Leicester**	0-1 Man City

Crossan, Johnny (3, 1)

BC59	**N Ireland**	1-2 England
BC63 (1)	**N Ireland**	3-8 England
BC65	**N Ireland**	1-2 England

Crossley, Mark (1, 0)

FAC91	**Nottm F**	1-2 Spurs

Crowe, Charlie (1, 0)

FAC51	**Newcastle Utd**	2-0 Blackpool

Crowe, Vic (1, 0)

BC60 (C)	**Wales**	1-5 England

As Manager

FLC71	**Aston Villa**	0-2 Spurs

Crowther, Stan (3, 0)

FAC57	**Aston Villa**	2-1 Man Utd
U23I57	**England**	3-2 Romania
FAC58	**Man Utd**	0-2 Bolton

Crum, John (1, 0)

BC36	**Scotland**	1-1 England

Cruyff, Jordi (5, 0)

ECH96	**Netherlands**	1-4 England
CS96 (S)	**Man Utd**	4-0 Newcastle Utd
CS97 (S)	**Man Utd**	1-1 Chelsea
CS98 (S)	**Man Utd**	0-3 Arsenal
CS99 (W)	**Man Utd**	1-2 Arsenal

Cullis, Stan (9, 0)

BC38	**England**	0-1 Scotland
FAC39 (C)	**Wolves**	1-4 Portsmouth
WI40	**England**	0-1 Wales
WI41	**England**	2-0 Scotland
WI42	**England**	3-0 Scotland
WI42	**England**	0-0 Scotland
WI43	**England**	5-3 Wales
WI43	**England**	8-3 Wales
WI44 (C)	**England**	6-2 Scotland

As Manager

FAC49	**Wolves**	3-1 Leicester
FAC60	**Wolves**	3-0 Blackburn

Cumbes, Jim (1, 0)

FLC75	**Aston Villa**	1-0 Norwich

Cumming, David (2, 0)

BC38	**Scotland**	1-0 England
WI44	**Scotland**	2-6 England

Cumming, John (1, 0)

BC55	**Scotland**	2-7 England

Cummings, George (2, 0)

BC36	**Scotland**	1-1 England
WI44	**Scotland**	2-6 England

Cummings, Tommy (1, 0)

FAC62	**Burnley**	1-3 Spurs

Cummins, George (1, 0)

FAC59	**Luton**	1-2 Nottm F

Cunningham, Andy (1, 0)

BC24	**Scotland**	1-1 England

Cunningham, Laurie (3, 0)

BC79	**England**	0-0 Wales
ECQ80	**England**	2-0 R of Ireland
FAC88 (S)	**Wimbledon**	1-0 Liverpool

Cunningham, Willie (2, 0)

FAC54	**PNE**	2-3 WBA
BC55 (C)	**Scotland**	2-7 England

Cunningham, Willie (2, 0)

BC55	**N Ireland**	0-3 England
BC59	**N Ireland**	1-2 England

Curle, Keith (3, 0)

FRT86	**Bristol C**	3-0 Bolton
FRT87 (S)	**Bristol C**	1-1 Mansfield
SC88	**Reading**	4-1 Luton

Curran, Hugh (1, 1)

BC71 (1, W)	**Scotland**	1-3 England

Curran, Terry (1, 0)

FLC79	**Southampton**	2-3 Nottm F

Currie, Tony (12, 2)

BC72 (W)	**England**	0-1 N Ireland
INT73 (1)	**England**	7-0 Austria
WCQ73	**England**	1-1 Poland
INT73	**England**	0-1 Italy
INT78	**England**	1-1 Brazil
BC78	**England**	1-0 N Ireland
INT78 (S, 1)	**England**	4-1 Hungary
INT78	**England**	1-0 Czechoslovakia
ECQ79	**England**	4-0 N Ireland
BC79	**England**	0-0 Wales
FAC82	**QPR**	1-1 Spurs
FAC82 (C)	**QPR**	0-1 Spurs

Curtis, Alan (1, 0)

BC79	**Wales**	0-0 England

Curtis, Dermot (1, 1)

WCQ57 (1)	**R of Ireland**	1-5 England

Curtis, Ernie (2, 0)

FAC27	**Cardiff**	1-0 Arsenal
FAC31	**Birmingham**	1-2 WBA

Cush, Wilbur (1, 0)

BC59	**N Ireland**	1-2 England

Cutbush, John (1, 0)

FAC75	**Fulham**	0-2 West Ham

Dabizas, Nikos (3, 0)

FAC98	**Newcastle Utd**	0-2 Arsenal
FAC99	**Newcastle Utd**	0-2 Man Utd
FAC00	**Newcastle Utd**	1-2 Chelsea

Dailly, Christian (1, 0)

ECQ99	**Scotland**	1-0 England

Dale, Billy (2, 0)

FAC33	**Man City**	0-3 Everton
FAC34	**Man City**	2-1 Portsmouth

Daley, Tony (5, 0)

LCT88	**Aston Villa**	0-0 Blackburn
MT90	**Aston Villa**	0-2 Arsenal
MT90	**Aston Villa**	0-1 Real Sociedad
INT92 (W)	**England**	1-1 Brazil
CCC94	**Aston Villa**	3-1 Man Utd

Dalglish, Kenny (19, 3)

BC73	**Scotland**	0-1 England
BC75	**Scotland**	1-5 England
BC77 (1)	**Scotland**	2-1 England
CS77	**Liverpool**	0-0 Man Utd
FLC78	**Liverpool**	0-0 Nottm F
EC78 (1)	**Liverpool**	1-0 Bruges
BC79 (C)	**Scotland**	1-3 England
CS79 (1)	**Liverpool**	3-1 Arsenal
CS80	**Liverpool**	1-0 West Ham
FLC81	**Liverpool**	1-1 West Ham
FLC82	**Liverpool**	3-1 Spurs
CS82 (W)	**Liverpool**	1-0 Spurs
MC83	**Liverpool**	2-1 Man Utd
CS83	**Liverpool**	0-2 Man Utd
MC84	**Liverpool**	0-1 Everton
CS84	**Liverpool**	0-1 Everton
FAC86	**Liverpool**	3-1 Everton
CS86 (S)	**Liverpool**	1-1 Everton
LC87 (S)	**Liverpool**	1-2 Arsenal

As Player-Manager

FAC86	**Liverpool**	3-1 Everton
CS86	**Liverpool**	1-1 Everton
LC87	**Liverpool**	1-2 Arsenal

As Manager

LCT88	**Liverpool**	0-0 Newcastle Utd
FAC88	**Liverpool**	0-1 Wimbledon
CS88	**Liverpool**	2-1 Wimbledon
FAC89	**Liverpool**	3-2 Everton
MT89	**Liverpool**	2-0 Dynamo Kiev
MT89	**Liverpool**	0-1 Arsenal
CS89	**Liverpool**	1-0 Arsenal
CS90	**Liverpool**	1-1 Man Utd
PPO92	**Blackburn**	1-0 Leicester
CS94	**Blackburn**	0-2 Man Utd
FAC98	**Newcastle Utd**	0-2 Arsenal

Daly, Gerry (3, 1)

FAC76	**Man Utd**	0-1 Southampton
INT76 (1)	**R of Ireland**	1-1 England
ECQ80	**R of Ireland**	0-2 England

Daniel, Peter (2, 0)

FLC80	**Wolves**	1-0 Nottm F
MC85	**Sunderland**	0-1 Norwich

Daniel, Ray (4, 0)

FAC52	**Arsenal**	0-1 Newcastle Utd
BC52	**Wales**	2-5 England
BC54	**Wales**	2-3 England
BC56	**Wales**	1-3 England

Darracott, Terry (1, 0)

FLC77	**Everton**	0-0 Aston Villa

Davenport, Peter (6, 2)

INT85 (S)	**England**	2-1 R of Ireland
LCT88 (1)	**Man Utd**	2-0 Luton
LCT88	**Man Utd**	1-0 Everton
LCT88 (1)	**Man Utd**	1-2 Sheffield W
ZC90	**Middlesbrough**	0-1 Chelsea
FAC92	**Sunderland**	0-2 Liverpool

Davidson, Callum (1, 0)

ECQ99	**Scotland**	1-0 England

Davidson, Dave (1, 0)

FAC32	**Newcastle Utd**	2-1 Arsenal

Davidson, James (1, 0)

BC55	**Scotland**	2-7 England

Davies, Alan (2, 0)

FAC83	**Man Utd**	2-2 Brighton
FAC83	**Man Utd**	4-0 Brighton

Davies, Billy (1, 0)

FAC25	**Cardiff**	0-1 Sheffield Utd

Davies, Dai (4, 0)

BC75	**Wales**	2-2 England
BC77	**Wales**	1-0 England
BC79	**Wales**	0-0 England
BC81	**Wales**	0-0 England

Davies, Gordon (1, 0)

BC83	**Wales**	1-2 England

Davies, Harry (1, 0)

FAC30	**Huddersfield**	0-2 Arsenal

Davies, Len (1, 0)

FAC27	**Cardiff**	1-0 Arsenal

Davies, Reg (1, 0)

BC52	**Wales**	2-5 England

Davies, Ron (4, 1)

BC64	**Wales**	1-2 England
ECQ66	**Wales**	1-5 England
BC69 (1)	**Wales**	1-2 England
BC71	**Wales**	0-0 England

Davies, Wyn (3, 1)

BC64	**Wales**	1-2 England
ECQ66 (1)	**Wales**	1-5 England
BC69	**Wales**	1-2 England

Davis, Paul (12, 0)

LC87	**Arsenal**	2-1 Liverpool
LC88	**Arsenal**	2-3 Luton
WIT88	**Arsenal**	4-0 Spurs
WIT88	**Arsenal**	3-0 Bayern Munich
MT90	**Arsenal**	2-0 Aston Villa
MT90	**Arsenal**	0-1 Sampdoria
FAC91	**Arsenal**	1-3 Spurs
CS91	**Arsenal**	0-0 Spurs
CCC93	**Arsenal**	2-1 Sheffield W
FAC93	**Arsenal**	1-1 Sheffield W
FAC93	**Arsenal**	2-1 Sheffield W
CS93	**Arsenal**	1-1 Man Utd

Dawes, Ian (3, 0)

SI78	**England**	3-3 France
SI78	**England**	3-0 Scotland
MC86	**QPR**	0-3 Oxford

383

Dawson, Alex (3, 3)
SI55 (2)	**England** 6-0 Wales
FAC58	**Man Utd** 0-2 Bolton
FAC64 (1)	**PNE** 2-3 West Ham

Dawson, Jerry (4, 0)
BC36	**Scotland** 1-1 England
WI41	**Scotland** 0-2 England
WI42	**Scotland** 0-3 England
WI42	**Scotland** 0-0 England

Dawson, Tommy (1, 0)
| FAC47 | **Charlton** 1-0 Burnley |

Day, Mervyn (3, 0)
FAC75	**West Ham** 2-0 Fulham
CS75	**West Ham** 0-2 Derby
LCT88	**Leeds** 0-3 Nottm F

As Manager
| AWS97 | **Carlisle** 0-0 Colchester United |

Deacy, Nick (1, 0)
| BC77 | **Wales** 1-0 England |

Dean, Dixie (2, 1)
| BC28 | **England** 1-5 Scotland |
| FAC33 (C, 1) | **Everton** 3-0 Man City |

Deane, Brian (2, 0)
| FAC93 | **Sheffield Utd** 1-2 Sheffield W |
| CCC96 (S) | **Leeds** 0-3 Aston Villa |

Dear, Brian (1, 0)
| ECW65 | **West Ham** 2-0 TSV Munich |

Deehan, John (2, 0)
| FLC77 | **Aston Villa** 0-0 Everton |
| MC85 | **Norwich** 1-0 Sunderland |

Deeley, Norman (1, 2)
| FAC60 (2) | **Wolves** 3-0 Blackburn |

De Goey, Ed (6, 0)
WCQ93	**Netherlands** 2-2 England
CS97	**Chelsea** 1-1 Man Utd
CCC98	**Chelsea** 2-0 Middlesbrough
FAC00	**Chelsea** 2-1 Newcastle Utd
FAC00	**Chelsea** 1-0 Aston Villa
CS00	**Chelsea** 2-0 Man Utd

Delaney, Mark (2, 0)
| FAC00 (D) | **Aston Villa** 0-0 Bolton |
| FAC00 | **Aston Villa** 0-1 Chelsea |

Delaney, Jimmy (2, 0)
| BC47 | **Scotland** 1-1 England |
| FAC48 | **Man Utd** 4-2 Blackpool |

Dempsey, John (2, 0)
| FAC70 | **Chelsea** 2-2 Leeds |
| FLC72 | **Chelsea** 1-2 Stoke |

Desailly, Marcel (4, 0)
INT99	**France** 2-0 England
FAC00	**Chelsea** 2-1 Newcastle Utd
FAC00	**Chelsea** 1-0 Aston Villa
CS00	**Chelsea** 2-0 Man Utd

Deschamps, Didier (3, 0)
INT99 (C, W)	**France** 2-0 England
FAC00	**Chelsea** 2-1 Newcastle Utd
FAC00	**Chelsea** 1-0 Aston Villa

Devine, John (1, 0)
| FAC80 (W) | **Arsenal** 0-1 West Ham |

Devonshire, Alan (8, 0)
FAC80	**West Ham** 1-0 Arsenal
BC80	**England** 1-1 N Ireland
CS80	**West Ham** 0-1 Liverpool
FLC81	**West Ham** 1-1 Liverpool
INT82 (W)	**England** 2-0 Netherlands
INT82	**England** 1-2 W Germany
BC83	**England** 2-1 Wales
ECQ83 (W)	**England** 0-0 Greece

Dewar, Neil (1, 0)
| BC32 | **Scotland** 0-3 England |

Dibble, Andy (2, 0)
| LCT88 | **Luton** 0-2 Man Utd |
| LC88 | **Luton** 3-2 Arsenal |

Dick, George (1, 0)
| FAC48 | **Blackpool** 2-4 Man Utd |

Dick, John (1, 0)
| BC59 | **Scotland** 0-1 England |

Dickinson, Jimmy (10, 0)
INT51	**England** 2-2 Austria
BC52	**England** 5-2 Wales
INT52	**England** 5-0 Belgium
BC53	**England** 2-2 Scotland
NIN53	**England** 4-4 FIFA
INT53	**England** 3-6 Hungary
BC55	**England** 3-0 N Ireland
INT55	**England** 4-1 Spain
BC56	**England** 3-1 Wales
INT56	**England** 3-0 Yugoslavia

Di Matteo, Roberto (7, 3)
WCQ97	**Italy** 1-0 England
FAC97 (1)	**Chelsea** 2-0 Middlesbrough
CS97	**Chelsea** 1-1 Man Utd
CCC98 (1)	**Chelsea** 2-0 Middlesbrough
FAC00	**Chelsea** 2-1 Newcastle Utd
FAC00 (1)	**Chelsea** 1-0 Aston Villa
CS00 (W)	**Chelsea** 2-0 Man Utd

Ditchburn, Ted (5, 0)
WI44	**England** 6-2 Scotland
CHA44	**C Services** 5-2 Met Police
EFC55	**London** 3-2 Frankfurt
BC56	**England** 3-1 Wales
INT56	**England** 3-0 Yugoslavia

Dixon, Johnny (1, 0)
| FAC57 (C) | **Aston Villa** 2-1 Man Utd |

Dixon, Kerry (3, 0)
WCQ85	**England** 0-0 N Ireland
ZC90	**Chelsea** 1-0 Middlesbrough
FAC94	**Luton** 0-2 Chelsea

Dixon, Lee (35, 2)
WIT88	**Arsenal** 4-0 Spurs
WIT88 (1)	**Arsenal** 3-0 Bayern Munich
MT89	**Arsenal** 1-0 Porto
MT89	**Arsenal** 1-0 Liverpool
CS89	**Arsenal** 0-1 Liverpool
INT90	**England** 4-2 Czechoslovakia

MT90	**Arsenal**	2-0 Aston Villa
MT90	**Arsenal**	0-1 Sampdoria
INT90	**England**	1-0 Hungary
ECQ90	**England**	2-0 Poland
INT91	**England**	2-0 Cameroon
ECQ91 (1)	**England**	1-1 R of Ireland
FAC91	**Arsenal**	1-3 Spurs
INT91	**England**	2-2 Argentina
CS91	**Arsenal**	0-0 Spurs
INT91	**England**	0-1 Germany
ECQ91	**England**	1-0 Turkey
WCQ92 (W)	**England**	1-1 Norway
WCQ92	**England**	4-0 Turkey
WCQ93	**England**	6-0 San Marino
FAC93 (D)	**Arsenal**	1-0 Spurs
WCQ93	**England**	2-2 Netherlands
FAC93	**Arsenal**	1-1 Sheffield W.
FAC93	**Arsenal**	2-1 Sheffield W.
CS93 (W)	**Arsenal**	1-1 Man Utd
FAC98	**Arsenal**	2-0 Newcastle Utd
CS98	**Arsenal**	3-0 Man Utd
EC98	**Arsenal**	2-1 Panathinaikos
EC98	**Arsenal**	1-1 Dynamo Kiev
EC98	**Arsenal**	0-1 Lens
INT99 (W)	**England**	0-2 France
CS99	**Arsenal**	2-1 Man Utd
EC99	**Arsenal**	3-1 AIK Stockholm
EC99	**Arsenal**	2-4 Barcelona
EC99 (W)	**Arsenal**	0-1 Fiorentina

Dobing, Peter (2, 0)

FAC60	**Blackburn**	0-3 Wolves
FLC72 (C)	**Stoke**	2-1 Chelsea

Dobson, Martin (2, 0)

ECQ74 (W)	**England**	3-0 Czechoslovakia
FLC77	**Everton**	0-0 Aston Villa

Docherty, Tommy (5, 1)

BC53	**Scotland**	2-2 England
FAC54	**PNE**	2-3 WBA
BC55 (1)	**Scotland**	2-7 England
BC57	**Scotland**	1-2 England
BC59	**Scotland**	0-1 England

As Manager

FAC67	**Chelsea**	1-2 Spurs
FAC76	**Man Utd**	0-1 Southampton
FAC77	**Man Utd**	2-1 Liverpool

Dodds, Billy (1, 0)

ECQ99	**Scotland**	1-0 England

Dodds, Jock (3, 2)

FAC36	**Sheffield Utd**	0-1 Arsenal
WI42	**Scotland**	0-0 England
WI44 (2)	**Scotland**	2-6 England

Doherty, Peter (1, 1)

FAC46 (1)	**Derby**	4-1 Charlton

As Manager

BC55	**N Ireland**	0-3 England
BC57	**N Ireland**	3-2 England
BC59	**N Ireland**	1-2 England
BC61	**N Ireland**	1-1 England

Domi, Didier (2, 0)

FAC99	**Newcastle Utd**	0-2 Man Utd
FAC00 (S)	**Newcastle Utd**	1-2 Chelsea

Donachie, Willie (3, 0)

FLC74	**Man City**	1-2 Wolves
FLC76	**Man City**	2-1 Newcastle Utd
BC77	**Scotland**	2-1 England

Donaghy, Mal (9, 0)

BC80	**N Ireland**	1-1 England
BC82	**N Ireland**	0-4 England
BC84	**N Ireland**	0-1 England
WCQ85	**N Ireland**	0-0 England
ECQ86	**N Ireland**	0-3 England
SC88	**Luton**	1-4 Reading
LCT88 (W)	**Luton**	0-2 Man Utd
LC88	**Luton**	3-2 Arsenal
CS90	**Man Utd**	1-1 Liverpool

Donovan, Don (1, 0)

WCQ57	**R of Ireland**	1-5 England

Donowa, Louie (2, 0)

MC85	**Norwich**	1-0 Sunderland
AWS95 (S)	**Birmingham**	1-0 Carlisle

Dorigo, Tony (10, 2)

INT89 (S)	**England**	2-1 Yugoslavia
ZC90 (1)	**Chelsea**	1-0 Middlesbrough
INT90 (S)	**England**	4-2 Czechoslovakia
INT90 (S)	**England**	1-0 Denmark
INT90 (S)	**England**	1-0 Hungary
INT91	**England**	3-1 USSR
INT91	**England**	0-1 Germany
INT92 (W)	**England**	1-1 Brazil
CS92 (1)	**Leeds**	4-3 Liverpool
WCQ93	**England**	6-0 San Marino

Dorrell, Arthur (1, 0)

FAC24	**Aston Villa**	0-2 Newcastle Utd

Dorsett, Dickie (1, 1)

FAC39 (1)	**Wolves**	1-4 Portsmouth

Dougal, Jim (2, 0)

FAC37	**PNE**	1-3 Sunderland
FLWC41	**PNE**	1-1 Arsenal

Dougan, Derek (5, 0)

FAC60	**Blackburn**	0-3 Wolves
BC65	**N Ireland**	1-2 England
BC70	**N Ireland**	1-3 England
BC72 (C)	**N Ireland**	1-0 England
FLC74	**Wolves**	2-1 Man City

Douglas, Bryan (15, 7)

BC57	**England**	2-3 N Ireland
INT57	**England**	4-0 France
INT58	**England**	2-1 Portugal
INT58	**England**	5-0 USSR
BC59	**England**	1-0 Scotland
FAC60	**Blackburn**	0-3 Wolves
INT60 (1)	**England**	3-3 Yugoslavia
INT60 (1)	**England**	4-2 Spain
BC60	**England**	5-1 Wales
BC61 (1)	**England**	9-3 Scotland
INT61 (2)	**England**	8-0 Mexico

WCQ61	**England** 2-0 Portugal	
BC61	**England** 1-1 N Ireland	
BC63 (1)	**England** 1-2 Scotland	
INT63 (1)	**England** 1-1 Brazil	

Dowd, Harry (1, 0)
FAC69 — **Man City** 1-0 Leicester

Dowie, Iain (2, 1)
MCC88 (1) — **Hendon** 2-0 Wembley
ZC92 — **Southampton** 2-3 Nottm F

Downs, Greg (2, 0)
FAC87 — **Coventry** 3-2 Spurs
CS87 — **Coventry** 0-1 Everton

Downsborough, Peter (1, 0)
FLC69 — **Swindon** 3-1 Arsenal

Doyle, Mike (5, 1)
FAC69 — **Man City** 1-0 Leicester
FLC70 (1) — **Man City** 2-1 WBA
FLC74 — **Man City** 1-2 Wolves
FLC76 (C) — **Man City** 2-1 Newcastle Utd
INT77 — **England** 0-2 Netherlands

Drake, Ted (5, 9)
FAC36 (1) — **Arsenal** 1-0 Sheffield Utd
CHA42 (3) — **Royal Air Force** 6-3 Met Police
LSC43 (2) — **Arsenal** 7-1 Charlton
CHA43 — **Royal Air Force** 4-3 Met Police
CHA44 (3) — **C Services** 5-2 Met Police

Draper, Mark (3, 0)
PPO91 — **Notts County** 3-1 Brighton
AIC94 (W) — **Notts County** 0-1 Brescia
CCC96 — **Aston Villa** 3-0 Leeds

Dreyer, John (1, 0)
FAC94 — **Luton** 0-2 Chelsea

Duberry, Michael (1, 0)
CCC98 — **Chelsea** 2-0 Middlesbrough

Dublin, Dion (6, 1)
PPO90 (1) — **Cambridge Utd** 1-0 Chesterfield
FAC94 (W) — **Man Utd** 1-1 Oldham
INT98 — **England** 0-2 Chile
INT98 — **England** 2-0 Czech Republic
FAC00 (S) — **Aston Villa** 0-0 Bolton
FAC00 — **Aston Villa** 0-1 Chelsea

Dudley, Jimmy (1, 0)
FAC54 — **WBA** 3-2 PNE

Duffy, Chris (3, 1)
LSC44 — **Charlton** 3-1 Chelsea
FAC46 — **Charlton** 1-4 Derby
FAC47 (1) — **Charlton** 1-0 Burnley

Dugdale, Jimmy (2, 0)
FAC54 — **WBA** 3-2 PNE
FAC57 — **Aston Villa** 2-1 Man Utd

Dumitrescu, Ilie (1, 1)
INT94 (1) — **Romania** 1-1 England

Duncan, Arthur (1, 0)
BC75 — **Scotland** 1-5 England

Duncan, Dally (2, 0)
BC36 — **Scotland** 1-1 England
FAC46 — **Derby** 4-1 Charlton

As Manager
FAC60 — **Blackburn** 0-3 Wolves

Dunn, Jimmy (2, 1)
BC28 — **Scotland** 5-1 England
FAC33 (1) — **Everton** 3-0 Man City

Dunn, Jimmy (1, 0)
FAC49 — **Wolves** 3-1 Leicester

Dunn, John (1, 0)
FLC71 — **Aston Villa** 0-2 Spurs

Dunne, Tony (2, 0)
FAC63 — **Man Utd** 3-1 Leicester
EC68 — **Man Utd** 4-1 Benfica

Duns, Len (1, 0)
FAC37 — **Sunderland** 3-1 PNE

Durban, Alan (2, 0)
BC69 (C) — **Wales** 1-2 England
BC71 (C) — **Wales** 0-0 England

Durie, Gordon (2, 0)
ZC90 — **Chelsea** 1-0 Middlesbrough
ECH96 (W) — **Scotland** 0-2 England

Duxbury, Mike (11, 0)
MC83 — **Man Utd** 1-2 Liverpool
FAC83 — **Man Utd** 2-2 Brighton & Hove A.
FAC83 — **Man Utd** 4-0 Brighton & Hove A.
CS83 — **Man Utd** 0-2 Liverpool
INT84 — **England** 0-2 USSR
INT84 — **England** 1-0 E Germany
WCQ84 (W) — **England** 5-0 Finland
FAC85 (S) — **Man Utd** 1-0 Everton
CS85 (W) — **Man Utd** 0-2 Everton
LCT88 — **Man Utd** 2-0 Luton
LCT88 (W) — **Man Utd** 1-0 Everton

Dwight, Roy (2, 2)
CYC50 (1) — **Middlesex** 1-2 Essex
FAC59 (1) — **Nottm F** 2-1 Luton

Dwyer, Phil (2, 0)
SI69 (C) — **Wales** 0-3 England
BC79 — **Wales** 0-0 England

Dyer, Kieron (5, 0)
ECQ99 (W) — **England** 6-0 Luxembourg
INT00 (W) — **England** 0-0 Argentina
FAC00 — **Newcastle Utd** 1-2 Chelsea
INT00 (S) — **England** 2-0 Ukraine
WCQ00 (S) — **England** 0-1 Germany

Dyson, Jack (1, 1)
FAC56 (1) — **Man City** 3-1 Birmingham

Dyson, Terry (1, 1)
FAC61 (1) — **Spurs** 2-0 Leicester

Easson, Jim (1, 0)
FAC34 — **Portsmouth** 1-2 Man City

Eastham, George (6, 1)
INT63 — **England** 1-1 Brazil
CEN63 — **England** 2-1 FIFA
BC63 — **England** 8-3 N Ireland
INT64 — **England** 2-1 Uruguay
INT65 — **England** 1-0 Hungary
FLC72 (1) — **Stoke** 2-1 Chelsea

Eckersley, Bill (5, 0)
BC 51	**England**	2-3 Scotland
INT51	**England**	2-1 Argentina
INT51	**England**	2-2 Austria
NIN53	**England**	4-4 FIFA
INT53	**England**	3-6 Hungary

Edinburgh, Justin (4, 0)
FAC91	**Spurs**	3-1 Arsenal
FAC91	**Spurs**	2-1 Nottm F
FAC93	**Spurs**	0-1 Arsenal
WLC99 (D)	**Spurs**	1-0 Leicester

Edwards, Bryan (1, 0)
FAC58	**Bolton**	2-0 Man Utd

Edwards, Duncan (9, 2)
SI51	**England**	3-0 Wales
SI52 (C)	**England**	1-0 Scotland
BC55	**England**	7-2 Scotland
INT56	**England**	4-2 Brazil
BC57 (1)	**England**	2-1 Scotland
FAC57	**Man Utd**	1-2 Aston Villa
WCQ57	**England**	5-1 R of Ireland
BC57 (1)	**England**	2-3 N Ireland
INT57	**England**	4-0 France

Edwards, Jimmy (2, 0)
FAC31	**WBA**	2-1 Birmingham
FAC35	**WBA**	2-4 Sheffield W

Edwards, Willis (1, 0)
BC28	**England**	1-5 Scotland

Ehiogu, Ugo (3, 0)
CCC96	**Aston Villa**	3-0 Leeds
FAC00	**Aston Villa**	0-0 Bolton
FAC00	**Aston Villa**	0-1 Chelsea

Ekoku, Efan (1, 0)
INT94 (S)	**Nigeria**	0-1 England

Elder, Alex (4, 0)
BC61	**N Ireland**	1-1 England
FAC62	**Burnley**	1-3 Spurs
BC65	**N Ireland**	1-2 England
ECQ67	**N Ireland**	0-2 England

Elliott, Billy (2, 2)
BC52	**England**	5-2 Wales
INT52 (2)	**England**	5-0 Belgium

Elliott, Matt (2, 2)
WLC99	**Leicester**	0-1 Spurs
WLC00 (C, 2)	**Leicester**	2-1 Tranmere

Elliott, Robbie (2, 0)
PPO99	**Bolton**	0-2 Watford
FAC00	**Bolton**	0-0 Aston Villa

Ellis, Sam (1, 0)
FAC66	**Sheffield W**	2-3 Everton

Emanuel, John (1, 0)
BC73 (S)	**Wales**	0-3 England

Emerson (2, 0)
CCC97	**Middlesbrough**	1-1 Leicester
FAC97	**Middlesbrough**	0-2 Chelsea

England, Mike (6, 0)
BC64 (C)	**Wales**	1-2 England

ECQ66 (C)	**Wales**	1-5 England
FAC67	**Spurs**	2-1 Chelsea
WCQ73 (C)	**Wales**	1-1 England
FLC73	**Spurs**	1-0 Norwich
BC73 (C, W)	**Wales**	0-3 England

As Manager
BC81	**Wales**	0-0 England
BC83	**Wales**	1-2 England

Eustace, Peter (1, 0)
FAC66	**Sheffield W**	2-3 Everton

Evans, Allan (3, 0)
CS81	**Aston Villa**	2-2 Spurs
LCT88 (C)	**Aston Villa**	0-0 Blackburn
LCT88 (C)	**Aston Villa**	0-0 Nottm F

Evans, Alun (2, 1)
SI65 (1)	**England**	3-0 Scotland
FAC71 (W)	**Liverpool**	1-2 Arsenal

Evans, Bobby (3, 0)
BC49	**Scotland**	3-1 England
BC51	**Scotland**	3-2 England
BC59 (C)	**Scotland**	0-1 England

Evans, Brian (2, 0)
WCQ73	**Wales**	1-1 England
BC73	**Wales**	0-3 England

Evans, Ian (1, 0)
BC77	**Wales**	1-0 England

Evans, Jack (1, 0)
FAC25	**Cardiff**	0-1 Sheffield Utd

Eves, Mel (1, 0)
FLC80	**Wolves**	1-0 Nottm F

Ewing, Dave (2, 0)
FAC55	**Man City**	1-3 Newcastle Utd
FAC56	**Man City**	3-1 Birmingham

Fagan, Fionan (1, 0)
FAC55	**Man City**	1-3 Newcastle Utd

Fagan, Willie (2, 0)
FAC37	**PNE**	1-3 Sunderland
FAC50	**Liverpool**	0-2 Arsenal

Fairbrother, Jack (2, 0)
LSC41	**PNE**	1-1 Arsenal
FAC51	**Newcastle Utd**	2-0 Blackpool

Fairclough, Chris (3, 0)
WIT88	**Spurs**	0-4 Arsenal
WIT88	**Spurs**	1-2 AC Milan
CS92	**Leeds**	4-3 Liverpool

Fairclough, David (4, 0)
CS77	**Liverpool**	0-0 Man Utd
FLC78 (S)	**Liverpool**	0-0 Nottm F
EC78	**Liverpool**	1-0 Bruges
MC83 (S)	**Liverpool**	2-1 Man Utd

Fairhurst, David (1, 0)
FAC32	**Newcastle Utd**	2-1 Arsenal

Fairweather, Carlton (1, 0)
CS88	**Wimbledon**	1-2 Liverpool

Falco, Mark (2, 2)
CS81	**Spurs**	2-2 Aston V
CS82 (S)	**Spurs**	0-1 Liverpool

Fantham, Johnny (1, 0)
FAC66   **Sheffield W**   2-3 Everton

Farm, George (3, 0)
FAC51   **Blackpool**   0-2 Newcastle Utd
BC53   **Scotland**   2-2 England
FAC53   **Blackpool**   4-3 Bolton

Farquharson, Tom (2, 0)
FAC25   **Cardiff**   0-1 Sheffield Utd
FAC27   **Cardiff**   1-0 Arsenal

Farrell, Peter (1, 0)
WCQ57 (C)   **Rep of Ireland**   1-5 England

Fashanu, John (4, 1)
LCT88   **Wimbledon**   0-1 Tranmere
FAC88   **Wimbledon**   1-0 Liverpool
CS88 (1, W)   **Wimbledon**   1-2 Liverpool
RC89 (W)   **England**   0-0 Chile

Fell, Leslie (1, 0)
FAC46   **Charlton**   1-4 Derby

Fenton, Ewan (1, 0)
FAC53   **Blackpool**   4-3 Bolton

Fenton, Graham (1, 0)
CCC94   **Aston Villa**   3-1 Man Utd

Fenton, Micky (1, 0)
BC38   **England**   0-1 Scotland

Fenwick, Terry (10, 2)
FAC82 (1)   **QPR**   1-1 Spurs
FAC82   **QPR**   0-1 Spurs
INT84   **England**   0-2 U.S.S.R.
WCQ85   **England**   1-1 Romania
WCQ85   **England**   5-0 Turkey
WCQ85   **England**   0-0 N Ireland
MC86 (C)   **QPR**   0-3 Oxford
WIT88   **Spurs**   0-4 Arsenal
WIT88 (1)   **Spurs**   1-2 AC Milan
CS91   **Spurs**   0-0 Arsenal

Ferdinand, Les (14, 3)
FAV86   **Southall**   0-3 Halesowen
WCQ93 (1)   **England**   6-0 San Marino
WCQ93   **England**   2-2 Netherlands
WCQ93 (1)   **England**   3-0 Poland
INT94 (S)   **England**   2-0 U.S.A.
INT95 (W)   **England**   1-1 Portugal
INT96 (1, W)   **England**   1-0 Bulgaria
INT96 (W)   **England**   3-0 Hungary
CS 96   **Newcastle Utd**   0-4 Man Utd
WCQ96   **England**   2-1 Poland
WCQ97 (S)   **England**   0-1 Italy
WCQ97 (W)   **England**   4-0 Moldova
INT98 (S)   **England**   0-0 Saudi Arabia
WLC99   **Spurs**   1-0 Leicester

Ferdinand, Rio (5, 0)
INT97 (S)   **England**   2-0 Cameroon
INT98   **England**   2-0 Czech Rep
INT99 (S)   **England**   0-2 France
ECQ99 (S)   **England**   0-0 Sweden
INT00 (S)   **England**   0-0 Argentina

Ferguson, Barry (1, 0)
ECQ99   **Scotland**   1-0 England

Ferguson, Duncan (3, 0)
FAC95 (S)   **Everton**   1-0 Man Utd
FAC99 (S)   **Newcastle Utd**   0-2 Man Utd
FAC00 (W)   **Newcastle Utd**   1-2 Chelsea

Ferguson, Hugh (1, 1)
FAC27 (1)   **Cardiff**   1-0 Arsenal

Fern, Rodney (1, 0)
FAC69   **Leicester**   0-1 Man City

Fernie, Willie (1, 0)
BC57   **Scotland**   1-2 England

Ferrer, Albert (1, 0)
FAC00 (W)   **Chelsea**   2-1 Newcastle Utd

Festa, Gianluca (3, 0)
CCC97   **Middlesbrough**   1-1 Leicester
FAC97   **Middlesbrough**   0-2 Chelsea
CCC98   **Middlesbrough**   0-2 Chelsea

Finlayson, Malcolm (1, 0)
FAC60   **Wolves**   3-0 Blackburn

Finney, Alex (2, 0)
FAC23   **Bolton**   2-0 West Ham
FAC29   **Bolton**   2-0 Portsmouth

Finney, Sir Tom (18, 5)
FFLWC41   **PNE**   1-1 Arsenal
BC49   **England**   1-3 Scotland
BC51 (1)   **England**   2-3 Scotland
INT51   **England**   2-1 Argentina
BC52 (1)   **England**   5-2 Wales
INT52   **England**   5-0 Belgium
BC53   **England**   2-2 Scotland
FAC54 (C)   **PNE**   2-3 WBA
INT54   **England**   3-1 W Germany
BC55 (1)   **England**   3-0 N Ireland
INT55 (1)   **England**   4-1 Spain
BC56 (1)   **England**   3-1 Wales
INT56   **England**   3-0 Yugoslavia
BC57   **England**   2-1 Scotland
WCQ57   **England**   5-1 Rep of Ireland
INT57   **England**   4-0 France
INT58   **England**   2-1 Portugal
INT58   **England**   5-0 USSR

Finney, Tom (1, 0)
BC80   **N Ireland**   1-1 England

Fish, Mark (2, 0)
PPO99 (C)   **Bolton**   0-2 Watford
FAC00 (C)   **Bolton**   0-0 Aston Villa

Fisher, Hugh (1, 0)
CS76 (S)   **Southampton**   0-1 Liverpool

Fitzsimons, Arthur (1, 0)
WCQ57   **Rep of Ireland**   1-5 England

Fjortoft, Jan-Aage (1, 0)
INT94 (W)   **Norway**   0-0 England
PPO97   **Sheffield Utd**   0-1 Crystal P

Flanagan, Mike (2, 0)
FAC82   **QPR**   1-1 Spurs
FAC82   **QPR**   0-1 Spurs

Fleming, Craig (1, 0)
FAC94   **Oldham**   1-1 Man Utd

Fleming, Curtis (2, 0)
CCC97　　**Middlesbrough** 1-1 Leicester
FAC97　　**Middlesbrough** 0-2 Chelsea

Fleming, Gary (5, 0)
ECQ86　　**N Ireland** 0-3 England
LCT88　　**Nottm F** 3-0 Leeds
LCT88　　**Nottm F** 0-0 Aston Villa
LCT88　　**Nottm F** 2-2 Tranmere
LCT88　　**Nottm F** 0-0 Sheffield W

Fleming, Jimmy (1, 2)
BC30 (2)　　**Scotland** 2-5 England

Flo, Jostein (2, 0)
WCQ92 (S)　　**Norway** 1-1 England
INT94　　**Norway** 0-0 England

Flo, Tore Andre (3, 0)
CCC98 (S)　　**Chelsea** 2-0 Middlesbrough
FAC00 (S)　　**Chelsea** 2-1 Newcastle Utd
FAC00 (S)　　**Chelsea** 1-0 Aston Villa

Flowers, Ron (18, 3)
BC59　　**England** 1-0 Scotland
INT59　　**England** 2-2 Italy
INT59　　**England** 2-3 Sweden
BC59　　**England** 2-1 N Ireland
FAC60　　**Wolves** 3-0 Blackburn
INT60　　**England** 3-3 Yugoslavia
INT60　　**England** 4-2 Spain
BC60　　**England** 5-1 Wales
BC61　　**England** 9-3 Scotland
INT61 (1)　　**England** 8-0 Mexico
WCQ61　　**England** 2-0 Portugal
BC61　　**England** 1-1 N Ireland
INT62 (1)　　**England** 3-1 Austria
INT62 (1)　　**England** 3-1 Switzerland
BC62　　**England** 4-0 Wales
BC63　　**England** 1-2 Scotland
BC64 (C)　　**England** 2-1 Wales
FAT70 (C)　　**Telford** 0-2 Macclesfield
As Player-Manager
FAT70　　**Telford** 0-2 Macclesfield
As Manager
FAT71　　**Telford** 3-2 Hillingdon

Flowers, Tim (9, 0)
ZC92　　**Southampton** 2-3 Nottm F
INT94　　**England** 5-0 Greece
CS94　　**Blackburn** 0-2 Man Utd
INT94　　**England** 1-0 Nigeria
INT95　　**England** 0-0 Uruguay
UC95　　**England** 2-1 Japan
UC95　　**England** 1-3 Brazil
CS95　　**Blackburn** 0-1 Everton
WLC00　　**Leicester** 2-1 Tranmere

Flynn, Brian (5, 0)
BC75　　**Wales** 2-2 England
BC77　　**Wales** 1-0 England
BC79　　**Wales** 0-0 England
BC81 (C)　　**Wales** 0-0 England
BC83　　**Wales** 1-2 England

Forbes, Alex (3, 0)
BC47　　**Scotland** 1-1 England

FAC50　　**Arsenal** 2-0 Liverpool
FAC52　　**Arsenal** 0-1 Newcastle Utd

Forbes, Duncan (2, 0)
FLC73 (C)　　**Norwich** 0-1 Spurs
FLC75 (C)　　**Norwich** 0-1 Aston Villa

Forbes, Willie (1, 0)
FAC54　　**PNE** 2-3 WBA

Ford, David (1, 1)
FAC66 (1)　　**Sheffield W** 2-3 Everton

Ford, Mark (1, 0)
CCC96 (W)　　**Leeds** 0-3 Aston Villa

Ford, Trevor (2, 2)
BC52 (2)　　**Wales** 2-5 England
BC54　　**Wales** 2-3 England

Forsyth, Alex (1, 0)
FAC76　　**Man Utd** 0-1 Southampton

Forsyth, Tommy (1, 0)
BC77　　**Scotland** 2-1 England

Fortune, Quinton (1, 0)
CS00 (S)　　**Man Utd** 0-2 Chelsea

Forward, Fred (1, 0)
FAC29　　**Portsmouth** 0-2 Bolton

Foster, Bob (1, 0)
FAC54　　**PNE** 2-3 WBA

Foster, Steve (7, 0)
BC82　　**England** 4-0 N Ireland
INT82　　**England** 2-0 Netherlands
FAC83 (C)　　**Brighton** 0-4 Man Utd
SC88 (C)　　**Luton** 1-4 Reading
LCT88 (C)　　**Luton** 0-2 Man Utd
LC88 (C)　　**Luton** 3-2 Arsenal
LC89 (C)　　**Luton** 1-3 Nottm F

Foulkes, Bill (4, 0)
FAC57　　**Man Utd** 1-2 Aston Villa
FAC58 (C)　　**Man Utd** 0-2 Bolton
FAC63　　**Man Utd** 3-1 Leicester
EC68　　**Man Utd** 4-1 Benfica

Foulkes, Billy (2, 0)
FAC52　　**Newcastle Utd** 1-0 Arsenal
BC52　　**Wales** 2-5 England

Fowler, Robbie (12, 3)
CCC95　　**Liverpool** 2-1 Bolton
INT96 (S)　　**England** 1-0 Bulgaria
INT96　　**England** 0-0 Croatia
FAC96　　**Liverpool** 0-1 Man Utd
ECH96 (S)　　**England** 4-1 Netherlands
ECH96 (S)　　**England** 0-0 Spain
INT97 (1)　　**England** 2-0 Mexico
INT97 (1)　　**England** 2-0 Cameroon
INT98 (S)　　**England** 2-0 Czech Rep
ECQ99　　**England** 6-0 Luxembourg
INT00 (S)　　**England** 1-1 Brazil
INT00 (1, W)　　**England** 2-0 Ukraine

Francis, Gerry (5, 3)
ECQ74　　**England** 3-0 Czechoslovakia
ECQ74　　**England** 0-0 Portugal
BC75　　**England** 2-2 Wales
BC75 (2)　　**England** 5-1 Scotland

BC76 (C, 1)   **England** 4-0 N Ireland
As Manager
LDT90   **Bristol R** 1-2 Tranmere

Francis, Steve (4, 0)
FMC86   **Chelsea** 5-4 Man City
SC88   **Reading** 4-1 Luton
AT94   **Huddersfield** 1-1 Swansea
PPO95   **Huddersfield** 2-1 Bristol R

Francis, Trevor (21, 3)
INT77   **England** 0-2 Netherlands
WCQ77 (1)   **England** 5-0 Luxembourg
BC77   **England** 1-2 Scotland
INT77   **England** 0-0 Switzerland
WCQ77 (S)   **England** 2-0 Italy
INT78   **England** 1-1 Brazil
INT78 (1)   **England** 4-1 Hungary
ECQ79   **England** 2-0 Bulgaria
FLC80   **Nottm F** 0-1 Wolves
INT81 (W)   **England** 1-2 Spain
WCQ81   **England** 0-0 Romania
BC81 (S)   **England** 0-1 Scotland
BC82 (W)   **England** 4-0 N Ireland
ECQ83   **England** 0-0 Greece
ECQ83 (1)   **England** 2-0 Hungary
BC83   **England** 2-0 Scotland
ECQ83   **England** 0-1 Denmark
BC84   **England** 1-0 N Ireland
INT84 (W)   **England** 0-2 USSR
INT84 (S)   **England** 1-0 E Germany
RC86   **England** 2-1 Scotland
As Manager
FAC93   **Sheffield W** 2-1 Sheffield Utd
CCC93   **Sheffield W** 1-2 Arsenal
FAC93   **Sheffield W** 1-1 Arsenal
FAC93   **Sheffield W** 1-2 Arsenal

Franklin, Neil (5, 0)
VI45   **England** 2-2 France
VI46   **England** 2-0 Belgium
IT46   **FA** 3-5 Army PT Corps
BC47   **England** 1-1 Scotland
BC49   **England** 1-3 Scotland

Fraser, Doug (3, 0)
FLC67   **WBA** 2-3 QPR
FAC68   **WBA** 1-0 Everton
FLC70   **WBA** 1-2 Man City

Fraser, John (1, 0)
FAC75   **Fulham** 0-2 West Ham

Freund, Steffen (2, 0)
EC96 (W)   **Germany** 1-1 England
WLC99   **Spurs** 1-0 Leicester

Froggatt, Jack (5, 1)
BC51   **England** 2-3 Scotland
INT51   **England** 2-2 Austria
BC52 (1)   **England** 5-2 Wales
INT52   **England** 5-0 Belgium
BC53   **England** 2-2 Scotland

Froggatt, Redfern (3, 1)
BC52   **England** 5-2 Wales
INT52 (1)   **England** 5-0 Belgium

BC53   **England** 2-2 Scotland

Furnell, Jim (1, 0)
FLC68   **Arsenal** 0-1 Leeds

Gabriel, Jimmy (2, 0)
SI56   **Scotland** 2-1 England
FAC66   **Everton** 3-2 Sheffield W

Gage, Kevin (5, 0)
LCT88   **Aston Villa** 0-0 Blackburn
LCT88   **Aston Villa** 0-0 Nottm F
MT90   **Aston Villa** 0-2 Arsenal
MT90   **Aston Villa** 0-1 R Sociedad
FAC93   **Sheffield Utd** 1-2 Sheffield W

Gale, Tony (1, 0)
CS94   **Blackburn** 0-2 Man Utd

Gallacher, Hughie (2, 0)
BC28   **Scotland** 5-1 England
BC34   **Scotland** 0-3 England

Gallacher, Kevin (2, 0)
RC88 (S)   **Scotland** 0-1 England
CS95   **Blackburn** 0-1 Everton

Gallacher, Patsy (1, 0)
FAC37   **Sunderland** 3-1 PNE

Galley, Tom (1, 0)
FAC39   **Wolves** 1-4 Portsmouth

Gallimore, Len (2, 0)
FAC37   **PNE** 1-3 Sunderland
FAC38   **PNE** 1-0 Huddersfield
FFLWC41   **PNE** 1-1 Arsenal

Galvin, Tony (10, 0)
FAC81   **Spurs** 1-1 Man City
FAC81   **Spurs** 3-2 Man City
CS81   **Spurs** 2-2 Aston Villa
FLC82   **Spurs** 1-3 Liverpool
FAC82   **Spurs** 1-1 QPR
FAC82   **Spurs** 1-0 QPR
CS82   **Spurs** 0-1 Liverpool
LCT88   **Sheffield W** 0-0 Crystal P
LCT88   **Sheffield W** 1-1 Wigan
LCT88 (W)   **Sheffield W** 2-1 Man Utd

Gannon, John (1, 0)
FAC93   **Sheffield Utd** 1-2 Sheffield W

Gardiner, Joe (1, 0)
FAC39   **Wolves** 1-4 Portsmouth

Garland, Chris (1, 0)
FLC72   **Chelsea** 1-2 Stoke

Garner, Simon (4, 1)
FMC87   **Blackburn** 1-0 Charlton
LCT88   **Blackburn** 0-0 Aston Villa
PPO93 (S)   **WBA** 3-0 Port V
PPO94 (1)   **Wycombe** 4-2 Preston

Garrett, Tom (2, 0)
FAC51   **Blackpool** 0-2 Newcastle Utd
FAC53   **Blackpool** 4-3 Bolton

Gascoigne, Paul (39, 8)
LCT88   **Newcastle Utd** 0-0 Liverpool
LCT88   **Newcastle Utd** 0-2 Tranmere
WIT88   **Spurs** 0-4 Arsenal

WIT88	**Spurs** 1-2 AC Milan	
INT88 (S)	**England** 1-0 Denmark	
WCQ89 (S, 1)	**England** 5-0 Albania	
RC89	**England** 0-0 Chile	
INT90 (S)	**England** 1-0 Brazil	
INT90 (1)	**England** 4-2 Czechoslovakia	
INT90	**England** 1-0 Denmark	
INT90	**England** 1-2 Uruguay	
INT90	**England** 1-0 Hungary	
ECQ90	**England** 2-0 Poland	
INT91 (W)	**England** 2-0 Cameroon	
FAC91 (1, W)	**Spurs** 3-1 Arsenal	
FAC91 (W)	**Spurs** 2-1 Nottm F	
WCQ92	**England** 1-1 Norway	
WCQ92 (2)	**England** 4-0 Turkey	
WCQ93	**England** 6-0 San Marino	
WCQ93 (W)	**England** 2-2 Netherlands	
WCQ93 (1)	**England** 3-0 Poland	
INT94 (W)	**England** 1-0 Denmark	
UC95 (S)	**England** 2-1 Japan	
UC95 (S)	**England** 1-3 Brazil	
INT95 (W)	**England** 0-0 Colombia	
INT95	**England** 3-1 Switzerland	
INT95	**England** 1-1 Portugal	
INT96 (W)	**England** 1-0 Bulgaria	
INT96	**England** 0-0 Croatia	
ECH96 (W)	**England** 1-1 Switzerland	
ECH96 (1)	**England** 2-0 Scotland	
ECH96	**England** 4-1 Netherlands	
ECH96	**England** 0-0 Spain	
ECH96	**England** 1-1 Germany	
WCQ96	**England** 2-1 Poland	
WCQ97 (1)	**England** 4-0 Moldova	
INT97 (W)	**England** 2-0 Cameroon	
CCC98 (S)	**Middlesbrough** 0-2 Chelsea	
INT98 (S)	**England** 0-0 Saudi Arabia	

Gaskell, Dave (2, 0)
| SI56 | **England** 1-2 Scotland |
| FAC63 | **Man Utd** 3-1 Leicester |

Gates, Eric (4, 0)
CS78	**Ipswich** 0-5 Nottm F
WCQ80	**England** 4-0 Norway
LCT88	**Sunderland** 0-0 Wigan
PPO90 (W)	**Sunderland** 0-1 Swindon

Gatting, Steve (3, 0)
FAC83	**Brighton** 2-2 Man Utd
FAC83	**Brighton** 0-4 Man Utd
PPO91 (W)	**Brighton** 1-3 Notts C

Gayle, Brian (1, 0)
| FAC93 (C) | **Sheffield Utd** 1-2 Sheffield W |

Gayle, Howard (1, 0)
| MC85 (S) | **Sunderland** 0-1 Norwich |

Gaynor, Tommy (5, 0)
LCT88 (S)	**Nottm F** 3-0 Leeds
LCT88 (S)	**Nottm F** 2-2 Tranmere
LCT88 (W)	**Nottm F** 0-0 Sheffield W
LC89	**Nottm F** 3-1 Luton
SC89 (W)	**Nottm F** 4-3 Everton

Geddis, David (2, 0)
| FAC78 | **Ipswich** 1-0 Arsenal |
| CS81 | **Aston Villa** 2-2 Spurs |

Geldard, Albert (1, 0)
| FAC33 | **Everton** 3-0 Man City |

Gemmell, Tommy (2, 0)
| ECQ67 | **Scotland** 3-2 England |
| BC69 | **Scotland** 1-4 England |

Gemmill, Archie (4, 0)
CS75	**Derby** 2-0 West Ham
BC77 (S)	**Scotland** 2-1 England
CS78	**Nottm F** 5-0 Ipswich
FLC79	**Nottm F** 3-2 Southampton
As Manager	
AWS96	**Rotherham** 2-1 Shrewsbury

Gemmill, Scot (2, 2)
| ZC92 (2) | **Nottm F** 3-2 Southampton |
| RLC92 | **Nottm F** 0-1 Man Utd |

Gennoe, Terry (2, 0)
| FLC79 | **Southampton** 2-3 Nottm F |
| LCT88 | **Blackburn** 0-0 Aston Villa |

George, Charlie (4, 1)
FAC71 (1)	**Arsenal** 2-1 Liverpool
FAC72	**Arsenal** 0-1 Leeds
CS75	**Derby** 2-0 West Ham
INT76 (W)	**England** 1-1 Rep of Ireland

Gerrard, Steven (1, 0)
| INT00 (W) | **England** 2-0 Ukraine |

Gibb, Tommy (1, 0)
| FAC74 (S) | **Newcastle Utd** 0-3 Liverpool |

Gibson, Colin (5, 0)
CS81	**Aston Villa** 2-2 Spurs
LCT88	**Man Utd** 2-0 Luton
LCT88	**Man Utd** 1-0 Everton
LCT88	**Man Utd** 1-2 Sheffield W
PPO94	**Leicester** 2-1 Derby

Gibson, David (2, 0)
| FAC63 | **Leicester** 1-3 Man Utd |
| FAC69 | **Leicester** 0-1 Man City |

Gibson, George (1, 0)
| FAC29 | **Bolton** 2-0 Portsmouth |

Gibson, Jimmy (1, 0)
| BC28 | **Scotland** 5-1 England |

Gibson, Terry (3, 0)
LCT88	**Wimbledon** 0-1 Tranmere
FAC88 (W)	**Wimbledon** 1-0 Liverpool
CS88	**Wimbledon** 1-2 Liverpool

Gibson, Willie (1, 0)
| FAC24 | **Newcastle Utd** 2-0 Aston Villa |

Gidman, John (5, 0)
FLC77	**Aston Villa** 0-0 Everton
WCQ77	**England** 5-0 Luxembourg
CS83 (S)	**Man Utd** 2-0 Liverpool
FAC85	**Man Utd** 1-0 Everton
CS85	**Man Utd** 0-2 Everton

Giggs, Ryan (15, 1)
| SI89 (C, 1) | **England** 3-1 Belgium |

SI89 (C) **England** 1-3 W Germany
RLC92 **Man Utd** 1-0 Nottm F
CS93 (W) **Man Utd** 1-1 Arsenal
CCC94 (W) **Man Utd** 1-3 Aston Villa
FAC94 **Man Utd** 1-1 Oldham
FAC94 **Man Utd** 4-0 Chelsea
CS94 **Man Utd** 2-0 Blackburn
FAC95 (S) **Man Utd** 0-1 Everton
FAC96 **Man Utd** 1-0 Liverpool
CS96 **Man Utd** 4-0 Newcastle Utd
CS97 (W) **Man Utd** 1-1 Chelsea
CS98 (W) **Man Utd** 0-3 Arsenal
FAC99 **Man Utd** 2-0 Newcastle Utd
CS00 (W) **Man Utd** 0-2 Chelsea

Gilchrist, Paul (2, 0)
FAC76 **Southampton** 1-0 Man Utd
CS76 **Southampton** 0-1 Liverpool

Giles, David (1, 0)
BC81 (S) **Wales** 0-0 England

Giles, Johnny (9, 0)
FAC63 **Man Utd** 3-1 Leicester
FAC65 **Leeds** 1-2 Liverpool
FLC68 **Leeds** 1-0 Arsenal
FAC70 **Leeds** 2-2 Chelsea
FAC72 **Leeds** 1-0 Arsenal
EEC73 **The Three** 2-0 The Six
FAC73 **Leeds** 0-1 Sunderland
CS74 **Leeds** 1-1 Liverpool
INT76 (C) **Rep of Ireland** 1-1 England
As Player-Manager
INT76 **Rep of Ireland** 1-1 England
As Manager
ECQ80 **Rep of Ireland** 0-2 England

Gilfillan, John (2, 0)
FAC29 **Portsmouth** 0-2 Bolton
FAC34 **Portsmouth** 1-2 Man City

Gilkes, Michael (2, 1)
SC88 (1) **Reading** 4-1 Luton
PPO95 **Reading** 3-4 Bolton

Gill, Jimmy (1, 0)
FAC25 **Cardiff** 0-1 Sheffield Utd

Gillard, Ian (4, 0)
INT75 **England** 2-0 W Germany
BC75 **England** 2-2 Wales
FAC82 **QPR** 1-1 Spurs
FAC82 **QPR** 0-1 Spurs

Gillespie, Billy (1, 0)
FAC25 (C) **Sheffield Utd** 1-0 Cardiff

Gillespie, Gary (5, 0)
LC87 **Liverpool** 1-2 Arsenal
LCT88 **Liverpool** 0-0 Newcastle Utd
FAC88 **Liverpool** 0-1 Wimbledon
CS88 **Liverpool** 2-1 Wimbledon
MT89 **Liverpool** 0-1 Arsenal

Gillespie, Keith (1, 0)
CS96 (S) **Newcastle Utd** 0-4 Man Utd

Gilzean, Alan (4, 0)
FAC67 **Spurs** 2-1 Chelsea

BC69 (W) **Scotland** 1-4 England
FLC71 **Spurs** 2-0 Aston Villa
FLC73 **Spurs** 1-0 Norwich

Ginola, David (2, 0)
CS96 (W) **Newcastle Utd** 0-4 Man Utd
WLC99 (W) **Spurs** 1-0 Leicester

Given, Shay (2, 0)
FAC98 **Newcastle Utd** 0-2 Arsenal
FAC00 **Newcastle Utd** 1-2 Chelsea

Givens, Don (1, 0)
INT76 **Rep of Ireland** 1-1 England

Glass, Stephen (1, 0)
FAC99 (S) **Newcastle Utd** 0-2 Man Utd

Glidden, Tommy (2, 0)
FAC31 (C) **WBA** 2-1 Birmingham
FAC35 (C) **WBA** 2-4 Sheffield W

Glover, Lee (2, 0)
FAC91 (W) **Nottm F** 1-2 Spurs
AIC96 (W) **Port V** 2-5 Genoa

Glover, Len (1, 0)
FAC69 (W) **Leicester** 0-1 Man City

Goddard, Paul (3, 0)
FLC81 (W) **West Ham** 1-1 Liverpool
LCT88 **Newcastle Utd** 0-0 Liverpool
LCT88 **Newcastle Utd** 0-2 Tranmere

Godfrey, Brian (1, 0)
FLC71 (C) **Aston Villa** 0-2 Spurs

Golac, Ivan (1, 0)
FLC79 **Southampton** 2-3 Nottm F

Goodall, Roy (4, 0)
BC28 (C) **England** 1-5 Scotland
FAC28 **Huddersfield** 1-3 Blackburn
BC30 **England** 5-2 Scotland
FAC30 **Huddersfield** 0-2 Arsenal

Goodchild, Jim (1, 0)
FAC26 **Man City** 0-1 Bolton

Goodlass, Ronnie (2, 2)
SI69 (2) **England** 3-0 Wales
FLC77 **Everton** 0-0 Aston Villa

Goodwin, Freddie (1, 0)
FAC58 **Man Utd** 0-2 Bolton

Goodyear, Clive (1, 0)
FAC88 **Wimbledon** 1-0 Liverpool

Goram, Andy (1, 0)
ECH96 **Scotland** 0-2 England

Goring, Peter (1, 0)
FAC50 **Arsenal** 2-0 Liverpool

Gorman, Jimmy (1, 0)
FAC37 **Sunderland** 3-1 PNE

Gough, Richard (5, 0)
BC83 **Scotland** 0-2 England
RC86 **Scotland** 1-2 England
FAC87 (C) **Spurs** 2-3 Coventry
LCEN87 (W) **Football League** 3-0 Rest of World
RC88 **Scotland** 0-1 England

Gould, Bobby (2, 1)
FLC69 (1) **Arsenal** 1-3 Swindon

CS75	West Ham 0-2 Derby
As Manager	
LCT88	Wimbledon 0-1 Tranmere
FAC88	Wimbledon 1-0 Liverpool
CS88	Wimbledon 1-2 Liverpool

Govan, Alex (1, 0)

| FAC56 | Birmingham 1-3 Man City |

Gow, Gerry (2, 0)

| FAC81 | Man City 1-1 Spurs |
| FAC81 | Man City 2-3 Spurs |

Gowling, Alan (1, 1)

| FLC76 | Newcastle Utd 1-2 Man City |

Graham, Arthur (2, 0)

| BC79 | Scotland 1-3 England |
| CS83 | Man Utd 2-0 Liverpool |

Graham, George (6, 2)

SI60 (1)	Scotland 3-5 England
YI63 (1)	Rest of UK 2-5 England
FLC68	Arsenal 0-1 Leeds
FLC69 (S)	Arsenal 1-3 Swindon
FAC71	Arsenal 2-1 Liverpool
FAC72	Arsenal 0-1 Leeds
As Manager	
LC87	Arsenal 2-1 Liverpool
LC88	Arsenal 2-3 Luton
WIT88	Arsenal 4-0 Spurs
WIT88	Arsenal 3-0 Bayern Munich
MT89	Arsenal 1-0 Porto
MT89	Arsenal 1-0 Liverpool
CS89	Arsenal 0-1 Liverpool
MT90	Arsenal 2-0 Aston Villa
MT90	Arsenal 0-1 Sampdoria
FAC91	Arsenal 1-3 Spurs
CS91	Arsenal 0-0 Spurs
FAC93	Arsenal 1-0 Spurs
CCC93	Arsenal 2-1 Sheffield W
FAC93	Arsenal 1-1 Sheffield W
FAC93	Arsenal 2-1 Sheffield W
CS93	Arsenal 1-1 Man Utd
WLC99	Spurs 1-0 Leicester

Graham, Len (1, 0)

| BC55 | N Ireland 0-3 England |

Grainger, Colin (3, 2)

INT56 (2)	England 4-2 Brazil
BC56	England 3-1 Wales
BC57	England 2-1 Scotland

Grant, Tony (1, 0)

| CS95 (W) | Everton 1-0 Blackburn |

Granville, Danny (1, 0)

| CS97 | Chelsea 1-1 Man Utd |

Gray, Andy (5, 2)

FLC77	Aston Villa 0-0 Everton
FLC80 (1)	Wolves 1-0 Nottm F
BC83	Scotland 0-2 England
FAC84 (1)	Everton 2-0 Watford
FAC85	Everton 0-1 Man Utd

Gray, Andy (5, 0)

| LCT88 (W) | Aston Villa 0-0 Blackburn |

LCT88	Aston Villa 0-0 Nottm F
FAC90 (W)	Crystal P 3-3 Man Utd
FAC90	Crystal P 0-1 Man Utd
ZC91 (W)	Crystal P 4-1 Everton

Gray, Andy (1, 0)

| CCC96 | Leeds 0-3 Aston Villa |

Gray, Billy (1, 0)

| FAC59 | Nottm F 2-1 Luton |

Gray, Dougie (1, 0)

| BC30 | Scotland 2-5 England |

Gray, Eddie (6, 0)

FLC68 (W)	Leeds 1-0 Arsenal
BC69	Scotland 1-4 England
FAC70	Leeds 2-2 Chelsea
FAC72	Leeds 1-0 Arsenal
FAC73 (W)	Leeds 0-1 Sunderland
CS74	Leeds 1-1 Liverpool

Gray, Frankie (6, 0)

SI70	Scotland 0-2 England
BC79	Scotland 1-3 England
FLC80	Nottm F 0-1 Wolves
BC81	Scotland 1-0 England
BC83	Scotland 0-2 England
LCT88	Sunderland 0-0 Wigan

Gray, Michael (2, 0)

| PPO98 | Sunderland 4-4 Charlton |
| ECQ99 (S) | England 0-0 Sweden |

Graydon, Ray (1, 1)

| FLC75 (1) | Aston Villa 1-0 Norwich |

Grayson, Simon (5, 0)

LCT88	Leeds 0-3 Nottm F
PPO92	Leicester 0-1 Blackburn
PPO94 (C)	Leicester 2-1 Derby
PPO96	Leicester 2-1 Crystal P
CCC97	Leicester 1-1 Middlesbrough

Grealish, Tony (3, 0)

ECQ80	Rep of Ireland 0-2 England
FAC83 (C)	Brighton 2-2 Man Utd
FAC83	Brighton 0-4 Man Utd

Greaves, Ian (1, 0)

FAC58	Man Utd 0-2 Bolton
As Manager	
FRT87	Mansfield 1-1 Bristol C

Greaves, Jimmy (25, 20)

U23I57 (2)	England 3-2 Romania
INT59	England 2-3 Sweden
INT60 (1)	England 3-3 Yugoslavia
INT60 (1)	England 4-2 Spain
BC60 (2)	England 5-1 Wales
BC61 (3)	England 9-3 Scotland
FAC62 (1)	Spurs 3-1 Burnley
INT62	England 3-1 Switzerland
BC62 (1)	England 4-0 Wales
BC63	England 1-2 Scotland
INT63	England 1-1 Brazil
CEN63 (1)	England 2-1 F.I.FA.
BC63 (4)	England 8-3 N Ireland
INT64	England 2-1 Uruguay

INT64	**England**	2-2 Belgium
BC65 (1)	**England**	2-2 Scotland
INT65 (1)	**England**	1-0 Hungary
INT65	**England**	2-3 Austria
INT66 (1)	**England**	2-0 Yugoslavia
WC66	**England**	0-0 Uruguay
WC66	**England**	2-0 Mexico
WC66	**England**	2-0 France
ECQ67	**England**	2-3 Scotland
FAC67	**Spurs**	2-1 Chelsea
INT67 (1)	**England**	2-0 Spain

Green, Colin (1, 0)

ECQ66	**Wales**	1-5 England

Green, George (1, 0)

FAC25	**Sheffield Utd**	1-0 Cardiff

Green, Ken (1, 0)

FAC56	**Birmingham**	1-3 Man City

Green, Scott (4, 0)

PPO91 (S)	**Bolton**	0-1 Tranmere
CCC95 (W)	**Bolton**	1-2 Liverpool
PPO95	**Bolton**	4-3 Reading
PPO00	**Wigan**	2-3 Gillingham

Green, Tony (1, 0)

BC71 (W)	**Scotland**	1-3 England

Greenhalgh, Harry (1, 0)

FAC26	**Bolton**	1-0 Man City

Greenhoff, Brian (12, 0)

FAC76	**Man Utd**	0-1 Southampton
BC76	**England**	4-0 N Ireland
INT76	**England**	1-1 Ireland
WCQ76	**England**	2-1 Finland
INT77 (W)	**England**	0-2 Netherlands
FAC77	**Man Utd**	2-1 Liverpool
BC77	**England**	0-1 Wales
BC77 (W)	**England**	1-2 Scotland
CS77	**Man Utd**	0-0 Liverpool
INT78	**England**	1-1 Brazil
BC78	**England**	1-0 N Ireland
INT78 (S)	**England**	4-1 Hungary

Greenhoff, Jimmy (5, 1)

FLC68	**Leeds**	1-0 Arsenal
FLC72	**Stoke**	2-1 Chelsea
FAC77 (1)	**Man Utd**	2-1 Liverpool
CS77 (W)	**Man Utd**	0-0 Liverpool
FAC79	**Man Utd**	2-3 Arsenal

Gregg, Bob (1, 0)

FAC31	**Birmingham**	1-2 WBA

Gregg, Harry (4, 0)

BC57	**N Ireland**	3-2 England
FAC58	**Man Utd**	0-2 Bolton
BC59	**N Ireland**	1-2 England
BC63	**N Ireland**	3-8 England

Gregory, John (3, 0)

FAC82	**QPR**	1-1 Spurs
FAC82	**QPR**	0-1 Spurs
ECQ83	**England**	0-1 Denmark
As Manager		
FAC00	**Aston Villa**	0-0 Bolton
FAC00	**Aston Villa**	0-1 Chelsea

Gregory, Tony (1, 0)

FAC59	**Luton**	1-2 Nottm F

Greig, John (4, 0)

BC65	**Scotland**	2-2 England
ECQ67 (C)	**Scotland**	3-2 England
BC69	**Scotland**	1-4 England
BC71	**Scotland**	1-3 England

Griffin, Andy (1, 0)

FAC99	**Newcastle Utd**	0-2 Man Utd

Griffin, Frank (1, 1)

FAC54 (1)	**WBA**	3-2 PNE

Griffiths, Arfon (1, 1)

BC75 (1)	**Wales**	2-2 England

Griffiths, Mal (1, 1)

FAC49 (1)	**Leicester**	1-3 Wolves

Grimandi, Gilles (2, 0)

CS98 (S)	**Arsenal**	3-0 Man Utd
CS99	**Arsenal**	2-1 Man Utd
EC99 (W)	**Arsenal**	3-1 AIK Stockholm

Grimes, Ashley (4, 0)

ECQ80	**Rep of Ireland**	0-2 England
SC88	**Luton**	1-4 Reading
LC88 (S)	**Luton**	3-2 Arsenal
LC89 (W)	**Luton**	1-3 Nottm F

Grobbelaar, Bruce (18, 0)

FLC82	**Liverpool**	3-1 Spurs
CS82	**Liverpool**	1-0 Spurs
MC83	**Liverpool**	2-1 Man Utd
CS83	**Liverpool**	0-2 Man Utd
MC84	**Liverpool**	0-0 Everton
CS84	**Liverpool**	1-0 Everton
FAC86	**Liverpool**	3-1 Everton
CS86 (W)	**Liverpool**	1-1 Everton
LC87	**Liverpool**	1-2 Arsenal
FAC88	**Liverpool**	0-1 Wimbledon
CS88	**Liverpool**	2-1 Wimbledon
FAC89	**Liverpool**	3-2 Everton
MT89	**Liverpool**	2-0 Dynamo Kiev
MT89	**Liverpool**	0-1 Arsenal
CS89	**Liverpool**	1-0 Arsenal
CS90	**Liverpool**	1-1 Man Utd
FAC92	**Liverpool**	2-0 Sunderland
CS92	**Liverpool**	3-4 Leeds

Grodas, Frode (1, 0)

FAC97	**Chelsea**	2-0 Middlesbrough

Groves, John (1, 0)

FAC59	**Luton**	1-2 Nottm F

Groves, Perry (4, 0)

LC87 (S)	**Arsenal**	2-1 Liverpool
LC88 (W)	**Arsenal**	2-3 Luton
MT90 (S)	**Arsenal**	2-0 Aston Villa
FAC91 (S)	**Arsenal**	1-3 Spurs

Gudjohnsen, Eidur (3, 0)

PPO99	**Bolton**	0-2 Watford
FAC00	**Bolton**	0-0 Aston Villa
CS00 (S)	**Chelsea**	2-0 Man Utd

Guentchev, Bontcho (1, 0)

INT96 (S)	**Bulgaria**	0-1 England

Guppy, Steve (6, 0)
FAT91 (W)	**Wycombe**	2-1 Kidderminster
FAT93	**Wycombe**	4-1 Runcorn
PPO94	**Wycombe**	4-2 PNE
AIC96 (W)	**Port V**	2-5 Genoa
WLC99	**Leicester**	0-1 Spurs
WLC00	**Leicester**	2-1 Tranmere

Gurney, Bobby (1, 1)
FAC37 (1)	**Sunderland**	3-1 PNE

Guthrie, Jimmy (1, 0)
FAC39 (C)	**Portsmouth**	4-1 Wolves
LWC42 (C)	**Portsmouth**	0-2 Brentford

Guthrie, Ron (1, 0)
FAC73	**Sunderland**	1-0 Leeds

Gynn, Micky (2, 0)
FAC87	**Coventry**	3-2 Leeds
CS87 (W)	**Coventry**	0-1 Everton

Haaland, Alf-Inge (1, 0)
INT94 (S)	**Norway**	0-0 England

Haddock, Harry (1, 0)
BC55	**Scotland**	2-7 England

Haffey, Frank (1, 0)
BC61	**Scotland**	3-9 England

Hall, Alex (1, 0)
FAC37	**Sunderland**	3-1 PNE

Hall, Brian (3, 0)
FAC71	**Liverpool**	1-2 Arsenal
FAC74	**Liverpool**	3-0 Newcastle Utd
CS74	**Liverpool**	1-1 Leeds

Hall, Gareth (3, 0)
SI84	**England**	1-0 Scotland
SI84 (S)	**England**	4-1 Netherlands
ZC90	**Chelsea**	1-0 Middlesbrough

Hall, Jeff (8, 0)
BC55	**England**	3-0 N Ireland
INT55	**England**	4-1 Spain
FAC56	**Birmingham**	1-3 Man City
INT56	**England**	4-2 Brazil
BC56	**England**	3-1 Wales
INT56	**England**	3-0 Yugoslavia
BC57	**England**	2-1 Scotland
WCQ57	**England**	5-1 Rep of Ireland

Hall, Willie (2, 0)
BC38	**England**	0-1 Scotland
WI40	**England**	0-1 Wales

Halle, Gunnar (1, 0)
WCQ92	**Norway**	1-1 England

Hallworth, Jon (1, 0)
FAC94	**Oldham**	1-1 Man Utd

Halom, Vic (1, 0)
FAC73	**Sunderland**	1-0 Leeds

Hamann, Dietmar (2, 1)
FAC99 (W)	**Newcastle Utd**	0-2 Man Utd
WCQ00 (1)	**Germany**	1-0 England

Hamilton, Alex (2, 0)
BC63	**Scotland**	2-1 England
BC65	**Scotland**	2-2 England

Hamilton, Billy (3, 0)
BC80 (W)	**N Ireland**	1-1 England
BC82	**N Ireland**	0-4 England
BC84	**N Ireland**	0-1 England

Hamilton, Bryan (4, 0)
BC74 (W)	**N Ireland**	0-1 England
BC76	**N Ireland**	0-4 England
FLC77	**Everton**	0-0 Aston Villa
BC78 (C)	**N Ireland**	0-1 England

As Manager
FRT85	**Wigan**	3-1 Brentford

Hamilton, Ian (2, 0)
FLC71	**Aston Villa**	0-2 Spurs
FLC75	**Aston Villa**	1-0 Norwich

Hamilton, Tom (1, 0)
BC32	**Scotland**	0-3 England

Hampson, Billy (1, 0)
FAC24	**Newcastle Utd**	2-0 Aston Villa

Hancocks, Johnny (1, 0)
FAC49	**Wolves**	3-1 Leicester

Hannah, George (1, 1)
FAC55 (1)	**Newcastle Utd**	3-1 Man City

Hansen, Alan (16, 0)
EC78	**Liverpool**	1-0 Bruges
CS79	**Liverpool**	3-1 Arsenal
CS80	**Liverpool**	1-0 West Ham
FLC81	**Liverpool**	1-1 West Ham
CS82	**Liverpool**	1-0 Spurs
MC83	**Liverpool**	2-1 Man Utd
CS83	**Liverpool**	0-2 Man Utd
MC84	**Liverpool**	0-0 Everton
CS84	**Liverpool**	0-1 Everton
FAC86 (C)	**Liverpool**	3-1 Everton
CS86 (C)	**Liverpool**	1-1 Everton
LC87 (C)	**Liverpool**	1-2 Arsenal
FAC88 (C)	**Liverpool**	0-1 Wimbledon
FAC89	**Liverpool**	3-2 Everton
MT89	**Liverpool**	2-0 Dynamo Kiev
CS89 (C)	**Liverpool**	1-0 Arsenal

Hanson, Stan (1, 0)
FAC53	**Bolton**	3-4 Blackpool

Hapgood, Eddie (13, 0)
FAC30	**Arsenal**	2-0 Huddersfield
FAC32	**Arsenal**	1-2 Newcastle Utd
BC34	**England**	3-0 Scotland
BC36 (C)	**England**	1-1 Scotland
FAC36	**Arsenal**	1-0 Sheffield Utd
BC38 (C)	**England**	0-1 Scotland
WI40 (C)	**England**	0-1 Wales
FLWC41 (C)	**Arsenal**	1-1 PNE
WI41 (C)	**England**	2-0 Scotland
WI42 (C)	**England**	3-0 Scotland
CHA42 (C)	**RAF**	6-3 Met Police
WI42 (C)	**England**	0-0 Scotland
WI43 (C)	**England**	5-3 Wales

Hardwick, George (11, 0)
CHA42	**RAF**	6-3 Met Police
CHA43	**RAF**	4-3 Met Police

WI43   **England** 8-3 Wales
WI44   **England** 6-2 Scotland
LSC44   **Chelsea** 1-3 Charlton
WI44   **England** 6-2 Scotland
LSC45   **Chelsea** 2-0 Millwall
VI45   **England** 2-2 France
VI46   **England** 2-0 Belgium
IT46   **FA** 3-5 Army PT Corps
BC47   **England** 1-1 Scotland

Hardy, Billy (2, 0)
FAC25   **Cardiff** 0-1 Sheffield Utd
FAC27   **Cardiff** 1-0 Arsenal

Hardyman, Paul (1, 0)
FAC92 (S)   **Sunderland** 0-2 Liverpool

Harford, Mick (5, 2)
SC88 (1)   **Luton** 1-4 Reading
LCT88 (W)   **Luton** 0-2 Man Utd
LC88 (W)   **Luton** 3-2 Arsenal
INT88 (W)   **England** 1-0 Denmark
LC89 (1)   **Luton** 1-3 Nottingham F

Harkes, John (6, 1)
RLC91 (W)   **Sheffield W** 1-0 Man Utd
FAC93   **Sheffield W** 2-1 Sheffield Utd
CCC93 (1)   **Sheffield W** 1-2 Arsenal
FAC93   **Sheffield W** 1-1 Arsenal
FAC93   **Sheffield W** 1-2 Arsenal
PPO94   **Derby** 1-2 Leicester

Harkness, Jack (2, 0)
BC28   **Scotland** 5-1 England
BC30   **Scotland** 2-5 England

Harland, Stan (1, 0)
FLC69 (S)   **Swindon** 3-1 Arsenal

Harley, Jon (1, 0)
FAC00   **Chelsea** 2-1 Newcastle Utd

Harper, Alan (6, 0)
MC84 (S)   **Everton** 0-0 Liverpool
CS86   **Everton** 1-1 Liverpool
CS87   **Everton** 1-0 Coventry
LCT88   **Everton** 1-1 Wolves
LCT88 (W)   **Everton** 0-1 Man Utd
FAC94   **Luton** 0-2 Chelsea

Harper, Bill (1, 0)
BC24   **Scotland** 1-1 England

Harper, Steve (1, 0)
FAC99   **Newcastle Utd** 0-2 Man Utd

Harrington, Alan (2, 0)
BC56   **Wales** 1-3 England
BC60   **Wales** 1-5 England

Harris, Allan (1, 0)
FAC67   **Chelsea** 1-2 Spurs

Harris, Brian (1, 0)
FAC66   **Everton** 3-2 Sheffield W

Harris, Carl (2, 0)
BC79 (S)   **Wales** 0-0 England
BC81 (W)   **Wales** 0-0 England

Harris, Gerry (2, 0)
U23I57   **England** 3-2 Romania
FAC60   **Wolves** 3-0 Blackburn

Harris, Gordon (1, 0)
FAC62   **Burnley** 1-3 Spurs

Harris, Neil (2, 1)
BC24   **Scotland** 1-1 England
FAC24 (1)   **Newcastle Utd** 2-0 Aston Villa

Harris, Ron (6, 1)
SI60 (1)   **England** 5-3 Scotland
EYT63   **England** 4-0 N Ireland
YI63   **England** 5-2 Rest of UK
FAC67 (C)   **Chelsea** 1-2 Spurs
FAC70 (C, W) **Chelsea** 2-2 Leeds
FLC72 (C)   **Chelsea** 1-2 Stoke

Harrison, Jim (1, 0)
FAC49   **Leicester** 1-3 Wolves

Harrison, Ray (1, 0)
FAC47   **Burnley** 0-1 Charlton

Harrison, Reg (1, 0)
FAC46   **Derby** 4-1 Charlton

Harrison, Walter (1, 0
FAC49   **Leicester** 1-3 Wolves

Hart, Ernie (1, 0)
BC34   **England** 3-0 Scotland

Hartford, Asa (7, 0)
FLC70 (W)   **WBA** 1-2 Man City
FLC76   **Man City** 2-1 Newcastle Utd
BC77   **Scotland** 2-1 England
BC79   **Scotland** 1-3 England
BC81 (W)   **Scotland** 1-0 England
MC85   **Norwich** 1-0 Sunderland
FRT86   **Bolton** 0-3 Bristol C

Hartle, Roy (1, 0)
FAC58   **Bolton** 2-0 Man Utd

Hartson, John (1, 0)
FAC94 (S)   **Luton** 0-2 Chelsea

Harvey, Colin (2, 0)
FAC66   **Everton** 3-2 Sheffield W
FAC68   **Everton** 0-1 WBA
As Manager
CS87   **Everton** 1-0 Coventry
LCT88   **Everton** 1-1 Wolves
LCT88   **Everton** 0-1 Man Utd
SC89   **Everton** 3-4 Nottingham F
FAC89   **Everton** 2-3 Liverpool
ZC91   **Everton** 1-4 Crystal P

Harvey, David (3, 0)
FAC72   **Leeds** 1-0 Arsenal
FAC73   **Leeds** 0-1 Sunderland
CS74   **Leeds** 1-1 Liverpool

Harvey, Joe (2, 0)
FAC51 (C)   **Newcastle Utd** 2-0 Blackpool
FAC52 (C)   **Newcastle Utd** 1-0 Arsenal
As Manager
FAC74   **Newcastle Utd** 0-3 Liverpool

Harvey, Martin (3, 0)
BC63   **N Ireland** 3-8 England
BC65   **N Ireland** 1-2 England
ECQ67   **N Ireland** 0-2 England

Hassall, Harold (3, 1)
BC51 (1)	England	2-3 Scotland
INT51	England	2-1 Argentina
FAC53	Bolton	3-4 Blackpool

Hasselbaink, Jimmy Floyd (1, 1)
CS00 (1)	Chelsea	2-0 Man Utd

Hateley, Mark (10, 2)
INT84 (S)	England	0-2 USSR
INT84 (S)	England	1-0 E Germany
WCQ84 (2)	England	5-0 Finland
INT85 (W)	England	2-1 Rep of Ireland
WCQ85	England	1-1 Romania
WCQ85 (W)	England	5-0 Turkey
RC86	England	2-1 Scotland
RC87 (S)	England	1-1 Brazil
INT88 (S)	England	2-2 Netherlands
RC88 (S)	England	1-1 Colombia

Hateley, Tony (1, 0)
FAC67	Chelsea	1-2 Spurs

Haverty, Joe (1, 0)
WCQ57	Rep of Ireland	1-5 England

Hawke, Warren (1, 0)
FAC92 (S)	Sunderland	0-2 Liverpool

Hawkes, Ken (1, 0)
FAC59	Luton	1-2 Nottingham F

Haworth, Bob (3, 0)
FAC23	Bolton	2-0 West Ham
FAC26	Bolton	1-0 Man City
FAC29	Bolton	2-0 Portsmouth

Hay, David (1, 0)
BC73	Scotland	0-1 England

Hayes, Austin (1, 0)
FLC79 (W)	Southampton	2-3 Nottingham F

Hayes, Joe (2, 1)
FAC55	Man City	1-3 Newcastle Utd
FAC56 (1)	Man City	3-1 Birmingham

Hayes, Martin (6, 1)
LC87 (W)	Arsenal	2-1 Liverpool
LC88 (S, 1)	Arsenal	2-3 Luton
WIT88 (S)	Arsenal	4-0 Spurs
WIT88 (S)	Arsenal	3-0 Bayern Munich
MT89 (S)	Arsenal	1-0 Porto
MT89 (S)	Arsenal	1-0 Liverpool

Haylock, Paul (1, 0)
MC85	Norwich	1-0 Sunderland

Haynes, Johnny (23, 10)
SI50 (2)	England	8-2 Scotland
BC55	England	3-0 N Ireland
INT55	England	4-1 Spain
INT56	England	4-2 Brazil
BC56 (1)	England	3-1 Wales
INT56 (W)	England	3-0 Yugoslavia
WCQ57	England	5-1 Rep of Ireland
BC57	England	2-3 N Ireland
INT57	England	4-0 France
INT58	England	2-1 Portugal
INT58 (3)	England	5-0 USSR
BC59	England	1-0 Scotland

INT59	England	2-2 Italy
BC59	England	2-1 N Ireland
INT60 (1)	England	3-3 Yugoslavia
INT60 (C)	England	4-2 Spain
BC60 (C, 1)	England	5-1 Wales
BC61 (C, 2)	England	9-3 Scotland
INT61 (C)	England	8-0 Mexico
WCQ61 (C)	England	2-0 Portugal
BC61 (C)	England	1-1 N Ireland
INT62 (C)	England	3-1 Austria
INT62 (C)	England	3-1 Switzerland

Hayward, Eric (2, 0)
FAC48	Blackpool	2-4 Man Utd
FAC51	Blackpool	0-2 Newcastle Utd

Hazard, Mike (5, 0)
FLC82 (W)	Spurs	1-3 Liverpool
FAC82 (W)	Spurs	1-1 QPR
FAC82 (W)	Spurs	1-0 QPR
CS82 (W)	Spurs	0-1 Liverpool
PPO93 (S)	Swindon	4-3 Leicester

Hazell, Bob (2, 0)
FAC82	QPR	1-1 Spurs
FAC82	QPR	0-1 Spurs

Hazell, Reuben (1, 0)
WLC00	Tranmere	1-2 Leicester

Hazell, Tony (1, 0)
FLC67	QPR	3-2 WBA

Healey, Ron (1, 0)
ECQ80 (S)	Rep of Ireland	0-2 England

Healless, Harry (2, 0)
BC28	England	1-5 Scotland
FAC28 (C)	Blackburn	3-1 Huddersfield

Heath, Adrian (11, 2)
MC84	Everton	0-0 Liverpool
FAC84	Everton	2-0 Watford
CS84	Everton	1-0 Liverpool
CS85 (S, 1)	Everton	2-0 Man Utd
FAC86 (S)	Everton	1-3 Liverpool
CS86 (1)	Everton	1-1 Liverpool
CS87	Everton	1-0 Coventry
LCT88	Everton	1-1 Wolves
LCT88	Everton	0-1 Man Utd
AT92	Stoke	1-0 Stockport
PPO94	Burnley	2-1 Stockport

Heath, Don (1, 0)
FLC69	Swindon	3-1 Arsenal

Hebberd, Trevor (1, 1)
MC86 (1)	Oxford	3-0 QPR

Hector, Kevin (3, 1)
WCQ73 (S)	England	1-1 Poland
INT73 (S)	England	0-1 Italy
CS75 (1)	Derby	2-0 West Ham

Hedman, Magnus (1, 0)
ECQ99	Sweden	0-0 England

Hegan, Danny (1, 0)
BC72	N Ireland	1-0 England

Hegarty, Paul (1, 0)
BC79	Scotland	1-3 England

Heighway, Steve (10, 2)
FAC71 (1) **Liverpool** 1-2 Arsenal
FAC74 (1) **Liverpool** 3-0 Newcastle Utd
CS74 **Liverpool** 1-1 Leeds
CS76 **Liverpool** 1-0 Southampton
INT76 **Rep of Ireland** 1-1 England
FAC77 **Liverpool** 1-2 Man Utd
FLC78 **Liverpool** 0-0 Nottingham F
EC78 (S) **Liverpool** 1-0 Bruges
ECQ80 **Rep of Ireland** 0-2 England
FLC81 (W) **Liverpool** 1-1 West Ham

Henderson, Billy (1, 0)
FAC23 **West Ham** 0-2 Bolton

Henderson, Willie (3, 0)
BC63 **Scotland** 2-1 England
BC65 **Scotland** 2-2 England
BC69 **Scotland** 1-4 England

Hendrie, Lee (3, 0)
INT98 (S) **England** 2-0 Czech Rep
FAC00 (S) **Aston Villa** 0-0 Bolton
FAC00 (S) **Aston Villa** 0-1 Chelsea

Hendry, Colin (6, 1)
FMC87 (1) **Blackburn** 1-0 Charlton
LCT88 **Blackburn** 0-0 Aston Villa
PPO92 **Blackburn** 1-0 Leicester
CS94 **Blackburn** 0-2 Man Utd
ECH96 **Scotland** 0-2 England
ECQ99 (C) **Scotland** 1-0 England

Hennessey, Terry (3, 0)
BC62 **Wales** 0-4 England
BC64 **Wales** 1-2 England
ECQ66 **Wales** 1-5 England

Hennin, Derek (1, 0)
FAC58 **Bolton** 2-0 Man Utd

Henry, Nick (3, 0)
LC90 **Oldham** 0-1 Nottingham F
FAC94 **Oldham** 1-1 Man Utd
WLC00 **Tranmere** 1-2 Leicester

Henry, Ron (2, 0)
FAC61 **Spurs** 2-0 Leicester
FAC62 **Spurs** 3-1 Burnley

Henry, Tony (1, 0)
FAC81 (S) **Man City** 1-1 Spurs

Herd, Alec (2, 0)
FAC33 **Man City** 0-3 Everton
FAC34 **Man City** 2-1 Portsmouth

Herd, David (2, 2)
BC59 **Scotland** 0-1 England
FAC63 (2) **Man Utd** 3-1 Leicester

Herriot, Jim (1, 0)
BC69 **Scotland** 1-4 England

Hesford, Bob (1, 0)
FAC38 **Huddersfield** 0-1 PNE

Heskey, Emile (7, 1)
PPO96 **Leicester** 2-1 Crystal P
CCC97 (1) **Leicester** 1-1 Middlesbrough
WLC99 (W) **Leicester** 0-1 Spurs
ECQ99 (S) **England** 0-1 Scotland

Heslop, George (1, 0)
FLC70 **Man City** 2-1 WBA

Hewie, John (1, 0)
BC57 **Scotland** 1-2 England

Hibbitt, Kenny (2, 1)
FLC74 (1) **Wolves** 2-1 Man City
FLC80 **Wolves** 1-0 Nottingham F

Hibbitt, Terry (1, 0)
FAC74 **Newcastle Utd** 0-3 Liverpool

Hibbs, Harry (2, 0)
BC30 **England** 5-2 Scotland
FAC31 **Birmingham** 1-2 Man City

Hicks, George (1, 0)
FAC26 **Man City** 0-1 Bolton

Hicks, Martin (1, 0)
SC88 **Reading** 4-1 Luton

Higgins, John (1, 0)
FAC58 **Bolton** 2-0 Man Utd

Hignett, Craig (3, 1)
CCC97 **Middlesbrough** 1-1 Leicester
FAC97 (W) **Middlesbrough** 0-2 Chelsea
PPO00 (C, 1) **Barnsley** 2-4 Ipswich

Hill, Clint (1, 0)
WLC00 (D) **Tranmere** 1-2 Leicester

Hill, Freddie (1, 0)
BC62 **England** 4-0 Wales

Hill, Gordon (7, 0)
FAC76 (W) **Man Utd** 0-1 Southampton
INT76 (S) **England** 1-1 Rep of Ireland
WCQ76 (S) **England** 2-1 Finland
WCQ77 **England** 5-0 Luxembourg
FAC77 (W) **Man Utd** 2-1 Liverpool
CS77 **Man Utd** 0-0 Liverpool
INT77 (S) **England** 0-0 Switzerland

Hill, Jimmy (1, 0)
BC63 **N Ireland** 3-8 England

Hill, Ricky (4, 0)
INT82 **England** 1-2 W Germany
LCT88 **Luton** 0-2 Man Utd
LC88 **Luton** 3-2 Arsenal
LC89 **Luton** 1-3 Nottingham F

Hillier, David (2, 0)
CS91 **Arsenal** 0-0 Spurs
FAC93 **Arsenal** 1-0 Spurs

Hinchcliffe, Andy (7, 0)
ZC91 **Everton** 1-4 Crystal P
FAC95 **Everton** 1-0 Man Utd
CS95 **Everton** 1-0 Blackburn
WCQ96 **England** 2-1 Poland
INT97 **England** 2-0 Cameroon
INT98 (W) **England** 0-0 Saudi Arabia
ECQ98 (W) **England** 0-0 Bulgaria

Hinton, Alan (2, 1)

INT64 (1)	England	2-2 Belgium
BC64	England	2-1 Wales

Hinton, Marvin (2, 0)

FAC67	Chelsea	1-2 Spurs
FAC70 (S)	Chelsea	2-2 Leeds

Hirst, David (10, 1)

LCT88 (W)	Sheffield W	0-0 Crystal P
LCT88 (W)	Sheffield W	1-1 Wigan
LCT88	Sheffield W	2-1 Man Utd
LCT88 (S)	Sheffield W	0-0 Nottingham F
RLC91	Sheffield W	1-0 Man Utd
INT92 (W)	England	2-0 France
FAC93 (S)	Sheffield W	2-1 Sheffield Utd
CCC93 (S)	Sheffield W	1-2 Arsenal
FAC93 (1)	Sheffield W	1-1 Arsenal
FAC93	Sheffield W	1-2 Arsenal

Hitchens, Gerry (2, 2)

INT61 (1)	England	8-0 Mexico
INT62 (1)	England	3-1 Switzerland

Hoar, Sid (1, 0)

FAC27	Arsenal	0-1 Cardiff

Hockey, Trevor (2, 0)

WCQ73	Wales	1-1 England
BC73	Wales	0-3 England

Hoddle, Glenn (27, 9)

ECQ79 (1)	England	2-0 Bulgaria
INT81 (1)	England	1-2 Spain
FAC81	Spurs	1-1 Man City
FAC81	Spurs	3-2 Man City
BC81	England	0-0 Wales
BC81	England	0-1 Scotland
CS81	Spurs	2-2 Aston Villa
BC82 (1)	England	4-0 N Ireland
FLC82	Spurs	1-3 Liverpool
FAC82 (1)	Spurs	1-1 QPR
FAC82 (1)	Spurs	1-0 QPR
CS82 (C)	Spurs	0-1 Liverpool
ECQ82 (S, 1)	England	9-0 Luxembourg
BC83	England	2-0 Scotland
INT85 (S)	England	2-1 Rep of Ireland
WCQ85 (1)	England	1-1 Romania
WCQ85	England	5-0 Turkey
WCQ85	England	0-0 N Ireland
RC86 (1)	England	2-1 Scotland
ECQ86	England	3-0 N Ireland
ECQ86	England	2-0 Yugoslavia
FAC87	Spurs	2-3 Coventry
ECQ87 (S)	England	8-0 Turkey
INT88 (S)	England	2-2 Netherlands
RC88 (S)	England	1-1 Colombia
PPO93 (1)	Swindon	4-3 Leicester
FAC94 (S)	Chelsea	0-4 Man Utd

As Player-Manager

PPO93	Swindon	4-3 Leicester
FAC94	Chelsea	0-4 Man Utd

As Coach

WCQ96	England	2-1 Poland
WCQ97	England	0-1 Italy

INT97	England	2-0 Mexico
WCQ97	England	2-0 Georgia
WCQ97	England	4-0 Moldova
INT97	England	2-0 Cameroon
INT98	England	0-2 Chile
INT98	England	3-0 Portugal
INT98	England	0-0 Saudi Arabia
ECQ98	England	0-0 Bulgaria
INT98	England	2-0 Czech Rep

Hodge, Steve (16, 0)

RC86 (W)	England	2-1 Scotland
ECQ86	England	3-0 N Ireland
ECQ86 (W)	England	2-0 Yugoslavia
FAC87	Spurs	2-3 Coventry
INT88	England	1-0 Denmark
LC89	Nottingham F	3-1 Luton
SC89 (W)	Nottingham F	4-3 Everton
INT89 (S)	England	0-0 Italy
INT89 (S)	England	2-1 Yugoslavia
INT90	England	4-2 Czechoslovakia
LC90	Nottingham F	1-0 Oldham
INT90	England	1-0 Denmark
INT90 (W)	England	1-2 Uruguay
INT91 (S)	England	2-0 Cameroon
FAC91 (S)	Nottingham F	1-2 Spurs
CS92 (S)	Leeds	4-3 Liverpool

Hodges, Glyn (1, 0)

FAC93 (W)	Sheffield Utd	1-2 Sheffield W

Hodgkinson, Alan (4, 0)

BC57	England	2-1 Scotland
WCQ57	England	5-1 Rep of Ireland
U23I57	England	3-2 Romania
BC60	England	5-1 Wales

Hodgson, David (3, 0)

CS82 (S)	Liverpool	1-0 Spurs
CS83 (S)	Liverpool	0-2 Man Utd
MC85	Sunderland	0-1 Norwich

As Manager

PPO00	Darlington	0-1 Peterborough

Hogg, Graeme (1, 0)

CS85	Man Utd	0-2 Everton

Holdcroft, Harry (1, 0)

FAC38	Preston	1-0 Huddersfield

Holden, Doug (5, 1)

FAC53	Bolton	3-4 Blackpool
FAC58	Bolton	2-0 Man Utd
BC59	England	1-0 Scotland
INT59	England	2-2 Italy
FAC64 (1)	PNE	2-3 West Ham

Holden, Rick (2, 0)

LC90	Oldham	0-1 Nottingham F
FAC94	Oldham	1-1 Man Utd

Holdsworth, Dean (1, 0)

FAC00	Bolton	0-0 Aston Villa

Hole, Barrie (2, 0)

BC64	Wales	1-2 England
ECQ66	Wales	1-5 England

Holland, Pat (3, 0)
FAC75	**West Ham**	2-0 Fulham
CS75 (C)	**West Ham**	0-2 Derby
CS80	**West Ham**	0-1 Liverpool

Holliday, Eddie (2, 0)
INT59	**England**	2-3 Sweden
BC59	**England**	2-1 N Ireland

Hollins, John (5, 0)
FAC67	**Chelsea**	1-2 Spurs
INT67	**England**	2-0 Spain
FAC70	**Chelsea**	2-2 Leeds
FLC72	**Chelsea**	1-2 Stoke
CS79 (S)	**Arsenal**	1-3 Liverpool

As Manager
FMC86	**Chelsea**	5-4 Man City

Holmes, Jimmy (1, 0)
INT76	**Rep of Ireland**	1-1 England

Holmes, Nick (3, 1)
FAC76	**Southampton**	1-0 Man Utd
CS76	**Southampton**	0-1 Liverpool
FLC79 (1)	**Southampton**	2-3 Nottingham F

Holton, Cliff (1, 0)
FAC52	**Arsenal**	0-1 Newcastle Utd

Holton, Jim (1, 0)
BC73	**Scotland**	0-1 England

Hooper, Harry (1, 0)
FAC36 (C)	**Sheffield Utd**	0-1 Arsenal

Hooper, Mark (1, 1)
FAC35 (1)	**Sheffield W**	4-2 WBA

Hooper, Mike (2, 0)
CS86 (S)	**Liverpool**	1-1 Everton
LCT88	**Liverpool**	0-0 Newcastle Utd

Hope, Bobby (3, 0)
FLC67	**WBA**	2-3 QPR
FAC68	**WBA**	1-0 Everton
FLC70	**WBA**	1-2 Man City

Hopkins, Mel (1, 0)
BC56	**Wales**	1-3 England

Hopkinson, Eddie (7, 0)
BC57	**England**	2-3 N Ireland
INT57	**England**	4-0 France
FAC58	**Bolton**	2-0 Man Utd
INT58	**England**	2-1 Portugal
BC59	**England**	1-0 Scotland
INT59	**England**	2-2 Italy
INT59	**England**	2-3 Sweden

Horne, Barry (3, 0)
ZC92	**Southampton**	2-3 Nottingham F
FAC95	**Everton**	1-0 Man Utd
CS95 (C)	**Everton**	1-0 Blackburn

Horne, Des (1, 0)
FAC60	**Wolves**	3-0 Blackburn

Horswill, Mick (1, 0)
FAC73	**Sunderland**	1-0 Leeds

Hottiger, Marc (1, 0)
INT95	**Switzerland**	1-3 England

Houchen, Keith (2, 1)
FAC87 (1)	**Coventry**	3-2 Spurs
CS87	**Coventry**	0-1 Everton

Houghton, Eric (2, 0)
BC32	**England**	3-0 Scotland
CHA41	**RAF**	6-3 Met Police

As Manager
FAC57	**Asron Villa**	2-1 Man Utd

Houghton, Ray (9, 1)
MC86 (1)	**Oxford**	3-0 QPR
FAC88	**Liverpool**	0-1 Wimbledon
CS88	**Liverpool**	2-1 Wimbledon
FAC89	**Liverpool**	3-2 Everton
MT89	**Liverpool**	2-0 Dynamo Kiev
CS90	**Liverpool**	1-1 Man Utd
ECQ91	**Rep of Ireland**	1-1 England
FAC92	**Liverpool**	2-0 Sunderland
PPO96	**Crystal P**	1-2 Leicester

Houliston, Billy (1, 0)
BC49	**Scotland**	3-1 England

Houseman, Peter (2, 1)
FAC70 (1)	**Chelsea**	2-2 Leeds
FLC72	**Chelsea**	1-2 Stoke

Houston, Stewart (1, 0)
FAC76	**Man Utd**	0-1 Southampton

Howard, Pat (2, 0)
FAC74	**Newcastle**	0-3 Liverpool
FLC76	**Newcastle**	1-2 Man City

Howard, Trevor (1, 0)
FLC73 (S)	**Norwich**	0-1 Spurs

Howe, Don (8, 0)
BC57	**England**	2-3 N Ireland
INT57	**England**	4-0 France
INT58	**England**	2-1 Portugal
INT58	**England**	5-0 USSR
BC59	**England**	1-0 Scotland
INT59	**England**	2-2 Italy
INT59	**England**	2-3 Sweden
BC59	**England**	2-1 N Ireland

Howe, Jack (2, 0)
FAC46	**Derby**	4-1 Charlton
BC49	**England**	1-3 Scotland

Howells, David (4, 0)
WIT88 (S)	**Spurs**	0-4 Arsenal
FAC91	**Spurs**	3-1 Arsenal
FAC91	**Spurs**	2-1 Nottingham F
CS91	**Spurs**	0-0 Arsenal

Howey, Steve (6, 0)
INT94	**England**	1-0 Nigeria
INT95	**England**	0-0 Colombia
INT95	**England**	1-1 Portugal
INT96	**England**	1-0 Bulgaria
FAC98	**Newcastle Utd**	0-2 Arsenal
FAC00	**Newcastle Utd**	1-2 Chelsea

Howlett, Gary (2, 0)
FAC83	**Brighton**	2-2 Man Utd
FAC83 (W)	**Brighton**	0-4 Man Utd

Hoyland, Jamie (1, 0)
FAC93 (S)   **Sheffield Utd** 1-2 Sheffield W
Hucker, Peter (2, 0)
FAC82   **QPR** 1-1 Spurs
FAC82   **QPR** 0-1 Spurs
Hudson, Alan (4, 0)
FLC72   **Chelsea** 1-2 Stoke
INT75   **England** 2-0 W Germany
ECQ75   **England** 5-0 Cyprus
FAC78   **Arsenal** 0-1 Ipswich
Hudspeth, Frank (1, 0)
FAC24 (C)   **Newcastle Utd** 2-0 Aston Villa
Hufton, Ted (2, 0)0
FAC23   **West Ham** 0-2 Bolton
BC28   **England** 1-5 Scotland
Hughes, Aaron (1, 0)
FAC00 (W)   **Newcastle Utd** 1-2 Chelsea
Hughes, Billy (1, 0)
FAC73   **Sunderland** 1-0 Leeds
Hughes, Ceri (1, 0)
FAC94   **Luton** 0-2 Chelsea
Hughes, Emlyn (39, 0)
INT69   **England** 1-0 Portugal
BC70   **England** 3-1 N Ireland
INT70   **England** 3-1 E Germany
ECQ71   **England** 3-0 Greece
FAC71   **Liverpool** 1-2 Arsenal
ECQ71   **England** 5-0 Malta
BC71   **England** 0-0 Wales
ECQ71   **England** 1-1 Switzerland
ECQ72   **England** 1-3 W Germany
BC72   **England** 0-1 N Ireland
EEC73   **The Three** 2-0 The Six
WCQ73   **England** 1-1 Wales
BC73   **England** 3-0 Wales
BC73   **England** 1-0 Scotland
INT73   **England** 7-0 Austria
WCQ73   **England** 1-1 Poland
INT73   **England** 0-1 Italy
FAC74 (C)   **Liverpool** 3-0 Newcastle Utd
BC74 (C)   **England** 1-0 N Ireland
INT74 (C)   **England** 2-2 Argentina
CS74 (C)   **Liverpool** 1-1 Leeds
ECQ74 (C)   **England** 3-0 Czechoslovakia
ECQ74 (C)   **England** 0-0 Portugal
CS76 (C)   **Liverpool** 1-0 Southampton
WCQ77   **England** 5-0 Luxembourg
FAC77 (C)   **Liverpool** 1-2 Man Utd
BC77   **England** 0-1 Wales
BC77 (C)   **England** 1-2 Scotland
CS77 (C)   **Liverpool** 0-0 Man Utd
INT77 (C)   **England** 0-0 Switzerland
WCQ77 (C)   **England** 2-0 Italy
FLC78 (C)   **Liverpool** 0-0 Nottingham F
EC78 (C)   **Liverpool** 1-0 Bruges
BC78 (C)   **England** 1-0 N Ireland
INT78 (C)   **England** 4-1 Hungary
ECQ79 (C)   **England** 4-0 N Ireland
BC79 (C)   **England** 0-0 Wales

FLC80 (C)   **Wolves** 1-0 Nottingham F
BC80 (C)   **England** 1-1 N Ireland
Hughes, Mark (17, 7)
SI79   **Wales** 1-1 England
FAC85   **Man Utd** 1-0 Everton
CS85   **Man Utd** 0-2 Everton
FAC90 (2)   **Man Utd** 3-3 Crystal P
FAC90   **Man Utd** 1-0 Crystal P
CS90   **Man Utd** 1-1 Liverpool
RLC91   **Man Utd** 0-1 Sheffield W
RLC92   **Man Utd** 1-0 Nottingham F
CS93 (1)   **Man Utd** 1-1 Arsenal
CCC94 (1)   **Man Utd** 1-3 Aston Villa
FAC94 (1)   **Man Utd** 1-1 Oldham
FAC94 (1)   **Man Utd** 4-0 Chelsea
CS94   **Man Utd** 2-0 Blackburn
FAC95   **Man Utd** 0-1 Everton
FAC97   **Chelsea** 2-0 Middlesbrough
CS97 (1, W)   **Chelsea** 1-1 Man Utd
CCC98 (W)   **Chelsea** 2-0 Middlesbrough
Hughes, Laurie (1, 0)
FAC50   **Liverpool** 0-2 Arsenal
Hughes, Phil (3, 0)
ECQ86   **N Ireland** 0-3 England
LCT88   **Wigan** 0-0 Sunderland
LCT88   **Wigan** 1-1 Sheffield W
Hughton, Chris (11, 0)
ECQ80   **Rep of Ireland** 0-2 England
FAC81   **Spurs** 1-1 Man City
FAC81   **Spurs** 3-2 Man City
CS81   **Spurs** 2-2 Aston Villa
FLC82   **Spurs** 1-3 Liverpool
FAC82   **Spurs** 1-1 QPR
FAC82   **Spurs** 1-0 QPR
CS82   **Spurs** 0-1 Liverpool
INT85   **Rep of Ireland** 1-2 England
FAC87 (W)   **Spurs** 2-3 Coventry
WIT88   **Spurs** 1-2 AC Milan
Hulme, Joe (6, 0)
FAC27   **Arsenal** 0-1 Cardiff
BC28   **England** 1-5 Scotland
FAC30   **Arsenal** 2-0 Huddersfield
FAC32   **Arsenal** 1-2 Newcastle Utd
FAC36   **Arsenal** 1-0 Sheffield Utd
FAC38   **Huddersfield** 0-1 PNE
Humphrey, John (2, 0)
FMC87   **Charlton** 0-1 Blackburn
ZC91   **Crystal P** 4-1 Everton
Humphries, Willie (1, 0)
BC63   **N Ireland** 3-8 England
Hunt, Roger (18, 7)
INT62 (1)   **England** 3-1 Austria
BC64   **England** 2-1 Wales
FAC65 (1)   **Liverpool** 2-1 Leeds
INT66   **England** 1-0 W Germany
WC66   **England** 0-0 Uruguay
WC66 (1)   **England** 2-0 Mexico
WC66 (2)   **England** 2-0 France
WC66   **England** 1-0 Argentina

401

WC66	**England** 2-1 Portugal	
WC66	**England** 4-2 W Germany	
INT66	**England** 0-0 Czechoslovakia	
ECQ66	**England** 5-1 Wales	
INT67 (1)	**England** 2-0 Spain	
ECQ67	**England** 2-0 N Ireland	
INT67	**England** 2-2 USSR	
ECQ68	**England** 1-0 Spain	
INT68 (1)	**England** 3-1 Sweden	
INT69	**England** 1-1 Romania	

Hunt, Ron (1, 0)

FLC67	**QPR** 3-2 WBA	

Hunt, Steve (1, 0)

INT84 (S)	**England** 0-2 USSR	

Hunter, Allan (5, 0)

BC72	**N Ireland** 1-0 England	
EEC73	**The Three** 2-0 The Six	
BC74	**N Ireland** 0-1 England	
BC76	**N Ireland** 0-4 England	
FAC78	**Ipswich** 1-0 Arsenal	

Hunter, Ally (1, 0)

BC73	**Scotland** 0-1 England	

Hunter, Norman (19, 1)

FAC65	**Leeds** 1-2 Liverpool	
INT66	**England** 1-0 W Germany	
INT66	**England** 2-0 Yugoslavia	
FLC68	**Leeds** 1-0 Arsenal	
INT68	**England** 3-1 Sweden	
INT69	**England** 1-1 Romania	
BC69	**England** 2-1 Wales	
INT70	**England** 0-0 Netherlands	
FAC70	**Leeds** 2-2 Chelsea	
ECQ72	**England** 1-3 W Germany	
FAC72	**Leeds** 1-0 Arsenal	
BC72	**England** 0-1 N Ireland	
WCQ73 (1)	**England** 1-1 Wales	
FAC73	**Leeds** 0-1 Sunderland	
INT73	**England** 7-0 Austria	
WCQ73	**England** 1-1 Poland	
BC74 (S)	**England** 1-0 N Ireland	
CS74	**Leeds** 1-1 Liverpool	
ECQ74	**England** 3-0 Czechoslovakia	

Hunter, Victor (1, 0)

BC61	**N Ireland** 1-1 England	

Hurlock, Terry (2, 0)

FRT85	**Brentford** 1-3 Wigan	
ZC92	**Southampton** 2-3 Nottingham F	

Hurst, Sir Geoff (26, 17)

FAC64 (1)	**West Ham** 3-2 PNE	
ECW65	**West Ham** 2-0 TSV Munich	
INT66	**England** 1-0 W Germany	
INT66	**England** 2-0 Yugoslavia	
WC66 (1)	**England** 1-0 Argentina	
WC66	**England** 2-1 Portugal	
WC66 (3)	**England** 4-2 W Germany	
INT66	**England** 0-0 Czechoslovakia	
ECQ66 (2)	**England** 5-1 Wales	
ECQ67 (1)	**England** 2-3 Scotland	
INT67	**England** 2-0 Spain	

ECQ67 (1)	**England** 2-0 N Ireland	
INT67	**England** 2-2 USSR	
INT68 (S)	**England** 3-1 Sweden	
INT68 (1)	**England** 1-1 Bulgaria	
INT69	**England** 1-1 Romania	
INT69 (3)	**England** 5-0 France	
BC69 (2)	**England** 4-1 Scotland	
INT70 (S)	**England** 0-0 Netherlands	
BC70 (1)	**England** 3-1 N Ireland	
INT70	**England** 3-1 E Germany	
ECQ71 (1)	**England** 3-0 Greece	
BC71	**England** 0-0 Wales	
BC71	**England** 3-1 Scotland	
ECQ71	**England** 1-1 Switzerland	
ECQ72 (W)	**England** 1-3 W Germany	

Hurst, Gordon (1, 0)

FAC47	**Charlton** 1-0 Burnley	

Hurst, John (2, 0)

SI62	**England** 1-2 W Germany	
FAC68	**Everton** 0-1 WBA	

Husband, Jimmy (2, 0)

SI63	**England** 4-1 Wales	
FAC68	**Everton** 0-1 WBA	

Hutchinson, Ian (1, 1)

FAC70 (1)	**Chelsea** 2-2 Leeds	

Hutchison, Don (3, 1)

CS92 (S)	**Liverpool** 3-4 Leeds	
PPO97 (W)	**Sheffield Utd** 0-1 Crystal P	
ECQ99 (1)	**Scotland** 1-0 England	

Hutchison, Tommy (3, 1)

BC75 (S)	**Scotland** 1-5 England	
FAC81 (1, W)	**Man City** 1-1 Spurs	
FAC81	**Man City** 2-3 Spurs	

Hutton, Jock (1, 0)

FAC28	**Blackburn** 3-1 Huddersfield	

Hyde, Graham (4, 0)

FAC93 (S)	**Sheffield W** 2-1 Sheffield Utd	
CCC93 (S)	**Sheffield W** 1-2 Arsenal	
FAC93 (S)	**Sheffield W** 1-1 Arsenal	
FAC93 (S)	**Sheffield W** 1-2 Arsenal	

Hysen, Glenn (4, 0)

LCEN87	**Rest of World** 0-3 Football League	
WCQ88 (C)	**Sweden** 0-0 England	
CS89	**Liverpool** 1-0 Arsenal	
CS90	**Liverpool** 1-1 Man Utd	

Imlach, Stuart (1, 0)

FAC59	**Nottingham F** 2-1 Luton	

Impey, Andrew (2, 0)

FAV90	**Yeading** 0-0 Bridlington	
WLC00 (S)	**Leicester** 2-1 Tranmere	

Ince, Paul (35, 1)

FAC90	**Man Utd** 3-3 Crystal P	
FAC90	**Man Utd** 1-0 Crystal P	
CS90	**Man Utd** 1-1 Liverpool	
RLC91	**Man Utd** 0-1 Sheffield W	
RLC92	**Man Utd** 1-0 Nottingham F	
WCQ92	**England** 1-1 Norway	
WCQ92	**England** 4-0 Turkey	

WCQ93	**England** 2-2 Netherlands	
CS93	**Man Utd** 1-1 Arsenal	
WCQ93	**England** 3-0 Poland	
INT94 (W)	**England** 1-0 Denmark	
CCC94	**Man Utd** 1-3 Aston Villa	
FAC94	**Man Utd** 1-1 Oldham	
FAC94	**Man Utd** 4-0 Chelsea	
INT94 (W)	**England** 0-0 Norway	
CS94 (1)	**Man Utd** 2-0 Blackburn	
INT94	**England** 1-1 Romania	
FAC95	**Man Utd** 0-1 Everton	
INT96	**England** 1-0 Bulgaria	
INT96	**England** 0-0 Croatia	
INT96 (W)	**England** 3-0 Hungary	
ECH96	**England** 1-1 Switzerland	
ECH96 (W)	**England** 2-0 Scotland	
ECH96 (W)	**England** 4-1 Netherlands	
ECH96	**England** 1-1 Germany	
WCQ96	**England** 2-1 Poland	
WCQ97	**England** 0-1 Italy	
INT97 (C)	**England** 2-0 Mexico	
WCQ97 (W)	**England** 2-0 Georgia	
INT97 (C)	**England** 2-0 Cameroon	
INT98 (S)	**England** 0-2 Chile	
INT98	**England** 3-0 Portugal	
INT99	**England** 0-2 France	
ECQ99	**England** 0-1 Scotland	
INT00 (W)	**England** 1-1 Brazil	

Irvine, Alan (1, 0)
MC84   **Everton** 0-0 Liverpool

Irvine, Willie (3, 1)
BC65	**N Ireland** 1-2 England
ECQ67	**N Ireland** 0-2 England
BC72	**N Ireland** 1-0 England

Irving, Sam (1, 0)
FAC27   **Cardiff** 1-0 Arsenal

Irwin, Colin (1, 0)
FLC81   **Liverpool** 1-1 West Ham

Irwin, Denis (16, 0)
LC90	**Oldham** 0-1 Nottingham F
CS90	**Man Utd** 1-1 Liverpool
ECQ91	**Rep of Ireland** 1-1 England
RLC91	**Man Utd** 0-1 Sheffield W
RLC92	**Man Utd** 1-0 Nottingham F
CS93	**Man Utd** 1-1 Arsenal
CCC94	**Man Utd** 1-3 Aston Villa
FAC94	**Man Utd** 1-1 Oldham
FAC94 (W)	**Man Utd** 4-0 Chelsea
FAC95	**Man Utd** 0-1 Everton
FAC96	**Man Utd** 1-0 Liverpool
CS96 (W)	**Man Utd** 4-0 Newcastle Utd
CS97	**Man Utd** 1-1 Chelsea
CS98	**Man Utd** 0-3 Arsenal
CS99 (C)	**Man Utd** 1-2 Arsenal
CS00	**Man Utd** 0-2 Chelsea

Isaac, Jimmy (1, 0)
FAC38   **Huddersfield** 0-1 PNE

Iversen, Steffen (1, 0)
WLC99   **Spurs** 1-0 Leicester

Izzet, Muzzy (4, 0)
PPO96	**Leicester** 2-1 Crystal P
CCC97 (W)	**Leicester** 1-1 Middlesbrough
WLC99	**Leicester** 0-1 Spurs
WLC00	**Leicester** 2-1 Tranmere

Jaaskelainen, Jussi (1, 0)
FAC00   **Bolton** 0-0 Aston Villa

Jack, David (6, 3)
FAC23 (1)	**Bolton** 2-0 West Ham
BC24	**England** 1-1 Scotland
FAC26 (1)	**Bolton** 1-0 Man City
BC30 (C, 1)	**England** 5-2 Scotland
FAC30	**Arsenal** 2-0 Huddersfield
FAC32	**Arsenal** 1-2 Newcastle Utd

Jackett, Kenny (2, 0)
| BC83 | **Wales** 1-2 England |
| FAC84 | **Watford** 0-2 Everton |

Jackson, Alec (4, 4)
BC28 (3)	**Scotland** 5-1 England
FAC28 (1)	**Huddersfield** 1-3 Blackburn
BC30	**Scotland** 2-5 England
FAC30	**Huddersfield** 0-2 Arsenal

Jackson, Ernie (1, 0)
FAC36   **Sheffield Utd** 0-1 Arsenal

Jackson, John (1, 0)
BC34   **Scotland** 0-3 England

Jackson, Matt (1, 0)
FAC95   **Everton** 1-0 Man Utd

Jackson, Tommy (1, 0)
FAC24   **Aston Villa** 0-2 Newcastle Utd

Jackson, Tommy (2, 0)
| BC72 | **N Ireland** 1-0 England |
| BC74 (S) | **N Ireland** 0-1 England |

James, Alex (4, 3)
BC28	**Scotland** 5-1 England
BC30	**Scotland** 2-5 England
FAC30	**Arsenal** 2-0 Huddersfield
FAC36	**Arsenal** 1-0 Sheffield Utd

James, David (5, 0)
CCC95	**Liverpool** 2-1 Bolton
FAC96	**Liverpool** 0-1 Man Utd
INT97	**England** 2-0 Mexico
FAC00	**Aston Villa** 0-0 Bolton
FAC00	**Aston Villa** 0-1 Chelsea

James, Glyn (1, 0)
BC71   **Wales** 0-0 England

James, Julian (1, 0)
FAC94   **Luton** 0-2 Chelsea

James, Leighton (7, 1)
WCQ73	**Wales** 1-1 England
BC73	**Wales** 0-3 England
BC75	**Wales** 2-2 England
BC77 (1)	**Wales** 1-0 England
BC81 (W)	**Wales** 0-0 England
BC83 (S)	**Wales** 1-2 England
SVT88 (S)	**Burnley** 0-2 Wolves

James, Robbie (3, 0)
BC79	**Wales**	0-0 England
BC83	**Wales**	1-2 England
MC86	**QPR**	0-3 Oxford

Jardine, Sandy (2, 0)
BC73	**Scotland**	0-1 England
BC75 (C)	**Scotland**	1-5 England

Jarvie, Drew (1, 0)
BC71 (S)	**Scotland**	1-3 England

Jarvis, Alan (1, 0)
ECQ66	**Wales**	1-5 England

Jelly, Horace (1, 0)
FAC49	**Leicester**	1-3 Wolves

Jemson, Nigel (2, 3)
LC90 (1)	**Nottingham F**	1-0 Oldham

Jenkins, David (1, 0)
FLC68	**Arsenal**	0-1 Leeds

Jennings, Billy (2, 0)
FAC23	**Bolton**	2-0 West Ham
FAC26	**Bolton**	1-0 Man City

Jennings, Billy (2, 0)
FAC75	**West Ham**	2-0 Fulham
CS75 (W)	**West Ham**	0-2 Derby

Jennings, Pat (19, 0)
EYT63	**N Ireland**	0-4 England
YI63	**Rest of UK**	2-5 England
BC65	**N Ireland**	1-2 England
FAC67	**Spurs**	2-1 Chelsea
ECQ67	**N Ireland**	0-2 England
BC70	**N Ireland**	1-3 England
FLC71	**Spurs**	2-0 Aston Villa
BC72	**N Ireland**	0-4 England
EEC73	**The Three**	2-0 The Six
FLC73	**Spurs**	1-0 Norwich
BC74	**N Ireland**	0-1 England
BC76	**N Ireland**	0-4 England
FAC78	**Arsenal**	0-1 Ipswich
ECQ79 (C)	**N Ireland**	0-4 England
FAC79	**Arsenal**	3-2 Man Utd
CS79	**Arsenal**	1-3 Liverpool
FAC80	**Arsenal**	0-1 West Ham
BC82	**N Ireland**	0-4 England
WCQ85	**N Ireland**	0-0 England

Jensen, Claus (2, 0)
PPO99	**Bolton**	0-2 Watford
FAC00 (W)	**Bolton**	0-0 Aston Villa

Jensen, John (6, 0)
INT88 (W)	**Denmark**	0-1 England
INT90	**Denmark**	0-1 England
FAC93	**Arsenal**	1-1 Sheffield W.
FAC93	**Arsenal**	2-1 Sheffield W.
CS93	**Arsenal**	1-1 Manchester United
INT94	**Denmark**	0-1 England

Jess, Eoin (1, 0)
ECH96 (S)	**Scotland**	0-2 England

Jezzard, Bedford (2, 2)
EFC55 (2)	**London**	3-2 Frankfurt
BC55	**England**	3-0 N Ireland

Joachim, Julian (4, 1)
PPO93 (1)	**Leicester**	3-4 Swindon
PPO94 (W)	**Leicester**	2-1 Derby
FAC00	**Aston Villa**	0-0 Bolton
FAC00 (S)	**Aston Villa**	0-1 Chelsea

Jobson, Richard (1, 0)
FAC94	**Oldham**	1-1 Man Utd

Johanneson, Albert (1, 0)
FAC65	**Leeds**	1-2 Liverpool

Johansen, Michael (2, 0)
PPO99 (W)	**Bolton**	0-2 Watford
FAC00	**Bolton**	0-0 Aston Villa

John, Bob (3, 1)
FAC27	**Arsenal**	0-1 Cardiff
FAC30	**Arsenal**	2-0 Huddersfield
FAC32 (1)	**Arsenal**	1-2 Newcastle Utd

Johnsen, Erland (4, 0)
ZC90	**Chelsea**	1-0 Middlesbrough
FAC94	**Chelsea**	2-0 Luton
FAC94	**Chelsea**	0-4 Man Utd
INT94	**Norway**	0-0 England

Johnsen, Ronny (4, 1)
CS97 (1)	**Man Utd**	1-1 Chelsea
CS98	**Man Utd**	0-3 Arsenal
FAC99	**Man Utd**	2-0 Newcastle Utd
CS00	**Man Utd**	0-2 Chelsea

Johnson, Bert (2, 0)
FAC46	**Charlton**	1-4 Derby
FAC47	**Charlton**	1-0 Burnley

Johnson, Bert (1, 0)
FAC37	**Sunderland**	3-1 PNE

Johnson, David (9, 6)
BC75 (2)	**England**	2-2 Wales
BC75 (1)	**England**	5-1 Scotland
FAC77 (W)	**Liverpool**	1-2 Man Utd
CS79	**Liverpool**	3-1 Arsenal
ECQ80 (W)	**England**	2-0 Rep of Ireland
INT80 (2, W)	**England**	3-1 Argentina
BC80 (1)	**England**	1-1 N Ireland
CS80	**Liverpool**	1-0 West Ham
FLC82 (S)	**Liverpool**	3-1 Spurs

Johnson, Harry (1, 0)
FAC25	**Sheffield Utd**	1-0 Cardiff

Johnson, Marvin (3, 0)
SC88 (S)	**Luton**	1-4 Reading
LCT88 (S)	**Luton**	0-2 Man Utd
LC88	**Luton**	3-2 Arsenal

Johnson, Tom (1, 0)
FAC36	**Sheffield Utd**	0-1 Arsenal

Johnson, Tommy (3, 0)
FAC26	**Man City**	0-1 Bolton
BC32	**England**	3-0 Scotland
FAC33	**Everton**	3-0 Man City

Johnston, Allan (2, 0)
PPO98	**Sunderland**	4-4 Charlton
FAC00	**Bolton**	0-0 Aston Villa

Johnston, Craig (8, 1)
MC83 (W)	**Liverpool**	2-1 Man Utd
CS83 (S)	**Liverpool**	0-2 Man Utd
MC84 (W)	**Liverpool**	0-0 Everton
FAC86 (1)	**Liverpool**	3-1 Everton
CS86	**Liverpool**	1-1 Everton
LC87	**Liverpool**	1-2 Arsenal
LCT88	**Liverpool**	0-0 Newcastle Utd
FAC88 (S)	**Liverpool**	0-1 Wimbledon

Johnston, Harry (6, 0)
BC47	**England**	1-1 Scotland
FAC48 (C)	**Blackpool**	2-4 Man Utd
BC51	**England**	2-3 Scotland
FAC51 (C)	**Blackpool**	0-2 Newcastle Utd
FAC53 (C)	**Blackpool**	4-3 Bolton
INT53	**England**	3-6 Hungary

Johnston, Maurice (2, 0)
FAC84	**Watford**	0-2 Everton
RC88	**Scotland**	0-1 England

Johnston, Willie (1, 0)
BC77	**Scotland**	2-1 England

Johnstone, Bobby (5, 3)
BC51 (1)	**Scotland**	3-2 England
BC53	**Scotland**	2-2 England
BC55	**Scotland**	2-7 England
FAC55 (1)	**Man City**	1-3 Newcastle Utd
FAC56 (1)	**Man City**	3-1 Birmingham

Johnstone, Derek (1, 0)
BC73	**Scotland**	0-1 England

Johnstone, Jimmy (1, 0)
BC71	**Scotland**	1-3 England

Jones, Barrie (2, 0)
BC62	**Wales**	0-4 England
BC69	**Wales**	1-2 England

Jones, Bill (1, 0)
FAC50	**Liverpool**	0-2 Arsenal

Jones, Charlie (1, 0)
FAC32	**Arsenal**	1-2 Newcastle Utd

Jones, Cliff (7, 1)
BJC51	**Army Cadet Force**	2-4 NABC
BC56	**Wales**	1-3 England
BC60	**Wales**	1-5 England
FAC61	**Spurs**	2-0 Leicester
FAC62	**Spurs**	3-1 Burnley
BC64 (1)	**Wales**	1-2 England
ECQ66	**Wales**	1-5 England

Jones, Cobi (1, 0)
INT94	**USA**	0-2 England

Jones, Dave (1, 0)
FLC77	**Everton**	0-0 Aston Villa

Jones, Gary (1, 0)
WLC00	**Tranmere**	1-2 Leicester

Jones, Herbert (2, 0)
BC28	**England**	1-5 Scotland
FAC28	**Blackburn**	3-1 Huddersfield

Jones, Joey (7, 0)
CS76	**Liverpool**	1-0 Southampton

FAC77	**Liverpool**	1-2 Man Utd
BC77	**Wales**	1-0 England
CS77	**Liverpool**	0-0 Man Utd
BC79	**Wales**	0-0 England
BC81	**Wales**	0-0 England
BC83 (W)	**Wales**	1-2 England

Jones, Linden (1, 0)
SC88 (W)	**Reading**	4-1 Luton

Jones, Mick (4, 1)
INT70 (W)	**England**	0-0 Netherlands
FAC70 (1)	**Leeds**	2-2 Chelsea
FAC72	**Leeds**	1-0 Arsenal
FAC73	**Leeds**	0-1 Sunderland

Jones, Rob (11, 0)
INT92	**England**	2-0 France
FAC92	**Liverpool**	2-0 Sunderland
WCQ93	**England**	3-0 Poland
INT94 (W)	**England**	5-0 Greece
INT94	**England**	0-0 Norway
INT94	**England**	2-0 USA
INT94 (W)	**England**	1-1 Romania
INT94	**England**	1-0 Nigeria
INT95	**England**	0-0 Uruguay
CCC95	**Liverpool**	2-1 Bolton
FAC96 (W)	**Liverpool**	0-1 Man Utd

Jones, Vinnie (1, 0)
FAC88	**Wimbledon**	1-0 Liverpool

Jordan, Joe (7, 0)
BC73 (S)	**Scotland**	0-1 England
CS74	**Leeds**	1-1 Liverpool
BC77 (W)	**Scotland**	2-1 England
FAC79	**Man Utd**	2-3 Arsenal
BC79	**Scotland**	1-3 England
BC81	**Scotland**	1-0 England
FRT87 (C)	**Bristol C**	1-1 Mansfield

Judge, Alan (1, 0)
MC86	**Oxford**	3-0 QPR

Juninho (3, 1)
UC95 (1, W)	**Brazil**	3-1 England
CCC97	**Middlesbrough**	1-1 Leicester
FAC97	**Middlesbrough**	0-2 Chelsea

Kaamark, Pontus (3, 0)
CCC97	**Leicester**	1-1 Middlesbrough
ECQ99	**Sweden**	0-0 England
EC99 (W)	**AIK Stockholm**	1-3 Arsenal

Kanchelskis, Andrei (8, 1)
MT89 (S)	**Dynamo Kiev**	0-2 Liverpool
MT89 (1)	**Dynamo Kiev**	1-0 Porto
INT91	**USSR**	1-3 England
RLC92 (W)	**Man Utd**	1-0 Nottingham F
CS93	**Man Utd**	1-1 Arsenal
CCC94 (D)	**Man Utd**	1-3 Aston Villa
FAC94 (W)	**Man Utd**	4-0 Chelsea
CS94	**Man Utd**	2-0 Blackburn

Kanu, Nwankwo (5, 1)
INT94 (S)	**Nigeria**	0-1 England
CS99 (1)	**Arsenal**	2-1 Man Utd
EC99 (S)	**Arsenal**	3-1 AIK Stockholm

EC99 (W)   **Arsenal** 2-4 Barcelona
EC99   **Arsenal** 0-1 Fiorentina

Kay, George (1, 0)
FAC23 (C)   **West Ham** 0-2 Bolton

Kaye, John (3, 0)
FLC67   **WBA** 2-3 QPR
FAC68 (W)   **WBA** 1-0 Everton
FLC70   **WBA** 1-2 Man City

Kean, Fred (1, 0)
FAC29   **Bolton** 2-0 Portsmouth

Keane, Roy (13, 1)
FAC91   **Nottingham F** 1-2 Spurs
ZC92   **Nottingham F** 3-2 Southampton
RLC92   **Nottingham F** 0-1 Man Utd
CS93   **Man Utd** 1-1 Arsenal
CCC94   **Man Utd** 1-3 Aston Villa
FAC94   **Man Utd** 4-0 Chelsea
FAC95   **Man Utd** 0-1 Everton
FAC96   **Man Utd** 1-0 Liverpool
CS96 (1)   **Man Utd** 4-0 Newcastle Utd
CS97 (C)   **Man Utd** 1-1 Chelsea
CS98 (C, W)   **Man Utd** 0-3 Arsenal
FAC99 (C, W)   **Man Utd** 2-0 Newcastle Utd
CS00 (C, D)   **Man Utd** 0-2 Chelsea

Kearns, Mick (1, 0)
INT76   **Rep of Ireland** 1-1 England

Keeble, Vic (1, 0)
FAC55   **Newcastle Utd** 3-1 Man City

Keegan, Ged (1, 0)
FLC76   **Man City** 2-1 Newcastle Utd

Keegan, Kevin (31, 12)
WCQ73   **England** 1-1 Wales
FAC74 (2)   **Liverpool** 3-0 Newcastle Utd
BC74   **England** 1-0 N Ireland
INT74   **England** 2-2 Argentina
CS74 (D)   **Liverpool** 1-1 Leeds
ECQ74   **England** 3-0 Czechoslovakia
INT75   **England** 2-0 W Germany
ECQ75   **England** 5-0 Cyprus
BC75 (W)   **England** 5-1 Scotland
BC76 (W)   **England** 4-0 N Ireland
CS76   **Liverpool** 1-0 Southampton
INT76 (C)   **England** 1-1 Rep of Ireland
WCQ76 (C)   **England** 2-1 Finland
INT77 (C)   **England** 0-2 Netherlands
WCQ77 (C, 1)   **England** 5-0 Luxembourg
FAC77   **Liverpool** 1-2 Man Utd
BC77 (C)   **England** 0-1 Wales
INT77   **England** 0-0 Switzerland
WCQ77 (1, W)   **England** 2-0 Italy
INT78 (C, 1)   **England** 1-1 Brazil
INT78   **England** 4-1 Hungary
INT78 (C)   **England** 1-0 Czechoslovakia
ECQ79 (1)   **England** 4-0 N Ireland
BC79 (W)   **England** 0-0 Wales
BC79 (C, 1)   **England** 3-1 Scotland
ECQ79 (C, 1)   **England** 1-0 Denmark
ECQ80 (C, 2)   **England** 2-0 Rep of Ireland
INT80 (C, 1)   **England** 3-1 Argentina

INT81 (C)   **England** 1-2 Spain
WCQ81 (C)   **England** 1-0 Hungary
BC82 (C, 1)   **England** 4-0 N Ireland
As Manager
CS96   **Newcastle Utd** 0-4 Man Utd
As Head Coach
ECQ99   **England** 3-1 Poland
ECQ99   **England** 0-0 Sweden
ECQ99   **England** 6-0 Luxembourg
ECQ99   **England** 0-1 Scotland
INT00   **England** 0-0 Argentina
INT00   **England** 1-1 Brazil
INT00   **England** 2-0 Ukraine
WCQ00   **England** 0-1 Germany

Keelan, Kevin (2, 0)
FLC73   **Norwich** 0-1 Spurs
FLC75   **Norwich** 0-1 Aston Villa

Keeley, Glenn (2, 0)
FLC76   **Newcastle Utd** 1-2 Man City
FMC87 (C)   **Blackburn** 1-0 Charlton

Keen, Mike (1, 0)
FLC67 (C)   **QPR** 3-2 WBA

Keenor, Fred (2, 0)
FAC25 (C)   **Cardiff** 0-1 Sheffield Utd
FAC27 (C)   **Cardiff** 1-0 Arsenal

Keith, Richard (2, 0)
BC57   **N Ireland** 3-2 England
BC59   **N Ireland** 1-2 England

Keller, Kasey (2, 0)
CCC97   **Leicester** 1-1 Middlesbrough
WLC99   **Leicester** 0-1 Spurs

Kelly, Alan (2, 0)
WCQ57   **Rep of Ireland** 1-5 England
FAC64   **PNE** 2-3 West Ham

Kelly, Alan (1, 0)
FAC93   **Sheffield Utd** 1-2 Sheffield W

Kelly, Bob (3, 1)
BC28 (1)   **England** 1-5 Scotland
FAC28   **Huddersfield** 1-3 Blackburn
FAC30   **Huddersfield** 0-2 Arsenal

Kelly, David (1, 1)
WLC00 (C, 1)   **Tranmere** 1-2 Leicester

Kelly, Eddie (1, 1)
FAC71 (S, 1)   **Arsenal** 2-1 Liverpool

Kelly, Gary (1, 0)
CCC96   **Leeds** 0-3 Aston Villa

Kelly, Hugh (2, 0)
FAC48   **Blackpool** 2-4 Man Utd
FAC51   **Blackpool** 0-2 Newcastle Utd

Kelsey, Jack (2, 0)
BC56   **Wales** 1-3 England
BC60   **Wales** 1-5 England

Kendall, Howard (2, 0)
FAC64   **PNE** 2-3 West Ham
FAC68   **Everton** 0-1 WBA
As Manager
MC84   **Everton** 0-0 Liverpool
FAC84   **Everton** 2-0 Watford

CS84	**Everton** 1-0 Liverpool
FAC85	**Everton** 0-1 Man Utd
CS85	**Everton** 2-0 Man Utd
FAC86	**Everton** 1-3 Liverpool
CS86	**Everton** 1-1 Liverpool
AIC95	**Notts C** 2-1 Ascoli
PPO97	**Sheffield Utd** 0-1 Crystal P

Kenna, Jeff (2, 0)

ZC92	**Southampton** 2-3 Nottingham F
CS95 (W)	**Blackburn** 0-1 Everton

Kennedy, Alan (14, 1)

FAC74	**Newcastle Utd** 0-3 Liverpool
FLC76	**Newcastle Utd** 1-2 Man City
CS79	**Liverpool** 3-1 Arsenal
CS80	**Liverpool** 1-0 West Ham
FLC81 (1)	**Liverpool** 1-1 West Ham
FLC82	**Liverpool** 3-1 Spurs
CS82	**Liverpool** 1-0 Spurs
MC83 (1)	**Liverpool** 2-1 Man Utd
CS83	**Liverpool** 0-2 Man Utd
MC84	**Liverpool** 0-0 Everton
BC84	**England** 1-0 N Ireland
CS84	**Liverpool** 0-1 Everton
LCT88	**Wigan** 0-0 Sunderland
LCT88	**Wigan** 1-1 Sheffield W

Kennedy, Andy (1, 0)

FAC27	**Arsenal** 0-1 Cardiff

Kennedy, Joe (1, 0)

FAC54	**WBA** 3-2 PNE

Kennedy, Ray (17, 1)

FAC71	**Arsenal** 2-1 Liverpool
FAC72 (S)	**Arsenal** 0-1 Leeds
BC76	**England** 4-0 N Ireland
CS76	**Liverpool** 1-0 Southampton
WCQ77 (1)	**England** 5-0 Luxembourg
FAC77	**Liverpool** 1-2 Man Utd
BC77	**England** 0-1 Wales
BC77 (W)	**England** 1-2 Scotland
CS77	**Liverpool** 0-0 Man Utd
INT77	**England** 0-0 Switzerland
FLC78 (W)	**Liverpool** 0-0 Nottingham F
EC78	**Liverpool** 1-0 Bruges
CS79	**Liverpool** 3-1 Arsenal
ECQ79	**England** 2-0 Bulgaria
INT80 (W)	**England** 3-1 Argentina
CS80	**Liverpool** 1-0 West Ham
FLC81 (C)	**Liverpool** 1-1 West Ham

Kennedy, Stewart (1, 0)

BC75	**Scotland** 1-5 England

Keown, Martin (25, 1)

LCT88	**Aston Villa** 0-0 Blackburn
LCT88	**Aston Villa** 0-0 Nottingham F
ZC91 (W)	**Everton** 1-4 Crystal P
INT92	**England** 2-0 France
INT92	**England** 1-1 Brazil
WCQ93	**England** 2-2 Netherlands
CS93 (S)	**Arsenal** 1-1 Man Utd
INT97	**England** 2-0 Mexico
FAC98	**Arsenal** 2-0 Newcastle Utd

CS98	**Arsenal** 3-0 Man Utd
EC98 (1)	**Arsenal** 2-1 Panathinaikos
EC98	**Arsenal** 1-1 Dynamo Kiev
INT98	**England** 2-0 Czech Rep
EC98	**Arsenal** 0-1 Lens
INT99 (W)	**England** 0-2 France
ECQ99	**England** 3-1 Poland
ECQ99 (W)	**England** 0-0 Sweden
CS99	**Arsenal** 2-1 Man Utd
ECQ99	**England** 6-0 Luxembourg
EC99	**Arsenal** 3-1 AIK Stockholm
EC99 (W)	**Arsenal** 2-4 Barcelona
EC99	**Arsenal** 0-1 Fiorentina
INT00 (W)	**England** 0-0 Argentina
INT00	**England** 1-1 Brazil
WCQ00	**England** 0-1 Germany

Kernaghan, Alan (1, 0)

ZC90	**Middlesbrough** 0-1 Chelsea

Kerr, Bobby (1, 0)

FAC73 (C)	**Sunderland** 1-0 Leeds

Ketsbaia, Temuri (4, 0)

WCQ97	**Georgia** 0-2 England
FAC98 (W)	**Newcastle Utd** 0-2 Arsenal
FAC99 (W)	**Newcastle Utd** 0-2 Man Utd
FAC00 (S)	**Newcastle Utd** 1-2 Chelsea

Kevan, Derek (4, 1)

BC57 (1)	**England** 2-1 Scotland
BC57	**England** 2-3 N Ireland
INT58	**England** 2-1 Portugal
INT61	**England** 8-0 Mexico

Keyworth, Ken (2, 1)

FAC61	**Leicester** 0-2 Spurs
FAC63 (1)	**Leicester** 1-3 Man Utd

Kharine, Dimitri (2, 0)

FAC94	**Chelsea** 2-0 Luton
FAC94	**Chelsea** 0-4 Man Utd

Kidd, Brian (2, 1)

EC68 (1)	**Man Utd** 4-1 Benfica
BC70	**England** 3-1 N Ireland

Kilcline, Brian (2, 0)

FAC87 (C, W)	**Coventry** 3-2 Spurs
CS87 (C)	**Coventry** 0-1 Everton

Kinder, Vladimir (2, 0)

FAC97 (S)	**Middlesbrough** 0-2 Chelsea
CCC98	**Middlesbrough** 0-2 Chelsea

King, Andy (1, 0)

FLC77	**Everton** 0-0 Aston Villa

King, Ian (3, 0)

SI52 (C)	**Scotland** 0-1 England
FAC61	**Leicester** 0-2 Spurs
FAC63	**Leicester** 1-3 Man Utd

King, John (1, 0)

FAC49	**Leicester** 1-3 Wolves

King, Johnny (1, 0)

BC54	**Wales** 2-3 England

King, Phil (2, 0)

RLC91	**Sheffield W** 1-0 Man Utd
CCC93 (W)	**Sheffield W** 1-2 Arsenal

King, Seth (1, 0)
FAC25   **Sheffield Utd**   1-0 Cardiff

Kinkladze, Georgi (1, 0)
WCQ97 (W)   **Georgia**   0-2 England

Kinnear, Joe (3, 0)
FAC67   **Spurs**   2-1 Chelsea
FLC71   **Spurs**   2-0 Aston Villa
FLC73   **Spurs**   1-0 Norwich

Kinsey, Noel (1, 1)
FAC56 (1)   **Birmingham**   1-3 Man City

Kinsey, Steve (1, 1)
FMC86 (1)   **Man City**   4-5 Chelsea

Kippax, Peter (2, 0)
FAC47   **Burnley**   0-1 Charlton
OLY48   **Great Britain**   1-3 Yugoslavia

Kirkup, Joe (1, 0)
ECW65   **West Ham**   2-0 TSV Munich

Kirton, Billy (1, 0)
FAC24   **Aston Villa**   0-2 Newcastle Utd

Kjeldbjerg, Jakob (3, 0)
INT94   **Denmark**   0-1 England
FAC94   **Chelsea**   2-0 Luton
FAC94   **Chelsea**   0-4 Man Utd

Knowles, Cyril (6, 0)
FAC67   **Spurs**   2-1 Chelsea
INT67   **England**   2-2 USSR
ECQ68   **England**   1-0 Spain
INT68   **England**   3-1 Sweden
FLC71   **Spurs**   2-0 Aston Villa
FLC73   **Spurs**   1-0 Norwich
As Manager
SVT89   **Torquay**   1-4 Bolton

Kozma, Istvan (2, 0)
INT90   **Hungary**   0-1 England
CS92 (S)   **Liverpool**   3-4 Leeds

Krzywicki, Dick (1, 0)
FLC70 (S)   **WBA**   1-2 Man City

Labone, Brian (7, 0)
BC62   **England**   4-0 Wales
FAC66 (C)   **Everton**   3-2 Sheffield W
INT67   **England**   2-0 Spain
FAC68 (C)   **Everton**   0-1 WBA
INT68   **England**   3-1 Sweden
INT68   **England**   1-1 Bulgaria
BC69   **England**   4-1 Scotland

Lacy, John (2, 0)
FAC75   **Fulham**   0-2 West Ham
CS82   **Spurs**   0-1 Liverpool

Lahtinen, Aki (1, 0)
WCQ84   **Finland**   0-5 England

Lambert, Jack (2, 1)
FAC30 (1)   **Arsenal**   2-0 Huddersfield
FAC32   **Arsenal**   1-2 Newcastle Utd

Lambert, Mick (1, 0)
FAC78 (S)   **Ipswich**   1-0 Arsenal

Lambert, Ray (2, 0)
WI43   **Wales**   3-8 England

FAC50   **Liverpool**   0-2 Arsenal

Lampard, Frank (5, 0)
INT72   **England**   1-1 Yugoslavia
FAC75   **West Ham**   2-0 Fulham
CS75   **West Ham**   0-2 Derby
FAC80   **West Ham**   1-0 Arsenal
FLC81   **West Ham**   1-1 Liverpool

Lang, Tommy (1, 0)
FAC32   **Newcastle Utd**   2-1 Arsenal

Langan, David (1, 0)
MC86   **Oxford**   3-0 QPR

Langford, Len (1, 0)
FAC33   **Man City**   0-3 Everton

Langley, Jim (3, 0)
INT58   **England**   2-1 Portugal
FLC67   **QPR**   3-2 WBA
FAT71   **Hillingdon**   2-3 Telford
As Player-Manager
FAT71   **Hillingdon**   2-3 Telford

Langley, Kevin (2, 0)
FRT85   **Wigan**   3-1 Brentford
CS86   **Everton**   1-1 Liverpool

Langton, Bobby (1, 0)
FAC53   **Bolton**   3-4 Blackpool

Larsson, Henrik (1, 0)
ECQ99 (W)   **Sweden**   0-0 England

Latchford, Bob (7, 2)
FLC77   **Everton**   0-0 Aston Villa
WCQ77 (W)   **England**   2-0 Italy
INT78   **England**   1-1 Brazil
INT78 (S)   **England**   1-0 Czechoslovakia
ECQ79 (2)   **England**   4-0 N Ireland
BC79   **England**   0-0 Wales
BC79   **England**   3-1 Scotland

Law, Denis (7, 4)
BC61   **Scotland**   3-9 England
BC63   **Scotland**   2-1 England
FAC63 (1)   **Man Utd**   3-1 Leicester
CEN63 (1)   **FIFA**   1-2 England
BC65 (1)   **Scotland**   2-2 England
ECQ67 (1)   **Scotland**   3-2 England
FLC74   **Man City**   1-2 Wolves

Law, Tommy (2, 0)
BC28   **Scotland**   5-1 England
BC30   **Scotland**   2-5 England

Lawler, Chris (5, 1)
FAC65   **Liverpool**   2-1 Leeds
FAC71   **Liverpool**   1-2 Arsenal
ECQ71 (1)   **England**   5-0 Malta
BC71   **England**   0-0 Wales
BC71   **England**   3-1 Scotland

Lawrence, Tommy (1, 0)
FAC65   **Liverpool**   2-1 Leeds

Lawrenson, Mark (10, 0)
ECQ80   **Rep of Ireland**   0-2 England
FLC82   **Liverpool**   3-1 Spurs
CS82   **Liverpool**   1-0 Spurs
MC83   **Liverpool**   2-1 Man Utd

CS83	**Liverpool**	0-2 Man Utd
MC84	**Liverpool**	0-0 Everton
CS84	**Liverpool**	0-1 Everton
INT85	**Rep of Ireland**	1-2 England
FAC86	**Liverpool**	3-1 Everton
CS86	**Liverpool**	1-1 Everton

Laws, Brian (5, 0)

LC89	**Nottingham F**	3-1 Luton
SC89	**Nottingham F**	4-3 Everton
LC90	**Nottingham F**	1-0 Oldham
FAC91 (S)	**Nottingham F**	1-2 Spurs
RLC92 (S)	**Nottingham F**	0-1 Man Utd
As Manager		
PPO99	**Scunthorpe**	1-0 Leyton Orient

Lawson, David (1, 0)

FLC77	**Everton**	0-0 Aston Villa

Lawton, Nobby (1, 0)

FAC64 (C)	**PNE**	2-3 West Ham

Lawton, Tommy (8, 8)

WI42 (2)	**England**	3-0 Scotland
WI42	**England**	0-0 Scotland
WI44 (1)	**England**	6-2 Scotland
WI44 (3)	**England**	6-2 Scotland
VI45 (1)	**England**	2-2 France
VI46	**England**	2-0 Belgium
IT46 (1)	**Army PT Corps**	5-3 FA
BC47	**England**	1-1 Scotland

Lazarus, Mark (1, 1)

FLC67 (1)	**QPR**	3-2 WBA

Leboeuf, Frank (7, 0)

FAC97	**Chelsea**	2-0 Middlesbrough
CS97	**Chelsea**	1-1 Man Utd
CCC98	**Chelsea**	2-0 Middlesbrough
INT99 (S)	**France**	2-0 England
FAC00	**Chelsea**	2-1 Newcastle Utd
FAC00	**Chelsea**	1-0 Aston Villa
CS00	**Chelsea**	2-0 Man Utd

Lee, Colin (1, 2)

FMC86 (2)	**Chelsea**	5-4 Man City

Lee, David (1, 0)

CCC95	**Bolton**	1-2 Liverpool

Lee, Francis (17, 6)

INT68	**England**	1-1 Bulgaria
INT69 (1)	**England**	5-0 France
FAC69	**Man City**	1-0 Leicester
BC69 (1)	**England**	2-1 Wales
BC69	**England**	4-1 Scotland
INT69	**England**	1-0 Portugal
INT70 (W)	**England**	0-0 Netherlands
FLC70	**Man City**	2-1 WBA
INT70 (1)	**England**	3-1 E Germany
ECQ71 (1)	**England**	3-0 Greece
ECQ71 (1)	**England**	5-0 Malta
BC71	**England**	0-0 Wales
BC71 (W)	**England**	3-1 Scotland
ECQ71 (W)	**England**	1-1 Switzerland
ECQ72 (1)	**England**	1-3 W Germany
FLC74	**Man City**	1-2 Wolves
CS75	**Derby**	2-0 West Ham

Lee, George (1, 0)

FAC54	**WBA**	3-2 PNE

Lee, Jack (1, 0)

FAC49	**Leicester**	1-3 Wolves

Lee, Robert (16, 2)

FMC87	**Charlton**	0-1 Blackburn
INT94 (1, W)	**England**	1-1 Romania
INT94 (W)	**England**	1-0 Nigeria
INT95 (S)	**England**	0-0 Colombia
INT95	**England**	3-1 Switzerland
INT96 (S)	**England**	1-0 Bulgaria
INT96	**England**	3-0 Hungary
CS 96	**Newcastle Utd**	0-4 Man Utd
INT97	**England**	2-0 Mexico
WCQ97	**England**	2-0 Georgia
INT97 (S)	**England**	2-0 Cameroon
INT98	**England**	0-2 Chile
FAC98 (C)	**Newcastle Utd**	0-2 Arsenal
ECQ98	**England**	0-0 Bulgaria
FAC99	**Newcastle Utd**	0-2 Man Utd
FAC00 (1)	**Newcastle Utd**	1-2 Chelsea

Lee, Sammy (14, 0)

FLC81	**Liverpool**	1-1 West Ham
FLC82	**Liverpool**	3-1 Spurs
CS82	**Liverpool**	1-0 Spurs
ECQ82	**England**	9-0 Luxembourg
BC83	**England**	2-1 Wales
MC83	**Liverpool**	2-1 Man Utd
ECQ83	**England**	0-0 Greece
ECQ83	**England**	2-0 Hungary
BC83	**England**	2-0 Scotland
CS83	**Liverpool**	0-2 Man Utd
ECQ83 (W)	**England**	1-1 Denmark
MC84	**Liverpool**	0-0 Everton
BC84	**England**	1-0 N Ireland
CS84 (W)	**Liverpool**	0-1 Everton

Leek, Ken (2, 1)

BC60	**Wales**	1-5 England
BC62	**Wales**	0-4 England

Leggat, Graham (1, 0)

BC59	**Scotland**	0-1 England

Leighton, Jim (3, 0)

BC83	**Scotland**	0-2 England
RC88	**Scotland**	0-1 England
FAC90	**Man Utd**	3-3 Crystal P

Leivers, Bill (1, 0)

FAC56	**Man City**	3-1 Birmingham

Lennon, Neil (5, 0)

PPO93	**Crewe**	1-1 York
PPO96	**Leicester**	2-1 Crystal P
CCC97	**Leicester**	1-1 Middlesbrough
WLC99	**Leicester**	0-1 Spurs
WLC00	**Leicester**	2-1 Tranmere

Lennox, Bobby (1, 1)

ECQ67 (1)	**Scotland**	3-2 England

Leonard, Keith (1, 0)

FLC75	**Aston Villa**	1-0 Norwich

Le Saux, Graeme (25, 1)

INT94	**England**	1-0 Denmark
INT94	**England**	5-0 Greece
INT94	**England**	0-0 Norway
CS94	**Blackburn**	0-2 Man Utd
INT94	**England**	2-0 USA
INT94	**England**	1-1 Romania
INT94	**England**	1-0 Nigeria
INT95 (W)	**England**	0-0 Uruguay
UC95 (1)	**England**	1-3 Brazil
CS95	**Blackburn**	0-1 Everton
INT95	**England**	0-0 Colombia
INT95 (S)	**England**	1-1 Portugal
WCQ97	**England**	0-1 Italy
INT97	**England**	2-0 Mexico
WCQ97	**England**	2-0 Georgia
INT98 (S)	**England**	0-2 Chile
CCC98	**Chelsea**	2-0 Middlesbrough
INT98	**England**	3-0 Portugal
ECQ98 (S)	**England**	0-0 Bulgaria
INT98	**England**	2-0 Czech Rep
INT99	**England**	0-2 France
ECQ99	**England**	3-1 Poland
ECQ99 (W)	**England**	0-0 Sweden
CS00 (S)	**Chelsea**	2-0 Man Utd
WCQ00 (W)	**England**	0-1 Germany

Leslie, Alec (1, 0)

FAC31	**Birmingham**	1-2 WBA

Le Tissier, Matthew (7, 1)

ZC92 (1)	**Southampton**	2-3 Nottingham F
INT94 (S)	**England**	1-0 Denmark
INT94 (S)	**England**	5-0 Greece
INT94 (S)	**England**	0-0 Norway
INT94	**England**	1-1 Romania
INT94 (S)	**England**	1-0 Nigeria
WCQ97 (W)	**England**	0-1 Italy

Leuty, Leon (1, 0)

FAC46	**Derby**	4-1 Charlton

Lewis, Dan (1, 0)

FAC27	**Arsenal**	0-1 Cardiff

Lewis, Reg (2, 6)

LSC43 (4)	**Arsenal**	7-1 Charlton
FAC50 (2)	**Arsenal**	2-0 Liverpool

Leyland, Harry (1, 0)

FAC60	**Blackburn**	0-3 Wolves

Liddell, Billy (4, 1)

WI42	**Scotland**	0-0 England
FAC50	**Liverpool**	0-2 Arsenal
BC51 (1)	**Scotland**	3-2 England
BC53	**Scotland**	2-2 England

Liddell, George (1, 0)

FAC31	**Birmingham**	1-2 WBA

Lillis, Mark (1, 2)

FMC86 (2)	**Man City**	4-5 Chelsea

Limpar, Anders (6, 1)

MT90 (1)	**Arsenal**	2-0 Aston Villa
MT90	**Arsenal**	0-1 Sampdoria
FAC91 (W)	**Arsenal**	1-3 Spurs

CS93 (W)	**Arsenal**	1-1 Man Utd
FAC95 (W)	**Everton**	1-0 Man Utd
CS95	**Everton**	1-0 Blackburn

Lindsay, Alec (4, 0)

FAC71	**Liverpool**	1-2 Arsenal
FAC74	**Liverpool**	3-0 Newcastle Utd
INT74	**England**	2-2 Argentina
CS74	**Liverpool**	1-1 Leeds

Lineker, Gary (35, 25)

INT85 (1)	**England**	2-1 Rep of Ireland
CS85 (W)	**Everton**	2-0 Man Utd
WCQ85 (W)	**England**	1-1 Romania
WCQ85 (3)	**England**	5-0 Turkey
WCQ85	**England**	0-0 N Ireland
FAC86 (1)	**Everton**	1-3 Liverpool
ECQ86 (2)	**England**	3-0 N Ireland
ECQ86	**England**	2-0 Yugoslavia
RC87 (1, W)	**England**	1-1 Brazil
LCEN87 (W)	**Rest of World**	0-3 Football League
ECQ87 (3)	**England**	8-0 Turkey
INT88 (1)	**England**	2-2 Netherlands
RC88	**England**	1-0 Scotland
RC88 (1)	**England**	1-1 Colombia
WCQ88	**England**	0-0 Sweden
WCQ89 (1)	**England**	5-0 Albania
WCQ89 (1)	**England**	3-0 Poland
INT89	**England**	0-0 Italy
INT89	**England**	2-1 Yugoslavia
INT90 (1)	**England**	1-0 Brazil
INT90	**England**	4-2 Czechoslovakia
INT90 (1, W)	**England**	1-0 Denmark
INT90 (W)	**England**	1-2 Uruguay
INT90 (C, 1)	**England**	1-0 Hungary
ECQ90 (C, 1, W)	**England**	2-0 Poland
INT91 (2)	**England**	2-0 Cameroon
ECQ91 (W)	**England**	1-1 Rep of Ireland
FAC91 (2)	**Spurs**	3-1 Arsenal
FAC91	**Spurs**	2-1 Nottingham F
INT91 (C, 1)	**England**	2-2 Argentina
CS91	**Spurs**	0-0 Arsenal
INT91 (C)	**England**	0-1 Germany
ECQ91 (C)	**England**	1-0 Turkey
INT92 (S, 1)	**England**	2-0 France
INT92 (C)	**England**	1-1 Brazil

Linighan, Andy (8, 1)

MT90	**Arsenal**	2-0 Aston Villa
MT90 (W)	**Arsenal**	0-1 Sampdoria
FAC93	**Arsenal**	1-0 Spurs
CCC93	**Arsenal**	2-1 Sheffield W
FAC93	**Arsenal**	1-1 Sheffield W
FAC93 (1)	**Arsenal**	2-1 Sheffield W
CS93	**Arsenal**	1-1 Man Utd
PPO97	**Crystal P**	1-0 Sheffield Utd

Linton, Des (1, 0)

FAC94 (W)	**Luton**	0-2 Chelsea

Lishman, Doug (1, 0)

FAC52	**Arsenal**	0-1 Newcastle Utd

Little, Brian (3, 0)

FLC75	**Aston Villa**	1-0 Norwich

BC75 (S)	**England** 2-2 Wales	
FLC77	**Aston Villa** 0-0 Everton	

As Manager

PPO92	**Leicester** 0-1 Blackburn
PPO93	**Leicester** 3-4 Swindon
PPO94	**Leicester** 2-1 Derby
CCC96	**Aston Villa** 3-0 Leeds

Little, Roy (2, 0)

FAC55	**Man City** 1-3 Newcastle Utd
FAC56	**Man City** 3-1 Birmingham

Littlejohn, Adrian (1, 0)

U16l86 (S)	**England** 0-1 France
FAC93 (S)	**Sheffield Utd** 1-2 Sheffield W
PPO96	**Plymouth** 1-0 Darlington

Livermore, Doug (1, 0)

FLC73	**Norwich** 0-1 Spurs

As Coach

FAC93	**Spurs** 0-1 Arsenal

Ljungberg, Freddie (5, 1)

ECQ99	**Sweden** 0-0 England
CS99	**Arsenal** 2-1 Man Utd
EC99 (1, W)	**Arsenal** 3-1 AIK Stockholm
EC99 (W)	**Arsenal** 2-4 Barcelona
EC99 (S)	**Arsenal** 0-1 Fiorentina

Lloyd, Larry (7, 1)

FAC71	**Liverpool** 1-2 Arsenal
BC71	**England** 0-0 Wales
ECQ71	**England** 1-1 Switzerland
BC72	**England** 0-1 N Ireland
FLC78	**Nottingham F** 0-0 Liverpool
CS78 (1)	**Nottingham F** 5-0 Ipswich
FLC79	**Nottingham F** 3-2 Southampton

Lochhead, Andy (2, 0)

FAC69	**Leicester** 0-1 Man City
FLC71	**Aston Villa** 0-2 Spurs

Lock, Kevin (2, 0)

FAC75	**West Ham** 2-0 Fulham
CS75	**West Ham** 0-2 Derby

Lofthouse, Nat (10, 11)

INT51 (1)	**England** 2-2 Austria
BC 52 (2)	**England** 5-2 Wales
INT52 (2)	**England** 5-0 Belgium
BC53	**England** 2-2 Scotland
FAC53 (1)	**Bolton** 3-4 Blackpool
NIN53	**England** 4-4 FIFA
BC55 (2)	**England** 7-2 Scotland
INT55	**England** 4-1 Spain
FAC58 (C, 2)	**Bolton** 2-0 Man Utd
INT58 (1)	**England** 5-0 USSR

Logie, Jimmy (2, 0)

FAC50	**Arsenal** 2-0 Liverpool
FAC52	**Arsenal** 0-1 Newcastle Utd

Lorimer, Peter (7, 0)

FLC68	**Leeds** 1-0 Arsenal
FAC70	**Leeds** 2-2 Chelsea
FAC72	**Leeds** 1-0 Arsenal
EEC73	**The Three** 2-0 The Six
FAC73	**Leeds** 0-1 Sunderland

BC73 (W)	**Scotland** 0-1 England	
CS74	**Leeds** 1-1 Liverpool	

Lovett, Graham (1, 0)

FAC68	**WBA** 1-0 Everton

Low, James (1, 0)

FAC24	**Newcastle Utd** 2-0 Aston Villa

Lucas, Malcolm (1, 0)

BC62	**Wales** 0-4 England

Lukic, John (9, 0)

LC87	**Arsenal** 2-1 Liverpool
LC88	**Arsenal** 2-3 Luton
WIT88	**Arsenal** 4-0 Spurs
WIT88	**Arsenal** 3-0 Bayern Munich
MT89	**Arsenal** 1-0 Porto
MT89	**Arsenal** 1-0 Liverpool
CS89	**Arsenal** 0-1 Liverpool
CS92	**Leeds** 4-3 Liverpool
CCC96	**Leeds** 0-3 Aston Villa

Lutton, Bertie (1, 0)

BC70 (W)	**N Ireland** 1-3 England

Luzhny, Oleg (3, 0)

EC98 (C)	**Dynamo Kiev** 1-1 Arsenal
CS99 (S)	**Arsenal** 2-1 Man Utd
INT00 (C)	**Ukraine** 0-2 England

Lynn, Stan (1, 0)

FAC57	**Aston Villa** 2-1 Man Utd

Lyons, Mick (1, 0)

FLC77 (C)	**Everton** 0-0 Aston Villa

Mabbutt, Gary (16, 0)

CS82	**Spurs** 0-1 Liverpool
INT82	**England** 1-2 W Germany
ECQ82 (W)	**England** 9-0 Luxembourg
BC83	**England** 2-1 Wales
ECQ83	**England** 0-0 Greece
ECQ83	**England** 2-0 Hungary
BC83 (S)	**England** 2-0 Scotland
ECQ86	**England** 2-0 Yugoslavia
FAC87	**Spurs** 2-3 Coventry
WIT88 (C)	**Spurs** 0-4 Arsenal
WIT88 (C)	**Spurs** 1-2 AC Milan
FAC91 (C)	**Spurs** 3-1 Arsenal
FAC91 (C)	**Spurs** 2-1 Nottingham F
CS91 (C)	**Spurs** 0-0 Arsenal
ECQ91	**England** 1-0 Turkey
FAC93 (C)	**Spurs** 0-1 Arsenal

Macari, Lou (8, 0)

BC73 (W)	**Scotland** 0-1 England
BC75 (S)	**Scotland** 1-5 England
FAC76	**Man Utd** 0-1 Southampton
FAC77	**Man Utd** 2-1 Liverpool
BC77 (S)	**Scotland** 2-1 England
CS77	**Man Utd** 0-0 Liverpool
FAC79	**Man Utd** 2-3 Arsenal
MC83 (S)	**Man Utd** 1-2 Liverpool

As Manager

LDC91	**Birmingham** 3-2 Tranmere
AT92	**Stoke** 1-0 Stockport

Macaulay, Archie (4, 0)
FLWC40	West Ham	1-0 Blackburn
WI44	Scotland	2-6 England
WI44	Scotland	2-6 England
BC47	Scotland	1-1 England

MacDonald, Kevin (3, 0)
FAC86	Liverpool	3-1 Everton
CS86 (W)	Liverpool	1-1 Everton
LCT88	Liverpool	0-0 Newcastle Utd

Macdonald, Malcolm (6, 6)
BC72 (W)	England	0-1 N Ireland
FAC74	Newcastle Utd	0-3 Liverpool
INT75 (1)	England	2-0 W Germany
ECQ75 (5)	England	5-0 Cyprus
FLC76	Newcastle Utd	1-2 Man City
FAC78	Arsenal	0-1 Ipswich

MacDougall, Ted (2, 0)
FLC75	Norwich	0-1 Aston V
BC75 (W)	Scotland	1-5 England

Machin, Mel (1, 0)
FLC75	Norwich	0-1 Aston V

As Manager
AWS98	Bournemouth	1-2 Grimsby

Mackay, Dave (7, 1)
SI50 (S)	Scotland	2-8 England
BC59	Scotland	0-1 England
BC61 (1)	Scotland	3-9 England
FAC61	Spurs	2-0 Leicester
FAC62	Spurs	3-1 Burnley
BC63	Scotland	2-1 England
FAC67 (C)	Spurs	2-1 Chelsea

As Manager
CS75	Derby	2-0 West Ham

Mackenzie, Steve (2, 1)
FAC81	Man City	1-1 Spurs
FAC81 (1)	Man City	2-3 Spurs

Mackey, Gerry (1, 0)
WCQ57	Rep of Ireland	1-5 England

Mackie, Alex (2, 0)
FAC29	Portsmouth	0-2 Bolton
FAC34	Portsmouth	1-2 Man City

MacLeod, John (1, 0)
BC61	Scotland	3-9 England

MacLeod, Murdo (1, 0)
RC88	Scotland	0-1 England

MacRae, Keith (1, 0)
FLC74	Man City	1-2 Wolves

Madden, David (2, 0)
FAC90 (S)	Crystal P	3-3 Man Utd
FAC90 (S)	Crystal P	0-1 Man Utd

Madden, Lawrie (5, 0)
LCT88	Sheffield W	0-0 Crystal P
LCT88	Sheffield W	1-1 Wigan
LCT88	Sheffield W	2-1 Man Utd
LCT88	Sheffield W	0-0 Nottingham F
RLC91 (S)	Sheffield W	1-0 Man Utd

Maddison, Neil (1, 0)
CCC98 (W)	Middlesbrough	0-2 Chelsea

Madeley, Paul (14, 0)
FLC68	Leeds	1-0 Arsenal
FAC70	Leeds	2-2 Chelsea
ECQ71	England	1-1 Switzerland
ECQ72	England	1-3 W Germany
FAC72	Leeds	1-0 Arsenal
FAC73	Leeds	0-1 Sunderland
INT73	England	7-0 Austria
WCQ73	England	1-1 Poland
INT73	England	0-1 Italy
ECQ74	England	3-0 Czechoslovakia
ECQ74	England	0-0 Portugal
ECQ75	England	5-0 Cyprus
INT76	England	1-1 Rep of Ireland
INT77 (W)	England	0-2 Netherlands

Magee, Tommy (1, 0)
FAC31	WBA	2-1 Birmingham

Magill, Ted (3, 0)
BC61	N Ireland	1-1 England
BC63	N Ireland	3-8 England
BC65	N Ireland	1-2 England

Maguire, Teddy (1, 0)
FAC39	Wolves	1-4 Portsmouth

Mahon, Alan (1, 0)
WLC00	Tranmere	1-2 Leicester

Mahoney, John (7, 0)
FLC72 (S)	Stoke	2-1 Chelsea
WCQ73	Wales	1-1 England
BC73	Wales	0-3 England
BC75	Wales	2-2 England
BC77	Wales	1-0 England
BC79	Wales	0-0 England
BC83 (W)	Wales	1-2 England

Mahoney, Mike (1, 0)
FLC76	Newcastle Utd	1-2 Man City

Mail, David (3, 0)
FMC87	Blackburn	1-0 Charlton
LCT88	Blackburn	0-0 Aston V
FAV96 (S)	Brigg	3-0 Clitheroe

Makel, Lee (1, 0)
CS95 (S)	Blackburn	0-1 Everton

Makin, Chris (4, 0)
U16I88 (S)	England	1-1 Israel
U17I90	England	1-3 France
FAC94	Oldham	1-1 Man Utd
PPO98 (S)	Sunderland	4-4 Charlton

Male, George (6, 0)
FAC32	Arsenal	1-2 Newcastle Utd
BC36	England	1-1 Scotland
FAC36	Arsenal	1-0 Sheffield Utd
LSC43	Arsenal	7-1 Charlton
CHA43	RAF	4-3 Met Police
CHA44	Combined Services	5-2 Met Police

Malone, Dick (1, 0)
FAC73	Sunderland	1-0 Leeds

Malpas, Maurice (1, 0)
RC86	Scotland	1-2 England

Manley, Malcolm (2, 0)
SI65 (C)   **Scotland** 0-3 England
FAC69 (S)   **Leicester** 0-1 Man City

Mann, Arthur (1, 0)
FLC70   **Man City** 2-1 WBA

Manninger, Alex (2, 0)
CS99   **Arsenal** 2-1 Man Utd
EC99   **Arsenal** 3-1 AIK Stockholm

Mannion, Wilf (4, 0)
WI41   **England** 2-0 Scotland
WI42   **England** 3-0 Scotland
BC47   **England** 1-1 Scotland
BC51   **England** 2-3 Scotland

Mapson, Johnny (1, 0)
FAC37   **Sunderland** 3-1 PNE

Maric, Silvio (1, 0)
FAC99 (S)   **Newcastle Utd** 0-2 Man Utd

Mariner, Paul (13, 4)
WCQ77 (S)   **England** 5-0 Luxembourg
FAC78   **Ipswich** 1-0 Arsenal
CS78   **Ipswich** 0-5 Nottingham F
BC80 (S)   **England** 1-1 N Ireland
WCQ80 (1)   **England** 4-0 Norway
WCQ80 (1)   **England** 2-1 Switzerland
INT81   **England** 1-2 Spain
WCQ81 (1)   **England** 1-0 Hungary
INT82 (1, W) **England** 2-0 Netherlands
INT82 (W)   **England** 1-2 W Germany
BC83   **England** 2-1 Wales
ECQ83   **England** 0-1 Denmark
INT84 (W)   **England** 1-0 E Germany

Marker, Nicky (1, 0)
CS95 (S)   **Blackburn** 0-1 Everton

Marriott, Andrew (6, 0)
SI86   **England** 1-0 Netherlands
SI86   **England** 2-1 Italy
U16I86   **England** 0-1 France
U17I87   **England** 3-1 Netherlands
ZC92   **Nottingham F** 3-2 Southampton
RLC92   **Nottingham F** 0-1 Man Utd

Marsden, Billy (1, 0)
BC30   **England** 5-2 Scotland

Marsh, John (1, 0)
FLC72   **Stoke** 2-1 Chelsea

Marsh, Mike (1, 0)
CS92 (W)   **Liverpool** 3-4 Leeds

Marsh, Rodney (7, 1)
FLC67 (1)   **QPR** 3-2 WBA
ECQ71 (S)   **England** 1-1 Switzerland
ECQ72 (S)   **England** 1-3 W Germany
BC72   **England** 0-1 N Ireland
INT72   **England** 1-1 Yugoslavia
WCQ73   **England** 1-1 Wales
FLC74   **Man City** 1-2 Wolves

Marshall, Bobby (2, 0)
FAC33   **Man City** 0-3 Everton
FAC34   **Man City** 2-1 Portsmouth

Marshall, Ian (3, 0)

CS86   **Everton** 1-1 Liverpool
WLC99 (S)   **Leicester** 0-1 Spurs
WLC00 (S)   **Leicester** 2-1 Tranmere

Marshall, James (2, 0)
BC32   **Scotland** 0-3 England
BC34   **Scotland** 0-3 England

Marston, Joe (1, 0)
FAC54   **PNE** 2-3 WBA

Martin, Alvin (10, 0)
FAC80   **West Ham** 1-0 Arsenal
CS80   **West Ham** 0-1 Liverpool
FLC81   **West Ham** 0-1 Liverpool
INT81   **England** 0-1 Brazil
BC81 (S)   **England** 0-1 Scotland
WCQ81   **England** 1-0 Hungary
ECQ82   **England** 9-0 Luxembourg
BC83   **England** 2-1 Wales
ECQ83   **England** 0-0 Greece
ECQ83   **England** 2-0 Hungary

Martin, Fred (1, 0)
BC55   **Scotland** 2-7 England

Martin, Lee (2, 1)
FAC90 (W)   **Man Utd** 3-3 Crystal P
FAC90 (1)   **Man Utd** 1-0 Crystal P

Martin, Mick (1, 0)
INT76   **Rep of Ireland** 1-1 England

Martyn, Nigel (10, 0)
FAC90   **Crystal P** 3-3 Man Utd
FAC90   **Crystal P** 0-1 Man Utd
ZC91   **Crystal P** 4-1 Everton
PPO96   **Crystal P** 1-2 Leicester
INT97   **England** 2-0 Cameroon
INT98   **England** 0-2 Chile
INT98   **England** 2-0 Czech Rep
INT99 (S)   **England** 0-2 France
ECQ99   **England** 6-0 Luxembourg
INT00   **England** 2-0 Ukraine

Marwood, Brian (3, 2)
WIT88 (2)   **Arsenal** 4-0 Spurs
WIT88   **Arsenal** 3-0 Bayern Munich
CS89 (S)   **Arsenal** 0-1 Liverpool

Mason, Jimmy (2, 1)
LSC43   **Charlton** 1-7 Arsenal
BC49 (1)   **Scotland** 3-1 England

Massie, Alex (2, 0)
BC34 (C)   **Scotland** 0-3 England
BC36   **Scotland** 1-1 England

Masson, Don (1, 0)
BC77 (W)   **Scotland** 2-1 England

Mather, Harold (1, 0)
FAC47   **Burnley** 0-1 Charlton

Matthews, Reg (1, 0)
INT56   **England** 4-2 Brazil

Matthews, Sir Stanley (27, 0)
BC38   **England** 0-1 Scotland
WI40   **England** 0-1 Wales
WI41   **England** 2-0 Scotland
WI42   **England** 3-0 Scotland

WI42	**England**	0-0 Scotland
WI43	**England**	5-3 Wales
WI43	**England**	8-3 Wales
WI44	**England**	6-2 Scotland
WI44	**England**	6-2 Scotland
WI45	**England**	2-2 France
VI46	**England**	2-0 Belgium
BC47	**England**	1-1 Scotland
FAC48	**Blackpool**	2-4 Man Utd
BC49	**England**	1-3 Scotland
BC51	**England**	2-3 Scotland
FAC51	**Blackpool**	0-2 Newcastle Utd
FAC53	**Blackpool**	4-3 Bolton
NIN53	**England**	4-4 FIFA
INT53	**England**	3-6 Hungary
BC54	**England**	3-2 Wales
INT54	**England**	3-1 W Germany
BC55	**England**	7-2 Scotland
INT56	**England**	4-2 Brazil
BC56	**England**	3-1 Wales
INT56	**England**	3-0 Yugoslavia
BC57	**England**	2-1 Scotland
WCQ57	**England**	5-1 Rep of Ireland

Maxwell, Bud (1, 0)
FAC38	**PNE**	1-0 Huddersfield

May, Andy (1, 0)
FMC86	**Man City**	4-5 Chelsea

May, David (6, 0)
PPO92	**Blackburn**	1-0 Leicester
CS94	**Man Utd**	2-0 Blackburn
FAC96	**Man Utd**	1-0 Liverpool
CS96	**Man Utd**	4-0 Newcastle Utd
FAC99	**Man Utd**	2-0 Newcastle Utd
CS99 (S)	**Man Utd**	1-2 Arsenal

McAdams, Billy (1, 0)
BC61	**N Ireland**	1-1 England

McAlinden, Jimmy (1, 0)
FAC39	**Portsmouth**	4-1 Wolves

McAlle, John (1, 0)
FLC74	**Wolves**	2-1 Man City

McAllister, Gary (3, 0)
CS92 (C)	**Leeds**	4-3 Liverpool
CCC96 (C)	**Leeds**	0-3 Aston V
ECH96 (C)	**Scotland**	0-2 England

McAllister, Kevin (2, 0)
FMC86	**Chelsea**	5-4 Man City
ZC90	**Chelsea**	1-0 Middlesbrough

McAteer, Jason (3, 0)
CCC95	**Bolton**	1-2 Liverpool
PPO95	**Bolton**	4-3 Reading
FAC96	**Liverpool**	0-1 Man Utd

McCall, Stuart (4, 2)
SC89 (S)	**Everton**	3-4 Nottingham F
FAC89 (S, 2)	**Everton**	2-3 Liverpool
ZC91	**Everton**	1-4 Crystal P
ECH96	**Scotland**	0-2 England

McCalliog, Jim (4, 2)
FAC66 (1)	**Sheffield W**	2-3 Everton

ECQ67 (1)	**Scotland**	3-2 England
FAC76	**Southampton**	1-0 Man Utd
CS76	**Southampton**	0-1 Liverpool

McCann, Neil (1, 0)
ECQ99 (W)	**Scotland**	1-0 England

McCann, Robert (1, 0)
BC61	**Scotland**	3-9 England

McCarthy, Mick (2, 0)
INT85	**Rep of Ireland**	1-2 England
FMC86	**Man City**	4-5 Chelsea

McCavana, William (1, 0)
BC55	**N Ireland**	0-3 England

McClair, Brian (13, 3)
LCT88 (1)	**Man Utd**	2-0 Luton
LCT88	**Man Utd**	1-0 Everton
LCT88	**Man Utd**	1-2 Sheffield W
FAC90	**Man Utd**	3-3 Crystal P
FAC90	**Man Utd**	1-0 Crystal P
CS90	**Man Utd**	1-1 Liverpool
RLC91	**Man Utd**	0-1 Sheffield W.
RLC92 (1)	**Man Utd**	1-0 Nottingham F
CCC94 (S)	**Man Utd**	1-3 Aston V
FAC94	**Man Utd**	1-1 Oldham
FAC94 (S, 1)	**Man Utd**	4-0 Chelsea
CS94	**Man Utd**	2-0 Blackburn
FAC95	**Man Utd**	0-1 Everton

McClelland, Jim (1, 0)
FAC29	**Bolton**	2-0 Portsmouth

McClelland, John (3, 0)
BC84	**N Ireland**	0-1 England
ECQ86 (C)	**N Ireland**	0-3 England
LCEN87	**Football League**	3-0 Rest of World

McCloy, Philip (2, 0)
BC24	**Scotland**	1-1 England
FAC26	**Man City**	0-1 Bolton

McCoist, Ally (2, 0)
RC88 (W)	**Scotland**	0-1 England
ECH96 (S)	**Scotland**	0-2 England

McColl, Ian (1, 0)
BC57	**Scotland**	1-2 England

As Manager
BC61	**Scotland**	3-9 England
BC63	**Scotland**	2-1 England
BC65	**Scotland**	2-2 England

McCreadie, Eddie (5, 0)
BC65	**Scotland**	2-2 England
ECQ67	**Scotland**	3-2 England
FAC67	**Chelsea**	1-2 Spurs
BC69	**Scotland**	1-4 England
FAC70	**Chelsea**	2-2 Leeds

McCreery, David (10, 0)
FAC76 (S)	**Man Utd**	0-1 Southampton
BC76	**N Ireland**	0-4 England
FAC77 (S)	**Man Utd**	2-1 Liverpool
CS77 (S)	**Man Utd**	0-0 Liverpool
BC78	**N Ireland**	0-1 England
ECQ79	**N Ireland**	0-4 England
BC80 (S)	**N Ireland**	1-1 England

BC82 (S) **N Ireland** 0-4 England
WCQ85 **N Ireland** 0-0 England
LCT88 (W) **Newcastle Utd** 0-0 Liverpool

McCrory, Sammy (1, 1)
BC57 (1) **N Ireland** 3-2 England

McCulloch, David (1, 0)
BC36 **Scotland** 1-1 England

McCullough, Bill (1, 0)
BC63 **N Ireland** 3-8 England

McDermott, Terry (20, 5)
FAC74 **Newcastle Utd** 0-3 Liverpool
FAC77 **Liverpool** 1-2 Man Utd
CS77 **Liverpool** 0-0 Man Utd
INT77 **England** 0-0 Switzerland
FLC78 **Liverpool** 0-0 Nottingham F
EC78 **Liverpool** 1-0 Bruges
BC79 **England** 0-0 Wales
CS79 (2) **Liverpool** 3-1 Arsenal
ECQ79 **England** 1-0 Denmark
ECQ80 **England** 2-0 Rep of Ireland
BC80 **England** 1-1 N Ireland
CS80 (1) **Liverpool** 1-0 West Ham
WCQ80 (2) **England** 4-0 Norway
WCQ80 **England** 2-1 Switzerland
FLC81 **Liverpool** 1-1 West Ham
WCQ81 (S) **England** 0-0 Romania
INT81 **England** 0-1 Brazil
WCQ81 **England** 1-0 Hungary
FLC82 (W) **Liverpool** 3-1 Spurs
INT82 **England** 2-0 Netherlands

McDonald, Alan (3, 0)
WCQ85 **N Ireland** 0-0 England
MC86 **QPR** 0-3 Oxford
ECQ86 **N Ireland** 0-3 England

McDonald, Bobby (3, 0)
FLC75 **Aston Villa** 1-0 Norwich
FAC81 **Man City** 1-1 Spurs
FAC81 (W) **Man City** 2-3 Spurs

McDonald, Colin (1, 0)
INT58 **England** 5-0 U.S.S.R.

McDonald, Joe (1, 0)
FAC59 **Nottingham F** 2-1 Luton

McDonald, Neil (7, 0)
SI81 **England** 1-2 W Germany
LCT88 **Newcastle Utd** 0-0 Liverpool
LCT88 **Newcastle Utd** 0-2 Tranmere
SC89 **Everton** 3-4 Nottingham F
FAC89 **Everton** 2-3 Liverpool
ZC91 **Everton** 1-4 Crystal P
PPO95 (W) **Bolton** 4-3 Reading

McDonald, Tommy (1, 0)
FAC24 **Newcastle Utd** 2-0 Aston V

McDonough, Darron (2, 0)
SC88 **Luton** 1-4 Reading
LC89 (S) **Luton** 1-3 Nottingham F

McDowell, John (2, 0)
FAC75 **West Ham** 2-0 Fulham
CS75 **West Ham** 0-2 Derby

McElhinney, Gerry (1, 0)
BC84 **N Ireland** 0-1 England

McFadyen, Willie (1, 0)
FAC38 **Huddersfield** 0-1 PNE

McFarland, Roy (12, 1)
ECQ71 **England** 3-0 Greece
ECQ71 **England** 5-0 Malta
BC71 **England** 3-1 Scotland
WCQ73 **England** 1-1 Wales
BC73 **England** 3-0 Wales
BC73 **England** 1-0 Scotland
INT73 **England** 7-0 Austria
WCQ73 **England** 1-1 Poland
INT73 **England** 0-1 Italy
BC74 (W) **England** 1-0 N Ireland
CS75 (C, 1) **Derby** 2-0 West Ham
INT76 **England** 1-1 Rep of Ireland
As Manager
PPO94 **Derby** 1-2 Leicester

McFaul, Willie (1, 0)
FAC74 **Newcastle Utd** 0-3 Liverpool
As Manager
LCT88 **Newcastle Utd** 0-0 Liverpool

McGee, Owen (1, 0)
ZC90 **Middlesbrough** 0-1 Chelsea

McGinlay, John (1, 0)
CCC95 **Bolton** 1-2 Liverpool
PPO95 **Bolton** 4-3 Reading

McGoldrick, Eddie (2, 0)
ZC91 (S) **Crystal P** 4-1 Everton
CS93 (S) **Arsenal** 1-1 Man Utd

McGonagle, Peter (1, 0)
BC34 **Scotland** 0-3 England

McGovern, John (4, 0)
FLC78 (C, W) **Nottingham F** 0-0 Liverpool
CS78 (C) **Nottingham F** 5-0 Ipswich
FLC79 (C) **Nottingham F** 3-2 Southampton
FLC80 (C) **Nottingham F** 0-1 Wolves
As Manager
AWS96 **Rotherham** 2-1 Shrewsbury

McGrain, Danny (4, 0)
BC73 **Scotland** 0-1 England
BC75 **Scotland** 1-5 England
BC77 **Scotland** 2-1 England
BC81 (C) **Scotland** 1-0 England

McGrath, Chris (3, 0)
BC74 **N Ireland** 0-1 England
BC78 (W) **N Ireland** 0-1 England
ECQ79 (S) **N Ireland** 0-4 England

McGrath, Lloyd (2, 0)
FAC87 **Coventry** 3-2 Spurs
CS87 (W) **Coventry** 0-1 Everton

McGrath, Mick (1, 0)
FAC60 **Blackburn** 0-3 Wolves

McGrath, Paul (11, 0)
INT85 (W) **Rep of Ireland** 1-2 England
FAC85 **Man Utd** 1-0 Everton
CS85 **Man Utd** 0-2 Everton

LCEN87	**Football League**	3-0 Rest of World
LCT88	**Man Utd**	2-0 Luton
LCT88	**Man Utd**	1-0 Everton
LCT88	**Man Utd**	1-2 Sheffield W
MT90	**Aston Villa**	0-2 Arsenal
ECQ91	**Rep of Ireland**	1-1 England
CCC94	**Aston Villa**	3-1 Man Utd
CCC96	**Aston Villa**	3-0 Leeds

McIlmoyle, Hugh (1, 0)

FAC61	**Leicester**	0-2 Spurs

McIlroy, Jimmy (6, 2)

BC55	**N Ireland**	0-3 England
BC57 (1)	**N Ireland**	3-2 England
BC59	**N Ireland**	1-2 England
BC61 (1)	**N Ireland**	1-1 England
FAC62	**Burnley**	1-3 Spurs
BC65	**N Ireland**	1-2 England

McIlroy, Sammy (13, 1)

BC74	**N Ireland**	0-1 England
FAC76	**Man Utd**	0-1 Southampton
BC76	**N Ireland**	0-4 England
FAC77	**Man Utd**	2-1 Liverpool
CS77	**Man Utd**	0-0 Liverpool
BC78	**N Ireland**	0-1 England
ECQ79	**N Ireland**	0-4 England
FAC79 (1)	**Man Utd**	2-3 Arsenal
BC80 (C)	**N Ireland**	1-1 England
BC82	**N Ireland**	0-4 England
BC84	**N Ireland**	0-1 England
WCQ85 (C)	**N Ireland**	0-0 England
ECQ86 (S)	**N Ireland**	0-3 England
As Manager		
FAT96	**Macclesfield**	3-1 Northwich

McIlwaine, Johnny (1, 0)

FAC29 (C)	**Portsmouth**	0-2 Bolton

McInroy, Albert (1, 0)

FAC32	**Newcastle Utd**	2-1 Arsenal

McIntosh, Alex (1, 0)

FAC39	**Wolves**	1-4 Portsmouth

McKay, Duncan (1, 0)

BC59	**Scotland**	0-1 England

McKenzie, Duncan (2, 0)

CS74 (S)	**Leeds**	1-1 Liverpool
FLC77	**Everton**	0-0 Aston V

McKenzie, John (1, 0)

BC55	**Scotland**	2-7 England

McKenzie, Roddie (1, 0)

FAC32	**Newcastle**	2-1 Arsenal

McKimmie, Stewart (1, 0)

ECH96	**Scotland**	0-2 England

McKinlay, Bobby (1, 0)

FAC59	**Nottingham F**	2-1 Luton

McKinlay, Tosh (1, 0)

ECH96 (W)	**Scotland**	0-2 England

McKinnon, Ron (1, 0)

ECQ67	**Scotland**	3-2 England

McLachlan, George (1, 0)

FAC27	**Cardiff**	1-0 Arsenal

McLaren, Andy (2, 2)

FLWC41 (1)	**PNE**	1-1 Arsenal
BC47 (1)	**Scotland**	1-1 England

McLaughlin, Jimmy (1, 0)

BC61	**N Ireland**	1-1 England

McLaughlin, Joe (1, 0)

FMC86	**Chelsea**	5-4 Man City

McLean, Tom (1, 1)

FAC28 (1)	**Blackburn**	3-1 Huddersfield

McLeish, Alex (4, 0)

BC81	**Scotland**	1-0 England
BC83	**Scotland**	0-2 England
RC86	**Scotland**	1-2 England
RC88	**Scotland**	0-1 England

McLeod, Ally (1, 0)

FAC60	**Blackburn**	0-3 Wolves
As Manager		
BC77	**Scotland**	2-1 England

McLintock, Frank (7, 0)

FAC61	**Leicester**	0-2 Spurs
FAC63	**Leicester**	1-3 Man Utd
FLC68 (C)	**Arsenal**	0-1 Leeds
FLC69 (C)	**Arsenal**	1-3 Swindon
FAC71 (C)	**Arsenal**	2-1 Liverpool
BC71	**Scotland**	1-3 England
FAC72 (C)	**Arsenal**	0-1 Leeds
As Manager		
FRT85	**Brentford**	1-3 Wigan

McMahon, Pat (1, 0)

FLC71	**Aston Villa**	0-2 Spurs

McMahon, Steve (16, 0)

CS86	**Liverpool**	1-1 Everton
LC87 (W)	**Liverpool**	1-2 Arsenal
LCT88	**Liverpool**	0-0 Newcastle Utd
FAC88	**Liverpool**	0-1 Wimbledon
RC88	**England**	1-1 Colombia
CS88	**Liverpool**	2-1 Wimbledon
FAC89	**Liverpool**	3-2 Everton
MT89 (W)	**Liverpool**	2-0 Dynamo Kiev
MT89 (W)	**Liverpool**	0-1 Arsenal
CS89	**Liverpool**	1-0 Arsenal
INT89 (W)	**England**	0-0 Italy
INT89 (S)	**England**	2-1 Yugoslavia
INT90	**England**	1-0 Brazil
INT90 (S)	**England**	4-2 Czechoslovakia
INT90 (W)	**England**	1-0 Denmark
CS90	**Liverpool**	1-1 Man Utd

McManaman, Steve (24, 4)

U19I91 (S)	**England**	1-1 Spain
FAC92	**Liverpool**	2-0 Sunderland
INT94 (S)	**England**	1-0 Nigeria
INT95 (S)	**England**	0-0 Uruguay
CCC95 (2)	**Liverpool**	2-1 Bolton
UC95 (S)	**England**	2-1 Japan
INT95	**England**	0-0 Colombia
INT95	**England**	3-1 Switzerland
INT95 (S)	**England**	1-1 Portugal
INT96	**England**	1-0 Bulgaria

INT96	**England**	0-0 Croatia
FAC96	**Liverpool**	0-1 Man Utd
ECH96 (W)	**England**	1-1 Switzerland
ECH96	**England**	2-0 Scotland
ECH96	**England**	4-1 Netherlands
ECH96 (W)	**England**	0-0 Spain
ECH96	**England**	1-1 Germany
WCQ96	**England**	2-1 Poland
WCQ97 (W)	**England**	0-1 Italy
INT97 (W)	**England**	2-0 Mexico
INT97	**England**	2-0 Cameroon
ECQ99 (W)	**England**	3-1 Poland
ECQ99 (2)	**England**	6-0 Luxembourg
INT00	**England**	2-0 Ukraine

McMenemy, Harry (1, 0)

FAC32	**Newcastle Utd**	2-1 Arsenal

McMichael, Alf (3, 0)

FAC52	**Newcastle Utd**	1-0 Arsenal
BC57	**N Ireland**	3-2 England
BC59	**N Ireland**	1-2 England

McMillan, John (1, 0)

BC55	**Scotland**	2-7 England

McMordie, Eric (2, 0)

BC70	**N Ireland**	1-3 England
BC72	**N Ireland**	1-0 England

McMullan, Jimmy (4, 0)

BC24 (C)	**Scotland**	1-1 England
FAC26 (C)	**Man City**	0-1 Bolton
BC28 (C)	**Scotland**	5-1 England
FAC33	**Man City**	0-3 Everton

McNab, Alex (1, 0)

FAC37	**Sunderland**	3-1 PNE

McNab, Bob (6, 0)

FLC68	**Arsenal**	0-1 Leeds
INT68	**England**	1-1 Bulgaria
INT69	**England**	1-1 Romania
FLC69	**Arsenal**	1-3 Swindon
FAC71	**Arsenal**	2-1 Liverpool
FAC72	**Arsenal**	0-1 Leeds

McNab, Colin (1, 0)

BC32	**Scotland**	0-3 England

McNab, Neil (4, 0)

FMC86	**Man City**	4-5 Chelsea
LDC90	**Tranmere**	2-1 Bristol R
PPO90	**Tranmere**	0-2 Notts C
PPO91 (W)	**Tranmere**	1-0 Bolton

McNally, Brendan (1, 0)

FAC59	**Luton**	1-2 Nottingham F

McNaught, Ken (2, 0)

FLC77	**Everton**	0-0 Aston V
CS81	**Aston Villa**	2-2 Spurs

McNeil, Mick (4, 0)

INT60	**England**	4-2 Spain
BC60	**England**	5-1 Wales
BC61	**England**	9-3 Scotland
INT61	**England**	8-0 Mexico

McNeill, Billy (3, 0)

BC61	**Scotland**	3-9 England

BC65 (C)	**Scotland**	2-2 England
BC69	**Scotland**	1-4 England
As Manager		
FMC86	**Man City**	4-5 Chelsea

McParland, Peter (4, 2)

BC55	**N Ireland**	0-3 England
FAC57 (2)	**Aston Villa**	2-1 Man Utd
BC57	**N Ireland**	3-2 England
BC59	**N Ireland**	1-2 England

McPherson, Archie (1, 0)

FAC36	**Sheffield Utd**	0-1 Arsenal

McQueen, Gordon (9, 2)

CS74	**Leeds**	1-1 Liverpool
BC75	**Scotland**	1-5 England
BC77 (1)	**Scotland**	2-1 England
FAC79 (1)	**Man Utd**	2-3 Arsenal
BC79	**Scotland**	1-3 England
MC83	**Man Utd**	1-2 Liverpool
FAC83	**Man Utd**	2-2 Brighton
FAC83	**Man Utd**	4-0 Brighton
CS83	**Man Utd**	2-0 Liverpool

McStay, Paul (2, 2)

SI80 (2)	**Scotland**	5-4 England
RC88	**Scotland**	0-1 England

Meadows, Jimmy (2, 0)

BC55	**England**	7-2 Scotland
FAC55	**Man City**	1-3 Newcastle Utd

Medley, Les (1, 0)

INT51	**England**	2-2 Austria

Medwin, Terry (4, 0)

BC56	**Wales**	1-3 England
BC60	**Wales**	1-5 England
FAC62	**Spurs**	3-1 Burnley
BC62	**Wales**	0-4 England

Megson, Don (1, 0)

FAC66 (C)	**Sheffield W**	2-3 Everton

Meiklejohn, David (1, 0)

BC30	**Scotland**	2-5 England

Melchiot, Mario (2, 1)

FAC00	**Chelsea**	1-0 Aston V
CS00 (1)	**Chelsea**	2-0 Man Utd

Melia, Jimmy (1, 0)

BC63	**England**	1-2 Scotland
As Manager		
FAC83	**Brighton**	2-2 Man Utd
FAC83	**Brighton**	0-4 Man Utd

Mellor, Peter (1, 0)

FAC75	**Fulham**	0-2 West Ham

Melrose, Jim (1, 0)

FMC87	**Charlton**	0-1 Blackburn

Mendham, Peter (2, 1)

MC85	**Norwich**	1-0 Sunderland
FAV94 (1)	**Diss**	2-1 Taunton

Mercer, Billy (1, 0)

FAC28	**Huddersfield**	1-3 Blackburn

Mercer, Dave (1, 0)

FAC25	**Sheffield Utd**	1-0 Cardiff

Mercer, Joe (10, 1)

WI41	**England** 2-0	Scotland
WI42	**England** 0-0	Scotland
WI43	**England** 5-3	Wales
WI44 (1)	**England** 6-2	Scotland
WI44 (C)	**England** 6-2	Scotland
VI45 (C)	**England** 2-2	France
VI46 (C)	**England** 2-0	Belgium
IT46 (C)	**Army PT Corps** 5-3	FA
FAC50 (C)	**Arsenal** 2-0	Liverpool
FAC52 (C)	**Arsenal** 0-1	Newcastle Utd
As Manager		
FAC69	**Man City** 1-0	Leicester
FLC70	**Man City** 2-1	WBA
BC74	**England** 1-0	N Ireland
INT74	**England** 2-2	Argentina

Merrick, Gil (9, 0)

CHA44	**Met Police** 2-5	Combined Services
IT46	**Army PT Corps** 5-3	FA
INT51	**England** 2-2	Austria
BC52	**England** 5-2	Wales
INT52	**England** 5-0	Belgium
BC53	**England** 2-2	Scotland
NIN53	**England** 4-4	FIFA
INT53	**England** 3-6	Hungary
FAC56	**Birmingham** 1-3	Man City

Merson, Paul (25, 3)

WIT88 (1, W)	**Arsenal** 4-0	Spurs
WIT88 (W)	**Arsenal** 3-0	Bayern Munich
MT89	**Arsenal** 1-0	Porto
MT89	**Arsenal** 1-0	Liverpool
CS89	**Arsenal** 0-1	Liverpool
MT90 (W)	**Arsenal** 2-0	Aston V
MT90 (W)	**Arsenal** 0-1	Sampdoria
FAC91	**Arsenal** 1-3	Spurs
CS91	**Arsenal** 0-0	Spurs
INT91 (S)	**England** 0-1	Germany
INT92 (S)	**England** 1-1	Brazil
WCQ92 (S)	**England** 1-1	Norway
FAC93	**Arsenal** 1-0	Spurs
CCC93 (1)	**Arsenal** 2-1	Sheffield W
WCQ93 (S)	**England** 2-2	Netherlands
FAC93	**Arsenal** 1-1	Sheffield W
FAC93	**Arsenal** 2-1	Sheffield W
CS93	**Arsenal** 1-1	Man Utd
INT94	**England** 5-0	Greece
WCQ97 (S)	**England** 0-1	Italy
CCC98	**Middlesbrough** 0-2	Chelsea
INT98 (S)	**England** 3-0	Portugal
INT98 (1, W)	**England** 2-0	Czech Rep
FAC00	**Aston Villa** 0-0	Bolton
FAC00	**Aston Villa** 0-1	Chelsea

Metcalfe, Vic (1, 0)

INT51	**England** 2-1	Argentina

Micklewhite, Gary (3, 0)

FAC82 (S)	**QPR** 1-1	Spurs
FAC82 (W)	**QPR** 0-1	Spurs
AIC93	**Derby** 1-3	Cremonese

Mikhailov, Boris (1, 0)

INT96 (C, W)	**Bulgaria** 0-1	England

Miklosko, Ludek (1, 0)

INT90	**Czechoslovakia** 2-4	England

Milburn, Jackie (5, 5)

BC49 (1)	**England** 1-3	Scotland
FAC51 (2)	**Newcastle Utd** 2-0	Blackpool
INT51 (1)	**England** 2-1	Argentina
FAC52	**Newcastle Utd** 1-0	Arsenal
FAC55 (1)	**Newcastle Utd** 3-1	Man City

Millard, Len (1, 0)

FAC54 (C)	**WBA** 3-2	PNE

Miller, Brian (1, 0)

FAC62	**Burnley** 1-3	Spurs
As Manager		
SVT88	**Burnley** 0-2	Wolves

Miller, Ian (2, 0)

FMC87	**Blackburn** 1-0	Charlton
LCT88	**Blackburn** 0-0	Aston V

Miller, John (1, 0)

BC34	**Scotland** 0-3	England

Miller, Johnny (1, 0)

FLC75	**Norwich** 0-1	Aston V

Miller, Paul (8, 0)

FAC81	**Spurs** 1-1	Man City
FAC81	**Spurs** 3-2	Man City
CS81	**Spurs** 2-2	Aston V
FLC82	**Spurs** 1-3	Liverpool
FAC82	**Spurs** 1-1	QPR
FAC82	**Spurs** 1-0	QPR
CS82	**Spurs** 0-1	Liverpool
FMC87	**Charlton** 0-1	Blackburn

Miller, Willie (1, 0)

BC47	**Scotland** 1-1	England

Miller, Willie (4, 0)

BC81	**Scotland** 1-0	England
BC83	**Scotland** 0-2	England
RC86	**Scotland** 1-0	England
RC88	**Scotland** 0-1	England

Millership, Walter (1, 0)

FAC35	**Sheffield W** 4-2	WBA

Milligan, Mike (3, 0)

LC90 (C)	**Oldham** 0-1	Nottingham F
ZC91	**Everton** 1-4	Crystal P
FAC94 (C)	**Oldham** 1-1	Man Utd

Millington, Tony (3, 0)

BC62	**Wales** 0-4	England
BC64	**Wales** 1-2	England
ECQ66	**Wales** 1-5	England

Mills, Mick (15, 0)

INT72	**England** 1-1	Yugoslavia
BC76	**England** 4-0	N Ireland
WCQ76 (S)	**England** 2-1	Finland
BC77	**England** 0-1	Wales
BC77	**England** 1-2	Scotland
INT78	**England** 1-1	Brazil
FAC78 (C)	**Ipswich** 1-0	Arsenal
BC78	**England** 1-0	N Ireland

INT78	**England**	4-1 Hungary
CS78 (C)	**Ipswich**	0-5 Nottingham F
ECQ79	**England**	4-0 N Ireland
BC79	**England**	3-1 Scotland
ECQ79	**England**	1-0 Denmark
WCQ80 (C)	**England**	2-1 Switzerland
WCQ81	**England**	1-0 Hungary

Milne, Gordon (5, 0)

INT63	**England**	1-1 Brazil
CEN63	**England**	2-1 FIFA
BC63	**England**	8-3 N Ireland
INT64	**England**	2-1 Uruguay
INT64	**England**	2-2 Belgium

Milne, Jimmy (1, 0)

FAC37	**Preston**	1-3 Sunderland

As Manager

FAC64	**PNE**	2-3 West Ham

Milne, John (1, 0)

BC38	**Scotland**	1-0 England

Milne, Ralph (1, 0)

FMC87	**Charlton**	0-1 Blackburn

Milne, Victor (1, 0)

FAC24	**Aston Villa**	0-2 Newcastle Utd

Milosevic, Savo (1, 1)

CCC96 (1)	**Aston Villa**	3-0 Leeds

Milton, Arthur (1, 0)

INT51	**England**	2-2 Austria

Milton, Ernest (1, 0)

FAC25	**Sheffield Utd**	1-0 Cardiff

Mimms, Bobby (6, 0)

FAC86	**Everton**	1-3 Liverpool
CS86	**Everton**	1-1 Liverpool
CS87	**Everton**	1-0 Coventry
WIT88	**Spurs**	0-4 Arsenal
WIT88	**Spurs**	1-2 AC Milan
PPO92	**Blackburn**	1-0 Leicester

Minto, Scott (3, 0)

YI90	**England**	0-0 Denmark
U19I91	**England**	1-1 Spain
FAC97	**Chelsea**	2-0 Middlesbrough

Mitchell, Bobby (3, 1)

FAC51	**Newcastle Utd**	2-0 Blackpool
FAC52	**Newcastle Utd**	1-0 Arsenal
FAC55 (1)	**Newcastle Utd**	3-1 Man City

Mitchell, John (1, 0)

FAC75	**Fulham**	0-2 West Ham

Mitten, Charlie (3, 0)

LSC44	**Chelsea**	1-3 Charlton
FAC48	**Man Utd**	4-2 Blackpool
EFC55	**London**	3-2 Frankfurt

Mjallby, Johan (1, 0)

ECQ99 (W)	**Sweden**	0-0 England

Moir, Willie (1, 1)

FAC53 (C, 1)	**Bolton**	3-4 Blackpool

Molby, Jan (10, 0)

ECQ83 (S)	**Denmark**	1-0 England
FAC86	**Liverpool**	3-1 Everton

CS86	**Liverpool**	1-1 Everton
LC87	**Liverpool**	1-2 Arsenal
FAC88 (S)	**Liverpool**	0-1 Wimbledon
INT88	**Denmark**	0-1 England
MT89 (S)	**Liverpool**	2-0 Dynamo Kiev
MT89	**Liverpool**	0-1 Arsenal
FAC92	**Liverpool**	2-0 Sunderland
PPO97	**Swansea**	0-1 Northampton

As Player-Manager

PPO97	**Swansea**	0-1 Northampton

Moncur, Bobby (3, 0)

SI60	**Scotland**	3-5 England
BC71 (C)	**Scotland**	1-3 England
FAC74 (C)	**Newcastle Utd**	0-3 Liverpool

Monkou, Ken (1, 0)

ZC90	**Chelsea**	1-0 Middlesbrough

Montgomery, Jim (1, 0)

FAC73	**Sunderland**	1-0 Leeds

Mooney, Peter (1, 0)

FAC24	**Newcastle Utd**	2-0 Aston V

Moore, Billy (1, 0)

FAC23	**West Ham**	0-2 Bolton

Moore, Bobby (47, 0)

BC62	**England**	4-0 Wales
BC63	**England**	1-2 Scotland
INT63	**England**	1-1 Brazil
CEN63	**England**	2-1 FIFA
BC63	**England**	8-3 N Ireland
FAC64 (C)	**West Ham**	3-2 PNE
INT64 (C)	**England**	2-1 Uruguay
INT64 (C)	**England**	2-2 Belgium
BC65 (C)	**England**	2-2 Scotland
INT65 (C)	**England**	1-0 Hungary
ECW65 (C)	**West Ham**	2-0 TSV Munich
INT65 (C)	**England**	2-3 Austria
BC65 (C)	**England**	2-1 N Ireland
INT66 (C)	**England**	1-0 W Germany
WC66 (C)	**England**	0-0 Uruguay
WC66 (C)	**England**	2-0 Mexico
WC66 (C)	**England**	2-0 France
WC66 (C)	**England**	1-0 Argentina
WC66 (C)	**England**	2-1 Portugal
WC66 (C)	**England**	4-2 W Germany
INT66 (C)	**England**	0-0 Czechoslovakia
ECQ66 (C)	**England**	5-1 Wales
ECQ67 (C)	**England**	2-3 Scotland
INT67 (C)	**England**	2-0 Spain
ECQ67 (C)	**England**	2-0 N Ireland
INT67 (C)	**England**	2-2 U.S.S.R.
ECQ68 (C)	**England**	1-0 Spain
INT68 (C)	**England**	3-1 Sweden
INT68 (C)	**England**	1-1 Bulgaria
INT69 (C)	**England**	5-0 France
BC69 (C)	**England**	2-1 Wales
BC69 (C)	**England**	4-1 Scotland
INT69 (C)	**England**	1-0 Portugal
BC70 (C)	**England**	3-1 N Ireland
INT70 (C)	**England**	3-1 E Germany
ECQ71 (C)	**England**	3-0 Greece

ECQ71 (C)	**England** 5-0 Malta	
BC71 (C)	**England** 3-1 Scotland	
ECQ71 (C)	**England** 1-1 Switzerland	
ECQ72 (C)	**England** 1-3 W Germany	
INT72 (C)	**England** 1-1 Yugoslavia	
EEC73	**The Three** 2-0 The Six	
WCQ73 (C)	**England** 1-1 Wales	
BC73 (C)	**England** 3-0 Wales	
BC73 (C)	**England** 1-0 Scotland	
INT73 (C)	**England** 0-1 Italy	
FAC75	**Fulham** 0-2 West Ham	

Moore, Graham (1, 0)
BC69   **Wales** 1-2 England

Moore, Kevin (1, 1)
ZC92 (1)   **Southampton** 2-3 Nottingham F

Moran, Kevin (7, 0)
MC83 (W)   **Man Utd** 1-2 Liverpool
FAC83   **Man Utd** 2-2 Brighton
FAC83   **Man Utd** 4-0 Brighton
CS83   **Man Utd** 2-0 Liverpool
FAC85 (D)   **Man Utd** 1-0 Everton
ECQ91 (C)   **Rep of Ireland** 1-1 England
PPO92 (C)   **Blackburn** 1-0 Leicester

Morgan, Lew (1, 0)
FAC39   **Portsmouth** 4-1 Wolves

Morgan, Nicky (1, 0)
CS80 (S)   **West Ham** 0-1 Liverpool

Morgan, Roger (1, 1)
FLC67 (1)   **QPR** 3-2 WBA

Morgan, Sammy (1, 0)
BC74   **N Ireland** 0-1 England

Morgan, Willie (1, 0)
BC73   **Scotland** 0-1 England

Morley, Tony (3, 0)
CS81   **Aston Villa** 2-2 Spurs
WCQ81 (S)   **England** 1-0 Hungary
BC82 (W)   **England** 4-0 N Ireland

Morrall, George (1, 0)
FAC31   **Birmingham** 1-2 WBA

Morris, Billy (1, 0)
FAC39   **Wolves** 1-4 Portsmouth

Morris, Billy (1, 0)
FAC47   **Burnley** 0-1 Charlton

Morris, David (1, 0)
BC24   **Scotland** 1-1 England

Morris, Jody (3, 0)
CS97 (W)   **Chelsea** 1-1 Man Utd
FAC00 (S)   **Chelsea** 1-0 Aston V
CS00 (S)   **Chelsea** 2-0 Man Utd

Morris, Johnny (1, 0)
FAC48   **Man Utd** 4-2 Blackpool

Morris, Peter (1, 0)
FLC75   **Norwich** 0-1 Aston V

Morrison, Angus (1, 1)
FAC54 (1)   **PNE** 2-3 WBA

Morrissey, Johnny (1, 0)
FAC68   **Everton** 0-1 WBA

Morrow, Steve (2, 1)
FAC93 (S)   **Arsenal** 1-0 Spurs
CCC93 (1)   **Arsenal** 2-1 Sheffield W

Mort, Tommy (1, 0)
FAC24   **Aston Villa** 0-2 Newcastle Utd

Mortensen, Stan (10, 9)
WI43 (S)   **Wales** 3-8 England
CHA45 (2)   **Combined Services** 3-1 Nat Police
FAC48 (1)   **Blackpool** 2-4 Man Utd
BC49   **England** 1-3 Scotland
BC51   **England** 2-3 Scotland
FAC51   **Blackpool** 0-2 Newcastle Utd
INT51 (1)   **England** 2-1 Argentina
FAC53 (3)   **Blackpool** 4-3 Bolton
NIN53 (1)   **England** 4-4 FIFA
INT53 (1)   **England** 3-6 Hungary

Mortimer, Dennis (2, 0)
FLC77   **Aston Villa** 0-0 Everton
CS81 (C, W)   **Aston Villa** 2-2 Spurs

Morton, Alan (4, 0)
BC24   **Scotland** 1-1 England
BC28   **Scotland** 5-1 England
BC30   **Scotland** 2-5 England
BC32   **Scotland** 0-3 England

Morton, Bob (1, 0)
FAC59   **Luton** 1-2 Nottingham F

Moseley, Graham (2, 0)
FAC83   **Brighton** 2-2 Man Utd
FAC83   **Brighton** 0-4 Man Utd

Moses, Remi (2, 0)
MC83   **Man Utd** 1-2 Liverpool
CS85 (S)   **Man Utd** 0-2 Everton
LCT88 (S)   **Man Utd** 1-2 Sheffield W

Moss, Frank (2, 0)
BC24 (C)   **England** 1-1 Scotland
FAC24 (C)   **Aston Villa** 0-2 Newcastle Utd

Moss, Frank (2, 0)
FAC32   **Arsenal** 1-2 Newcastle Utd
BC34   **England** 3-0 Scotland

Mountfield, Derek (9, 0)
MC84   **Everton** 0-0 Liverpool
FAC84   **Everton** 2-0 Watford
CS84   **Everton** 1-0 Liverpool
FAC85   **Everton** 0-1 Man Utd
CS85   **Everton** 2-0 Man Utd
FAC86   **Everton** 1-3 Liverpool
MT90   **Aston Villa** 0-2 Arsenal
MT90   **Aston Villa** 0-1 Real Sociedad
AWS95 (W)   **Carlisle** 0-1 Birmingham

Mountford, Reg (1, 0)
FAC38   **Huddersfield** 0-1 PNE

Mudie, Jackie (3, 0)
FAC51   **Blackpool** 0-2 Newcastle Utd
FAC53   **Blackpool** 4-3 Bolton
BC57   **Scotland** 1-2 England

Muhren, Arnold (6, 1)
INT82   **Netherlands** 0-2 England

MC83	**Man Utd** 1-2 Liverpool	
FAC83	**Man Utd** 2-2 Brighton	
FAC83 (1)	**Man Utd** 4-0 Brighton	
CS83 (W)	**Man Utd** 2-0 Liverpool	
INT88	**Netherlands** 2-2 England	

Mullen, Jimmy (4, 2)
VI46	**England** 2-0 Belgium
BC47	**England** 1-1 Scotland
FAC49	**Wolves** 3-1 Leicester
NIN53 (2)	**England** 4-4 FIFA

Mullery, Alan (16, 0)
FAC67	**Spurs** 2-1 Chelsea
INT67	**England** 2-0 Spain
ECQ67	**England** 2-0 N Ireland
INT67	**England** 2-2 U.S.S.R.
ECQ68	**England** 1-0 Spain
INT68	**England** 3-1 Sweden
INT68	**England** 1-1 Bulgaria
INT69	**England** 5-0 France
BC69	**England** 4-1 Scotland
INT69	**England** 1-0 Portugal
INT70 (S)	**England** 0-0 Netherlands
BC70	**England** 3-1 N Ireland
INT70	**England** 3-1 E Germany
FLC71 (C)	**Spurs** 2-0 Aston V
ECQ71	**England** 3-0 Greece
FAC75 (C)	**Fulham** 0-2 West Ham

Mulligan, Paddy (2, 0)
FLC72 (W)	**Chelsea** 1-2 Stoke
INT76	**Rep of Ireland** 1-1 England

Munro, Alex (1, 0)
FAC48	**Blackpool** 2-4 Man Utd

Munro, Frank (3, 0)
BC71 (S)	**Scotland** 1-3 England
FLC74	**Wolves** 2-1 Man City
BC75	**Scotland** 1-5 England

Murdoch, Bobby (1, 0)
BC69	**Scotland** 1-4 England

Murphy, Jimmy (1, 0)
FAC35	**WBA** 2-4 Sheffield W

As Manager
BC60	**Wales** 1-5 England
BC62	**Wales** 0-4 England

Murphy, Joe (1, 0)
WLC00	**Tranmere** 1-2 Leicester

Murphy, Peter (1, 0)
FAC56	**Birmingham** 1-3 Man City

Murray, Jimmy (1, 0)
FAC60	**Wolves** 3-0 Blackburn

Musson, Chick (1, 0)
FAC46	**Derby** 4-1 Charlton

Mustoe, Robbie (3, 0)
CCC97	**Middlesbrough** 1-1 Leicester
FAC97 (W)	**Middlesbrough** 0-2 Chelsea
CCC98	**Middlesbrough** 0-2 Chelsea

Mutch, George (2, 1)
BC38	**Scotland** 1-0 England
FAC38 (1)	**PNE** 1-0 Huddersfield

Myerscough, Bill (1, 0)
FAC57	**Aston Villa** 2-1 Man Utd

Napier, Charlie (1, 0)
BC32	**Scotland** 0-3 England

Narey, David (2, 0)
BC81 (S)	**Scotland** 1-0 England
BC83	**Scotland** 0-2 England

Nattrass, Irving (1, 0)
FLC76	**Newcastle Utd** 1-2 Man City

Nayim (4, 0)
FAC91 (S)	**Spurs** 3-1 Arsenal
FAC91 (S)	**Spurs** 2-1 Nottingham F
CS91	**Spurs** 0-0 Arsenal
FAC93	**Spurs** 0-1 Arsenal

Naylor, Jimmy (1, 0)
FAC30	**Huddersfield** 0-2 Arsenal

Neal, Phil (36, 4)
CS76	**Liverpool** 1-0 Southampton
FAC77	**Liverpool** 1-2 Man Utd
BC77	**England** 0-1 Wales
BC77	**England** 1-2 Scotland
CS77	**Liverpool** 0-0 Man Utd
INT77	**England** 0-0 Switzerland
WCQ77	**England** 2-0 Italy
FLC78	**Liverpool** 0-0 Nottingham F
EC78	**Liverpool** 1-0 Bruges
BC78 (1)	**England** 1-0 N Ireland
INT78 (1)	**England** 4-1 Hungary
ECQ79	**England** 4-0 N Ireland
BC79	**England** 3-1 Scotland
CS79	**Liverpool** 3-1 Arsenal
ECQ79	**England** 1-0 Denmark
INT80 (W)	**England** 3-1 Argentina
CS80	**Liverpool** 1-0 West Ham
WCQ80	**England** 2-1 Switzerland
FLC81	**Liverpool** 1-1 West Ham
INT81	**England** 1-2 Spain
INT81	**England** 0-1 Brazil
WCQ81	**England** 1-0 Hungary
FLC82	**Liverpool** 3-1 Spurs
INT82	**England** 2-0 Netherlands
CS82	**Liverpool** 1-0 Spurs
ECQ82 (1)	**England** 9-0 Luxembourg
BC83 (1)	**England** 2-1 Wales
MC83	**Liverpool** 2-1 Man Utd
ECQ83	**England** 0-0 Greece
ECQ83	**England** 2-0 Hungary
BC83	**England** 2-0 Scotland
CS83	**Liverpool** 0-2 Man Utd
ECQ83	**England** 0-1 Denmark
MC84	**Liverpool** 0-0 Everton
CS84 (C)	**Liverpool** 0-1 Everton
FRT86 (C)	**Bolton** 0-3 Bristol C

As Player-Manager
FRT86	**Bolton** 0-3 Bristol C

As Manager
SVT89	**Bolton** 4-1 Torquay
PPO91	**Bolton** 0-1 Tranmere

Needham, David (3, 0)

CS78 (S)	**Nottingham F**	5-0 Ipswich
FLC79	**Nottingham F**	3-2 Southampton
FLC80	**Nottingham F**	0-1 Wolves

Neighbour, Jimmy (2, 0)

FLC71	**Spurs**	2-0 Aston V
FLC81	**West Ham**	1-1 Liverpool

Neill, Terry (6, 1)

BC61	**N Ireland**	1-1 England
BC63	**N Ireland**	3-8 England
BC65 (C)	**N Ireland**	1-2 England
ECQ67 (C)	**N Ireland**	0-2 England
BC70 (C)	**N Ireland**	1-3 England
BC72 (1)	**N Ireland**	1-0 England

As Player-Manager

BC72	**N Ireland**	1-0 England

As Manager

BC74	**N Ireland**	0-1 England
FAC78	**Arsenal**	0-1 Ipswich
FAC79	**Arsenal**	3-2 Man Utd
CS79	**Arsenal**	1-3 Liverpool
FAC80	**Arsenal**	0-1 West Ham

Neill, Warren (3, 0)

SI78 (S)	**England**	3-3 France
FAC82	**QPR**	0-1 Spurs
MC86	**QPR**	0-3 Oxford

Nelson, Jimmy (4, 0)

FAC25	**Cardiff**	0-1 Sheffield Utd
FAC27	**Cardiff**	1-0 Arsenal
BC28	**Scotland**	5-1 England
FAC32 (C)	**Newcastle Utd**	2-1 Arsenal

Nelson, Sammy (10, 0)

BC70 (S)	**N Ireland**	1-3 England
BC72	**N Ireland**	1-0 England
BC74 (W)	**N Ireland**	0-1 England
BC76 (W)	**N Ireland**	0-4 England
FAC78	**Arsenal**	0-1 Ipswich
ECQ79	**N Ireland**	0-4 England
FAC79	**Arsenal**	3-2 Man Utd
CS79 (W)	**Arsenal**	1-3 Liverpool
FAC80 (S)	**Arsenal**	0-1 West Ham
BC82	**N Ireland**	0-4 England

Neville, Gary (30, 0)

FAC95	**Man Utd**	0-1 Everton
UC95	**England**	2-1 Japan
UC95	**England**	1-3 Brazil
INT95	**England**	0-0 Colombia
INT95	**England**	3-1 Switzerland
INT95	**England**	1-1 Portugal
INT96	**England**	1-0 Bulgaria
INT96	**England**	0-0 Croatia
FAC96 (S)	**Man Utd**	1-0 Liverpool
INT96	**England**	3-0 Hungary
ECH96	**England**	1-1 Switzerland
ECH96	**England**	2-0 Scotland
ECH96	**England**	4-1 Netherlands
ECH96	**England**	0-0 Spain
CS96 (S)	**Man Utd**	4-0 Newcastle Utd
WCQ96	**England**	2-1 Poland

WCQ97	**England**	0-1 Italy
WCQ97	**England**	2-0 Georgia
WCQ97	**England**	4-0 Moldova
INT98	**England**	0-2 Chile
INT98 (W)	**England**	3-0 Portugal
INT98	**England**	0-0 Saudi Arabia
CS98	**Man Utd**	0-3 Arsenal
ECQ98	**England**	0-0 Bulgaria
ECQ99	**England**	3-1 Poland
FAC99	**Man Utd**	2-0 Newcastle Utd
ECQ99 (S)	**England**	6-0 Luxembourg
INT00	**England**	1-1 Brazil
CS00	**Man Utd**	0-2 Chelsea
WCQ00 (W)	**England**	0-1 Germany

Neville, Phil (20, 0)

SI92	**England**	0-0 Netherlands
SI92	**England**	1-1 Italy
FAC96	**Man Utd**	1-0 Liverpool
CS96	**Man Utd**	4-0 Newcastle Utd
CS97	**Man Utd**	1-1 Chelsea
WCQ97	**England**	4-0 Moldova
INT97	**England**	2-0 Cameroon
INT98 (W)	**England**	0-2 Chile
INT98 (S)	**England**	3-0 Portugal
INT98 (S)	**England**	0-0 Saudi Arabia
CS98 (S)	**Man Utd**	0-3 Arsenal
ECQ99 (S)	**England**	3-1 Poland
FAC99	**Man Utd**	2-0 Newcastle Utd
ECQ99	**England**	0-0 Sweden
CS99	**Man Utd**	1-2 Arsenal
ECQ99 (S)	**England**	6-0 Luxembourg
ECQ99	**England**	0-1 Scotland
INT00 (S)	**England**	0-0 Argentina
INT00	**England**	1-1 Brazil
INT00 (W)	**England**	2-0 Ukraine

Nevin, Pat (6, 0)

FMC86	**Chelsea**	5-4 Man City
RC86 (S)	**Scotland**	1-2 England
LCEN87 (S)	**Football League**	3-0 Rest of World
SC89	**Everton**	3-4 Nottingham F
FAC89	**Everton**	2-3 Liverpool
ZC91 (S)	**Everton**	1-4 Crystal P

Newell, Mike (4, 2)

FRT85 (1)	**Wigan**	3-1 Brentford
ZC91	**Everton**	1-4 Crystal P
PPO92 (1)	**Blackburn**	1-0 Leicester
CS95	**Blackburn**	0-1 Everton

Newman, John (1, 0)

FAC56	**Birmingham**	1-3 Man City

Newsome, Jon (1, 0)

CS92 (W)	**Leeds**	4-3 Liverpool

Newton, Eddie (4, 1)

FAC94	**Chelsea**	2-0 Luton
FAC94	**Chelsea**	0-4 Man Utd
FAC97 (1)	**Chelsea**	2-0 Middlesbrough
CCC98	**Chelsea**	2-0 Middlesbrough

Newton, Henry (1, 0)

CS75	**Derby**	2-0 West Ham

Newton, Keith (9, 0)
INT66 (W)	**England** 1-0 W Germany
INT67	**England** 2-0 Spain
INT68	**England** 3-1 Sweden
INT68 (W)	**England** 1-1 Bulgaria
INT69	**England** 5-0 France
BC69	**England** 2-1 Wales
BC69	**England** 4-1 Scotland
INT70	**England** 0-0 Netherlands
BC70 (W)	**England** 3-1 N Ireland

Nibloe, Joe (2, 0)
| BC32 | **Scotland** 0-3 England |
| FAC35 | **Sheffield W** 4-2 WBA |

Nichol, Jimmy (2, 0)
| FAC29 | **Portsmouth** 0-2 Bolton |
| FAC34 | **Portsmouth** 1-2 Man City |

Nicholas, Charlie (3, 2)
BC83 (W)	**Scotland** 0-2 England
RC86 (W)	**Scotland** 1-2 England
LC87 (2)	**Arsenal** 2-1 Liverpool

Nicholas, Jack (2, 0)
| CHA43 | **Met Police** 3-4 RAF |
| FAC46 (C) | **Derby** 4-1 Charlton |

Nicholas, Peter (2, 0)
| BC81 | **Wales** 0-0 England |
| ZC90 (C) | **Chelsea** 1-0 Middlesbrough |

Nicholl, Chris (8, 0)
FLC75	**Aston Villa** 1-0 Norwich
BC76	**N Ireland** 0-4 England
FLC77 (C)	**Aston Villa** 0-0 Everton
BC78	**N Ireland** 0-1 England
ECQ79	**N Ireland** 0-4 England
FLC79	**Southampton** 2-3 Nottingham F
BC80	**N Ireland** 1-1 England
BC82	**N Ireland** 0-4 England

Nicholl, Jimmy (9, 0)
FAC77	**Man Utd** 2-1 Liverpool
CS77	**Man Utd** 0-0 Liverpool
BC78	**N Ireland** 0-1 England
ECQ79	**N Ireland** 0-4 England
FAC79	**Man Utd** 2-3 Arsenal
BC80	**N Ireland** 1-1 England
BC82	**N Ireland** 0-4 England
BC84	**N Ireland** 0-1 England
WCQ85	**N Ireland** 0-0 England

Nicholls, Johnny (1, 0)
| FAC54 | **WBA** 3-2 PNE |

Nicholson, Jimmy (4, 0)
BC61	**N Ireland** 1-1 England
BC65	**N Ireland** 1-2 England
ECQ67	**N Ireland** 0-2 England
BC70	**N Ireland** 1-3 England

Nicholson, Joe (1, 0)
| FAC25 | **Cardiff** 0-1 Sheffield Utd |

Nicol, Steve (11, 0)
CS84	**Liverpool** 0-1 Everton
RC86	**Scotland** 1-2 England
FAC86	**Liverpool** 3-1 Everton
LCT88 (C)	**Liverpool** 0-0 Newcastle Utd
FAC88	**Liverpool** 0-1 Wimbledon
RC88	**Scotland** 0-1 England
FAC89	**Liverpool** 3-2 Everton
MT89	**Liverpool** 2-0 Dynamo Kiev
MT89	**Liverpool** 0-1 Arsenal
CS89	**Liverpool** 1-0 Arsenal
FAC92	**Liverpool** 2-0 Sunderland

Nielsen, Allan (1, 1)
| WLC99 (1) | **Spurs** 1-0 Leicester |

Nielsen, Kent (3, 0)
INT88	**Denmark** 0-1 England
INT90	**Denmark** 0-1 England
MT90 (W)	**Aston Villa** 0-2 Arsenal

Nilsen, Roger (3, 0)
WCQ92	**Norway** 1-1 England
INT94 (W)	**Norway** 0-0 England
PPO97	**Sheffield Utd** 0-1 Crystal P

Nilsson, Roland (7, 0)
WCQ88 (W)	**Sweden** 0-0 England
RLC91	**Sheffield W** 1-0 Man Utd
FAC93	**Sheffield W** 2-1 Sheffield Utd
CCC93	**Sheffield W** 1-2 Arsenal
FAC93	**Sheffield W** 1-1 Arsenal
FAC93 (W)	**Sheffield W** 1-2 Arsenal
ECQ99	**Sweden** 0-0 England

Nish, David (3, 0)
FAC69 (C)	**Leicester** 0-1 Man City
BC74	**England** 1-0 N Ireland
CS75	**Derby** 2-0 West Ham

Nixon, Eric (8, 0)
FMC86	**Man City** 4-5 Chelsea
LCT88	**Tranmere** 1-0 Wimbledon
LCT88	**Tranmere** 2-0 Newcastle Utd
LCT88	**Tranmere** 2-2 Nottingham F
LDC90	**Tranmere** 2-1 Bristol R
PPO90	**Tranmere** 0-2 Notts C
LDC91 (C)	**Tranmere** 2-3 Birmingham
PPO91 (C)	**Tranmere** 1-0 Bolton

Noble, Peter (1, 0)
| FLC69 | **Swindon** 3-1 Arsenal |

Norman, Maurice (8, 0)
FAC61	**Spurs** 2-0 Leicester
FAC62	**Spurs** 3-1 Burnley
BC63	**England** 1-2 Scotland
INT63	**England** 1-1 Brazil
CEN63	**England** 2-1 F.I.F.A.
BC63	**England** 8-3 N Ireland
INT64	**England** 2-1 Uruguay
INT64	**England** 2-2 Belgium

Norman, Richie (2, 0)
| FAC61 | **Leicester** 0-2 Spurs |
| FAC63 | **Leicester** 1-3 Man Utd |

Norman, Tony (2, 0)
| PPO90 | **Sunderland** 0-1 Swindon |
| FAC92 | **Sunderland** 0-2 Liverpool |

Nurse, Mel (3, 0)
| SI53 | **Wales** 3-3 England |

423

BC60   **Wales** 1-5 England
BC62   **Wales** 0-4 England

Nuttall, Harry (3, 0)
FAC23   **Bolton** 2-0 West Ham
FAC26   **Bolton** 1-0 Man City
FAC29   **Bolton** 2-0 Portsmouth

Oakes, Alan (3, 0)
FAC69   **Man City** 1-0 Leicester
FLC70   **Man City** 2-1 WBA
FLC76   **Man City** 2-1 Newcastle Utd

Oakes, John (6, 0)
CHA42   **RAF** 6-3 Met Police
LSC43   **Charlton** 1-7 Arsenal
CHA43   **RAF** 4-3 Met Police
LSC44   **Charlton** 3-1 Chelsea
CHA44   **Combined Services** 5-2 Met Police
FAC46   **Charlton** 1-4 Derby

Oakes, Scott (1, 0)
FAC94   **Luton** 0-2 Chelsea

Oakes, Stefan (1, 0)
WLC00 (W)   **Leicester** 2-1 Tranmere

O'Brien, Fran (1, 0)
ECQ80   **Rep of Ireland** 0-2 England

O'Callaghan, Kevin (1, 0)
INT85 (S)   **Rep of Ireland** 1-2 England

O'Doherty, Tony (1, 0)
BC70   **N Ireland** 1-3 England

O'Donnell, Frank (2, 1)
FAC37 (1)   **PNE** 1-3 Sunderland
BC38   **Scotland** 1-0 England

O'Donnell, Hugh (3, 0)
FAC37   **PNE** 1-3 Sunderland
FAC38   **PNE** 1-0 Huddersfield
FLWC41   **PNE** 1-1 Arsenal

O'Dowd, Peter (1, 0)
BC32   **England** 3-0 Scotland

O'Grady, Mike (1, 1)
INT69 (1)   **England** 5-0 France

Ogrizovic, Steve (3, 0)
FAC87   **Coventry** 3-2 Spurs
CS87   **Coventry** 0-1 Everton
LCEN87 (S)   **Football League** 3-0 Rest of World

O'Hare, John (1, 0)
FLC78 (S)   **Nottingham F** 0-0 Liverpool

O'Kane, John (1, 0)
FAC00 (S)   **Bolton** 0-0 Aston V

O'Kane, Liam (2, 0)
BC70   **N Ireland** 1-3 England
BC74   **N Ireland** 0-1 England

O'Keefe, Eamonn (1, 0)
INT85 (W)   **Rep of Ireland** 1-2 England

O'Keefe, Vince (1, 0)
FMC87   **Blackburn** 1-0 Charlton

O'Leary, David (17, 0)
INT76   **Rep of Ireland** 1-1 England
FAC78   **Arsenal** 0-1 Ipswich
FAC79   **Arsenal** 3-2 Man Utd

CS79   **Arsenal** 1-3 Liverpool
ECQ80 (W)   **Rep of Ireland** 0-2 England
FAC80   **Arsenal** 0-1 West Ham
INT85 (S)   **Rep of Ireland** 1-2 England
LC87   **Arsenal** 2-1 Liverpool
WIT88 (W)   **Arsenal** 4-0 Spurs
MT89   **Arsenal** 1-0 Porto
MT89   **Arsenal** 1-0 Liverpool
CS89   **Arsenal** 0-1 Liverpool
ECQ91   **Rep of Ireland** 1-1 England
CS91   **Arsenal** 0-0 Spurs
CCC93   **Arsenal** 2-1 Sheffield W
FAC93 (S)   **Arsenal** 1-1 Sheffield W
FAC93 (S)   **Arsenal** 2-1 Sheffield W

O'Leary, Pierce (1, 0)
ECQ80 (S)   **Rep of Ireland** 0-2 England

Olsen, Jesper (6, 0)
ECQ83   **Denmark** 1-0 England
FAC85   **Man Utd** 1-0 Everton
CS85   **Man Utd** 0-2 Everton
LCT88   **Man Utd** 2-0 Luton
LCT88   **Man Utd** 1-0 Everton
LCT88 (W)   **Man Utd** 1-2 Sheffield W

O'Neill, John (3, 0)
BC80   **N Ireland** 1-1 England
BC82   **N Ireland** 0-4 England
WCQ85   **N Ireland** 0-0 England

O'Neill, Martin (9, 2)
BC74 (S)   **N Ireland** 0-1 England
FLC78   **Nottingham F** 0-0 Liverpool
BC78   **N Ireland** 0-1 England
CS78 (2, W)   **Nottingham F** 5-0 Ipswich
ECQ79   **N Ireland** 0-4 England
FLC79   **Nottingham F** 3-2 Southampton
FLC80   **Nottingham F** 0-1 Wolves
BC82 (C, W)   **N Ireland** 0-4 England
BC84 (C)   **N Ireland** 0-1 England
As Manager
FAT91   **Wycombe** 2-1 Kidderminster
FAT93   **Wycombe** 4-1 Runcorn
PPO94   **Wycombe** 4-2 PNE
PPO96   **Leicester** 2-1 Crystal P
CCC97   **Leicester** 1-1 Middlesbrough
WLC99   **Leicester** 0-1 Spurs
WLC00   **Leicester** 2-1 Tranmere

O'Reilly, Gary (3, 1)
CS82 (W)   **Spurs** 0-1 Liverpool
FAC90 (1)   **Crystal P** 3-3 Man Utd
FAC90   **Crystal P** 0-1 Man Utd

Ormond, Willie (1, 0)
BC59   **Scotland** 0-1 England
As Manager
BC73   **Scotland** 0-1 England
BC75   **Scotland** 1-5 England

Osborne, John (2, 0)
FAC68   **WBA** 1-0 Everton
FLC70   **WBA** 1-2 Man City

Osborne, Roger (1, 1)
FAC78 (1, W)   **Ipswich** 1-0 Arsenal

Osgood, Peter (5, 1)
FAC70	**Chelsea**	2-2 Leeds
FLC72 (1)	**Chelsea**	1-2 Stoke
INT73	**England**	0-1 Italy
FAC76	**Southampton**	1-0 Man Utd
CS76	**Southampton**	0-1 Liverpool

Osman, Russell (4, 0)
CS78	**Ipswich**	0-5 Nottingham F
INT81	**England**	1-2 Spain
WCQ81	**England**	0-0 Romania
ECQ83	**England**	0-1 Denmark

Overmars, Marc (9, 3)
WCQ93	**Netherlands**	2-2 England
FAC98 (1)	**Arsenal**	2-0 Newcastle Utd
CS98 (1)	**Arsenal**	3-0 Man Utd
EC98	**Arsenal**	2-1 Panathinaikos
EC98	**Arsenal**	1-1 Dynamo Kiev
EC98	**Arsenal**	0-1 Lens
EC99 (W)	**Arsenal**	3-1 AIK Stockholm
EC99 (1)	**Arsenal**	2-4 Barcelona
EC99	**Arsenal**	0-1 Fiorentina

Owen, Michael
(9, 4)
SI95 (1)	**England**	1-0 Brazil
SI95 (1)	**England**	2-4 W Germany
INT98	**England**	0-2 Chile
INT98 (S)	**England**	3-0 Portugal
ECQ98	**England**	0-0 Bulgaria
INT99	**England**	0-2 France
ECQ99 (S, 1)	**England**	6-0 Luxembourg
ECQ99	**England**	0-1 Scotland
INT00 (1)	**England**	1-1 Brazil
WCQ00	**England**	0-1 Germany

Owen, Syd (1, 0)
FAC59 (C)	**Luton**	1-2 Nottingham F

Owers, Gary (3, 0)
LCT88	**Sunderland**	0-0 Wigan
PPO90	**Sunderland**	0-1 Swindon
FAC92	**Sunderland**	0-2 Liverpool

Paatelainen, Mixu (2, 1)
CCC95	**Bolton**	1-2 Liverpool
PPO95 (1)	**Bolton**	4-3 Reading

Pacey, Dave (1, 1)
FAC59 (1)	**Luton**	1-2 Nottingham F

Paddon, Graham (3, 0)
FLC73	**Norwich**	0-1 Spurs
FAC75	**West Ham**	2-0 Fulham
CS75	**West Ham**	0-2 Derby

Page, Malcolm (3, 0)
WCQ73 (S)	**Wales**	1-1 England
BC73 (W)	**Wales**	0-3 England
BC75	**Wales**	2-2 England

Paine, Terry (7, 4)
CEN63 (1)	**England**	2-1 FIFA
BC63 (3)	**England**	8-3 N Ireland
INT64	**England**	2-1 Uruguay
INT65	**England**	1-0 Hungary
INT65	**England**	2-3 Austria

INT66	**England**	2-0 Yugoslavia
WC66	**England**	2-0 Mexico

Palethorpe, Jack (1, 1)
FAC35 (1)	**Sheffield W**	4-2 WBA

Pallister, Gary (23, 0)
FAC90 (W)	**Man Utd**	3-3 Crystal P
FAC90	**Man Utd**	1-0 Crystal P
CS90	**Man Utd**	1-1 Liverpool
INT91 (S)	**England**	2-0 Cameroon
RLC91	**Man Utd**	0-1 Sheffield W
INT91	**England**	0-1 Germany
RLC92	**Man Utd**	1-0 Nottingham F
CS93	**Man Utd**	1-1 Arsenal
WCQ93	**England**	3-0 Poland
INT94	**England**	1-0 Denmark
CCC94	**Man Utd**	1-3 Aston V
FAC94	**Man Utd**	1-1 Oldham
FAC94	**Man Utd**	4-0 Chelsea
CS94	**Man Utd**	2-0 Blackburn
INT94	**England**	2-0 USA
INT94	**England**	1-1 Romania
INT95	**England**	0-0 Uruguay
FAC95	**Man Utd**	0-1 Everton
INT95	**England**	3-1 Switzerland
FAC96	**Man Utd**	1-0 Liverpool
CS96	**Man Utd**	4-0 Newcastle Utd
WCQ96 (S)	**England**	2-1 Poland
CS97	**Man Utd**	1-1 Chelsea

Palmer, Carlton (10, 1)
INT92	**England**	1-1 Brazil
WCQ92 (S)	**England**	1-1 Norway
WCQ92	**England**	4-0 Turkey
WCQ93 (1)	**England**	6-0 San Marino
FAC93	**Sheffield W**	2-1 Sheffield Utd
CCC93	**Sheffield W**	1-2 Arsenal
WCQ93	**England**	2-2 Netherlands
FAC93	**Sheffield W**	1-1 Arsenal
FAC93 (C)	**Sheffield W**	1-2 Arsenal
CCC96	**Leeds**	0-3 Aston V

Palmer, Geoff (2, 0)
FLC74	**Wolves**	2-1 Man City
FLC80	**Wolves**	1-0 Nottingham F

Palmer, Roger (1, 0)
LC90 (S)	**Oldham**	0-1 Nottingham F

Pantling, Harry (1, 0)
FAC25	**Sheffield Utd**	1-0 Cardiff

Pardew, Alan (3, 0)
FAC90	**Crystal P**	3-3 Man Utd
FAC90	**Crystal P**	0-1 Man Utd
ZC91	**Crystal P**	4-1 Everton

Pardoe, Glyn (4, 5)
SI61 (4)	**England**	8-1 Wales
FAC69	**Man City**	1-0 Leicester
FLC70 (1)	**Man City**	2-1 WBA
FLC74	**Man City**	1-2 Wolves

Parke, John (2, 0)
BC63	**N Ireland**	3-8 England
ECQ67	**N Ireland**	0-2 England

Parker, Cliff (2, 2)

| FAC39 (2) | **Portsmouth** 4-1 Wolves |
| LWC42 | **Portsmouth** 0-2 Brentford |

Parker, Garry (7, 4)

LCT88 (S, 1)	**Nottingham F** 3-0 Leeds
LC89	**Nottingham F** 3-1 Luton
SC89 (2)	**Nottingham F** 4-3 Everton
LC90	**Nottingham F** 1-0 Oldham
FAC91	**Nottingham F** 1-2 Spurs
PPO96 (1)	**Leicester** 2-1 Crystal P
CCC97	**Leicester** 1-1 Middlesbrough

Parker, Paul (14, 0)

WCQ89 (S)	**England** 5-0 Albania
RC89	**England** 0-0 Chile
INT89	**England** 2-1 Yugoslavia
INT90	**England** 1-2 Uruguay
INT90	**England** 1-0 Hungary
ECQ90	**England** 2-0 Poland
INT91	**England** 3-1 USSR
INT91	**England** 0-1 Germany
RLC92	**Man Utd** 1-0 Nottingham F
CS93	**Man Utd** 1-1 Arsenal
INT94	**England** 1-0 Denmark
CCC94	**Man Utd** 1-3 Aston V
FAC94 (W)	**Man Utd** 1-1 Oldham
FAC94	**Man Utd** 4-0 Chelsea

Parker, Tom (3, 0)

FAC27	**Arsenal** 0-1 Cardiff
FAC30 (C)	**Arsenal** 2-0 Huddersfield
FAC32 (C)	**Arsenal** 1-2 Newcastle Utd

Parkes, Phil (3, 0)

FAC80	**West Ham** 1-0 Arsenal
CS80	**West Ham** 0-1 Liverpool
FLC81	**West Ham** 1-1 Liverpool

Parkin, Derek (2, 0)

| FLC74 | **Wolves** 2-1 Man City |
| FLC80 | **Wolves** 1-0 Nottingham F |

Parkin, Tommy (1, 0)

| CS78 | **Ipswich** 0-5 Nottingham F |

Parkinson, Andy (1, 0)

| WLC00 (W) | **Tranmere** 1-2 Leicester |

Parkinson, Gary (2, 1)

| ZC90 | **Middlesbrough** 0-1 Chelsea |
| PPO94 (1) | **Burnley** 2-1 Stockport |

Parkinson, Joe (2, 0)

| FAC95 | **Everton** 1-0 Man Utd |
| CS95 | **Everton** 1-0 Blackburn |

Parlane, Derek (1, 0)

| BC75 | **Scotland** 1-5 England |

Parlour, Ray (17, 1)

FAC93	**Arsenal** 1-0 Spurs
CCC93	**Arsenal** 2-1 Sheffield W
FAC93 (W)	**Arsenal** 1-1 Sheffield W
FAC98	**Arsenal** 2-0 Newcastle Utd
CS98	**Arsenal** 3-0 Man Utd
EC98	**Arsenal** 1-1 Dynamo Kiev
EC98 (D)	**Arsenal** 0-1 Lens
ECQ99 (S)	**England** 3-1 Poland

ECQ99 (S)	**England** 0-0 Sweden
CS99 (1, W)	**Arsenal** 2-1 Man Utd
ECQ99	**England** 6-0 Luxembourg
EC99	**Arsenal** 2-4 Barcelona
EC99 (W)	**Arsenal** 0-1 Fiorentina
ECQ99 (S)	**England** 0-1 Scotland
INT00 (S)	**England** 0-0 Argentina
INT00 (S, W)	**England** 1-1 Brazil
WCQ00 (S)	**England** 0-1 Germany

Parry, Ray (5, 3)

SI50	**England** 8-2 Scotland
SI51 (C, 1)	**England** 3-0 Wales
U23I57	**England** 3-2 Romania
FAC58	**Bolton** 2-0 Man Utd
BC59 (1)	**England** 2-1 N Ireland

Pates, Colin (2, 0)

| FMC86 (C) | **Chelsea** 5-4 Man City |
| PPO91 | **Brighton** 1-3 Notts C |

Patterson, Mark (1, 0)

| FMC87 (S) | **Blackburn** 1-0 Charlton |

Paul, Roy (4, 0)

BC52	**Wales** 2-5 England
BC54	**Wales** 2-3 England
FAC55 (C)	**Man City** 1-3 Newcastle Utd
FAC56 (C)	**Man City** 3-1 Birmingham

Payne, Clive (1, 0)

| FLC73 | **Norwich** 0-1 Spurs |

Payne, Jimmy (1, 0)

| FAC50 | **Liverpool** 0-2 Arsenal |

Peach, David (3, 1)

FAC76	**Southampton** 1-0 Man Utd
CS76	**Southampton** 0-1 Liverpool
FLC79 (1)	**Southampton** 2-3 Nottingham F

Peacock, Alan (3, 3)

BC62 (2)	**England** 4-0 Wales
FAC65	**Leeds** 1-2 Liverpool
BC65 (1)	**England** 2-1 N Ireland

Peacock, Bertie (3, 0)

BC55	**N Ireland** 0-3 England
BC57	**N Ireland** 3-2 England
BC59	**N Ireland** 1-2 England
As Manager	
BC63	**N Ireland** 3-8 England
BC65	**N Ireland** 1-2 England

Peacock, Darren (1, 0)

| CS96 | **Newcastle Utd** 0-4 Man Utd |

Peacock, Gavin (4, 2)

SI83	**England** 1-0 W Germany
SI83 (W)	**England** 3-3 Scotland
FAC94 (2)	**Chelsea** 2-0 Luton
FAC94	**Chelsea** 0-4 Man Utd

Peake, Andy (1, 0)

| FMC87 | **Charlton** 0-1 Blackburn |

Peake, Trevor (3, 0)

FAC87	**Coventry** 3-2 Spurs
CS87	**Coventry** 0-1 Everton
FAC94 (C)	**Luton** 0-2 Chelsea

Pearce, Graham (2, 0)
FAC83   **Brighton** 2-2 Man Utd
FAC83   **Brighton** 0-4 Man Utd

Pearce, Ian (2, 0)
CS94   **Blackburn** 0-2 Man Utd
CS95   **Blackburn** 0-1 Everton

Pearce, Jimmy (2, 0)
SI63   **England** 4-1 Wales
FLC73   **Spurs** 1-0 Norwich

Pearce, Stuart (51, 6)
RC87   **England** 1-1 Brazil
LCT88 (C, 1)   **Nottingham F** 3-0 Leeds
LCT88 (C)   **Nottingham F** 0-0 Aston V
LCT88 (C)   **Nottingham F** 2-2 Tranmere
LCT88 (C)   **Nottingham F** 0-0 Sheffield W
INT88   **England** 1-0 Denmark
WCQ88   **England** 0-0 Sweden
LC89 (C)   **Nottingham F** 3-1 Luton
WCQ89   **England** 5-0 Albania
SC89 (C)   **Nottingham F** 4-3 Everton
RC89   **England** 0-0 Chile
WCQ89   **England** 3-0 Poland
INT89 (W)   **England** 0-0 Italy
INT89 (W)   **England** 2-1 Yugoslavia
INT90   **England** 1-0 Brazil
INT90 (1, W)   **England** 4-2 Czechoslovakia
LC90 (C)   **Nottingham F** 1-0 Oldham
INT90 (W)   **England** 1-0 Denmark
INT90   **England** 1-2 Uruguay
INT90 (W)   **England** 1-0 Hungary
ECQ90   **England** 2-0 Poland
INT91   **England** 2-0 Cameroon
ECQ91   **England** 1-1 Rep of Ireland
FAC91 (C, 1)   **Nottingham F** 1-2 Spurs
INT91   **England** 2-2 Argentina
ECQ91   **England** 1-0 Turkey
INT92 (C)   **England** 2-0 France
ZC92 (C, W)   **Nottingham F** 3-2 Southampton
INT92 (S)   **England** 1-1 Brazil
WCQ92 (C)   **England** 1-1 Norway
WCQ92 (C, 1)   **England** 4-0 Turkey
WCQ93 (C, 1)   **England** 3-0 Poland
INT94 (S)   **England** 5-0 Greece
INT94 (S)   **England** 1-1 Romania
UC95   **England** 2-1 Japan
UC95   **England** 1-3 Brazil
INT95 (1)   **England** 3-1 Switzerland
INT95 (W)   **England** 1-1 Portugal
INT96 (C)   **England** 1-0 Bulgaria
INT96   **England** 0-0 Croatia
INT96   **England** 3-0 Hungary
ECH96   **England** 1-1 Switzerland
ECH96 (W)   **England** 2-0 Scotland
ECH96   **England** 4-1 Netherlands
ECH96   **England** 0-0 Spain
ECH96   **England** 1-1 Germany
WCQ96   **England** 2-1 Poland
WCQ97   **England** 0-1 Italy
INT97   **England** 2-0 Mexico

FAC98 (W)   **Newcastle Utd** 0-2 Arsenal
ECQ99   **England** 6-0 Luxembourg

Pears, Stephen (1, 0)
ZC90   **Middlesbrough** 0-1 Chelsea

Pearson, Harold (3, 0)
FAC31   **WBA** 2-1 Birmingham
BC32   **England** 3-0 Scotland
FAC35   **WBA** 2-4 Sheffield W

Pearson, Nigel (4, 0)
RLC91 (C)   **Sheffield W** 1-0 Man Utd
CCC97 (C)   **Middlesbrough** 1-1 Leicester
FAC97 (C)   **Middlesbrough** 0-2 Chelsea
CCC98 (C)   **Middlesbrough** 0-2 Chelsea

Pearson, Stan (2, 1)
FAC48 (1)   **Man Utd** 4-2 Blackpool
BC49   **England** 1-3 Scotland

Pearson, Stuart (12, 3)
FAC76   **Man Utd** 0-1 Southampton
BC76 (1)   **England** 4-0 N Ireland
INT76 (1)   **England** 1-1 Rep of Ireland
INT77 (S)   **England** 0-2 Netherlands
FAC77 (1)   **Man Utd** 2-1 Liverpool
BC77   **England** 0-1 Wales
BC77   **England** 1-2 Scotland
CS77   **Man Utd** 0-0 Liverpool
WCQ77 (S)   **England** 2-0 Italy
BC78   **England** 1-0 N Ireland
FAC80   **West Ham** 1-0 Arsenal
FLC81 (S)   **West Ham** 1-1 Liverpool

Pearson, Tommy (1, 0)
BC47   **Scotland** 1-1 England

Pegg, David (2, 0)
SI51   **England** 3-0 Wales
FAC57   **Man Utd** 1-2 Aston V

Pejic, Mike (2, 0)
FLC72   **Stoke** 2-1 Chelsea
BC74   **England** 1-0 N Ireland

Pemberton, John (4, 0)
FAC90   **Crystal P** 3-3 Man Utd
FAC90   **Crystal P** 0-1 Man Utd
FAC93   **Sheffield Utd** 1-2 Sheffield W
CCC96   **Leeds** 0-3 Aston V

Penman, Willie (1, 0)
FLC69 (S)   **Swindon** 3-1 Arsenal

Penney, Steve (2, 0)
WCQ85 (W)   **N Ireland** 0-0 England
ECQ86 (W)   **N Ireland** 0-3 England

Perry, Bill (4, 3)
FAC51   **Blackpool** 0-2 Newcastle Utd
FAC53 (1)   **Blackpool** 4-3 Bolton
BC55   **England** 3-0 N Ireland
INT55 (2)   **England** 4-1 Spain

Perryman, Steve (10, 0)
SI67   **England** 0-2 Scotland
FLC71   **Spurs** 2-0 Aston V
FLC73   **Spurs** 1-0 Norwich
FAC81 (C)   **Spurs** 1-1 Man City
FAC81 (C)   **Spurs** 3-2 Man City

CS81 (C)	**Spurs** 2-2 Aston V	
FLC82 (C)	**Spurs** 1-3 Liverpool	
FAC82 (C)	**Spurs** 1-1 QPR	
FAC82 (C)	**Spurs** 1-0 QPR	
CS82 (S)	**Spurs** 0-1 Liverpool	

Persson, Orjan (1, 0)
INT68	**Sweden** 1-3 England

Peters, Gary (1, 0)
SC88 (S)	**Reading** 4-1 Luton

Peters, Martin (35, 10)
SI59	**England** 2-0 W Germany
ECW65	**West Ham** 2-0 TSV Munich
INT66	**England** 2-0 Yugoslavia
WC66	**England** 2-0 Mexico
WC66	**England** 2-0 France
WC66	**England** 1-0 Argentina
WC66	**England** 2-1 Portugal
WC66 (1)	**England** 4-2 W Germany
INT66	**England** 0-0 Czechoslovakia
ECQ66	**England** 5-1 Wales
ECQ67	**England** 2-3 Scotland
ECQ67	**England** 2-0 N Ireland
INT67 (1)	**England** 2-2 USSR
ECQ68	**England** 1-0 Spain
INT68 (1)	**England** 3-1 Sweden
INT68	**England** 1-1 Bulgaria
INT69	**England** 5-0 France
BC69 (2)	**England** 4-1 Scotland
INT69 (S)	**England** 1-0 Portugal
INT70	**England** 0-0 Netherlands
BC70 (1)	**England** 3-1 N Ireland
INT70 (1)	**England** 3-1 E Germany
FLC71	**Spurs** 2-0 Aston V
ECQ71	**England** 3-0 Greece
ECQ71 (W)	**England** 5-0 Malta
BC71 (C)	**England** 0-0 Wales
BC71 (1)	**England** 3-1 Scotland
ECQ72	**England** 1-3 W Germany
BC72 (S)	**England** 0-1 N Ireland
FLC73 (C)	**Spurs** 1-0 Norwich
BC73 (1)	**England** 3-0 Wales
BC73 (1)	**England** 1-0 Scotland
INT73 (C)	**England** 7-0 Austria
WCQ73 (C)	**England** 1-1 Poland
INT73	**England** 0-1 Italy

Petit, Emmanuel (6, 0)
FAC98	**Arsenal** 2-0 Newcastle Utd
CS98 (W)	**Arsenal** 3-0 Man Utd
EC98	**Arsenal** 1-1 Panathinaikos
INT99	**France** 2-0 England
CS99	**Arsenal** 2-1 Man Utd
EC99 (W)	**Arsenal** 0-1 Fiorentina

Petrescu, Dan (5, 0)
INT94	**Romania** 1-1 England
FAC97	**Chelsea** 2-0 Middlesbrough
CS97 (S)	**Chelsea** 1-1 Man Utd
CCC98 (W)	**Chelsea** 2-0 Middlesbrough
FAC00 (S)	**Chelsea** 2-1 Newcastle Utd

Peyton, Gerry (1, 0)
ECQ80 (W)	**Rep of Ireland** 0-2 England

Phelan, Mike (6, 0)
INT89 (S)	**England** 0-0 Italy
FAC90	**Man Utd** 3-3 Crystal P
FAC90	**Man Utd** 1-0 Crystal P
CS90	**Man Utd** 1-1 Liverpool
RLC91 (S)	**Man Utd** 0-1 Sheffield W
RLC92	**Man Utd** 1-0 Nottingham F

Phelan, Terry (3, 0)
LCT88	**Wimbledon** 0-1 Tranmere
FAC88	**Wimbledon** 1-0 Liverpool
CS88	**Wimbledon** 1-2 Liverpool

Phillips, David (3, 0)
FMC86 (W)	**Man City** 4-5 Chelsea
FAC87	**Coventry** 3-2 Spurs
CS87	**Coventry** 0-1 Everton

Phillips, Jimmy (3, 0)
FRT86	**Bolton** 0-3 Bristol C
CCC95	**Bolton** 1-2 Liverpool
PPO95	**Bolton** 4-3 Reading

Phillips, John (1, 0)
BC73	**Wales** 0-3 England

Phillips, Kevin (3, 1)
PPO98 (1, W)	**Sunderland** 4-4 Charlton
INT00 (S)	**England** 0-0 Argentina
INT00 (S)	**England** 1-1 Brazil

Phillips, Leighton (6, 0)
BC71	**Wales** 0-0 England
BC75	**Wales** 2-2 England
FLC77	**Aston V** 0-0 Everton
BC77 (W)	**Wales** 1-0 England
BC79	**Wales** 0-0 England
BC81	**Wales** 0-0 England

Phillips, Len (2, 0)
BC54	**England** 3-2 Wales
INT54	**England** 3-1 W Germany

Phillips, Les (1, 0)
MC86	**Oxford** 3-0 QPR

Phipps, Harold (3, 0)
LSC43	**Charlton** 1-7 Arsenal
FAC46	**Charlton** 1-4 Derby
FAC47	**Charlton** 1-0 Burnley

Pickering, Fred (1, 1)
INT64 (1)	**England** 2-2 Belgium

Pickering, Jack (1, 0)
FAC36	**Sheffield Utd** 0-1 Arsenal

Pickering, Nick (3, 0)
MC85	**Sunderland** 0-1 Norwich
FAC87	**Coventry** 3-2 Spurs
CS87	**Coventry** 0-1 Everton

Pierce, Gary (1, 0)
FLC74	**Wolves** 2-1 Man City

Pike, Geoff (3, 0)
FAC80	**West Ham** 1-0 Arsenal
CS80 (W)	**West Ham** 0-1 Liverpool
FLC81	**West Ham** 1-1 Liverpool

Pistone, Alessandro (1, 0)
FAC98   **Newcastle Utd**   0-2 Arsenal

Pitt, Richie (2, 0)
SI67   **England** 0-2 Scotland
FAC73   **Sunderland** 1-0 Leeds

Platt, David (35, 16)
LCT88   **Aston V** 0-0 Blackburn
LCT88   **Aston V** 0-0 Nottingham F
INT89 (S)   **England** 0-0 Italy
INT89 (S)   **England** 2-1 Yugoslavia
INT90   **England** 1-0 Brazil
INT90 (S)   **England** 1-0 Denmark
INT90   **England** 1-0 Hungary
ECQ90   **England** 2-0 Poland
ECQ91   **England** 1-1 Rep of Ireland
INT91 (2)   **England** 3-1 USSR
INT91 (1)   **England** 2-2 Argentina
INT91   **England** 0-1 Germany
ECQ91   **England** 1-0 Turkey
INT92 (1)   **England** 1-1 Brazil
WCQ92 (1)   **England** 1-1 Norway
WCQ92   **England** 4-0 Turkey
WCQ93 (C, 4)   **England** 6-0 San Marino
WCQ93 (C, 1)   **England** 2-2 Netherlands
WCQ93   **England** 3-0 Poland
INT94 (C, 1)   **England** 1-0 Denmark
INT94 (C, 2)   **England** 5-0 Greece
INT94 (C)   **England** 0-0 Norway
INT94 (C)   **England** 2-0 USA
INT94 (C, 1)   **England** 1-0 Nigeria
INT95 (C)   **England** 0-0 Uruguay
UC95 (C, 1)   **England** 2-1 Japan
UC95 (C)   **England** 1-3 Brazil
INT96 (S)   **England** 1-0 Bulgaria
INT96 (C)   **England** 0-0 Croatia
INT96 (C, 1, W)   **England** 3-0 Hungary
ECH96 (S)   **England** 1-1 Switzerland
ECH96 (S)   **England** 4-1 Netherlands
ECH96   **England** 0-0 Spain
ECH96   **England** 1-1 Germany
FAC98 (S)   **Arsenal** 2-0 Newcastle Utd

Platt, Jim (3, 0)
BC78   **N Ireland** 0-1 England
BC80   **N Ireland** 1-1 England
BC84   **N Ireland** 0-1 England
As Manager
PPO96   **Darlington** 0-1 Plymouth

Plummer, Norman (1, 0)
FAC49 (C)   **Leicester** 1-3 Wolves

Poborsky, Karel (3, 0)
ECH96 (W)   **Czech Rep** 1-2 Germany
CS96 (S)   **Man Utd** 4-0 Newcastle Utd
INT98   **Czech Rep** 0-2 England

Pointer, Ray (2, 1)
WCQ61 (1)   **England** 2-0 Portugal
FAC62   **Burnley** 1-3 Spurs

Pointon, Neil (4, 1)
CS87 (S)   **Everton** 1-0 Coventry
LCT88   **Everton** 1-1 Wolves

LCT88   **Everton** 0-1 Man Utd
FAC94 (1)   **Oldham** 1-1 Man Utd

Popescu, Gheorghe (1, 0)
INT94   **Romania** 1-1 England

Porterfield, Ian (1, 1)
FAC73 (1)   **Sunderland** 1-0 Leeds

Potts, Harry (1, 0)
FAC47   **Burnley** 0-1 Charlton
As Manager
FAC62   **Burnley** 1-3 Spurs

Powell, Barry (1, 0)
FLC74 (S)   **Wolves** 2-1 Man City

Powell, David (1, 0)
BC69   **Wales** 1-2 England

Powell, Tony (1, 0)
FLC75   **Norwich** 0-1 Aston V

Power, Paul (7, 0)
FAC81 (C)   **Man City** 1-1 Spurs
FAC81 (C)   **Man City** 2-3 Spurs
FMC86 (C)   **Man City** 4-5 Chelsea
CS86   **Everton** 1-1 Liverpool
CS87   **Everton** 1-0 Coventry
LCT88 (S)   **Everton** 1-1 Wolves
LCT88 (S)   **Everton** 0-1 Man Utd

Poyet, Gustavo (4, 2)
CS97   **Chelsea** 1-1 Man Utd
FAC00 (2)   **Chelsea** 2-1 Newcastle Utd
FAC00   **Chelsea** 1-0 Aston V
CS00 (W)   **Chelsea** 2-0 Man Utd

Pratt, John (1, 0)
FLC73 (W)   **Spurs** 1-0 Norwich

Preece, David (3, 0)
LC88 (W)   **Luton** 3-2 Arsenal
LC89   **Luton** 1-3 Nottingham F
FAC94   **Luton** 0-2 Chelsea

Preedy, Charlie (1, 0)
FAC30   **Arsenal** 2-0 Huddersfield

Price, Chris (4, 0)
FMC87   **Blackburn** 1-0 Charlton
LCT88   **Blackburn** 0-0 Aston V
MT90 (W)   **Aston V** 0-2 Arsenal
PPO92   **Blackburn** 1-0 Leicester

Price, David (5, 0)
SI70   **England** 2-0 Scotland
FAC78   **Arsenal** 0-1 Ipswich
FAC79 (W)   **Arsenal** 3-2 Man Utd
CS79 (W)   **Arsenal** 1-3 Liverpool
FAC80   **Arsenal** 0-1 West Ham

Price, Neil (1, 0)
FAC84 (W)   **Watford** 0-2 Everton

Price, Paul (5, 0)
BC81   **Wales** 0-0 England
FLC82   **Spurs** 1-3 Liverpool
FAC82   **Spurs** 1-1 QPR
FAC82   **Spurs** 1-0 QPR
BC83 (C)   **Wales** 1-2 England

Pringle, Charlie (1, 0)
FAC26   **Man City** 0-1 Bolton
Prior, Spencer (1, 0)
CCC97   **Leicester** 1-1 Middlesbrough
Pritchard, Roy (1, 0)
FAC49   **Wolves** 3-1 Leicester
Proctor, Mark (5, 0)
LCT88   **Sheffield W** 0-0 Crystal P
LCT88   **Sheffield W** 1-1 Wigan
LCT88   **Sheffield W** 2-1 Man Utd
LCT88 (W)   **Sheffield W** 0-0 Nottingham F
ZC90 (C)   **Middlesbrough** 0-1 Chelsea
Provan, Davie (1, 0)
BC81 (W)   **Scotland** 1-0 England
Puddefoot, Syd (1, 0)
FAC28   **Blackburn** 3-1 Huddersfield
Pugh, Graham (1, 0)
FAC66   **Sheffield W** 2-3 Everton
Pye, Jesse (3, 3)
VI46 (1)   **England** 2-0 Belgium
IT46   **FA** 3-5 Army PT Corps
FAC49 (2)   **Wolves** 3-1 Leicester
Pym, Dick (3, 0)
FAC23   **Bolton** 2-0 West Ham
FAC26   **Bolton** 1-0 Man City
FAC29   **Bolton** 2-0 Portsmouth
Quigley, John (1, 0)
FAC59   **Nottingham F** 2-1 Luton
Quinn, Jimmy (3, 1)
WCQ85   **N Ireland** 0-0 England
ECQ86 (S)   **N Ireland** 0-3 England
PPO95 (S, 1)   **Reading** 3-4 Bolton
As Player-Manager
PPO95   **Reading** 3-4 Bolton
Quinn, Johnny (1, 0)
FAC66   **Sheffield W** 2-3 Everton
Quinn, Niall (4, 3)
LC87 (W)   **Arsenal** 2-1 Liverpool
CS89 (S)   **Arsenal** 0-1 Liverpool
ECQ91 (1)   **Rep of Ireland** 1-1 England
PPO98 (2)   **Sunderland** 4-4 Charlton
Quinn, Pat (1, 1)
BC61 (1)   **Scotland** 3-9 England
Quixall, Albert (2, 0)
NIN53   **England** 4-4 FIFA
FAC63   **Man Utd** 3-1 Leicester
Radebe, Lucas (1, 0)
CCC96 (W)   **Leeds** 0-3 Aston V
Radford, John (6, 0)
FLC68   **Arsenal** 0-1 Leeds
INT69   **England** 1-1 Romania
FLC69   **Arsenal** 1-3 Swindon
FAC71   **Arsenal** 2-1 Liverpool
FAC72 (W)   **Arsenal** 0-1 Leeds
FAT81   **Bishop's Stortford** 1-0 Sutton
Ramsey, Sir Alf (8, 3)
BC51   **England** 2-3 Scotland

INT51   **England** 2-1 Argentina
INT51 (1)   **England** 2-2 Austria
BC52   **England** 5-2 Wales
INT52   **England** 5-0 Belgium
BC53   **England** 2-2 Scotland
NIN53 (1)   **England** 4-4 FIFA
INT53 (1)   **England** 3-6 Hungary
As Manager
BC63   **England** 1-2 Scotland
INT63   **England** 1-1 Brazil
CEN63   **England** 2-1 FIFA
BC63   **England** 8-3 N Ireland
INT64   **England** 2-1 Uruguay
INT64   **England** 2-2 Belgium
BC64   **England** 2-1 Wales
BC65   **England** 2-2 Scotland
INT65   **England** 1-0 Hungary
INT65   **England** 2-3 Austria
BC65   **England** 2-1 N Ireland
INT66   **England** 1-0 W Germany
INT66   **England** 2-0 Yugoslavia
WC66   **England** 0-0 Uruguay
WC66   **England** 2-0 Mexico
WC66   **England** 2-0 France
WC66   **England** 1-0 Argentina
WC66   **England** 2-1 Portugal
WC66   **England** 4-2 W Germany
INT66   **England** 0-0 Czechoslovakia
ECQ66   **England** 5-1 Wales
ECQ67   **England** 2-3 Scotland
INT67   **England** 2-0 Spain
ECQ67   **England** 2-0 N Ireland
INT67   **England** 2-2 USSR
ECQ68   **England** 1-0 Spain
INT68   **England** 3-1 Sweden
INT68   **England** 1-1 Bulgaria
INT69   **England** 1-1 Romania
INT69   **England** 5-0 France
BC69   **England** 2-1 Wales
BC69   **England** 4-1 Scotland
INT69   **England** 1-0 Portugal
INT70   **England** 0-0 Netherlands
BC70   **England** 3-1 N Ireland
INT70   **England** 3-1 E Germany
ECQ71   **England** 3-0 Greece
ECQ71   **England** 5-0 Malta
BC71   **England** 0-0 Wales
BC71   **England** 3-1 Scotland
ECQ71   **England** 1-1 Switzerland
ECQ72   **England** 1-3 W Germany
BC72   **England** 0-1 N Ireland
INT72   **England** 1-1 Yugoslavia
EEC73   **The Three** 2-0 The Six
WCQ73   **England** 1-1 Wales
BC73   **England** 3-0 Wales
BC73   **England** 1-0 Scotland
INT73   **England** 7-0 Austria
WCQ73   **England** 1-1 Poland
INT73   **England** 0-1 Italy

Ramsey, Chris (1, 0)
FAC83 (W)   **Brighton** 2-2 Man Utd
Rankin, Willie (1, 0)
FAC28   **Blackburn** 3-1 Huddersfield
Ranson, Ray (4, 0)
SI75   **England** 4-0 Netherlands
SI75   **England** 0-1 Scotland
FAC81   **Man City** 1-1 Spurs
FAC81   **Man City** 2-3 Spurs
Ratcliffe, Kevin (14, 0)
SI76   **Wales** 1-4 England
BC81   **Wales** 0-0 England
BC83   **Wales** 1-2 England
MC84 (C)   **Everton** 0-0 Liverpool
FAC84 (C)   **Everton** 2-0 Watford
CS84 (C)   **Everton** 1-0 Liverpool
FAC85 (C)   **Everton** 0-1 Man Utd
CS85 (C)   **Everton** 2-0 Man Utd
FAC86 (C)   **Everton** 1-3 Liverpool
CS86 (C)   **Everton** 1-1 Liverpool
CS87 (C)   **Everton** 1-0 Coventry
SC89 (C)   **Everton** 3-4 Nottingham F
FAC89 (C)   **Everton** 2-3 Liverpool
ZC91 (S)   **Everton** 1-4 Crystal P
Ravanelli, Fabrizio (3, 1)
WCQ97 (S)   **Italy** 1-0 England
CCC97 (1)   **Middlesbrough** 1-1 Leicester
FAC97 (W)   **Middlesbrough** 0-2 Chelsea
Raw, Harry (1, 0)
FAC30   **Huddersfield** 0-2 Arsenal
Reaney, Paul (7, 0)
FAC65   **Leeds** 1-2 Liverpool
FLC68   **Leeds** 1-0 Arsenal
INT68 (S)   **England** 1-1 Bulgaria
INT69   **England** 1-0 Portugal
FAC72   **Leeds** 1-0 Arsenal
FAC73   **Leeds** 0-1 Sunderland
CS74   **Leeds** 1-1 Liverpool
Redfern, Levi (1, 0)
FAC28   **Huddersfield** 1-3 Blackburn
Redknapp, Jamie (12, 0)
U17I90 (S)   **England** 1-3 France
CCC95   **Liverpool** 2-1 Bolton
INT95 (W)   **England** 0-0 Colombia
INT95 (W)   **England** 3-1 Switzerland
FAC96   **Liverpool** 0-1 Man Utd
ECH96 (S, W)   **England** 2-0 Scotland
INT97 (S)   **England** 2-0 Mexico
WCQ97 (S)   **England** 2-0 Georgia
ECQ98   **England** 0-0 Bulgaria
INT99 (W)   **England** 0-2 France
ECQ99 (S)   **England** 3-1 Poland
ECQ99   **England** 0-1 Scotland
Redmond, Steve (1, 0)
FMC86   **Man City** 4-5 Chelsea
Redpath, Willie (1, 0)
BC51   **Scotland** 3-2 England

Reece, Gil (1, 0)
BC71 (W)   **Wales** 0-0 England
Rees, Ronnie (3, 0)
BC64   **Wales** 1-2 England
ECQ66   **Wales** 1-5 England
BC71 (S)   **Wales** 0-0 England
Reeves, Kevin (4, 1)
ECQ79   **England** 2-0 Bulgaria
BC80 (W)   **England** 1-1 N Ireland
FAC81   **Man City** 1-1 Spurs
FAC81 (1)   **Man City** 2-3 Spurs
Regis, Cyrille (4, 0)
BC82 (S)   **England** 4-0 N Ireland
INT82 (W)   **England** 1-2 W Germany
FAC87   **Coventry** 3-2 Spurs
ECQ87 (S)   **England** 8-0 Turkey
Reid, Bobby (1, 0)
BC38   **Scotland** 1-0 England
Reid, Mark (1, 0)
FMC87   **Charlton** 0-1 Blackburn
Reid, Nicky (6, 1)
FAC81   **Man City** 1-1 Spurs
FAC81   **Man City** 2-3 Spurs
FMC86 (W)   **Man City** 4-5 Chelsea
LCT88 (C)   **Blackburn** 0-0 Aston V
PPO93 (1)   **WBA** 3-0 Port V
PPO94   **Wycombe** 4-2 PNE
Reid, Peter (12, 0)
MC84   **Everton** 0-0 Liverpool
FAC84   **Everton** 2-0 Watford
CS84   **Everton** 1-0 Liverpool
FAC85   **Everton** 0-1 Man Utd
CS85   **Everton** 2-0 Man Utd
WCQ85   **England** 1-1 Romania
RC86 (S)   **England** 2-1 Scotland
FAC86   **Everton** 1-3 Liverpool
RC87   **England** 1-1 Brazil
CS87   **Everton** 1-0 Coventry
LCT88   **Everton** 1-1 Wolves
LCT88   **Everton** 0-1 Man Utd
As Manager
PPO98   **Sunderland** 4-4 Charlton
Reilly, George (1, 0)
FAC84   **Watford** 0-2 Everton
Reilly, Lawrie (5, 5)
BC49 (1)   **Scotland** 3-1 England
BC51 (1)   **Scotland** 3-2 England
BC53 (2)   **Scotland** 2-2 England
BC55 (1)   **Scotland** 2-7 England
BC57   **Scotland** 1-2 England
Revie, Don (3, 1)
BC55 (1)   **England** 7-2 Scotland
FAC55   **Man City** 1-3 Newcastle Utd
FAC56   **Man City** 3-1 Birmingham
As Manager
FAC65   **Leeds** 1-2 Liverpool
FLC68   **Leeds** 1-0 Arsenal
FAC70   **Leeds** 2-2 Chelsea

FAC72	**Leeds** 1-0 Arsenal
FAC73	**Leeds** 0-1 Sunderland
ECQ74	**England** 3-0 Czechoslovakia
ECQ74	**England** 0-0 Portugal
INT75	**England** 2-0 W Germany
ECQ75	**England** 5-0 Cyprus
BC75	**England** 2-2 Wales
BC75	**England** 5-1 Scotland
BC76	**England** 4-0 N Ireland
INT76	**England** 1-1 Rep of Ireland
WCQ76	**England** 2-1 Finland
INT77	**England** 0-2 Netherlands
WCQ77	**England** 5-0 Luxembourg
BC77	**England** 0-1 Wales
BC77	**England** 1-2 Scotland

Rhodes, Andy (1, 0)

LC90	**Oldham** 0-1 Nottingham F

Ricard, Hamilton (1, 0)

CCC98 (W)	**Middlesbrough** 0-2 Chelsea

Rice, Pat (10, 0)

FAC71	**Arsenal** 2-1 Liverpool
FAC72	**Arsenal** 0-1 Leeds
BC72	**N Ireland** 1-0 England
BC74	**N Ireland** 0-1 England
BC76	**N Ireland** 0-4 England
FAC78 (C)	**Arsenal** 0-1 Ipswich
ECQ79	**N Ireland** 0-4 England
FAC79 (C)	**Arsenal** 3-2 Man Utd
CS79 (C)	**Arsenal** 1-3 Liverpool
FAC80 (C)	**Arsenal** 0-1 West Ham

Richards, Dick (1, 0)

FAC23	**West Ham** 0-2 Bolton

Richards, John (2, 1)

FLC74 (1)	**Wolves** 2-1 Man City
FLC80	**Wolves** 1-0 Nottingham F

Richardson, Bill (2, 0)

FAC31	**WBA** 2-1 Birmingham
FAC35	**WBA** 2-4 Sheffield W

Richardson, Billy (4, 4)

FAC31 (2)	**WBA** 2-1 Birmingham
FAC35	**WBA** 2-4 Sheffield W
CHA43 (2)	**Met Police** 3-4 RAF
CHA45	**Nat Police** 1-3 Combined Services

Richardson, Jimmy (1, 0)

FAC32	**Newcastle Utd** 2-1 Arsenal

Richardson, Kevin (13, 0)

MC84	**Everton** 0-0 Liverpool
FAC84	**Everton** 2-0 Watford
CS84	**Everton** 1-0 Liverpool
CS86	**Everton** 1-1 Liverpool
LC88	**Arsenal** 2-3 Luton
WIT88 (S)	**Arsenal** 3-0 Bayern Munich
MT89	**Arsenal** 1-0 Porto
MT89	**Arsenal** 1-0 Liverpool
CS89	**Arsenal** 0-1 Liverpool
MT90 (W)	**Real Sociedad** 1-1 Sampdoria
MT90	**Real Sociedad** 1-0 Aston V
CCC94 (C)	**Aston V** 3-1 Man Utd
INT94	**England** 5-0 Greece

Richardson, Steve (1, 0)

SC88	**Reading** 4-1 Luton

Rickett, Walter (1, 0)

FAC48	**Blackpool** 2-4 Man Utd

Rideout, Paul (5, 6)

SI79 (1)	**England** 2-2 W Germany
SI80 (1)	**England** 2-0 Switzerland
SI80 (3)	**England** 4-5 Scotland
FAC95 (1, W)	**Everton** 1-0 Man Utd
CS95	**Everton** 1-0 Blackburn

Rigby, Arthur (1, 0)

FAC28	**Blackburn** 3-1 Huddersfield

Riley, Howard (2, 0)

FAC61	**Leicester** 0-2 Spurs
FAC63	**Leicester** 1-3 Man Utd

Rimmer, Ellis (2, 4)

BC30 (2)	**England** 5-2 Scotland
FAC35 (2)	**Sheffield W** 4-2 WBA

Rimmer, Jimmy (1, 0)

CS81	**Aston V** 2-2 Spurs

Ring, Tommy (2, 1)

BC55	**Scotland** 2-7 England
BC57 (1)	**Scotland** 1-2 England

Ringstead, Alf (1, 0)

WCQ57	**Rep of Ireland** 1-5 England

Rioch, Bruce (4, 1)

FLC71	**Aston V** 0-2 Spurs
BC75 (1)	**Scotland** 1-5 England
CS75	**Derby** 2-0 West Ham
BC77 (C)	**Scotland** 2-1 England

As Manager

CCC95	**Bolton** 1-2 Liverpool
PPO95	**Bolton** 4-3 Reading

Ripley, Stuart (4, 0)

ZC90	**Middlesbrough** 0-1 Chelsea
CS94	**Blackburn** 0-2 Man Utd
CS95 (W)	**Blackburn** 0-1 Everton
WCQ97 (S, W)	**England** 4-0 Moldova

Ritchie, Andy (3, 3)

SI76 (2)	**England** 4-1 Wales
SI76 (1)	**England** 6-1 France
LC90	**Oldham** 0-1 Nottingham F

Ritchie, John (2, 0)

FLC72	**Stoke** 2-1 Chelsea
FAT76 (S)	**Stafford** 2-3 Scarborough

Ritchie, Paul (2, 0)

VS91 (C)	**Scotland** 1-2 England
FAC00	**Bolton** 0-0 Aston V

Rix, Graham (13, 0)

FAC78 (S)	**Arsenal** 0-1 Ipswich
FAC79	**Arsenal** 3-2 Man Utd
CS79	**Arsenal** 1-3 Liverpool
FAC80	**Arsenal** 0-1 West Ham
WCQ80	**England** 4-0 Norway
WCQ80 (S)	**England** 2-1 Switzerland
INT81	**England** 0-1 Brazil
BC81	**England** 0-0 Wales
BC81	**England** 0-1 Scotland

INT82 (S)   **England** 2-0 Netherlands
INT82 (S)   **England** 1-2 W Germany
ECQ83 (S)   **England** 0-0 Greece
BC84   **England** 1-0 N Ireland

Robb, Davie (1, 0)
BC71   **Scotland** 1-3 England

Robb, George (2, 0)
AI52   **England** 1-2 Scotland
INT53   **England** 3-6 Hungary

Roberts, Ben (1, 0)
FAC97   **Middlesbrough** 0-2 Chelsea

Roberts, Bobby (1, 0)
FAC69   **Leicester** 0-1 Man City

Roberts, Dave (2, 0)
BC73 (S)   **Wales** 0-3 England
BC77 (S)   **Wales** 1-0 England

Roberts, Frank (1, 0)
FAC26   **Man City** 0-1 Bolton

Roberts, Gareth (1, 0)
WLC00   **Tranmere** 1-2 Leicester

Roberts, Graham (8, 0)
FAC81   **Spurs** 1-1 Man City
FAC81   **Spurs** 3-2 Man City
CS81   **Spurs** 2-2 Aston V
FAC82   **Spurs** 1-1 QPR
FAC82   **Spurs** 1-0 QPR
BC83   **England** 2-0 Scotland
BC84   **England** 1-0 N Ireland
INT84   **England** 0-2 USSR

Roberts, Herbie (2, 0)
FAC32   **Arsenal** 1-2 Newcastle Utd
FAC36   **Arsenal** 1-0 Sheffield Utd

Roberts, John (4, 0)
BC71   **Wales** 0-0 England
WCQ73   **Wales** 1-1 England
BC73   **Wales** 0-3 England
BC75 (C)   **Wales** 2-2 England

Robertson, Jimmy (1, 1)
FAC67 (1)   **Spurs** 2-1 Chelsea

Robertson, John (5, 2)
FLC78   **Nottingham F** 0-0 Liverpool
CS78 (1)   **Nottingham F** 5-0 Ipswich
FLC79   **Nottingham F** 3-2 Southampton
FLC80   **Nottingham F** 0-1 Wolves
BC81 (1)   **Scotland** 1-0 England

Robins, Mark (5, 0)
U16I85 (S)   **England** 3-2 Yugoslavia
FAC90 (S)   **Man Utd** 3-3 Crystal P
CS90 (S)   **Man Utd** 1-1 Liverpool
PPO96 (S)   **Leicester** 2-1 Crystal P
CCC97 (S)   **Leicester** 1-1 Middlesbrough

Robinson, Bill (2, 0)
LSC44   **Charlton** 3-1 Chelsea
FAC47   **Charlton** 1-0 Burnley

Robinson, Cyril (1, 0)
FAC53   **Blackpool** 4-3 Bolton

Robinson, Joe (1, 0)
FAC48   **Blackpool** 2-4 Man Utd

Robinson, Michael (5, 0)
FAC83   **Brighton** 2-2 Man Utd
FAC83   **Brighton** 0-4 Man Utd
CS83 (W)   **Liverpool** 0-2 Man Utd
MC84 (S)   **Liverpool** 0-0 Everton
MC86   **QPR** 0-3 Oxford

Robledo, George (2, 1)
FAC51   **Newcastle Utd** 2-0 Blackpool
FAC52 (1)   **Newcastle Utd** 1-0 Arsenal

Robledo, Ted (1, 0)
FAC52   **Newcastle Utd** 1-0 Arsenal

Robson, Sir Bobby (9, 5)
EFC55 (1)   **London** 3-2 Frankfurt
INT57 (2)   **England** 4-0 France
INT60   **England** 4-2 Spain
BC60   **England** 5-1 Wales
BC61 (1)   **England** 9-3 Scotland
INT61 (1)   **England** 8-0 Mexico
WCQ61   **England** 2-0 Portugal
BC61   **England** 1-1 N Ireland
INT62   **England** 3-1 Switzerland

As Manager
FAC78   **Ipswich** 1-0 Arsenal
CS78   **Ipswich** 0-5 Nottingham F
INT82   **England** 1-2 W Germany
ECQ82   **England** 9-0 Luxembourg
BC83   **England** 2-1 Wales
ECQ83   **England** 0-0 Greece
ECQ83   **England** 2-0 Hungary
BC83   **England** 2-0 Scotland
ECQ83   **England** 0-1 Denmark
BC84   **England** 1-0 N Ireland
INT84   **England** 0-2 USSR
INT84   **England** 1-0 E Germany
WCQ84   **England** 5-0 Finland
INT85   **England** 2-1 Rep of Ireland
WCQ85   **England** 0-0 Romania
WCQ85   **England** 5-0 Turkey
WCQ85   **England** 0-0 N Ireland
RC86   **England** 2-1 Scotland
ECQ86   **England** 3-0 N Ireland
ECQ86   **England** 2-0 Yugoslavia
RC87   **England** 1-1 Brazil
LCEN87   **Football League** 3-0 Rest of World
ECQ87   **England** 8-0 Turkey
INT88   **England** 2-2 Netherlands
RC88   **England** 1-0 Scotland
RC88   **England** 1-1 Colombia
INT88   **England** 1-0 Denmark
WCQ88   **England** 0-0 Sweden
WCQ89   **England** 5-0 Albania
RC89   **England** 0-0 Chile
WCQ89   **England** 3-0 Poland
INT89   **England** 0-0 Italy
INT89   **England** 2-1 Yugoslavia
INT90   **England** 1-0 Brazil
INT90   **England** 4-2 Czechoslovakia

INT90	**England** 1-0 Denmark
INT90	**England** 1-2 Uruguay
FAC00	**Newcastle Utd** 1-2 Chelsea

Robson, Bryan (52, 15)

ECQ80	**England** 2-0 Rep of Ireland
WCQ80	**England** 4-0 Norway
WCQ80	**England** 2-1 Switzerland
INT81	**England** 1-2 Spain
WCQ81	**England** 0-0 Romania
INT81	**England** 0-1 Brazil
BC81	**England** 0-0 Wales
BC81	**England** 0-1 Scotland
WCQ81	**England** 1-0 Hungary
BC82 (1)	**England** 4-0 N Ireland
INT82	**England** 2-0 Netherlands
ECQ82 (C)	**England** 9-0 Luxembourg
FAC83 (C)	**Man Utd** 2-2 Brighton
FAC83 (C, 2)	**Man Utd** 4-0 Brighton
BC83 (C, 1, W)	**England** 2-0 Scotland
CS83 (C, 2)	**Man Utd** 2-0 Liverpool
BC84 (C)	**England** 1-0 N Ireland
INT84 (C)	**England** 0-2 USSR
INT84 (C, 1)	**England** 1-0 E Germany
WCQ84 (C, 1, W)	**England** 5-0 Finland
INT85 (C, W)	**England** 2-1 Rep of Ireland
FAC85 (C)	**Man Utd** 1-0 Everton
CS85 (C)	**Man Utd** 0-2 Everton
WCQ85 (C)	**England** 1-1 Romania
WCQ85 (C, 1, W)	**England** 5-0 Turkey
ECQ86 (C)	**England** 3-0 N Ireland
RC87 (C)	**England** 1-1 Brazil
LCEN87 (C, 2)	**Football League** 3-0 Rest of World
ECQ87 (C, 1)	**England** 8-0 Turkey
INT88 (C)	**England** 2-2 Netherlands
LCT88 (C)	**Man Utd** 2-0 Luton
LCT88 (C)	**Man Utd** 1-0 Everton
LCT88 (C)	**Man Utd** 1-2 Sheffield W
RC88 (C)	**England** 1-0 Scotland
RC88 (C)	**England** 1-1 Colombia
INT88 (C)	**England** 1-0 Denmark
WCQ88 (C)	**England** 0-0 Sweden
WCQ89 (C)	**England** 5-0 Albania
RC89 (C)	**England** 0-0 Chile
WCQ89 (C)	**England** 3-0 Poland
INT89 (C, W)	**England** 0-0 Italy
INT89 (C, 2, W)	**England** 2-1 Yugoslavia
INT90 (C, W)	**England** 4-2 Czechoslovakia
FAC90 (C, 1)	**Man Utd** 3-3 Crystal P
FAC90 (C)	**Man Utd** 1-0 Crystal P
INT90 (C)	**England** 1-2 Uruguay
INT91 (C, W)	**England** 2-0 Cameroon
ECQ91 (C)	**England** 1-1 Rep of Ireland
RLC91 (C)	**Man Utd** 0-1 Sheffield W
ECQ91	**England** 1-0 Turkey
CS93 (S)	**Man Utd** 1-1 Arsenal
FAC94 (S)	**Man Utd** 1-1 Oldham Athletic

As Manager

CCC97	**Middlesbrough** 1-1 Leicester
FAC97	**Middlesbrough** 0-2 Chelsea
CCC98	**Middlesbrough** 0-2 Chelsea

Robson, Jimmy (1, 1)

FAC62 (1)	**Burnley** 1-3 Spurs

Robson, John (2, 0)

FLC75	**Aston V** 1-0 Norwich
FLC77	**Aston V** 0-0 Everton

Robson, Keith (1, 0)

CS75 (S)	**West Ham** 0-2 Derby

Rocastle, David (16, 0)

LC87	**Arsenal** 2-1 Liverpool
LC88	**Arsenal** 2-3 Luton
WIT88	**Arsenal** 4-0 Spurs
WIT88 (W)	**Arsenal** 3-0 Bayern Munich
INT88	**England** 1-0 Denmark
WCQ89 (W)	**England** 5-0 Albania
WCQ89 (S)	**England** 3-0 Poland
MT89 (W)	**Arsenal** 1-0 Porto
MT89	**Arsenal** 1-0 Liverpool
CS89	**Arsenal** 0-1 Liverpool
INT89 (W)	**England** 2-1 Yugoslavia
INT90 (S)	**England** 1-0 Denmark
MT90 (W)	**Arsenal** 2-0 Aston V
MT90	**Arsenal** 0-1 Sampdoria
CS91 (W)	**Arsenal** 0-0 Spurs
INT92 (S)	**England** 1-1 Brazil

Rochford, Bill (2, 0)

FAC39	**Portsmouth** 4-1 Wolves
LWC42	**Portsmouth** 0-2 Brentford

Rodger, Graham (1, 0)

FAC87 (S)	**Coventry** 3-2 Spurs

Rodrigues, Peter (7, 0)

FAC69	**Leicester** 0-1 Man City
BC69	**Wales** 1-2 England
BC71	**Wales** 0-0 England
WCQ73 (W)	**Wales** 1-1 England
BC73	**Wales** 0-3 England
FAC76 (C)	**Southampton** 1-0 Man Utd
CS76 (C)	**Southampton** 0-1 Liverpool

Roeder, Glenn (3, 0)

FAC82 (C)	**QPR** 1-1 Spurs
LCT88 (C)	**Newcastle Utd** 0-0 Liverpool
LCT88 (C)	**Newcastle Utd** 0-2 Tranmere

Rogan, Anton (1, 0)

FAC92	**Sunderland** 0-2 Liverpool

Rogers, Don (1, 2)

FLC69 (2)	**Swindon** 3-1 Arsenal

Roper, Don (1, 0)

FAC52	**Arsenal** 0-1 Newcastle Utd

Roscamp, Jack (1, 2)

FAC28 (2)	**Blackburn** 3-1 Huddersfield

Rosenior, Leroy (1, 0)

MC86 (S)	**QPR** 0-3 Oxford

Rosenthal, Ronnie (2, 0)

CS90 (S)	**Liverpool** 1-1 Man Utd
CS92 (W)	**Liverpool** 3-4 Leeds

Ross, George (1, 0)

FAC64	**PNE** 2-3 WBA

Ross, Ian (1, 0)
FLC75 (C)   **Aston V** 1-0 Norwich

Rough, Alan (3, 0)
BC77   **Scotland** 2-1 England
BC81   **Scotland** 1-0 England
RC86   **Scotland** 1-2 England

Rougvie, Doug (1, 0)
FMC86   **Chelsea** 5-4 Man City

Rowe, Tommy (1, 0)
FAC39   **Portsmouth** 4-1 Wolves

Rowley, Jack (1, 2)
FAC48 (2)   **Man Utd** 4-2 Blackpool

Royle, Joe (6, 2)
FAC68   **Everton** 0-1 WBA
INT72 (1)   **England** 1-1 Yugoslavia
FLC76   **Man City** 2-1 Newcastle Utd
BC76 (S)   **England** 4-0 N Ireland
WCQ76 (1)   **England** 2-1 Finland
WCQ77 (W)   **England** 5-0 Luxembourg
As Manager
LC90   **Oldham** 0-1 Nottingham F
FAC94   **Oldham** 1-1 Man Utd
FAC95   **Everton** 1-0 Man Utd
CS95   **Everton** 1-0 Blackburn
PPO99   **Man City** 2-2 Gillingham

Ruddock, Neil (4, 0)
ZC92   **Southampton** 2-3 Nottingham F
FAC93   **Spurs** 0-1 Arsenal
INT94   **England** 1-0 Nigeria
CCC95   **Liverpool** 2-1 Bolton

Ruffell, Jimmy (1, 0)
FAC23   **West Ham** 0-2 Bolton

Rush, David (1, 0)
FAC92 (W)   **Sunderland** 0-2 Liverpool

Rush, Ian (20, 11)
BC81 (S)   **Wales** 0-0 England
FLC82 (1)   **Liverpool** 3-1 Spurs
CS82 (1)   **Liverpool** 1-0 Spurs
BC83 (1)   **Wales** 1-2 England
MC83   **Liverpool** 2-1 Man Utd
CS83   **Liverpool** 0-2 Man Utd
MC84   **Liverpool** 0-0 Everton
CS84   **Liverpool** 0-1 Everton
FAC86 (2)   **Liverpool** 3-1 Everton
CS86 (1)   **Liverpool** 1-1 Everton
LC87 (1)   **Liverpool** 1-2 Arsenal
FAC89 (S, 2)   **Liverpool** 3-2 Everton
MT89   **Liverpool** 2-0 Dynamo Kiev
MT89 (S)   **Liverpool** 0-1 Arsenal
CS89   **Liverpool** 1-0 Arsenal
CS90   **Liverpool** 1-1 Man Utd
FAC92 (1)   **Liverpool** 2-0 Sunderland
CS92 (1)   **Liverpool** 3-4 Leeds
CCC95 (C)   **Liverpool** 2-1 Bolton
FAC96 (S)   **Liverpool** 0-1 Man Utd

Rutherford, Sep (1, 1)
FAC34   **Portsmouth** 1-2 Man City

Ryan, Gerry (2, 0)
FAC83 (S)   **Brighton** 2-2 Man Utd
FAC83 (S)   **Brighton** 0-4 Man Utd

Ryan, Reg (1, 0)
FAC54   **WBA** 3-2 PNE

Ryan, Vaughan (2, 0)
LCT88   **Wimbledon** 0-1 Tranmere
CS88   **Wimbledon** 1-2 Liverpool

Sadler, David (4, 0)
ECQ67   **England** 2-0 N Ireland
INT67   **England** 2-2 USSR
EC68   **Man Utd** 4-1 Benfica
INT70   **England** 3-1 E Germany

Sagar, Ted (2, 0)
FAC33   **Everton** 3-0 Man City
BC36   **England** 1-1 Scotland

St John, Ian (4, 2)
BC61   **Scotland** 3-9 England
BC63   **Scotland** 2-1 England
BC65 (1)   **Scotland** 2-2 England
FAC65 (1)   **Liverpool** 2-1 Leeds

Salako, John (4, 1)
FAC90   **Crystal P** 3-3 Man Utd
FAC90 (W)   **Crystal P** 0-1 Man Utd
ZC91 (1)   **Crystal P** 4-1 Everton
INT91 (W)   **England** 0-1 Germany

Sammels, Jon (4, 2)
EYT63 (1)   **England** 4-0 N Ireland
YI63 (1)   **England** 5-2 Rest of UK
FLC68   **Arsenal** 0-1 Leeds
FLC69   **Arsenal** 1-3 Swindon

Samways, Vinny (6, 1)
WIT88 (W)   **Spurs** 0-4 Arsenal
FAC91 (W)   **Spurs** 3-1 Arsenal
FAC91 (W)   **Spurs** 2-1 Nottingham F
CS91   **Spurs** 0-0 Arsenal
FAC93 (W)   **Spurs** 0-1 Arsenal
CS95 (1)   **Everton** 1-0 Blackburn

Sanchez, Lawrie (2, 1)
FAC88 (1)   **Wimbledon** 1-0 Liverpool
CS88   **Wimbledon** 1-2 Liverpool

Sanders, Jim (1, 0)
FAC54   **WBA** 3-2 PNE

Sanderson, Keith (3, 0)
IV61   **Cambridge** 2-0 Oxford
IV62   **Cambridge** 5-2 Oxford
FLC67   **QPR** 3-2 WBA

Sandford, Ted (2, 1)
FAC31   **WBA** 2-1 Birmingham
FAC35 (1)   **WBA** 2-4 Sheffield W

Sansom, Kenny (39, 1)
SI74   **England** 5-2 France
SI74 (W)   **England** 4-0 W Germany
BC79   **England** 0-0 Wales
ECQ79   **England** 2-0 Bulgaria
ECQ80   **England** 2-0 Rep of Ireland
INT80   **England** 3-1 Argentina
BC80   **England** 1-1 N Ireland

WCQ80	**England**	4-0 Norway
WCQ80	**England**	2-1 Switzerland
INT81	**England**	1-2 Spain
WCQ81	**England**	0-0 Romania
INT81	**England**	0-1 Brazil
BC81	**England**	0-0 Wales
BC81	**England**	0-1 Scotland
BC82	**England**	4-0 N Ireland
INT82	**England**	2-0 Netherlands
INT82	**England**	1-2 W Germany
ECQ82	**England**	9-0 Luxembourg
ECQ83	**England**	0-0 Greece
ECQ83	**England**	2-0 Hungary
BC83	**England**	2-0 Scotland
ECQ83	**England**	0-1 Denmark
INT84	**England**	0-2 USSR
INT84	**England**	1-0 E Germany
WCQ84 (1)	**England**	5-0 Finland
INT85	**England**	2-1 Rep of Ireland
WCQ85	**England**	1-1 Romania
WCQ85	**England**	5-0 Turkey
WCQ85	**England**	0-0 N Ireland
RC86	**England**	2-1 Scotland
ECQ86	**England**	3-0 N Ireland
ECQ86	**England**	2-0 Yugoslavia
LC87 (C)	**Arsenal**	2-1 Liverpool
LCEN87	**Football League**	3-0 Rest of World
ECQ87	**England**	8-0 Turkey
INT88	**England**	2-2 Netherlands
LC88	**Arsenal**	2-3 Luton
RC88	**England**	1-0 Scotland
RC88	**England**	1-1 Colombia

Saul, Frank (2, 1)

FAC67 (1)	**Spurs**	2-1 Chelsea
FAT77	**Dagenham**	1-2 Scarborough

Saunders, Dean (3, 3)

FAC92	**Liverpool**	2-0 Sunderland
CS92 (1)	**Liverpool**	3-4 Leeds
CCC94 (2)	**Aston Villa**	3-1 Man Utd

Savage, Robbie (2, 0)

WLC99 (W)	**Leicester**	0-1 Spurs
WLC00	**Leicester**	2-1 Tranmere

Saward, Pat (2, 0)

FAC57	**Aston Villa**	2-1 Man Utd
WCQ57	**Rep of Ireland**	1-5 England

Sayer, Peter (1, 0)

BC77	**Wales**	1-0 England

Scales, John (7, 0)

LCT88	**Wimbledon**	0-1 Tranmere
FAC88 (S)	**Wimbledon**	1-0 Liverpool
CS88 (W)	**Wimbledon**	1-2 Liverpool
CCC95	**Liverpool**	2-1 Bolton
UC95	**England**	2-1 Japan
UC95 (W)	**England**	1-3 Brazil
FAC96	**Liverpool**	0-1 Man Utd

Schmeichel, Peter (13, 0)

INT90	**Denmark**	0-1 England
RLC92	**Man Utd**	1-0 Nottingham F
CS93	**Man Utd**	1-1 Arsenal

INT94	**Denmark**	0-1 England
FAC94	**Man Utd**	1-1 Oldham
FAC94	**Man Utd**	4-0 Chelsea
CS94	**Man Utd**	2-0 Blackburn
FAC95	**Man Utd**	0-1 Everton
FAC96	**Man Utd**	1-0 Liverpool
CS96	**Man Utd**	4-0 Newcastle Utd
CS97	**Man Utd**	1-1 Chelsea
CS98	**Man Utd**	0-3 Arsenal
FAC99	**Man Utd**	2-0 Newcastle Utd

Scholes, Paul (21, 6)

FAC95 (S)	**Man Utd**	0-1 Everton
FAC96 (S)	**Man Utd**	1-0 Liverpool
CS96 (W)	**Man Utd**	4-0 Newcastle Utd
CS97	**Man Utd**	1-1 Chelsea
WCQ97 (1)	**England**	4-0 Moldova
INT97 (1, W)	**England**	2-0 Cameroon
INT98	**England**	3-0 Portugal
INT98	**England**	0-0 Saudi Arabia
CS98 (W)	**Man Utd**	0-3 Arsenal
ECQ98 (W)	**England**	0-0 Bulgaria
INT99 (S)	**England**	0-2 France
ECQ99 (3, W)	**England**	3-1 Poland
FAC99 (1, W)	**Man Utd**	2-0 Newcastle Utd
ECQ99 (D)	**England**	0-0 Sweden
CS99	**Man Utd**	1-2 Arsenal
ECQ99 (W)	**England**	0-1 Scotland
INT00	**England**	0-0 Argentina
INT00	**England**	1-1 Brazil
INT00 (W)	**England**	2-0 Ukraine
CS00	**Man Utd**	0-2 Chelsea
WCQ00	**England**	0-1 Germany

Schwarzer, Mark (2, 0)

CCC97	**Middlesbrough**	1-1 Leicester
CCC98	**Middlesbrough**	0-2 Chelsea

Scott, Alex (1, 0)

FAC66	**Everton**	3-2 Sheffield W

Scott, Laurie (11, 0)

FLWC41	**Arsenal**	1-1 PNE
CHA41	**RAF**	6-3 Met Police
LSC43	**Arsenal**	7-1 Charlton
WI43	**England**	8-3 Wales
WI44	**England**	6-2 Scotland
WI44	**England**	6-2 Scotland
VI45	**England**	2-2 France
VI46	**England**	2-0 Belgium
IT46	**FA**	3-5 Army PT Corps
BC47	**England**	1-1 Scotland
FAC50	**Arsenal**	2-0 Liverpool

Scott, Peter (2, 0)

BC76 (S)	**N Ireland**	0-4 England
BC78	**N Ireland**	0-1 England

Scott, Robert (1, 0)

FAC39	**Wolves**	1-4 Portsmouth

Scott, Sandy (1, 0)

FAC49	**Leicester**	1-3 Wolves

Scoular, Jimmy (1, 0)

FAC55 (C)	**Newcastle Utd**	3-1 Man City

Seagraves, Mark (4, 0)

SI82 (C)	**England** 7-0	Netherlands
SI82	**England** 0-0	Scotland
PPO91	**Bolton** 0-1	Tranmere
CCC95	**Bolton** 1-2	Liverpool

Sealey, Alan (1, 2)

ECW65 (2)	**West Ham** 2-0	TSV Munich

Sealey, Les (6, 0)

SC88	**Luton** 1-4	Reading
LC89	**Luton** 1-3	Nottingham F
FAC90	**Man Utd** 1-0	Crystal P
CS90	**Man Utd** 1-1	Liverpool
RLC91	**Man Utd** 0-1	Sheffield W
CCC94	**Man Utd** 1-3	Aston Villa

Sealy, Tony (1, 0)

FLC79 (S)	**Southampton** 2-3	Nottingham F

Seaman, David (49, 0)

INT90 (S)	**England** 4-2	Czechoslovakia
MT90	**Arsenal** 2-0	Aston Villa
MT90	**Arsenal** 0-1	Sampdoria
INT91	**England** 2-0	Cameroon
ECQ91	**England** 1-1	Rep of Ireland
FAC91	**Arsenal** 1-3	Spurs
INT91	**England** 2-2	Argentina
CS91	**Arsenal** 0-0	Spurs
FAC93	**Arsenal** 1-0	Spurs
CCC93	**Arsenal** 2-1	Sheffield W
FAC93	**Arsenal** 1-1	Sheffield W
FAC93	**Arsenal** 2-1	Sheffield W
CS93	**Arsenal** 1-1	Man Utd
WCQ93	**England** 3-0	Poland
INT94	**England** 1-0	Denmark
INT94	**England** 0-0	Norway
INT94	**England** 2-0	USA
INT94	**England** 1-1	Romania
INT95	**England** 0-0	Colombia
INT95	**England** 3-1	Switzerland
INT95	**England** 1-1	Portugal
INT96	**England** 1-0	Bulgaria
INT96	**England** 0-0	Croatia
INT96 (W)	**England** 3-0	Hungary
ECH96	**England** 1-1	Switzerland
ECH96	**England** 2-0	Scotland
ECH96	**England** 4-1	Netherlands
ECH96	**England** 0-0	Spain
ECH96	**England** 1-1	Germany
WCQ96	**England** 2-1	Poland
WCQ97	**England** 2-0	Georgia
WCQ97 (C)	**England** 4-0	Moldova
INT98	**England** 3-0	Portugal
FAC98	**Arsenal** 2-0	Newcastle Utd
INT98	**England** 0-0	Saudi Arabia
CS98	**Arsenal** 3-0	Man Utd
ECQ98	**England** 0-0	Bulgaria
EC98	**Arsenal** 2-1	Panathinaikos
EC98	**Arsenal** 1-1	Dynamo Kiev
EC98	**Arsenal** 0-1	Lens
INT99 (W)	**England** 0-2	France
ECQ99	**England** 3-1	Poland
ECQ99	**England** 0-0	Sweden
EC99	**Arsenal** 2-4	Barcelona
EC99	**Arsenal** 0-1	Fiorentina
ECQ99	**England** 0-1	Scotland
INT00	**England** 0-0	Argentina
INT00	**England** 1-1	Brazil
WCQ00	**England** 0-1	Germany

Sear, Cliff (1, 0)

BC62	**Wales** 0-4	England

Seddon, Bill (1, 0)

FAC30	**Arsenal** 2-0	Huddersfield

Seddon, Jimmy (3, 0)

FAC23	**Bolton** 2-0	West Ham
FAC26	**Bolton** 1-0	Man City
FAC29 (C)	**Bolton** 2-0	Portsmouth

Sedgley, Steve (5, 0)

CS87 (S)	**Coventry** 0-1	Everton
FAC91	**Spurs** 3-1	Arsenal
FAC91	**Spurs** 2-1	Nottingham F
CS91	**Spurs** 0-0	Arsenal
FAC93 (W)	**Spurs** 0-1	Arsenal

Sellars, Scott (4, 0)

FMC87 (W)	**Blackburn** 1-0	Charlton
LCT88	**Blackburn** 0-0	Aston Villa
PPO92 (W)	**Blackburn** 1-0	Leicester
PPO99 (S)	**Bolton** 0-2	Watford

Selley, Ian (1, 0)

FAC93	**Arsenal** 1-0	Spurs

Setters, Maurice (2, 0)

U23I57	**England** 3-2	Romania
FAC63	**Man Utd** 3-1	Leicester

Sewell, Jackie (2, 1)

INT53 (1)	**England** 3-6	Hungary
FAC57	**Aston Villa** 2-1	Man Utd

Seymour, Stan (1, 1)

FAC24 (1)	**Newcastle Utd** 2-0	Aston Villa
As Manager		
FAC51	**Newcastle Utd** 2-0	Arsenal
FAC52	**Newcastle Utd** 1-0	Blackpool

Shackleton, Len (3, 2)

IT46 (1)	**FA** 3-5	Army PT Corps
BC54	**England** 3-2	Wales
INT54 (1)	**England** 3-1	W Germany

Shankly, Bill (8, 0)

FAC37	**PNE** 1-3	Sunderland
BC38	**Scotland** 1-0	England
FAC38	**PNE** 1-0	Huddersfield
FLWC41	**PNE** 1-1	Arsenal
WI41	**Scotland** 0-2	England
WI42	**Scotland** 0-3	England
WI42	**Scotland** 0-0	England
CHA43	**RAF** 4-3	Met Police
As Manager		
FAC65	**Liverpool** 2-1	Leeds
FAC71	**Liverpool** 1-2	Arsenal
FAC74	**Liverpool** 3-0	Newcastle Utd

Sharp, Graeme (11, 2)

MC84	**Everton** 0-0	Liverpool

FAC84 (1)	**Everton** 2-0 Watford
CS84	**Everton** 1-0 Liverpool
FAC85	**Everton** 0-1 Man Utd
CS85	**Everton** 2-0 Man Utd
FAC86	**Everton** 1-3 Liverpool
CS86	**Everton** 1-1 Liverpool
CS87	**Everton** 1-0 Coventry
SC89 (1)	**Everton** 3-4 Nottingham F
FAC89	**Everton** 2-3 Liverpool
FAC94	**Oldham** 1-1 Manchester Utd

Sharp, Wilf (1, 0)

FAC35	**Sheffield W** 4-2 WBA

Sharpe, Lee (9, 0)

ECQ91 (S)	**England** 1-1 Rep of Ireland
RLC91	**Man Utd** 0-1 Sheffield W
RLC92 (S)	**Man Utd** 1-0 Nottingham F
WCQ93	**England** 3-0 Poland
CCC94 (S)	**Man Utd** 1-3 Aston Villa
FAC94	**Man Utd** 1-1 Oldham
FAC94 (S)	**Man Utd** 4-0 Chelsea
CS94	**Man Utd** 2-0 Blackburn
FAC95 (W)	**Man Utd** 0-1 Everton

Shaw, George (3, 0)

FAC31	**WBA** 2-1 Birmingham
BC32	**England** 3-0 Scotland
FAC35	**WBA** 2-4 Sheffield W

Shaw, Graham (4, 0)

INT58	**England** 5-0 USSR
BC59	**England** 1-0 Scotland
INT59	**England** 2-2 Italy
BC62	**England** 4-0 Wales

Shaw, John (1, 0)

BC47 (C)	**Scotland** 1-1 England

Shaw, Richard (3, 0)

FAC90	**Crystal P** 3-3 Man Utd
FAC90	**Crystal P** 0-1 Man Utd
ZC91	**Crystal P** 4-1 Everton

Shearer, Alan (41, 18)

INT92 (1)	**England** 2-0 France
ZC92	**Southampton** 2-3 Nottingham F
WCQ92	**England** 1-1 Norway
WCQ92 (1)	**England** 4-0 Turkey
INT94	**England** 1-0 Denmark
INT94 (1)	**England** 5-0 Greece
INT94	**England** 0-0 Norway
INT94 (2, W)	**England** 2-0 USA
INT94	**England** 1-1 Romania
INT94 (W)	**England** 1-0 Nigeria
UC95	**England** 2-1 Japan
UC95	**England** 1-3 Brazil
CS95	**Blackburn** 0-1 Everton
INT95 (W)	**England** 0-0 Colombia
INT95	**England** 3-1 Switzerland
INT95	**England** 1-1 Portugal
INT96 (S)	**England** 3-0 Hungary
ECH96 (1)	**England** 1-1 Switzerland
ECH96 (1)	**England** 2-0 Scotland
ECH96 (2, W)	**England** 4-1 Netherlands
ECH96	**England** 0-0 Spain

ECH96 (1)	**England** 1-1 Germany
CS96	**Newcastle Utd** 0-4 Man Utd
WCQ96 (C, 2)	**England** 2-1 Poland
WCQ97 (C)	**England** 0-1 Italy
WCQ97 (C, 1)	**England** 2-0 Georgia
INT98 (S)	**England** 0-2 Chile
INT98 (C, 2)	**England** 3-0 Portugal
FAC98	**Newcastle Utd** 0-2 Arsenal
INT98 (C, W)	**England** 0-0 Saudi Arabia
ECQ98 (C)	**England** 0-0 Bulgaria
INT99 (C)	**England** 0-2 France
ECQ99 (C)	**England** 3-1 Poland
FAC99 (C)	**Newcastle Utd** 0-2 Man Utd
ECQ99 (C)	**England** 0-0 Sweden
ECQ99 (C, 3)	**England** 6-0 Luxembourg
ECQ99 (C)	**England** 0-1 Scotland
INT00 (C, W)	**England** 0-0 Argentina
FAC00 (C)	**Newcastle Utd** 1-2 Chelsea
INT00 (C, W)	**England** 1-1 Brazil
INT00 (C)	**England** 2-0 Ukraine

Shearer, Bobby (1, 0)

BC61	**Scotland** 3-9 England

Sheedy, Kevin (10, 0)

MC84 (W)	**Everton** 0-0 Liverpool
FAC85	**Everton** 0-1 Man Utd
CS85	**Everton** 2-0 Man Utd
FAC86	**Everton** 1-3 Liverpool
CS86 (W)	**Everton** 1-1 Liverpool
CS87 (W)	**Everton** 1-0 Coventry
SC89	**Everton** 3-4 Nottingham F
FAC89 (W)	**Everton** 2-3 Liverpool
ECQ91	**Rep of Ireland** 1-1 England
ZC91	**Everton** 1-4 Crystal P

Sheppard, Rick (1, 0)

FLC67	**WBA** 2-3 QPR

Sheridan, John (6, 1)

LCT88	**Leeds** 0-3 Nottingham F
RLC91 (1)	**Sheffield W** 1-0 Man Utd
FAC93 (W)	**Sheffield W** 2-1 Sheffield Utd
CCC93	**Sheffield W** 1-2 Arsenal
FAC93	**Sheffield W** 1-1 Arsenal
FAC93	**Sheffield W** 1-2 Arsenal

Sheringham, Teddy (30, 7)

ZC92	**Nottingham F** 3-2 Southampton
RLC92	**Nottingham F** 0-1 Man Utd
FAC93	**Spurs** 0-1 Arsenal
INT94 (W)	**England** 2-0 USA
INT94 (S)	**England** 1-1 Romania
INT94 (S)	**England** 1-0 Nigeria
INT95 (W)	**England** 0-0 Uruguay
UC95 (S)	**England** 2-1 Japan
UC95 (W)	**England** 1-3 Brazil
INT95 (S)	**England** 0-0 Colombia
INT95 (1)	**England** 3-1 Switzerland
INT96 (W)	**England** 1-0 Bulgaria
INT96	**England** 0-0 Croatia
INT96	**England** 3-0 Hungary
ECH96 (W)	**England** 1-1 Switzerland
ECH96	**England** 2-0 Scotland

ECH96 (2, W)	**England** 4-1 Netherlands	
ECH96 (W)	**England** 0-0 Spain	
ECH96	**England** 1-1 Germany	
INT97 (1, W)	**England** 2-0 Mexico	
WCQ97 (1)	**England** 2-0 Georgia	
CS97 (W)	**Man Utd** 1-1 Chelsea	
INT98 (W)	**England** 0-2 Chile	
INT98 (1, W)	**England** 3-0 Portugal	
INT98 (W)	**England** 0-0 Saudi Arabia	
CS98 (S)	**Man Utd** 0-3 Arsenal	
ECQ98 (S)	**England** 0-0 Bulgaria	
FAC99 (S, 1)	**Man Utd** 2-0 Newcastle Utd	
CS99 (S)	**Man Utd** 1-2 Arsenal	
CS00 (W)	**Man Utd** 0-2 Chelsea	

Sherwood, Alf (3, 0)

BC52	**Wales** 2-5 England
BC54 (C)	**Wales** 2-3 England
BC56 (C)	**Wales** 1-3 England

Sherwood, Steve (1, 0)

FAC84	**Watford** 0-2 Everton

Sherwood, Tim (4, 0)

CS94 (C)	**Blackburn** 0-2 Man Utd
CS95 (C)	**Blackburn** 0-1 Everton
ECQ99	**England** 3-1 Poland
ECQ99	**England** 0-0 Sweden

Shilton, Peter (58, 0)

SI65	**England** 3-0 Scotland
FAC69	**Leicester** 0-1 Man City
INT70	**England** 3-1 E Germany
BC71	**England** 0-0 Wales
ECQ71	**England** 1-1 Switzerland
BC72	**England** 0-1 N Ireland
INT72	**England** 1-1 Yugoslavia
BC73	**England** 3-0 Wales
BC73	**England** 1-0 Scotland
INT73	**England** 7-0 Austria
WCQ73	**England** 1-1 Poland
INT73	**England** 0-1 Italy
BC74	**England** 1-0 N Ireland
INT74	**England** 2-2 Argentina
ECQ75	**England** 5-0 Cyprus
BC77	**England** 0-1 Wales
INT78	**England** 4-1 Hungary
CS78	**Nottingham F** 5-0 Ipswich
INT78	**England** 1-0 Czechoslovakia
FLC79	**Nottingham F** 3-2 Southampton
FLC80	**Nottingham F** 0-1 Wolves
WCQ80	**England** 4-0 Norway
WCQ80	**England** 2-1 Switzerland
WCQ81	**England** 0-0 Romania
WCQ81	**England** 1-0 Hungary
INT82 (C)	**England** 2-0 Netherlands
INT82	**England** 1-2 W Germany
BC83 (C)	**England** 2-1 Wales
ECQ83 (C)	**England** 0-0 Greece
ECQ83 (C)	**England** 2-0 Hungary
BC83	**England** 2-0 Scotland
ECQ83	**England** 0-1 Denmark
BC84	**England** 1-0 N Ireland

INT84	**England** 0-2 USSR
INT84	**England** 1-0 E Germany
WCQ84	**England** 5-0 Finland
WCQ85	**England** 1-1 Romania
WCQ85	**England** 5-0 Turkey
WCQ85	**England** 0-0 N Ireland
RC86	**England** 2-1 Scotland
ECQ86	**England** 3-0 N Ireland
RC87	**England** 1-1 Brazil
LCEN87 (W)	**Football League** 3-0 Rest of World
ECQ87	**England** 8-0 Turkey
INT88	**England** 2-2 Netherlands
RC88	**England** 1-0 Scotland
RC88	**England** 1-1 Colombia
INT88 (W)	**England** 1-0 Denmark
WCQ88	**England** 0-0 Sweden
WCQ89	**England** 5-0 Albania
RC89	**England** 0-0 Chile
WCQ89	**England** 3-0 Poland
INT89 (W)	**England** 0-0 Italy
INT89 (W)	**England** 2-1 Yugoslavia
INT90 (W)	**England** 1-0 Brazil
INT90 (W)	**England** 4-2 Czechoslovakia
INT90 (W)	**England** 1-0 Denmark
INT90	**England** 1-2 Uruguay

Shimwell, Eddie (3, 1)

FAC48 (1)	**Blackpool** 2-4 Man Utd
FAC51	**Blackpool** 0-2 Newcastle Utd
FAC53	**Blackpool** 4-3 Bolton

Shipley, George (1, 0)

FMC87	**Charlton** 0-1 Blackburn

Shirtliff, Peter (1, 0)

RLC91	**Sheffield W** 1-0 Man Utd

Shorthouse, Bill (1, 0)

FAC49	**Wolves** 3-1 Leicester

Shortt, Bill (1, 0)

BC52	**Wales** 2-5 England

Shotton, Malcolm (1, 0)

MC86 (C)	**Oxford** 3-0 QPR

Showell, George (1, 0)

FAC60	**Wolves** 3-0 Blackburn

Showers, Derek (1, 0)

BC75 (S)	**Wales** 2-2 England

Shreeve, Jack (4, 0)

LSC43	**Charlton** 1-7 Arsenal
LSC44	**Charlton** 3-1 Chelsea
FAC46	**Charlton** 1-4 Derby
FAC47	**Charlton** 1-0 Burnley

Sibley, Frank (1, 0)

FLC67	**QPR** 3-2 WBA

Sidlow, Cyril (3, 0)

WI40	**Wales** 1-0 England
WI43	**Wales** 3-8 England
FAC50	**Liverpool** 0-2 Arsenal

Silvestre, Mikael (1, 0)

CS00 (W)	**Man Utd** 0-2 Chelsea

Silvinho (2, 0)

CS99 (W)	**Arsenal** 2-1 Man Utd

| EC99 (S) | **Arsenal** 3-1 AIK Stockholm |
| INT00 (W) | **Brazil** 1-1 England |

Simpson, Billy (1, 1)

| BC57 (1) | **N Ireland** 3-2 England |

Simpson, Jimmy (1, 0)

| BC36 (C) | **Scotland** 1-1 England |

Simpson, Neil (1, 0)

| RC88 (W) | **Scotland** 0-1 England |

Simpson, Paul (3, 0)

FMC86 (S)	**Man City** 4-5 Chelsea
AIC93 (S)	**Derby** 1-3 Cremonese
PPO94	**Derby** 1-2 Leicester

Simpson, Peter (4, 0)

FLC68	**Arsenal** 0-1 Leeds
FLC69 (W)	**Arsenal** 1-3 Swindon
FAC71	**Arsenal** 2-1 Liverpool
FAC72	**Arsenal** 0-1 Leeds

Simpson, Ronnie (4, 0)

OLY48	**Great Britain** 3-5 Denmark
FAC52	**Newcastle Utd** 1-0 Arsenal
FAC55	**Newcastle Utd** 3-1 Man City
ECQ67	**Scotland** 3-2 England

Sims, Nigel (1, 0)

| FAC57 | **Aston Villa** 2-1 Man Utd |

Sinclair, Frank (6, 1)

FAC94	**Chelsea** 2-0 Luton
FAC94	**Chelsea** 0-4 Manchester Utd
FAC97	**Chelsea** 2-0 Middlesbrough
CS97	**Chelsea** 1-1 Manchester Utd
CCC98 (1)	**Chelsea** 2-0 Middlesbrough
WLC00	**Leicester** 2-1 Tranmere

Singleton, Tony (1, 0)

| FAC64 | **PNE** 2-3 West Ham |

Sinnott, Lee (2, 0)

| FAC84 | **Watford** 0-2 Everton |
| PPO95 (C) | **Huddersfield** 2-1 Bristol R |

Sinton, Andy
(4, 1)

VS81 (1)	**England** 4-0 N Ireland
SI81 (S)	**England** 1-2 W Germany
INT92	**England** 1-1 Brazil
WLC99 (S)	**Spurs** 1-0 Leicester

Sissons, John
(5, 5)

SI61 (2)	**England** 8-1 Wales
EYT63 (1)	**England** 4-0 N Ireland
YI63 (1)	**England** 5-2 Rest of UK
FAC64 (1)	**West Ham** 3-2 PNE
ECW65	**West Ham** 2-0 TSV Munich

Sjoberg, John (2, 0)

| SI56 | **Scotland** 2-1 England |
| FAC63 | **Leicester** 1-3 Man Utd |

Slater, Bill (7, 0)

FAC51	**Blackpool** 0-2 Newcastle Utd
AI52	**England** 1-2 Scotland
BC54	**England** 3-2 Wales
INT54	**England** 3-1 West Germany
INT58	**England** 2-1 Portugal

| INT58 | **England** 5-0 USSR |
| FAC60 (C) | **Wolves** 3-0 Blackburn |

Slater, Robbie (1, 0)

| CS94 | **Blackburn** 0-2 Man Utd |

Slaven, Bernie (3, 0)

ZC90	**Middlesbrough** 0-1 Chelsea
AT93 (1)	**Port V** 2-1 Stockport
PPO93	**Port V** 0-3 WBA

Sloan, Tommy (1, 0)

| FAC27 | **Cardiff** 1-0 Arsenal |

Slough, Alan (1, 0)

| FAC75 | **Fulham** 0-2 West Ham |

Smallman, David (1, 0)

| BC75 (W) | **Wales** 2-2 England |

Smart, Roger (1, 1)

| FLC69 (1) | **Swindon** 3-1 Arsenal |

Smart, Tom (2, 0)

| BC24 | **England** 1-1 Scotland |
| FAC24 | **Aston Villa** 0-2 Newcastle Utd |

Smillie, Neil (3, 1)

FAC83	**Brighton** 2-2 Man Utd
FAC83	**Brighton** 0-4 Man Utd
SC88 (1)	**Reading** 4-1 Luton

Smith, Alan (19, 7)

LCEN87 (S)	**Football League** 3-0 Rest of World
LC88 (1)	**Arsenal** 2-3 Luton
WIT88 (1)	**Arsenal** 4-0 Spurs
WIT88 (2)	**Arsenal** 3-0 Bayern Munich
WCQ89 (S)	**England** 3-0 Poland
MT89 (W)	**Arsenal** 1-0 Porto
MT89	**Arsenal** 1-0 Liverpool
CS89 (W)	**Arsenal** 0-1 Liverpool
MT90	**Arsenal** 2-0 Aston Villa
MT90	**Arsenal** 0-1 Sampdoria
FAC91 (1)	**Arsenal** 1-3 Spurs
INT91 (1)	**England** 3-1 USSR
INT91	**England** 2-2 Argentina
CS91	**Arsenal** 0-0 Spurs
INT91	**England** 0-1 Germany
ECQ91 (1)	**England** 1-0 Turkey
FAC93 (S)	**Arsenal** 1-0 Spurs
FAC93 (S)	**Arsenal** 1-1 Sheffield W
FAC93	**Arsenal** 2-1 Sheffield W

Smith, Billy (3, 0)

BC28	**England** 1-5 Scotland
FAC28	**Huddersfield** 1-3 Blackburn
FAC30	**Huddersfield** 0-2 Arsenal

Smith, Billy (1, 0)

| FAC34 | **Portsmouth** 1-2 Man City |

Smith, Bobby (10, 8)

CYC50	**Middlesex** 1-2 Essex
INT60 (2)	**England** 4-2 Spain
BC60 (1)	**England** 5-1 Wales
BC61 (2)	**England** 9-3 Scotland
FAC61 (1)	**Spurs** 2-0 Leicester
FAC62 (1)	**Spurs** 3-1 Burnley
BC63	**England** 1-2 Scotland
INT63	**England** 1-1 Brazil

CEN63   **England** 2-1 FIFA
BC63 (1)   **England** 8-3 N Ireland

Smith, Denis (1, 0)
FLC72   **Stoke** 2-1 Chelsea
As Manager
LCT88   **Sunderland** 0-0 Wigan
PPO90   **Sunderland** 0-1 Swindon

Smith, Gordon (2, 0)
WI44   **Scotland** 2-6 England
BC47   **Scotland** 1-1 England

Smith, Gordon (2, 1)
FAC83 (1)   **Brighton** 2-2 Man Utd
FAC83   **Brighton** 0-4 Man Utd

Smith, Jack (2, 0)
FAC29   **Portsmouth** 0-2 Bolton
FAC34   **Portsmouth** 1-2 Man City

Smith, Jack (1, 0)
FAC36   **Sheffield Utd** 0-1 Arsenal

Smith, Jim (1, 0)
FAC64   **PNE** 2-3 West Ham

Smith, Jimmy (1, 0)
FAC74 (W)   **Newcastle Utd** 0-3 Liverpool

Smith, Jock (1, 0)
BC24   **Scotland** 1-1 England

Smith, Joe (2, 0)
FAC23 (C)   **Bolton** 2-0 West Ham
FAC26   **Bolton** 1-0 Man City
As Manager
FAC48   **Blackpool** 2-4 Man Utd
FAC51   **Blackpool** 0-2 Newcastle Utd
FAC53   **Blackpool** 4-3 Bolton

Smith, John (2, 1)
FAC23 (1)   **Bolton** 2-0 West Ham
FAC26   **Bolton** 1-0 Man City

Smith, John (1, 0)
FLC69   **Swindon** 3-1 Arsenal

Smith, Les (1, 0)
FAC57   **Aston Villa** 2-1 Man Utd

Smith, Lionel (4, 0)
FAC52   **Arsenal** 0-1 Newcastle Utd
BC52   **England** 5-2 Wales
INT52   **England** 5-0 Belgium
BC53   **England** 2-2 Austria

Smith, Tom (4, 0)
BC34   **Scotland** 0-3 England
BC38   **Scotland** 1-0 England
FAC38 (C)   **PNE** 1-0 Huddersfield
FLWC41 (C)   **PNE** 1-1 Arsenal

Smith, Tommy (9, 2)
EYT63   **England** 4-0 N Ireland
YI63 (2)   **England** 5-2 Rest of UK
FAC65   **Liverpool** 2-1 Leeds Utd
FAC71 (C)   **Liverpool** 1-2 Arsenal
BC71   **England** 0-0 Wales
FAC74   **Liverpool** 3-0 Newcastle Utd
CS74   **Liverpool** 1-1 Leeds
FAC77   **Liverpool** 1-2 Manchester Utd
FLC78   **Liverpool** 0-0 Nottingham F

Smith, Trevor (3, 0)
FAC56   **Birmingham** 1-3 Man City
U23I57 (C)   **England** 3-2 Romania
INT59   **England** 2-3 Sweden

Smith, Wilf (1, 0)
FAC66   **Sheffield W** 2-3 Everton

Smyth, Sammy (1, 1)
FAC49 (1)   **Wolves** 3-1 Leicester

Sneekes, Richard (1, 0)
CCC95   **Bolton** 1-2 Liverpool

Solano, Nolberto (2, 0)
FAC99 (W)   **Newcastle Utd** 0-2 Man Utd
FAC00   **Newcastle Utd** 1-2 Chelsea

Solskjaer, Ole-Gunnar (4, 0)
CS98 (S)   **Man Utd** 0-3 Arsenal
FAC99   **Man Utd** 2-0 Newcastle Utd
CS99 (S)   **Man Utd** 1-2 Arsenal
CS00 (W)   **Man Utd** 0-2 Chelsea

Sommer, Juergen (2, 0)
FAC94   **Luton** 0-2 Chelsea
INT94 (S)   **USA** 0-2 England

Souness, Graeme (12, 1)
EC78   **Liverpool** 1-0 Bruges
BC79   **Scotland** 1-3 England
CS79   **Liverpool** 3-1 Arsenal
CS80   **Liverpool** 1-0 West Ham
FLC81   **Liverpool** 1-1 West Ham
FLC82 (C)   **Liverpool** 3-1 Spurs
CS82 (C)   **Liverpool** 1-0 Spurs
MC83 (C)   **Liverpool** 2-1 Manchester Utd
BC83 (C)   **Scotland** 0-2 England
CS83 (C)   **Liverpool** 0-2 Man Utd
MC84 (C)   **Liverpool** 0-0 Everton
RC86 (C, 1)   **Scotland** 1-2 England
As Manager
FAC92   **Liverpool** 2-0 Sunderland
CS92   **Liverpool** 3-4 Leeds

Southall, Neville (13, 0)
BC83   **Wales** 1-2 England
MC84   **Everton** 0-0 Liverpool
FAC84   **Everton** 2-0 Watford
CS84   **Everton** 1-0 Liverpool
FAC85   **Everton** 0-1 Man Utd
CS85   **Everton** 2-0 Man Utd
LCT88   **Everton** 1-1 Wolves
LCT88   **Everton** 0-1 Man Utd
SC89   **Everton** 3-4 Nottingham F
FAC89   **Everton** 2-3 Liverpool
ZC91   **Everton** 1-4 Crystal P
FAC95   **Everton** 1-0 Man Utd
CS95   **Everton** 1-0 Blackburn

Southgate, Gareth (22, 0)
INT95 (S)   **England** 1-1 Portugal
CCC96   **Aston Villa** 3-0 Leeds
INT96   **England** 1-0 Bulgaria
INT96 (S)   **England** 3-0 Hungary
ECH96   **England** 1-1 Switzerland
ECH96   **England** 2-0 Scotland
ECH96   **England** 4-1 Netherlands

ECH96	**England**	0-0 Spain
ECH96	**England**	1-1 Germany
WCQ96 (W)	**England**	2-1 Poland
INT97	**England**	2-0 Mexico
WCQ97 (S)	**England**	2-0 Georgia
WCQ97	**England**	4-0 Moldova
INT97 (W)	**England**	2-0 Cameroon
INT98	**England**	0-0 Saudi Arabia
ECQ98	**England**	0-0 Bulgaria
ECQ99	**England**	0-1 Sweden
INT00	**England**	0-0 Argentina
FAC00 (C)	**Aston Villa**	0-0 Bolton
FAC00 (C)	**Aston Villa**	0-1 Chelsea
INT00	**England**	2-0 Ukraine
WCQ00	**England**	0-1 Germany

Spackman, Nigel (3, 0)

FMC86	**Chelsea**	5-4 Man City
LC87	**Liverpool**	1-2 Arsenal
FAC88 (W)	**Liverpool**	0-1 Wimbledon

Spavin, Alan (1, 0)

FAC64	**PNE**	2-3 West Ham

Speed, Gary (5, 0)

CS92	**Leeds**	4-3 Liverpool
CCC96	**Leeds**	0-3 Aston Villa
FAC98	**Newcastle Utd**	0-2 Arsenal
FAC99	**Newcastle Utd**	0-2 Manchester Utd
FAC00	**Newcastle Utd**	1-2 Chelsea

Speedie, David (4, 3)

FMC86 (3)	**Chelsea**	5-4 Man City
RC86	**Scotland**	1-2 England
CS87	**Coventry**	0-1 Everton
PPO92	**Blackburn**	1-0 Leicester

Spence, Bonwell (1, 0)

FAC30	**Huddersfield**	0-2 Arsenal

Spence, Derek (2, 0)

BC76	**N Ireland**	0-4 England
ECQ79 (S)	**N Ireland**	0-4 England

Spencer, Charlie (2, 0)

BC24	**England**	1-1 Scotland
FAC24	**Newcastle Utd**	2-0 Aston Villa

Spencer, John (3, 0)

FAC94	**Chelsea**	2-0 Luton
FAC94	**Chelsea**	0-4 Man Utd
ECH96 (W)	**Scotland**	0-2 England

Spicer, Eddie (1, 0)

FAC50	**Liverpool**	0-2 Arsenal

Sprake, Gary (6, 0)

FAC65	**Leeds**	1-2 Liverpool
FLC68	**Leeds**	1-0 Arsenal
BC69	**Wales**	1-2 England
FAC70	**Leeds**	2-2 Chelsea
BC71	**Wales**	0-0 England
WCQ73	**Wales**	1-1 England

Springett, Peter (1, 0)

FLC67	**QPR**	3-2 WBA

Springett, Ron (12, 0)

BC59	**England**	2-1 N Ireland
INT60	**England**	3-3 Yugoslavia
INT60	**England**	4-2 Spain
BC61	**England**	9-3 Scotland
INT61	**England**	8-0 Mexico
WCQ61	**England**	2-0 Portugal
BC61	**England**	1-1 N Ireland
INT62	**England**	3-1 Austria
INT62	**England**	3-1 Switzerland
BC62	**England**	4-0 Wales
INT65	**England**	2-3 Austria
FAC66	**Sheffield W**	2-3 Everton

Springthorpe, Terry (1, 0)

FAC49	**Wolves**	3-1 Leicester

Sproston, Bert (1, 0)

BC38	**England**	0-1 Scotland

Spurdle, Bill (1, 0)

FAC55	**Man City**	1-3 Newcastle

Srnicek, Pavel (1, 0)

CS96	**Newcastle Utd**	0-4 Man Utd

Stainrod, Simon (2, 0)

FAC82	**QPR**	1-1 Spurs
FAC82	**QPR**	0-1 Spurs

Stam, Jaap (4, 0)

CS98	**Man Utd**	0-3 Arsenal
FAC99 (S)	**Man Utd**	2-0 Newcastle Utd
CS99 (W)	**Man Utd**	1-2 Arsenal
CS00 (S)	**Man Utd**	0-2 Chelsea

Stamp, Phil (1, 0)

FAC97	**Middlesbrough**	0-2 Chelsea

Stamps, Jack (1, 2)

FAC46 (2)	**Derby**	4-1 Charlton

Standen, Jim (2, 0)

FAC64	**West Ham**	3-2 PNE
ECW65	**West Ham**	2-0 TSV Munich

Stanic, Mario (2, 0)

INT96 (S)	**Croatia**	0-0 England
CS00	**Chelsea**	2-0 Man Utd

Staniforth, Ron (2, 0)

BC54	**England**	3-2 Wales
INT54	**England**	3-1 W Germany

Stapleton, Frank (12, 2)

FAC78	**Arsenal**	0-1 Ipswich
FAC79 (1)	**Arsenal**	3-2 Man Utd
CS79	**Arsenal**	1-3 Liverpool
ECQ80	**Rep of Ireland**	0-2 England
FAC80	**Arsenal**	0-1 West Ham
MC83	**Man Utd**	1-2 Liverpool
FAC83 (1)	**Man Utd**	2-2 Brighton
FAC83	**Man Utd**	4-0 Brighton
CS83	**Man Utd**	2-0 Liverpool
INT85 (C)	**Rep of Ireland**	1-2 England
FAC85	**Man Utd**	1-0 Everton
CS85	**Man Utd**	0-2 Everton

Starling, Ronnie (1, 0)

FAC35 (C)	**Sheffield W**	4-2 WBA

Statham, Derek (1, 0)

BC83	**England**	2-1 Wales

Staunton, Steve (4, 0)

LCT88	**Liverpool**	0-0 Newcastle Utd

FAC89 (W) **Liverpool** 3-2 Everton
ECQ91 **Rep of Ireland** 1-1 England
CCC94 (W) **Aston Villa** 3-1 Man Utd

Steel, Billy (4, 1)
BC47 **Scotland** 1-1 England
BC49 (1) **Scotland** 3-1 England
BC51 **Scotland** 3-2 England
BC53 **Scotland** 2-2 England

Steele, David (1, 0)
FAC28 **Huddersfield** 1-3 Blackburn

Steele, Jim (2, 0)
FAC76 **Southampton** 1-0 Man Utd
CS76 **Southampton** 0-1 Liverpool

Stein, Brian (3, 2)
SC88 (W) **Luton** 1-4 Reading
LCT88 **Luton** 0-2 Man Utd
LC88 (2) **Luton** 3-2 Arsenal

Stein, Colin (3, 2)
BC69 (1) **Scotland** 1-4 England
EEC73 (1) **The Three** 2-0 The Six
BC73 (S) **Scotland** 0-1 England

Stein, Jimmy (1, 1)
FAC33 (1) **Everton** 3-0 Man City

Stein, Mark (6, 1)
SC88 (W) **Luton** 1-4 Reading
LCT88 (S) **Luton** 0-2 Man Utd
LC88 (S) **Luton** 3-2 Arsenal
AT92 (1) **Stoke** 1-0 Stockport
FAC94 (W) **Chelsea** 0-4 Man Utd
AWS98 **Bournemouth** 1-2 Grimsby

Stephenson, Clem (1, 0)
FAC28 (C) **Huddersfield** 1-3 Blackburn
As Manager
FAC30 **Huddersfield** 0-2 Arsenal
FAC38 **Huddersfield** 0-1 PNE

Stephenson, Eric (1, 0)
BC38 **England** 0-1 Scotland

Stepney, Alex (5, 0)
INT68 **England** 3-1 Sweden
EC68 **Man Utd** 4-1 Benfica
FAC76 **Man Utd** 0-1 Southampton
FAC77 **Man Utd** 2-1 Liverpool
CS77 **Man Utd** 0-0 Liverpool

Steven, Trevor (20, 2)
SI79 **England** 1-1 Wales
FAC84 **Everton** 2-0 Watford
CS84 **Everton** 1-0 Liverpool
INT85 (1) **England** 2-1 Rep of Ireland
FAC85 **Everton** 0-1 Man Utd
CS85 (1) **Everton** 2-0 Man Utd
WCQ85 (S) **England** 5-0 Finland
FAC86 **Everton** 1-3 Liverpool
CS86 **Everton** 1-1 Liverpool
ECQ86 (S) **England** 2-0 Yugoslavia
CS87 **Everton** 1-0 Coventry
ECQ87 (W) **England** 8-0 Turkey
INT88 **England** 2-2 Netherlands
RC88 (W) **England** 1-0 Scotland

SC89 **Everton** 3-4 Nottingham F
FAC89 **Everton** 2-3 Liverpool
INT90 **England** 4-2 Czechoslovakia
INT91 **England** 2-0 Cameroon
INT91 (W) **England** 0-1 Germany
INT92 (W) **England** 1-1 Brazil

Stevens, Dennis (1, 0)
FAC58 **Bolton** 2-0 Man Utd

Stevens, Gary (5, 1)
FAC83 (1) **Brighton** 2-2 Man Utd
FAC83 **Brighton** 0-4 Man Utd
WCQ84 (S) **England** 5-0 Finland
RC86 (S) **England** 2-1 Scotland
FAC87 (S) **Spurs** 2-3 Coventry

Stevens, Gary (25, 0)
MC84 **Everton** 0-0 Liverpool
FAC84 **Everton** 2-0 Watford
CS84 **Everton** 1-0 Liverpool
FAC85 **Everton** 0-1 Man Utd
CS85 **Everton** 2-0 Man Utd
WCQ85 **England** 1-1 Romania
WCQ85 **England** 5-0 Turkey
WCQ85 **England** 0-0 N Ireland
RC86 **England** 2-1 Scotland
FAC86 (W) **Everton** 1-3 Liverpool
RC87 **England** 1-1 Brazil
ECQ87 **England** 8-0 Turkey
INT88 **England** 2-2 Netherlands
LCT88 **Everton** 1-1 Wolves
LCT88 **Everton** 0-1 Man Utd
RC88 **England** 1-0 Scotland
INT88 **England** 1-0 Denmark
WCQ88 **England** 0-0 Sweden
WCQ89 (W) **England** 5-0 Albania
WCQ89 **England** 3-0 Poland
INT89 **England** 0-0 Italy
INT90 **England** 1-0 Brazil
INT90 **England** 1-0 Denmark
INT91 **England** 3-1 USSR
INT92 **England** 1-1 Brazil

Stevenson, Byron (1, 0)
BC79 **Wales** 0-0 England

Stevenson, George (2, 0)
BC30 **Scotland** 2-5 England
BC34 **Scotland** 0-3 England

Stevenson, Willie (1, 0)
FAC65 **Liverpool** 2-1 Leeds

Stewart, Arthur (1, 0)
ECQ67 **N Ireland** 0-2 England

Stewart, Ian (3, 0)
BC84 **N Ireland** 0-1 England
WCQ85 (W) **N Ireland** 0-0 England
ECQ86 **N Ireland** 0-3 England

Stewart, Paul (7, 1)
WIT88 (W) **Spurs** 0-4 Arsenal
WIT88 **Spurs** 1-2 AC Milan
FAC91 **Spurs** 3-1 Arsenal
FAC91 (1) **Spurs** 2-1 Nottingham F
CS91 **Spurs** 0-0 Arsenal

INT91 (S)	**England** 0-1 Germany	
CS92	**Liverpool** 3-4 Leeds	

Stewart, Ray (4, 1)

FAC80	**West Ham** 1-0 Arsenal
CS80	**West Ham** 0-1 Liverpool
FLC81 (1)	**West Ham** 1-1 Liverpool
BC81	**Scotland** 1-0 England

Stiles, Nobby (18, 1)

SI57	**England** 2-0 Wales
BC65	**England** 2-2 Scotland
INT65	**England** 1-0 Hungary
INT65	**England** 2-3 Austria
BC65	**England** 2-1 N Ireland
INT66 (1)	**England** 1-0 W Germany
WC66	**England** 0-0 Uruguay
WC66	**England** 2-0 Mexico
WC66	**England** 2-0 France
WC66	**England** 1-0 Argentina
WC66	**England** 2-1 Portugal
WC66	**England** 4-2 W Germany
INT66	**England** 0-0 Czechoslovakia
ECQ66	**England** 5-1 Wales
ECQ67	**England** 2-3 Scotland
EC68	**Man Utd** 4-1 Benfica
INT69	**England** 1-1 Romania
BC70	**England** 3-1 N Ireland

Stimac, Igor (1, 0)

INT96 (W)	**Croatia** 0-0 England

Stitfall, Ron (1, 0)

BC52	**Wales** 2-5 England

Stobart, Barry (1, 0)

FAC60	**Wolves** 3-0 Blackburn

Stoker, Lewis (1, 0)

BC34	**England** 3-0 Scotland

Stokoe, Bob (1, 0)

FAC55	**Newcastle Utd** 3-1 Man City
As Manager	
FAC73	**Sunderland** 1-0 Leeds

Stokes, Bobby (2, 1)

FAC76 (1)	**Southampton** 1-0 Man Utd
CS76	**Southampton** 0-1 Liverpool

Stone, Steve (9, 2)

INT95 (S, 1)	**England** 3-1 Switzerland
INT95 (1)	**England** 1-1 Portugal
INT96	**England** 1-0 Bulgaria
INT96	**England** 0-0 Croatia
ECH96 (S)	**England** 1-1 Switzerland
ECH96 (S)	**England** 2-0 Scotland
ECH96 (S)	**England** 0-0 Spain
FAC00 (S)	**Aston Villa** 0-0 Bolton
FAC00 (S)	**Aston Villa** 0-1 Chelsea

Storey, Peter (14, 0)

SI61 (S)	**England** 8-1 Wales
FLC68	**Arsenal** 0-1 Leeds
FLC69	**Arsenal** 1-3 Swindon
ECQ71	**England** 3-0 Greece
FAC71 (W)	**Arsenal** 2-1 Liverpool
BC71	**England** 3-1 Scotland

ECQ71	**England** 1-1 Switzerland
FAC72	**Arsenal** 0-1 Leeds
BC72	**England** 0-1 N Ireland
INT72	**England** 1-1 Yugoslavia
EEC73	**The Three** 2-0 The Six
WCQ73	**England** 1-1 Wales
BC73	**England** 3-0 Wales
BC73	**England** 1-0 Scotland

Storey-Moore, Ian (1, 0)

INT70	**England** 0-0 Netherlands

Storrie, Jim (1, 0)

FAC65	**Leeds** 1-2 Liverpool

Strachan, Gordon (6, 0)

BC83	**Scotland** 0-2 England
FAC85	**Man Utd** 1-0 Everton
LCT88	**Man Utd** 2-0 Luton
LCT88	**Man Utd** 1-0 Everton
LCT88 (W)	**Man Utd** 1-2 Sheffield W
CS92 (S)	**Leeds** 4-3 Liverpool

Strange, Alf (2, 0)

BC30	**England** 5-2 Scotland
BC32	**England** 3-0 Scotland

Stringer, Dave (2, 0)

FLC73	**Norwich** 0-1 Spurs
FLC75	**Norwich** 0-1 Aston Villa

Stringfellow, Mike (1, 0)

FAC63	**Leicester** 1-3 Man Utd

Strong, Geoff (1, 0)

FAC65	**Liverpool** 2-1 Leeds

Strong, Jim (1, 0)

FAC47	**Burnley** 0-1 Charlton

Stuart, Graham (3, 0)

U16I86	**England** 0-1 France
U17I87	**England** 3-1 Netherlands
FAC95	**Everton** 1-0 Man Utd

Stubbins, Albert (2, 1)

IT46 (1)	**FA** 3-5 Army PT Corps
FAC50	**Liverpool** 0-2 Arsenal

Stubbs, Alan (3, 0)

PPO91	**Bolton** 0-1 Tranmere
CCC95 (C)	**Bolton** 1-2 Liverpool
PPO95 (C)	**Bolton** 4-3 Reading

Sturrock, Paul (1, 0)

BC81 (S)	**Scotland** 1-0 England

Suggett, Colin (3, 1)

SI64 (1)	**England** 1-1 W Germany
FLC70	**WBA** 1-2 Man City
FLC75	**Norwich** 0-1 Aston Villa

Sulley, Chris (1, 0)

FMC87	**Blackburn** 1-0 Charlton

Sullivan, Colin (1, 0)

FLC75	**Norwich** 0-1 Aston Villa

Sullivan, Derrick (2, 0)

BC54	**Wales** 2-3 England
BC56	**Wales** 1-3 England

Sullivan, Neil (1, 0)

ECQ99	**Scotland** 1-0 England

Summerbee, Mike (6, 1)
ECQ68	**England**	1-0 Spain
FAC69	**Man City**	1-0 Leicester City
FLC70 (W)	**Man City**	2-1 WBA
ECQ71 (1, W)	**England**	1-1 Switzerland
BC72	**England**	0-1 N Ireland
FLC74 (C)	**Man City**	1-2 Wolves

Sunderland, Alan (5, 2)
FLC74	**Wolves**	2-1 Man City
FAC78	**Arsenal**	0-1 Ipswich
FAC79 (1)	**Arsenal**	3-2 Man Utd
CS79 (1)	**Arsenal**	1-3 Liverpool
FAC80	**Arsenal**	0-1 West Ham

Surtees, Jack (1, 0)
FAC35	**Sheffield W**	4-2 WBA

Sutcliffe, Charles (1, 0)
FAC25	**Sheffield Utd**	1-0 Cardiff

Sutton, Chris (3, 0)
CS95	**Blackburn**	0-1 Everton
INT97 (S)	**England**	2-0 Cameroon
FAC00 (W)	**Chelsea**	2-1 Newcastle Utd

Sutton, Steve (7, 0)
LCT88	**Nottingham F**	3-0 Leeds
LCT88	**Nottingham F**	0-0 Aston Villa
LCT88	**Nottingham F**	2-2 Tranmere
LCT88	**Nottingham F**	0-0 Sheffield W
LC89	**Nottingham F**	3-1 Luton
SC89	**Nottingham F**	4-3 Everton
LC90	**Nottingham F**	1-0 Oldham

Swain, Kenny (1, 0)
CS81	**Aston Villa**	2-2 Spurs

Swan, Peter (10, 0)
INT60	**England**	3-3 Yugoslavia
INT60	**England**	4-2 Spain
BC60	**England**	5-1 Wales
BC61	**England**	9-3 Scotland
INT61	**England**	8-0 Mexico
WCQ61	**England**	2-0 Portugal
BC61	**England**	1-1 N Ireland
INT62	**England**	3-1 Austria
INT62	**England**	3-1 Switzerland
FAT75	**Matlock**	4-0 Scarborough

Swift, Frank (5, 0)
FAC34	**Man City**	2-1 Portsmouth
WI44	**England**	6-2 Scotland
VI46	**England**	2-0 Belgium
BC47	**England**	1-1 Scotland
BC49	**England**	1-3 Scotland

Swindin, George (2, 0)
FAC50	**Arsenal**	2-0 Liverpool
FAC52	**Arsenal**	0-1 Newcastle Utd

Taggart, Gerry (2, 0)
WLC99	**Leicester**	0-1 Spurs
WLC00	**Leicester**	2-1 Tranmere

Tait, Mick (1, 1)
SC88 (1, W)	**Reading**	4-1 Luton

Talbot, Brian (6, 1)
BC77	**England**	1-2 Scotland

FAC78	**Ipswich**	1-0 Arsenal
CS78	**Ipswich**	0-5 Nottingham F
FAC79 (1)	**Arsenal**	3-2 Man Utd
CS79	**Arsenal**	1-3 Liverpool
FAC80	**Arsenal**	0-1 West Ham

Talbot, John (2, 0)
FAC68	**WBA**	1-0 Everton
FLC70	**WBA**	1-2 Man City

Tambling, Bobby (4, 1)
SI57	**England**	2-0 Wales
BC62	**England**	4-0 Wales
INT66	**England**	2-0 Yugoslavia
FAC67 (1)	**Chelsea**	1-2 Spurs

Tanner, Nick (1, 0)
CS92	**Liverpool**	3-4 Leeds

Tapscott, Derek (1, 0)
BC54	**Wales**	2-3 England

Taylor, Alan (2, 2)
FAC75 (2)	**West Ham**	2-0 Fulham
CS75	**West Ham**	0-2 Derby

Taylor, Ernie (4, 0)
FAC51	**Newcastle Utd**	2-0 Blackpool
FAC53	**Blackpool**	4-3 Bolton
INT53	**England**	3-6 Hungary
FAC58	**Man Utd**	0-2 Bolton

Taylor, Ian (3, 1)
CCC96 (1)	**Aston Villa**	3-0 Leeds
FAC00 (W)	**Aston Villa**	0-0 Bolton
FAC00 (W)	**Aston Villa**	0-1 Chelsea

Taylor, Jack (1, 0)
FAC39	**Wolves**	1-4 Portsmouth

Taylor, Jim (1, 0)
INT51	**England**	2-1 Argentina

Taylor, Les (2, 0)
FAC84 (C)	**Watford**	0-2 Everton
SC88	**Reading**	4-1 Luton

Taylor, Peter (1, 0)
BC76 (W)	**England**	4-0 N Ireland

As Manager
PPO00	**Gillingham**	3-2 Wigan

Taylor, Phil (1, 0)
FAC50 (C)	**Liverpool**	0-2 Arsenal

Taylor, Scott (1, 0)
PPO95	**Reading**	3-4 Bolton
PPO96 (W)	**Leicester**	2-1 Crystal P
CCC97 (S)	**Leicester**	1-1 Middlesbrough

Taylor, Scott (1, 0)
WLC00	**Tranmere**	1-2 Leicester

Taylor, Ted (1, 0)
BC24	**England**	1-1 Scotland

Taylor, Tommy (6, 10)
INT56 (2)	**England**	4-2 Brazil
INT56 (S, 2)	**England**	3-0 Yugoslavia
FAC57 (1)	**Man Utd**	1-2 Aston Villa
WCQ57 (3)	**England**	5-1 Rep of Ireland
BC57	**England**	2-3 N Ireland
INT57 (2)	**England**	4-0 France

Taylor, Tommy (3, 0)
SI67 (C)	**England**	0-2 Scotland
FAC75	**West Ham**	2-0 Fulham
CS75	**West Ham**	0-2 Derby
As Manager		
PPO99	**Leyton Orient**	0-1 Scunthorpe

Teale, Shaun (1, 0)
CCC94	**Aston Villa**	3-1 Man Utd

Telfer, Paul (1, 0)
FAC94	**Luton**	0-2 Chelsea

Temple, Derek (1, 1)
FAC66 (1)	**Everton**	3-2 Sheffield W

Terry, Steve (1, 0)
FAC84	**Watford**	0-2 Everton

Thackeray, David (2, 0)
FAC29	**Portsmouth**	0-2 Bolton
FAC34	**Portsmouth**	1-2 Man City

Thomas, Dave (6, 1)
SI66 (1)	**England**	2-1 W Germany
ECQ74 (S)	**England**	3-0 Czechoslovakia
ECQ74	**England**	0-0 Portugal
ECQ75 (S)	**England**	5-0 Cyprus
BC75	**England**	2-2 Wales
BC75 (S)	**England**	5-1 Scotland

Thomas, Geoff (7, 1)
LCT88	**Crystal P**	0-0 Sheffield W
FAC90 (C)	**Crystal P**	3-3 Man Utd
FAC90 (C)	**Crystal P**	0-1 Man Utd
ZC91 (C, 1)	**Crystal P**	4-1 Everton
INT91	**England**	3-1 USSR
INT91	**England**	2-2 Argentina
INT92	**England**	2-0 France

Thomas, Michael (18, 1)
SI82 (W)	**England**	7-0 Netherlands
SI82	**England**	0-0 Scotland
SI83 (C)	**England**	1-0 W Germany
SI83 (C)	**England**	3-3 Scotland
LC87 (S)	**Arsenal**	2-1 Liverpool
LC88	**Arsenal**	2-3 Luton
WIT88	**Arsenal**	4-0 Spurs
WIT88	**Arsenal**	3-0 Bayern Munich
MT89	**Arsenal**	1-0 Porto
MT89	**Arsenal**	1-0 Liverpool
CS89	**Arsenal**	0-1 Liverpool
INT89 (W)	**England**	2-1 Yugoslavia
MT90	**Arsenal**	2-0 Aston Villa
MT90	**Arsenal**	0-1 Sampdoria
FAC91	**Arsenal**	1-3 Spurs
CS91 (S)	**Arsenal**	0-0 Spurs
FAC92 (1)	**Liverpool**	2-0 Sunderland
FAC96 (S)	**Liverpool**	0-1 Man Utd

Thomas, Mickey (3, 0)
FAC79	**Man Utd**	2-3 Arsenal
BC81	**Wales**	0-0 England
BC83	**Wales**	1-2 England

Thomas, Mitchell (2, 0)
FAC87	**Spurs**	2-3 Coventry
WIT88	**Spurs**	0-4 Arsenal

Thomas, Rod (8, 0)
FLC69	**Swindon**	3-1 Arsenal
BC69	**Wales**	1-2 England
BC71	**Wales**	0-0 England
WCQ73	**Wales**	1-1 England
BC73	**Wales**	0-3 England
BC75	**Wales**	2-2 England
CS75	**Derby**	2-0 West Ham
BC77	**Wales**	1-0 England

Thompson, Alan (2, 1)
CCC95 (1)	**Bolton**	1-2 Liverpool
PPO95	**Bolton**	4-3 Reading

Thompson, Garry (3, 0)
LCT88	**Aston Villa**	0-0 Blackburn
LCT88	**Aston Villa**	0-0 Nottingham F
ZC91 (S)	**Crystal P**	4-1 Everton

Thompson, George (1, 0)
FAC54	**PNE**	2-3 WBA

Thompson, Peter (8, 0)
SI58	**England**	3-1 Scotland
INT64	**England**	2-2 Belgium
BC64	**England**	2-1 Wales
BC65	**England**	2-2 Scotland
FAC65	**Liverpool**	2-1 Leeds
BC65	**England**	2-1 N Ireland
ECQ67	**England**	2-0 N Ireland
FAC71 (S)	**Liverpool**	1-2 Arsenal

Thompson, Phil (23, 0)
FAC74	**Liverpool**	3-0 Newcastle Utd
CS74	**Liverpool**	1-1 Leeds
BC76	**England**	4-0 N Ireland
CS76	**Liverpool**	1-0 Southampton
WCQ76	**England**	2-1 Finland
CS77	**Liverpool**	0-0 Man Utd
FLC78	**Liverpool**	0-0 Nottingham F
EC78	**Liverpool**	1-0 Bruges
INT78	**England**	1-0 Czechoslovakia
BC79	**England**	3-1 Scotland
CS79 (C)	**Liverpool**	3-1 Arsenal
ECQ79	**England**	1-0 Denmark
ECQ79 (C)	**England**	2-0 Bulgaria
ECQ80	**England**	2-0 Rep of Ireland
INT80	**England**	3-1 Argentina
CS80 (C)	**Liverpool**	1-0 West Ham
WCQ80 (C)	**England**	4-0 Norway
WCQ81	**England**	1-0 Hungary
FLC82	**Liverpool**	3-1 Spurs
INT82	**England**	2-0 Netherlands
CS82	**Liverpool**	1-0 Spurs
INT82	**England**	1-2 W Germany
CS83 (W)	**Liverpool**	0-2 Man Utd

Thompson, Steve (1, 0)
FMC87 (C)	**Charlton**	0-1 Blackburn

Thompson, Tommy (1, 0)
BC57	**England**	2-1 Scotland

Thomson, Bobby (3, 0)
BC63	**England**	8-3 N Ireland
INT64	**England**	2-2 Belgium
BC64	**England**	2-1 Wales

Thomson, Charlie (1, 0)
FAC37   **Sunderland** 3-1 PNE

Thomson, Chick (1, 0)
FAC59   **Nottingham F** 2-1 Luton

Thomson, Jock (1, 0)
FAC33   **Everton** 3-0 Man City

Thorn, Andy (4, 0)
FAC88   **Wimbledon** 1-0 Liverpool
FAC90   **Crystal P** 3-3 Man Utd
FAC90   **Crystal P** 0-1 Man Utd
ZC91   **Crystal P** 4-1 Everton

Thorne, Peter (2, 1)
CS94 (S)   **Blackburn** 0-2 Man Utd
AWS00 (1) **Stoke** 2-1 Bristol C

Thornewell, George (1, 0)
FAC28   **Blackburn** 3-1 Huddersfield

Thorstvedt, Erik (6, 0)
FAC91   **Spurs** 3-1 Arsenal
FAC91   **Spurs** 2-1 Nottingham F
CS91   **Spurs** 0-0 Arsenal
WCQ92   **Norway** 1-1 England
FAC93   **Spurs** 0-1 Arsenal
INT94 (W) **Norway** 0-0 England

Tiler, Brian (1, 0)
FLC71   **Aston Villa** 0-2 Spurs

Tilson, Fred (1, 2)
FAC34 (2) **Man City** 2-1 Portsmouth

Todd, Colin (13, 0)
BC72   **England** 0-1 N Ireland
BC74   **England** 1-0 N Ireland
INT74   **England** 2-2 Argentina
ECQ74 (S) **England** 0-0 Portugal
INT75   **England** 2-0 W Germany
ECQ75   **England** 5-0 Cyprus
BC75   **England** 2-2 Wales
BC75   **England** 5-1 Scotland
CS75   **Derby** 2-0 West Ham
BC76   **England** 4-0 N Ireland
INT76   **England** 1-1 Rep of Ireland
WCQ76   **England** 2-1 Finland
INT77 (S) **England** 0-2 Netherlands
As Manager
ZC90   **Middlesbrough** 0-1 Chelsea
PP090   **Bolton** 0-2 Watford

Toseland, Ernie (2, 0)
FAC33   **Man City** 0-3 Everton
FAC34   **Man City** 2-1 Portsmouth

Toshack, John (9, 3)
BC69   **Wales** 1-2 England
FAC71   **Liverpool** 1-2 Arsenal
BC71   **Wales** 0-0 England
WCQ73 (1) **Wales** 1-1 England
BC73   **Wales** 0-3 England
FAC74   **Liverpool** 3-0 Newcastle Utd
BC75 (1)   **Wales** 2-2 England
CS76 (1)   **Liverpool** 1-0 Southampton
BC79 (W)   **Wales** 0-0 England

Towers, Tony (3, 0)
SI67   **England** 0-2 Scotland
FLC74   **Man City** 1-2 Wolves
BC76 (S)   **England** 4-0 N Ireland

Townsend, Andy (4, 0)
ECQ91   **Rep of Ireland** 1-1 England
CCC94   **Aston Villa** 3-1 Man Utd
CCC96 (C) **Aston Villa** 3-0 Leeds
CCC98   **Middlesbrough** 0-2 Chelsea

Tracey, Simon (2, 0)
CS88   **Wimbledon** 1-2 Liverpool
PPO97   **Sheffield Utd** 0-1 Crystal P

Trautmann, Bert (2, 0)
FAC55   **Man City** 1-3 Newcastle Utd
FAC56   **Man City** 3-1 Birmingham

Trebilcock, Mike (1, 2)
FAC66 (2) **Everton** 3-2 Sheffield W

Tremelling, Billy (1, 0)
FAC37 (C) **PNE** 1-3 Sunderland

Trentham, Bert (2, 0)
FAC31   **WBA** 2-1 Birmingham
FAC35   **WBA** 2-4 Sheffield W

Tresadern, Jack (1, 0)
FAC23   **West Ham** 0-2 Bolton

Trewick, John (2, 1)
SI72 (1)   **England** 4-0 W Germany
MC86   **Oxford** 3-0 QPR
As Coach
YAC00   **WBA** 0-0 Scunthorpe

Trollope, John (1, 0)
FLC69   **Swindon** 3-1 Arsenal

Tudor, John (1, 0)
FAC74   **Newcastle Utd** 0-3 Liverpool

Tueart, Dennis (6, 2)
FAC73   **Sunderland** 1-0 Leeds
FLC76 (1)   **Man City** 2-1 Newcastle Utd
WCQ76 (1, W) **England** 2-1 Finland
BC77 (S)   **England** 0-1 Wales
BC77 (S)   **England** 1-2 Scotland
FAC81 (S)   **Man City** 2-3 Spurs

Tully, Charlie (1, 0)
BC55   **N Ireland** 0-3 England

Tunstall, Fred (2, 1)
BC24   **England** 1-1 Scotland
FAC25 (1) **Sheffield Utd** 1-0 Cardiff

Turnbull, Fred (1, 0)
FLC71   **Aston Villa** 0-2 Spurs

Turner, Chris (5, 0)
MC85   **Sunderland** 0-1 Norwich
LCT88   **Man Utd** 2-0 Luton
LCT88   **Man Utd** 1-0 Everton
LCT88   **Man Utd** 1-2 Sheffield W
RLC91   **Sheffield W** 1-0 Man Utd

Turner, Hugh (1, 0)
FAC30   **Huddersfield** 0-2 Arsenal

447

Turner, Arthur (1, 0)
FAC46   **Charlton** 1-4 Derby

Turner, Bert (3, 1)
WI40 (C)   **Wales** 1-0 England
WI43 (C)   **Wales** 3-5 England
FAC46 (1)   **Charlton** 1-4 Derby

Turner, Ian (2, 0)
FAC76   **Southampton** 1-0 Man Utd
CS76   **Southampton** 0-1 Liverpool

Turner, Rob (1, 0)
CS88 (S)   **Wimbledon** 1-2 Liverpool

Turner, Robin (1, 0)
CS78 (S)   **Ipswich** 0-5 Nottingham F

Ufton, Derek (1, 0)
NIN53   **England** 4-4 FIFA

Ullathorne, Robert (2, 0)
YI90 (W)   **England** 1-1 Czechoslovakia
WLC99   **Leicester** 0-1 Spurs

Unsworth, David (3, 0)
FAC95   **Everton** 1-0 Man Utd
UC95   **England** 2-1 Japan
CS95   **Everton** 1-0 Blackburn

Uprichard, Norman
(1, 0)
BC55   **N Ireland** 0-3 England

Ure, Ian (3, 0)
BC63   **Scotland** 2-1 England
FLC68   **Arsenal** 0-1 Leeds
FLC69   **Arsenal** 1-3 Swindon

Van den Hauwe, Pat (10, 0)
FAC85   **Everton** 0-1 Man Utd
CS85 (W)   **Everton** 2-0 Man Utd
FAC86   **Everton** 1-3 Liverpool
LCT88   **Everton** 1-1 Wolves
LCT88   **Everton** 0-1 Man Utd
SC89   **Everton** 3-4 Nottingham F
FAC89   **Everton** 2-3 Liverpool
FAC91   **Spurs** 3-1 Arsenal
FAC91   **Spurs** 2-1 Nottingham F
CS91   **Spurs** 0-0 Arsenal

Van Wyk, Dennis (1, 0)
MC85   **Norwich** 1-0 Sunderland

Vega, Ramon (3, 0)
INT95 (S)   **Switzerland** 1-3 England
ECH96   **Switzerland** 1-1 England
WLC99   **Spurs** 1-0 Leicester

Venables, Terry (3, 0)
SI58   **England** 3-1 Scotland
INT64   **England** 2-2 Belgium
FAC67   **Spurs** 2-1 Chelsea
As Manager
FAC82   **QPR** 1-1 Spurs
FAC82   **QPR** 0-1 Spurs
LCEN87   **Rest of World** 0-3 Football League
WIT88   **Spurs** 0-4 Arsenal
WIT88   **Spurs** 1-2 AC Milan
FAC91   **Spurs** 3-1 Arsenal
FAC91   **Spurs** 2-1 Nottingham F

INT94   **England** 1-0 Denmark
INT94   **England** 5-0 Greece
INT94   **England** 0-0 Norway
INT94   **England** 2-0 USA
INT94   **England** 1-1 Romania
INT94   **England** 1-0 Nigeria
INT95   **England** 0-0 Uruguay
UC95   **England** 2-1 Japan
UC95   **England** 1-3 Brazil
INT95   **England** 0-0 Colombia
INT95   **England** 3-1 Switzerland
INT95   **England** 1-1 Portugal
INT96   **England** 1-0 Bulgaria
INT96   **England** 0-0 Croatia
INT96   **England** 3-0 Hungary
ECH96   **England** 1-1 Switzerland
ECH96   **England** 2-0 Scotland
ECH96   **England** 4-1 Netherlands
ECH96   **England** 0-0 Spain
ECH96   **England** 1-1 Germany

Venison, Barry (11, 0)
MC85 (C)   **Sunderland** 0-1 Norwich
CS86   **Liverpool** 1-1 Everton
LC87   **Liverpool** 1-2 Arsenal
CS88   **Liverpool** 2-1 Wimbledon
FAC89 (S)   **Liverpool** 3-2 Everton
MT89   **Liverpool** 2-0 Dynamo Kiev
MT89   **Liverpool** 0-1 Arsenal
CS89   **Liverpool** 1-0 Arsenal
CS90   **Liverpool** 1-1 Man Utd
INT94   **England** 2-0 USA
INT95   **England** 0-0 Uruguay

Venters, Alex (1, 0)
BC36   **Scotland** 1-1 England

Vernon, Roy (2, 0)
BC60   **Wales** 1-5 England
BC62   **Wales** 0-4 England

Vialli, Gianluca (6, 1)
INT89 (W)   **Italy** 0-0 England
MT90 (1, W)   **Sampdoria** 1-1 Real Sociedad
MT90   **Sampdoria** 1-0 Arsenal
EC92 (W)   **Sampdoria** 0-1 Barcelona
FAC97 (S)   **Chelsea** 2-0 Middlesbrough
CS97 (S)   **Chelsea** 1-1 Man Utd
As Manager
CCC98   **Chelsea** 2-0 Middlesbrough
FAC00   **Chelsea** 2-1 Newcastle Utd
FAC00   **Chelsea** 1-0 Aston Villa
CS00   **Chelsea** 2-0 Man Utd

Vickers, Steve (8, 0)
LCT88   **Tranmere** 1-0 Wimbledon
LCT88   **Tranmere** 2-0 Newcastle Utd
LCT88   **Tranmere** 2-2 Nottingham F
LDC90   **Tranmere** 2-1 Bristol R
PPO90   **Tranmere** 0-2 Notts C
PPO91 (W)   **Tranmere** 1-0 Bolton
FAC97 (S)   **Middlesbrough** 0-2 Chelsea
CCC98   **Middlesbrough** 0-2 Chelsea

Vieira, Patrick (8, 0)
FAC98   **Arsenal** 2-0 Newcastle Utd
CS98 (W)   **Arsenal** 3-0 Man Utd
EC98   **Arsenal** 2-1 Panathinaikos
INT99 (S)   **France** 2-0 England
CS99   **Arsenal** 2-1 Man Utd
EC99   **Arsenal** 3-1 AIK Stockholm
EC99   **Arsenal** 2-4 Barcelona
EC99   **Arsenal** 0-1 Fiorentina

Viljoen, Colin (1, 0)
BC75   **England** 2-2 Wales

Villa, Ricardo (4, 2)
FAC81 (W)   **Spurs** 1-1 Man City
FAC81 (2)   **Spurs** 3-2 Man City
CS81   **Spurs** 2-2 Aston Villa
FLC82 (S)   **Spurs** 1-3 Liverpool

Viollet, Dennis (1, 0)
FAC58   **Man Utd** 0-2 Bolton

Vivas, Nelson (5, 0)
EC98 (S)   **Arsenal** 2-1 Panathinaikos
EC98 (S)   **Arsenal** 1-1 Dynamo Kiev
EC98 (S)   **Arsenal** 0-1 Lens
EC99 (S)   **Arsenal** 0-1 Fiorentina
INT00 (S)   **Argentina** 0-0 England

Vizard, Ted (2, 0)
FAC23   **Bolton** 2-0 West Ham
FAC26   **Bolton** 1-0 Man City

Waddell, Willie (3, 0)
WI42   **Scotland** 0-0 England
BC49   **Scotland** 3-1 England
BC51   **Scotland** 3-2 England

Waddle, Chris (30, 5)
INT85   **England** 2-1 Rep of Ireland
WCQ85 (W)   **England** 1-1 Romania
WCQ85 (1)   **England** 5-0 Turkey
WCQ85   **England** 0-0 N Ireland
RC86   **England** 2-1 Scotland
ECQ86 (1)   **England** 3-0 N Ireland
ECQ86 (W)   **England** 2-0 Yugoslavia
FAC87   **Spurs** 2-3 Coventry
RC87   **England** 1-1 Brazil
LCEN87   **Football League** 3-0 Rest of World
RC88 (S)   **England** 1-0 Scotland
RC88 (W)   **England** 1-1 Colombia
WCQ88   **England** 0-0 Sweden
WIT88   **Spurs** 0-4 Arsenal
WIT88   **Spurs** 1-2 AC Milan
WCQ89 (1)   **England** 5-0 Albania
RC89   **England** 0-0 Chile
WCQ89 (W)   **England** 3-0 Poland
INT89   **England** 0-0 Italy
INT89   **England** 2-1 Yugoslavia
INT90   **England** 1-0 Brazil
INT90 (W)   **England** 1-0 Denmark
INT90   **England** 1-2 Uruguay
INT90 (S)   **England** 1-0 Hungary
ECQ90 (S)   **England** 2-0 Poland
ECQ91   **England** 1-0 Turkey
FAC93 (1)   **Sheffield W** 2-1 Sheffield Utd

CCC93   **Sheffield W** 1-2 Arsenal
FAC93 (W)   **Sheffield W** 1-1 Arsenal
FAC93 (1)   **Sheffield W** 1-2 Arsenal

Waddock, Gary (3, 0)
FAC82   **QPR** 1-1 Spurs
FAC82   **QPR** 0-1 Spurs
INT85   **Rep of Ireland** 1-2 England

Wadsworth, Sam (1, 0)
BC24   **England** 1-1 Scotland

Wagstaffe, Dave (1, 0)
FLC74 (W)   **Wolves** 2-1 Man City

Waiters, Tony (2, 0)
INT64   **England** 2-2 Belgium
BC64   **England** 2-1 Wales

Wake, Harry (1, 0)
FAC25   **Cardiff** 0-1 Sheffield Utd

Waldron, Malcolm (1, 0)
FLC79   **Southampton** 2-3 Nottingham F

Walford, Steve (2, 0)
FAC79 (S)   **Arsenal** 3-2 Man Utd
CS79   **Arsenal** 1-3 Liverpool

Walker, Billy (2, 1)
BC24 (1)   **England** 1-1 Scotland
FAC24   **Aston Villa** 0-2 Newcastle Utd
As Manager
FAC35   **Sheffield W** 4-2 WBA
FAC59   **Nottingham F** 2-1 Luton

Walker, Clive (6, 0)
MC85   **Sunderland** 0-1 Norwich
PPO91   **Brighton** 1-3 Notts C
FAT94   **Woking** 2-1 Runcorn
FAT95   **Woking** 2-1 Kidderminster
FAT97   **Woking** 1-0 Dagenham
FAT98 (W)   **Cheltenham** 1-0 Southport

Walker, Des (29, 0)
INT88 (S)   **England** 1-0 Denmark
WCQ88 (S)   **England** 0-0 Sweden
LC89   **Nottingham F** 3-1 Luton
WCQ89   **England** 5-0 Albania
SC89   **Nottingham F** 4-3 Everton
RC89   **England** 0-0 Chile
WCQ89   **England** 3-0 Poland
INT89   **England** 0-0 Italy
INT89   **England** 2-1 Yugoslavia
INT90   **England** 1-0 Brazil
INT90 (W)   **England** 4-2 Czechoslovakia
LC90   **Nottingham F** 1-0 Oldham
INT90   **England** 1-0 Denmark
INT90   **England** 1-2 Uruguay
INT90   **England** 1-0 Hungary
ECQ90   **England** 2-0 Poland
INT91   **England** 2-0 Cameroon
ECQ91   **England** 1-1 Rep of Ireland
FAC91   **Nottingham F** 1-2 Spurs
INT91   **England** 2-2 Argentina
ECQ91   **England** 1-0 Turkey
INT92   **England** 2-0 France
ZC92   **Nottingham F** 3-2 Southampton

RLC92 (C)	**Nottingham F** 0-1	Man Utd
INT92	**England** 1-1	Brazil
WCQ92	**England** 1-1	Norway
WCQ92	**England** 4-0	Turkey
WCQ93	**England** 6-0	San Marino
WCQ93	**England** 2-2	Netherlands

Walker, George (1, 0)

FAC39	**Portsmouth** 4-1	Wolves
LWC42	**Portsmouth** 0-2	Brentford

Walker, Ian (8, 0)

U16I87 (W)	**England** 2-1	Denmark
YI90	**England** 0-0	Denmark
YI90	**England** 1-1	Czechoslovakia
YI90 (W)	**England** 3-0	Poland
U19I91 (W)	**England** 1-1	Spain
INT96 (S)	**England** 3-0	Hungary
WCQ97	**England** 0-1	Italy
WLC99	**Spurs** 1-0	Leicester

Walker, Tommy (6, 3)

BC36 (1)	**Scotland** 1-1	England
BC38 (1)	**Scotland** 1-0	England
WI41	**Scotland** 0-2	England
WI42	**Scotland** 0-3	England
WI42	**Scotland** 0-0	England
WI44 (1)	**Scotland** 2-6	England

Walker, Tommy (2, 0)

FAC51	**Newcastle Utd** 2-0	Blackpool
FAC52	**Newcastle Utd** 1-0	Arsenal

Wallace, Danny (3, 0)

FAC90	**Man Utd** 3-3	Crystal P
FAC90	**Man Utd** 1-0	Crystal P
CS90 (W)	**Man Utd** 1-1	Liverpool

Wallace, Ian (1, 0)

MC85	**Sunderland** 0-1	Norwich

Wallace, Rod (1, 0)

CS92	**Leeds** 4-3	Liverpool

Wallace, Willie (2, 0)

ECQ67	**Scotland** 3-2	England
BC69 (S)	**Scotland** 1-4	England

Walsh, Colin (2, 0)

SI77	**Scotland** 0-2	England
FMC87	**Charlton** 0-1	Blackburn

Walsh, Ian (1, 0)

BC81	**Wales** 0-0	England

Walsh, Jimmy (1, 0)

FAC61 (C)	**Leicester** 0-2	Spurs

Walsh, Paul (4, 0)

CS84 (S)	**Liverpool** 0-1	Everton
LC87 (W)	**Liverpool** 1-2	Arsenal
WIT88	**Spurs** 0-4	Arsenal
WIT88 (W)	**Spurs** 1-2	AC Milan
FAC91 (S)	**Spurs** 3-1	Arsenal
FAC91 (S)	**Spurs** 2-1	Nottingham F

Walsh, Steve (7, 3)

FRT85	**Wigan** 3-1	Brentford
PPO92 (C)	**Leicester** 0-1	Blackburn
PPO93 (1)	**Leicester** 3-4	Swindon
PPO94 (2)	**Leicester** 2-1	Derby

PPO96 (C, W)	**Leicester** 2-1	Crystal P
CCC97 (C)	**Leicester** 1-1	Middlesbrough
WLC99 (C)	**Leicester** 0-1	Spurs

Walters, Mark (3, 0)

SI79	**England** 1-1	Wales
SI79	**England** 2-2	W Germany
CS92	**Liverpool** 3-4	Leeds

Walton, Joe (1, 0)

FAC54	**PNE** 2-3	WBA

Ward, Mitch (1, 0)

FAC93	**Sheffield Utd** 1-2	Sheffield W
PPO97	**Sheffield Utd** 0-1	Crystal P

Warhurst, Paul (6, 0)

LC90	**Oldham** 0-1	Nottingham F
FAC93 (W)	**Sheffield W** 2-1	Sheffield Utd
CCC93	**Sheffield W** 1-2	Arsenal
FAC93	**Sheffield W** 1-1	Arsenal
FAC93	**Sheffield W** 1-2	Arsenal
FAC00 (S)	**Bolton** 0-0	Aston Villa

Waring, Pongo (1, 1)

BC32 (1)	**England** 3-0	Scotland

Wark, John (6, 1)

FAC78	**Ipswich** 1-0	Arsenal
CS78	**Ipswich** 0-5	Nottingham F
BC79 (1)	**Scotland** 1-3	England
BC83 (S)	**Scotland** 0-2	England
CS84	**Liverpool** 0-1	Everton
LC87 (S)	**Liverpool** 1-2	Arsenal

Warzycha, Robert (3, 1)

ECQ90	**Poland** 0-2	England
ZC91 (1)	**Everton** 1-4	Crystal P
WCQ93	**Poland** 0-3	England

Wassall, Darren
(2, 0)

ZC92	**Nottingham F** 3-2	Southampton
RLC92	**Nottingham F** 0-1	Man Utd

Watmough, Dickie (1, 0)

FAC38	**PNE** 1-0	Huddersfield

Watson, Alex (3, 0)

LCT88	**Liverpool** 0-0	Newcastle Utd
CS88	**Liverpool** 2-1	Wimbledon
PPO98 (C)	**Torquay** 0-1	Colchester

Watson, Dave (33, 2)

FAC73	**Sunderland** 1-0	Leeds
INT74	**England** 2-2	Argentina
ECQ74	**England** 3-0	Czechoslovakia
ECQ74	**England** 0-0	Portugal
INT75	**England** 2-0	W Germany
ECQ75	**England** 5-0	Cyprus
BC75	**England** 2-2	Wales
BC75	**England** 5-1	Scotland
FLC76	**Man City** 2-1	Newcastle Utd
INT77	**England** 0-2	Netherlands
WCQ77	**England** 5-0	Luxembourg
BC77	**England** 0-1	Wales
BC77	**England** 1-2	Scotland
INT77	**England** 0-0	Switzerland
WCQ77	**England** 2-0	Italy

INT78	**England**	1-1 Brazil
BC78	**England**	1-0 N Ireland
INT78 (W)	**England**	4-1 Hungary
INT78	**England**	1-0 Czechoslovakia
ECQ79 (1)	**England**	4-0 N Ireland
BC79	**England**	0-0 Wales
BC79	**England**	3-1 Scotland
ECQ79	**England**	1-0 Denmark
ECQ79 (1)	**England**	2-0 Bulgaria
ECQ80	**England**	2-0 Rep of Ireland
INT80	**England**	3-1 Argentina
BC80	**England**	1-1 N Ireland
WCQ80	**England**	4-0 Norway
WCQ80	**England**	2-1 Switzerland
WCQ81 (C)	**England**	0-0 Romania
BC81 (C)	**England**	0-0 Wales
BC81 (C, W)	**England**	0-1 Scotland
BC82	**England**	4-0 N Ireland

Watson, Dave (13, 0)

MC85 (C)	**Norwich**	1-0 Sunderland
RC86	**England**	2-1 Scotland
ECQ86	**England**	3-0 N Ireland
CS87	**Everton**	1-0 Coventry
INT88 (W)	**England**	2-2 Netherlands
LCT88 (C)	**Everton**	1-1 Wolves
LCT88 (C)	**Everton**	0-1 Man Utd
RC88	**England**	1-0 Scotland
SC89	**Everton**	3-4 Nottingham F
FAC89	**Everton**	2-3 Liverpool
ZC91 (C)	**Everton**	1-4 Crystal P
FAC95 (C)	**Everton**	1-0 Man Utd
CS95 (S)	**Everton**	1-0 Blackburn

Watson, David (1, 0)

FAC29	**Portsmouth**	0-2 Bolton

Watson, Steve (3, 0)

U19I91 (W)	**England**	1-1 Spain
CS96	**Newcastle Utd**	0-4 Man Utd
FAC98 (S)	**Newcastle Utd**	0-2 Arsenal

Watson, Tommy (1, 0)

FAC27	**Cardiff**	1-0 Arsenal

Watson, Vic (2, 2)

FAC23	**West Ham**	0-2 Bolton
BC30 (2)	**England**	5-2 Scotland

Wayman, Charlie (1, 1)

FAC54 (1)	**PNE**	2-3 WBA

Wdowczyk, Dariusz (3, 0)

WCQ89	**Poland**	0-3 England
ECQ90	**Poland**	0-2 England
PPO95	**Reading**	3-4 Bolton

Weah, George (2, 0)

FACOO (W)	**Chelsea**	2-1 Newcastle Utd
FACOO (W)	**Chelsea**	1-0 Aston Villa

Weaver, Sam (2, 0)

BC32	**England**	3-0 Scotland
FAC32	**Newcastle Utd**	2-1 Arsenal

Webb, David (2, 0)

FAC70	**Chelsea**	2-2 Leeds
FLC72	**Chelsea**	1-2 Stoke

As Manager

PPO97	**Brentford**	0-1 Crewe

Webb, Neil (20, 4)

LCEN87 (W)	**Football League**	3-0 Rest of World
ECQ87 (1)	**England**	8-0 Turkey
INT88 (W)	**England**	2-2 Netherlands
LCT88 (W)	**Nottingham F**	3-0 Leeds
LCT88	**Nottingham F**	0-0 Aston Villa
LCT88	**Nottingham F**	2-2 Tranmere
LCT88	**Nottingham F**	0-0 Sheffield W
RC88	**England**	1-0 Scotland
INT88 (1)	**England**	1-0 Denmark
WCQ88	**England**	0-0 Sweden
LC89 (1)	**Nottingham F**	3-1 Luton
WCQ89	**England**	5-0 Albania
SC89	**Nottingham F**	4-3 Everton
RC89	**England**	0-0 Chile
WCQ89 (1)	**England**	3-0 Poland
FAC90	**Man Utd**	3-3 Crystal P
FAC90	**Man Utd**	1-0 Crystal P
RLC91 (W)	**Man Utd**	0-1 Sheffield W
INT92	**England**	2-0 France
INT92 (S)	**England**	1-1 Brazil

Webster, Colin (1, 0)

FAC58	**Man Utd**	0-2 Bolton

Webster, Maurice (1, 0)

BC30	**England**	5-2 Scotland

Weddle, Jack (3, 0)

FAC29	**Portsmouth**	0-2 Bolton
FAC34	**Portsmouth**	1-2 Man City
FLWC40	**Blackburn**	0-1 West Ham

Wegerle, Roy (1, 0)

LC89	**Luton**	1-3 Nottingham F

Weir, David (1, 0)

ECQ99	**Scotland**	1-0 England

Weller, Keith (2, 1)

BC74 (1)	**England**	1-0 N Ireland
INT74	**England**	2-2 Argentina

Welsh, Don (8, 7)

WI41 (1)	**England**	2-0 Scotland
WI42	**England**	3-0 Scotland
LSC43 (C)	**Charlton**	1-7 Chelsea
WI43 (3)	**England**	8-3 Wales
LSC44 (C, 1)	**Charlton**	3-1 Chelsea
IT46 (2)	**Army PT Corps**	5-3 FA
FAC46 (C)	**Charlton**	1-4 Derby
FAC47 (C)	**Charlton**	1-0 Burnley

West, Gordon (4, 0)

FAC66	**Everton**	3-2 Sheffield W
FAC68	**Everton**	0-1 WBA
INT68	**England**	1-1 Bulgaria
BC69	**England**	2-1 Wales

Westcott, Dennis (3, 3)

FAC39	**Wolves**	1-4 Portsmouth
WI40	**England**	0-1 Wales
WI43 (3)	**England**	8-3 Wales

Wetherall, David (1, 0)

CCC96	**Leeds**	0-3 Aston Villa

451

Whare, Bill (1, 0)
FAC59   **Nottingham F**   2-1 Luton

Wharton, Guy (2, 0)
FAC39   **Portsmouth**   4-1 Wolves
LWC42   **Portsmouth**   0-2 Brentford

Wheeler, Johnny (1, 0)
FAC53   **Bolton**   3-4 Blackpool

Whelan, Dave (1, 0)
FAC60   **Blackburn**   0-3 Wolves

Whelan, Liam (2, 0)
FAC57   **Man Utd**   1-2 Aston Villa
WCQ57   **Rep of Ireland**   1-5 England

Whelan, Ronnie (16, 3)
FLC82 (2)   **Liverpool**   3-1 Spurs
CS82   **Liverpool**   1-0 Spurs
MC83 (1)   **Liverpool**   2-1 Man Utd
MC84   **Liverpool**   0-0 Everton
CS84   **Liverpool**   0-1 Everton
INT85 (W)   **Rep of Ireland**   1-2 England
FAC86   **Liverpool**   3-1 Everton
CS86   **Liverpool**   1-1 Everton
LC87   **Liverpool**   1-2 Arsenal
CS88 (C)   **Liverpool**   2-1 Wimbledon
FAC89 (C)   **Liverpool**   3-2 Everton
MT89 (C)   **Liverpool**   2-0 Dynamo Kiev
MT89 (C)   **Liverpool**   0-1 Arsenal
CS89   **Liverpool**   1-0 Arsenal
CS90 (C)   **Liverpool**   1-1 Man Utd
CS92   **Liverpool**   3-4 Leeds

White, John (3, 0)
FAC61   **Spurs**   2-0 Leicester
FAC62   **Spurs**   3-1 Burnley
BC63   **Scotland**   2-1 England

White, Len (1, 0)
FAC55   **Newcastle Utd**   3-1 Man City

White, Tommy (1, 0)
FAC33   **Everton**   3-0 Man City

Whitefoot, Jeff (1, 0)
FAC59   **Nottingham F**   2-1 Luton

Whitehouse, Dane (1, 0)
FAC93   **Sheffield Utd**   1-2 Sheffield W
PPO97   **Sheffield Utd**   0-1 Crystal P

Whiteside, Norman (13, 4)
MC83 (1)   **Man Utd**   1-2 Liverpool
FAC83   **Man Utd**   2-2 Brighton
FAC83 (1)   **Man Utd**   4-0 Brighton
CS83   **Man Utd**   2-0 Liverpool
BC84   **N Ireland**   0-1 England
FAC85 (1)   **Man Utd**   1-0 Everton
CS85   **Man Utd**   0-2 Everton
WCQ85   **N Ireland**   0-0 England
ECQ86 (W)   **N Ireland**   0-3 England
LCEN87 (S, 1)   **Football League**   3-0 Rest of World
LCT88   **Man Utd**   2-0 Luton
LCT88 (W)   **Man Utd**   1-0 Everton
LCT88   **Man Utd**   1-2 Sheffield W

Whitlow, Mike (6, 0)
PPO92   **Leicester**   0-1 Blackburn

PPO93   **Leicester**   3-4 Swindon
PPO94   **Leicester**   2-1 Derby
PPO96   **Leicester**   2-1 Crystal P
CCC97 (W)   **Leicester**   1-1 Middlesbrough
FAC00   **Bolton**   0-0 Aston Villa

Whittaker, Bill (1, 0)
FAC47   **Charlton**   1-0 Burnley

Whitworth, Steve (3, 0)
INT75   **England**   2-0 W Germany
BC75   **England**   2-2 Wales
BC75   **England**   5-1 Scotland

Whymark, Trevor (1, 0)
CS78 (W)   **Ipswich**   0-5 Nottingham F

Whyte, Chris (1, 0)
CS92   **Leeds**   4-3 Liverpool

Wicks, Steve (1, 0)
MC86   **QPR**   0-3 Oxford

Wignall, Frank (1, 2)
BC64 (2)   **England**   2-1 Wales

Wilcox, Jason (4, 0)
CS94   **Blackburn**   0-2 Man Utd
INT96   **England**   3-0 Hungary
INT99 (S)   **England**   0-2 France
INT00   **England**   0-0 Argentina

Wilkins, Ray (36, 2)
SI72 (W)   **England**   4-0 W Germany
INT76   **England**   1-1 Rep of Ireland
WCQ76   **England**   2-1 Finland
INT77 (S)   **England**   0-0 Switzerland
WCQ77   **England**   2-0 Italy
BC78   **England**   1-0 N Ireland
INT78   **England**   4-1 Hungary
INT78   **England**   1-0 Czechoslovakia
BC79 (W)   **England**   0-0 Wales
BC79   **England**   3-1 Scotland
ECQ79   **England**   1-0 Denmark
ECQ79   **England**   2-0 Bulgaria
INT80   **England**   3-1 Argentina
BC80   **England**   1-1 N Ireland
INT81 (S)   **England**   1-2 Spain
WCQ81   **England**   0-0 Romania
INT81   **England**   0-1 Brazil
BC81   **England**   0-0 Wales
BC81   **England**   0-1 Scotland
BC82 (1)   **England**   4-0 N Ireland
INT82   **England**   2-0 Netherlands
INT82 (C)   **England**   1-2 W Germany
MC83 (C)   **Man Utd**   1-2 Liverpool
FAC83 (1)   **Man Utd**   2-2 Brighton
FAC83   **Man Utd**   4-0 Brighton
CS83   **Man Utd**   2-0 Liverpool
ECQ83 (C)   **England**   0-1 Denmark
BC84   **England**   1-0 N Ireland
INT84   **England**   0-2 USSR
INT84   **England**   1-0 E Germany
WCQ84   **England**   5-0 Finland
INT85   **England**   2-1 Rep of Ireland
WCQ85   **England**   5-0 Turkey
WCQ85 (C)   **England**   0-0 N Ireland

RC86 (C, W)   **England** 2-1 Scotland
ECQ86 (S)   **England** 2-0 Yugoslavia

Wilkinson, Charlie (1, 0)
FAC36   **Sheffield Utd** 0-1 Arsenal

Wilkinson, Paul (1, 0)
CS86 (S)   **Everton** 1-1 Liverpool

Williams, Bert (7, 0)
WI45   **England** 2-2 France
IT46   **FA** 3-5 Army PT Corps
FAC49   **Wolves** 3-1 Leicester
BC51   **England** 2-3 Scotland
INT51   **England** 2-1 Argentina
INT54   **England** 3-1 W Germany
BC55   **England** 7-2 Scotland

Williams, Bertie (1, 0)
FAC36   **Sheffield Utd** 0-1 Arsenal

Williams, Brett (1, 0)
RLC92   **Nottingham F** 0-1 Man Utd

Williams, Graham (5, 0)
BC60   **Wales** 1-5 England
BC64   **Wales** 1-2 England
ECQ66   **Wales** 1-5 England
FLC67 (C)   **WBA** 2-3 QPR
FAC68 (C)   **WBA** 1-0 Everton

Williams, Jeremy (1, 0)
SC88 (S)   **Reading** 4-1 Luton

Williams, Paul (1, 0)
RLC91   **Sheffield W** 1-0 Man Utd

Williams, Steve (4, 0)
FLC79   **Southampton** 2-3 Nottingham F
INT84   **England** 1-0 E Germany
WCQ84   **England** 5-0 Finland
LC87   **Arsenal** 2-1 Liverpool

Williams, Stuart (3, 0)
BC54   **Wales** 2-3 England
BC62 (C)   **Wales** 0-4 England
BC64   **Wales** 1-2 England

Willingham, Ken (4, 0)
BC38   **England** 0-1 Scotland
FAC38   **Huddersfield** 0-1 PNE
WI40   **England** 0-1 Wales
WI42   **England** 3-0 Scotland

Wilshaw, Dennis (2, 6)
BC55 (4)   **England** 7-2 Scotland
BC55 (2)   **England** 3-0 N Ireland

Wilson, Alex (1, 0)
FAC36   **Arsenal** 1-0 Sheffield Utd

Wilson, Bob (2, 0)
FLC69   **Arsenal** 1-3 Swindon
FAC71   **Arsenal** 2-1 Liverpool

Wilson, Clive (1, 0)
FMC86   **Man City** 4-5 Chelsea

Wilson, Danny (8, 1)
SC88   **Luton** 1-4 Reading
LCT88   **Luton** 0-2 Man Utd
LC88 (1)   **Luton** 3-2 Arsenal
LC89   **Luton** 1-3 Nottingham F

RLC91   **Sheffield W** 1-0 Man Utd
FAC93   **Sheffield W** 2-1 Sheffield Utd
CCC93 (W)   **Sheffield W** 1-2 Arsenal
FAC93 (W)   **Sheffield W** 1-2 Arsenal

Wilson, David (1, 0)
FAC64   **PNE** 2-3 West Ham

Wilson, Davie (3, 1)
BC61 (1)   **Scotland** 3-9 England
BC63   **Scotland** 2-1 England
BC65   **Scotland** 2-2 England

Wilson, Ian (3, 0)
LCT88 (W)   **Everton** 1-1 Wolves
LCT88 (W)   **Everton** 0-1 Man Utd
FAC89 (S)   **Everton** 2-3 Liverpool

Wilson, Kevin (2, 0)
ZC90   **Chelsea** 1-0 Middlesbrough
AIC94   **Notts C** 0-1 Brescia

Wilson, Ray (28, 0)
INT60   **England** 3-3 Yugoslavia
WCQ61   **England** 2-0 Portugal
BC61   **England** 1-1 N Ireland
INT62   **England** 3-1 Austria
INT62   **England** 3-1 Switzerland
INT63   **England** 1-1 Brazil
CEN63   **England** 2-1 FIFA
INT64   **England** 2-1 Uruguay
BC65   **England** 2-2 Scotland
INT65   **England** 1-0 Hungary
INT65   **England** 2-3 Austria
BC65   **England** 2-1 N Ireland
INT66 (S)   **England** 1-0 W Germany
INT66   **England** 2-0 Yugoslavia
FAC66   **Everton** 3-2 Sheffield W.
WC66   **England** 0-0 Uruguay
WC66   **England** 2-0 Mexico
WC66   **England** 2-0 France
WC66   **England** 1-0 Argentina
WC66   **England** 2-1 Portugal
WC66   **England** 4-2 W Germany
INT66   **England** 0-0 Czechoslovakia
ECQ66   **England** 5-1 Wales
ECQ67   **England** 2-3 Scotland
ECQ67   **England** 2-0 N Ireland
INT67   **England** 2-2 USSR
ECQ68   **England** 1-0 Spain
FAC68   **Everton** 0-1 WBA

Wilson, Ray (1, 0)
FLC70   **WBA** 1-2 Man City

Wilson, Sammy (2, 2)
BC63 (2)   **N Ireland** 3-8 England
ECQ67   **N Ireland** 0-2 England

Wilson, Terry (7, 0)
SI84 (W)   **Scotland** 0-1 England
LCT88   **Nottingham F** 3-0 Leeds
LCT88   **Nottingham F** 0-0 Aston Villa
LCT88   **Nottingham F** 2-2 Tranmere
LCT88   **Nottingham F** 0-0 Sheffield W
LC89   **Nottingham F** 3-1 Luton
SC89   **Nottingham F** 4-3 Everton

Wilson, Tommy (3, 0)
BC28	**England**	1-5 Scotland
FAC28	**Huddersfield**	1-3 Blackburn
FAC30 (C)	**Huddersfield**	0-2 Arsenal

Wilson, Tommy (1, 1)
FAC59 (1)	**Nottingham F**	2-1 Luton

Winterburn, Nigel (25, 0)
LC88	**Arsenal**	2-3 Luton
WIT88	**Arsenal**	4-0 Spurs
WIT88	**Arsenal**	3-0 Bayern Munich
MT89	**Arsenal**	1-0 Porto
MT89 (W)	**Arsenal**	1-0 Liverpool
CS89	**Arsenal**	0-1 Liverpool
INT89 (S)	**England**	0-0 Italy
MT90	**Arsenal**	2-0 Aston Villa
MT90	**Arsenal**	0-1 Sampdoria
FAC91	**Arsenal**	1-3 Spurs
CS91	**Arsenal**	0-0 Spurs
FAC93	**Arsenal**	1-0 Spurs
CCC93	**Arsenal**	2-1 Sheffield W
FAC93	**Arsenal**	1-1 Sheffield W
FAC93	**Arsenal**	2-1 Sheffield W
CS93	**Arsenal**	1-1 Man Utd
FAC98	**Arsenal**	2-0 Newcastle Utd
CS98	**Arsenal**	3-0 Man Utd
EC98	**Arsenal**	2-1 Panathinaikos
EC98	**Arsenal**	1-1 Dynamo Kiev
EC98	**Arsenal**	0-1 Lens
CS99 (C)	**Arsenal**	2-1 Man Utd
EC99	**Arsenal**	3-1 AIK Stockholm
EC99	**Arsenal**	2-4 Barcelona
EC99	**Arsenal**	0-1 Fiorentina

Wise, Dennis (20, 0)
LCT88	**Wimbledon**	0-1 Tranmere
FAC88	**Wimbledon**	1-0 Liverpool
CS88 (C)	**Wimbledon**	1-2 Liverpool
INT91 (W)	**England**	3-1 USSR
FAC94 (C)	**Chelsea**	2-0 Luton
FAC94 (C)	**Chelsea**	0-4 Man Utd
INT94	**England**	0-0 Norway
INT94 (S)	**England**	1-1 Romania
INT94	**England**	1-0 Nigeria
INT95	**England**	0-0 Colombia
INT95 (W)	**England**	1-1 Portugal
INT96 (S)	**England**	3-0 Hungary
FAC97 (C)	**Chelsea**	2-1 Middlesbrough
CS97 (C)	**Chelsea**	1-1 Man Utd
CCC98 (C)	**Chelsea**	2-0 Middlesbrough
INT00	**England**	0-0 Argentina
FAC00 (C)	**Chelsea**	2-1 Newcastle Utd
FAC00 (C)	**Chelsea**	1-0 Aston Villa
INT00	**England**	1-1 Brazil
CS00 (C)	**Chelsea**	2-0 Man Utd

Withe, Peter (8, 4)
FLC78	**Nottingham F**	0-0 Liverpool
CS78 (1)	**Nottingham F**	5-0 Ipswich
INT81	**England**	0-1 Brazil
BC81 (W)	**England**	0-0 Wales
BC81	**England**	0-1 Scotland

CS81 (2)	**Aston Villa**	2-2 Spurs
ECQ83 (1)	**England**	2-0 Hungary
BC83 (W)	**England**	2-0 Scotland

Woan, Ian (1, 0)
FAC91 (W)	**Nottingham F**	1-2 Spurs

Wood, Darren (3, 1)
SI79 (C, 1)	**England**	1-1 Wales
SI79 (C)	**England**	2-2 W Germany
FMC86	**Chelsea**	5-4 Man City

Wood, George (1, 0)
BC79	**Scotland**	1-3 England

Wood, Ray (2, 0)
BC54	**England**	3-2 Wales
FAC57	**Man Utd**	1-2 Aston Villa

Wood, Stan (1, 0)
FAC31	**WBA**	2-1 Birmingham

Woodburn, Willie (3, 0)
BC47	**Scotland**	1-1 England
BC49	**Scotland**	3-1 England
BC51	**Scotland**	3-2 England

Woodcock, Tony (23, 7)
FLC78	**Nottingham F**	0-0 Liverpool
BC78	**England**	1-0 N Ireland
CS78	**Nottingham F**	5-0 Ipswich
INT78 (W)	**England**	1-0 Czechoslovakia
FLC79 (1)	**Nottingham F**	3-2 Southampton
ECQ79	**England**	2-0 Bulgaria
ECQ80	**England**	2-0 Rep of Ireland
INT80	**England**	3-1 Argentina
WCQ80 (1)	**England**	4-0 Norway
WCQ80	**England**	2-1 Switzerland
WCQ81	**England**	0-0 Romania
BC81 (S)	**England**	0-0 Wales
BC81 (W)	**England**	0-1 Scotland
BC82 (S)	**England**	4-0 N Ireland
INT82 (1)	**England**	2-0 Netherlands
INT82 (S, 1)	**England**	1-2 W Germany
ECQ82 (1)	**England**	9-0 Luxembourg
ECQ83 (W)	**England**	0-0 Greece
BC84 (1)	**England**	1-0 N Ireland
INT84 (W)	**England**	1-0 E Germany
WCQ84 (1)	**England**	5-0 Finland
WCQ85 (S)	**England**	1-1 Romania
WCQ85 (S)	**England**	5-0 Turkey

Woodley, Vic (3, 0)
BC38	**England**	0-1 Scotland
LSC44	**Chelsea**	1-3 Charlton
FAC46	**Derby**	4-1 Charlton

Woodruff, Arthur (1, 0)
FAC47	**Burnley**	0-1 Charlton

Woods, Chris (21, 0)
FLC78	**Nottingham F**	0-0 Liverpool
MC85	**Norwich**	1-0 Sunderland
ECQ86	**England**	2-0 Yugoslavia
INT88 (S)	**England**	1-0 Denmark
INT90 (S)	**England**	1-0 Brazil
INT90 (S)	**England**	1-0 Denmark
INT90	**England**	1-0 Hungary

ECQ90	**England** 2-0 Poland
INT91	**England** 3-1 USSR
INT91	**England** 0-1 Germany
ECQ91	**England** 1-0 Turkey
INT92	**England** 2-0 France
INT92	**England** 1-1 Brazil
WCQ92	**England** 1-1 Norway
WCQ92	**England** 4-0 Turkey
WCQ93	**England** 6-0 San Marino
FAC93	**Sheffield W** 2-1 Sheffield Utd
CCC93	**Sheffield W** 1-2 Arsenal
WCQ93	**England** 2-2 Netherlands
FAC93	**Sheffield W** 1-1 Arsenal
FAC93	**Sheffield W** 1-2 Arsenal

Woods, Clive (2, 0)
FAC78	**Ipswich** 1-0 Arsenal
CS78	**Ipswich** 0-5 Nottingham F

Woods, Matt (1, 0)
FAC60	**Blackburn** 0-3 Wolves

Woollett, Alan (1, 0)
FAC69	**Leicester** 0-1 Man City

Woosnam, Phil (1, 0)
BC60	**Wales** 1-5 England

Worrall, Fred (2, 0)
FAC34	**Portsmouth** 1-2 Man City
FAC39	**Portsmouth** 4-1 Wolves

Worthington, Frank (4, 1)
BC74 (S)	**England** 1-0 N Ireland
INT74 (1)	**England** 2-2 Argentina
ECQ74 (W)	**England** 3-0 Czechoslovakia
ECQ74 (S)	**England** 0-0 Portugal

Worthington, Nigel (10, 1)
WCQ85 (S)	**N Ireland** 0-0 England
ECQ86	**N Ireland** 0-3 England
LCT88	**Sheffield W** 0-0 Crystal P
LCT88 (1)	**Sheffield W** 1-1 Wigan
LCT88	**Sheffield W** 2-1 Man Utd
LCT88	**Sheffield W** 0-0 Nottingham F
RLC91	**Sheffield W** 1-0 Man Utd
FAC93	**Sheffield W** 2-1 Sheffield Utd
FAC93	**Sheffield W** 1-1 Arsenal
FAC93	**Sheffield W** 1-2 Arsenal

Wreh, Christopher (3, 1)
FAC98 (W)	**Arsenal** 2-0 Newcastle Utd
CS98 (S, 1)	**Arsenal** 3-0 Man Utd
EC98	**Arsenal** 0-1 Lens

Wright, Alan (7, 0)
SI87	**England** 2-0 W Germany
VS87 (C)	**England** 1-1 Scotland
PPO91	**Blackpool** 1-1 Torquay
PPO92	**Blackburn** 1-0 Leicester
CCC96	**Aston Villa** 3-0 Leeds
FAC00	**Aston Villa** 0-0 Bolton
FAC00 (W)	**Aston Villa** 0-1 Chelsea

Wright, Billy (29, 0)
VI46	**England** 2-0 Belgium
IT46	**Army PT Corps** 5-3 FA
BC47	**England** 1-1 Scotland

BC49 (C)	**England** 1-3 Scotland
FAC49 (C)	**Wolves** 3-1 Leicester
BC51 (C)	**England** 2-3 Scotland
INT51 (C)	**England** 2-1 Argentina
INT51 (C)	**England** 2-2 Austria
BC52 (C)	**England** 5-2 Wales
INT52 (C)	**England** 5-0 Belgium
BC53 (C)	**England** 2-2 Scotland
NIN53 (C)	**England** 4-4 FIFA
INT53 (C)	**England** 3-6 Hungary
BC54 (C)	**England** 3-2 Wales
INT54 (C)	**England** 3-1 W Germany
BC55 (C)	**England** 7-2 Scotland
BC55 (C)	**England** 3-0 N Ireland
INT55 (C)	**England** 4-1 Spain
INT56 (C)	**England** 4-2 Brazil
BC56 (C)	**England** 3-1 Wales
INT56 (C)	**England** 3-0 Yugoslavia
BC57 (C)	**England** 2-1 Scotland
WCQ57 (C)	**England** 5-1 Rep of Ireland
BC57 (C)	**England** 2-3 N Ireland
INT57 (C)	**England** 4-0 France
INT58 (C)	**England** 2-1 Portugal
INT58 (C)	**England** 5-0 USSR
BC59 (C)	**England** 1-0 Scotland
INT59 (C)	**England** 2-2 Italy

Wright, Ian (24, 9)
LCT88	**Crystal P** 0-0 Sheffield W
FAC90 (S, 2)	**Crystal P** 3-3 Man Utd
FAC90 (S)	**Crystal P** 0-1 Man Utd
INT91	**England** 2-0 Cameroon
ECQ91 (S)	**England** 1-1 Rep of Ireland
ZC91 (2)	**Crystal P** 4-1 Everton
INT91 (W)	**England** 3-1 USSR
WCQ92 (W)	**England** 1-1 Norway
WCQ92	**England** 4-0 Turkey
FAC93 (W)	**Arsenal** 1-0 Spurs
CCC93	**Arsenal** 2-1 Sheffield W
FAC93 (1, W)	**Arsenal** 1-1 Sheffield W
FAC93 (1, W)	**Arsenal** 2-1 Sheffield W
CS93 (1)	**Arsenal** 1-1 Man Utd
WCQ93	**England** 3-0 Poland
INT94 (S)	**England** 5-0 Greece
INT94 (S)	**England** 0-0 Norway
INT94 (S)	**England** 2-0 USA
INT94 (W)	**England** 1-1 Romania
WCQ97 (S)	**England** 0-1 Italy
INT97 (S)	**England** 2-0 Mexico
WCQ97 (2)	**England** 4-0 Moldova
INT98 (S)	**England** 0-0 Saudi Arabia
INT98 (W)	**England** 2-0 Czech Rep

Wright, Mark (22, 0)
INT84	**England** 1-0 E Germany
WCQ84	**England** 5-0 Finland
INT85	**England** 2-1 Rep of Ireland
WCQ85	**England** 1-1 Romania
WCQ85	**England** 5-0 Turkey
WCQ85	**England** 0-0 N Ireland
ECQ86	**England** 2-0 Yugoslavia
INT88 (S)	**England** 2-2 Netherlands

RC88   **England** 1-1 Colombia
INT90 (S)   **England** 4-2 Czechoslovakia
INT90   **England** 1-0 Hungary
ECQ90   **England** 2-0 Poland
INT91   **England** 2-0 Cameroon
ECQ91   **England** 1-1 Rep of Ireland
INT91 (C)   **England** 3-1 USSR
INT91   **England** 2-2 Argentina
INT92   **England** 2-0 France
FAC92 (C)   **Liverpool** 2-0 Sunderland
CS92 (C)   **Liverpool** 3-4 Leeds
INT96   **England** 0-0 Croatia
FAC96   **Liverpool** 0-1 Man Utd
INT96 (W)   **England** 3-0 Hungary

Wright, Tommy (1, 0)
BC53   **Scotland** 2-2 England

Wright, Tommy (3, 0)
FAC66   **Everton** 3-2 Sheffield W
FAC68   **Everton** 0-1 WBA
INT69   **England** 1-1 Romania

Yates, Steve (2, 0)
LDC90   **Bristol R** 1-2 Tranmere
WLC00 (S)   **Tranmere** 1-2 Leicester

Yeats, Ron (1, 0)
FAC65 (C)   **Liverpool** 2-1 Leeds

Yeboah, Tony (1, 0)
CCC96   **Leeds** 0-3 Aston Villa

Yorath, Terry (5, 0)
BC71   **Wales** 0-0 England
WCQ73   **Wales** 1-1 England
FAC73 (S)   **Leeds** 0-1 Sunderland
BC77 (C)   **Wales** 1-0 England
BC79 (C)   **Wales** 0-0 England

York, Dick (1, 0)
FAC24   **Aston Villa** 0-2 Newcastle Utd

Yorke, Dwight (6, 1)
MT90   **Aston Villa** 0-2 Arsenal
MT90 (W)   **Aston Villa** 0-1 Real Sociedad
CCC96 (1)   **Aston Villa** 3-0 Leeds
FAC99 (S)   **Man Utd** 2-0 Newcastle Utd
CS99   **Man Utd** 1-2 Arsenal
CS00 (S)   **Man Utd** 0-2 Chelsea

Young, Alex (1, 0)
FAC66   **Everton** 3-2 Sheffield W

Young, Alf (1, 0)
FAC38 (C)   **Huddersfield** 0-1 PNE

Young, Eric (4, 0)
LCT88   **Wimbledon** 0-1 Tranmere
FAC88   **Wimbledon** 1-0 Liverpool
CS88   **Wimbledon** 1-2 Liverpool
ZC91 (W)   **Crystal P** 4-1 Everton

Young, George (5, 0)
BC47   **Scotland** 1-1 England
BC49 (C)   **Scotland** 3-1 England
BC51 (C)   **Scotland** 3-2 England
BC53 (C)   **Scotland** 2-2 England
BC57 (C)   **Scotland** 1-2 England

Young, Gerry (2, 0)
BC64   **England** 2-1 Wales
FAC66   **Sheffield W** 2-3 Everton

Young, Jack (1, 0)
FAC23   **West Ham** 0-2 Bolton

Young, Neil (1, 1)
FAC69 (1)   **Man City** 1-0 Leicester

Young, Willie (4, 0)
FAC78   **Arsenal** 0-1 Ipswich
FAC79   **Arsenal** 3-2 Man Utd
CS79 (S)   **Arsenal** 1-3 Liverpool
FAC80   **Arsenal** 0-1 West Ham

Younger, Tommy (1, 0)
BC57   **Scotland** 1-2 England

Zagorakis, Theo (1, 0)
WLC99 (S)   **Leicester** 0-1 Spurs

Ziege, Christian (3, 0)
ECQ96   **Germany** 1-1 England
ECQ96   **Germany** 2-1 Czech Rep
WCQ00 (S)   **Germany** 1-0 England

Zola, Gianfranco (7, 1)
WCQ97 (1, W)   **Italy** 1-0 England
FAC97 (W)   **Chelsea** 2-0 Middlesbrough
CS97   **Chelsea** 1-1 Man Utd
CCC98   **Chelsea** 2-0 Middlesbrough
FAC00 (S)   **Chelsea** 2-1 Newcastle Utd
FAC00 (W)   **Chelsea** 1-0 Aston Villa
CS00 (W)   **Chelsea** 2-0 Man Utd

Top 20 scorers at Wembley Stadium

27 – Sir Bobby Charlton (50 apps)
  Man Utd (2)
  England Schoolboys (2)
  England (23)
25 – Gary Lineker (35 apps)
  Everton (1)
  Tottenham Hotspur (2)
  England (22)
20 – Jimmy Greaves (25 apps)
  Tottenham Hotspur (1)
  England Under-23 (2)
  England (17)
18 – Alan Shearer (41 apps)
  England (18)
17 – Sir Geoff Hurst (26 apps)
  West Ham United (1)
  England (16)
16 – David Platt (33 apps)
  England (16)
15 – Bryan Robson (49 apps)
  Manchester United (5)
  Football League (2)
  England (8)
12 – Kevin Keegan (31 apps)
  Liverpool (2)
  England (10)
11 – Nat Lofthouse (10 apps)
  Bolton Wanderers (3)
  England (8)
11 – Ian Rush (20 apps)
  Liverpool (10)
  Wales (1)
10 – Mike Channon (23 apps)
  England (10)
10 – Johnny Haynes (23 apps)
  England Schoolboys (2)
  England (8)
10 – Martin Peters (35 apps)
  England (10)
10 – Tommy Taylor (6 apps)
  Manchester United (1)
  England (9)
9 – Raich Carter (9 apps)
  Sunderland (1)
  England (8)
9 – Martin Chivers (13 apps)
  Tottenham Hotspur (2)
  England (7)
9 – Ted Drake (5 apps)
  Arsenal (3)
  Royal Air Force (3)
  Combined Services (3)
9 – Glenn Hoddle (27 apps)
  Tottenham Hotspur (2)
  Swindon Town (1)
  England (6)
9 – Stan Mortensen (10 apps)
  Blackpool (4)
  Combined Services (2)
  England (3)
9 – Ian Wright (23 apps)
  Crystal Palace (4)
  Arsenal (3)
  England (2)

Most appearances by a Non-English player:
Ian Rush – 20 (1981-96)

Most appearances by a Non-League player:
Bob Hardisty – 9 (1948-57)
Played in six FA Amateur Cup finals for Bishop Auckland
And three times for the Great Britain Olympic Team,
captaining them in the 1948 Games.

**Most appearances by a professional from outside
the top flight:**
Steve Hayward – 7 (1990-97)
Played in three England Youth internationals, an under-19
international, an Anglo-Italian Cup final for Derby County
and two Auto Windscreens Shield finals for Carlisle United,
captaining them to penalty shootout success in 1997.

Most appearances by a foreign-based player:
Mario Coluna – 6 (1958-68)
Eusebio – 6 (1961-68)
Both played for Benfica and Portugal, with Eusebio also
representing FIFA at the FA Centenary match In 1963.

Wembley Dismissals:

1948	Boris Stankovic (Yugoslavia)
1966	Antonio Rattin (Argentina)
1974	Billy Bremner (Leeds)
1974	Kevin Keegan (Liverpool)
1977	Gilbert Dresch (Luxembourg)
1985	Kevin Moran (Man Utd)
1989	Mike Henry (Sudbury)
1992	Jason Cook (Colchester)
1993	Lee Dixon (Arsenal)
1993	Peter Swan (Port V)
1994	Andrei Kanchelskis (Man Utd)
1994	Michael Wallace (Stockport)
1994	Chris Beaumont (Stockport)
1995	Tetsuji Hashiratani (Japan)
1996	Derek Ward (Northwich)
1997	Tony Rogers (Dagenham)
1997	Brian Statham (Brentford)
1998	Rubinho (Brazil)
1998	Capucho (Portugal)
1998	Tony Nelson (Tow Law)
1998	Ray Parlour (Arsenal)
1998	Tony Vairelles (Lens)
1999	Justin Edinburgh (Tottenham)
1999	Paul Scholes (England)
2000	Clint Hill (Tranmere)
2000	Mark Delaney (Aston V)
2000	Kevin Sharp (Wigan)
2000	Roy Keane (Man Utd)

THE MATCHES

The full list of abbreviations of competitions referenced in this index is as follows:

Date	Comp	Match
28/04/23	FAC	Bolton 2-0 West Ham
12/04/24	BC	England 1-1 Scotland
26/04/24	FAC	Aston Villa 0-2 Newcastle
02/05/24		RAF Senior Cup Final
25/04/25	FAC	Cardiff 0-1 Sheffield U
24/04/26	FAC	Bolton 1-0 Man City
23/04/27	FAC	Arsenal 0-1 Cardiff
31/03/28	BC	England 1-5 Scotland
21/04/28	FAC	Blackburn 3-1 Huddersfield
29/09/28		Ealing 1-0 Hastings
13/10/28		Ealing 0-4 Ipswich
20/10/28		Ealing 0-4 Midland Bank
27/10/28		Ealing 1-5 Bank of England
03/11/28		Ealing 0-3 Westminster Bank
10/11/28		Ealing 4-2 Barclays Bank
17/11/28		Cambridge Un 5-2 Casuals
01/12/28		Ealing 0-3 Aquarius
08/12/28		Ealing 0-3 Old Lyonians
12/01/29		Old Malvernians 1-2 Barclays Bank
26/01/29		London Un 0-3 Cambridge Un
09/02/29		Old Malvernians 4-2 Old Cholmeleians
09/03/29		Middlesex 1-5 London
27/04/29	FAC	Bolton 2-0 Portsmouth
22/02/30		Glacier Sports 4-5 Harrow St Mary *aet*
05/04/30	BC	England 5-2 Scotland
26/04/30	FAC	Arsenal 2-0 Huddersfield
22/11/30		Clapton Orient 3-0 Brentford
06/12/30		Clapton Orient 3-1 Southend
25/04/31	FAC	Birmingham 1-2 WBA
09/04/32	BC	England 3-0 Scotland
23/04/32	FAC	Arsenal 1-2 Newcastle
29/04/33	FAC	Everton 3-0 Man City
21/03/34		Greenwich 0-1 Walthamstow
14/04/34	BC	England 3-0 Scotland
28/04/34	FAC	Man City 2-1 Portsmouth
27/04/35	FAC	Sheffield W 4-2 WBA
04/04/36	BC	England 1-1 Scotland
25/04/36	FAC	Arsenal 1-0 Sheffield Utd
07/01/37	UI	Great Britain 1-0 Germany
01/05/37	FAC	PNE 1-3 Sunderland
09/04/38	BC	England 0-1 Scotland
30/04/38	FAC	Huddersfield 0-1 PNE *aet*
29/04/39	FAC	Portsmouth 4-1 Wolves

Key

AC	FA Amateur Cup Final	LCEN	Football League Centenary Match
AI	Amateur International	LCT	Football League Centenary Tournament
AIC	Anglo-Italian Cup Final	LDC	Leyland Daf Cup Final
AT	Autoglass Trophy Final	LSC	Football League South Cup Final
AWS	Auto Windscreens Shield Final	LWC	London War Cup Final
BAC	British Amateur Championship	MC	Milk Cup Final
BC	British Championship	MCC	Middlesex Charity Cup Final
CEN	FA Centenary Match	MT	Makita Tournament
CHA	Charity Matches	NIN	FA 90th Anniversary Match
CCC	Coca-Cola Cup Final	OLY	Olympic Games
CS	FA Charity Shield	OQ	Olympic Qualifying
CYC	FA County Youth Cup Final Second Leg	PPO	Football League Promotion Play-Off Final
D3S	Football League Third Division South	RC	Rous Cup
EACQ	European Amateur	RLC	Rumbelows Cup Final
	Championship Qualifying	SC	Simod Cup Final
EC	European Cup	SI	Schoolboy Internationals
ECH	European Championship	SVT	Sherpa Van Trophy Final
ECQ	European Championship Qualifying	UC	Umbro Cup
ECW	European Cup-Winners Cup Final	UI	University International
EEC	European Economic	U16I	Under-16 Internationals
	Community Celebration Match	U17I	Under-17 Internationals
EFC	European Fairs Cup	U18SI	Under-18 Schoolboy Internationals
EYT	European Youth Tournament Final	U19I	Under-19 International
FAC	FA Cup	U23I	Under-23 International
FAT	FA Trophy Final	VI	Victory International
FAV	FA Vase Final	VS	Victory Shield Schoolboy Internationals
FLC	Football League Cup Final	WC	World Cup
FLWC	Football League War Cup Final	WCQ	World Cup Qualifying
FMC	Full Members Cup Final	WI	Wartime Internationals
FRT	Freight Rover Trophy Final	WIT	Wembley International Tournament
INT	Internationals	WLC	Worthington Cup
IT	International Trial	YAC	Football League Youth Alliance Cup Final
IV	Inter-Varsity Matches	YI	Youth Internationals
LC	Littlewoods Cup Final	ZC	Zenith Cup Final

13/04/40	WI	England 0-1 Wales		03/05/52	FAC	Arsenal 0-1 Newcastle
08/06/40	FLWC	Blackburn 0-1 West Ham		10/05/52		ATC 3-5 NABC
10/05/41	FLWC	Arsenal 1-1 PNE		12/11/52	BC	England 5-2 Wales
04/06/41	CHA	Met Police 3-6 RAF		26/11/52	INT	England 5-0 Belgium
04/10/41	WI	England 2-0 Scotland		07/03/53	IV	Cambridge Un 0-0 Oxford Un
11/10/41	WI	Belgium 5-4 Netherlands		28/03/53	SI	England 3-3 Wales
17/01/42	WI	England 3-0 Scotland		11/04/53	AC	Harwich 0-6 Pegasus
22/04/42		Geipel Cup Final		18/04/53	BC	England 2-2 Scotland
06/05/42	CHA	Met Police 3-6 RAF		02/05/53	FAC	Blackpool 4-3 Bolton
30/05/42	LWC	Brentford 2-0 Portsmouth		09/05/53		ATC 1-3 NABC
03/06/42	MCC	RAF Uxbridge 2-5 Wealdstone *aet*		21/10/53	NIN	England 4-4 FIFA
10/10/42	WI	England 0-0 Scotland		25/11/53	INT	England 3-6 Hungary
27/02/43	WI	England 5-3 Wales		05/12/53	IV	Cambridge Un 1-1 Oxford Un
01/05/43	FLSC	Arsenal 7-1 Charlton		27/03/54	AI	England 1-4 Scotland
05/05/43	CHA	Met Police 3-4 RAF		03/04/54	SI	England 1-0 Scotland
12/05/43	MCC	Finchley 1-0 Southall		10/04/54	AC	Bishop Auckland 2-2 Crook *aet*
13/05/43		Wembley Youth Committee League Cup Finals		01/05/54	FAC	PNE 2-3 WBA
25/09/43	WI	England 8-3 Wales		08/05/54		ATC 1-0 NABC
19/02/44	WI	England 6-2 Scotland		10/11/54	INT	England 3-2 Wales
15/04/44	FLSC	Charlton 3-1 Chelsea		01/12/54	INT	England 3-1 West Germany
10/05/44	CHA	Combined Serv 5-2 Met Police/Defence		04/12/54	IV	Cambridge Un 3-2 Oxford Un
17/05/44	MCC	QPR Juniors 2-3 Tufnell Park		02/04/55	BC	England 7-2 Scotland
14/10/44	WI	England 6-2 Scotland		16/04/55	AC	Bishop Auckland 2-0 Hendon
07/04/45	FLSC	Chelsea 2-0 Millwall		23/04/55	SI	England 6-0 Wales
18/04/45		Wembley Youth Committee League Cup Finals		07/05/55	FAC	Man City 1-3 Newcastle
25/04/45		Greenwich 10-1 Paddington		26/10/55	EFC	London 3-2 Frankfurt
09/05/45	CHA	Combined Serv 3-1 Nat Police/Defence		02/11/55	BC	England 3-0 N Ireland
16/05/45	MCC	Golders Green 4-1 Tufnell Park		30/11/55	INT	England 4-1 Spain
26/05/45	WI	England 2-2 France		07/12/55	IV	Cambridge Un 4-2 Oxford Un
19/01/46	VI	England 2-0 Belgium		24/03/56	AI	England 4-2 Scotland
30/03/46		ATC 4-2 NABC		07/04/56	AC	Bishop Auckland 1-1 Corinthian Cas *aet*
06/04/46	IT	FA 3-5 Army PT Corps		21/04/56	SI	England 1-2 Scotland
27/04/46	FAC	Charlton 1-4 Derby *aet*		05/05/56	FAC	Birmingham 1-3 Man City
12/04/47	BC	England 1-1 Scotland		09/05/56	INT	England 4-2 Brazil
26/04/47	FAC	Burnley 0-1 Charlton *aet*		12/05/56		Army Cadets 1-2 NABC
03/04/48		ATC 2-0 Army Cadets		12/05/56	OLY	Great Britain 3-3 Bulgaria
24/04/48	FAC	Blackpool 2-4 Man Utd		14/11/56	BC	England 3-1 Wales
10/08/48	OLY	Denmark 2-4 Sweden		28/11/56	INT	England 3-0 Yugoslavia
11/08/48	OLY	Great Britain 1-3 Yugoslavia		08/12/56	IV	Cambridge Un 1-4 Oxford Un
13/08/48	OLY	Denmark 5-3 Great Britain		30/03/57	SI	England 2-0 Wales
13/08/48	OLY	Sweden 3-1 Yugoslavia		06/04/57	BC	England 2-1 Scotland
19/03/49		ATC 2-2 NABC *aet*		13/04/57	AC	Bishop Auckland 3-1 Wycombe
09/04/49	BC	England 1-3 Scotland		04/05/57	FAC	Aston Villa 2-1 Man Utd
23/04/49	AC	Bromley 1-0 Romford		08/05/57	WCQ	England 5-1 Rep of Ireland
30/04/49	FAC	Leicester 1-3 Wolves		16/10/57	U23	England 3-2 Romania
15/04/50	SI	England 8-2 Scotland		06/11/57	BC	England 2-3 N Ireland
22/04/50	AC	Bishop Auckland 0-4 Willington		27/11/57	INT	England 4-0 France
29/04/50	FAC	Arsenal 2-0 Liverpool		07/12/57	IV	Cambridge Un 1-1 Oxford Un
13/05/50		Army Cadets 1-4 NABC		29/03/58	AI	England 2-3 Scotland
20/05/50	CYC	Middlesex 1-2 Essex *aet*		12/04/58	AC	Ilford 0-3 Woking
07/04/51	SI	England 3-0 Wales		26/04/58	SI	England 3-1 Scotland
14/04/51	BC	England 2-3 Scotland		03/05/58	FAC	Bolton 2-0 Man Utd
21/04/51	AC	Bishop Auckland 1-2 Pegasus		07/05/58	INT	England 2-1 Portugal
28/04/51	FAC	Blackpool 0-2 Newcastle		22/10/58	INT	England 5-0 USSR
19/05/51		Army Cadets 2-4 NABC		06/12/58	IV	Cambridge Un 1-1 Oxford Un
09/05/51	INT	England 2-1 Argentina		11/04/59	BC	England 1-0 Scotland
28/11/51	INT	England 2-2 Austria		18/04/59	AC	Barnet 2-3 Crook
15/03/52	AI	England 1-2 Scotland		25/04/59	SI	England 2-0 West Germany
05/04/52	SI	England 1-0 Scotland		02/05/59	FAC	Luton 1-2 Nottingham F
26/04/52	AC	Leyton 1-2 Walthamstow Ave *aet*		06/05/59	INT	England 2-2 Italy

28/10/59	INT	England 2-3 Sweden		19/07/66	WC	Mexico 0-0 Uruguay
18/11/59	BC	England 2-1 N Ireland		20/07/66	WC	England 2-0 France
05/12/59	IV	Cambridge Un 6-2 Oxford Un		23/07/66	WC	Argentina 0-1 England
23/04/60	AC	Hendon 2-1 Kingstonian		26/07/66	WC	England 2-1 Portugal
30/04/60	SI	England 5-3 Scotland		28/07/66	WC	Portugal 2-1 USSR
07/05/60	FAC	Blackburn 0-3 Wolves		30/07/66	WC	England 4-2 West Germany *aet*
11/05/60	INT	England 3-3 Yugoslavia		02/11/66	INT	England 0-0 Czechoslovakia
26/10/60	INT	England 4-2 Spain		16/11/66	ECQ	England 5-1 Wales
23/11/60	BC	England 5-1 Wales		07/12/66	IV	Cambridge Un 1-0 Oxford Un
03/12/60	IV	Cambridge Un 2-2 Oxford Un		04/03/67	FLC	QPR 3-2 WBA
15/04/61	BC	England 9-3 Scotland		15/04/67	ECQ	England 2-3 Scotland
22/04/61	AC	Walthamstow Ave 2-1 West Auckland		22/04/67	AC	Enfield 0-0 Skelmersdale *aet*
29/04/61	SI	England 8-1 Wales		29/04/67	SI	England 0-2 Scotland
06/05/61	FAC	Leicester 0-2 Spurs		20/05/67	FAC	Chelsea 1-2 Spurs
10/05/61	INT	England 8-0 Mexico		24/05/67	INT	England 2-0 Spain
25/10/61	WCQ	England 2-0 Portugal		22/11/67	ECQ	England 2-0 N Ireland
22/11/61	BC	England 1-1 N Ireland		06/12/67	INT	England 2-2 USSR
09/12/61	IV	Cambridge Un 2-0 Oxford Un		13/12/67	IV	Cambridge Un 1-0 Oxford Un
04/04/62	INT	England 3-1 Austria		02/03/68	FLC	Arsenal 0-1 Leeds
14/04/62	AC	Crook 1-1 Hounslow *aet*		03/04/68	ECQ	England 1-0 Spain
30/04/62	SI	England 1-2 West Germany		20/04/68	AC	Chesham 0-1 Leytonstone
05/05/62	FAC	Burnley 1-3 Spurs		27/04/68	SI	England 1-2 West Germany
09/05/62	INT	England 3-1 Switzerland		18/05/68	FAC	Everton 0-1 WBA *aet*
21/11/62	BC	England 4-0 Wales		22/05/68	INT	England 3-1 Sweden
08/12/62	IV	Cambridge Un 5-2 Oxford Un		29/05/68	EC	Benfica 1-4 Man Utd *aet*
06/04/63	BC	England 1-2 Scotland		04/12/68	IV	Cambridge Un 3-1 Oxford Un
23/04/63	EYT	England 4-0 N Ireland		11/12/68	INT	England 1-1 Bulgaria
27/04/63	SI	England 4-1 Wales		15/01/69	INT	England 1-1 Romania
04/05/63	AC	Sutton 2-4 Wimbledon		12/03/69	INT	England 5-0 France
08/05/63	INT	England 1-1 Brazil		15/03/69	FLC	Arsenal 1-3 Swindon *aet*
22/05/63	EC	Benfica 1-2 Milan		12/04/69	AC	North Shields 2-1 Sutton
25/05/63	FAC	Leicester 1-3 Man Utd		19/04/69	SI	England 3-0 Wales
23/10/63	CEN	England 2-1 FIFA		26/04/69	FAC	Leicester 0-1 Man City
06/11/63	YI	England 5-2 Rest of UK		07/05/69	BC	England 2-1 Wales
20/11/63	BC	England 8-3 N Ireland		10/05/69	BC	England 4-1 Scotland
07/12/63	IV	Cambridge Un 4-2 Oxford Un		03/12/69	IV	Cambridge Un 1-1 Oxford Un
18/04/64	AC	Crook 2-1 Enfield		10/12/69	INT	England 1-0 Portugal
25/04/64	SI	England 1-1 West Germany		14/01/70	INT	England 0-0 Netherlands
02/05/64	FAC	PNE 2-3 West Ham		07/03/70	FLC	Man City 2-1 WBA *aet*
06/05/64	INT	England 2-1 Uruguay		21/03/70	SI	England 2-0 Scotland
21/10/64	INT	England 2-2 Belgium		04/04/70	AC	Dagenham 1-5 Enfield
18/11/64	BC	England 2-1 Wales		11/04/70	FAC	Chelsea 2-2 Leeds *aet*
05/12/64	IV	Cambridge Un 1-3 Oxford Un		21/04/70	BC	England 3-1 N Ireland
03/04/65	SI	England 3-0 Scotland		02/05/70	FAT	Macclesfield 2-0 Telford
10/04/65	BC	England 2-2 Scotland		16/05/70	SI	England 3-0 West Germany
24/04/65	AC	Hendon 3-1 Whitby		25/11/70	INT	England 3-1 East Germany
01/05/65	FAC	Leeds 1-2 Liverpool *aet*		09/12/70	IV	Cambridge Un 1-0 Oxford Un
05/05/65	INT	England 1-0 Hungary		27/02/71	FLC	Aston Villa 0-2 Spurs
19/05/65	ECW	Munich 0-2 West Ham		06/03/71	SI	England 1-0 N Ireland
20/10/65	INT	England 2-3 Austria		24/03/71	OLY	Great Britain 1-0 Bulgaria
10/11/65	BC	England 2-1 N Ireland		03/04/71	SI	England 5-1 Netherlands
08/12/65	IV	Cambridge Un 3-2 Oxford Un		21/04/71	ECQ	England 3-0 Greece
23/02/66	INT	England 1-0 West Germany		24/04/71	AC	Dagenham 1-4 Skelmersdale
16/04/66	AC	Hendon 1-3 Wealdstone		01/05/71	FAT	Hillingdon 2-3 Telford
30/04/66	SI	England 2-1 West Germany		08/05/71	FAC	Arsenal 2-1 Liverpool *aet*
04/05/66	INT	England 2-0 Yugoslavia		12/05/71	ECQ	England 5-0 Malta
14/05/66	FAC	Everton 3-2 Sheffield W		19/05/71	BC	England 0-0 Wales
11/07/66	WC	England 0-0 Uruguay		22/05/71	BC	England 3-1 Scotland
13/07/66	WC	France 1-1 Mexico		02/06/71	EC	Ajax 2-0 Panathinaikos
16/07/66	WC	England 2-0 Mexico		10/11/71	ECQ	England 1-1 Switzerland

08/12/71	IV	Cambridge Un 0-0 Oxford Un		13/10/76	WCQ	England 2-1 Finland
04/03/72	FLC	Chelsea 1-2 Stoke		08/12/76	IV	Cambridge Un 0-0 Oxford Un
15/04/72	FAT	Barnet 0-3 Stafford		09/02/77	INT	England 0-2 Netherlands
22/04/72	AC	Enfield 0-2 Hendon		12/03/77	FLC	Aston Villa 0-0 Everton
29/04/72	ECQ	England 1-3 West Germany		19/03/77	SI	England 2-0 Scotland
06/05/72	FAC	Arsenal 0-1 Leeds		30/03/77	WCQ	England 5-0 Luxembourg
20/05/72	SI	England 4-0 West Germany		30/04/77	FAV	Billericay 1-1 Sheffield *aet*
23/05/72	BC	England 0-1 N Ireland		14/05/77	FAT	Dagenham 1-2 Scarborough
11/10/72	INT	England 1-1 Yugoslavia		21/05/77	FAC	Liverpool 1-2 Man Utd
06/12/72	IV	Cambridge Un 2-1 Oxford Un		31/05/77	BC	England 0-1 Wales
03/01/73	EEC	The Three 2-0 The Six		04/06/77	BC	England 1-2 Scotland
24/01/73	WCQ	England 1-1 Wales		18/06/77	SI	England 1-2 West Germany
03/03/73	FLC	Norwich 0-1 Spurs		13/08/77	CS	Liverpool 0-0 Man Utd
07/04/73	SI	England 3-1 Netherlands		07/09/77	INT	England 0-0 Switzerland
14/04/73	AC	Slough 0-1 Walton & Hersham		16/11/77	WCQ	England 2-0 Italy
28/04/73	FAT	Scarborough 2-1 Wigan *aet*		07/12/77	IV	Cambridge Un 0-4 Oxford Un
05/05/73	FAC	Leeds 0-1 Sunderland		04/03/78	SI	England 3-3 France
15/05/73	BC	England 3-0 Wales		18/03/78	FLC	Liverpool 0-0 Nottingham F *aet*
19/05/73	BC	England 1-0 Scotland		19/04/78	INT	England 1-1 Brazil
09/06/73	SI	England 2-4 Scotland		22/04/78	FAV	Barton 1-2 Blue Star
26/09/73	INT	England 7-0 Austria		29/04/78	FAT	Altrincham 3-1 Leatherhead
17/10/73	WCQ	England 1-1 Poland		06/05/78	FAC	Arsenal 0-1 Ipswich
31/10/73	EAC	England 1-0 West Germany		10/05/78	EC	Bruges 0-1 Liverpool
14/11/73	INT	England 0-1 Italy		16/05/78	BC	England 1-0 N Ireland
05/12/73	IV	Cambridge Un 0-0 Oxford Un		24/05/78	INT	England 4-1 Hungary
02/03/74	FLC	Man City 1-2 Wolves		27/05/78	SI	England 3-0 Scotland
06/04/74	SI	England 5-2 France		12/08/78	CS	Ipswich 0-5 Nottingham F
20/04/74	AC	B. Stortford 4-1 Ilford		29/11/78	INT	England 1-0 Czechoslovakia
27/04/74	FAT	Dartford 1-2 Morecambe		06/12/78	IV	Cambridge Un 2-1 Oxford Un
04/05/74	FAC	Liverpool 3-0 Newcastle		07/02/79	ECQ	England 4-0 N Ireland
15/05/74	BC	England 1-0 N Ireland		17/03/79	FLC	Nottingham F 3-2 Southampton
22/05/74	INT	England 2-2 Argentina		24/03/79	SI	England 1-1 Wales
01/06/74	SI	England 4-0 West Germany		28/04/79	FAV	Almondsbury 1-4 Billericay
09/06/74		Plymouth 3-1 Sheffield		12/05/79	FAC	Arsenal 3-2 Man Utd
10/08/74	CS	Leeds 1-1 Liverpool (5-6)		19/05/79	FAT	Kettering 0-2 Stafford
30/10/74	ECQ	England 3-0 Czechoslovakia		23/05/79	BC	England 0-0 Wales
20/11/74	ECQ	England 0-0 Portugal		26/05/79	BC	England 3-1 Scotland
04/12/74	IV	Cambridge Un 1-3 Oxford Un		09/06/79	SI	England 2-2 West Germany
01/03/75	FLC	Aston Villa 1-0 Norwich		11/08/79	CS	Arsenal 1-3 Liverpool
12/03/75	INT	England 2-0 West Germany		12/09/79	ECQ	England 1-0 Denmark
22/03/75	SI	England 4-0 Netherlands		22/11/79	ECQ	England 2-0 Bulgaria
16/04/75	ECQ	England 5-0 Cyprus		05/12/79	IV	Cambridge Un 1-3 Oxford Un
19/04/75	FAV	Epsom & Ewell 1-2 Hoddesdon		06/02/80	ECQ	England 2-0 Rep of Ireland
26/04/75	FAT	Matlock 4-0 Scarborough		15/03/80	FLC	Nottingham F 0-1 Wolves
03/05/75	FAC	Fulham 0-2 West Ham		22/03/80	SI	England 2-0 Switzerland
21/05/75	BC	England 2-2 Wales		26/04/80	FAV	Guisborough 0-2 Stamford
24/05/75	BC	England 5-1 Scotland		10/05/80	FAC	Arsenal 0-1 West Ham
07/06/75	SI	England 0-1 Scotland		13/05/80	INT	England 3-1 Argentina
14/06/75		Merseyside 1-3 Plymouth		17/05/80	FAT	Dagenham 2-1 Mossley
09/08/75	CS	Derby 2-0 West Ham		20/05/80	BC	England 1-1 N Ireland
03/12/75	IV	Cambridge Un 0-2 Oxford Un		07/06/80	SI	England 4-5 Scotland
28/02/76	FLC	Man City 2-1 Newcastle		09/08/80	CS	Liverpool 1-0 West Ham
20/03/76	SI	England 4-1 Wales		10/09/80	WCQ	England 4-0 Norway
10/04/76	FAV	Billericay 1-0 Stamford *aet*		19/11/80	WCQ	England 2-1 Switzerland
24/04/76	FAT	Scarborough 3-2 Stafford *aet*		10/12/80	IV	Cambridge Un 0-2 Oxford Un
01/05/76	FAC	Man Utd 0-1 Southampton		14/03/81	FLC	Liverpool 1-1 West Ham *aet*
11/05/76	BC	England 4-0 N Ireland		25/03/81	INT	England 1-2 Spain
05/06/76	SI	England 6-1 France		28/03/81	VS	England 4-0 N Ireland
14/08/76	CS	Liverpool 1-0 Southampton		25/04/81	FAV	Whickham 3-2 Willenhall
08/09/76	INT	England 1-1 Rep of Ireland		29/04/81	WCQ	England 0-0 Romania

461

09/05/81	FAC	Man City 1-1 Spurs *aet*
12/05/81	INT	England 0-1 Brazil
14/05/81	FAC	Man City 2-3 Spurs
16/05/81	FAT	B. Stortford 1-0 Sutton
20/05/81	BC	England 0-0 Wales
23/05/81	BC	England 0-1 Scotland
13/06/81	SI	England 1-2 West Germany
22/08/81	CS	Aston Villa 2-2 Spurs
18/11/81	WCQ	England 1-0 Hungary
09/12/81	IV	Cambridge Un 0-2 Oxford Un
23/02/82	BC	England 4-0 N Ireland
13/03/82	FLC	Liverpool 3-1 Spurs *aet*
27/03/82	SI	England 7-0 Netherlands
08/05/82	FAV	Forest Green 3-0 Rainworth
15/05/82	FAT	Altrincham 0-1 Enfield *aet*
22/05/82	FAC	QPR 1-1 Spurs *aet*
25/05/82	INT	England 2-0 Netherlands
27/05/82	FAC	QPR 0-1 Spurs
05/06/82	SI	England 0-0 Scotland
21/08/82	CS	Liverpool 1-0 Spurs
13/10/82	INT	England 1-2 West Germany
08/12/82	IV	Cambridge Un 2-4 Oxford Un
15/12/82	ECQ	England 9-0 Luxembourg
23/02/83	BC	England 2-1 Wales
19/03/83	SI	England 1-0 West Germany
26/03/83	MC	Liverpool 2-1 Man Utd *aet*
30/03/83	ECQ	England 0-0 Greece
27/04/83	ECQ	England 2-0 Hungary
30/04/83	FAV	Halesowen 0-1 V Rugby
14/05/83	FAT	Northwich 1-2 Telford
21/05/83	FAC	Brighton 2-2 Man Utd *aet*
26/05/83	FAC	Brighton 0-4 Man Utd
01/06/83	BC	England 2-0 Scotland
11/06/83	SI	England 3-3 Scotland
20/08/83	CS	Liverpool 0-2 Man Utd
21/09/83	ECQ	England 0-0 Denmark
07/12/83	IV	Cambridge Un 2-2 Oxford Un
17/03/84	SI	England 1-0 Scotland
25/03/84	MC	Everton 0-0 Liverpool *aet*
04/04/84	BC	England 1-0 N Ireland
28/04/84	FAV	Stamford 2-3 Stansted
12/05/84	FAT	Bangor 1-1 Northwich *aet*
19/05/84	FAC	Everton 2-0 Watford
02/06/84	INT	England 0-2 USSR
09/06/84	SI	England 4-1 Netherlands
18/08/84	CS	Everton 1-0 Liverpool
12/09/84	INT	England 1-0 East Germany
17/10/84	WCQ	England 5-0 Finland
12/12/84	IV	Cambridge Un 2-4 Oxford Un
16/03/85	SI	England 0-1 West Germany
24/03/85	MC	Norwich 1-0 Sunderland
26/03/85	INT	England 2-1 Rep of Ireland
27/04/85	FAV	Fleetwood 1-3 Halesowen
11/05/85	FAT	Boston 1-2 Wealdstone
18/05/85	FAC	Everton 0-1 Man Utd *aet*
01/06/85	FRT	Brentford 1-3 Wigan
08/06/85	SI	England 2-0 Switzerland
10/08/85	U16	England 3-2 Yugoslavia
10/08/85	CS	Everton 2-0 Man Utd
11/09/85	WCQ	England 1-1 Romania
16/10/85	WCQ	England 5-0 Turkey
13/11/85	WCQ	England 0-0 N Ireland
11/12/85	IV	Cambridge Un 2-0 Oxford Un
08/03/86	SI	England 1-0 Netherlands
24/03/86	FMC	Chelsea 5-4 Man City
20/04/86	MC	Oxford Utd 3-0 QPR
23/04/86	RC	England 2-1 Scotland
26/04/86	FAV	Halesowen 3-0 Southall
10/05/86	FAC	Everton 1-3 Liverpool
17/05/86	FAT	Altrincham 1-0 Runcorn
24/05/86	FRT	Bolton 0-3 Bristol C
31/05/86	SI	England 2-1 Italy
16/08/86	U16	England 0-1 France
16/08/86	CS	Everton 1-1 Liverpool
15/10/86	ECQ	England 3-0 N Ireland
12/11/86	ECQ	England 2-0 Yugoslavia
10/12/86	IV	Cambridge Un 4-3 Oxford Un
14/03/87	SI	England 2-0 West Germany
29/03/87	FMC	Blackburn 1-0 Charlton
05/04/87	LC	Arsenal 2-1 Liverpool
25/04/87	FAV	St. Helens 3-2 Warrington
09/05/87	FAT	Burton 0-0 Kidderminster *aet*
16/05/87	FAC	Coventry 3-2 Spurs *aet*
19/05/87	RC	England 1-1 Brazil
24/05/87	FRT	Bristol C 1-1 Mansfield *aet* 4-5
30/05/87	VS	England 1-1 Scotland
31/05/87		Brent Leisure Action Sport Cup Final
16/07/87		London International Youth Festival
01/08/87	U17	England 3-1 Netherlands
01/08/87	CS	Coventry 0-1 Everton
08/08/87	U16	England 2-1 Denmark
08/08/87	LCEN	Football League 3-0 Rest of World
14/10/87	ECQ	England 8-0 Turkey
09/12/87	IV	Cambridge Un 2-1 Oxford Un
12/03/88	SI	England 2-0 Brazil
23/03/88	INT	England 2-2 Netherlands
27/03/88	SC	Luton 1-4 Reading
16/04/88		Football League Centenary Tournament
17/04/88		Football League Centenary Tournament
23/04/88	FAV	Colne 1-0 Emley *aet*
24/04/88	LC	Arsenal 2-3 Luton
07/05/88	FAT	Enfield 0-0 Telford *aet*
14/05/88	FAC	Liverpool 0-1 Wimbledon
21/05/88	RC	England 1-0 Scotland
24/05/88	RC	England 1-1 Colombia
28/05/88	SI	England 4-1 Italy
29/05/88	SVT	Burnley 0-2 Wolves
02/06/88	MCC	Hendon 2-0 Wembley
13/08/88	WIT	Arsenal 4-0 Spurs
13/08/88	WIT	Bayern Munich 0-1 Milan
14/08/88	WIT	Milan 2-1 Spurs
14/08/88	WIT	Arsenal 3-0 Bayern Munich
20/08/88	U16	England 1-1 Israel
20/08/88	CS	Liverpool 2-1 Wimbledon
14/09/88	INT	England 1-0 Denmark
19/10/88	WCQ	England 0-0 Sweden
11/03/89	SI	England 3-1 Belgium
09/04/89	LC	Luton 1-3 Nottingham F
26/04/89	WCQ	England 5-0 Albania
30/04/89	SC	Everton 3-4 Nottingham F *aet*

Date	Comp	Match
06/05/89	FAV	Sudbury 1-1 Tamworth *aet*
13/05/89	FAT	Macclesfield 0-1 Telford *aet*
20/05/89	FAC	Everton 2-3 Liverpool *aet*
23/05/89		England Women 0-2 Sweden Women
23/05/89	RC	England 0-0 Chile
28/05/89	SVT	Bolton 4-1 Torquay
03/06/89	WCQ	England 3-0 Poland
10/06/89	SI	England 1-3 West Germany
29/07/89	MT	Arsenal 1-0 Porto
29/07/89	MT	Dynamo Kiev 0-2 Liverpool
30/07/89	MT	Dynamo Kiev 1-0 Porto
30/07/89	MT	Arsenal 1-0 Liverpool
12/08/89	U16	England 2-1 Scandinavia
12/08/89	CS	Arsenal 0-1 Liverpool
15/11/89	INT	England 0-0 Italy
13/12/89	INT	England 2-1 Yugoslavia
10/03/90	SI	England 1-1 France
25/03/90	ZC	Chelsea 1-0 Middlesbrough
28/03/90	YI	England 0-0 Denmark
28/03/90	INT	England 1-0 Brazil
25/04/90	YI	England 1-1 Czechoslovakia
25/04/90	INT	England 4-2 Czechoslovakia
29/04/90	LC	Nottingham F 1-0 Oldham
05/05/90	FAV	Bridlington 0-0 Yeading *aet*
12/05/90	FAC	Crystal P 3-3 Man Utd *aet*
15/05/90	YI	England 3-0 Poland
15/05/90	INT	England 1-0 Denmark
17/05/90	FAC	Crystal P 0-1 Man Utd
19/05/90	FAT	Barrow 3-0 Leek
20/05/90	LDT	Bristol R 1-2 Tranmere
22/05/90	U17	England 1-3 France
22/05/90	INT	England 1-2 Uruguay
26/05/90	PPO	Cambridge 1-0 Chesterfield
27/05/90	PPO	Notts C 2-0 Tranmere
28/05/90	PPO	Sunderland 0-1 Swindon
02/06/90	SI	England 1-0 Netherlands
10/08/90	MT	Real Sociedad 1-1 Sampdoria (3-5)
10/08/90	MT	Arsenal 2-0 Aston Villa
11/08/90	MT	Aston Villa 0-1 Real Sociedad
11/08/90	MT	Arsenal 0-1 Sampdoria
18/08/90		England Women 1 Italy 4
18/08/90	CS	Liverpool 1-1 Man Utd
12/09/90	INT	England 1-0 Hungary
17/10/90	ECQ	England 2-0 Poland
06/02/91	INT	England 2-0 Cameroon
09/03/91	SI	England 2-1 Scotland
27/03/91	ECQ	England 1-1 Rep of Ireland
07/04/91	ZC	Crystal P 4-1 Everton *aet*
14/04/91	FAC	Arsenal 1-3 Spurs
21/04/91	RLC	Man Utd 0-1 Sheffield W
04/05/91	FAV	Gresley 4-4 Guiseley *aet*
11/05/91	FAT	Kidderminster 1-2 Wycombe
18/05/91	FAC	Nottingham F 1-2 Spurs *aet*
21/05/91	INT	England 3-1 USSR
25/05/91	U19	England 1-1 Spain
25/05/91	INT	England 2-2 Argentina
26/05/91	LDT	Birmingham 3-2 Tranmere
31/05/91	PPO	Blackpool 2-2 Torquay *aet* 4-5
01/06/91	PPO	Bolton 0-1 Tranmere *aet*
02/06/91	PPO	Brighton 1-3 Notts C
08/06/91	SI	England 1-3 West Germany
10/08/91	CS	Arsenal 0-0 Spurs
11/09/91	INT	England 0-1 Germany
16/10/91	ECQ	England 1-0 Turkey
19/02/92	INT	England 2-0 France
07/03/92	SI	England 0-0 Netherlands
29/03/92	ZC	Nottingham F 3-2 Southampton *aet*
12/04/92	RLC	Man Utd 1-0 Nottingham F
25/04/92	FAV	Guiseley 3-5 Wimborne
09/05/92	FAC	Liverpool 2-0 Sunderland
10/05/92	FAT	Colchester 3-1 Witton
16/05/92	AT	Stockport 0-1 Stoke
17/05/92	INT	England 1-1 Brazil
20/05/92	EC	Barcelona 1-0 Sampdoria *aet*
23/05/92	PPO	Blackpool 1-1 Scunthorpe *aet* 4-3
24/05/92	PPO	Peterborough 2-1 Stockport
25/05/92	PPO	Blackburn 1-0 Leicester
06/06/92	SI	England 1-1 Italy
08/08/92	CS	Leeds 4-3 Liverpool
14/10/92	WCQ	England 1-1 Norway
18/11/92	WCQ	England 4-0 Turkey
17/02/93	WCQ	England 6-0 San Marino
13/03/93	VS	England 1-2 Scotland
27/03/93	AIC	Cremonese 3-1 Derby
03/04/93	FAC	Sheffield U 1-2 Sheffield W *aet*
04/04/93	FAC	Arsenal 1-0 Spurs
18/04/93	CCC	Arsenal 2-1 Sheffield W
28/04/93	WCQ	England 2-2 Netherlands
08/05/93	FAV	Bridlington 1-0 Tiverton
09/05/93	FAT	Runcorn 1-4 Wycombe
12/05/93	ECW	Parma 3-1 Royal Antwerp
15/05/93	FAC	Arsenal 1-1 Sheffield W *aet*
20/05/93	FAC	Arsenal 2-1 Sheffield W *aet*
22/05/93	AT	Port Vale 2-1 Stockport
29/05/93		Arsenal Women 3-0 Knowsley Women
29/05/93	PPO	Crewe 1-1 York *aet* 3-5
30/05/93	PPO	Port Vale 0-3 WBA
31/05/93	PPO	Leicester 3-4 Swindon
05/06/93	SI	England 0-0 Germany
07/08/93	CS	Arsenal 1-1 Man Utd (4-5)
08/09/93	WCQ	England 3-0 Poland
09/03/94	INT	England 1-0 Denmark
12/03/94	SI	England 3-0 Switzerland
20/03/94	AIC	Brescia 1-0 Notts C
27/03/94	CCC	Aston Villa 3-1 Man Utd
09/04/94	FAC	Chelsea 2-0 Luton
10/04/94	FAC	Man Utd 1-1 Oldham *aet*
24/04/94	AT	Huddersfield 1-1 Swansea *aet* 1-3
07/05/94	FAV	Diss 2-1 Taunton *aet*
14/05/94	FAC	Chelsea 0-4 Man Utd
17/05/94	INT	England 5-0 Greece
21/05/94	FAT	Runcorn 1-2 Woking
22/05/94	INT	England 0-0 Norway
28/05/94	PPO	PNE 2-4 Wycombe
29/05/94	PPO	Burnley 2-1 Stockport
30/05/94	PPO	Derby 1-2 Leicester
11/06/94	SI	England 2-1 France
14/08/94	CS	Blackburn 0-2 Man Utd
07/09/94	INT	England 2-0 USA
12/10/94	INT	England 1-1 Romania

463

Wembley – The Complete Record

Date	Comp	Match
16/11/94	INT	England 1-0 Nigeria
11/03/95	SI	England 1-0 Brazil
19/03/95	AIC	Ascoli 1-2 Notts C
29/03/95	INT	England 0-0 Uruguay
02/04/95	CCC	Bolton 1-2 Liverpool
15/04/95		Littlewoods Wembley Challenge Tournament
23/04/95	AWS	Birmingham 1-0 Carlisle iet
13/05/95	FAV	Arlesey 2-1 Oxford C.
14/05/95	FAT	Kidderminster 1-2 Woking *aet*
20/05/95	FAC	Everton 1-0 Man Utd
27/05/95	PPO	Bury 0-2 Chesterfield
28/05/95	PPO	Bristol R 1-2 Huddersfield
29/05/95	PPO	Bolton 4-3 Reading *aet*
03/06/95	UC	England 2-1 Japan
10/06/95	SI	England 2-4 Germany
11/06/95	UC	Brazil 3-1 England
13/08/95	CS	Blackburn 0-1 Everton
06/09/95	INT	England 0-0 Colombia
15/11/95	INT	England 3-1 Switzerland
12/12/95	INT	England 1-1 Portugal
02/03/96		Littlewoods Wembley Challenge Tournament
09/03/96	SI	England 2-3 Spain
17/03/96	AIC	Genoa 5-2 Port Vale
24/03/96	CCC	Aston Villa 3-0 Leeds
27/03/96	INT	England 1-0 Bulgaria
14/04/96	AWS	Rotherham 2-1 Shrewsbury
24/04/96	INT	England 0-0 Croatia
11/05/96	FAC	Liverpool 0-1 Man Utd
12/05/96	FAV	Brigg 3-0 Clitheroe
18/05/96	INT	England 3-0 Hungary
19/05/96	FAT	Macclesfield 3-1 Northwich
25/05/96	PPO	Darlington 0-1 Plymouth
26/05/96	PPO	Bradford 2-0 Notts C
27/05/96	PPO	Crystal P 1-2 Leicester *aet*
08/06/96	ECH	England 1-1 Switzerland
15/06/96	ECH	England 2-0 Scotland
18/06/96	ECH	England 4-1 Netherlands
22/06/96	ECH	England 0-0 Spain *aet* 4-2
26/06/96	ECH	England 1-1 Germany *aet* 5-6
30/06/96	ECH	Czech Republic 1-2 Germany iet
11/08/96	CS	Man Utd 4-0 Newcastle
22/09/96		Brigade Bodega 1-0 Dawlish
09/10/96	WCQ	England 2-1 Poland
12/02/97	WCQ	England 0-1 Italy
29/03/97	INT	England 2-0 Mexico
06/04/97	CCC	Leicester 1-1 Middlesbrough *aet*
20/04/97	AWS	Carlisle 0-0 Colchester *aet* 4-3
30/04/97	WCQ	England 2-0 Georgia
10/05/97		Corby 1-3 Poulton
10/05/97	FAV	North Ferriby 0-3 Whitby
17/05/97	FAC	Chelsea 2-0 Middlesbrough
18/05/97	FAT	Dagenham 0-1 Woking *aet*
24/05/97	PPO	Northampton 1-0 Swansea
25/05/97	PPO	Brentford 0-1 Crewe
26/05/97	PPO	Crystal P 1-0 Sheffield U
07/06/97	SI	England 2-1 Germany
03/08/97	CS	Chelsea 1-1 Man Utd (2-4)
10/09/97	WCQ	England 4-0 Moldova
15/11/97	INT	England 2-0 Cameroon
11/02/98	INT	England 0-2 Chile
14/03/98	SI	England 0-0 Brazil
29/03/98	CCC	Chelsea 2-0 Middlesbrough *aet*
19/04/98	AWS	Bournemouth 1-2 Grimsby iet
22/04/98	INT	England 3-0 Portugal
09/05/98		Honiton Clyst 1-1 West Hendon (1-3)
09/05/98	FAV	Tiverton 1-0 Tow Law
16/05/98	FAC	Arsenal 2-0 Newcastle
17/05/98	FAT	Cheltenham 1-0 Southport
22/05/98	PPO	Colchester 1-0 Torquay
23/05/98	INT	England 0-0 Saudi Arabia
24/05/98	PPO	Grimsby 1-0 Northampton
25/05/98	PPO	Charlton 4-4 Sunderland *aet* 7-6
13/06/98		Vagns Krostue 0-1 West Hendon
09/08/98	CS	Arsenal 3-0 Man Utd
30/09/98	EC	Arsenal 2-1 Panathinaikos
10/10/98	ECQ	England 0-0 Bulgaria
21/10/98	EC	Arsenal 1-1 Dynamo Kiev
18/11/98	INT	England 2-0 Czech Republic
25/11/98	EC	Arsenal 0-1 Lens
10/02/99	INT	England 0-2 France
21/03/99	WLC	Leicester 0-1 Spurs
27/03/99	ECQ	England 3-1 Poland
18/04/99	AWS	Millwall 0-1 Wigan
08/05/99	U18SI	England 1-2 Netherlands
15/05/99	FAT	Forest Green 0-1 Kingstonian
16/05/99		Sizewell 2-0 West Hendon
16/05/99	FAV	Bedlington 0-1 Tiverton
22/05/99	FAC	Man Utd 2-0 Newcastle
29/05/99	PPO	Leyton Orient 0-1 Scunthorpe
30/05/99	PPO	Gillingham 2-2 Man City *aet* 1-3
31/05/99	PPO	Bolton 0-2 Watford
05/06/99	ECQ	England 0-0 Sweden
04/07/99		England Girls 5-0 Scotland Girls
04/07/99	U16	England 2-1 Argentina
01/08/99	CS	Arsenal 2-1 Man Utd
04/09/99	ECQ	England 6-0 Luxembourg
22/09/99	EC	Arsenal 3-1 Stockholm
19/10/99	EC	Arsenal 2-4 Barcelona
27/10/99	EC	Arsenal 0-1 Fiorentina
17/11/99	ECQ	England 0-1 Scotland
25/11/99		Burton Wembley Challenge Tournament
23/02/00	INT	England 0-0 Argentina
27/02/00	WLC	Leicester 2-1 Tranmere
25/03/00	U18SI	England 0-1 Hungary
02/04/00	FAC	Aston V. 0-0 Bolton *aet* 4-1
09/04/00	FAC	Chelsea 2-1 Newcastle
16/04/00	AWS	Bristol C 1-2 Stoke
16/04/00	FLYAC	Scunthorpe 0-0 WBA (2-3)
06/05/00		Earl Soham 2-1 Eastleigh
06/05/00	FAV	Chippenham 0-1 Deal
13/05/00	FAT	Kettering 2-3 Kingstonian
20/05/00	FAC	Aston V. 0-1 Chelsea
26/05/00	PPO	Darlington 0-1 Peterborough
27/05/00	INT	England 1-1 Brazil
28/05/00	PPO	Gillingham 3-2 Wigan *aet*
29/05/00	PPO	Barnsley 2-4 Ipswich
31/05/00	INT	England 2-0 Ukraine
03/06/00		Nike Park
13/08/00	CS	Chelsea 2-0 Man Utd
07/10/00	WCQ	England 0-1 Germany

SUMMARY OF LEAGUE CLUBS' APPEARANCES

(Note – first team only and does not include penalty shoot-outs or 1988 Football League Centenary Tournament)

	Years	P	W	D	L	F	A
Arsenal	1927-1999	41	20	5	16	59	42
Aston Villa	1924-2000	12	4	3	5	11	12
Barnsley	2000	1	0	0	1	2	4
Birmingham	1931-1995	4	2	0	2	6	7
Blackburn R	1928-1995	7	3	0	4	5	8
Blackpool	1948-1992	5	1	2	2	9	12
Bolton W	1923-2000	12	6	1	5	19	16
Bournemouth	1998	1	0	0	1	1	2
Bradford City	1996	1	1	0	0	2	0
Brentford	1930-1997	4	1	0	3	3	7
Brighton	1983-1991	3	0	1	2	3	9
Bristol City	1986-2000	3	1	1	1	5	3
Bristol R	1990-1995	2	0	0	2	2	4
Burnley	1947-1994	4	1	0	3	3	7
Bury	1995	1	0	0	2	0	2
Cambridge Utd	1990	1	1	0	0	1	0
Cardiff City	1925-1927	2	1	0	1	1	1
Carlisle Utd	1995-1997	2	0	1	1	0	1
Charlton A	1943-1998	6	2	1	3	10	17
Chelsea	1944-2000	15	9	2	4	25	19
Chesterfield	1990-1995	2	1	0	1	2	1
Colchester Utd	1992-1998	3	2	1	0	4	1
Coventry City	1987	2	1	0	1	3	3
Crewe A	1993-1997	2	1	1	0	2	1
Crystal P	1990-1997	5	2	1	2	9	7
Darlington	1996-2000	2	0	0	2	0	2
Derby County	1946-1994	4	2	0	2	8	6
Everton	1933-1995	17	8	3	6	22	19
Fulham	1975	1	0	0	1	0	2
Gillingham	1999-2000	2	1	1	0	5	4
Grimsby Town	1998	2	2	0	0	3	1
Huddersfield Town	1928-1995	5	1	1	3	4	8
Ipswich Town	1928-2000	4	3	0	1	9	7
Leeds Utd	1965-1996	8	3	2	3	10	12
Leicester City	1949-2000	11	3	1	7	12	19
Leyton Orient	1930-1999	3	2	0	1	6	2
Liverpool	1950-1996	33	16	7	10	42	31
Luton Town	1959-1994	5	1	0	4	6	13
Manchester City	1926-1999	13	5	2	6	21	24
Manchester Utd	1948-2000	33	14	7	12	52	38
Mansfield Town	1987	1	0	1	0	1	1
Middlesbrough	1990-1998	4	0	1	3	1	6
Millwall	1945-1999	2	0	0	2	0	3
Newcastle Utd	1924-2000	11	5	0	6	12	17
Northampton Town	1997-1998	2	1	0	1	1	1

Norwich City	1973-1985	3	1	0	2	1	2
Nottingham F	1959-1992	11	7	1	3	22	13
Notts County	1990-1996	5	3	0	2	7	5
Oldham A	1990-1994	2	0	1	1	1	2
Oxford Utd	1986	1	1	0	0	3	0
Peterborough Utd	1992-2000	2	2	0	0	3	1
Plymouth A	1996	1	1	0	0	1	0
Portsmouth	1929-1942	4	1	0	3	5	7
Port Vale	1993-1996	3	1	0	2	4	9
Preston	1937-1994	6	1	1	4	9	14
QPR	1967-1986	4	1	1	2	4	7
Reading	1988-1995	2	1	0	1	7	5
Rotherham Utd	1996	1	1	0	0	2	1
Scunthorpe Utd	1992-1999	2	1	1	0	2	1
Sheffield Utd	1925-1997	4	1	0	3	2	4
Sheffield W	1935-1993	7	3	1	3	12	11
Shrewsbury Town	1996	1	0	0	1	1	2
Southampton	1976-1992	4	1	0	3	5	7
Southend Utd	1930	1	0	0	1	1	3
Stockport County	1992-1994	4	0	0	4	3	7
Stoke City	1972-2000	3	3	0	0	5	2
Sunderland	1937-1998	6	2	1	3	8	9
Swansea City	1994-1997	2	0	1	1	1	2
Swindon Town	1969-1993	3	3	0	0	8	4
Torquay Utd	1989-1998	3	0	1	2	3	7
Tottenham H	1961-1999	20	10	4	6	28	24
Tranmere R	1990-2000	5	2	0	3	6	8
Watford	1984-1999	2	1	0	1	2	2
WBA	1931-1993	7	4	0	3	14	12
West Ham Utd	1923-1981	9	5	1	3	10	8
Wigan A	1973-2000	4	2	0	2	7	6
Wimbledon	1963-1988	3	2	0	1	6	4
Wolverhampton W	1939-1988	6	5	0	1	12	6
Wycombe W	1957-1994	4	3	0	1	11	7
York City	1993	1	0	1	0	1	1

THE TEAMS

Appearances and scorers do not include the 1988 Football League Centenary Tournament. If no player has appeared more than once, most appearances are not listed for that team

ABERDEEN
International appearances
Scotland: 4, McLeish, Miller; 1, Clark, Leighton, Martin, McKimmie, Robb, Simpson, Strachan

ACF
British Junior Cup final
03/04/48 lost to ATC 0-2
13/05/50 lost to NABC 1-4
19/05/51 lost to NABC 2-4
12/05/56 lost to NABC 1-2

	P	W	D	L	F	A
British Junior Cup	4	0	0	4	4	12

AIRDRIEONIANS
International appearances
Scotland: 1, Crapnell, Jarvie (s), McMillan

AJAX AMSTERDAM (see NETHERLANDS)

ALBANIA
World Cup Qualifying
26/04/89 lost to England 0-5

ALMONDSBURY GREENWAY
FA Vase final
28/04/79 lost to Billericay T 1-4

ALTRINCHAM
FA Trophy final
29/04/78 beat Leatherhead 3-1
15/05/82 lost to Enfield 0-1 aet
17/05/86 beat Runcorn 1-0

	P	W	D	L	F	A
FA Trophy	3	2	0	1	4	2

AQUARIUS
Southern Amateur League First Division
01/12/28 beat Ealing Association 3-0

ARGENTINA
World Cup Quarter-final
23/07/66 lost to England 0-1
Internationals
09/05/51 lost to England 1-2
22/05/74 drew with England 2-2
13/05/80 lost to England 1-3
25/05/91 drew with England 2-2
23/02/00 drew with England 0-0
U-16
04/07/99 lost to England 1-2

	P	W	D	L	F	A
World Cup	1	0	0	1	0	1
Internationals	5	0	3	2	6	9
Senior Total	6	0	3	3	6	10
Under-16	1	0	0	1	1	2

Most appearances: 2, Perfumo, Simeone
Scorers: 2, Kempes (1 pen); 1, Boye, Franco, Garcia, Passarella (pen)

ARLESEY TOWN
FA Vase final
13/05/95 beat Oxford C 2-1

ARMY PHYSICAL TRAINING CORPS
International Trial
06/04/46 beat FA 5-3

ARSENAL
European Cup
30/09/98 beat Panathinaikos 2-1
21/10/98 drew with Dynamo Kiev 1-1
25/11/98 lost to Lens 0-1
22/09/99 beat AIK Stockholm 3-1
19/10/99 lost to Barcelona 2-4
27/10/99 lost to Fiorentina 0-1
FA Cup final
23/04/27 lost to Cardiff 0-1
26/04/30 beat Huddersfield T 2-0
23/04/32 lost to Newcastle Utd 1-2
25/04/36 beat Sheffield Utd 1-0
29/04/50 beat Liverpool 2-0
03/05/52 lost to Newcastle Utd 0-1
08/05/71 beat Liverpool 2-1 aet
06/05/72 lost to Leeds 0-1
06/05/78 lost to Ipswich 0-1
12/05/79 beat Man Utd 3-2
10/05/80 lost to West Ham 0-1
15/05/93 drew with Sheffield W 1-1 aet
16/05/98 beat Newcastle Utd 2-0
FA Cup final replay
20/05/93 beat Sheffield W 2-1 aet
FA Cup semi-final
14/04/91 lost to Spurs 1-3
04/04/93 beat Spurs 1-0
League Cup/Littlewoods/Coca Cola Cup final
02/03/68 lost to Leeds 0-1
15/03/69 lost to Swindon 1-3 aet
05/04/87 beat Liverpool 2-1
24/04/88 lost to Luton 2-3
18/04/93 beat Sheffield W 2-1
Charity Shield
11/08/79 lost to Liverpool 1-3
12/08/89 lost to Liverpool 0-1
10/08/91 drew with Spurs 0-0
07/08/93 drew with Man Utd 1-1 (lost 5-4 on pens)
09/08/98 beat Man Utd 3-0
01/08/99 beat Man Utd 2-1
Wembley International Tournament
13/08/88 beat Spurs 4-0
14/08/88 beat Bayern Munich 3-0
Makita Tournament
semi-final: 29/07/89 beat Porto 1-0; 10/08/90 beat

Aston Villa 2-0; **final**: 30/07/89 beat Liverpool 1-0;
11/08/90 lost to Sampdoria 0-1

League War Cup final
10/05/41 drew with PNE 1-1

League South Cup final
01/05/43 beat Charlton 7-1

Women's League Cup final
29/05/93 beat Knowsley Utd 3-0

	P	W	D	L	F	A
European Cup	6	2	1	3	8	9
FA Cup final	14	7	1	6	16	12
FA Cup semi-final	2	1	0	1	2	3
FA Cup Total	16	8	1	7	18	15
League Cup	5	2	0	3	7	9
Charity Shield	6	2	2	2	7	6
Makita Tournament	6	5	0	1	11	1
League War Cup	1	0	1	0	1	1
League South Cup	1	1	0	0	7	1
v Liverpool	6	4	0	2	8	6
Total	41	20	5	16	59	42
Women's League Cup	1	1	0	0	3	0

Most appearances: 24, Adams, Winterburn; 22, Dixon;
16, Seaman; 14, Merson,; 13, OLeary (2s), A Smith (2s);
12 Davis; 11, Thomas (2s); 10, Campbell (3s), Keown
(1s), Parlour, Rocastle; 8, Bould (4s), Overmars; 7,
Linighan, Lukic, Viera; 6, Bergkamp, Hayes (5s), Rice; 5,
Anelka, Bastin, Petit, Richardson (1s); Wright
Scorers: 6, R Lewis; 5, A Smith; 3, Drake, Overmars,
Wright; 2, Adams, Anelka, Bergkamp, D Compton,
Marwood, Merson, C Nicholas, Sunderland

International appearances
England: 36, Adams; 32, Seaman; 29, Sansom; 13,
Dixon; 11, Wright (6s); 10, Keown; 9, Ball, Rix (4s); 8,
Storey, Woodcock (3s); 7, Parlour (6s), Platt (3s); 6,
Merson (5s), Rocastle (3s); 5, Eastham, A Smith (1s); 3,
Anderson, Bastin, Hapgood, L Smith; 2, Bould, McNab;
1, Baker, Blockley, Copping, Crayston, Hulme, Jack,
Male, Mariner, Milton, Moss, Radford, Scott, Thomas,
Winterburn (s)
N Ireland: 5, Neill, Nelson (1s); 4, Rice; 3, Magill; 2,
Jennings; 1, McCullough
Scotland: 1, Docherty, Herd, James, McLintock, Nicholas
Wales: 2, Kelsey; 1, Daniel, P Nicholas, J Roberts,
Tapscott
Republic of Ireland: 4, O'Leary (1s); 2, Brady; 1, Haverty,
Stapleton
Argentina: 1, Vivas (s)
Brazil: 1, Silvinho
Denmark: 1, Jensen
France: 1, Anelka, Petit, Vieira (s)
Netherlands: 1, Bergkamp
Sweden: 1, Ljungberg
Ukraine: 1, Luzhny
International Scorers: England: 4, Woodcock; 2, Adams,
A Smith, Wright; 1, Anderson, Baker, Bastin, Dixon, Jack,
Platt, Sansom
France: 2, Anelka

ASCOLI (see ITALY)

ASTON VILLA
FA Cup final
26/04/24 lost to Newcastle Utd 0-2
04/05/57 beat Man Utd 2-1
20/05/00 lost to Chelsea 0-1

FA Cup semi-final
02/04/00 drew with Bolton 0-0 aet (won 4-1 on pens)

League Cup/Coca-Cola Cup final
27/02/71 lost to Spurs 0-2
01/03/75 beat Norwich 1-0
12/03/77 drew with Everton 0-0
27/03/94 beat Man Utd 3-1
24/03/96 beat Leeds 3-0

Charity Shield
22/08/81 drew with Spurs 2-2

Makita Tournament
semi-final: 10/08/90 lost to Arsenal 0-2; **3rd & 4th
place:** 11/08/90 lost to Real Sociedad 0-1

League Centenary Tournament
1st round: 16/04/88 drew with Blackburn 0-0 (won 2-1
on pens); **quarter-final:** 16/04/88 drew with Nottingham
F 0-0 (lost 1-0 on pens)

	P	W	D	L	F	A
FA Cup final	3	1	0	2	2	4
FA Cup semi-final	1	0	1	0	0	0
FA Cup Total	4	1	1	2	2	4
League Cup	5	3	1	1	7	3
Charity Shield	1	0	1	0	2	2
Makita Tournament	2	0	0	2	0	3
Total	12	4	3	5	11	12
League Centenary Tournament	2	0	2	0	0	0

Most appearances: 3, Cowans, Daley, Ehiogu, McGrath,
Southgate, Taylor, Wright, Yorks
Scorers: 2, McParland, Saunders (1 pen), Withe; 1,
Atkinson, Graydon, Milosevic, Taylor, Yorke

International appearances
England: 19, Southgate (3s); 9, Platt (3s); 5, Withe; 3,
Cowans, Hodge; 2, Barry (s), Morley (1s); 1, Collymore
(s), Daley, Dublin, Gidman, Hendrie (s), Hitchens,
Houghton, Little (s), Merson, Moss, Richardson, Smart,
Walker, Waring
N Ireland: 3, McParland; 1, Morgan, Nicholl
Scotland: 1, Cummings, Gibson, Massie
Wales: 2, Phillips; 1, Crowe
Republic of Ireland: 1, Cascarino (s), McGrath, Saward
Denmark: 1, Nielsen
International Scorers: England: 3, Platt (1 pen); 1,
Cowans, Hitchens, Merson, Walker, Waring, Withe

ATC
British Junior Cup final
30/03/46 beat NABC 4-2
03/04/48 beat ACF 2-0
19/03/49 drew with NABC 2-2 aet
10/05/52 lost to NABC 3-5
09/05/53 lost to NABC 1-3
08/05/54 beat NABC 1-0

	P	W	D	L	F	A
British Junior Cup	6	3	1	2	13	12
v Boys Clubs	5	2	1	2	11	12
Total	6	3	1	2	13	12

AUSTRIA
Internationals
28/11/51 drew with England 2-2
04/04/62 lost to England 1-3
20/10/65 beat England 3-2
26/09/73 lost to England 0-7

	P	W	D	L	F	A
Internationals	4	1	1	2	6	14

Most appearances: 2, Buzek, Fluegel (1s), Fraydl, Sara
Scorers: 2, Fritsch; 1, Buzek, Fluegel, Melchior, Stojaspol (pen)
FIFA appearances
Rest of Europe
1, Hanappi, Ocwirk, Zeman

AYR UNITED
International appearances
Scotland: 1, McCloy, Smith

BALLYMENA UNITED
International appearances
N Ireland: 1, Platt

BANGOR CITY
FA Vase final
12/05/84 drew with Northwich V 1-1 aet

BANK OF ENGLAND
Southern Amateur League First Division
27/10/28 beat Ealing Association 5-1

BARCELONA (see SPAIN)

BARCLAYS BANK
FA Amateur Cup 2nd round
12/01/29 beat Old Malvernians 2-1
Southern Amateur League First Division
10/11/28 lost to Ealing Association 2-4

	P	W	D	L	F	A
FA Amateur Cup	1	1	0	0	2	1
S Amateur League	1	0	0	1	2	4
Total	2	1	0	1	4	5

BARI (see ITALY)

BARNET
FA Amateur Cup final
18/04/59 lost to Crook Town 2-3
FA Trophy final
15/04/72 lost to Stafford Rangers 0-3

	P	W	D	L	F	A
FA Amateur Cup	1	0	0	1	2	3
FA Trophy	1	0	0	1	0	3
Total	2	0	0	2	2	6

BARNSLEY
First Division promotion play-off final
29/05/00 lost to Ipswich 2-4

BARROW
FA Trophy final
19/05/90 beat Leek Town 3-0

BARTON ROVERS
FA Vase final
22/04/78 lost to Blue Star 1-2

BAYERN MUNICH (see GERMANY)

BEDLINGTON TERRIERS
FA Vase final
16/05/99 lost to Tiverton Town 0-1

BELGIUM
Internationals
26/11/52 lost to England 0-5
21/10/64 drew with England 2-2
Wartime
11/10/41 beat Netherlands 5-4
Victory International
19/01/46 lost to England 0-2
Schoolboy
11/03/89 lost to England 1-3

	P	W	D	L	F	A
Internationals	2	0	1	1	2	7
Total (official)	2	0	1	1	2	7
Wartime	1	1	0	0	5	4
Victory International	1	0	0	1	0	2
Senior Total	4	1	1	2	7	13
Schoolboy	1	0	0	1	1	3

Scorers: 1, Cornelis, Van Himst
Clubs
Bruges
10/05/78 lost to Liverpool 0-1
Royal Antwerp
European Cup-Winners Cup final
12/05/93 lost to Parma 1-3
Scorers: 1, Severeyns

BENFICA (see PORTUGAL)

BILLERICAY TOWN
FA Vase final
10/04/76 beat Stamford 1-0 aet
30/04/77 drew with Sheffield 1-1 aet
28/04/79 beat Almondsbury Greenway 4-1

	P	W	D	L	F	A
FA Vase	3	2	1	0	6	2

BIRMINGHAM CITY
FA Cup final
12, 25/04/31 lost to WBA 1-2
50 - 05/05/56 lost to Man City 1-3
Leyland DAF Cup/Auto Windscreenss Shield final
26/05/91 beat Tranmere 3-2
23/04/95 beat Carlisle 1-0 iet

	P	W	D	L	F	A
FA Cup	2	0	0	2	2	5
Leyland DAF/ Auto Windscreenss	2	2	0	0	4	2
Total	4	2	0	2	6	7

Scorers: 2, Gayle
International appearances
England: 7, Francis (1s), Hall; 6, Merrick; 2, Bradford; 1, Barton, Hibbs, Smith, Stoker
Scotland: 1, Herriot
Wales: 3, Page (1s), Roberts; 2, Hennessey; 1, Green, Leek
International Scorers: England: 2, Francis

BISHOP AUCKLAND
FA Amateur Cup final

22/04/50 lost to Willington 0-4
21/04/51 lost to Pegasus 1-2
10/04/54 drew with Crook Town 2-2 aet
16/04/55 beat Hendon 2-0
07/04/56 drew with Corinthian Casuals 1-1 aet
13/04/57 beat Wycombe W 3-1

	P	W	D	L	F	A
FA Amateur Cup	6	2	2	2	9	10

BISHOP'S STORTFORD
FA Amateur Cup final
20/04/74 beat Ilford 4-1
FA Trophy final
16/05/81 beat Sutton Utd 1-0

	P	W	D	L	F	A
FA Amateur Cup	1	1	0	0	4	1
FA Trophy	1	1	0	0	1	0
Total	2	2	0	0	5	1

BLACKBURN ROVERS
FA Cup final
21/04/28 beat Huddersfield T 3-1
07/05/60 lost to Wolves 0-3
Full Members Cup final
29/03/87 beat Charlton 1-0
Charity Shield
14/08/94 lost to Man Utd 0-2
13/08/95 lost to Everton 0-1
Second Division promotion play-off final
25/05/92 beat Leicester 1-0
League War Cup final
08/06/40 lost to West Ham 0-1
League Centenary Tournament
1st round: - 16/04/88 drew with Aston Villa 0-0 (lost 2-1 on pens)

	P	W	D	L	F	A
FA Cup	2	1	0	1	3	4
Full Members Cup	1	1	0	0	1	0
Charity Shield	2	0	0	2	0	3
Promotion play-off	1	1	0	0	1	0
League War Cup	1	0	0	1	0	1
Full match Total	7	3	0	4	5	8
League Centenary	1	0	1	0	0	0

Most appearances: 3, Atkins (1s), Hendry
Scorers: 2, Roscamp; 1, Hendry, McLean, Newell (pen)
International appearances
England: 19, Shearer (1s); 16, Clayton; 14, Douglas; 13, Le Saux (1s); 7, Newton; 5, Eckersley, Flowers; 3, Batty (1s); 2, Wilcox (1s); 1, Healless, Jones, Ripley (s), Sutton (s)
N Ireland: 2, Brotherston, Quinn (1s)
Scotland: 1, Dailly, Davidson, Hendry
Wales: 1, England, Hole
Republic of Ireland: 1, Moran
Norway: 1, Berg
International Scorers: England: 9, Shearer (1 pen); 7, Douglas; 1, Le Saux

BLACKPOOL
FA Cup final
24/04/48 lost to Man Utd 2-4
28/04/51 lost to Newcastle Utd 0-2
02/05/53 beat Bolton 4-3
Fourth Division promotion play-off final

31/05/91 drew with Torquay 2-2 aet (lost 5-4 on pens)
23/05/92 drew with Scunthorpe 1-1 aet (won 4-3 on pens)

	P	W	D	L	F	A
FA Cup	3	1	0	2	6	9
Promotion play-offs	2	0	2	0	3	3
Total	5	1	2	2	9	12

Most appearances: 3, Johnston, Matthews, Mortensen, Shimwell
Scorers: 4, Mortensen; 1, Bamber, Groves, Perry, Shimwell (pen), own goal
International appearances
England: 15, Armfield; 12, Matthews; 5, Ball, Mortensen; 3, Johnston; 2, Perry, Waiters; 1, Taylor
N Ireland: 1, Spence (s)
Scotland: 1, Farm, Green, Mudie
Wales: 1, James
International Scorers: England: 3, Mortensen; 2, Perry

BLUE STAR
FA Vase final
22/04/78 beat Barton Rovers 2-1

BOLTON WANDERERS
FA Cup final
28/04/23 beat West Ham 2-0
24/04/26 beat Man City 1-0
27/04/29 beat Portsmouth 2-0
02/05/53 lost to Blackpool 3-4
03/05/58 beat Man Utd 2-0
FA Cup semi-final
02/04/00 drew with Aston Villa 0-0 aet (lost 4-1 on pens)
Coca-Cola Cup final
02/04/95 lost to Liverpool 1-2
First Division promotion play-off final
29/05/95 beat Reading 4-3 aet
31/05/99 lost to Watford 0-2
Third Division promotion play-off final
01/06/91 lost to Tranmere 0-1 aet
Freight Rover/Sherpa Van Trophy final
24/05/86 lost to Bristol City 0-3
28/05/89 beat Torquay 4-1

	P	W	D	L	F	A
FA Cup final	5	4	0	1	10	4
FA Cup semi-final	1	0	1	0	0	0
FA Cup Total	6	4	1	1	10	4
Coca-Cola Cup	1	0	0	1	1	2
First Division Play-offs	2	1	0	1	4	5
Third Division Play-off	1	0	0	1	0	1
Promotion play-offs Total	3	1	0	2	4	6
Freight Rover/sherpa Van	2	1	0	1	4	4
Total	12	6	1	5	19	16

Most appearances: 3, Bergsson (1s), Butler, Haworth, Nuttall, Phillips, Pym, Seddon
Scorers: 3, Lofthouse; 2, De Freitas, Jack; 1, Bell, Blackmore, Butler, Moir, J R Smith, Thompson
International appearances
England: 8, Lofthouse; 6, Hopkinson; 2, Holden; 1, Barrass, Butler, Hill, Jack, Parry
N Ireland: 1, McAdams, McElhinney
Scotland: 1, Cook
Wales: 1, Davies
International Scorers: England: 8, Lofthouse; 1, Parry

BORUSSIA DORTMUND (see GERMANY)

BOSTON UNITED
FA Trophy final
11/05/85 lost to Wealdstone 1-2

BOURNEMOUTH
Auto Windscreens Shield final
19/04/98 lost to Grimsby 1-2 iet

BRADFORD CITY
Second Division promotion play-off final
26/05/96 beat Notts County 2-0

BRAZIL
Rous Cup
19/05/87 drew with England 1-1
Umbro Cup
11/06/95 beat England 3-1
Internationals
09/05/56 lost to England 2-4
08/05/63 drew with England 1-1
19/04/78 drew with England 1-1
12/05/81 beat England 1-0
28/03/90 lost to England 0-1
17/05/92 drew with England 1-1
27/05/00 drew with England 1-1
Schoolboy
12/03/88 lost to England 0-2
11/03/95 lost to England 0-1
14/03/98 drew with England 0-0

	P	W	D	L	F	A
Rous Cup	1	0	1	0	1	1
Umbro Cup	1	1	0	0	3	1
Internationals	7	1	4	2	7	9
Senior Total	9	2	5	2	11	11
Schoolboy	3	0	1	2	0	3

Most appearances: 3, Aldair (1s), Dunga (1s), Valdo
Scorers: 1, Bebeto, Didi, Edmundo, Franca, Gil, Juninho, Mirandinha, Paulinho, Pepe, Ronaldo, Zico
FIFA appearances
  Rest of World: 1, D Santos

BRENTFORD
Second Division promotion play-off final
25/05/97 lost to Crewe 0-1
League Third Division South
22/11/30 lost to Clapton Orient 0-3
Freight Rover Trophy final
01/06/85 lost to Wigan 1-3
London War Cup final
30/05/42 beat Portsmouth 2-0

	P	W	D	L	F	A
Promotion play-off	1	0	0	1	0	1
Third Division South	1	0	0	1	0	3
League Total	2	0	0	2	0	4
Freight Rover Trophy	1	0	0	1	1	3
London War Cup	1	1	0	0	2	0
Total	4	1	0	3	3	7

International appearances
  Scotland: 1, Macaulay, McCulloch, Reid

BRESCIA (see ITALY)

BRIDLINGTON TOWN
FA Vase final
05/05/90 drew with Yeading 0-0 aet
08/05/93 beat Tiverton Town 1-0

	P	W	D	L	F	A
FA Vase	2	1	1	0	1	0

BRIGADE BODEGA (see DENMARK)

BRIGG TOWN
FA Vase final
12/05/96 beat Clitheroe 3-0

BRIGHTON AND HOVE ALBION
FA Cup final
21/05/83 drew with Man Utd 2-2 aet
FA Cup final replay
26/05/83 lost to Man Utd 0-4
Second Division promotion play-off final
02/06/91 lost to Notts County 1-3

	P	W	D	L	F	A
FA Cup	2	0	1	1	2	6
Promotion play-off	1	0	0	1	1	3
Total	3	0	1	2	3	9

Most appearances: 3, Gatting, 2, Case, Grealish, Howlett, Moseley, Pearce, Robinson, Ryan (s), Smillie, Smith, Stevens
Scorers: 1, Smith, Stevens
International appearances
  England: 2, Foster
  N Ireland: 2, Penney; 1, Irvine, Nelson
  Republic of Ireland: 1, Lawrenson

BRISTOL CITY
Freight Rover Trophy/Auto Windscreens Shield final
24/05/86 beat Bolton 3-0
24/05/87 drew with Mansfield 1-1 aet (lost 5-4 on pens)
16/04/00 lost to Stoke 1-2

	P	W	D	L	F	A
Freight Rover Trophy/ Auto Windscreens Shield	3	1	1	1	5	3
Total	3	1	1	1	5	3

International appearances
  England: 3, Atyeo
  Wales: 1, Emanuel (s)
  Republic of Ireland: 1, Curtis
  International Scorers: England: 3, Atyeo
  Republic of Ireland: 1, Curtis

BRISTOL ROVERS
Second Division promotion play-off final
28/05/95 lost to Huddersfield T 1-2
Leyland DAF Cup final
20/05/90 lost to Tranmere 1-2

	P	W	D	L	F	A
Promotion play-off	1	0	0	1	1	2
Leyland DAF Cup	1	0	0	1	1	2
Total	2	0	0	2	2	4

BROMLEY
FA Amateur Cup final
23/04/49 beat ROMFORD 1-0

BRUGES (see BELGIUM)

BULGARIA
European Championship Qualifying
22/11/79 lost to England 0-2
10/10/98 drew with England 0-0
Internationals
11/12/68 drew with England 1-1
27/03/96 lost to England 0-1
Olympic Q - 2nd leg
12/05/56 drew with Great Britain 3-3
Olympic Q - 1st leg
24/03/71 lost to Great Britain 0-1

	P	W	D	L	F	A
European Championship	2	0	1	1	0	2
Internationals	2	0	1	1	1	2
v England	4	0	2	2	1	4
Olympics	2	0	1	1	3	4

Most appearances: 2, Iordanov, Kishishev (1s)
Scorers: 1, Asparoukhov

BURNLEY
FA Cup final
27, 26/04/47 lost to Charlton 0-1 aet
77, 05/05/62 lost to Spurs 1-3
Second Division promotion play-off final
29/05/94 beat Stockport County 2-1
Sherpa Van Trophy final
29/05/88 lost to Wolves 0-2

	P	W	D	L	F	A
FA Cup	2	0	0	2	1	4
Promotion play-off	1	1	0	0	2	1
Sherpa Van Trophy	1	0	0	1	0	2
Total	4	1	0	3	3	7

Scorers: 1, Eyres, Parkinson, Robson
International appearances
England: 6, Connelly; 2, Coates (1s), Elliott; 1, McDonald, Pointer
N Ireland: 4, McIlroy; 3, Hamilton; 2, Elder, Irvine; 1, Cochrane (s)
Wales: 3, Flynn, James
International Scorers: England: 4, Connelly; 2, Elliott; 1, Pointer
N Ireland: 2, McIlroy (1 pen); 1, Irvine

BURTON ALBION
FA Trophy final
09/05/87 drew with Kidderminster 0-0 aet

BURY
Third Division promotion play-off final
27/05/95 lost to Chesterfield 0-2
International appearances
N Ireland: 1, Hughes, Spence
Scotland: 1, Bradshaw

CAMBRIDGE UNITED
Fourth Division promotion play-off final
26/05/90 beat Chesterfield 1-0
International appearances
N Ireland: 1, Finney

CAMBRIDGE UNIVERSITY
Inter-Varsity
26/01/29 beat London Uni 3-0

07/03/53 drew with Oxford Uni 0-0
05/12/53 drew with Oxford Uni 1-1
04/12/54 beat Oxford Uni 3-2
07/12/55 beat Oxford Uni 4-2
08/12/56 lost to Oxford Uni 1-4
07/12/57 drew with Oxford Uni 1-1
06/12/58 drew with Oxford Uni 1-1
05/12/59 beat Oxford Uni 6-2
03/12/60 drew with Oxford Uni 2-2
09/12/61 beat Oxford Uni 2-0
08/12/62 beat Oxford Uni 5-2
07/12/63 beat Oxford Uni 4-2
05/12/64 lost to Oxford Uni 1-3
08/12/65 beat Oxford Uni 3-2
07/12/66 beat Oxford Uni 1-0
13/12/67 beat Oxford Uni 1-0
04/12/68 beat Oxford Uni 3-1
03/12/69 drew with Oxford Uni 1-1
09/12/70 beat Oxford Uni 1-0
08/12/71 drew with Oxford Uni 0-0
06/12/72 beat Oxford Uni 2-1
05/12/73 drew with Oxford Uni 0-0
04/12/74 lost to Oxford Uni 1-3
03/12/75 lost to Oxford Uni 0-2
08/12/76 drew with Oxford Uni 0-0
07/12/77 lost to Oxford Uni 0-4
06/12/78 beat Oxford Uni 2-1
05/12/79 lost to Oxford Uni 1-3
10/12/80 lost to Oxford Uni 0-2
09/12/81 lost to Oxford Uni 0-2
08/12/82 lost to Oxford Uni 2-4
07/12/83 drew with Oxford Uni 2-2
12/12/84 beat Oxford Uni 4-2
11/12/85 beat Oxford Uni 2-0
10/12/86 beat Oxford Uni 4-3
09/12/87 beat Oxford Uni 2-1
Friendly
17/11/28 beat Casuals 5-2

	P	W	D	L	F	A
Inter-Varsity	37	18	10	9	66	56
Friendly	1	1	0	0	5	2
v Oxford Uni	36	17	10	9	63	56
Total	38	19	10	9	71	58

CAMEROON
International
06/02/91 lost to England 0-2
15/11/97 lost to England 0-2

	P	W	D	L	F	A
Internationals	2	0	0	2	0	4
Total	2	0	0	2	0	4

CARDIFF CITY
FA Cup final
25/04/25 lost to Sheffield Utd 0-1
23/04/27 beat Arsenal 1-0

	P	W	D	L	F	A
FA Cup	2	1	0	1	1	1
Total	2	1	0	1	1	1

Most appearances: 2, Farquharson, Hardy, Keenor, Nelson
Scorers: 1, Ferguson

International appearances
Wales: 2, Allchurch, Harrington, Sherwood, Sullivan; 1, Baker, Dwyer, Ford, Hole, Jones, Phillips, Sayer, Showers (s), Stitfall, Toshack
Scotland: 1, Nelson
Republic of Ireland: 1, Healey (s)

CARLISLE UNITED
Auto Windscreens Shield final
23/04/95 lost to Birmingham C 0-1 iet
20/04/97 drew with Colchester 0-0 aet (won 4-3 on pens)

	P	W	D	L	F	A
Auto Windscreens Shield	2	0	1	1	0	1
Total	2	0	1	1	0	1

CASUALS
Friendly
17/11/28 lost to Cambridge Uni 2-5

CELTIC
International appearances
Scotland: 4, McGrain; 3, Dalglish, Evans, McNeill; 2, Aitken, Gemmell, Wallace (1s); 1, Boyd, Brogan, Burchill (s), Burley, Burns (s), J Collins, R Collins, Crum, Fernie, Haffey, Hay, Hunter, Johnstone, Lennox, McGonagle, McKay, McKinlay, McStay, Miller, Murdoch, Napier, Nicholas, Provan, Simpson
N Ireland: 3, Peacock; 1, Tully
Republic of Ireland: 2, Bonner
Poland: 1, Wdowczyk
Sweden: 1, Larsson, Mjallby
International Scorers: Scotland: 1, Dalglish, Lennox

CHARLTON ATHLETIC
FA Cup final
27/04/46 lost to Derby County 1-4 aet
26/04/47 beat Burnley 1-0 aet
Full Members Cup final
29/03/87 lost to Blackburn 0-1
First Division promotion play-off final
25/05/98 drew with Sunderland 4-4 aet (won 7-6 on pens)
League South Cup final
01/05/43 lost to Arsenal 1-7
15/04/44 beat Chelsea 3-1

	P	W	D	L	F	A
FA Cup	2	1	0	1	2	4
Full Members Cup	1	0	0	1	0	1
Promotion play-off	1	0	1	0	4	4
League South Cup	2	1	0	1	4	8
Total	6	2	1	3	10	17

Most appearances: 4, Shreeve, Welsh, 2, Bartram, Duffy, Johnson, Phipps
Scorers: 3, Mendonca, 1, Duffy, H Turner
International appearances
England: 1, Bailey, Ufton
Scotland: 1, Hewie
Wales: 1, Moore

CHELSEA
FA Cup final
20/05/67 lost to Spurs 1-2
11/04/70 drew with Leeds 2-2 aet
14/05/94 lost to Man Utd 0-4

17/05/97 beat Middlesbrough 2-0
20/05/00 beat Aston Villa 1-0
FA Cup semi-final
09/04/94 beat Luton 2-0
09/04/00 beat Newcastle Utd 2-1
League Cup/Coca-Cola Cup final
04/03/72 lost to Stoke 1-2
29/03/98 beat Middlesbrough 2-0 aet
Charity Shield
03/08/97 drew with Man Utd 1-1 (lost 4-2 on pens)
13/08/00 beat Man Utd 2-0
Full Members/Zenith Cup final
23/03/86 beat Man City 5-4
25/03/90 beat Middlesbrough 1-0
League South Cup final
15/04/44 lost to Charlton 1-3
07/04/45 beat Millwall 2-0

	P	W	D	L	F	A
FA Cup final	5	2	1	2	6	8
FA Cup semi-finalS	2	2	0	0	4	1
FA Cup Total	7	4	1	2	10	9
League Cup/Coca-Cola Cup	2	1	0	1	3	2
Charity Shield	2	1	1	0	3	1
Full Members/Zenith Cup	2	2	0	0	6	4
League South Cup	2	1	0	1	3	3
Total	15	9	2	4	25	19

Most appearances: 8, Wise; 6, Di Matteo, Lebeouf, Zola (1s); 5, Clarke (1s), De Goey, Sinclair
Scorers: 3, Di Matteo, Speedie; 2, Lee, Peacock, Poyet; 1, Dorigo, Hasselbaink, Houseman, Hughes, Hutchinson, McDonald, Melchiot, Osgood, Payne, Sinclair, Tambling, Wardle
International appearances
England: 9, Wilkins (1s), Wise (2s); 8, Le Saux (2s); 5, Dorigo (4s), Greaves; 4, Bentley; 3, Blunstone, Bridges; 2, Beasant (s), Bonetti, Tambling; 1, Armstrong, Dixon, Hollins, Lawton, O'Dowd, Osgood, Venables, Woodley
Scotland: 3, McCreadie; 2, Law; 1, Burley (s), Gallacher, Jackson, Nevin (s), Speedie, Spencer
Wales: 1, Jones, Phillips
Republic of Ireland: 1, Townsend
Denmark: 1, Kjeldbjerg
France: 1, Desailly, Lebeouf (s)
Italy: 1, Di Matteo, Zola
Norway: 1, Johnsen
International Scorers: England: 7, Greaves; 5, Bentley
Italy: 1, Zola

CHELTENHAM TOWN
FA Trophy final
17/05/98 beat Southport 1-0

CHESHAM UNITED
FA Amateur Cup final
20/04/68 lost to Leytonstone 0-1

CHESTERFIELD
Fourth/Third Division promotion play-off final
26/05/90 lost to Cambridge Utd 0-1
27/05/95 beat Bury 2-0

	P	W	D	L	F	A
Promotion play-offs	2	1	0	1	2	1
Total	2	1	0	1	2	1

CHILE
Rous Cup
23/05/89 drew with England 0-0
International
11/02/98 beat England 2-0

	P	W	D	L	F	A
Rous Cup	1	0	1	0	0	0
International	1	1	0	0	2	0
Total	2	1	1	0	2	0

Scorers: 2, Salas
FIFA appearances
Rest of World: 1, Eyzaguirre (s)

CHIPPENHAM TOWN
FA Vase final
06/05/00 lost to Deal Town 0-1

CLAPTON ORIENT (see LEYTON ORIENT)

CLITHEROE
FA Vase final
12/05/96 lost to Brigg Town 0-3

CLYDE
International appearances
Scotland: 2, Ring; 1, Haddock
International Scorers: Scotland: 1, Ring

COLCHESTER UNITED
Third Division promotion play-off final
22/05/98 beat Torquay 1-0
Auto Windscreens Shield final
20/04/97 drew with Carlisle 0-0 aet (lost 4-3 on pens)
FA Trophy final
10/05/92 beat Witton Albion 3-1

	P	W	D	L	F	A
Promotion play-off	1	1	0	0	1	0
Auto Windscreens Shield	1	0	1	0	0	0
FA Trophy	1	1	0	0	3	1
Total	3	2	1	0	4	1

COLERAINE
International appearances
N Ireland: 1, Coyle, Hunter, McCavana, O'Doherty

COLNE DYNAMOES
FA Vase final
23/04/88 beat Emley 1-0 aet

COLOGNE (see GERMANY)

COLOMBIA
Rous Cup
24/05/88 drew with England 1-1
International
06/09/95 drew with England 0-0

	P	W	D	L	F	A
Rous Cup	1	0	1	0	1	1
International	1	0	1	0	0	0
Total	2	0	2	0	1	1

Most appearances: 2, Alvarez, Higuita, Valderrama
Scorers: 1, Escobar

COMBINED SERVICES
Charity matches
10/05/44 beat Met Police and Civil Defence 5-2
09/05/45 beat Met Police and Civil Defence 3-1

	P	W	D	L	F	A
Charity matches	2	2	0	0	8	3
Total	2	2	0	0	8	3

CORBY CALEDONIAN
Carlsberg Pub Cup final
10/05/97 lost to Poulton Victoria 1-3

CORINTHIAN-CASUALS
FA Amateur Cup final
07/04/56 drew with Bishop Auckland 1-1 aet

COVENTRY CITY
FA Cup final
258, 16/05/87 beat Spurs 3-2 aet
Charity Shield
260 - 01/08/87 lost to Everton 0-1

	P	W	D	L	F	A
FA Cup	1	1	0	0	3	2
Charity Shield	1	0	0	1	0	1
Total	2	1	0	1	3	3

Most appearances: 2, Bennett, Downs, Gynn, Houchen, Kilcline, McGrath, Ogrizovic, Peake, Phillips, Pickering
Scorers: 1, Bennett, Houchen, own goal
International appearances
England: 1, Dublin, Matthews, Regis (s)
N Ireland: 2, Clements; 1, Humphries
Scotland: 1, Hutchison (s), Jess (s), Stein (s)
Wales: 2, Rees, Yorath
Republic of Ireland: 1, Holmes
Sweden: 1, Hedman
USA: 1, Jones

CREMONESE (see ITALY)

CREWE ALEXANDRA
Second Division promotion play-off final
25/05/97 beat Brentford 1-0
Third Division promotion play-off final
29/05/93 drew with York City 1-1 aet (lost 5-3 on pens)

	P	W	D	L	F	A
Second Division Play-off	1	1	0	0	1	0
Third Division Play-off	1	0	1	0	1	1
Promotion play-offs Total	2	1	1	0	2	1
Total	2	1	1	0	2	1

CROATIA (see also YUGOSLAVIA)
International
343, 24/04/96 drew with England 0-0

CROOK TOWN
FA Amateur Cup final
10/04/54 drew with Bishop Auckland 2-2 aet
18/04/59 beat Barnet 3-2
14/04/62 drew with Hounslow Town 1-1 aet
18/04/64 beat Enfield 2-1

	P	W	D	L	F	A
FA Amateur Cup	4	2	2	0	8	6
Total	4	2	2	0	8	6

CRYSTAL PALACE
FA Cup final
12/05/90 drew with Man Utd 3-3 aet
FA Cup final replay
17/05/90 lost to Man Utd 0-1

Zenith Cup final
07/04/91 beat Everton 4-1 aet
First Division promotion play-off final
27/05/96 lost to Leicester 1-2 aet
26/05/97 beat Sheffield Utd 1-0
League Centenary Tournament
1st round: - 16/04/88 drew with Sheffield W 0-0 (lost 2-1 on pens)

	P	W	D	L	F	A
FA Cup	2	0	1	1	3	4
Zenith Cup	1	1	0	0	4	1
Promotion play-offs	2	1	0	1	2	2
Full match Total	5	2	1	2	9	7
League Centenary	1	0	1	0	0	0

Most appearances: 4, Martyn, 3, Bright, Gray, Pardew, Salako, Shaw, Thomas, Wright (2s)
Scorers: 4, Wright; 1, Hopkin, O'Reilly, Roberts, Salako, Thomas
International appearances
England: 5, Sansom; 3, Thomas, Wright (1s); 1, Byrne, Salako, Taylor
Wales: 1, Evans, Millington, Walsh

CYPRUS
European Championship Qualifying
164, 16/04/75 lost to England 0-5

CZECHOSLOVAKIA (see also CZECH REPUBLIC)
European Championship Qualifying
30/10/74 lost to England 0-3
Internationals
02/11/66 drew with England 0-0
29/11/78 lost to England 0-1
25/04/90 lost to England 2-4
Youth
25/04/90 drew with England 1-1

	P	W	D	L	F	A
European Championship	1	0	0	1	0	3
Internationals	3	0	1	2	2	5
Senior Total	4	0	1	3	2	8
Youth	1	0	1	0	1	1

Most appearances: 2, Gajdusek, Kuna (s), Masny, Viktor, Vojacek (1s)
Scorers: 1, Kubik, Skuhravy
FIFA appearances
Rest of World: 1, Masopust, Pluskal, Popluhar

CZECH REPUBLIC (see also CZECHOSLOVAKIA)
European Championship final
30/06/96 lost to Germany 1-2 iet
International
18/11/98 lost to England 0-2

	P	W	D	L	F	A
European Championship	1	0	0	1	1	2
International	1	0	0	1	0	2
Total	2	0	0	2	1	4

Most appearances: 2, Bejbl, Berger, Kouba, Kuka, Nemec, Poborsky, Smicer (1s)
Scorers: 1, Berger (pen)

DAGENHAM AND REDBRIDGE
FA Amateur Cup final (Dagenham)
04/04/70 lost to Enfield 1-5
24/04/71 lost to Skelmersdale 1-4

FA Trophy final
14/05/77 lost to Scarborough 1-2 (Dagenham)
17/05/80 beat Mossley 2-1 (Dagenham)
18/05/97 lost to Woking 0-1 aet

	P	W	D	L	F	A
FA Amateur Cup	2	0	0	2	2	9
FA Trophy	3	1	0	2	3	4
Total	5	1	0	4	5	13

DARLINGTON
Third Division promotion play-off final
25/05/96 lost to Plymouth Argyle 0-1
26/05/00 lost to Peterborough 0-1

	P	W	D	L	F	A
Promotion play-offs	2	0	0	2	0	2
Total	2	0	0	2	0	2

DARTFORD
FA Trophy final
27/04/74 lost to Morecambe 1-2

DAWLISH TOWN
Carlsberg Pub Cup International
22/09/96 lost to Brigade Bodega 0-1

DEAL TOWN
FA Vase final
06/05/00 beat Chippenham Town 1-0

DENMARK
European Championship Qualifying
12/09/79 lost to England 0-1
21/09/83 beat England 1-0
Internationals
14/09/88 lost to England 0-1
15/05/90 lost to England 0-1
09/03/94 lost to England 0-1
Olympic semi-final
10/08/48 lost to Sweden 2-4
Olympic 3rd & 4th place: - 13/08/48 beat Great Britain 5-3
Youth
28/03/90 drew with England 0-0
U-16
08/08/87 lost to England 1-2

	P	W	D	L	F	A
European Championship	2	1	0	1	1	1
Internationals	3	0	0	3	0	3
v England	5	1	0	4	1	4
Olympics	2	1	0	1	7	7
Youth	1	0	1	0	0	0
U-16	1	0	0	1	1	2

Most appearances: 4, M Laudrup
Scorers: 1, Simonsen (pen)
Clubs
Brigade Bodega
Carlsberg Pub Cup International
22/09/96 beat Dawlish Town 1-0
Vagns Krostue
Carlsberg Pub Cup International
13/06/98 lost to West Hendon Ex-Servicemen 0-1

DERBY COUNTY
FA Cup final
27/04/46 beat Charlton 4-1 aet
Charity Shield
09/08/75 beat West Ham 2-0
First Division promotion play-off final
30/05/94 lost to Leicester 1-2
Anglo-Italian Cup final
27/03/93 lost to Cremonese 1-3

	P	W	D	L	F	A
FA Cup	1	1	0	0	4	1
Charity Shield	1	1	0	0	2	0
Promotion play-off	1	0	0	1	1	2
Anglo-Italian Cup	1	0	0	1	1	3
Total	4	2	0	2	8	6

Scorers: 2, Stamps; 1, Doherty, Gabbiadini, Hector, Johnson, McFarland, own goal
International appearances
England: 15, Shilton; 12, Todd (2s); 11, McFarland; 9, Wright (2s), 4, Crooks; 2, Hector (s); 1, Barker, Bowers, Carter, Cooper, George, Howe, Nish
N Ireland: 1, Caskey
Scotland: 1, Duncan, Gemmill (s), Rioch, Steel
Wales: 2, Durban, Thomas; 1, James
Republic of Ireland: 1, Daly
Croatia: 1, Stimac
International Scorers: England: 1, Bowers, Carter, Crooks
Scotland: 1, Rioch (pen), Steel
Wales: 1, James (pen)

DISS TOWN
FA Vase final
07/05/94 beat Taunton Town 2-1 aet

DONCASTER ROVERS
International appearances
N Ireland: 1, Graham, Gregg

DRUMCONDRA
International appearances
Republic of Ireland: 1, Kelly

DUNDEE
International appearances
Scotland: 2, Hamilton, Steel; 1, Brown, Cowie, McNab, Ure
N Ireland: 1, Campbell, Wilson
Poland: 1, Adamczuk

DUNDEE UNITED
International appearances
Scotland: 2, Bannon, Gough, Narey (1s); 1, Dodds, Gallacher (s), Hegarty, Malpas, Sturrock (s)

DUNFERMLINE ATHLETIC
International appearances
Hungary: 1, Kozma

DYNAMO KIEV (see USSR)

EALING ASSOCIATION
Southern Amateur League First Division
29/09/28 beat Hastings and St Leonards 1-0

13/10/28 lost to Ipswich 0-4
20/10/28 lost to Midland Bank 0-4
27/10/28 lost to Bank of England 1-5
03/11/28 lost to Westminster Bank 0-3
10/11/28 beat Barclays 4-2
01/12/28 lost to Aquarias 0-3
08/12/28 lost to Old Lyonians 0-3

	P	W	D	L	F	A
Southern Amateur League	8	2	0	6	5	24
Total	8	2	0	6	5	24

EARL SOHAM VICTORIA
Carlsberg Pub Cup final
06/05/00 beat Eastleigh 2-1

	P	W	D	L	F	A
Carlsberg Pub Cup	1	1	0	0	2	1
Total	1	1	0	0	2	1

EAST FIFE
International appearances
Scotland: 1, Aitken

EAST GERMANY (see GERMANY)

EASTLEIGH
Carlsberg Pub Cup final
06/05/00 lost to Earl Soham Victoria 1-2

EMLEY
FA Vase final
23/04/88 lost to Colne Dynamoes 0-1 aet

ENFIELD
FA Amateur Cup final
18/04/64 lost to Crook Town 1-2
22/04/67 drew with Skelmersdale 0-0 aet
04/04/70 beat Dagenham 5-1
22/04/72 lost to Hendon 0-2
FA Trophy final
15/05/82 beat Altrincham 1-0 aet
07/05/88 drew with Telford 0-0 aet

	P	W	D	L	F	A
FA Amateur Cup	4	1	1	2	6	5
FA Trophy	2	1	1	0	1	0
Total	6	2	2	2	7	5

ENGLAND
World Cup
11/07/66 drew with Uruguay 0-0
16/07/66 beat Mexico 2-0
20/07/66 beat France 2-0
World Cup quarter-final
23/07/66 beat Argentina 1-0
World Cup semi-final
26/07/66 beat Portugal 2-1
World Cup final
30/07/66 beat West Germany 4-2 aet
World Cup Qualifying
08/05/57 beat R of Ireland 5-1
25/10/61 beat Portugal 2-0
24/01/73 drew with Wales 1-1
17/10/73 drew with Poland 1-1
13/10/76 beat Finland 2-1
30/03/77 beat Luxembourg 5-0

16/11/77 beat Italy 2-0
10/09/80 beat Norway 4-0
19/11/80 beat Switzerland 2-1
29/04/81 drew with Romania 0-0
18/11/81 beat Hungary 1-0
17/10/84 beat Finland 5-0
11/09/85 drew with Romania 1-1
16/10/85 beat Turkey 5-0
13/11/85 drew with N Ireland 0-0
19/10/88 drew with Sweden 0-0
26/04/89 beat Albania 5-0
03/06/89 beat Poland 3-0
14/10/92 drew with Norway 1-1
18/11/92 beat Turkey 4-0
17/02/93 beat San Marino 6-0
28/04/93 drew with Netherlands 2-2
08/09/93 beat Poland 3-0
09/10/96 beat Poland 2-1
12/02/97 lost to Italy 0-1
30/04/97 beat Georgia 2-0
10/09/97 beat Moldova 4-0
07/10/00 lost to Germany 0-1
European Championship
08/06/96 drew with Switzerland 1-1
15/06/96 beat Scotland 2-0
18/06/96 beat Netherlands 4-1
European Championship quarter-final
03/04/68 beat Spain 1-0 (1st leg)
29/04/72 lost to West Germany 1-3 (1st leg)
22/06/96 drew with Spain 0-0 aet (won 4-2 on pens)
European Championship semi-final
26/06/96 drew with Germany 1-1 aet (lost 6-5 on pens)
European Championship Play-off 2nd leg
17/11/99 lost to Scotland 0-1
European Championship Qualifying
16/11/66 beat Wales 5-1
15/04/67 lost to Scotland 2-3
22/11/67 beat N Ireland 2-0
21/04/71 beat Greece 3-0
12/05/71 beat Malta 5-0
10/11/71 drew with Switzerland 1-1
30/10/74 beat Czechoslovakia 3-0
20/11/74 drew with Portugal 0-0
16/04/75 beat Cyprus 5-0
07/02/79 beat N Ireland 4-0
12/09/79 beat Denmark 1-0
22/11/79 beat Bulgaria 2-0
06/02/80 beat R of Ireland 2-0
15/12/82 beat Luxembourg 9-0
30/03/83 drew with Greece 0-0
27/04/83 beat Hungary 2-0
21/09/83 lost to Denmark 0-1
15/10/86 beat N Ireland 3-0
12/11/86 beat Yugoslavia 2-0
14/10/87 beat Turkey 8-0
17/10/90 beat Poland 2-0
27/03/91 drew with R of Ireland 1-1
16/10/91 beat Turkey 1-0
10/10/98 drew with Bulgaria 0-0
27/03/99 beat Poland 3-1

05/06/99 drew with Sweden 0-0
04/09/99 beat Luxembourg 6-0
British Championship
12/04/24 drew with Scotland 1-1
31/03/28 lost to Scotland 1-5
05/04/30 beat Scotland 5-2
09/04/32 beat Scotland 3-0
14/04/34 beat Scotland 3-0
04/04/36 drew with Scotland 1-1
09/04/38 lost to Scotland 0-1
12/04/47 drew with Scotland 1-1
09/04/49 lost to Scotland 1-3
14/04/51 lost to Scotland 2-3
12/11/52 beat Wales 5-2
18/04/53 drew with Scotland 2-2
10/11/54 beat Wales 3-2
02/04/55 beat Scotland 7-2
02/11/55 beat N Ireland 3-0
14/11/56 beat Wales 3-1
06/04/57 beat Scotland 2-1
06/11/57 lost to N Ireland 2-3
11/04/59 beat Scotland 1-0
18/11/59 beat N Ireland 2-1
23/11/60 beat Wales 5-1
15/04/61 beat Scotland 9-3
22/11/61 drew with N Ireland 1-1
21/11/62 beat Wales 4-0
06/04/63 lost to Scotland 1-2
20/11/63 beat N Ireland 8-3
18/11/64 beat Wales 2-1
10/04/65 drew with Scotland 2-2
10/11/65 beat N Ireland 2-1
16/11/66 beat Wales 5-1
15/04/67 lost to Scotland 2-3
22/11/67 beat N Ireland 2-0
07/05/69 beat Wales 2-1
10/05/69 beat Scotland 4-1
21/04/70 beat N Ireland 3-1
19/05/71 drew with Wales 0-0
22/05/71 beat Scotland 3-1
23/05/72 lost to N Ireland 0-1
15/05/73 beat Wales 3-0
19/05/73 beat Scotland 1-0
15/05/74 beat N Ireland 1-0
21/05/75 drew with Wales 2-2
24/05/75 beat Scotland 5-1
11/05/76 beat N Ireland 4-0
31/05/77 lost to Wales 0-1
04/06/77 lost to Scotland 1-2
16/05/78 beat N Ireland 1-0
23/05/79 drew with Wales 0-0
26/05/79 beat Scotland 3-1
20/05/80 drew with N Ireland 1-1
20/05/81 drew with Wales 0-0
23/05/81 lost to Scotland 0-1
23/02/82 beat N Ireland 4-0
23/02/83 beat Wales 2-1
01/06/83 beat Scotland 2-0
04/04/84 beat N Ireland 1-0

Rous Cup
23/04/86 beat Scotland 2-1
19/05/87 drew with Brazil 1-1
21/05/88 beat Scotland 1-0
24/05/88 drew with Colombia 1-1
23/05/89 drew with Chile 0-0

Umbro Cup
03/06/95 beat Japan 2-1
11/06/95 lost to Brazil 1-3

FA 90th Anniversary Match
21/10/53 drew with FIFA 4-4

FA Centenary match
23/10/63 beat FIFA 2-1

Internationals
09/05/51 beat Argentina 2-1
28/11/51 drew with Austria 2-2
26/11/52 beat Belgium 5-0
25/11/53 lost to Hungary 3-6
01/12/54 beat West Germany 3-1
30/11/55 beat Spain 4-1
09/05/56 beat Brazil 4-2
28/11/56 beat Yugoslavia 3-0
27/11/57 beat France 4-0
07/05/58 beat Portugal 2-1
22/10/58 beat USSR 5-0
06/05/59 drew with Italy 2-2
28/10/59 lost to Sweden 2-3
11/05/60 drew with Yugoslavia 3-3
26/10/60 beat Spain 4-2
10/05/61 beat Mexico 8-0
04/04/62 beat Austria 3-1
09/05/62 beat Switzerland 3-1
08/05/63 drew with Brazil 1-1
06/05/64 beat Uruguay 2-1
21/10/64 drew with Belgium 2-2
05/05/65 beat Hungary 1-0
20/10/65 lost to Austria 2-3
23/02/66 beat West Germany 1-0
04/05/66 beat Yugoslavia 2-0
02/11/66 drew with Czechoslovakia 0-0
24/05/67 beat Spain 2-0
06/12/67 drew with USSR 2-2
22/05/68 beat Sweden 3-1
11/12/68 drew with Bulgaria 1-1
15/01/69 drew with Romania 1-1
12/03/69 beat France 5-0
10/12/69 beat Portugal 1-0
14/01/70 drew with Netherlands 0-0
25/11/70 beat East Germany 3-1
11/10/72 drew with Yugoslavia 1-1
26/09/73 beat Austria 7-0
14/11/73 lost to Italy 0-1
22/05/74 drew with Argentina 2-2
12/03/75 beat West Germany 2-0
08/09/76 drew with R of Ireland 1-1
09/02/77 lost to Netherlands 0-2
07/09/77 drew with Switzerland 0-0
19/04/78 drew with Brazil 1-1
24/05/78 beat Hungary 4-1
29/11/78 beat Czechoslovakia 1-0

13/05/80 beat Argentina 3-1
25/03/81 lost to Spain 1-2
12/05/81 lost to Brazil 0-1
25/05/82 beat Netherlands 2-0
13/10/82 lost to West Germany 1-2
02/06/84 lost to USSR 0-2
12/09/84 beat East Germany 1-0
26/03/85 beat R of Ireland 2-1
23/03/88 drew with Netherlands 2-2
14/09/88 beat Denmark 1-0
15/11/89 drew with Italy 0-0
13/12/89 beat Yugoslavia 2-1
28/03/90 beat Brazil 1-0
25/04/90 beat Czechoslovakia 4-2
15/05/90 beat Denmark 1-0
22/05/90 lost to Uruguay 1-2
12/09/90 beat Hungary 1-0
06/02/91 beat Cameroon 2-0
21/05/91 beat USSR 3-1
25/05/91 drew with Argentina 2-2
11/09/91 lost to Germany 0-1
19/02/92 beat France 2-0
17/05/92 drew with Brazil 1-1
09/03/94 beat Denmark 1-0
17/05/94 beat Greece 5-0
22/05/94 drew with Norway 0-0
07/09/94 beat USA 2-0
12/10/94 drew with Romania 1-1
16/11/94 beat Nigeria 1-0
29/03/95 drew with Uruguay 0-0
06/09/95 drew with Colombia 0-0
15/11/95 beat Switzerland 3-1
12/12/95 drew with Portugal 1-1
27/03/96 beat Bulgaria 1-0
24/04/96 drew with Croatia 0-0
18/05/96 beat Hungary 3-0
29/03/97 beat Mexico 2-0
15/11/97 beat Cameroon 2-0
11/02/98 lost to Chile 0-2
22/04/98 beat Portugal 3-0
23/05/98 drew with Saudi Arabia 0-0
18/11/98 beat Czech Republic 2-0
10/02/99 lost to France 0-2
23/02/00 drew with Argentina 0-0
27/05/00 drew with Brazil 1-1
31/05/00 beat Ukraine 2-0

Wartime
13/04/40 lost to Wales 0-1
04/10/41 beat Scotland 2-0
17/01/42 beat Scotland 3-0
10/10/42 drew with Scotland 0-0
27/02/43 beat Wales 5-3
25/09/43 beat Wales 8-3
19/02/44 beat Scotland 6-2
14/10/44 beat Scotland 6-2
26/05/45 drew with France 2-2

Victory International
19/01/46 beat Belgium 2-0

U-23
16/10/57 beat Romania 3-2

International Trial (FA)
06/04/46 lost to Army PTC 3-5
Amateur (see also Great Britain)
15/03/52 lost to Scotland 1-2
European Amateur Championship
31/10/73 beat West Germany 1-0
British Amateur Championship
27/03/54 lost to Scotland 1-4
24/03/56 beat Scotland 4-2
29/03/58 lost to Scotland 2-3
U-19
25/05/91 drew with Spain 1-1
Youth (U-18)
06/11/63 beat Rest of United Kingdom 5-2
28/03/90 drew with Denmark 0-0
25/04/90 drew with Czechoslovakia 1-1
15/05/90 beat Poland 3-0
European Youth Tournament final
23/04/63 beat N Ireland 4-0
U-17
01/08/87 beat Netherlands 3-1
22/05/90 lost to France 1-3
U-16
10/08/85 beat Yugoslavia 3-2
16/08/86 lost to France 0-1
08/08/87 beat Denmark 2-1
20/08/88 drew with Israel 1-1
12/08/89 beat Scandinavia 2-1
04/07/99 beat Argentina 2-1
U-18 Schoolboy
08/05/99 lost to Netherlands 1-2
25/03/00 lost to Hungary 0-1
Schoolboy
15/04/50 beat Scotland 8-2
07/04/51 beat Wales 3-0
05/04/52 beat Scotland 1-0
28/03/53 drew with Wales 3-3
03/04/54 beat Scotland 1-0
23/04/55 beat Wales 6-0
21/04/56 lost to Scotland 1-2
30/03/57 beat Wales 2-0
26/04/58 beat Scotland 3-1
25/04/59 beat West Germany 2-0
30/04/60 beat Scotland 5-3
29/04/61 beat Wales 8-1
30/04/62 lost to West Germany 1-2
27/04/63 beat Wales 4-1
25/04/64 drew with West Germany 1-1
03/04/65 beat Scotland 3-0
30/04/66 beat West Germany 2-1
29/04/67 lost to Scotland 0-2
27/04/68 lost to West Germany 1-2
19/04/69 beat Wales 3-0
21/03/70 beat Scotland 2-0
16/05/70 beat West Germany 3-0
06/03/71 beat N Ireland 1-0
03/04/71 beat Netherlands 5-1
20/05/72 beat West Germany 4-0
07/04/73 beat Netherlands 3-1
09/06/73 lost to Scotland 2-4

06/04/74 beat France 5-2
01/06/74 beat West Germany 4-0
22/03/75 beat Netherlands 4-0
07/06/75 lost to Scotland 0-1
20/03/76 beat Wales 4-1
05/06/76 beat France 6-1
19/03/77 beat Scotland 2-0
18/06/77 lost to West Germany 1-2
04/03/78 drew with France 3-3
27/05/78 beat Scotland 3-0
24/03/79 drew with Wales 1-1
09/06/79 drew with West Germany 2-2
22/03/80 beat Switzerland 2-0
07/06/80 lost to Scotland 4-5
13/06/81 lost to West Germany 1-2
27/03/82 beat Netherlands 7-0
05/06/82 drew with Scotland 0-0
19/03/83 beat West Germany 1-0
11/06/83 drew with Scotland 3-3
17/03/84 beat Scotland 1-0
09/06/84 beat Netherlands 4-1
16/03/85 lost to West Germany 0-1
08/06/85 beat Switzerland 2-0
08/03/86 beat Netherlands 1-0
31/05/86 beat Italy 2-1
14/03/87 beat West Germany 2-0
12/03/88 beat Brazil 2-0
28/05/88 beat Italy 4-1
11/03/89 beat Belgium 3-1
10/06/89 lost to West Germany 1-3
10/03/90 drew with France 1-1
02/06/90 beat Netherlands 1-0
08/06/91 lost to West Germany 1-3
07/03/92 drew with Netherlands 0-0
06/06/92 drew with Italy 1-1
05/06/93 drew with Germany 0-0
12/03/94 beat Switzerland 3-0
11/06/94 beat France 2-1
11/03/95 beat Brazil 1-0
10/06/95 lost to Germany 2-4
09/03/96 lost to Spain 2-3
07/06/97 beat Germany 2-1
14/03/98 drew with Brazil 0-0
Victory Shield
28/03/81 beat N Ireland 4-0
30/05/87 drew with Scotland 1-1
09/03/91 beat Scotland 2-1
13/03/93 lost to Scotland 1-2
Women
23/05/89 lost to Sweden 0-2
U-16 Girls
04/07/99 beat Scotland 5-0

	P	W	D	L	F	A
World Cup	6	5	1	0	11	3
World Cup Q	28	18	8	2	68	12
World Cup Total	34	23	9	2	79	15
European Championship	5	2	3	0	8	3
quarter-final 1st leg	2	1	0	1	2	3
Play-off 2nd leg	1	0	0	1	0	1
Qualifying	27	19	6	2	72	8

(includes three in British Championship)

European Championship Total	35	22	9	4	82	15
British Championship	56	34	11	11	134	64
Rous Cup	5	2	3	0	5	3
Umbro Cup	2	1	0	1	3	4
FA 90th Anniversary Match	1	0	1	0	4	4
FA Centenary Match	1	1	0	0	2	1
Internationals	92	51	28	13	173	77
Total (official)	223	132	61	30	473	179
v N Ireland (British Championship)	15	11	2	2	32	12
v N Ireland (Total)	18	13	3	2	39	12
v Scotland (British Championship)	26	13	5	8	63	39
v Scotland (official Total)	30	16	5	9	68	41
v Scotland (Wartime)	5	4	1	0	17	4
v Scotland (Senior Total)	35	20	6	9	85	45
v Wales (British Championship)	15	10	4	1	36	13
v Wales (official Total)	16	10	5	1	37	14
v Wales (Senior Total)	19	12	5	2	50	21
v R of Ireland	5	3	2	0	11	4
v Argentina	6	3	3	0	10	6
v Brazil	9	2	5	2	11	11
v Denmark	5	4	0	1	4	1
v France (official Total)	5	4	0	1	13	2
v France (Senior Total)	6	4	1	1	15	4
v Netherlands	6	2	3	1	10	7
v Hungary	7	6	0	1	15	7
v Italy	5	1	2	2	4	4
v Poland	6	5	1	0	14	3
v Portugal	7	5	2	0	11	3
v Spain	6	4	1	1	12	5
v Switzerland	6	3	3	0	10	5
v West Germany	6	4	0	2	12	8
v Yugoslavia	6	4	2	0	13	5
Wartime Total	9	6	2	1	32	13
Victory International	1	1	0	0	2	0
Senior Total	233	139	63	31	507	192
U-23	1	1	0	0	3	2
International Trial (FA)	1	0	0	1	3	5
European Amateur	1	1	0	0	1	0
British Amateur	3	1	0	2	7	9
Amateur Total	5	2	0	3	9	11
U-19	1	0	1	0	1	1
European Youth Tournament	1	1	0	0	4	0
Youth Total	5	3	2	0	13	3
U-17	2	1	0	1	4	4
U-16	6	4	1	1	10	7
U-18 Schoolboy	2	0	0	2	1	3
Victory Shield	4	2	1	1	8	4
Schoolboy Total	74	46	13	15	177	76
v Scotland (Schoolboy)	20	11	3	6	43	27
v Wales (Schoolboy)	9	7	2	0	34	7
v France (Schoolboy)	5	3	2	0	17	8
v Netherlands (Schoolboy)	8	7	1	0	25	3
v West Germany (Schoolboy)	16	7	2	7	27	19
Women	1	0	0	1	0	2
U-16 Girls	1	1	0	0	5	0

Most appearances: 52, Shilton; 44, R Charlton; 43, Moore; 41, Pearce (3s); 38, B Robson; 36, Adams; 35, Shearer (2s); 34, Sansom; 33, Seaman (1s); 32, Gascoigne (6s), Platt (6s); 31, Banks, Peters (2s), D V Watson, Wilkins (3s); 29, Ball (1s), J Barnes (2s), Hughes, Lineker (1s); 28, Butcher; 27, Keegan; 26, R Wilson (1s), W Wright; 25, Clemence; 24, Beardsley (4s), Hurst (2s), Ince (1s),

G Neville (1s); 23, Bell (1s), D Walker (2s); 22, Greaves, Haynes, Sheringham (5s), Waddle (3s); 21, J Charlton, Le Saux (3s), Neal; 20, Channon, T Francis (3s), McManaman (4s), Woodcock (5s); 19, Batty (3s), Brooking (3s), Cohen, Coppell (2s), Southgate (3s), M Wright (2s); 17, Anderton, Beckham, Hoddle (5s), R Hunt, M G Stevens; 16, Campbell (2s), Clayton, Finney, R Flowers, Stiles; 15, Armfield, Woods (3s), I Wright (7s); 14, Douglas, S Matthews; 13, L Dixon, Hunter (1s), F Lee, Mills (1s), Mullery (2s), Scholes (1s); 12, V Anderson, R Byrne, Keown, P Neville (5s), P B Thompson, Todd (2s); 11, P Barnes (2s), Cherry (2s), Chivers (2s), L Ferdinand (3s), R Lee (3s), Mariner (2s), McDermott (1s), McFarland, Springett; 10, Clarke (2s), Connelly, T Cooper, Currie (1s), Dickinson, Fowler (5s), Hateley (5s), Hodge (3s), Madeley, Steven (2s), Webb (1s); 9, Barmby (6s), Greenhoff (1s), Newton, Pallister (2s), Parker (1s), Redknapp (4s), Rix (4s), Swan, Wise (2s); 8, Blissett (4s), Dorigo (4s), D Howe, R Jones, Lofthouse, Mabbutt (1s), Merson (6s), Owen (2s), Ramsey, R Robson, Storey; 7, J Hall, R Kennedy, S Lee, Martin (1s), Paine, Parlour (6s), J S Pearson (2s), R Smith, Stone (4s); 6, Bull (2s), Cole (3s), D Edwards, Hopkinson, Latchford (1s), Le Tissier (4s), Martyn (1s), McMahon (2s), Merrick, Norman, Rocastle (3s); 5, Corrigan, Devonshire, Eastham, Eckersley, R Ferdinand (4s), T Flowers, G Francis, J Froggatt, D Johnson, Labone, Marsh (2s), Milne, Mortensen, Palmer (1s), A Smith (1s), T Taylor (1s), D Thomas (3s), P Thompson, Withe

Scorers: 23, R Charlton (1 pen), 22, Lineker (2 pens); 18, Shearer (2 pens); 17, Greaves; 16, Hurst (3 pens); Platt (3 pens); 10, Channon (3 pens), Keegan, Peters; 9, T Taylor; 8, Haynes, Lofthouse, B Robson; 7, Chivers, Douglas, Gascoigne; 6, Beardsley, Hoddle, Hunt, D Johnson, F Lee, Macdonald, Sheringham (1 pen), R Smith, Wilshaw, Woodcock; 5, Anderton, J Barnes, Bell, Bentley, Clarke (2 pens), Connelly, Finney, Scholes; 4, J Charlton, Mariner, Neal (2 pens), Paine, Pearce, R Robson; 3, Atyeo, Blissett, Coppell, L Ferdinand, R Flowers (2 pens), Fowler, G Francis, T Francis, Mortensen, Peacock, Ramsey (pens), Waddle, Webb, own goals, 2, Adams, Baker, P Barnes, Broadis, Brooks, Bull, Butcher, J Byrne, Currie, D Edwards, Elliott, Grainger, Hateley, Hitchens, Latchford, McDermott (1 pen), McManaman, Milburn, Mullen, Owen, J S Pearson, Perry, Rimmer, Royle, A Smith, Stone, D V Watson, V Watson, Wignall, I Wright; 1, A'Court, R Allen, V Anderson, Ball, Barclay, Bastin, Beattie, Bowers, Bradley, Brook, Brooking, Camsell, Carter, Chamberlain, Cowans, Crawford, Crooks, L Dixon, J Froggatt, R Froggatt, Hassall, Hinton, Hunter, Jack, Kelly, R Kennedy, Kevan, Lawler, R Lee, Le Saux, Mabbutt, Merson, O'Grady, Palmer, Parry, Pickering, Pointer, Revie, Sansom, Sewell, Shackleton, Steven, Stiles, Summerbee, Tueart, W Walker, Waring, Weller, Wilkins, Withe, Worthington

EPSOM and EWELL
FA Vase final
19/04/75 lost to Hoddesdon Town 1-2

ESSEX
FA County Youth Cup final 2nd leg
20/05/50 beat Middlesex 2-1 aet

EVERTON
FA Cup final
29/04/33 beat Man City 3-0
14/05/66 beat Sheffield W 3-2
18/05/68 lost to WBA 0-1 aet
19/05/84 beat Watford 2-0
18/05/85 lost to Man Utd 0-1 aet
10/05/86 lost to Liverpool 1-3
20/05/89 lost to Liverpool 2-3 aet
20/05/95 beat Man Utd 1-0
League/Milk Cup final
12/03/77 drew with Aston Villa 0-0
25/03/84 drew with Liverpool 0-0 aet
Simod/Zenith Cup final
30/04/89 lost to Nottingham F 3-4 aet
07/04/91 lost to Crystal Palace 1-4 aet
Charity Shield
18/08/84 beat Liverpool 1-0
10/08/85 beat Man Utd 2-0
16/08/86 drew with Liverpool 1-1
01/08/87 beat Coventry 1-0
13/08/95 beat Blackburn 1-0
League Centenary Tournament
1st round: 16/04/88 drew with Wolves 1-1 (won 3-2 on pens), **quarter-final:** - 16/04/88 lost to Man Utd 0-1

	P	W	D	L	F	A
FA Cup	8	4	0	4	12	10
League/Milk Cup	2	0	2	0	0	0
Simod/Zenith Cup	2	0	0	2	4	8
Charity Shield	5	4	1	0	6	1
v Liverpool	5	1	2	2	5	7
Full match Total	17	8	3	6	22	19
League Centenary	2	0	1	1	1	2

Most appearances: 11, Ratcliffe (1s); 10, Sharp, Southall; 9, Sheedy, Steven; 7, Heath (2s), Reid; 6, Bracewell, Mountfield, Stevens, Watson (1s); 5, Van den Hauwe
Scorers: 2, Cottee, Heath, McCall, Sharp, Trebilcock; 1, Clarke, Dean, Dunn, Gray, Lineker, Rideout, Samways, Stein, Steven, Temple, Warzycha, own goal
International appearances
England: 18, Wilson (1s); 15, Ball (1s); 8, Stevens; 6, Latchford (1s), Steven (2s); 5, Labone; 3, Cottee (s); Lineker, Reid (1s), Watson; 2, Barmby (s), Hinchcliffe, Keown, Newton, West; 1, Bracewell, Dean, Dobson, Johnson, Pickering, Royle, Sagar, Unsworth, Wright
N Ireland: 1, Bingham, Clements, Hamilton, Hill
Scotland: 2, Collins; 1, Hartford, Hutchison, Rioch, Weir, Wood
Wales: 2, Davies, Ratcliffe, Vernon; 1, Smallman, Southall
Republic of Ireland: 1, Donovan, Farrell, Sheedy
Nigeria: 1, Amokachi
Poland: 1, Warzycha
International Scorers: England: 3, Lineker; 2, Latchford; 1, Ball, Pickering, Royle, Steven
Scotland: 1, Hutchison

FALKIRK
International appearances
N Ireland: 1, Wilson
International Scorers: N Ireland: 2, Wilson

FIFA (see also REST OF THE WORLD)
FA 90th Anniversary Match (Rest of Europe)
21/10/53 drew with England 4-4
FA Centenary Match (Rest Of The World)
23/10/63 lost to England 1-2

	P	W	D	L	F	A
FA 90th Anniversary	1	0	1	0	4	4
FA Centenary	1	0	0	1	1	2
Total	2	0	1	1	5	6

Scorers: 2, Boniperti, Kubala (1 pen); 1, Law

FINCHLEY
Middlesex Charity Cup final
12/05/43 beat Southall 1-0

FINLAND
World Cup Qualifying
13/10/76 lost to England 1-2
17/10/84 lost to England 0-5

	P	W	D	L	F	A
World Cup Q	2	0	0	2	1	7
Total	2	0	0	2	1	7

Scorers: 1, Nieminen

FIORENTINA (see ITALY)

FLEETWOOD TOWN
FA Vase final
27/04/85 lost to Halesown Town 1-3

FOOTBALL LEAGUE
League Centenary Match
08/08/87 beat Rest of the World 3-0

FOREST GREEN ROVERS
FA Trophy final
15/05/99 lost to Kingstonian 0-1
FA Vase final
08/05/82 beat Rainworth Miners Welfare 3-0

	P	W	D	L	F	A
FA Trophy	1	0	0	1	0	1
FA Vase	1	1	0	0	3	0
Total	2	1	0	1	3	1

FRANCE
World Cup
13/07/66 drew with Mexico 1-1
20/07/66 lost to England 0-2
Internationals
27/11/57 lost to England 0-4
12/03/69 lost to England 0-5
19/02/92 lost to England 0-2
10/02/99 beat England 2-0
Wartime
26/05/45 drew with England 2-2
U-17
22/05/90 beat England 3-1
U-16
16/08/86 beat England 1-0
Schoolboy
06/04/74 lost to England 2-5
05/06/76 lost to England 1-6
04/03/78 drew with England 3-3
10/03/90 drew with England 1-1
11/06/94 lost to England 1-2

	P	W	D	L	F	A
World Cup	2	0	1	1	1	3
Internationals	4	1	0	3	2	11
v England	5	1	0	4	2	13
Total (official)	6	1	1	4	3	14
Wartime	1	0	1	0	2	2
v England (Senior Total)	6	1	1	4	4	15
Senior Total	7	1	2	4	5	16
U-17	1	1	0	0	3	1
U-16	1	1	0	0	1	0
Schoolboy	5	0	2	3	8	17

Most appearances: 3, Bonnel, Bosquier, J Djorkaeff
Scorers: 2, Anelka; 1, Hausser
FIFA appearances
  Rest of World: 1, Kopa
Clubs
Lens
European Cup
  25/11/98 beat Arsenal 1-0
  Monaco
  British & Irish International appearances
  England: 3, Hoddle (s); 2, Hateley (s)
Nantes
  British & Irish International appearances
  Scotland: 1, Johnston
Olympique Marseille
  British & Irish International appearances
  England: 8, Waddle (2s); 2, Steven

FRANKFURT (see GERMANY)

FULHAM
FA Cup final
  03/05/75 lost to West Ham 0-2
International appearances
  England: 22, Haynes; 19, Cohen; 1, Jezzard, Langley, Taylor
  Scotland: 1, Leggat
  Wales: 1, Davies
  Republic of Ireland: 1, Peyton
  International Scorers: England: 8, Haynes

GENOA (see ITALY)

GEORGIA (see also USSR)
World Cup Qualifying
  30/04/97 lost to England 0-2

GERMANY
World Cup Qualifying
  07/10/00 beat England 1-0
European Championship semi-final
  26/06/96 drew with England 1-1 (won 6-5 on pens)
European Championship final
  30/06/96 beat Czech Republic 2-1 iet
International
  11/09/91 beat England 1-0
University
  07/01/37 lost to Great Britain 0-1
Schoolboy
  05/06/93 drew with England 0-0
  10/06/95 beat England 4-2
  07/06/97 lost to England 1-2

World Cup final (West)
  30/07/66 lost to England 2-4 aet
European Championship quarter-final 1st leg (West)
  29/04/72 beat England 3-1
Internationals (West)
  01/12/54 lost to England 1-3
  23/02/66 lost to England 0-1
  12/03/75 lost to England 0-2
  13/10/82 beat England 2-1
European Amateur Championship (West)
  31/10/73 lost to England 0-1
Schoolboy (West)
  25/04/59 lost to England 0-2
  30/04/62 beat England 2-1
  25/04/64 drew with England 1-1
  30/04/66 lost to England 1-2
  27/04/68 beat England 2-1
  16/05/70 lost to England 0-3
  20/05/72 lost to England 0-4
  01/06/74 lost to England 0-4
  18/06/77 beat England 2-1
  09/06/79 drew with England 2-2
  13/06/81 beat England 2-1
  19/03/83 lost to England 0-1
  16/03/85 beat England 1-0
  14/03/87 lost to England 0-2
  10/06/89 beat England 3-1
  08/06/91 beat England 3-1
Internationals (East)
  25/11/70 lost to England 1-3
  12/09/84 lost to England 0-1

	P	W	D	L	F	A
World Cup Q	1	1	0	0	1	0
European Championship	2	1	1	0	3	2
International	1	1	0	0	1	0
Senior Total	4	3	1	0	5	2
University	1	0	0	1	0	1
Schoolboy	3	1	1	1	5	4
World Cup (West)	1	0	0	1	2	4
European Champs (West)	1	1	0	0	3	1
Internationals (West)	4	1	0	3	3	7
Senior Total (West)	6	2	0	4	8	12
Amateur (West)	1	0	0	1	0	1
Schoolboy (West)	16	7	2	7	19	27
Internationals (East)	2	0	0	2	1	4
Total (East)	2	0	0	2	1	4

Most appearances: 3, Bode (1s), Hassler (1s), Scholl, Ziege (1s)
Most appearances (West): 4, Beckenbauer
Scorers: 2, Bierhoff; 1, Hamann, Kuntz, Riedle
Scorers (West): 2, Rummenigge; 1, Beck, Haller, Hoeness, Muller, Netzer, Weber
Scorers (East): 1, Vogel
FIFA appearances
Rest of Europe
  1, Posipal
  Rest of World: 1, Schnellinger, Seeler (s)
Clubs
Bayern Munich
  Wembley International Tournament
  13/08/88 lost to Milan 0-1
  14/08/88 lost to Arsenal 0-3

	P	W	D	L	F	A
International Tournament	2	0	0	2	0	4
Total	2	0	0	2	0	4

Borussia Dortmund
British & Irish International appearances
Scotland: 1, MacLeod
Cologne
British & Irish International appearances
England: 10, Woodcock (2s)
British & Irish International Scorers: England: 2,
Woodcock
Eintracht Frankfurt
European Fairs Cup
26/10/55 lost to London 2-3
Hamburg
British & Irish International appearances
England: 11, Keegan
British & Irish International Scorers: England: 8,
Keegan
TSV Munich
European Cup-Winners Cup final
19/05/65 lost to West Ham 0-2
Werder Bremen
British & Irish International appearances
England: 1, Watson

GILLINGHAM
Second Division promotion play-off final
30/05/99 drew with Man City 2-2 aet (lost 3-1 on pens)
28/05/00 beat Wigan 3-2

	P	W	D	L	F	A
Play-offs	2	1	1	0	5	4
Total	2	1	1	0	5	4

GLACIER SPORTS
Wembley Hospital Cup final
22/02/30 lost to Harrow St Mary's 4-5 aet

GLENTORAN
International appearances
N Ireland: 1, Stewart

GOLDERS GREEN (see HENDON)

GREAT BRITAIN (see also REST of UNITED KINGDOM)
Olympic semi-final
11/08/48 lost to Yugoslavia 1-3
Olympic 3rd & 4th place: - 13/08/48 lost to Denmark
3-5
Olympic Q - 2nd leg (England)
12/05/56 drew with Bulgaria 3-3
Olympic Q - 1st leg
24/03/71 beat Bulgaria 1-0
University (England)
07/01/37 beat Germany 1-0

	P	W	D	L	F	A
Olympics	2	0	0	2	4	8
Olympic Qualifying	2	1	1	0	4	3
Olympic Total	4	1	1	2	8	11
University	1	1	0	0	1	0

GREECE
European Championship Qualifying
21/04/71 lost to England 0-3
30/03/83 drew with England 0-0
International
17/05/94 lost to England 0-5

	P	W	D	L	F	A
European Championship	2	0	1	1	0	3
International	1	0	0	1	0	5
Total	3	0	1	2	0	8

Most appearances: 2, Mitropoulos (1s)
Clubs
Panathinaikos
European Cup final
02/06/71 lost to Ajax Amsterdam 0-2
European Cup
30/09/98 lost to Arsenal 1-2

	P	W	D	L	F	A
European Cup final	1	0	0	1	0	2
European Cup	1	0	0	1	1	2
Total	2	0	0	2	1	4

GREENOCK MORTON
International appearances
Scotland: 2, Cowan; 1, Steel

GREENWICH
London Civil Defence Cup final
25/04/45 beat Paddington 10-1

GREENWICH TRAFALGAR
London Occupational League final
21/03/34 lost to Walthamstow Fellowship 0-1

GRESLEY ROVERS
FA Vase final
04/05/91 drew with Guisley 4-4 aet

GRIMSBY TOWN
Second Division promotion play-off final
24/05/98 beat Northampton 1-0
Auto Windscreens Shield final
19/04/98 beat Bournemouth 2-1 iet

	P	W	D	L	F	A
Promotion play-off	1	1	0	0	1	0
Auto Windscreens Shield	1	1	0	0	2	1
Total	2	2	0	0	3	1

GUISBOROUGH TOWN
FA Vase final
26/04/80 lost to Stamford 0-2

GUISELEY
FA Vase final
04/05/91 drew with Gresley Rovers 4-4 aet
25/04/92 lost to Wimborne Town 3-5

	P	W	D	L	F	A
FA Vase	2	0	1	1	7	9
Total	2	0	1	1	7	9

HALESOWEN TOWN
FA Vase final
30/04/83 lost to VS Rugby 0-1
27/04/85 beat Fleetwood Town 3-1
26/04/86 beat Southall 3-0

	P	W	D	L	F	A
FA Vase	3	2	0	1	6	2
Total	3	2	0	1	6	2

HAMBURG (see GERMANY)

HARROW ST MARY'S
Wembley Hospital Cup final
22/02/30 beat Glacier Sports 5-4 aet

HARWICH AND PARKESTON
FA Amateur Cup final
11/04/53 lost to Pegasus 0-6

HASTINGS AND ST LEONARDS
Southern Amateur League First Division
29/09/28 lost to Ealing Association 0-1

HEART OF MIDLOTHIAN
International appearances
  Scotland: 3, Anderson; 2, Walker; 1, Cumming,
  Harkness, Massie
  International Scorers: Scotland: 2, Walker (1 pen)

HENDON
FA Amateur Cup final
16/04/55 lost to Bishop Auckland 0-2
23/04/60 beat Kingstonian 2-1
24/04/65 beat Whitby Town 3-1
16/04/66 lost to Wealdstone 1-3
22/04/72 beat Enfield 2-0
Middlesex Charity Cup final
16/05/45 beat Tufnell Park 4-1 (Golders Green)
02/06/88 beat Wembley 2-0

	P	W	D	L	F	A
FA Amateur Cup	5	3	0	2	8	7
Middlesex Charity Cup	2	2	0	0	6	1
Total	7	5	0	2	14	8

HIBERNIAN
International appearances
  Scotland: 5, Reilly; 2, Johnstone; 1, Duncan, Dunn,
  Harper, MacLeod, Ormond, Rough, Smith
  England: 2, Baker
  N Ireland: 1, Parke
  International Scorers: Scotland: 5, Reilly; 1, Johnstone
  England: 1, Baker

HILLINGDON BOROUGH
FA Trophy final
01/05/71 lost to Telford 2-3

HODDESDON TOWN
FA Vase final
19/04/75 beat Epsom & Ewell 2-1

HONITON CLYST
Carlsberg Pub Cup final
09/05/98 drew with West Hendon Ex-Servicemen 1-1
(lost 3-1 on pens)

HOUNSLOW TOWN
FA Amateur Cup final
14/04/62 drew with Crook Town 1-1 aet

HUDDERSFIELD TOWN
FA Cup final
21/04/28 lost to Blackburn 1-3
26/04/30 lost to Arsenal 0-2
30/04/38 lost to PNE 0-1 aet
Second Division promotion play-off final
28/05/95 beat Bristol Rovers 2-1
Autoglass Trophy final
24/04/94 drew with Swansea 1-1 aet (lost 3-1 on pens)

	P	W	D	L	F	A
FA Cup	3	0	0	3	1	6
Promotion play-off	1	1	0	0	2	1
Autoglass Trophy	1	0	1	0	1	1
Total	5	1	1	3	4	8

  Most appearances: 2, Billy, Booth, Bullock, Cowan,
  Dunn (s), Francis, Goodall, Jackson, Kelly, Scully, Smith,
  T Wilson
  Scorers: 1, Billy, Booth, Jackson, Logan
International appearances
  England: 8, R Wilson; 2, Goodall, Hassall, Staniforth; 1,
  Kelly, Metcalfe, Smith, Taylor, Wadsworth, Willingham,
  T Wilson
  N Ireland: 3, Nicholson
  Scotland: 2, Jackson
  International Scorers: England: 1, Hassall, Kelly
  Scotland: 3, Jackson

HULL CITY
International appearances
  N Ireland: 1, Neill
  Wales: 1, Jarvis, Roberts (s)
  International Scorers: N Ireland: 1, Neill

HUNGARY
World Cup Qualifying
18/11/81 lost to England 0-1
European Championship Qualifying
27/04/83 lost to England 0-2
Internationals
25/11/53 beat England 6-3
05/05/65 lost to England 0-1
24/05/78 lost to England 1-4
12/09/90 lost to England 0-1
18/05/96 lost to England 0-3
U-18 Schoolboy
25/03/00 beat England 1-0

	P	W	D	L	F	A
World Cup Q	1	0	0	1	0	1
European Championship	1	0	0	1	0	2
Internationals	5	1	0	4	7	12
Senior Total	7	1	0	6	7	15
U-18 Schoolboy	1	0	0	1	0	1

  Most appearances: 3, Garaba, Torocsik (1s), Toth
  Scorers: 3, Hidegkuti; 2, Puskas; 1, Bozsik, Nagy
FIFA appearances
  Rest of World: 1, Puskas (s)

ILFORD
FA Amateur Cup final
12/04/58 lost to Woking 0-3
20/04/74 lost to Bishop's Stortford 1-4

	P	W	D	L	F	A
FA Amateur Cup	2	0	0	2	1	7
Total	2	0	0	2	1	7

INTERNAZIONALE (see ITALY)

IPSWICH TOWN

FA Cup final
06/05/78 beat Arsenal 1-0
Charity Shield
12/08/78 lost to Nottingham F 0-5
First Division promotion play-off final
29/05/00 beat Barnsley 4-2
Southern Amateur League First Division
13/10/28 beat Ealing Association 4-0

	P	W	D	L	F	A
FA Cup	1	1	0	0	1	0
Charity Shield	1	0	0	1	0	5
Play-off	1	1	0	0	4	2
Southern Amateur League	1	1	0	0	4	0
Total	4	3	0	1	9	7

Most appearances: 2, Burley, Cooper, Mariner, Mills, Talbot, Wark, Woods
Scorers: 1, Mowbray, Naylor, Osborne, Reuser, Stewart
International appearances
England: 13, Butcher, Mills (1s); 10, Mariner (2s); 4, Beattie; 3, Osman; 2, Crawford, Johnson; 1, Gates, Talbot, Viljoen
N Ireland: 3, Hunter; 1, Hamilton
Scotland: 2, Wark (1s); 1, Burley
Republic of Ireland: 1, O'Callaghan (s)
Netherlands: 1, Muhren
International Scorers: England: 4, Mariner; 3, Johnson; 2, Butcher; 1, Beattie, Crawford
Scotland: 1, Wark

ISRAEL

U-16
20/08/88 drew with England 1-1

ITALY

World Cup Qualifying
16/11/77 lost to England 0-2
12/02/97 beat England 1-0
Internationals
06/05/59 drew with England 2-2
14/11/73 beat England 1-0
15/11/89 drew with England 0-0
Schoolboy
31/05/86 lost to England 1-2
28/05/88 lost to England 1-4
06/06/92 drew with England 1-1

	P	W	D	L	F	A
World Cup Q	2	1	0	1	1	2
Internationals	3	1	2	0	3	2
Senior Total	5	2	2	1	4	4
Schoolboy	3	0	1	2	3	7

Most appearances: 2, Benetti, Causio, Facchetti, Maldini, Zoff
Scorers: 1, Brighenti, Capello, Mariani, Zoff
FIFA appearances
Rest of Europe: 1, Boniperti
FIFA Scorers: Rest of Europe: 2, Boniperti
Clubs
Ascoli
Anglo-Italian Cup final
19/03/95 lost to Notts County 1-2

Bari
British & Irish International appearances
England: 3, Platt
British & Irish International Scorers: England: 1, Platt
Brescia
Anglo-Italian Cup final
20/03/94 beat Notts County 1-0
Cremonese
Anglo-Italian Cup final
27/03/93 beat Derby County 3-1
Fiorentina
European Cup
27/10/99 beat Arsenal 1-0
Genoa
Anglo-Italian Cup final
17/03/96 beat Port Vale 5-2
Internazionale
British & Irish International appearances
England: 11, Ince; 1, Hitchens
Republic of Ireland: 1, Brady
British & Irish International Scorers: England: 1, Hitchens
Republic of Ireland: 1, Brady
Juventus
British & Irish International appearances
England: 4, Platt
British & Irish International Scorers: England: 6, Platt
Lazio
British & Irish International appearances
England: 8, Gascoigne (2s)
British & Irish International Scorers: England: 3, Gascoigne
AC Milan
European Cup final
22/05/63 beat Benfica 2-1
Wembley International Tournament
13/08/88 beat Bayern Munich 1-0
14/08/88 beat Spurs 2-1

	P	W	D	L	F	A
European Cup	1	1	0	0	2	1
International Tournament	2	2	0	0	3	1
Total	3	3	0	0	5	2

Scorers: 2, Altafini
British & Irish International appearances
England: 7, Hateley (2s), Wilkins (1s); 2, Blissett (1s)
British & Irish International Scorers: England: 2, Hateley
Parma
European Cup-Winners Cup final
12/05/93 beat Royal Antwerp 3-1
Scorers: 1, Cuoghi, Melli, Minotti
Sampdoria
European Cup final
20/05/92 lost to Barcelona 0-1 aet
Makita Tournament
semi-final: - 10/08/90 drew with Real Sociedad 1-1 (won 5-3 on pens); **final:** - 11/08/90 beat Arsenal 1-0

	P	W	D	L	F	A
European Cup	1	0	0	1	0	1
Makita Tournament	2	1	1	0	2	1
Total	3	1	1	1	2	2

British & Irish International appearances
England: 9, Platt; 8, Francis (1s); 4, Walker
Scotland: 1, Souness
British & Irish International Scorers: England: 5, Platt
(2 pens); 1, Francis
Scotland: 1, Souness (pen)

JAPAN
Umbro Cup
335, 03/06/95 lost to England 1-2
Scorers: 1, Ihara

JUVENTUS (see ITALY)

KETTERING TOWN
FA Trophy final
19/05/79 lost to Stafford Rangers 0-2
13/05/00 lost to Kingstonian 2-3

	P	W	D	L	F	A
FA Trophy	2	0	0	2	2	5
Total	2	0	0	2	2	5

KIDDERMINSTER HARRIERS
FA Trophy final
09/05/87 drew with Burton Albiion 0-0 aet
11/05/91 lost to Wycombe W 1-2
14/05/95 lost to Woking 1-2 aet

	P	W	D	L	F	A
FA Trophy	3	0	1	2	2	4
Total	3	0	1	2	2	4

KILMARNOCK
International appearances
   Scotland: 1, Nibloe, Smith

KINGSTONIAN
FA Amateur Cup final
23/04/60 lost to Hendon 1-2
FA Trophy final
15/05/99 beat Forest Green Rovers 1-0
13/05/00 beat Kettering 3-2

	P	W	D	L	F	A
FA Amateur Cup	1	0	0	1	1	2
FA Trophy	2	2	0	0	4	2
Total	3	2	0	1	5	4

KNOWSLEY UNITED
Women's League Cup final
29/05/93 lost to Arsenal 0-3

LEATHERHEAD
FA Trophy final
29/04/78 lost to Altrincham 1-3

LEEDS UNITED
FA Cup final
01/05/65 lost to Liverpool 1-2 aet
11/04/70 drew with Chelsea 2-2 aet
06/05/72 beat Arsenal 1-0
05/05/73 lost to Sunderland 0-1
League Cup/Coca-Cola Cup final
02/03/68 beat Arsenal 1-0
27/03/96 lost to Aston Villa 0-3
Charity Shield
10/08/74 drew with Liverpool 1-1 (lost 6-5 on pens)
08/08/92 beat Liverpool 4-3

League Centenary Tournament
1st round: - 16/04/88 lost to Nottingham F 0-3

	P	W	D	L	F	A
FA Cup	4	1	1	2	4	5
League Cup/Coca-Cola Cup	2	1	0	1	1	3
Charity Shield	2	1	1	0	5	4
Full match Total	8	3	2	3	10	12
League Centenary	1	0	0	1	0	3

Most appearances: 6, Bremner, Giles, Hunter; 5, E Gray, Lorimer, Reaney
Scorers: 3, Cantona; 1, Bremner, Charlton, Cherry, Clarke, Cooper, Dorigo, Jones
International appearances
   England: 21, Charlton; 13, Hunter (1s); 11, Cherry (2s); 10, Clarke (2s), Cooper, Madeley; 8, Batty (1s); 6, Currie (1s), Martyn (1s), 3, Dorigo; 2, Reaney (1s); 1, Barnes (s), Copping, Edwards, Hart, Jones, O'Grady, , Peacock, Sproston, Stephenson, Wilcox
   N Ireland: 1, Cush
   Scotland: 4, Bremner; 2, F Gray, Jordan (s), McQueen; 1, Collins, Graham, E Gray, Lorimer, McAllister
   Wales: 3, Sprake; 2, Charles, Flynn, Harris (1s), Yorath; 1, Stevenson
   France: 1, Cantona
   International Scorers: England: 5, Clarke (2 pens); 4, Charlton; 1, Currie, Hunter, O'Grady, Peacock
   Scotland: 1, McQueen
   Wales: 3, Charles

LEEK TOWN
FA Trophy final
19/05/90 lost to Barrow 0-3

LEICESTER CITY
FA Cup final
30/04/49 lost to Wolves 1-3
06/05/61 lost to Spurs 0-2
25/05/63 lost to Man Utd 1-3
26/04/69 lost to Man City 0-1
Coca-Cola/Worthington Cup final
06/04/97 drew with Middlesbrough 1-1 aet
21/03/99 lost to Spurs 0-1
27/02/00 beat Tranmere 2-1
Second/First Division promotion play-off final
25/05/92 lost to Blackburn 0-1
31/05/93 lost to Swindon 3-4
30/05/94 beat Derby County 2-1
27/05/96 beat Crystal Palace 2-1 aet

	P	W	D	L	F	A
FA Cup	4	0	0	4	2	9
Coca-Cola/Worthington Cup	3	1	1	1	3	3
Promotion play-offs	4	2	0	2	7	7
Total	11	3	1	7	12	19

Most appearances: 6, S Walsh, 3, Heskey, Izzet, Lennon
Scorers: 3, S Walsh; 2, Elliott; 1, Griffiths, Heskey, Keyworth
International appearances
   England: 19, Banks; 12, Shilton; 4, Worthington (2s); 3, Whitworth; 2, Heskey (1s), Weller; 1, Lineker
   N Ireland: 3, O'Neill; 2, Cunningham; 1, Dougan
   Wales: 1, Leek, Rodrigues
   Sweden: 1, Kaamark

International Scorers: England: 1, Lineker, Weller, Worthington
Wales: 1, Leek

LENS (see FRANCE)

LEYTON
FA Amateur Cup final
26/04/52 lost to Walthamstow Avenue 1-2 aet

LEYTON ORIENT
Third Division promotion play-off final
29/05/99 lost to Scunthorpe 0-1
League Third Division South (Clapton Orient)
22/11/30 beat Brentford 3-0
06/12/30 beat Southend United 3-1

	P	W	D	L	F	A
Promotion play-off	1	0	0	1	0	1
Third Division South	2	2	0	0	6	1
Total	3	2	0	1	6	2

International appearances
Wales: 1, Lucas

LEYTONSTONE
FA Amateur Cup final
20/04/68 beat Chesham United 1-0

LINFIELD
International appearances
N Ireland: 1, Barr

LIVERPOOL
European Cup final
187, 10/05/78 beat Bruges 1-0
FA Cup final
29/04/50 lost to Arsenal 0-2
01/05/65 beat Leeds 2-1 aet
08/05/71 lost to Arsenal 1-2 aet
04/05/74 beat Newcastle Utd 3-0
21/05/77 lost to Man Utd 1-2
10/05/86 beat Everton 3-1
14/05/88 lost to Wimbledon 0-1
20/05/89 beat Everton 3-2 aet
09/05/92 beat Sunderland 2-0
11/05/96 lost to Man Utd 0-1
League/Milk/Littlewoods/Coca-Cola Cup final
18/03/78 drew with Nottingham F 0-0 aet
14/03/81 drew with West Ham 1-1 aet
13/03/82 beat Spurs 3-1 aet
26/03/83 beat Man Utd 2-1 aet
25/03/84 drew with Everton 0-0 aet
05/04/87 lost to Arsenal 1-2
02/04/95 beat Bolton 2-1
Charity Shield
10/08/74 drew with Leeds 1-1 (won 6-5 on pens)
14/08/76 beat Southampton 1-0
13/08/77 drew with Man Utd 0-0
11/08/79 beat Arsenal 3-1
09/08/80 beat West Ham 1-0
21/08/82 beat Spurs 1-0
20/08/83 lost to Man Utd 0-2
18/08/84 lost to Everton 0-1
16/08/86 drew with Everton 1-1

20/08/88 beat Wimbledon 2-1
12/08/89 beat Arsenal 1-0
18/08/90 drew with Man Utd 1-1
08/08/92 lost to Leeds 3-4
Makita Tournament
semi-final: - 29/07/89 beat Dynamo Kiev 2-0; final:
30/07/89 lost to Arsenal 0-1
League Centenary Tournament
1st round: - 16/04/88 drew with Newcastle Utd 0-0 (lost 1-0 on pens)

	P	W	D	L	F	A
European Cup	1	1	0	0	1	0
FA Cup	10	5	0	5	15	12
League Cup	7	3	3	1	9	6
Charity Shield	13	6	4	3	15	12
Makita Tournament	2	1	0	1	2	1
v Arsenal	6	2	0	4	6	8
v Everton	5	2	2	1	7	5
v Man Utd	6	1	2	3	4	7
Full match Total	33	16	7	10	42	31
League Centenary	1	0	1	0	0	0

Most appearances: 18, Grobbelaar, Rush (3s); 16, Hansen; 15, Dalglish (2s), Whelan; 14, Neal; 11, Clemence, P B Thompson; 9, Barnes, A Kennedy, McMahon, Souness; 8, Callaghan (1s), Case (1s), Heighway (1s), E Hughes, R Kennedy, Lawrenson, McDermott, Nicol, Venison (1s); 7, Beardsley, Johnston (2s), Lee, Molby (2s); 6, Burrows, Houghton, Smith; 5, Ablett, Aldridge (1s)
Scorers: 10, Rush; 4, Aldridge; 3, McDermott, Whelan; 2, Barnes (pens), Dalglish, Heighway, Keegan, A Kennedy, McManaman; 1, Beardsley, Boersma, Case, Hunt, Johnston, St John, Saunders, Thomas, Toshack, own goal
International appearances
England: 28, E Hughes, 23, Barnes (1s), Clemence, 21, Neal; 18, McManaman (4s), 17, Hunt; 14, Beardsley (3s); 13, Keegan; 12, P B Thompson; 11, McDermott (1s); 10, Fowler (5s); 9, Redknapp (4s); 8, R Jones, Owen (2s); 7, R Kennedy, Lee; 6, McMahon (2s); 5, Milne, P Thompson; 4, Ince (1s); 3, Johnson, Lawler, Lloyd, Wright; 2, Callaghan, Scales; 1, A'Court, Barmby, Byrne, Gerrard, Heskey (s), James, A Kennedy, Lindsay, Melia, Ruddock, Smith
Scotland: 2, Liddell, Nicol, St John, Souness; 1, Dalglish, Younger
Wales: 3, Toshack; 2, Rush (1s); 1, J Jones
Republic of Ireland: 2, Heighway; 1, Beglin, Houghton, Lawrenson, Staunton, Whelan
Czech Republic: 1, Berger
Denmark: 1, Molby
Germany: 1, Hamann, Ziege (s)
International Scorers: England: 6, Hunt; 5, Barnes, Beardsley; 4, Neal (2 pens); 3, Fowler, Johnson; 2, McDermott (1 pen), Owen; 1, A'Court, Keegan, R Kennedy, Lawler
Scotland: 1, Liddell, St John
Wales: 2, Toshack; 1, Rush
Germany: 1, Hamann

LONDON
European Fairs Cup
26/10/55 beat Frankfurt 3-2

Schoolboy Charity match
09/03/29 beat Middlesex 5-1

	P	W	D	L	F	A
European Fairs Cup	1	1	0	0	3	2
Senior Total	1	1	0	0	3	2
Schoolboy	1	1	0	0	5	1

LONDON UNIVERSITY
Inter-Varsity match
26/01/29 lost to Cambridge Uni 0-3

LUTON TOWN
FA Cup final
02/05/59 lost to Nottingham F 1-2
FA Cup semi-final
09/04/94 lost to Chelsea 0-2
Littlewoods Cup final
24/04/88 beat Arsenal 3-2
09/04/89 lost to Nottingham F 1-3
Simod Cup final
27/03/88 lost to Reading 1-4
League Centenary Tournament
1st round: - 16/04/88 lost to Man Utd 0-2

	P	W	D	L	F	A
FA Cup final	1	0	0	1	1	2
FA Cup semi-final	1	0	0	1	0	2
FA Cup Total	2	0	0	2	1	4
Littlewoods Cup	2	1	0	1	4	5
Simod Cup	1	0	0	1	1	4
Full match Total	5	1	0	4	6	13
League Centenary	1	0	0	1	0	2

Most appearances: 3, Black (1s), Breacker, Foster, Grimes (1s), Harford, Preece, Wilson
Scorers: 2, Harford, B Stein; 1, Pacey, Wilson
International appearances
England: 2, Baynham; 1, Harford, Hill
N Ireland: 5, Donaghy; 1, Bingham
Wales: 1, Price
Republic of Ireland: 1, Grealish
USA: 1, Sommer (s)
Bulgaria: 1, Guentchev (s)
International Scorers: N Ireland: 1, Bingham

LUXEMBOURG
World Cup Qualifying
30/03/77 lost to England 0-5
European Championship Qualifying
15/12/82 lost to England 0-9
04/09/99 lost to England 0-6

	P	W	D	L	F	A
World Cup Q	1	0	0	1	0	5
European Championship	2	0	0	2	0	15
Total	3	0	0	3	0	20

Most appearances: 2, Di Domenico, Dresch

MACCLESFIELD TOWN
FA Trophy final
02/05/70 beat Telford 2-0
13/05/89 lost to Telford 0-1 aet
19/05/96 beat Northwich V 3-1

	P	W	D	L	F	A
FA Trophy	3	2	0	1	5	2
Total	3	2	0	1	5	2

MALTA
European Championship Qualifying
12/05/71 lost to England 0-5

MANCHESTER CITY
FA Cup final
24/04/26 lost to Bolton 0-1
29/04/33 lost to Everton 0-3
28/04/34 beat Portsmouth 2-1
07/05/55 lost to Newcastle Utd 1-3
05/05/56 beat Birmingham C 3-1
26/04/69 beat Leicester 1-0
09/05/81 drew with Spurs 1-1 aet
FA Cup final replay
14/05/81 lost to Spurs 2-3
League Cup final
07/03/70 beat WBA 2-1 aet
02/03/74 lost to Wolves 1-2
28/02/76 beat Newcastle Utd 2-1
Full Members Cup final
23/03/86 lost to Chelsea 4-5
Second Division promotion play-off final
30/05/99 drew with Gillingham 2-2 aet (won 3-1 on pens)

	P	W	D	L	F	A
FA Cup	8	3	1	4	10	13
League Cup	3	2	0	1	5	4
Full Members Cup	1	0	0	1	4	5
Play-off	1	0	1	0	2	2
Total	13	5	2	6	21	24

Most appearances: 4, Booth, Corrigan, Doyle
Scorers: 2, Johnstone, Lillis (1 pen), Tilson; 1, P Barnes, Bell, Dickov, Doyle, Hayes, Horlock, Hutchison, Kinsey, Mackenzie, Pardoe, Reeves (pen), Tueart, Young, own goal
International appearances
England: 23, Bell (1s); 13, Lee, Watson; 6, P Barnes; 5, Corrigan; 4, Marsh (1s); 3, Royle (1s), Summerbee, Tueart (2s); 2, Broadis, Brook, Swift; 1, Bray, Channon, Doyle, Francis, Meadows, Reeves, Revie
N Ireland: 2, McIlroy (1s); 1, Crossan
Scotland: 2, Hartford; 1, Donachie, Johnstone, Law, McMullan
Wales: 2, Clarke, Paul, Sear
Republic of Ireland: 1, McCarthy, Quinn
Georgia: 1, Kinkladze
International Scorers: England: 6, Lee; 5, Bell; 2, P Barnes, Broadis; 1, Brook, Revie, Royle, Summerbee, Tueart, Watson
Republic of Ireland: 1, Quinn

MANCHESTER UNITED
European Cup final
29/05/68 beat Benfica 4-1 aet
FA Cup final
24/04/48 beat Blackpool 4-2
04/05/57 lost to Aston Villa 1-2
03/05/58 lost to Bolton 0-2
25/05/63 beat Leicester 3-1
01/05/76 lost to Southampton 0-1
21/05/77 beat Liverpool 2-1
12/05/79 lost to Arsenal 2-3

21/05/83 drew with Brighton 2-2 aet
18/05/85 beat Everton 1-0 aet
12/05/90 drew with Crystal Palace 3-3 aet
14/05/94 beat Chelsea 4-0
20/05/95 lost to Everton 0-1
11/05/96 beat Liverpool 1
22/05/99 beat Newcastle Utd 2-0

FA Cup final replay
26/05/83 beat Brighton 4-0
17/05/90 beat Crystal Palace 1-0

FA Cup semi-final
10/04/94 drew with Oldham 1-1 aet

Milk/Rumbelows/Coca-Cola Cup final
26/03/83 lost to Liverpool 1-2 aet
21/04/91 lost to Sheffield W 0-1
12/04/92 beat Nottingham F 1-0
27/03/94 lost to Aston Villa 1-3

Charity Shield
13/08/77 drew with Liverpool 0-0
20/08/83 beat Liverpool 2-0
10/08/85 lost to Everton 0-2
18/08/90 drew with Liverpool 1-1
07/08/93 drew with Arsenal 1-1 (won 5-4 on pens)
14/08/94 beat Blackburn 2-0
11/08/96 beat Newcastle Utd 4-0
03/08/97 drew with Chelsea 1-1 (won 4-2 on pens)
09/08/98 lost to Arsenal 0-3
01/08/99 lost to Arsenal 1-2
13/08/00 lost to Chelsea 0-2

League Centenary Tournament
1st round: - 16/04/88 beat Luton 2-0; **quarter-final:**
16/04/88 beat Everton 1-0; **semi-final:** 17/04/88 lost to
Sheffield W 1-2

	P	W	D	L	F	A
European Cup	1	1	0	0	4	1
FA Cup final	16	9	2	5	30	18
FA Cup semi-final	1	0	1	0	1	1
FA Cup Total	17	9	3	5	31	19
Milk/Rumbelows/						
Coca-Cola Cup	1	0	3	3	6	
Charity Shield	11	3	4	4	12	12
v Liverpool	6	3	2	1	7	4
Full match Total	33	14	7	12	52	38
League Centenary	3	2	0	1	4	2

Most appearances: 14, Irwin, Pallister, 13, Giggs (1s),
Hughes; 11, Bruce, Ince, Schmeichel, 10, Keane, McClair
(2s), Robson (2s),9, Albiston; 8, Scholes (2s); 7, Bailey,
Beckham (1s), Butt (1s), Sharpe (3s); 6, Cantona,
Cole (1s), Duxbury (1s), G Neville (2s), P Neville (1s),
Stapleton, Whiteside; 5, Coppell, Kanchelskis, Macari
(1s), May (1s), McQueen, Moran, Parker, Phelan (1s),
Sheringham (3s)
Scorers: 6, Hughes; 5, Cantona (3 pens), Robson; 3,
Whiteside; 2, Beckham, Charlton, Herd, McClair, Rowley;
1, J Anderson, Best, Blackmore, J Greenhoff, Ince,
Johnsen, Keane, Kidd, Law, Martin, McIlroy, McQueen,
Muhren (pen), J S Pearson, S Pearson, Scholes,
Sheringham, Stapleton, T Taylor, Wilkins
International appearances
England: 44, Charlton, 30 - Robson, 24, G Neville (1s);
19, Coppell (2s), 17, Beckham; 16, Stiles, 15, Wilkins

(1s); 13, Scholes (1s), 12, Byrne, P Neville (5s); 9,
B Greenhoff (1s), Pallister (2s); 7, Ince, J S Pearson
(2s), 6, Cole (3s), Edwards; 5, T Taylor (1s); 4, Butt
(2s), Connelly, Hill (3s), Sheringham (1s); 3, Duxbury,
Sadler; 2, Cockburn, Parker, Sharpe (1s), Webb (1s); 1,
V Anderson, Aston Snr , Bailey, Bradley, Kidd, S Pearson,
Phelan (s), Stepney, Wood
N Ireland: 5, McIlroy; 4, Nicholl; 3, McCreery, Whiteside;
2, Best, Gregg, C McGrath (1s); 1, Blanchflower,
Nicholson
Scotland: 3, Law, Macari (2s); 2, Jordan; 1, Crerand,
Delaney, Holton, Leighton, McQueen, Morgan
Republic of Ireland: 1, Daly, Grimes, Irwin, P McGrath,
Stapleton, Whelan
FIFA (Rest of the World): 1, Law
Denmark: 1, Schmeichel
International Scorers: England: 23, Charlton (1 pen); 9,
T Taylor; 8, Robson; 5, Scholes; 3, Coppell; 2, Edwards, J
S Pearson; 1, Bradley, Connelly, Sheringham, Wilkins
N Ireland: 1, Best
Scotland: 2, Law
Republic of Ireland: 1, Daly (pen)
FIFA (Rest of the World): 1, Law

MANSFIELD TOWN
Freight Rover Trophy final
24/05/87 drew with Bristol City 1-1 aet (won 5-4 on
pens)

MATLOCK TOWN
FA Trophy final
26/04/75 beat Scarborough 4-0

MERSEYSIDE
National Association of Youth Clubs Cup final
14/06/75 lost to Plymouth 1-3

MET POLICE AND CIVIL DEFENCE (see POLICE)
MEXICO
World Cup
13/07/66 drew with France 1-1
16/07/66 lost to England 0-2
19/07/66 drew with Uruguay 0-0
International
10/05/61 lost to England 0-8
29/03/97 lost to England 0-2

	P	W	D	L	F	A
World Cup	3	0	2	1	1	3
Internationals	2	0	0	2	0	10
Total	5	0	2	3	1	13

Most appearances: 4, Pena, Reyes
Scorers: 1, Borja

MIDDLESBROUGH
FA Cup final
17/05/97 lost to Chelsea 0-2
Coca-Cola Cup final
06/04/97 drew with Leicester 1-1 aet
29/03/98 lost to Chelsea 0-2 aet
Zenith Cup final
25/03/90 lost to Chelsea 0-1

	P	W	D	L	F	A
FA Cup	1	0	0	1	0	2
Coca-Cola Cup	2	0	1	1	1	3
Zenith Cup	1	0	0	1	0	1
Total	4	0	1	3	1	6

Most appearances: 3, Beck (2s), Festa, Mustoe, Pearson
Scorers: 1, Ravanelli
International appearances
England: 5, Barmby (3s); 4, McNeil; 2, Holliday, Ince, Mannion; 1, Camsell, Clough, Fenton, Gascoigne (s), Hardwick, Merson (s), Peacock, Webster
N Ireland: 3, Cochrane (2s); 2, McMordie, Platt
Scotland: 1, Cumming, Milne
Wales: 1, Mahoney, Nurse
Republic of Ireland: 1, Fitzsimons
Italy: 1, Ravanelli (s)
International Scorers: England: 2, Peacock; 1, Camsell
N Ireland: 1, Cochrane

MIDDLESEX
FA County Youth Cup final 2nd leg
20/05/50 lost to Essex 1-2 aet
Schoolboy Charity match
09/03/29 lost to London 1-5

	P	W	D	L	F	A
FA County Youth Cup	1	0	0	1	1	2
Youth Total	1	0	0	1	1	2
Schoolboy	1	0	0	1	1	5

MIDLAND BANK
Southern Amateur League First Division
20/10/28 beat Ealing Association 4-0

MILAN (see ITALY)

MILLWALL
Auto Windscreens Shield final
18/04/99 lost to Wigan 0-1
League South Cup final
07/04/45 lost to Chelsea 0-2

	P	W	D	L	F	A
Auto Windscreens Shield	1	0	0	1	0	1
League South Cup	1	0	0	1	0	2
Total	2	0	0	2	0	3

International appearances
N Ireland: 1, Hamilton

MOLDOVA (see also USSR)
World Cup Qualifying
360 - 10/09/97 lost to England 0-4

MONACO (see FRANCE)

MORECAMBE
FA Trophy final
27/04/74 beat DARTFORD 2-1

MOSSLEY
FA Trophy final
17/05/80 lost to Dagenham 1-2

MOTHERWELL
International appearances
Scotland: 2, Stevenson; 1, Craig, McCann, Quinn, Redpath, St John
International Scorers: Scotland: 1, Quinn

MUNICH (see GERMANY)

NANTES (see FRANCE)

NABC
British Junior Cup final
30/03/46 lost to ATC 2-4
19/03/49 drew with ATC 2-2 aet
13/05/50 beat ACF 4-1
19/05/51 beat ACF 4-2
10/05/52 beat ATC 5-3
09/05/53 beat ATC 3-1
08/05/54 lost to ATC 0-1
12/05/56 beat ACF 2-1

	P	W	D	L	F	A
British Junior Cup	8	5	1	2	22	15
v ATC	5	2	1	2	12	11
Total	8	5	1	2	22	15

NATIONAL POLICE and CIVIL DEFENCE (see POLICE)

NETHERLANDS
World Cup Qualifying
28/04/93 drew with England 2-2
European Championship
18/06/96 lost to England 1-4
Internationals
14/01/70 drew with England 0-0
09/02/77 beat England 2-0
25/05/82 lost to England 0-2
23/03/88 drew with England 2-2
Wartime
11/10/41 lost to Belgium 4-5
Youth
08/05/99 beat England 2-1
U-17
01/08/87 lost to England 1-3
Schoolboy
03/04/71 lost to England 1-5
07/04/73 lost to England 1-3
22/03/75 lost to England 0-4
27/03/82 lost to England 0-7
09/06/84 lost to England 1-4
08/03/86 lost to England 0-1
02/06/90 lost to England 0-1
07/03/92 drew with England 0-0

	P	W	D	L	F	A
World Cup Q	1	0	1	0	2	2
European Championship	1	0	0	1	1	4
Internationals	4	1	2	1	4	4
Total (official)	6	1	3	2	7	10
Wartime	1	0	0	1	4	5
Senior Total	7	1	3	3	11	15
Youth	1	1	0	0	2	1
U-17	1	0	0	1	1	3
Schoolboy	8	0	1	7	3	25

Most appearances: 3, Krol
Scorers: 2, Peters; 1, Bergkamp, Bosman, Kluivert, Van Vossen (pen), own goal
Clubs
Ajax Amsterdam
European Cup final

02/06/71 beat Panathinaikos 2-0
Scorers: 1, Van Dijk, own goal
PSV Eindhoven
British & Irish International appearances
Wales: 1, Deacy
Sparta Rotterdam
British & Irish International appearances
N Ireland: 1, Crossan

NEWCASTLE UNITED
FA Cup final
26/04/24 beat Aston Villa 2-0
23/04/32 beat Arsenal 2-1
28/04/51 beat Blackpool 2-0
03/05/52 beat Arsenal 1-0
07/05/55 beat Man City 3-1
04/05/74 lost to Liverpool 0-3
16/05/98 lost to Arsenal 0-2
22/05/99 lost to Man Utd 0-2
FA Cup semi-final
09/04/00 lost to Chelsea 1-2
League Cup final
28/02/76 lost to Man City 1-2
Charity Shield
11/08/96 lost to Man Utd 0-4
League Centenary Tournament
1st round: - 16/04/88 drew with Liverpool 0-0 (won 1-0 on pens); **quarter-final:** 16/04/88 lost to Tranmere 0-2

	P	W	D	L	F	A
FA Cup final	8	5	0	3	10	9
FA Cup semi-final	1	0	0	1	1	2
FA Cup Total	9	5	0	4	11	11
League Cup	1	0	0	1	1	2
Charity Shield	1	0	0	1	0	4
Full match Total	11	5	0	6	12	17
League Centenary	2	0	1	1	0	2

Most appearances: 4, Lee, Shearer
Scorers: 3, Milburn; 2, Allen; 1, Gowling, Hannah, Harris, Lee, Mitchell, G Robledo, Seymour
International appearances
England: 15, Shearer (1s); 11, Lee (3s); 10, Beardsley (1s); 8, Batty (1s); 5, Ferdinand (1s); 4, Dyer (2s), Howey, 3, Macdonald; 2, Milburn, Venison; 1, Barton (s), Spencer, Waddle, Weaver
N Ireland: 3, Cassidy; 2, Keith, McMichael, Stewart; 1, J Cowan (s), D Craig, McCreery
Scotland: 1, Brennan, W Cowan, Gallacher, Harris, Moncur, Pearson
Wales: 3, Davies; 1, Burton, Foulkes
Switzerland: 1, Hottiger
International Scorers: England: 8, Shearer (1 pen); 6, Macdonald; 2, Milburn; 1, Beardsley, Ferdinand, Lee
Wales: 1, Davies

NEWPORT COUNTY
International appearances
Wales: 1, Sherwood

NEW YORK COSMOS (see USA)

NIGERIA
International
16/11/94, lost to England 0-1

NORTHAMPTON TOWN
Second Division promotion play-off final
24/05/98 lost to Grimsby 0-1
Third Division promotion play-off final
24/05/97 beat Swansea 1-0

	P	W	D	L	F	A
Second Division Play-off	1	0	0	1	0	1
Third Division Play-off	1	1	0	0	1	0
Total	2	1	0	1	1	1

NORTHERN IRELAND
World Cup Qualifying
13/11/85 drew with England 0-0
European Championship Qualifying
22/11/67 lost to England 0-2
07/02/79 lost to England 0-4
15/10/86 lost to England 0-3
British Championship
02/11/55 lost to England 0-3
06/11/57 beat England 3-2
18/11/59 lost to England 1-2
22/11/61 drew with England 1-1
20/11/63 lost to England 3-8
10/11/65 lost to England 1-2
22/11/67 lost to England 0-2
21/04/70 lost to England 1-3
23/05/72 beat England 1-0
15/05/74 lost to England 0-1
11/05/76 lost to England 0-4
16/05/78 lost to England 0-1
20/05/80 drew with England 1-1
23/02/82 lost to England 0-4
04/04/84 lost to England 0-1
European Youth Tournament final
23/04/63 lost to England 0-4
Schoolboy
06/03/71 lost to England 0-1
Victory Shield
28/03/81 lost to England 0-4

	P	W	D	L	F	A
World Cup Q	1	0	1	0	0	0
European Championship	3	0	0	3	0	9
(includes one in British Championship)						
British Championship	15	2	2	11	12	32
Senior Total	18	2	3	13	12	39
European Youth Tournament	1	0	0	1	0	4
Victory Shield	1	0	0	1	0	4
Schoolboy Total	2	0	0	2	0	5

Most appearances: 9, Jennings, S McIlroy (1s); 6, Armstrong (1s), McCreery (2s), Neill, Nelson (1s), J Nicholl; 5, Bingham, Clements, Donaghy, J McIlroy, C Nicholl, M O'Neill (1s)
Scorers: 2, J McIlroy (1 pen), Wilson; 1, Best, Bingham, Cochrane, Crossan, Irvine, McCrory, Neill, Simpson

NORTH FERRIBY UNITED
FA Vase final
10/05/97 lost to Whitby Town 0-3

NORTH SHIELDS
FA Amateur Cup final
12/04/69 beat Sutton Utd 2-1

NORTHWICH VICTORIA
FA Trophy final
14/05/83 lost to Telford 1-2
12/05/84 drew with Bangor City 1-1 aet
19/05/96 lost to Macclesfield 1-3

	P	W	D	L	F	A
FA Trophy	3	0	1	2	3	6
Total	3	0	1	2	3	6

NORWAY
World Cup Qualifying
10/09/80 lost to England 0-4
14/10/92 drew with England 1-1
International
22/05/94 drew with England 0-0

	P	W	D	L	F	A
World Cup Q	2	0	1	1	1	5
International	1	0	1	0	0	0
Total	3	0	2	1	1	5

Most appearances: 2, H Berg (1s), Bratseth, Flo (1s), Ingebrigtsen (1s), Jakobsen, Nilsen, Rekdal, Sorloth (1s), Thorstvedt
Scorers: 1, Rekdal

NORWICH CITY
League/Milk Cup final
03/03/73 lost to Spurs 0-1
01/03/75 lost to Aston Villa 0-1
24/03/85 beat Sunderland 1-0

	P	W	D	L	F	A
League/Milk Cup	3	1	0	2	1	2
Total	3	1	0	2	1	2

Most appearances: 2, Forbes, Keelan, Stringer
Scorers: 1, own goal
International appearances
England: 1, Reeves, Watson
N Ireland: 1, O'Neill
Scotland: 1, MacDougall
Wales: 1, Davies

NOTTINGHAM FOREST
FA Cup final
02/05/59 beat Luton 2-1
18/05/91 lost to Spurs 1-2 aet
League/Littlewoods/Rumbelows Cup final
18/03/78 drew with Liverpool 0-0 aet
17/03/79 beat Southampton 3-2
15/03/80 lost to Wolves 0-1
09/04/89 beat Luton 3-1
29/04/90 beat Oldham 1-0
12/04/92 lost to Man Utd 0-1
Simod/Zenith Cup final
30/04/89 beat Everton 4-3 aet
29/03/92 beat Southampton 3-2 aet
Charity Shield
12/08/78 beat Ipswich 5-0
League Centenary Tournament
1st round: - 16/04/88 beat Leeds 3-0; **quarter-final:** 16/04/88 drew with Aston Villa 0-0 (won 1-0 on pens); **semi-final:** 17/04/88 drew with Tranmere 2-2 (won 1-0 on pens); **final:** 17/04/88 drew with Sheffield W 0-0 (won 3-2 on pens)

	P	W	D	L	F	A
FA Cup	2	1	0	1	3	3
League/Littlewoods/ Rumbelows	6	3	1	2	7	5
Simod/Zenith Cup	2	2	0	0	7	5
Charity Shield	1	1	0	0	5	0
Full match Total	11	7	1	3	22	13
League Centenary	4	1	3	0	5	2

Most appearances: 6, Clough, Walker; 5, Laws (2s), Pearce
Scorers: 2, Birtles, Chapman, Clough (1 pen), S Gemmill, O'Neill, Parker; 1, Black, Dwight, Jemson, Lloyd, Pearce, Robertson, Webb, Th Wilson, Withe, Woodcock
International appearances
England: 40 - Pearce (2s); 19, Walker (2s); 8, Anderson, Webb; 7, Hodge (3s), Shilton, Stone (4s); 4, Francis (1s); 3, Clough (1s); 2, Collymore (1s), Hinton, Woodcock; 1, Birtles (s), Cooper, Davenport (s), Storey-Moore, Wignall
N Ireland: 3, O'Neill (1s); 2, Jackson (1s), O'Kane; 1, Campbell, Fleming
Scotland: 1, Cormack, F Gray, Robertson
Wales: 1, Hennessey, Rees (s)
Norway: 1, Bohinen, Haland (s)
International Scorers: England: 4, Pearce; 3, Webb; 2, Stone, Wignall; 1, Hinton
Scotland: 1, Robertson (pen)

NOTTS COUNTY
Anglo-Italian Cup final
20/03/94 lost to Brescia 0-1
19/03/95 beat Ascoli 2-1
Second Division promotion play-off final
02/06/91 beat Brighton 3-1
Third/Second Division promotion play-off final
27/05/90 beat Tranmere 2-0
26/05/96 lost to Bradford City 0-2

	P	W	D	L	F	A
Anglo-Italian Cup	2	1	0	1	2	2
Second Division Play-off	1	1	0	0	3	1
Third/Second Division	2	1	0	1	2	2
Promotion play-offs Total	3	2	0	1	5	3
Total	5	3	0	2	7	5

International appearances
N Ireland: 1, O'Neill
Finland: 1, Lahtinen

OLD CHOLMELEIANS
Arthur Dunn Cup 2nd round replay
09/02/29 lost to Old Malvernians 2-4

OLDHAM ATHLETIC
FA Cup semi-final
324, 10/04/94 drew with Man Utd 1-1 aet
Littlewoods Cup final
283, 29/04/90 lost to Nottingham F 0-1

	P	W	D	L	F	A
FA Cup	1	0	1	0	1	1
Littlewoods Cup	1	0	0	1	0	1
Total	2	0	1	1	1	2

Most appearances: 2, Henry, Holden, Milligan
Scorers: 1, Pointon
International appearances
Norway: 1, Halle

OLD LYONIANS
Southern Amateur League First Division
08/12/28 beat Ealing Association 3-0

OLD MALVERNIANS
FA Amateur Cup 2nd round
12/01/29 lost to Barclays 1-2
Arthur Dunn Cup 2nd round replay
09/02/29 beat Old Cholmeleians 4-2

	P	W	D	L	F	A
FA Amateur Cup	1	0	0	1	1	2
Arthur Dunn Cup	1	1	0	0	4	2
Total	2	1	0	1	5	4

OLYMPIQUE MARSEILLE (see FRANCE)

OXFORD CITY
FA Vase final
13/05/95 lost to Arlesey Town 1-2

OXFORD UNITED
Milk Cup final
20/04/86 beat QPR 3-0
Scorers: 1, Charles, Hebberd, Houghton
International appearances
Wales: 1, Roberts (s)

OXFORD UNIVERSITY
Inter-Varsity
07/03/53 drew with Cambridge Uni 0-0
05/12/53 drew with Cambridge Uni 1-1
04/12/54 lost to Cambridge Uni 2-3
07/12/55 lost to Cambridge Uni 2-4
08/12/56 beat Cambridge Uni 4-1
07/12/57 drew with Cambridge Uni 1-1
06/12/58 drew with Cambridge Uni 1-1
05/12/59 lost to Cambridge Uni 2-6
03/12/60 drew with Cambridge Uni 2-2
09/12/61 lost to Cambridge Uni 0-2
08/12/62 lost to Cambridge Uni 2-5
07/12/63 lost to Cambridge Uni 2-4
05/12/64 beat Cambridge Uni 3-1
08/12/65 lost to Cambridge Uni 2-3
07/12/66 lost to Cambridge Uni 0-1
13/12/67 lost to Cambridge Uni 0-1
04/12/68 lost to Cambridge Uni 1-3
03/12/69 drew with Cambridge Uni 1-1
09/12/70 lost to Cambridge Uni 0-1
08/12/71 drew with Cambridge Uni 0-0
06/12/72 lost to Cambridge Uni 1-2
05/12/73 drew with Cambridge Uni 0-0
04/12/74 beat Cambridge Uni 3-1
03/12/75 beat Cambridge Uni 2-0
08/12/76 drew with Cambridge Uni 0-0
07/12/77 beat Cambridge Uni 4-0
06/12/78 lost to Cambridge Uni 1-2
05/12/79 beat Cambridge Uni 3-1
10/12/80 beat Cambridge Uni 2-0
09/12/81 beat Cambridge Uni 2-0
08/12/82 beat Cambridge Uni 4-2
07/12/83 drew with Cambridge Uni 2-2
12/12/84 lost to Cambridge Uni 2-4
11/12/85 lost to Cambridge Uni 0-2
10/12/86 lost to Cambridge Uni 3-4
09/12/87 lost to Cambridge Uni 1-2

	P	W	D	L	F	A
Inter-Varsity	36	9	10	17	56	63
Total	36	9	10	17	56	63

PADDINGTON
London Civil Defence Cup final
25/04/45 lost to Greenwich 1-10

PANATHINAIKOS (see GREECE)

PARMA (see ITALY)

PARTICK THISTLE
International appearances
Scotland: 2, Rough; 1, Davidson, McKenzie, McMullan

PEGASUS
FA Amateur Cup final
21/04/51 beat Bishop Auckland 2-1
11/04/53 beat Harwich & Parkeston 6-0

	P	W	D	L	F	A
FA Amateur Cup	2	2	0	0	8	1
Total	2	2	0	0	8	1

PETERBOROUGH
(old) **Third Division promotion play-off final**
24/05/92 beat Stockport County 2-1
(new) **Third Division promotion play-off final**
26/05/00 beat Darlington 1-0

	P	W	D	L	F	A
(old) Third Division Play-off	1	1	0	0	2	1
(new) Third Division Play-off	1	1	0	0	1	0
Total	2	2	0	0	3	1

International appearances
N Ireland: 1, Anderson
Wales: 1, Millington

PHILADELPHIA FURY (see USA)

PLYMOUTH
National Association of Youth Clubs Cup final
09/06/74 beat Sheffield 3-1
14/06/75 beat Merseyside 3-1

	P	W	D	L	F	A
NAYC Cup	2	2	0	0	6	2
Total	2	2	0	0	6	2

PLYMOUTH ARGYLE
Third Division promotion play-off final
25/05/96 beat Darlington 1-0
International appearances
Wales: 1, Shortt

POLAND
World Cup Qualifying
17/10/73 drew with England 1-1
03/06/89 lost to England 0-3
08/09/93 lost to England 0-3
09/10/96 lost to England 1-2
European Championship Qualifying
17/10/90 lost to England 0-2
27/03/99 lost to England 1-3

493

Youth
15/05/90 lost to England 0-3

	P	W	D	L	F	A
World Cup Q	4	0	1	3	2	9
European Championship	2	0	0	2	1	5
Senior Total	6	0	1	5	3	14
Youth	1	0	0	1	0	3

Most appearances: 3, Furtok, Kosecki (1s), K Warzycha (1s)

Scorers: 1, Brzeczek, Citko, Domarski

POLICE
Charity matches
(Met Police)
04/06/41 lost to RAF 3-6
06/05/42 lost to RAF 3-6
05/05/43 lost to RAF 3-4
(and Civil Defence)
10/05/44 lost to Combined Services 2-5
(National Police and Civil Defence)
09/05/45 lost to Combined Services 1-3

	P	W	D	L	F	A
Charity (Met Police)	3	0	0	3	8	16
Charity (and Civil Defence)	1	0	0	1	2	5
Charity (National & Defence)	1	0	0	1	1	3
Total	5	0	0	5	11	24

PORTO (see PORTUGAL)

PORTSMOUTH
FA Cup final
27/04/29 lost to Bolton 0-2
28/04/34 lost to Man City 1-2
29/04/39 beat Wolves 4-1
London War Cup final
30/05/42 lost to Brentford 0-2

	P	W	D	L	F	A
FA Cup	3	1	0	2	5	5
London War Cup	1	0	0	1	0	2
Total	4	1	0	3	5	7

Most appearances: 2, Barlow, Gilfillan, Guthrie, Mackie, Nichol, Parker, Rochford, J Smith, Thackeray, Walker, Weddle, Wharton. Worrall

Scorers: 2, Parker; 1, Anderson, Barlow, Rutherford

International appearances
England: 10, Dickinson; 5, Froggatt; 2, Phillips; 1, Hateley (s)
N Ireland: 1, Uprichard
International Scorers: England: 1, Froggatt

PORTUGAL
World Cup semi-final
26/07/66 lost to England 1-2
World Cup 3rd & 4th place
28/07/66 beat USSR 2-1
World Cup Qualifying
25/10/61 lost to England 0-2
European Championship Qualifying
20/11/74 drew with England 0-0
Internationals
07/05/58 lost to England 1-2
10/12/69 lost to England 0-1
12/12/95 drew with England 1-1
22/04/98 lost to England 0-3

	P	W	D	L	F	A
World Cup	2	1	0	1	3	3
World Cup Q	1	0	0	1	0	2
European Championship	1	0	1	0	0	0
Internationals	4	0	1	3	2	7
v England	7	0	2	5	3	11
Total	8	1	2	5	5	12

Most appearances: 4, Coluna
Scorers: 2, Eusebio (pens); 1, Alves, Duarte, Torres
FIFA appearances
Rest of World: 1, Eusebio
Clubs
Benfica
European Cup final
22/05/63 lost to AC Milan 1-2
29/05/68 lost to Man Utd 1-4 aet

	P	W	D	L	F	A
European Cup	2	0	0	2	2	6
Total	2	0	0	2	2	6

Most appearances: 2, Augusto, Coluna, Cruz, Eusebio, Humberto, Simoes, Torres
Scorers: 1, Eusebio, Graca
Porto
Makita Tournament
semi-final: - 29/07/89 lost to Arsenal 0-1; **3rd & 4th place:** - 30/07/89 lost to Dynamo Kiev 0-1

	P	W	D	L	F	A
Makita Tournament	2	0	0	2	0	2
Total	2	0	0	2	0	2

PORT VALE
Anglo-Italian Cup final
17/03/96 lost to Genoa 2-5
Second Division promotion play-off final
30/05/93 lost to WBA 0-3
Autoglass Trophy final
22/05/93 beat Stockport County 2-1

	P	W	D	L	F	A
Anglo-Italian Cup	1	0	0	1	2	5
Promotion play-off	1	0	0	1	0	3
Autoglass Trophy	1	1	0	0	2	1
Total	3	1	0	2	4	9

International appearances
N Ireland: 1, Bingham
Republic of Ireland: 1, O'Keefe

POULTON VICTORIA
Carlsberg Pub Cup final
10/05/97 beat Corby Caledonian 3-1

PRESTON NORTH END
FA Cup final
01/05/37 lost to Sunderland 1-3
30/04/38 beat Huddersfield T 1-0 aet
01/05/54 lost to WBA 2-3
02/05/64 lost to West Ham 2-3
Third Division promotion play-off final
28/05/94 lost to Wycombe W 2-4
League War Cup final
10/05/41 drew with Arsenal 1-1

	P	W	D	L	F	A
FA Cup	4	1	0	3	6	9
Promotion play-off	1	0	0	1	2	4
League War Cup	1	0	1	0	1	1
Total	6	1	1	4	9	14

Most appearances: 3, A Beattie, Gallimore, H O'Donnell, Shankly

Scorers: 1, Bryson, Dawson, Holden, McLaren, Morrison, Mutch (pen), F O'Donnell, Raynor, Wayman

International appearances
England: 16, Finney; 1, Thompson
Scotland: 3, Docherty; 1, A Beattie, Cunningham, James, McLaren, Mutch, F O'Donnell, Shankly, T Smith
International Scorers: England: 5, Finney
Scotland: 2, James; 1, Docherty, McLaren

PSV EINDHOVEN (see NETHERLANDS)

QUEEN OF THE SOUTH
International appearances
Scotland: 1, Houliston

QUEENS PARK
International appearances
Scotland: 1, Harkness

QUEENS PARK RANGERS
FA Cup final
22/05/82 drew with Spurs 1-1 aet
FA Cup final replay
27/05/82 lost to Spurs 0-1
League/Milk Cup final
04/03/67 beat WBA 3-2
20/04/86 lost to Oxford Utd 0-3
Middlesex Charity Cup final (Juniors)
17/05/44 lost to Tufnell Park 2-3

	P	W	D	L	F	A
FA Cup	2	0	1	1	1	2
League/Milk Cup	2	1	0	1	3	5
Senior Total	4	1	1	2	4	7
Middlesex Charity Cup	1	0	0	1	2	3

Most appearances: 3, Fenwick
Scorers: 1, Fenwick, Lazarus, Marsh, Morgan
International appearances
England: 7, Parker (1s); 5, Francis, Thomas (3s); 4, Fenwick, Ferdinand (1s); 2, Bowles, Gillard; 1, Clement, Gregory, Marsh (s), Seaman (s), Sinton
N Ireland: 2, McDonald; 1, McCreery (s), Stewart
Scotland: 1, Masson
Republic of Ireland: 1, Byrne (s), Givens, Waddock
International Scorers: England: 3, Francis; 2, Ferdinand

RAF UXBRIDGE
Middlesex Charity Cup final
03/06/42 lost to Wealdstone 2-5 aet

RAINWORTH MINERS WELFARE
FA Vase final
08/05/82 lost to Forest Green Rovers 0-3

RAITH ROVERS
International appearances
Scotland: 1, Morris

RANGERS
International appearances
FIFA (Rest of the World): 1, Baxter (s)
Scotland: 5, Young; 4, Caldow, Greig, Morton; 3, Brown, Cox, Henderson, Wilson, Woodburn; 2, Archibald, Jardine,

Marshall, McCoist (1s), Waddell; 1, Baxter, Buchanan, Craig, Cunningham, Dawson, Durie, Ferguson, Fleming, Forsyth, Goram, Gough, Gray, Hamilton, Hendry, Johnstone, Kennedy, McCall, McCann, McColl, McKinnon, Meiklejohn, Parlane, Shaw, Shearer, J Simpson, Stein, Venters
England: 15, Butcher; 13, Gascoigne; 9, Stevens; 7, Woods (3s); 2, Steven
N Ireland: 1, McClelland, Nicholl, W Simpson
Sweden: 1, Persson
International Scorers: Scotland: 2, Baxter (1 pen), Fleming; 1, Stein, Wilson
England: 2, Gascoigne
N Ireland: 1, W Simpson

READING
Simod Cup final
27/03/88 beat Luton 4-1
First Division promotion play-off final
29/05/95 lost to Bolton 3-4 aet

	P	W	D	L	F	A
Simod Cup	1	1	0	0	4	1
Promotion play-off	1	0	0	1	3	4
Total	2	1	0	1	7	5

Scorers: 1, Beavon (pen), Gilkes, Nogan, Quinn, Smillie, Tait, A Williams
International appearances
Bulgaria: 1, Mikhailov

REAL MADRID (see SPAIN)

REAL MALLORCA (see SPAIN)

REAL SOCIEDAD (see SPAIN)

REPUBLIC OF IRELAND
World Cup Qualifying
08/05/57 lost to England 1-5
European Championship Qualifying
06/02/80 lost to England 0-2
27/03/91 drew with England 1-1
Internationals
08/09/76 drew with England 1-1
26/03/85 lost to England 1-2

	P	W	D	L	F	A
World Cup Q	1	0	0	1	1	5
European Championship	2	0	1	1	1	3
Internationals	2	0	1	1	2	3
Total	5	0	2	3	4	11

Most appearances: 4, D O'Leary (1s)
Scorers: 1, Brady, Curtis, Daly (pen), Quinn

REST OF EUROPE (see FIFA)

REST OF THE WORLD (see also FIFA)
League Centenary Match
08/08/87 lost to League 0-3

REST OF UNITED KINGDOM
Youth
06/11/63 lost to England 2-5

ROMANIA
World Cup Qualifying
29/04/81 drew with England 0-0
11/09/85 drew with England 1-1
Internationals

15/01/69 drew with England 1-1
12/10/94 drew with England 1-1

U-23
16/10/57 lost to England 2-3

	P	W	D	L	F	A
World Cup Q	2	0	2	0	1	1
Internationals	2	0	2	0	2	2
Senior Total	4	0	4	0	3	3
U-23	1	0	0	1	2	3

Most appearances: 2, Camataru, Hagi, Negrila, Stefanescu
Scorers: 1, Camataru, Dumitrache (pen), Dumitrescu

ROMFORD
FA Amateur Cup final
23/04/49 lost to Bromley 0-1

ROTHERHAM UNITED
Auto Windscreens Shield final
14/04/96 beat Shrewsbury Town 2-1

ROYAL AIR FORCE
Charity matches
04/06/41 beat Met Police 6-3
06/05/42 beat Met Police 6-2
05/05/43 beat Met Police 4-3

	P	W	D	L	F	A
Charity matches	3	3	0	0	16	8
Total	3	3	0	0	16	8

ROYAL ANTWERP (see BELGIUM)

RUNCORN
FA Trophy final
17/05/86 lost to Altrincham 0-1
09/05/93 lost to Wycombe W 1-4
21/05/94 lost to Woking 1-2

	P	W	D	L	F	A
FA Trophy	3	0	0	3	2	7
Total	3	0	0	3	2	7

ST HELENS TOWN
FA Vase final
25/04/87 beat Warrington Town 3-2

ST MIRREN
International appearances
Scotland: 1, Miller

SAMPDORIA (see ITALY)

SAN MARINO
World Cup Qualifying
311, 17/02/93 lost to England 0-6

SAUDI ARABIA
International
23/05/98 drew with England 0-0

SCANDINAVIA
U-16
12/08/89 lost to England 1-2

SCARBOROUGH
FA Trophy final
28/04/73 beat Wigan 2-1 aet
26/04/75 lost to Matlock Town 0-4

24/04/76 beat Stafford Rangers 3-2 aet
14/05/77 beat Dagenham 2-1

	P	W	D	L	F	A
FA Trophy	4	3	0	1	7	8
Total	4	3	0	1	7	8

SCOTLAND
European Championship
15/06/96 lost to England 0-2
European Championship Play-off 2nd leg
17/11/99 beat England 1-0
European Championship Qualifying
15/04/67 beat England 3-2
British Championship
12/04/24 drew with England 1-1
31/03/28 beat England 5-1
05/04/30 lost to England 2-5
09/04/32 lost to England 0-3
14/04/34 lost to England 0-3
04/04/36 drew with England 1-1
09/04/38 beat England 1-0
12/04/47 drew with England 1-1
09/04/49 beat England 3-1
14/04/51 beat England 3-2
18/04/53 drew with England 2-2
02/04/55 lost to England 2-7
06/04/57 lost to England 1-2
11/04/59 lost to England 0-1
15/04/61 lost to England 3-9
06/04/63 beat England 2-1
10/04/65 drew with England 2-2
15/04/67 beat England 3-2
10/05/69 lost to England 1-4
22/05/71 lost to England 1-3
19/05/73 lost to England 0-1
24/05/75 lost to England 1-5
04/06/77 beat England 2-1
26/05/79 lost to England 1-3
23/05/81 beat England 1-0
01/06/83 lost to England 0-2
Rous Cup
23/04/86 lost to England 1-2
21/05/88 lost to England 0-1
Wartime
04/10/41 lost to England 0-2
17/01/42 lost to England 0-3
10/10/42 drew with England 0-0
19/02/44 lost to England 2-6
14/10/44 lost to England 2-6
Amateur
15/03/52 beat England 2-1
British Amateur Championship
27/03/54 beat England 4-1
24/03/56 lost to England 2-4
29/03/58 beat England 3-2
Schoolboy
15/04/50 lost to England 2-8
05/04/52 lost to England 0-1
03/04/54 lost to England 0-1
21/04/56 beat England 2-1
26/04/58 lost to England 1-3

30/04/60 lost to England 3-5
03/04/65 lost to England 0-3
29/04/67 beat England 2-0
21/03/70 lost to England 0-2
09/06/73 beat England 4-2
07/06/75 beat England 1-0
19/03/77 lost to England 0-2
27/05/78 lost to England 0-3
07/06/80 beat England 5-4
05/06/82 drew with England 0-0
11/06/83 drew with England 3-3
17/03/84 lost to England 0-1

Victory Shield
30/05/87 drew with England 1-1
09/03/91 lost to England 1-2
13/03/93 beat England 2-1

U-16 Girls
04/07/99 lost to England 0-5

	P	W	D	L	F	A
European Championship	1	0	0	1	0	2
Play-off 2nd leg	1	1	0	0	1	0
Qualifying	1	1	0	0	3	2
(also British Championship)						
European Championship Total	3	2	0	1	4	4
British Championship	26	8	5	13	39	63
Rous Cup	2	0	0	2	1	3
Total (official)	30	9	5	16	41	68
Wartime	5	0	1	4	4	17
Senior Total	35	9	6	20	45	85
British Amateur Champs	3	2	0	1	9	7
Amateur Total	4	3	0	1	11	8
Victory Shield	3	1	1	1	4	4
Schoolboy Total	20	6	3	11	27	43
U-16 Girls	1	0	0	1	0	5

Most appearances: 5, Reilly, Young
Scorers: 5, Reilly; 3, A Jackson; 2, Baxter (1 pen), Fleming, James, D Law, Walker (1 pen); 1, Curran, Dalglish, Docherty, D Hutchison, R Johnstone, Lennox, Liddell, Mackay, Mason, McCalliog, McLaren, McQueen, Quinn, Ring, Rioch (pen), Robertson (pen), St John, Souness (pen), Steel, Stein, Wark, Wilson, own goal

FIFA appearances
Rest of World: 1, Baxter (s), D Law
FIFA Scorers: Rest of World: 1, D Law

SCUNTHORPE UNITED
Fourth/Third Division promotion play-off final
23/05/92 drew with Blackpool 1-1 aet (lost 4-3 on pens)
29/05/99 beat Leyton Orient 1-0
League Youth Alliance Cup final
16/04/00 drew with WBA 0-0 (lost 3-2 on pens)

	P	W	D	L	F	A
Promotion play-offs	2	1	1	0	2	1
Senior Total	2	1	1	0	2	1
League Youth Alliance Cup	1	0	1	0	0	0

SHAMROCK ROVERS
International appearances
Republic of Ireland: 1, Mackey, O'Leary (s)

SHEFFIELD
FA Vase final
30/04/77 drew with Billericay T 1-1 aet

SHEFFIELD
National Association of Youth Clubs Cup final
09/06/74 lost to Plymouth 1-3

SHEFFIELD UNITED
FA Cup final
25/04/25 beat Cardiff 1-0
25/04/36 lost to Arsenal 0-1
FA Cup semi-final
03/04/93 lost to Sheffield W 1-2 aet
First Division promotion play-off final
26/05/97 lost to Crystal Palace 0-1

	P	W	D	L	F	A
FA Cup final	2	1	0	1	1	1
FA Cup semi-final	1	0	0	1	1	2
FA Cup Total	3	1	0	2	2	3
Promotion play-off	1	0	0	1	0	1
Total	4	1	0	3	2	4

Scorers: 1, Cork, Tunstall
International appearances
England: 4, Currie, Shaw; 3, Hodgkinson; 2, Barclay, Grainger; 1, Tunstall
Scotland: 1, Forbes
Wales: 2, Hockey; 1, Powell, Reece
Republic of Ireland: 1, Ringstead
Norway: 1, Flo, Nilsen
International Scorers: England: 2, Grainger; 1, Barclay, Currie

SHEFFIELD WEDNESDAY
FA Cup final
27/04/35 beat WBA 4-2
14/05/66 lost to Everton 2-3
15/05/93 drew with Arsenal 1-1 aet
FA Cup final replay
20/05/93 lost to Arsenal 1-2 aet
FA Cup semi-final
03/04/93 beat Sheffield Utd 2-1 aet
Rumbelows/Coca-Cola Cup final
21/04/91 beat Man Utd 1-0
18/04/93 lost to Arsenal 1-2
League Centenary Tournament
1st round: - 16/04/88 drew with Crystal Palace 0-0 (won 2-1 on pens); **quarter-final:** 16/04/88 drew with Wigan 1-1 (won 3-2 on pens); **semi-final:** 17/04/88 beat Man Utd 2-1; **final:** - 17/04/88 drew with Nottingham F 0-0 (lost 3-2 on pens)

	P	W	D	L	F	A
FA Cup final	4	1	1	2	8	8
FA Cup semi-final	1	1	0	0	2	1
FA Cup Total	5	2	1	2	10	9
Rumbelows/Coca-Cola Cup	2	1	0	1	2	2
Full match Total	7	3	1	3	12	11
League Centenary	4	1	3	0	3	2

Most appearances: 5, Harkes, Hirst (2s), Nilsson, Sheridan
Scorers: 2, Rimmer, Waddle; 1, Bright, Ford, Harkes, Hirst, Hooper, McCalliog, Palethorpe, Sheridan
International appearances
England: 11, Springett; 9, Swan; 8, Woods; 5, Palmer (1s); 3, Froggatt; 2, Blenkinsop, Hinchcliffe, Strange; 1, Hirst, Marsden, Quixall, Rimmer, Sewell, Young

N Ireland: 2, Worthington (1s); 1, Clements
Scotland: 1, McCalliog
Wales: 2, Rodrigues
Romania: 1, Petrescu
Sweden: 1, Alexandersson (s)
International Scorers: England: 2, Rimmer; 1, Froggatt, Palmer, Sewell
Scotland: 1, McCalliog

SHREWSBURY TOWN
Auto Windscreens Shield final
14/04/96 lost to Rotherham 1-2
International appearances
N Ireland: 1, McLaughlin

THE SIX
EEC Celebration match
03/01/73 lost to The Three 0-2

SIZEWELL
Carlsberg Pub Cup final
16/05/99 beat West Hendon Ex-Servicemen 2-0

SKELMERSDALE
FA Amateur Cup final
22/04/67 drew with Enfield 0-0 aet
24/04/71 beat Dagenham 4-1

	P	W	D	L	F	A
FA Amateur Cup	2	1	1	0	4	1
Total	2	1	1	0	4	1

SLOUGH TOWN
FA Amateur Cup final
14/04/73 lost to Walton and Hersham 0-1

SOUTHALL
FA Vase final
26/04/86 lost to Halesowen Town 0-3
Middlesex Charity Cup final
12/05/43 lost to Finchley 0-1

	P	W	D	L	F	A
FA Vase	1	0	0	1	0	3
Middlesex Charity Cup	1	0	0	1	0	1
Total	2	0	0	2	0	4

SOUTHAMPTON
FA Cup final
170 - 01/05/76 beat Man Utd 1-0
League Cup final
193, 17/03/79 lost to Nottingham F 2-3
Zenith Cup final
303, 29/03/92 lost to Nottingham F 2-3 aet
Charity Shield
172, 14/08/76 lost to Liverpool 0-1

	P	W	D	L	F	A
FA Cup	1	1	0	0	1	0
League Cup	1	0	0	1	2	3
Zenith Cup	1	0	0	1	2	3
Charity Shield	1	0	0	1	0	1
Total	4	1	0	3	5	7

Most appearances: 3, Holmes, Peach
Scorers: 1, Holmes, Le Tissier, Moore, Peach, Stokes
International appearances
England: 19, Channon; 16, Shilton; 9, Watson; 7, Paine,

Wright; 6, Le Tissier (4s); 3, Keegan; 2, S C Williams; 1, Armstrong, Shearer
N Ireland: 4, Nicholl; 1, Clarke
Wales: 3, Davies; 2, S G Williams
International Scorers: England: 10, Channon (3 pens); 4, Paine; 1, Keegan, Shearer, Watson
Wales: 1, Davies

SOUTHEND UNITED
League Third Division South
06/12/30 lost to Clapton Orient 1-3
International appearances
N Ireland: 1, McCrory
International Scorers: N Ireland: 1, McCrory

SOUTHPORT
FA Trophy final
17/05/98 lost to Cheltenham 0-1

SPAIN
European Championship quarter-final
03/04/68 lost to England 0-1 (1st leg)
22/06/96 drew with England 0-0 (lost 4-2 on pens)
Internationals
30/11/55 lost to England 1-4
26/10/60 lost to England 2-4
24/05/67 lost to England 0-2
25/03/81 beat England 2-1
U-19
25/05/91 drew with England 1-1
Schoolboy
09/03/96 beat England 3-2

	P	W	D	L	F	A
European Championship	2	0	1	1	0	1
Internationals	4	1	0	3	5	11
Senior Total	6	1	0	4	5	12
U-19	1	0	1	0	1	1
Schoolboy	1	1	0	0	3	2

Most appearances: 2, Amancio, Gallego, Gento, Grosso, Pirri
Scorers: 1, Arieta, Del Sol, Satrustegui, Suarez, Zamora
FIFA appearances
Rest of Europe: 1, Kubala, Navarro
Rest of World: 1, Di Stefano, Gento
FIFA Scorers: Rest of Europe: 2, Kubala (1 pen)
Clubs
Barcelona
European Cup final
20/05/92 beat Sampdoria 1-0 aet
European Cup
19/10/99 beat Arsenal 4-2

	P	W	D	L	F	A
European Cup final	1	1	0	0	1	0
European Cup	1	1	0	0	4	2
Total	2	2	0	0	5	2

Scorers: 1, Koeman
British & Irish International appearances
England: 10, Lineker
British & Irish International Scorers: England: 10, Lineker
Real Madrid
British & Irish International appearances

England: 2, McManaman; 1, Cunningham
British & Irish International Scorers: England: 2, McManaman
Real Mallorca
British & Irish International appearances
N Ireland: 1, Armstrong
Real Sociedad
Makita Tournament
semi-final: - 10/08/90 drew with Sampdoria 1-1 (lost 5-3 on pens); **3rd & 4th place:** - 11/08/90 beat Aston Villa 1-0

	P	W	D	L	F	A
Makita Tournament	2	1	1	0	2	1
Total	2	1	1	0	2	1

British & Irish International appearances
Republic of Ireland: 1, Aldridge

SPARTA ROTTERDAM (see NETHERLANDS)

STAFFORD RANGERS
FA Trophy final
15/04/72 beat Barnet 3-0
24/04/76 lost to Scarborough 2-3 aet
19/05/79 beat Kettering 2-0

	P	W	D	L	F	A
FA Trophy	3	2	0	1	7	3
Total	3	2	0	1	7	3

STAMFORD
FA Vase final
10/04/76 lost to Billericay T 0-1 aet
26/04/80 beat Guisborough Town 2-0
28/04/84 lost to Stansted 2-3

	P	W	D	L	F	A
FA Vase	3	1	0	2	4	4
Total	3	1	0	2	4	4

STANSTED
FA Vase final
28/04/84 beat Stamford 3-2

STOCKHOLM (see SWEDEN)

STOCKPORT COUNTY
Third/Second Division promotion play-off final
24/05/92 lost to Peterborough 1-2
29/05/94 lost to Burnley 1-2
Autoglass Trophy final
16/05/92 lost to Stoke 0-1
22/05/93 lost to Port Vale 1-2

	P	W	D	L	F	A
Promotion play-offs	2	0	0	2	2	4
Autoglass Trophy	2	0	0	2	1	3
Total	4	0	0	4	3	7

STOKE CITY
League Cup final
142, 04/03/72 beat Chelsea 2-1
Autoglass Trophy/Auto Windscreens Shield final
16/05/92 beat Stockport County 1-0
16/04/00 beat Bristol City 2-1

	P	W	D	L	F	A
League Cup	1	1	0	0	2	1
Autoglass/Auto Windscreens	2	2	0	0	3	1
Total	3	3	0	0	5	2

Scorers: 1, Conroy, Eastham, Kavanagh, Stein, Thorne
International appearances
England: 12, Banks; 4, Chamberlain (3s); 2, Allen, Franklin, Hudson, Matthews, Shilton; 1, Pejic, Watson
N Ireland: 2, S McIlroy; 1, Elder, J McIlroy
Wales: 4, Mahoney; 1, Berry (s), Thomas
Republic of Ireland: 1, Conroy
International Scorers: England: 1, Chamberlain

SUDBURY TOWN
FA Vase final
06/05/89 drew with Tamworth 1-1 aet

SUNDERLAND
FA Cup final
01/05/37 beat PNE 3-1
05/05/73 beat Leeds 1-0
09/05/92 lost to Liverpool 0-2
Milk Cup final
24/03/85 lost to Norwich 0-1
Second/First Division promotion play-off final
28/05/90 lost to Swindon 0-1
25/05/98 drew with Charlton 4-4 aet (lost 7-6 on pens)
League Centenary Tournament
1st round: - 16/04/88 drew with Wigan 0-0 (lost 2-1 on pens)

	P	W	D	L	F	A
FA Cup	3	2	0	1	4	3
Milk Cup	1	0	0	1	0	1
Promotion play-offs	2	0	1	1	4	5
Full match Total	6	2	1	3	8	9
League Centenary	1	0	1	0	0	0

Most appearances: 3, Bennett
Scorers: 2, Quinn; 1, Burbanks, Carter, Gurney, Porterfield
International appearances
England: 7, Watson; 2, Phillips (s), Shackleton; 1, Anderson, Buchan, Carter, Grainger, Gray (s), Towers (s)
N Ireland: 3, Harvey; 2, Bingham; 1, Crossan, Parke
Scotland: 1, Baxter, Clunas, Connor, Wright
Wales: 2, Daniel; 1, Ford, James (s)
International Scorers: England: 1, Shackleton
N Ireland: 1, Crossan
Wales: 2, Ford

SUTTON UNITED
FA Amateur Cup final
04/05/63 lost to Wimbledon 2-4
12/04/69 lost to North Shields 1-2
FA Trophy final
16/05/81 lost to Bishop's Stortford 0-1

	P	W	D	L	F	A
FA Amateur Cup	2	0	0	2	3	6
FA Trophy	1	0	0	1	0	1
Total	3	0	0	3	3	7

SWANSEA
Third Division promotion play-off final
24/05/97 lost to Northampton 0-1
Autoglass Trophy final
24/04/94 drew with Huddersfield T 1-1 aet (won 3-1 on pens)

	P	W	D	L	F	A
Promotion play-off	1	0	0	1	0	1
Autoglass Trophy	1	0	1	0	1	1
Total	2	0	1	1	1	2

International appearances
Wales: 3, Allchurch; 2, Evans, R James, Phillips; 1, Charles, Curtis, Giles (s), L James, B Jones, C Jones, King, Mahoney, Nurse, Toshack

SWEDEN
World Cup Qualifying
19/10/88 drew with England 0-0
European Championship Qualifying
05/06/99 drew with England 0-0
Internationals
28/10/59 beat England 3-2
22/05/68 lost to England 1-3
Olympic semi-final
10/08/48 beat Denmark 4-2
Olympic final
13/08/48 beat Yugoslavia 3-1
Women
23/05/89 beat England 2-0

	P	W	D	L	F	A
World Cup Q	1	0	1	0	0	0
European Championship	1	0	1	0	0	0
Internationals	2	1	0	1	4	5
v England	4	1	2	1	4	5
Olympics	2	2	0	0	7	3
Women	1	1	0	0	2	0

Most appearances: 2, R Nilsson
Scorers: 2, Simonsson; 1, R Andersson, Salomonsson
FIFA appearances
Rest of Europe
1, G Nordahl
Clubs
AIK Stockholm
European Cup
22/09/99 lost to Arsenal 1-3

SWINDON TOWN
League Cup final
124, 15/03/69 beat Arsenal 3-1 aet
Second/First Division promotion play-off final
28/05/90 beat Sunderland 1-0
31/05/93 beat Leicester 4-3

	P	W	D	L	F	A
League Cup	1	1	0	0	3	1
Promotion play-offs	2	2	0	0	5	3
Total	3	3	0	0	8	4

Scorers: 2, Rogers; 1, Bodin (pen), Hoddle, Maskell, McLoughlin, Smart, Taylor
International appearances
Wales: 4, Thomas
Norway: 1, Fjortoft

SWITZERLAND
World Cup Qualifying
19/11/80 lost to England 1-2
European Championship
08/06/96 drew with England 1-1
European Championship Qualifying
10/11/71 drew with England 1-1
Internationals
09/05/62 lost to England 1-3
07/09/77 drew with England 0-0
15/11/95 lost to England 1-3
Schoolboy
22/03/80 lost to England 0-2
08/06/85 lost to England 0-2
12/03/94 lost to England 0-3

	P	W	D	L	F	A
World Cup Q	1	0	0	1	1	2
European Championship	1	0	1	0	1	1
Qualifying	1	0	1	0	1	1
European Champs Total	2	0	2	0	2	2
Internationals	3	0	1	2	2	6
Senior Total	6	0	3	3	5	10
Schoolboy	3	0	0	3	0	7

Most appearances: 3, Geiger
Scorers: 1, Allemann, Knup, Odermatt, Pfister, Turkyilmaz (Pen)

TAMWORTH
FA Vase final
06/05/89 drew with Sudbury Town 1-1 aet

TAUNTON TOWN
FA Vase final
07/05/94 lost to Diss Town 1-2 aet

TELFORD
FA Trophy final
02/05/70 lost to Macclesfield Town 0-2
01/05/71 beat Hillingdon Borough 3-2
14/05/83 beat Northwich V 2-1
07/05/88 drew with Enfield 0-0 aet
13/05/89 beat Maccesfield 1-0 aet

	P	W	D	L	F	A
FA Trophy	5	3	1	1	6	5
Total	5	3	1	1	6	5

THIRD LANARK
International appearances
Scotland: 1, Dewar, Mason
International Scorers: Scotland: 1, Mason

THE THREE
EEC Celebration match
03/01/73 beat The Six 2-0

TIVERTON TOWN
FA Vase final
08/05/93 lost to Bridlington Town 0-1
09/05/98 beat Tow Law Town 1-0
16/05/99 beat Bedlington Terriers 1-0

	P	W	D	L	F	A
FA Vase	3	2	0	1	2	1
Total	3	2	0	1	2	1

TORQUAY
Fourth/Third Division promotion play-off final
31/05/91 drew with Blackpool 2-2 aet (won 5-4 on pens)
22/05/98 lost to Colchester 0-1
Sherpa Van Trophy final
28/05/89 lost to Bolton 1-4

	P	W	D	L	F	A
Promotion play-offs	2	0	1	1	2	3
Sherpa Van Trophy	1	0	0	1	1	4
Total	3	0	1	2	3	7

TOTTENHAM HOTSPUR
FA Cup final
06/05/61 beat Leicester 2-0
05/05/62 beat Burnley 3-1
20/05/67 beat Chelsea 2-1
09/05/81 drew with Man City 1-1 aet
22/05/82 drew with QPR 1-1 aet
16/05/87 lost to Coventry 2-3 aet
18/05/91 beat Nottingham F 2-1 aet
FA Cup final replay
14/05/81 beat Man City 3-2
27/05/82 beat QPR 1-0
FA Cup semi-final
14/04/91 beat Arsenal 3-1
04/04/93 lost to Arsenal 0-1
League/Milk/Worthington Cup final
27/02/71 beat Aston Villa 2-0
03/03/73 beat Norwich 1-0
13/03/82 lost to Liverpool 1-3 aet
21/03/99 beat Leicester 1-0
Charity Shield
22/08/81 drew with Aston Villa 2-2
21/08/82 lost to Liverpool 0-1
10/08/91 drew with Arsenal 0-0
Wembley International Tournament
13/08/88 lost to Arsenal 0-4
14/08/88 lost to Milan 1-2

	P	W	D	L	F	A
FA Cup final	9	6	2	1	17	10
FA Cup semi-final	2	1	0	1	3	2
FA Cup Total	11	7	2	2	20	12
League/Milk/ Worthington Cup	4	3	0	1	5	3
Charity Shield	3	0	2	1	2	3
International Tournament	2	0	0	2	1	6
Total	20	10	4	6	28	24

Most appearances: 9, Hughton, Perryman (1s); 8, Hoddle, Mabbutt; 7, P Allen, Archibald, Galvin, Miller; 6, Clemence, Crooks; 5, Ardiles, Roberts, Samways, Stewart
Scorers: 3, own goals; 2, Chivers, Falco, Hoddle (1 pen), Lineker, Smith, Villa; 1, C Allen, Archibald, Blanchflower (pen), Coates, Crooks, Dyson, Fenwick, Gascoigne, Greaves, Nielsen, Robertson, Saul, Stewart
International appearances
England: 18, Sheringham (4s), 17, Anderton, Greaves; 16, Campbell (2s); 15, Lineker (1s); 14, Hoddle (2s); 13, Mullery (1s), Peters (1s), Waddle (1s); 11, Chivers (2s); 10, Gascoigne (3s); 8, Mabbutt (1s), Ramsey; 7, Smith; 6, Norman; 3, Knowles, Roberts; 2, Brooks, Clemence, Coates, Ditchburn, Ferdinand (1s), Sherwood, Stevens (s), Walker (s); 1, Baily, Barmby (s), Hall, Medley, Robb, Stewart (s)
N Ireland: 7, Jennings; 4, Blanchflower; 3, Armstrong; 1, McGrath
Scotland: 3, Mackay; 2, Brown; 1, Archibald, Brazil (s), Calderwood, Conn, Gilzean, White
Wales: 3, England, Jones, Medwin; 1, Burgess, Hopkins, Price
Republic of Ireland: 2, Hughton
Norway: 2, Thorstvedt
Romania: 1, Dumitrescu, Popescu

International Scorers: England: 10, Greaves; 8, Lineker (2 pens); 7, Chivers; 6, Hoddle, Smith, 5, Anderton, Peters, Sheringham (1 pen); 3, Ramsey (pens), Waddle; 2, Brooks, Gascoigne; 1, Mabbutt
Scotland: 1, Mackay
Wales: 1, Jones
Romania: 1, Dumitrescu

TOW LAW TOWN
FA Vase final
09/05/98 lost to Tiverton Town 0-1

TRANMERE ROVERS
Worthington Cup final
27/02/00 lost to Leicester 1-2
Third Division promotion play-off final
27/05/90 lost to Notts County 0-2
01/06/91 beat Bolton 1-0 aet
Leyland DAF Cup final
20/05/90 beat Bristol Rovers 2-1
26/05/91 lost to Birmingham C 2-3
League Centenary Tournament
1st round: - 16/04/88 beat Wimbledon 1-0; **quarter-final:** - 16/04/88 beat Newcastle Utd 2-0; **semi-final:** 17/04/88 drew with Nottingham F 2-2 (lost 1-0 on pens)

	P	W	D	L	F	A
Worthington Cup	1	0	0	1	1	2
Promotion play-offs	2	1	0	1	1	2
Leyland DAF Cup	2	1	0	1	4	4
Full match Total	5	2	0	3	6	8
League Centenary	3	2	1	0	5	2

Scorers: 2, Steel

TUFNELL PARK
Middlesex Charity Cup final
17/05/44 beat QPR Juniors 3-2
16/05/45 lost to Golders Green 1-4

	P	W	D	L	F	A
Middlesex Charity Cup	2	1	0	1	4	6
Total	2	1	0	1	4	6

TULSA ROUGHNECKS (see USA)

TURKEY
World Cup Qualifying
16/10/85 lost to England 0-5
18/11/92 lost to England 0-4
European Championship Qualifying
14/10/87 lost to England 0-8
16/10/91 lost to England 0-1

	P	W	D	L	F	A
World Cup Q	2	0	0	2	0	9
European Championship	2	0	0	2	0	9
Total	4	0	0	4	0	18

Most appearances: 3, Riza (1s)

UKRAINE (see also USSR)
International
31/05/00 lost to England 0-2
Clubs
Dynamo Kiev
European Cup
21/10/98 drew with Arsenal 1-1
Makita Tournament

501

semi-final: 29/07/89 lost to Liverpool 0-2
3rd & 4th place: - 30/07/89 beat Porto 1-0

	P	W	D	L	F	A
European Cup	1	0	1	0	1	1
Makita Tournament	2	1	0	1	1	2
Total	3	1	1	1	2	3

URUGUAY
World Cup
11/07/66 drew with England 0-0
19/07/66 drew with Mexico 0-0
Internationals
06/05/64 lost to England 1-2
22/05/90 beat England 2-1
29/03/95 drew with England 0-0

	P	W	D	L	F	A
World Cup	2	0	2	0	0	0
Internationals	3	1	1	1	3	3
Total	5	1	3	1	3	3

Most appearances: 3, Cortes
Scorers: 1, Ostolaza, Perdomo, Spencer

USA
International
07/09/94 lost to England 0-2
Clubs
New York Cosmos
  British & Irish International appearances
  N Ireland: 1, Clements
Philadelphia Fury
  British & Irish International appearances
  Republic of Ireland: 1, O'Brien
Tulsa Roughnecks
  British & Irish International appearances
  N Ireland: 1, McCreery (s)

USSR (see also GEORGIA, MOLDOVA and UKRAINE)
World Cup 3rd & 4th place: 106, 28/07/66 lost to
Portugal 1-2
Internationals
22/10/58 lost to England 0-5
06/12/67 drew with England 2-2
02/06/84 beat England 2-0
21/05/91 lost to England 1-3

	P	W	D	L	F	A
World Cup	1	0	0	1	1	2
Internationals	4	1	1	2	5	10
Total	5	1	1	3	6	12

Most appearances: 2, Banichevski, Khurtsilava,
Malafeev, Metreveli, Voronin
Scorers: 2, Chislenko; 1, Gotsmanov, Malafeev, Protasov,
own goal
FIFA appearances
  Rest of World: 1, Yashin

VAGNS KROSTUE (see DENMARK)

VS RUGBY
FA Vase final
30/04/83 beat Halesown Town 1-0

WALES
World Cup Qualifying
24/01/73 drew with England 1-1

European Championship Qualifying
16/11/66 lost to England 1-5
British Championship
12/11/52 lost to England 2-5
10/11/54 lost to England 2-3
14/11/56 lost to England 1-3
23/11/60 lost to England 1-5
21/11/62 lost to England 0-4
18/11/64 lost to England 1-2
16/11/66 lost to England 1-5
07/05/69 lost to England 1-2
19/05/71 drew with England 0-0
15/05/73 lost to England 0-3
21/05/75 drew with England 2-2
31/05/77 beat England 1-0
23/05/79 drew with England 0-0
20/05/81 drew with England 0-0
23/02/83 lost to England 1-2
Wartime
13/04/40 beat England 1-0
27/02/43 lost to England 3-5
25/09/43 lost to England 3-8
Schoolboy
07/04/51 lost to England 0-3
28/03/53 drew with England 3-3
23/04/55 lost to England 0-6
30/03/57 lost to England 0-2
29/04/61 lost to England 1-8
27/04/63 lost to England 1-4
19/04/69 lost to England 0-3
20/03/76 lost to England 1-4
24/03/79 drew with England 1-1

	P	W	D	L	F	A
World Cup Q	1	0	1	0	1	1
European Championship Qualifying (also British Championship)	1	0	0	1	1	5
British Championship	15	1	4	10	13	36
Total (official)	16	1	5	10	14	37
Wartime	3	1	0	2	7	13
Senior Total	19	2	5	12	21	50
Schoolboy	9	0	2	7	7	34

Most appearances: 6, L James (1s), Mahoney, R Thomas,
Toshack; 5, Allchurch, Flynn, L Phillips
Scorers: 3, J Charles; 2, Ford, Toshack; 1, R Davies, W
Davies, Griffiths, L James (pen), C Jones, Leek, Rush

WALSALL
International appearances
  Republic of Ireland: 1, Kearns

WALTHAMSTOW AVENUE
FA Amateur Cup final
26/04/52 beat Leyton 2-1 aet
22/04/61 beat West Auckland Town 2-1

	P	W	D	L	F	A
FA Amateur Cup	2	2	0	0	4	2
Total	2	2	0	0	4	2

WALTHAMSTOW FELLOWSHIP
London Occupational League final
21/03/34 beat Greenwich Trafalgar 1-0

WALTON AND HERSHAM
FA Amateur Cup final
14/04/73 beat Slough Town 1-0

WARRINGTON TOWN
FA Vase final
25/04/87 lost to St Helens Town 2-3

WATFORD
FA Cup final
19/05/84 lost to Everton 0-2
First Division promotion play-off final
31/05/99 beat Bolton 2-0

	P	W	D	L	F	A
FA Cup	1	0	0	1	0	2
Promotion play-off	1	1	0	0	2	0
Total	2	1	0	1	2	2

International appearances
England: 6, Barnes (1s), Blissett (3s)
N Ireland: 1, Armstrong, McClelland
Wales: 1, Jackett
International Scorers: England: 3, Blissett

WEALDSTONE
FA Amateur Cup final
16/04/66 beat Hendon 3-1
FA Trophy final
11/05/85 beat Boston United 2-1
Middlesex Charity Cup final
03/06/42 beat RAF Uxbridge 5-2 aet

	P	W	D	L	F	A
FA Amateur Cup	1	1	0	0	3	1
FA Trophy	1	1	0	0	2	1
Middlesex Charity Cup	1	1	0	0	5	2
Total	3	3	0	0	10	4

WERDER BREMEN (see GERMANY)

WEST AUCKLAND TOWN
FA Amateur Cup final
22/04/61 lost to Walthamstow Avenue 1-2

WEST BROMWICH ALBION
FA Cup final
25/04/31 beat Birmingham C 2-1
27/04/35 lost to Sheffield W 2-4
01/05/54 beat PNE 3-2
18/05/68 beat Everton 1-0 aet
League Cup final
04/03/67 lost to QPR 2-3
07/03/70 lost to Man City 1-2 aet
Second Division promotion play-off final
30/05/93 beat Port Vale 3-0
League Youth Alliance Cup final
16/04/00 drew with Scunthorpe 0-0 (won 3-2 on pens)

	P	W	D	L	F	A
FA Cup	4	3	0	1	8	7
League Cup	2	0	0	2	3	5
Promotion play-off	1	1	0	0	3	0
Senior Total	7	4	0	3	14	12
League Youth Alliance Cup	1	0	1	0	0	0

Most appearances: 3, Astle, Brown, Fraser, Hope, Kaye
Scorers: 2, Allen (1 pen), Astle, Clark, W G Richardson;
1, Boyes, Donovan, Griffin, Hunt, Reid, Sandford

International appearances
England: 8, Howe, B Robson, R Robson; 4, Barnes
(1s), Kevan; 2, Allen, Astle, Regis (1s); 1, Brown,
Cunningham, Hunt (s), Pearson, Shaw, Statham
N Ireland: 1, Armstrong (s), Nicholl
Scotland: 1, Johnston
Wales: 3, G Williams; 1, Millington, S Williams
Republic of Ireland: 1, Giles, Martin, Mulligan
International Scorers: England: 4, R Robson; 1, Allen,
Kevan

WEST GERMANY (see GERMANY)

WEST HAM UNITED
European Cup-Winners Cup final
19/05/65 beat Munich 2-0
FA Cup final
28/04/23 lost to Bolton 0-2
02/05/64 beat PNE 3-2
03/05/75 beat Fulham 2-0
10/05/80 beat Arsenal 1-0
League Cup final
14/03/81 drew with Liverpool 1-1 aet
Charity Shield
09/08/75 lost to Derby County 0-2
09/08/80 lost to Liverpool 0-1
League War Cup final
13/04/40 beat Blackburn 1-0

	P	W	D	L	F	A
European Cup-Winners Cup	1	1	0	0	2	0
FA Cup	4	3	0	1	6	4
League Cup	1	0	1	0	1	1
Charity Shield	2	0	0	2	0	3
League War Cup	1	1	0	0	1	0
Total	9	5	1	3	10	8

Most appearances: 5, Brooking
Scorers: 2, Sealey, A Taylor; 1, Boyce, Brooking, Hurst,
Sissons, Small, Stewart (pen)

International appearances
England: 43, R Moore, 24, Hurst (2s); 19, Brooking (3s);
18, Peters (1s); 7, Martin (1s), 5, Devonshire, Ferdinand
(4s), 3, Byrne; 1, K Brown, Cottee (s), Hufton, Lampard,
Pearce, Watson, Wright
Scotland: 1, Dick, Stewart
Wales: 1, Woosnam
Republic of Ireland: 1, Cantwell
Croatia: 1, Bilic
Czechoslovakia: 1, Miklosko
International Scorers: England: 16, Hurst (3 pens); 5,
Peters; 2, Byrne, Watson; 1, Brooking

WEST HENDON EX-SERVICEMEN
Carlsberg Pub Cup International
13/06/98 beat Vagns Krostue 1-0
Carlsberg Pub Cup final
09/05/98 drew with Honiton Clyst 1-1 (won 3-1 on pens)
16/05/99 lost to Sizewell 0-2

	P	W	D	L	F	A
Pub Cup International	1	1	0	0	1	0
Carlsberg Pub Cup	2	0	1	1	1	3
Total	3	1	1	1	2	3

503

WESTMINSTER BANK
Southern Amateur League First Division
03/11/28 beat Ealing Association 3-0

WHICKHAM
FA Vase final
25/04/81 beat Willenhall Town 3-2 aet

WHITBY TOWN
FA Amateur Cup final
24/04/65 lost to Hendon 1-3
FA Vase final
10/05/97 beat North Ferriby United 3-0

	P	W	D	L	F	A
FA Amateur Cup	1	0	0	1	1	3
FA Vase	1	1	0	0	3	0
Total	2	1	0	1	4	3

WIGAN ATHLETIC
Second Division promotion play-off final
28/05/00 lost to Gillingham 2-3
Freight Rover Trophy/Auto Windscreens Shield final
01/06/85 beat Brentford 3-1
18/04/99 beat Millwall 1-0
FA Trophy final
28/04/73 lost to Scarborough 1-2 aet
League Centenary Tournament
1st round: - 16/04/88 drew with Sunderland 0-0 (won 2-1 on pens); **quarter-final:** - 16/04/88 drew with Sheffield W 1-1 (lost 3-2 on pens)

	P	W	D	L	F	A
Play-off	1	0	0	1	2	3
Freight Rover Trophy/ Auto Windscreens Shield	2	2	0	0	4	1
FA Trophy	1	0	0	1	1	2
Full match Total	4	2	0	2	7	6
League Centenary	2	0	2	0	1	1

WILLENHALL TOWN
FA Vase final
25/04/81 lost to Whickham 2-3 aet

WILLINGTON
FA Amateur Cup final
22/04/50 beat Bishop Auckland 4-0

WIMBLEDON
FA Cup final
14/05/88 beat Liverpool 1-0
Charity Shield
20/08/88 lost to Liverpool 1-2
FA Amateur Cup final
04/05/63 beat Sutton Utd 4-2
League Centenary Tournament
1st round: - 16/04/88 lost to Tranmere 0-1

	P	W	D	L	F	A
FA Cup	1	1	0	0	1	0
Charity Shield	1	0	0	1	1	2
FA Amateur Cup	1	1	0	0	4	2
Full match Total	3	2	0	1	6	4
League Centenary	1	0	0	1	0	1

Most appearances: 2, Fashanu, Gibson, Phelan, Sanchez, Scales (1s), Wise, Young
Scorers: 4 Reynolds

International appearances
England: 1, Fashanu
Scotland: 1, Sullivan
Nigeria: 1, Ekoku (s)

WIMBORNE TOWN
FA Vase final
25/04/92 beat Guiseley 5-3

WITTON ALBION
FA Trophy final
10/05/92 lost to Colchester 1-3

WOKING
FA Amateur Cup final
12/04/58 beat Ilford 3-0
FA Trophy final
21/05/94 beat Runcorn 2-1
14/05/95 beat Kidderminster 2-1 aet
18/05/97 beat Dagenham and Redbridge 1-0 aet

	P	W	D	L	F	A
FA Amateur Cup	1	1	0	0	3	0
FA Trophy	3	3	0	0	5	2
Total	4	4	0	0	8	2

WOLVERHAMPTON WANDERERS
FA Cup final
29/04/39 lost to Portsmouth 1-4
30/04/49 beat Leicester 3-1
07/05/60 beat Blackburn 3-0
League Cup final
02/03/74 beat Man City 2-1
15/03/80 beat Nottingham F 1-0
Sherpa Van Trophy final
29/05/88 beat Burnley 2-0
League Centenary Tournament
1st round: - 16/04/88 drew with Everton 1-1 (lost 3-2 on pens)

	P	W	D	L	F	A
FA Cup	3	2	0	1	7	5
League Cup	2	2	0	0	3	1
Sherpa Van Trophy	1	1	0	0	2	0
Full match Total	6	5	0	1	12	6
League Centenary	1	0	1	0	1	1

Most appearances: 2, Hibbitt, Palmer, Parkin, Richards
Scorers: 2, Deeley, Pye; 1, Dennison, Dorsett, Gray, Hibbitt, Mutch, Richards, Smyth, own goal
International appearances
England: 26, Wright; 16, Flowers; 6, Bull (2s); 4, Slater, Williams; 3, Thomson; 2, Broadbent, Mullen, Wilshaw; 1, Cullis, Hughes
N Ireland: 2, Dougan; 1, Hegan, Lutton
Scotland: 2, Munro (1s); 1, Curran, Gray
International Scorers: England: 6, Wilshaw; 3, Flowers (2 pens); 2, Bull, Mullen
Scotland: 1, Curran

WREXHAM
International appearances
Wales: 2, Davies, Jones; 1, Griffiths
International Scorers: Wales: 1, Griffiths

WYCOMBE WANDERERS
Third Division promotion play-off final
28/05/94 beat PNE 4-2
FA Amateur Cup final
13/04/57 lost to Bishop Auckland 1-3
FA Trophy final
11/05/91 beat Kidderminster 2-1
09/05/93 beat Runcorn 4-1

	P	W	D	L	F	A
Promotion play-off	1	1	0	0	4	2
FA Amateur Cup	1	0	0	1	1	3
FA Trophy	2	2	0	0	6	2
Total	4	3	0	1	11	7

YEADING
FA Vase final
05/05/90 drew with Bridlington Town 0-0 aet

YORK CITY
Third Division promotion play-off final
29/05/93 drew with Crewe 1-1 aet (won 5-3 on pens)
International appearances
N Ireland: 2, Scott (1s)

YUGOSLAVIA (see also CROATIA)
European Championship Qualifying
12/11/86 lost to England 0-2
Internationals
28/11/56 lost to England 0-3
11/05/60 drew with England 3-3
04/05/66 lost to England 0-2
11/10/72 drew with England 1-1
13/12/89 lost to England 1-2
Olympic semi-final
11/08/48 beat Great Britain 3-1
Olympic final
13/08/48 lost to Sweden 1-3
U-16
10/08/85 lost to England 2-3

	P	W	D	L	F	A
European Championship	1	0	0	1	0	2
Internationals	5	0	2	3	5	11
v England	6	0	2	4	5	13
Olympics	2	1	0	1	4	4
U-16	1	0	0	1	2	3

Most appearances: 2, Dzajic, Hadzibegic, Skoro, Soskic, Zebec

Scorers: 2, Galic; 1, Kostic, Skoro, Vladic

FIFA appearances
Rest of Europe
1, Beara (s), Caikowski, Vukas, Zebec
Rest of World: 1, Soskic (s)

NOT JUST A FOOTBALL STADIUM...

WEMBLEY STADIUM was built for the British Empire Exhibition of 1924, but was ready in time for the 1923 FA Cup Final and so began a rich football history. This book covers the complete football record, but it is by no means, the whole story, for the stadium also became a household name in a variety of other sports and entertainments, thanks to its ambitious owner, Arthur Elvin.

It did not take long for other sports to appear. Three months after the 'White Horse Final', an athletics event was staged when a combined team from Oxford and Cambridge Universities defeated a team from the American universities of Yale and Harvard. The home side starred sprinter Harold Abrahams, who won gold at the following year's Olympics in Paris and whose name became immortalised in the 1981 movie, *Chariots of Fire*.

The British Empire Exhibition was opened in the stadium on St George's Day, 1924, three days before Wembley's second FA Cup Final, by King George V. It was to be a celebration of the diverse cultures and resources of the British Empire following the hardships of the First World War. The stadium had become the centrepiece of a huge theme park with fairground rides, lakes and palaces. Over the next two summers, it was visited by more than 27 million people. The stadium was used to host such diverse attractions as the first rodeos to be held in England, the Boy Scouts' Imperial Jamboree and a re-enactment of the Great Fire of London, with the pitch being transformed into a burning network of streets!

Greyhound racing was introduced to Wembley in 1927 and a dog named Spin won the first race. The stadium rapidly became one of the premier venues in the sport and meetings were held two or three nights a week for over 70 years. The twice Derby winner, Mick the Miller, won the St Leger at Wembley in 1931 in his last race and 1985 saw a showdown between BBC Television Trophy winner, Scurlogue Champ, and the seemingly unbeatable Ballyregan Bob. Unfortunately for the promoters, Scurlogue Champ broke down after less than half the race and Ballyregan Bob romped home, going on to complete a world record 32 consecutive wins. The last race was in December 1998, won by a dog called Ballistic Missile.

The Rugby League Challenge Cup Final made its Wembley debut in 1929, with Wigan beating Dewsbury, 13-2 and the fixture was to become an annual pilgrimage to the capital for thousands of northern fans. Wigan returned many times to lift the famous Cup. In 1959, they became the first to retain the trophy at Wembley and won it for an unprecedented eight consecutive years from 1988-95. Leeds Rhinos won the last Wembley final in 1999 with a record victory of 52-16 against London Broncos. Leroy Rivett became the first man to score four tries in the final.

International Rugby League took a little longer to establish itself at Wembley, probably because of the lack of home success. Australia beat Wales 26-10 in 1930 and England lost to France in 1949. Great Britain took their First Test with Australia to Wembley in 1963 but had to wait another ten years for their first victory, though they eventually lost the series. Britain won again in 1990, but failed again to maintain their challenge when the ultimate prize was at stake. A world record 73,631 crowd saw Australia lift the World Cup at Wembley in 1992 following a 10-6 victory against Britain, who managed another First Test success in 1994 against the Aussies. The following year saw a new-style World Cup tournament kick-off at Wembley, with a lavish opening ceremony which included performances from Diana Ross and Carol Decker. This time, it was England who defeated Australia 20-16 to raise hopes that the old enemy could at last be vanquished. But three weeks later the invincible Aussie machine exacted its revenge by 16-8 in the final.

Speedway was the next sport to receive the Wembley treatment in May 1929 as Wembley Lions joined the Southern League. Despite an inauspicious start, when they lost nine of their first 11 fixtures, they turned things around and won the title. By 1932 they were National champions and the stadium had become an international venue with England defeating Australia in the 1930 Fifth Test.

A World championship was introduced to the fledgling sport in 1936. Wembley was the natural choice as host and the Lions' Australian captain, Lionel Van Praag, became the first World champion. The first Englishman to win the title was Tommy Price, also of Wembley Lions, in 1949 and the Lions dominated the National League, winning seven of the first eight post-war championships. Perhaps, it would have been eight in a row, if they hadn't had to vacate the stadium for the 1948 Olympics.

In the 1950s, the sport went into decline and the club was disbanded in 1957 although the World championship continued to be held at Wembley each year. Other venues were used to alternate with Wembley in the 1960s but Great Britain won the first World Team championship at the stadium in 1968 and the Wembley Lions returned in 1970 for a couple of years before the advent of more football fixtures and continual relaying of the pitch across the corners forced them out again. There was more World Team championship success for Britain in 1973 but Wembley finally bowed out as a speedway venue after Bruce Penhall's World title success in 1981. The track was narrowed to accommodate more seating and speedway was no longer possible.

Wembley was used to stage all manner of festivals, ceremonies, pageants and tattoos right from the early days of the British Empire Exhibition. In June 1937, 6,000 members of the Women's League of Health and Beauty gave a display of exercise to music as part of the Coronation Pageant and four months later the Lord Mayor of London was at the stadium to present the charter as Wembley officially became a London borough. The stadium had originally been built in the countryside around London but the area developed rapidly to become part of the capital city. In 1945, Wembley marked the end of the Second World War with a thanksgiving service.

Having played an important role in wartime – housing refugees and staging numerous football matches for war charities – it then gave the world a long-overdue chance to celebrate sporting excellence by hosting the 1948 Olympic Games.

They began on July 29th and were formally opened by King George VI. The following day, the athletics began with a bang as Emil Zatopek smashed the 10,000 metres world record by 12 seconds, finishing an astonishing 45 seconds ahead of the silver medallist. Three days later, Dutch housewife Fanny Blankers-Koen won the 100 metres, the first of her four gold medals in. As well as the athletics and football, the stadium was also used for the closing stages of the hockey tournament, won by India, who thrashed Great Britain 4-0 in the final. As an exhibition sport, lacrosse was played at Wembley for the one and only time. England drew 5-5 with Rensellaer Polytechnic Institute from the state of New York. The Olympics ended with the equestrian events on the famous turf. Great Britain was unable to win any gold medals at the stadium, but the Games were a huge success.

After the men's hockey at the Olympics, the women's game made its Wembley debut in 1951, with England beating Ireland 6-1. Like the schoolboy international football games, they became annual fixtures and the terraces echoed to high-pitched voices. Forty years later, England made their last Wembley appearance, losing to France for the first time. Despite Wembley's plush green grass, the future of hockey was now on artificial surfaces.

Wembley tried its hand with American sports before, during and after the war, as played by the American forces. Two teams from the USS New Orleans played baseball in 1934 and in 1942 the US Air Force met the US Army twice. American football was played in the stadium during the war and in 1952 the final of a competition for the US Forces in Europe ended at Wembley with the German-based Furstenfeldbruck Eagles beating Burtonwood Bullets 26-7.

Gridiron returned to the stadium in 1983 as Minnesota Vikings defeated St. Louis Cardinals in the first of six demonstration games capitalising on renewed interest in the UK, thanks to TV coverage of the American sport. In 1991, it had grown so much that a World League was created to give European fans a chance to support a team of their own. London Monarchs became the first World champions when they trounced Barcelona Dragons, 21-0 but the game had reached its peak and Wembley saw only one more year of the World League.

Irish fans living in London were treated to their national sports when Wembley began staging an annual double bill from 1958. Galway beat Derry at Gaelic football and All-Ireland Hurling champions, Kilkenny, defeated Clare. Different teams were invited each year in May and the event ran until 1976 when dwindling attendances brought the games to an end.

In 1954, the American evangelist, Billy Graham managed to fill Wembley with 120,000 people on the first of several visits. Only the 1923 FA Cup Final saw more people in the stadium. There was a crowd of under 100,000 when Pope John Paul II celebrated mass at Wembley in 1982.

Possibly the most bizarre event the stadium ever staged was the ski-jumping on May 31st and June 1st 1961. Two nights of fund-raising for British skiing were made possible with artificial snow.

Boxing was first staged at Wembley in 1924 when the American heavyweight Tommy Gibbons knocked out Jack Bloomfield in a poorly attended fight. Commonwealth champion Jack Petersen was defeated by the German heavyweight Walter Neusel in 1935 and Wembley Arena staged many bouts, but it was not until 1963 that the stadium made boxing history. Cassius Clay, the Olympic Light-Heavyweight champion of 1960, beat the British and Commonwealth Heavyweight champion, Henry Cooper in the fifth round. Cooper had knocked down Clay at the end of the previous round but his own cut eye ruined his chances. Clay (who became World Heavyweight champion three times and changed his name to Muhammad Ali) had predicted he would win in the fifth. 'Our 'Enry' became Sir Henry Cooper and Ali acquired a fame which went far beyond the world of boxing.

It was not until July 1986, that Wembley finally staged a World championship fight but the great British hope was once more defeated. In a fight held in the early hours of Sunday morning to suit American TV audiences, Frank Bruno was defeated by the WBA Heavyweight champion Tim Witherspoon. Nine years later, after two more failed attempts to win the title, Bruno eventually realised his dream when he returned to Wembley to take the WBC title from Oliver McCall on points. Nigel Benn successfully defended his WBC Super-Middleweight title on the same bill.

Equestrianism returned to the stadium in 1968 and '69, with the Royal International Horse Show. The effect of six consecutive nights of horses pounding the turf was blamed for the state of the pitch in subsequent cup finals, although Wembley's groundsman Percy Young also blamed the new roof because it prevented the wind from drying the grass. Nevertheless, by 1971, it was back in pristine condition.

Speedway wasn't the only motor sport to be held beneath the twin towers. In 1974, two stock-car meetings were held, including the Formula Two World championship and the following year, motorcycle stunt rider Evel Knievel attempted to jump a world record 13 buses but clipped the last one and crashed, fracturing his spine. Injuries were nothing new to him, however, and he recovered to clear 13 buses in Ohio five months later.

The World Wrestling Federation staged its 'Summerslam' outside the US for the first time, in 1992 and a packed Wembley saw the British Bulldog Davey 'Boy' Smith become the Intercontinental champion.

Rugby Union was first played at Wembley in 1925, with the Army and the RAF sharing the points in a 5-5 draw. Scotland beat England, 8-5 in 1942 and a five-a-side tournament, won by Heriot's Former Pupils, was held in 1979, but it was not until the 1990's that the stadium staged the big games. England beat Canada in 1992 while Twickenham was undergoing rebuilding work and Wales made Wembley their home from 1997-99, so that Cardiff Arms Park could be transformed into the Millennium Stadium for the World Cup. Cardiff subsequently repaid the favour by stepping in to host several football and Rugby League finals, when Wembley was being rebuilt. Although Wales were swept aside by the New Zealand All Blacks on their first appearance and suffered a 51-0 humiliation as France retained the 'Grand Slam', they left Wembley with the sweet memory of an injury-time victory against England, to deny the 'visitors' their own 'Grand Slam'.

One more great British sport was attempted at Wembley. A cricket match between England and the Rest of the World was scheduled for September 1991. Artificial turf had been laid across the track to take the pitch right up to the spectators. Alas, the great British weather scuppered the event. It was rained off without a ball being bowled.

On Saturday 5th August 1972, a new chapter in Wembley's history began. The London Rock 'n' Roll Show opened with the Houseshakers, followed by Billy Fury, the first solo performer. British acts, Gary Glitter and Screaming Lord Sutch appeared, but topping the bill were Bill Haley and his Comets, Little Richard and Chuck Berry, who closed the show. Crosby Stills Nash and Young had the honour of performing at the second concert, two years later and The Who became the first British band to top the bill in 1979, but it was the 1980s, when the venue really established itself in the music world. Live Aid became the biggest music event of all-time and Wembley subsequently became the stage on which all the world's great artists performed. Almost every summer, a succession of megastars filled the stadium. These were the headline acts:

1982
Simon and Garfunkel, Rolling Stones (two nights)
1984
Bob Dylan
Having appeared a month earlier as chairman of FA Cup finalists' Watford, Elton John topped the bill at the 'Summer of '84' concert,. He was supported by Paul Young, Nik Kershaw and Kool and the Gang.
1985
Live Aid was a ten-hour extravaganza of popular music, broadcast live to the world, to raise money for the starving millions in Africa. Status Quo was the opening act and amongst the numerous highlights were the Boomtown Rats, with lead singer, Bob Geldof, who had instigated the Band Aid charity and co-wrote the single, 'Do They Know It's Christmas?'. Also appearing, in duets were Sting and Phil Collins, Paul Young and Alison Moyet, and Elton John and Kiki Dee. There were memorable performances from U2, Dire Straits, David Bowie, Wham! and The Who, who had re-formed for the occasion. Freddie Mercury and Queen gave an unforgettable performance and Paul McCartney sang 'Let It Be', before all the performers returned to sing the original Band Aid hit in an emotional finale. The event raised over £70 million.
Bruce Springsteen (three nights)
1986
Concerts by Wham!, Rod Stewart and Electric Light Orchestra, Feargal Sharkey, Queen and Status Quo
1987
Concerts by Madonna (three nights), U2, David Bowie, Genesis (four nights)
1988
Another mammoth ten-hour concert was held as a 70th birthday tribute to Nelson Mandela, the South African anti-apartheid leader, who had been

imprisoned for the previous 25 years. A wide range of musical styles was represented and artists included Sting, George Michael, The Eurythmics, Natalie Cole, Bryan Adams, The Bee Gees, Phil Collins, Paul Young, Midge Ure, Wet Wet Wet, Aswad, UB40, Chrissie Hynde and Simple Minds. Stevie Wonder made a guest appearance before Whitney Houston and then Dire Straits provided the climax to the event.

Bruce Springsteen

Pink Floyd (two nights)

Michael Jackson (seven sell-out concerts, a world record for one venue)

On the 40th anniversary of the Universal Declaration of Human Rights, Amnesty International began a six-week tour of the world, raising awareness with a series of concerts. The performers were Tracy Chapman, Peter Gabriel, Youssou N'Dour, Sting and Bruce Springsteen.

1989

Concerts by Cliff Richard (two nights), Bros, Simple Minds

1990

A hastily arranged five-hour concert began with Nelson Mandela's first public speech to a worldwide audience after his release from prison in South Africa. Many of the artists from his 70th birthday tribute were at Wembley again.

Concerts by Amitabh Bachchan (first Asian music concert), Rolling Stones (five nights), Madonna, Fleetwood Mac

1991

Australian band, Inxs topped the bill at an all-day concert, which also included Hothouse Flowers and Debbie Harry.

Rod Stewart and Status Quo (with Joe Cocker supporting)

1992

Freddie Mercury, with Queen, had stolen the show at Live Aid and his death at the age of 45 from AIDS in November 1991 had been a devastating blow to British music. This concert was held as a tribute and also to raise awareness for AIDS research. Numerous artists performed their own versions of Queen hits, accompanied by the three surviving members of the band. Among the highlights were David Bowie and Annie Lennox performing 'Under Pressure'. Five tracks from the concert, performed by George Michael and Lisa Stansfield, with Queen, were released as a single, which became Wembley Stadium's first chart topper. 'Bohemian Rhapsody' was sung by Elton John and Axl Rose, a most unlikely pairing, while Liza Minnelli led all the performers in a rousing finale with 'We Are The Champions'.

Concerts by Guns 'n' Roses, Elton John and Eric Clapton (three nights), Simply Red (two nights), Bryan Adams, Michael Jackson (five nights)

1993

Concerts by Jean Michel Jarre, Prince, U2 (four nights), Madonna (two nights)

1995

Concerts by Bon Jovi (three nights, with Van Halen supporting), Rolling Stones (three nights), Rod Stewart

1996
The Three Tenors (Jose Carreras, Placido Domingo and Luciano Pavarotti)
Concerts by Tina Turner (two nights), Eagles (three nights), Bryan Adams
1997
'Songs and Visions', sponsored by Carling, was a celebration of 40 years of popular music, held on the 20th anniversary of the death of Elvis Presley. Ten major artists took turns to perform a song from each year, with video images portraying news events of that year. The performers were Rod Stewart, k.d. lang, Steve Winwood, Seal, Jon Bon Jovi, Toni Braxton, Mary J. Blige, Chaka Khan, Robert Palmer and Yazawa.
Concerts by Michael Jackson (three nights), U2 (two nights). The stadium also staged the country's biggest ever Christian Praise concert.
1998
Concerts by Spice Girls (two nights), Bee Gees, Sir Elton John (two nights, billed with Billy Joel, who pulled out because of illness)
1999
The netaid concert was staged to raise awareness of the web site, which aimed to eradicate world poverty. The stadium had never staged a concert as late as October before, but the quality of performers ensured a warm atmosphere. The Eurythmics began the show, and Catatonia, The Corrs, George Michael, David Bowie and Bryan Adams were all on top form, before Robbie Williams provided a memorable climax.
Concerts by Rolling Stones (two nights), Celine Dion (two nights), Aerosmith
2000
Concerts by Tina Turner (two nights), Oasis (two nights)
Bon Jovi (two nights) had the honour of performing the stadium's last concert on August 20th, though there was also the AXA Final Ball on November 2nd, where 2,000 guests in a specially-built structure on what was left of the pitch, watched Sir Elton John performing a charity show for the NSPCC. He was joined on stage by Chris De Burgh, Jools Holland, The Bootleg Beatles and Lesley Garrett. This was the stadium's very last event.